Pro EJB 3

Java Persistence API

Mike Keith

Merrick Schincariol

Apress®

Pro EJB 3: Java Persistence API

Copyright © 2006 by Mike Keith and Merrick Schincariol

ISBN-13 (pbk): 978-1-59059-645-6

ISBN-10 (pbk): 1-59059-645-5

Printed and bound in the United States of America 9 8 7 6 5 4 3 2

Lead Editor: Steve Anglin
Technical Reviewer: Jason Haley, Huyen Nguyen, Shahid Shah
Editorial Board: Steve Anglin, Ewan Buckingham, Gary Cornell, Jason Gilmore, Jonathan Gennick,
    Jonathan Hassell, James Huddleston, Chris Mills, Matthew Moodie, Dominic Shakeshaft, Jim Sumser,
    Keir Thomas, Matt Wade
Project Manager: Julie M. Smith
Copy Edit Manager: Nicole LeClerc
Copy Editor: Hastings Hart
Assistant Production Director: Kari Brooks-Copony
Production Editor: Laura Esterman
Compositors: Pat Christenson and Susan Glinert Stevens
Proofreader: Elizabeth Berry
Indexer: Julie Grady
Artist: Kinetic Publishing Services, LLC
Cover Designer: Kurt Krames
Manufacturing Director: Tom Debolski

Distributed to the book trade worldwide by Springer-Verlag New York, Inc., 233 Spring Street, 6th Floor, New York, NY 10013. Phone 1-800-SPRINGER, fax 201-348-4505, e-mail orders-ny@springer-sbm.com, or visit http://www.springeronline.com.

For information on translations, please contact Apress directly at 2560 Ninth Street, Suite 219, Berkeley, CA 94710. Phone 510-549-5930, fax 510-549-5939, e-mail info@apress.com, or visit http://www.apress.com.

The source code for this book is available to readers at http://www.apress.com in the Source Code section. You will need to answer questions pertaining to this book in order to successfully download the code.

To the memory of my mother, who touched so many lives, and to my wife Darleen,
who touches my life each and every day. —Mike

To my parents, for always supporting me in all of my adventures,
and my wife Natalie, whose love and support kept me going to the end. —Merrick

Contents at a Glance

Contents

Foreword

I believe that the Java Persistence API (JPA) is the most important advance in the Java EE 5 platform revision. It offers a simple yet powerful standard for object-relational mapping (ORM). Leading persistence vendors have united to develop it, and developers should unite in adopting it.

Up to and including EJB 2.1, the persistence technology (entity beans) was the weakest part of the overall EJB specification—complex yet lacking in essential capabilities such as inheritance modelling, and unusable in isolation. JPA is now a fine model that can stand on its own and works in a range of environments. In future revisions, JPA's independence from its runtime environment is likely to become explicit, with JPA split into a separate specification from EJB. Thus JPA is relevant to *all* Java developers who work with relational databases, not merely those who work with the EJB component model overall.

Since the release of EJB 2.0 in 2001, enterprise Java has been revolutionized by a switch to a simpler, POJO-based programming model. This switch has been equally marked in the Fortune 500 as it has amongst developers of simple web applications. The focus is increasingly on the Java language itself rather than complex container contracts. Modern infrastructure can apply enterprise services to POJOs without their needing to be polluted by infrastructure concerns.

Unlike the former entity bean model, JPA offers the ability to persist POJOs. The JPA specification has been drawn from collective experience from more than 10 years, across products such as TopLink, Kodo, and Hibernate. POJO-based persistence offers many important benefits lacking in the former entity bean model: a simple, productive development experience; ease of testing; and the ability to build and persist true domain models capturing business concepts. The rise of POJO persistence will gradually change for the better how we design applications, enabling greater object orientation in place of the often procedural style traditionally associated with J2EE development.

Of course, ORM is not new, and many developers have been successfully working with ORM products for years. The importance of JPA lies in the fact that it offers users choices between implementations without subjecting them to a lowest common denominator. All leading ORM products will support the JPA in addition to their proprietary APIs (or other standards, such as JDO); users who choose to move to the JPA API will not be forced to switch persistence products but will gain greater choice in the future.

As leader of the Spring Framework open source project, I am particularly pleased that the leading JPA implementations are all open source. The Spring Framework 2.0 release integrates with JPA, and we aim to make it easy for Spring users to work with JPA in any environment. We are excited about working with the communities around the open source JPA implementations to help make the Spring/JPA experience still better.

Thus this is an important topic. Hopefully I have convinced you that you should read a book on JPA, but why should you read this one?

Mike Keith is ideally qualified to write such a book. He was co-lead of the EJB 3.0 specification, and he not only has intimate knowledge of the specification but also played a vital role in bringing it to completion. His experience with persistence engines dates back almost 15 years. He has been a key member of the TopLink team for five years, championing what would now be called POJO persistence before it become fashionable, during the persistence Dark Ages of J2EE 1.3 and 1.4.

Most important, Mike and Merrick Schincariol have turned their experience into a clear, readable book providing a thorough introduction to JPA. While you won't be disappointed as you grow in your experience with JPA, and while you will find valuable content on more advanced questions and best practices, the book never feels bogged down in detail. The authors clearly convey the big picture of how you can use JPA effectively. The many code examples ensure that the discussion always comes back to practice, with examples that are directly relevant to developers.

I encourage you to browse for yourself and am confident you will my share my high opinion of *Pro EJB 3: Java Persistence API.*

Rod Johnson
Founder, Spring Framework
CEO, Interface21

About the Authors

 **MIKE KEITH** is the co-specification lead of EJB 3.0 and a member of the Java EE 5 expert group. He holds a Master of Science degree in computing from Carleton University and has over 15 years of teaching, research, and practical experience in object persistence. He has implemented persistence systems for Fortune 100 corporations on a host of technologies, including relational and object databases, XML, directory services, and custom data formats. Since the fledgling EJB days he has worked on EJB implementations and integrations to multiple application servers. He has written various papers and articles and spoken at numerous conferences about EJB 3.0. He is currently employed at Oracle as a persistence architect.

 **MERRICK SCHINCARIOL** is a senior engineer at Oracle and a reviewer of the EJB 3.0 specification. He has a Bachelor of Science degree in computer science from Lakehead University and has over seven years of experience in the industry. He spent some time consulting in the pre-Java enterprise and business intelligence fields before moving on to write Java and J2EE applications. His experience with large-scale systems and data warehouse design gave him a mature and practiced perspective on enterprise software, which later propelled him into doing EJB container implementation work. He was a lead engineer for Oracle's EJB 3.0 offering.

About the Technical Reviewers

JASON HALEY is a senior engineer at Oracle and a reviewer of the EJB 3.0 specification. He has a Bachelor of Science degree in computing from Carleton University and has been working with the EJB internals, and Java and J2EE applications for over seven years. He has done consulting and training but spent much of his time designing and implementing EJB container infrastructure both on the session and persistence sides. He has extensive experience with the inner workings of BEA WebLogic Server and Oracle Application Server, and has devised multiple session and persistence manager interfaces. He is a lead engineer for Oracle's EJB container.

HUYEN NGUYEN is quality assurance manager at Oracle in the Server Technologies group. He has a Bachelor of Applied Science degree in Systems Design Engineering from the University of Waterloo. In the field of object persistence, he has been working as an instructor and consultant for 11 years and a quality assurance manager for the past four years.

SHAHID N. SHAH is the Founder and CEO of Netspective Communications. Netspective is a software development firm that provides the tools and skills necessary for creating service-oriented systems using Java and .NET. He has recently built a large health-care informatics framework using EJB 3.0 and Java 5.0. Shahid has held the positions of VP of Technology, CTO, Chief Software Architect, and Lead Engineer at large enterprises for the past 15 years. Shahid's key technology expertise areas are service-oriented architectures, distributed object services, Java, J2EE, .NET, XML, UML, and object- and aspect-oriented software development. Shahid runs three successful blogs. At http://shahid.shah.org he writes about architecture issues, at http://www.healthcareguy.com he provides valuable insights on how to apply technology in health care, and at http://www.hitsphere.com he gives a glimpse of the health-care IT blogosphere as an aggregator. He can be reached at shahid@shah.org.

Acknowledgments

I want to thank all of the members of the expert group who contributed to the EJB 3.0 specification. Numerous conference calls, countless hours on the phone with Linda, Gavin, Patrick, and others, and bucket-loads of email produced a result that we all hope is worth the two years of our lives that we sacrificed for it.

I want to thank the four D's (Dennis Leung, Dan Lesage, Doug Clarke, and Donald Smith) for their support and friendship at various stages of the book. Thanks to Shahid for reviewing the early drafts of the chapters and to a host of other casual reviewers that looked at the occasional chapter. I especially owe huge thanks to three great friends: Jason for agreeing to tirelessly put all of the examples into code (and fix my bugs!), for reviewing, and even writing some of the early chapter drafts; Huyen for going above and beyond the call of duty by spending night after late night reviewing to meet a tight schedule; and of course Merrick for being great to work with and taking up the slack when I was out of commission or not able to keep up. Tony, Julie, Hastings, and Laura at Apress really helped out along the way and performed miracles getting this book to print. Last of all, and most important, my wife Darleen and my kids Cierra, Ariana, Jeremy, and Emma. I love them all without bounds. It is they who sacrificed the most for this book by being so very patient over months of having a distant husband and father slouched in a chair clacking away on a laptop.

Mike Keith

Writing a book involves many more people than will ever have their names printed on the cover. Over the last year I have been blessed with the support of many people, who offered advice, reviewed my work, and encouraged me along the way. First of all I'd like to thank Mike for giving me the opportunity to collaborate with him on this book. It was a true partnership from beginning to end. But it could not have been done without the loving support of my wife Natalie and the remarkable patience of my young son Anthony, who had to put up with a daddy who was often hidden away in his office writing. At Oracle, special thanks to Jason Haley for shouldering more than his fair share of senior engineering responsibilities while I worked on this project, and thanks for the support of Dennis Leung, Rob Campbell, and the entire EJB container team. At Apress, Julie Smith, Hastings Hart, and Laura Esterman pulled out all the stops to get things done on time. And finally, thanks to the many reviewers who looked over the drafts of this book. Huyen Nguyen and Jason Haley in particular were instrumental in helping us refine and make this book both accurate and readable.

Merrick Schincariol

Preface

The Java Persistence API has been a long time in coming, some might even say overdue. The arrival of an enterprise Java persistence standard based on a "POJO" development model fills a gap in the platform that has needed to be filled for a long time. The previous attempt missed the mark and advocated EJB entity beans that were awkward to develop and too heavy for many applications. It never reached the level of widespread adoption or general approval in many sectors of the industry. But in the absence of a standard, proprietary persistence products such as JBoss Hibernate and Oracle TopLink gained popularity in the industry and have been thriving. With the emergence of the Java Persistence API, developers can now create portable persistence code that will run on any compliant Java EE 5 server, as well as in a stand-alone JVM outside the server.

It could be argued that the result of waiting until the persistence market had matured was that a superior standard emerged based on product and user experience instead of theory and design. Contained in the Java Persistence API (abbreviated by some as "JPA") are the basic notions and interfaces that all persistence connoisseurs will recognize from their experience with existing products. This will make it easier for people who are already using these products to adopt the Java Persistence API while still allowing novice persistence developers to pick up the API and quickly learn it.

The specification was written for architects and developers alike, but it is still a specification. Few people enjoy sitting down with a tersely worded specification to find out how to use an API. It does not delve into the intricacies of applying the API, nor does it explain any of the peripheral issues that you may encounter during development. In this book we wanted to bring a more practical approach to the topic and highlight some of the usage patterns that we think are of value.

Our original intent was to write about the entire EJB 3.0 specification. We also wanted to produce a book that would fit in someone's laptop bag and not outweigh the laptop. It didn't take us long to realize that in order to provide adequate coverage of the topic and write a book that offered value to the average developer, we needed to focus on only half of the specification. Given our own persistence experience and the lack of existing outside knowledge of the Java Persistence API, the choice was an easy one.

Over the course of this book we will go into detail on all of the elements of the API. We will explain the concepts and illustrate their usage by providing practical examples of how to apply them in your own applications. We begin the journey with a quick tour of the API by creating a very simple application in the Java SE environment. We then move into the enterprise and provide an overview of the features in the EJB 3.0 and Java EE 5 standards that apply to persistence in enterprise applications.

Object-relational mapping is at the heart of storing object state in a relational database, and we go into detail on ORM technology and the mappings and features supported by the API. The EntityManager is the main interface used to interact with entities. Different aspects of using the entity manager are explored, and we open the hood to expose the internals of the implementation to help you understand some of the important nuances. We also explore the queries that can be obtained from entity managers, and make distinctions between the different kinds of dynamic, static, or named queries that are available. We assess the query capabilities that may be accessed and present ideas about when the different kinds of queries should be used. Java Persistence Query Language is discussed in its entirety, with examples of all of its features.

Next we tackle some of the intermediate and advanced topics of ORM, such as inheritance, and show how to map different kinds of class hierarchies to a variety of data schemas. We also delve into the important subject of locking and explain how to best make use of locking strategies in your application. For those who like to use XML for metadata, we describe how XML mappings are specified and explain how they can be used to override annotations. The development life cycle is then completed by a discussion of how to configure the persistence unit and package it up in different categories of enterprise application components.

Much has been written about testing, and much is still being written. Another strength of the API is its ability to support unit testing and some of the other current testing methodologies and patterns that are being used today. We spend some time discussing some of the ways that you can test entities and the application logic that invokes them, both inside and outside the application server.

Finally, for those who are coming to the API from existing persistence systems, we devote some time to going over the migration issues. We offer some suggestions, through the use of some of the common design patterns, of ways to migrate different kinds of architected applications to use the Java Persistence API.

We hope that you enjoy both reading this book and learning how to use the Java Persistence API. We still couldn't fit everything that we wanted to fit in this book, but hopefully, like Indiana Jones, we "chose wisely" about what was important and what didn't need to be included. We welcome any suggestions for additional topics as well as any comments about the topics that we did include.

Who This Book Is For

We have written this book for everybody who wants to use persistence in enterprise and desktop applications. We do not assume that you have any experience with persistence products, although we do assume that you have some Java programming experience, as well as some exposure to the J2EE platform. Experience with the new Java EE 5 standard may be helpful but is certainly not required. Knowledge of previous versions of EJB is also not required.

A persistence API that maps objects and stores data in a relational database expects some amount of basic understanding of databases and SQL. In addition, since the API is implemented on top of Java Database Connectivity (JDBC) API that accesses the database, any knowledge of that API will also be an asset but is not absolutely needed.

About the Code Examples

Sometimes a single code example is worth more than the number of words that can fit in a chapter. We have tried to use inlined code examples when it is practical and when it suits the purpose. Although we tend to prefer learning from code rather than reading paragraphs of text, we find it frustrating when a code example goes on for pages, and by the time you reach the end of it you have forgotten what it was you were trying to learn from it. We have attempted to alleviate the distraction of the nonrelevant code bits by using ellipses and eliding the parts that do not contribute to the point of the example. Our hope is that you will agree with us and think that it makes the examples more meaningful, not that the examples are only half-baked.

The API is somewhat flexible about the access modifier of persistent state in that it may be package, protected, or private. We have defined entity state to consistently be private in the examples to highlight how the state should be encapsulated within the entity. For the record, we are not dogmatic about state being private. We just happened to start out doing it that way and never bothered to change.

To ensure that the focus remains on understanding the technology and not puzzling over the sample domain, we have adopted the simplest and most prevalent domain model that we could think of, the tried and true Employee model. While being a bit on the dull side, we had to admit that it was ubiquitous to the point where it was a sure bet that virtually every developer on the planet would understand and be able to relate to it. It contains all of the necessary modeling variability (although admittedly we did have to stretch it a bit in some cases) that is needed to illustrate the concepts and practices of the API.

The examples that accompany the book have been implemented using the official Reference Implementation (RI) of the Java EE 5 application server and the Java Persistence API. The Java EE 5 RI is called "Glassfish" and is a fully featured open source application server that can be obtained and used under the Common Development and Distribution License (CDDL). The RI for the Java Persistence API is called "TopLink Essentials" and is an open source and freely available product derived from the commercially distributed Oracle TopLink enterprise data integration stack. GlassFish and TopLink Essentials can be obtained from the GlassFish project downloads link on java.net, but we recommend going to the persistence page at `http://glassfish. dev.java.net/javaee5/persistence`. TopLink Essentials can also be obtained from the TopLink page on the Oracle Technology Network at `http://www.oracle.com/technology/products/ias/ toplink`.

The examples are available for download on the Apress website at `http://www.apress.com`. We recommend downloading them and poking around. The best way to learn the API is to try it out on your own, and taking an existing model and tweaking it is a great way to get started. The API is its own best selling point. Once you develop with it, you will see that it really does make persistence development much easier than it has ever been before!

Contacting Us

We can be contacted at `michael.keith@oracle.com` and `merrick.schincariol@oracle.com`.

CHAPTER 1

■■■

Introduction

The word *enterprise* is arguably one of the most overused terms in software development today. And yet, when someone states that they are developing an enterprise application, invariably a single word comes to mind: information. Enterprise applications are defined by their need to collect, transform and report on vast amounts of information. And, of course, that information does not simply exist in the ether. Storing and retrieving data is a multibillion dollar business, as evidenced by the burgeoning enterprise integration systems (EIS) and enterprise application integration (EAI) companies that have sprung up in recent years.

Many ways of persisting data have come and gone over the years, and no concept has had more staying power than the relational database. It turns out that the vast majority of the world's corporate data is now stored in relational databases. They are the starting point for every enterprise application with a lifespan that may continue long after the application has faded away.

Understanding the relational data is key to successful enterprise development. Developing applications to work well with database systems has become the primary business of software development. For Java in particular, part of its success can be attributed to the widespread adoption of the language for building enterprise database systems. From consumer web sites to automated gateways, Java applications are at the heart of enterprise data development.

Despite the success the Java platform has had in working with database systems, it still suffers from a problem. Moving data back and forth between a database system and the object model of a Java application is a lot harder than it needs to be. Java developers either seem to spend a lot of time converting row and column data into objects, or they find themselves tied to proprietary frameworks that try to hide the database from the developer.

Fortunately, a solution is finally at hand. Recently standardized and backed by both commercial and open source interests from across the spectrum, the Java Persistence API is set to have a major impact on the way we handle persistence within Java. For the first time, developers have a standard way of bridging the gap between object-oriented domain models and relational database systems.

Over the course of this book we will introduce the Java Persistence API and explore everything that it has to offer developers. Whether you are building client-server applications to collect form data in a Swing application or building a web site using the latest application framework, the Java Persistence API is a framework you can use to be more effective with persistence. One of its major strengths is that it can be slotted into whichever layer, tier, or framework that an application needs it to be in.

To set the stage for the Java Persistence API, this chapter first takes a step back to show where we've been and what problems we are trying to solve. From there we will look at the history of the specification and provide a high-level view of the value it brings to developers.

Java Support for Persistence

The Java platform is well supported for managing persistence to relational databases. From the earliest days of the platform, programming interfaces have existed to provide gateways into the database and even to abstract away much of the vendor-specific persistence requirements of business applications. In the next few sections we will look at the current set of Java standards for persistence and their role in enterprise applications.

JDBC

The second release of the Java platform ushered in the first major support for database persistence with the Java Database Connectivity specification, better known as JDBC. Offering a simple and portable abstraction of the proprietary client programming interfaces offered by database vendors, JDBC allows Java programs to fully interact with the database. This interaction is heavily reliant on SQL, offering developers the chance to write queries and data manipulation statements in the language of the database, but executed and processed using a simple Java programming model.

The irony of JDBC is that while the programming interfaces are portable, the SQL language is not. Despite many attempts to standardize the SQL language, it is still rare to write SQL of any complexity that will run unchanged on any two major database platforms. Even where the languages are the same, each database performs differently depending on the structure of the query, necessitating vendor-specific tuning in most cases.

There is also the issue of tight coupling between Java source and SQL text. Developers are constantly tempted by the lure of ready-to-run SQL queries either dynamically constructed at runtime or simply stored in variables or fields. This is a very effective programming model until the minute you realize that the application has to support a new database vendor and that it doesn't support the dialect of SQL you have been using.

Even with SQL text relegated to property files or other application metadata, there comes a point in working with JDBC where it not only feels wrong, but also becomes a cumbersome exercise to take tabular row and column data and continuously have to convert it back and forth into objects. The application has an object model—why does it have to be so hard to use with the database?

Enterprise JavaBeans

The first release of the Java 2 Enterprise Edition (J2EE) platform introduced a new solution for Java persistence in the form of the *entity bean*, part of the Enterprise JavaBean (EJB) family of components. Intended to fully insulate developers from dealing directly with persistence, it introduced an interface-based approach, where the concrete bean class is never directly used by client code. Instead, a specialized bean compiler generates an implementation of the bean interface that facilitates persistence, security, transaction management, and more, delegating only the business logic to the entity bean implementation. Entity beans are configured using a combination of standard and vendor-specific XML deployment descriptors which have become famous for their complexity and verbosity.

It's probably fair to say that entity beans were over-engineered for the problem they were trying to solve; yet ironically the first release of the technology lacked many features necessary to implement realistic business applications. Relationships between entities had to be managed by the application, requiring foreign key fields to be stored and managed on the bean class. The actual mapping of the entity bean to the database was done entirely using vendor-specific configurations, as was the definition of finders, the entity bean term for queries. Finally, entity beans were modeled as remote objects that used RMI and CORBA, introducing network overhead and restrictions that should never have been added to a persistent object to begin with. The entity bean seemed to have begun by solving the distributed persistent component problem that never existed to begin with, leaving behind the common case of locally accessed lightweight persistent objects.

The EJB 2.0 specification solved many of the problems identified in the early releases. The notion of container-managed entity beans was introduced, where bean classes became abstract and the server was responsible for generating a subclass to manage the persistent data. Local interfaces and container-managed relationships were introduced, allowing associations to be defined between entity beans and automatically kept consistent by the server. This release also saw the introduction of Enterprise JavaBeans Query Language (EJB QL), a query language designed to work with entities that could be portably compiled to any SQL dialect.

Despite the improvements introduced with EJB 2.0, there is one problem that could not be overcome by the EJB expert group: complexity. The specification assumed that development tools would insulate the developer from the challenge of configuring and managing the sheer number of artifacts that were required for each bean. Unfortunately, these tools took too long to materialize, and the development burden fell squarely on the shoulders of the developer even as the size and scope of EJB applications increased. Developers felt abandoned in a sea of complexity without the promised infrastructure to keep them afloat.

Java Data Objects

Due in part to some of the failures of the EJB persistence model, and some amount of frustration at not having a standardized persistence API that was satisfactory, another persistence specification effort was attempted. Java Data Objects (JDO) was inspired and supported primarily by the object-oriented database (OODB) community at the outset and probably at least partly because it did not garner the support that a specification needed to become adopted by the community. It required that vendors enhance the bytecode of the domain objects to produce class files that were binary-compatible across all vendors, and every compliant vendor had to be capable of both producing and consuming them. It also had a query language that was decidedly object-oriented in nature, which did not sit well with the relational database users, who as it turned out were the majority.

JDO reached the status of being an extension of the Java Development Kit (JDK) but never became an integrated part of the enterprise Java platform. It had a great many good features in it and was adopted by a small community of devoted and loyal users who stuck by it and tried to promote it. Unfortunately the major commercial vendors did not share the same view of how a persistence framework should be implemented. Few supported the specification, and as a result JDO spent most of its time in the persistence underground.

Some might argue that it was slightly ahead of its time and that its reputation for enhancement caused it to be unfairly stigmatized. This was probably true, and if it had been introduced three years later, it might have been much more accepted by a developer community that now thinks nothing of using frameworks that make extensive use of bytecode enhancement. Once the EJB 3.0 persistence movement was in motion, however, and the major vendors all signed up to be a part of the new enterprise persistence standard, the writing was on the wall for JDO. People soon complained to Sun that they now had two persistence specifications, one that was part of its enterprise platform and also worked in Java SE, and one that was standardized only for Java SE. Shortly thereafter Sun announced that JDO would be reduced to specification maintenance mode and that the Java Persistence API would draw from both JDO and the other persistence vendors and become the single supported standard going forward.

Why Another Standard?

Software developers knew what they wanted, but many could not find it in the existing standards, so they decided to look elsewhere. What they found was proprietary persistence frameworks, both in the commercial and open source domains. The products that implemented these technologies adopted a persistence model that did not intrude upon the domain objects. Persistence was nonintrusive to the business objects in that, unlike entity beans, they did not have to be aware of the technology that was persisting them. They did not have to implement any type of interface or extend a special class. The developer could simply develop the persistent object as with any other Java object, and then map it to a persistent store and use a persistence API to persist the object. Because the objects were regular Java objects, this persistence model came to be known as POJO (Plain Old Java Object) persistence.

The two most popular of these persistence APIs were TopLink in the commercial space and Hibernate in the open source community. These and other products grew to support all the major application servers and provided applications with all of the persistence features they needed. Application developers were quite satisfied to use a third-party product for their persistence needs.

As Hibernate, TopLink, and other persistence APIs became ensconced in applications and met the needs of the application perfectly well, the question was often asked, "Why bother updating the EJB standard to match what these products already did? Why not just continue to use these products as has already been done for years, or why not even just standardize on an open source product like Hibernate?" There are actually a great many reasons why this is not only infeasible but also unpalatable.

A standard goes far deeper than a product, and a single product (even a product as successful as Hibernate or TopLink) cannot embody a specification, even though it can implement one. At its very core, the intention of a specification is that it be implemented by different vendors and that it have different products offer standard interfaces and semantics that can be assumed by applications without coupling the application to any one product.

Binding a standard to an open source project like Hibernate would be problematic for the standard and probably even worse for the Hibernate project. Imagine a specification that was based on a specific version or checkpoint of the code base of an open source project, and how confusing that would be. Now imagine an open source software (OSS) project that could not change or could change only in discrete versions controlled by a special committee every two years, as opposed to the changes being decided by the project itself. Hibernate, and indeed any open source project, would likely be suffocated.

Standardization may not be valued by the consultant or the five-person software shop, but to a corporation it is huge. Software technologies are a big investment for most corporate IT shops, and when large sums of money are involved, risk must be measured. Using a standard technology reduces that risk substantially and allows the corporation to be able to switch vendors if the initial choice turns out not to have met the need.

Besides portability, the value of standardizing a technology is manifested in all sorts of other areas as well. Education, design patterns, and industry communication are just some of the many other benefits that standards bring to the table.

Object-Relational Mapping

"The domain model has a class. The database has a table. They look pretty similar. It should be simple to convert from one to the other automatically." This is a thought we've probably all had at one point or another while writing yet another Data Access Object to convert JDBC result sets into something object-oriented. The domain model looks similar enough to the relational model of the database that it seems to cry out for a way to make the two models talk to each other.

The science of bridging the gap between the object model and the relational model is known as *object-relational mapping*, often referred to as O-R mapping or simply ORM. The term comes from the idea that we are in some way mapping the concepts from one model onto another, with the goal of introducing a mediator to manage the automatic transformation of one to the other.

Before going into the specifics of object-relational mapping, let's define a brief manifesto of sorts for what the ideal solution *should* be:

- **Objects, not tables.** Applications should be written in terms of the domain model and not be bound to the relational model. It must be possible to operate on and query against the domain model without having to express it in the relational language of tables, columns, and foreign keys.

- **Convenience, not ignorance.** The task of mapping will be and should be done by someone familiar with relational technology. O-R mapping is not for someone who does not want to understand the mapping problems or have them hidden from their view. It is meant for those who have an understanding of the issues and know what they want but who just don't want to have to write thousands of lines of code that somebody has already written to solve the problem.

- **Unobtrusive, not transparent.** It is unreasonable to expect that persistence be transparent since an application always needs to have control of the objects that it is persisting and be aware of the entity life cycle. The persistence solution should not intrude on the domain model, however, and domain classes must not be required to extend classes or implement interfaces in order to be persistable.

- **Legacy data, new objects.** It is far more likely that an application will target an existing relational database schema instead of creating a new one. Support for legacy schemas is one of the most relevant use cases that will arise, and it is quite possible that such databases will outlive every one of us.

- **Enough, but not too much.** Enterprise applications have problems to solve, and they need features sufficient to solve those problems. What they don't like is being forced to eat a heavyweight persistence model that introduces large overhead because it is solving problems that many do not even agree are problems.

- **Local, but mobile.** A persistent representation of data does not need to be modeled as a full-fledged remote object. Distribution is something that exists as part of the application, not part of the persistence layer. The entities that contain the persistent state, however, must be able to travel to whichever layer needs them.

This would appear to be a somewhat demanding set of requirements, but it is one born of both practical experience and necessity. Enterprise applications have very specific persistence needs, and this shopping list of items is a fairly specific representation of the experience of the enterprise community.

The Impedance Mismatch

Advocates for object-relational mapping often describe the difference between the object model and the relational model as the *impedance mismatch* between the two. This is an apt description because the challenge of mapping one to the other lies not in the similarities between the two, but in the many concepts in both for which there is no logical equivalent in the other.

In the following sections we will present some basic object-oriented domain models and a variety of relational models to persist the same set of data. As you are about to see, the challenge in object-relational mapping is not so much the complexity of a single mapping but that there are so many possible mappings. The goal is not to explain how to get from one point to the other but to understand the roads that may have to be taken to arrive at an intended destination.

Class Representation

Let's begin this discussion with a simple class. Figure 1-1 shows an `Employee` class with four attributes: employee id, employee name, date they started, and current salary.

Figure 1-1. *The* `Employee` *class*

Now consider the relational model shown in Figure 1-2. The ideal representation of this class in the database corresponds to scenario (A). Each field in the class maps directly to a column in the table. The employee number becomes the primary key. With the exception of some slight naming differences, this is a straightforward mapping.

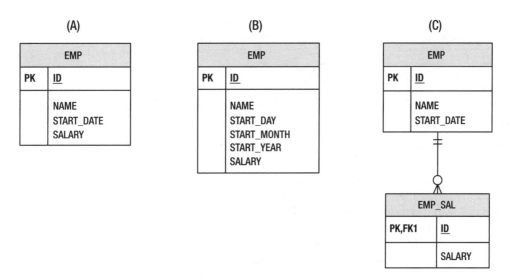

Figure 1-2. *Three scenarios for storing employee data*

In scenario (B), we see that the start date of the employee is actually stored as three separate columns, one each for the day, month, and year. Recall that the class used a Date object to represent this value. As database schemas are much harder to change, should the class be forced to adopt the same storage strategy in order to keep parity with the relational model? Also consider the inverse of the problem, where the class had used three fields and the table used a single date column. Even a single field becomes complex to map when the database and object model differ in representation.

Salary information is considered sensitive information, so it may be unwise to place the salary value directly in the EMP table, which may be used for a number of purposes. In scenario (C), the EMP table has been split so that the salary information is stored in a separate EMP_SAL table. This allows the database administrator to restrict SELECT access on salary information to only those users who genuinely require it. With such a mapping, even a single store operation for the Employee class now requires inserts or updates to two different tables.

Clearly, even storing the data from a single class in a database can be a challenging exercise. We concern ourselves with these scenarios because real database schemas in production systems were never designed with object models in mind. The rule of thumb in enterprise applications is that the needs of the database trump the wants of the application. It's up to the object model to adapt and find ways to work with the database schema without letting the physical design overpower the logical application model.

Relationships

Objects rarely exist in isolation. Just like relationships in a database, domain classes depend on and associate themselves with other domain classes. Consider the Employee class introduced in Figure 1-1. There are many domain concepts we could associate with an employee, but for now let's introduce the Address domain class, for which an Employee may have at most one instance. We say in this case that Employee has a one-to-one relationship with Address, represented in the Unified Modeling Language (UML) model by the 0..1 notation. Figure 1-3 demonstrates this relationship.

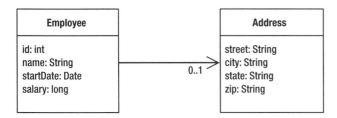

Figure 1-3. *The* Employee *and* Address *relationship*

We discussed different scenarios for representing the Employee state in the previous section, and likewise there are several approaches to representing a relationship in a database schema. Figure 1-4 demonstrates three different scenarios for a one-to-one relationship between an employee and an address.

The building block for relationships in the database is the foreign key. Each scenario involves foreign key relationships between the various tables, but in order for there to be a foreign key relationship, the target table must have a primary key. And so before we even get to associate employees and addresses with each other we have a problem. The domain class Address does not have an identifier, yet the table that it would be stored in must have one if it is to be part of relationships. We could construct a primary key out of all of the columns in the ADDRESS table, but this is considered bad practice. Therefore the ID column is introduced and the object relational mapping will have to adapt in some way.

In scenario (A) of Figure 1-4 we have the ideal mapping of this relationship. The EMP table has a foreign key to the ADDRESS table stored in the ADDRESS_ID column. If the domain class holds onto an instance of the Address class, then the primary key value for the address can be set during store operations.

And yet consider scenario (B), which is only slightly different yet suddenly much more complex. In our domain model, Address did not hold onto the Employee instance that owned it, and yet the employee primary key must be stored in the ADDRESS table. The object-relational mapping must either account for this mismatch between domain class and table or a reference back to the employee will have to be added for every address.

To make matters worse, scenario (C) introduces a join table to relate the EMP and ADDRESS tables. Instead of storing the foreign keys directly in one of the domain tables, the join table instead holds onto the pair of keys. Every database operation involving the two tables must now traverse the join table and keep it consistent. We could introduce an EmployeeAddress association class into our domain model to compensate, but that defeats the logical representation we are trying to achieve.

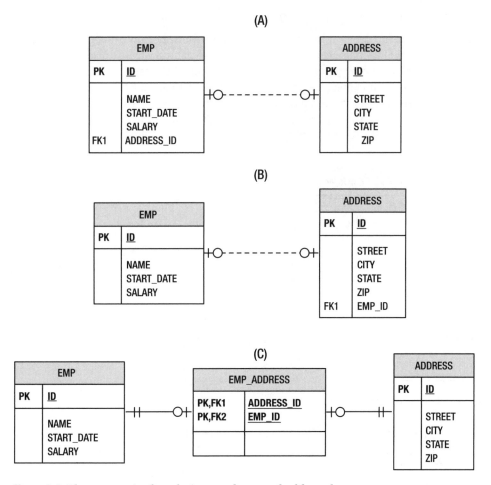

Figure 1-4. *Three scenarios for relating employee and address data*

Relationships present a challenge in any object-relational mapping solution. In this introduction we have covered only one-to-one relationships, and yet we have been faced with the need for primary keys not in the object model and the possibility of having to introduce extra relationships into the model or even association classes to compensate for the database schema.

Inheritance

A defining element of an object-oriented domain model is the opportunity to introduce generalized relationships between like classes. Inheritance is the natural way to express these relationships and allows for polymorphism in the application. Let's revisit the `Employee` class shown in Figure 1-1 and imagine a company that needs to distinguish between full-time and part-time employees. Part-time employees work off of an hourly rate, while full-time employees are assigned a salary. This is a good opportunity for inheritance, moving wage information to `PartTimeEmployee` and `FullTimeEmployee` subclasses. Figure 1-5 shows this arrangement.

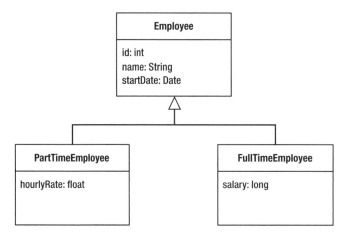

Figure 1-5. *Inheritance relationships between full-time and part-time employees*

   Inheritance presents a genuine problem for object-relational mapping. We are no longer dealing with a situation where there is a natural mapping from a class to a table. Consider the relational models shown in Figure 1-6. Once again we demonstrate three different strategies for persisting the same set of data.

   Arguably the easiest solution for someone mapping an inheritance structure to a database would be to put all of the data necessary for each class (including parent classes) into separate tables. This strategy is demonstrated by scenario (A) in Figure 1-6. Note that there is no relationship between the tables. This means that queries against these tables are now much more complicated if the user needs to operate on both full-time and part-time employees in a single step.

   An efficient but denormalized alternative is to place all of the data required for every class in the model in a single table. That makes it very easy to query, but note the structure of the table shown in scenario (B) of Figure 1-6. There is a new column, `TYPE`, which does not exist in any part of the domain model. The `TYPE` column indicates whether or not the employee is part-time or full-time. This information must now be interpreted by an object-relational mapping solution to know what kind of domain class to instantiate for any given row in the table.

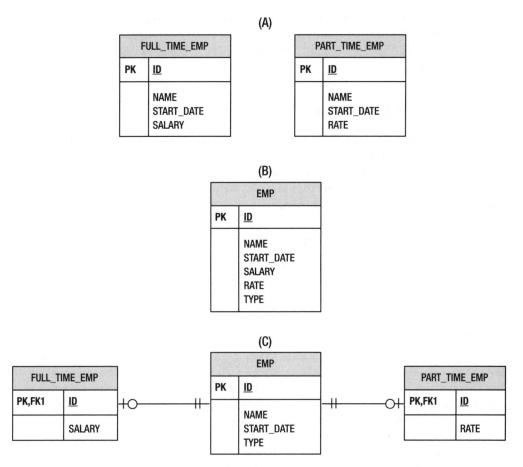

Figure 1-6. *Inheritance strategies in a relational model*

Scenario (C) takes this one step further, this time normalizing the data into separate tables each for full-time and part-time employees. Unlike scenario (A), however, these tables are related by a common EMP table that stores all of the data common to both employee types. It might seem like an excessive solution for a single column of extra data, but a real schema with many columns specific to each type of employee would likely use this type of table structure. It presents the data in a logical form and also simplifies querying by allowing the tables to be joined together. Unfortunately, what works well for the database does not necessarily work well for an object model mapped to such a schema. Even without associations to other classes, the object-relational mapping of the domain class must now take joins between multiple tables into account.

When you start to consider abstract superclasses or parent classes with no persistent form, inheritance rapidly becomes a complex issue in object-relational mapping. Not only is there a challenge with storage of the class data, but the complex table relationships are difficult to query efficiently.

The Java Persistence API

The Java Persistence API is a lightweight, POJO-based framework for Java persistence. Although object-relational mapping is a major component of the API, it also offers solutions to the architectural challenges of integrating persistence into scalable enterprise applications. In the following sections we will look at the evolution of the specification and provide an overview of the major aspects of this technology.

History of the Specification

The Java Persistence API is remarkable not only for what it offers developers but also for the way in which it came to be. The following sections outline the prehistory of object-relational persistence solutions and the genesis of the Java Persistence API as part of EJB 3.0.

The Early Years

It may come as a surprise to learn that object-relational mapping solutions have been around for a long time, longer even than the Java language itself. Products such as Oracle TopLink originally got their start in the Smalltalk world before making the switch to Java. Perhaps one of the greatest ironies in the history of Java persistence solutions is that one of the first implementations of entity beans, which have long been criticized for their complexity, was actually demonstrated by mapping the bean class and persisting it using TopLink.

Commercial object-relational mapping products like TopLink have been available since the earliest days of the Java language. They were successful, but the techniques were never standardized for the Java platform. An approach similar to object-relational mapping was standardized in the form of JDO, but as we mentioned previously, that standard failed to gain any significant market penetration.

It was actually the popularity of open source object-relational mapping solutions such as Hibernate that led to some surprising changes in the direction of persistence in the Java platform and brought about a convergence towards object-relational mapping as the preferred solution.

EJB 3.0

After years of complaints about the complexity of building enterprise applications with Java, "ease of development" was adopted as the theme for the Java EE 5.0 platform release. The members of the EJB 3.0 expert group were charged with finding ways to make Enterprise JavaBeans easier and more productive to use.

In the case of session beans and message-driven beans, solutions for usability issues were largely cosmetic in scope. By simply removing some of the more onerous implementation requirements and letting components look more like plain Java objects, the goal was largely achieved early on.

In the case of entity beans, however, a more serious problem faced the expert group. If the definition of "ease of use" is to keep implementation interfaces and descriptors out of application code and to embrace the natural object model of the Java language, how do you make coarse-grained, interface-driven, container-managed entity beans look and feel like a domain model?

The conclusion reached by the expert group was nothing short of remarkable: *start over*. Leave entity beans alone and introduce a new model for persistence. And start over we did, but not from scratch. The Java Persistence API was born out of recognition of the demands of practitioners and the existing proprietary solutions that they were using to solve their problems. To ignore that experience would have been folly.

The expert group reached out to the leading vendors of object-relational mapping solutions and invited them to come forward and standardize the best practices represented by their products. Hibernate and TopLink were the first to sign on with the existing EJB vendors, followed later by the JDO vendors.

Years of industry experience coupled with a mission to simplify development combined to produce the first specification to truly embrace the new programming models offered by the Java SE 5 platform. The use of annotations in particular resulted in a new way of using persistence in applications that had never been seen before.

The resulting EJB 3.0 specification ended up being divided into three distinct pieces and split across three separate documents. The first includes the existing EJB 2.1 APIs and the traditional contracts from the perspectives of the container, the bean provider, and the client. This content was incremented by the additional Java EE injection features as well as the new EJB 3.0 interceptor specifications and lifecycle callback changes. This is the heavy document that describes the "old school" of EJB development plus some of the new features that have been made available to the old API.

The second document describes a simplified API that people can use to develop new session and message-driven components against. It is essentially an overview of the ease-of-use features that were introduced for EJB components by EJB 3.0. It outlines the basic ideas of how to define and annotate beans, use them without home interfaces, add callback methods and interceptors, and apply these new features.

The third document is the Java Persistence API, a stand-alone specification that describes the persistence model in both the Java SE and Java EE environments, and the subject of this book. In the next iteration the Java Persistence API will become a separate specification in the Java EE platform, distinct from the Enterprise JavaBeans specification.

Overview

The model of the Java Persistence API is simple and elegant, powerful and flexible. It is natural to use, and easy to learn, especially if you have used any of the existing persistence products on the market today on which the API was based. The main operational API that an application will be exposed to is contained within only a few classes.

POJO Persistence

Perhaps the most important aspect of the Java Persistence API is the fact that the objects are POJOs, meaning that there is nothing special about any object that is made persistent. In fact, any existing application object can be made persistent without so much as changing a single line of code. Object-relational mapping with the Java Persistence API is entirely metadata-driven. It can be done either by adding annotations to the code or using externally defined

XML. The objects that are persisted are lightweight in memory and as light as the user happens to define and map them in the database.

Non-intrusiveness

The persistence API exists as a separate layer from the persistent objects. The persistence API is called by the application business logic and is passed the persistence objects and instructed to operate upon them. So even though the application must be aware of the persistence API, since it has to call into it, the persistent objects themselves need not be aware. This is noteworthy because some people are under the misconception that transparent persistence means that objects magically get persisted, the way that object databases of yesteryear used to do when a transaction got committed. This is an incorrect notion and even more irrational when you think about querying. You need to have some way of retrieving the objects from the data store. This requires a separate API object and, in fact, even object databases used separate Extent objects to issue queries. Applications absolutely need to manage their persistent objects in very explicit ways, and they require a designated API to do it. Because the API does not intrude upon the persistent objects themselves, we call this *non-intrusive persistence*.

Object Queries

A powerful query framework offers the ability to query across entities and their relationships without having to use concrete foreign keys or database columns. Queries are expressed in Java Persistence Query Language, a query language that is derived from EJB QL and modeled after SQL for its familiarity, but it is not tied to the database schema. Queries use a schema abstraction that is based on the state of an entity as opposed to the columns in which the entity is stored. Creating a query does not require knowledge of the database mapping information and typically returns results that are in the form of entities.

A query may be defined statically in metadata or created dynamically by passing query criteria when constructing it. It is also possible to escape to SQL if a special query requirement exists that cannot be met by the SQL generation from the persistence framework. These queries can all return results that are entities and are valuable abstractions that enable querying across the Java domain model instead of across database tables.

Mobile Entities

Client/server and web applications and other distributed architectures are clearly the most popular types of applications in a connected world. To acknowledge this fact meant acknowledging that persistent entities must be mobile in the network. Objects must be able to be moved from one virtual machine to another and then back again, and must still be usable by the application.

The detachment model provides a way of reconciling any newly relocated or deserialized instance that may have changed state along the way, with the instance or state that was left behind. Objects that leave the persistence layer are called detached, and a key feature of the persistence model is the ability to reattach such detached entities upon their return.

Simple Configuration

There are a great number of persistence features that the specification has to offer and which we will explain in the chapters of this book. All of the features are configurable through the use of Java SE 5 annotations, or XML, or a combination of the two. Annotations offer ease of use that is unparalleled in the history of Java metadata. They are convenient to write and painless to read, and they make it possible for beginners to get an application going quickly and easily. Configuration may also be done in XML for those who like XML or are more comfortable with it. Of greater significance than the metadata language is the fact that the Java Persistence API 3.0 makes heavy use of defaults. This means that no matter which method is chosen, the amount of metadata that will be required just to get running is the absolute minimum. In some cases, if the defaults are good enough almost no metadata will be required at all.

Integration and Testability

Multitier applications hosted on an application server have become the de facto standard for application architectures. Testing on an application server is a challenge that few relish. It can bring pain and hardship, and it is often prohibitive to unit testing and white box testing.

This is solved by defining the API to work outside as well as inside the application server. While it is not as common a use case, those applications that do run on two tiers (the application talking directly to the database tier) can use the persistence API without the existence of an application server at all. The more common scenario is for unit tests and automated testing frameworks that can be run easily and conveniently in Java SE environments.

The Java Persistence API really has introduced a new era in standardized integrated persistence. When running inside a container, all of the benefits of container support and superior ease of use apply, but the same application may also be configured to run outside the container as well.

Summary

In this chapter we presented an introduction to the Java Persistence API. We began with an overview of current standards for persistence, looking at JDBC, EJB, and JDO. In each case, we looked at the conditions forced on us by these frameworks and developed a view of what a better solution could be.

In the Object-Relational Mapping section we introduced the primary problem facing developers trying to use object-oriented domain models in concert with a relational database: the impedance mismatch. To demonstrate the complexity bridging the gap, we presented three small object models and nine different ways to represent the same information.

We concluded the chapter with a brief look at the Java Persistence API. We looked at the history of the specification and the vendors who came together to create it. We then looked at the role it plays in enterprise application development and introduced the feature set offered by the specification.

In the next chapter we will get our feet wet with the Java Persistence API, taking a whirlwind tour of the API basics and building a simple application in the process.

CHAPTER 2

■■■

Getting Started

From the outset, one of the main goals when creating the Java Persistence API was to ensure that it is simple to use and easy to understand. Although the problem domain cannot be trivialized or watered down, the technology that enables one to deal with it can be straightforward and intuitive. In this chapter we will show how effortless it is to develop and use entities.

We will start this chapter off by describing the basic characteristics of entities. We'll define what an entity is and how to create, read, update, and delete them. We'll also introduce entity managers and how they are obtained and used. Then we'll take a quick look at queries and how to specify and execute a query using the `EntityManager` and `Query` objects. The chapter will conclude by showing a simple working application that runs in a standard Java SE 5 environment and that demonstrates all of the example code in action.

Entity Overview

The entity is not a new thing. In fact, entities have been around longer than many programming languages and certainly longer than Java. They were first introduced by Peter Chen in his seminal paper on entity-relationship modeling.[1] He described entities as things that have attributes and relationships. The expectation was that the attributes were going to be persisted in a relational database, as were the relationships.

Even now, the definition still holds true. An *entity* is essentially a noun, or a grouping of state associated together as a single unit. It may participate in relationships to any number of other entities in a number of standard ways. In the object-oriented paradigm, we would add behavior to it and call it an object. In the Java Persistence API, any application-defined object can be an entity, so the important question might be, What are the characteristics of an object that has been turned into an entity?

Persistability

The first and most basic characteristic of entities is that they are *persistable*. This generally just means that they can be made persistent. More specifically it means that their state can be represented in a data store and can be accessed at a later time, perhaps well after the end of the process that created it.

---

1. Peter C. Chen, "The entity-relationship model—toward a unified view of data," *ACM Transactions on Database Systems* 1, no. 1 (1976): 9–36.

We could call them persistent objects, and many people do, but it is not technically correct. Strictly speaking, a persistent object becomes persistent the moment it is instantiated. If a persistent object exists, then by definition it is already persistent.

An entity is persistable because it *can* be created in a persistent store. The difference is that it is not automatically persisted and that in order for it to have a persistent representation the application must actively invoke an API method to initiate the process. This is an important distinction because it leaves control over persistence firmly in the hands of the application. It offers the application the flexibility to manipulate data and perform business logic on the entity, and then only when the application decides that it is the right time to persist the entity, actually causing it to be persistent. The lesson is that entities may be manipulated without necessarily having persistent repercussions, and it is the application that decides whether or not they do.

Identity

Like any other Java object, an entity has an object identity, but when it exists in the data store it also has a *persistent identity*. Persistent identity, or an *identifier*, is the key that uniquely identifies an entity instance and distinguishes it from all of the other instances of the same entity type. An entity has a persistent identity when there exists a representation of it in the data store, that is, a row in a database table. If it is not in the database then even though the in-memory entity may have its identity set in a field, it does not have a persistent identity. The entity identifier, then, is equivalent to the primary key in the database table that stores the entity state.

Transactionality

Entities are what we might call *quasi-transactional*. They are normally only created, updated, and deleted within a transaction,[2] and a transaction is required for the changes to be committed in the database. Changes made to the database either succeed or fail atomically, so the persistent view of an entity should indeed be transactional.

In memory it is a slightly different story in the sense that entities may be changed without the changes ever being persisted. Even when enlisted in a transaction, they may be left in an undefined or inconsistent state in the event of a rollback or transaction failure. The in-memory entities are simple Java objects that obey all of the rules and constraints that are applied by the Java virtual machine to other Java objects.

Granularity

Finally, we can also learn something about what entities are by describing what they are *not*. They are not primitives, primitive wrappers, or built-in objects. These are no more than scalars and do not have any designated semantic meaning to an application. A string, for example is too fine-grained an object to be an entity because it does not have any domain-specific connotation. Rather, a string is well-suited and very often used as a type for an entity attribute and given meaning according to the entity attribute that it is typing.

---

2. In most cases this is a requirement, but in certain configurations the transaction may not be present until later.

Entities are fine-grained objects that have a set of aggregated state that is normally stored in a single place, such as a row in a table, and typically have relationships to other entities. In the most general sense they are business domain objects that have specific meaning to the application that accesses them.

While it is certainly true that entities may be defined in exaggerated ways to be as fine-grained as storing a single string or coarse-grained enough to contain 500 columns' worth of data, the suggested granularity of an entity is definitely on the smaller end of the spectrum. Ideally, entities should be designed and defined as fairly lightweight objects of equal or smaller size than that of the average Java object.

Entity Metadata

Associated with every entity is metadata in some amount, possibly small, that describes it. This metadata enables the persistence layer to recognize, interpret, and properly manage the entity from the time it is loaded through to its runtime invocation.

The metadata that is actually required for each entity is minimal, rendering entities easy to define and use. However, like any sophisticated technology with its share of switches, levers, and buttons, there is also the possibility to specify much, much more metadata than is required. It may be extensive amounts, depending upon the application requirements, and may be used to customize every detail of the entity configuration or state mappings.

Entity metadata may be specified in one of two ways—annotations or XML. Each is equally valid, but the one that you use will depend upon your development preferences or process.

Annotations

Annotation metadata is a language feature that allows structured and typed metadata to be attached to the source code. It was introduced as part of Java SE 5 and is a key part of the EJB 3.0 and Java EE 5 specifications.[3] Although annotations are not required by the Java Persistence API, they are a convenient way to learn and use the API. Because annotations co-locate the metadata with the program artifacts, it is not necessary to escape to an additional file and additional language (XML) just to specify the metadata.

Annotations are used throughout both the examples and the accompanying explanations in this book. All of the API annotations that are shown and described, except for Chapter 3, which talks about Java EE annotations, are defined in the `javax.persistence` package. Example code snippets can be assumed to have an implicit import of the form `import javax.persistence.*;`.

XML

For those who prefer to use the traditional XML descriptors, this option is still available. It should be a fairly straightforward process to switch to using XML descriptors after having learned and understood the annotations since the XML has in large part been patterned after the annotations. Chapter 10 describes how to use XML to specify or override entity mapping metadata.

---

3. The Java EE 5 platform specification and all of its sub-specifications require the use of Java SE 5.

ANNOTATIONS

Java annotations are specially defined types that may annotate (be attached to or placed in front of) Java programming elements including classes, methods, fields, and variables. When they annotate a program element, the compiler reads the information contained in them and may retain it in the class files or dispose of it according to what was specified in the annotation type definition. When retained in the class files the elements contained in the annotation may be queried at runtime through a reflection-based API. A running program can in this way obtain the metadata that exists on a Java program element. An example of a custom annotation type definition that could be used to indicate classes that should be validated (whatever validate means to the application or tool that is processing it) is:

```
@Target(TYPE) @Retention(RUNTIME)
public @interface Validate {
    boolean flag;
}
```

This annotation definition is in fact itself annotated by @Target and @Retention built-in annotations that determine what kinds of program elements the annotation may annotate and at what point the annotation metadata should be discarded from the class. The annotation defined above may annotate any type and will not be discarded from the class (that is, it will be retained in the class file even at runtime). This annotation may, for example, annotate any given class definition. An example usage of this annotation could be:

```
@Validate(flag=true)
public class MyClass {
    ...
}
```

An application that looks at all classes in the system for this annotation will be able to determine that MyClass should be validated and perform that validation whenever it makes sense. The semantic meaning of @Validate is completely up to the component that defines the annotation type and the one that reads and processes the annotation.

Configuration by Exception

The notion of *configuration by exception* means that the persistence engine defines defaults that apply to the majority of applications and that users need to supply values only when they want to override the default value. In other words, having to supply a configuration value is the exception to the rule, not a requirement.

Configuration by exception is ingrained in the Java Persistence API and is a strong contributing factor to its usability. The majority of configuration values have defaults, rendering the metadata that does have to be specified more relevant and concise.

The extensive use of defaults and the ease of use that it brings to configuration comes with a price, however. When defaults are embedded into the API and do not have to be specified, then they are not visible or obvious to users. This *can* make it possible for users to be unaware of the complexity of developing persistence applications, making it slightly more difficult to debug or to change the behavior when it becomes necessary.

Defaults are not meant to shield users from the often complex issues surrounding persistence. They are meant to allow a developer to get started easily and quickly with something that will work and then iteratively improve and implement additional functionality as the complexity of their application increases. Even though the defaults may be what you want to have happen most of the time, it is still fairly important for developers to be familiar with the default values that are being applied. For example, if a table name default is being assumed, then it is important to know what table the runtime is expecting, or if schema generation is used, what table will be generated.

For each of the annotations we will also discuss the default value so that it is clear what will be applied if the annotation is not specified. We recommend that you remember these defaults as you learn them. After all, a default value is still part of the configuration of the application; it was just really easy to configure!

Creating an Entity

Regular Java classes are easily transformed into entities simply by annotating them. In fact, by adding a couple of annotations, virtually any class with a no-arg constructor can become an entity.

Let's start by creating a regular Java class for an employee. Listing 2-1 shows a simple Employee class.

Listing 2-1. Employee *Class*

```
public class Employee {
    private int id;
    private String name;
    private long salary;

    public Employee() {}
    public Employee(int id) { this.id = id; }

    public int getId() { return id; }
    public void setId(int id) { this.id = id; }
    public String getName() { return name; }
    public void setName(String name) { this.name = name; }
    public long getSalary() { return salary; }
    public void setSalary (long salary) { this.salary = salary; }
}
```

You may notice that this class resembles a JavaBean-style class with three properties: id, name, and salary. Each of these properties is represented by a pair of accessor methods to get and set the property and is backed by a member field. Properties or member fields are the units of state within the entity that we want to persist.

To turn Employee into an entity we first need to annotate the class with @Entity. This is primarily just a marker annotation to indicate to the persistence engine that the class is an entity.

The second annotation that we need to add is @Id. This annotates the particular field or property that holds the persistent identity of the entity (the primary key) and is needed so the provider knows which field or property to use as the unique identifying key in the table.

Adding these two annotations to our Employee class, we end up with pretty much the same class that we had before, except that now it is an entity. Listing 2-2 shows the entity class.

Listing 2-2. Employee *Entity*

```
@Entity
public class Employee {
    @Id private int id;
    private String name;
    private long salary;

    public Employee() {}
    public Employee(int id) { this.id = id; }

    public int getId() { return id; }
    public void setId(int id) { this.id = id; }
    public String getName() { return name; }
    public void setName(String name) { this.name = name; }
    public long getSalary() { return salary; }
    public void setSalary (long salary) { this.salary = salary; }
}
```

When we say that the @Id annotation is placed on the field or property, we mean that the user can choose to annotate either the declared field, or the getter method[4] of a JavaBean-style property. Either field or property strategy is allowed, depending upon the needs and tastes of the entity developer, but whichever strategy is chosen, it must be followed for all persistent state annotations in the entity. We have chosen in this example to annotate the field because it is simpler; in general, this will be the easiest and most direct approach. We will learn more about the details of annotating persistent state using field or property access in subsequent chapters.

Automatic State Mapping

The fields in the entity are automatically made persistable by virtue of their existence in the entity. Default mapping and loading configuration values apply to these fields and enable them to be persisted when the object is persisted. Given the questions that were brought up in the last chapter, one might be led to ask, "How did the fields get mapped, and where do they get persisted to?"

To find the answer we must first take a quick detour to dig inside the @Entity annotation and look at an element called name that uniquely identifies the entity. The entity name may be explicitly specified for any entity by using this name element in the annotation, as in @Entity(name="Emp"). In practice this is seldom specified because it gets defaulted to be the unqualified name of the entity class. This is almost always both reasonable and adequate.

Now we can get back to the question about where the data gets stored. It turns out that the default name of the table used to store any given entity of a particular entity type is the name

---

4. Annotations on setter methods will just be ignored.

of the entity. If we have specified the name of the entity, then that will be the default table name, but if we have not, then the default value of the entity name will be used. We just stated that the default entity name was the unqualified name of the entity class, so that is effectively the answer to the question of which table gets used. In our Employee example all entities of type Employee will get stored in a table called EMPLOYEE.

Each of the fields or properties has individual state in it and needs to be directed to a particular column in the table. We know to go to the EMPLOYEE table, but we don't know which column to use for any given field or property. When no columns are explicitly specified, then the default column is used for a field or property, which is just the name of the field or property itself. So our employee id will get stored in the ID column, the name in the NAME column, and the salary in the SALARY column of the EMPLOYEE table.

Of course these values can all be overridden to match an existing schema. We will discuss how to override them when we get to Chapter 4 and discuss mapping in more detail.

Entity Manager

In the Entity Overview section, it was stated that a specific API call needs to be invoked before an entity actually gets persisted to the database. In fact, separate API calls are needed to perform many of the operations on entities. This API is implemented by the entity manager and encapsulated almost entirely within a single interface called EntityManager. When all is said and done, it is to an entity manager that the real work of persistence is delegated. Until an entity manager is used to actually create, read, or write an entity, the entity is nothing more than a regular (non-persistent) Java object.

When an entity manager obtains a reference to an entity, either by having it explicitly passed in or because it was read from the database, that object is said to be *managed* by the entity manager. The set of managed entity instances within an entity manager at any given time is called its *persistence context*. Only one Java instance with the same persistent identity may exist in a persistence context at any time. For example, if an Employee with a persistent identity (or id) of 158 exists in the persistence context, then no other object with its id set to 158 may exist within that same persistence context.

Entity managers are configured to be able to persist or manage specific types of objects, read and write to a given database, and be implemented by a particular *persistence provider* (or *provider* for short). It is the provider that supplies the backing implementation engine for the entire Java Persistence API, from the EntityManager through to Query implementation and SQL generation.

All entity managers come from factories of type EntityManagerFactory. The configuration for an entity manager is bound to the EntityManagerFactory that created it, but it is defined separately as a *persistence unit*. A persistence unit dictates either implicitly or explicitly the settings and entity classes used by all entity managers obtained from the unique EntityManagerFactory instance bound to that persistence unit. There is, therefore, a one-to-one correspondence between a persistence unit and its concrete EntityManagerFactory.

Persistence units are named to allow differentiation of one EntityManagerFactory from another. This gives the application control over which configuration or persistence unit is to be used for operating on a particular entity.

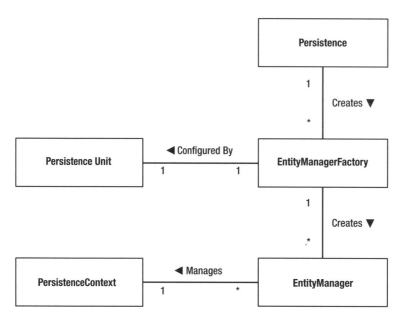

Figure 2-1. *Relationships between Java Persistence API concepts*

Figure 2-1 shows that for each persistence unit there is an EntityManagerFactory and that many entity managers can be created from a single EntityManagerFactory. The part that may come as a surprise is that many entity managers can point to the same persistence context. We have talked only about an entity manager and its persistence context, but later on we will see that this is indeed the case and that there may be multiple references to different entity managers which all point to the same group of managed entities.

Obtaining an Entity Manager

An entity manager is always obtained from an EntityManagerFactory. The factory from which it was obtained determines the configuration parameters that govern its operation. While there are shortcuts that veil the factory from the user view when running in a Java EE application server environment, in the Java SE environment we can use a simple bootstrap class called Persistence. The static createEntityManagerFactory() method in the Persistence class returns the EntityManagerFactory for the specified persistence unit name. The following example demonstrates creating an EntityManagerFactory for the persistence unit named "EmployeeService":

```
EntityManagerFactory emf =
    Persistence.createEntityManagerFactory("EmployeeService");
```

The name of the specified persistence unit "EmployeeService" passed into the createEntityManagerFactory() method identifies the given persistence unit configuration that determines such things as the connection parameters that entity managers generated from this factory will use when connecting to the database.

Now that we have a factory, we can easily obtain an entity manager from it. The following example demonstrates creating an entity manager from the factory that we acquired in the previous example:

```
EntityManager em = emf.createEntityManager();
```

With this entity manager, we are now in a position to start working with persistent entities.

Persisting an Entity

Persisting an entity is the operation of taking a transient entity, or one that does not yet have any persistent representation in the database, and storing its state so that it can be retrieved later. This is really the basis of persistence—creating state that may outlive the process that created it. We are going to start by using the entity manager to persist an instance of Employee. Here is a code example that does just that:

```
Employee emp = new Employee(158);
em.persist(emp);
```

The first line in this code segment is simply creating an Employee instance that we want to persist. If we ignore the sad fact that we seem to be employing a nameless individual and paying them nothing (we are setting only the id, not the name or salary) the instantiated Employee is just a regular Java object.

The next line obtains an entity manager and uses it to persist the entity. Calling persist() is all that is required to initiate it being persisted in the database. If the entity manager encounters a problem doing this, then it will throw an unchecked PersistenceException; otherwise the employee will be stored in the database. When the persist() call returns, emp will be a managed entity within the entity manager's persistence context.

Listing 2-3 shows how to incorporate this into a simple method that creates a new employee and persists it to the database.

Listing 2-3. *Method for Creating an Employee*

```
public Employee createEmployee(int id, String name, long salary) {
    Employee emp = new Employee(id);
    emp.setName(name);
    emp.setSalary(salary);
    em.persist(emp);
    return emp;
}
```

This method assumes the existence of an entity manager in the em field of the instance and uses it to persist the Employee. Note that we do not need to worry about the failure case in this example. It will result in a runtime PersistenceException being thrown, which will get propagated up to the caller.

Finding an Entity

Once an entity is in the database, then the next thing one typically wants to do is find it again. In this section we will show how an entity can be found using the entity manager. There is really only one line that we need to show:

```
Employee emp = em.find(Employee.class, 158);
```

We are passing in the class of the entity that is being sought (in this example we are looking for an instance of Employee) and the id or primary key that identifies the particular entity (in our case we want to find the entity that we just created). This is all the information needed by the entity manager to find the instance in the database, and when the call completes, the employee that gets returned will be a managed entity, meaning that it will exist in the current persistence context associated with the entity manager.

PARAMETERIZED TYPES

Another of the principal features included in Java SE 5 was the introduction of generics. The abstraction of Java types allowed them to be parameterized and used generically by a class or method. Such classes or methods that make use of type parameterization are called generic types or generic methods. An example of a generic class is one that defines a parameterized type variable in its definition. It could then use that type in the signature of its methods just as does the following generic class:

```
public class Holder<T> {
    T contents;
    public void setContents(T obj) { contents = obj; }
    public T getContents() { return contents; }
}
```

This Holder class is parameterized by the T type variable making it possible to create an instance that can hold a given type. Why is this better than simply using Object everywhere where T is used? The reason is because once the type is supplied and the Holder is instantiated to be of a given type, then only instances of that type will be allowed to be stored. This makes any given Holder instance strongly typed for the type of our choice. For example, we can do the following:

```
Holder<String> stringHolder = new Holder<String>();
stringHolder.setContents("MyOwnString");
Holder<Integer> intHolder = new Holder<Integer>();
intHolder.setContents(100);
String s = stringHolder.getContents();
stringHolder.setContents(101); // compile error
```

We have a Holder that stores String objects or anything we want, but once we define it then we get the strong compile-time type checking that frees us from having to type-check at runtime. ClassCastExceptions can be a thing of the past (well, almost!). As an added bonus, we don't have to cast. The getContents() generic method returns precisely the type that was passed to Holder as the type parameter, so the compiler can type-check and safely assign as needed.

You may have noticed that there is no cast required to make the return result an Employee object, even though the find() method call can be used for any type of entity. Those who have used Java SE 5 will recognize that this is just because the return type of the find() method is parameterized to return the same class that was passed in, so if Employee was passed as the entity class, then it will also be the return type.

What happens if the object has been deleted or if we supplied the wrong id by accident? In the event that the object was not found, then the find() call simply returns null. We would need to ensure that a null check is performed before the next time the emp variable is used.

The code for a method that looks up and returns the Employee with a given id is now trivial and shown in Listing 2-4.

Listing 2-4. *Method for Finding an Employee*

```
public Employee findEmployee(int id) {
    return em.find(Employee.class, id);
}
```

In the case where no employee exists for the id that is passed in, then the method will return null, since that is what find() will return.

Removing an Entity

Removal of an entity from the database is not as common a thing as some might think. Many applications simply never delete objects, or if they do they just flag the data as being out of date or no longer valid and then just keep it out of sight of clients. We are not talking about that kind of application-level logical removal, where the data is not actually even removed from the database. We are talking about something that results in a DELETE statement being made across one or more tables.

In order to remove an entity, the entity itself must be managed, meaning that it is present in the persistence context. This means that the calling application should have already loaded or accessed the entity and is now issuing a command to remove it. This is not normally a problem given that most often the application will have caused it to become managed as part of the process of determining that this was the object that it wanted to remove.

A simple example for removing an employee is:

```
Employee emp = em.find(Employee.class, 158);
em.remove(emp);
```

In this example we are first finding the entity using the find() call, which returns a managed instance of Employee, and then removing the entity using the remove() call on the entity manager. Of course, we learned in the previous section that if the entity was not found then the find() method will return null. We would get a java.lang.IllegalArgumentException if it turned out that we passed null into the remove() call because we forgot to include a null check before calling remove().

In our application method for removing an employee, we can fix the problem by checking for the existence of the employee before we issue the remove() call, as shown in Listing 2-5.

Listing 2-5. *Method for Removing an Employee*

```
public void removeEmployee(int id) {
    Employee emp = em.find(Employee.class, id);
    if (emp != null) {
        em.remove(emp);
    }
}
```

This method will ensure that the employee with the given id is removed from the database. It will return successfully whether the employee exists or not.

Updating an Entity

An entity may be updated in a few different ways, but for now we will illustrate the most common and simple case. This is the case where we have a managed entity and want to make changes to it. If we do not have a reference to the managed entity, then we must first obtain one using find() and then perform our modifying operations on the managed entity. This code adds $1,000 to the salary of the employee with id 158:

```
Employee emp = em.find(Employee.class, 158);
emp.setSalary(emp.getSalary() + 1000);
```

Note the difference between this operation and the others. In this case we are not calling into the entity manager to modify the object but directly on the object itself. For this reason it is important that the entity be a managed instance, otherwise the persistence provider will have no means of detecting the change, and no changes will be made to the persistent representation of the employee.

Our method to raise the salary of a given employee will take the id and amount of the raise, find the employee, and change the salary to the adjusted one. Listing 2-6 demonstrates this approach.

Listing 2-6. *Method for Updating an Employee*

```
public Employee raiseEmployeeSalary(int id, long raise) {
    Employee emp = em.find(Employee.class, id);
    if (emp != null) {
        emp.setSalary(emp.getSalary() + raise);
    }
    return emp;
}
```

If we can't find the employee, then we return null so the caller will know that no change could be made. We indicate success by returning the updated employee.

Transactions

The keen reader may have noticed something in the code to this point that was inconsistent with earlier statements made about transactionality when working with entities. There were no transactions in any of the above examples, even though we said that changes to entities must be made persistent using a transaction.

In all the examples except the one that only called find(), we assume that a transaction enclosed each method. The find() call is not a mutating operation, so it may be called any time, with or without a transaction.

Once again, the key is the environment in which the code is being executed. The typical situation when running inside the Java EE container environment is that the standard Java Transaction API (JTA) is used. The transaction model when running in the container is to assume the application will ensure that a transactional context is present when one is required. If a transaction is not present, then either the modifying operation will throw an exception or the change will simply never be persisted to the data store. We will come back to discussing transactions in the Java EE environment in more detail in Chapter 3.

In our example in this chapter, though, we are not running in Java EE. We are in a Java SE environment, and the transaction service that should be used in Java SE is the EntityTransaction service. When executing in Java SE we either need to begin and to commit the transaction in the operational methods, or we need to begin and to commit the transaction before and after calling an operational method. In either case, a transaction is started by calling getTransaction() on the entity manager to get the EntityTransaction and then invoking begin() on it. Likewise, to commit the transaction the commit() call is invoked on the EntityTransaction obtained from the entity manager. For example, starting and committing before and after the method would produce code that creates an employee the way it is done in Listing 2-7.

Listing 2-7. *Beginning and Committing an* EntityTransaction

```
em.getTransaction().begin();
createEmployee(158, "John Doe", 45000);
em.getTransaction().commit();
```

Further detail about resource-level transactions and the EntityTransaction API are contained in Chapter 5.

Queries

In general, given that most developers have used a relational database at some point or other in their lives, most of us pretty much know what a database query is. In the Java Persistence API, a query is similar to a database query, except that instead of using Structured Query Language (SQL) to specify the query criteria, we are querying over entities and using a language called Java Persistence Query Language (which we will abbreviate as JPQL).

A query is implemented in code as a Query object. Query objects are constructed using the EntityManager as a factory. The EntityManager interface includes a variety of API calls that return a new Query object. As a first class object, this query can in turn be customized according to the needs of the application.

A query can be defined either *statically* or *dynamically*. A static query is defined in either annotation or XML metadata, and it must include both the query criteria as well as a user-assigned name. This kind of query is also called a *named query*, and it is later looked up by its name at the time it is executed.

A dynamic query can be issued at runtime by supplying only the JPQL query criteria. These may be a little more expensive to execute because the persistence provider cannot do any query preparation beforehand, but they are nevertheless very simple to use and can be issued in response to program logic or even user logic.

Following is an example showing how to create a query and then execute it to obtain all of the employees in the database. Of course this may not be a very good query to execute if the database is large and contains hundreds of thousands of employees, but it is nevertheless a legitimate example. The simple query is as follows:

```
Query query = em.createQuery("SELECT e FROM Employee e");
Collection emps = query.getResultList();
```

We create a `Query` object by issuing the `createQuery()` call on the `EntityManager` and passing in the JPQL string that specifies the query criteria. The JPQL string refers not to an `EMPLOYEE` database table but the `Employee` entity, so this query is selecting all `Employee` objects without filtering them any further. We will be diving into queries in Chapter 6 and JPQL in Chapters 6 and 7. You will see that you can be far more discretionary about which objects you want to be returned.

To execute the query we simply invoke `getResultList()` on it. This returns a `List` (a sub-interface of `Collection`) containing the `Employee` objects that matched the query criteria. Note that a `List<Employee>` is not returned. Unfortunately this is not possible, since no class is passed into the call, so no parameterization of the type is able to occur. The return type is inferred by the persistence provider as it processes the JPQL string. We could cast the result to a `Collection<Employee>`, however, to make a neater return type for the caller. Doing so, we can easily create a method that returns all of the employees, as shown in Listing 2-8.

Listing 2-8. *Method for Issuing a Query*

```
public Collection<Employee> findAllEmployees() {
    Query query = em.createQuery("SELECT e FROM Employee e");
    return (Collection<Employee>) query.getResultList();
}
```

This example shows how simple queries are to create, execute, and process, but what this example does not show is how powerful they are. In Chapter 6 we will examine many other extremely useful and interesting ways of defining and using queries in an application.

Putting It All Together

We can now take all of the methods that we have created and combine them into a class. The class will act like a service class, which we will call `EmployeeService`, and will allow us to perform operations on employees. The code should be pretty familiar by now. Listing 2-9 shows the complete implementation.

Listing 2-9. *Service Class for Operating on* Employee *Entities*

```
import javax.persistence.*;
import java.util.Collection;
```

```java
public class EmployeeService {
    protected EntityManager em;

    public EmployeeService(EntityManager em) {
        this.em = em;
    }

    public Employee createEmployee(int id, String name, long salary) {
        Employee emp = new Employee(id);
        emp.setName(name);
        emp.setSalary(salary);
        em.persist(emp);
        return emp;
    }

    public void removeEmployee(int id) {
        Employee emp = findEmployee(id);
        if (emp != null) {
            em.remove(emp);
        }
    }

    public Employee raiseEmployeeSalary(int id, long raise) {
        Employee emp = em.find(Employee.class, id);
        if (emp != null) {
            emp.setSalary(emp.getSalary() + raise);
        }
        return emp;
    }

    public Employee findEmployee(int id) {
        return em.find(Employee.class, id);
    }

    public Collection<Employee> findAllEmployees() {
        Query query = em.createQuery("SELECT e FROM Employee e");
        return (Collection<Employee>) query.getResultList();
    }
}
```

This is a simple yet fully functional class that can be used to issue the typical CRUD (create, read, update, and delete) operations on Employee entities. This class requires that an entity manager is created and passed into it by the caller and also that any required transactions are begun and committed by the caller. This may seem strange at first, but decoupling the transaction logic from the operation logic makes this class more portable to the Java EE environment. We will revisit this example in the next chapter, where we focus on Java EE applications.

A simple main program that uses this service and performs all of the required entity manager creation and transaction management is shown in Listing 2-10.

Listing 2-10. *Using* EmployeeService

```
import javax.persistence.*;
import java.util.Collection;

public class EmployeeTest {

    public static void main(String[] args) {
        EntityManagerFactory emf =
                Persistence.createEntityManagerFactory("EmployeeService");
        EntityManager em = emf.createEntityManager();
        EmployeeService service = new EmployeeService(em);

        // create and persist an employee
        em.getTransaction().begin();
        Employee emp = service.createEmployee(158, "John Doe", 45000);
        em.getTransaction().commit();
        System.out.println("Persisted " + emp);

        // find a specific employee
        emp = service.findEmployee(158);
        System.out.println("Found " + emp);

        // find all employees
        Collection<Employee> emps = service.findAllEmployees();
        for (Employee e : emps)
            System.out.println("Found employee: " + e);

        // update the employee
        em.getTransaction().begin();
        emp = service.raiseEmployeeSalary(158, 1000);
        em.getTransaction().commit();
        System.out.println("Updated " + emp);

        // remove an employee
        em.getTransaction().begin();
        service.removeEmployee(158);
        em.getTransaction().commit();
        System.out.println("Removed Employee 158");

        // close the EM and EMF when done
        em.close();
        emf.close();
    }
}
```

Packaging It Up

Now that we know the basic building blocks of the Java Persistence API, we are ready to organize the pieces into an application that runs in Java SE. The only thing left to discuss is how to put it together so that it runs.

Persistence Unit

The configuration that describes the persistence unit is defined in an XML file called persistence.xml. Each persistence unit is named, so when a referencing application wants to specify the configuration for an entity it need only reference the name of the persistence unit that defines that configuration. A single persistence.xml file may contain one or more named persistence unit configurations, but each persistence unit is separate and distinct from the others, and they can be logically thought of as being in separate persistence.xml files.

Many of the persistence unit elements in the persistence.xml file apply to persistence units that are deployed within the Java EE container. The only ones that we need to specify for our example are name, transaction-type, class, and properties. There are a number of other elements that can be specified in the persistence unit configuration in the persistence.xml file, but these will be discussed in more detail in Chapter 11. Listing 2-11 shows the relevant part of the persistence.xml file for this example.

Listing 2-11. *Elements in the* persistence.xml *File*

```
<persistence>
    <persistence-unit name="EmployeeService" transaction-type="RESOURCE_LOCAL">
        <class>examples.model.Employee</class>
        <properties>
            <property name="toplink.jdbc.driver"
                      value="org.apache.derby.jdbc.ClientDriver"/>
            <property name="toplink.jdbc.url"
                      value="jdbc:derby://localhost:1527/EmpServDB;create=true"/>
            <property name="toplink.jdbc.user" value="APP"/>
            <property name="toplink.jdbc.password" value="APP"/>
        </properties>
    </persistence-unit>
</persistence>
```

The name element indicates the name of our persistence unit and is the string that we specify when we create the EntityManagerFactory. We have used "EmployeeService" as the name. The transaction-type element indicates that our persistence unit uses resource level EntityTransaction instead of JTA transactions. The class element lists the entity that is part of the persistence unit. Multiple class elements may be specified when there is more than one entity. These would not normally be needed when deploying in a Java EE container, but they are needed for portable execution when running in Java SE. We only have a single Employee entity.

The last part that we use is a list of properties that are vendor-specific. The login parameters to a database must be specified when running in a Java SE environment, so these properties exist to tell the provider what to connect to. Other provider properties, such as logging options, are also useful.

Persistence Archive

The persistence artifacts are packaged in what we will loosely call a *persistence archive*. This is really just a JAR-formatted file that contains the `persistence.xml` file in the `META-INF` directory and normally the entity class files.

Since we are running as a simple Java SE application, all we have to do is put the application JAR, the persistence provider JARs, and the Java Persistence API JAR on the classpath when the program is executed.

Summary

In this chapter we discussed just enough of the basics of the Java Persistence API to develop and run a simple application in a Java SE runtime.

We started out discussing the entity, how to define one, and how to turn an existing Java class into one. We discussed entity managers and how they are obtained and constructed in the Java SE environment.

The next step was to instantiate an entity instance and use the entity manager to persist it in the database. After we inserted some new entities, we were able to retrieve them again and then remove them. We also made some updates and ensured that the changes were written back to the database.

We talked about the resource-local transaction API and how to use it. We then went over some of the different types of queries and how to define and execute them. Finally, we aggregated all of these techniques and combined them into a simple application that we can execute in isolation from an enterprise environment.

In the next chapter, we will look at the impact of the Java EE environment when developing enterprise applications using the Java Persistence API.

CHAPTER 3

■ ■ ■

Enterprise Applications

No technology exists in a vacuum, and the Java Persistence API is no different than any other in this regard. Although the fat-client style of application demonstrated in the previous chapter is a viable use of the Java Persistence API, the vast majority of enterprise Java applications are deployed to a Java EE application server. Therefore it is essential to understand the components that make up a Java EE application and the role of the Java Persistence API in this environment.

We will begin with an overview of the major Java EE technologies relevant to persistence. As part of this overview, we will also detour into the EJB component model, demonstrating the new syntax for stateless, stateful, and message-driven beans. Even if you have experience with previous versions of these components, you may find this section helpful to get up to speed with the changes in EJB 3.0 and Java EE 5. As part of the ease-of-development initiative for Java EE 5, EJBs have undergone a major revision and have become considerably easier to implement in the process.

Although this chapter is not a complete or detailed exploration of Java EE, it will hopefully serve as a sufficient overview to the new simplified programming interfaces. We will introduce features only briefly and spend the bulk of the chapter focusing on the elements relevant to developing applications that use persistence.

Next we will look at the other application server technologies that are going to have a major impact on applications using the Java Persistence API: transactions and dependency management. Transactions, of course, are a fundamental element of any enterprise application that needs to ensure data integrity. The new dependency-management facilities of Java EE 5 are also key to understanding how the entity manager is acquired by enterprise components and how these components can be linked together.

Finally, we will demonstrate how to use the Java EE components described in this chapter, with a focus on how persistence integrates into each component technology. We will also revisit the Java SE application from the previous chapter and retarget it to the Java EE 5 platform.

Application Component Models

The word *component* has taken on many meanings in software development, so let's begin with a definition. A component is a self-contained, reusable software unit that can be integrated into an application. Clients interact with components via a well-defined contract. In Java, the simplest form of software component is the JavaBean, commonly referred to as just a *bean*. Beans are components implemented in terms of a single class whose contract is defined by the naming patterns of the methods on the bean. The JavaBean naming patterns are so common now that it is easy to forget that they were originally intended to give user-interface builders a standard way of dealing with third-party components.

In the enterprise space, components focus more on implementing business services, with the contract of the component defined in terms of the business operations that may be carried out by that component. The standard component model for Java EE is the Enterprise JavaBeans model, which defines ways to package, deploy, and interact with self-contained business services. The EJB's type determines the contract required to interact with it. Session beans use standard Java interfaces to define the set of business methods that may be invoked, while message-driven bean behavior is determined by the type and format of the messages the bean is designed to receive.

Choosing whether or not to use a component model in your application is largely a personal preference. With some exceptions, most of the container services available to session beans are also available to servlets. As a result, many web applications today sidestep EJBs entirely, going directly from servlets to the database. Using components requires organizing the application into layers, with business services living in the component model and presentation services layered on top of it.

Historically, one of the challenges in adopting components in Java EE was the complexity of implementing them. With that problem largely solved, we are left with the benefits that a well-defined set of business services brings to an application:

- **Loose coupling.** Using components to implement services encourages loose coupling between layers of an application. The implementation of a component may change without any impact to the clients or other components that depend on it.

- **Dependency management.** Dependencies for a component may be declared in metadata and automatically resolved by the container.

- **Life cycle management.** The life cycle of components is well defined and managed by the application server. Component implementations can participate in life cycle operations to acquire and release resources or perform other initialization and shutdown behavior.

- **Declarative container services.** Business methods for components are intercepted by the application server in order to apply services such as concurrency, transaction management, security, and remoting.

- **Portability.** Components that comply to Java EE standards and that are deployed to standards-based servers can be more easily ported from one compliant server to another.

- **Scalability and reliability.** Application servers are designed to ensure that components are managed efficiently with an eye to scalability. Depending on the component type and server configuration, business operations implemented using components can retry failed method calls or even fail over to another server in a cluster.

One of the themes you will encounter as you read this book is the tendency for example code to be written often in terms of session beans. This is intentional. Not only are session beans easy to write and a good way to organize application logic, but they are also a natural fit for interacting with the Java Persistence API. In fact, as web application frameworks continue to push application code further away from the servlet, the ability for session beans to seamlessly integrate and acquire the services of other components makes them more valuable today than ever before.

Session Beans

Session beans are a component technology designed to encapsulate business services. The operations supported by the service are defined using a regular Java interface, referred to as the *business interface* of the session bean, that clients use to interact with the bean. The bean implementation is little more than a regular Java class which implements the business interface. And yet, by virtue of being part of the Enterprise JavaBeans component model, the bean has access to a wide array of container services that it can leverage to implement the business service. The significance of the name *session bean* has to do with the way in which clients access and interact with them. Once a client acquires a reference to a session bean from the server, it starts a session with that bean and may invoke business operations on it.

There are two types of session bean, *stateless* and *stateful*. Interaction with a stateless session bean begins at the start of a business method call and ends when the method call completes. There is no state that carries over from one business operation to the other. An interaction with stateful session beans becomes more of a conversation that begins from the moment the client acquires a reference to the session bean and ends when the client explicitly releases it back to the server. Business operations on a stateful session bean may maintain state on the bean instance across calls. We will provide more detail on the implementation considerations of this difference in interaction style as we describe each type of session bean.

Clients never interact directly with a session bean instance. The client references and invokes an implementation of the business interface provided by the server. This implementation class acts as a proxy to the underlying bean implementation. This decoupling of client from bean allows the server to intercept method calls in order to provide the services required by the bean, such as transaction management. It also allows the server to optimize and reuse instances of the session bean class as necessary.

Stateless Session Beans

As we mentioned, a stateless session bean sets out to accomplish the goals of an operation entirely within the lifetime of a single method. Stateless beans may implement many business operations, but each method cannot assume that any other was invoked before it.

This might sound like a limitation of the stateless bean, but it is by far the most common form of business service implementation. Unlike stateful session beans, which are good for accumulating state during a conversation (such as the shopping cart of a retail application), stateless session beans are designed to carry out independent operations very efficiently. Stateless session beans may scale to large numbers of clients with minimal impact to overall server resources.

Defining a Stateless Session Bean

A session bean is defined in two parts:

- One or more business interfaces that define what methods a client may invoke on the bean

- A class that implements these interfaces, called the bean class, which is marked with the @Stateless annotation

Most session beans have only a single business interface, but there is no restriction on the number of interfaces that a session bean may expose to its clients. When the server encounters the @Stateless annotation, it knows to treat the bean class as a session bean. It will configure the bean in the EJB container and make it available for use by other components in the application. The @Stateless annotation and other annotations described in this chapter are defined in the javax.ejb and javax.annotation packages.

Let's look at a complete implementation of a stateless session bean. Listing 3-1 shows the business interface that will be supported by this session bean. In this example, the service consists of a single method, sayHello(), which accepts a String argument corresponding to a person's name and returns a String response. There is no annotation or parent interface to indicate that this is a business interface. When implemented by the session bean, it will be automatically treated as a local business interface, meaning that it is accessible only to clients within the same application server. A second type of business interface for remote clients is discussed later in the section Remote Business Interfaces. To emphasize that an interface is a local business interface, the @Local annotation may be optionally added to the interface.

Listing 3-1. *The Business Interface for a Session Bean*

```
public interface HelloService {
    public String sayHello(String name);
}
```

Now let's consider the implementation, which is shown in Listing 3-2. This is a regular Java class that implements the HelloService business interface. The only thing unique about this class is the @Stateless annotation that marks it as a stateless session bean. The business method is implemented without any special constraints or requirements. This is a regular class that just happens to be an EJB.

Listing 3-2. *The Bean Class Implementing the* HelloService *Interface*

```
@Stateless
public class HelloServiceBean implements HelloService {
    public String sayHello(String name) {
        return "Hello, "  + name;
    }
}
```

There are only a couple of caveats about the stateless session bean class definition. The first is that it needs a no-arg constructor, but the compiler normally generates this automatically when no other constructors are supplied. The second is that static fields should not be used, primarily because of bean redeployment issues.

Many EJB containers create a pool of stateless session bean instances and then select an arbitrary instance to service each client request. Therefore there is no guarantee that the same state will be used between calls, and hence it cannot be relied on. Any state placed on the bean class should be restricted to factory classes that are inherently stateless, such as `DataSource`.

Lifecycle Callbacks

Unlike a regular Java class used in application code, the server manages the life cycle of a stateless session bean. This impacts the implementation of a bean in two ways.

First, the server decides when to create and remove bean instances. The application has no control over when or even how many instances of a particular stateless session bean are created or how long they will stay around.

Second, the server has to initialize services for the bean after it is constructed but before the business logic of the bean is invoked. Likewise, the bean may have to acquire a resource such as a JDBC data source before business methods can be used. However, in order for the bean to acquire a resource, the server must first have completed initializing its services for the bean. This limits the usefulness of the constructor for the class since the bean won't have access to any resources until server initialization has completed.

To allow both the server and the bean to achieve their initialization requirements, EJBs support lifecycle callback methods that are invoked by the server at various points in the bean's life cycle. For stateless session beans there are two lifecycle callbacks, PostConstruct and PreDestroy. The server will invoke the PostConstruct callback as soon as it has completed initializing all of the container services for the bean. In effect, this replaces the constructor as the location for initialization logic since it is only here that container services are guaranteed to be available. The server invokes the PreDestroy callback immediately before the server releases the bean instance to be garbage-collected. Any resources acquired during PostConstruct that require explicit shutdown should be released during PreDestroy.

Listing 3-3 shows a stateless session bean that acquires a reference to a `java.util.logging.Logger` instance during the PostConstruct callback. A bean may have at most one PostConstruct callback method[1] that is identified by the `@PostConstruct` marker annotation. Likewise, the PreDestroy callback is identified by the `@PreDestroy` annotation.

---

1. In inheritance situations, additional callback methods from parent classes may also be invoked.

Listing 3-3. *Using the PostConstruct Callback to Acquire a Logger*

```
@Stateless
public class LoggerBean implements Logger {
    private java.util.logging.Logger logger;

    @PostConstruct
    public void init() {
        logger = Logger.getLogger("notification");
    }

    public void logMessage(String message) {
        logger.info(message);
    }
}
```

Remote Business Interfaces

So far we have only discussed session beans that use a local business interface. Local in this case means that a dependency on the session bean may be declared only by Java EE components that are running together in the same application server instance. It is not possible to use a session bean with a local interface from a remote client, for example.

To accommodate remote clients, session beans may mark their business interface with the @Remote annotation to declare that it should be useable remotely. Listing 3-4 demonstrates this syntax for a remote version of the HelloService interface shown in Listing 3-1. Marking an interface as being remote is equivalent to having it extend the java.rmi.Remote interface. The reference to the bean that gets acquired by a client is no longer a local reference on the server but a Remote Method Invocation (RMI) stub that will invoke operations on the session bean from across the network. No special support is required on the bean class to use remote interfaces.

Listing 3-4. *A Remote Business Interface*

```
@Remote
public interface HelloServiceRemote {
    public String sayHello(String name);
}
```

Making an interface remote has consequences both in terms of performance and how arguments to business methods are handled. Remote business interfaces may be used locally within a running server, but doing so may still result in network overhead if the method call is routed through the RMI layer. Arguments to methods on remote interfaces are also *passed by value* instead of *passed by reference*. This means that the argument is serialized even when the client is local to the session bean. Local interfaces for local clients are generally a better approach. Local interfaces preserve the semantics of regular Java method calls and avoid the costs associated with networking and RMI.

■**Tip** Many application servers provide options to improve the performance of remote interfaces when used locally within an application server. This may include the ability to disable serialization of method arguments or may go so far as to sidestep RMI entirely. Use caution when relying on these features in application code, as they are not portable across different application servers.

Stateful Session Beans

In our introduction to session beans we described the difference between stateless and stateful beans as being based on the interaction style between client and server. In the case of stateless session beans, that interaction started and ended with a single method call. Sometimes clients need to issue multiple requests to a service and have each request be able to access or consider the results of previous requests. Stateful session beans are designed to handle this scenario by providing a dedicated service to a client that starts when the client obtains a reference to the bean and ends only when the client chooses to end the conversation.

The quintessential example of the stateful session bean is the shopping cart of an e-commerce application. The client obtains a reference to the shopping cart, starting the conversation. Over the span of the user session, the client adds or removes items from the shopping cart, which maintains state specific to the client. Then, when the session is complete, the client completes the purchase, causing the shopping cart to be removed.

This is not unlike using a non-managed Java object in application code. We create an instance, invoke operations on the object that accumulate state, and then dispose of the object when we no longer need it. The only difference with the stateful session bean is that the server manages the actual object instance and the client interacts with that instance indirectly through the business interface of the bean.

Stateful session beans offer a superset of the functionality available in stateless session beans. The features that we covered for stateless session beans such as remote interfaces apply equally to stateful session beans.

Defining a Stateful Session Bean

Now that we have established the use case for a stateful session bean, let's look at how to define one. Similar to the stateless session bean, a stateful session bean is comprised of one or more business interfaces implemented by a single bean class. A sample local business interface for a shopping cart bean is demonstrated in Listing 3-5.

Listing 3-5. *Business Interface for a Shopping Cart*

```
public interface ShoppingCart {
    public void addItem(String id, int quantity);
    public void removeItem(String id, int quantity);
    public Map<String,Integer> getItems();
    public void checkout(int paymentId);
    public void cancel();
}
```

Listing 3-6 shows the bean class that implements the ShoppingCart interface. The bean class has been marked with the @Stateful annotation to indicate to the server that the class is a stateful session bean.

Listing 3-6. *Implementing a Shopping Cart Using a Stateful Session Bean*

```
@Stateful
public class ShoppingCartBean implements ShoppingCart {
    private HashMap<String,Integer> items = new HashMap<String,Integer>();

    public void addItem(String item, int quantity) {
        Integer orderQuantity = items.get(item);
        if (orderQuantity == null) {
            orderQuantity = 0;
        }
        orderQuantity += quantity;
        items.put(item, orderQuantity);
    }

    // ...

    @Remove
    public void checkout(int paymentId) {
        // store items to database
        // ...
    }

    @Remove
    public void cancel() {
    }
}
```

There are two things different in this bean compared to the stateless session beans we have been dealing with so far.

The first difference is that the bean class has state fields that are modified by the business methods of the bean. This is allowed because the client that uses the bean effectively has access to a private instance of the session bean on which to make changes.

The second difference is that there are methods marked with the @Remove annotation. These are the methods that the client will use to end the conversation with the bean. After one of these methods has been called, the server will destroy the bean instance, and the client reference will throw an exception if any further attempt is made to invoke business methods. Every stateful session bean must define at least one method marked with the @Remove annotation, even if the method doesn't do anything other than serve as an end to the conversation. In Listing 3-6, the checkout() method is called if the user completes the shopping transaction, while cancel() is called if the user decides not to proceed. The session bean is removed in either case.

Lifecycle Callbacks

Like the stateless session bean, the stateful session bean also supports lifecycle callbacks in order to facilitate bean initialization and cleanup. It also supports two additional callbacks to allow the bean to gracefully handle passivation and activation of the bean instance. Passivation is the process by which the server serializes the bean instance so that it can either be stored offline to free up resources or so that it can be replicated to another server in a cluster. Activation is the process of deserializing a passivated session bean instance and making it active in the server once again. Because stateful session beans hold state on behalf of a client and are not removed until the client invokes one of the remove methods on the bean, the server cannot destroy a bean instance to free up resources. Passivation allows the server to reclaim resources while preserving session state.

Before a bean is passivated, the server will invoke the PrePassivate callback. The bean uses this callback to prepare the bean for serialization, usually by closing any live connections to other server resources. The PrePassivate method is identified by the @PrePassivate marker annotation. After a bean has been activated, the server will invoke the PostActivate callback. With the serialized instance restored, the bean must then reacquire any connections to other resources that the business methods of the bean may be depending on. The PostActivate method is identified by the @PostActivate marker annotation. Listing 3-7 shows a session bean that makes full use of the lifecycle callbacks in order to maintain a JDBC connection. Note that only the JDBC Connection is explicitly managed. As a resource connection factory, the server automatically saves and restores the data source during passivation and activation.

Listing 3-7. *Using Lifecycle Callbacks on a Stateful Session Bean*

```
@Stateful
public class OrderBrowserBean implements OrderBrowser {
    DataSource ds;
    Connection conn;

    @PostConstruct
    public void init() {
        // acquire the data source
        // ...

        acquireConnection();
    }

    @PrePassivate
    public void passivate() { releaseConnection(); }

    @PostActivate
    public void activate() { acquireConnection(); }

    @PreDestroy
    public void shutdown() { releaseConnection(); }
```

```
    private void acquireConnection() {
        try {
            conn = ds.getConnection();
        } catch (SQLException e) {
            throw new EJBException(e);
        }
    }

    private void releaseConnection() {
        try {
            conn.close();
        } catch (SQLException e) {
        }
        conn = null;
    }

    public Collection<Order> listOrders() {
        // ...
    }
}
```

Message-Driven Beans

So far we have been looking at components that are synchronous in nature. The client invokes a method through the business interface, and the server completes that method invocation before returning control to the client. For the majority of services, this is the most natural approach. There are cases, however, where it is not necessary for the client to wait for a response from the server. We would like the client to be able to issue a request and continue while the server processes the request asynchronously.

The *message-driven bean* (MDB) is the EJB component for asynchronous messaging. Clients issue requests to the MDB using a messaging system such as Java Message Service (JMS). These requests are queued and eventually delivered to the MDB by the server. The server invokes the business interface of the MDB whenever it receives a message sent from a client. Whereas the component contract of a session bean is defined by its business interface, the component contract of an MDB is defined by the structure of the messages it is designed to receive.

Defining a Message-Driven Bean

When defining a session bean, the developer creates a business interface, and the bean class implements it. In the case of message-driven beans, the bean class implements an interface specific to the messaging system the MDB is based on. The most common case is JMS, but other messaging systems are possible with the Java Connector Architecture. For JMS message-driven beans, the business interface is `javax.jms.MessageListener`, which defines a single method, `onMessage()`.

Listing 3-8 shows the basic structure of a message-driven bean. The `@MessageDriven` annotation marks the class as an MDB. The activation configuration properties, defined using the `@ActivationConfigProperty` annotations, tell the server the type of messaging system and any configuration details required by that system. In this case the MDB will be invoked only if the JMS message has a property named RECIPIENT where the value is ReportProcessor. Whenever the server receives a message, it invokes the onMessage() method with the message as the argument. Because there is no synchronous connection with a client, the onMessage() method does not return anything. However, the MDB can use session beans, data sources, or even other JMS resources to process and carry out an action based on the message.

Listing 3-8. *Defining a JMS Message-Driven Bean*

```
@MessageDriven(
  activationConfig = {
    @ActivationConfigProperty(propertyName="destinationType",
                             propertyValue="javax.jms.Queue"),
    @ActivationConfigProperty(propertyName="messageSelector",
                             propertyValue="RECIPIENT='ReportProcessor'")
})
public class ReportProcessorBean implements javax.jms.MessageListener {
    public void onMessage(javax.jms.Message message) {
        // ...
    }
}
```

Servlets

Servlets are a component technology designed to serve the needs of web developers who need to respond to HTTP requests and generate dynamic content in return. Servlets are the oldest and most popular technology introduced as part of the Java EE platform. They are the foundation for technologies such as JavaServer Pages (JSP) and the backbone of web frameworks such as Apache Struts and JavaServer Faces (JSF).

Although it is quite likely that readers will have some experience with servlets, it is worth describing the impact that web application models have had on enterprise application development. The web, due to its reliance on the HTTP protocol, is inherently a stateless medium. Much like the stateless session beans we described earlier, a client makes a request, the server triggers the appropriate service method in the servlet, and content is generated and returned to the client. Each request is entirely independent from the last.

This presents a challenge, because many web applications involve some kind of conversation between the client and the server in which the previous actions of the user influence the results returned on subsequent pages. To maintain that conversational state, many early applications attempted to dynamically embed context information into URLs. Unfortunately not only does this technique not scale very well, it requires a dynamic element to all content generation that makes it difficult for non-developers to write content for a web application.

Servlets solve the problem of conversational state with the *session*. Not to be confused with the session bean, the HTTP session is a map of data associated with a session id. When the application requests that a session be created, the server generates a new id and returns an HTTPSession object that the application can use to store key/value pairs of data. It then uses techniques such as browser cookies to link the session id with the client, tying the two together into a conversation. For web applications, the client is largely ignorant of the conversational state that is tracked by the server.

Using the HTTP session effectively is an important element of servlet development. Listing 3-9 demonstrates the steps required to request a session and store conversational data in it. In this example, assuming that the user has logged in, the servlet stores the user id in the session, making it available for use in all subsequent requests by the same client. The getSession() call on the HttpServletRequest object will either return the active session or create a new one if one does not exist. Once obtained, the session acts like a map, with key/value pairs set and retrieved with the setAttribute() and getAttribute() methods respectively. As we see later in this chapter, the servlet session, which stores unstructured data, is sometimes paired with a stateful session bean in order to manage session information with the benefit of a well-defined business interface.

Listing 3-9. *Maintaining Conversational State with a Servlet*

```
public class LoginServlet extends HttpServlet {

    protected void doPost(HttpServletRequest request, HttpServletResponse response)
            throws ServletException, IOException {
        String userId = request.getParameter("user");
        HttpSession session = request.getSession();
        session.setAttribute("user", userId);

        // ...
    }
}
```

The rise of application frameworks targeted to the web has also changed the way in which we develop web applications. Application code written in servlets is rapidly being replaced with application code further abstracted from the base model using frameworks like JavaServer Faces. When working in an environment such as this, basic application persistence issues such as where to acquire and store the entity manager and how to effectively use transactions quickly become more challenging.

Although we will explore some of these issues, persistence in the context of a framework such as JavaServer Faces is beyond the scope of this book. As a general solution, we recommend adopting a session bean component model in which to focus persistence operations. Session beans are easily accessible from anywhere within a Java EE application, making them perfect neutral ground for business services. The ability to exchange entities inside and outside of the session bean model means that the results of persistence operations will be directly usable in web frameworks without having to tightly couple your presentation code to the persistence API.

Dependency Management

The business logic of a Java EE component is not always self-contained. More often than not, the implementation depends on other resources hosted by the application server. This may include server resources such as a JDBC data source or JMS message queue, or application-defined resources such as a session bean or entity manager for a specific persistence unit.

To manage these dependencies, Java EE components support the notion of *references* to resources that are defined in metadata for the component. A reference is a named link to a resource that may be resolved dynamically at runtime from within application code or resolved automatically by the container when the component instance is created. We'll cover each of these scenarios shortly.

A reference consists of two parts: a name and a target. The name is used by application code to resolve the reference dynamically while the server uses target information to find the resource the application is looking for. The type of resource to be located determines the type of information required to match the target. Each resource reference requires a different set of information specific to the resource type it refers to.

A reference is declared using one of the resource reference annotations: `@Resource`, `@EJB`, `@PersistenceContext`, or `@PersistenceUnit`. These annotations may be placed on a class, field, or setter method. The choice of location determines the default name of the reference and whether or not the server resolves the reference automatically.

Dependency Lookup

The first strategy for resolving dependencies in application code that we will discuss is called *dependency lookup*. This is the traditional form of dependency management in Java EE, where the application code is responsible for using the Java Naming and Directory Interface (JNDI) to look up a named reference.

All of the resource annotations support an element called `name` that defines the name of the reference. When the resource annotation is placed on the class definition, this element is mandatory. If the resource annotation is placed on a field or a setter method, the server will generate a default name. When using dependency lookup, annotations are typically placed at the class level, and the name is explicitly specified. Placing a resource reference on a field or setter method has other effects besides generating a default name that we will discuss in the next section.

The role of the name is to provide a way for the client to resolve the reference dynamically. Every Java EE application server supports JNDI, and each component has its own locally scoped JNDI naming context called the environment naming context. The name of the reference is bound into the environment naming context, and when it is looked up using the JNDI API, the server resolves the reference and returns the target of the reference.

Consider the DeptServiceBean session bean shown in Listing 3-10. It has declared a dependency on a session bean using the @EJB annotation and given it the name "audit". The beanInterface element of the @EJB annotation references the business interface of the session bean that the client is interested in. In the PostConstruct callback, the audit bean is looked up and stored in the audit field. The Context and InitialContext interfaces are both defined by the JNDI API. The lookup() method of the Context interface is the primary way to retrieve objects from a JNDI context. To find the reference named "audit", the application looks up the name "java:comp/env/audit" and casts the result to the AuditService business interface. The prefix "java:comp/env/" that was added to the reference name indicates to the server that the environment naming context should be searched to find the reference. If the name is incorrectly specified, an exception will be thrown when the lookup fails.

Listing 3-10. *Looking Up an EJB Dependency*

```
@Stateless
@EJB(name="audit", beanInterface=AuditService.class)
public class DeptServiceBean implements DeptService {
    private AuditService audit;

    @PostConstruct
    public void init() {
        try {
            Context ctx = new InitialContext();
            audit = (AuditService) ctx.lookup("java:comp/env/audit");
        } catch (NamingException e) {
            throw new EJBException(e);
        }
    }

    // ...
}
```

Using the JNDI API to look up resource references from the environment naming context is supported by all Java EE components. It is, however, a somewhat cumbersome method of finding a resource due to the exception-handling requirements of JNDI. EJBs also support an alternative syntax using the lookup() method of the EJBContext interface. The EJBContext interface (and subinterfaces such as SessionContext and MessageDrivenContext) is available to any EJB and provides the bean with access to runtime services such as the timer service. Listing 3-11 shows the same example as Listing 3-10 using the lookup() method. The SessionContext instance in this example is provided via a setter method. We will revisit this example later in the section called Referencing Server Resources to see how it is invoked.

Listing 3-11. *Using the* `EJBContext lookup()` *Method*

```
@Stateless
@EJB(name="audit", beanInterface=AuditService.class)
public class DeptServiceBean implements DeptService {
    SessionContext context;
    AuditService audit;

    public void setSessionContext(SessionContext context) {
        this.context = context;
    }

    @PostConstruct
    public void init() {
        audit = (AuditService) context.lookup("audit");
    }

    // ...
}
```

The `EJBContext lookup()` method has two advantages over the JNDI API. The first is that the argument to the method is the name exactly as it was specified in the resource reference. The second is that only runtime exceptions are thrown from the `lookup()` method so the checked exception handling of the JNDI API can be avoided. Behind the scenes the exact same sequence of JNDI API calls from Listing 3-10 is being made, but the JNDI exceptions are handled automatically.

Dependency Injection

When a resource annotation is placed on a field or setter method, two things occur. First, a resource reference is declared just as if it had been placed on the bean class (similar to the example in Listing 3-10), and the name for that resource will be bound into the environment naming context when the component is created. Second, the server does the lookup automatically on your behalf and sets the result into the instantiated class.

The process of automatically looking up a resource and setting it into the class is called *dependency injection* because the server is said to inject the resolved dependency into the class. This technique, one of several commonly referred to as *inversion of control*, removes the burden of manually looking up resources from the JNDI environment context.

Dependency injection is rapidly being considered a best practice for application development, not only because it reduces the need for JNDI lookups (and the associated Service Locator[2] pattern), but also because it simplifies testing. Without any JNDI API code in the class that has dependencies on the application server runtime environment, the bean class may be instantiated directly in a unit test. The developer can then manually supply the required dependencies and test the functionality of the class in question instead of worrying about how to work around the JNDI APIs.

---

2. Alur, Deepak, John Crupi, and Dan Malks. *Core J2EE Patterns: Best Practices and Design Strategies, Second Edition.* Upper Saddle River, N.J.: Prentice Hall PTR, 2003.

Field Injection

The first form of dependency injection is called *field injection.* Injecting a dependency into a field means that after the server looks up the dependency in the environment naming context, it assigns the result directly into the annotated field of the class. Listing 3-12 revisits the example from Listing 3-10 and demonstrates the @EJB annotation, this time by injecting the result into the audit field. All of the directory interface code we demonstrated before is gone, and the business methods of the bean can assume that the audit field holds a reference to the AuditService bean.

Listing 3-12. *Using Field Injection*

```
@Stateless
public class DeptServiceBean implements DeptService {
    @EJB AuditService audit;

    // ...
}
```

Field injection is certainly the easiest to implement, and the examples in this book use this form exclusively to conserve space. The only thing to consider with field injection is that if you are planning on unit testing, then you need either to add a setter method or to make the field accessible to your unit tests in order to manually satisfy the dependency. Private fields, though legal, require unpleasant hacks if there is no accessible way to set their value. Consider package scope for field injection if you want to unit test without having to add a setter.

We mentioned in the previous section that a name is automatically generated for the reference when a resource annotation is placed on a field or setter method. For completeness, we will describe the format of this name, but it is unlikely that you will find many opportunities to use it. The generated name is the fully qualified class name followed by a forward slash and then the name of the field or property. This means that if the AuditService bean is located in the persistence.session package, then the injected EJB referenced in Listing 3-12 would be accessible in the environment naming context under the name "persistence.session.AuditService/audit". Specifying the name element for the resource annotation will override this default value.

Setter Injection

The second form of dependency injection is called *setter injection* and involves annotating a setter method instead of a class field. When the server resolves the reference, it will invoke the annotated setter method with the result of the lookup. Listing 3-13 revisits Listing 3-10 for the last time to demonstrate using setter injection.

Listing 3-13. *Using Setter Injection*

```
@Stateless
public class DeptServiceBean implements DeptService {
    private AuditService audit;

    @EJB
    public void setAuditService(AuditService audit) {
        this.audit = audit;
    }

    // ...
}
```

This style of injection allows for private fields yet also works well with unit testing. Each test can simply instantiate the bean class and manually perform the dependency injection by invoking the setter method, usually by providing an implementation of the required resource that is tailored to the test.

Declaring Dependencies

The following sections describe the resource annotations defined by the Java EE and EJB specifications. Each annotation has a name element for optionally specifying the reference name for the dependency. Other elements on the annotations are specific to the type of resource that needs to be acquired.

Referencing a Persistence Context

In the previous chapter we demonstrated how to create an entity manager for a persistence context using an EntityManagerFactory returned from the Persistence class. In the Java EE environment, the @PersistenceContext annotation may be used to declare a dependency on a persistence context and have the entity manager for that persistence context acquired automatically.

Listing 3-14 demonstrates using the @PersistenceContext annotation to acquire an entity manager through dependency injection. The unitName element specifies the name of the persistence unit on which the persistence context will be based.

■**Tip** If the unitName element is omitted, it is vendor-specific how the unit name for the persistence context is determined. Some vendors may provide a default value if there is only one persistence unit for an application, while others may require that the unit name be specified in a vendor-specific configuration file.

Listing 3-14. *Injecting an* EntityManager *Instance*

```
@Stateless
public class EmployeeServiceBean implements EmployeeService {
    @PersistenceContext(unitName="EmployeeService")
    EntityManager em;

    // ...
}
```

After the warnings about using a state field in a stateless session bean, you may be wondering how this code is legal. After all, entity managers must maintain their own state in order to be able to manage a specific persistence context. The good news is that the specification was designed with Java EE integration in mind, so what actually gets injected in Listing 3-14 is not an entity manager instance like the ones we used in the previous chapter. The value injected into the bean is a container-managed proxy that acquires and releases persistence contexts on behalf of the application code. This is a powerful feature of the Java Persistence API in Java EE and one we will cover extensively in Chapter 5. For now it is safe to assume that the injected value will "do the right thing." It does not have to be disposed of and works automatically with the transaction management of the application server.

Referencing a Persistence Unit

The EntityManagerFactory for a persistence unit may be referenced using the @PersistenceUnit annotation. Like the @PersistenceContext annotation, the unitName element identifies the persistence unit for the EntityManagerFactory instance we wish to access. If the persistent unit name is not specified in the annotation, then it is vendor-specific how the name is determined.

Listing 3-15 demonstrates injection of an EntityManagerFactory instance into a stateful session bean. The bean then creates an EntityManager instance from the factory during the PostConstruct lifecycle callback. An injected EntityManagerFactory instance may be safely stored on any component instance. It is thread-safe and does not need to be disposed of when the bean instance is removed.

Listing 3-15. *Injecting an* EntityManagerFactory *Instance*

```
@Stateful
public class EmployeeServiceBean implements EmployeeService {
    @PersistenceUnit(unitName="EmployeeService")
    private EntityManagerFactory emf;
    private EntityManager em;

    @PostConstuct
    public void init() {
        em = emf.createEntityManager();
    }

    // ...
}
```

The EntityManagerFactory for a persistence unit is not used very often in the Java EE environment since injected entity managers are easier to acquire and use. As we will see in Chapter 5, there are important differences between the entity managers returned from the factory and the ones provided by the server in response to the @PersistenceContext annotation.

Referencing Enterprise JavaBeans

When a component needs to access an EJB, it declares a reference to that bean with the @EJB annotation. The target of this reference type is typically a session bean. Message-driven beans have no client interface, so they cannot be accessed directly and cannot be injected. We have already demonstrated the beanInterface element for specifying the business interface of the session bean that the client is interested in. The server will search through all deployed session beans to find the one that implements the requested business interface.

In the rare case that two session beans implement the same business interface or if the client needs to access a session bean located in a different EJB jar, then the beanName element may also be specified to identify the session bean by its name. The name of a session bean defaults to the unqualified class name of the bean class, or it may be set explicitly by using the name element of the @Stateless and @Stateful annotations. Listing 3-16 revisits the example shown in Listing 3-12, this time specifying the beanName element on the injected value. Sharing the same business interface across multiple bean implementations is not recommended. The beanName element should almost never be required.

Listing 3-16. *Qualifying an EJB Reference Using the Bean Name*

```
@Stateless
public class DeptServiceBean implements DeptService {
    @EJB(beanName="AuditServiceBean")
    AuditService audit;

    // ...
}
```

Referencing Server Resources

The @Resource annotation is the catchall reference for all resource types that don't correspond to one of the types we have described so far. It is used to define references to resource factories, message destinations, data sources, and other server resources. The @Resource annotation is also the simplest to define, as the only additional element is resourceType, which allows you to specify the type of resource if the server can't figure it out automatically. For example, if the field you are injecting into is of type Object, then there is no way for the server to know that you wanted a data source instead. The resourceType element can be set to javax.sql.DataSource to make the need explicit.

One of the features of the @Resource annotation is that it is used to acquire logical resources specific to the component type. This includes EJBContext implementations as well as services such as the EJB timer service. Without defining it as such, we used setter injection to acquire the EJBContext instance in Listing 3-11. To make that example complete, the @Resource annotation would be placed on the setSessionContext() method. Listing 3-17 revisits the example from Listing 3-11, this time demonstrating field injection to acquire a SessionContext instance.

Listing 3-17. *Injecting a* SessionContext *instance*

```
@Stateless
@EJB(name="audit", beanInterface=AuditService.class)
public class DeptServiceBean implements DeptService {
    @Resource SessionContext context;
    AuditService audit;

    @PostConstruct
    public void init() {
        audit = (AuditService) context.lookup("audit");
    }

    // ...
}
```

Transaction Management

More than any other type of enterprise application, applications that use persistence require careful attention to issues of transaction management. When transactions start, when they end, and how the entity manager participates in container-managed transactions are all essential topics for developers using the Java Persistence API. In the following sections we will lay out the foundation for transactions in Java EE and then revisit this topic in detail again in Chapter 5 as we look at the entity manager and how it participates in transactions. Advanced transaction topics are beyond the scope of this book. We recommend *Java Transaction Processing*[3] for an in-depth discussion on using and implementing transactions in Java.

Transaction Review

A transaction is an abstraction that is used to group together a series of operations. Once grouped together, the set of operations is treated as a single unit, and all of the operations must succeed or none of them can succeed. The consequence of only some of the operations being successful would produce an inconsistent view of the data that would be harmful or undesirable to the application. The term used to describe whether the operations succeed together or not at all is called *atomicity* and is arguably the most important of the four basic properties that

---

3. Little, Mark, Jon Maron, and Greg Pavlik. *Java Transaction Processing: Design and Implementation.* Upper Saddle River, N.J.: Prentice Hall PTR, 2004.

are used to characterize how transactions behave. Understanding these four properties is fundamental to understanding transactions. The following list summarizes these properties:

- **Atomicity:** All of the operations in a transaction are successful or none of them are. The success of every individual operation is tied to the success of the entire group.

- **Consistency:** The resulting state at the end of the transaction adheres to a set of rules that define acceptability of the data. The data in the entire system is legal or valid with respect to the rest of the data in the system.

- **Isolation:** Changes made within a transaction are visible only to the transaction that is making the changes. Once a transaction commits the changes they are atomically visible to other transactions.

- **Durability:** The changes made within a transaction endure beyond the completion of the transaction.

A transaction that meets all of these requirements is said to be an ACID transaction (the familiar ACID term being obtained by combining the first letter of each of the four properties).

Not all transactions are ACID transactions, and those that are often offer some flexibility in the fulfillment of the ACID properties. For example, the isolation level is a common setting that can be configured to provide either looser or tighter degrees of isolation than what was described earlier. These are typically done for reasons of either increased performance or, on the other side of the spectrum, if an application has more stringent data consistency requirements. The transactions that we discuss in the context of Java EE are normally of the ACID variety.

Enterprise Transactions in Java

Transactions actually exist at different levels within the enterprise application server. The lowest and most basic transaction is at the level of the resource, which in our discussion is assumed to be a relational database fronted by a DataSource interface. This is called a *resource-local transaction* and is equivalent to a database transaction. These types of transactions are manipulated by interacting directly with the JDBC DataSource that is obtained from the application server. Resource-local transactions are used much more infrequently than container transactions.

The broader *container transaction* uses the Java Transaction API (JTA) that is available in every compliant Java EE application server. This is the typical transaction that is used for enterprise applications and may involve or *enlist* a number of resources including data sources as well as other types of transactional resources. Resources defined using Java Connector Architecture (J2C) components may also be enlisted in the container transaction.

Containers typically add their own layer on top of the JDBC DataSource to perform functions such as connection management and pooling that make more efficient use of the resources and provide a seamless integration with the transaction-management system. This is also necessary because it is the responsibility of the container to perform the commit or rollback operation on the data source when the container transaction completes.

Because container transactions use JTA and because they may span multiple resources, they are also called *JTA transactions* or *global transactions*. The container transaction is a central aspect of programming within Java EE application servers.

Transaction Demarcation

Every transaction has a beginning and an end. Beginning a transaction will allow subsequent operations to become a part of the same transaction until the transaction has completed. Transactions may be completed in one of two ways. They may be committed, causing all of the changes to be persisted to the data store, or rolled back, indicating that the changes should be discarded. The act of causing a transaction to either begin or complete is termed *transaction demarcation*. This is a critical part of writing enterprise applications, since doing transaction demarcation incorrectly is one of the most common sources of performance degradation.

Resource-local transactions are always demarcated explicitly by the application, while container transactions may either be demarcated automatically by the container or by using a JTA interface that supports application-controlled demarcation. In the first case, when the container takes over the responsibility of transaction demarcation, we call it container-managed transaction management, but when the application is responsible for demarcation we call it bean-managed transaction management.

EJBs may use either container-managed transactions or bean-managed transactions. Servlets are limited to the somewhat poorly named bean-managed transaction. The default transaction management style for an EJB component is container-managed. To configure an EJB to have its transactions demarcated one way or the other, the @TransactionManagement annotation should be specified on the session or message-driven bean class. The TransactionManagementType enumerated type defines BEAN for bean-managed transactions and CONTAINER for container-managed transactions. Listing 3-18 demonstrates how to enabled bean-managed transactions using this approach.

Listing 3-18. *Changing the Transaction Management Type of a Bean*

```
@Stateless
@TransactionManagement(TransactionManagementType.BEAN)
public class ProjectServiceBean implements ProjectService {
    // methods in this class manually control transaction demarcation
}
```

Since the default transaction management for a bean is container-managed, this annotation needs to be specified only if bean-managed transactions are desired.

Container-Managed Transactions

The most common way to demarcate transactions is to use container-managed transactions (CMTs). This spares the application the effort and code to begin and commit transactions explicitly.

Transaction requirements are determined by metadata on session and message-driven beans and are configurable at the granularity of method execution. For example, a session bean may declare that whenever any specific method on that bean gets invoked, then the container must ensure that a transaction is started before the method begins. The container would also be responsible for committing the transaction after the completion of the method.

It is quite common for one bean to invoke another bean from one or more of its methods. In this case a transaction that may have been started by the calling method would not have been committed, because the calling method will not be completed until its call to the second bean has completed. This leads to the requirement to have settings for defining how the container should behave when a method is invoked within a specific transactional context.

For example, if a transaction is already in progress when a method is called, then the container may be expected to just make use of that transaction, whereas it may be directed to start a new one if no transaction is active. These settings are called *transaction attributes*, and they determine exactly what the container-managed transactional behavior is.

The defined transaction attributes choices are

- MANDATORY: If this attribute is specified for a method, then a transaction is expected to have already been started and be active when the method is called. If no transaction is active, then an exception is thrown. This attribute is seldom used but can be a development tool to catch transaction demarcation errors in cases where it is expected that a transaction should already have been started.

- REQUIRED: This is the most common case where a method is expected to be in a transaction. The container provides a guarantee that a transaction is active for the method. If one is already active, then that one is used, but if one does not exist, then a new transaction is created for the method execution.

- REQUIRES_NEW: This is used when the method always needs to be in its own transaction, that is, the method should be committed or rolled back independent of methods further up the call stack. It should be used with caution, as it can lead to excessive transaction overhead.

- SUPPORTS: Methods marked with Supports are not dependent upon a transaction but will tolerate running inside one if it exists. This is an indicator that no transactional resources are accessed in the method.

- NOT_SUPPORTED: A method marked to not support transactions will cause the container to suspend the current transaction if one is active when the method is called. It implies that the method does not perform transactional operations but may fail in other ways that could undesirably affect the outcome of a transaction. This is not a commonly used attribute.

- NEVER: A method marked to never support transactions will cause the container to throw an exception if a transaction is active when the method is called. This attribute is very seldom used but can be a development tool to catch transaction demarcation errors in cases when it is expected that transactions should already have been completed.

Any time the container starts a transaction for a method, the container is assumed to also attempt to commit the transaction at the end of the method. Each time the current transaction must be suspended, then the container is responsible for resuming the suspended transaction at the conclusion of the method.

The transaction attribute for a method may be indicated by annotating a session or message-driven bean class, or one of its methods that is part of the business interface, with the @TransactionAttribute annotation. This annotation requires a single argument of the enumerated type TransactionAttributeType, the values of which are defined in the preceding list. Annotating the bean class will cause the transaction attribute to apply to all of the business methods in the class, while annotating a method applies the attribute only to the method. If both class-level and method-level annotations exist, then the method-level annotation takes precedence. In the absence of class-level or method-level `@TransactionAttribute` annotations, the default attribute of `REQUIRED` will be applied.

Listing 3-19 shows how the `addItem()` method from the shopping cart bean in Listing 3-6 might use a transaction attribute. No transaction management setting was supplied, so container-managed transactions will be used. No attribute was specified on the class, so the default behavior of `REQUIRED` will apply to all of the methods of the class. The exception is that the `addItem()` method has declared a transaction attribute of `SUPPORTS`, which overrides the `REQUIRED` setting. Whenever a call to add an item is made, then that item will be added to the cart, but if no transaction was active then none will need to be started.

Listing 3-19. *Specifying a Transaction Attribute*

```
@Stateful
public class ShoppingCartBean implements ShoppingCart {

    @TransactionAttribute(TransactionAttributeType.SUPPORTS)
    public void addItem(String item, Integer quantity) {
        verifyItem(item, quantity);
        // ...
    }

    // ...
}
```

Furthermore, before the `addItem()` method adds the item to the cart, it does some validation in a private method called `verifyItem()` that is not shown in the example. When this method is invoked from `verifyItem()`, it will run in whatever transactional context `addItem()` was invoked.

Any bean wanting to cause a container-managed transaction to roll back may do so by invoking the `setRollbackOnly()` method on the `EJBContext` object. While this will not cause the immediate rollback of the transaction, it is an indication to the container that the transaction should be rolled back when the time comes. Note that entity managers will also cause the current transaction to be set to roll back when an exception is thrown during an entity manager invocation or when the transaction completes.

Bean-Managed Transactions

The other way of demarcating transactions is to use bean-managed transactions (BMT). Declaring that a bean is using bean-managed transactions means that the bean class is assuming the responsibility to begin and commit the transactions whenever it deems it's necessary. With this responsibility, however, comes the expectation that the bean class will get it right. Beans that use BMT must ensure that any time a transaction has been started, it must also be completed before returning from the method that started it. Failure to do so will result in the container rolling back the transaction automatically and an exception being thrown.

One penalty of transactions being managed by the application instead of by the container is that they do not get propagated to methods called on another BMT bean. For example, if Bean A begins a transaction and then calls Bean B, which is using bean-managed transactions, then the transaction will not get propagated to the method in Bean B. Any time a transaction is active when a BMT method is invoked, the active transaction will be suspended until control returns to the calling method.

BMT is not generally recommended for use in EJBs because it adds complexity to the application and requires the application to do work that the server can already do for it. It is necessary, though, when transactions must be initiated from the web tier, since it is the only supported way that non-EJB components can use container transactions.

UserTransaction

In order to be able to manually begin and commit container transactions, the application must have an interface that supports it. The UserTransaction interface is the designated object in the JTA that applications can hold on to and invoke to manage transaction boundaries. An instance of UserTransaction is not actually the current transaction instance but is a sort of proxy that provides the transaction API and represents the current transaction. A UserTransaction instance may be injected into BMT components by using the @Resource annotation. When using dependency lookup, it is found in the environment naming context using the reserved name "java:comp/UserTransaction". The UserTransaction interface is shown in Listing 3-20.

Listing 3-20. *The* UserTransaction *Interface*

```
public interface javax.transaction.UserTransaction {
    public abstract void begin();
    public abstract void commit();
    public abstract int getStatus();
    public abstract void rollback();
    public abstract void setRollbackOnly();
    public abstract void setTransactionTimeout(int seconds);
}
```

Each JTA transaction is associated with an execution thread, so it follows that no more than one transaction can be active at any given time. So if one transaction is active, the user cannot start another one in the same thread until the first one has committed or rolled back. Alternatively, the transaction may time out, causing the transaction to roll back.

We discussed earlier that in certain CMT conditions the container will suspend the current transaction. From the previous API you can see that there is no UserTransaction method for suspending a transaction. Only the container can do this using an internal transaction management API. In this way multiple transactions can be associated with a single thread, even though only one can ever be active at a time.

Rollbacks may occur in several different scenarios. The setRollbackOnly() method indicates that the current transaction may not be committed, leaving rollback as the only possible outcome. The transaction may be rolled back immediately by calling the rollback() method. Alternately, a time limit for the transaction may be set with the setTransactionTimeout() method, causing the transaction to roll back when the limit is reached. The only catch with transaction timeouts is that the time limit must be set before the transaction starts and it cannot be changed once the transaction is in progress.

In JTA every thread has a transactional status that can be accessed through the getStatus() call. The return value of this method is one of the constants defined on the java.transaction.Status interface. If no transaction is active, for example, then the value returned by getStatus() will be the STATUS_NO_TRANSACTION. Likewise if setRollbackOnly() has been called on the current transaction, then the status will be STATUS_MARKED_ROLLBACK until the transaction has begun rolling back.

Listing 3-21 shows a fragment from a servlet using the ShoppingCart bean in order to demonstrate using UserTransaction to invoke multiple EJB methods within a single transaction. The doPost() method uses the UserTransaction instance injected with the @Resource annotation to start and commit a transaction. Note the try ... finally block required around the transaction operations in order to ensure that the transaction is correctly cleaned up in the event of a failure.

Listing 3-21. *Using the* UserTransaction *Interface*

```
public class ProjectServlet extends HttpServlet {
    @Resource UserTransaction tx;
    @EJB ProjectService bean;

    protected void doPost(HttpServletRequest request, HttpServletResponse response)
        throws ServletException, IOException {
        // ...

        try {
            tx.begin();
            try {
                bean.assignEmployeeToProject(projectId, empId);
                bean.updateProjectStatistics();
            } finally {
                tx.commit();
            }
        } catch (Exception e) {
            // handle exceptions from UserTransaction methods
            // ...
        }

        // ...
    }
}
```

Using Java EE Components

Now that we have described how to define Java EE components and make use of services such as transaction management that are provided by the application server, we can demonstrate how to put these components to work. Once again we must caution that this is not an exhaustive overview of these technologies but is provided to put the upcoming persistence examples in context and preview the new features in Java EE 5 for developers who may be new to the platform.

Using a Stateless Session Bean

A client of a stateless session bean is any Java EE component that can declare a dependency on the bean. This includes other session beans, message-driven beans, and servlets. Two-tier access from a remote client is also possible if the bean defines a remote business interface.

Consider the servlet shown in Listing 3-22, which uses the EJB from Listing 3-2 to obtain a message and then generates a simple HTML page. As we discussed earlier in the section on Dependency Management, the @EJB annotation causes the HelloService bean to be automatically injected into the servlet. Therefore when the doGet() method is invoked, methods on the business interface can be invoked without any extra steps.

Listing 3-22. *A Servlet That Uses a Session Bean*

```
public class HelloServlet extends HttpServlet {
    @EJB HelloService bean;

    protected void doGet(HttpServletRequest request, HttpServletResponse response)
        throws IOException {
        String name = request.getParameter("name");
        String message = bean.sayHello(name);

        PrintWriter out = response.getWriter();
        out.println("<html>" +
                    "<head><title>Hello</title></head>" +
                    "<body><p>" + message + "</p></body>" +
                    "</html>");
    }
}
```

The use of annotations to manage dependencies is an important change in Java EE 5 that significantly reduces the complexity of weaving together components within applications. In the case of session beans that depend on other session beans, note that it is always safe to declare a reference to a stateless session bean and store it in a field on the bean. The bean reference in the case of a stateless session bean is itself a stateless and thread-safe object.

Using a Stateful Session Bean

There are a few basic things to keep in mind when working with stateful session beans:

1. When a client obtains a reference to a stateful session bean, a private instance of that bean is created for the client. In other words, there is one bean instance per client reference.

2. The bean does not go away until the client invokes a method annotated with @Remove. If the client forgets or is unable to end the conversation with the bean, it will hang around until the server can determine that it is safe to remove it.

3. A reference to a stateful session bean cannot be shared between threads.

A consequence of these rules is that clients need to plan carefully on when they need to start the session and when it can be ended. It also means that using the @EJB annotation to inject a stateful session bean is not a good solution. Servlets, stateless session beans, and message-driven beans are all stateless components. As we stated before in the description of stateless session beans, that means that any state placed on a stateless component must also be stateless as well. A stateful session bean reference is itself stateful because it references a private instance of the bean managed by the server. If @EJB were used to inject a stateful session bean into a stateless session bean where the server had pooled 100 bean instances, then there would be 100 stateful session bean instances created as well. The only time it is ever safe to inject a stateful session bean is into another stateful session bean.

Dependency lookup is the preferred method for acquiring a stateful session bean instance for a stateless client. The EJBContext lookup() method is the easiest way to accomplish this, but JNDI will be required if the client is a servlet. Listing 3-23 demonstrates a typical pattern for servlets using stateful session beans. A reference is declared to the bean, it is looked up lazily when needed, and the result is bound to the HTTP session. The stateful session bean and HTTP session have similar life cycles, making them good candidates to work together.

Listing 3-23. *Creating and Using a Stateful Session Bean*

```
@EJB(name="cart", beanInterface=ShoppingCart.class)
public class ShoppingCartServlet extends HttpServlet {

    protected void doPost(HttpServletRequest request, HttpServletResponse response)
        throws ServletException, IOException {
        HttpSession session = request.getSession(true);
        ShoppingCart cart = (ShoppingCart) session.getAttribute("cart");
        if (cart == null) {
            try {
                Context ctx = new InitialContext();
                cart = (ShoppingCart) ctx.lookup("java:comp/env/cart");
                session.setAttribute("cart", cart);
            } catch (NamingException e) {
                throw new ServletException(e);
            }
        }

        if (request.getParameter("action").equals("add")) {
            String itemId = request.getParameter("item");
            String quantity = request.getParameter("quantity");
            cart.addItem(itemId, Integer.parseInt(quantity));
        }
```

```
        if (request.getParameter("action").equals("cancel")) {
            cart.cancel();
            session.removeAttribute("cart");
        }

        // ...
    }
}
```

When the server receives a request to look up a stateful session bean, it asks the EJB container to create a new instance of the bean, which is then assigned a unique identifier. The reference to the bean that is returned keeps track of this identifier and uses it when communicating with the server to ensure that the right bean instance is used to invoke each business method.

Using a Message-Driven Bean

As an asynchronous component, clients of a message-driven bean can't directly invoke business operations. Instead they send messages, which are then delivered to the MDB by the messaging system being used. The client needs to know only the format of the message that the MDB is expecting and the messaging destination where the message must be sent. Listing 3-24 demonstrates sending a message to the MDB we defined in Listing 3-8. The ReportProcessor MDB expects an employee id as its message format. Therefore the session bean client in this example creates a text message with the employee id and sends it through the JMS API. The same criteria that was specified on the MDB to filter the messages is also specified here on the client.

Listing 3-24. *Sending a Message to an MDB*

```
@Stateless
public class EmployeeServiceBean implements EmployeeService {
    @Resource Queue destinationQueue;
    @Resource QueueConnectionFactory factory;

    public void generateReport() {
        try {
            QueueConnection connection = factory.createQueueConnection();
            QueueSession session =
                connection.createQueueSession(false, 0);
            QueueSender sender = session.createSender(destinationQueue);

            Message message = session.createTextMessage("12345");
            message.setStringProperty("RECIPIENT", "ReportProcessor");

            sender.send(message);
```

```
                sender.close();
                session.close();
                connection.close();
            } catch (JMSException e) {
                // ...
            }
        }

        // ...
    }
```

Adding the Entity Manager

Using stateless session beans as components to manage persistence operations is the pre-ferred strategy for Java EE applications. Clients gain the benefit of working with a session façade that presents a business interface that is decoupled from the specifics of the implemen-tation. The bean is able to leverage the dependency-management capabilities of the server to access the entity manager and can make use of services such as container-managed transac-tions to precisely specify the transaction requirements of each business operation. Finally, the POJO nature of entities allows them to be easily returned from and passed as arguments to a session bean method.

Leveraging the stateless session bean for persistence is largely a case of injecting an entity manager. Listing 3-25 demonstrates a typical session bean that injects an entity manager and uses it to implement its business operations.

Listing 3-25. *Using the Entity Manager with a Stateless Session Bean*

```
@Stateless
public class DepartmentServiceBean {
    @PersistenceContext(unitName="EmployeeService")
    EntityManager em;

    public void addEmployeeToDepartment(int empId, int deptId) {
        Employee emp = em.find(Employee.class, empId);
        Department dept = em.find(Deptartment.class, deptId);
        dept.getEmployees().add(emp);
        emp.setDept(dept);
    }

    // ...
}
```

Stateful session beans are also well suited to managing persistence operations within an application component model. The ability to store state on the session bean means that query criteria or other conversational state can be constructed across multiple method calls before being acted upon. The results of entity manager operations may also be cached on the bean instance in some situations.

Listing 3-26 revisits the shopping cart bean from Listing 3-6. In this example `Order` and `Item` are entities representing a sales transaction. The order is built up incrementally over the life of the session and then persisted to the database using the injected entity manager when payment has been confirmed.

Listing 3-26. *Using the Entity Manager with a Stateful Session Bean*

```
@Stateful
public class ShoppingCartBean implements ShoppingCart {
    @PersistenceContext(unitName="order")
    private EntityManager em;
    private Order order = new Order();

    public void addItem(Item item, int quantity) {
        order.addItem(item, quantity);
    }

    // ...

    @Remove
    public void checkout(int paymentId) {
        order.setPaymentId(paymentId);
        em.persist(order);
    }
}
```

From the perspective of using the entity manager with message-driven beans, the main question is whether or not the MDB should use the Java Persistence API directly or delegate to another component such as a session bean. A common pattern in many applications is to treat the MDB as an asynchronous façade for session beans in situations where the business logic does not produce results that are customer-facing, that is, where the results of the business operation are stored in a database or propagated to another messaging system. This is largely an issue of personal taste, as message-driven beans fully support injecting the entity manager and can leverage container-managed transactions.

Putting It All Together

Now that we have discussed the application component model and services available as part of a Java EE application server, we can revisit the `EmployeeService` example from the previous chapter and port it to the Java EE environment. Along the way, we'll provide example code to show how the components fit together and how they relate back to the Java SE example.

Defining the Component

To begin, let's consider the definition of the `EmployeeService` class from Listing 2-9 in the previous chapter. The goal of this class is to provide business operations related to the mainte-nance of employee data. In doing so, it encapsulates all of the persistence operations. To introduce this class into the Java EE environment, we must first decide how it should be represented. The service pattern exhibited by the class suggests the session bean as the ideal component. Since the business methods of the bean have no dependency on each other, we can further decide that a stateless session bean is suitable. In fact, this bean demonstrates a very typical design pattern called a Session Façade,[4] in which a stateless session bean is used to shield clients from dealing with a particular persistence API. Our first step is to extract a business interface from the original bean. Listing 3-27 shows the EmployeeService business interface.

Listing 3-27. *The* EmployeeService *Business Interface*

```
public interface EmployeeService {
    public Employee createEmployee(int id, String name, long salary);
    public void removeEmployee(int id);
    public Employee changeEmployeeSalary(int id, long newSalary);
    public Employee findEmployee(int id);
    public Collection<Employee> findAllEmployees();
}
```

In the Java SE example, the EmployeeService class must create and maintain its own entity manager instance. We can replace this logic with dependency injection to acquire the entity manager automatically. Having decided on a stateless session bean and dependency injection, the converted stateless session bean is demonstrated in Listing 3-28. With the exception of how the entity manager is acquired, the business methods are identical. This is an important feature of the Java Persistence API, as the same EntityManager interface can be used both inside and outside of the application server.

Listing 3-28. *The* EmployeeService *Session Bean*

```
@Stateless
public class EmployeeServiceBean implements EmployeeService {
    @PersistenceContext(unitName="EmployeeService")
    protected EntityManager em;

    public EntityManager getEntityManager() {
        return em;
    }

    public Employee createEmployee(int id, String name, long salary) {
        Employee emp = new Employee(id);
        emp.setName(name);
        emp.setSalary(salary);
        getEntityManager().persist(emp);
        return emp;
    }
```

---

4. Alur et al., *Core J2EE Patterns.*

```
    public void removeEmployee(int id) {
        Employee emp = findEmployee(id);
        if (emp != null) {
            getEntityManager().remove(emp);
        }
    }

    public Employee changeEmployeeSalary(int id, long newSalary) {
        Employee emp = findEmployee(id);
        if (emp != null) {
            emp.setSalary(newSalary);
        }
        return emp;
    }

    public Employee findEmployee(int id) {
        return getEntityManager().find(Employee.class, id);
    }

    public Collection<Employee> findAllEmployees() {
        Query query = getEntityManager().createQuery("SELECT e FROM Employee e");
        return (Collection<Employee>) query.getResultList();
    }
}
```

Defining the User Interface

The next question to consider is how the bean will be accessed. A web interface is the standard presentation method for modern enterprise applications. To demonstrate how this stateless session bean might be used by a servlet, consider Listing 3-29. The request parameters are interpreted to determine the action, which is then carried out by invoking methods on the injected EmployeeService bean. Although only the first action is described, you can see how this could easily be extended to handle each of the operations defined on the EmployeeService business interface.

Listing 3-29. *Using the* EmployeeService *Session Bean from a Servlet*

```
public class EmployeeServlet extends HttpServlet {
    @EJB EmployeeService bean;

    protected void doPost(HttpServletRequest request,
                          HttpServletResponse response) {
        String action = request.getParameter("action");
```

```
    if (action.equals("create")) {
        String id = request.getParameter("id");
        String name = request.getParameter("name");
        String salary = request.getParameter("salary");
        bean.createEmployee(Integer.parseInt(id), name,
                            Long.parseLong(salary));
    }

    // ...
}
}
```

Packaging It Up

In the Java EE environment, many properties required in the `persistence.xml` file for Java SE may be omitted. In Listing 3-30 we see the `persistence.xml` file from Listing 2-11 in the previous chapter converted for deployment as part of a Java EE application. Instead of JDBC properties for creating a connection, we now declare that the entity manager should use the data source name "jdbc/EmployeeDS". The `transaction-type` attribute has also been removed to allow the persistence unit to default to JTA. The application server will automatically find entity classes, so even the list of classes has been removed. This example represents the ideal minimum Java EE configuration.

Since the business logic that uses this persistence unit is implemented in a stateless session bean, the `persistence.xml` file would typically be located in the `META-INF` directory of the corresponding EJB JAR. We will fully describe the `persistence.xml` file and its placement within a Java EE application later in Chapter 11.

Listing 3-30. *Defining a Persistence Unit in Java EE*

```
<persistence>
    <persistence-unit name="EmployeeService">
        <jta-data-source>jdbc/EmployeeDS</jta-data-source>
    </persistence-unit>
</persistence>
```

Summary

It would be impossible to provide details on all of the features of the Java EE platform in a single chapter. However, is it likewise difficult to put the Java Persistence API in context without understanding the application server environment in which it will be used. Therefore over the course of this chapter we have attempted to introduce the technologies that are of the most relevance to the developer using persistence in enterprise applications.

We began with an introduction to software component models and introduced the Enterprise JavaBeans model for enterprise components. We argued that the use of components is more important than ever before and identified some of the benefits that come from leveraging this approach.

In the section on session beans, we introduced the fundamentals and then looked in detail at both stateless and stateful session beans. We learned about the difference in interaction style between the two session types and looked at the syntax for declaring beans. We also looked at the difference between local and remote business interfaces.

We next looked at dependency management in Java EE application servers. We discussed the reference annotation types and how to declare them. We also looked at the difference between dependency lookup and dependency injection. In the case of injection we looked at the difference between field and setter injection. Finally, we explored each of the resource types demonstrating how to acquire server and Java Persistence API resources.

In the section on transaction management, we looked at the Java Transaction API and its role in building datacentric applications. We then looked at the difference between bean-managed transactions and container-managed transactions for EJBs. We documented the different types of transaction attributes for CMT beans and showed how to manually control bean-managed transactions.

Finally, we concluded the chapter by exploring how to use Java EE components in applications and how they can leverage the Java Persistence API. We also discussed an end-to-end example of the Java Persistence API in the Java EE environment, converting the example application introduced in the previous chapter from a command-line Java SE application to a web-based application running on an application server.

Now that we have introduced the Java Persistence API in both the Java SE and Java EE environments, it's time to dive into the specification in detail. In the next chapter we begin this journey with the central focus of the Java Persistence API, object-relational mapping.

CHAPTER 4

Object-Relational Mapping

The largest part of an API that persists objects to a relational database ends up being the object-relational mapping component. The topic of object-relational mapping usually includes everything from how the object state is mapped to the database columns to how to issue queries across the objects. We are focusing this chapter primarily on how to define and map entity state to the database, emphasizing the simple manner in which it may be done.

In this chapter we will introduce the basics of mapping fields to database columns and then go on to show how to map and automatically generate entity identifiers. We will go into some detail about different kinds of relationships and show examples that demonstrate how they are mapped from the domain model to the data model.

Persistence Annotations

We have shown in previous chapters how annotations have been used extensively both in the EJB 3.0 and Java Persistence API specifications. We are going to discuss in significant detail persistence and mapping metadata, and since we use annotations to explain the concepts, it is worth reviewing a few things about the annotations before we get started.

Persistence annotations may be applied at three different levels: at the class, method, and field levels. To annotate any of these, the annotation must be placed in front of the code definition of the artifact being annotated. In some cases we will put them on the same line just before the class, method, or field, and in other cases we will put them on the line above. It is based completely upon the preferences of the person applying the annotations, and if you have not already noticed, we think it makes sense to do one thing in some cases and the other in other cases. It depends on how long the annotation is and what the most readable format seems to be.

The Java Persistence API annotations were designed to provide maximum readability, be easy to specify, and be flexible enough to allow different combinations of metadata. Most annotations are specified as siblings instead of being nested inside each other. As with all trade-offs, the piper must be paid however, and the cost of flexibility is that many possible permutations of top-level metadata will be syntactically correct but semantically invalid. The compiler will be of no use, but the provider runtime will often do some basic checking for some improper annotation groupings. The nature of annotations, however, is that when they are unexpected, then they will often just not get noticed at all. This is worth remembering when attempting to understand behavior that may not match what you thought you specified in the annotations. It could be that one or more of the annotations are just being ignored.

The mapping annotations can be categorized as being in one or the other of the two categories: logical annotations and physical annotations. The annotations in the logical group are those that describe the entity model from an object modeling view. They are tightly bound to the domain model and are the sort of metadata that you might want to specify in UML or any other object modeling language or framework. The physical annotations relate to the concrete data model in the database. They deal with tables, columns, constraints, and other database-level artifacts that the object model might never otherwise be aware of.

We will make use of both types of annotations throughout the examples and to demonstrate the mapping metadata. Understanding and being able to distinguish between these two levels of metadata will better qualify you to make decisions about where to declare metadata, and where to use annotations and XML. As we will see in Chapter 10, there are XML equivalents to all of the mapping annotations described in this chapter, giving you the freedom to use the approach that best suits your development needs.

Accessing Entity State

The mapped state of an entity must be accessible to the provider at runtime, so that when it comes time to write the data out, it can be obtained from the entity instance and stored in the database. Similarly, when the state is loaded from the database, the provider runtime must be able to insert it into a new entity instance. The way the state is accessed in the entity is called the *access mode*.

In Chapter 2 we saw briefly that there were two different ways that could be used to specify persistent entity state: we could either annotate the fields or annotate the JavaBean-style properties. The mechanism that we use to designate the persistent state is the same as the access mode that the provider uses to access that state. If we annotate fields, then the provider will get and set the fields of the entity using reflection. If the annotations are set on the getter methods of properties, then those getter and setter methods will be invoked by the provider to access and set the state.

■**Tip** Some vendors may support annotating a mixture of fields and properties on the same entity class. Be careful of relying upon this kind of behavior, as it could cause your entity class definitions to be non-portable.

Field Access

Annotating the fields of the entity will cause the provider to use field access to get and set the state of the entity. Getter and setter methods may or may not be present, but if they are present, they are ignored by the provider. All fields must be declared as either protected, package, or private. Public fields are disallowed because it would open up the state fields to access by any unprotected class in the VM. Doing so is not just an obviously bad practice but could also defeat the provider implementation. Other classes must use the methods of an entity in order to access its persistent state.

The example in Listing 4-1 shows the Employee entity being mapped using field access. The @Id annotation indicates not only that the id field is the persistent identifier or primary key for the entity but also that field access should be assumed. The name and salary fields are then defaulted to being persistent, and they get mapped to columns of the same name.

Listing 4-1. *Using Field Access*

```
@Entity
public class Employee {
    @Id private int id;
    private String name;
    private long salary;

    public int getId() { return id; }
    public void setId(int id) { this.id = id; }

    public String getName() { return name; }
    public void setName(String name) { this.name = name; }

    public long getSalary() { return salary; }
    public void setSalary(long salary) { this. salary = salary; }
}
```

Property Access

When property access mode is used, the same contract as for JavaBeans applies, and there must be getter and setter methods for the persistent properties. The type of the property is determined by the return type of the getter method and must be the same as the type of the single parameter passed into the setter method. Both methods must be either public or protected visibility. The mapping annotations for a property must be on the getter method.

In Listing 4-2 the Employee class has an @Id annotation on the getId() getter method so the provider will use property access to get and set the state of the entity. The name and salary properties will be made persistent by virtue of the getter and setter methods that exist for them and will be mapped to NAME and SALARY columns respectively. Note that the salary property is backed by the wage field, which does not share the same name. This goes unnoticed by the provider, since by specifying property access, we are telling the provider to ignore the entity fields and use only the getter and setter methods for naming.

Listing 4-2. *Using Property Access*

```
@Entity
public class Employee {
    private int id;
    private String name;
    private long wage;
```

```
    @Id public int getId() { return id; }
    public void setId(int id) { this.id = id; }

    public String getName() { return name; }
    public void setName(String name) { this.name = name; }

    public long getSalary() { return wage; }
    public void setSalary(long salary) { this.wage = salary; }
}
```

Mapping to a Table

We saw in Chapter 2 that mapping an entity to a table in the simplest case does not need any mapping annotations at all. Only the @Entity and @Id annotations need to be specified to create and map an entity to a database table.

In those cases the default table name, which is just the unqualified name of the entity class, was perfectly suitable. If it happens that the default table name is not the name that we like, or if a suitable table that contains the state already exists in our database with a different name, then we must specify the name of the table. We do this by annotating the entity class with the @Table annotation and by including the name of the table using the name element. Many databases have terse names for tables. Listing 4-3 shows an entity that is mapped to a table that has a name different than its class name.

Listing 4-3. *Overriding the Default Table Name*

```
@Entity
@Table(name="EMP")
public class Employee { ... }
```

■**Tip** Default names are not specified to be either uppercase or lowercase. Most databases are not case-sensitive, so it won't generally matter whether a vendor uses the case of the entity name or converts it to uppercase.

The @Table annotation provides the ability to not only name the table that the entity state is being stored in but also to name a database schema or catalog. The schema name is commonly used to differentiate one set of tables from another and is indicated by using the schema element. Listing 4-4 shows an Employee entity that is mapped to the EMP table in the HR schema.

Listing 4-4. *Setting a Schema*

```
@Entity
@Table(name="EMP", schema="HR")
public class Employee { ... }
```

When specified, the schema name will be prepended to the table name when the persistence runtime goes to the database to access the table. In this case the HR schema will be prepended to the EMP table each time the table is accessed.

■**Tip** Some vendors may allow the schema to be included in the name element of the table without having to specify the schema element—for example, @Table(name="HR.EMP"). Support for inlining the name of the schema with the table name is non-standard.

Some databases support the notion of a catalog. For these databases, the catalog element of the @Table annotation may be specified. Listing 4-5 shows a catalog being explicitly set for the EMP table.

Listing 4-5. *Setting a Catalog*

```
@Entity
@Table(name="EMP", catalog="HR")
public class Employee { ... }
```

Mapping Simple Types

Simple Java types are mapped as part of the immediate state of an entity in its fields or properties. The list of persistable types is quite lengthy and includes pretty much every type that you would want to persist. They are

- **Primitive Java types:** byte, int, short, long, boolean, char, float, double

- **Wrapper classes of primitive Java types:** Byte, Integer, Short, Long, Boolean, Character, Float, Double

- **Byte and character array types:** byte[], Byte[], char[], Character[]

- **Large numeric types:** java.math.BigInteger, java.math.BigDecimal

- **Strings:** java.lang.String

- **Java temporal types:** java.util.Date, java.util.Calendar

- **JDBC temporal types:** java.sql.Date, java.sql.Time, java.sql.Timestamp

- **Enumerated types:** Any system or user-defined enumerated type

- **Serializable objects:** Any system or user-defined serializable type

Sometimes the type of the database column being mapped to is not exactly the same as the Java type. In almost all cases the provider runtime can convert the type returned by JDBC into the correct Java type of the attribute. If the type from the JDBC layer cannot be converted to the Java type of the field or property, then an exception will normally be thrown, although it is not guaranteed.

■**Tip** When the persistent type does not match the JDBC type, some providers may choose to take proprietary action or make a best guess to convert between the two. In other cases, the JDBC driver may be
performing the conversion on its own.

When persisting a field or property, the provider looks at the type and ensures that it is
one of the persistable types listed earlier. If it is in the list, the provider will persist it using the
appropriate JDBC type and pass it through to the JDBC driver. At that point, if the field or property is not serializable, the result is unspecified. The provider may choose to throw an
exception or just try and pass the object through to JDBC.

An optional @Basic annotation may be placed on a field or property to explicitly mark it as
being persistent. This annotation is mostly for documentation purposes and is not required for
the field or property to be persistent. Because of the annotation, we call mappings of simple
types *basic mappings*.

Now that we have seen how we can persist either fields or properties and how they are
virtually equivalent in terms of persistence, we will just call them *attributes*. An attribute is a
field or property of a class, and we will use the term *attribute* from now on to avoid having to
continually refer to fields or properties in specific terms when one or the other may apply.

Column Mappings

Where the persistent attributes can be thought of as being logical mappings that indicate that
a given attribute is persistent, the physical annotation that is the companion annotation to the
basic mapping is the @Column annotation. Specifying @Column on the attribute indicates specific characteristics of the physical database column that the object model is less concerned
about. In fact, the object model might never even need to know to which column it is mapped,
and the column name and physical mapping metadata may be located in a separate XML file.

A number of annotation elements may be specified as part of @Column, but most of them
apply only to schema generation and will be covered in Chapter 9. The only one that is of consequence is the name element, which is just a string that specifies the name of the column that
the attribute has been mapped to. This is used when the default column name is not appropriate or does not apply to the schema being used. We can think of the name element of the
@Column annotation as a means of overriding the default column name that would have otherwise been applied.

The example in Listing 4-6 shows how we can override the default column name for an
attribute.

Listing 4-6. *Mapping Attributes to Columns*

```
@Entity
public class Employee {
    @Id
    @Column(name="EMP_ID")
    private int id;
    private String name;
    @Column(name="SAL")
    private long salary;
    @Column(name="COMM")
    private String comments;
    // ...
}
```

To put these annotations in context, let's look at the full table mapping represented by this entity. The first thing that we notice is that no @Table annotation exists on the class, so the default table name of "EMPLOYEE" will be applied to it.

The next thing we see is that @Column can be used with @Id mappings as well as with basic mappings. The id field is being overridden to map to the EMP_ID column instead of the default ID column. The name field is not annotated with @Column, so the default column name NAME would be used to store and retrieve the employee name. The salary and comments fields, however, are annotated to map to the SAL and COMM columns, respectively. The Employee entity is therefore mapped to the table that is shown in Figure 4-1.

Figure 4-1. EMPLOYEE *entity table*

Lazy Fetching

On occasion, we know that certain portions of an entity will be seldom accessed. In these situations we can optimize the performance when retrieving the entity by fetching only the data that we expect to be frequently accessed. We would like the remainder of the data to be fetched only when or if it is required. There are many names for this kind of feature, including lazy loading, deferred loading, lazy fetching, on-demand fetching, just-in-time reading, indirection, and others. They all mean pretty much the same thing, which is just that some data may not be loaded when the object is initially read from the database but will be fetched only when it is referenced or accessed.

The *fetch type* of a basic mapping can be configured to be lazily or eagerly loaded by specifying the fetch element in the corresponding @Basic annotation. The FetchType enumerated type defines the values for this element, which may be either EAGER or LAZY. Setting the fetch type of a basic mapping to LAZY means that the provider may defer loading the state for that attribute until it is referenced. The default is to eagerly load all basic mappings. Listing 4-7 shows an example of overriding a basic mapping to be lazily loaded.

Listing 4-7. *Lazy Field Loading*

```
@Entity
public class Employee {
    // ...
    @Basic(fetch=FetchType.LAZY)
    @Column(name="COMM")
    private String comments;
    // ...
}
```

We are assuming in this example that applications will seldom access the comments in an employee record, so we mark it as being lazily fetched. Note that in this case the @Basic annotation is not only present for documentation purposes but also required in order to specify the fetch type for the field. Configuring the comments field to be fetched lazily will allow an Employee instance returned from a query to have the comments field empty. The application does not have to do anything special to get it, however. By simply accessing the comments field, it will be transparently read and filled in by the provider if it was not already loaded.

Before you use this feature you should be aware of a few pertinent points about lazy attribute fetching. First and foremost, the directive to lazily fetch an attribute is meant only to be a hint to the persistence provider to help the application achieve better performance. The provider is not required to respect the request, since the behavior of the entity is not compromised if the provider goes ahead and loads the attribute. The converse is not true, though, since specifying that an attribute be eagerly fetched may be critical to being able to access the entity state once the entity is detached from the persistence context. We will discuss detachment more in Chapter 5 and explore the connection between lazy loading and detachment.

Second, on the surface it may appear that this is a good idea for certain attributes of an entity, but in practice it is almost never a good idea to lazily fetch simple types. The reason is that there is little to be gained in only returning part of a database row unless you are certain that the state will not be accessed in the entity later on. The only times when lazy loading of a basic mapping should be considered are when either there are many columns in a table (for example, dozens or hundreds) or when the columns are large (for example, very large character strings or byte strings). It could take significant resources to load the data, and not loading it could save quite a lot of effort, time, and resources. Unless either of these two cases is true, then in the majority of cases this will cause lazily fetching a subset of object attributes to end up being more expensive than eagerly fetching them.

Lazy fetching is quite relevant when it comes to relationship mappings, though, so we will be discussing this topic more later in the chapter.

Large Objects

A common database term for a character or byte-based object that can be very large (up to the gigabyte range) is *large object*, or *LOB* for short. Database columns that can store these types of large objects require special JDBC calls to be accessed from Java. To signal to the provider that it should use the LOB methods when passing and retrieving this data to and from the JDBC driver, an additional annotation must be added to the basic mapping. The @Lob annotation acts as the marker annotation to fulfill this purpose and may appear in conjunction with the @Basic annotation, or it may appear when @Basic is absent and implicitly assumed to be on the mapping.

Since a LOB mapping is just a specialized kind of basic mapping, it can also be accompanied by an @Column annotation when the name of the LOB column needs to be overridden from the assumed default name.

LOBs come in two flavors in the database: character large objects, called *CLOBs*, and binary large objects, or *BLOBs*. As their names imply, a CLOB column holds a large character sequence, and a BLOB column can store a large byte sequence. The Java types mapped to BLOB columns are byte[], Byte[], and Serializable types, while char[], Character[], and String objects are mapped to CLOB columns. The provider is responsible for making this distinction based upon the type of the attribute being mapped.

An example of mapping an image to a BLOB column is shown in Listing 4-8. Here, the PIC column is assumed to be a BLOB column to store the employee picture that is in the picture field. We have also marked this field to be loaded lazily, a common practice applied to LOBs that do not get referenced often.

Listing 4-8. *Mapping a BLOB Column*

```
@Entity
public class Employee {
    @Id
    private int id;
    @Basic(fetch=FetchType.LAZY)
    @Lob @Column(name="PIC")
    private byte[] picture;
    // ...
}
```

Enumerated Types

Another of the simple types that may be treated specially is the enumerated type. The values of an enumerated type are constants that can be handled differently depending upon the application needs.

As with enumerated types in other languages, the values of an enumerated type in Java have an implicit ordinal assignment that is determined by the order in which they were declared. This ordinal cannot be modified at runtime and can be used to represent and store the values of the enumerated type in the database. Interpreting the values as ordinals is the default way that providers will map enumerated types to the database, and the provider will assume that the database column is an integer type.

Consider the following enumerated type:

```
public enum EmployeeType {
    FULL_TIME_EMPLOYEE,
    PART_TIME_EMPLOYEE,
    CONTRACT_EMPLOYEE
}
```

The ordinals assigned to the values of this enumerated type at compile time would be 0 for `FULL_TIME_EMPLOYEE`, 1 for `PART_TIME_EMPLOYEE`, and 2 for `CONTRACT_EMPLOYEE`. In Listing 4-9 we define a persistent field of this type.

Listing 4-9. *Mapping an Enumerated Type Using Ordinals*

```
@Entity
public class Employee {
    @Id private int id;
    private EmployeeType type;
    // ...
}
```

We can see that mapping `EmployeeType` is trivially easy to the point where we don't actually have to do anything at all. The defaults are applied, and everything will just work. The `type` field will get mapped to an integer `TYPE` column, and all full-time employees will have an ordinal of 0 assigned to them. Similarly the other employees will have their types stored in the `TYPE` column accordingly.

If an enumerated type changes, however, then we have a problem. The persisted ordinal data in the database will no longer apply to the correct value. For example, if the company benefits policy changed and we started giving additional benefits to part-time employees who worked over 20 hours a week, then we would want to differentiate between the two types of part-time employees. By adding a `PART_TIME_BENEFITS_EMPLOYEE` value after `PART_TIME_EMPLOYEE`, we would be causing a new ordinal assignment to occur, where our new value would get assigned the ordinal of 2 and `CONTRACT_EMPLOYEE` would get 3. This would have the effect of causing all of the contract employees on record to suddenly become part-time employees with benefits, clearly not the result that we were hoping for.

We could go through the database and adjust all of the `Employee` entities to have their correct type, but if the employee type is used elsewhere, then we would need to make sure that they were all fixed as well. This is not a good maintenance situation to be in.

A better solution would be to store the name of the value as a string instead of storing the ordinal. This would isolate us from any changes in declaration and allow us to add new types without having to worry about the existing data. We can do this by adding an `@Enumerated` annotation on the attribute and specifying a value of `STRING`.

The @Enumerated annotation actually allows an EnumType to be specified, and the EnumType is itself an enumerated type that defines values of ORDINAL and STRING. While it is somewhat ironic that an enumerated type is being used to indicate how the provider should represent enumerated types, it is wholly appropriate. Since the default value of @Enumerated is ORDINAL, specifying @Enumerated(ORDINAL) is useful only when you want to make this mapping explicit.

In Listing 4-10 we are storing strings for the enumerated values. Now the TYPE column must be a string-based type, and all of the full-time employees will have the string "FULL_TIME_EMPLOYEE" stored in their corresponding TYPE column.

Listing 4-10. *Mapping an Enumerated Type Using Strings*

```
@Entity
public class Employee {
    @Id
    private int id;
    @Enumerated(EnumType.STRING)
    private EmployeeType type;
    // ...
}
```

Note that using strings will solve the problem of inserting additional values in the middle of the enumerated type, but it will leave the data vulnerable to changes in the names of the values. For instance, if we wanted to change PART_TIME_EMPLOYEE to PT_EMPLOYEE, then we would be in trouble. This is a less likely problem, though, because changing the names of an enumerated type would cause all of the code that uses the enumerated type to have to change also. This would be a bigger bother than reassigning values in a database column.

In general, storing the ordinal is going to be the best and most efficient way to store enumerated types as long as the likelihood of additional values inserted in the middle is not high. New values could still be added on the end of the type without any negative consequences.

One final note about enumerated types is that they are defined quite flexibly in Java. In fact, it is even possible to have values that contain state. There is currently no support within the Java Persistence API for mapping state contained within enumerated values.

Temporal Types

Temporal types are the set of time-based types that may be used in persistent state mappings. The list of supported temporal types includes the three java.sql types java.sql.Date, java.sql.Time, and java.sql.Timestamp, and it includes the two java.util types java.util.Date and java.util.Calendar.

The java.sql types are completely hassle-free. They act just like any other simple mapping type and do not need any special consideration. The two java.util types need additional metadata, however, to indicate which of the JDBC java.sql types to use when communicating with the JDBC driver. This is done by annotating them with the @Temporal annotation and specifying the JDBC type as a value of the TemporalType enumerated type. There are three enumerated values of DATE, TIME, and TIMESTAMP to represent each of the java.sql types.

Listing 4-11 shows how java.util.Date and java.util.Calendar may be mapped to date columns in the database.

Listing 4-11. *Mapping Temporal Types*

```
@Entity
public class Employee {
    @Id
    private int id;
    @Temporal(TemporalType.DATE)
    private Calendar dob;
    @Temporal(TemporalType.DATE)
    @Column(name="S_DATE")
    private Date startDate;
    // ...
}
```

Like the other varieties of basic mappings, the @Column annotation may be used to override the default column name.

Transient State

Attributes that are part of a persistent entity but not intended to be persistent can either be modified with the transient modifier in Java or be annotated with the @Transient annotation. If either of these is specified, then the provider runtime will not apply its default mapping rules to the attribute it was specified on.

Transient fields are used for various reasons. One might be when you want to cache some in-memory state that you don't want to have to recompute, rediscover, or reinitialize. For example, in Listing 4-12 we are using a transient field to save the correct locale-specific word for "Employee" so that we print it correctly wherever it is being displayed. We have used the transient modifier instead of the @Transient annotation so that if the Employee gets serialized from one VM to another then the translated name will get reinitialized to correspond to the locale of the new VM. In cases where the non-persistent value should be retained across serialization, the annotation should be used instead of the modifier.

Listing 4-12. *Using a Transient Field*

```
@Entity
public class Employee {
    @Id private int id;
    private String name;
    private long salary;
    transient private String translatedName;
    // ...
```

```
    public String toString() {
        if (translatedName == null) {
            translatedName =
                ResourceBundle.getBundle("EmpResources").getString("Employee");
        }
        return translatedName + ": " id + " " + name;
    }
}
```

Mapping the Primary Key

Every entity that is mapped to a relational database must have a mapping to a primary key in the table. We have already learned the basics of how the @Id annotation indicates the identifier of the entity. In this section we explore simple identifiers and primary keys in a little more depth and learn how we can let the persistence provider generate unique identifier values for us.

Except for its special significance in designating the mapping to the primary key column, an id mapping is almost the same as the basic mapping. Another difference is that id mappings are generally restricted to the following types:

- **Primitive Java types:** byte, int, short, long, char

- **Wrapper classes of primitive Java types:** Byte, Integer, Short, Long, Character

- **Arrays of primitive or wrapper types:** Byte, Integer, Short, Long, Character

- **Strings:** java.lang.String

- **Large numeric types:** java.math.BigInteger

- **Temporal types:** java.util.Date, java.sql.Date

Floating point types like float and double are permitted, as well as the Float and Double wrapper classes and java.math.BigDecimal, but these are discouraged because of the nature of rounding error and the untrustworthiness of the equals() operator when applied to them. Using floating types for primary keys is a risky endeavor and definitely not recommended.

Just as with basic mappings, the @Column annotation may be used to override the column name that the id attribute is mapped to. The same defaulting rules apply to id mappings as apply to basic mappings, which is that the name of the column is assumed to be the same as the name of the attribute.

Identifier Generation

Sometimes applications do not want to be bothered with trying to define and ensure uniqueness in some aspect of their domain model and are content to let the identifier values be automatically generated for them. This is called id generation and is specified by the @GeneratedValue annotation.

When id generation is enabled, the persistence provider will generate an identifier value for every entity instance of that type. Once the identifier value is obtained, the provider will insert it into the newly persisted entity; however, depending upon the way it is generated, it may not actually be present in the object until the entity has been inserted in the database. In other words, the application cannot rely upon being able to access the identifier until after either a flush has occurred or the transaction has completed.

Applications can choose one of four different id generation strategies by specifying a strategy in the strategy element. The value may be any one of AUTO, TABLE, SEQUENCE, or IDENTITY enumerated values of the GenerationType enumerated type.

Table and sequence generators may be specifically defined and then reused by multiple entity classes. These generators are named and are globally accessible to all of the entities in the persistence unit.

Automatic Id Generation

If an application does not care what kind of generation is used by the provider but wants generation to occur, then it can specify a strategy of AUTO. This means that the provider will use whatever strategy it wants to generate identifiers. Listing 4-13 shows an example of using automatic id generation. This will cause an identifier value to be created by the provider and inserted into the id field of each Employee entity that gets persisted.

Listing 4-13. *Using Auto Id Generation*

```
@Entity
public class Employee {
    @Id @GeneratedValue(strategy=GenerationType.AUTO)
    private int id;
    // ...
}
```

There is a catch to using AUTO, though. The provider gets to pick its own strategy to store the identifiers, but it needs to have some kind of persistent resource in order to do so. For example, if it chooses a table-based strategy, then it needs to create a table; if it chooses a sequence-based strategy, then it needs to create a sequence. The provider can't always rely upon the database connection that it obtains from the server to have permissions to create a table in the database. This is normally a privileged operation that is often restricted to the DBA. There will need to be some kind of creation phase or schema generation to cause the resource to be created before the AUTO strategy is able to function.

The AUTO mode is really a generation strategy for development or prototyping. It works well as a means of getting you up and running more quickly when the database schema is being generated. In any other situation it would be better to use one of the other generation strategies discussed in the later sections.

Id Generation Using a Table

The most flexible and portable way to generate identifiers is to use a database table. Not only will it port to different databases, but it also allows for storing multiple different identifier sequences for different entities within the same table. The easiest way to use a table to generate identifiers is to simply specify the generation strategy to be TABLE in the strategy element:

```
@Id GeneratedValue(strategy=GenerationType.TABLE)
private int id;
```

Since the generation strategy is indicated but no generator has been specified, the provider will assume a table of its own choosing. If schema generation is used, then it will be created, but if not, then the default table assumed by the provider must be known and must exist in the database.

A more explicit approach would be to actually specify the table that is to be used for id storage. This is done by defining a table generator that, contrary to what its name implies, does not actually generate tables. Rather, it is an identifier generator that uses a table to store them. We can define one by using a @TableGenerator annotation and then refer to it by name in the @GeneratedValue annotation:

```
@TableGenerator(name="Emp_Gen")
@Id @GeneratedValue(generator="Emp_Gen")
private int id;
```

Although we are showing the @TableGenerator annotating the identifier attribute, it can actually be defined on any attribute or class. Regardless of where it is defined, it will be available to the entire persistence unit. A good practice would be to define it locally on the id attribute if only one class is using it but to define it in XML, as described in Chapter 10, if it will be used for multiple classes.

The name element globally names the generator, which then allows us to reference it in @GeneratedValue. This is functionally equivalent to the previous example where we simply said that we wanted to use table generation but did not specify the generator. Now we are specifying the name of the generator but not supplying any of the generator details, leaving them to be defaulted by the provider.

A further qualifying approach would be to specify the table details, as in the following:

```
@TableGenerator(name="Emp_Gen",
    table="ID_GEN",
    pkColumnName="GEN_NAME",
    valueColumnName="GEN_VAL")
```

We have included some additional elements after the name of the generator. Following the name are three elements, table, pkColumnName, and valueColumnName, which define the actual table that stores the identifiers for "Emp_Gen". The table element just indicates the name of the table.

Every table that is used for id generation should have two columns. It could have more than two columns, but only two will be used. The first column is of a string type and is used to identify the particular generator sequence. It is the primary key for all of the generators in the table. The name of this column is specified by pkColumnName. The second column is of an integer type and stores the actual id sequence that is being generated. The value stored in this column is the last identifier that was allocated in the sequence. The name of this column is specified by valueColumnName. In our case our table is named "ID_GEN". The name of the primary key column of the table, or the column that stores the generator names, is named "GEN_NAME", and the column that stores the id sequence values is named "GEN_VAL".

Each defined generator represents a row in the table. The name of the generator becomes the value stored in the pkColumnName column for that row and is used by the provider to look up the generator to obtain its last allocated value.

In our example we named our generator "Emp_Gen" so our table would look like the one in Figure 4-2.

ID_GEN

GEN_NAME	GEN_VAL
Emp_Gen	0

Figure 4-2. *Table for identifier generation*

We can see that the last allocated Employee identifier is 0, which tells us that no identifiers have been generated yet. An initialValue element representing the last allocated identifier may be specified as part of the generator definition, but the default setting of 0 will suffice in almost every case. This setting is used only during schema generation when the table is created. During subsequent executions, the provider will read the contents of the value column to determine the next identifier to give out.

To avoid updating the row for every single identifier that gets requested, an allocation size is used. This will cause the provider to pre-allocate a block of identifiers and then give out identifiers from memory as requested until the block is used up. Once this block is used up, the next request for an identifier triggers another block of identifiers to be pre-allocated, and the identifier value is incremented by the allocation size. By default, the allocation size is set to 50. This value can be overridden to be larger or smaller through the use of the allocationSize element when defining the generator.

■**Tip** The provider may allocate identifiers within the same transaction as the entity being persisted or in a separate transaction. It is not specified, but you should check your provider documentation to see how it can avoid the risk of deadlock when concurrent threads are creating entities and locking resources.

Shown in Listing 4-14 is an example of defining a second generator to be used for Address entities but that uses the same ID_GEN table to store the identifier sequence. In this case we are actually explicitly dictating the value we are storing in the identifier table's primary key column by specifying the pkColumnvalue element. This element allows the name of the generator to be different from the column value, although doing so is rarely needed. The example shows an Address id generator named "Address_Gen" but then defines the value stored in the table for Address id generation as "Addr_Gen". The generator also sets the initial value to 10000 and the allocation size to 100.

Listing 4-14. *Using Table Id Generation*

```
@TableGenerator(name="Address_Gen",
    table="ID_GEN",
    pkColumnName="GEN_NAME",
    valueColumnName="GEN_VAL",
    pkColumnValue="Addr_Gen",
    initialValue=10000,
    allocationSize=100)
```

```
@Id @GeneratedValue(generator="Address_Gen")
private int id;
```

If both "Emp_Gen" and "Address_Gen" generators were defined, then on application startup the ID_GEN table would look like Figure 4-3. As the application allocates identifiers, the values stored in the GEN_VAL column will increase.

ID_GEN

GEN_NAME	GEN_VAL
Emp_Gen	0
Addr_Gen	10000

Figure 4-3. *Table for generating* Address *and* Employee *identifiers*

If schema generation has not been run, then the table must exist in the database and be configured to be in this state when the application starts up for the first time. The following SQL could be applied to create and initialize this table:

```
CREATE TABLE id_gen (
    gen_name VARCHAR(80),
    gen_val INTEGER,
    CONSTRAINT pk_id_gen
        PRIMARY KEY (gen_name)
);
INSERT INTO id_gen (gen_name, gen_val) VALUES ('Emp_Gen', 0);
INSERT INTO id_gen (gen_name, gen_val) VALUES ('Addr_Gen', 10000);
```

Id Generation Using a Database Sequence

Many databases support an internal mechanism for id generation called sequences. A database sequence may be used to generate identifiers when the underlying database supports them.

As we saw with table generators, if it is known that a database sequence should be used for generating identifiers and we are not concerned that it be any particular sequence, then specifying the generator type alone should be sufficient:

```
@Id @GeneratedValue(strategy=GenerationType.SEQUENCE)
private int id;
```

In this case no generator is named, so the provider will use a default sequence object of its own choosing. Note that if multiple sequence generators are defined but not named, then it is not specified whether they use the same default sequence or different ones. The only difference between using one sequence for multiple entity types and using one for each entity would be the ordering of the sequence numbers and possible contention on the sequence. The safer route would be to define a named sequence generator and refer to it in the @GeneratedValue annotation:

```
@SequenceGenerator(name="Emp_Gen", sequenceName="Emp_Seq")
@Id @GeneratedValue(generator="Emp_Gen")
private int getId;
```

Unless schema generation is enabled, this would require that the sequence be defined and already exist. The SQL to create such a sequence would be:

```
CREATE SEQUENCE Emp_Seq
    MINVALUE 1
    START WITH 1
    INCREMENT BY 50
```

The initial value and allocation size can also be used in sequence generators and would need to be reflected in the SQL to create the sequence. We can see that the default allocation size is 50, just as it is with table generators. If schema generation is not being used and the sequence is being manually created, then the INCREMENT BY clause would need to be configured to match the setting or default value of the allocation size.

Id Generation Using Database Identity

Some databases support a primary key identity column sometimes referred to as an autonumber column. Whenever a row is inserted into the table, then the identity column will get a unique identifier assigned to it. This can be used to generate the identifiers for objects, but once again is available only when the underlying database supports it.

To indicate that IDENTITY generation should occur, the @GeneratedValue annotation should specify a generation strategy of IDENTITY. This will indicate to the provider that it must reread the inserted row from the table after an INSERT has occurred. This will allow it to obtain the newly generated identifier from the database and put it into the in-memory entity that was just persisted:

```
@Id @GeneratedValue(strategy=GenerationType.IDENTITY)
private int id;
```

There is no generator annotation for IDENTITY since it must be defined as part of the database schema for the primary key column itself. Identity generation obviously may not be shared across multiple entity types.

Another difference, hinted at earlier, between using IDENTITY and other id generation strategies is that the identifier will not be accessible until after the insert has occurred. While no guarantee is made as to the accessibility of the identifier before the transaction has completed, it is at least possible for other types of generation to eagerly allocate the identifier, but when using identity, it is the action of inserting that causes the identifier to be generated. It would be impossible for the identifier to be available before the entity is inserted into the database, and because insertion of entities is most often deferred until commit time, the identifier would not be available until after the transaction has been committed.

Relationships

If entities contained only simple persistent state then the business of object-relational mapping would be a trivial one indeed. Most entities need to be able to reference, or have relationships with, other entities. This is what produces the domain model graphs that are common in business applications.

In the following sections we will explore the different kinds of relationships that can exist and show how to define and map them using Java Persistence API mapping metadata.

Relationship Concepts

Before we go off and start mapping relationships we should really take a quick tour through some of the basic relationship concepts and terminology. Having a firm grasp on these concepts will make it easier to understand the remainder of the relationship mapping sections.

Roles

There is an old adage that says every story has three sides: yours, mine, and the truth. Relationships are kind of the same in that there are three different perspectives. The first is the view from one side of the relationship, the second is from the other side, and the third is from a global perspective that knows about both sides. The "sides" are called *roles*. In every relationship there are two entities that are related to one another, and each entity is said to play a role in the relationship.

Relationships are everywhere, so examples are not hard to come by. An employee has a relationship to the department that he or she works in. The Employee entity plays the role of working in the department, while the Department entity plays the role of having an employee working in it.

Of course the role a given entity is playing differs according to the relationship, and an entity may be participating in many different relationships with many different entities. We can conclude, therefore, that any entity may be playing a number of different roles in any given model. If we think of an Employee entity, we realize that it does in fact play other roles in other relationships, such as the role of working for a manager in its relationship with another Employee entity, working on a project in its relationship with the Project entity, and so forth.

Unlike EJB 2.1, where the roles all had to be enumerated in metadata for every relationship, the Java Persistence API does not have metadata requirements to declare the role an entity is playing. Nevertheless, roles are still helpful as a means of understanding the nature and structure of relationships.

Directionality

In order to have relationships at all, there has to be a way to create, remove, and maintain them. The basic way this is done is by an entity having a relationship attribute that refers to its related entity in a way that identifies it as playing the other role of the relationship. It is often the case that the other entity in turn has an attribute that points back to the original entity. When each entity points to the other, the relationship is *bidirectional*. If only one entity has a pointer to the other, the relationship is said to be *unidirectional*.

A relationship from an Employee to the Project that they work on would be bidirectional. The Employee should know its Project, and the Project should point to the Employee working on it. A UML model of this relationship is shown in Figure 4-4. The arrows going in both directions indicate the bidirectionality of the relationship.

An Employee and its Address would likely be modeled as a unidirectional relationship because the Address is not expected to ever need to know its resident. If it did, of course, then it would need to become a bidirectional relationship. Figure 4-5 shows this relationship. Because the relationship is unidirectional the arrow points from the Employee to the Address.

Figure 4-4. Employee *and* Project *in a bidirectional relationship*

Figure 4-5. Employee *in a unidirectional relationship with* Address

As we will see later in the chapter, although they both share the same concept of directionality, the object and data models each see it a little differently because of the paradigm difference. In some cases, unidirectional relationships in the object model can pose a problem in the database model.

Source and Target

Even though we can use the directionality of a relationship to help describe and explain a model, when it comes to actually discussing it in concrete terms, it makes sense to think of every bidirectional relationship as a pair of unidirectional relationships.

So instead of having a single bidirectional relationship of an Employee working on a Project, we would have one unidirectional "project" relationship where the Employee points to the Project they work on, and another unidirectional "worker" relationship where the Project points to the Employee that works on it. Each of these relationships has an entity that is the *source* or referring role, and the side that is the *target* or referred-to role. The beauty of this is that we can use the same terms no matter which relationship we are talking about and no matter what the roles are in the relationship. Figure 4-6 shows how the two relationships have source and target entities, and how from each relationship perspective the source and target entities are different.

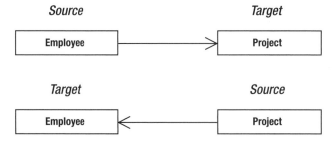

Figure 4-6. *Unidirectional relationships between* Employee *and* Project

Cardinality

It isn't very often that a project has only a single employee working on it. We would like to be able to capture the aspect of how many entities exist on each side of the same relationship instance. This is called the *cardinality* of the relationship. Each role in a relationship will have its own cardinality, which indicates whether there can be only one instance of the entity or many instances.

In our employee and department example, we might first say that one employee works in one department, so the cardinality of both sides would be *one*. But chances are that more than one employee works in the department. Because of this we would make the relationship have a *many* cardinality on the Employee or source side, meaning that many Employee instances could each point to the same Department. The target or Department side would keep its cardinality of one. Figure 4-7 shows this many-to-one relationship. The "many" side is marked with a "*".

Figure 4-7. *Unidirectional many-to-one relationship*

In our Employee and Project example, we have a bidirectional relationship, or two relationship directions. If an employee can work on multiple projects and a project can have multiple employees working on it, then we would end up with cardinalities of "many" on the sources and targets of both directions. Figure 4-8 shows the UML diagram of this relationship.

Figure 4-8. *Bidirectional many-to-many relationship*

A picture is worth a thousand words, and describing these relationships in text is quite a lot harder than simply showing a picture. In words, though, this picture indicates the following:

- Each employee can work on a number of projects

- Many employees can work on the same project

- Each project can have a number of employees working on it

- Many projects can have the same employee working on them

Implicit in this model is the fact that there can be sharing of Employee and Project instances across multiple relationship instances.

Ordinality

A role may be further specified by determining whether or not it may be present at all. This is called the *ordinality* and serves to show whether the target entity needs to be specified when the source entity is created. Because the ordinality is really just a Boolean value, we also refer to it as the *optionality* of the relationship.

In cardinality terms, ordinality would be indicated by the cardinality being a range instead of a simple value, and the range would begin with 0 or 1 depending upon the ordinality. It is simpler, though, to merely state that the relationship is either optional or mandatory. If optional, then the target may not be present, but if mandatory, then a source entity without a reference to its associated target entity is in an invalid state.

Mappings Overview

Now that we know enough theory and have the conceptual background to be able to discuss relationships, we can go on to explaining and using relationship mappings.

Each one of the mappings is named for the cardinality of the source and target roles. As we saw in the previous sections, we can view a bidirectional relationship as a pair of two unidirectional mappings. Each of these mappings is really a unidirectional relationship mapping, and if we take the cardinalities of the source and target of the relationship and combine them together in that order, permuting them with the two possible values of "one" and "many", we end up with the following names given to the mappings:

1. Many-to-one

2. One-to-one

3. One-to-many

4. Many-to-many

These mapping names are also the names of the annotations that are used to indicate the relationship types on the attributes that are being mapped. They are the basis for the logical relationship annotations, and they contribute to the object modeling aspects of the entity.

Like basic mappings, relationship mappings may be applied to either fields or properties of the entity.

Single-Valued Associations

An association from an entity instance to another entity instance (where the cardinality of the target is "one") is called a single-valued association. The many-to-one and one-to-one relationship mappings fall into this category because the source entity refers to at most one target entity. We will discuss these relationships and some of their variants first.

Many-to-One Mappings

In our cardinality discussion of the Employee and Department relationship (shown in Figure 4-7) we first thought of an employee working in a department, so we just assumed that it was a one-to-one relationship. However, when we realized that more than one employee works in the same department, we changed it to a many-to-one relationship mapping. It turns out that many-to-one is the most common mapping and is the one that is normally used when creating an association to an entity.

In Figure 4-9 we show a many-to-one relationship between Employee and Department. Employee is the "many" side and the source of the relationship, and Department is the "one" side and the target. Once again, because the arrow points in only one direction, from Employee to Department, the relationship is unidirectional. Note that in UML, the source class has an implicit attribute of the target class type if it can be navigated to. For example, Employee has an attribute called department that will contain a reference to a single Department instance.

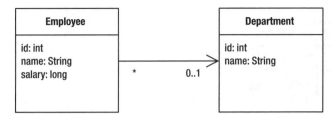

Figure 4-9. *Many-to-one relationship from* Employee *to* Department

A many-to-one mapping is defined by annotating the attribute in the source entity (the attribute that refers to the target entity) with the @ManyToOne annotation. In Listing 4-15 we can see how the @ManyToOne annotation is used to map this relationship. The department field in Employee is the source attribute that is annotated.

Listing 4-15. *Many-to-One Relationship from* Employee *to* Department

```
@Entity
public class Employee {
    // ...
    @ManyToOne
    private Department department;
    // ...
}
```

We have included only the bits of the class that are relevant to our discussion, but we see from the previous example that the code was rather anticlimactic. A single annotation was all that was required to map the relationship, and it turned out to be quite dull, really.

The same kinds of attribute flexibility and modifier requirements that were described for basic mappings also apply to relationship mappings. The annotation may be present on either the field or property, depending upon the strategy used for the entity.

Using Join Columns

In the database, a relationship mapping means that one table has a reference to another table. The database term for a column that refers to a key (usually the primary key) in another table is a *foreign key* column. In the Java Persistence API we call them *join columns*, and the @JoinColumn annotation is the primary annotation used to configure these types of columns.

Consider the EMPLOYEE and DEPARTMENT tables shown in Figure 4-10 that correspond to the Employee and Department entities. The EMPLOYEE table has a foreign key column named DEPT_ID that references the DEPARTMENT table. From the perspective of the entity relationship, DEPT_ID is the join column that associates the Employee and Department entities.

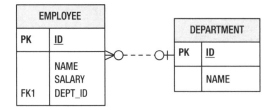

Figure 4-10. EMPLOYEE *and* DEPARTMENT *tables*

In almost every relationship, independent of source and target sides, one of the two sides is going to have the join column in its table. That side is called the *owning side* or the *owner* of the relationship. The side that does not have the join column is called the non-owning or *inverse* side.

Ownership is important for mapping because the physical annotations that define the mappings to the columns in the database (for example, @JoinColumn) are always defined on the owning side of the relationship. If they are not there, then the values are defaulted from the perspective of the attribute on the owning side.

Many-to-one mappings are always on the owning side of a relationship, so if there is a @JoinColumn to be found in the relationship that has a many-to-one side, then that is where it will be located. To specify the name of the join column, the name element is used. For example, the @JoinColumn(name="DEPT_ID") annotation means that the DEPT_ID column in the source entity table is the foreign key to the target entity table, whatever the target entity of the relationship happens to be.

If no @JoinColumn annotation accompanies the many-to-one mapping, then a default column name will be assumed. The name that is used as the default is formed from a combination of both the source and target entities. It is the name of the relationship attribute in the source entity, which is department in our example, plus an underscore character ("_"), plus the name of the primary key column of the target entity. So if the Department entity were mapped to a table that had a primary key column named ID, then the join column in the EMPLOYEE table would be assumed to be named DEPARTMENT_ID. If this is not actually the name of the column, then the @JoinColumn annotation must be defined to override the default.

Going back to Figure 4-10, the foreign key column is named DEPT_ID instead of the defaulted DEPARTMENT_ID column name. Listing 4-16 shows the @JoinColumn annotation being used to override the join column name to be DEPT_ID.

Listing 4-16. *Many-to-One Relationship Overriding the Join Column*

```
@Entity
public class Employee {
    @Id private int id;
    @ManyToOne
    @JoinColumn(name="DEPT_ID")
    private Department department;
    // ...
}
```

Annotations allow us to specify @JoinColumn on either the same line as @ManyToOne or on a separate line, above or below it. By convention the logical mapping should appear first and then the physical mapping. This makes the object model clear since the physical part is less important to the object model.

One-to-One Mappings

If it really was the case that only one employee could work in a department, then we would be back to the one-to-one association again. A more realistic example of a one-to-one association, however, would be an employee who has a parking space. Assuming that every employee got his or her own parking space, then we would create a one-to-one relationship from Employee to ParkingSpace. Figure 4-11 shows this relationship.

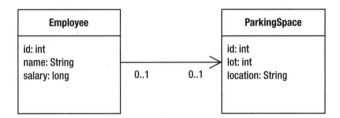

Figure 4-11. *One-to-one relationship from* Employee *to* ParkingSpace

We define the mapping in a similar way to the way we define a many-to-one mapping, except that we use the @OneToOne annotation on the parkingSpace attribute instead of a @ManyToOne annotation. Just as with a many-to-one mapping, the one-to-one mapping has a join column in the database and needs to override the name of the column in an @JoinColumn annotation when the default name does not apply. The default name is composed the same way as for many-to-one mappings using the name of the source attribute and the target primary key column name.

Figure 4-12 shows the tables mapped by the Employee and ParkingSpace entities. The foreign key column in the EMPLOYEE table is named PSPACE_ID and refers to the PARKING_SPACE table.

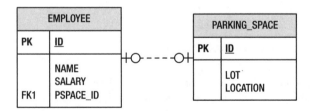

Figure 4-12. EMPLOYEE *and* PARKING_SPACE *tables*

As it turns out, one-to-one mappings are almost the same as many-to-one mappings except for the fact that only one instance of the source entity is able to refer to the same target entity instance. In other words, the target entity instance is not shared amongst the source entity instances. In the database, this equates to having a uniqueness constraint on the source foreign key column (that is, the foreign key column in the source entity table). If there were more than one foreign key value that was the same, then it would contravene the rule that no more than one source entity instance can refer to the same target entity instance.

In Listing 4-17 we see the mapping for this relationship. The `@JoinColumn` annotation has been used to override the default join column name of `PARKINGSPACE_ID` to be `PSPACE_ID`.

Listing 4-17. *One-to-One Relationship from* `Employee` *to* `ParkingSpace`

```
@Entity
public class Employee {
    @Id private int id;
    private String name;
    @OneToOne
    @JoinColumn(name="PSPACE_ID")
    private ParkingSpace parkingSpace;
    // ...
}
```

Bidirectional One-to-One Mappings

It often happens that the target entity of the one-to-one has a relationship back to the source entity; for example, `ParkingSpace` has a reference back to the `Employee` that uses it. When this is the case, we call it a bidirectional one-to-one relationship. As we saw previously, we actually have two separate one-to-one mappings, one in each direction, but we call the combination of the two a bidirectional one-to-one relationship. To make our existing one-to-one employee and parking space example bidirectional, we need only change the `ParkingSpace` to point back to the `Employee`. Figure 4-13 shows the bidirectional relationship.

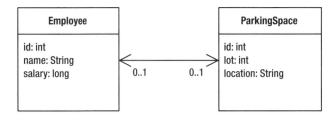

Figure 4-13. *One-to-one relationship between* `Employee` *and* `ParkingSpace`

We already learned that the entity table that contains the join column determines the entity that is the owner of the relationship. In a bidirectional one-to-one relationship both of the mappings are one-to-one mappings, and either side may be the owner, so the join column may end up being on one side or the other. This would normally be a data modeling decision and not a Java programming decision, and it would likely be decided based upon the most frequent direction of traversal.

Consider the `ParkingSpace` entity class shown in Listing 4-18. This example assumes the table mapping shown in Figure 4-12, and it assumes that `Employee` is the owning side of the relationship. We now have to add a reference from `ParkingSpace` back to `Employee`. This is achieved by adding the `@OneToOne` relationship annotation on the employee field. As part of the annotation we must add a `mappedBy` element to indicate that the owning side is the `Employee` and not the `ParkingSpace`. Because `ParkingSpace` is the inverse side of the relationship, it does not have to supply the join column information.

Listing 4-18. *Inverse Side of a Bidirectional One-to-One Relationship*

```
@Entity
public class ParkingSpace {
    @Id private int id;
    private int lot;
    private String location;
    @OneToOne(mappedBy="parkingSpace")
    private Employee employee;
    // ...
}
```

The `mappedBy` element in the one-to-one mapping of the `employee` attribute of `ParkingSpace` is needed to refer to the `parkingSpace` attribute in the `Employee` class. The value of `mappedBy` is the name of the attribute in the owning entity that points back to the inverse entity.

The two rules, then, for bidirectional one-to-one associations are:

1. The `@JoinColumn` annotation goes on the mapping of the entity that is mapped to the table containing the join column, or the owner of the relationship. This may be on either side of the association.

2. The `mappedBy` element should be specified in the `@OneToOne` annotation in the entity that does not define a join column, or the inverse side of the relationship.

It would not be legal to have a bidirectional association that had `mappedBy` on both sides just as it would be incorrect to not have it on either side. The difference is that if it were absent on both sides of the relationship, then the provider would treat each side as an independent unidirectional relationship. This would be fine except that it would assume that each side was the owner and that each had a join column.

Bidirectional many-to-one relationships are explained later as part of the discussion of multi-valued bidirectional associations.

One-to-One Primary Key Mappings

A specific case of a unique one-to-one relationship is when the primary keys of the related entities are always guaranteed to match. The two entities must always have been created with the same identifiers, and in the database each primary key could also be used as a foreign key to the other entity. Of course the direction in which the actual constraint occurs should dictate which side is the owner since the owner is the one with the foreign key constraint in its table.

Imagine if every time an employee got hired, his or her employee id was used as their parking space id (and employees were never allowed to change parking spaces!). This relationship would be modeled in the database as shown in Figure 4-14.

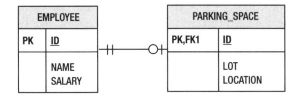

Figure 4-14. EMPLOYEE *and* PARKING_SPACE *tables with shared primary keys*

The difference between mapping this kind of one-to-one relationship and the previous kind is that there is no additional foreign key column in either table. The primary key in the PARKING_SPACE table is also a foreign key to the EMPLOYEE table. When this is the case, then an @PrimaryKeyJoinColumn is used instead of an @JoinColumn annotation. Because the foreign key is now defined from ParkingSpace to Employee, we need to reverse the ownership of the relationship and make ParkingSpace the owner. We specify the @PrimaryKeyJoinColumn annotation on the employee field of the ParkingSpace entity.

Listing 4-19 shows the revised Employee and ParkingSpace entities. Note that since the Employee is now the inverse side of the relationship, the join column mapping is removed, and the @OneToOne annotation must now specify the mappedBy element.

Listing 4-19. *One-to-One Primary Key Relationship*

```
@Entity
public class Employee {
    @Id private int id;
    private String name;
    @OneToOne(mappedBy="employee")
    private ParkingSpace parkingSpace;
    // ...
}

@Entity
public class ParkingSpace {
    @Id private int id;
    private int lot;
    private String location;
    @OneToOne
    @PrimaryKeyJoinColumn
    private Employee employee;
    // ...
}
```

We did not have to specify anything more than the @PrimaryKeyJoinColumn annotation since the entities had simple primary keys. If compound primary keys had been used, then additional information would need to be specified in the @PrimaryKeyJoinColumn annotation. We will discuss this case in Chapter 8.

Collection-Valued Associations

When the source entity references one or more target entity instances, a many-valued association or associated collection is used. Both the one-to-many and many-to-many mappings fit the criteria of having many target entities, and although the one-to-many association is the most frequently used, many-to-many mappings are useful as well when there is sharing in both directions.

One-to-Many Mappings

When an entity is associated with a `Collection` of other entities, it is most often in the form of a one-to-many mapping. For example, a department would normally have a number of employees. Figure 4-15 shows the `Employee` and `Department` relationship that we showed earlier in the section Many-to-One Mappings, only this time the relationship is bidirectional in nature.

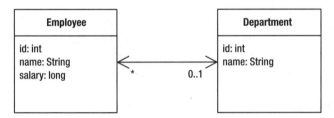

Figure 4-15. *Bidirectional* Employee *and* Department *relationship*

When a relationship is bidirectional, there are actually two mappings, one for each direction. A bidirectional one-to-many relationship always implies a many-to-one mapping back to the source, so in our `Employee` and `Department` example there is a one-to-many mapping from `Department` to `Employee` and a many-to-one mapping from `Employee` back to `Department`. We could just as easily say that the relationship is a bidirectional many-to-one if we were looking at it from the `Employee` perspective. They are equivalent, since bidirectional many-to-one relationships imply a one-to-many mapping back from the target to source, and vice versa.

When a source entity has an arbitrary number of target entities stored in its collection, there is no scalable way to store those references in the database table that it maps to. How would it store an arbitrary number of foreign keys in a single row? It must, rather, let the tables of the entities in the collection have foreign keys back to the source entity table. This is why the one-to-many association is almost always bidirectional and never the owning side.

Furthermore, if the target entity tables have foreign keys that point back to the source entity table then the target entities themselves should have many-to-one associations back to the source entity object. Having a foreign key in a table for which there is no association in the corresponding entity object model is not in keeping with the data model and not supported by the API.

Let's look at a concrete example of a one-to-many mapping based on the `Employee` and `Department` example shown in Figure 4-15. The tables for this relationship are exactly the same as those shown in Figure 4-10, where we talked about many-to-one relationships. The only difference between the many-to-one example and this one is that we are now implementing the inverse side of the relationship. Because `Employee` has the join column and is the owner of the relationship, the `Employee` class is unchanged from Listing 4-16.

On the Department side of the relationship, we need to map the employees collection of Employee entities as a one-to-many association using the @OneToMany annotation. Listing 4-20 shows the Department class that uses this annotation. Note that because this is the inverse side of the relationship, we need to include the mappedBy element just as we did in the bidirectional one-to-one relationship example.

Listing 4-20. *One-to-Many Relationship*

```
@Entity
public class Department {
    @Id private int id;
    private String name;
    @OneToMany(mappedBy="department")
    private Collection<Employee> employees;
    // ...
}
```

There are a couple of noteworthy points to mention about this class. The first is that a generic type-parameterized Collection is being used to store the Employee entities. This provides the strict typing that guarantees that only objects of type Employee will exist in the Collection. This, in and of itself, is quite useful since it not only provides compile-time checking of our code but also saves us having to perform cast operations when we retrieve the Employee instances from the collection.

The Java Persistence API assumes the availability of generics; however, it is still perfectly acceptable to use a Collection that is not type-parameterized. We might just as well have defined the Department class without using generics but defining only a simple Collection type, as we would have done in releases of standard Java previous to Java SE 5 (except for JDK 1.0 or 1.1 when java.util.Collection was not even standardized!). If we did, then we would need to specify the type of entity that will be stored in the Collection that is needed by the persistence provider. The code is shown in Listing 4-21 and looks almost identical, except for the targetEntity element that indicates the entity type.

Listing 4-21. *Using* targetEntity

```
@Entity
public class Department {
    @Id private int id;
    private String name;
    @OneToMany(targetEntity=Employee.class, mappedBy="department")
    private Collection employees;
    // ...
}
```

There are two important points to remember when defining bidirectional one-to-many (or many-to-one) relationships:

1. The many-to-one side is the owning side, so the join column is defined on that side.

2. The one-to-many mapping is the inverse side, so the mappedBy element must be used.

Failing to specify the mappedBy element in the @OneToMany annotation will cause the provider to treat it as a unidirectional one-to-many relationship that is defined to use a join table (described later). This is an easy mistake to make and should be the first thing you look for if you see a missing table error with a name that has two entity names concatenated together.

Many-to-Many Mappings

When one or more entities are associated with a Collection of other entities and the entities have overlapping associations with the same target entities, then we must model it as a many-to-many relationship. Each of the entities on each side of the relationship will have a collection-valued association that contains entities of the target type. Figure 4-16 shows a many-to-many relationship between Employee and Project. Each employee can work on multiple projects, and each project can be worked on by multiple employees.

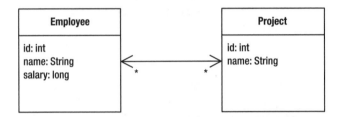

Figure 4-16. *Bidirectional many-to-many relationship*

A many-to-many mapping is expressed on both the source and target entities as an @ManyToMany annotation on the collection attributes. For example, in Listing 4-22 the Employee has a projects attribute that has been annotated with @ManyToMany. Likewise, the Project entity has an employees attribute that has also been annotated with @ManyToMany.

Listing 4-22. *Many-to-Many Relationship Between* Employee *and* Project

```
@Entity
public class Employee {
    @Id private int id;
    private String name;
    @ManyToMany
    private Collection<Project> projects;
    // ...
}

@Entity
public class Project {
    @Id private int id;
    private String name;
    @ManyToMany(mappedBy="projects")
    private Collection<Employee> employees;
    // ...
}
```

There are some important differences between this many-to-many relationship and the one-to-many relationship that we discussed earlier. The first is just a mathematical inevitability and is that when a many-to-many relationship is bidirectional, both sides of the relationship are many-to-many mappings.

The second difference is that there are no join columns on either side of the relationship. We will see in the next section that the only way to implement a many-to-many relationship is with a separate join table. The consequence of not having any join columns in either of the entity tables is that there is no way to determine which side is the owner of the relationship. Because every bidirectional relationship has to have both an owning side and an inverse side, we must pick one of the two entities to be the owner. In this example we have picked Employee to be owner of the relationship, but we could have just as easily picked Project instead. As in every other bidirectional relationship, the inverse side must use the mappedBy element to identify the owning attribute.

Note that no matter which side is designated as the owner, the other side should include the mappedBy element, otherwise the provider will think that both sides are the owner and that the mappings are separate unidirectional relationships.

Using Join Tables

Since the multiplicity of both sides of a many-to-many relationship is plural, neither of the two entity tables can store an unlimited set of foreign key values in a single entity row. We must use a third table to associate the two entity types. We call this association table a *join table*, and each many-to-many relationship must have one.

A join table consists simply of two foreign key or join columns to refer to each of the two entity types in the relationship. A collection of entities is then mapped as multiple rows in the table, each of which associates one entity with another. The set of rows that contains the same value in the foreign key column to an entity represents the associations that entity instance has with entity instances that it is related to.

In Figure 4-17 we see the EMPLOYEE and PROJECT tables for the Employee and Project entities and the EMP_PROJ join table that associates them. The EMP_PROJ table contains only foreign key columns that make up its compound primary key. The EMP_ID column refers to the EMPLOYEE primary key, while the PROJ_ID column refers to the PROJECT primary key.

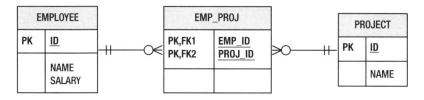

Figure 4-17. *Join table for a many-to-many relationship*

In order to map the tables described in Figure 4-17 we need to add some additional metadata to the Employee class that we have designated as the owner of the relationship. Listing 4-23 shows the many-to-many relationship with the accompanying join table annotations.

Listing 4-23. *Using a Join Table*

```
@Entity
public class Employee {
    @Id private int id;
    private String name;
    @ManyToMany
    @JoinTable(name="EMP_PROJ",
           joinColumns=@JoinColumn(name="EMP_ID"),
           inverseJoinColumns=@JoinColumn(name="PROJ_ID"))
    private Collection<Project> projects;
    // ...
}
```

The @JoinTable annotation is used to configure the join table for the relationship. The two join columns in the join table are distinguished by means of the owning and inverse sides. The join column to the owning side is described in the joinColumns element while the join column to the inverse side is specified by the inverseJoinColumns element. We can see from the previous example that the values of these elements are actually @JoinColumn annotations embedded within the @JoinTable annotation. This provides the ability to declare all of the information about the join columns within the table that defines them. The names are plural for the case when there may be multiple columns for each foreign key when either the owning entity or the inverse entity has a multipart primary key. This more complicated case will be discussed in Chapter 8.

In our example we fully specified the names of the join table and its columns because this is the most common case. But if we were generating the database schema from the entities, then we would not actually need to specify this information. We could have relied upon the default values that would be assumed and used when the persistence provider generates the table for us. When no @JoinTable annotation is present on the owning side, then a default join table named <Owner>_<Inverse> is assumed, where <Owner> is the name of the owning entity and <Inverse> is the name of the inverse or non-owning entity. Of course, the owner is basically picked at random by the developer so these defaults will apply according to the way the relationship is mapped and whichever entity is designated as the owning side.

The join columns will be defaulted according to the join column defaulting rules that were previously described in the section Using Join Columns. The default name of the join column that points to the owning entity is the name of the attribute on the inverse entity that points to the owning entity, appended by an underscore and the name of the primary key column of the owning entity table. So in our example the Employee is the owning entity, and the Project has an employees attribute that contains the collection of Employee instances. The Employee entity maps to the EMPLOYEE table and has a primary key column of ID, so the defaulted name of the join column to the owning entity would be EMPLOYEES_ID. The inverse join column would be likewise defaulted to be PROJECTS_ID.

It is fairly clear that the defaulted names of a join table and the join columns within it are not likely to match up with an existing table. This is why we mentioned that the defaults are really useful only if the database schema being mapped to was generated by the provider.

Unidirectional Collection Mappings

When an entity has a one-to-many mapping to a target entity but the @OneToMany annotation does not include the mappedBy element, it is assumed to be in a unidirectional relationship with the target entity. This means that the target entity does not have a many-to-one mapping back to the source entity. Figure 4-18 shows a unidirectional one-to-many association between Employee and Phone.

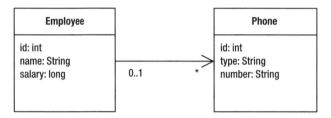

Figure 4-18. *Unidirectional one-to-many relationship*

Consider the data model in Figure 4-19. There is no join column to store the association back from Phone to Employee. Therefore, we have used a join table to associate the Phone entity with the Employee entity.

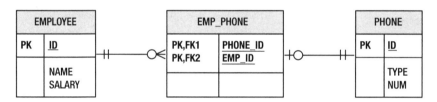

Figure 4-19. *Join table for a unidirectional one-to-many relationship*

   Similarly, when one side of a many-to-many relationship does not have a mapping to the other, then it is a unidirectional relationship. The join table must still be used; the only difference is that only one of the two entity types actually uses the table to load its related entities or updates it to store additional entity associations.

   In both of these two unidirectional collection-valued cases the source code is similar to the earlier examples, but there is no collection attribute in the target entity, and the mappedBy element will not be present in the @OneToMany annotation on the source entity. The join table must now be specified as part of the mapping. Listing 4-24 shows Employee with a one-to-many relationship to Phone using a join table.

Listing 4-24. *Unidirectional One-to-Many Relationship*

```
@Entity
public class Employee {
    @Id private int id;
    private String name;
    @OneToMany
    @JoinTable(name="EMP_PHONE",
        joinColumns=@JoinColumn(name="EMP_ID"),
        inverseJoinColumns=@JoinColumn(name="PHONE_ID"))
    private Collection<Phone> phones;
    // ...
}
```

Note that when generating the schema, default naming for the join columns is slightly different in the unidirectional case because there is no inverse attribute. The name of the join table would default to EMPLOYEE_PHONE and would have a join column named EMPLOYEE_ID after the name of the Employee entity and its primary key column. The inverse join column would be named PHONES_ID, which is the concatenation of the phones attribute in the Employee entity and the ID primary key column of the PHONE table.

■**Tip** Some vendors may provide support for a unidirectional one-to-many target foreign key mapping, where a join column exists in the target table but no relationship exists from the target entity back to the source entity. This is not supported in the current version of the Java Persistence API.

Using Different Collections

Different types of collections may be used to store multivalued entity associations. Depending upon the needs of the application, any of Collection, Set, List, and Map may be used for multivalued associations. There are only a couple of basic rules that guide their usage.

The first step is to define the collection to be any one of the interface types just mentioned. Implementation classes may not be used in the definition of the attribute but may be used as initial values set by the constructor or in an initialization method of the entity class.

The implementation class may be invoked through its implementation API at any time on a new object until the entity becomes managed or has been persisted by means of an EntityManager.persist() call. After that point, the interface must always be used when operating on the collection, whether it has been read in from the database or has been detached from the entity manager. This is because when the entity instance becomes managed, the persistence provider may have replaced the initial concrete instance with an alternate Collection implementation class of its own.

Using a Set or a Collection

The most common collection type used in associations is the standard Collection superinterface. This is used when it doesn't matter which implementation is underneath and when the common Collection methods are all that are required to access the entities stored in it.

A Set will prevent duplicate elements from being inserted and may be a simpler and more concise collection model, while a vanilla Collection interface is the most generic. Neither of these interfaces require accompanying annotations to further specify them. They are used the same way that they would be used if they held non-persistent objects.

Using a List

Another common collection type is the List. A List is often used when the entities are to be retrieved in some user-defined order, which may be optionally specified using an @OrderBy annotation. The value of the annotation is a string that indicates one or more fields or properties that are to be used to determine the order of the results, each of which may be optionally followed by an ASC or DESC keyword to define whether the attribute should be ordered in ascending or descending order. If the sequence direction is not specified, then the property will be listed in ascending order. Multiple attributes may be specified, each with their own ascending or descending sequence. If none are included then the list will be ordered using the primary keys of the entities. If the annotation is not present then the List will be in some undefined order, typically in the order returned by the database in the absence of any ORDER BY clause.

Let's take our example in Listing 4-20 and use a List instead of a Collection interface in the employees attribute of Department. By adding an @OrderBy annotation on the mapping, we will indicate that we want the employees to be ordered in ascending order according to the name attribute of the Employee. Listing 4-25 shows the updated example.

Listing 4-25. *One-to-Many Relationship Using a List*

```
@Entity
public class Department {
    // ...
    @OneToMany(mappedBy="department")
    @OrderBy("name ASC")
    private List<Employee> employees;
    // ...
}
```

We needn't have included the ASC in the @OrderBy annotation since it would be ascending by default, but it is good documentation style to include it.

We might also want to have sub-orderings using multiple attributes, and we could do that by specifying comma-separated <attribute name ASC/DESC> pairs in the annotation. For example, if Employee had a status, then we might have ordered by status and then by name by using an @OrderBy annotation of @OrderBy("status DESC, name ASC"). Of course the prerequisite for using an attribute in an @OrderBy annotation is that the attribute type be comparable.

Order is not preserved, however, when writing the List out to the database. Since database rows do not have any inherent order, the entities in a Java List cannot retain their order unless a designated database column has been created to store it. Then when an entity gets added to the front of the List, each of the other entities in the List must be updated to reflect their new order assignment in the List.

The Java Persistence API does not include support for persistent order preservation that is not based upon some state of the entity, so changing the order of the items in a List in memory will not cause that order to be stored in the database at commit time. The order specified in

@OrderBy, which depends upon some aspect of the entity state, will be used only when reading the List back into memory. The rule of thumb, then, is that the entity List order should always be kept consistent by the application logic. Persisting the order of the List is being considered for inclusion in a subsequent version of the specification.

Using a Map

Sometimes a collection of entities is stored as a Map keyed by some attribute of the target entity type. When this is the case, the collection type may be declared to be of type Map, and the @MapKey annotation may be applied to the collection.

The map key designates the attribute of the target entity that is to be used to key on. It may be any persistent attribute on the target entity that is comparable and responds appropriately to the hashCode() and equals() methods. It should also be unique, at least in the collection domain, so that values are not lost or overwritten in memory.

If, for example, we want to use a Map instead of a List to store our employees in a department, then we could key the map on the employee name for quick employee lookup. The relevant Department code would look like Listing 4-26.

Listing 4-26. *One-to-Many Relationship Using a* Map

```
@Entity
public class Department {
    // ...
    @OneToMany(mappedBy="department")
    @MapKey(name="name")
    private Map<String, Employee> employees;
    // ...
}
```

If, for some reason we did not want or were not able to use the generic version of Map<KeyType, ValueType>, then we would instead define it using an old-style non-parameterized Map as shown in Listing 4-27.

Listing 4-27. *One-to-Many Relationship Using a Non-parameterized* Map

```
@Entity
public class Department {
    // ...
    @OneToMany(targetEntity=Employee.class, mappedBy="department")
    @MapKey(name="name")
    private Map employees;
    // ...
}
```

When the collection is of type Map but no @MapKey annotation is specified, the entities will be keyed by their primary key attributes. Entities that have multiple primary key fields will be keyed on instances of the primary key class.

Lazy Relationships

In previous sections we saw how we could configure an attribute to be loaded when it got accessed and not necessarily before. We learned that lazy loading at the attribute level is not normally going to be very beneficial.

At the relationship level, however, lazy loading can be a big boon to enhancing performance. It can reduce the amount of SQL that gets executed and speed up queries and object loading considerably.

The fetch mode can be specified on any of the four relationship mapping types. When not specified on a single-valued relationship the related object is guaranteed to be loaded eagerly. Collection-valued relationships default to be lazily loaded, but because lazy loading is only a hint to the provider, they may be loaded eagerly if the provider decides to do so.

In bidirectional relationship cases, the fetch mode may be lazy on one side but eager on the other. This kind of configuration is actually quite common since relationships are often accessed in different ways depending upon the direction from which navigation occurs.

An example of overriding the default fetch mode would be if we didn't want to load the ParkingSpace for an Employee every time we loaded the Employee. Listing 4-28 shows the parkingSpace attribute configured to use lazy loading.

Listing 4-28. *Changing the Fetch Mode on a Relationship*

```
@Entity
public class Employee {
    @Id private int id;
    @OneToOne(fetch=FetchType.LAZY)
    private ParkingSpace parkingSpace;
    // ...
}
```

▨**Tip**   A relationship that is specified or defaulted to be lazily loaded may or may not cause the related object to be loaded when the getter method is used to access the object. The object may be a proxy, so it may take actually invoking a method on it to cause it to be faulted in.

Summary

Mapping objects to relational databases is of critical importance to persistence applications. Dealing with the impedance mismatch requires a sophisticated suite of metadata. The Java Persistence API not only provides this metadata, but also facilitates easy and convenient development.

In this chapter we went through the process of mapping entity state that included simple Java types, large objects, enumerated types, and temporal types. We also used the metadata to do meet-in-the-middle mapping to specific table names and columns.

We went over how identifiers are generated and described four different strategies of generation. We saw the different strategies in action and differentiated them from each other.

We then reviewed some of the relationship concepts and applied them to object-relational mapping metadata. We used join columns and join tables to map single-valued and collection-valued associations and went over some examples of using different kinds of `Collection` types.

In the next chapter we will discuss using entity managers and persistence contexts in more advanced ways than we did previously, delving into the practices and nuances of injecting and using them in Java EE and Java SE environments.

CHAPTER 5

■■■

Entity Manager

Entities do not persist themselves when they are created. Nor do they remove themselves from the database when they are garbage-collected. It is the business logic of the application that must manipulate entities to manage their persistent life cycle. The Java Persistence API provides the EntityManager interface for this purpose in order to let applications manage and search for entities in the relational database. At first this might seem like a limitation of the Java Persistence API. If the persistence runtime knows which objects are persistent, why should the application have to be involved in the process? Rest assured that this design is both deliberate and far more beneficial to the application than any transparent persistence solution. Persistence applications are a partnership between the application and persistence provider. The Java Persistence API brings a level of control and flexibility that cannot otherwise be achieved without the active participation of the application.

In Chapter 2 we introduced the EntityManager interface and described some of the basic operations that it provides for operating on entities. We extended that discussion in Chapter 3 to include an overview of the Java EE environment and the types of services that impact persistence applications. Finally, in the previous chapter we described object-relational mapping, the key to building entities out of objects. With that groundwork in place we are ready to revisit entity managers, persistence contexts, and persistence units, and to begin a more in-depth discussion of these concepts.

Persistence Contexts

Let's begin by reintroducing the core terms of the Java Persistence API. A persistence unit is a named configuration of entity classes. A persistence context is a managed set of entity instances. Every persistence context is associated with a persistence unit, restricting the classes of the managed instances to the set defined by the persistence unit. Saying that an entity instance is managed means that it is contained within a persistence context and that it may be acted upon by an entity manager. It is for this reason that we say an entity manager manages a persistence context.

Understanding the persistence context is the key to understanding the entity manager. An entity's inclusion or exclusion from a persistence context will determine the outcome of any persistent operations on it. If the persistence context participates in a transaction, then the in-memory state of the managed entities will get synchronized to the database. Yet despite the important role that it plays, the persistence context is never actually visible to the application. It is always accessed indirectly through the entity manager and assumed to be there when we need it.

So far so good, but how does the persistence context get created and when does this occur? How does the entity manager figure into the equation? This is where it starts to get interesting.

Entity Managers

Up to this point we have demonstrated only basic entity manager operations in both the Java SE and Java EE environments. We have reached a point, however, where we can finally reveal the full range of entity manager configurations. The Java Persistence API defines no less than *three* different types of entity managers, each of which has a different approach to persistence context management that is tailored to a different application need. As we will see, the persistence context is just one part of the puzzle.

Container-Managed Entity Managers

In the Java EE environment, the most common way to acquire an entity manager is by using the @PersistenceContext annotation to inject one. An entity manager obtained in this way is called *container-managed*, because the container manages the life cycle of the entity manager. The application does not have to create it or close it. This is the style of entity manager we demonstrated in Chapter 3.

Container-managed entity managers come in two varieties. The style of a container-managed entity manager determines how it works with persistence contexts. The first and most common style is called *transaction-scoped*. This means that the persistence contexts managed by the entity manager are determined by the active JTA transaction. The second style is called *extended*. Extended entity managers work with a single persistence context that is tied to the life cycle of a stateful session bean.

Transaction-Scoped

All of the entity manager examples that we have shown so far for the Java EE environment have been transaction-scoped entity managers. A transaction-scoped entity manager is returned whenever the reference created by the @PersistenceContext annotation is resolved. As we mentioned in Chapter 3, a transaction-scoped entity manager is stateless, meaning that it can be safely stored on any Java EE component. Because the container manages it for us, it is also basically maintenance-free.

Once again, let's introduce a stateless session bean that uses a transaction-scoped entity manager. Listing 5-1 shows the bean class for a session bean that manages project information. The entity manager is injected into the em field using the @PersistenceContext annotation and is then used in the business methods of the bean.

Listing 5-1. *The* ProjectService *Session Bean*

```
@Stateless
public class ProjectServiceBean implements ProjectService {
    @PersistenceContext(unitName="EmployeeService")
    EntityManager em;
```

```
public void assignEmployeeToProject(int empId, int projectId) {
    Project project = em.find(Project.class, projectId);
    Employee employee = em.find(Employee.class, empId);
    project.getEmployees().add(employee);
    employee.getProjects().add(project);
}

// ...
}
```

We described the transaction-scoped entity manager as stateless. If that is the case, how can it work with a persistence context? The answer lies with the JTA transaction. All container-managed entity managers depend on JTA transactions. The reason for this is because they can use the transaction as a way to track persistence contexts. Every time an operation is invoked on the entity manager, it checks to see if a persistence context is associated with the transaction. If it finds one, the entity manager will use this persistence context. If it doesn't find one, then it creates a new persistence context and associates it with the transaction. When the transaction ends, the persistence context goes away.

Let's walk through an example. Consider the `assignEmployeeToProject()` method from Listing 5-1. The first thing the method does is search for the `Employee` and `Project` instances using the `find()` operation. When the first `find()` method is invoked, the container checks for a transaction. By default, the container will ensure that a transaction is active whenever a session bean method starts, so the entity manager in this example will find one ready. It then checks for a persistence context. This is the first time any entity manager call has occurred, so there isn't a persistence context yet. The entity manager creates a new one and uses it to find the employee.

When the entity manager is used to search for the employee, it checks the transaction again and this time finds the one it created when searching for the project. It then reuses this persistence context to search for the employee. At this point `employee` and `project` are both managed entity instances. The employee is then added to the project, updating both the `employee` and `project` entities. When the method call ends, the transaction is committed. Because the `employee` and `project` instances were managed, the persistence context is able to detect any state changes in them, and it updates the database during the commit. When the transaction is over, the persistence context goes away.

This process is repeated every time one or more entity manager operations are invoked within a transaction.

Extended

In order to describe the extended entity manager, we must first talk a little about stateful session beans. As we learned in Chapter 3, stateful session beans are designed to hold conversational state. Once acquired by a client, the same bean instance is used for the life of the conversation until the client invokes one of the methods marked @Remove on the bean. While the conversation is active, the business methods of the client may store and access information using the fields of the bean.

Let's try using a stateful session bean to help manage a department. Our goal is to create a business object for a Department entity that provides business operations relating to that entity. Listing 5-2 shows our first attempt. The business method init() is called by the client to initialize the department id. We then store this department id on the bean instance, and the addEmployee() method uses it to find the department and make the necessary changes. From the perspective of the client, they only have to set the department id once, and then subsequent operations always refer to the same department.

Listing 5-2. *First Attempt at Department Manager Bean*

```
@Stateful
public class DepartmentManagerBean implements DepartmentManager {
    @PersistenceContext(unitName="EmployeeService")
    EntityManager em;
    int deptId;

    public void init(int deptId) {
        this.deptId = deptId;
    }

    public void setName(String name) {
        Department dept = em.find(Department.class, deptId);
        dept.setName(name);
    }

    public void addEmployee(int empId) {
        Department dept = em.find(Department.class, deptId);
        Employee emp = em.find(Employee.class, empId);
        dept.getEmployees().add(emp);
        emp.setDepartment(dept);
    }

    // ...

    @Remove
    public void finished() {
    }
}
```

The first thing that should stand out when looking at this bean is that it seems unnecessary to have to search for the department every time. After all, we have the department id, why not just store the Department entity instance as well? Listing 5-3 revises our first attempt by searching for the department once during the init() method and then reusing the entity instance for each business method.

Listing 5-3. *Second Attempt at Department Manager Bean*

```
@Stateful
public class DepartmentManagerBean implements DepartmentManager {
    @PersistenceContext(unitName="EmployeeService")
    EntityManager em;
    Department dept;

    public void init(int deptId) {
        dept = em.find(Department.class, deptId);
    }

    public void setName(String name) {
        dept.setName(name);
    }

    public void addEmployee(int empId) {
        Employee emp = em.find(Employee.class, empId);
        dept.getEmployees().add(emp);
        emp.setDepartment(dept);
    }

    // ...

    @Remove
    public void finished() {
    }
}
```

This version looks better-suited to the capabilities of a stateful session bean. It is certainly more natural to reuse the Department entity instance instead of searching for it each time. But there is a problem. The entity manager in Listing 5-3 is transaction-scoped. Assuming there is no active transaction from the client, every method on the bean will start and commit a new transaction since the default transaction attribute for each method is REQUIRED. Because there is a new transaction for each method, the entity manager will use a different persistence context each time.

Even though the Department instance still exists, the persistence context that used to manage it went away when the transaction associated with the init() call ended. We refer to the Department entity in this case as being *detached* from a persistence context. The instance is still around and can be used, but any changes to its state will be ignored. For example, invoking setName() will change the name in the entity instance, but the changes will never be reflected in the database.

This is the situation that the extended entity manager is designed to solve. Designed specifically for stateful session beans, it prevents entities from becoming detached when transactions end. Before we go too much further, let's introduce our third and final attempt at a department manager bean. Listing 5-4 shows our previous example updated to use an extended persistence context.

Listing 5-4. *Using an Extended Entity Manager*

```
@Stateful
public class DepartmentManagerBean implements DepartmentManager {
    @PersistenceContext(unitName="EmployeeService",
                        type=PersistenceContextType.EXTENDED)
    EntityManager em;
    Department dept;

    public void init(int deptId) {
        dept = em.find(Department.class, deptId);
    }

    public void setName(String name) {
        dept.setName(name);
    }

    public void addEmployee(int empId) {
        Employee emp = em.find(Employee.class, empId);
        dept.getEmployees().add(emp);
        emp.setDepartment(dept);
    }

    // ...

    @Remove
    public void finished() {
    }
}
```

As you can see, we changed only one line. The `@PersistenceContext` annotation that we introduced in Chapter 3 has a special `type` element that may be set to either `TRANSACTION` or `EXTENDED`. These constants are defined by the `PersistenceContextType` enumerated type. `TRANSACTION` is the default and corresponds to the transaction-scoped entity managers we have been using up to now. `EXTENDED` means that an extended entity manager should be used.

With this change made, the department manager bean now works as expected. Extended entity managers create a persistence context when a stateful session bean instance is created that lasts until the bean is removed. Unlike the persistence context of a transaction-scoped entity manager that begins when the transaction begins and lasts until the end of a transaction, the persistence context of an extended entity manager will last for the entire length of the conversation. Because the `Department` entity is still managed by the same persistence context, any time it is used in a transaction, any changes will be automatically written to the database.

The extended persistence context allows stateful session beans to be written in a way that is more natural with respect to their capabilities. Later we will discuss special limitations on the transaction management of extended entity managers, but by and large they are well-suited to the type of example we have shown here.

The biggest limitation of the extended entity manager is that it requires a stateful session bean. Despite having been available in the EJB specification for many years, stateful session beans are still not widely used. Partly due to the poor quality of early vendor implementations, stateful session beans gained a reputation for poor performance and poor scalability. Even though modern servers are very efficient in their management of stateful session beans, developer skepticism remains. Given that the HTTP session offers similar capabilities and is readily available without developing new beans, developers have traditionally chosen that route over stateful session beans for conversational data.

More importantly, Java EE applications are largely stateless in nature. Many business operations do not require the kind of conversational state that stateful session beans provide. But that said, with the new ease-of-use features introduced in EJB 3.0 and the extended persistence context as a major new feature custom-tailored to stateful session beans, they may see more use in the future.

Application-Managed Entity Managers

In Chapter 2 we introduced the Java Persistence API with an example written using Java SE. The entity manager in that example, and any entity manager that is created from the createEntityManager() call of an EntityManagerFactory instance, is what we call an *application-managed* entity manager. This name comes from the fact that the application manages the life cycle of the entity manager instead of the container.

Although we expect the majority of applications to be written using container-managed entity managers, application-managed entity managers still have a role to play. They are the only entity manager type available in Java SE, and as we will see, they can be used in Java EE as well.

Creating an application-managed entity manager is simple enough. All you need is an EntityManagerFactory to create the instance. What separates Java SE and Java EE for application-managed entity managers is not how you create the entity manager but how you get the factory. Listing 5-5 demonstrates use of the Persistence class to bootstrap an EntityManagerFactory instance that is then used to create an entity manager.

Listing 5-5. *Application-Managed Entity Managers in Java SE*

```
public class EmployeeClient {
    public static void main(String[] args) {
        EntityManagerFactory emf =
            Persistence.createEntityManagerFactory("EmployeeService");
        EntityManager em = emf.createEntityManager();

        Collection emps = em.createQuery("SELECT e FROM Employee e")
                            .getResultList();
        for (Iterator i = emps.iterator(); i.hasNext();) {
            Employee e = (Employee) i.next();
            System.out.println(e.getId() + ", " + e.getName());
        }

        em.close();
        emf.close();
    }
}
```

The `Persistence` class offers two variations of the same `createEntityManager()` method that may be used to create an `EntityManagerFactory` instance for a given persistence unit name. The first, specifying only the persistence unit name, returns the factory created with the default properties defined in the `persistence.xml` file. The second form of the method call allows a map of properties to be passed in, adding to or overriding the properties specified in `persistence.xml`. This form is useful when required JDBC properties may not be known until the application is started, perhaps with information provided as command-line parameters. We will discuss persistence unit properties in Chapter 11.

Creating an application-managed entity manager in Java EE requires using the `@PersistenceUnit` annotation to declare a reference to the `EntityManagerFactory` for a persistence unit. Once acquired, the factory can be used to create an entity manager, which may be used just as it would in Java SE. Listing 5-6 demonstrates injection of an `EntityManagerFactory` into a servlet and the use of it to create a short-lived entity manager in order to verify a user id.

Listing 5-6. *Application-Managed Entity Managers in Java EE*

```
public class LoginServlet extends HttpServlet {
    @PersistenceUnit(unitName="EmployeeService")
    EntityManagerFactory emf;

    protected void doPost(HttpServletRequest request, HttpServletResponse response)
{
        String userId = request.getParameter("user");

        // check valid user
        EntityManager em = emf.createEntityManager();
        try {
            User user = em.find(User.class, userId);
            if (user == null) {
                // return error page
                // ...
            }
        } finally {
            em.close();
        }

        // ...
    }
}
```

One thing in common in both of these examples is that the entity manager is explicitly closed with the `close()` call when it is no longer needed. This is one of the lifecycle requirements of an entity manager that must be performed manually in the case of application-managed entity managers and that is normally taken care of automatically by container-managed entity managers. Likewise, the `EntityManagerFactory` instance must also be closed, but only in the Java SE application. In Java EE, the container closes the factory automatically, so no extra steps are required.

In terms of the persistence context, the application-managed entity manager is similar to an extended container-managed entity manager. When an application-managed entity manager is created, it creates it own private persistence context that lasts until the entity manager is closed. This means that any entities managed by the entity manager will remain that way, independent of any transactions.

The role of the application-managed entity manager in Java EE is somewhat specialized. If resource-local transactions are required for an operation, an application-managed entity manager is the only type of entity manager that can be configured with that transaction type within the server. As we will describe in the next section, the transaction requirements of an extended entity manager can make them difficult to deal with in some situations. Application-managed entity managers can be safely used on stateful session beans to accomplish similar goals.

Transaction Management

Developing a persistence application is as much about transaction management as it is about object-relational mapping. Transactions define when new, changed, or removed entities are synchronized to the database. Understanding how persistence contexts interact with transactions is a fundamental part of working with the Java Persistence API.

Note that we said persistence contexts, not entity managers. There are several different entity manager types, but all use a persistence context internally. The entity manager type determines the lifetime of a persistence context, but all persistence contexts behave the same way when they are associated with a transaction.

There are two transaction-management types supported by the Java Persistence API. The first is resource-local transactions. These are the native transactions of the JDBC drivers that are referenced by a persistence unit. The second transaction-management type is the Java Transaction API, or JTA transactions. These are the transactions of the Java EE server, supporting multiple participating resources, transaction lifecycle management, and distributed XA transactions.

Container-managed entity managers always use JTA transactions, while application-managed entity managers may use either type. Because JTA is not typically available in Java SE applications, the provider need only support resource-local transactions in that environment. The default and preferred transaction type for Java EE applications is JTA. As we will describe in the next section, propagating persistence contexts with JTA transactions is a major benefit to enterprise persistence applications.

The transaction type is defined for a persistence unit and is configured using the `persistence.xml` file. We will discuss this setting and how to apply it in Chapter 11.

JTA Transaction Management

In order to talk about JTA transactions, we must first discuss the difference between transaction synchronization, transaction association, and transaction propagation. *Transaction synchronization* is the process by which a persistence context is registered with a transaction so that the persistence context may be notified when a transaction commits. The provider uses this notification to ensure that a given persistence context is correctly flushed to the database. *Transaction association* is the act of binding a persistence context to a transaction. You can also think of this as the *active* persistence context within the scope of that transaction. *Transaction propagation* is the process of sharing a persistence context between multiple container-managed entity managers in a single transaction.

There can be only one persistence context associated with and propagated across a JTA transaction. All container-managed entity managers in the same transaction must share the same propagated persistence context.

Transaction-Scoped Persistence Contexts

As the name suggests, a transaction-scoped persistence context is tied to the life cycle of the transaction. It is created by the container during a transaction and will be closed when the transaction completes. Transaction-scoped entity managers are responsible for creating transaction-scoped persistence contexts automatically when needed. We say only when needed because transaction-scoped persistence context creation is *lazy*. An entity manager will create a persistence context only when a method is invoked on the entity manager and when there is no persistence context available.

When a method is invoked on the transaction-scoped entity manager, it must first check if there is a propagated persistence context. If one exists, the entity manager uses this persistence context to carry out the operation. If one does not exist, the entity manager requests a new persistence context from the persistence provider and then marks this new persistence context as the propagated persistence context for the transaction before carrying out the method call. All subsequent transaction-scoped entity manager operations, in this component or any other, will thereafter use this newly created persistence context. This behavior works independently of whether or not container-managed or bean-managed transaction demarcation has been used.

Propagation of the persistence context simplifies the building of enterprise applications. When an entity is updated by a component inside of a transaction, any subsequent references to the same entity will always correspond to the correct instance, no matter what component obtains the entity reference. Propagating the persistence context gives developers the freedom to build loosely coupled applications knowing that they will always get the right data even though they are not sharing the same entity manager instance.

To demonstrate propagation of a transaction-scoped persistence context, let's introduce an audit service bean that stores information about a successfully completed transaction. Listing 5-7 shows the complete bean implementation. The logTransaction() method ensures that an employee id is valid by attempting to find the employee using the entity manager.

Listing 5-7. AuditService *Session Bean*

```
@Stateless
public class AuditServiceBean implements AuditService {
    @PersistenceContext(unitName="EmployeeService")
    EntityManager em;

    public void logTransaction(int empId, String action) {
        // verify employee number is valid
        if (em.find(Employee.class, empId) == null) {
            throw new IllegalArgumentException("Unknown employee id");
        }
        LogRecord lr = new LogRecord(empId, action);
        em.persist(lr);
    }
}
```

Now consider the fragment from the EmployeeService session bean example shown in Listing 5-8. After an employee is created, the logTransaction() method of the AuditService session bean is invoked to record the "created employee" event.

Listing 5-8. *Logging* EmployeeService *Transactions*

```
@Stateless
public class EmployeeServiceBean implements EmployeeService {
    @PersistenceContext(unitName="EmployeeService")
    EntityManager em;

    @EJB AuditService audit;

    public void createEmployee(Employee emp) {
        em.persist(emp);
        audit.logTransaction(emp.getId(), "created employee");
    }

    // ...
}
```

Even though the newly created Employee is not yet in the database, the audit bean is able to find the entity and verify that it exists. This works because the two beans are actually sharing the same persistence context. The transaction attribute of the createEmployee() method is REQUIRED by default since no attribute has been explicitly set. The container will guarantee that a transaction is started before the method is invoked. When persist() is called on the entity manager, the container checks to see if a persistence context is already associated with the transaction. Let's assume in this case that this was the first entity manager operation in the transaction, so the container creates a new persistence context and marks it as the propagated one.

When the logTransaction() method starts, it issues a find() call on the entity manager from the AuditServiceBean. We are guaranteed to be in a transaction, since the transaction attribute is also REQUIRED and the container-managed transaction from createEmployee() has been extended to this method by the container. When the find() method is invoked, the container again checks for an active persistence context. It finds the one created in the createEmployee() method and uses that persistence context to search for the entity. Since the newly created Employee instance is managed by this persistence context, it is returned successfully.

Now consider the case where logTransaction() has been declared with the REQUIRES_NEW transaction attribute instead of the default REQUIRED. Before the logTransaction() method call starts, the container will suspend the transaction inherited from createEmployee() and start a new transaction. When the find() method is invoked on the entity manager, it will check the current transaction for an active persistence context only to determine that one does not exist. A new persistence context will be created starting with the find() call, and this persistence context will be the active persistence context for the remainder of the logTransaction() call. Since the transaction started in createEmployee() has not yet committed, the newly created Employee instance is not in the database and therefore is not visible to this new persistence context. The find() method will return null, and the logTransaction() method will throw an exception as a result.

The rule of thumb for persistence context propagation is that the persistence context propagates as the JTA transaction propagates. Therefore it is important to understand not only when transactions begin and end, but also when a business method expects to inherit the transaction context from another method and when doing so would be incorrect. Having a clear plan for transaction management in your application is key to getting the most out of persistence context propagation.

Extended Persistence Contexts

The life cycle of an extended persistence context is tied to the stateful session bean to which it is bound. Unlike a transaction-scoped entity manager that creates a new persistence context for each transaction, the extended entity manager of a stateful session bean always uses the same persistence context. The stateful session bean is associated with a single extended persistence context that is created when the bean instance is created and closed when the bean instance is removed. This has implications for both the association and propagation characteristics of the extended persistence context.

Transaction association for extended persistence contexts is *eager*. In the case of container-managed transactions, as soon as a method call starts on the bean, the container automatically associates the persistence context with the transaction. Likewise in the case of bean-managed transactions; as soon as UserTransaction.begin() is invoked within a bean method, the container intercepts the call and performs the same association.

Because a transaction-scoped entity manager will use an existing persistence context associated with the transaction before it will create a new persistence context, it is possible to share an extended persistence context with other transaction-scoped entity managers. So long as the extended persistence context is propagated before any transaction-scoped entity managers are accessed, the same extended persistence context will be shared by all components.

Similar to the auditing EmployeeServiceBean we demonstrated in Listing 5-8, consider the same change made to a stateful session bean DepartmentManagerBean to audit when an employee is added to a department. Listing 5-9 shows this example.

Listing 5-9. *Logging Department Changes*

```
@Stateful
public class DepartmentManagerBean implements DepartmentManager {
    @PersistenceContext(unitName="EmployeeService",
                        type=PersistenceContextType.EXTENDED)
    EntityManager em;
    Department dept;
    @EJB AuditService audit;

    public void init(int deptId) {
        dept = em.find(Department.class, deptId);
    }
```

```
    public void addEmployee(int empId) {
        Employee emp = em.find(Employee.class, empId);
        dept.getEmployees().add(emp);
        emp.setDepartment(dept);
        audit.logTransaction(emp.getId(),
                            "added to department " + dept.getName());
    }

    // ...
}
```

The addEmployee() method has a default transaction attribute of REQUIRED. Since the container eagerly associates extended persistence contexts, the extended persistence context stored on the session bean will be immediately associated with the transaction when the method call starts. This will cause the relationship between the managed Department and Employee entities to be persisted to the database when the transaction commits. It also means that the extended persistence context will now be shared by other transaction-scoped persistence contexts used in methods called from addEmployee().

The logTransaction() method in this example will inherit the transaction context from addEmployee() since its transaction attribute is the default REQUIRED and a transaction is active during the call to addEmployee(). When the find() method is invoked, the transaction-scoped entity manager checks for an active persistence context and will find the extended persistence context from the DepartmentManagerBean. It will then use this persistence context to execute the operation. All of the managed entities from the extended persistence context become visible to the transaction-scoped entity manager.

Persistence Context Collision

We said earlier that only one persistence context could be propagated with a JTA transaction. We also said that the extended persistence context would always try to make itself the active persistence context. This can quickly lead to situations where the two persistence contexts collide with each other. Consider, for example, that a stateless session bean with a transaction-scoped entity manager creates a new persistence context and then invokes a method on a stateful session bean with an extended persistence context. During the eager association of the extended persistence context, the container will check to see if there is already an active persistence context. If there is, it must be the same as the extended persistence context that it is trying to associate, or an exception will be thrown. In this example, the stateful session bean will find the transaction-scoped persistence context created by the stateless session bean, and the call into the stateful session bean method will fail. There can only be one active persistence context for a transaction.

While extended persistence context propagation is useful if a stateful session bean with an extended persistence context is the first EJB to be invoked in a call chain, it limits the situations in which other components can call into the stateful session bean if they too are using entity managers. This may or may not be common depending on your application architecture, but it is something to keep in mind when planning dependencies between components.

One way to work around this problem is to change the default transaction attribute for the stateful session bean that uses the extended persistence context. If the default transaction attribute is REQUIRES_NEW, then any active transaction will be suspended before the stateful session bean method starts, allowing it to associate its extended persistence context with the new transaction. This is a good strategy if the stateful session bean calls in to other stateless session beans and needs to propagate the persistence context. Note that excessive use of the REQUIRES_NEW transaction attribute can lead to application performance problems as many more transactions than normal will be created and active transactions will be suspended and resumed.

If the stateful session bean is largely self-contained, that is, it does not call other session beans and does not need its persistence context propagated, then a default transaction attribute type of NOT_SUPPORTED may be worth considering. In this case, any active transaction will be suspended before the stateful session bean method starts, but no new transaction will be started. If there are some methods that need to write data to the database, then those methods can be overridden to use the REQUIRES_NEW transaction attribute.

Listing 5-10 repeats the DepartmentManager bean, this time with some additional getter methods and customized transaction attributes. We have set the default transaction attribute to REQUIRES_NEW to force a new transaction by default when a business method is invoked. For the getName() method, we don't need a new transaction since no changes are being made, so it has been set to NOT_SUPPORTED. This will suspend the current transaction but won't result in a new transaction being created. With these changes, the DepartmentManager bean may be accessed in any situation, even if there is already an active persistence context.

Listing 5-10. *Customizing Transaction Attributes to Avoid Collision*

```
@Stateful
@TransactionAttribute(TransactionAttributeType.REQUIRES_NEW)
public class DepartmentManagerBean implements DepartmentManager {
    @PersistenceContext(unitName="EmployeeService",
                        type=PersistenceContextType.EXTENDED)
    EntityManager em;
    Department dept;
    @EJB AuditService audit;

    public void init(int deptId) {
        dept = em.find(Department.class, deptId);
    }

    @TransactionAttribute(TransactionAttributeType.NOT_SUPPORTED)
    public String getName() { return dept.getName(); }
    public void setName(String name) { dept.setName(name); }

    public void addEmployee(int empId) {
        Employee emp = em.find(empId, Employee.class);
        dept.getEmployees().add(emp);
        emp.setDepartment(dept);
        audit.logTransaction(emp.getId(),
                             "added to department " + dept.getName());
    }

    // ...
}
```

Finally, one last option to consider is using an application-managed entity manager instead of an extended entity manager. If there is no need to propagate the persistence context, then the extended entity manager is not adding a lot of value over an application-managed entity manager. The stateful session bean can safely create an application-managed entity manager, store it on the bean instance, and use it for persistence operations without having to worry about whether or not an active transaction already has a propagated persistence context. An example of this technique is demonstrated later in the section Application-Managed Persistence Contexts.

Persistence Context Inheritance

The restriction of only one stateful session bean with an extended persistence context being able to participate in a JTA transaction can be a limitation in some situations. For example, the pattern we followed earlier in this chapter for the extended persistence context was to encapsulate the behavior of an entity behind a stateful session façade. In our example, clients worked with a DepartmentManager session bean instead of the actual Department entity instance. Since a department has a manager, it makes sense to extend this façade to the Employee entity as well.

Listing 5-11 shows changes to the DepartmentManager bean so that it returns an EmployeeManager stateful session bean from the getManager() method in order to represent the manager of the department. The EmployeeManager stateful session bean is injected and then initialized during the invocation of the init() method.

Listing 5-11. *Creating and Returning a Stateful Session Bean*

```
@Stateful
public class DepartmentManagerBean implements DepartmentManager {
    @PersistenceContext(unitName="EmployeeService",
                        type=PersistenceContextType.EXTENDED)
    EntityManager em;
    Department dept;
    @EJB EmployeeManager manager;

    public void init(int deptId) {
        dept = em.find(Department.class, deptId);
        manager.init();
    }

    public EmployeeManager getManager() {
        return manager;
    }

    // ...
}
```

Should the init() method succeed or fail? So far based on what we have described, it looks like it should fail. When init() is invoked on the DepartmentManager bean, its extended persistence context will be propagated with the transaction. In the subsequent call to init() on the EmployeeManager bean, it will attempt to associate its own extended persistence context with the transaction, causing a collision between the two.

Perhaps surprisingly, this example actually works. When a stateful session bean with an extended persistence context creates another stateful session bean that also uses an extended persistence context, the child will inherit the parent's persistence context. The EmployeeManager bean inherits the persistence context from the DepartmentManager bean when it is injected into the DepartmentManager instance. The two beans can now be used together within the same transaction.

Application-Managed Persistence Contexts

Like container-managed persistence contexts, application-managed persistence contexts may be synchronized with JTA transactions. Synchronizing the persistence context with the transaction means that a flush will occur if the transaction commits, but the persistence context will not be considered associated by any container-managed entity managers. There is no limit to the number of application-managed persistence contexts that may be synchronized with a transaction, but only one container-managed persistence context will ever be associated. This is one of the most important differences between application-managed and container-managed entity managers.

An application-managed entity manager participates in a JTA transaction in one of two ways. If the persistence context is created inside the transaction, then the persistence provider will automatically synchronize the persistence context with the transaction. If the persistence context was created earlier (outside of a transaction or in a transaction that has since ended), the persistence context may be manually synchronized with the transaction by calling joinTransaction() on the EntityManager interface. Once synchronized, the persistence context will automatically be flushed when the transaction commits.

Listing 5-12 shows a variation of the DepartmentManagerBean from Listing 5-11 that uses an application-managed entity manager instead of an extended entity manager.

Listing 5-12. *Using Application-Managed Entity Managers with JTA*

```
@Stateful
public class DepartmentManagerBean implements DepartmentManager {
    @PersistenceUnit(unitName="EmployeeService")
    EntityManagerFactory emf;
    EntityManager em;
    Department dept;

    public void init(int deptId) {
        em = emf.createEntityManager();
        dept = em.find(Department.class, deptId);
    }

    public String getName() {
        return dept.getName();
    }
```

```
    public void addEmployee(int empId) {
        em.joinTransaction();
        Employee emp = em.find(Employee.class, empId);
        dept.getEmployees().add(emp);
        emp.setDepartment(dept);
    }

    // ...

    @Remove
    public void finished() {
        em.close();
    }
}
```

Instead of injecting an entity manager, we are injecting an entity manager factory. Prior to searching for the entity, we manually create a new application-managed entity manager using the factory. Because the container does not manage its life cycle, we have to close it later when the bean is removed during the call to finished(). Like the container-managed extended persistence context, the Department entity remains managed after the call to init(). When addEmployee() is called, there is the extra step of calling joinTransaction() to notify the persistence context that it should synchronize itself with the current JTA transaction. Without this call, the changes to Department would not be flushed to the database when the transaction commits.

Because application-managed entity managers do not propagate, the only way to share managed entities with other components is to share the EntityManager instance. This can be achieved by passing the entity manager around as an argument to local methods or by storing the entity manager in a common place such as an HTTP session. Listing 5-13 demonstrates a servlet creating an application-managed entity manager and using it to instantiate the EmployeeService class we defined in Chapter 2. In these cases, care must be taken to ensure that access to the entity manager is done in a thread-safe manner. While EntityManagerFactory instances are thread-safe, EntityManager instances are not. Also, application code must not call joinTransaction() on the same entity manager in multiple concurrent transactions.

Listing 5-13. *Sharing an Application-Managed Entity Manager*

```
public class EmployeeServlet extends HttpServlet {
    @PersistenceUnit(unitName="EmployeeService")
    EntityManagerFactory emf;
    @Resource UserTransaction tx;

    protected void doPost(HttpServletRequest request, HttpServletResponse response)
            throws ServletException, IOException {
        // ...
        int id = Integer.parseInt(request.getParameter("id"));
        String name = request.getParameter("name");
        long salary = Long.parseLong(request.getParameter("salary"));
        tx.begin();
```

```
        EntityManager em = emf.createEntityManager();
        try {
            EmployeeService service = new EmployeeService(em);
            service.createEmployee(id, name, salary);
        } finally {
            em.close();
        }
        tx.commit();
        // ...
    }
}
```

Listing 5-13 demonstrates an additional characteristic of the application-managed entity manager in the presence of transactions. If the persistence context becomes synchronized with a transaction, changes will still be written to the database when the transaction commits, even if the entity manager is closed. This allows entity managers to be closed at the point where they are created without the need to worry about closing them after the transaction ends. Note that closing an application-managed entity manager still prevents any further use of the entity manager. It is only the persistence context that continues until the transaction has completed.

There is a danger in mixing multiple persistence contexts in the same JTA transaction. This occurs when multiple application-managed persistence contexts become synchronized with the transaction or when application-managed persistence contexts become mixed with container-managed persistence contexts. When the transaction commits, each persistence context will receive notification from the transaction manager that changes should be written to the database. This will cause each persistence context to be flushed.

What happens if an entity with the same primary key is used in more than one persistence context? Which version of the entity gets stored? The unfortunate answer is that there is no way to know for sure. The container does not guarantee any ordering when notifying persistence contexts of transaction completion. As a result, it is critical for data integrity that entities never be used by more than one persistence context in the same transaction. When designing your application, we recommend picking a single persistence context strategy (container-managed or application-managed) and sticking to that strategy consistently.

Resource-Local Transactions

Resource-local transactions are controlled explicitly by the application. The application server, if there is one, has no part in the management of the transaction. Applications interact with resource-local transactions by acquiring an implementation of the EntityTransaction interface from the entity manager. The getTransaction() method of the EntityManager interface is used for this purpose.

The EntityTransaction interface is designed to imitate the UserTransaction interface defined by the Java Transaction API, and the two behave very similarly. The main difference is that EntityTransaction operations are implemented in terms of the transaction methods on the JDBC Connection interface. Listing 5-14 shows the complete EntityTransaction interface.

Listing 5-14. *The* EntityTransaction *Interface*

```
public interface EntityTransaction {
    public void begin();
    public void commit();
    public void rollback();
    public void setRollbackOnly();
    public void getRollbackOnly();
    public void isActive();
}
```

There are only six methods on the EntityTransaction interface. The begin() method starts a new resource transaction. If a transaction is active, isActive() will return true. Attempting to start a new transaction while a transaction is active will result in an IllegalStateException being thrown. Once active, the transaction may be committed by invoking commit() or rolled back by invoking rollback(). Both operations will fail with an IllegalStateException if there is no active transaction. A PersistenceException will be thrown if an error occurs during rollback, while a RollbackException will be thrown if the commit fails.

If a persistence operation fails while an EntityTransaction is active, the provider will mark it for rollback. It is the application's responsibility to ensure that the rollback actually occurs by calling rollback(). If the transaction is marked for rollback and a commit is attempted, a RollbackException will be thrown. To avoid this exception, the getRollbackOnly() method may be called to determine whether the transaction is in a failed state. Until the transaction is rolled back, it is still active and will cause any subsequent commit or begin operation to fail.

Listing 5-15 shows a Java SE application that uses the EntityTransaction API to perform a password change for users who failed to update their passwords before they expired.

Listing 5-15. *Using the* EntityTransaction *Interface*

```
public class ExpirePasswords {
    public static void main(String[] args) {
        int maxAge = Integer.parseInt(args[0]);
        String defaultPassword = args[1];

        EntityManagerFactory emf =
            Persistence.createEntityManagerFactory("admin");
        try {
            EntityManager em = emf.createEntityManager();

            Calendar cal = Calendar.getInstance();
            cal.add(Calendar.DAY_OF_YEAR, -maxAge);

            em.getTransaction().begin();
            Collection expired =
                em.createQuery("SELECT u FROM User u WHERE u.lastChange > ?1")
                    .setParameter(1, cal)
                    .getResultList();
```

```
            for (Iterator i = expired.iterator(); i.hasNext();) {
                User u = (User) i.next();
                System.out.println("Expiring password for " + u.getName());
                u.setPassword(defaultPassword);
            }
            em.getTransaction().commit();
            em.close();
        } finally {
            emf.close();
        }
    }
}
```

Within the application server, JTA transaction management is the default and should be used by most applications. One example use of resource-local transactions in the Java EE environment might be for logging. If your application requires an audit log stored in the database that must be written regardless of the outcome of any JTA transactions, then a resource-local entity manager may be used to persist data outside of the current transaction. Resource transactions may be freely started and committed any number of times within a JTA transaction without impacting the state of the JTA transactions.

Listing 5-16 shows an example of a stateless session bean that provides audit logging that will succeed even if the active JTA transaction fails.

Listing 5-16. *Using Resource-Local Transactions in the Java EE Environment*

```
@Stateless
public class LogServiceBean implements LogService {
    @PersistenceUnit(unitName="logging")
    EntityManagerFactory emf;

    public void logAccess(int userId, String action) {
        EntityManager em = emf.createEntityManager();
        try {
            LogRecord lr = new LogRecord(userId, action);
            em.getTransaction().begin();
            em.persist(lr);
            em.getTransaction().commit();
        } finally {
            em.close();
        }
    }
}
```

Of course, you could make the argument that this is overkill for a simple logging bean. Direct JDBC would probably work just as easily, but these same log records may have uses elsewhere in the application. It is a trade-off in configuration (defining a completely separate persistence unit in order to enable the resource-local transactions) versus the convenience of having an object-oriented representation of a log record.

Transaction Rollback and Entity State

When a database transaction is rolled back, all of the changes made during the transaction are abandoned. The database reverts to whatever state it was in before the transaction began. But as mentioned in Chapter 2, the Java memory model is not transactional. There is no way to take a snapshot of object state and revert to it later if something goes wrong. One of the harder parts of using an object-relational mapping solution is that while we can use transactional semantics in our application to control whether or not data is committed to the database, we can't truly apply the same techniques to the in-memory persistence context that manages our entity instances.

Any time we are working with changes that must be persisted to the database, we are working with a persistence context synchronized with a transaction. At some point during the life of the transaction, usually just before it commits, the changes we require will be translated into the appropriate SQL statements and sent to the database. Whether we are using JTA transactions or resource-local transactions is irrelevant. We have a persistence context participating in a transaction with changes that need to be made.

If that transaction rolls back, two things happen. The first is that the database transaction will be rolled back. The next thing that happens is that the persistence context is cleared, detaching all of our managed entity instances. If the persistence context was transaction-scoped, then it is removed.

Because the Java memory model is not transactional, we are basically left with a bunch of detached entity instances. More importantly, these detached instances reflect the entity state exactly as it was at the point when the rollback occurred. Faced with a rolled-back transaction and detached entities, you might be tempted to start a new transaction, merge the entities into the new persistence context, and start over. The following issues need to be considered in this case:

- If there is a new entity that uses automatic primary key generation, there may be a primary key value assigned to the detached entity. If this primary key was generated from a database sequence or table, the operation to generate the number may have been rolled back with the transaction. This means that the same sequence number could be given out again to a different object. Clear the primary key before attempting to persist the entity again, and do not rely on the primary key value in the detached entity.

- If your entity uses a version field for locking purposes that is automatically maintained by the persistence provider, it may be set to an incorrect value. The value in the entity will not match the correct value stored in the database. We will cover locking and versioning in Chapter 9.

If you need to reapply some of the changes that failed and are currently sitting in the detached entities, consider selectively copying the changed data into new managed entities. This guarantees that the merge operation will not be compromised by stale data left in the detached entity. To merge failed entities into a new persistence context, some providers may offer additional options that avoid some or all of these issues.

Choosing an Entity Manager

With three different entity manager types, each with a different life cycle and different rules about transaction association and propagation, it can all be a little overwhelming. What style is right for your application? Application-managed or container-managed? Transaction-scoped or extended?

Generally speaking, we believe that container-managed, transaction-scoped entity managers are the best model for most applications. This is the design that originally inspired the Java Persistence API and is the model that commercial persistence providers have been using for years. The selection of this style to be the default for Java EE applications was no accident. It offers the best combination of flexible transaction propagation with easy-to-understand semantics.

Extended persistence contexts are effectively a new programming model introduced by this specification. Although commercial vendors have had similar features to allow entities to remain managed after commit, never before has such a feature been fully integrated into the life cycle of a Java EE component, in this case the stateful session bean. There are some interesting new techniques possible with the extended persistence context (some of which we will describe later in this chapter), but these may not apply to all applications.

In most enterprise applications, application-managed entity managers are unlikely to see much use. There is rarely a need for persistence contexts that are not associated with a container transaction and that remain isolated from the rest of the container-managed persistence contexts. The lack of propagation means that application-managed entity managers must be passed around as method arguments or stored in a shared object in order to share the persistence context. Evaluate application-managed entity managers based on your expected transactional needs and the size and complexity of your application.

More than anything, we recommend that you try to be consistent in how entity managers are selected and applied. Mixing all three entity manager types into an application is likely to be frustrating as the different entity manager types can intersect in unexpected ways.

Entity Manager Operations

Armed with information about the different entity manager types and how they work with persistence contexts, we can now revisit the basic entity manager operations we introduced in Chapter 2 and reveal more of the details. The following sections describe the entity manager operations with respect to the different entity manager and persistence context types.

Persisting an Entity

The `persist()` method of the `EntityManager` interface accepts a new entity instance and causes it to become managed. If the entity to be persisted is already managed by the persistence context, then it is ignored. The `contains()` operation can be used to check whether an entity is already managed, but it is very rare that this should be required. It should not come as a surprise to the application to find out which entities are managed and which are not. The design of the application dictates when entities become managed.

For an entity to be managed does not mean that it is persisted to the database right away. The actual SQL to create the necessary relational data will not be generated until the persistence context is synchronized with the database, typically only when the transaction commits. However, once a new entity is managed, any changes to that entity may be tracked by the persistence context. Whatever state exists on the entity when the transaction commits is what will be written to the database.

When `persist()` is invoked outside of a transaction, the behavior depends on the type of entity manager. A transaction-scoped entity manager will throw a `TransactionRequiredException` as there is no persistence context available in which to make the entity managed. Application-managed and extended entity managers will accept the persist request, causing the entity to become managed, but no immediate action will be taken until a new transaction begins and the persistence context becomes synchronized with the transaction. In effect, this queues up the change to happen at a later point in time. It is only when the transaction commits that changes will be written out to the database.

The `persist()` operation is intended for new entities that do not already exist in the database. If the provider immediately determines that this is not true, then an `EntityExistsException` will be thrown. If the provider does not make this determination and the primary key is in fact a duplicate, then an exception will be thrown when the persistence context is synchronized to the database.

Up to this point we have been discussing the persistence of entities only without relationships. But, as we learned in Chapter 4, the Java Persistence API supports a wide variety of relationship types. In practice, most entities are in a relationship with at least one other entity. Consider the following sequence of operations:

```
Department dept = em.find(Department.class, 30);
Employee emp = new Employee();
emp.setId(53);
emp.setName("Peter");
emp.setDepartment(dept);
dept.getEmployees().add(emp);
em.persist(emp);
```

Despite the brevity of this example, we have covered a lot of points relating to persisting a relationship. We begin by retrieving a pre-existing `Department` instance. A new `Employee` instance is then created, supplying the primary key and basic information about the `Employee`. We then assign the employee to the department, by setting the `department` attribute of the `Employee` to point to the `Department` instance we retrieved earlier. Because the relationship is bidirectional, we then add the new `Employee` instance to the `employees` collection in the `Department` instance. Finally the new `Employee` instance is persisted with the call to `persist()`. Assuming a transaction then commits, the new entity will be stored in the database.

An interesting thing about this example is that the `Department` is a passive participant despite the `Employee` instance being added to its collection. The `Employee` entity is the owner of the relationship because it is in a many-to-one relationship with the `Department`. As we mentioned in the previous chapter, the source side of the relationship is the owner, while the target is the inverse in this type of relationship. When the `Employee` is persisted, the foreign key to the `Department` is written out to the table mapped by the `Employee`, and no actual change is made to the `Department` entity's physical representation. Had we only added the employee to the collection and not updated the other side of the relationship, nothing would have been persisted to the database.

Finding an Entity

The ever-present `find()` method is the workhorse of the entity manager. Whenever an entity needs to be located by its primary key, `find()` is usually the best way to go. Not only does it have simple semantics, but most persistence providers will also optimize this operation to use an in-memory cache that minimizes trips to the database.

The `find()` operation returns a managed entity instance in all cases except when invoked outside of a transaction on a transaction-scoped entity manager. In this case, the entity instance is returned in a detached state. It is not associated with any persistence context.

There exists a special version of `find()` that may be used in one particular situation. That situation is when a relationship is being created between two entities in a one-to-one or many-to-one relationship where the target entity already exists and its primary key is well-known. Since we are only creating a relationship, it may not be necessary to fully load the target entity in order to create the foreign key reference to it. Only its primary key is required. The `getReference()` operation may be used for this purpose. Consider the following example:

```
Department dept = em.getReference(Department.class, 30);
Employee emp = new Employee();
emp.setId(53);
emp.setName("Peter");
emp.setDepartment(dept);
dept.getEmployees().add(emp);
em.persist(emp);
```

The only difference between this sequence of operations and the ones we demonstrated earlier is that the `find()` call has been replaced with a call to `getReference()`. When the `getReference()` call is invoked, the provider may return a proxy to the `Department` entity without actually retrieving it from the database. So long as only its primary key is accessed, `Department` data does not need to be fetched. Instead, when the `Employee` is persisted, the primary key value will be used to create the foreign key to the corresponding `Department` entry. The `getReference()` call is effectively a performance optimization that removes the need to retrieve the target entity instance.

There are some drawbacks to using `getReference()` that must be understood. The first is that if a proxy is used, then it may throw an `EntityNotFoundException` exception if it is unable to locate the real entity instance when an attribute other the primary key is accessed. The assumption with `getReference()` is that you are sure the entity with the correct primary key exists. If, for some reason, an attribute other than the primary key is accessed and the entity does not exist, then an exception will be thrown. A corollary to this is that the object returned from `getReference()` may not be safe to use if it is no longer managed. If the provider returns a proxy, it will be dependent on there being an active persistence context to load entity state.

Given the very specific situation in which `getReference()` may be used, `find()` should be used in virtually all cases. The in-memory cache of a good persistence provider is effective enough that the performance cost of accessing an entity via its primary key will not usually be noticed. In the case of TopLink Essentials, it has a fully integrated shared object cache, so not only is local persistence context management efficient, but also all threads on the same server can benefit from the shared contents of the cache. The `getReference()` call is a performance optimization that should be used only when there is evidence to suggest that it will actually benefit the application.

Removing an Entity

Removing an entity is not a complex task, but it can require several steps depending on the number of relationships in the entity to be removed. At its most basic, removing an entity is simply a case of passing a managed entity instance to the remove() method of an entity manager. As soon as the associated persistence context becomes synchronized with a transaction and commits, the entity is removed. At least that is what we would like to happen. As we will soon show, removing an entity requires some attention to the relationships of an entity, or the integrity of the database can be compromised in the process.

Let's walk through a simple example. Consider the Employee and ParkingSpace relationship that we demonstrated in Chapter 4. The Employee has a unidirectional one-to-one relationship with the ParkingSpace entity. Now imagine that we execute the following code inside a transaction, where empId corresponds to an Employee primary key:

```
Employee emp = em.find(Employee.class, empId);
em.remove(emp.getParkingSpace());
```

When the transaction commits, we see the DELETE statement for the PARKING_SPACE table get generated, but then we get an exception containing a database error that shows that we have violated a foreign key constraint. It turns out that a referential integrity constraint exists between the EMPLOYEE table and the PARKING_SPACE table. The row was deleted from the PARKING_SPACE table, but the corresponding foreign key in the EMPLOYEE table was not set to NULL. To correct the problem we have to explicitly set the parkingSpace attribute of the Employee entity to null before the transaction commits:

```
Employee emp = em.find(Employee.class, empId);
ParkingSpace ps = em.getParkingSpace();
em.setParkingSpace(null);
em.remove(ps);
```

Relationship maintenance is the responsibility of the application. We are going to repeat this statement over the course of this book, but it cannot be emphasized enough. Almost every problem related to removing an entity always comes back to this issue. If the entity to be removed is the target of foreign keys in other tables, then those foreign keys must be cleared in order for the remove to succeed. The remove operation will either fail as it did here, or it will result in stale data being left in the foreign key columns referring to the removed entity in the event that there is no referential integrity.

An entity may be removed only if it is managed by a persistence context. This means that a transaction-scoped entity manager may be used to remove an entity only if there is an active transaction. Attempting to invoke remove() when there is no transaction will result in a TransactionRequiredException exception. Like the persist() operation we described earlier, application-managed and extended entity managers can remove an entity outside of a transaction, but the change will not take place in the database until a transaction involving the persistence context is committed.

After the transaction has committed, all entities that were removed in that transaction are left in the state that they were in before they were removed. A removed entity instance can be persisted again with the persist() operation, but the same issues with generated state that we discussed in the Transaction Rollback and Entity State section apply here as well.

Cascading Operations

By default, every entity manager operation applies only to the entity supplied as an argument to the operation. The operation will not cascade to other entities that have a relationship with the entity that is being operated on. For some operations, such as remove(), this is usually the desired behavior. We wouldn't want the entity manager to make incorrect assumptions about which entity instances should be removed as a side effect from some other operation. But the same does not hold true for operations such as persist(). Chances are that if we have a new entity and it has a relationship to another new entity, the two must be persisted together.

Consider the sequence of operations in Listing 5-17 that are required to create a new Employee entity with an associated Address entity and make the two persistent. The second call to persist() that makes the Address entity managed is bothersome. An Address entity is coupled to the Employee entity that holds on to it. Whenever a new Employee is created, it makes sense to cascade the persist() operation to the Address entity if it is present.

Listing 5-17. *Persisting Employee and Address Entities*

```
Employee emp = new Employee();
emp.setId(2);
emp.setName("Rob");
Address addr = new Address();
addr.setStreet("645 Stanton Way");
addr.setCity("Manhattan");
addr.setState("NY");
emp.setAddress(addr);
em.persist(addr);
em.persist(emp);
```

Fortunately the Java Persistence API provides a mechanism to define when operations such as persist() should be cascaded across relationships. The cascade element, in all of the logical relationship annotations (@OneToOne, @OneToMany, @ManyToOne, and @ManyToMany), defines the list of entity manager operations to be cascaded.

Entity manager operations are identified using the CascadeType enumerated type when listed as part of the cascade element. The PERSIST, REFRESH, REMOVE, and MERGE constants pertain to the entity manager operation of the same name. The constant ALL is shorthand for declaring that all four operations should be cascaded.

The following sections will define the cascading behavior of the persist() and remove() operations. We will introduce the merge() operation and its cascading behavior later in this chapter in the section Merging Detached Entities. Likewise, we will introduce the refresh() operation and its cascading behavior in Chapter 9.

Cascade Persist

To begin, let's consider the changes required to make the persist() operation cascade from Employee to Address. In the definition of the Employee class, there is an @ManyToOne annotation defined for the address relationship. To enable the cascade, we must add the PERSIST operation to the list of cascading operations for this relationship. Listing 5-18 shows a fragment of the Employee entity that demonstrates this change.

Listing 5-18. *Enabling Cascade Persist*

```
@Entity
public class Employee {
    // ...
    @ManyToOne(cascade=CascadeType.PERSIST)
    Address address;
    // ...
}
```

To leverage this change, we need only ensure that the Address entity has been set on the Employee instance before invoking persist() on it. As the entity manager encounters the Employee instance and adds it to the persistence context, it will navigate across the address relationship looking for a new Address entity to manage as well. In comparison to the approach in Listing 5-16, this change frees us from having to persist the Address separately.

Cascade settings are unidirectional. This means that it must be explicitly set on both sides of a relationship if the same behavior is intended for both situations. For example, in Listing 5-17, we only added the cascade setting to the address relationship in the Employee entity. If Listing 5-16 were changed to persist only the Address entity and not the Employee entity, then the Employee entity would not become managed, because the entity manager has not been instructed to navigate out from any relationships defined on the Address entity.

Even though it is legal to do so, it is still unlikely that we would add cascading operations from the Address entity to the Employee entity, because it is a child of the Employee entity. While causing the Employee instance to become managed as a side effect of persisting the Address instance is harmless, application code would not expect the same from the remove() operation, for example. Therefore we must be judicious in applying cascades, because there is an expectation of ownership in relationships that influences what developers expect when interacting with these entities.

In the Persisting an Entity section, we mentioned that the entity instance is ignored if it is already persisted. This is true, but the entity manager will still honor the PERSIST cascade in this situation. For example, consider our Employee entity again. If the Employee instance is already managed and a new Address instance is set in it, then invoking persist() again on the Employee instance will cause the Address instance to become managed. No changes will be made to the Employee instance since it is already managed.

As adding the PERSIST cascade is a very common and desirable behavior for relationships, it is possible to make this the default cascade setting for all relationships in the persistence unit. We will discuss this technique in Chapter 10.

Cascade Remove

At first glance, having the entity manager automatically cascade remove() operations may sound attractive. Depending on the cardinality of the relationship, it could eliminate the need to explicitly remove multiple entity instances. And yet, while we could cascade this operation in a number of situations, this should be applied only in certain cases. There are really only two cases where cascading the remove() operation makes sense: one-to-one and one-to-many relationships where there is a clear parent-child relationship. It can't be blindly applied to all one-to-one and one-to-many relationships because the target entities might also be participating in other relationships or might make sense as stand-alone entities. Because there is no way in the logical annotations of the Java Persistence API to declare private ownership of the entities across a relationship, care must be taken when using the REMOVE cascade option.

With that warning out of the way, let's look at a situation where cascading the remove() operation makes sense. If an Employee entity is removed (hopefully an uncommon occurrence), it makes sense to cascade the remove() operation to both the ParkingSpace and Phone entities related to the Employee. These are both cases in which the Employee is the parent of the target entities. Listing 5-19 demonstrates the changes to the Employee entity class that enables this behavior. Note that we have added the REMOVE cascade in addition to the existing PERSIST option. Chances are, if an owning relationship is safe to use REMOVE, then it is also safe to use PERSIST.

Listing 5-19. *Enabling Cascade Remove*

```
@Entity
public class Employee {
    // ...
    @OneToOne(cascade={CascadeType.PERSIST, CascadeType.REMOVE})
    ParkingSpace parkingSpace;
    @OneToMany(mappedBy="employee",
                cascade={CascadeType.PERSIST, CascadeType.REMOVE})
    Collection<Phone> phones;
    // ...
}
```

Now let's take a step back and look at what it means to cascade the remove() operation. As it processes the Employee instance, the entity manager will navigate across the parkingSpace and phones relationships and invoke remove() on those entity instances as well. Like the remove() operation on a single entity, this is a database operation and has no effect at all on the in-memory links between the object instances. When the Employee instance becomes detached, its phones collection will still contain all of the Phone instances that were there before the remove() operation took place. The Phone instances are detached because they were removed as well, but the link between the two instances remains.

Because the remove() operation can be safely cascaded only from parent to child, it can't help the situation we encountered earlier in the Removing an Entity section. There is no setting that can be applied to a relationship from one entity to another that will cause it to be removed from a parent without also removing the parent in the process. For example, when trying to remove the ParkingSpace entity, we hit an integrity constraint violation from the database unless the parkingSpace field in the Employee entity is set to null. Setting the REMOVE cascade option on the @OneToOne annotation in the ParkingSpace entity would not cause it to be removed from the Employee; rather it would cause the Employee instance itself to become removed. Clearly this is not the behavior we desire. There are no shortcuts to relationship maintenance.

Clearing the Persistence Context

Occasionally it may be necessary to clear a persistence context of its managed entities. This is usually required only for application-managed and extended persistence contexts that are long-lived and have grown too large in size. For example, consider an application-managed entity manager that issues a query returning several hundred entity instances. Once changes are made to a handful of these instances and the transaction is committed, you have left in memory hundreds of objects that you have no intention of changing any further. If you don't want to close the persistence context, then you need to be able to clear out the managed entities, or else the persistence context will continue to grow over time.

The `clear()` method of the `EntityManager` interface can be used to clear the persistence context. In many respects this is semantically equivalent to a transaction rollback. All entity instances managed by the persistence context become detached with their state left exactly as it was when the `clear()` operation was invoked. If a transaction was started at this point and then committed, nothing would be written out to the database because the persistence context is empty. The `clear()` operation is all or nothing. You cannot selectively cancel the management of any particular entity instance while the persistence context is still open.

While technically possible, clearing the persistence context when there are uncommitted changes is a dangerous operation. The persistence context is an in-memory structure, and clearing it simply detaches the managed entities. If you are in a transaction and changes have already been written to the database, they will not be rolled back when the persistence context is cleared. The detached entities that result from clearing the persistence context also suffer from all of the negative effects caused by a transaction rollback even though the transaction is still active. For example, identifier generation and versioning should be considered suspect for any entities detached as a result of using the `clear()` operation.

Synchronization with the Database

Any time the persistence provider generates SQL and writes it out to the database over a JDBC connection, we say that the persistence context has been flushed. All pending changes that require a SQL statement to become part of the transactional changes in the database have been written out and will be made permanent when the database transaction commits. It also means that any subsequent SQL operation that takes place after the flush will incorporate these changes. This is particularly important for SQL queries that are executed in a transaction that is also changing entity data.

If there are managed entities with changes pending, a flush is guaranteed to occur in two situations. The first is when the transaction commits. A flush of any required changes will occur before the database transaction has completed. The only other time a flush is guaranteed to occur is when the entity manager `flush()` operation is invoked. This method allows developers to manually trigger the same process that the entity manager internally uses to flush the persistence context.

That said, a flush of the persistence context could occur at any time if the persistence provider deems it necessary. An example of this is when a query is about to be executed and it depends on new or changed entities in the persistence context. Some providers will flush the persistence context to ensure that the query incorporates all pending changes. A provider might also flush the persistence context often if it uses an eager-write approach to entity updates. Most persistence providers defer SQL generation to the last possible moment for performance reasons, but this is not guaranteed.

Now that we have covered the circumstances where a flush can occur, let's look at exactly what it means to flush the persistence context. A flush basically consists of three components: new entities that need to be persisted, changed entities that need to be updated, and removed entities that need to be deleted from the database. All of this information is managed by the persistence context. It maintains links to all of the managed entities that will be created or changed as well as the list of entities that need to be removed.

When a flush occurs, the entity manager first iterates over the managed entities and looks for new entities that have been added to relationships with cascade persist enabled. This is logically equivalent to invoking persist() again on each managed entity just before the flush occurs. The entity manager also checks to ensure the integrity of all of the relationships. If an entity points to another entity that is not managed or has been removed, then an exception may be thrown.

The rules for determining whether or not the flush fails in the presence of an unmanaged entity can be complicated. Let's walk through an example that demonstrates the most common issues. Figure 5-1 shows an object diagram for an Employee instance and some of the objects that it is related to. The emp and ps entity objects are managed by the persistence context. The addr object is a detached entity from a previous transaction, and the Phone objects are new objects that have not been part of any persistence operation so far.

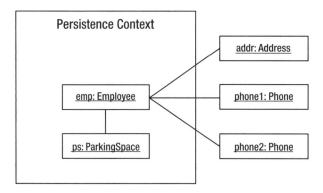

Figure 5-1. *Links to unmanaged entities from a persistence context*

To determine the outcome of flushing the persistence context given the arrangement shown in Figure 5-1, we must first look at the cascade settings of the Employee entity. Listing 5-20 shows the relationships as implemented in the Employee entity. Only the phones relationship has the PERSIST cascade option set. The other relationships are all defaulted so they will not cascade.

Listing 5-20. *Relationship Cascade Settings for Employee*

```
@Entity
public class Employee {
    // ...
    @OneToOne
    ParkingSpace parkingSpace;
    @OneToMany(mappedBy="employee", cascade=CascadeType.PERSIST)
    Collection<Phone> phones;
    @ManyToOne
    Address address;
    // ...
}
```

Starting with the emp object, let's walk through the flush process as if we are the persistence provider. The emp object is managed and has links to four other objects. The first step in the process is to navigate the relationships from this entity as if we are invoking persist() on it. The first object we encounter in this process is the ps object across the parkingSpace relationship. Since ps is also managed, we don't have to do anything further.

Next we navigate the phones relationship to the two Phone objects. These entities are new, and this would normally cause an exception, but since the PERSIST cascade option has been set, we perform the equivalent of invoking persist() on each Phone object. This makes the objects managed, making them part of the persistence context. The Phone objects do not have any further relationships to cascade the persist operation, so we are done here as well.

Next we reach the addr object across the address relationship. Since this object is detached, we would normally throw an exception, but this particular relationship is a special case in the flush algorithm. Any time a detached object that is the target of the one-to-one or many-to-one relationship is encountered where the source entity is the owner, the flush will still proceed because the act of persisting the owning entity does not depend on the target. The owning entity has the foreign key column and needs to store only the primary key value of the target entity.

This completes the flush of the emp object. The algorithm then moves to the ps object and starts the process again. Since there are no relationships from the ps object to any other, the flush process completes. So in this example even though three of the objects pointed to from the emp object are not managed, the overall flush completes successfully due to the cascade settings and rules of the flush algorithm.

Ideally during a flush all of the objects pointed to by a managed entity will also be managed entities themselves. If this is not the case, the next thing we need to be aware of is the PERSIST cascade setting. If the relationship has this setting, target objects in the relationship will also be persisted, making them managed before the flush completes. If the PERSIST cascade option is not set, an IllegalStateException exception will be thrown whenever the target of the relationship is not managed, except in the special case related to one-to-one and many-to-one relationships that we described previously.

In light of how the flush operation works, it is always safer to update relationships pointing to entities that will be removed before carrying out the remove() operation. A flush may occur at any time, so invoking remove() on an entity without clearing any relationships that point to the removed entity could result in an unexpected IllegalStateException exception if the provider decides to flush the persistence context before you get around to updating the relationships.

In Chapter 6, we will also discuss techniques to configure the data integrity requirements of queries so that the persistence provider is better able to determine when a flush of the persistence context is really necessary.

Detachment and Merging

Simply put, a detached entity is one that is no longer associated with a persistence context. It was managed at one point, but the persistence context may have ended or the entity may have been transformed in such a way that it has lost its association with the persistence context that used to manage it. The persistence context, if there still is one, is no longer tracking the entity. Any changes made to the entity won't be persisted to the database, but all of the state that was there on the entity when it was detached can still be used by the application. A detached entity cannot be used with any entity manager operation that requires a managed instance.

The opposite of detachment is merging. Merging is the process by which an entity manager integrates detached entity state into a persistence context. Any changes to entity state that were made on the detached entity overwrite the current values in the persistence context. When the transaction commits, those changes will be persisted. Merging allows entities to be changed "offline" and then have those changes incorporated later on.

The following sections will describe detachment and how detached entities can be merged back into a persistence context.

Detachment

There are two views on detachment. On one hand, it is a powerful tool that can be leveraged by applications in order to work with remote applications or to support access to entity data long after a transaction has ended. On the other hand, it can be a frustrating problem when the domain model contains lots of lazy-loading attributes and clients using the detached entities need to access this information.

There are many ways in which an entity can become detached. Each of the following situations will lead to detached entities:

- When the transaction that a transaction-scoped persistence context is associated with commits, all of the entities managed by the persistence context become detached.

- If an application-managed persistence context is closed, all of its managed entities become detached.

- If a stateful session bean with an extended persistence context is removed, all of its managed entities become detached.

- If the clear() method of an entity manager is used, it detaches all of the entities in the persistence context managed by that entity manager.

- When transaction rollback occurs, it causes all entities in all persistence contexts associated with the transaction to become detached.

- When an entity is serialized, the serialized form of the entity is detached from its persistence context.

Some of these situations may be intentional and planned for, such as detachment after the end of the transaction or serialization. Others may be unexpected, such as detachment due to rollback.

In Chapter 4, we introduced the LAZY fetch type that can be applied to any basic mapping or relationship. This has the effect of hinting to the provider that the loading of a basic or relationship attribute should be deferred until it is accessed for the first time. Although not commonly used on basic mappings, marking relationship mappings to be lazy loaded is an important part of performance tuning.

We need to consider, however, the impact of detachment on lazy loading. Consider the Employee entity shown in Listing 5-21. The address relationship will eagerly load because many-to-one relationships eagerly load by default. In the case of the parkingSpace attribute, which would also normally eagerly load, we have explicitly marked the relationship as being lazy loading. The phones relationship, as a one-to-many relationship, will also lazy load by default.

Listing 5-21. *Employee with Lazy-Loading Mappings*

```
@Entity
public class Employee {
    // ...
    @ManyToOne
    private Address address;
    @OneToOne(fetch=FetchType.LAZY)
    private ParkingSpace parkingSpace;
    @OneToMany(mappedBy="employee")
    private Collection<Phone> phones;
    // ...
}
```

So long as the Employee entity is managed, everything works as we expect. When the entity is retrieved from the database, only the associated Address entity will be eagerly loaded. The provider will fetch the necessary entities the first time the parkingSpace and phones relationships are accessed.

If this entity becomes detached, the outcome of accessing the parkingSpace and phones relationships is suddenly a more complex issue. If the relationships were accessed while the entity was still managed, the target entities may also be safely accessed while the Employee entity is detached. If the relationships were not accessed while the entity was managed, then we have a problem.

The behavior of accessing an unloaded attribute when the entity is detached is not defined. Some vendors may attempt to resolve the relationship, while others may simply throw an exception or leave the attribute uninitialized. If the entity was detached due to serialization, there is virtually no hope of resolving the relationship. The only portable thing to do with attributes that are unloaded is leave them alone.

In the case where entities have no lazy-loading attributes, detachment is not a big deal. All of the entity state that was there in the managed version is still available and ready to use in the detached version of the entity. In the presence of lazy-loading attributes, care must be taken to ensure that all of the information you need to access offline is triggered while the entity is still managed. Later in the chapter we will demonstrate a number of strategies for planning for, and working with, detached entities.

Merging Detached Entities

The merge() operation is used to merge the state of a detached entity into a persistence context. The method is straightforward to use, requiring only the detached entity instance as an argument. There are some subtleties to using merge() that make it different to use than other entity manager methods. Consider the following example, which shows a session bean method that accepts a detached Employee parameter and merges it into the current persistence context:

```
public void updateEmployee(Employee emp) {
    em.merge(emp);
    emp.setLastAccessTime(new Date());
}
```

Assuming that a transaction begins and ends with this method call, any changes made to the Employee instance while it was detached will be written to the database. What will not be written, however, is the change to the last access time. The argument to merge() does not become managed as a result of the merge. A different managed entity (either a new instance or an existing managed version already in the persistence context) is updated to match the argument, and then this instance is returned from the merge() method. Therefore to capture this change, we need to use the return value from merge() since it is the managed entity. The following example shows the correct implementation:

```
public void updateEmployee(Employee emp) {
    Employee managedEmp = em.merge(emp);
    managedEmp.setLastAccessTime(new Date());
}
```

Returning a managed instance other than the original entity is a critical part of the merge process. If an entity instance with the same identifier already exists in the persistence context, the provider will overwrite its state with the state of the entity that is being merged, but the managed version that existed already must be returned to the client so that it can be used. If the provider did not update the Employee instance in the persistence context, then any references to that instance will become inconsistent with the new state being merged in.

When merge() is invoked on a new entity, it behaves similarly to the persist() operation. It adds the entity to the persistence context, but instead of adding the original entity instance, it creates a new copy and manages that instance instead. The copy that is created by the merge() operation is persisted as if the persist() method was invoked on it.

In the presence of relationships, the merge() operation will attempt to update the managed entity to point to managed versions of the entities referenced by the detached entity. If the entity has a relationship to an object that has no persistent identity, then the outcome of the merge operation is undefined. Some providers may allow the managed copy to point to the non-persistent object, while others may throw an exception immediately. The merge() operation may be optionally cascaded in these cases to prevent an exception from occurring. We will cover cascading of the merge() operation later in this section. If an entity being merged points to a removed entity, an IllegalArgumentException exception will be thrown.

Lazy-loading relationships are a special case in the merge operation. If a lazy-loading relationship was not triggered on an entity before it became detached, then that relationship will be ignored when the entity is merged. If the relationship was triggered while managed and then set to null while the entity was detached, then the managed version of the entity will likewise have the relationship cleared during the merge.

To illustrate the behavior of merge() with relationships, consider the object diagram shown in Figure 5-2. The detached emp object has relationships to three other objects. The addr and dept objects are detached entities from a previous transaction, while the phone1 entity was recently created and persisted using the persist() operation and is now managed as a result. Inside the persistence context there is currently an Employee instance with a relationship to another managed Address. The existing managed Employee instance does not have a relationship to the newly managed Phone instance.

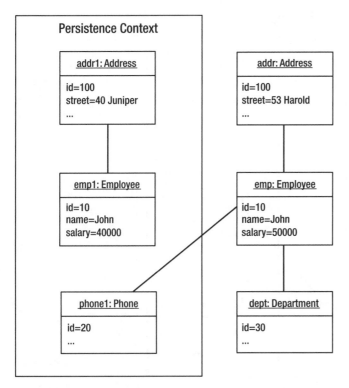

Figure 5-2. *Entity state prior to merge*

Let's consider the effect of invoking merge() on the emp object. The first thing that happens is that the provider checks the persistence context for a pre-existing entity instance with the same identifier. In this example, the emp1 object from the persistence context matches the identifier from the emp object we are trying to merge. Therefore the basic state of the emp object overwrites the state of the emp1 object in the persistence context, and the emp1 object will be returned from the merge() operation.

The provider next considers the Phone and Department entities pointed to from emp. The phone1 object is already managed, so the provider can safely update emp1 to point to this instance. In the case of the dept object, the provider checks to see if there is already a persistent Department entity with the same identifier. In this case it finds one in the database and loads it into the persistence context. The emp1 object is then updated to point to this version of the Department entity. The detached dept object does not become managed again.

Finally the provider checks the addr object referenced from emp. In this case it finds a pre-existing managed object addr1 with the same identifier. Since the emp1 object already points to the addr1 object, no further changes are made. At this point let's look at the state of the object model after the merge. Figure 5-3 shows these changes.

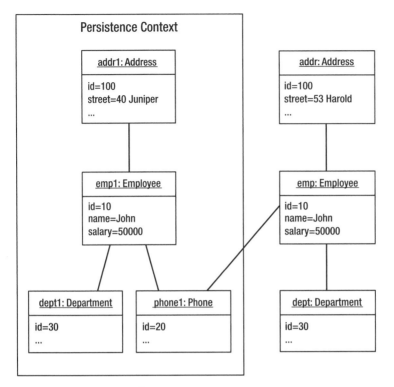

Figure 5-3. *Entity state after merge*

In Figure 5-3 we see that the emp1 object has been updated to reflect the state changes from emp. The dept1 object is new to the persistence context after being loaded from the database. The emp1 object now points to both the phone1 object and the dept1 object in order to match the relationships of the emp object. The addr1 object has not changed at all. The fact that the addr1 object has not changed might come as a surprise. After all, the addr object had pending changes and it was pointed to by the emp object that was merged.

To understand why, we must return to the issue of cascading operations with the entity manager. By default, no operations are cascaded when an entity manager operation is applied to an entity instance. The merge() operation is no different in this regard. In order for the merge to be cascaded across relationships from an Employee, the MERGE cascade setting must be set on the relationship mappings. Otherwise we would have to invoke merge() on each related object.

Looking back at our example, the problem with the updated Address entity was that the Employee entity did not cascade the merge() operation to it. This had the unfortunate side effect of effectively discarding the changes we had made to the Address entity in favor of the version already in the persistence context. To obtain the behavior that we intended, we must either invoke merge() explicitly on the addr object or change the relationship mappings of the Employee entity to include the MERGE cascade option. Listing 5-22 shows the changed Employee class.

Listing 5-22. *Employee Entity with Merge Cascade Setting*

```
@Entity
public class Employee {
    @Id private int id;
    private String name;
    private long salary;
    @ManyToOne(cascade=CascadeType.MERGE)
    private Address address;
    @ManyToOne
    private Department department;
    @OneToMany(mappedBy="employee", cascade=CascadeType.MERGE)
    private Collection<Phone> phones;
    // ...
}
```

With the `Employee` entity changed in this way, the merge operation will be cascaded to the `Address` and `Phone` entities pointed to by any `Employee` instances. This is equivalent to invoking `merge()` on each instance individually. Note that we did not cascade the merge operation to the `Department` entity. We generally only cascade operations down from parent to child, not upwards from child to parent. Doing so is not harmful but requires more effort from the persistence provider to search out changes. If the `Department` entity changes as well, it is better to cascade the merge from the `Department` to its associated `Employee` instances and then merge only a single `Department` instance instead of multiple `Employee` instances.

Merging detached entities with relationships can be a tricky operation. Ideally we want to merge the root of an object graph and have all related entities get merged in the process. This can work, but only if the `MERGE` cascade setting has been applied to all relationships in the graph. If it hasn't, you must merge each instance that is the target of a non-cascaded relationship one at a time.

Before we leave the topic of merging, we must mention that locking and versioning plays a vital role in ensuring data integrity in these situations. We will explore this topic in Chapter 9.

Working with Detached Entities

Let's begin with a scenario that is very common with modern web applications. A servlet calls out to a session bean in order to execute a query and receives a collection of entities in return. The servlet then places these entities into the request map and forwards the request to a JSP for presentation. This pattern is called Page Controller,[1] a variation of the Front Controller[2] pattern in which there is a single controller for each view instead of one central controller for all views. In the context of the familiar Model-View-Controller (MVC) architecture, the session bean provides the model, the JSP page is the view, and the servlet is our controller.

First consider the session bean that will produce the results that will be rendered by the JSP page. Listing 5-23 shows the bean implementation. In this example we are looking only at the `findAll()` method, which returns all of the `Employee` instances stored in the database.

---

1. Fowler, Martin. *Patterns of Enterprise Application Architecture.* Boston: Addison-Wesley, 2002.
2. Alur, Deepak, John Crupi, and Dan Malks. *Core J2EE Patterns: Best Practices and Design Strategies, Second Edition.* Upper Saddle River, N.J.: Prentice Hall PTR, 2003.

Listing 5-23. *The* EmployeeService *Session Bean*

```
@Stateless
public class EmployeeServiceBean implements EmployeeService {
    @PersistenceContext(unitName="EmployeeService")
    private EntityManager em;

    public List findAll() {
        return em.createQuery("SELECT e FROM Employee e")
                .getResultList();
    }

    // ...
}
```

Listing 5-24 shows the source code for a simple servlet that invokes the findAll() method of the EmployeeService session bean to fetch all of the Employee entities in the database. It then places the results in the request map and delegates to the "listEmployees.jsp" JSP page to render the result.

Listing 5-24. *The View Employees Servlet*

```
public class EmployeeServlet extends HttpServlet {
    @EJB EmployeeService bean;

    protected void doGet(HttpServletRequest request, HttpServletResponse response)
            throws ServletException, IOException {
        List emps = bean.findAll();
        request.setAttribute("employees", emps);
        getServletContext().getRequestDispatcher("/listEmployees.jsp")
                            .forward(request, response);
    }
}
```

Finally, Listing 5-25 shows the last part of our MVC architecture, the JSP page to render the results. It uses the JavaServer Pages Standard Tag Library (JSTL) to iterate over the collection of Employee instances and display the name of each employee as well as the name of the department to which that employee is assigned. The employees variable accessed by the <c:forEach/> tag is the List of Employee instances that was placed in the request map by the servlet.

Listing 5-25. *JSP Page to Display Employee Information*

```
<!DOCTYPE HTML PUBLIC "-//W3C//DTD HTML 4.01 Transitional//EN">
<%@ taglib uri="http://java.sun.com/jsp/jstl/core" prefix="c"%>
<html>
  <head>
    <title>All Employees</title>
  </head>
```

```
<body>
  <table>
    <thead>
      <tr>
        <th>Name</th>
        <th>Department</th>
      </tr>
    </thead>
    <tbody>
      <c:forEach items="${employees}" var="emp">
        <tr>
          <td><c:out value="${emp.name}"/></td>
          <td><c:out value="${emp.department.name}"/></td>
        </tr>
      </c:forEach>
    </tbody>
  </table>
</body>
</html>
```

The findAll() method of the EmployeeService session bean uses REQUIRED container-managed transactions by default. Since the servlet invoking the method has not started a transaction, the container will start a new transaction before findAll() is invoked and commit the transaction after it finishes executing. As a result, the results of the query become detached before they are returned to the servlet.

This causes us a problem. In this example, the department relationship of the Employee class has been configured to use lazy fetching. As we learned previously in the section on Detachment, the only portable thing to do is leave them alone. In this example, however, we don't want to leave them alone. In order to display the department name for the employee, the JSP expression navigates to the Department entity from the Employee entity. Since this is a lazy-loading relationship, the results are unpredictable. It might work, but then it might not.

This scenario forms the basis of our challenge. In the following sections we will look at a number of strategies to either prepare the entities needed by the JSP page for detachment or avoid detachment altogether.

Planning for Detachment

Knowing that the results of the findAll() method will be used to display employee information and that the department name will be required as part of this process, we need to ensure that the department relationship of the Employee entity has been resolved before the entities become detached. There are several strategies that can be used to resolve lazy loaded associations in preparation for detachment. We will discuss two of them here, focusing on how to structure application code to plan for detachment. A third strategy, for Java Persistence QL queries called fetch joins, will be discussed in Chapter 7.

Triggering Lazy Loading

The first strategy to consider in resolving lazy-loading associations is to simply trigger the lazy loading behavior by accessing the field or relationship. It looks slightly odd in code since the return values of the getter methods are discarded, but nevertheless it has the desired effect. Listing 5-26 shows an alternate implementation of the `findAll()` method of the `EmployeeService` session bean. In this case we iterate over the `Employee` entities, triggering the `department` relationship before returning the original list from the method. Because `findAll()` is executed inside of a transaction, the `getDepartment()` call completes successfully, and the `Department` entity instance is guaranteed to be available when the `Employee` instance is detached.

Listing 5-26. *Triggering a Lazy-Loading Relationship*

```
@Stateless
public class EmployeeServiceBean implements EmployeeService {
    @PersistenceContext(unitName="EmployeeService")
    private EntityManager em;

    public List findAll() {
        List<Employee> emps = (List<Employee>)
            em.createQuery("SELECT e FROM Employee e")
              .getResultList();
        for (Employee emp : emps) {
            Department dept = emp.getDepartment();
            if (dept != null) {
                dept.getName();
            }
        }
        return emps;
    }

    // ...
}
```

One thing that might look odd from Listing 5-26 is that we not only invoked `getDepartment()` on the `Employee` instance, but we also invoked `getName()` on the `Department` instance. If you recall from Chapter 4, the entity returned from a lazy-loading relationship may actually be a proxy that further waits until a method is invoked on the proxy before the entity is faulted in. We have to invoke a method on the entity to guarantee that it is actually retrieved from the database. If this were a collection-valued relationship, the `size()` method of the `Collection` would be commonly used to force eager loading.

If lazy-loading basic mappings were used on either the `Employee` or `Department` entities, then those attributes would not be guaranteed to be present after detachment as well. This is another reason why configuring basic mappings to use lazy loading is not recommended. Developers often expect that a relationship is not eagerly loaded but can be caught off guard if a basic state field such as the `name` attribute of the `Employee` instance is missing.

Configuring Eager Loading

When an association is continuously being triggered for detachment scenarios, at some point it is worth revisiting whether or not the association should be lazy loaded in the first place. Carefully switching some relationships to eager loading can avoid a lot of special cases in code that attempt to trigger the lazy loading.

In this example, `Employee` has a many-to-one relationship with `Department`. The default fetch type for a many-to-one relationship is eager loading, but the class was modeled by explicitly using lazy loading. By removing the `LAZY` fetch type from the `department` relationship or by specifying the `EAGER` fetch type explicitly, we ensure that the `Department` instance is always available to the `Employee` instance.

Collection-valued relationships lazy load by default, so the `EAGER` fetch type must be explicitly applied to those mappings if eager loading is desired. Be judicious in configuring collection-valued relationships to be eagerly loaded, however, as it may cause excessive database access in cases where detachment is not a requirement.

Avoiding Detachment

The only complete solution to any detachment scenario is not to detach at all. If your code methodically triggers every lazy-loaded relationship or has marked every association on an entity to be eagerly loaded in anticipation of detachment, then this is probably a sign that an alternative approach is required.

Avoiding detachment really only boils down to two approaches. Either we don't work with entities in our JSP page, or we must keep a persistence context open for the duration of the JSP rendering process so that lazy-loading relationships can be resolved.

Not using entities means copying entity data into a different data structure that does not have the same lazy-loading behavior. One approach would be to use the Transfer Object[3] pattern, but that seems highly redundant given the POJO nature of entities. A better approach, which we will discuss in Chapters 6 and 7, is to use projection queries to retrieve only the entity state that will be displayed on the JSP page instead of retrieving full entity instances.

Keeping a persistence context open requires additional planning but allows the JSP page to work with entity data using the JavaBean properties of the entity class. In practical terms, keeping a persistence context open means that there is either an active transaction for entities fetched from transaction-scoped persistence contexts or that an application-managed or extended persistence context is in use. This obviously isn't an option when entities must be serialized to a separate tier or remote client, but it suits the web application scenario we described earlier. We'll cover each of these strategies here.

Transaction View

The persistence context created by a transaction-scoped entity manager remains open only as long as the transaction in which it was created has not ended. Therefore, in order to use a transaction-scoped entity manager to execute a query and be able to render the query results while resolving lazy-loading relationships, both operations must be part of the same transaction. When a transaction is started in the web tier and includes both session bean invocation and JSP page rendering before it is committed, we call this pattern a Transaction View.

---

3. Ibid.

The benefit of this approach is that any lazy-loading relationships encountered during the rendering of the view will be resolved because the entities are still managed by a persistence context. To implement this pattern in our example scenario, we start a bean-managed transaction before the `findAll()` method is invoked and commit the transaction after the JSP page has rendered the results. Listing 5-27 demonstrates this approach. Note that to conserve space we have omitted the handling of the checked exceptions thrown by the `UserTransaction` operations. The `commit()` method alone throws no less than six checked exceptions.

Listing 5-27. *Combining a Session Bean Method and JSP in a Single Transaction*

```
public class EmployeeServlet extends HttpServlet {
    @Resource UserTransaction tx;
    @EJB EmployeeService bean;

    protected void doGet(HttpServletRequest request, HttpServletResponse response)
            throws ServletException, IOException {
        // ...
        try {
            tx.begin();
            List emps = bean.findAll();
            request.setAttribute("employees", emps);
            getServletContext().getRequestDispatcher("/listEmployees.jsp")
                               .forward(request, response);
        } finally {
            tx.commit();
        }
        // ...
    }
}
```

With this solution in place, the lazy-loading relationships of the `Employee` entity do not have to be eagerly resolved before the JSP page renders the results. The only downside to this approach is that the servlet must now manage transactions and recover from transaction failures. A lot of logic also has to be duplicated between all of the servlet controllers that need this behavior.

One way to work around this duplication is to introduce a common superclass for servlets that use the Transaction View pattern that encapsulates the transaction behavior. If, however, you are using the Front Controller pattern and controller actions are implemented using the Command[4] pattern, this may become more difficult to manage, particularly if the page flow is complex and multiple controllers collaborate to build a composite view. Then not only does each controller need to start transactions, but they also need to be aware of any transactions that were started earlier in the rendering sequence.

---

4. Gamma, Erich, Richard Helms, Ralph Johnson, and John Vlissades. *Design Patterns: Elements of Reusable Object-Oriented Software*. Boston: Addison-Wesley, 1995.

Another possible, though non-portable, solution is to move the transaction logic into a servlet filter. It allows us to intercept the HTTP request before the first controller servlet is accessed and wrap the entire request in a transaction. Such coarse-grained use of transactions is something that needs to be managed carefully, however. If applied to all HTTP requests equally, it may also cause trouble for requests that involve updates to the database. Assuming that these operations are implemented as session beans, the REQUIRES_NEW transaction attribute may be required in order to isolate entity updates and handle transaction failure without impacting the overriding global transaction.

Entity Manager per Request

For applications that do not encapsulate their query operations behind session bean façades, an alternative approach to the Transaction View pattern is to create a new application-managed entity manager to execute reporting queries, closing it only after the JSP page has been rendered. Because the entities returned from the query on the application-managed entity manager will remain managed until the entity manager is closed, it offers the same benefits as the Transaction View pattern without requiring an active transaction.

Listing 5-28 revisits our EmployeeServlet servlet again, this time creating an application-managed entity manager to execute the query. The results are placed in the map as before, and the entity manager is closed after the JSP page has finished rendering.

Listing 5-28. *Using an Application-Managed Entity Manager for Reporting*

```java
public class EmployeeServlet extends HttpServlet {
    @PersistenceUnit(unitName="EmployeeService")
    EntityManagerFactory emf;

    protected void doGet(HttpServletRequest request, HttpServletResponse response)
            throws ServletException, IOException {
        EntityManager em = emf.createEntityManager();
        try {
            List emps = em.createQuery("SELECT e FROM Employee e")
                        .getResultList();
            request.setAttribute("employees", emps);
            getServletContext().getRequestDispatcher("/listEmployees.jsp")
                            .forward(request, response);
        } finally {
            em.close();
        }
    }
}
```

Unfortunately, we now have query logic embedded in our servlet implementation. The query is also no longer reusable the way it was when it was part of a stateless session bean. There are a couple of other options we can explore as a solution to this problem. Instead of executing the query directly, we could create a POJO service class that uses the application-managed entity manager created by the servlet to execute queries. This is similar to the first example we created in Chapter 2. We gain the benefit of encapsulating the query behavior inside business methods while being decoupled from a particular style of entity manager.

Alternatively we can place our query methods on a stateful session bean that uses an extended entity manager. When a stateful session bean uses an extended entity manager, its persistence context lasts for the lifetime of the session bean, which ends only when the user invokes a remove method on the bean. If a query is executed against the extended persistence context of a stateful session bean, the results of that query can continue to resolve lazy-loading relationships so long as the bean is still available.

Let's explore this option and see how it would look instead of the application-managed entity manager we showed in Listing 5-28. Listing 5-29 introduces a stateful session bean equivalent to the EmployeeService stateless session bean that we have been using so far. In addition to using the extended entity manager, we have also set the default transaction type to be NOT_SUPPORTED. There is no need for transactions because the results of the query will never be modified, only displayed.

Listing 5-29. *Stateful Session Bean with Query Methods*

```
@Stateful
@TransactionAttribute(TransactionAttributeType.NOT_SUPPORTED)
public class EmployeeQueryBean implements EmployeeQuery {
    @PersistenceContext(type=PersistenceContextType.EXTENDED,
                        unitName="EmployeeService")
    EntityManager em;

    public List findAll() {
        return em.createQuery("SELECT e FROM Employee e")
                .getResultList();
    }

    // ...

    @Remove
    public void finished() {
    }
}
```

Using this bean is very similar to using the application-managed entity manager. We create an instance of the bean, execute the query, and then remove the bean when the JSP page has finished rendering. Listing 5-30 shows this approach.

Listing 5-30. *Using an Extended Entity Manager for Reporting*

```
@EJB(name="queryBean", beanInterface=EmployeeQuery.class)
public class EmployeeServlet extends HttpServlet {

    protected void doGet(HttpServletRequest request, HttpServletResponse response)
            throws ServletException, IOException {
        EmployeeQuery bean = createQueryBean();
        try {
            List emps = bean.findAll();
            request.setAttribute("employees", emps);
            getServletContext().getRequestDispatcher("/listEmployees.jsp")
                            .forward(request, response);
        } finally {
            bean.finished();
        }
    }

    private EmployeeQuery createQueryBean() throws ServletException {
        // look up queryBean
        // ...
    }
}
```

At first glance this might seem like an overengineered solution. We gain the benefit of decoupling queries from the servlet, but we have introduced a new session bean just to accomplish this goal. Furthermore, we are using stateful session beans with very short lifetimes. Doesn't that go against the accepted practice of how to use a stateful session bean?

To a certain extent this is true, but the extended persistence context invites us to experiment with new approaches. In practice, stateful session beans do not add a significant amount of overhead to an operation, even when used for short durations. As we will see later in the section Edit Session, moving the stateful session bean to the HTTP session instead of limiting it to a single request also opens up new possibilities for web application design.

Merge Strategies

Creating or updating information is a regular part of most enterprise applications. Users typically interact with an application via the web, using forms to create or change data as required. The most common strategy to handle these changes in a Java EE application that uses the Java Persistence API is to place the results of the changes into detached entity instances and merge the pending changes into a persistence context so that they can be written to the database.

Let's revisit our simple web application scenario again. This time, instead of simply viewing Employee information, the user is able to select an Employee and update basic information about that employee. The entities are queried for presentation in a form in one request and then updated in a second request when the user submits the form with changes entered.

Using a Session Façade, this operation is straightforward. The changed entity is updated and handed off to a stateless session bean to be merged. The only complexity involved is making sure that relationships properly merge by identifying cases where the MERGE cascade setting is required.

Similar to the question of whether we can avoid detaching entities to compensate for lazy loading concerns, the long-lived nature of application-managed and extended persistence contexts suggests that there may also be a way to apply a similar technique to this situation. Instead of querying entities in one HTTP request and throwing the entity instances away after the view has been rendered, we want to keep these entities around in a managed state so that they can be updated in a subsequent HTTP request and persisted merely by starting and committing a new transaction.

In the following sections we will revisit the traditional Session Façade approach to merging and then look at new techniques possible with the extended entity manager that will keep entities managed for the life of a user's editing session.

Session Façade

To use a Session Façade to capture changes to entities, we provide a business method that will merge changes made to a detached entity instance. In our example scenario, this means accepting an Employee instance and merging it into a transaction-scoped persistence context. Listing 5-31 shows an implementation of this technique in our EmployeeService session bean.

Listing 5-31. *Business Method to Update Employee Information*

```
@Stateless
public class EmployeeServiceBean implements EmployeeService {
    @PersistenceContext(unitName="EmployeeService")
    private EntityManager em;

    public void updateEmployee(Employee emp) {
        if (em.find(Employee.class, emp.getId()) == null) {
            throw new IllegalArgumentException("Unknown employee id: " + ➥
emp.getId());
        }
        em.merge(emp);
    }

    // ...
}
```

The updateEmployee() method in Listing 5-31 is straightforward. Given the detached Employee instance, it first attempts to check whether a matching identifier already exists. If no matching Employee is found, then an exception is thrown since we don't want to allow new Employee records to be created. Then we use the merge() operation to copy the changes into the persistence context, which are then saved when the transaction commits.

Using the façade from a servlet is a two-step approach. During the initial HTTP request to begin an editing session, the Employee instance is queried (typically using a separate method on the same façade) and used to create a web form on which the user can make their desired changes. The detached instance is then stored in the HTTP session so it can be updated when the user submits the form from their browser. We need to keep the detached instance around in order to preserve any relationships or other state that will remain unchanged by the edit. Creating a new `Employee` instance and supplying only partial values could have many negative side effects when the instance is merged.

Listing 5-32 shows an `EmployeeUpdateServlet` servlet that collects the id, name, and salary information from the request parameters and invokes the session bean method to perform the update. The previously detached `Employee` instance is retrieved from the HTTP session, and then the changes indicated by the request parameters are set into it. We have omitted validation of the request parameters to conserve space, but ideally this should happen before the business method on the session bean is invoked.

Listing 5-32. *Using a Session Bean to Perform Entity Updates*

```
public class EmployeeUpdateServlet extends HttpServlet {
    @EJB EmployeeService bean;

    protected void doPost(HttpServletRequest request, HttpServletResponse response)
            throws ServletException, IOException {
        int id = Integer.parseInt(request.getParameter("id"));
        String name = request.getParameter("name");
        long salary = Long.parseLong(request.getParameter("salary"));
        HttpSession session = request.getSession();
        Employee emp = (Employee) session.getAttribute("employee.edit");
        emp.setId(id);
        emp.setName(name);
        emp.setSalary(salary);
        bean.updateEmployee(emp);
        // ...
    }
}
```

If the amount of information being updated is very small, we can avoid the detached object and `merge()` operation entirely by locating the managed version and manually copying the changes into it. Consider the following example:

```
public void updateEmployee(int id, String name, long salary) {
    Employee emp = em.find(Employee.class, id);
    if (emp == null) {
        throw new IllegalArgumentException("Unknown employee id: " + id);
    }
    emp.setEmpName(name);
    emp.setSalary(salary);
}
```

The beauty of this approach is its simplicity, but that is also its primary limitation. Typical web applications today offer the ability to update large amounts of information in a single operation. To accommodate these situations with this pattern, there would either have to be business methods taking large numbers of parameters or many business methods that would have to be invoked in sequence to completely update all of the necessary information. And, of course, once you have more than one method involved, then it becomes important to maintain a transaction across all of the update methods so that the changes are committed as a single unit.

As a result, despite the availability of this approach, the web tier still commonly collects changes into detached entities or transfer objects and passes the changed state back to session beans to be merged and written to the database.

Edit Session

With the introduction of the extended entity manager, we can take a different approach to building web applications that update entities. As we have discussed in this chapter, entities associated with an extended entity manager remain managed so long as the stateful session bean holding the extended entity manager is not removed. By placing a stateful session bean in a central location such as the HTTP session, we can operate on entities managed by the extended entity manager without having to merge in order to persist changes. We will refer to this as the Edit Session pattern to reflect the fact that the primary goal of this pattern is to encapsulate editing use cases using stateful session beans.

Listing 5-33 introduces a stateful session bean that represents an employee editing session. Unlike the EmployeeService session bean that contains a number of reusable business methods, this style of stateful session bean is targeted to a single application use case. In addition to using the extended entity manager, we have also set the default transaction type to be NOT_SUPPORTED with the exception of the save() method. There is no need for transactions for methods that simply access the Employee instance. It is only when we want to persist the changes that we need a transaction.

Listing 5-33. *Stateful Session Bean to Manage an Employee Editing Session*

```
@Stateful
@TransactionAttribute(TransactionAttributeType.NOT_SUPPORTED)
public class EmployeeEditBean implements EmployeeEdit {
    @PersistenceContext(type=PersistenceContextType.EXTENDED,
                        unitName="EmployeeService")
    EntityManager em;
    Employee emp;

    public void begin(int id) {
        emp = em.find(Employee.class, id);
        if (emp == null) {
            throw new IllegalArgumentException("Unknown employee id: " + id);
        }
    }

    public Employee getEmployee() {
        return emp;
    }
```

```
@Remove
@TransactionAttribute(TransactionAttributeType.REQUIRES_NEW)
public void save() {}

@Remove
public void cancel() {}
}
```

Let's start putting the operations of the EmployeeEdit bean in context. When the HTTP request arrives and starts the editing session, we will create a new EmployeeEdit stateful session bean and invoke begin() using the id of the Employee instance that will be edited. The session bean then loads the Employee instance and caches it on the bean. The bean is then bound to the HTTP session so that it can be accessed again in a subsequent request once the user has changed the Employee information. Listing 5-34 shows the EmployeeEditServlet servlet that handles the HTTP request to begin a new editing session.

Listing 5-34. *Beginning an Employee Editing Session*

```
@EJB(name="EmployeeEdit", beanInterface=EmployeeEdit.class)
public class EmployeeEditServlet extends HttpServlet {

    protected void doPost(HttpServletRequest request, HttpServletResponse response)
            throws ServletException, IOException {
        int id = Integer.parseInt(request.getParameter("id"));
        EmployeeEdit bean = getBean();
        bean.begin(id);
        HttpSession session = request.getSession();
        session.setAttribute("employee.edit", bean);
        request.setAttribute("employee", bean.getEmployee());
        getServletContext().getRequestDispatcher("/editEmployee.jsp")
                        .forward(request, response);
    }

    public EmployeeEdit getBean() throws ServletException {
        // lookup EmployeeEdit bean
        // ...
    }
}
```

Now let's look at the other half of the editing session, where we wish to commit the changes. When the user submits the form that contains the necessary Employee changes, the EmployeeUpdateServlet is invoked. It begins by retrieving the EmployeeEdit bean from the HTTP session. The request parameters with the changed values are then copied into the Employee instance obtained from called getEmployee() on the EmployeeEdit bean. If everything is in order, the save() method is invoked to write the changes to the database. Listing 5-35 shows the EmployeeUpdateServlet implementation. Note that we need to remove the bean from the HTTP session once the editing session has completed.

Listing 5-35. *Completing an Employee Editing Session*

```
public class EmployeeUpdateServlet extends HttpServlet {

    protected void doPost(HttpServletRequest request, HttpServletResponse response)
            throws ServletException, IOException {
        String name = request.getParameter("name");
        long salary = Long.parseLong(request.getParameter("salary"));
        HttpSession session = request.getSession();
        EmployeeEdit bean = (EmployeeEdit) session.getAttribute("employee.edit");
        session.removeAttribute("employee.edit");
        Employee emp = bean.getEmployee();
        emp.setName(name);
        emp.setSalary(salary);
        bean.save();
        // ...
    }
}
```

The pattern for using stateful session beans and extended entity managers in the web tier is as follows:

1. For each application use case that modifies entity data, we create a stateful session bean with an extended persistence context. This bean will hold onto all entity instances necessary to make the desired changes.

2. The HTTP request that initiates the editing use case creates an instance of the stateful session bean and binds it to the HTTP session. The entities are retrieved at this point and used to populate the web form for editing.

3. The HTTP request that completes the editing use case obtains the previously bound stateful session bean instance and writes the changed data from the web form into the entities stored on the bean. A method is then invoked on the bean to commit the changes to the database.

In our simple editing scenario this may seem somewhat excessive, but the beauty of this technique is that it can easily scale to accommodate editing sessions of any complexity. Department, Project, and other information may all be edited in one or even multiple sessions with the results accumulated on the stateful session bean until the application is ready to persist the results.

Another major benefit of this approach is that web application frameworks like JavaServer Faces can directly access the bean bound in the HTTP session from within JSP pages. The entity can be accessed both to display the form for editing and as the target of the form when the user submits the results. In this scenario the developer only has to ensure that the necessary save and cancel methods are invoked at the correct point in the application page flow.

There are a couple of other points that we need to mention about this approach. Once bound to the HTTP session, the session bean will remain there until it is explicitly removed or until the HTTP session expires. It is therefore important to ensure that the bean is removed once the editing session is complete, regardless of whether the changes will be saved or abandoned. The `HttpSessionBindingListener` callback interface can be used by applications to track when the HTTP session is destroyed and clean up corresponding session beans appropriately.

The HTTP session is not thread-safe, and neither are stateful session bean references. In some circumstances it may be possible for multiple HTTP requests from the same user to access the HTTP session concurrently. This is mostly an issue when requests take a long time to process and an impatient user refreshes the page or abandons their editing session for another part of the web application. In these circumstances the web application will either have to deal with possible exceptions occurring if the stateful session bean is accessed by more than one thread, or proxy the stateful session bean with a synchronized wrapper.

Summary

In this chapter we have presented a thorough treatment of the entity manager and its interactions with entities, persistence contexts, and transactions. As we have seen, the entity manager can be used in many different ways to accommodate a wide variety of application requirements.

We began by reintroducing the core terminology of the Java Persistence API and explored the persistence context. We then covered the three different types of entity manager: transaction-scoped, extended, and application-managed. We looked at how to acquire and use each type and the types of problems they are designed to solve.

In the Transaction Management section we looked at each of the entity manager types and how they relate to container-managed JTA transactions and the resource-local transactions of the JDBC driver. Transactions play an important role in all aspects of enterprise application development with the Java Persistence API.

Next we revisited the basic operations of the entity manager, this time armed with the full understanding of the different entity manager types and transaction-management strategies. We introduced the notion of cascading and looked at the impact of relationships on persistence.

In our discussion of detachment, we introduced the problem and looked at it both from the perspective of mobile entities to remote tiers and the challenge of merging offline entity changes back into a persistence context. We presented several strategies to minimize the impact of detachment and merging on application design by adopting design patterns specific to the Java Persistence API.

In the next chapter we will turn our attention to the query facilities of the Java Persistence API, showing how to create, execute, and work with the results of query operations.

CHAPTER 6

■ ■ ■

Using Queries

For most enterprise applications, getting data out of the database is at least as important as the ability to put new data in. From searching, to sorting, to analytics and business intelligence, efficiently moving data from the database to the application and presenting it to the user is a regular part of enterprise development. Doing so requires the ability to issue bulk queries against the database and interpret the results for the application. Although high-level languages and expression frameworks have attempted to insulate developers from the task of dealing with database queries at a low level, it's probably fair to say that most enterprise developers have worked with at least one SQL dialect at some point in their career.

Object-relational mapping adds another level of complexity to this task. Most of the time, the developer will want the results converted to entities so that the query results may be used directly by application logic. Similarly, if the domain model has been abstracted from the physical model via object-relational mapping, then it makes sense to also abstract queries away from SQL, which is not only tied to the physical model but also difficult to port between vendors. Fortunately, as we will see, the Java Persistence API can handle a diverse set of query requirements.

The Java Persistence API supports two query languages for retrieving entities and other persistent data from the database. The primary language is Java Persistence QL (JPQL), a database-independent query language that operates on the logical entity model as opposed to the physical data model. Queries may also be expressed in SQL in order to take advantage of the underlying database. We will discuss SQL queries with the Java Persistence API later in Chapter 9.

We will begin our discussion of queries with an introduction to Java Persistence QL, followed by an exploration of the query facilities provided by the `EntityManager` and `Query` interfaces.

Java Persistence QL

Before discussing JPQL, we must first look to its roots in the EJB specification. The EJB Query Language (EJB QL) was first introduced in the EJB 2.0 specification to allow developers to write portable finder and select methods for container-managed entity beans. Based on a small subset of SQL, it introduced a way to navigate across entity relationships both to select data and to filter the results. Unfortunately it placed strict limitations on the structure of the query, limiting results to either a single entity or a persistent field from an entity. Inner joins between entities were possible but used an odd notation. The initial release didn't even support sorting.

The EJB 2.1 specification tweaked EJB QL a little bit, adding support for sorting, and introduced basic aggregate functions; but again the limitation of a single result type hampered the use of aggregates. You could filter the data, but there was no equivalent to SQL GROUP BY and HAVING expressions.

Java Persistence Query Language significantly extends EJB QL, eliminating many weaknesses of the previous versions while preserving backwards compatibility. The following features are available above and beyond EJB QL:

- Single and multiple value result types

- Aggregate functions, with sorting and grouping clauses

- A more natural join syntax, including support for both inner and outer joins

- Conditional expressions involving subqueries

- Update and delete queries for bulk data changes

- Result projection into non-persistent classes

The next few sections provide a quick introduction to Java Persistence QL intended for readers familiar with SQL or previous versions of EJB QL. A complete tutorial and reference for Java Persistence QL can be found in Chapter 7.

Getting Started

The simplest JPQL query selects all of the instances of a single entity type. Consider the following query:

```
SELECT e
FROM Employee e
```

If this looks similar to SQL, it should. JPQL uses SQL syntax where possible in order to give developers experienced with SQL a head start in writing queries. The key difference between SQL and JPQL for this query is that instead of selecting from a table, an entity from the application domain model has been specified instead. The SELECT clause of the query is also slightly different, listing only the Employee alias e. This indicates that the result type of the query is the Employee entity, so executing this statement will result in a list of zero or more Employee instances.

Starting with an alias, we can navigate across entity relationships using the dot (.) operator. For example, if we want just the names of the employees, the following query will suffice:

```
SELECT e.name
FROM Employee e
```

Each part of the expression corresponds to a persistent field of the entity or an association leading to another entity or collection of entities. Since the Employee entity has a persistent field named name of type String, this query will result in a list of zero or more String objects.

We can also select an entity we didn't even list in the FROM clause. Consider the following example:

```
SELECT e.department
FROM Employee e
```

An employee has a many-to-one relationship with his or her department named `department`, so therefore the result type of the query is the `Department` entity.

Filtering Results

Just like SQL, JPQL supports the WHERE clause to set conditions on the data being returned. The majority of operators commonly available in SQL are available in JPQL, including basic comparison operators; IN, LIKE, and BETWEEN expressions; numerous function expressions (such as SUBSTRING and LENGTH); and subqueries. The key difference for JPQL is that entity expressions and not column references are used. Listing 6-1 demonstrates filtering using entity expressions in the WHERE clause.

Listing 6-1. *Filtering Criteria Using Entity Expressions*

```
SELECT e
FROM Employee e
WHERE e.department.name = 'NA42' AND
      e.address.state IN ('NY','CA')
```

Projecting Results

For applications that need to produce reports, a common scenario is selecting large numbers of entity instances, but only using a portion of that data. Depending on how an entity is mapped to the database, this can be an expensive operation if much of the entity data is discarded. It would be useful to return only a subset of the properties from an entity. The following query demonstrates selecting only the name and salary of each `Employee` instance:

```
SELECT e.name, e.salary
FROM Employee e
```

Joins Between Entities

The result type of a select query cannot be a collection; it must be a single valued object such as an entity instance or persistent field type. This means that expressions such as `e.phones` are illegal in the SELECT clause because they would result in `Collection` instances. Therefore, just as with SQL and tables, if we want to navigate along a collection association and return elements of that collection, then we must join the two entities together. Listing 6-2 demonstrates a join between `Employee` and `Phone` entities in order to retrieve all of the cell phone numbers for a specific department.

Listing 6-2. *Joining Two Entities Together*

```
SELECT p.number
FROM Employee e, Phone p
WHERE e = p.employee AND
      e.department.name = 'NA42' AND
      p.type = 'Cell'
```

In JPQL, joins may also be expressed in the FROM clause using the JOIN operator. The advantage of this operator is that the join can be expressed in terms of the association itself, and the query engine will automatically supply the necessary join criteria when it generates the SQL. Listing 6-3 shows the same query rewritten to use the JOIN operator. Just as in the previous query, the alias p is of type Phone, only this time it refers to each of the phones in the e.phones collection.

Listing 6-3. *Joining Two Entities Together Using the JOIN Operator*

```
SELECT p.number
FROM Employee e JOIN e.phones p
WHERE e.department.name = 'NA42' AND
      p.type = 'Cell'
```

JPQL supports multiple join types, including inner and outer joins, as well as a technique called fetch joins for eagerly loading data associated to the result type of a query but not directly returned. See the Joins section in Chapter 7 for more information.

Aggregate Queries

The syntax for aggregate queries in JPQL is very similar to that of SQL. There are five supported aggregate functions (AVG, COUNT, MIN, MAX, and SUM), and results may be grouped in the GROUP BY clause and filtered using the HAVING clause. Once again, the difference is the use of entity expressions when specifying the data to be aggregated. Listing 6-4 demonstrates an aggregate query with JPQL.

Listing 6-4. *Query Returning Statistics for Departments with Five or More Employees*

```
SELECT d, COUNT(e), MAX(e.salary), AVG(e.salary)
FROM Department d JOIN d.employees e
GROUP BY d
HAVING COUNT(e) >= 5
```

Query Parameters

JPQL supports two types of parameter binding syntax. The first is positional binding, where parameters are indicated in the query string by a question mark followed by the parameter number. When the query is executed, the developer specifies the parameter number that should be replaced. Listing 6-5 demonstrates positional parameter syntax.

Listing 6-5. *Positional Parameter Notation*

```
SELECT e
FROM Employee e
WHERE e.department = ?1 AND
      e.salary > ?2
```

Named parameters may also be used and are indicated in the query string by a colon followed by the parameter name. When the query is executed, the developer specifies the parameter name that should be replaced. Listing 6-6 demonstrates named parameter syntax.

Listing 6-6. *Named Parameter Notation*

```
SELECT e
FROM Employee e
WHERE e.department = :dept AND
      e.salary > :base
```

Defining Queries

The Java Persistence API provides the Query interface to configure and execute queries. An implementation of the Query interface for a given query is obtained through one of the factory methods in the EntityManager interface. The choice of factory method depends on the type of query (JPQL or SQL) and whether or not the query has been predefined. For now, we will restrict our discussion to JPQL queries. SQL query definition is discussed in Chapter 9.

There are two approaches to defining a query. A query may either be dynamically specified at runtime or configured in persistence unit metadata (annotation or XML) and referenced by name. Dynamic queries are nothing more than strings, and therefore may be defined on the fly as the need arises. Named queries, on the other hand, are static and unchangeable but are more efficient to execute as the persistence provider can translate the JPQL string to SQL once when the application starts as opposed to every time the query is executed.

The following sections compare the two approaches and discuss when one should be used instead of the other.

Dynamic Query Definition

A query may be defined dynamically by passing the JPQL query string to the createQuery() method of the EntityManager interface. There are no restrictions on the query definition. All JPQL query types are supported, as well as the use of parameters. The ability to build up a string at runtime and use it for a query definition is useful, particularly for applications where the user may specify complex criteria and the exact shape of the query cannot be known ahead of time.

An issue to consider with dynamic queries, however, is the cost of translating the JPQL string to SQL for execution. A typical query engine will have to parse the JPQL string into a syntax tree, get the object-relational mapping metadata for each entity in each expression, and then generate the equivalent SQL. For applications that issue many queries, the performance cost of dynamic query processing can become an issue.

Many query engines will cache the translated SQL for later use, but this can easily be defeated if the application does not use parameter binding and concatenates parameter values directly into query strings. This has the effect of generating a new and unique query every time a query that requires parameters is constructed.

Consider the session bean method shown in Listing 6-7 that searches for salary information given the name of a department and the name of an employee. There are two problems with this example, one performance-related and one security-related. Because the names are concatenated into the string instead of using parameter binding, it is effectively creating a new and unique query each time. One hundred calls to this method could potentially generate one hundred different query strings. This not only requires excessive parsing of JPQL but also almost certainly makes it difficult for the persistence provider if it attempts to build a cache of converted queries.

Listing 6-7. *Defining a Query Dynamically*

```
@Stateless
public class QueryServiceBean implements QueryService {
    @PersistenceContext(unitName="DynamicQueries")
    EntityManager em;

    public long queryEmpSalary(String deptName, String empName) {
        String query = "SELECT e.salary " +
                       "FROM Employee e " +
                       "WHERE e.department.name = '" + deptName + "' AND " +
                       "      e.name = '" + empName + "'";
        return (Long) em.createQuery(query).getSingleResult();
    }
}
```

The second problem with this example is that a malicious user could pass in a value that alters the query to his advantage. Consider a case where the department argument was fixed by the application but the user was able to specify the employee name (the manager of the department is querying the salaries of his or her employees, for example). If the name argument were actually the text "`'_UNKNOWN' OR e.name = 'Roberts'`". The actual query parsed by the query engine would be as follows:

```
SELECT e.salary
FROM Employee e
WHERE e.department.name = 'NA65' AND
      e.name = '_UNKNOWN' OR
      e.name = 'Roberts'
```

By introducing the OR condition, the user has effectively given himself access to the salary value for any employee in the company, since the original AND condition has a higher precedence than OR and the fake employee name is unlikely to belong to a real employee in that department.

Parameter binding defeats this type of security threat, because the original query string is never altered. The parameters are marshaled using the JDBC API and handled directly by the database. The text of a parameter string is effectively quoted by the database, so the malicious attack would actually end up producing the following query:

```
SELECT e.salary
FROM Employee e
WHERE e.department.name = 'NA65' AND
      e.name = '_UNKNOWN'' OR e.name = ''Roberts'
```

The single quotes used in the query parameter here have been escaped by prefixing them with an additional single quote. This removes any special meaning from them, and the entire sequence is treated as a single string value.

This type of problem may sound unlikely, but in practice many web applications take text submitted over a GET or POST request and blindly construct queries of this sort without considering side effects. One or two attempts that result in a parser stack trace displayed to the web page and the attacker will learn everything he needs to know about how to alter the query to his advantage.

Listing 6-8 shows the same method as in Listing 6-7 except that it uses named parameters instead. This not only reduces the number of unique queries parsed by the query engine, but it also eliminates the chance of the query being altered.

Listing 6-8. *Using Parameters with a Dynamic Query*

```
@Stateless
public class QueryServiceBean implements QueryService {
    private static final String QUERY =
        "SELECT e.salary " +
        "FROM Employee e " +
        "WHERE e.department.name = :deptName AND " +
        "      e.name = :empName ";

    @PersistenceContext(unitName="DynamicQueries")
    EntityManager em;

    public long queryEmpSalary(String deptName, String empName) {
        return (Long) em.createQuery(QUERY)
                        .setParameter("deptName", deptName)
                        .setParameter("empName", empName)
                        .getSingleResult();
    }
}
```

We recommend statically defined named queries in general, particularly for queries that are executed frequently. If dynamic queries are a necessity, take care to use parameter binding instead of concatenating parameter values into query strings in order to minimize the number of distinct query strings parsed by the query engine.

Named Query Definition

Named queries are a powerful tool for organizing query definitions and improving application performance. A named query is defined using the @NamedQuery annotation, which may be placed on the class definition for any entity. The annotation defines the name of the query, as well as the query text. Listing 6-9 shows how the query string used in Listing 6-8 would be declared as a named query.

Listing 6-9. *Defining a Named Query*

```
@NamedQuery(name="findSalaryForNameAndDepartment",
            query="SELECT e.salary " +
                  "FROM Employee e " +
                  "WHERE e.department.name = :deptName AND " +
                  "      e.name = :empName")
```

Note the use of string concatenation in the annotation definition. Formatting your queries visually aids in the readability of the query definition. Named queries are typically placed on the entity class that most directly corresponds to the query result, so the Employee entity would be a good location for this named query.

The name of the query is scoped to the persistence unit and must be unique within that scope. This is an important restriction to keep in mind, as commonly used query names such as "findAll" will have to be qualified for each entity. A common practice is to prefix the query name with the entity name. For example, the "findAll" query for the Employee entity would be named "Employee.findAll". It is undefined what should happen if two queries in the same persistence unit have the same name, but it is likely that either deployment of the application will fail or one will overwrite the other, leading to unpredictable results at runtime. Entity-scoped query names are planned for the next release of the Java Persistence API and will remove the need for this kind of prefixing.

If more than one named query is to be defined for a class, they must be placed inside of a @NamedQueries annotation, which accepts an array of one or more @NamedQuery annotations. Listing 6-10 shows the definition of several queries related to the Employee entity. Queries may also be defined (or redefined) using XML. This technique is discussed in Chapter 10.

Listing 6-10. *Multiple Named Queries for an Entity*

```
@NamedQueries({
    @NamedQuery(name="Employee.findAll",
                query="SELECT e FROM Employee e"),
    @NamedQuery(name="Employee.findByPrimaryKey",
                query="SELECT e FROM Employee e WHERE e.id = :id"),
    @NamedQuery(name="Employee.findByName",
                query="SELECT e FROM Employee e WHERE e.name = :name")
})
```

Because the query string is defined in the annotation, it cannot be altered by the application at runtime. This contributes to the performance of the application and helps to prevent the kind of security issues we discussed in the previous section. Due to the static nature of the query string, any additional criteria that are required for the query must be specified using query parameters. Listing 6-11 demonstrates using the `createNamedQuery()` call on the `EntityManager` interface to create and execute a named query that requires a query parameter.

Listing 6-11. *Executing a Named Query*

```
@Stateless
public class EmployeeServiceBean implements EmployeeService {
    @PersistenceContext(unitName="EmployeeService")
    EntityManager em;

    public Employee findEmployeeByName(String name) {
        return (Employee) em.createNamedQuery("Employee.findByName")
                             .setParameter("name", name)
                             .getSingleResult();
    }

    // ...
}
```

Named parameters are the most practical choice for named queries as it effectively self-documents the application code that invokes the queries. Positional parameters are still supported, however, and may be used instead.

Parameter Types

As mentioned earlier, the Java Persistence API supports both named and positional parameters for JPQL queries. The query factory methods of the entity manager return an implementation of the `Query` interface. Parameter values are then set on this object using the `setParameter()` methods of the `Query` interface.

There are three variations of this method for both named parameters and positional parameters. The first argument is always the parameter name or number. The second argument is the object to be bound to the named parameter. `Date` and `Calendar` parameters also require a third argument that specifies whether the type passed to JDBC is a `java.sql.Date`, `java.sql.Time`, or `java.sql.TimeStamp` value.

Consider the following named query definition, which requires two named parameters:

```
@NamedQuery(name="findEmployeesAboveSal",
            query="SELECT e " +
                  "FROM Employee e " +
                  "WHERE e.department = :dept AND " +
                  "       e.salary > :sal")
```

This query highlights one of the nice features of JPQL in that entity types may be used as parameters. When the query is translated to SQL, the necessary primary key columns will be inserted into the conditional expression and paired with the primary key values from the parameter. It is not necessary to know how the primary key is mapped in order to write the query. Binding the parameters for this query is a simple case of passing in the required `Department` entity instance as well as a `long` representing the minimum salary value for

the query. Listing 6-12 demonstrates how to bind the entity and primitive parameters required
by this query.

Listing 6-12. *Binding Named Parameters*

```
@Stateless
public class EmployeeServiceBean implements EmployeeService {
    @PersistenceContext(unitName="EmployeeService")
    EntityManager em;

    public List findEmployeesAboveSal(Department dept, long minSal) {
        return em.createNamedQuery("findEmployeesAboveSal")
                    .setParameter("dept", dept)
                    .setParameter("sal", minSal)
                    .getResultList();
    }

    // ...
}
```

Date and Calendar parameters are a special case because they represent both dates and
times. In Chapter 4, we discussed mapping temporal types by using the @Temporal annotation
and the TemporalType enumeration. This enumeration indicates whether the persistent field is
a date, time, or timestamp. When a query uses a Date or Calendar parameter, it must select the
appropriate temporal type for the parameter. Listing 6-13 demonstrates binding parameters
where the value should be treated as a date.

Listing 6-13. *Binding Date Parameters*

```
@Stateless
public class EmployeeServiceBean implements EmployeeService {
    @PersistenceContext(unitName="EmployeeService")
    EntityManager em;

    public List findEmployeesHiredDuringPeriod(Date start, Date end) {
        return em.createQuery("SELECT e " +
                                "FROM Employee e " +
                                "WHERE e.startDate BETWEEN ?1 AND ?2")
                    .setParameter(1, start, TemporalType.DATE)
                    .setParameter(2, end, TemporalType.DATE)
                    .getResultList();
    }

    // ...
}
```

One thing to keep in mind with query parameters is that the same parameter can be used
multiple times in the query string yet only needs to be bound once using the setParameter()

method. For example, consider the following named query definition, where the "dept" parameter is used twice in the WHERE clause:

```
@NamedQuery(name="findHighestPaidByDepartment",
            query="SELECT e " +
                  "FROM Employee e " +
                  "WHERE e.department = :dept AND " +
                  "      e.salary = (SELECT MAX(e.salary) " +
                  "                  FROM Employee e " +
                  "                  WHERE e.department = :dept)")
```

To execute this query, the "dept" parameter only needs to be set once with `setParameter()` as in the following example:

```
public Employee findHighestPaidByDepartment(Department dept) {
    return (Employee) em.createNamedQuery("findHighestPaidByDepartment")
                        .setParameter("dept", dept)
                        .getSingleResult();
}
```

Executing Queries

The Query interface provides three different ways to execute a query, depending on whether or not the query returns results and how many results should be expected. For queries that return values, the developer may choose to call either getSingleResult() if the query is expected to return a single result or getResultList() if more than one result may be returned. The executeUpdate() method of the query interface is used to invoke bulk update and delete queries. We will discuss this method later in the section Bulk Update and Delete.

The simplest form of query execution is via the getResultList() method. It returns a collection containing the query results. If the query did not return any data, then the collection is empty. The return type is specified as a List instead of Collection in order to support queries that specify a sort order. If the query uses the ORDER BY clause to specify a sort order, then the results will be put into the result list in the same order. Listing 6-14 demonstrates how a query might be used to generate a menu for a command line application that displays the name of each employee working on a project as well as the name of the department that the employee is assigned to. The results are sorted by the name of the employee. Queries are unordered by default.

Listing 6-14. *Iterating over Sorted Results*

```
public void displayProjectEmployees(String projectName) {
    List result = em.createQuery("SELECT e " +
                                 "FROM Project p JOIN p.employees e " +
                                 "WHERE p.name = ?1 " +
                                 "ORDER BY e.name")
                    .setParameter(1, projectName)
                    .getResultList();
    int count = 0;
```

```
    for (Iterator i = result.iterator(); i.hasNext();) {
        Employee e = (Employee) i.next();
        System.out.println(++count + ": " + e.getName() + ", " +
                            e.getDepartment().getName());
    }
}
```

The getSingleResult() method is provided as a convenience for queries that return only a single value. Instead of iterating to the first result in a collection, the object is directly returned. It is important to note, however, that getSingleResult() behaves differently than getResultList() in how it handles unexpected results. Whereas getResultList() returns an empty collection when no results are available, getSingleResult() throws a NoResultException exception. Therefore if there is a chance that the desired result may not be found, then this exception needs to be handled.

If multiple results are available after executing the query instead of the single expected result, getSingleResult() will throw a NonUniqueResultException exception. Again, this can be problematic for application code if the query criteria may result in more than one row being returned in certain circumstances. Although getSingleResult() is convenient to use, be sure that the query and its possible results are well understood, otherwise application code may have to deal with an unexpected runtime exception. Unlike other exceptions thrown by entity manager operations, these exceptions will not cause the provider to roll back the current transaction, if there is one.

Query objects may be reused as often as needed so long as the same persistence context that was used to create the query is still active. For transaction-scoped entity managers, this limits the lifetime of the Query object to the life of the transaction. Other entity manager types may reuse Query objects until the entity manager is closed or removed.

Listing 6-15 demonstrates caching a Query object instance on the bean class of a stateful session bean that uses an extended persistence context. Whenever the bean needs to find the list of employees who are currently not assigned to any project, it reuses the same unassignedQuery object that was initialized during PostConstruct.

Listing 6-15. *Reusing a Query Object*

```
@Stateful
public class ProjectManagerBean implements ProjectManager {
    @PersistenceContext(unitName="EmployeeService",
                        type=PersistenceContextType.EXTENDED)
    EntityManager em;

    Query unassignedQuery;

    @PostConstruct
    public void init() {
        unassignedQuery =
            em.createQuery("SELECT e " +
                           "FROM Employee e " +
                           "WHERE e.projects IS EMPTY");
    }
```

```
    public List findEmployeesWithoutProjects() {
        return unassignedQuery.getResultList();
    }

    // ...
}
```

Working with Query Results

The *result type* of a query is determined by the expressions listed in the SELECT clause of the query. If the result type of a query is the Employee entity, then executing getResultList() will result in a collection of zero or more Employee entity instances. There is a wide variety of results possible depending on the makeup of the query. The following are just some of the types that may result from JPQL queries:

- Basic types, such as String, the primitive types, and JDBC types

- Entity types

- An array of Object

- User-defined types created from a constructor expression

For developers used to JDBC, the most important thing to remember when using the Query interface is that the results are not encapsulated in a ResultSet. The collection or single result corresponds directly to the result type of the query.

Whenever an entity instance is returned, it becomes managed by the active persistence context. If that entity instance is modified and the persistence context is part of a transaction, then the changes will be persisted to the database. The only exception to this rule is the use of transaction-scoped entity managers outside of a transaction. Any query executed in this situation returns detached entity instances instead of managed entity instances. To make changes on these detached entities, they must first be merged into a persistence context before they can be synchronized with the database.

A consequence of the long-term management of entities with application-managed and extended persistence contexts is that executing large queries will cause the persistence context to grow as it stores all of the managed entity instances that are returned. If many of these persistence contexts are holding onto large numbers of managed entities for long periods of time, then memory use may become a concern. The clear() method of the EntityManager interface may be used to clear application-managed and extended persistence contexts, removing unnecessary managed entities.

Optimizing Read-Only Queries

When the query results will not be modified, queries using transaction-scoped entity managers outside of a transaction are typically more efficient than queries executed within a transaction when the result type is an entity. When query results are prepared within a transaction, the persistence provider has to take steps to convert the results into managed entities. This usually entails taking a snapshot of the data for each entity in order to have a baseline to compare against when the transaction is committed. If the managed entities are never modified, then the effort of converting the results into managed entities is wasted.

Outside of a transaction, in some circumstances the persistence provider may be able to optimize the case where the results will be detached immediately. Therefore it can avoid the overhead of creating the managed versions. Note that this technique does not work on application-managed or extended entity managers, since their persistence context outlives the transaction. Any query result from this type of persistence context may be modified for later synchronization to the database even if there is no transaction.

When encapsulating query operations behind a stateless session façade, the easiest way to execute non-transactional queries is to use the NOT_SUPPORTED transaction attribute for the session bean method. This will cause any active transaction to be suspended, forcing the query results to be detached and enabling this optimization. Listing 6-16 shows an example of this technique.

Listing 6-16. *Executing a Query Outside of a Transaction*

```
@Stateless
public class QueryServiceBean implements QueryService {
    @PersistenceContext(unitName="EmployeeService")
    EntityManager em;

    @TransactionAttribute(TransactionAttributeType.NOT_SUPPORTED)
    public List findAllDepartmentsDetached() {
        return em.createQuery("SELECT d FROM Department d")
                .getResultList();
    }

    // ...
}
```

Special Result Types

The array of Object result occurs whenever a query involves more than one expression in the SELECT clause. Common examples include projection of entity fields and aggregate queries where grouping expressions or multiple functions are used. Listing 6-17 revisits the menu generator from Listing 6-14 using a projection query instead of returning full Employee entity instances. Each element of the List is cast to an array of Object that is then used to extract the employee and department name information.

Listing 6-17. *Handling Multiple Result Types*

```
public void displayProjectEmployees(String projectName) {
    List result = em.createQuery("SELECT e.name, e.department.name " +
                                 "FROM Project p JOIN p.employees e " +
                                 "WHERE p.name = ?1 " +
                                 "ORDER BY e.name")
                    .setParameter(1, projectName)
                    .getResultList();
    int count = 0;
    for (Iterator i = result.iterator(); i.hasNext();) {
        Object[] values = (Object[]) i.next();
        System.out.println(++count + ": " + values[0] + ", " + values[1]);
    }
}
```

Constructor expressions provide developers with a way to map array of Object result types to custom objects. Typically this is used to convert the results into JavaBean-style classes that provide getters for the different returned values. This makes the results easier to work with and makes it possible to use the results directly in an environment such as JavaServer Faces without additional translation.

A constructor expression is defined in JPQL using the NEW operator in the SELECT clause. The argument to the NEW operator is the fully qualified name of the class that will be instantiated to hold the results for each row of data returned. The only requirement on this class is that it has a constructor with arguments matching the exact type and order that will be specified in the query. Listing 6-18 shows an EmpMenu class defined in the package example that could be used to hold the results of the query that was executed in Listing 6-17.

Listing 6-18. *Defining a Class for Use in a Constructor Expression*

```
package example;

public class EmpMenu {
    private String employeeName;
    private String departmentName;

    public EmpMenu(String employeeName, String departmentName) {
        this.employeeName = employeeName;
        this.departmentName = departmentName;
    }

    public String getEmployeeName() { return employeeName; }
    public String getDepartmentName() { return departmentName; }
}
```

Listing 6-19 shows the same example as Listing 6-17 using the fully qualified EmpMenu class name in a constructor expression. Instead of working with array indexes, each result is cast to the EmpMenu class and used like a regular Java object.

Listing 6-19. *Using Constructor Expressions*

```
public void displayProjectEmployees(String projectName) {
    List result =
        em.createQuery("SELECT NEW example.EmpMenu(e.name, e.department.name) " +
                        "FROM Project p JOIN p.employees e " +
                        "WHERE p.name = ?1 " +
                        "ORDER BY e.name")
            .setParameter(1, projectName)
            .getResultList();
    int count = 0;
    for (Iterator i = result.iterator(); i.hasNext();) {
        EmpMenu menu = (EmpMenu) i.next();
        System.out.println(++count + ": " + menu.getEmployeeName() + ", " +
                            menu.getDepartmentName());
    }
}
```

Query Paging

Large result sets from queries are often a problem for many applications. In cases where it would be overwhelming to display the entire result set, or if the application medium makes displaying many rows inefficient (web applications, in particular), applications must be able to display ranges of a result set and provide users with the ability to control the range of data that they are viewing. The most common form of this technique is to present the user with a fixed-size table that acts as a sliding window over the result set. Each increment of results displayed is called a *page*, and the process of navigating through the results is called *pagination*.

Efficiently paging through result sets has long been a challenge for both application developers and database vendors. Before support existed at the database level, a common technique was to first retrieve all of the primary keys for the result set and then issue separate queries for the full results using ranges of primary key values. Later, database vendors added the concept of logical row number to query results, guaranteeing that so long as the result was ordered, the row number could be relied on to retrieve portions of the result set. More recently, the JDBC specification has taken this even further with the concept of scrollable result sets, which can be navigated forwards and backwards as required.

The Query interface provides support for pagination via the setFirstResult() and setMaxResults() methods. These methods specify the first result to be received (numbered from zero) and the maximum number of results to return relative to that point. A persistence provider may choose to implement support for this feature in a number of different ways, as not all databases benefit from the same approach. It's a good idea to become familiar with how your vendor approaches pagination and what level of support exists in the target database platform for your application.

■**Caution** The setFirstResult() and setMaxResults() methods should not be used with queries that join across collection relationships (one-to-many and many-to-many) because these queries may return duplicate values. The duplicate values in the result set make it impossible to use a logical result position.

To better illustrate pagination support, consider the stateful session bean shown in Listing 6-20. Once created, it is initialized with the name of a query to count the total results and the name of a query to generate the report. When results are requested, it uses the page size and current page number to calculate the correct parameters for the setFirstResult() and setMaxResults() methods. The total number of results possible is calculated by executing the count query. By using the next(), previous(), and getCurrentResults() methods, presentation code can page through the results as required. If this session bean were bound into an HTTP session, it could be directly used by a JSP or JavaServer Faces page presenting the results in a data table.

Listing 6-20. *Stateful Session Report Pager*

```
@Stateful
public class ResultPagerBean implements ResultPager {
    @PersistenceContext(unitName="QueryPaging")
    private EntityManager em;

    private String reportQueryName;
    private int currentPage;
    private int maxResults;
    private int pageSize;

    public int getPageSize() {
        return pageSize;
    }

    public int getMaxPages() {
        return maxResults / pageSize;
    }

    public void init(int pageSize, String countQueryName,
                     String reportQueryName) {
        this.pageSize = pageSize;
        this.reportQueryName = reportQueryName;
        maxResults = (Long) em.createNamedQuery(countQueryName)
                            .getSingleResult();
        maxResults = resultCount.longValue();
        currentPage = 0;
    }
```

```
    public List getCurrentResults() {
        return em.createNamedQuery(reportQueryName)
                .setFirstResult(currentPage * pageSize)
                .setMaxResults(pageSize)
                .getResultList();
    }

    public void next() {
        currentPage++;
    }

    public void previous() {
        currentPage--;
        if (currentPage < 0) {
            currentPage = 0;
        }
    }

    public int getCurrentPage() {
        return currentPage;
    }

    public void setCurrentPage(int currentPage) {
        this.currentPage = currentPage;
    }

    @Remove
    public void finished() {
    }
}
```

Queries and Uncommitted Changes

Executing queries against entities that have been created or changed in a transaction is a topic that requires special consideration. As we discussed in Chapter 5, the persistence provider will attempt to minimize the number of times the persistence context must be flushed within a transaction. Optimally this will occur only once, when the transaction commits. While the transaction is open and changes are being made, the provider relies on its own internal cache synchronization to ensure that the right version of each entity is used in entity manager operations. At most the provider may have to read new data from the database in order to fulfill a request. All entity operations other than queries can be satisfied without flushing the persistence context to the database.

Queries are a special case because they are executed directly as SQL against the database. Because the database executes the query and not the persistence provider, the active persistence context cannot usually be consulted by the query. As a result, if the persistence context has not been flushed and the database query would be impacted by the changes pending in the persistence context, incorrect data is likely to be retrieved from the query. The entity manager find() operation, on the other hand, always checks the persistence context before going to the database, so this is not a concern.

The good news is that by default, the persistence provider will ensure that queries are able to incorporate pending transactional changes in the query result. It might accomplish this by flushing the persistence context to the database, or it might leverage its own runtime information to ensure the results are correct.

And yet, there are times when having the persistence provider ensure query integrity is not necessarily the behavior we need. The problem is that it is not always easy for the provider to determine the best strategy to accommodate the integrity needs of a query. There is no way the provider can logically determine at a fine-grained level which objects have changed and therefore need to be incorporated into the query results. If the provider solution to ensuring query integrity is to flush the persistence context to the database, then you might have a performance problem if this is a frequent occurrence.

To put this issue in context, consider a message board application, which has modeled conversation topics as Conversation entities. Each Conversation entity refers to one or more messages represented by a Message entity. Periodically, conversations are archived when the last message added to the conversation is more than 30 days old. This is accomplished by changing the status of the Conversation entity from "ACTIVE" to "INACTIVE". The two queries to obtain the list of active conversations and the last message date for a given conversation are shown in Listing 6-21.

Listing 6-21. *Conversation Queries*

```
@NamedQueries({
    @NamedQuery(name="findActiveConversations",
                query="SELECT c " +
                    "FROM Conversation c " +
                    "WHERE c.status = 'ACTIVE'"),
    @NamedQuery(name="findLastMessageDate",
                query="SELECT MAX(m.postingDate) " +
                    "FROM Conversation c JOIN c.messages m " +
                    "WHERE c = :conversation")
})
```

Listing 6-22 shows the session bean method used to perform this maintenance, accepting a Date argument that specifies the minimum age for messages in order to still be considered an active conversation. In this example, we see that two queries are being executed. The "findAllActiveConversations" query collects all of the active conversations, while the "findLastMessageDate" returns the last date that a message was added to a Conversation entity. As the code iterates over the Conversation entities, it invokes the "findLastMessage-Date" query for each one. As these two queries are related, it is reasonable for a persistence provider to assume that the results of the "findLastMessageDate" query will depend on the changes being made to the Conversation entities. If the provider ensures the integrity of the "findLastMessageDate" query by flushing the persistence context, this could become a very expensive operation if hundreds of active conversations are being checked.

Listing 6-22. *Archiving Conversation Entities*

```
@Stateless
public class ConversationMaintenanceBean implements ConversationMaintenance {
    @PersistenceContext(unitName="MessageBoard")
    EntityManager em;

    public void archiveConversations(Date minAge) {
        List<Conversation> active = (List<Conversation>)
            em.createNamedQuery("findActiveConversations")
              .getResultList();
        Query maxAge = em.createNamedQuery("findLastMessageDate");
        for (Conversation c : active) {
            maxAge.setParameter("conversation", c);
            Date lastMessageDate  = (Date) maxAge.getSingleResult();
            if (lastMessageDate.before(minAge)) {
                c.setStatus("INACTIVE");
            }
        }
    }

    // ...
}
```

To give developers more control over the integrity requirements of queries, the `EntityManager` and `Query` interfaces support a `setFlushMode()` method to set the *flush mode*, an indicator to the provider how it should handle pending changes and queries. There are two possible flush mode settings, `AUTO` and `COMMIT`, which are defined by the `FlushModeType` enumerated type. The default setting is `AUTO`, which means that the provider should ensure that pending transactional changes are included in query results. If a query might overlap with changed data in the persistence context, then this setting will ensure that the results are correct.

The `COMMIT` flush mode tells the provider that queries don't overlap with changed data in the persistence context, so it does not need to do anything in order to get correct results. Depending on how the provider implements its query integrity support, this might mean that it does not have to flush the persistence context before executing a query since you have indicated that there is nothing in memory that will be queried from the database.

Although the flush mode is set on the entity manager, the flush mode is really a property of the persistence context. For transaction-scoped entity managers, that means the flush mode has to be changed in every transaction. Extended and application-managed entity managers will preserve their flush-mode setting across transactions.

Setting the flush mode on the entity manager applies to all queries, while setting the flush mode for a query limits the setting to that scope. Setting the flush mode on the query overrides the entity manager setting as you would expect. If the entity manager setting is `AUTO` and one query has the `COMMIT` setting, then the provider will guarantee query integrity for all of the queries other than the one with the COMMIT setting. Likewise if the entity manager setting is COMMIT and one query has an AUTO setting, then only the query with the AUTO setting is guaranteed to incorporate pending changes from the persistence context.

Generally speaking, if you are going to execute queries in transactions where data is being changed, AUTO is the right answer. If you are concerned about the performance implications of ensuring query integrity, consider changing the flush mode to COMMIT on a per-query basis. Changing the value on the entity manager, while convenient, can lead to problems if more queries are added to the application later and they require AUTO semantics.

Coming back to the example at the start of this section, we can set the flush mode on the Query object for the "findLastMessageDate" query to COMMIT because it does not need to see the changes being made to the Conversation entities. The following fragment shows how this would be accomplished for the archiveConversations() method shown in Listing 6-22:

```
public void archiveConversations(Date minAge) {
    // ...
    Query maxAge = em.createNamedQuery("findLastMessageDate");
    maxAge.setFlushMode(FlushModeType.COMMIT);
    // ...
}
```

Bulk Update and Delete

Like their SQL counterparts, JPQL bulk update and delete statements are designed to make changes to large numbers of entities in a single operation without requiring the individual entities to be retrieved and modified using the entity manager. Unlike SQL, which operates on tables, JPQL update and delete statements must take the full range of mappings for the entity into account. These operations are challenging for vendors to implement correctly, and as a result, there are restrictions on the use of these operations that must be well understood by developers.

The full syntax for UPDATE and DELETE statements is described in Chapter 7. The following sections will describe how to use these operations effectively and the issues that may result when used incorrectly.

Using Bulk Update and Delete

Bulk update of entities is accomplished with the UPDATE statement. This statement operates on a single entity type and sets one or more single-valued properties of the entity (either a state field or a single-valued association) subject to the conditions in the WHERE clause. In terms of syntax, it is nearly identical to the SQL version with the exception of using entity expressions instead of tables and columns. Listing 6-23 demonstrates using a bulk update statement. Note that the use of the REQUIRES_NEW transaction attribute type is significant and will be discussed following the examples.

Listing 6-23. *Bulk Update of Entities*

```
@Stateless
public class EmployeeServiceBean implements EmployeeService {
    @PersistenceContext(unitName="BulkQueries")
    EntityManager em;

    @TransactionAttribute(TransactionAttributeType.REQUIRES_NEW)
    public void assignManager(Department dept, Employee manager) {
        em.createQuery("UPDATE Employee e " +
                        "SET e.manager = ?1 " +
                        "WHERE e.department = ?2 ")
            .setParameter(1, manager)
            .setParameter(2, dept)
            .executeUpdate();
    }
}
```

Bulk removal of entities is accomplished with the DELETE statement. Again, the syntax is the same as the SQL version except that the target in the FROM clause is an entity instead of a table and the WHERE clause is composed of entity expressions instead of column expressions. Listing 6-24 demonstrates bulk removal of entities.

Listing 6-24. *Bulk Removal of Entities*

```
@Stateless
public class ProjectServiceBean implements ProjectService {
    @PersistenceContext(unitName="BulkQueries")
    EntityManager em;

    @TransactionAttribute(TransactionAttributeType.REQUIRES_NEW)
    public void removeEmptyProjects() {
        em.createQuery("DELETE FROM Project p " +
                        "WHERE p.employees IS EMPTY ")
            .executeUpdate();
    }
}
```

The first issue for developers to consider when using these statements is that the persistence context is not updated to reflect the results of the operation. Bulk operations are issued as SQL against the database, bypassing the in-memory structures of the persistence context. Therefore updating the salary of all of the employees will not change the current values for any entities managed in memory as part of a persistence context. The developer can rely only on entities retrieved after the bulk operation completes.

For developers using transaction-scoped persistence contexts, this means that the bulk operation should either execute in a transaction all by itself or be the first operation in the transaction. Running the bulk operation in its own transaction is the preferred approach as it minimizes the chance of the developer accidentally fetching data before the bulk change occurs. Executing the bulk operation and then working with entities after it completes is also safe, because then any `find()` operation or query will go to the database to get current results. The examples in Listing 6-23 and Listing 6-24 used the `REQUIRES_NEW` transaction attribute to ensure that the bulk operations occurred within their own transactions.

A typical strategy for persistence providers dealing with bulk operations is to invalidate any in-memory cache of data related to the target entity. This forces data to be fetched from the database the next time it is required. How much cached data gets invalidated depends on the sophistication of the persistence provider. If the provider can detect that the update impacts only a small range of entities, then those specific entities may be invalidated, leaving other cached data in place. Such optimizations are limited, however, and if the provider cannot be sure of the scope of the change, then the entire cache must be invalidated. This can have performance impacts on the application if bulk changes are a frequent occurrence.

■**Caution** SQL update and delete operations should never be executed on tables mapped by an entity. The JPQL operations tell the provider what cached entity state must be invalidated in order to remain consistent with the database. Native SQL operations bypass such checks and can quickly lead to situations where the in-memory cache is out of date with respect to the database.

The danger present in bulk operations and the reason they must occur first in a transaction is that any entity actively managed by a persistence context will remain that way, oblivious to the actual changes occurring at the database level. The active persistence context is separate and distinct from any data cache that the provider may use for optimizations. Consider the following sequence of operations:

1. A new transaction starts.

2. Entity A is created by calling `persist()` to make the entity managed.

3. Entity B is retrieved from a `find()` operation and modified.

4. A bulk remove deletes entity A.

5. A bulk update changes the same properties on entity B that were modified in step 3.

6. The transaction commits.

What should happen to entities A and B in this sequence? In the case of entity A, the provider has to assume that the persistence context is correct and so will still attempt to insert the new entity even though it should have been removed. In the case of entity B, again the provider has to assume that managed version is the correct version and will attempt to update the version in the database, undoing the bulk update change.

This brings us to the issue of extended persistence contexts. Bulk operations and extended persistence contexts are a particularly dangerous combination because the persistence context survives across transaction boundaries, but the provider will never refresh the persistence context to reflect the changed state of the database after a bulk operation has completed. When the extended persistence context is next associated with a transaction, it will attempt to synchronize its current state with the database. Since the managed entities in the persistence context are now out of date with respect to the database, any changes made since the bulk operation could result in incorrect results being stored. In this situation, the only option is to refresh the entity state or ensure that the data is versioned in such a way that the incorrect change can be detected. Locking strategies and refreshing of entity state are discussed in Chapter 9.

Bulk Delete and Relationships

In our discussion of the `remove()` operation in the previous chapter, we emphasized that relationship maintenance is always the responsibility of the developer. The only time a cascading remove occurs is when the `REMOVE` cascade option is set for a relationship. Even then, the persistence provider won't automatically update the state of any managed entities that refer to the removed entity. As we are about to see, the same requirement holds true when using DELETE statements as well.

A DELETE statement in JPQL corresponds more or less to a DELETE statement in SQL. Writing the statement in JPQL gives you the benefit of working with entities instead of tables, but the semantics are exactly the same. This has implications in how applications must write DELETE statements in order to ensure that they execute correctly and leave the database in a consistent state.

DELETE statements do not cascade to related entities. Even if the `REMOVE` cascade option is set on a relationship, it will not be followed. It is your responsibility to ensure that relationships are correctly updated with respect to the entities that have been removed. The persistence provider also has no control over constraints in the database. If you attempt to remove data that is the target of a foreign key relationship in another table, you will get a referential integrity constraint violation in return.

Let's look at an example that puts these issues in context. Consider, for example, that a company wishes to reorganize its department structure. We want to delete a number of departments and then assign the employees to new departments. The first step is to delete the old departments, so the following statement is to be executed:

```
DELETE FROM Department d
WHERE d.name IN ('CA13', 'CA19', 'NY30')
```

This is a straightforward operation. We want to remove the department entities that match the given list of names using a DELETE statement instead of querying for the entities and using the `remove()` operation to dispose of them. But when this query is executed, a `PersistenceException` exception is thrown, reporting that a foreign key integrity constraint has been violated. Therefore, another table has a foreign key reference to one of the rows we are trying to delete. Checking the database, we see that the table mapped by the `Employee` entity has a foreign key constraint against the table mapped by the `Department` entity. Since the foreign key value in the `Employee` table is not NULL, the parent key from the `Department` table can't be removed.

Therefore we need to first update the `Employee` entities in question to make sure that they do not point to the department we are trying to delete:

```
UPDATE Employee e
SET e.department = null
WHERE e.department.name IN ('CA13', 'CA19', 'NY30')
```

With this change the original DELETE statement will work as expected. Now consider what would have happened if the integrity constraint had not been in the database. The DELETE operation would have completed successfully, but the foreign key values would still be sitting in the Employee table. The next time the persistence provider tried to load the Employee entities with dangling foreign keys, it would be unable to resolve the target entity. The outcome of this operation is vendor-specific but will most likely lead to a PersistenceException exception being thrown, complaining of the invalid relationship.

Query Hints

Query hints are the Java Persistence API extension point for vendor-specific query features. A hint is simply a string name and object value. The meaning of both the name and value is entirely up to the persistence provider. Every query may be associated with any number of hints, set either in persistence unit metadata as part of the @NamedQuery annotation, or on the Query interface itself using the setHint() method.

We left query hints until the end of this chapter because they are the only feature in the query API that has no standard usage. Everything about hints is vendor-specific. The only guarantee provided by the specification is that providers must ignore hints that they do not understand. Listing 6-25 demonstrates the "toplink.cache-usage" hint supported by the Reference Implementation of the Java Persistence API to indicate that the cache should not be checked when reading an Employee from the database. Unlike the refresh() method of the EntityManager interface, this hint will not cause the query result to override the current cached value.

Listing 6-25. *Using Query Hints*

```java
public Employee findEmployeeNoCache(int empId) {
    Query q = em.createQuery("SELECT e FROM Employee e WHERE e.id = ?1");
    // force read from database
    q.setHint("toplink.cache-usage", "DoNotCheckCache");
    q.setParameter(1, empId);
    try {
        return (Employee) q.getSingleResult();
    } catch (NoResultException e) {
        return null;
    }
}
```

If this query were to be executed frequently, a named query would be more efficient. The following named query definition incorporates the cache hint used earlier:

```java
@NamedQuery(name="findEmployeeNoCache",
            query="SELECT e FROM Employee e WHERE e.id = :empId",
            hints={@QueryHint(name="toplink.cache-usage", value="DoNotCheckCache")})
```

The hints element accepts an array of @QueryHint annotations, allowing any number of hints to be set for a query.

Query Best Practices

The typical application using the Java Persistence API is going to have many queries defined. It is the nature of enterprise applications that information is constantly being queried from the database, for everything from complex reports to drop-down lists in the user interface. Therefore efficiently using queries can have a major impact on your application as a whole.

Named Queries

First and foremost, we recommend named queries whenever possible. Persistence providers will often take steps to precompile JPQL named queries to SQL as part of the deployment or initialization phase of an application. This avoids the overhead of continuously parsing JPQL and generating SQL. Even with a cache for converted queries, dynamic query definition will always be less efficient than using named queries.

Named queries also enforce the best practice of using query parameters. Query parameters help to keep the number of distinct SQL strings parsed by the database to a minimum. Since databases typically keep a cache of SQL statements on hand for frequently accessed queries, this is an essential part of ensuring peak database performance.

As we discussed in the Dynamic Query Definition section, query parameters also help to avoid security issues caused by concatenating values into query strings. For applications exposed to the web, security has to be a concern at every level of an application. You can either spend a lot of effort trying to validate input parameters, or you can use query parameters and let the database do the work for you.

When naming queries, decide on a naming strategy early in the application development cycle with the understanding that the query namespace is global for each persistence unit. Collisions between query names are likely to be a common frustration if there is no established naming pattern.

Finally, using named queries allows for JPQL queries to be overridden with SQL queries or even with vendor-specific languages and expression frameworks. For applications migrating from an existing object-relational mapping solution, it is quite likely that the vendor will provide some support for invoking their existing query solution using the named query facility in the Java Persistence API. We will discuss SQL named queries in Chapter 9.

Report Queries

If you are executing queries that return entities for reporting purposes and have no intention of modifying the results, consider executing queries using a transaction-scoped entity manager but outside of a transaction. The persistence provider may be able to detect the lack of a transaction and optimize the results for detachment, often by skipping some of the steps required to create an interim managed version of the entity results.

Likewise, if an entity is expensive to construct due to eager relationships or a complex table mapping, consider selecting individual entity properties using a projection query instead of retrieving the full entity result. If all you need is the name and office phone number for 500 employees, selecting only those two fields is likely to be far more efficient than fully constructing 1,000 entity instances.

Query Hints

It is quite likely that vendors will entice you with a variety of hints to enable different performance optimizations for queries. Query hints may well be an essential tool in meeting your performance expectations. We strongly advise, however, that you resist the urge to embed query hints in your application code. The ideal location for query hints is in an XML mapping file (which we will be describing in Chapter 10), or at the very least as part of a named query definition. Hints are often highly dependent on the target platform and may well change over time as different aspects of the application impact the overall balance of performance. Keep hints decoupled from your code if at all possible.

Stateless Session Beans

We tried to demonstrate as many examples as possible in the context of a stateless session bean method, as we believe that this is the best way to organize queries in a Java EE application. Using the stateless session bean has a number of benefits over simply embedding queries all over the place in application code:

- Clients can execute queries by invoking an appropriately named business method instead of relying on a cryptic query name or multiple copies of the same query string.

- Stateless session bean methods can optimize their transaction usage depending on whether or not the results need to be managed or detached.

- Using a transaction-scoped persistence context ensures that large numbers of entity instances don't remain managed long after they are needed.

- For existing entity bean applications, the stateless session bean is the ideal vehicle for migrating finder queries away from the entity bean home interface. We will discuss this technique in Chapter 13.

This is not to say that other components are unsuitable locations for queries, but stateless session beans are a well-established best practice for hosting queries in the Java EE environment.

Bulk Update and Delete

If bulk update and delete operations must be used, ensure that they are executed only in an isolated transaction where no other changes are being made. There are many ways in which these queries can negatively impact an active persistence context. Interweaving these queries with other non-bulk operations requires careful management by the application.

Entity versioning and locking requires special consideration when bulk update operations are used. Bulk delete operations can have wide ranging ramifications depending on how well the persistence provider can react and adjust entity caching in response. Therefore we view bulk update and delete operations as being highly specialized, to be used with care.

Provider Differences

Take time to become familiar with the SQL that your persistence provider generates for different JPQL queries. Although understanding SQL is not necessary for writing JPQL queries, knowing what happens in response to the various JPQL operations is an essential part of performance tuning. Joins in JPQL are not always explicit, and you may find yourself surprised at the complex SQL generated for a seemingly simple JPQL query.

The benefits of features such as query paging are also dependent on the approach used by your persistence provider. There are a number of different techniques that can be used to accomplish pagination, many of which suffer from performance and scalability issues. Because the Java Persistence API can't dictate a particular approach that will work well in all cases, become familiar with the approach used by your provider and whether or not it is configurable.

Finally, understanding the provider strategy for when and how often it flushes the persistence context is necessary before looking at optimizations such as changing the flush mode. Depending on the caching architecture and query optimizations used by a provider, changing the flush mode may or may not make a difference to your application.

Summary

We began this chapter with an introduction to JPQL, the query language defined by the Java Persistence API. We briefly discussed the origins of JPQL and its role in writing queries that interact with entities. We also provided an overview of major JPQL features for developers already experienced with SQL or previous versions of EJB QL.

In the discussion on executing queries, we introduced the methods for defining queries both dynamically at runtime and statically as part of persistence unit metadata. We looked at the Query interface and the types of query results possible using JPQL. We also looked at parameter binding, strategies for handling large result sets and how to ensure that queries in transactions with modified data complete successfully.

In the section on bulk update and delete we looked at how to execute these types of queries and how to ensure that they are used safely by the application. We provided details on how persistence providers deal with bulk operations and the impact that they have on the active persistence context.

We ended our discussion of query features with a look at query hints. We showed how to specify hints and provided an example using hints supported by the Reference Implementation of the Java Persistence API.

Finally, we summarized our view of best practices relating to queries, looking at named queries, different strategies for the various query types, as well as the implementation details that need to be understood for different persistence providers.

In the next chapter, we will continue to focus on queries by examining JPQL in detail.

■ ■ ■

CHAPTER 7

Query Language

Based on the EJB Query Language (EJB QL) first introduced in EJB 2.0, the Java Persistence Query Language (JPQL), is a portable query language designed to combine the syntax and simple query semantics of SQL with the expressiveness of an object-oriented expression language. Queries written using this language can be portably compiled to SQL on all major database servers.

In the last chapter, we looked at programming using the query interfaces and presented a brief introduction to JPQL for users already experienced with SQL. This chapter will explore the query language in detail, breaking the language down piece by piece with examples to demonstrate all of its features.

Introduction

In order to describe what JPQL is, it is important to make clear what it is not. JPQL is not SQL. Despite the similarities between the two languages in terms of keywords and overall structure, there are very important differences. Attempting to write JPQL as if it were SQL is the easiest way to get frustrated with the language. The similarities between the two languages are intentional in order to give developers a feel for what the language can accomplish, but the object-oriented nature of the language requires a different mode of thinking.

If JPQL is not SQL, then what is it? Put simply, JPQL is a language for querying entities. Instead of tables and rows, the currency of the language is entities and objects. It provides us with a way to express queries in terms of entities and their relationships, operating on the persistent state of the entity as defined in the object model, not in the physical database model.

If the Java Persistence API supports SQL queries, why introduce a new query language? There are a couple of important reasons to consider JPQL over SQL. The first is portability. It may be translated into the SQL dialect of all major database vendors. The second reason is that queries are literally written against the domain model of persistent entities. Queries may be written without any need to know exactly how the entities are mapped to the database. We hope that the examples in this chapter will demonstrate the power present in even the simplest JPQL expressions.

Adopting JPQL does not mean losing all of the SQL features you have grown accustomed to using. A broad selection of SQL features are directly supported, including subqueries, aggregate queries, update and delete statements, numerous SQL functions, and more.

Terminology

Queries fall into one of four categories: select, aggregate, update, and delete queries. Select queries retrieve persistent state from one or more entities, filtering results as required. Aggregate queries are variations of select queries that group the results and produce summary data. Together, select and aggregate queries are sometimes called *report queries*, since they are primarily focused on generating data for reporting. Update and delete queries are used to conditionally modify or remove entire sets of entities. Each query type will be described in detail in its own section as the chapter progresses.

Queries operate on the set of entities defined by a persistence unit. This set of entities is known as the *abstract persistence schema*, the collection of which defines the overall domain from which results may be retrieved.

■**Note** To allow this chapter to be used as a companion to the Query Language chapter of the Java Persistence API specification, the same terminology is used where possible.

In query expressions, entities are referred to by name. If an entity has not been explicitly named (using the name attribute of the @Entity annotation, for example) the unqualified class name is used by default. This name is the *abstract schema name* of the entity in the context of a query.

Entities are composed of one or more persistence properties implemented as fields or JavaBean properties. The *abstract schema type* of a persistent property on an entity refers to the class or primitive type used to implement that property. For example, if the Employee entity has a property name of type String, then the abstract schema type of that property in query expressions is String as well. Simple persistent properties with no relationship mapping comprise the persistent state of the entity and are referred to as *state fields*. Persistent properties that are also relationships are called *association fields*.

As we saw in the last chapter, queries may be defined dynamically or statically. The examples in this chapter will consist of queries that may be used either dynamically or statically depending on the needs of the application.

Finally, it is important to note that queries are not case sensitive except in two cases. Entity names and property names must be specified exactly as they are named.

Example Data Model

Figure 7-1 shows the domain model for the queries in this chapter. Continuing the examples we have been using throughout the book, it demonstrates many different relationship types, including unidirectional, bidirectional, and self-referencing relationships. We have added the role names to this diagram to make the relationship property names explicit.

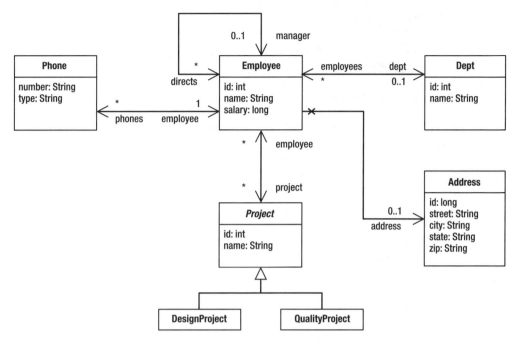

Figure 7-1. *Example application domain model*

The object relational mappings for this model are not included in this chapter except where we describe the SQL equivalent of a particular query. Knowing how a mapping is implemented is only a performance concern and is not necessary to write queries since the query language is based entirely on the object model and the logical relationships between entities. It is the job of the query translator to take the object-oriented query expressions and interpret the mapping metadata in order to produce the SQL required to execute the query on the database.

Example Application

Learning a new language can be a challenging experience. It's one thing to read through page after page of text describing the features of the language, but it's another thing completely to put these features into practice. To get used to writing queries, consider using an application like the one shown in Listing 7-1. This simple application reads queries from the console and executes them against the entities from a particular persistence unit.

Listing 7-1. *Application for Testing Queries*

```
package persistence;

import java.io.*;
import java.util.*;
import javax.persistence.*;
import org.apache.commons.lang.builder.*;
```

```java
public class QueryTester {

    public static void main(String[] args) throws Exception {
        String unitName = args[0];

        EntityManagerFactory emf =
            Persistence.createEntityManagerFactory(unitName);
        EntityManager em = emf.createEntityManager();
        BufferedReader reader =
            new BufferedReader(new InputStreamReader(System.in));

        for (;;) {
            System.out.print("JPQL> ");
            String query = reader.readLine();
            if (query.equals("quit")) {
                break;
            }
            if (query.length() == 0) {
                continue;
            }

            try {
                List result = em.createQuery(query).getResultList();
                if (result.size() > 0) {
                    int count = 0;
                    for (Object o : result) {
                        System.out.print(++count + " ");
                        printResult(o);
                    }
                } else {
                    System.out.println("0 results returned");
                }
            } catch (Exception e) {
                e.printStackTrace();
            }
        }
    }

    private static void printResult(Object result) throws Exception {
        if (result == null) {
            System.out.print("NULL");
        } else if (result instanceof Object[]) {
            Object[] row = (Object[]) result;
            System.out.print("[");
            for (int i = 0; i < row.length; i++) {
                printResult(row[i]);
            }
```

```
            System.out.print("]");
        } else if (result instanceof Long ||
                    result instanceof Double ||
                    result instanceof String) {
            System.out.print(result.getClass().getName() + ": " + result);
        } else {
            System.out.print(ReflectionToStringBuilder.toString(result, ➥
ToStringStyle.SHORT_PREFIX_STYLE));
        }
        System.out.println();
    }
}
```

The only requirement for using this application is the name of a persistence unit containing the entities you wish to query against. The application will read the persistence unit name from the command line and attempt to create an EntityManagerFactory for that name. If initialization is successful, queries may be typed at the JPQL> prompt. The query will be executed and the results printed out. The format of each result is the class name followed by each of the properties for that class. This example uses the Apache Jakarta Commons-Lang library to generate the object summary. Listing 7-2 demonstrates a sample session with the application.

Listing 7-2. *Example Session with* QueryTester

```
JPQL> SELECT p FROM Phone p WHERE p.type NOT IN ('office', 'home')
1 Phone[id=5,number=516-555-1234,type=cell,employee=Employee@13c0b53]
2 Phone[id=9,number=650-555-1234,type=cell,employee=Employee@193f6e2]
3 Phone[id=12,number=650-555-1234,type=cell,employee=Employee@36527f]
4 Phone[id=18,number=585-555-1234,type=cell,employee=Employee@bd6a5f]
5 Phone[id=21,number=650-555-1234,type=cell,employee=Employee@979e8b]
JPQL> SELECT d.name, AVG(e.salary) FROM Department d JOIN d.employees e ➥
GROUP BY d.name
1 [java.lang.String: QA
java.lang.Double: 52500.0
]
2 [java.lang.String: Engineering
java.lang.Double: 56833.333333333336
]
JPQL> quit
```

Select Queries

Select queries are the primary query type and facilitate the bulk retrieval of data from the database. Not surprisingly, select queries are also the most common form of query used in applications. The overall form of a select query is as follows:

```
SELECT <select_expression>
FROM <from_clause>
[WHERE <conditional_expression>]
[ORDER BY <order_by_clause>]
```

The simplest form of a select query consists of two mandatory parts, the SELECT clause and the FROM clause. The SELECT clause defines the format of the query results, while the FROM clause defines the entity or entities from which the results will be obtained. Consider the following complete query that retrieves all of the employees in the company:

```
SELECT e
FROM Employee e
```

The structure of this query is very similar to a SQL query but with a couple of important differences. The first difference is that the domain of the query defined in the FROM clause is not a table but an entity, in this case the Employee entity. As in SQL, it has been aliased to the identifier e. This aliased value is known as an *identification variable* and is the key by which the entity will be referred to in the rest of the select statement. Unlike queries in SQL, where a table alias is optional, the use of identification variables is mandatory in JPQL.

The second difference is that the SELECT clause does not enumerate the fields of the table or use a wildcard to select all of the fields. Instead, only the identification variable is listed in order to indicate that the result type of the query is the Employee entity, not a tabular set of rows.

As the query processor iterates over the result set returned from the database, it converts the tabular row and column data into a set of entity instances. The getResultList() method of the Query interface will return a collection of zero or more Employee objects after evaluating the query.

Despite the differences in structure and syntax, every query is translatable to SQL. In order to execute a query, the query engine first builds an optimal SQL representation of the JPQL query. The resulting SQL query is what actually gets executed on the database. In this simple example the resulting SQL would look something like this:

```
SELECT id, name, salary, manager_id, dept_id, address_id
FROM emp
```

The SQL statement must read in all of the mapped columns required to create the entity instance, including foreign key columns. Even if the entity is cached in memory, the query engine will still typically read all required data in order to ensure that the cached version is up to date. Note that, had the relationships between the Employee and the Department or Address entities required eager loading, the SQL statement would either be extended to retrieve the extra data or multiple statements would have been batched together in order to completely construct the Employee entity. Every vendor will provide some method for displaying the SQL it generates from translating JPQL. For performance tuning in particular, being familiar with how your vendor approaches SQL generation can help you write more efficient queries.

Now that we have looked at a simple query and covered the basic terminology, the following sections will move through each of the clauses of the select query, explaining the syntax and features available.

The SELECT Clause

The SELECT clause of a query can take several forms, including simple and complex path expressions, transformation functions, multiple expressions (including constructor expressions), and aggregate functions. The following sections introduce path expressions and discuss the different styles of SELECT clauses and how they determine the result type of the query. Aggregate functions are detailed later in the chapter in the section on Aggregate Queries.

Path Expressions

Path expressions are the building blocks of queries. They are used to navigate out from an entity, either across a relationship to another entity (or collection of entities) or to one of the persistent properties of an entity. Navigation that results in one of the persistent state fields (either field or property) of an entity is referred to as a *state field path*. Navigation that leads to a single entity is referred to as a *single-valued association path*, while navigation to a collection of entities is referred to as a *collection-valued association path*.

The dot operator (.) signifies path navigation in an expression. For example, if the Employee entity has been mapped to the identification variable e, then e.name is a state field path expression resolving to the employee name. Likewise, the path expression e.department is a single-valued association from the employee to the department to which he or she is assigned. Finally, e.directs is a collection-valued association that resolves to the collection of employees reporting to an employee who is also a manager.

What makes path expressions so powerful is that they are not limited to a single navigation. Rather, navigation expressions can be chained together to traverse complex entity graphs, so long as the path moves from left to right across single-valued associations. A path cannot continue from a state field or collection-valued association. Using this technique, we can construct path expressions such as e.department.name, which is the name of the department to which the employee belongs.

Path expressions are used in every clause of a select query, determining everything from the result type of the query to the conditions under which the results should be filtered. Experience with path expressions is the key to writing effective queries.

Entities and Objects

The first and simplest form of the SELECT clause is a single identification variable. The result type for a query of this style is the entity to which the identification variable is associated. For example, the following query returns all of the departments in the company:

```
SELECT d
FROM Department d
```

The keyword OBJECT may be used to indicate that the result type of the query is the entity bound to the identification variable. It has no impact on the query, but it may be used as a visual clue:

```
SELECT OBJECT(d)
FROM Department d
```

The only problem with using OBJECT is that even though path expressions can resolve to an entity type, the syntax of the OBJECT keyword is limited to identification variables. The expression OBJECT(e.department) is illegal even though Department is an entity type. For that reason, we do not recommend the OBJECT syntax. It exists primarily for compatibility with previous versions of the language that required the OBJECT keyword on the assumption that a future revision to SQL would include the same terminology.

A path expression resolving to a state field or single-valued association may also be used in the SELECT clause. The result type of the query in this case becomes the type of the path expression, either the state field type or the entity type of a single-valued association. The following query returns the names for all employees:

```
SELECT e.name
FROM Employee e
```

The result type of the path expression in the SELECT clause is String, so executing this query using getResultList() will produce a collection of zero or more String objects.

Entities reached from a path expression may also be returned. The following query demonstrates returning a different entity as a result of path navigation:

```
SELECT e.department
FROM Employee e
```

The result type of this query is the Department entity since that is the result of traversing the department relationship from Employee to Department. Executing the query will therefore result in a collection of zero or more Department objects, including duplicates.

To remove the duplicates, the DISTINCT operator must be used:

```
SELECT DISTINCT e.department
FROM Employee e
```

The DISTINCT operator is functionally equivalent to the SQL operator of the same name. Once the result set is collected, duplicate values (using entity identity if the query result type is an entity) are removed so that only unique results are returned.

The result type of a select query is the type corresponding to each row in the result set produced by executing the query. This may include entities, primitive types and other persistent attribute types, but never a collection type. The following query is illegal:

```
SELECT d.employees
FROM Department d
```

The path expression d.employees is a collection-valued path that produces a collection type. Restricting queries in this way prevents the provider from having to combine successive rows from the database into a single result object.

Combining Expressions

Multiple expressions may be specified in the same SELECT clause by separating them with commas. The result type of the query in this case is an array of type Object, where the elements of the array are the results of resolving the expressions in the order in which they appeared in the query.

Consider the following query that returns only the name and salary of an employee:

```
SELECT e.name, e.salary
FROM Employee e
```

When executed, a collection of zero or more instances of arrays of type `Object` will be returned. Each array in this example has two elements, the first being a `String` containing the employee name and the second being a `Double` containing the employee salary. The practice of reporting only a subset of the state fields from an entity is called *projection* because the entity data is projected out from the entity into tabular form.

Projection is a useful technique for web applications where only a few pieces of information are displayed from a large set of entity instances. Depending on how the entity has been mapped, it may require a complex SQL query to fully retrieve the entity state. If only two fields are required, then the extra effort spent constructing the entity instance may have been wasted. A projection query that returns only the minimum amount of data is more useful in these cases.

Constructor Expressions

A more powerful form of SELECT clause involving multiple expressions is the constructor expression, which specifies that the results of the query are to be stored using a user-specified object type. Consider the following query:

```
SELECT NEW example.EmployeeDetails(e.name, e.salary, e.department.name)
FROM Employee e
```

The result type of this query is the type `example.EmployeeDetails`. As the query processor iterates over the results of the query, it instantiates new instances of `EmployeeDetails` using the constructor that matches the expression types listed in the query. In this case the expression types are `String`, `Double`, and `String`, so the query engine will search for a constructor with those class types for arguments. Each row in the resulting query collection is therefore an instance of `EmployeeDetails` containing the employee name, salary, and department name.

The result object type must be referred to using the fully qualified name of the object. The class does not have to be mapped to the database in any way, however. Any class with a constructor compatible with the expressions listed in the SELECT clause can be used in a constructor expression.

Constructor expressions are powerful tools for constructing coarse-grained data transfer objects or view objects for use in other application tiers. Instead of manually constructing these objects, a single query can be used to gather together view objects ready for presentation on a web page.

Inheritance and Polymorphism

The Java Persistence API supports inheritance between entities. As a result, the query language supports polymorphic results where multiple subclasses of an entity can be returned by the same query.

In the example model, `Project` is an abstract base class for `QualityProject` and `DesignProject`. If an identification variable is formed from the `Project` entity, then the query results will include a mixture of `QualityProject` and `DesignProject` objects, and the results may be cast to these classes as necessary. There is no special syntax to enable this behavior. The following query retrieves all projects with at least one employee:

```
SELECT p
FROM Project p
WHERE p.employees IS NOT EMPTY
```

The impact that inheritance between entities has on the generated SQL is important to understand for performance reasons and will be described in Chapter 8.

The FROM Clause

The FROM clause is used to declare one or more identification variables, optionally derived from joined relationships, that form the domain over which the query should draw its results. The syntax of the FROM clause consists of one or more identification variables and join clause declarations.

Identification Variables

The identification variable is the starting point for all query expressions. Every query must have at least one identification variable defined in the FROM clause, and that variable must correspond to an entity type. When an identification variable declaration does not use a path expression (that is, when it is a single entity name), it is referred to as a *range variable declaration*. This terminology comes from set theory as the variable is said to range over the entity.

Range variable declarations use the following syntax: `<entity_name> [AS] <identifier>`. The identifier must follow the standard Java naming rules and may be referenced throughout the query in a case-insensitive manner. Multiple declarations may be specified by separating them with commas.

Path expressions may also be aliased to identification variables in the case of joins and subqueries. The syntax for identification variable declarations in these cases will be covered in their respective sections next.

Joins

A join is a query that combines results from multiple entities. Joins in JPQL queries are logically equivalent to SQL joins. Ultimately, once the query is translated to SQL, it is quite likely that the joins between entities will produce similar joins amongst the tables to which the entities are mapped. Understanding when joins occur is therefore important to writing efficient queries.

Joins occur whenever any of the following conditions are met in a select query:

1. Two or more range variable declarations are listed in the FROM clause

2. The JOIN operator is used to extend an identification variable using a path expression

3. A path expression anywhere in the query navigates across an association field, to the same or a different entity

The semantics of a join between entities are the same as SQL joins between tables. Most queries contain a series of join conditions, expressions that define the rules for matching one entity to another. Join conditions may be specified explicitly, such as using the JOIN operator in the FROM clause of a query, or implicitly as a result of path navigation.

An *inner join* between two entities returns the objects from both entity types that satisfy all of the join conditions. Path navigation from one entity to another is a form of inner join. The *outer join* of two entities is the set of objects from both entity types that satisfy the join conditions plus the set of objects from one entity type (designated as the *left* entity) that have no matching join condition in the other.

In the absence of join conditions between two entities, queries will produce a Cartesian product. Each object of the first entity type is paired with each object of the second entity type, squaring the number of results. Cartesian products are rare with JPQL queries given the navigation capabilities of the language, but they are possible if two range variable declarations in the FROM clause are specified without additional conditions specified in the WHERE clause.

Further discussion and examples of each join style are provided in the following sections.

Inner Joins

All of the example queries so far have been using the simplest form of FROM clause, a single entity type aliased to an identification variable. However, as a relational language, JPQL supports queries that draw on multiple entities and the relationships between them.

Inner joins between two entities may be specified in one of two ways. The first and preferred form is the JOIN operator in the FROM clause. The second form requires multiple range variable declarations in the FROM clause and WHERE clause conditions to provide the join conditions.

The JOIN Operator and Collection Association Fields The syntax of an inner join using the JOIN operator is [INNER] JOIN <path_expression> [AS] <identifier>. Consider the following query:

```
SELECT p
FROM Employee e JOIN e.phones p
```

This query uses the JOIN operator to join the Employee entity to the Phone entity across the phones relationship. The join condition in this query is defined by the object-relational mapping of the phones relationship. No additional criteria need to be specified in order to link the two entities. By joining the two entities together, this query returns all of the Phone entity instances associated with employees in the company.

The syntax for joins is similar to the JOIN expressions supported by ANSI SQL. For readers who may not be familiar with this syntax, consider the equivalent SQL form of the previous query written using the traditional join form:

```
SELECT p.id, p.phone_num, p.type, p.emp_id
FROM emp e, phone p
WHERE e.id = p.emp_id
```

The table mapping for the Phone entity replaces the expression e.phones. The WHERE clause also includes the criteria necessary to join the two tables together across the join columns defined by the phones mapping.

Note that the phones relationship has been mapped to the identification variable p. Even though the Phone entity does not directly appear in the query, the target of the phones relationship is the Phone entity, and this determines the identification variable type. This implicit determination of the identification variable type can take some getting used to. Familiarity with how relationships are defined in the object model is necessary to navigate through a written query.

Each occurrence of p outside of the FROM clause now refers to a single phone owned by an employee. Even though a collection association field was specified in the JOIN clause, the identification variable is really referring to entities reached by that association, not the collection itself. The variable can now be used as if the Phone entity was listed directly in the FROM clause. For example, instead of returning Phone entity instances, phone numbers can be returned instead:

```
SELECT p.number
FROM Employee e JOIN e.phones p
```

In the definition of path expressions earlier, it was noted that a path couldn't continue from a state field or collection association field. To work around this situation, the collection association field must be joined in the FROM clause so that a new identification variable is created for the path, allowing it to be the root for new path expressions.

IN VS. JOIN

The JOIN operator is new with the Java Persistence API. Previous versions of EJB QL defined by the EJB 2.0 and EJB 2.1 specifications used a special operator IN in the FROM clause to map collection associations to identification variables. The equivalent form of the query used earlier in this section may be specified as:

```
SELECT DISTINCT p
FROM Employee e, IN(e.phones) p
```

The IN operator is intended to indicate that the variable p is an enumeration of the phones collection. We believe that the JOIN operator is a more powerful and expressive way to declare relationships in a query. The IN operator is still supported, but use of the JOIN operator is recommended.

The JOIN Operator and Single-Valued Association Fields The JOIN operator works with both collection-valued association path expressions and single-valued association path expressions. Consider the following example:

```
SELECT d
FROM Employee e JOIN e.department d
```

This query defines a join from Employee to Department across the department relationship. This is semantically equivalent to using a path expression in the SELECT clause to obtain the department for the employee. For example, the following query should result in similar if not identical SQL representations involving a join between the Employee and Department entities:

```
SELECT e.department
FROM Employee e
```

The primary use case for using a single-valued association path expression in the FROM clause as opposed to just using a path expression in the SELECT clause is for outer joins. Path navigation is equivalent to the inner join of all associated entities traversed in the path expression.

Implicit inner joins resulting from path expressions is something that developers should be aware of. Consider the following example that returns the distinct departments based in California that are participating in the "Release1" project:

```
SELECT DISTINCT e.department
FROM Project p JOIN p.employees e
WHERE p.name = 'Release1' AND
      e.address.state = 'CA'
```

There are actually four logical joins here, not two. The translator will treat the query as if it had been written with explicit joins between the various entities. We will cover the syntax for multiple joins later, but for now consider the following query that is equivalent to the previous query, reading the join conditions from left to right:

```
SELECT DISTINCT d
FROM Project p JOIN p.employees e JOIN e.department d JOIN e.address a
WHERE p.name = 'Release1' AND
      a.state = 'CA'
```

We say four logical joins because the actual physical mapping may involve more tables. In this case the Employee and Project entities are related via a many-to-many association using a join table. Therefore the actual SQL for such a query uses five tables, not four:

```
SELECT DISTINCT d.id, d.name
FROM project p, emp_projects ep, emp e, dept d, address a
WHERE p.id = ep.project_id AND
      ep.emp_id = e.id AND
      e.dept_id = d.id AND
      e.address_id = a.id AND
      p.name = 'Release1' AND
      a.state = 'CA'
```

The first form of the query is certainly easier to read and understand. However, during performance tuning it may be helpful to understand how many joins can occur as the result of seemingly trivial path expressions.

Join Conditions in the WHERE Clause SQL queries have traditionally joined tables together by listing the tables to be joined in the FROM clause and supplying criteria in the WHERE clause of the query to determine the join conditions. To join two entities without using a relationship, use a range variable declaration for each entity in the FROM clause.

The previous join example between the Employee and Department entities could also have been written like this:

```
SELECT DISTINCT d
FROM Department d, Employee e
WHERE d = e.department
```

This style of query is usually used to compensate for the lack of an explicit relationship between two entities in the domain model. For example, there is no association between the `Department` entity and the `Employee` who is the manager of the department. We can use a join condition in the WHERE clause to make this possible:

```
SELECT d, m
FROM Department d, Employee m
WHERE d = m.department AND
      m.directs IS NOT EMPTY
```

In this example we are using one of the special collection expressions, IS NOT EMPTY, to check that the collection of direct reports to the employee is not empty. Any employee with a non-empty collection of directs is by definition a manager.

Multiple Joins More than one join may be cascaded if necessary. For example, the following query returns the distinct set of projects belonging to employees who belong to a department:

```
SELECT DISTINCT p
FROM Department d JOIN d.employees e JOIN e.projects p
```

The query processor interprets the FROM clause from left to right. Once a variable has been declared, it may be subsequently referenced by other JOIN expressions. In this case the `projects` relationship of the `Employee` entity is navigated once the employee variable has been declared.

Outer Joins

An outer join between two entities produces a domain where only one side of the relationship is required to be complete. In other words, the outer join of `Employee` to `Department` across the employee `department` relationship returns all employees and the department to which the employee has been assigned, but the department is returned only if it is available.

An outer join is specified using the following syntax: LEFT [OUTER] JOIN <path_expression> [AS] <identifier>. The following query demonstrates an outer join between two entities:

```
SELECT e, d
FROM Employee e LEFT JOIN e.department d
```

If the employee has not been assigned to a department, then the department object (the second element of the `Object` array) will be null. For readers familiar with Oracle SQL, the previous query would be equivalent to the following:

```
SELECT e.id, e.name, e.salary, e.manager_id, e.dept_id, e.address_id,
       d.id, d.name
FROM emp e, dept d
WHERE e.dept_id = d.id (+)
```

Fetch Joins

Fetch joins are intended to help application designers optimize their database access and prepare query results for detachment. They allow queries to specify one or more relationships that should be navigated and prefetched by the query engine so that they are not lazy loaded later at runtime.

For example, if we have an Employee entity with a lazy loading relationship to its address, the following query can be used to indicate that the relationship should be resolved eagerly during query execution:

```
SELECT e
FROM Employee e JOIN FETCH e.address
```

Note that no identification variable is set for the e.address path expression. This is because even though the Address entity is being joined in order to resolve the relationship, it is not part of the result type of the query. The result of executing the query is still a collection of Employee entity instances, except that the address relationship on each entity will not cause a secondary trip to the database when it is accessed. This also allows the address relationship to be accessed safely if the Employee entity becomes detached. A fetch join is distinguished from a regular join by adding the FETCH keyword to the JOIN operator.

In order to implement fetch joins, the query is rewritten to turn the fetched association into a regular join of the appropriate type: inner by default or outer if the LEFT keyword was specified. The SELECT expression of the query is then expanded to include the joined relationship.

Consider the changes required to the previous example in order to implement the fetch join:

```
SELECT e, a
FROM Employee e JOIN e.address a
```

As the results are processed from this query, the query engine creates the Address entity in memory and assigns it to the Employee entity but then drops it from the result collection that it builds for the client. This eagerly loads the address relationship, which may then get accessed normally via the Employee entity.

A consequence of implementing fetch joins in this way is that fetching a collection association results in duplicate results. For example, consider a department query where the employees relationship of the Department entity is eagerly fetched. The fetch join query, this time using an outer join to ensure that departments without employees are retrieved, would be written as follows:

```
SELECT d
FROM Department d LEFT JOIN FETCH d.employees
```

The actual query executed replaces the fetch with an outer join across the employees relationship:

```
SELECT d, e
FROM Department d LEFT JOIN d.employees e
```

Once again, as the results are processed the Employee entity is constructed in memory but dropped from the result collection. Each Department entity now has a fully resolved employees collection, but the client receives one reference to each department per employee. For example, if four departments with five employees each were retrieved, the result would be a collection of 20 Department instances, with each department duplicated five times. The actual entity instances all point back to the same managed versions, but the results are somewhat odd at the very least.

To eliminate the duplicate values, either the DISTINCT operator must be used or the results must be placed into a data structure such as a Set. Since it is not possible to write a SQL query that uses the DISTINCT operator while preserving the semantics of the fetch join, the provider will have to eliminate duplicates in memory after the results have been fetched. This could have performance implications for large result sets.

Given the somewhat peculiar results generated from a fetch join to a collection, it may not be the most appropriate way to eagerly load related entities in all cases. If a collection requires eager fetching on a regular basis, then it is worth considering making the relationship eager by default. Some persistence providers also offer batch reads as an alternative to fetch joins that issue multiple queries in a single batch and then correlate the results to eagerly load relationships.

The WHERE Clause

The WHERE clause of a query is used to specify filtering conditions to reduce the result set. In this section we will explore the features of the WHERE clause and the types of expressions that can be formed to filter query results.

The definition of the WHERE clause is deceptively simple. It is simply the keyword WHERE, followed by a conditional expression. However, as the following sections demonstrate, JPQL supports a powerful set of conditional expressions to filter the most sophisticated of queries.

Input Parameters

Input parameters for queries may be specified using either positional or named notation. Positional notation is defined by prefixing the variable number with a question mark. Consider the following query:

```
SELECT e
FROM Employee e
WHERE e.salary > ?1
```

Using the Query interface, any double value can be bound into the first parameter in order to indicate the lower bound for employee salaries in this query. The same positional parameter may occur more than once in the query. The value bound into the parameter will be substituted for each of its occurrences.

Named parameters are specified using a colon followed by an identifier. Here is the same query, this time using a named parameter:

```
SELECT e
FROM Employee e
WHERE e.salary > :sal
```

Input parameters were covered in detail in Chapter 6.

Basic Expression Form

Much of the conditional expression support in JPQL is borrowed directly from SQL. This is intentional and serves to ease the transition for developers already familiar with SQL. The key difference between conditional expressions in JPQL and SQL is that JPQL expressions can leverage identification variables and path expressions to navigate relationships during expression evaluation.

Conditional expressions are constructed in the same style as SQL conditional expressions, using a combination of logical operators, comparison expressions, primitive and function operations on fields, and so on. Although a summary of the operators is provided later, the grammar for conditional expressions is not repeated here. The Java Persistence API specification contains the grammar in Backus-Naur form (BNF) and is the place to look for the exact rules about using basic expressions. The following sections do, however, explain the higher-level operators and expressions, particularly those unique to JPQL, and they provide examples for each.

Literal syntax is also similar to SQL. Single quotes are used for string literals and escaped within a string by prefixing the quote with another single quote. Numeric expressions are defined according to the conventions of the Java programming language. Boolean values are represented by the literals TRUE and FALSE. There is no support in the query language for date literals.

Operator precedence is as follows:

1. Navigation operator (.)

2. Unary +/−

3. Multiplication (*) and division (/)

4. Addition (+) and subtraction (−)

5. Comparison operators: =, >, >=, <, <=, <>, [NOT] BETWEEN, [NOT] LIKE, [NOT] IN, IS [NOT] NULL, IS [NOT] EMPTY, [NOT] MEMBER [OF]

6. Logical operators (AND, OR, NOT)

BETWEEN Expressions

The BETWEEN operator may be used in conditional expressions to determine whether or not the result of an expression falls within an inclusive range of values. Numeric, string, and date expressions may be evaluated in this way. Consider the following example:

```
SELECT e
FROM Employee e
WHERE e.salary BETWEEN 40000 AND 45000
```

Any employee making $40,000 to $45,000 inclusively is included in the results. This is identical to the following query using basic comparison operators:

```
SELECT e
FROM Employee e
WHERE e.salary >= 40000 AND e.salary <= 45000
```

The BETWEEN operator may also be negated with the NOT operator.

LIKE Expressions

JPQL supports the SQL LIKE condition to provide for a limited form of string pattern matching. Each LIKE expression consists of a string expression to be searched and a pattern string and optional escape sequence that defines the match conditions. The wildcard characters used by the pattern string are the underscore (_) for single character wildcards and the percent sign (%) for multicharacter wildcards.

```
SELECT d
FROM Department d
WHERE d.name LIKE '__Eng%'
```

Example department names to match this query would be "CAEngOtt" or "USEngCal", but not "CADocOtt". Note that pattern matches are case-sensitive.

If the pattern string contains an underscore or percent sign that should be literally matched, the ESCAPE clause may be used to specify a character that, when prefixing a wildcard character, indicates that it should be treated literally:

```
SELECT d
FROM Department d
WHERE d.name LIKE 'QA\_%' ESCAPE '\'
```

By escaping the underscore, it becomes a mandatory part of the expression. For example, "QA_East" would match, but "QANorth" would not.

Subqueries

Subqueries may be used in the WHERE and HAVING clauses of a query. A subquery is a complete select query inside a pair of parentheses that is embedded within a conditional expression. The results of executing the subquery (which will either be a scalar result or a collection of values) are then evaluated in the context of the conditional expression. Subqueries are a powerful technique for solving the most complex query scenarios.

Consider the following query:

```
SELECT e
FROM Employee e
WHERE e.salary = (SELECT MAX(e.salary)
                  FROM Employee e)
```

This query returns the employee with the highest salary from among all employees. A subquery consisting of an aggregate query (described later in this chapter) is used to return the maximum salary value, and then this result is used as the key to filter the employee list by salary. A subquery may be used in most conditional expressions and may appear on either the left or right side of an expression.

The scope of an identifier variable name begins in the query where it is defined and extends down into any subqueries. Identifiers in the main query may be referenced by a subquery, and identifiers introduced by a subquery may be referenced by any subquery that it creates. If a subquery declares an identifier variable of the same name, then it overrides the parent declaration and prevents the subquery from referring to the parent variable. In the previous example, the declaration of the identification variable e in the subquery overrides the same declaration from the parent query.

■**Note** Overriding an identification variable name in a subquery is not guaranteed to be supported by all providers. Unique names should be used to ensure portability.

The ability to refer to a variable from the main query in the subquery allows the two queries to be correlated. Consider the following example:

```
SELECT e
FROM Employee e
WHERE EXISTS (SELECT p
              FROM Phone p
              WHERE p.employee = e AND p.type = 'Cell')
```

This query returns all of the employees who have a cell phone number. This is also an example of a subquery that returns a collection of values. The EXISTS expression in this example returns true if any results are returned by the subquery. Note that the WHERE clause of the subquery references the identifier variable e from the main query and uses it to filter the subquery results. Conceptually, the subquery can be thought of as executing once for each employee. In practice, many database servers will optimize these types of queries into joins or inline views in order to maximize performance.

This query could also have been written using a join between the Employee and Phone entities with the DISTINCT operator used to filter the results. The advantage in using the correlated subquery is that the main query remains unburdened by joins to other entities. Quite often if a join is used only to filter the results, there is an equivalent subquery condition that may alternately be used in order to remove constraints on the join clause of the main query or even to improve query performance.

The FROM clause of a subquery may also create new identification variables out of path expressions using an identification variable from the main query. For example, the previous query could also have been written as follows:

```
SELECT e
FROM Employee e
WHERE EXISTS (SELECT p
              FROM e.phones p
              WHERE p.type = 'Cell')
```

In this version of the query, the subquery uses the collection association path phones from the Employee identification variable e in the subquery. This is then mapped to a local identification variable p that is used to filter the results by phone type. Each occurrence of p refers to a single phone associated with the employee.

To better illustrate how the translator handles this query, consider the equivalent query written in SQL:

```
SELECT e.id, e.name, e.salary, e.manager_id, e.dept_id, e.address_id
FROM emp e
WHERE EXISTS (SELECT 1
              FROM phone p
              WHERE p.emp_id = e.id AND
                    p.type = 'Cell')
```

The expression e.phones is converted to the table mapped by the Phone entity. The WHERE clause for the subquery then adds the necessary join condition to correlate the subquery to the primary query, in this case the expression p.emp_id = e.id. The join criteria applied to the PHONE table results in all of the phones owned by the related employee. Returning the literal 1 from the subquery is a standard practice with SQL EXISTS expressions because the actual columns selected by the subquery do not matter; only the number of rows is relevant. Because literals are not allowed in the SELECT clause, the entity must still be selected even though it will be ignored when the SQL is generated.

IN Expressions

The IN expression may be used to check whether a single-valued path expression is a member of a collection. The collection may be defined inline as a set of literal values or may be derived from a subquery. The following query demonstrates the literal notation by selecting all of the employees who live in New York or California:

```
SELECT e
FROM Employee e
WHERE e.address.state IN ('NY', 'CA')
```

The subquery form of the expression is similar, replacing the literal list with a nested query. The following query returns employees who work in departments that are contributing to projects beginning with the prefix "QA":

```
SELECT e
FROM Employee e
WHERE e.department IN (SELECT DISTINCT d
                       FROM Department d JOIN d.employees de JOIN de.projects p
                       WHERE p.name LIKE 'QA%')
```

The IN expression may also be negated using the NOT operator. For example, the following query returns all of the Phone entities with a phone number other than office or home:

```
SELECT p
FROM Phone p
WHERE p.type NOT IN ('Office', 'Home')
```

Collection Expressions

The IS EMPTY operator is the logical equivalent of IS NULL for collections. Queries may use the IS EMPTY operator or its negated form IS NOT EMPTY to check whether a collection association path resolves to an empty collection or has at least one value. For example, the following query returns all employees who are managers by virtue of having at least one direct report:

```
SELECT e
FROM Employee e
WHERE e.directs IS NOT EMPTY
```

Note that IS EMPTY expressions are translated to SQL as subquery expressions. The query translator may make use of an aggregate subquery or use the SQL EXISTS expression. Therefore the following query is equivalent to the previous one:

```
SELECT m
FROM Employee m
WHERE (SELECT COUNT(e)
       FROM Employee e
       WHERE e.manager = m) > 0
```

The MEMBER OF operator and its negated form NOT MEMBER OF are a shorthand way of checking whether an entity is a member of or not a member of a collection association path. The following query returns all managers who are incorrectly entered as reporting to themselves:

```
SELECT e
FROM Employee e
WHERE e MEMBER OF e.directs
```

A more typical use of the MEMBER OF operator is in conjunction with an input parameter. For example, the following query selects all employees who are assigned to a designated project:

```
SELECT e
FROM Employee e
WHERE :project MEMBER OF e.projects
```

Like the IS EMPTY expression, the MEMBER OF expression will be translated to SQL using either an EXISTS expression or the subquery form of the IN expression. The previous example is equivalent to the following query:

```
SELECT e
FROM Employee e
WHERE :project IN (SELECT p
                   FROM e.projects p)
```

EXISTS Expressions

The EXISTS condition returns true if a subquery returns any rows. Examples of EXISTS were demonstrated earlier in the introduction to subqueries. The EXISTS operator may also be negated with the NOT operator. The following query selects all employees who do not have a cell phone:

```
SELECT e
FROM Employee e
WHERE NOT EXISTS (SELECT p
                  FROM e.phones p
                  WHERE p.type = 'Cell')
```

ANY, ALL, and SOME Expressions

The ANY, ALL, and SOME operators may be used to compare an expression to the results of a subquery. Consider the following example:

```
SELECT e
FROM Employee e
WHERE e.directs IS NOT EMPTY AND
      e.salary < ALL (SELECT d.salary
                      FROM e.directs d)
```

This query returns all of the managers who are paid less than all of the employees who work for them. The subquery is evaluated, and then each value of the subquery is compared to the left-hand expression, in this case the manager salary. When the ALL operator is used, the comparison between the left side of the equation and all subquery results must be true for the overall condition to be true.

The ANY operator behaves similarly, but the overall condition is true so long as at least one of the comparisons between the expression and the subquery result are true. For example, if ANY were specified instead of ALL in the previous example, then the result of the query would be all of the managers who were paid less than at least one of their employees. The SOME operator is an alias for the ANY operator.

There is symmetry between IN expressions and the ANY operator. Consider the following variation of the project department example used previously:

```
SELECT e
FROM Employee e
WHERE e.department = ANY (SELECT DISTINCT d
                          FROM Department d JOIN d.employees de JOIN de.projects p
                          WHERE p.name LIKE 'QA%')
```

Function Expressions

Conditional expressions may leverage a number of functions that can be used to modify query results in the WHERE and HAVING clauses of a select query. Table 7-1 summarizes the syntax for each of the supported function expressions.

Table 7-1. *Supported Function Expressions*

Function	Description
ABS(*number*)	The ABS function returns the unsigned version of the *number* argument. The result type is the same as the argument type (integer, float, or double).
CONCAT(string1, string2)	The CONCAT function returns a new string that is the concatenation of its arguments, *string1* and *string2*.
CURRENT_DATE	The CURRENT_DATE function returns the current date as defined by the database server.
CURRENT_TIME	The CURRENT_TIME function returns the current time as defined by the database server.

Function	Description
CURRENT_TIMESTAMP	The CURRENT_TIMESTAMP function returns the current timestamp as defined by the database server.
LENGTH(*string*)	The LENGTH function returns the number of characters in the *string* argument.
LOCATE(*string1, string2* [, *start*])	The LOCATE function returns the position of *string2* in *string1*, optionally starting at the position indicated by *start*. The result is zero if the string cannot be found.
LOWER(*string*)	The LOWER function returns the lowercase form of the *string* argument.
MOD(*number1, number2*)	The MOD function returns the modulus of numeric arguments *number1* and *number2* as an integer.
SIZE(*collection*)	The SIZE function returns the number of elements in the collection, or zero if the collection is empty.
SQRT(*number*)	The SQRT function returns the square root of the *number* argument as a double.
SUBSTRING(*string, start, end*)	The SUBSTRING function returns a portion of the input *string*, starting at the index indicated by *start* up to *length* characters. String indexes are measured starting from one.
UPPER(*string*)	The UPPER function returns the uppercase form of the *string* argument.
TRIM([[LEADING|TRAILING|BOTH] [*char*] FROM] *string*)	The TRIM function removes leading and/or trailing characters from a string. If the optional LEADING, TRAILING, or BOTH keyword is not used, then both leading and trailing characters are removed. The default trim character is the space character.

The SIZE function requires special attention, as it is shorthand notation for an aggregate subquery. For example, consider the following query that returns all departments with only two employees:

```
SELECT d
FROM Department d
WHERE SIZE(d.employees) = 2
```

Similar to the collection expressions IS EMPTY and MEMBER OF, the SIZE function will be translated to SQL using a subquery. The equivalent form of the previous example using a subquery is as follows:

```
SELECT d
FROM Department d
WHERE (SELECT COUNT(e)
       FROM d.employees e) = 2
```

The ORDER BY Clause

Queries may optionally be sorted using one or more expressions comprised of identification variables, a path expression resolving to a single entity, or a path expression resolving to a persistent state field. The optional keywords ASC or DESC after the expression may be used to indicate ascending or descending sorts respectively. The default sort order is ascending.

The following example demonstrates sorting by a single field:

```
SELECT e
FROM Employee e
ORDER BY e.name DESC
```

Multiple expressions may also be used to refine the sort order:

```
SELECT e
FROM Employee e JOIN e.department d
ORDER BY d.name, e.name DESC
```

If the SELECT clause of the query uses state field path expressions, then the ORDER BY clause is limited to the same path expressions used in the SELECT clause. For example, the following query is not legal:

```
SELECT e.name
FROM Employee e
ORDER BY e.salary DESC
```

Because the result type of the query is the employee name, which is of type `String`, the remainder of the `Employee` state fields are no longer available for ordering.

Aggregate Queries

An aggregate query is a variation of a normal select query. An aggregate query groups results and applies aggregate functions to obtain summary information about query results. A query is considered an aggregate query if it uses an aggregate function or possesses a GROUP BY clause and/or a HAVING clause. The most typical form of aggregate query involves the use of one or more grouping expressions and aggregate functions in the SELECT clause paired with grouping expressions in the GROUP BY clause. The syntax of an aggregate query is as follows:

```
SELECT <select_expression>
FROM <from_clause>
[WHERE <conditional_expression>]
[GROUP BY <group_by_clause>]
[HAVING <conditional_expression>]
[ORDER BY <order_by_clause>]
```

The SELECT, FROM, and WHERE clauses behave largely the same as previously described under select queries, with the exception of some restrictions on how the SELECT clause is formulated.

The power of an aggregate query comes from the use of aggregate functions over grouped data. Consider the following simple aggregate example:

```
SELECT AVG(e.salary)
FROM Employee e
```

This query returns the average salary of all employees in the company. AVG is an aggregate function that takes a numeric state field path expression as an argument and calculates the average over the group. Because there was no GROUP BY clause specified, the group here is the entire set of employees. This was the only form of aggregate query supported by EJB QL as defined in the EJB 2.1 specification.

Now consider this variation, where the result has been grouped by the department name:

```
SELECT d.name, AVG(e.salary)
FROM Department d JOIN d.employees e
GROUP BY d.name
```

This query returns the names of all departments and the average salary of the employees in that department. The Department entity is joined to the Employee entity across the employees relationship and then formed into a group defined by the department name. The AVG function then calculates its result based on the employee data in this group.

This can be extended further to filter the data so that manager salaries are not included:

```
SELECT d.name, AVG(e.salary)
FROM Department d JOIN d.employees e
WHERE e.directs IS EMPTY
GROUP BY d.name
```

Finally, we can extend this one last time to return only the departments where the average salary is greater than $50,000. Consider the following version of the previous query:

```
SELECT d.name, AVG(e.salary)
FROM Department d JOIN d.employees e
WHERE e.directs IS EMPTY
GROUP BY d.name
HAVING AVG(e.salary) > 50000
```

To better understand this query, let's go through the logical steps that took place to execute it. Databases use many techniques to optimize these types of queries, but conceptually the same process is being followed. First, the following non-grouping query is executed:

```
SELECT d.name, e.salary
FROM Department d JOIN d.employees e
WHERE e.directs IS EMPTY
```

This will produce a result set consisting of all department name and salary value pairs. The query engine then starts a new result set and makes a second pass over the data, collecting all of the salary values for each department name and handing them off to the AVG function. This function then returns the group average, which is then checked against the criteria from the HAVING clause. If the average value is greater than $50,000 then the query engine generates a result row consisting of the department name and average salary value.

The following sections describe the aggregate functions available for use in aggregate queries and the use of the GROUP BY and HAVING clauses.

Aggregate Functions

There are five aggregate functions that may be placed in the select clause of a query: AVG, COUNT, MAX, MIN, and SUM.

AVG

The AVG function takes a state field path expression as an argument and calculates the average value of that state field over the group. The state field type must be numeric, and the result is returned as a Double.

COUNT

The COUNT function takes either an identification variable or a path expression as its argument. This path expression may resolve to a state field or a single-valued association field. The result of the function is a Long value representing the number of values in the group. The argument to the COUNT function may optionally be preceded with the keyword DISTINCT, in which case duplicate values are eliminated before counting.

The following query counts the number of phones associated with each employee as well as the number of distinct number types (cell, office, home, and so on):

```
SELECT e, COUNT(p), COUNT(DISTINCT p.type)
FROM Employee e JOIN e.phones p
GROUP BY e
```

MAX

The MAX function takes a state field expression as an argument and returns the maximum value in the group for that state field.

MIN

The MIN function takes a state field expression as an argument and returns the minimum value in the group for that state field.

SUM

The SUM function takes a state field expression as an argument and calculates the sum of the values in that state field over the group. The state field type must be numeric, and the result type must correspond to the field type. For example, if a Double field is summed, then the result will be returned as a Double. If a Long field is summed, then the response will be returned as a Long.

The GROUP BY Clause

The GROUP BY clause defines the grouping expressions over which the results will be aggregated. A grouping expression must either be a single-valued path expression (state field or single-valued association field) or an identification variable. If an identification variable is used, the entity must not have any serialized state or large object fields.

The following query counts the number of employees in each department:

```
SELECT d.name, COUNT(e)
FROM Department d JOIN d.employees e
GROUP BY d.name
```

Note that the same field expression used in the SELECT clause is repeated in the GROUP BY clause. All non-aggregate expressions must be listed this way. More than one aggregate function may be applied to the same GROUP BY clause:

```
SELECT d.name, COUNT(e), AVG(e.salary)
FROM Department d JOIN d.employees e
GROUP BY d.name
```

This variation of the query calculates the average salary of all employees in each department in addition to counting the number of employees in the department.

Multiple grouping expressions may also be used to further break down the results:

```
SELECT d.name, e.salary, COUNT(p)
FROM Department d JOIN d.employees e JOIN e.projects p
GROUP BY d.name, e.salary
```

Because there are two grouping expressions, the department name and employee salary must be listed in both the SELECT clause and GROUP BY clause. For each department, this query counts the number of projects assigned to employees based on their salary.

In the absence of a GROUP BY clause, the entire query is treated as one group, and the SELECT list may contain only aggregate functions. For example, the following query returns the number of employees and their average salary across the entire company:

```
SELECT COUNT(e), AVG(e.salary)
FROM Employee e
```

The HAVING Clause

The HAVING clause defines a filter to be applied after the query results have been grouped. It is effectively a secondary WHERE clause, and its definition is the same, the keyword HAVING followed by a conditional expression. The key difference with the HAVING clause is that its conditional expressions are limited to state fields or single-valued association fields previously identified in the GROUP BY clause.

Conditional expressions in the HAVING clause may also make use of aggregate functions. In many respects, the primary use of the HAVING clause is to restrict the results based on the aggregate result values. The following query uses this technique to retrieve all employees assigned to two or more projects:

```
SELECT e, COUNT(p)
FROM Employee e JOIN e.projects p
GROUP BY e
HAVING COUNT(p) >= 2
```

Update Queries

Update queries are a new feature in the Java Persistence API. They provide an equivalent to the SQL UPDATE statement but with JPQL conditional expressions. The form of an update query is:

```
UPDATE <entity name> [[AS] <identification variable>]
SET <update_statement> {, <update_statement>}*
[WHERE <conditional_expression>]
```

Each UPDATE statement consists of a single-valued path expression, assignment operator (=), and an expression. Expression choices for the assignment statement are slightly restricted compared to regular conditional expressions. The right side of the assignment must resolve to a literal, simple expression resolving to a basic type, function expression, identification variable, or input parameter. The result type of that expression must be compatible with the simple association path or persistent state field on the left side of the assignment.

The following simple example demonstrates the update query by giving employees who make $55,000 a year a raise to $60,000:

```
UPDATE Employee e
SET e.salary = 60000
WHERE e.salary = 55000
```

The WHERE clause of an UPDATE statement functions the same as a SELECT statement and may use the identification variable defined in the UPDATE clause in expressions. A slightly more complex but more realistic update query would be to award a $5,000 raise to employees who worked on a particular project:

```
UPDATE Employee e
SET e.salary = e.salary + 5000
WHERE EXISTS (SELECT p
              FROM e.projects p
              WHERE p.name = 'Release2')
```

More than one property of the target entity may be modified with a single UPDATE statement. For example, the following query updates the phone exchange for employees in the city of Ottawa and changes the terminology of the phone type from "Office" to "Business":

```
UPDATE Phone p
SET p.number = CONCAT('288', SUBSTRING(p.number, LOCATE(p.number, '-'), 4)),
    p.type = 'Business'
WHERE p.employee.address.city = 'Ottawa' AND
      p.type = 'Office'
```

Delete Queries

Like the update query, the delete query is a new feature in the Java Persistence API. It provides equivalent capability as the SQL DELETE statement but with JPQL conditional expressions. The form of a delete query is:

```
DELETE FROM <entity name> [[AS] <identification variable>]
[WHERE <condition>]
```

The following example demonstrates removes all employees who are not assigned to a department:

```
DELETE FROM Employee e
WHERE e.department IS NULL
```

The WHERE clause for a DELETE statement functions the same as it would for a SELECT statement. All conditional expressions are available to filter the set of entities to be removed. If the WHERE clause is not provided, all entities of the given type are removed.

Delete queries are polymorphic. Any entity subclass instances that meet the criteria of the delete query will also be deleted. Delete queries do not honor cascade rules, however. No entities other than the type referenced in the query and its subclasses will be removed, even if the entity has relationships to other entities with cascade removes enabled.

Summary

In this chapter we have taken a complete tour of the Java Persistence Query Language, looking at the numerous query types and the syntax for each. We covered the history of the language, from its roots in the EJB 2.0 specification to the major enhancements introduced by the Java Persistence API.

In the section on select queries, we explored each query clause and incrementally built up more complex queries as the full syntax was described. We discussed identification variables and path expressions, which are used to navigate through the domain model in query expressions. We also looked at the various conditional expressions supported by the language.

In our discussion of aggregate queries we introduced the additional grouping and filtering clauses that extend select queries. We also demonstrated the various aggregate functions.

In the sections on update and delete queries, we described the full syntax for bulk update and delete statements, the runtime behavior of which was described in the previous chapter.

In the next chapter we switch back to object-relational mapping and cover advanced concepts such as inheritance, composite primary keys and associations, and multiple table mappings.

■■■

CHAPTER 8

Advanced Object-Relational Mapping

Every application is different, and while most have some elements of complexity in them, the difficult parts in one application will tend to be different than those in other types of applications. Chances are that whichever application you are working on at any given time will need to make use of at least one advanced feature of the API. This chapter will introduce and explain some of these more advanced ORM features.

As it turns out, an entity is just one of three different types of persistable classes that can be used with the Java Persistence API. The provider must also manage classes called mapped superclasses and embeddable classes. Collectively we refer to these three types as *managed classes* because they are the classes that must be managed by the provider in order for them to be made persistent.

Some of the features in this chapter are targeted at applications that need to reconcile the differences between an existing data model and an object model. For example, when the data in an entity table would be better decomposed in the object model as an entity and a dependent sub-object that is referenced by the entity, then the mapping infrastructure should be able to support that. Likewise, when the entity data is spread across multiple tables, the mapping layer should allow for this kind of configuration to be specified.

There has been no shortage of discussion in this book about how entities in the Java Persistence API are just regular Java classes and not the heavy persistent objects that were generated by EJB 2.1 entity bean compilers. One of the benefits of entities being regular Java classes is that they can adhere to already established concepts and practices that exist in object-oriented systems. One of the traditional object-oriented innovations is the use of inheritance and creating objects in a hierarchy in order to inherit state and behavior.

This chapter will discuss some of the more advanced mapping features and delve into some of the diverse possibilities offered by the API and the mapping layer. We will see how inheritance works within the framework of the Java Persistence API and how inheritance affects the model.

Embedded Objects

An *embedded object* is one that is dependent upon an entity for its identity. It has no identity of its own but is merely part of the entity state that has been carved off and stored in a separate Java object hanging off of the entity. In Java, embedded objects appear similar to relationships in that they are referenced by an entity and appear in the Java sense to be the target of an asso-ciation. In the database, however, the state of the embedded object is stored with the rest of the entity state in the database row, with no distinction between the state in the Java entity and that in its embedded object.

If the database row contains all of the data for both the entity and its embedded object, why have such an object anyway? Why not just define the fields of the entity to reference all of its persistence state instead of splitting it up into one or more sub-objects that are second-class persistent objects dependent upon the entity for their existence?

This brings us back to the object-relational impedance mismatch. Since the database record contains more than one logical type, it makes sense to make that relationship explicit in the object model of the application even though the physical representation is different. You could almost say that the embedded object is a more natural representation of the domain concept than a simple collection of attributes on the entity. Furthermore, once we have identi-fied a grouping of entity state that makes up an embedded object, we can share the same embedded object type with any other entity that also has the same internal representation.[1]

An example of such reuse might be address information. Figure 8-1 shows an EMPLOYEE table that contains a mixture of basic employee information as well as columns that correspond to the home address of the employee.

EMPLOYEE	
PK	ID
	NAME
	SALARY
	STREET
	CITY
	STATE
	ZIP_CODE

Figure 8-1. EMPLOYEE *table with embedded address information*

The STREET, CITY, STATE, and ZIP_CODE columns combine logically to form the address. In the object model this is an excellent candidate to be abstracted into a separate Address embed-ded type instead of listing each attribute on the entity class itself. The entity class would then simply have an address attribute pointing to an embedded object of type Address. Figure 8-2 shows the relationship between Employee and Address. The UML composition association is used to denote that the Employee wholly owns the Address and that an instance of Address may not be shared by any other object other than the Employee instance that owns it.

With this representation, not only is the address information neatly encapsulated within an object, but if another entity such as Company also has address information, then it can also have an attribute that points to its own embedded Address object. We will describe this scenario in the next section.

---

1. Even though embedded types can be shared or reused, the instances cannot. An embedded object instance belongs to the entity that references it, and no other entity instance, of that entity type or any other, may reference the same embedded instance.

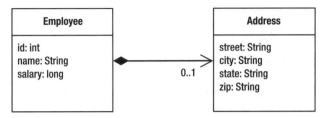

Figure 8-2. Employee *and* Address *relationship*

An embedded type is marked as such by adding the @Embeddable annotation to the class definition. This annotation serves to distinguish the class from other regular Java types. Once a class has been designated as embeddable, then its fields and properties will be persistable as part of an entity. Basic column mappings such as @Basic, @Temporal, @Enumerated, @Lob, and @Column may be added to the attributes of the embedded class, but it may not contain any relationships or other advanced mappings. Listing 8-1 shows the definition of the Address embedded type.

Listing 8-1. *Embeddable Address Type*

```
@Embeddable
public class Address {
    private String street;
    private String city;
    private String state;
    @Column(name="ZIP_CODE")
    private String zip;
    // ...
}
```

To use this class in an entity, the entity must have an attribute of the same type annotated with the @Embedded annotation. Listing 8-2 shows the Employee class using an embedded Address object.

Listing 8-2. *Using an Embedded Object*

```
@Entity
public class Employee {
    @Id private int id;
    private String name;
    private long salary;
    @Embedded private Address address;
    // ...
}
```

When the provider persists an instance of Employee, it will access the attributes of the Address object just as if they were present on the entity instance itself. Column mappings on the Address type really pertain to columns on the EMPLOYEE table, even though they are listed in a different type.

Support for an entity having a collection of embedded objects, an embedded object referencing other embedded objects, or an embedded object having relationships to entities is not in the current version of the Java Persistence API. It is also not portable to use embedded objects as part of inheritance hierarchies. These are features that some persistence providers support and that may be in future versions of the API.

The decision to use embedded objects or entities depends upon whether you think you will ever need to create relationships to them or from them. Embedded objects are not meant to be entities, and as soon as you start to treat them as entities then you should probably make them first-class entities instead of embedded objects if the data model permits it.

Sharing Embedded Object Classes

Before we got to our example we mentioned that an Address class could be reused in both Employee and Company entities. Ideally we would like the representation shown in Figure 8-3. Even though both the Employee and Company classes compose the Address class, this is not a problem, because each instance of Address will be used by only a single Employee or Company instance.

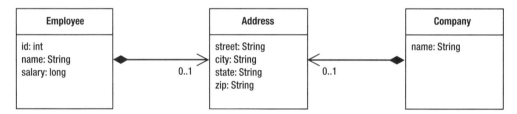

Figure 8-3. *Address shared by two entities*

Given that the column mappings of the Address embedded type apply to the columns of the containing entity, you might be wondering how sharing could be possible in the case where the two entity tables may have different column names for the same fields. Figure 8-4 demonstrates this problem. The COMPANY table matches the default and mapped attributes of the Address type we defined earlier, but the EMPLOYEE table in this example has been changed to match the address requirements of a person living in Canada. We need a way for an entity to map the embedded object according to its own entity table needs, and we have one in the @AttributeOverride annotation.

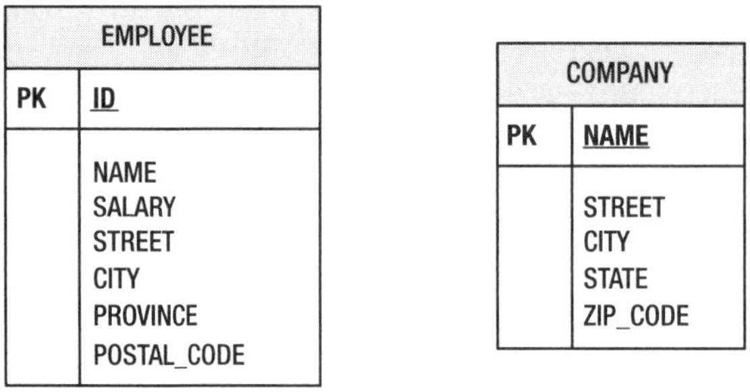

Figure 8-4. EMPLOYEE *and* COMPANY *tables*

We use an @AttributeOverride annotation for each attribute of the embedded object that we want to override in the entity. We annotate the embedded field or property in the entity and specify in the name element the field or property in the embedded object that we are overriding. The column element allows us to specify the column that the attribute is being mapped to in the entity table. We indicate this in the form of a nested @Column annotation. If we are overriding multiple fields or properties, then we can use the plural @AttributeOverrides annotation and nest multiple @AttributeOverride annotations inside of it.

In Listing 8-3 is an example of using Address in both Employee and Company. The Company entity uses the Address type without change, but the Employee entity specifies two attribute overrides to map the state and zip attributes of the Address to the PROVINCE and POSTAL_CODE columns of the EMPLOYEE table.

Listing 8-3. *Reusing an Embedded Object in Multiple Entities*

```
@Entity
public class Employee {
    @Id private int id;
    private String name;
    private long salary;
    @Embedded
    @AttributeOverrides({
        @AttributeOverride(name="state", column=@Column(name="PROVINCE")),
        @AttributeOverride(name="zip", column=@Column(name="POSTAL_CODE"))
    })
    private Address address;
    // ...
}
@Entity
public class Company {
    @Id private String name;
    @Embedded
    private Address address;
    // ...
    }
```

Compound Primary Keys

In some cases an entity needs to have a primary key or identifier that is composed of multiple fields, or from the database perspective the primary key in its table is made up of multiple columns. This is more common for legacy databases and also occurs when a primary key is composed of a relationship, a topic that we will discuss later in this chapter.

We have two options available to us for having compound primary keys in our entity, depending on how we want to structure our entity class. Both of them require that we use a separate class containing the primary key fields called a *primary key class*; the difference between the two options is determined by what the entity class contains.

Primary key classes must include method definitions for equals() and hashCode() in order to be able to stored and keyed upon by the persistence provider, and their fields or properties must be in the set of valid identifier types listed in the previous chapter. They must also be public, implement `Serializable`, and have a no-arg constructor.

As an example of a compound primary key, we will look at the `Employee` entity again, only this time the employee number is specific to the country where he or she works. Two employees in different countries can have the same employee number, but only one can be used within any given country. Figure 8-5 shows the `EMPLOYEE` table structured with a compound primary key to capture this requirement. Given this table definition, we will now look at how to map the `Employee` entity using the two different styles of primary key class.

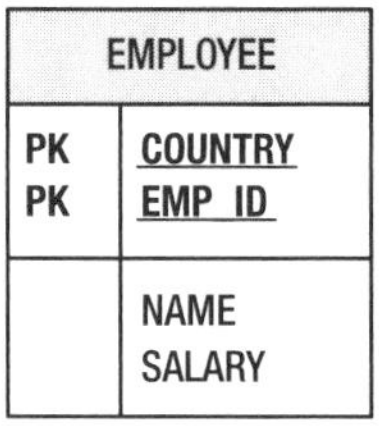

Figure 8-5. `EMPLOYEE` *table with a compound primary key*

Id Class

The first and most basic type of primary key class is an *id class*. Each field of the entity that makes up the primary key is marked with the `@Id` annotation. The primary key class is defined separately and associated with the entity by using the `@IdClass` annotation on the entity class definition. Listing 8-4 demonstrates an entity with a compound primary key that uses an id class.

Listing 8-4. *Using an Id Class*

```
@Entity
@IdClass(EmployeeId.class)
public class Employee {
    @Id private String country;
    @Id
    @Column(name="EMP_ID")
    private int id;
    private String name;
    private long salary;
    // ...
}
```

The primary key class must contain fields or properties that match the primary key attributes in the entity in both name and type. Listing 8-5 shows the `EmployeeId` primary key class. It has two fields, one to represent the country and one to represent the employee number. We have also supplied `equals()` and `hashCode()` methods to allow the class to be used in sorting and hashing operations.

Listing 8-5. *The* EmployeeId *Id Class*

```
public class EmployeeId implements Serializable {
    private String country;
    private int id;

    public EmployeeId() {}
    public EmployeeId(String country, int id) {
      this.country = country;
      this.id = id;
    }

    public String getCountry() { return country; }
    public int getId() { return id; }

    public boolean equals(Object o) {
        return ((o instanceof EmployeeId) &&
                country.equals(((EmployeeId)o).getCountry()) &&
                id == ((EmployeeId)o).getId());
    }

    public int hashCode() {
        return country.hashCode() + id;
    }
}
```

Note that there are no setter methods on the EmployeeId class. Once it has been constructed using the primary key values, it can't be changed. We do this to enforce the notion that a primary key value cannot be changed, even when it is made up of multiple fields. Because the @Id annotation was placed on the fields of the entity, the provider will also use field access when it needs to work with the primary key class.

The id class is useful as a structured object that encapsulates all of the primary key information. For example, when doing a query based upon the primary key, such as the find() method of the EntityManager interface, an instance of the id class can be used as an argument instead of some unstructured and unordered collection of primary key data. Listing 8-6 shows the definition of a method to search for an Employee instance given the name of the country and the employee number. A new instance of the EmployeeId class is constructed using the method arguments and then used as the argument to the find() method.

Listing 8-6. *Invoking a Primary Key Query on an Entity with an Id Class*

```
public Employee findEmployee(String country, int id) {
    return em.find(Employee.class, new EmployeeId(country, id));
}
```

■**Tip** Because the argument to find() is of type Object, vendors may support passing in simple arrays or collections of primary key information. Passing arguments that are not primary key classes is nonportable.

Embedded Id Class

An entity that contains a single field of the same type as the primary key class is said to use an *embedded id class*. The embedded id class is just an embedded object that happens to be composed of the primary key components. Instead of annotating the embedded id class with an @Embedded annotation, though, we use an @EmbeddedId annotation to indicate that it is not just a regular embedded object but also a primary key class. When we use this approach there are no @Id annotations on the class, nor is the @IdClass annotation used. You can think of @EmbeddedId as the logical equivalent to putting both @Id and @Embedded on the field.

Like other embedded objects, the embedded id class must be annotated with @Embeddable, and access type must also match the access type of the entity that uses it. If the entity annotates its fields, then the embedded id class should also annotate its fields if such annotations are required. Listing 8-7 shows the EmployeeId class again, this time as an embeddable primary key class. The getter methods, equals() and hashCode() implementations, are the same as the previous version from Listing 8-5.

Listing 8-7. *Embeddable Primary Key Class*

```
@Embeddable
public class EmployeeId {
    private String country;
    @Column(name="EMP_ID")
    private int id;

    public EmployeeId() {}
    public EmployeeId(String country, int id) {
        this.country = country;
        this.id = id;
    }

    // ...
}
```

Using the embedded primary key class is no different than using a regular embedded type. Listing 8-8 shows the Employee entity adjusted to use the embedded version of the EmployeeId class. Note that since the column mappings are present on the embedded type, we do not specify the mapping for EMP_ID as was done in the case of the id class. If the embedded primary key class is used by more than one entity, then the @AttributeOverride annotation can be used to customize mappings just as you would for a regular embedded type. To return the country and id attributes of the primary key from getter methods, we must delegate to the embedded id object to obtain the values.

Listing 8-8. *Using an Embedded Id Class*

```
@Entity
public class Employee {
    @EmbeddedId private EmployeeId id;
    private String name;
    private long salary;

    public Employee() {}
    public Employee(String country, int id) {
        this.id = new EmployeeId(country, id);
    }

    public String getCountry() { return id.getCountry(); }
    public int getId() { return id.getId(); }
    // ...
}
```

We can create an instance of `EmployeeId` and pass it to the `find()` method just as we did for the id class example, but if we want to create the same query using JPQL and reference the primary key, then we have to traverse the embedded id class explicitly. Listing 8-9 shows this technique. Even though `id` is not a relationship, we still traverse it using the dot notation in order to access the members of the embedded class.

Listing 8-9. *Referencing an Embedded Id Class in a Query*

```
public Employee findEmployee(String country, int id) {
    return (Employee)
        em.createQuery("SELECT e " +
                       "FROM Employee e " +
                       "WHERE e.id.country = ?1 AND e.id.id = ?2")
          .setParameter(1, country)
          .setParameter(2, id)
          .getSingleResult();
}
```

Advanced Mapping Elements

Various other metadata may be specified on the `@Column` and `@JoinColumn` annotations, some of which applies to schema generation that will be discussed in Chapter 9. Other parts we can describe separately as applying to columns and join columns in the following sections.

Read-Only Mappings

The Java Persistence API does not really define any kind of read-only entity, although it will likely show up in a future release. The API does, however, define options to set individual mappings to be read-only using the `insertable` and `updatable` elements of the `@Column` and `@JoinColumn` annotations. These two settings default to true but may be set to false if we want to ensure that the provider will not insert or update information in the table in response to changes in the entity instance. If the data in the mapped table already exists and we want to ensure that it will not be modified at runtime, then the `insertable` and `updatable` elements can be set to false, effectively preventing the provider from doing anything other than reading the entity from the database. Listing 8-10 demonstrates the `Employee` entity with read-only mappings.

Listing 8-10. *Making Entity Mappings Read-Only*

```
@Entity
public class Employee {
    @Id private int id;
    @Column(insertable=false, updatable=false)
    private String name;
    @Column(insertable=false, updatable=false)
    private long salary;

    @ManyToOne
    @JoinColumn(name="DEPT_ID", insertable=false, updatable=false)
    private Department department;
    // ...
}
```

We don't need to worry about the identifier mapping being modified, because it is illegal to modify identifiers. The other mappings, though, are marked as not being able to be inserted or updated, so we are assuming that there are already entities in the database to be read in and used. No new entities will be persisted, and existing entities will never be updated.

Note that this does not guarantee that the entity state will not change in memory. `Employee` instances could still get changed either inside or outside a transaction, but at transaction commit time or whenever the entities get flushed to the database, this state will not be saved. Be careful modifying read-only mappings in memory, however, as changing the entities may cause them to become inconsistent with the state in the database and could wreak havoc on any vendor-specific cache.

Even though all of these mappings are not updatable, the entity as a whole could still be deleted. A proper read-only feature will solve this problem once and for all in a future release.

Optionality

As we will see in Chapter 9 when we talk about schema generation, there exists metadata that either permits the database columns to be null or requires them to have values. While this setting will affect the physical database schema, there are also settings on some of the logical mappings that allow a basic mapping or a single-valued association mapping to be left empty or required to be specified in the object model. The element that requires or permits such behavior is the `optional` element in the `@Basic`, `@ManyToOne`, and `@OneToOne` annotations.

When the `optional` element is specified as false, it indicates to the provider that the field or property mapping may not be null. The API does not actually define what the behavior is in the case when it is, but the provider may choose to throw an exception or simply do something else. For basic mappings, it is only a hint and may be completely ignored. The `optional` element may also be used by the provider when doing schema generation, since if optional is set to true, then the column in the database must also be nullable.

Because the API does not go into any detail about ordinality of the object model, there is a certain amount of nonportability associated with using it. An example of setting the manager to be a required attribute is shown in Listing 8-11. The default value for optional is true, making it necessary to be specified only if a false value is needed.

Listing 8-11. *Using Optional Mappings*

```
@Entity
public class Employee {
    // ...
    @ManyToOne(optional=false)
    @JoinColumn(name="DEPT_ID", insertable=false, updatable=false)
    private Department department;
    // ...
}
```

Advanced Relationships

If your object model is able to dictate your physical schema, then it is likely that you will not need to use many of the advanced relationship features that are offered by the API. The flexibility of being able to define a data model usually makes for a less demanding mapping configuration. It is when the tables are already in place that an object model must work around the data schema and go beyond the rudimentary relationship mappings that we have been using thus far. The following sections describe a few of the more common relationship issues that you may encounter.

Compound Join Columns

Now that we know how to create entities with compound primary keys it is not a far stretch to figure out that as soon as we have a relationship to an entity with a compound identifier, we will need some way to extend the way we currently reference it.

Up to this point we have dealt with the physical relationship mapping only as a join column, but if the primary key that we are referencing is composed of multiple fields, then we will need multiple join columns. This is why we have the plural @JoinColumns annotation that can hold as many join columns as we need to put into it.

There are no default values for join column names when we have multiple join columns. The simplest answer is to simply require that the user assign them, so when multiple join columns are used, both the name element and the referencedColumnName element, which indicates the name of the primary key column in the target table, must be specified.

Now that we are getting into more complex scenarios, let's add a more interesting relationship to the mix. Let's say that employees have managers and that each manager has a number of employees that work for him or her. You may not find that very interesting until you realize that managers are themselves employees, so the join columns are actually self-referential, that is, referring to the same table they are stored in. Figure 8-6 shows the EMPLOYEE table with this relationship.

	EMPLOYEE	
PK PK	<u>COUNTRY</u> <u>EMP_ID</u>	
  FK1 FK1	NAME SALARY MGR_COUNTRY MGR_ID	

Figure 8-6. EMPLOYEE *table with self-referencing compound foreign key*

Listing 8-12 shows a version of the Employee entity that has a manager relationship, which is many-to-one from each of the managed employees to the manager, and a one-to-many directs relationship from the manager to its managed employees.

Listing 8-12. *Self-Referencing Compound Relationships*

```
@Entity
@IdClass(EmployeeId.class)
public class Employee {
    @Id private String country;
    @Id
    @Column(name="EMP_ID")
    private int id;

    @ManyToOne
    @JoinColumns({
        @JoinColumn(name="MGR_COUNTRY", referencedColumnName="COUNTRY"),
        @JoinColumn(name="MGR_ID", referencedColumnName="EMP_ID")
    })
    private Employee manager;

    @OneToMany(mappedBy="manager")
    private Collection<Employee> directs;
    // ...
}
```

Any number of join columns can be specified, although in practice very seldom are there more than two. The plural form of @JoinColumns may be used on many-to-one or one-to-one relationships or more generally whenever the single @JoinColumn annotation is valid.

Another example to consider is in the join table of a many-to-many relationship. We can revisit the Employee and Project relationship described in Chapter 4 to take into account our compound primary key in Employee. The new table structure for this relationship is shown in Figure 8-7.

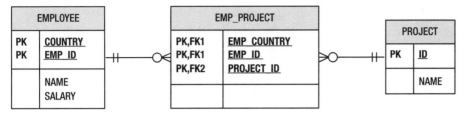

Figure 8-7. *Join table with a compound primary key*

If we keep the Employee entity as the owner, where the join table is defined, then the mapping for this relationship will be as shown in Listing 8-13.

Listing 8-13. *Join Table with Compound Join Columns*

```
@Entity
@IdClass(EmployeeId.class)
public class Employee {
    @Id private String country;
    @Id
    @Column(name="EMP_ID")
    private int id;

    @ManyToMany
    @JoinTable(
        name="EMP_PROJECT",
        joinColumns={
            @JoinColumn(name="EMP_COUNTRY", referencedColumnName="COUNTRY"),
            @JoinColumn(name="EMP_ID", referencedColumnName="EMP_ID")},
        inverseJoinColumns=@JoinColumn(name="PROJECT_ID"))
    private Collection<Project> projects;
    // ...
}
```

Identifiers That Include a Relationship

It is possible for a compound primary key to actually include a relationship, which implies that the object cannot exist without participating in the relationship that is part of its identifier. Being that primary key fields may not be changed once they have been set, a relationship that is part of a primary key is likewise immutable. Such a relationship must be set in order for the entity to be created and must not be changed once the entity exists.

To demonstrate, let's reconsider our Project entity. Instead of having a unique numeric identifier, it will now consist of a name and a reference to the Department entity. Multiple projects of the same name may exist, but only one name can be used with a given department. Figure 8-8 shows the data model for this relationship.

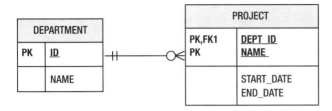

Figure 8-8. *Compound primary key with a foreign key dependency*

We first need to create a primary key class that will store the compound primary key. This primary key class will not contain the relationship mapping. Instead, it will just contain the basic mappings for the actual primary key columns. Listing 8-14 shows the `ProjectId` id class.

Listing 8-14. *The* `ProjectId` *Id Class*

```
public class ProjectId implements Serializable {
    private int deptId;
    private String name;

    public ProjectId() {}
    public ProjectId(int deptId, String name) {
        this.deptId = deptId;
        this.name = name;
    }
    // ...
}
```

Now we can update the `Project` entity to reference the `ProjectId` id class and declare the compound primary key. Listing 8-15 shows the `Project` entity. Note that we are placing the `@Id` annotations on the basic attributes, not on the relationship. We have introduced an `@ManyToOne` relationship to the `Department` entity that maps to the same `DEPT_ID` column as the `deptId` basic mapping. Because the basic mapping has been changed so that it is not insertable or updatable, it will be ignored when the entity is persisted. Instead, the foreign key mapped by the department relationship will be inserted into the `DEPT_ID` column. Structuring it in this way prevents the two mappings from colliding with each other when the provider writes entity changes to the database.

Listing 8-15. *Primary Key That Includes a Relationship*

```
@Entity
@IdClass(ProjectId.class)
public class Project {
    @Id
    @Column(name="DEPT_ID", insertable=false, updatable=false)
    private int deptId;
    @Id private String name;
```

```
@ManyToOne
@JoinColumn(name="DEPT_ID")
private Department department;

@Temporal(TemporalType.DATE)
@Column(name="START_DATE")
private Date startDate;
@Temporal(TemporalType.DATE)
@Column(name="END_DATE")
private Date endDate;
// ...
}
```

■Tip Support for primary keys that include relationships or foreign keys is not explicitly mentioned in the current version of the Java Persistence API even though the specifics of doing so are not disallowed. It may be that some vendors will not support the duplicate mapping case that is described in this section or that a slightly different mapping practice from the one described here is required.

Mapping Relationship State

There are times when a relationship actually has state associated with it. For example, let's say that we want to maintain the date an employee was assigned to work on a project. Storing the state on the employee is possible but less helpful, since the date is really coupled to the employee's relationship to a particular project (a single entry in the many-to-many association). Taking an employee off of a project should really just cause the assignment date to go away, so storing it as part of the employee means that we have to ensure that the two are consistent with each other, which is kind of bothersome. In UML, we would show this kind of relationship using an association class. Figure 8-9 shows an example of this technique.

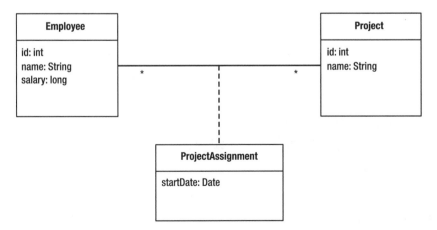

Figure 8-9. *Modeling state on a relationship using an association class*

In the database everything is rosy, since we can simply add a column to the join table. The data model provides natural support for relationship state. Figure 8-10 shows the many-to-many relationship between EMPLOYEE and PROJECT with an expanded join table.

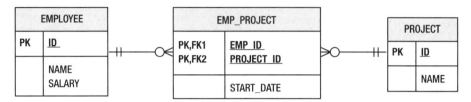

Figure 8-10. *Join table with additional state*

When we get to the object model, however, it becomes much more problematic. The issue is that Java has no inherent support for relationship state. Relationships are just object references or pointers, hence no state can ever exist on them. State exists on objects only, and relationships are not first-class objects.

The Java solution is to turn the relationship into an entity that contains the desired state and map the new entity to what was previously the join table. The new entity will have a many-to-one relationship to each of the existing entity types, and each of the entity types will have a one-to-many relationship back to the new entity representing the relationship. The primary key of the new entity will be the combination of the two relationships to the two entity types. Listing 8-16 shows all of the participants in the Employee and Project relationship.

Listing 8-16. *Mapping Relationship State with an Intermediate Entity*

```
@Entity
public class Employee {
    @Id private int id;
    // ...
    @OneToMany(mappedBy="employee")
    private Collection<ProjectAssignment> assignments;
    // ...
}

@Entity
public class Project {
    @Id private int id;
    // ...
    @OneToMany(mappedBy="project")
    private Collection<ProjectAssignment> assignments;
    // ...
}

@Entity
@Table(name="EMP_PROJECT")
@IdClass(ProjectAssignmentId.class)
```

```
public class ProjectAssignment {
    @Id
    @Column(name="EMP_ID", insertable=false, updatable=false)
    private int empId;
    @Id
    @Column(name="PROJECT_ID", insertable=false, updatable=false)
    private int projectId;

    @ManyToOne
    @JoinColumn(name="EMP_ID")
    private Employee employee;
    @ManyToOne
    @JoinColumn(name="PROJECT_ID")
    private Project project;

    @Temporal(TemporalType.DATE)
    @Column(name="START_DATE", updatable=false)
    private Date startDate;
    // ...
}

public class ProjectAssignmentId implements Serializable {
    private int empId;
    private int projectId;
    // ...
}
```

Here we have the two foreign key columns making up the primary key in the EMP_PROJECT join table, so in reality the primary key is actually entirely composed of relationships. The date at which the assignment was made could be manually set when the assignment is created, or it could be associated with a trigger that causes it to be set when the assignment is created in the database. Note that if a trigger were used, then the entity would need to be refreshed from the database in order to populate the assignment date field in the Java object.

Multiple Tables

The most common mapping scenarios are of the so-called *meet-in-the-middle* variety. This means that the data model and the object model already exist, or if one does not exist, then it is not created based on requirements from the other model. This is relevant because there are a number of features in the Java Persistence API that attempt to address concerns that arise in this case.

Up to this point we have assumed that an entity gets mapped to a single table and that a single row in that table represents an entity. In an existing or legacy data model, it was actually quite common to spread data, even data that was tightly coupled, across multiple tables. This was done for different administrative as well as performance reasons, one of which was to decrease table contention when specific subsets of the data were accessed or modified.

To account for this, entities may be mapped across multiple tables by making use of the @SecondaryTable annotation and its plural @SecondaryTables form. We call the default table or the table defined by the @Table annotation the *primary table* and any additional ones *secondary tables*. We can then distribute the data in an entity across rows in both the primary table and the secondary tables simply by defining the secondary tables as annotations on the entity and then specifying when we map each field or property which table the column is in. We do this by specifying the name of the table in the table element in @Column or @JoinColumn. We did not need to use this element earlier, because the default value of table is the name of the primary table.

The only bit that is left is to specify how to join the secondary table or tables to the primary table. We saw in Chapter 4 how the primary key join column is a special case of a join column where the join column is just the primary key column (or columns in the case of composite primary keys). Support for joining secondary tables to the primary table is limited to primary key join columns and is specified as an @PrimaryKeyJoinColumn annotation as part of the @SecondaryTable annotation.

To demonstrate the use of a secondary table, consider the data model shown in Figure 8-11. There is a primary key relationship between the EMP and EMP_ADDRESS tables. The EMP table stores the primary employee information, while address information has been moved to the EMP_ADDRESS table.

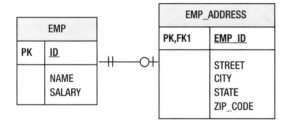

Figure 8-11. EMP *and* EMP_ADDRESS *tables*

To map this table structure to the Employee entity, we must declare EMP_ADDRESS as a secondary table and use the table element of the @Column annotation for every attribute stored in that table. Listing 8-17 shows the mapped entity. The primary key of the EMP_ADDRESS table is in the EMP_ID column. If it had been named ID then we would not have needed to use the name element in the @PrimaryKeyJoinColumn annotation. It defaults to the name of the primary key column in the primary table.

Listing 8-17. *Mapping an Entity Across Two Tables*

```
@Entity
@Table(name="EMP")
@SecondaryTable(name="EMP_ADDRESS",
    pkJoinColumns=@PrimaryKeyJoinColumn(name="EMP_ID"))
public class Employee {
    @Id private int id;
    private String name;
    private long salary;
```

```
    @Column(table="EMP_ADDRESS")
    private String street;
    @Column(table="EMP_ADDRESS")
    private String city;
    @Column(table="EMP_ADDRESS")
    private String state;
    @Column(name="ZIP_CODE", table="EMP_ADDRESS")
    private String zip;
    // ...
}
```

In Chapter 4 we learned how to use the schema or catalog elements in @Table to qualify the primary table to be in a particular database schema or catalog. This is also valid in the @SecondaryTable annotation.

Previously when discussing embedded objects, we mapped the address fields of the Employee entity into an Address embedded type. With the address data in a secondary table, it is still possible to do this by specifying the mapped table name as part of the column information in the @AttributeOverride annotation. Listing 8-18 demonstrates this approach. Note that we have to enumerate all of the fields in the embedded type even though the column names may match the correct default values.

Listing 8-18. *Mapping an Embedded Type to a Secondary Table*

```
@Entity
@Table(name="EMP")
@SecondaryTable(name="EMP_ADDRESS",
                pkJoinColumns=@PrimaryKeyJoinColumn(name="EMP_ID"))
public class Employee {
    @Id private int id;
    private String name;
    private long salary;
    @Embedded
    @AttributeOverrides({
        @AttributeOverride(name="street", column=@Column(table="EMP_ADDRESS")),
        @AttributeOverride(name="city", column=@Column(table="EMP_ADDRESS")),
        @AttributeOverride(name="state", column=@Column(table="EMP_ADDRESS")),
        @AttributeOverride(name="zip",
                           column=@Column(name="ZIP_CODE", table="EMP_ADDRESS"))
    })
    private Address address;
    // ...
}
```

Let's consider a more complex example involving multiple tables and compound primary keys. Figure 8-12 shows the table structure we wish to map. In addition to the EMPLOYEE table, we have two secondary tables, ORG_STRUCTURE and EMP_LOB. The ORG_STRUCTURE table stores employee and manger reporting information. The EMP_LOB table stores large objects that are infrequently fetched during normal query options. Moving large objects to a secondary table is a common design technique in many database schemas.

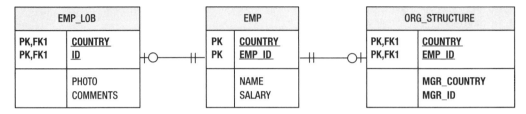

Figure 8-12. *Secondary tables with compound primary key relationships*

Listing 8-19 shows the Employee entity mapped to this table structure. We have reused the EmployeeId id class from Listing 8-5 in this example.

Listing 8-19. *Mapping an Entity with Multiple Secondary Tables*

```
@Entity
@IdClass(EmployeeId.class)
@SecondaryTables({
    @SecondaryTable(name="ORG_STRUCTURE", pkJoinColumns={
        @PrimaryKeyJoinColumn(name="COUNTRY", referencedColumnName="COUNTRY"),
        @PrimaryKeyJoinColumn(name="EMP_ID", referencedColumnName="EMP_ID")})
    @SecondaryTable(name="EMP_LOB", pkJoinColumns={
        @PrimaryKeyJoinColumn(name="COUNTRY", referencedColumnName="COUNTRY"),
        @PrimaryKeyJoinColumn(name="ID", referencedColumnName="EMP_ID")})
})
public class Employee {
    @Id private String country;
    @Id
    @Column(name="EMP_ID")
    private int id;

    @Basic(fetch=FetchType.LAZY)
    @Lob
    @Column(table="EMP_LOB")
    private byte[] photo;

    @Basic(fetch=FetchType.LAZY)
    @Lob
    @Column(table="EMP_LOB")
    private char[] comments;
```

```
@ManyToOne
@JoinColumns({
    @JoinColumn(name="MGR_COUNTRY", referencedColumnName="COUNTRY",
                table="ORG_STRUCTURE"),
    @JoinColumn(name="MGR_ID", referencedColumnName="EMP_ID",
                table="ORG_STRUCTURE")
})
private Employee manager;
// ...
}
```

We have thrown a few curves into this example to make it more interesting. The first is that we have defined Employee to have a composite primary key. This requires additional information to be provided for the EMP_LOB table, because its primary key is not named the same as the primary table. The next difference is that we are storing a relationship in the ORG_STRUCTURE secondary table. The MGR_COUNTRY and MGR_ID columns combine to reference the id of the manager for this employee. Since the employee has a composite primary key, the manager relationship must also specify a set of join columns instead of only one, and the referencedColumnName elements in those join columns refer to the primary key columns COUNTRY and EMP_ID in the entity's own primary table EMPLOYEE.

Inheritance

One of the common mistakes made by novice object-oriented developers is that they catch the vision of reuse and create complex inheritance hierarchies all for the sake of sharing a few methods. This will often lead to pain and hardship down the road as the application becomes difficult to debug and a challenge to maintain.

Most applications do enjoy the benefits of at least some inheritance in the object model. As with most things, moderation should be used, however, especially when it comes to mapping the classes to relational databases. Large hierarchies can often lead to significant performance reduction, and it may be that the cost of code reuse is higher than what you might want to pay.

In the following sections we will explain the support that exists in the API to map inheritance hierarchies and outline some of the repercussions.

Class Hierarchies

Being that this is a book about the Java Persistence API, the first and most obvious place to start talking about inheritance is in the Java object model. Entities are objects, after all, and should be able to inherit state and behavior from other entities. This is not only expected but also essential for the development of object-oriented applications.

What does it mean when one entity inherits state from its entity superclass? It may imply different things in the data model, but in the Java model it simply means that when a subclass entity is instantiated, then it has its own version or copy of both its locally defined state and its inherited state, all of which is persistent. While this basic premise is not at all surprising, it introduces the less obvious notion of what happens when an entity inherits from something other than another entity. Which classes is an entity allowed to extend, and what happens when it does?

Consider the class hierarchy shown in Figure 8-13. As we saw in Chapter 1 there are a number of ways that class inheritance can be represented in the database. In the object model there may even be a number of different ways to implement a hierarchy, some of which may include non-entity classes. We will use this example as we explore ways to persist inheritance hierarchies in the sections that follow.

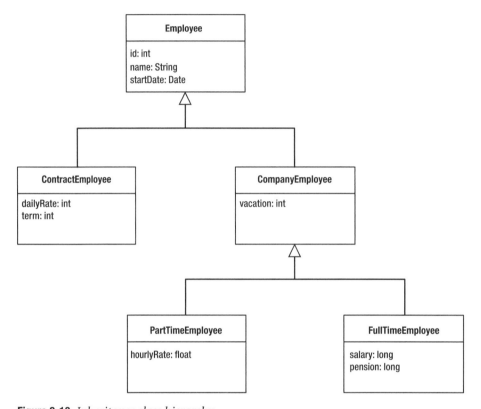

Figure 8-13. *Inheritance class hierarchy*

We differentiate between a class hierarchy, which is a set of various types of Java classes that extend each other in a tree, and an entity hierarchy, which is a tree consisting of persistent entity classes interspersed with non-entity classes. An entity hierarchy is rooted at the first entity class in the hierarchy.

Mapped Superclasses

The Java Persistence API defines a special kind of class called a *mapped superclass* that is quite useful as a superclass for entities. A mapped superclass provides a convenient class on which to store shared state and behavior that entities can inherit from, but it is itself not a persistent class and cannot act in the capacity of an entity. It cannot be queried over and cannot be the target of a relationship. Annotations such as @Table are not permitted on mapped superclasses since the state defined in them applies only to its entity subclasses.

Mapped superclasses can be compared to entities in somewhat the same way that an abstract class is compared to a concrete class; they can contain state and behavior but just can't be instantiated as persistent entities. An abstract class is of use only in relation to its concrete subclasses, and a mapped superclass is useful only as state and behavior that is inherited by the entity subclasses that extend it. They do not play a role in an entity inheritance hierarchy other than contributing that state and behavior to the entities that inherit from them.

Mapped superclasses may or may not be defined as abstract in their class definitions, but it is good practice to make them actual abstract Java classes. We don't know of any good use cases for creating concrete Java instances of them without ever being able to persist them, and chances are that if you happen to find one, then you probably want the mapped superclass to be an entity.

All of the default mapping rules that apply to entities also apply to the basic and relationship state in mapped superclasses. The biggest advantage of using mapped superclasses is being able to define partial shared state that should not be accessed on its own without the additional state that its entity subclasses add to it. If you are not sure whether to make a class an entity or a mapped superclass, then you need only ask yourself if you will ever need to query across or access an instance that is only exposed as an instance of that mapped class. This also includes relationships, since a mapped superclass can't be used as the target of a relationship. If you answer yes to any variant of that question, then you should probably make it a first class entity.

If we look back at Figure 8-13 we could conceivably treat the CompanyEmployee class as a mapped superclass instead of an entity. It defines shared state, but perhaps we have no reason to query over it.

A class is indicated as being a mapped superclass by annotating it with the @MappedSuperclass annotation. The class fragments from Listing 8-20 show how the hierarchy would be mapped with CompanyEmployee as a mapped superclass.

Listing 8-20. *Entities Inheriting from a Mapped Superclass*

```
@Entity
public class Employee {
    @Id private int id;
    private String name;
    @Temporal(TemporalType.DATE)
    @Column(name="S_DATE")
    private Date startDate;
    // ...
}

@Entity
public class ContractEmployee extends Employee {
    @Column(name="D_RATE")
    private int dailyRate;
    private int term;
    // ...
}
```

```
@MappedSuperclass
public abstract class CompanyEmployee extends Employee {
    private int vacation;
    // ...
}

@Entity
public class FullTimeEmployee extends CompanyEmployee {
    private long salary;
    private long pension;
    // ...
}

@Entity
public class PartTimeEmployee extends CompanyEmployee {
    @Column(name="H_RATE")
    private float hourlyRate;
    // ...
}
```

Transient Classes in the Hierarchy

We call classes in an entity hierarchy that are not entities or mapped superclasses *transient classes*. Entities may extend transient classes either directly or indirectly through a mapped superclass. When an entity inherits from a transient class, then the state defined in the transient class is still inherited in the entity, but it is not persistent. In other words, the entity will have space allocated for the inherited state, according to the usual Java rules, but that state will not be managed by the persistence provider. It will be effectively ignored during the life cycle of the entity. The entity may manage that state manually through the use of lifecycle callback methods that we describe in Chapter 9, or other approaches, but the state will not be persisted as part of the provider-managed entity life cycle.

One could conceive of having a hierarchy that is composed of an entity that has a transient subclass, which in turn has one or more entity subclasses. While this case is not really a common one, it is nonetheless possible and can be achieved in the rare circumstances when having shared transient state or common behavior is desired. It would normally be more convenient, though, to declare the transient state or behavior in the entity superclass than to create an intermediate transient class. Listing 8-21 shows an entity that inherits from a superclass that defines transient state that is the time an entity was created in memory.

Listing 8-21. *Entity Inheriting from a Transient Superclass*

```java
public abstract class CachedEntity {
    private long createTime;

    public CachedEntity() { createTime = System.currentTimeMillis(); }

    public long getCacheAge() { return System.currentTimeMillis() - createTime; }
}

@Entity
public class Employee extends CachedEntity {
    public Employee() { super(); }
    // ...
}
```

In this example we moved the transient state from the entity class into a transient superclass, but the end result is really quite the same. The previous example might have been a little neater without the extra class, but this example allows us to share the transient state and behavior across any number of entities that need only extend CachedEntity.

Abstract and Concrete Classes

We have mentioned the notion of abstract versus concrete classes in the context of mapped superclasses, but we didn't go into any more detail about entity and transient classes. Most people, depending upon their philosophy, might expect that all non-leaf classes in an object hierarchy should be abstract, or at the very least that some of them would be. A restriction that entities always be concrete classes would mess this up quite handily, and fortunately this is not the case. It is perfectly acceptable for entities, mapped superclasses, or transient classes to be either abstract or concrete at any level of the inheritance tree. Like mapped superclasses, making transient classes concrete in the hierarchy doesn't really serve any purpose and as a general rule should be avoided.

The case that we have not talked about is the one where an entity is an abstract class. The only difference between an entity that is an abstract class and one that is a concrete class is the Java rule that prohibits abstract classes from being instantiated. They can still define persistent state and behavior that will be inherited by the concrete entity subclasses below them. They can be queried, the result of which will be composed of concrete entity subclass instances. They can also bear the inheritance mapping metadata for the hierarchy.

Our hierarchy in Figure 8-13 had an Employee class that was a concrete class. It does not make any sense to instantiate this class, so we would likely want it to be abstract. We would then end up with all of our non-leaf classes being abstract and the leaf classes being persistent.

Inheritance Models

The Java Persistence API provides support for three different data representations. The use of two of them is fairly widespread, while the third is less common and not required to be supported, though it is still fully defined with the intention that it be required to be supported by providers in the future.

When an entity hierarchy exists, it is always rooted at an entity class. Recall that mapped superclasses do not count as levels in the hierarchy since they contribute only to the entities beneath them. The root entity class must signify the inheritance hierarchy by being annotated with the @Inheritance annotation. This annotation indicates the strategy that should be used for mapping and must be one of the three strategies described in the following sections.

Every entity in the hierarchy must either define or inherit its identifier, which means that the identifier must be defined either in the root entity or in a mapped superclass above it. A mapped superclass may be higher up in the class hierarchy than where the identifier is defined.

Single-Table Strategy

The most common and performant way of storing the state of multiple classes is to define a single table to contain a superset of all of the possible state in any of the entity classes. This approach is called, not surprisingly, a *single-table* strategy. It has the consequence that for any given table row representing an instance of a concrete class, there may be columns that do not have values because they apply only to a sibling class in the hierarchy.

From Figure 8-13 we see that the id is located in the root Employee entity class and is shared by the rest of the persistence classes. All of the persistent entities in an inheritance tree must use the same type of identifier. We don't need to think about it very long before we see why this makes sense at both levels. In the object layer it wouldn't be possible to issue a polymorphic find() operation on a superclass if there were not a common identifier type that we could pass in. Similarly at the table level we would need multiple primary key columns but without being able to fill them all in on any given insertion of an instance that only made use of one of them.

The table must contain enough columns to store all of the state in all of the classes. An individual row stores the state of an entity instance of a concrete entity type, which would normally imply that there would be some columns left unfilled in every row. Of course this leads to the conclusion that the columns mapped to concrete subclass state should be nullable, which is normally not a big issue but could be a problem for some database administrators.

In general, the single-table approach tends to be more wasteful of database tablespace, but it does offer peak performance for both polymorphic queries and write operations. The SQL that is needed to issue these operations is simple, optimized, and does not require joining.

To specify the single-table strategy for the inheritance hierarchy, the root entity class is annotated with the @Inheritance annotation with its strategy set to SINGLE_TABLE. In our previous model this would mean annotating the Employee class as follows:

```
@Entity
@Inheritance(strategy=InheritanceType.SINGLE_TABLE)
public abstract class Employee { ... }
```

As it turns out, though, the single-table strategy is the default one, so we wouldn't strictly even need to include the strategy element at all. An empty @Inheritance annotation, or even no @Inheritance annotation at all, would work just just as well.

In Figure 8-14 we see the single-table representation of our Employee hierarchy model. In terms of the table structure and schema architecture for the single-table strategy, it makes no difference whether CompanyEmployee is a mapped superclass or an entity.

EMPLOYEE	
PK	ID
	NAME
	S_DATE
	D_RATE
	TERM
	VACATION
	H_RATE
	SALARY
	PENSION
	EMP_TYPE

Figure 8-14. *A single-table inheritance data model*

Discriminator Column

You may have noticed an extra column named EMP_TYPE in Figure 8-13 that was not mapped to any field in any of the classes. This field has a special purpose and is required when using a single table to model inheritance. It is called a *discriminator column* and is mapped using the @DiscriminatorColumn annotation in conjunction with the @Inheritance annotation we have already learned about. The name element of this annotation specifies the name of the column that should be used as the discriminator column, and if not specified will be defaulted to a column named DTYPE.

A discriminatorType element dictates the type of the discriminator column. Some applications prefer to use strings to discriminate between the entity types, while others like using integer values to indicate the class. The type of the discriminator column may be one of three predefined discriminator column types: INTEGER, STRING, or CHAR. If the discriminatorType element is not specified, then the default type of STRING will be assumed.

Discriminator Value

Every row in the table will have a value in the discriminator column called a *discriminator value*, or a *class indicator*, to indicate the type of entity that is stored in that row. Every concrete entity in the inheritance hierarchy, therefore, needs a discriminator value specific to that entity type so that the provider can process or assign the correct entity type when it loads and stores the row. The way this is done is to use an @DiscriminatorValue annotation on each concrete entity class. The string value in the annotation specifies the discriminator value that instances of the class will get assigned when they are inserted into the database. This will allow the provider to recognize instances of the class when it issues queries. This value should be of the same type as was specified or defaulted as the discriminatorType element in the @DiscriminatorColumn annotation.

If no `@DiscriminatorValue` annotation is specified, then the provider will use a provider-specific way of obtaining the value. If the `discriminatorType` was `STRING`, then the provider will just use the entity name as the class indicator string. If the `discriminatorType` is `INTEGER`, then we would either have to specify the discriminator values for every entity class or none of them. If we were to specify some but not others, then we could not guarantee that a provider-generated value would not overlap with one that we specified.

Listing 8-22 shows how our `Employee` hierarchy is mapped to a single-table strategy.

Listing 8-22. *Entity Hierarchy Mapped Using Single-Table Strategy*

```
@Entity
@Table(name="EMP")
@Inheritance
@DiscriminatorColumn(name="EMP_TYPE")
public abstract class Employee { ... }

@Entity
public class ContractEmployee extends Employee { ... }

@MappedSuperclass
public abstract class CompanyEmployee extends Employee { ... }

@Entity
@DiscriminatorValue("FTEmp")
public class FullTimeEmployee extends CompanyEmployee { ... }

@Entity(name="PTEmp")
public class PartTimeEmployee extends CompanyEmployee { ... }
```

The `Employee` class is the root class, so it establishes the inheritance strategy and discriminator column. We have assumed the default strategy of `SINGLE_TABLE` and discriminator type of `STRING`.

Neither the `Employee` nor the `CompanyEmployee` classes have discriminator values, because discriminator values should not be specified for abstract entity classes, mapped superclasses, transient classes, or any abstract classes for that matter. Only concrete entity classes use discriminator values since they are the only ones that actually get stored and retrieved from the database.

The `ContractEmployee` entity does not use an `@DiscriminatorValue` annotation, because the default string "ContractEmployee", which is the default entity name that is given to the class, is just what we want. The `FullTimeEmployee` class explicitly lists its discriminator value to be "FTEmp", so that is what is stored in each row for instances of `FullTimeEmployee`. Meanwhile, the `PartTimeEmployee` class will get "PTEmp" as its discriminator value since it set its entity name to be "PTEmp", and that is the name that gets used as the discriminator value when none is specified.

In Figure 8-15 we can see a sample of some of the data that we might find given the earlier model and settings. We can see from the `EMP_TYPE` discriminator column that there are three different types of concrete entities. We also see null values in the columns that do not apply to an entity instance.

EMPLOYEE

ID	NAME	S_DATE	D_RATE	TERM	VACATION	H_RATE	SALARY	PENSION	EMP_TYPE
1	John	020101	500	12					ContractEmployee
2	Paul	020408	600	24					ContractEmployee
3	Sarah	030610	700	18					ContractEmployee
4	Patrick	040701			15		55000	100000	FTEmp
5	Joan	030909			15		59000	200000	FTEmp
6	Sam	000312			20		60000	450000	FTEmp
7	Mark	041101			15	17.00			PTEmp
8	Ryan	051205			15	16.00			PTEmp
9	Jackie	060103			10	15.00			PTEmp

Figure 8-15. *Sample of single-table inheritance data*

Joined Strategy

From the perspective of a Java developer, a data model that maps each entity to its own table makes a lot of sense. Every entity, whether it is abstract or concrete, will have its state mapped to a different table. Consistent with our earlier description, mapped superclasses do not get mapped to their own tables but are mapped as part of their entity subclasses.

Mapping a table per entity provides the data reuse that a *normalized*[2] data schema offers and is the most efficient way to store data that is shared by multiple subclasses in a hierarchy. The problem is that when it comes time to reassemble an instance of any of the subclasses, the tables of the subclasses must be joined together with the superclass tables. It makes fairly obvious the reason why this strategy is called the *joined* strategy. It is also somewhat more expensive to insert an entity instance, because a row must be inserted in each of its superclass tables along the way.

Recall from the single-table strategy that the identifier must be of the same type for every class in the hierarchy. In a joined approach we will have the same type of primary key in each of the tables, and the primary key of a subclass table also acts as a foreign key that joins to its superclass table. This should ring a bell because of its similarity to the multiple-table case earlier in the chapter where we joined the tables together using the primary keys of the tables and used the @PrimaryKeyJoinColumn annotation to indicate it. We use this same annotation in the joined inheritance case since we have multiple tables that each contain the same primary key type and each potentially has a row that contributes to the final combined entity state.

While joined inheritance is both intuitive and efficient in terms of data storage, the joining that it requires makes it somewhat expensive to use when hierarchies are deep or wide. The deeper the hierarchy the more joins it will take to assemble instances of the concrete entity at the bottom. The broader the hierarchy the more joins it will take to query across an entity superclass.

In Figure 8-16 we see our Employee example mapped to a joined table architecture. The data for an entity subclass is spread across the tables in the same way that it is spread across the class hierarchy. When using a joined architecture, the decision as to whether CompanyEmployee

---

2. Normalization of data is a database practice that attempts to remove redundantly stored data. For the seminal paper on data normalization, see "A Relational Model of Data for Large Shared Databanks" by E. F. Codd (*Communications of the ACM*, 13(6) June 1970). Also, any database design book or paper should have an overview.

is a mapped superclass or an entity makes a difference, since mapped superclasses do not get mapped to tables. An entity, even if it is an abstract class, always does. Figure 8-13 shows it as a mapped superclass, but if it were an entity then an additional COMPANY_EMP table would exist with ID and VACATION columns in it, and the VACATION column in the FT_EMP and PT_EMP tables would not be present.

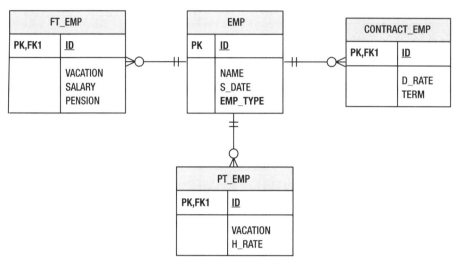

Figure 8-16. *Joined inheritance data model*

To map an entity hierarchy to a joined model, the @Inheritance annotation need only specify JOINED as the strategy. Like the single-table example, the subclasses will adopt the same strategy that is specified in the root entity superclass.

Even though there are multiple tables to model the hierarchy, the discriminator column is only defined on the root table, so the @DiscriminatorColumn annotation is placed on the same class as the @Inheritance annotation.

■**Tip** Some vendors offer implementations of joined inheritance without the use of a discriminator column. Discriminator columns should be used if portability is required.

Our Employee hierarchy example can be mapped using the joined approach shown in Listing 8-23. In this example we have used integer discriminator columns instead of the default string type.

Listing 8-23. *Entity Hierarchy Mapped Using the Joined Strategy*

```
@Entity
@Table(name="EMP")
@Inheritance(strategy=InheritanceType.JOINED)
@DiscriminatorColumn(name="EMP_TYPE", discriminatorType=DiscriminatorType.INTEGER)
public abstract class Employee { ... }

@Entity
@Table(name="CONTRACT_EMP")
@DiscriminatorValue("1")
public class ContractEmployee extends Employee { ... }

@MappedSuperclass
public abstract class CompanyEmployee extends Employee { ... }

@Entity
@Table(name="FT_EMP")
@DiscriminatorValue("2")
public class FullTimeEmployee extends CompanyEmployee { ... }

@Entity
@Table(name="PT_EMP")
@DiscriminatorValue("3")
public class PartTimeEmployee extends CompanyEmployee { ... }
```

Table-per-Concrete-Class Strategy

A third approach to mapping an entity hierarchy is to use a strategy where a *table per concrete class* is defined. This data architecture goes in the reverse direction of non-normalization of entity data and maps each concrete entity class and all of its inherited state to a separate table. This has the effect of causing all shared state to be redefined in the tables of all of the concrete entities that inherit it. This strategy is not required to be supported by providers but is included because it is anticipated that it will be required in a future release of the API. We will describe it briefly for completeness.

The negative side of using this strategy is that it makes polymorphic querying across a class hierarchy more expensive than the other strategies. The problem is that it must query across all of the subclass tables using a UNION operation, which is generally regarded as being expensive when lots of data is involved.

The bright side of table-per-concrete-class hierarchies when compared to joined hierarchies is seen in cases of querying over instances of a single concrete entity. In the joined case, every query requires a join, even when querying across a single concrete entity class. In the table-per-concrete-class case, it is kind of like the single-table hierarchy because the query is confined to a single table. Another advantage is that the discriminator column goes away. Every concrete entity has its own separate table, and there is no mixing or sharing of schema, so no class indicator is ever needed.

Mapping our example to this type of hierarchy is a matter of specifying the strategy as TABLE_PER_CLASS and making sure there is a table for each of the concrete classes. If a legacy database is being used, then the inherited columns could be named differently in each of the concrete tables and the @AttributeOverride annotation would come in handy. In this case the CONTRACT_EMP table didn't have the NAME and S_DATE columns but instead had FULLNAME and SDATE for the name and startDate fields defined in Employee.

If the attribute that we wanted to override was an association instead of a simple state mapping, then we could still override the mapping, but we would need to use an @AssociationOverride annotation instead of @AttributeOverride. The @AssociationOverride annotation allows us to override the join columns used to reference the target entity of a many-to-one or one-to-one association defined in a mapped superclass. To show this, we need to add a manager attribute to the CompanyEmployee mapped superclass. The join column is mapped by default in the CompanyEmployee class to the MANAGER column in the two FT_EMP and PT_EMP subclass tables, but in PT_EMP the name of the join column is actually MGR. We override the join column by adding the @AssociationOverride annotation to the PartTimeEmployee entity class and specifying the name of the attribute we are overriding and the join column that we are overriding it to be. Listing 8-24 shows a complete example of the entity mappings, including the overrides.

Listing 8-24. *Entity Hierarchy Mapped Using Table-per-Concrete-Class Strategy*

```
@Entity
@Inheritance(strategy=InheritanceType.TABLE_PER_CLASS)
public abstract class Employee {
    @Id private int id;
    private String name;
    @Temporal(TemporalType.DATE)
    @Column(name="S_DATE")
    private Date startDate;
    // ...
}

@Entity
@Table(name="CONTRACT_EMP")
@AttributeOverrides({
    @AttributeOverride(name="name", column=@Column(name="FULLNAME")),
    @AttributeOverride(name="startDate", column=@Column(name="SDATE"))
})
public class ContractEmployee extends Employee {
    @Column(name="D_RATE")
    private int dailyRate;
    private int term;
    // ...
}
```

```java
@MappedSuperclass
public abstract class CompanyEmployee extends Employee {
    private int vacation;
    @ManyToOne
    private Employee manager;
    // ...
}

@Entity @Table(name="FT_EMP")
public class FullTimeEmployee extends CompanyEmployee {
    private long salary;
    @Column(name="PENSION")
    private long pensionContribution;
    // ...
}

@Entity
@Table(name="PT_EMP")
@AssociationOverride(name="manager",
                     joinColumns=@JoinColumn(name="MGR"))
public class PartTimeEmployee extends CompanyEmployee {
    @Column(name="H_RATE")
    private float hourlyRate;
    // ...
}
```

The table organization shows how these columns are mapped to the concrete tables. See Figure 8-17 for a clear picture of what the tables would look like and how the different types of employee instances would be stored.

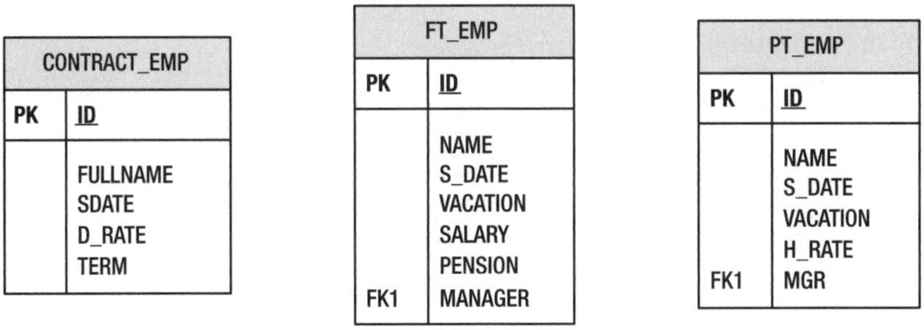

Figure 8-17. *Table-per-concrete-class data model*

Mixed Inheritance

We should begin this section by saying that the practice of mixing inheritance types within a single inheritance hierarchy is currently outside the specification. We are including it because it is both useful and interesting, but we are offering a warning that it may not be portable to rely on such behavior, even if your vendor supports it.

Furthermore, it really makes sense to mix only single-table and joined inheritance types. We will show an example of mixing these two, bearing in mind that support for them is vendor-specific. The intent is that in future releases of the specification, the more useful cases will be standardized and required to be supported by compliant implementations.

The premise for mixing inheritance types is that it is well within the realm of possibilities that a data model includes a combination of single-table and joined-table designs within a single entity hierarchy. This can be illustrated by taking our joined example in Figure 8-16 and storing the FullTimeEmployee and PartTimeEmployee instances in a single table. This would produce a model that looks like the one shown in Figure 8-18.

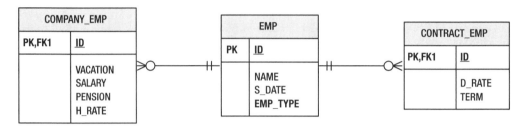

Figure 8-18. *Mixed inheritance data model*

In this example the joined strategy is used for the Employee and ContractEmployee classes, while the CompanyEmployee, FullTimeEmployee, and PartTimeEmployee classes revert to a single-table model. To make this inheritance strategy switch at the level of the CompanyEmployee, we need to make a simple change to the hierarchy. We need to turn CompanyEmployee into an abstract entity instead of a mapped superclass so that it can bear the new inheritance metadata. Note that this is simply an annotation change, not making any change to the domain model.

The inheritance strategies can be mapped as shown in Listing 8-25. Notice that we do not need to have a discriminator column for the single-table subhierarchy since we already have one in the superclass EMP table.

Listing 8-25. *Entity Hierarchy Mapped Using Mixed Strategies*

```
@Entity
@Table(name="EMP")
@Inheritance(strategy=InheritanceType.JOINED)
@DiscriminatorColumn(name="EMP_TYPE")
public abstract class Employee {
    @Id private int id;
    private String name;
    @Temporal(TemporalType.DATE)
    @Column(name="S_DATE")
    private Date startDate;
    // ...
}
```

```
@Entity
@Table(name="CONTRACT_EMP")
public class ContractEmployee extends Employee {
    @Column(name="D_RATE") private int dailyRate;
    private int term;
    // ...
}

@Entity
@Table(name="COMPANY_EMP")
@Inheritance(strategy=InheritanceType.SINGLE_TABLE)
public abstract class CompanyEmployee extends Employee {
    private int vacation;
    // ...
}

@Entity
public class FullTimeEmployee extends CompanyEmployee {
    private long salary;
    @Column(name="PENSION")
    private long pensionContribution;
    // ...
}

@Entity
public class PartTimeEmployee extends CompanyEmployee {
    @Column(name="H_RATE")
    private float hourlyRate;
    // ...
}
```

Summary

Entity mapping requirements often go well beyond the simplistic mappings that map a field or a relationship to a named column. In this chapter we addressed some of the more varied and diverse mapping practices that are supported by the Java Persistence API.

We discussed defining secondary objects called embedded objects and storing them into the tables of the entities that own them. We showed how the embedded object class definitions can be reused by multiple entities and how to override the mappings within any given entity.

Identifiers may be composed of multiple columns. We revealed the two approaches for defining and using compound primary keys and demonstrated using them in a way that is compatible with EJB 2.1 primary key classes. We established how other entities can have foreign key references to entities with compound identifiers and explained how multiple join columns can be used in any context when a single join column applies. We also showed an example of mapping an identifier that included a relationship as part of its identity.

We went on to show how to distribute entity state across multiple tables and how to use the secondary tables with relationships. We even saw how an embedded object can map to a secondary table of an entity.

Finally we went into detail about the three different inheritance strategies that can be used to map inheritance hierarchies to tables. We explained mapped superclasses and how they can be used to define shared state and behavior. We went over the data models that differentiate the various approaches and showed how to map an entity hierarchy to the tables in each case. We finished off by illustrating how to mix inheritance types within a single hierarchy.

In the next chapter we will continue our discussion of advanced topics, looking at issues such as SQL queries, optimistic locking, and schema generation.

■ ■ ■

Advanced Topics

Having a chapter called "Advanced Topics" is always a bit dicey because not everybody's definition of "advanced" is going to correspond to the same topics. What one person sees as advanced may be another person's basic bread-and-butter feature. It very much depends upon the background and experience of the developer as well as the complexity of applications that one is involved in developing.

What we can say is that, in large part, the topics in this chapter are those that we intended during development of the specification to be of a more advanced nature or to be used by more advanced developers. There are a few exceptions to this rule, though. For example, we included optimistic locking in this chapter even though most applications do need to be aware of and make use of optimistic locking. Generally, we think that most applications will not use more than a few of the features described in this chapter. With this in mind, let us explore some of the other features of the Java Persistence API.

SQL Queries

With all of the effort that has gone into abstracting away the physical data model, both in terms of object-relational mapping and JPQL, it might be surprising to learn that SQL is alive and well in the Java Persistence API. Although JPQL is the preferred method of querying over entities, SQL cannot be overlooked as a necessary element in many enterprise applications. The sheer size and scope of the SQL features supported by the major database vendors means that a portable language like JPQL will never be able to fully encompass all of their features.

Note SQL queries are also known as *native* queries. EntityManager methods and query annotations related to SQL queries also use this terminology. While this allows other query languages to be supported in the future, any query string in a native query operation is assumed to be SQL.

Before discussing the mechanics of SQL queries, let's first consider some of the reasons a developer using JPQL might want to integrate SQL queries into their application.

First, JPQL, despite the enhancements made by the Java Persistence API, still contains only a subset of the features supported by many database vendors. Inline views (subqueries in the FROM clause), hierarchical queries, access to stored procedures, and function expressions to manipulate date and time values are just some of the features missing from JPQL.

Second, although vendors may provide hints to assist with optimizing a JPQL expression, there are cases where the only way to achieve the performance required by an application is to replace the JPQL query with a hand-optimized SQL version. This may be a simple restructuring of the query that the persistence provider was generating, or it may be a vendor-specific version that leverages query hints and features specific to a particular database.

Of course, just because you can use SQL doesn't mean you should. Persistence providers have become very skilled at generating high-performance queries, and many of the limitations of JPQL can often be worked around in application code. We recommend avoiding SQL initially if possible and then introducing it only when necessary.

In the following sections we will discuss how SQL queries are defined using the Java Persistence API and how their result sets may be mapped back to entities. One of the major benefits of SQL query support is that it uses the same Query interface used for JPQL queries. With some small exceptions that will be described later, all of the Query interface operations discussed earlier in the chapter apply equally to both JPQL and SQL queries.

Native Queries vs. JDBC

A perfectly valid question for anyone investigating SQL support in the Java Persistence API is whether or not it is needed at all. JDBC has been in use for years, provides a broad feature set, and works well. It's one thing to introduce a persistence API that works on entities, but another thing entirely to introduce a new API for issuing SQL queries.

The main reason to consider using SQL queries with the Java Persistence API is when the result of the query will be converted back into entities. As an example, let's consider a typical use case for SQL in an application that uses the Java Persistence API. Given the employee id for a manager, the application needs to determine all of the employees that report to that manager either directly or indirectly. For example, if the query were for a senior manager, then the results would include all of the managers who report to that senior manager as well as the employees who report to those managers. This type of query cannot be implemented using JPQL, but a database such as Oracle natively supports hierarchical queries for just this purpose. Listing 9-1 demonstrates the typical sequence of JDBC calls to execute this query and transform the results into entities for use by the application.

Listing 9-1. *Querying Entities Using SQL and JDBC*

```
@Stateless
public class OrgStructureBean implements OrgStructure {
    private static final String ORG_QUERY =
        "SELECT emp_id, name, salary " +
        "FROM emp " +
        "START WITH manager_id = ? " +
        "CONNECT BY PRIOR emp_id = manager_id";

    @Resource
    DataSource hrDs;

    public List findEmployeesReportingTo(int managerId) {
        Connection conn = null;
        PreparedStatement sth = null;
```

```
        try {
            conn = hrDs.getConnection();
            sth = conn.prepareStatement(ORG_QUERY);
            sth.setLong(1, managerId);
            ResultSet rs = sth.executeQuery();

            ArrayList<Employee> result = new ArrayList<Employee>();
            while (rs.next()) {
                Employee emp = new Employee();
                emp.setId(rs.getInt(1));
                emp.setName(rs.getString(2));
                emp.setSalary(rs.getLong(3));
                result.add(emp);
            }
            return result;
        } catch (SQLException e) {
            throw new EJBException(e);
        }
    }
}
```

Now consider the alternative syntax supported by the Java Persistence API as shown in Listing 9-2. By simply indicating that the result of the query is the Employee entity, the query engine uses the object-relational mapping of the entity to figure out which result columns map to the entity properties and builds the result set accordingly.

Listing 9-2. *Querying Entities Using SQL and the* Query *Interface*

```
@Stateless
public class OrgStructureBean implements OrgStructure {
    private static final String ORG_QUERY =
        "SELECT emp_id, name, salary, manager_id, dept_id, address_id " +
        "FROM emp " +
        "START WITH manager_id = ? " +
        "CONNECT BY PRIOR emp_id = manager_id";

    @PersistenceContext(unitName="EmployeeService")
    EntityManager em;

    public List findEmployeesReportingTo(int managerId) {
        return em.createNativeQuery(ORG_QUERY, Employee.class)
                .setParameter(1, managerId)
                .getResultList();
    }
}
```

Not only is the code much easier to read, but it also makes use of the same Query interface used for JPQL queries. This helps to keep application code consistent, as it only needs to concern itself with the EntityManager and Query interfaces.

Defining and Executing SQL Queries

SQL queries may be defined dynamically at runtime or named in persistence unit metadata, similar to the JPQL query definitions we discussed in Chapter 6. The key difference between defining JPQL and SQL queries lies in the understanding that the query engine should not parse and interpret vendor-specific SQL. In order to execute a SQL query and get entity instances in return, additional mapping information about the query result is required.

The first and simplest form of dynamically defining a SQL query that returns an entity result is to use the createNativeQuery() method of the EntityManager interface, passing in the query string and the entity type that will be returned. Listing 9-2 in the previous section demonstrated this approach to map the results of an Oracle hierarchical query to the Employee entity. The query engine uses the object-relational mapping of the entity to figure out which result column aliases map to which entity properties. As each row is processed, the query engine instantiates a new entity instance and sets the available data into it.

If the column aliases of the query do not match up with the object-relational mapping for an entity, or if the results contain both entity and non-entity results, then SQL result set mapping metadata is required. SQL result set mappings are defined as persistence unit metadata and are referenced by name. When the createNativeQuery() method is invoked with a SQL query string and a result set mapping name, the query engine uses this mapping to build the result set. SQL result set mappings are discussed in the next section.

Named SQL queries are defined using the @NamedNativeQuery annotation. This annotation may be placed on any entity and defines the name of the query as well as the query text. Like JPQL named queries, the name of the query must be unique within the persistence unit. If the result type is an entity, the resultClass element may be used to indicate the entity class. If the result requires a SQL mapping, the resultSetMapping element may be used to specify the mapping name. Listing 9-3 shows how the hierarchical query demonstrated earlier would be defined as a named query.

Listing 9-3. *Using an Annotation to Define a Named Native Query*

```
@NamedNativeQuery(
    name="orgStructureReportingTo",
    query="SELECT emp_id, name, salary, manager_id, dept_id, address_id " +
        "FROM emp " +
        "START WITH manager_id = ? " +
        "CONNECT BY PRIOR emp_id = manager_id",
    resultClass=Employee.class
)
```

The advantage of using named SQL queries is that the application can use the createNamedQuery() method on the EntityManager interface to create and execute the query. The fact that the named query was defined using SQL instead of JPQL is not important. Listing 9-4 demonstrates the reporting structure bean again, this time using a named query. The other advantage of using named queries instead of dynamic queries is that they can be overridden using XML mapping files. A query originally specified in JPQL can be overridden with a SQL version and vice versa. This technique is described in Chapter 10.

Listing 9-4. *Executing a Named SQL Query*

```
@Stateless
public class OrgStructureBean implements OrgStructure {
    @PersistenceContext(unitName="EmployeeService")
    EntityManager em;

    public List findEmployeesReportingTo(int managerId) {
        return em.createNamedQuery("orgStructureReportingTo")
                .setParameter(1, managerId)
                .getResultList();
    }
}
```

One thing to be careful of with SQL queries that return entities is that the resulting entity instances become managed by the persistence context, just like the results of a JPQL query. If you modify one of the returned entities, it will be written to the database when the persistence context becomes associated with a transaction. This is normally what you want, but it requires that any time you select data that corresponds to existing entity instances, it is important to ensure that all of the necessary data required to fully construct the entity is part of the query. If you leave out a field from the query, or default it to some value and then modify the resulting entity, you will most likely overwrite the correct version already stored in the database.

There are two benefits to getting managed entities back from a SQL query. The first is that a SQL query can replace an existing JPQL query and that application code should still work without changes. The second benefit is that it allows the developer to use SQL queries as a method of constructing new entity instances from tables that may not have any object-relational mapping. For example, in many database architectures, there is a staging area to hold data that has not yet been verified or requires some kind of transformation before it can be moved to its final location. Using the Java Persistence API, a developer could start a transaction, query the staged data to construct entities, perform any required changes, and then commit. The newly created entities will get written to the tables mapped by the entity, not the staging tables used in the SQL query.

SQL data-manipulation statements (INSERT, UPDATE, and DELETE) are also supported as a convenience so that JDBC calls do not have to be introduced in an application otherwise restricted to the Java Persistence API. To define such a query, use the `createNativeQuery()` method, but without any mapping information. Listing 9-5 demonstrates these types of queries in the form of a session bean that logs messages to a table. Note that the bean methods run in a `REQUIRES_NEW` transaction context to ensure that the message is logged even if an active transaction rolls back.

Listing 9-5. *Using SQL INSERT and DELETE Statements*

```
@Stateless
@TransactionAttribute(TransactionAttributeType.REQUIRES_NEW)
public class LoggerBean implements Logger {
    private static final String INSERT_SQL =
        "INSERT INTO message_log (id, message, log_dttm) " +
        "        VALUES(id_seq.nextval, ?, SYSDATE)";
    private static final String DELETE_SQL =
        "DELETE FROM message_log";

    @PersistenceContext(unitName="Logger")
    EntityManager em;

    public void logMessage(String message) {
        em.createNativeQuery(INSERT_SQL)
          .setParameter(1, message)
          .executeUpdate();
    }

    public void clearMessageLog() {
        em.createNativeQuery(DELETE_SQL)
          .executeUpdate();
    }
}
```

Executing SQL statements that make changes to data in tables mapped by entities is generally discouraged. Doing so may cause cached entities to be inconsistent with the database, as the provider is not able to track changes made to entity state that has been modified by data-manipulation statements.

SQL Result Set Mapping

In the SQL query examples shown so far, the result mapping was straightforward. The column aliases in the SQL string matched up directly with the object-relational column mapping for a single entity. It is not always the case that the names match up, nor is it always the case that only a single entity type is returned. The Java Persistence API provides SQL result set mappings to handle these scenarios.

A SQL result set mapping is defined using the @SqlResultSetMapping annotation. It may be placed on an entity class and consists of a name (unique within the persistence unit) and one or more entity and column mappings. The entity result class argument on the createNativeQuery() method is really a shortcut to specifying a simple SQL result set mapping. The following mapping is equivalent to specifying Employee.class in a call to createNativeQuery():

```
@SqlResultSetMapping(
    name="employeeResult",
    entities=@EntityResult(entityClass=Employee.class)
)
```

Here we have defined a SQL result set mapping called employeeResult that may be referenced by any query returning Employee entity instances. The mapping consists of a single entity result, specified by the @EntityResult annotation, that references the Employee entity class. The query must supply values for all columns mapped by the entity, including foreign keys. It is vendor-specific whether the entity is partially constructed or whether an error occurs if any required entity state is missing.

Mapping Foreign Keys

When the query engine attempts to map the query results to an entity, it considers foreign key columns for single-valued associations as well. Let's look at the reporting structure query again:

```
SELECT emp_id, name, salary, manager_id, dept_id, address_id
FROM emp
START WITH manager_id IS NULL
CONNECT BY PRIOR emp_id = manager_id
```

The MANAGER_ID, DEPT_ID, and ADDRESS_ID columns all map to the join columns of associations on the Employee entity. An Employee instance returned from this query can use the methods getManager(), getDepartment(), and getAddress(), and the results will be as expected. The persistence provider will retrieve the associated entity based on the foreign key value read in from the query. There is no way to populate collection associations from a SQL query. Entity instances constructed from this example are effectively the same as they would have been had they been returned from a JPQL query.

Multiple Result Mappings

A query may return more than one entity at a time. This is most often useful if there is a one-to-one relationship between two entities, otherwise the query will result in duplicate entity instances. Consider the following query:

```
SELECT emp_id, name, salary, manager_id, dept_id, address_id,
       id, street, city, state, zip
FROM emp, address
WHERE address_id = id
```

The SQL result set mapping to return both the Employee and Address entities out of this query is defined in Listing 9-6. Each entity is listed in an @EntityResult annotation, an array of which is assigned to the entities element. The order in which the entities are listed is not important. The query engine uses the column names of the query to match against entity mapping data, not column position.

Listing 9-6. *Mapping a SQL Query That Returns Two Entity Types*

```
@SqlResultSetMapping(
    name="EmployeeWithAddress",
    entities={@EntityResult(entityClass=Employee.class),
             @EntityResult(entityClass=Address.class)}
)
```

Mapping Column Aliases

If the column aliases in the SQL statement do not directly match up with the names specified in the column mappings for the entity, then field result mappings are required for the query engine to make the correct association. Consider, for example, if both the EMP and ADDRESS tables listed in the previous example used the column ID for their primary key. The query would have to be altered to alias the ID columns so that they are unique:

```
SELECT emp.id AS emp_id, name, salary, manager_id, dept_id, address_id,
        address.id, street, city, state, zip
FROM emp, address
WHERE address_id = address.id
```

The @FieldResult annotation is used to map column aliases to the entity attributes in situations where the name in the query is not the same as the one used in the column mapping. Listing 9-7 shows the mapping required to convert the EMP_ID alias to the id attribute of the entity. More than one @FieldResult may be specified, but only the mappings that are different need to be specified. This can be a partial list of entity attributes.

Listing 9-7. *Mapping a SQL Query with Unknown Column Aliases*

```
@SqlResultSetMapping(
    name="EmployeeWithAddress",
    entities={@EntityResult(entityClass=Employee.class,
                            fields=@FieldResult(name="id", column="EMP_ID")),
              @EntityResult(entityClass=Address.class)}
)
```

Mapping Scalar Result Columns

SQL queries are not limited to returning only entity results, although it is expected that this will be the primary use case. Consider the following query:

```
SELECT e.name AS emp_name, m.name AS manager_name
FROM emp e,
     emp m
WHERE e.manager_id = m.emp_id (+)
START WITH e.manager_id IS NULL
CONNECT BY PRIOR e.emp_id = e.manager_id
```

Non-entity result types, called scalar result types, are mapped using the @ColumnResult annotation. One or more column mappings may be assigned to the columns attribute of the mapping annotation. The only attribute available for a column mapping is the column name. Listing 9-8 shows the SQL mapping for the employee and manager hierarchical query.

Listing 9-8. *Scalar Column Mappings*

```
@SqlResultSetMapping(
    name="EmployeeAndManager",
    columns={@ColumnResult(name="EMP_NAME"),
             @ColumnResult(name="MANAGER_NAME")}
)
```

Scalar results may also be mixed with entities. In this case the scalar results are typically providing additional information about the entity. Let's look at a more complex example where this would be the case. A report for an application needs to see information about each department, showing the manager, the number of employees, and the average salary. The following JPQL query produces the correct report:

```
SELECT d, m, COUNT(e), AVG(e.salary)
FROM Department d LEFT JOIN e.employees e
                 LEFT JOIN e.employees m
WHERE m IS NULL OR m IN (SELECT de.manager
                        FROM Employee de
                        WHERE de.department = d)
GROUP BY d, m
```

This query is particularly challenging, because there is no direct relationship from Department to the Employee who is the manager of the department. Therefore the employees relationship must be joined twice, once for the employees assigned to the department and once for the employee in that group who is also the manager. This is possible because the subquery reduces the second join of the employees relationship to a single result. We also need to accommodate the fact that there might not be any employees currently assigned to the department and further that a department might not have a manager assigned. This means that each of the joins must be an outer join and that we further have to use an OR condition to allow for the missing manager in the WHERE clause.

Once in production, it is determined that the SQL query generated by the provider is not performing well, so the DBA proposes an alternate query that takes advantage of the inline views possible with the Oracle database. The query to accomplish this result is shown in Listing 9-9.

Listing 9-9. *Department Summary Query*

```
SELECT d.id, d.name AS dept_name,
       e.emp_id, e.name, e.salary, e.manager_id, e.dept_id, e.address_id,
       s.tot_emp, s.avg_sal
FROM dept d,
     (SELECT *
      FROM emp e
      WHERE EXISTS(SELECT 1 FROM emp WHERE manager_id = e.emp_id)) e,
     (SELECT d.id, COUNT(*) AS tot_emp, AVG(e.salary) AS avg_sal
      FROM dept d, emp e
      WHERE d.id = e.dept_id (+)
      GROUP BY d.id) s
WHERE d.id = e.dept_id (+) AND
      d.id = s.id
```

Fortunately, mapping this query is a lot easier than reading it. The query results consist of a Department entity, an Employee entity, and two scalar results, the number of the employees and the average salary. Listing 9-10 shows the mapping for this query.

Listing 9-10. *Mapping for the Department Query*

```
@SqlResultSetMapping(
    name="DepartmentSummary",
    entities={
        @EntityResult(entityClass=Department.class,
                      fields=@FieldResult(name="name", column="DEPT_NAME")),
        @EntityResult(entityClass=Employee.class)
    },
    columns={@ColumnResult(name="TOT_EMP"),
             @ColumnResult(name="AVG_SAL")}
)
```

Mapping Compound Keys

When a primary or foreign key is comprised of multiple columns that have been aliased to unmapped names, then a special notation must be used in the `@FieldResult` annotations to identify each part of the key. Consider the query shown in Listing 9-11 that returns both the employee and the manager of the employee. The table in this example is the same one we demonstrated in Figure 8-6 of Chapter 8. Because each column is repeated twice, the columns for the manager state have been aliased to new names.

Listing 9-11. *SQL Query Returning Employee and Manager*

```
SELECT  e.country, e.emp_id, e.name, e.salary,
        e.manager_country, e.manager_id, m.country AS mgr_country,
        m.emp_id AS mgr_id, m.name AS mgr_name, m.salary AS mgr_salary,
        m.manager_country AS mgr_mgr_country, m.manager_id AS mgr_mgr_id
FROM    emp e,
        emp m
WHERE   e.manager_country = m.country AND
        e.manager_id = m.emp_id
```

The result set mapping for this query depends on the type of primary key class used by the target entity. Listing 9-12 shows the mapping in the case where an id class has been used. For the primary key, each attribute is listed as a separate field result. For the foreign key, each primary key attribute of the target entity (the `Employee` entity again in this example) is suffixed to the name of the relationship attribute.

Listing 9-12. *Mapping for Employee Query Using Id Class*

```
@SqlResultSetMapping(
    name="EmployeeAndManager",
    entities={
        @EntityResult(entityClass=Employee.class),
        @EntityResult(
            entityClass=Employee.class,
```

```
            fields={
                @FieldResult(name="country", column="MGR_COUNTRY"),
                @FieldResult(name="id", column="MGR_ID"),
                @FieldResult(name="name", column="MGR_NAME"),
                @FieldResult(name="salary", column="MGR_SALARY"),
                @FieldResult(name="manager.country", column="MGR_MGR_COUNTRY"),
                @FieldResult(name="manager.id", column="MGR_MGR_ID")
            }
        )
    }
)
```

If Employee uses an embedded id class instead of an id class, the notation is slightly different. We have to include the primary key attribute name as well as the individual attributes within the embedded type. Listing 9-13 shows the result set mapping using this notation.

Listing 9-13. *Mapping for Employee Query Using Embedded Id Class*

```
@SqlResultSetMapping(
    name="EmployeeAndManager",
    entities={
        @EntityResult(entityClass=Employee.class),
        @EntityResult(
            entityClass=Employee.class,
            fields={
                @FieldResult(name="id.country", column="MGR_COUNTRY"),
                @FieldResult(name="id.id", column="MGR_ID"),
                @FieldResult(name="name", column="MGR_NAME"),
                @FieldResult(name="salary", column="MGR_SALARY"),
                @FieldResult(name="manager.id.country", column="MGR_MGR_COUNTRY"),
                @FieldResult(name="manager.id.id", column="MGR_MGR_ID")
            }
        )
    }
)
```

Mapping Inheritance

In many respects, polymorphic queries in SQL are no different than regular queries returning a single entity type. All columns must be accounted for, including foreign keys and the discriminator column for single-table and joined inheritance strategies. The key thing to remember is that if the results include more than one entity type, then each of the columns for all of the possible entity types must be represented in the query. The field result mapping techniques we demonstrated earlier may be used to customize columns that use unknown aliases. These columns may be at any level in the inheritance tree. The only special element in the @EntityResult annotation for use with inheritance is the discriminatorColumn element. This element allows the name of the discriminator column to be specified in the unlikely event that it is different from the mapped version.

Assume that the Employee entity had been mapped to the table shown in Figure 8-14 from Chapter 8. To understand aliasing a discriminator column, consider the following query that returns data from another EMPLOYEE_STAGE table structured to use single-table inheritance:

```
SELECT id, name, start_date, daily_rate, term, vacation,
       hourly_rate, salary, pension, type
FROM employee_stage
```

To convert the data returned from this query to Employee entities, the following result set mapping would be used:

```
@SqlResultSetMapping(
    name="EmployeeStageMapping",
    entities=
        @EntityResult(
            entityClass=Employee.class,
            discriminatorColumn="TYPE",
            fields={
                @FieldResult(name="startDate", column="START_DATE"),
                @FieldResult(name="dailyRate", column="DAILY_RATE"),
                @FieldResult(name="hourlyRate", column="HOURLY_RATE")
            }
        )
)
```

Parameter Binding

SQL queries have traditionally supported only positional parameter binding. The JDBC specification itself did not introduce support for named parameters until version 3.0, and not all database vendors support this syntax. As a result, the Java Persistence API guarantees only the use of positional parameter binding for SQL queries. Check with your vendor to see if the named parameter methods of the Query interface are supported, but understand that using them may make your application non-portable between persistence providers.

Another limitation of parameter support for SQL queries is that entity parameters may not be used. The specification does not define how these parameter types should be treated. Be careful when converting or overriding a named JPQL query with a native SQL query that the parameter values are still interpreted correctly.

Lifecycle Callbacks

Every entity has the potential to go through one or more of a defined set of *lifecycle events*. Depending upon the operations invoked upon an entity, these events may or may not occur for that entity, but there is at least the potential for them to occur. In order to respond to any one or more of the events, an entity class or any of its superclasses may declare one or more methods that will be invoked by the provider when the event gets fired. These methods are called *callback methods*.

Lifecycle Events

The event types that make up the lifecycle fall into four categories: persisting, updating, removing, and loading. These are really data-level events that correspond to the database operations of inserting, updating, deleting, and reading, and except for loading, each has a "Pre" event and a "Post" event. In the load category there is only a PostLoad event, since it would not make any sense for there to be PreLoad on an entity that was not yet built. Thus the full suite of lifecycle events that can occur is composed of: PrePersist, PostPersist, PreUpdate, PostUpdate, PreRemove, PostRemove, and PostLoad.

PrePersist and PostPersist

The PrePersist event notifies an entity when persist() has been successfully invoked on it. PrePersist events may also occur on a merge() call when a new entity has been merged into the persistence context. If the PERSIST cascade option is set on a relationship of an object that is being persisted and the target object is also a new object, then the PrePersist event is triggered on the target object. If multiple entities are cascaded to during the same operation, then the order in which the PrePersist callbacks occur cannot be relied upon.

PostPersist events occur when an entity is inserted, which normally occurs during the transaction completion phase. Firing of a PostPersist event does not indicate that the entity has committed successfully to the database, since the transaction in which it was persisted may be subsequently rolled back.

PreRemove and PostRemove

When a remove() call is invoked on an entity, the PreRemove callback is triggered. This callback implies that an entity is being queued for deletion, and any related entities across relationships that have been configured with the REMOVE cascade option will also get a PreRemove notification. When the SQL for deletion of an entity finally does get sent to the database, the PostRemove event will get fired. As with the PostPersist lifecycle event, the PostRemove event does not guarantee success. The enclosing transaction may still be rolled back.

PreUpdate and PostUpdate

Updates to managed entities may occur at any time, either within a transaction, or in the case of an extended persistence context, outside a transaction. Because there is no explicit method on the EntityManager, the PreUpdate callback is guaranteed to be invoked only at some point before the database update. Some implementations may track changes dynamically and may invoke the callback on each change, while others may wait until the end of the transaction and just invoke the callback once.

Another difference between implementations is whether PreUpdate events get fired on entities that were persisted in a transaction and then modified in the same transaction before being committed. This would be a rather unfortunate choice because unless the writes were done eagerly on each entity call, there would be no symmetric PostUpdate call, since in the usual deferred writing case, a single persist to the database would occur when the transaction ends. The PostUpdate callback occurs right after the database update. The same potential rollback exists after PostUpdate callbacks as exist with PostPersist and PostRemove.

PostLoad

The `PostLoad` callback occurs after the data for an entity is read from the database and the entity instance is constructed. This can get triggered by any operation that causes an entity to be loaded, normally by either a query or traversal of a lazy relationship. It can also happen as a result of a `refresh()` call on the entity manager. When a relationship is set to cascade `REFRESH`, then the entities that get cascaded to will also get loaded. The order of invocation of entities in a single operation, be it a query or a refresh, is not guaranteed to be in any order, so we should not rely upon any observed order in any implementation.

Callback Methods

Callback methods may be defined a few different ways, the most basic of which is to simply define a method on the entity class. Designating the method as a callback method involves two steps: defining the method according to a given signature, and annotating the method with the appropriate lifecycle event annotation.

The required signature definition is very simple. The callback method may have any name but must have a signature that takes no parameters and has a return type of `void`. A method like `public void foo() {}` is an example of a valid method. Final or static methods are not valid callback methods, however.

Checked exceptions may not be thrown from callback methods, because the method definition of a callback method is not permitted to include a throws clause. Runtime exceptions may be thrown, though, and if they are thrown while in a transaction, they will cause the provider to not only abandon invocation of subsequent lifecycle event methods in that transaction but also mark the transaction for rollback.

A method is indicated as being a callback method by being annotated with a lifecycle event annotation. The relevant annotations match the names of the events listed earlier: `@PrePersist`, `@PostPersist`, `@PreUpdate`, `@PostUpdate`, `@PreRemove`, `@PostRemove`, and `@PostLoad`. A method may be annotated with multiple lifecycle event annotations, but only one lifecycle annotation of a given type may be present in an entity class.

Certain types of operations may not be portably performed inside callback methods. For example, invoking on an entity manager or executing queries obtained from an entity manager are not supported, as well as accessing entities other than the one to which the lifecycle event applies. Looking up resources in JNDI or using JDBC and JMS resources are allowed, so looking up and invoking EJB session beans is also allowed.

Now that we know all of the different kinds of lifecycle events that we can handle, let's look at an example that uses them. One common usage of lifecycle events is to maintain non-persistent state inside a persistent entity. If we want the entity to record its cached age or the time it was last synchronized with the database, then we could easily do this right inside the entity using callback methods. We consider that the entity is synchronized with the database each time it is read from or written to the database. Users of this `Employee` could check on the cached age of this object to see if it meets their freshness requirements. The entity is shown in Listing 9-14.

Listing 9-14. *Using Callback Methods on an Entity*

```
@Entity
public class Employee {
    @Id private int id;
    private String name;
    @Transient private long syncTime;

    // ...

    @PostPersist
    @PostUpdate
    @PostLoad
    private void resetSyncTime() {
        syncTime = System.currentTimeMillis();
    }

    public long getCachedAge() {
        return System.currentTimeMillis() - syncTime;
    }

    // ...
}
```

Enterprise Contexts

When a callback method is invoked, the provider will not take any particular action to suspend or establish any different kind of naming, transaction, or security context in the Java EE environment. Callback methods are executed in whatever contexts are active at the time they are invoked.

Remembering this fact is important, because it will most often be a session bean with a container-managed transaction that invokes calls on the entity manager, and it will be that session bean's contexts that will be in effect when the "Pre" calls are invoked. Depending upon where the transaction started and is committed, the "Post" calls will likely be invoked at the end of the transaction and could actually be in an entirely different set of contexts than the "Pre" methods. This is especially true in the case of an extended persistence context where the entities are managed and persisted outside a transaction, yet the next transaction commit will cause the entities that were persisted to be written out.

Entity Listeners

Callback methods in the entity are fine when you don't mind if the event callback logic is included in the entity, but what if you want to pull the event handling behavior out of the entity class into a different class? To do this you can use an *entity listener*. An entity listener is not an entity but is a class on which you can define one or more lifecycle callback methods to be invoked for the lifecycle events of an entity. Like the callback methods on the entity, however, each event type may have only one method annotated to be invoked.

When the callback is invoked on a listener, the listener typically needs to have access to the entity state. For example, if we were to implement the previous example of the cached age of an entity instance then we would want to get passed the entity instance. For this reason, the signature required of callback methods on entity listeners is slightly different than the one required on entities. On an entity listener, a callback method must have a similar signature as on an entity with the exception that it must also have a single defined parameter of a type that is compatible with the entity type, either as the entity class, a superclass (including `Object`) or an interface implemented by the entity. A method with the signature `public void foo(Object o) {}` is an example of a valid callback method on an entity listener. The method must then be annotated with the necessary event annotation(s).

Entity listener classes must be stateless, meaning that they should not declare any fields. A single instance may be shared amongst multiple entity instances and may even be invoked upon concurrently for multiple entity instances. In order for the provider to be able to create instances of the entity listener, every entity listener class must have a public no-argument constructor.

Attaching Entity Listeners to Entities

An entity designates the entity listeners that should be notified of its lifecycle events through the use of the `@EntityListeners` annotation. One or more entity listeners may be listed in the annotation. When a lifecycle event occurs, the provider will iterate through each of the entity listeners in the order in which they were listed and instantiate an instance of the entity listener class that has a method annotated with the annotation for the given event. It will invoke the callback method on the listener, passing in the entity to which the event applies. After it has done this for all of the listed entity listeners, then it will invoke the callback method on the entity if there is one. If any of the listeners throws an exception, then it will abort the callback process, causing the remaining listeners and the callback method on the entity to not be invoked.

Now let's look at our cached entity age example and add some entity listeners into the mix. Because we now have the ability to do multiple tasks in multiple listeners, we can add a listener to do some name validation as well as some extra actions on employee record changes. Listing 9-15 shows the entity with its added listeners.

Listing 9-15. *Using Multiple Entity Listeners*

```
@Entity
@EntityListeners({EmployeeDebugListener.class, NameValidator.class})
public class Employee implements NamedEntity {
    @Id private int id;
    private String name;
    @Transient private long syncTime;

    @PostPersist
    @PostUpdate
    @PostLoad
    private void resetSyncTime() {
        syncTime = System.currentTimeMillis();
    }
```

```java
    public long getCachedAge() {
        return System.currentTimeMillis() - syncTime;
    }

    // ...
}

public interface NamedEntity {
    public String getName();
}

public class NameValidator {
    static final int MAX_NAME_LEN = 40;

    @PrePersist
    public void validate(NamedEntity obj) {
        if (obj.getName().length()) > MAX_NAME_LEN)
            throw new ValidationException("Identifier out of range");
    }
}

public class EmployeeDebugListener {
    @PrePersist
    public void prePersist(Employee emp) {
        System.out.println("Persist on employee id: " + emp.getId());
    }

    @PreUpdate
    public void preUpdate(Employee emp) { ... }

    @PreRemove
    public void preRemove(Employee emp) { ... }

    @PostLoad
    public void postLoad(Employee emp) { ... }
}
```

As we can see, different listener callback methods take different types of parameters. The callback methods in the EmployeeDebugListener class take Employee as a parameter because they are being applied only to Employee entities. In the NameValidator class, the validate() method parameter is of type NamedEntity. The Employee entity and any number of other entities that have names may implement this interface. The validation logic may be needed because a particular aspect of the system may have a current name length limitation but may change in the future. It is preferable to centralize this logic in a single class than to duplicate the validation logic in each of the class setter methods if there is possibility of an inheritance hierarchy.

Even though entity listeners are convenient, we have decided to leave the cache age logic in the entity, because it is actually modifying the state of the entity and because putting it in a separate class would have required us to relax the access of the private resetSyncTime() method.

In general, when a callback method accesses state beyond what should be publicly accessible, then it is best suited to being on the entity and not in an entity listener.

Default Entity Listeners

A listener may be attached to more than one type of entity simply by being listed in the `@EntityListeners` annotation of more than one entity. This can be useful in cases where the listener provides a more general facility or wide-ranging runtime logic.

For even broader usage of an entity listener across all of the entities in a persistence unit, one or more *default entity listeners* may be declared. There is currently no standard annotation target for persistence unit scoped metadata, so this kind of metadata can be declared only in an XML mapping file. See Chapter 10 for the specifics of how to declare default entity listeners.

When a list of default entity listeners is declared, then it will be traversed in the order they were listed in the declaration, and each one that has a method annotated or declared for the current event will be invoked upon. Default entity listeners will always get invoked before any of the entity listeners listed in the `@EntityListeners` annotation for a given entity.

Any entity may opt out of having the default entity listeners applied to it by using the `@ExcludeDefaultListeners` annotation. When an entity is annotated with this annotation, then none of the declared default listeners will get invoked for the lifecycle events for instances of that entity type.

Inheritance and Lifecycle Events

The presence of events with class hierarchies requires that we explore the topic of lifecycle events in a little more depth. What happens when we have multiple entities that each define callback methods or entity listeners or both? Do they all get invoked on a subclass entity or only those that are defined on or in the subclass entity?

These and many other questions arise because of the added complexity of inheritance hierarchies. It follows that there must be rules for defining predictable behavior in the face of potentially complex hierarchies where lifecycle event methods are scattered throughout the hierarchy.

Inheriting Callback Methods

Callback methods may occur on any entity or mapped superclass, be it abstract or concrete. The rule is fairly simple. It is that every callback method for a given event type will be invoked in the order according to its place in the hierarchy, most general classes first. Thus, if in our `Employee` hierarchy that we saw in Figure 8-13 the `Employee` class contains a `PrePersist` callback method named `checkName()` and `FullTimeEmployee` also contains a `PrePersist` callback method named `verifyPension()`, then when the `PrePersist` event occurs, the `checkName()` method will get invoked followed by the `verifyPension()` method.

We could also have a method on the `CompanyEmployee` mapped superclass that we want to apply to all of the entities that subclassed it. If we add a `PrePersist` method named `checkVacation()` that verifies that the vacation carryover is less than a certain amount, then it will be executed after `checkName()` and before `verifyPension()`.

It gets more interesting if we define a `checkVacation()` method on the `PartTimeEmployee` class, because part-time employees don't get as much vacation. Annotating the overridden method with `PrePersist` would cause the `PartTimeEmployee.checkVacation()` method to be invoked instead of the one in `CompanyEmployee`.

Inheriting Entity Listeners

Like callback methods in an entity, the `@EntityListeners` annotation is also valid on entities or mapped superclasses in a hierarchy, whether they are concrete or abstract. Also similar to callback methods, the listeners listed in the entity superclass annotation get invoked before the listeners in the subclass entities. In other words, defining an `@EntityListeners` annotation on an entity is additive in that it only adds listeners; it does not redefine them or their order of invocation. Any listener defined on a superclass of the entity will be invoked before the listeners defined on the entity.

To redefine which entity listeners get invoked and their order of invocation, an entity or mapped superclass should be annotated with `@ExcludeSuperclassListeners`. This will cause the listeners defined in all of the superclasses to not be invoked for any of the lifecycle events of the annotated entity subclass. If we want a subset of the listeners to still be invoked, then they must be listed in the `@EntityListeners` annotation on the overriding entity and in the order that is appropriate.

Lifecycle Event Invocation Order

The rules for lifecycle event invocation are now a little more complex, so they warrant being laid out more carefully. Perhaps the best way to describe it is to outline the process that the provider must follow to invoke the event methods. If a given lifecycle event X occurs for entity A, the provider will do the following:

1. Check whether any default entity listeners exist (see Chapter 10). If they do, then iterate through them in the order they are defined and look for methods that are annotated with the lifecycle event X annotation. Invoke the lifecycle method on the listener if a method was found.

2. Check on the highest mapped superclass or entity in the hierarchy for classes that have an `@EntityListeners` annotation. Iterate through the entity listener classes that are listed in the annotation and look for methods that are annotated with the lifecycle event X annotation. Invoke the lifecycle method on the listener if a method was found.

3. Repeat step 2 going down the hierarchy on entities and mapped superclasses until entity A is reached, and then repeat it for entity A.

4. Check on the highest mapped superclass or entity in the hierarchy for methods that are annotated with the lifecycle event X annotation. Invoke the callback method on the entity if a method was found and the method is not also defined in entity A with the lifecycle event X annotation on it.

5. Repeat step 2 going down the hierarchy on entities and mapped superclasses until entity A is reached.

6. Invoke any methods that are defined on A and annotated with the lifecycle event X annotation.

This process might be easier to follow if we have code that includes these cases and we go through the order in which they are executed. Listing 9-16 shows our entity hierarchy with a number of listeners and callback methods on it.

Listing 9-16. *Using Entity Listeners and Callback Methods in a Hierarchy*

```
@Entity
@Inheritance(strategy=InheritanceType.JOINED)
@EntityListeners(NameValidator.class)
public class Employee implements NamedEntity {
    @Id private int id;
    private String name;
    @Transient private long syncTime;

    @PostPersist
    @PostUpdate
    @PostLoad
    private void resetSyncTime() { syncTime = System.currentTimeMillis(); }
    // ...
}

public interface NamedEntity {
    public String getName();
}

@Entity
@ExcludeSuperclassListeners
@EntityListeners(LongNameValidator.class)
public class ContractEmployee extends Employee {
    private int dailyRate;
    private int term;

    @PrePersist
    public void verifyTerm() { ... }
    // ...
}

@MappedSuperclass
@EntityListeners(EmployeeAudit.class)
public abstract class CompanyEmployee extends Employee {
    protected int vacation;
    // ...

    @PrePersist
    @PreUpdate
    public void verifyVacation() { ... }
}
```

```
@Entity
public class FullTimeEmployee extends CompanyEmployee {
    private long salary;
    private long pension;
    // ...
}

@Entity
@EntityListeners({})
public class PartTimeEmployee extends CompanyEmployee {
    private float hourlyRate;
    // ...

    @PrePersist
    @PreUpdate
    public void verifyVacation() { ... }
}

public class EmployeeAudit {
    @PostPersist
    public void auditNewHire(CompanyEmployee emp) { ... }
}

public class NameValidator {
    @PrePersist
    public void validateName(NamedEntity obj) { ... }
}

public class LongNameValidator {
    @PrePersist
    public void validateLongName(NamedEntity obj) { ... }
}

public class EmployeeDebugListener {
    @PrePersist
    public void prePersist(Employee emp) {
        System.out.println("Persist called on: " + emp);
    }

    @PreUpdate
    public void preUpdate(Employee emp) { ... }

    @PreRemove
    public void preRemove(Employee emp) { ... }

    @PostLoad
    public void postLoad(Employee emp) { ... }
}
```

We have a pretty complex example here to study, and the easiest way to make use of it is to say what happens when a given event occurs for a specific entity. We will assume that the EmployeeDebugListener class has been set in the XML mapping file as a default entity listener for all entities.

Let's see what happens when we create a new instance of PartTimeEmployee and pass it to em.persist(). Since the first step is always to invoke the default listeners and our default listener does indeed have a PrePersist method on it, the EmployeeDebugListener.prePersist() method will be invoked first.

The next step would be to traverse down the hierarchy looking for entity listeners. The first class we find is the Employee class, which defines a NameValidator entity listener. The NameValidator class does define a PrePersist method, so the next method to get executed would be NameValidator.validateName(). The next class we hit moving down the hierarchy is the CompanyEmployee class. This class defines an EmployeeAudit listener that does not happen to have a PrePersist method on it, so we skip past it.

Next we get to the PartTimeEmployee class that has an @EntityListeners annotation but does not define any listeners. This is essentially a false alarm that does not really override anything, but is simply a no-op in terms of adding listeners (probably a leftover of a listener that was once there but has since been removed).

The next phase in the process is to start looking for callback methods on entities and mapped superclasses. Once again we start at the top of the hierarchy and look at the Employee class to see if a PrePersist method exists, but none does. We have PostPersist and others, but no PrePersist. We continue on down to CompanyEmployee and see a PrePersist method called verifyVacation(), but looking down on the PartTimeEmployee entity we find that the method has been overridden by a verifyVacation() method there that also has an @PrePersist annotation on it. This is a case of overriding the callback method and will result in the PartTimeEmployee. verifyVacation() method being called instead of the CompanyEmployee.verifyVacation() method. We are finally done, and the entity will be persisted.

The next event might then be a PostPersist event on the same entity at commit time. This will bypass the default listener since there is no PostPersist method in EmployeeDebugListener and also bypass the NameValidator since there is no PostPersist event method there either. The next listener that it tries will be the EmployeeAudit listener class, which does include a PostPersist method called auditNewHire(), which will then get invoked. There are no more listeners to examine, so we move on to the callback methods and find the resetSyncTime() method in Employee. This one gets called, and since we find no more PostPersist callback methods in the hierarchy, we are done.

The next thing we can try is persisting a ContractEmployee. This is a simple persistence structure with only the Employee and ContractEmployee entities in it. When we create a ContractEmployee and the PrePersist event gets triggered, we first get our default EmployeeDebugListener.prePersist() callback and then move on to processing the entity listeners. The curve is that the @ExcludeSuperclassListeners annotation is present on the ContractEmployee, so the NameValidator.validateName() method that would otherwise have been invoked will not be considered. We instead go right to the @EntityListeners annotation on the ContractEmployee class and find that we need to look at LongNameValidator. When we do, we find that it has a validateLongName() method on it that we execute and then go on to executing the callback methods. There are callback methods in both classes in the hierarchy, and the Employee.resetSyncTime() method gets invoked first, followed by the ContractEmployee.verifyTerm() method.

Concurrency

The concurrency of entity access and entity operations is not heavily specified, but there are a few rules that dictate what we can and can't expect. We will go over these and leave the rest to the vendors to explain in the documentation for their respective implementations.

Entity Operations

A managed entity belongs to a single persistence context and should not be managed by more than one persistence context at any given time. This is an application responsibility, however, and may not necessarily be enforced by the persistence provider. Merging the same entity into two different open persistence contexts could produce undefined results.

Entity managers and the persistence contexts that they manage are not intended to be accessed by more than one concurrently executing thread. The application cannot expect it to be synchronized and is responsible for ensuring that it stays within the thread that obtained it.

Entity Access

Applications may not access an entity directly from multiple threads while it is managed by a persistence context. An application may choose, however, to allow entities to be accessed concurrently when they are detached. If it chooses to do so, the synchronization must be controlled through the methods coded on the entity. Concurrent entity state access is not recommended, however, since the entity model does not lend itself well to concurrent patterns. It would be preferable to simply copy the entity and pass the copied entity to other threads for access and then merge any changes back into a persistence context when they need to be persisted.

Refreshing Entity State

The refresh() method of the EntityManager interface can be useful in situations when we know or suspect that there are changes in the database that we do not have in our managed entity. The refresh operation applies only when an entity is managed, since when we are detached we typically only need to issue a query to get an updated version of the entity from the database.

Refreshing makes more sense the longer the duration of the persistence context that contains it. Refreshing is especially relevant when using an extended or application-managed persistence context, since it prolongs the interval of time that an entity is effectively cached in the persistence context in isolation from the database.

To refresh a managed entity, we simply call refresh() on the entity manager. If the entity that we try to refresh is not managed, then an IllegalArgumentException exception will be thrown. To clarify some of the issues around the refresh operation, we will use the example session bean shown in Listing 9-17.

Listing 9-17. *Periodic Refresh of a Managed Entity*

```
@Stateful
@TransactionAttribute(TransactionAttributeType.NOT_SUPPORTED)
public class EmployeeServiceBean implements EmployeeService {
    public static final long REFRESH_THRESHOLD = 300000;

    @PersistenceContext(unitName="EmployeeService",
                        type=PersistenceContextType.EXTENDED)
    EntityManager em;
    Employee emp;
    long loadTime;

    public void loadEmployee (int id) {
        emp = em.find(Employee.class, id);
        if (emp == null)
            throw new IllegalArgumentException("Unknown employee id: " + id);
        loadTime = System.currentTimeMillis();
    }

    public void deductEmployeeVacation(int days) {
        refreshEmployeeIfNeeded();
        emp.setVacationDays(emp.getVacationDays() - days);
    }

    public void adjustEmployeeSalary(long salary) {
        refreshEmployeeIfNeeded();
        emp.setSalary(salary);
    }

    @Remove
    @TransactionAttribute(TransactionAttributeType.REQUIRED)
    public void finished() {}

    private void refreshEmployeeIfNeeded() {
        if ((System.currentTimeMillis() Ð loadTime) > REFRESH_THRESHOLD) {
            em.refresh(emp);
            loadTime = System.currentTimeMillis();
        }
    }

    // ...
}
```

The stateful session bean in Listing 9-17 uses an extended persistence context in order to keep an `Employee` instance managed while various operations are applied to it via the business methods of the session bean. It might allow a number of modifying operations on it before it commits the changes, but we need to include only a couple of operations for this example.

Let's look at this bean in detail. The first thing to notice is that the default transaction attribute has been changed from REQUIRED to NOT_SUPPORTED. This means that as the Employee instance is changed by the various business methods of the bean, those changes will not be written to the database. This will occur only when the finished() method is invoked, which has a transaction attribute of REQUIRED. This is the only method on the bean that will associate the extended persistence context with a transaction and cause it to be synchronized with the database.

The second interesting thing about this bean is that it stores the time the Employee instance was last accessed from the database. Since the stateful session bean instance may exist for a long time, the business methods use the refreshEmployeeIfNeeded() method to see if it has been too long since the Employee instance was last refreshed. If the refresh threshold has been reached, the refresh() method is used to update the Employee state from the database.

Unfortunately, the refresh operation does not behave as the author of the session bean expected. When refresh is invoked, it will overwrite the managed entity with the state in the database, causing any changes that have been made to the entity to be lost. For example, if the salary is adjusted and five minutes later the vacation is adjusted, then the employee will get refreshed, causing the previous change to the salary to be lost. It turns out that although the example in Listing 9-17 does indeed do a periodic refresh of the managed entity, the result is not only an inappropriate use of refresh() but also a detrimental result to the application.

So when is refreshing valid for objects that we are modifying? The answer is, not as often as you think. One of the primary use cases is to "undo" or discard changes made in the current transaction, reverting them back to their original value. It may also be used in long-lived persistence contexts where read-only managed entities are being cached. In these scenarios, the refresh() operation can safely restore an entity to its currently recorded state in the database. This would have the effect of picking up changes made in the database since the entity had been last loaded into the persistence context. The stipulation is that the entity should be read-only or be guaranteed to not contain changes.

Recall our editing session in Listing 5-33. Using refresh(), we can add the ability to revert an entity when the user decides to cancel their changes to an Employee editing session. Listing 9-18 shows the bean with its additional revertEmployee() method.

Listing 9-18. *Employee Editing Session with Revert*

```
@Stateful
@TransactionAttribute(TransactionAttributeType.NOT_SUPPORTED)
public class EmployeeEditBean implements EmployeeEdit {
    @PersistenceContext(unitName="EmployeeService",
                        type=PersistenceContextType.EXTENDED)
    EntityManager em;
    Employee emp;

    public void begin(int id) {
        emp = em.find(Employee.class, id);
        if (emp == null) {
            throw new IllegalArgumentException("Unknown employee id: " + id);
        }
    }
}
```

```
    public Employee getEmployee() { return emp; }

    public Employee revertEmployee() {
        em.refresh(emp);
        return emp;
    }

    @Remove
    @TransactionAttribute(TransactionAttributeType.REQUIRES_NEW)
    public void save() {}

    @Remove
    public void cancel() {}
}
```

Refresh operations may also be cascaded across relationships. This is done on the relationship annotation by setting the cascade element to include the REFRESH value. If the REFRESH value is not present in the cascade element, then the refresh will stop at the source entity. Listing 9-19 demonstrates how to set the REFRESH cascade operation for a many-to-one relationship.

Listing 9-19. *Cascading a Refresh Operation*

```
@Entity
public class Employee {
    @Id private int id;
    private String name;
    @ManyToOne(cascade={CascadeType.REFRESH})
    private Employee manager;
    // ...
}
```

Locking

Locking surfaces at many different levels is intrinsic to the Java Persistence API. It is used and assumed at various points throughout the API and the specification. Whether your application is simple or complex, chances are that you will make use of locking somewhere along the way.

Optimistic Locking

When we talk about locking we are generally referring to optimistic locking,[1] which is essentially just what its name implies, that is, a model that takes an optimistic approach to locking the entity. The optimistic locking model subscribes to the philosophy that there is a good

---

1. Pessimistic locking means to eagerly obtain a lock on the resource before operating on it. This is typically very resource-restrictive and results in significant performance degradation. The Java Persistence API does not currently support a portable mechanism of pessimistic locking.

chance that the transaction in which changes are made to an entity will be the only one that actually changes the entity during that interval. This translates into the decision to not acquire a lock on the entity until the change is actually made to the database, usually at the end of the transaction.

When the data actually does get sent to the database to get updated at flush time or at the end of the transaction, then the entity lock is acquired and a check is made on the data in the database. The flushing transaction must see whether any other transaction has committed a change to the entity in the intervening time since this transaction read it in and changed it. If a change occurred, then it means that the flushing transaction has data that does not include those changes and should not write its own changes to the database lest it overwrite the changes from the intervening transaction. At this stage it must roll back the transaction and throw a special exception called OptimisticLockException. The example in Listing 9-20 shows how this could happen.

Listing 9-20. *Method That Adjusts Vacation Balance*

```
@Stateless
public class EmployeeServiceBean implements EmployeeService {
    @PersistenceContext(unitName="EmployeeService")
    EntityManager em;

    public void deductEmployeeVacation(int id, int days) {
        Employee emp = em.find(Employee.class, id);
        int currentDays = emp.getVacationDays();
        // Do some other stuff like notify HR system, etc.
        // ...
        emp.setVacationDays(currentDays Ð days);
    }
}
```

While this method may seem harmless enough, it is really just an accident waiting to happen. The problem is as follows. Imagine that two HR data-entry operators, Frank and Betty, were charged with entering a backlog of vacation adjustments into the system and they both happened to be entering an adjustment for the employee with id 14 at the same time. Frank is supposed to deduct 1 day from employee 14, while Betty is deducting 12 days. Frank's console calls deductEmployeeVacation() first, which immediately reads employee 14 in from the database, finds that employee 14 has 20 days, and then proceeds into the HR notification step. Meanwhile, Betty starts to enter her data on her console, which also calls deductEmployeeVacation(). It also reads employee 14 in from the database and finds that the employee has 20 vacation days, but Betty happens to have a much faster connection to the HR system. As a result Betty gets past the HR notification before Frank does and proceeds to set the vacation day count to 8 before committing her transaction and going on to the next item. Frank finally gets past the HR system notification and deducts 1 day from the 20, and then commits his transaction. If Frank commits, then he has overwritten Betty's deduction and employee 14 gets an extra 12 days of vacation.

Instead of committing Frank's transaction, though, an optimistic locking strategy would find out when it was time to commit that someone else had changed the vacation count. When Frank attempted to commit his transaction, an OptimisticLockException would have been thrown, and his transaction would have been rolled back instead. The result is that Frank would have to reenter his change and try again, which is far superior to getting an incorrect result for employee 14.

Versioning

The question that you might have been asking is how the provider can know if somebody made changes in the intervening time since the committing transaction read the entity? The answer is that the provider maintains a versioning system for the entity. In order for it to do this, the entity must have a dedicated persistent field or property declared in it to store the version number of the entity that was obtained in the transaction. The version number must also be stored in the database. When going back to the database to update the entity, the provider can check the version of the entity in the database to see if it matches the version that it obtained previously. If the version in the database is the same, then the change can be applied and everything goes on without any problems. If the version was greater, then somebody else changed the entity since it was obtained in the transaction, and an exception should be thrown. The version field will get updated both in the entity and in the database whenever an update to the entity is sent to the database.

Version fields are not required, but we recommend that version fields be in every entity that has any chance of being concurrently modified by more than one process. A version column is an absolute necessity whenever an entity gets modified as a detached entity and merged back into a persistence context again afterwards. The longer an entity stays in memory, the higher the chance that it will be changed in the database by another process, rendering the in-memory copy invalid. Version fields are at the core of optimistic locking and provide the best and most performant protection for infrequent concurrent entity modification.

Version fields are defined simply by annotating the field or property on the entity with an @Version annotation. In Listing 9-21 is an Employee entity annotated to have a version field.

Listing 9-21. *Using a Version Field*

```
@Entity
public class Employee {
    @Id private int id;
    @Version private int version;
    // ...
}
```

Version-locking fields defined on the entity may be of type int, Integer, short, Short, long, Long, or java.sql.Timestamp. The most common practice is just to use int or one of the numeric types, but some legacy databases use timestamps.

Like the identifier, the application should not set or change the version field once the entity has been created. It may access it, though, for its own purposes if it wants to make use of the version number for some application-dependent reason.

> ■**Tip** Some vendors do not require that the version field be defined and stored in the entity. Variations of storing it in the entity are storing it in a vendor-specific cache, or not storing anything at all but instead using field comparison. For example, a popular option is to compare some application-specified combination of the entity state in the database with the entity state being written and then use the results as criteria to decide whether state has been changed.

A final note about version fields is that they are not guaranteed to be updated, either in the managed entities or the database, as part of a bulk update operation. In fact, there should not be any managed entities before a bulk update. Some vendors offer support for automatic updating of the version field during bulk updates, but this cannot be portably relied upon. For those vendors that do not support automatic version updates, the entity version may be manually updated as part of the UPDATE statement, as exhibited by the following query:

```
UPDATE Employee e
SET e.salary = e.salary + 1000, e.version = e.version + 1
WHERE EXISTS (SELECT p
              FROM e.projects p
              WHERE p.name = 'Release2')
```

Additional Locking Strategies

By default, the Java Persistence API assumes what is defined in the ANSI/ISO SQL specification and known in transaction isolation parlance as *Read Committed* isolation. This standard isolation level simply guarantees that any changes made inside a transaction will not be visible to other transactions until the changing transaction has been committed. Optimistic locking works with Read Committed isolation to provide additional data-consistency checks in the face of interleaved writes. Satisfying tighter locking constraints than what optimistic locking offers requires that an additional locking strategy be used. To be portable, these strategies may be used only on entities with version fields.

Read Locking

The next level of transaction isolation is termed *Repeatable Read* and prevents the so-called non-repeatable read anomaly. This anomaly can be described a few different ways, but perhaps the simplest is to say that when a transaction queries for the same data twice in the same transaction, the second query returns a different version of the data than was returned the first time because another transaction modified it in the intervening time. Put another way, Repeatable Read isolation level means that once a transaction has accessed data and another transaction modifies that data, then at least one of the transactions must be prevented from committing. A *read lock* in the Java Persistence API provides this level of isolation.

To read-lock an entity, the `EntityManager.lock()` method must be invoked, passing the entity to lock and a lock mode of `LockModeType.READ`. Obviously this may be invoked only within a transaction, but in addition, the entity that is passed into the call must already be managed. The resulting lock will guarantee that both the transaction that obtains the entity read lock and any other that tries to change that entity instance will not both succeed. At least one will fail, but like the database isolation levels, which one fails depends upon the implementation.

The way read locking is implemented is entirely up to the provider. It may choose to be heavy-handed and obtain an eager write lock on the entity, in which case any other transaction that tries to change the entity will fail or block until the locking transaction completes. Often the provider will optimistically read-lock the object instead. This means that the provider will not actually go to the database for a lock when the `lock()` method is called. It will instead wait until the end of the transaction, and at commit time it will reread the entity to see if the entity has been changed since it was last read in the transaction. If it has not changed, then the read lock was honored, but if the entity has changed, then the gamble was lost and the transaction will be rolled back.

A corollary to this optimistic form of read-locking implementation is that it doesn't matter at which point `lock()` is actually invoked during the transaction. It may be invoked even right up until just before the commit, and the exact same results will be produced. All the `lock()` method does is flag the entity for being reread at commit time. It doesn't really matter when, during the transaction, the entity gets added to this list since the actual read operation will not occur until the end of the transaction. You can kind of think of the `lock()` call as being retroactive to the point at which the entity was read into the transaction to begin with since that is the point at which the version is read and recorded in the managed entity.

The quintessential case for using this kind of lock is when an entity has an intrinsic dependency on one or more other entities for consistency. There is often a relationship between the entities, but not always. To demonstrate this, think of a `Department` that has employees where we want to generate a salary report for a given set of departments and have the report indicate the salary expenditures of each department. We have a method called `generateDepartmentsSalaryReport()` that will iterate through the set of departments and use an internal method to find the total salary for each one. The method defaults to having a transaction attribute of `REQUIRED`, so it will be executed entirely within the context of a transaction. The code is in Listing 9-22.

Listing 9-22. *Department Salaries Report*

```
@Stateless
public class EmployeeServiceBean implements EmployeeService {
    @PersistenceContext(unitName="EmployeeService")
    EntityManager em;

    // ...

    public SalaryReport generateDepartmentsSalaryReport(List<Integer> deptIds) {
        SalaryReport report = new SalaryReport();
        long total = 0;
```

```
        for (Integer deptId : deptIds) {
            long deptTotal = totalSalaryInDepartment(deptId);
            report.addDeptSalaryLine(deptId, deptTotal);
            total += deptTotal;
        }
        report.addSummarySalaryLine(total);
        return report;
    }

    protected long totalSalaryInDepartment(int deptId) {
        long total = 0;
        Department dept = em.find(Department.class, deptId);
        for (Employee emp : dept.getEmployees())
            total += emp.getSalary();
        return total;
    }

    public void changeEmployeeDepartment(int deptId, int empId) {
        Employee emp = em.find(Employee.class, empId);
        emp.getDepartment().removeEmployee(emp);
        Department dept = em.find(Department.class, deptId);
        dept.addEmployee(emp);
        emp.setDepartment(dept);
    }
    // ...
}
```

The report will get generated fine, but is it correct? What happens if an employee gets moved from one department to another during the time we are computing the total salary? For example, we make a request for a report on departments 10, 11, and 12. The request starts to generate the report for department 10. It finishes department 10 and moves on to department 11. As it is iterating through all of the employees in department 11, employee with id 50 in department 10 gets changed to be in department 12. Somewhere a manager invokes the changeEmployeeDepartment() method, the transaction commits, and employee 50 is changed to be in department 12. Meanwhile the report generator has finished department 11 and is now going on to generate a salary total for department 12. When it iterates through the employees it will find employee 50 even though it already counted that employee in department 10, so employee 50 will be counted twice. We did everything in transactions but we still got an inconsistent view of the employee data. Why?

The problem was in the fact that we did not lock any of the employee objects from being modified during our operation. We issued multiple queries and were vulnerable to viewing the same object with different state in it, which is the non-repeatable read phenomenon. We could fix it in a number of ways, one of which would be to set the database isolation to Repeatable Read. Since we are explaining the lock() method, we will use it to lock each of the employees so that either they could not change while our transaction was active, or if one did, then our transaction would fail. Listing 9-23 shows the updated method that does the locking.

Listing 9-23. *Using a Read Lock*

```
protected long totalSalaryInDepartment(int deptId) {
    long total = 0;
    Department dept = em.find(Department.class, deptId);
    for (Employee emp : dept.getEmployees()) {
        em.lock(emp, LockModeType.READ);
        total += emp.getSalary();
    }
    return total;
}
```

We mentioned that the implementation is permitted to lock eagerly or defer acquisition of the locks until the end of the transaction. Most major implementations defer the locking until commit time and by doing so provide far superior performance and scalability without sacrificing any of the semantics.

Write Locking

The other level of locking is called a *write lock*, which by virtue of its name hints correctly that we are actually locking the object for writing. The write lock guarantees all that the read lock does but in addition pledges to increment the version field in the transaction regardless of whether a user updated the entity or not. This provides a promise of an optimistic lock failure if another transaction also tries to modify the same entity before this one commits. This is equivalent to making a forced update to the entity in order to trigger the version number to be augmented. The obvious conclusion is that if the entity is being updated or removed by the application, then it never needs to be write-locked and that write-locking it anyway would be redundant at best and at worst could lead to an additional update, depending upon the implementation.

The common case for using write locks is to guarantee consistency across entity relationship changes (often they are one-to-many relationships with target foreign keys) when in the object model the entity relationship pointers change but in the data model no columns in the entity table change.

For example, let's say an employee has a set of assigned uniforms that were given to him, and his company has a cheap cleaning service that bills him automatically through payroll deduction. So `Employee` has a one-to-many relationship to `Uniform`, and `Employee` has a `cleaningCost` field that contains the amount that will get deducted from his paycheck at the end of the month. If there are two different stateful session beans that have extended persistence contexts, one for managing employees (`EmployeeManagement`) and another that manages the cleaning fees (`CleaningFeeManagement`) for the company, then if the `Employee` exists in both of the persistence contexts, there is a possibility of inconsistency.

Both copies of the `Employee` entity start out the same, but let's say that an operator records that the employee has received an additional brand new uniform. This implies creation of a new `Uniform` entity and adding it to the one-to-many collection of the `Employee`. The transaction is committed and everything is fine, except that now the `EmployeeManagement` persistence context has a different version of the `Employee` than the `CleaningFeeManagement` persistence context has. The operator has done the first maintenance task and now goes on to computing the cleaning charge for clients. The `CleaningFeeManagement` session computes the cleaning charges based on the one-to-many relationship that it knows about (without the extra uniform) and writes out a new version of the Employee with the employee's cleaning charge based on one less uniform. The transaction commits successfully even though the first transaction had already committed and though the changes to the uniform relationship had already committed to the database. Now we have an inconsistency between the number of uniforms and the cost of cleaning them, and the CleaningFeeManagement persistence context could go on with its stale copy of the Employee without even knowing about the new uniform and never get a lock conflict.

The reason the change was not seen and no lock exception occurred for the second operation was because in the first operation no writes to the Employee actually occurred and thus the version column was not updated. The only changes to the Employee were to its relationship, and because it was owned by the uniform side there was no reason to make any updates to the Employee. Unfortunately for the company (though the employee may not be so unfortunate) this means they will be out a cleaning fee for the uniform.

The solution is to use the write lock, as shown in Listing 9-24, and force an update to the Employee when the relationship changed in the first operation. This will cause any updates in any other persistence contexts to fail if they make changes without knowing about the relationship update.

Listing 9-24. *Using a Write Lock*

```
@Stateful
public class EmployeeManagementBean implements EmployeeManagement {
    @PersistenceContext(unitName="EmployeeService",
                        type=PersistenceContextType.EXTENDED)
    EntityManager em;

    public void addUniform(int id, Uniform uniform) {
        Employee emp = em.find(Employee.class, id);
        em.lock(emp, LockModeType.WRITE);
        emp.addUniform(uniform);
        uniform.setEmployee(emp);
    }

    // ...
}

@Stateful
public class CleaningFeeManagementBean implements CleaningFeeManagement {
    static final Float UNIFORM_COST = 4.7f;

    @PersistenceContext(unitName="EmployeeService",
                        type=PersistenceContextType.EXTENDED)
    EntityManager em;
```

```
    public void calculateCleaningCost(int id) {
        Employee emp = em.find(Employee.class, id);
        Float cost = emp.getUniforms().size() * UNIFORM_COST;
        emp.setCost(emp.getCost() + cost);
    }

    // ...
}
```

Recovering from Optimistic Failures

An optimistic failure means that one or more of the entities that were modified were not *fresh*
enough to be allowed to record their changes. The version of the entity that was modified was
stale, and the entity had since been changed in the database, hence an OptimisticLockException
was thrown. There is not always an easy solution to recovering, and depending upon the application architecture, it may or may not even be possible, but if and when appropriate, one
solution may be to get a fresh copy of the entity and then re-apply the changes. In other cases
it may only be possible to give the client (such as a web browser) an indication that the changes
were in conflict with another transaction and must be reentered. The harsh reality of it is that
in the majority of cases it is neither practical nor feasible to handle optimistic lock problems
other than to simply retry the operation at a convenient transactional demarcation point.

The first problem you might encounter when an OptimisticLockException is thrown could
be the one you never see. Depending on what your settings are, for example whether the calling
bean is container-managed or bean-managed, and whether the interface is remote or local,
you may only get a container-initiated EJBException. This exception will not necessarily even
wrap the OptimisticLockException, since all that is formally required of the container is to log
it before throwing the exception.

Listing 9-25 shows how this could happen when invoking a method on a session bean that
initiates a new transaction.

Listing 9-25. *BMT Session Bean Client*

```
@Stateless
@TransactionManagement(TransactionManagementType.BEAN)
public class EmpServiceClientBean implements EmpServiceClient {
    @EJB EmployeeService empService;

    public void adjustVacation(int id, int days) {
        try {
            empService.deductEmployeeVacation(id, days);
        } catch (EJBException ejbEx) {
            System.out.println("Something went wrong, but I have no idea what!");
        } catch (OptimisticLockException olEx) {
            System.out.println("This exception would be nice, but I will ➡
```

probably never get it!");
```
        }
    }
}
```

The problem is that when an optimistic exception occurs down in the bowels of the persistence layer, it will get passed back to the `EmployeeService` session bean and get handled according to the rules of runtime exception handling by the container. Since the `EmpServiceClientBean` uses bean-managed transactions and does not start a transaction, and `EmployeeServiceBean` defaults to container-managed transactions with a `REQUIRED` attribute, a transaction will be initiated when the call to `deductVacationBalance()` occurs.

Once the method has completed and the changes have been made, the container will attempt to commit the transaction. In the process of doing this, the persistence provider will get a transaction synchronization notification from the transaction manager to flush its persistence context to the database. As the provider attempts its writes, it finds during its version number check that one of the objects has been modified by another process since being read by this one, so it throws an `OptimisticLockException`. The problem is that the container treats this exception the same way as any other runtime exception. The exception simply gets logged and the container throws an `EJBException`.

The solution to this problem is to perform a `flush()` operation from inside the container-managed transaction at the moment just before we are ready to complete the method. This forces a write to the database and locks the resources only at the end of the method so the effects on concurrency are minimized. It also allows us to handle an optimistic failure while we are in control, without the container interfering and potentially swallowing the exception. If we do get an exception from the `flush()` call, then we can throw an application exception that the caller can recognize. This is shown in Listing 9-26.

Listing 9-26. *Catching and Converting* `OptimisticLockException`

```
@Stateless
public class EmployeeServiceBean implements EmployeeService {
    @PersistenceContext(unitName="EmployeeService")
    EntityManager em;

    public void deductEmployeeVacation(int id, int days) {
        Employee emp = em.find(Employee.class, id);
        emp.setVacationDays(emp.getVacationDays() - days);
        // ...
        flushChanges();
    }

    public void adjustEmployeeSalary(int id, long salary) {
        Employee emp = em.find(Employee.class, id);
        emp.setSalary(salary);
        // ...
        flushChanges();
    }
```

```
    protected void flushChanges() {
        try {
            em.flush();
        } catch (OptimisticLockException optLockEx) {
            throw new ChangeCollisionException();
        }
    }
    // ...
}


@ApplicationException
public class ChangeCollisionException extends RuntimeException {
    public ChangeCollisionException() { super(); }
}
```

The `OptimisticLockException` may contain the object that caused the exception, but it is not guaranteed to. We have only one object that we know is the `Employee`, so we are not passing it on or looking at it. To access this object, we would have invoked `getObject()` on the exception that we caught to see whether the object was included.

We factor out the flushing as every method must flush and catch the exception and then rethrow a domain-specific application exception. The `ChangeCollisionException` class is annotated with `@ApplicationException`, which is an EJB 3.0 container annotation in the `javax.ejb` package to indicate to the container that the exception is not really a system-level exception but should be thrown back to the client as is. Normally, defining an application exception will cause the container to not roll back the transaction, but this is an EJB 3.0 container notion. The persistence provider that threw the `OptimisticLockException` does not know about the special semantics of designated application exceptions and seeing a runtime exception will go ahead and mark the transaction for rollback.

The client code that we saw earlier can now receive and handle the application exception and potentially do something about it. At the very least it is aware of the fact that the failure was a result of a data collision instead of some other more fatal error. The client bean is shown in Listing 9-27.

Listing 9-27. *Handling* `OptimisticLockException`

```
@Stateless
@TransactionManagement(TransactionManagementType.BEAN)
public class EmpServiceClientBean implements EmpServiceClient {
    @EJB EmployeeService empService;

    public void adjustVacation(int id, int days) {
        try {
            empService.deductEmployeeVacation(id, days);
        } catch (ChangeCollisionException ccEx) {
            System.out.println("Collision with other change Ð RetryingÉ");
            empService.deductEmployeeVacation(id, days);
        }
    }
}
```

When an `OptimisticLockException` occurs in this context, the easy answer is to retry. This was really quite a trivial case, so the decision to retry was not hard to make. If we are in an extended persistence context, however, we may have a much harder job of it since all of the entities in the extended persistence context become detached when a transaction rolls back. Essentially we would need to reenlist all of our objects after having reread them and then replay all of the changes that we had applied in the previous failed transaction. Not a very easy thing to do in most cases.

In general it is quite difficult to code for the optimistic exception case. When running in a server environment, chances are that any `OptimisticLockException` will be wrapped by an EJB exception or server exception. The best approach is to simply treat all transaction failures equally and retry the transaction from the beginning or to indicate to the browser client that they must restart and retry.

Schema Generation

When we touched on schema generation in Chapter 4 we promised to go over the mapping annotation elements that are considered when schema generation occurs. In this section we will make good on that pledge and explain which elements get applied to the generated schema for those vendors that support schema generation.[2]

A couple of comments are in order before we start into them, though. First, the elements that contain the schema-dependent properties are, with few exceptions, in the physical annotations. This is to try to keep them separate from the logical non-schema related metadata. Second, these annotations are ignored, for the most part,[3] if the schema is not being generated. This is one reason why using them is a little out of place in the usual case, since schema information about the database is of little use once the schema has been created and is being used.

One of the complaints around schema generation is that you can't specify everything that you need to be able to finely tune the schema. This was done on purpose. There are too many differences between databases and too many different settings to try to put in options for every database type. If every database-tuning option were exposed through the Java Persistence API then we would end up duplicating the features of Data Definition Language (DDL) in an API that was not meant to be a database schema generation facility. As we mentioned earlier, the majority of applications find themselves in a meet-in-the-middle mapping scenario in any case, and when they do have control over the schema, then the final schema will typically be tuned by a database administrator or someone with the appropriate level of database experience.

Unique Constraints

A unique constraint can be created on a generated column or join column by using the `unique` element in the `@Column` or `@JoinColumn` annotations. There are not actually very many cases where this will be necessary since most vendors will generate a unique constraint when it is appropriate, such as on the join column of one-to-one relationships. Otherwise the value of

---

2. Most vendors supporting the Java Persistence API support some kind of schema generation either in the runtime or in a tool.
3. The exception to this rule may be the `optional` element of the mapping annotations, which may result in a NON NULL constraint but which may also be used in memory to indicate that the value is or isn't allowed to be set to null.

the `unique` element defaults to false. Listing 9-28 shows an entity with a unique constraint defined for the `STR` column.

Listing 9-28. *Including Unique Constraints*

```
@Entity
public class Employee {
    @Id private int id;
    @Column(unique=true)
    private String name;
    // ...
}
```

Note that the `unique` element is unnecessary on the identifier column since a primary key constraint will always be generated for the primary key.

A second way of adding a unique constraint is to embed one or more `@UniqueConstraint` annotations in a `uniqueConstraints` element in the `@Table` or `@SecondaryTable` annotations. Any number of unique constraints may be added to the table definition, including compound constraints. The value passed to the `@UniqueConstraint` annotation is an array of one or more strings listing the column names that make up the constraint. Listing 9-29 demonstrates how to define a unique constraint as part of a table.

Listing 9-29. *Unique Constraints Specified in Table Definition*

```
@Entity
@Table(name="EMP",
        uniqueConstraints=@UniqueConstraint(columnNames={"NAME"}))
public class Employee {
    @Id private int id;
    private String name;
    // ...
}
```

Null Constraints

Constraints on a column may also be in the form of null constraints. A null constraint just indicates that the column may or may not be null. It is defined when the column is declared as part of the table.

Null constraints are defined on a column by using the `nullable` element in the `@Column` or `@JoinColumn` annotations. A column allows null values by default, so this element really needs to be used only when a value for the field or property is required. Listing 9-30 demonstrates how to set the `nullable` element of basic and relationship mappings.

Listing 9-30. *Null Constraints Specified in Column Definitions*

```
@Entity
public class Employee {
    @Id private int id;
    @Column(nullable=false)
    private String name;
    @ManyToOne
    @JoinColumn(nullable=false)
    private Address address;
    // ...
}
```

String-Based Columns

When no length is specified for a column that is being generated to store string values, then the length will be defaulted to 255. When a column is generated for a basic mapping of a field or property of type String, char[], or Character[], its length should be explicitly listed in the length element of the @Column annotation if 255 is not the desired maximum length. Listing 9-31 shows an entity with explicitly specified lengths for strings.

Listing 9-31. *Specifying the Length of Character-Based Column Types*

```
@Entity
public class Employee {
    @Id
    @Column(length=40)
    private String name;
    @ManyToOne
    @JoinColumn(name="MGR")
    private Employee manager;
    // ...
}
```

We can see from the previous example that there is no similar length element in the @JoinColumn annotation. When primary keys are string-based, the provider may set the join column length to the same length as the primary key column in the table that is being joined to. This is not required to be supported, however.

It is not defined for length to be used for large objects; some databases do not require or even allow the length of lobs to be specified.

Floating Point Columns

Columns containing floating point types have a precision and scale associated with them. The precision is just the number of digits that are used to represent the value, and the scale is the number of digits after the decimal point. These two values may be specified as precision and scale elements in the @Column annotation when mapping a floating point type. Like other schema generation elements, they have no effect on the entity at runtime. Listing 9-32 demonstrates how to set these values.

Listing 9-32. *Specifying the Precision and Scale of Floating Point Column Types*

```
@Entity
public class PartTimeEmployee {
    // ...
    @Column(precision=8, scale=2)
    private float hourlyRate;
    // ...
}
```

■**Tip** Precision may be defined differently for different databases. In some databases and for some floating point types it is the number of binary digits, while for others it is the number of decimal digits.

Defining the Column

There may be a time when you are happy with all of the generated columns except for one. It isn't what you want it to be, and you don't want to go through the trouble of manually generating the schema for the sake of one column. This is one instance when the `columnDefinition` element comes in handy. By hand-rolling the DDL for the column, we can include it as the column definition and let the provider use it to define the column.

The `columnDefinition` element is available in all of the column-oriented annotation types, including `@Column`, `@JoinColumn`, `@PrimaryKeyJoinColumn`, and `@DiscriminatorColumn`. Whenever a column is to be generated, the `columnDefinition` element may be used to indicate the DDL string that should be used to generate the type (not including the trailing comma). This gives the user complete control over what is generated in the table for the column being mapped. It also allows a database-specific type or format to be used that may supercede the generated type offered by the provider for the database being used.[4] Listing 9-33 shows some definitions specified for two columns and a join column.

Listing 9-33. *Using a Column Definition to Control DDL Generation*

```
@Entity
public class Employee {
    @Id
    @Column(columnDefinition="NVARCHAR2(40)")
    private String name;
    @Column(name="START_DATE", columnDefinition="DATE DEFAULT SYSDATE")
    private java.sql.Date startDate;
    @ManyToOne
```

---

4. The resulting column must be supported by the provider runtime to enable reading from and writing to the column.

```
    @JoinColumn(name="MGR", columnDefinition="NVARCHAR2(40)")
    private Employee manager;
    // ...
}
```

In this example we are using a Unicode character field for the primary key and then also for the join column that refers to the primary key. We also define the date to be assigned the default current date at the time the record was inserted (in case it was not specified).

Specifying the column definition is quite a powerful schema generation practice that allows overriding of the generated column to an application-defined custom column definition. But the power is accompanied by some risk as well. When a column definition is included, then other accompanying column-specific generation metadata is ignored. Specifying the precision, scale, or length in the same annotation as a column definition would be both unnecessary and confusing.

Not only does using columnDefinition in your code bind you to a particular schema, but it also binds you to a particular database since the DDL tends to be database-specific. This is just a flexibility-portability trade-off, and you have to decide whether it is appropriate for your application.

Summary

Over the course of this chapter we have covered a wide range of diverse topics, from SQL queries to schema generation. Not everything we have described will be immediately usable in a new application, but some features such as optimistic locking are likely to play a prominent role in many enterprise applications.

We began the chapter with a look at SQL queries. We looked at the role of SQL in applications that also use JPQL and the specialized situations where only SQL can be used. To bridge the gap between native SQL and entities, we described the result set mapping process in detail, showing a wide range of queries and how they translate back into the application domain model.

The Lifecycle Callbacks section introduced the life cycle of an entity and showed the points at which an application can monitor events that are fired as an entity moves through different stages of its life cycle. We looked at two different approaches to implementing callback methods, on the entity class and as part of a separate listener class.

In our discussion of locking and versioning, we introduced optimistic locking and described the vital role it plays in many applications, particularly those that use detached entities. We also looked at read and write locks for entities and how they correspond to isolation levels in the database. We described the difficulties of recovering from optimistic lock failures and when it is appropriate to refresh the state of a managed entity.

Finally we looked at schema generation and how to specify schema properties using different elements of the mapping annotations.

In the next chapter we will look at the XML mapping file, showing how to use XML with, or instead of, annotations and how annotation metadata can be overridden.

CHAPTER 10

■ ■ ■

XML Mapping Files

Since the release of Java SE 5 there has been a quiet, and sometimes not-so-quiet, ongoing debate about whether annotations are better or worse than XML. The defenders of annotations vigorously proclaim how annotations are so much simpler and provide in-lined metadata that is co-located with the code that it is describing. They claim that this avoids the need to replicate the source code context of where the metadata applies. The XML proponents then retort that annotations unnecessarily couple the metadata to the code and that changes to metadata should not require changes to the source code.

The truth is that both sides are right and that there are appropriate times for using annotation metadata and others for using XML. When the metadata really is coupled to the code, then it does make sense to use annotations since the metadata is just another aspect of the program. For example, specification of the identifier field of an entity is not only a relevant piece of information to the provider but also a necessary detail known and assumed by the referencing application code. Other kinds of metadata, such as which column a field is mapped to, can be safely changed without needing to change the code. This metadata is akin to configuration metadata and might be better expressed in XML, where it can be configured according to the usage pattern or execution environment.

These arguments also tend to unfairly compartmentalize the issue, because in reality it goes deeper than simply deciding when it might make sense to use one type of metadata or the other. In many talks and forums leading up to the release of the specification, we asked people whether they planned on using annotations or XML, and we consistently saw that there was a split. The reason is that there are other factors that have nothing to do with which is better, such as existing development processes, source control systems, developer experience, and so forth. Reasons for using XML go beyond whether or not it is a better or worse technique for specifying metadata.

With this controversy as a backdrop, it is easy to see that it was not by accident that mapping metadata was allowed to be specified in either format. In fact, XML mapping usage is defined in such a way as to allow annotations to be used and then overridden by XML. This provides the ability to use annotations for some things and XML for others, or to use annotations for an expected configuration but then supply an overriding XML file to suit a particular execution environment. The XML file may be sparse and supply only the information that is required to be overridden, and we will see later on in this chapter that the granularity with which this metadata may be specified offers a good deal of object-relational mapping flexibility.

Over the course of this chapter we will describe the structure and content of the mapping file and how it relates to the metadata annotations. We will also discuss how XML mapping metadata may combine with and override annotation metadata. We have tried to structure the chapter in a format that will allow it to be used as both a source of information and a reference for the mapping file format.

The Metadata Puzzle

The rules of XML and annotation usage and overriding can be a little confusing to say the least, especially given the permutation space of mixing annotations with XML. The trick to understanding the semantics and being able to properly specify metadata the way that you would like it to be specified is to understand the metadata collection process. Once you have a solid understanding of what the metadata processor does, you will be well on your way to understanding what you need to do to achieve a specific result.

The provider may choose to perform the metadata gathering process in any way it chooses, but the result is that it must honor the requirements of the specification. Developers understand algorithms, so we decided that it will be easier to understand if we present the logical functionality as an algorithm, even though the implementation may not actually implement it this way. The following algorithm can be considered as the simplified logic for obtaining the metadata for the persistence unit:

1. **Process the annotations.** The set of entities, mapped superclasses, and embedded objects is discovered (we'll call this set E) by looking for the `@Entity`, `@MappedSuperclass`, and `@Embeddable` annotations. The class and method annotations in all of the classes in E are processed, and the resulting metadata is stored in the set C. Any missing metadata that was not explicitly specified in the annotations is left empty.

2. **Add the classes defined in XML.** Look for all of the entities, mapped superclasses, and embedded objects that are defined in the mapping files and add them to E. If we find that one of the classes already exists in E, then we apply the overriding rules for class-level metadata that we found in the mapping file. Add or adjust the class-level metadata in C according to the overriding rules.

3. **Add the attribute mappings defined in XML.** For each class in E, look at the fields or properties in the mapping file and try to add the method metadata to C. If the field or property already exists there, then apply the overriding rules for attribute-level mapping metadata.

4. **Apply defaults.** Determine all default values according to the scoping rules and where defaults may have been defined (see the following for description of default rules). The classes, attribute mappings, and other settings that have not yet been filled in are assigned values and put in C.

Some of the following cases may cause this algorithm to be modified slightly, but in general this is what will logically happen when the provider needs to obtain the mapping metadata.

We already learned in the mapping chapters that annotations may be sparse and that not annotating a persistent attribute will cause it to default to being mapped as a basic mapping. Other mapping defaults were also explained, and we saw how much easier they made configuring and mapping entities. We notice in our algorithm that the defaults are applied at the end, so the same defaults that we saw for annotations will be applied when using mapping files as well. It should be of some comfort to XML users that mapping files may be sparsely specified in the same ways as annotations. They also have the same requirements for what needs to be specified; for example, an identifier must be specified, a relationship mapping must have at least its cardinality specified, and so forth.

The Mapping File

By this point you are well aware that if you don't want to use XML for mapping, then you don't need to use XML. In fact, as we will see in Chapter 11, any number of mapping files or none may be included in a persistence unit. If you do use one, however, each mapping file that is supplied must conform and be valid against the orm_1_0.xsd schema located at http://java.sun.com/xml/ns/persistence/orm_1_0.xsd. This schema defines a namespace called http://java.sun.com/xml/ns/persistence/orm that includes all of the ORM elements that can be used in a mapping file. A typical XML header for a mapping file is shown in Listing 10-1.

Listing 10-1. *XML Header for Mapping File*

```
<?xml version="1.0" encoding="UTF-8"?>
<entity-mappings xmlns="http://java.sun.com/xml/ns/persistence/orm"
    xmlns:xsi="http://www.w3.org/2001/XMLSchema-instance"
    xsi:schemaLocation="http://java.sun.com/xml/ns/persistence/orm
                        http://java.sun.com/xml/ns/persistence/orm_1_0.xsd"
    version="1.0">
```

The root element of the mapping file is called entity-mappings. All object-relational XML metadata is contained within this element, and as seen in the example, the header information is also specified as attributes in this element. The subelements of entity-mappings can be categorized into four main scoping and functional groups: persistence unit defaults, mapping files defaults, queries and generators, and managed classes and mappings. There is also a special setting that determines whether annotations should be considered in the metadata for the persistence unit. These groups are discussed in the following sections. For the sake of brevity we won't include the header information in the XML examples in these sections.

Disabling Annotations

For those who are perfectly happy with XML and don't feel the need for annotations, there are ways to skip the annotation processing phase (step 1 in the previous algorithm). The xml-mapping-metadata-complete element and metadata-complete attribute provide a convenient way to reduce the overhead that is required to discover and process all of the annotations on the classes in the persistence unit. It is also a way to effectively disable any annotations that do exist. These options will cause the processor to completely ignore them as if they did not exist at all.

xml-mapping-metadata-complete

When the `xml-mapping-metadata-complete` element is specified, all annotations in the entire persistence unit will be ignored, and only the mapping files in the persistence unit will be considered as the total set of provided metadata. Only entities, mapped superclasses, and embedded objects that have entries in a mapping file will be added to the persistence unit.

The `xml-mapping-metadata-complete` element needs to be in only one of the mapping files if there are multiple mapping files in the persistence unit. It is specified as an empty subelement of the `persistence-unit-metadata` element, which is the first[1] subelement of `entity-mappings`. An example of using this setting is in Listing 10-2.

Listing 10-2. *Disabling Annotation Metadata for the Persistence Unit*

```
<entity-mappings>
    <persistence-unit-metadata>
        <xml-mapping-metadata-complete/>
    </persistence-unit-metadata>
    ...
</entity-mappings>
```

If enabled, there is no way to portably override this setting. It will apply globally to the persistence unit, regardless of whether any `metadata-complete` attribute is set to false in an entity.

metadata-complete

The `metadata-complete` attribute is an attribute on the `entity`, `mapped-superclass`, and `embeddable` elements. If specified, all annotations on the specified class and on any fields or properties in the class will be ignored, and only the metadata in the mapping file will be considered as the set of metadata for the class.

■**Caution** Annotations defining queries, generators, or result set mappings are ignored if they are defined on a class that is marked as `metadata-complete` in an XML mapping file.

When `metadata-complete` is enabled, the same rules that apply to annotated entities will also apply to the XML-mapped entity. For example, the identifier must be mapped, and all relationships must be specified with their corresponding cardinality mappings inside the `entity` element.

An example of using the `metadata-complete` attribute is in Listing 10-3. The entity mappings in the annotated class are disabled by the `metadata-complete` attribute, and because the fields are not mapped in the mapping file, the default mapping values will be used. The `name` and `salary` fields will be mapped to the `NAME` and `SALARY` columns, respectively.

---

1. Technically there is a `description` element in many of the elements, just as there are in most of the standard schemas in Java EE, but these have little functional value and will not be mentioned here. They may be of some use to tools that parse XML schemas and use the descriptions for tooltips, and similar actions.

Listing 10-3. *Disabling Annotations for a Managed Class*

```
@Entity
public class Employee {
    @Id private int id;
    @Column(name="EMP_NAME")
    private String name;
    @Column(name="SAL")
    private long salary;
    // ...
}

<entity-mappings>
    ...
    <entity class="examples.model.Employee"
            metadata-complete="true">
        <attributes>
            <id name="id"/>
        </attributes>
    </entity>
    ...
</entity-mappings>
```

Persistence Unit Defaults

One of the conditions for using annotation metadata is that we need to have something to annotate. If we want to define metadata for a persistence unit, then we are in the unfortunate position of not having anything to annotate, since a persistence unit is just a logical grouping of Java classes, basically a configuration. This brings us back to the discussion that we had earlier when we decided that if metadata is not coupled to code, then maybe it shouldn't really be in the code. These are the reasons why persistence unit metadata may be specified only in an XML mapping file.

In general, a persistence unit default means that whenever a value for that setting is not specified at a more local scope, the persistence unit default value will apply. It is a convenient way to set default values that will apply to all entities, mapped superclasses, and embedded objects in the entire persistence unit, be they in any of the mapping files or annotated classes. The default values will not be applied if a value is present at any level below the persistence unit. This value may be in the form of a mapping file default value, some value in an entity element, or an annotation on one of the managed classes or persistent fields or properties.

The element that encloses all of the persistence unit level defaults is the aptly named persistence-unit-defaults element. It is the other subelement of the persistence-unit-metadata element (after xml-mapping-metadata-complete). If more than one mapping file exists in a persistence unit, then only one of the files should contain these elements.

There are five settings that can be configured to have default values for the persistence unit. They are specified using the schema, catalog, access, cascade-persist, and entity-listeners elements.

schema

The schema element is useful if you don't want to have to specify a schema in every @Table, @SecondaryTable, @JoinTable, or @TableGenerator annotation or table, secondary-table, join-table, or table-generator XML element in the persistence unit. When set here, it will apply to all tables in the persistence unit, whether they were actually defined or defaulted by the provider. The value of this element may be overridden by any of the following:

- schema element defined in the mapping file defaults (see the Mapping File Defaults section)

- schema attribute on any table, secondary-table, join-table, or table-generator element in a mapping file

- schema defined within an @Table, @SecondaryTable, @JoinTable, or @TableGenerator annotation or in an @TableGenerator annotation (unless xml-mapping-metadata-complete is set)

Listing 10-4 shows an example of how to set the schema for all of the tables in the persistence unit that do not already have their schema set.

Listing 10-4. *Setting the Default Persistence Unit Schema*

```
<entity-mappings>
    <persistence-unit-metadata>
        <persistence-unit-defaults>
            <schema>HR</schema>
        </persistence-unit-defaults>
    </persistence-unit-metadata>
    ...
</entity-mappings>
```

catalog

The catalog element is exactly analogous to the schema element except that it is for databases that support catalogs. It has the same behavior as schema and is overridden in exactly the same ways. The exact same rules may be applied to the catalog mapping file default as described in the preceding schema section.

access

The access element that is defined in the persistence-unit-defaults section is used to set the access type for all of the managed classes in the persistence unit that have XML entries but are not annotated. There is no corresponding annotation for this element. Its value may be either "FIELD" or "PROPERTY", indicating how the provider should access the persistent state.

The access setting is a subtly different default that does not affect any of the managed classes that have annotated fields or properties. It is a convenience for when XML is used and obviates having to specify the access for all of the entities listed in all of the XML mapping files.

This element affects only the managed classes defined in the mapping files, because a class with annotated fields or properties is considered to have overridden the access mode by virtue of its having annotations placed on its fields or properties. If the `xml-mapping-metadata-complete` element is enabled, then the persistence unit access default will be applied to these annotated classes that have entries in XML. Put another way, the annotations that would have otherwise overridden the access mode would no longer be considered, and the XML defaults, including the default access mode, would be applied.

The value of this element may be overridden only by one or more of the following:

- `access` element defined in the mapping file defaults (see the Mapping File Defaults section)

- `access` attribute on any `entity`, `mapped-superclass`, or `embeddable` element in a mapping file

- An annotated field or property in an entity, mapped superclass, or embedded object

In Listing 10-5 we show an example of setting the access mode to "PROPERTY" for all of the managed classes in the persistence unit that do not have annotated fields.

Listing 10-5. *Setting the Default Access Mode for the Persistence Unit*

```
<entity-mappings>
    <persistence-unit-metadata>
        <persistence-unit-defaults>
            <access>PROPERTY</access>
        </persistence-unit-defaults>
    </persistence-unit-metadata>
    ...
</entity-mappings>
```

cascade-persist

The `cascade-persist` element is unique in a different way. When the empty `cascade-persist` element is specified, it is analogous to adding the `PERSIST` cascade option to all of the relationships in the persistence unit. See Chapter 5 for a discussion about the cascade options on relationships.

The term *persistence-by-reachability* is often used to signify that when an object is persisted, all of the objects that are reachable from that object are also automatically persisted. The `cascade-persist` element provides the persistence-by-reachability semantics that some people are used to having. This setting cannot currently be overridden, but the intent is that it be overridable in future releases. The assumption is that when somebody is accustomed to persistence-by-reachability semantics, they don't normally want to be turning it off. If more fine-grained control over cascading of the persist operation is needed, then this element should not be specified, and the relationships should have their `PERSIST` cascade option specified explicitly.

An example of using the `cascade-persist` element is shown in Listing 10-6.

Listing 10-6. *Configuring for Persistence-by-Reachability Semantics*

```
<entity-mappings>
    <persistence-unit-metadata>
        <persistence-unit-defaults>
            <cascade-persist/>
        </persistence-unit-defaults>
    </persistence-unit-metadata>
    ...
</entity-mappings>
```

entity-listeners

This is the only place where a list of *default entity listeners* can be specified. A default entity listener is a listener that will be applied to every entity in the persistence unit. They will be invoked in the order that they are listed in this element, before any other listener or callback method is invoked on the entity. It is the logical equivalent of adding the listeners in this list to the front of the @EntityListeners list in the root superclass. We discussed entity listeners in the last chapter, so take a look at Chapter 9 to review the order of invocation if you need to. A description of how to specify an entity listener is given in the Entity Listeners section.

The entity-listeners element is composed of zero or more entity-listener elements that each defines an entity listener. They can be overridden or disabled in either of the following two ways:

- exclude-default-listeners element in an entity or mapped-superclass mapping file element

- @ExcludeDefaultListeners annotation on an entity or mapped superclass (unless xml-mapping-metadata-complete is set)

Mapping File Defaults

The next level of defaults after the ones defined for the entire persistence unit are those that pertain only to the entities, mapped superclasses, and embedded objects that are contained in a particular mapping file. In general, if there is a persistence unit default defined for the same setting, then this value will override the persistence unit default for the managed classes in the mapping file. Unlike the persistence unit defaults, the mapping file defaults do not affect managed classes that are annotated and not defined in the mapping file.

The mapping file defaults consist of four subelements of the entity-mappings element. They are package, schema, catalog, and access.

package

The package element is intended to be used by developers who don't want to have to repeat the fully qualified class name in all of the mapping file metadata. It may be overridden in the mapping file by fully qualifying a class name in any element or attribute where a class name is expected. These are the following:

- class attribute of id-class, entity-listener, entity, mapped-superclass, or embeddable elements

- target-entity attribute of many-to-one, one-to-one, one-to-many, and many-to-many elements

- result-class attribute of named-native-query element

- entity-class attribute of entity-result element

An example of using this element is shown in Listing 10-7. We set the default mapping file package name to examples.model for the entire mapping file and can just use the unqualified Employee and EmployeePK class names throughout the file. The package name will not be applied to OtherClass, though, as it is already fully specified.

Listing 10-7. *Using the* package *Element*

```
<entity-mappings>
    <package>examples.model</package>
    ...
    <entity class="Employee">
        <id-class class="EmployeePK"/>
        ...
    </entity>
    <entity class="examples.tools.OtherClass">
        ...
    </entity>
    ...
</entity-mappings>
```

schema

The schema element will set a default schema to be assumed for every table, secondary table, join table, or table generator defined or defaulted within the mapping file. This element may be overridden by the specification of the schema attribute on any table, secondary-table, join-table, or table-generator element in the mapping file.

Listing 10-8 shows the mapping file schema default set to "HR" so the EMP table that Employee is mapped to is assumed to be in the HR schema.

Listing 10-8. *Using the* schema *Element*

```
<entity-mappings>
    <package>examples.model</package>
    <schema>HR</schema>
    ...
    <entity class="Employee">
        <table name="EMP"/>
        ...
    </entity>
    ...
</entity-mappings>
```

The mapping file schema default will also affect @Table, @SecondaryTable, @JoinTable, and @TableGenerator annotations on classes that have entries in the mapping file. For example, since Employee is listed in the mapping file, it becomes part of the set of classes to which the default applies. If there was an @TableGenerator(name="EmpGen", table="IDGEN") annotation on Employee, then the mapping file default will be applied to it, and the IDGEN table will be assumed to be in the HR schema.

catalog

The catalog element is again exactly analogous to the schema element except it is for databases that support catalogs. It has the same behavior as schema at the mapping file default level and is overridden in exactly the same ways. As we mentioned in the persistence unit section, the exact same rules may be applied to the catalog mapping file default as described in the schema mapping file default section.

access

Setting a particular access mode as the mapping file default value affects only the managed classes that are defined in the mapping file. It is done through the use of the access element. As with annotations, it is not portable to use different access types for different classes in an entity hierarchy, although some vendors do allow it. Classes that have entries in the mapping file in addition to annotations must have matching access types if specified in XML. It is not portable to mix access types for the same entity.

Queries and Generators

Some persistence artifacts, such as id generators and queries, are defined as annotations on a class even though they are actually global to the persistence unit in scope. The reason for this is because they are annotations and there is no other place to put them other than on a class. In XML this global metadata does not need to be placed arbitrarily within a class but can be defined at the level of subelements of the entity-mappings element.

The global metadata elements are made up of generator and query elements that include sequence-generator, table-generator, named-query, named-native-query, and sql-result-set-mapping. These elements may appear in different contexts, but they are nevertheless still scoped to the persistence unit. There are three different persistence unit namespaces, one for queries, one for generators, and one for result set mappings that are used for native queries. When any of the elements that we just listed are defined in the mapping file, the artifacts they define will be added into the persistence unit namespace to which they apply. The namespaces will already contain all of the existing persistence unit artifacts that may have been defined in annotations or in another mapping file. Since these artifacts share the same global persistence unit namespace type, when one of the artifacts that is defined in XML shares the same name as one that already exists in the namespace of the same type, it is viewed as an override. The artifact that is defined in XML overrides the one that was defined by the annotation. There is no concept of overriding queries, generators, or result set mappings within the same or different mapping files. If one or more mapping files contains one of these objects defined with the same name, then it is undefined which overrides the other since the order that they are processed in is not specified.[2]

sequence-generator

The `sequence-generator` element is used to define a generator that uses a database sequence to generate identifiers. It corresponds to the `@SequenceGenerator` annotation (see Chapter 4) and may be used to define a new generator or override a generator of the same name that is defined by an `@SequenceGenerator` annotation in any class in the persistence unit. It may be specified either at the global level as a subelement of `entity-mappings`, at the entity level as a subelement of `entity`, or at the field or property level as a subelement of the `id` mapping element.

The attributes of `sequence-generator` line up exactly with the elements in the `@SequenceGenerator` annotation. Listing 10-9 shows an example of defining a sequence generator.

Listing 10-9. *Defining a Sequence Generator*

```
<entity-mappings>
    ...
    <sequence-generator name="empGen" sequence-name="empSeq"/>
    ...
</entity-mappings>
```

table-generator

The `table-generator` element defines a generator that uses a table to generate identifiers. Its annotation equivalent is the `@TableGenerator` annotation (see Chapter 4). This element may define a new generator, or it may be overriding a generator defined by an `@TableGenerator` annotation. Like the `sequence-generator` element, it may be defined within any of `entity-mappings`, `entity`, or `id` elements.

The attributes of `table-generator` also match the `@TableGenerator` annotation elements. Listing 10-10 shows an example of defining a sequence generator in annotation form but overriding it to be a table generator in XML.

Listing 10-10. *Overriding a Sequence Generator with a Table Generator*

```
@Entity
public class Employee {
    @SequenceGenerator(name="empGen")
    @Id @GeneratedValue(generator="empGen")
    private int id;
    // ...
}
```

---

2. It is possible, and even probable, that vendors will process the mapping files in the order that they are listed, but this is neither required nor standardized.

```
<entity-mappings>
    ...
    <table-generator name="empGen" table="ID_GEN" pk-column-value="EmpId"/>
    ...
</entity-mappings>
```

named-query

Static or named queries may be defined both in annotation form using @NamedQuery (see Chapter 6) or in a mapping file using the named-query element. A named-query element in the mapping file may also override an existing query of the same name but that was defined as an annotation. It makes sense, of course, when overriding a query to override it only with a query that has the same result type, be it an entity, data, or projection of data. Otherwise all of the code that executes the query and processes the results stands a pretty good chance of breaking.

A named-query element may appear as a subelement of entity-mappings or as a subelement of entity. Regardless of where it is defined, it will be keyed by its name in the persistence unit query namespace.

The name of the query is specified as an attribute of the named-query element, while the query string goes in a query subelement within it. Any number of query hints may also be provided as hint subelements.

In Listing 10-11 we see an example of two named queries, one of which uses a vendor-specific hint that bypasses the cache.

Listing 10-11. *Named Query in a Mapping File*

```
<entity-mappings>
    ...
    <named-query name="findEmpsWithName">
        <query>SELECT e FROM Employee e WHERE e.name LIKE :empName</query>
        <hint name="toplink.cache-usage" value="DoNotCheckCache"/>
    </named-query>
    <named-query name="findEmpsWithHigherSalary">
        <query><![CDATA[SELECT e FROM Employee e WHERE e.salary > :salary]]></query>
    </named-query>
    ...
</entity-mappings>
```

Query strings may also be expressed as CDATA within the query element. We can see in Listing 10-9 that this is helpful in cases when the query includes XML characters such as ">" that would otherwise need to be escaped.

named-native-query

Native SQL may also be used for named queries by defining an @NamedNativeQuery annotation (see Chapter 9) or by specifying a named-native-query element in a mapping file. Both named queries and native queries share the same query namespace in the persistence unit, so using either the named-query or named-native-query element will cause that query to override any query of the same name defined in annotation form.

Native queries are the same as named queries in that the `native-named-query` element may appear as a subelement of `entity-mappings` or as a subelement of `entity`. The name is specified using the `name` attribute, and the query string uses a `query` subelement. The hints are also specified in the same way. The only difference is that two additional attributes have been added to `named-native-query` to supply the result class or the result set mapping.

One use case for overriding queries is when the DBA comes to you and demands that your query run a certain way on a certain database. You can leave the query as generic JPQL for the other databases, but it turns out that the Oracle database can do this one particular thing very well using native syntax. By putting this query in a DB-specific XML file, it will be much easier to manage in the future. In Listing 10-12 we see an example of a vanilla named query in JPQL that is being overridden by a native SQL query.

Listing 10-12. *Overriding a JPQL Query with SQL*

```
@NamedQuery(name="findAllManagers"
            query="SELECT e FROM Employee e WHERE e.directs IS NOT EMPTY")
@Entity
public class Employee { ... }


<entity-mappings>
    ...
    <named-native-query name="findAllManagers"
                        result-class="examples.model.Employee">
        <query>
            SELECT /*+ FULL(m) */ e.id, e.name, e.salary,
                   e.manager_id, e.dept_id, e.address_id
            FROM   emp e,
                   (SELECT DISTINCT manager_id AS id FROM emp) m
            WHERE  e.id = m.id
        </query>
    </named-native-query>
    ...
</entity-mappings>
```

sql-result-set-mapping

A result set mapping is used by native queries to instruct the persistence provider how to map the results. The `sql-result-set-mapping` element corresponds to the `@SqlResultSetMapping` annotation. The name of the result set mapping is specified in the `name` attribute of the `sql-result-set-mapping` element. The result may be mapped as one or more entity types, projection data, or a combination of the two. Just as `@SqlResultSetMapping` encloses arrays of `@EntityResult` or `@ColumnResult` or both, so also can the `sql-result-set-mapping` element contain multiple `entity-result` and `column-result` elements. And similarly, as each `@EntityResult` contains an array of `@FieldResult`, the `entity-result` element may contain multiple `field-result` elements. The other `entityClass` and `discriminatorColumn` elements of the `@EntityResult` annotation map directly to the `entity-class` and `discriminator-column` attributes of the `entity-result` element.

Each `sql-result-set-mapping` may define a new mapping or override an existing one of the same name that was defined by an annotation. It is not possible to override only a part of the result set mapping. If you're overriding an annotation, then the entire annotation will be over-ridden, and the components of the result set mapping defined by the `sql-result-set-mapping` element will apply.

Having said all this about overriding, there is really not that much use in overriding an `@SqlResultSetMapping` since they are used to structure the result format from a static native query. As we mentioned earlier, queries tend to be executed with a certain expectation of the result that is being returned. Result set mappings are typically defined in a mapping file because that is also where the native query that it is defining the result is defined.

Listing 10-13 shows the "DepartmentSummary" result set mapping that we defined in Chapter 9 and its equivalent XML mapping file form.

Listing 10-13. *Specifying a Result Set Mapping*

```
@SqlResultSetMapping(
    name="DepartmentSummary",
    entities={
        @EntityResult(entityClass=Department.class,
                      fields=@FieldResult(name="name", column="DEPT_NAME")),
        @EntityResult(entityClass=Employee.class)
    },
    columns={@ColumnResult(name="TOT_EMP"),
            @ColumnResult(name="AVG_SAL")}
)

<entity-mappings>
    ...
    <sql-result-set-mapping name="DepartmentSummary">
        <entity-result entity-class="examples.model.Department">
            <field-result name="name" column="DEPT_NAME"/>
        </entity-result>
        <entity-result entity-class="examples.model.Employee"/>
        <column-result name="TOT_EMP"/>
        <column-result name="AVG_SAL"/>
    </sql-result-set-mapping>
    ...
</entity-mappings>
```

Managed Classes and Mappings

The main portion of every mapping file is typically going to be the managed classes in the persistence unit that are the `entity`, `mapped-superclass`, and `embeddable` elements and their state and relationship mappings. Each of these has their class specified as a `class` attribute of the element and their access type specified in an `access` attribute. The `access` attribute is required only when there are no annotations on the managed class or when `metadata-complete` (or `xml-mapping-metadata-complete`) has been specified for the class. If neither of these conditions apply and annotations do exist on the class, then the access attribute setting should match the access used by the annotations.

Queries and generators may be specified within an entity element. Generators may also be defined inside an id element in an entity or mapped superclass. These have already been described in the preceding Queries and Generators section.

Attributes

Unfortunately, the word *attribute* is grossly overloaded. It can be a general term for a field or property in a class, it can be a specific part of an XML element that can be inlined in the element tag, or it can be a generic term referring to a characteristic. Throughout these sections we have usually referred to it in the context of the second meaning because we have been talking a lot about XML elements. In this section, however, it refers to the first definition of a state attribute in the form of a field or property.

The attributes element is a subelement of the entity, mapped-superclass, and embeddable elements. It is an enclosing element that groups all of the mapping subelements for the fields or properties of the managed class. Because it is only a grouping element, it does not have an analogous annotation. It dictates which mappings are allowed for each type of managed class.

In the entity and mapped-superclass elements, there are a number of mapping subelements that may be specified. For identifiers, either multiple id subelements or a single embedded-id subelement may be included. The simple basic, version, and transient mapping subelements may also be specified, as well as the many-to-one, one-to-one, one-to-many, and many-to-many association subelements. The mapping mix is rounded out with the embedded subelement. An embeddable element is limited to containing only basic and transient mapping subelements. These elements will all be discussed separately in their own sections later, but each element has one thing in common. They each have a name attribute (in the XML attribute sense) that is required to indicate the name of the attribute (in this case we mean field or property) that it is mapping.

A first general comment about overriding that applies to all of these elements as attribute mappings is that overriding of XML over annotations is done at the level of the attribute (field or property) name. Our algorithm will apply to these mappings as they are keyed by attribute name, and XML overrides will be applied by attribute name alone. All of the annotated mapping information for the attribute will be overridden as soon as a mapping element for that attribute name is defined in XML.

The type of mapping that was defined in annotation form and the type that it is being overridden to are not really relevant to the provider at the time of overriding. The provider is responsible only for implementing the overriding rules. This leads us to our second comment about overriding, which is that when overriding annotations, we should use the correct and compatible XML mapping. There are some cases where it might be valid to actually map an attribute differently in XML, but these cases are few and far between and primarily for exceptional types of testing or debugging.

For example, one could imagine overriding a field mapped in annotation form as a basic mapping with a transient mapping in XML. This would be completely legal but not necessarily a good idea. At some point a client of the entity may actually be trying to access that state, and if it is not being persisted, then the client might get quite confused and fail in curious ways that are difficult to debug. Overriding an address association property that is mapped as a many-to-one mapping could conceivably be overridden to be stored serially as a blob, but this could not only break client access but also spill over to break other areas like JPQL queries that traverse the address.

The rule of thumb is that mappings should be overridden primarily to change the data-level mapping information. This would normally need to be done in the case, for example, where an application is developed on one database but deployed to another or must deploy to multiple different databases in production. In these cases the XML mappings would likely be `xml-mapping-metadata-complete` anyway, and the XML metadata would be used in its entirety rather than cobbling together bits of annotations and bits of XML and trying to keep it all straight across multiple database XML mapping configurations.

Tables

Specifying tables in XML works pretty much the same way as it does in annotation form. The same defaults are applied in both cases. There are two elements for specifying table information for a managed class: `table` and `secondary-table`.

table

A `table` element may occur as a subelement of `entity` and describes the table that the entity is mapped to. It corresponds to the `@Table` annotation (see Chapter 4) and has `name`, `catalog`, and `schema` attributes. One or more `unique-constraint` subelements may be included if unique column constraints are to be created in the table during schema generation.

If an `@Table` annotation exists on the entity, then the `table` element will override the table defined by the annotation. Overriding a table is usually accompanied also by the overridden mappings of the persistent state to the overridden table. In Listing 10-14 is an example that shows how an entity can be mapped to a different table than what it is mapped to by an annotation.

Listing 10-14. *Overriding a Table*

```
@Entity
@Table(name="EMP", schema="HR")
public class Employee { ... }

<entity class="examples.model.Employee">
    <table name="EMP_REC" schema="HR"/>
    ...
</entity>
```

secondary-table

Any number of secondary tables can be added to the entity by adding one or more `secondary-table` subelements to the `entity` element. This element corresponds to the `@SecondaryTable` annotation (see Chapter 8), and if it is present in an `entity` element, it will override any and all secondary tables that are defined in annotations on the entity class. The `name` attribute is required, just as the name is required in the annotation. The `schema` and `catalog` attributes and the `unique-constraint` subelements may be included just as with the `table` element.

Every secondary table needs to be joined to the primary table through a primary key join column (see Chapter 8). The primary-key-join-column element is a subelement of the secondary-table element and corresponds to the @PrimaryKeyJoinColumn annotation. As with the annotation, this is required only if the primary key column of the secondary table is different from that of the primary table. If the primary key happens to be a compound primary key, then multiple primary-key-join-column elements may be specified.

Listing 10-15 compares the specification of secondary tables in annotation and XML form.

Listing 10-15. *Specifying Secondary Tables*

```
@Entity
@Table(name="EMP")
@SecondaryTables({
    @SecondaryTable(name="EMP_INFO"),
    @SecondaryTable(name="EMP_HIST",
                    pkJoinColumns=@PrimaryKeyJoinColumn(name="EMP_ID"))
 })
public class Employee {
    @Id private int id;
    // ...
}

<entity class="examples.model.Employee">
    <table name="EMP"/>
    <secondary-table name="EMP_INFO"/>
    <secondary-table name="EMP_HIST">
        <primary-key-join-column name="EMP_ID"/>
    </secondary-table>
    ...
</entity>
```

Identifier Mappings

The three different types of identifier mappings may also be specified in XML. Overriding applies to the configuration information within a given identifier type, but the identifier type of a managed class should almost never be changed.

id

The id element is the most common method used to indicate the identifier for an entity. It corresponds to the @Id annotation but also encapsulates metadata that is relevant to identifiers. This includes a number of subelements, the first of which is the column subelement. It corresponds to the @Column annotation that might accompany an @Id annotation on the field or property. When not specified, the default column name will be assumed even if an @Column annotation exists on the field or property. As we discussed in the Attributes section previously, this is because the XML mapping of the attribute overrides the entire group of mapping metadata on the field or property.

A generated-value element corresponding to the @GeneratedValue annotation may also be included in the id element. This is used to indicate that the identifier will have its value automatically generated by the provider (see Chapter 4). This generated-value element has strategy and generator attributes that match those on the annotation. The named generator may be defined anywhere in the persistence unit. Sequence and table generators may also be defined within the id element. These were discussed in the Queries and Generators section.

An example of overriding an id mapping is to change the generator for a given database. This is shown in Listing 10-16.

Listing 10-16. *Overriding an Id Generator*

```
@Entity
public class Employee {
    @Id @GeneratedValue(strategy=GenerationType.TABLE, generator="empTab")
    @TableGenerator(name="empTab", table="ID_GEN")
    private long id;
    // ...
}

<entity class="examples.model.Employee">
    ...
    <attributes>
        <id name="id">
            <generated-value strategy="SEQUENCE" generator="empSeq"/>
            <sequence-generator name="empSeq" sequence-name="mySeq"/>
        </id>
        ...
    </attributes>
</entity>
```

embedded-id

An embedded-id element is used when a compound primary key class is used as the identifier (see Chapter 8). It corresponds to the @EmbeddedId annotation and is really just mapping an embedded class as the identifier. All of the state is actually mapped within the embedded object, so there are only attribute overrides available within the embedded-id element. As we will discuss in the Embedded Object Mappings section, attribute overrides allow mapping of the same embedded object in multiple entities. The zero or more attribute-override elements in the property or field mapping of the entity provide the local overrides that apply to the entity table. Listing 10-17 shows how to specify an embedded identifier in annotation and XML form.

Listing 10-17. *Specifying an Embedded Id*

```
@Entity
public class Employee {
    @EmbeddedId private EmployeePK id;
    // ...
}
```

```
<entity class="examples.model.Employee">
    ...
    <attributes>
        <embedded-id name="id"/>
        ...
    </attributes>
</entity>
```

id-class

An id class is one strategy that can be used for a compound primary key (see Chapter 8). The id-class subelement of an entity or mapped-superclass element corresponds to the @IdClass annotation, and when it is specified in XML, it will override any @IdClass annotation on the class. Overriding the id class should not normally be done in practice since code that uses the entities will typically assume a particular identifier class.

The name of the class is indicated as the value of the class attribute of the id-class element as shown in Listing 10-18.

Listing 10-18. *Specifying an Id Class*

```
@Entity
@IdClass(EmployeePK.class)
public class Employee { ... }

<entity class="examples.model.Employee">
    ...
    <id-class="examples.model.EmployeePK"/>
    ...
</entity>
```

Simple Mappings

A simple mapping takes an attribute and maps it to a single column in a table. The majority of persistent state mapped by an entity will be composed of simple mappings. In this section we will discuss basic mappings and also cover the metadata for versioning and transient attributes.

basic

Basic mappings were discussed in detail in the early part of the book; they map a simple state field or property to a column in the table. The basic element provides this same ability in XML and corresponds to the @Basic annotation. Unlike the @Basic annotation that we described in Chapter 4 and which is rarely used, the basic element is required when mapping persistent state to a specific column. Just as with annotations, when a field or property is not mapped, it will be assumed to be a basic mapping and will be defaulted as such. This will occur if the field or property is not annotated or has no named entry in the attributes element.

In addition to a name, the basic element has fetch and optional attributes that can be used for lazy loading and optionality. These are not required and not very useful at the level of a field or property.

The most important and useful subelement of basic is the column element. Three other subelements may optionally be included inside the basic element. These are used to indicate the type to use when communicating with the JDBC driver to the database column. The first is an empty lob element that corresponds to the @Lob annotation. This is used when the target column is a large object type. Whether it is a character or binary object depends upon the type of the field or property.

The next is the temporal element that contains as its content one of "DATE", "TIME", or "TIMESTAMP". It corresponds to the @Temporal annotation and is used for fields of type java.util.Date or java.util.Calendar.

Finally, if the field or property is an enumerated type and the enumerated values are to be mapped using strings instead of ordinals, then the enumerated element should be used. It corresponds to the @Enumerated annotation and contains either ORDINAL or STRING as its content.

Listing 10-19 shows some examples of basic mappings. By not specifying the column in the basic element mapping for the name field, the column is overridden from using the annotated EMP_NAME column to being defaulted to NAME. The comments field, however, is overridden from using the default to being mapped to the COMM column. It is also stored in a CLOB (character large object) column due to the lob element being present and the fact that the field is a String. The type field is overridden to be mapped to the STR_TYPE column, and the enumerated type of STRING is specified to indicate that the values should be stored as strings. The salary field does not have any metadata either in annotation or XML form and continues to be mapped to the default column name of SALARY.

Listing 10-19. *Overriding Basic Mappings*

```
@Entity
public class Employee {
    // ...
    @Column(name="EMP_NAME")
    private String name;
    private String comments;
    private EmployeeType type;
    private long salary;
    // ...
}

<entity class="examples.model.Employee">
    ...
    <attributes>
        ...
        <basic name="name"/>
        <basic name="comments">
            <column name="COMM"/>
            <lob/>
        </basic>
        <basic name="type">
            <column name="STR_TYPE"/>
            <enumerated>STRING</enumerated>
        </basic>
```

```
            ...
        </attributes>
    </entity>
```

transient

A transient element marks a field or property as being nonpersistent. It is equivalent to the @Transient annotation or having a transient qualifier on the field or property. Listing 10-20 shows an example of how to set a field to be transient.

Listing 10-20. *Setting a Transient Field in a Mapping File*

```
<entity-mappings>
    <entity class="examples.model.Employee">
        <attributes>
            <transient name="cacheAge"/>
            ...
        </attributes>
    </entity>
</entity-mappings>
```

version

The version element is used to map the version number field in the entity. It corresponds to the @Version annotation and is normally mapped to an integral field for the provider to increment when it makes persistent changes to the entity (see Chapter 9). The column subelement specifies the column that stores the version data. Only one version field should exist for each entity. Listing 10-21 shows how a version field is specified in annotations and XML.

Listing 10-21. *Specifying the Version*

```
@Entity
public class Employee {
    // ...
    @Version
    private int version;
    // ...
}

<entity-mappings>
    <entity class="examples.model.Employee">
        <attributes>
            ...
            <version name="version"/>
            ...
        </attributes>
    </entity>
    ...
</entity-mappings>
```

Relationship Mappings

Like their annotation counterparts, the XML relationship elements are used to map the associations between entities. The following sections discuss each of the relationship mapping types that exist in XML.

many-to-one

To create a many-to-one mapping for a field or property, the `many-to-one` element may be specified. This element corresponds to the `@ManyToOne` annotation and, like the basic mapping, has `fetch` and `optional` attributes. Normally the target entity is known by the provider since the field or property is almost always of the target entity type. The `target-entity` attribute may also be specified.

A `join-column` element may be specified as a subelement of the `many-to-one` element when the column name is different than the default. If the association is to an entity with a compound primary key, then multiple `join-column` elements will be required. Mapping an attribute using a `many-to-one` element causes the mapping annotations that may have been present on that attribute to be ignored. All of the mapping information for the relationship, including the join column information, must be specified or defaulted within the `many-to-one` XML element.

Instead of a join column, it is possible to have a many-to-one or one-to-many relationship that uses a join table. It is for this case that a `join-table` element may be specified as a subelement of the `many-to-one` element. The `join-table` element corresponds to the `@JoinTable` annotation and contains a collection of `join-column` elements that join to the owning entity, which is normally the many-to-one side. A second set of join columns joins the join table to the inverse side of the relationship. These are called `inverse-join-column` elements. In the absence of one or both of these, the default values will be applied.

Unique to relationships is the ability to cascade operations across them. The cascade settings for a relationship dictate which operations are cascaded to the target entity of the many-to-one mapping. To specify how cascading should occur, a cascade element should be included as a subelement of the `many-to-one` element. Within the cascade element, we can include our choice of empty `cascade-all`, `cascade-persist`, `cascade-merge`, `cascade-remove`, or `cascade-refresh` subelements that dictate that the given operations be cascaded. Of course, specifying cascade elements in addition to the `cascade-all` element is simply redundant.

Now we come to an exception to our rule that we gave earlier when we said that overriding of mappings will typically be for physical data overrides. When it comes to relationships, there are times where you will want to test the performance of a given operation and would like to be able to set certain relationships to load eagerly or lazily. You will not want to go through the code and have to keep changing these settings back and forth, however. It would be more practical to have the mappings that you are tuning in XML and just change them according to your whim.[3] Listing 10-22 shows overriding two many-to-one relationships to be lazily loaded.

---

3. Some have argued that these kinds of tuning exercises are precisely some of the reasons why XML should be used to begin with.

Listing 10-22. *Overriding Fetch Mode*

```
@Entity
public class Employee {
    // ...
    @ManyToOne
    private Address address;
    @ManyToOne
    @JoinColumn(name="MGR")
    private Employee manager;
    // ...
}

<entity class="examples.model.Employee">
    ...
    <attributes>
        ...
        <many-to-one name="address" fetch="LAZY"/>
        <many-to-one name="manager" fetch="LAZY">
            <join-column name="MGR"/>
        </many-to-one>
        ...
    </attributes>
</entity>
```

one-to-many

A one-to-many mapping is created by using a one-to-many element. This element corresponds to the @OneToMany annotation and has the same optional target-entity and fetch attributes that were described in the many-to-one mapping. It has an additional attribute called mapped-by, which indicates the field or property of the owning entity (see Chapter 4).

A one-to-many mapping is a collection-valued association, and the collection may be a List, Map, Set, or Collection. If it is a List, then the elements may be populated in a specific order by specifying an order-by subelement. This element corresponds to the @OrderBy annotation and will cause the contents of the list to be ordered by the specific field or property name that is specified in the element content.

If the collection is a Map, then an optional map-key subelement may be specified to indicate the name of the field or property to use as the key for the Map. This element corresponds to the @MapKey annotation and will default to the primary key field or property when none is specified.

A join table is used to map a unidirectional one-to-many association that does not store a join column in the target entity. To make use of this kind of mapping, the mapped-by attribute is omitted and the join-table element is included.

Finally, cascading across the relationship is specified through an optional cascade element. Listing 10-23 shows a bidirectional one-to-many mapping both in annotations and XML.

Listing 10-23. *Specifying a One-to-Many Mapping*

```
@Entity
public class Employee {
    // ...
    @OneToMany(mappedBy="manager")
    @OrderBy
    private List<Employee> directs;
    @ManyToOne
    private Employee manager;
    // ...
}

<entity class="examples.model.Employee">
    ...
    <attributes>
        ...
        <one-to-many name="directs" mapped-by="manager">
            <order-by/>
        </one-to-many>
        <many-to-one name="manager"/>
        ...
    </attributes>
</entity>
```

one-to-one

To map a one-to-one association, the one-to-one element must be used. This element corresponds to the @OneToOne annotation that we described in Chapter 4 and has the same target-entity, fetch, and optional attributes that the many-to-one element has. It also has the mapped-by attribute that we saw in the one-to-many mapping to refer to the owning entity.

A one-to-one element may contain a join-column element if it is the owner of the relationship, or it may have multiple join-column elements if the association is to an entity with a compound primary key.

When the one-to-one association is joined using the primary keys of the two entity tables, then the one-to-one element will contain a primary-key-join-column element, which corresponds to the @PrimaryKeyJoinColumn annotation. When it has a compound primary key, multiple primary-key-join-column elements will be present. Either of primary-key-join-column or join-column elements may be present, but not both.

The annotated classes and XML mapping file equivalents for a one-to-one mapping using a primary key join column are shown in Listing 10-24.

Listing 10-24. *One-to-One Primary Key Association*

```
@Entity
public class Employee {
    // ...
    @OneToOne(mappedBy="employee")
    private ParkingSpace parkingSpace;
    // ...
}

@Entity
public class ParkingSpace {
    // ...
    @OneToOne
    @PrimaryKeyJoinColumn
    private Employee employee;
    // ...
}

<entity-mappings>
    <entity class="examples.model.Employee">
        <attributes>
            ...
            <one-to-one name="parkingSpace" mapped-by="employee"/>
            ...
        </attributes>
    </entity>
    <entity class="examples.model.ParkingSpace">
        <attributes>
            ...
            <one-to-one name="employee">
                <primary-key-join-column/>
            </one-to-one>
            ...
        </attributes>
    </entity>
</entity-mappings>
```

many-to-many

Creating a many-to-many association is done through the use of a many-to-many element. This element corresponds to the @ManyToMany annotation (see Chapter 4) and has the same optional target-entity, fetch, and mapped-by attributes that were described in the one-to-many mapping.

Also, being a collection-valued association like the one-to-many mapping, it supports the same order-by, map-key, join-table, and cascade subelements as the one-to-many mapping. Listing 10-25 shows the entity classes and equivalent XML.

Listing 10-25. *Many-to-Many Mapping Annotations and XML*

```
@Entity
public class Employee {
    // ...
    @ManyToMany
    @MapKey(name="name")
    @JoinTable(name="EMP_PROJ",
            joinColumns=@JoinColumn(name="EMP_ID"),
            inverseJoinColumns=@JoinColumn(name="PROJ_ID"))
    private Map<String, Project> projects;
    // ...
}

@Entity
public class Project {
    // ...
    private String name;
    @ManyToMany(mappedBy="projects")
    private Collection<Employee> employees;
    // ...
}

<entity-mappings>
    <entity class="examples.model.Employee">
        <attributes>
            ...
            <many-to-many name="projects">
                <map-key name="name"/>
                <join-table name="EMP_PRJ">
                    <join-column name="EMP_ID"/>
                    <inverse-join-column name="PROJ_ID"/>
                </join-table>
            </many-to-many>
            ...
        </attributes>
    </entity>
    <entity class="examples.model.Project">
        <attributes>
            ...
            <many-to-many name="employee" mapped-by="projects"/>
            ...
        </attributes>
    </entity>
</entity-mappings>
```

Embedded Object Mappings

An embedded object is a class that depends upon its parent entity for its identity. Embedded objects are specified in XML using the embedded element and are customized using the attribute-override element.

embedded

An embedded element is used for mapping an embedded object contained within a field or property (see Chapter 8). It corresponds to the @Embedded annotation. Since the persistent state is mapped within the embedded object, only the attribute-override subelement is allowed within the embedded element.

There must be an embeddable class entry in a mapping file for the embedded object or it must be annotated as @Embeddable. An example of overriding an embedded Address is shown in Listing 12-26.

Listing 12-26. *Embedded Mappings in Annotations and XML*

```
@Entity
public class Employee {
    // ...
    @Embedded
    private Address address;
    // ...
}

@Embeddable
public class Address {
    private String street;
    private String city;
    private String state;
    private String zip;
    // ...
}

<entity-mappings>
    <entity class="examples.model.Employee">
        <attributes>
            ...
            <embedded name="address"/>
            ...
        </attributes>
    </entity>
    <embeddable class="examples.model.Address"/>
</entity-mappings>
```

attribute-override

When an embedded object is used by multiple entity types, it is likely that some of the basic mappings in the embedded object will need to be remapped by one or more of the entities (see Chapter 8). The attribute-override element may be specified as a subelement of embedded and embedded-id elements to accommodate this case.

The annotation that corresponds to the attribute-override element is the @AttributeOverride annotation. This annotation may be on the entity class or on a field or property that stores an embedded object or embedded id. When an @AttributeOverride annotation is present in the entity, it will be overridden only by an attribute-override element in the entity mapping file entry that specifies the same named field or property. Our earlier algorithm still holds if we think of the attribute overrides as keyed by the name of the field or property that they are overriding. All of the annotation overrides for an entity are gathered, then all of the XML overrides for the class are applied on top of the annotation overrides. If there is an override in XML for the same named field or property, it will overwrite the annotated one. The remaining non-overlapping overrides from annotations and XML will also be applied.

The attribute-override element stores the name of the field or property in its name attribute and the column that the field or property maps to as a column subelement. Listing 10-27 revisits Listing 10-26 and overrides the state and zip fields of the embedded address.

Listing 10-27. *Using Attribute Overrides*

```
@Entity
public class Employee {
    // ...
    @Embedded
    @AttributeOverrides({
        @AttributeOverride(name="state", column=@Column(name="PROV")),
        @AttributeOverride(name="zip", column=@Column(name="PCODE"))})
    private Address address;
    // ...
}

<entity class="examples.model.Employee">
    <attributes>
        ...
        <embedded name="address">
            <attribute-override name="state">
                <column name="PROV"/>
            </attribute-override>
            <attribute-override name="zip">
                <column name="PCODE"/>
            </attribute-override>
        </embedded>
        ...
    </attributes>
</entity>
```

Inheritance Mappings

An entity inheritance hierarchy is mapped using the inheritance, discriminator-column, and discriminator-value elements. If the inheritance strategy is changed, then it must be overridden for the entire entity hierarchy.

inheritance

The inheritance element is specified to indicate the root of an inheritance hierarchy. It corresponds to the @Inheritance annotation and indicates the inheritance mapping strategy that is to be used. When it is included in the entity element, it will override any inheritance strategy that is defined or defaulted in the @Inheritance annotation on the entity class.

Changing the inheritance strategy may cause repercussions that spill out into the other areas. For example, changing a strategy from single-table to joined will likely require adding a table to each of the entities below it. The example in Listing 10-28 overrides an entity hierarchy from using a single table to using a joined strategy.

Listing 10-28. *Overriding an Inheritance Strategy*

```
@Entity
@Table(name="EMP")
@Inheritance
@DiscriminatorColumn(name="TYPE")
public abstract class Employee { ... }

@Entity
@DiscriminatorValue("FT")
public class FullTimeEmployee { ... }

@Entity
@DiscriminatorValue("PT")
public class PartTimeEmployee { ... }

<entity-mappings>
    <entity class="examples.model.Employee">
        <table name="EMP"/>
        <inheritance strategy="JOINED"/>
        ...
    </entity>
    <entity class="examples.model.FullTimeEmployee">
        <table name="FT_EMP"/>
        ...
    </entity>
    <entity class="examples.model.PartTimeEmployee">
        <table name="PT_EMP"/>
        ...
    </entity>
</entity-mappings>
```

discriminator-column

Discriminator columns store values that differentiate between concrete entity subclasses in an inheritance hierarchy (see Chapter 8). The `discriminator-column` element is a subelement of the `entity` or `entity-result` elements and is used to define or override the discriminator column. It corresponds to and overrides the `@DiscriminatorColumn` annotation and has attributes that include the `name`, `discriminator-type`, `columnDefinition`, and `length`. It is an empty element that has no subelements.

The `discriminator-column` element is not typically used to override a column on its own but in conjunction with other inheritance and table overrides. Listing 10-29 demonstrates specifying a discriminator column.

Listing 10-29. *Specifying a Discriminator Column*

```
@Entity
@Inheritance
@DiscriminatorColumn(name="TYPE")
public abstract class Employee { ... }

<entity class="examples.model.Employee">
    <inheritance/>
    <discriminator-column name="TYPE"/>
    ...
</entity >
```

discriminator-value

A `discriminator-value` element is used to declare the value that identifies the concrete entity subclass that is stored in a database row (see Chapter 8). It exists only as a subelement of the `entity` element. The discriminator value is indicated by the content of the element. It has no attributes or subelements.

The `discriminator-value` element corresponds to the `@DiscriminatorValue` annotation and overrides it when it exists on the entity class. As with the other inheritance overrides, it is seldom used as an override. Even when a hierarchy is remapped to a different database or set of tables, it will not be normally be necessary to override the value. Listing 10-30 shows how to specify a discriminator value in annotation and XML form.

Listing 10-30. *Specifying a Discriminator Column*

```
@Entity
@DiscriminatorValue("FT")
public class FullTimeEmployee extends Employee { ... }

<entity class="examples.model.FullTimeEmployee">
    <discriminator-value>FT</discriminator-value>
    ...
</entity >
```

association-override

Association overrides are similar to attribute overrides except that they are used to override single-valued associations instead of simple persistent state. The `association-override` element is a subelement of `entity` and corresponds to the `@AssociationOverride` annotation (see Chapter 8). The XML override rules are the same as those for `attribute-override` elements described in the Embedded Object Mappings section and are based on the name of the association field or property. Association overrides do not apply to embedded objects, however, because embedded objects may not portably have relationships within them.

Simple mappings and associations may be overridden through the use of attribute overrides and association overrides, but only in the case of an entity that is the subclass of a mapped superclass. Simple persistent state or association state that is inherited from an entity superclass may not portably be overridden.

There is one other difference that distinguishes the `association-override` element from its `attribute-override` counterpart. Single-valued relationships have one or more join columns instead of a column, which requires that they contain one or more `join-column` elements instead of a single `column` element. There may be multiples because foreign keys may be compound and require more than one join column.

An example of overriding two simple `name` and `salary` persistent field mappings, and a `manager` association with a compound primary key, is shown in Listing 10-31.

Listing 10-31. *Using Attribute and Association Overrides*

```
@MappedSuperclass
@IdClass(EmployeePK.class)
public abstract class Employee {
    @Id private String name;
    @Id private java.sql.Date dob;
    private long salary;
    @ManyToOne
    private Employee manager;
    // ...
}

@Entity
@Table(name="PT_EMP")
@AttributeOverrides({
    @AttributeOverride(name="name", column=@Column(name="EMP_NAME")),
    @AttributeOverride(name="salary", column=@Column(name="SAL"))})
@AssociationOverride(name="manager",
    joinColumns={
        @JoinColumn(name="MGR_NAME", referencedName="EMP_NAME"),
        @JoinColumn(name="MGR_DOB", referencedName="DOB")})
public class PartTimeEmployee extends Employee { ... }
```

```
<entity class="examples.model.PartTimeEmployee">
    ...
    <attribute-override name="name">
        <column name="EMP_NAME"/>
    </attribute-override>
    <attribute-override name="salary">
        <column name="SAL"/>
    </attribute-override>
    <association-override name="manager">
        <join-column name="MGR_NAME"  referenced-column-name="EMP_NAME"/>
        <join-column name="MGR_DOB" referenced-column-name="DOB"/>
    </association-override>
    ...
</entity>
```

Lifecycle Events

All of the lifecycle events that can be associated with a method in an entity listener can also be associated directly with a method in an entity or mapped superclass (see Chapter 9). The pre-persist, post-persist, pre-update, post-update, pre-remove, post-remove, and post-load methods are all valid subelements of the entity or mapped-superclass elements. Each of these may occur only once in each class. Each lifecycle event element will override any entity callback method of the same event type that may be annotated in the entity class.

Before anyone goes out and overrides all their annotated callback methods with XML overrides, we should mention that the use case for doing such a thing borders on, if not completely falls off into, the non-existent. An example of specifying an entity callback method in annotations and in XML is shown in Listing 10-32.

Listing 10-32. *Specifying Lifecycle Callback Methods*

```
@Entity
public class Employee {
    // ...
    @PrePersist
    @PostLoad
    public void initTransientState() { ... }
    // ...
}

<entity class="examples.model.Employee">
    ...
    <pre-persist method-name="initTransientState"/>
    <post-load method-name="initTransientState"/>
    ...
</entity>
```

Entity Listeners

Lifecycle callback methods defined on a class other than the entity class are called entity listeners. The following sections describe how to configure entity listeners in XML using the entity-listeners element and how to exclude inherited and default listeners.

entity-listeners

One or more ordered entity listener classes may be defined in an @EntityListeners annotation on an entity or mapped superclass (see Chapter 9). When a lifecycle event fires, the listeners that have methods for the event will get invoked in the order in which they are listed. The entity-listeners element may be specified as a subelement of an entity or mapped-superclass element to accomplish exactly the same thing. It will also have the effect of overriding the entity listeners defined in an @EntityListeners annotation with the ones defined in the entity-listeners element.

An entity-listeners element includes a list of ordered entity-listener subelements, each of which defines an entity-listener class in its class attribute. For each listener, the methods corresponding to lifecycle events must be indicated as subelement events. The events may be one or more of pre-persist, post-persist, pre-update, post-update, pre-remove, post-remove, and post-load, which correspond to the @PrePersist, @PostPersist, @PreUpdate, @PostUpdate, @PreRemove, @PostRemove, and @PostLoad annotations, respectively. Each of the event subelements has a method-name attribute that names the method to be invoked when its lifecycle event is triggered. The same method may be supplied for multiple events, but no more than one event of the same type may be specified on a single listener class.

The entity-listeners element can be used to disable all of the entity listeners defined on a class or just add an additional listener. Disabling listeners is not recommended, of course, since listeners defined on a class tend to be fairly coupled to the class itself, and disabling them might introduce bugs into either the class or the system as a whole.

In Listing 10-33 we see that the XML mapping file is overriding the entity listeners on the Employee class. It is keeping the existing ones but also adding one more at the end of the order to notify the IT department to remove an employee's user accounts when he or she leaves the company.

Listing 10-33. *Overriding Entity Listeners*

```
@Entity
@EntityListeners({ EmployeeAuditListener.class, NameValidator.class })
public class Employee { ... }

public class EmployeeAuditListener {
    @PostPersist
    public void employeeCreated(Employee emp) { ... }
    @PostUpdate
    public void employeeUpdated(Employee emp) { ... }
    @PostRemove
    public void employeeRemoved(Employee emp) { ... }
}
```

```
public class NameValidator {
    @PrePersist
    public void validateName(Employee emp) { ... }
}
public class EmployeeExitListener {
    public void notifyIT(Employee emp) { ... }
}

<entity class="examples.model.Employee">
    ...
    <entity-listeners>
        <entity-listener class="examples.listeners.EmployeeAuditListener">
            <post-persist method-name="employeeCreated"/>
            <post-update method-name="employeeUpdated"/>
            <post-remove method-name="employeeRemoved"/>
        </entity-listener>
        <entity-listener class="examples.listeners.NameValidator">
            <pre-persist method-name="validateName"/>
        </entity-listener>
        <entity-listener class="examples.listeners.EmployeeExitListener">
            <post-remove method-name="notifyIT"/>
        </entity-listener>
    </entity-listeners>
    ...
</entity>
```

Note that we have fully specified each of the entity callback listeners in XML. Some vendors will find the lifecycle event annotations on the EmployeeAuditListener and NameValidator entity listener classes, but this is not required behavior. To be portable, the lifecycle event methods should be specified in each of the entity-listener elements.

exclude-default-listeners

The set of default entity listeners that applies to all entities is defined in the entity-listeners subelement of the persistence-unit-defaults element (see the entity-listeners section). These listeners can be turned off or disabled for a particular entity or hierarchy of entities by specifying an empty exclude-default-listeners element within the entity or mapped-superclass element. This is equivalent to the @ExcludeDefaultListeners annotation, and if either one is specified for a class, then default listeners are disabled for that class. Note that exclude-default-listeners is an empty element, not a Boolean. If default entity listeners are disabled for a class by an @ExcludeDefaultListeners annotation, then there is currently no way to re-enable them through XML.

exclude-superclass-listeners

Entity listeners defined on the superclass of an entity will normally be fired before the entity listeners defined on the entity class itself are fired (see Chapter 9). To disable the listeners defined on an entity superclass or mapped superclass, an empty exclude-superclass-listeners element may be supplied inside an `entity` or `mapped-superclass` element. This will disable the superclass listeners for the managed class and all of its subclasses.

The `exclude-superclass-listeners` element corresponds to the `@ExcludeSuperclassListeners` annotation and, like the `exclude-default-listeners`/`@ExcludeDefaultListeners` pair, either one of the two may be specified in order to disable the superclass listeners for the entity or mapped superclass and its subclasses.

Summary

With all of the XML mapping information under your belt, you should now be able to map entities using annotations, XML, or a combination of the two. In this chapter we went over all of the elements in the mapping file and compared them to their corresponding annotations. We discussed how each of the elements is used, what they override, and how they are overridden. We also used them in some short examples.

Defaults may be specified in the mapping files at different levels, from the global persistence unit level to the mapping file level. We covered what each of the defaulting scopes was and how they were applied.

In the next chapter we will look at how to package and deploy applications that use the Java Persistence API. We will also look at how XML mapping files are referenced as part of a persistence unit configuration.

CHAPTER 11

■ ■ ■

Packaging and Deployment

Configuring a persistence application involves specifying the bits of additional information that the execution environment or persistence platform may require in order for the code to function as a runtime application. Packaging means putting all of the pieces together in a way that makes sense and can be correctly interpreted and used by the infrastructure when the application is deployed into an application server or run in a stand-alone JVM. Deployment is the process of getting the application into an execution environment and running it.

One could view the mapping metadata as part of the overall configuration of an application, but that has already been discussed in previous chapters. In this chapter we will be discussing the primary runtime persistence configuration file, persistence.xml, which defines persistence units. We will go into detail about how to specify the different elements of this file, when they are required, and what the values should be.

Once the persistence unit has been configured, we will package a persistence unit with a few of the more common deployment units, such as EJB archives, web archives, and the application archives in a Java EE server. The resulting package will then be deployable into a compliant application server. We will also step through the packaging and deployment rules for Java SE applications.

Configuring Persistence Units

The persistence unit is the primary unit of runtime configuration. It defines the various pieces of information that the provider needs to know in order to manage the persistent classes during program execution and is configured within a persistence.xml file. There may be one or more persistence.xml files in an application, and each persistence.xml file may define multiple persistence units. There will normally be only one, though. Since there is one EntityManagerFactory for each persistence unit, you can think of the configuration of the persistence unit as the configuration of the factory for that persistence unit.

A common configuration file goes a long way to standardizing the runtime configuration, and the persistence.xml file offers exactly that. While some providers might still require an additional provider-specific configuration file, most will also support their properties being specified within the properties section (described in the Adding Vendor Properties section) of the persistence.xml file.

The persistence.xml file is the first step to configuring a persistence unit. All of the information required for the persistence unit should be specified in the persistence.xml file. Once a packaging strategy has been chosen, the persistence.xml file should be placed in the META-INF directory of the chosen archive.

Each persistence unit is defined by a `persistence-unit` element in the `persistence.xml` file. All of the information for that persistence unit is enclosed within that element. The following sections describe the metadata that a persistence unit may define when deploying to a Java EE server.

Persistence Unit Name

Every persistence unit must have a name that uniquely identifies it within the scope of its packaging. We will be discussing the different packaging options later, but in general, if a persistence unit is defined within a Java EE module, then there must not be any other persistence unit of the same name in that module. For example, if a persistence unit named "EmployeeService" is defined in an EJB JAR named `emp_ejb.jar`, then there should not be any other persistence units named "EmployeeService" in `emp_ejb.jar`. There may be persistence units named "EmployeeService" in a web module or even in another EJB module within the application though.

We have seen in some of the examples in previous chapters that the name of the persistence unit is just an attribute of the `persistence-unit` element, as in:

```
<persistence-unit name="EmployeeService"/>
```

This empty `persistence-unit` element is the minimal persistence unit definition. It may be all that is needed if the server defaults the remaining information, but not all servers will do this. Some may require other persistence unit metadata to be present, such as the data source to be accessed.

Transaction Type

The factory that is used to create entity managers for a given persistence unit will generate entity managers to be of a specific transactional type. We went into detail in Chapter 5 about the different types of entity managers, and one of the things that we saw was that every entity manager must either use JTA or resource-local transactions. Normally, when running in a managed server environment, the JTA transaction mechanism is used. It is the default transaction type that a server will assume when none is specified for a persistence unit and generally the only one that most applications will ever need, so in practice the transaction type will never need to be specified.

If the data source is required by the server, as it often will be, then a JTA-enabled data source should be supplied (see section Data Source). Specifying a data source that is not JTA-enabled may actually work in some cases, but the database operations will not be participating in the global JTA transaction or necessarily be atomic with respect to that transaction.

In situations like those described in Chapter 5, when you want to use resource-local transactions instead of JTA, the `transaction-type` attribute of the `persistence-unit` element is used to explicitly declare the transaction type of `RESOURCE_LOCAL` or `JTA`, as in the following example:

```
<persistence-unit name="EmployeeService" transaction-type="RESOURCE_LOCAL"/>
```

Here, we are overriding the default JTA transaction type to be resource-local, so all of the entity managers created in the "EmployeeService" persistence unit must use the `EntityTransaction` interface to control transactions.

Persistence Provider

The Java Persistence API has a pluggable Service Provider Interface (SPI) that allows any compliant Java EE server to communicate with any compliant persistence provider implementation. Servers normally have a default provider, though, that is native to the server, meaning that it is implemented by the same vendor or is shipped with the server. In most cases, this default provider will be used by the server, and no special metadata will be necessary to explicitly specify it.

In order to switch to a different provider, the provider-supplied class that implements the `javax.persistence.spi.PersistenceProvider` interface must be listed in the `provider` element. Listing 11-1 shows a simple persistence unit that explicitly defines the TopLink Essentials provider class. The only requirement is that the provider JARs be on the server or application classpath and accessible to the running application at deployment time.

Listing 11-1. *Specifying a Persistence Provider*

```
<persistence-unit name="EmployeeService">
    <provider>oracle.toplink.essentials.PersistenceProvider</provider>
</persistence-unit>
```

Data Source

A fundamental part of the persistence unit metadata is the description of where the provider should obtain database connections from in order to read and write entity data. The target database is specified in terms of the name of a JDBC data source that is usually in the server JNDI space. This data source must be globally accessible since the provider accesses it when the persistence application is deployed.

The typical case is that JTA transactions are used, so it is in the `jta-data-source` element that the name of the JTA data source should be specified. Similarly, if the transaction type of the persistence unit is resource-local, then the `non-jta-data-source` element should be used.

There is no standard format for specifying the name of the data source; it is totally vendor-specific. However, the *de facto* standard way that a data source is accessed is from JNDI. Normally, a data source is made available in JNDI by being configured in a server-specific configuration file or management console. Even though the name is not officially portable, at least the place where it can be specified is standard, and in practice the names will usually be of the form "jdbc/myDataSource". Listing 11-2 shows how a data source would normally be specified. This example assumes that the provider is being defaulted.

Listing 11-2. *Specifying JTA Data Source*

```
<persistence-unit name="EmployeeService">
    <jta-data-source>jdbc/EmployeeServiceDS</jta-data-source>
</persistence-unit>
```

Some servers actually provide a default data source at the deployed Java EE application level, and if the provider is a native implementation for the server, then it may make use of this default. In other cases the data source will need to be specified.

Some servers also offer high-performance reading through database connections that are not associated with the current JTA transaction. The query results are then returned and made conformant with the contents of persistence context. This improves the scalability of the application because the database connection does not get enlisted in the JTA transaction until later on when it absolutely needs to be, usually at commit time. To enable these types of scalable reads, the `non-jta-data-source` element value would be supplied in addition to the `jta-data-source` element. An example of specifying these two is in Listing 11-3.

Listing 11-3. *Specifying JTA and Non-JTA Data Sources*

```
<persistence-unit name="EmployeeService">
    <jta-data-source>jdbc/EmployeeServiceDS</jta-data-source>
    <non-jta-data-source>jdbc/NonTxEmployeeServiceDS</non-jta-data-source>
</persistence-unit>
```

Note that the "EmployeeServiceDS" is a regularly configured data source that accesses the employee database but that "NonTxEmployeeServiceDS" is a separate data source configured to access the same employee database but not be enlisted in JTA transactions.

Mapping Files

In Chapter 10 we used XML mapping files to supply mapping metadata. Part, or all of the mapping metadata for the persistence unit may be specified in mapping files. The union of all of the mapping files (and the annotations in the absence of `xml-mapping-metadata-complete`) will be the metadata that is applied to the persistence unit.

Some might wonder why multiple mapping files might be useful. There are actually numerous cases for using more than one mapping file in a single persistence unit, but it really comes down to preference and process. For example, you might want to define all of the persistence-unit-level artifacts in one file and then all of the entity metadata in another file. In another case it may make sense for you to group all of the queries together in a separate file to isolate them from the rest of the physical database mappings. Perhaps it suits the development process to even have a file for each entity, either to decouple them from each other or to reduce conflicts resulting from the version control and configuration management system. This can be a popular choice for a team that is working on different entities within the same persistence unit. Each may want to change the mappings for a particular entity without getting in the way of other team members who are modifying other entities. Of course this must be negotiated carefully when there really are dependencies across the entities such as relationships or embedded objects. It makes sense to group entity metadata together when the relationships between them are not static or when the object model may change. As a general rule, if there is strong coupling in the object model, then the coupling should be considered in the mapping configuration model.

Some might just prefer to have a single mapping file with all of the metadata contained within it. This is certainly a simpler deployment model and makes for easier packaging. There is built-in support available to those who are happy limiting their metadata to a single file and willing to name it "orm.xml". If a mapping file named "orm.xml" exists in a META-INF directory on the classpath, for example beside the `persistence.xml` file, then it does not need to be explicitly listed. The provider will automatically search for such a file and use it if one exists. Mapping files that are named differently or are in a different location must be listed in the `mapping-file` elements in the `persistence.xml` file.

Mapping files listed in the `mapping-file` elements are loaded as Java resources (using methods such as `ClassLoader.getResource()`, for example) from the classpath, so they should be specified in the same manner as any other Java resource that was intended to be loaded as such. The directory location component followed by the file name of the mapping file will cause it to be found, loaded, and processed at deployment time. For example, if we put all of our persistence-unit-level metadata in `META-INF/orm.xml`, all of our queries in `META-INF/employee_service_queries.xml`, and all of our entities in `META-INF/employee_service_entities.xml`, then we should end up with the persistence unit definition shown in Listing 11-4. Remember, we don't need to specify the `META-INF/orm.xml` file, because it will be found and processed by default. The other mapping files could be in any directory, not necessarily just the `META-INF` directory. We put them in `META-INF` just to keep them together with the `orm.xml` file.

Listing 11-4. *Specifying Mapping Files*

```
<persistence-unit name="EmployeeService">
    <jta-data-source>jdbc/EmployeeServiceDS</jta-data-source>
    <mapping-file>META-INF/employee_service_queries.xml</mapping-file>
    <mapping-file>META-INF/employee_service_entities.xml</mapping-file>
</persistence-unit>
```

Managed Classes

Typical deployments will put all of the entities and other managed classes in a single JAR, with the `persistence.xml` file in the `META-INF` directory and one or more mapping files also tossed in when XML mapping is used. The deployment process is optimized for these kinds of deployment scenarios to minimize the amount of metadata that a deployer has to specify.

The set of entities, mapped superclasses, and embedded objects that will be managed in a particular persistence unit is determined by the provider when it processes the persistence unit. At deployment time it may obtain managed classes from any of four sources. A managed class will be included if it is among the following:

1. **Local Classes:** the annotated classes in the deployment unit in which its `persistence.xml` file was packaged.

2. **Classes in Mapping Files:** the classes that have mapping entries in an XML mapping file.

3. **Explicitly Listed Classes:** the classes that are listed as `class` elements in the `persistence.xml` file.

4. **Additional JARs of Managed Classes:** the annotated classes in a named `JAR` listed in a `jar-file` element in the `persistence.xml` file.

As a deployer you may choose to use any one or a combination of these mechanisms to cause your managed classes to be included in the persistence unit. We will discuss each of them in turn.

Local Classes

The first category of classes that get included is the one that is the easiest and will likely be used the most often. We call these classes local classes because they are local to the deployment unit. When a JAR is deployed with a persistence.xml file in the META-INF directory, then that JAR will be searched for all of the classes that are annotated with @Entity, @MappedSuperclass, or @Embeddable. This will hold true for various types of deployment units that we will describe in more detail later in the chapter.

This method is clearly the simplest way to cause a class to be included because all that has to be done is to put the annotated classes into a JAR and add the persistence.xml file in the META-INF directory of the JAR. The provider will take care of going through the classes and finding the entities. Other classes may also be placed in the JAR with the entities and will have no effect on the finding process other than perhaps potentially slowing down the finding process if there are many such classes.

Classes in Mapping Files

Any class that has an entry in a mapping file is also going to be considered a managed class in the persistence unit. It need only be named in an entity, mapped-superclass, or embeddable element in one of the mapping files. The set of all of the classes from all of the listed mapping files (including the implicitly processed orm.xml file) will be added to the set of managed classes in the persistence unit. Nothing special has to be done apart from ensuring that the classes named in a mapping file are on the classpath of the unit being deployed. If they are in the deployed component archive, then they will already be on the classpath. But if they aren't, then they must be explicitly included in the classpath just as the explicitly listed ones are (see the following Explicitly Listed Classes section).

Explicitly Listed Classes

When the persistence unit is small or when there are not a large number of entities, then you may want to list classes explicitly in class elements in the persistence.xml file. This will cause the listed classes to be added to the persistence unit.

Since a class that is local to the deployment unit will already be included, we don't need to list them in the class elements. Explicitly listing the classes is really useful only in three main cases.

The first is when there are additional classes that are not local to the deployment unit JAR. For example, there is an embedded object class in a different JAR that you want to use in an entity in your persistence unit. You would list the fully qualified class in the class element in the persistence.xml file. You will also need to ensure that the JAR or directory that contains the class is on the classpath of the deployed component, for example, by adding it to the manifest classpath of the deployment JAR.

In the second case, we want to exclude one or more classes that may be annotated as an entity. Even though the class may be annotated with @Entity, we don't want it to be treated as an entity in this particular deployed context. For example, it may be used as a transfer object and need to be part of the deployment unit. In this case we need to make use of a special element called exclude-unlisted-classes in the persistence.xml file, which disables local classes from being added to the persistence unit. When exclude-unlisted-classes is used, then none of the classes in the local classes category described earlier will be included.

The third case is when we expect to be running the application in a Java SE environment and when we list the classes explicitly because that is the only portable way to do so in Java SE. We will explain deployment to the Java SE non-server environment later in the chapter.

Additional JARs of Managed Classes

The last way to get managed classes included in the persistence unit is to add them to another JAR and specify the name in a `jar-file` element in the `persistence.xml`. The `jar-file` element is used to indicate to the provider a JAR that may contain annotated classes. The provider will then treat the named JAR as if it were a deployment JAR, and it will look for any annotated classes and add them to the persistence unit. It will even search for an `orm.xml` file in the `META-INF` directory in the JAR and process it just as if it were an additionally listed mapping file.

Any JAR listed in a `jar-file` entry must be on the classpath of the deployment unit. You must do this manually, though, since the server will not automatically do it for you. Again this may be done by adding the JAR to the manifest classpath of the deployment unit or by some other vendor-specific means.

When listing a JAR in a `jar-file` element, it must be listed relative to the parent of the JAR file in which the `persistence.xml` file is located. This matches what you would put in the class-path entry in the manifest. For example, assume the enterprise archive (EAR), that we will call `emp.ear`, is structured as shown in Listing 11-5.

Listing 11-5. *Using Entities in an External JAR*

```
emp.ear
    emp-ejb.jar
        META-INF/persistence.xml
    employee/emp-classes.jar
        examples/model/Employee.class
```

The contents of the `persistence.xml` file should be as shown in Listing 11-6, with the `jar-file` element containing "employee/emp-classes.jar" to reference the `emp-classes.jar` in the employee directory in the EAR file. This would cause the provider to add the annotated classes it found in `emp-classes.jar` (`Employee.class`) to the persistence unit.

Listing 11-6. *Contents of* `persistence.xml`

```
<persistence-unit name="EmployeeService">
    <jta-data-source>jdbc/EmployeeServiceDS</jta-data-source>
    <jar-file>employee/emp-classes.jar</jar-file>
</persistence-unit>
```

Adding Vendor Properties

The last section in the `persistence.xml` file is the properties section. The `properties` element gives a deployer the chance to supply provider-specific settings for the persistence unit. To guarantee runtime compatibility, a provider must ignore properties it does not understand. While it is helpful to be able to use the same `persistence.xml` file across different providers, it also makes it easy to mistakenly type a property incorrectly and have it unintentionally and silently ignored. An example of adding some vendor properties is shown in Listing 11-7.

Listing 11-7. *Using Provider Properties*

```
<persistence-unit name="EmployeeService">
    ...
    <properties>
        <property name="toplink.logging.level" value="FINE"/>
        <property name="toplink.cache.size.default" value="500"/>
    </properties>
</persistence-unit>
```

Building and Deploying

One of the big wins that a standard persistence API brings is not only a portable runtime API but also a common way to compose, assemble, and configure an application that makes use of persistence. In this section we will describe some of the popular and practical choices that are used to deploy persistence-enabled applications.

Deployment Classpath

In some of the previous sections we say that a class or a JAR must be on the deployment classpath. When we say this we mean that the JAR must be accessible to the EJB JAR, the web archive (WAR), or the enterprise application archive (EAR). This may be achieved in a few ways.

The first is by putting the JAR in the manifest classpath of the EJB JAR or WAR. This is done by adding a classpath entry to the META-INF/MANIFEST.MF file in the JAR or WAR. One or more directories or JARs may be specified, as long as they are separated by spaces. For example, the following manifest file classpath entry will add the employee/emp-classes.jar and the employee/classes directory to the classpath of the JAR that contains the manifest file:

```
Class-Path: employee/emp-classes.jar employee/classes
```

Another way to get a JAR into the deployment unit classpath is to place the JAR in the library directory of the EAR. When a JAR is in the library directory, then it will be on the application classpath and accessible by all of the modules deployed within the EAR. By default this would just be the lib directory of the EAR, although it may be configured to be any directory in the EAR using the library-directory element in the application.xml deployment descriptor. The application.xml file would look something like the skeletal one shown in Listing 11-8.

Listing 11-8. *Setting the Application Library Directory*

```
<application ... >
    ...
    <library-directory>myDir/jars</library-directory>
</application>
```

Vendors usually provide their own vendor-specific way for deployers to add classes or JARs to the deployment classpath. This is usually offered at the application level and not at the level of a JAR or WAR; however some may provide both.

Packaging Options

A primary focus of the Java Persistence API is its integration with the Java EE platform. Not only has it been integrated in fine-grained ways, such as allowing injection of entity managers into Java EE components, but it also has special status in Java EE application packaging. Java EE allows for persistence to be supported in a variety of packaging configurations that offer flexibility and choice. We will divide them up into the different module types that the application might be deployed to: EJB modules, web modules, and persistence archives.

EJB JAR

Modularized business logic typically ends up in session bean components, which is why session beans have always been the primary clients of persistence. It is not only fitting but also an essential part of the integration of the Java Persistence API with Java EE. Because session beans provide such a natural home for code that operates on entities, the best supported way to access and package entities will be with session beans in an EJB JAR. We assume that the reader is familiar with packaging and deploying EJB components in an EJB JAR, but if not, there is a host of books and resources available to learn about it.

In EJB 3.0 you no longer need to have an ejb-jar.xml deployment descriptor, but if you choose to use one, then it must be in the META-INF directory. When defining a persistence unit in an EJB JAR, the persistence.xml file is not optional. It must be created and placed in the META-INF directory of the JAR alongside the ejb-jar.xml deployment descriptor, if it exists. Although the existence of persistence.xml is required, the contents may be very sparse indeed, in some cases including only the name of the persistence unit.

The only real work in defining a persistence unit is to decide where we want our entities and managed classes to reside. As we saw in the preceding sections, we have a number of options available to us. The simplest approach is to simply dump our managed classes into the EJB JAR along with the EJB components. As long as they are correctly annotated, the entities will be automatically discovered by the provider at deployment time and added to the persistence unit. Listing 11-9 shows a sample enterprise application archive file that does this.

Listing 11-9. *Packaging Entities in an EJB JAR*

```
emp.ear
    emp-ejb.jar
        META-INF/persistence.xml
        META-INF/orm.xml
        examples/ejb/EmployeeService.class
        examples/ejb/EmployeeServiceBean.class
        examples/model/Employee.class
        examples/model/Phone.class
        examples/model/Address.class
        examples/model/Department.class
        examples/model/Project.class
```

In this case the orm.xml file contains any mapping information that we might have at the persistence-unit level, for example, setting the schema for the persistence unit. In the persistence.xml file we would need to specify only the name of the persistence unit and the data source. Listing 11-10 shows the corresponding persistence.xml file in its entirety.

Listing 11-10. Persistence.xml *File for Entities Packaged in an EJB JAR*

```
<persistence xmlns="http://java.sun.com/xml/ns/persistence"
        xmlns:xsi="http://www.w3.org/2001/XMLSchema-instance"
        xsi:schemaLocation="http://java.sun.com/xml/ns/persistence
            http://java.sun.com/xml/ns/persistence/persistence_1_0.xsd"
        version="1.0">
    <persistence-unit name="EmployeeService">
        <jta-data-source>jdbc/EmployeeServiceDS</jta-data-source>
    </persistence-unit>
</persistence>
```

If we wanted to separate the entities from the EJB components, then we could put them in a different JAR and reference that JAR in a jar-file entry in the persistence.xml file. We showed a simple example of doing this in the Additional JARs of Managed Classes section, but we will show one again here with an additional orm.xml file and emp-mappings.xml mapping file. Listing 11-11 shows what the structure and contents of the EAR would look like.

Listing 11-11. *Packaging Entities in a Separate JAR*

```
emp.ear
    emp-ejb.jar
        META-INF/persistence.xml
        examples/ejb/EmployeeService.class
        examples/ejb/EmployeeServiceBean.class
    emp-classes.jar
        META-INF/orm.xml
        META-INF/emp-mappings.xml
        examples/model/Employee.class
        examples/model/Phone.class
        examples/model/Address.class
        examples/model/Department.class
        examples/model/Project.class
```

The emp-classes.jar file containing the entities would need to be on the classpath as described in the Deployment Classpath section. In addition to processing the entities found in the emp-classes.jar file, the orm.xml file in the META-INF directory will also be detected and processed automatically. We need to explicitly list the additional emp_mappings.xml mapping file in a mapping-file element, though, in order for the provider to find it as a resource. The persistence unit portion of the persistence.xml file is shown in Listing 11-12.

Listing 11-12. `Persistence.xml` *File for Entities Packaged in a Separate JAR*

```
<persistence-unit name="EmployeeService">
    <jta-data-source>jdbc/EmployeeServiceDS</jta-data-source>
    <mapping-file>META-INF/emp-mappings.xml</mapping-file>
    <jar-file>emp-classes.jar</jar-file>
</persistence-unit>
```

Web Archive

We have not been shy about the fact that we believe that session beans are the best way to access entities. Regardless of what we say, though, there will be people who for one reason or another don't want or are not able to use session beans. Operating on entities directly from the web tier is still a valid option and may continue to be popular for a subset of web developers.

The WAR is a little more complex than the EJB JAR is, and learning to package persistence units in web archives requires understanding the relevance of the `persistence.xml` file location. The location of the `persistence.xml` file determines the *persistence unit root*. The root of the persistence unit is defined as the JAR or directory that contains the `META-INF` directory where the `persistence.xml` file is located. For example, in an EJB JAR the `persistence.xml` file is located in the `META-INF` directory of the root of the JAR, so the root of the persistence unit is always the root of the EJB JAR file itself. In a WAR the persistence unit root is the `WEB-INF/classes` directory, so the `persistence.xml` file should be placed in the `WEB-INF/classes/META-INF` directory. Any annotated managed classes rooted in the `WEB-INF/classes` directory will be detected and added to the persistence unit. Similarly, if an `orm.xml` file is located in `WEB-INF/classes/META-INF`, then it will be processed. An example of packaging a persistence unit in the `WEB-INF/classes` directory is shown in Listing 11-13.

Listing 11-13. *Packaging Entities in the* `WEB-INF/classes` *Directory*

```
emp.ear
    emp.war
        WEB-INF/web.xml
        WEB-INF/classes/META-INF/persistence.xml
        WEB-INF/classes/META-INF/orm.xml
        WEB-INF/classes/examples/web/EmployeeServlet.class
        WEB-INF/classes/examples/model/Employee.class
        WEB-INF/classes/examples/model/Phone.class
        WEB-INF/classes/examples/model/Address.class
        WEB-INF/classes/examples/model/Department.class
        WEB-INF/classes/examples/model/Project.class
```

The `persistence.xml file` would be specified in exactly the same way as is shown in Listing 11-10. If we need to add another mapping file then we can put it anywhere on the deployment unit classpath. We just need to add a `mapping-file` element to the `persistence.xml` file. If, for example, we put `emp-mapping.xml` in the `WEB-INF/classes/mapping` directory, then we would add the following element to the `persistence.xml` file:

```
<mapping-file>mapping/emp-mapping.xml</mapping-file>
```

Since the `WEB-INF/classes` directory is automatically on the classpath of the WAR, the mapping file is specified relative to that directory.

Persistence Archive

If we want to allow a persistence unit to be shared or accessible by multiple components in different Java EE modules, then we should use a persistence archive. We saw a simple persistence archive back in Chapter 2 when we were first getting started and observed how it housed the `persistence.xml` file and the managed classes that were part of the persistence unit defined within it. By placing a persistence archive in the EAR, we can make it available to any component that needs to operate on the entities defined by its contained persistence unit.

The persistence archive is simple to create and easy to deploy. It is simply a JAR that contains a `persistence.xml` in its `META-INF` directory and the managed classes for the persistence unit defined by the `persistence.xml` file. In fact, an EJB JAR is really doubling as a persistence archive when it contains a `META-INF/persistence.xml` and the managed classes of the persistence unit. Now, with a persistence archive, we can define the persistence unit outside the EJB JAR but still use it from within the EJB JAR.

Listing 11-14 shows the contents of the simple persistence archive that defines the persistence unit that we have been using in the previous examples.

Listing 11-14. *Packaging Entities in a Persistence Archive*

```
emp.ear
    emp-persistence.jar
        META-INF/persistence.xml
        META-INF/orm.xml
        examples/model/Employee.class
        examples/model/Phone.class
        examples/model/Address.class
        examples/model/Department.class
        examples/model/Project.class
```

If this archive looks familiar it is because it is virtually the same as the structure that we defined in Listing 11-9 except that it is a persistence archive JAR instead of an EJB JAR. We just changed the name of the JAR and took out the session bean classes. The contents of the `persistence.xml` file are exactly the same as what is shown in Listing 11-10. Just like with the other archive types, the `orm.xml` file in the `META-INF` directory will be automatically detected and processed, and other XML mapping files may be placed within the JAR and referenced by the `persistence.xml` file as a `mapping-file` entry.

Once created, the persistence archive may be placed in either the root or the application library directory of the EAR. The advantage of placing it in the library directory is that it will automatically be on the application classpath and shared by all of the application components. If it is in the root directory of the EAR, then it will need to be incorporated into the application classpath in some vendor-specific way. In either case, though, the entity classes in the persistence archive will be loaded by the application class loader. This will enable the same class definition to be accessible to all of the components in the application.

As an alternative to putting the classes loose inside the web archive, a persistence archive may also be placed in the `WEB-INF/lib` directory of a WAR. This will make the persistence unit accessible only to the classes inside the WAR, but it allows the definition of the persistence unit to be decoupled from the web archive itself.

Managed classes may also be stored in a separate JAR external to the persistence archive, just as they could be in other packaging archive configurations. The external JAR would be referenced by the `persistence.xml` file as a `jar-file` entry with the same rules for specification as were described in the other cases. This is neither recommended nor useful, though, since the persistence archive itself is already separated from the other component classes. Seldom will there be a reason to create yet another JAR to store the managed classes, but there may be a case when the other JAR is pre-existing, and you need to reference it because you can't or don't want to put the `persistence.xml` file in the pre-existing JAR.

Persistence archives are actually a very tidy way of packaging a persistence unit. By keeping them self-contained (if they do not reference external JARs of classes using `jar-file` entries), they do not depend upon any other components of the application but can sit as a layer underneath those components to be used by them.

Persistence Unit Scope

For simplicity we have talked about a persistence unit in the singular. The truth is that any number of persistence units may be defined in the same `persistence.xml` file and be used in the scope within which they were defined. We saw in the preceding sections, when we discussed how managed classes get included in the persistence unit, that local classes in the same archive will be processed by default. If multiple persistence units are defined in the same `persistence.xml` file and `exclude-unlisted-classes` is not used on either one, then the same classes will be added to all of the defined persistence units. This may be a convenient way to import and transform data from one data source to another simply by reading in entities through one persistence unit and performing the transformation on them before writing them out through another persistence unit.

Now that we have defined and packaged our persistence units, we should outline the rules and ways to use them. There are only a few, but they are important to know.

The first rule is that persistence units are accessible only within the scope of their definition. We have already mentioned this in passing a couple of times, and we hinted at it again in the Persistence Archive section. We said that the persistence unit defined within a persistence archive at the EAR level was accessible to all of the components in the EAR, and that a persistence unit defined in a persistence archive in a WAR is accessible only to the components defined within that WAR. In fact, in general a persistence unit defined from an EJB JAR is seen by EJB components defined by that EJB JAR, and a persistence unit defined in a WAR will be seen only by the components defined within that WAR. Persistence units defined in a persistence archive that lives in the EAR will be seen by all of the components in the application.

The next part is that the names of persistence units must be unique within their scope. For example, there may be only one persistence unit of a given name within the same EJB JAR. Likewise there may be only one persistence unit of a given name in the same WAR, as well as only one persistence unit of the same name in all of the persistence archives at the EAR level. There may be a named persistence unit name in one EJB JAR and another that shares its name in another EJB JAR, or there may even be a persistence unit with the same name in an EJB JAR as there is in a persistence archive. It just means that whenever a persistence unit is referenced either within an `@PersistenceContext`, an `@PersistenceUnit` annotation, or a `createEntityManagerFactory()` method, then the most locally scoped one will get used.

A final note about naming is appropriate at this point. Just because it's possible to have multiple persistence units with the same name in different component archive namespaces doesn't mean that it is a good idea. As a general rule, you should always give persistence units unique names within the application.

Outside the Server

There are some obvious differences between deploying in a Java EE server and deploying to a Java SE runtime environment. For example, some of the Java EE container services are not going to be present, and this spills out into the runtime configuration information for a persistence unit. In this section we will outline the differences to consider when packaging and deploying to a Java SE environment.

Configuring the Persistence Unit

As before, the place to start is the configuration of the persistence unit, which is chiefly in the creation of the persistence.xml file. We will outline the differences between creating a persistence.xml file for a Java SE application and creating one for a Java EE application.

Transaction Type

When running in a server environment, the transaction-type attribute in the persistence unit defaults to being JTA. The JTA transaction layer was designed for use within the Java EE server and is intended to be fully integrated and coupled to the server components. There are currently no plans to make it pluggable, either, so the chances of getting a fully compliant JTA transaction manager to run in a Java SE environment are not only thin but also getting slimmer all the time. Given this fact, the Java Persistence API does not even provide support for using JTA outside the server. Some providers may offer this support, but it cannot be portably relied upon, and of course it relies upon the JTA component being present.

The transaction type does not normally need to be specified when deploying to Java SE. It will just default to being RESOURCE_LOCAL but may be specified explicitly to make the programming contract more clear.

Data Source

When we described configuration in the server, we illustrated how the jta-data-source element denotes the JNDI location of the data source that will be used to obtain connections. We also saw that some servers might even default the data source.

The non-jta-data-source element is used in the server to specify where resource-local connections can be obtained in JNDI. It may also be used by providers that do optimized reading through non-JTA connections.

When configuring for outside the server, not only can we not rely upon JTA, as we described in the Transaction Type section, but we cannot rely upon JNDI at all. We therefore cannot portably rely upon either of the data source elements in Java SE configurations.

When using resource-local transactions outside the server, the provider obtains database connections directly vended out by the JDBC driver. In order for it to get these connections it must obtain the driver-specific information, which typically includes the name of the driver class, the URL that the driver uses to connect to the database, and the user and password authentication that the driver also passes to the database. This metadata may be specified in whichever way the provider prefers it to be specified, but the most common method is to use the vendor-specific properties section. Listing 11-15 shows an example of using the TopLink Essentials properties that we use in the code example to connect to the Derby database through the Derby driver.

Listing 11-15. *Specifiying Resource-Level JDBC Properties*

```
<persistence-unit name="EmployeeService">
    ...
    <properties>
        <property name="toplink.jdbc.driver"
                  value="org.apache.derby.jdbc.ClientDriver"/>
        <property name="toplink.jdbc.url"
                  value="jdbc:derby://localhost:1527/EmpServDB;create=true"/>
        <property name="toplink.jdbc.user" value="APP"/>
        <property name="toplink.jdbc.password" value="APP"/>
    </properties>
</persistence-unit>
```

Providers

Many servers are going to have a default or native provider that they will use when the provider is not specified. It will automatically call into that provider to create an `EntityManagerFactory` at deployment time.

When not in a server, the factory is created programmatically using the `Persistence` class. When the `createEntityManagerFactory()` method is invoked, the `Persistence` class will begin a built-in pluggability protocol that goes out and finds the provider that is specified in the persistence unit configuration. If none was specified, then the first one that it finds will be used. Providers export themselves through a service that exists in the provider JAR that must be on the classpath. The net result is that the provider element is not required.

In the majority of cases when only one provider will be on the classpath, then the provider will be detected and used by the `Persistence` class to create an `EntityManagerFactory` for a given persistence unit. If you are ever in a situation where you have two providers on the classpath and you want a particular one to be used, then you should specify the provider class in the `provider` element. To prevent runtime and deployment errors, the `provider` element should be used if the application has a code dependency on a specific provider.

Listing the Entities

One of the benefits of deploying inside the server is that it is a highly controlled and structured environment. Because of this, the server can support the deployment process in ways that cannot be achieved by a simple Java SE runtime. The server already has to process all of the deployment units in an application and can do things like detecting all of the managed persistence classes in an EJB JAR or a persistence archive. This kind of class detection makes persistence archives a very convenient way to bundle a persistence unit.

The problem with this kind of detection outside the server is that the Java SE environment permits all kinds of different class resources to be added to the classpath, including network URLs or any other kind of resource that is acceptable to a classloader. This makes it difficult for the Java Persistence API to require providers to support doing automatic detection of the managed classes inside a persistence archive. The official position of the API is that for an application to be portable across all vendors it must explicitly list all of the managed classes in the persistence unit using class elements. When a persistence unit is large and includes a large number of classes, this task can become rather onerous.

In practice, however, most of the time the classes are sitting in a regular persistence archive JAR on the filesystem, and the provider runtime really can do the detection that the server would do in Java EE. For this reason all the major providers actually do support detecting the classes outside the server. This is really kind of an essential usability issue since the maintenance of a class list would be so cumbersome as to be a productivity bottleneck unless you had a tool manage the list for you.

A corollary to the official portability guideline to use class elements to enumerate the list of managed classes is that the exclude-unlisted-classes element is not guaranteed to have any impact in Java SE persistence units. Some providers may allow this element to be used outside the server, but it is not really very useful in the SE environment anyway given the flexibility of the classpath and packaging allowances in that environment.

Specifying Properties at Runtime

One of the benefits of running outside the server is the ability to specify provider properties at runtime. This is available because of the overloaded createEntityManagerFactory() method that accepts a Map of properties in addition to the name of the persistence unit. The properties passed to this method are combined with those already specified, normally in the persistence.xml file. They may be additional properties or they may override the value of a property that was already specified. This may not seem very useful to some applications, since putting runtime configuration information in code is not normally viewed as being better than isolating it in an XML file. However, one can imagine this being a convenient way to set properties obtained from a program input, such as the command line, as an even more dynamic configuration mechanism. In Listing 11-16 is an example of taking the user and password properties from the command line and passing them to the provider when creating the EntityManagerFactory.

Listing 11-16. *Using Command-Line Persistence Properties*

```
public class EmployeeService {
    public static void main(String[] args) {
        Map props = new HashMap();
        props.put("toplink.jdbc.user", args[0]);
        props.put("toplink.jdbc.password", args[1]);
        EntityManagerFactory emf = Persistence
            .createEntityManagerFactory("EmployeeService", props);
        // ...
        emf.close();
    }
}
```

System Classpath

In some ways configuring a persistence unit in a Java SE application is actually easier than configuring in the server because the classpath is simply the system classpath. Adding classes or jars on the system classpath is a trivial exercise. In the server we may have to manipulate the manifest classpath or add some vendor-specific application classpath configuration.

Summary

It is a simple exercise to package and deploy persistence applications using the Java Persistence API. In most cases it is just a matter of adding a very short `persistence.xml` file to the JAR containing the entity classes.

In this chapter we described how to configure the persistence unit in the Java EE server environment using the `persistence.xml` file and how in some cases the name may be the only setting required. We then explained when to apply and how to specify the transaction type, the persistence provider, and the data source. We showed how to use and specify the default `orm.xml` mapping file and then went on to use additional mapping files within the same persistence unit. We also discussed the various ways that classes may be included in the persistence unit and how to customize the persistence unit using vendor-specific properties.

We looked at the ways that persistence units may be packaged and deployed to a Java EE application as part of an EJB archive, a web archive, or a persistence archive that is accessible to all of the components in the application. We examined how persistence units may exist within different scopes of a deployed Java EE application and what the name-scoping rules were.

Finally we compared the configuration and deployment practices to deploying an application to a Java SE environment.

In the next chapter we will consider the accepted and best practices for testing applications that use persistence.

CHAPTER 12

■■■■

Testing

One of the major selling points of the Java Persistence API and EJB 3.0 has been the drive towards better testability. The use of plain Java classes where possible as well as the ability to use persistence outside of the application server has made enterprise applications much easier to test. This chapter will cover unit testing and integration testing with entities, with a mix of modern and traditional test techniques.

Testing Enterprise Applications

If we accept that testing is a good thing, then how exactly should we go about it? Almost all enterprise applications are hosted in some kind of server environment, whether it is a servlet container like Apache Tomcat or a full Java EE application server. Once deployed to such an environment, the developer is effectively cut off from the application. At this point it can only be tested using the public interface of the application, such as a browser using HTTP, RMI, or a messaging interface.

This presents an issue for developers, because we want to be able to focus on the components of an application in isolation. An elaborate sequence of operations through a web site may resolve to only a single method of a session bean that implements a particular business service. For example, to view an Employee record, a test client might have to log in using a user name and password, traverse through several menu options, execute a search, and then finally access the record. Afterwards the HTML output of the report must be verified to ensure that the operation completed as expected. In some applications this may be short-circuited by directly accessing the URL that retrieves a particular record. But with more and more information cached in HTTP session state, URLs are beginning to look like random sequences of letters and numbers. Direct access to a particular feature of an application may not be an easy process.

Java SE clients (so-called "fat" clients) that communicate with databases and other resources suffer from the same problem despite the ability to execute the program without the need for an application server. The user interface of a Java SE client may well be a Swing application requiring special tools to drive the user interface in order to do any kind of test automation. The application itself is still just a black box without any obvious way to get inside.

Numerous attempts have been made in recent years to expose the internals of an application to testing while deployed on a server. The Cactus[1] framework, for example, allows developers to write tests using JUnit, which are then deployed to the server along with the

---

1. Visit http://jakarta.apache.org/cactus/ for more information.

application and executed via a web interface provided by Cactus. Other frameworks have adopted a similar approach using RMI instead of a web interface to remotely control the tests.

Though effective, the downside to these approaches is that the application server still has to be up and running before we can attempt any kind of testing. For developers who use the test-driven development (TDD) methodology, where tests are written before code and the full unit test suite is executed after every development iteration (which can be as small as a change to a single method), any kind of interaction with the application server is a problem. Even for developers who practice a more traditional testing methodology, frequent test execution is hampered by the need to keep the application server running, with a packaging and deployment step before every test run.

Clearly, for developers who wish to break a Java EE application into its component parts and test those components in isolation, there is a need for tools that will let us directly execute portions of the application outside of the server environment in which it is normally hosted.

Terminology

Not everyone agrees about exactly what constitutes a unit test or an integration test. In fact, it is quite likely that any survey of a group of developers will yield a wide variety of results, some similar in nature with others venturing into completely different areas of testing. Therefore we feel it is important to define our terminology for testing so that you can translate it into whatever terms you are comfortable with.

We see tests falling into the following four categories:

1. **Unit Tests.** Unit tests are written by developers and focus on isolated components of an application. Depending on your approach, this may be a single class or a collection of classes. The only key defining element is that the unit test is not coupled to any server resources (these are typically stubbed out as part of the test process) and execute very quickly. It must be possible to execute an entire suite of unit tests from within an IDE and get the results in a matter of seconds. Unit test execution can be automated and is often configured to happen automatically as part of every merge to a configuration management system.

2. **Integration Tests.** Integration tests are also written by developers and focus on use cases within an application. They are still decoupled from the application server, but the difference between a unit test and an integration test is that the integration test makes full use of external resources such as a database. In effect, an integration test takes a component from an application and runs in isolation as if it were still inside the application server. Running the test locally makes it much faster than a test hosted in an application server but still slower than a unit test. Integration tests are also automated and often run at least daily to ensure that there are no regressions introduced by developers.

3. **Functional Tests.** Functional tests are the black box tests written and automated by quality engineers instead of developers. Quality engineers look at the functional specification for a product and its user interface and seek to automate tests that can verify product behavior without the understanding of how the application is implemented. Functional tests are a critical part of the application development process, but it is unrealistic to execute these tests as part of the day-to-day work done by a developer. Automated execution of these tests often happens at a different schedule relative to the regular development process.

4. **Acceptance Tests.** Acceptance tests are customer-driven. These tests, usually conducted manually, are carried out directly by customers or representatives who play the role of the customer. The goal of an acceptance test is to verify that the requirements set out by the customer are reflected in the user interface and behavior of the application.

In this chapter we will focus only on unit tests and integration tests. These tests are written by developers for the benefit of developers and constitute what is called white box testing. These tests are written with the full understanding of how the application is implemented and what it will take to test not only the successful path through an application but also how to trigger failure scenarios.

Testing Outside the Server

The common element between unit tests and integration tests is that they are executed without the need for an application server. Unfortunately for Java EE developers, this has traditionally been a very difficult task to accomplish. Applications developed before the Java EE 5 release are tightly coupled to the application server, often making it difficult and counterproductive to attempt replicating the required container services in a stand-alone environment.

To put this in perspective, let's look at Enterprise JavaBeans as they existed in EJB 2.1. On paper, testing a session bean class should be little more than a case of instantiating the bean class and invoking the business method. For trivial business methods, this is indeed the case, but things start to go downhill quickly once dependencies get involved. For example, let's consider a business method that needs to invoke another business method from a different session bean.

Dependency lookup was the only option in EJB 2.1, so if the business method has to access JNDI to obtain a reference to the other session bean, then either JNDI must be worked around or the bean class must be refactored so that the lookup code can be replaced with a test-specific version. If the code uses the Service Locator[2] pattern, then we have a bigger problem because a singleton static method is used to obtain the bean reference. The only solution for testing beans that use Service Locators outside the container is to refactor the bean classes so that the locator logic can be overridden in a test case.

2. Alur, Deepak, John Crupi, and Dan Malks. *Core J2EE Patterns: Best Practices and Design Strategies, Second Edition.* Upper Saddle River, N.J.: Prentice Hall PTR, 2003, p. 315.

Next we have the problem of the dependent bean itself. The bean class does not implement the business interface, so it cannot simply be instantiated and made available to the bean we are trying to test. Instead, it will have to be subclassed to implement the business interface, and stubs for a number of low-level EJB methods will have to be provided since the business interface in EJB 2.1 actually extends an interface that is implemented internally by the application server.

Even if we get that to work, what happens if we encounter a container-managed entity bean? Not only do we have the same issues with respect to the interfaces involved, but the bean class is abstract, with all of the persistent state properties unimplemented. We could implement these, but our test framework would rapidly start to outgrow the application code. We can't even just run them against the database like we can with JDBC code because so much of the entity bean logic, relationship maintenance and other persistence operations are only available inside of an EJB container.

The dirty secret of many applications written using older versions of Java EE is that there is little to no developer testing at all. Developers write, package, and deploy applications; test them manually through the user interface; and then hope that the quality assurance group can write a functional test that verifies each feature. It's just too much work to test individual components outside of the application server.

This is where EJB 3.0 and the Java Persistence API come in. Starting with EJB 3.0, a session bean class is a simple Java class that implements a regular Java interface. No special EJB interfaces need to be extended or implemented. To unit test a session bean, we can just implement it and execute it. If the bean depends on another bean, we can instantiate that bean and manually inject it into the bean being tested. The EJB 3.0 release was designed to encourage testing by breaking the hard dependencies between application code and the application server.

Likewise entities are a world apart from container-managed entity beans. If your session bean uses an entity, you can just instantiate it and use it like any other class. If you are testing code that uses the entity manager and want to verify that it is interacting with the database the way you expect it to, just bootstrap the entity manager in Java SE and make full use of the entity manager outside of the application server.

Over the course of this chapter, we will demonstrate how to take a session bean and Java Persistence API code from a Java EE application and run it outside the container, using unit testing and integration testing approaches. If you have worked with older versions of EJB and experienced the pain of developer testing, prepare yourself for a completely different look at testing enterprise applications.

Test Frameworks

In recent years, the JUnit test framework has become the de facto standard for testing Java applications. JUnit is a simple unit testing framework that allows tests to be written as Java classes. These Java classes are then bundled together and run in suites using a test runner that is itself a simple Java class. Out of this simple design, a whole community has emerged to provide extensions to JUnit and integrate it into all major development environments.

Despite its name, unit testing is now only one of the many things that JUnit can be used for. It has been extended to support testing of web sites, automatic stubbing of interfaces for testing, concurrency testing, and performance testing. Many quality assurance groups now use JUnit as part of the automation mechanism to run whole suites of end-to-end functional tests.

For our purposes we will look at JUnit in the context of its unit testing roots, and also at strategies that allow it to be used as an effective integration test framework. Collectively we look at these two approaches simply as developer tests, because they are written by developers to assist with the overall quality and development of an application.

In addition to the test framework itself, there are other libraries that can assist with the testing of Java EE components. There have been announcements for EJB 3.0 containers that can be used outside of the application server, providing developers with the full services of dependency injection even for isolated session bean testing. Frameworks like Spring also offer sophisticated dependency injection support even in the Java SE environment, allowing dependent classes to be woven together. Even though it may not directly support EJB 3.0 annotations, the fact that session beans are simple Java classes makes them usable with any lightweight container framework. As always, before writing these kinds of frameworks for testing, check to see that the problem hasn't already been solved. If nothing else, the Java community has shown a remarkable willingness to share solutions to problems, both in the open source community and even from the commercial vendors.

We will assume that you are familiar with JUnit at this point. Introductory articles and tutorials can be found on the JUnit website at `http://www.junit.org`. There are also a large number of books and other online resources that cover testing with JUnit in extensive detail.

Unit Testing

It might seem counterintuitive at first, but one of the most interesting things about entities is that they can participate in tests without requiring a running application server or live database. For years enterprise developers have been frustrated with container-managed entity beans because they were effectively untestable without a live application server. The component and home interfaces could conceivably be used in unit tests, but only if the developer provided implementations of those interfaces, duplicating effort already invested in writing the real bean classes and potentially introducing new bugs in the process. Because entities are plain Java classes, they can be used directly in tests without any additional effort required.

In the following sections we will look both at testing entity classes directly and using entities as part of tests for Java EE components. We will also discuss how to leverage dependency injection in unit tests and how to deal with the presence of Java Persistence API interfaces.

Testing Entities

Entities themselves are unlikely to be extensively tested in isolation. Most methods on entities are simple getters or setters that relate to the persistent state of the entity or to its relationships. Business methods may also appear on entities but are less common. In many applications, entities are little more than basic JavaBeans.

As a rule, property methods do not generally require explicit tests. Verifying that a setter assigns a value to a field and the corresponding getter retrieves the same value is not testing the application so much as the compiler. Unless there is a side effect in one or both of the methods, getters and setters are too simple to break and therefore too simple to warrant testing.

Key things to look for in determining whether or not an entity warrants individual testing are side effects from a getter or setter method (such as data transformation or validation rules) and the presence of business methods. The entity shown in Listing 12-1 contains non-trivial logic that warrants specific testing.

Listing 12-1. *An Entity That Validates and Transforms Data*

```
@Entity
public class Department {
    @Id private String id;
    private String name;
    @OneToMany(mappedBy="department")
    private Collection<Employee> employees;

    public String getId() { return id; }
    public void setId(String id) {
        if (id.length() != 4) {
            throw new IllegalArgumentException("Department identifiers must ➥
be four characters in length");
        }
        this.id = id.toUpperCase();
    }

    // ...
}
```

The setId() method both validates the format of the department identifier and transforms the string to uppercase. This type of logic and the fact that setting the identifier can actually cause an exception to be thrown suggests that tests would be worthwhile. Testing this behavior is simply a matter of instantiating the entity and invoking the setter with different values. Listing 12-2 shows one possible set of tests.

Listing 12-2. *Testing a Setter Method for Side Effects*

```
public class DepartmentTest extends TestCase {

    public void testValidDepartmentId() throws Exception {
        Department dept = new Department();
        dept.setId("NA65");
        assertEquals("NA65", dept.getId());
    }

    public void testDepartmentIdInvalidLength() throws Exception {
        Department dept = new Department();
        try {
            dept.setId("NA6");
            fail("Department identifiers must be four characters");
        } catch (IllegalArgumentException e) {
        }
    }
```

```
    public void testDepartmentIdCase() throws Exception {
        Department dept = new Department();
        dept.setId("na65");
        assertEquals("NA65", dept.getId());
    }
}
```

Testing Entities in Components

The most likely test scenario for entities is not the entities themselves but the application code that uses the entities as part of its business logic. For many applications this means testing session beans and other Java EE components. Just as with the entity test shown in Listing 12-1, these types of tests are made easy in the sense that the entity class can simply be instantiated, populated with entity data and set into the bean class for testing. When used as a domain object in application code, an entity is no different than any other Java class. You can effectively pretend that it's not an entity at all.

Of course, there is more to unit testing a session bean than simply instantiating entities to be used with a business method. We also need to concern ourselves with the dependencies that the session bean has in order to implement its business logic. These dependencies are usually manifested as fields on the bean class that are populated using a form of dependency injection or dependency lookup.

When writing unit tests, our goal is to introduce the minimum set of dependencies required to implement a particular test. If we are testing a business method that needs to invoke a method on the EJBContext interface, then we should worry only about providing a stubbed version of the interface. If the bean uses a data source but is not relevant to our testing, then ideally we would like to ignore it entirely.

Dependency injection is the key to effective unit testing. By removing the JNDI API from session bean code and eliminating the need for the Service Locator pattern, the bean class has few dependencies on the application server. We need only instantiate the bean instance and manually inject the required resources, the majority of which will either be other beans from the application or test-specific implementations of a standard interface.

As we discussed in Chapter 3, the setter injection form of dependency injection is the easiest to use in unit tests. Because the setter methods are almost always public, they can be invoked directly by the test case to assign a dependency to the bean class. Field injection is still easy to deal with so long as the field uses package scope since the convention for unit tests is to use the same package name as the class that is being tested.

When the dependency is another session bean, you must make a choice as to whether all of the dependencies of the required bean class must be met or whether a test-specific version of the business interface should be used instead. If the business method from the dependent business interface does not affect the outcome of the test, then it may not be worth the effort to establish the full dependency. As an example, consider the session bean shown in Listing 12-3. We have shown a single method for calculating years of service for an employee that retrieves an Employee instance using the EmployeeService session bean.

Listing 12-3. *Using the* EmployeeService *Bean in a Different Business Method*

```
@Stateless
public class VacationBean implements Vacation {
    public static final long MILLIS_PER_YEAR = 1000 * 60 * 60 * 24 * 365;
    @EJB EmployeeService empService;

    public int getYearsOfService(int empId) {
        Employee emp = empService.findEmployee(empId);
        long current = System.currentTimeMillis();
        long start = emp.getStartDate().getTime();
        return (int)((current - start) / MILLIS_PER_YEAR);
    }

    // ...
}
```

Since the only thing necessary to verify the getYearsOfService() method is a single Employee instance with a start date value, there is no need to use the real EmployeeService bean. An implementation of the EmployeeService interface that returns an entity instance pre-configured for the test is more than sufficient. In fact, the ability to specify a well-known return value from the findEmployee() method makes the overall test much easier to implement. Listing 12-4 demonstrates using a test-specific implementation of a session bean interface. Implementing an interface specifically for a test is called *mocking* the interface, and the instantiated instance is referred to as a *mock object*.

Listing 12-4. *Creating a Test-specific Version of a Business Interface*

```
public class VacationBeanTest extends TestCase {
    public void testYearsOfService() throws Exception {
        VacationBean bean = new VacationBean();
        bean.empService = new EmployeeService() {
            public Employee findEmployee(int id) {
                Employee emp = new Employee();
                emp.setStartDate(new Time(System.currentTimeMillis() -
                                          VacationBean.MILLIS_PER_YEAR * 5));
                return emp;
            }

            // ...
        };
        int yearsOfService = bean.getYearsOfService(0);
        assertEquals(5, yearsOfService);
    }

    // ...
}
```

The Entity Manager in Unit Tests

The EntityManager and Query interfaces present a challenge to developers writing unit tests. Code that interacts with the entity manager can vary from the simple (persisting an object) to the complex (issuing an JPQL query and obtaining the results). There are two basic approaches to dealing with the presence of standard interfaces:

- Introduce a subclass that replaces methods containing entity manager or query operations with test-specific versions that do not interact with the Java Persistence API.

- Provide custom implementations of standard interfaces that may be predictably used for testing.

Before covering these strategies in detail, consider the session bean implementation shown in Listing 12-5 that provides a simple authentication service. For such a simple class, it is surprisingly challenging to unit test. The entity manager operations are embedded directly within the authenticate() method, coupling the implementation to the Java Persistence API.

Listing 12-5. *Session Bean That Performs Basic Authentication*

```
@Stateless
public class UserServiceBean implements UserService {
    @PersistenceContext(unitName="EmployeeService")
    EntityManager em;

    public User authenticate(String userId, String password) {
        User user = em.find(User.class, userId);
        if (user != null) {
            if (password.equals(user.getPassword())) {
                return user;
            }
        }
        return null;
    }
}
```

The first technique we will demonstrate to make this class testable is to introduce a subclass that eliminates entity manager calls. For the UserServiceBean example shown in Listing 12-5, entity manager access must first be isolated to a separate method before it can be tested. Listing 12-6 demonstrates such a refactoring.

Listing 12-6. *Isolating Entity Manager Operations for Testing*

```
@Stateless
public class UserServiceBean implements UserService {
    @PersistenceContext(unitName="EmployeeService")
    EntityManager em;

    public User authenticate(String userId, String password) {
        User user = findUser(userId);
        // ...
    }

    User findUser(String userId) {
        return em.find(User.class, userId);
    }
}
```

With this refactoring complete, the authenticate() method no longer has any direct dependency on the entity manager. The UserServiceBean class can now be subclassed for testing, replacing the findUser() method with a test-specific version that returns a well-known result. Listing 12-7 demonstrates a complete test case using this technique.

Listing 12-7. *Using a Subclass to Eliminate Entity Manager Dependencies*

```
public class UserServiceTest extends TestCase {
    private static final String USER_ID = "test_id";
    private static final String PASSWORD = "test_password";
    private static final String INVALID_USER_ID = "test_user";

    public void testAuthenticateValidUser() throws Exception {
        TestUserService service = new TestUserService();
        User user = service.authenticate(USER_ID, PASSWORD);
        assertNotNull(user);
        assertEquals(USER_ID, user.getName());
        assertEquals(PASSWORD, user.getPassword());
    }

    public void testAuthenticateInvalidUser() throws Exception {
        TestUserService service = new TestUserService();
        User user = service.authenticate(INVALID_USER_ID, PASSWORD);
        assertNull(user);
    }

    class TestUserService extends UserServiceBean {
        private User user;
```

```
    public TestUserService() {
        user = new User();
        user.setName(USER_ID);
        user.setPassword(PASSWORD);
    }

    User findUser(String userId) {
        if (userId.equals(user.getName())) {
            return user;
        }
        return null;
    }
  }
}
```

This test case has the advantage of leaving the original authenticate() method implementation intact, only overriding the findUser() method for the test. This works well for classes that have been refactored to isolate persistence operations, but these changes cannot always be made. The alternative is to mock the EntityManager interface. Listing 12-8 demonstrates this approach.

Listing 12-8. *Using a Mock Entity Manager in a Unit Test*

```
public class UserServiceTest2 extends TestCase {
    private static final String USER_ID = "test_id";
    private static final String PASSWORD = "test_password";
    private static final String INVALID_USER_ID = "test_user";

    public void testAuthenticateValidUser() throws Exception {
        UserServiceBean service = new UserServiceBean();
        service.em = new TestEntityManager(USER_ID, PASSWORD);
        User user = service.authenticate(USER_ID, PASSWORD);
        assertNotNull(user);
        assertEquals(USER_ID, user.getName());
        assertEquals(PASSWORD, user.getPassword());
    }

    public void testAuthenticateInvalidUser() throws Exception {
        UserServiceBean service = new UserServiceBean();
        service.em = new TestEntityManager(USER_ID, PASSWORD);
        User user = service.authenticate(INVALID_USER_ID, PASSWORD);
        assertNull(user);
    }
```

```
class TestEntityManager extends MockEntityManager {
    private User user;

    public TestEntityManager(String user, String password) {
        this.user = new User();
        this.user.setName(user);
        this.user.setPassword(password);
    }

    public <T> T find(Class<T> entityClass, Object pk) {
        if (entityClass == User.class && ((String)pk).equals(user.getName())) {
            return (T) user;
        }
        return null;
    }
}
}
```

The advantage of this approach over subclassing is that it leaves the original bean class unchanged while allowing it to be unit tested. The MockEntityManager class referenced in the test is a concrete implementation of the EntityManager interface with empty method definitions. All methods that return a value return null or an equivalent instead. By defining it separately, it can be reused for other test cases. Many unit test suites contain a small set of mocked interfaces that can be reused across multiple tests.

Tip Check out http://www.mockobjects.com for further information on mock object techniques and open source tools to assist with mock object creation.

Integration Testing

Integration testing, for our purposes, is an extension of unit testing that takes components of a Java EE application and executes them outside of an application server. Unlike unit testing, where we went to great lengths to avoid the entity manager, in integration testing we embrace it and leverage the fact that it can be used in Java SE.

The following sections explore using the Java Persistence API outside of an application server in order to test application logic with a live database but without starting the application server.

Using the Entity Manager

In Listing 12-5 we demonstrated a session bean that performed basic authentication against a User object retrieved from the database. To unit test this class, a number of techniques were presented to replace or mock the entity manager operation. The downside to this approach is that the test code required to work around external dependencies in the application code can quickly reach a point where it is difficult to maintain and is a potential source of bugs.

Instead of mocking the entity manager, a resource-local, application-managed entity manager may be used to perform tests against a live database. Listing 12-9 demonstrates a functional test version of the UserServiceBean test cases.

Listing 12-9. *Integration Test for* UserServiceBean

```
public class UserServiceTest3 extends TestCase {
    private static final String USER_ID = "test_id";
    private static final String PASSWORD = "test_password";
    private static final String INVALID_USER_ID = "test_user";

    private EntityManagerFactory emf;
    private EntityManager em;

    public void setUp() {
        emf = Persistence.createEntityManagerFactory("hr");
        em = emf.createEntityManager();
        createTestData();
    }

    public void tearDown() {
        if (em != null) {
            removeTestData();
            em.close();
        }
        if (emf != null) {
            emf.close();
        }
    }

    private void createTestData() {
        User user = new User();
        user.setName(USER_ID);
        user.setPassword(PASSWORD);
        em.getTransaction().begin();
        em.persist(user);
        em.getTransaction().commit();
    }

    private void removeTestData() {
        em.getTransaction().begin();
        User user = em.find(User.class, USER_ID);
        if (user != null) {
            em.remove(user);
        }
        em.getTransaction().commit();
    }
```

```
public void testAuthenticateValidUser() throws Exception {
    UserServiceBean service = new UserServiceBean();
    service.em = em;
    User user = service.authenticate(USER_ID, PASSWORD);
    assertNotNull(user);
    assertEquals(USER_ID, user.getName());
    assertEquals(PASSWORD, user.getPassword());
}

public void testAuthenticateInvalidUser() throws Exception {
    UserServiceBean service = new UserServiceBean();
    service.em = em;
    User user = service.authenticate(INVALID_USER_ID, PASSWORD);
    assertNull(user);
}
}
```

This test case uses the fixture methods `setUp()` and `tearDown()` to create `EntityManagerFactory` and `EntityManager` instances using the Java SE bootstrap API and then closes them when the test completes. The test case also uses these methods to seed the database with test data and remove it when the test completes. The `tearDown()` method is guaranteed to be called even if a test fails due to an exception. Like any Java Persistence API application in the Java SE environment, a `persistence.xml` file will need to be on the classpath in order for the `Persistence` class to bootstrap an entity manager factory. This example demonstrates the basic pattern for all integration tests that use an entity manager.

The advantage of this style of test versus a unit test is that no effort was required to mock up persistence interfaces. Emulating the entity manager and query engine in order to test code that interacts directly with these interfaces suffers from diminishing returns as more and more effort is put into preparing a test environment instead of writing tests. In the worst-case scenario, incorrect test results occur because of bugs in the test harness, not in the application code. Given the ease with which the Java Persistence API can be used outside the application server, this type of effort may be better spent establishing a simple database test environment and writing automated functional tests.

However, despite the opportunity that testing outside the application server presents, care must be taken to ensure that such testing truly adds value. Quite often, developers fall into the trap of writing tests that do little more than test vendor functionality as opposed to true application logic. An example of this mistake is seeding a database, executing a query and verifying that the desired results are returned. It sounds valid at first, but all that it tests is the developer's understanding of how to write a query. Unless there is a bug in the database or the persistence provider, the test will never fail. A more valid variation of this test would be to start the scenario further up the application stack, by executing a business method on a session façade that initiates a query and then validating that the resulting transfer objects are formed correctly for later presentation by a JSP page.

Test Setup and Teardown

Many tests involving persistence require some kind of test data in the database before the test can be executed. If the business operation itself does not create and verify the result of a persistence operation, the database must already contain data that can be read and used by the test. Since tests should ideally be able to set and reset their own test data before and after each test, we must have a way to seed the database appropriately.

This sounds pretty straightforward; use JDBC to seed the database during `setUp()` and again during `tearDown()` to reset it. But there is a danger here. Most persistence providers employ some kind of data or object caching. Any time data changes in the database without the persistence provider knowing about it, its cache will get out of sync with the database. In the worst-case scenario, this could cause entity manager operations to return entities that have since been removed or that have stale data.

It's worth reiterating that this is not a problem with the persistence provider. Caching is a good thing and the reason that Java Persistence API solutions often significantly outperform direct JDBC access in read-mostly applications. The Reference Implementation, for example, uses a sophisticated shared-cache mechanism that is scoped to the entire persistence unit. When operations are completed in a particular persistence context, the results are merged back into the shared cache so that they can be used by other persistence contexts. This happens whether the entity manager and persistence context are created in Java SE or Java EE. Therefore you can't assume that closing an entity manager clears test data from the cache.

There are several approaches we can use to keep the cache consistent with our test database. The first, and easiest, is to create and remove test data using the entity manager. Any entity persisted or removed using the entity manager will always be kept consistent with the cache. For small data sets, this is very easy to accomplish. This is the approach we used in Listing 12-9.

For larger data sets, however, it can be cumbersome to create and manage test data using entities. JUnit extensions such as DbUnit[3] allow seed data to be defined in XML files and then loaded in bulk to the database before each test begins. So given that the persistence provider won't know about this data, how can we still make use of it? The first strategy is to establish a set of test data that is read-only. So long as the data is never changed, it doesn't matter if the entity exists in the provider cache or not. The second strategy is to either use special data sets for operations that need to modify test data without creating it, or to ensure that these changes are never permanently committed. If the transaction to update the database is rolled back, then the database and cache state will both remain consistent.

The last thing to consider is explicit cache invalidation. This is vendor-specific, but every vendor that supports a shared cache will also provide some mechanism to clear the cache. TopLink Essentials provides a number of options for controlling the cache. The following method demonstrates how to invalidate the entire shared cache in TopLink Essentials given any `EntityManager` instance:

```
public static void clearCache(EntityManager em) {
    em.clear();
    oracle.toplink.essentials.ejb.cmp3.EntityManager tlem =
        (oracle.toplink.essentials.ejb.cmp3.EntityManager) em;
    tlem.getActiveSession()
        .getIdentityMapAccessor()
        .initializeAllIdentityMaps();
}
```

---

3. Visit `http://dbunit.sourceforge.net/` for more information.

Note that we cleared the current persistence context as well as invalidated the cache. As we have discussed before, the persistence context is a localized set of transactional changes. It uses data from the shared cache but is actually a separate and distinct data structure.

Switching Configurations for Testing

One of the great advantages of the Java Persistence API is that metadata specified in annotation form may be overridden or replaced by metadata specified in XML form. This affords us a unique opportunity to develop an application targeting the production database platform and then provide an alternate set of mappings (even query definitions) targeted to a test environment. In the context of testing, the Java SE bootstrap mechanism will use the persistence.xml file located in the META-INF directory on the classpath. So long as the persistence unit definition inside this file has the same name as the one the application was written to, the test version can retarget it as necessary to suit the needs of the integration test.

There are two main uses for this approach. The first is to specify properties in the persistence.xml file that are specific to testing. For many developers, this will mean providing JDBC connection information to a local database so that tests do not collide with other developers on a shared database.

The second major use of a custom persistence.xml file is to customize the database mappings for deployment on a completely different database platform. For example, if Oracle is your production database and you don't wish to run the full database[4] on your local machine, you can adjust the mapping information to target an embedded database such as Apache Derby.

As an example of when this would be necessary, consider an application that uses the native sequencing of the Oracle database. Derby does not have an equivalent, so table generators must be used instead. First, let's consider an example entity that uses a native sequence generator:

```
@Entity
public class Phone {
    @SequenceGenerator(name="Phone_Gen", sequenceName="PHONE_SEQ")
    @Id @GeneratedValue(generator="Phone_Gen")
    private int id;
    // ...
}
```

The first step to getting this entity working on Derby is to create an XML mapping file that overrides the definition of the "Phone_Gen" generator to use a table generator. The following fragment of a mapping file demonstrates how to replace the sequence generator with a table generator:

```
<entity-mappings>
    ...
    <table-generator name="Phone_Gen" table="ID_GEN" pk-column-value="PhoneId"/>
    ...
</entity-mappings>
```

---

4. At the risk of sounding somewhat biased, might we humbly suggest Oracle XE. It represents the power of the Oracle database conveniently sized to an individual machine at no cost. All of the examples in this book (including the advanced SQL query examples in Chapter 9) were developed on Oracle XE.

This is the same technique we applied in Chapter 10 when we discussed overriding a sequence generator.

Finally we need to create a new `persistence.xml` file that references this mapping file. If the overrides were placed in a mapping file called `derby-overrides.xml`, then the following persistence unit configuration would apply the mapping overrides:

```
<persistence>
    <persistence-unit name="hr">

        ...

        <mapping-file>derby-overrides.xml</mapping-file>

        ...

    </persistence-unit>
</persistence>
```

Unlike the mapping file, which sparsely defines overrides, all of the information that was present in the production `persistence.xml` file must be copied into the test-specific version. The only exception to this is the JDBC connection properties, which will now have to be customized for the embedded Derby instance.

Minimizing Database Connections

Integration tests execute slower than unit tests due to the nature of the database interaction, but what may not be obvious from the test case shown in Listing 12-9 is that two separate connections are made to the database, one each for the `testAuthenticateValidUser()` and `testAuthenticateInvalidUser()` tests. JUnit actually instantiates a new instance of the test case class each time it runs a test method, running `setUp()` and `tearDown()` each time as well. The reason for this behavior is to minimize the chance of data stored in fields from one test case interfering with the execution of another.

While this works well for unit tests, it may lead to unacceptable performance for integration tests. To work around this limitation, an extension to JUnit called `TestSetup` may be used to create a fixture that runs `setUp()` and `tearDown()` only once for an entire test suite. Listing 12-10 demonstrates a test suite that uses this feature.

Listing 12-10. *One-time Database Setup for Integration Tests*

```
public class DatabaseTest {
    public static EntityManagerFactory emf;
    public static EntityManager em;

    public static Test suite() {
        TestSuite suite = new TestSuite();
        suite.addTestSuite(UserServiceTest3.class);

        TestSetup wrapper = new TestSetup(suite) {
```

```
            protected void setUp() throws Exception {
                emf = Persistence.createEntityManagerFactory("hr");
                em = emf.createEntityManager();
            }

            protected void tearDown() throws Exception {
                if (em != null) {
                    em.close();
                }
                if (emf != null) {
                    emf.close();
                }
            }
        };

        return wrapper;
    }
}
```

Using this test suite as a starting point, all child test cases or test suites that execute in the context of the TestSetup wrapper have access to the correctly populated EntityManager and EntityManagerFactory static fields on the DatabaseTest class. The setUp() method of each test case now only needs to reference this class to obtain the objects instead of creating them each time. The following example demonstrates the change required for the UnitServiceTest3 test case:

```
public void setUp() {
    emf = DatabaseTest.emf;
    em = DatabaseTest.em;
    createTestData();
}
```

This is a useful technique to minimize the cost of acquiring expensive resources, but care must be taken to ensure that side effects from one test do not accidentally interfere with the execution of other tests. Because all tests share the same entity manager instance, data may be cached or settings may be changed that have an unexpected impact later on. Just as it is necessary to keep the database tables clean between tests, any changes to the entity manager itself (including flushing the persistence context) must be reverted when the test ends, regardless of whether the outcome is a success or a failure.

Components and Persistence

More often than not, session beans in an integration test are no different than session beans in a unit test. You instantiate the bean, supply any necessary dependencies, and execute the test. Where we start to diverge is when we start to take into account issues such as transaction management and multiple session bean instances collaborating together to implement a single use case. In the following sections we will discuss techniques to handle more complex session bean scenarios when testing outside of the container.

Transaction Management

Transactions lie at the heart of every enterprise application. We made this statement back in Chapter 3 and tried to drive this point home in Chapter 5, demonstrating all of the different ways in which entity managers and persistence contexts can intersect with different transaction models. It might come as a surprise then to learn that when it comes to writing integration tests, we can often sidestep the stringent transactional requirements of the application to easily develop tests outside the container. The following sections will delve into when transactions are really required and how to translate the container-managed and bean-managed transaction models of the Java EE server into your test environment.

When to Use Transactions

Except for resource-local application-managed entity managers, which are rarely used in the Java EE environment, transaction management is the purview of session beans and other components that use the Java Persistence API. We will focus specifically on session beans, but the topics we cover apply equally to transactional persistence operations hosted by message-driven beans or servlets.

The transaction demarcation for a session bean method needs to be considered carefully when writing tests. Despite the default assumption that transactions are used everywhere in the application server, only a select number of methods actually require transaction management for the purpose of testing. Since we are focused on testing persistence, the situation we are concerned with is when the entity manager is being used to persist, merge, or remove entity instances. We also need to determine if these entities actually need to be persisted to the database.

In a test environment, we are using resource-local application-managed entity managers. Recall from Chapter 5 that an application-managed entity manager can perform all of its operations without an active transaction. In effect, invoking persist() queues up the entity to be persisted the next time a transaction starts and is committed. Furthermore, we also know that once an entity is managed, it can typically be located using the find() operation without the need to go to the database. Given these facts, we generally need a transacted entity manager only if the business method creates or modifies entities and executes a query that should include the results.

Although not required to satisfy business logic, a transaction may also be required if you wish the results of the operation to be persisted so that they can be analyzed using something other than the active entity manager. For example, the results of the operation may be read from the database using JDBC and compared to a known value using a test tool.

Overall, the main thing we want to stress here before we look into how to implement transactions for session bean tests is that more often than not, you don't really need them at all. Look at the sequence of operations you are testing and consider whether or not the outcome will be impacted one way or the other, first if the data must be written to the database and later if it truly must be committed as part of the test. Given the complexity that manual transaction management can sometimes require, use them only when they are necessary.

Container-Managed Transactions

One of the most important benefits of container-managed transactions is that they are configured for session bean methods entirely using metadata. There is no programming interface invoked by the session bean to control the transaction other than the setRollbackOnly() method on the EJBContext interface, and even this occurs only in certain circumstances.

Therefore, once we make a determination that a particular bean method requires a transaction to be active, we need only start a transaction at the start of the test and commit or roll back the results when the test ends.

Listing 12-11 shows a bean method that will require an open transaction during a test. The assignEmployeeToDepartment() method assigns an employee to a given department and then returns the list of employees currently assigned to the department by executing a query. Because the data modification and query occur in the same transaction, our test case will also require a transaction.

Listing 12-11. *Business Method Requiring a Transaction*

```
@Stateless
public class DepartmentServiceBean implements DepartmentService {
    private static final String QUERY =
        "SELECT e " +
        "FROM Employee e " +
        "WHERE e.department = ?1 ORDER BY e.name";

    @PersistenceContext(unitName="EmployeeService")
    EntityManager em;

    public List assignEmployeeToDepartment(int deptId, int empId) {
        Department dept = em.find(Department.class, deptId);
        Employee emp = em.find(Employee.class, empId);
        dept.getEmployees().add(emp);
        emp.setDepartment(dept);
        return em.createQuery(QUERY)
                .setParameter(1, dept)
                .getResultList();
    }

    // ...
}
```

Because we are using a resource-local entity manager, we will be simulating container-managed transactions with EntityTransaction transactions managed by the test case. Listing 12-12 shows the test case for the assignEmployeeToDepartment() method. We have followed the same template as in Listing 12-9, so the setUp() and tearDown() methods are not shown. Before the session bean method is invoked, we create a new transaction. When the test is complete, we roll back the changes since it isn't necessary to persist them in the database.

Listing 12-12. *Testing a Business Method That Requires a Transaction*

```
public class DepartmentServiceBeanTest extends TestCase {
    // ...

    private void createTestData() {
        Employee emp = new Employee(500, "Scott");
        em.persist(emp);
        emp = new Employee(600, "John");
        em.persist(emp);
        Department dept = new Department(700, "TEST");
        dept.getEmployees().add(emp);
        emp.setDepartment(dept);
        em.persist(dept);
    }

    public void testAssignEmployeeToDepartment() throws Exception {
        DepartmentServiceBean bean = new DepartmentServiceBean();
        bean.em = em;
        em.getTransaction().begin();
        List result = bean.assignEmployeeToDepartment(700, 500);
        em.getTransaction().rollback();
        assertEquals(2, result.size());
        assertEquals("John", ((Employee)result.get(0)).getName());
        assertEquals("Scott", ((Employee)result.get(1)).getName());
    }

    // ...
}
```

Bean-Managed Transactions

For a session bean that uses bean-managed transactions, the key issue we need to contend with is the UserTransaction interface. It may or may not be present in any given bean method and may be used for a number of purposes, from checking the transaction status to marking the current transaction for rollback, to committing and rolling back transactions. Fortunately, almost all of the UserTransaction methods have a direct correlation to one of the EntityTransaction methods. Since our test strategy involves a single entity manager instance for a test, we need to adapt its EntityTransaction implementation to the UserTransaction interface.

Listing 12-13 shows an implementation of the UserTransaction interface that delegates to the EntityTransaction interface of an EntityManager instance. Exception handling has been added to convert the unchecked exceptions thrown by EntityTransaction operations into the checked exceptions that clients of the UserTransaction interface will be expecting.

Listing 12-13. *Emulating* UserTransaction *Using* EntityTransaction

```
public class EntityUserTransaction implements UserTransaction {
    private EntityManager em;

    public EntityUserTransaction(EntityManager em) {
        this.em = em;
    }

    public void begin() throws NotSupportedException {
        if (em.getTransaction().isActive()) {
            throw new NotSupportedException();
        }
        em.getTransaction().begin();
    }

    public void commit() throws RollbackException {
        try {
            em.getTransaction().commit();
        } catch (javax.persistence.RollbackException e) {
            throw new RollbackException(e.getMessage());
        }
    }

    public void rollback() throws SystemException {.
        try {
            em.getTransaction().rollback();
        } catch (PersistenceException e) {
            throw new SystemException(e.getMessage());
        }
    }

    public void setRollbackOnly() {
        em.getTransaction().setRollbackOnly();
    }

    public int getStatus() {
        if (em.getTransaction().isActive()) {
            return Status.STATUS_ACTIVE;
        } else {
            return Status.STATUS_NO_TRANSACTION;
        }
    }

    public void setTransactionTimeout(int timeout) {
        throw new UnsupportedOperationException();
    }
}
```

Note that we have implemented setTransactionTimeout() to throw an exception, but this does not necessarily have to be the case. If the transaction timeout is set simply to prevent processes from taking too long to complete, it might be safe to ignore the setting in an integration test.

To demonstrate this wrapper, first consider Listing 12-14, which demonstrates a variation of the example from Listing 12-11 that uses bean-managed transactions instead of container-managed transactions.

Listing 12-14. *Using Bean-Managed Transactions*

```
@Stateless
@TransactionManagement(TransactionManagementType.BEAN)
public class DepartmentServiceBean implements DepartmentService {
    // ...
    @Resource UserTransaction tx;

    public List assignEmployeeToDepartment(int deptId, int empId) {
        try {
            tx.begin();
            Department dept = em.find(Department.class, deptId);
            Employee emp = em.find(Employee.class, empId);
            dept.getEmployees().add(emp);
            emp.setDepartment(dept);
            tx.commit();
            return em.createQuery(QUERY)
                    .setParameter(1, dept)
                    .getResultList();
        } catch (Exception e) {
            // handle transaction exceptions
            // ...
        }
    }

    // ...
}
```

Using the UserTransaction wrapper is simply a matter of injecting it into a session bean that has declared a dependency on UserTransaction. Since the wrapper holds onto an entity manager instance, it can begin and end EntityTransaction transactions as required from within the application code being tested. Listing 12-15 shows the revised test case from Listing 12-12 using this wrapper to emulate bean-managed transactions.

Listing 12-15. *Executing a Test with Emulated Bean-Managed Transactions*

```
public class DepartmentServiceBeanTest extends TestCase {
    // ...

    public void testAssignEmployeeToDepartment() throws Exception {
        DepartmentServiceBean2 bean = new DepartmentServiceBean2();
        bean.em = em;
        bean.tx = new EntityUserTransaction(em);
        List result = bean.assignEmployeeToDepartment(700, 500);
        assertEquals(2, result.size());
        assertEquals("John", ((Employee)result.get(0)).getName());
        assertEquals("Scott", ((Employee)result.get(1)).getName());
    }

    // ...
}
```

Note that just because the `UserTransaction` interface is used doesn't mean it's actually necessary for any particular test. If the transaction state doesn't affect the outcome of the test, consider using an implementation of the `UserTransaction` interface that doesn't actually do anything. For example, the implementation of `UserTransaction` shown in Listing 12-16 is fine for any case where transaction demarcation is declared but unnecessary.

Listing 12-16. *A Stubbed* `UserTransaction`

```
public class NullUserTransaction implements UserTransaction {
    public void begin() {}
    public void commit() {}
    public void rollback() {}
    public void setRollbackOnly() {}
    public int getStatus() {
        return Status.STATUS_NO_TRANSACTION;
    }
    public void setTransactionTimeout(int timeout) {}
}
```

The test case shown in Listing 12-12 could also have tested the bean from Listing 12-14 if the empty `UserTransaction` wrapper from Listing 12-16 was also injected into the bean instance. This would disable the bean-managed transactions of the actual business method, allowing the transactions of the test case to be used instead.

Container-Managed Entity Managers

The default entity manager type for a session bean is container-managed and transaction-scoped. Extended entity managers are an option only for stateful session beans. In either case, the goal of testing outside the container is to map the application-managed entity manager used by the test to one of these entity manager types.

The good news for testing code that uses the extended entity manager is that the application-managed entity manager offers nearly the exact same feature set. It can usually be injected into a stateful session bean instance in place of an extended entity manager, and the business logic should function without change in most cases.

Likewise, most of the time the transaction-scoped entity manager works just fine when an application-managed entity manager is used in its place. The only issue we need to deal with in the case of transaction-scoped entity managers is detachment. When a transaction ends, any managed entities become detached. In terms of a test, that just means that we need to ensure that clear() is invoked on the transaction boundary for our test entity manager.

We may also need to deal with the issue of propagation. In some respects, propagation is easy in a test environment. If you inject the same application-managed entity manager instance into two session bean instances, the beans share the same persistence context as if the entity manager were propagated with the transaction. In fact, it is far more likely that you will need to inject multiple entity managers to simulate the intentional lack of propagation (such as a bean that invokes a REQUIRES_NEW method on another bean) than that you will have to do anything special for propagation.

Let's look at a concrete example of transaction propagation using the examples we first introduced in Chapter 5. Listing 12-17 shows the implementation for the AuditService session bean that performs audit logging. We have used setter injection in this example to contrast it against the version from Chapter 5.

Listing 12-17. AuditService *Session Bean with Setter Injection*

```
@Stateless
public class AuditServiceBean implements AuditService {
    private EntityManager em;

    @PersistenceContext(unitName="hr")
    public void setEntityManager(EntityManager em) {
        this.em = em;
    }

    public void logTransaction(int empNo, String action) {
        // verify employee number is valid
        if (em.find(Employee.class, empNo) == null) {
            throw new IllegalArgumentException("Unknown employee id");
        }
        LogRecord lr = new LogRecord(empNo, action);
        em.persist(lr);
    }
}
```

Likewise, Listing 12-18 shows a fragment from the EmployeeService session bean that uses the AuditService session bean to record when a new Employee instance has been persisted. Because both the createEmployee() and logTransaction() methods are invoked in the same transaction without a commit in between, the persistence context must be propagated from one to the other. Again we have used setter injection instead of field injection to make the bean easier to test.

Listing 12-18. EmployeeService *Session Bean with Setter Injection*

```java
@Stateless
public class EmployeeServiceBean implements EmployeeService {
    EntityManager em;
    AuditService audit;

    @PersistenceContext
    public void setEntityManager(EntityManager em) {
        this.em = em;
    }

    @EJB
    public void setAuditService(AuditService audit) {
        this.audit = audit;
    }

    public void createEmployee(Employee emp) {
        em.persist(emp);
        audit.logTransaction(emp.getId(), "created employee");
    }

    // ...
}
```

Using the previous two session beans as an example, Listing 12-19 demonstrates how to emulate propagation between two transaction-scoped container-managed entity managers. The first step to make this testable is to instantiate each session bean. The AuditService bean is then injected into the EmployeeService bean, and the test entity manager instance is injected into both session beans. The injection of the same EntityManager instance effectively propagates any changes from the EmployeeService bean to the AuditService bean. Note that we have also used the entity manager in the test to locate and verify the results of the business method.

Listing 12-19. *Simulating Container-Managed Transaction Propagation*

```java
public class TestEmployeeServiceBean extends TestCase {
    // ...

    public void testCreateEmployee() throws Exception {
        EmployeeServiceBean bean = new EmployeeServiceBean();
        AuditServiceBean auditBean = new AuditServiceBean();
        bean.setEntityManager(em);
        bean.setAuditService(auditBean);
        auditBean.setEntityManager(em);
        Employee emp = new Employee();
```

```
        emp.setId(99);
        emp.setName("Wayne");
        bean.createEmployee(emp);
        emp = em.find(Employee.class, 99);
        assertNotNull(emp);
        assertEquals(99, emp.getId());
        assertEquals("Wayne", emp.getName());
    }

    // ...
}
```

Other Services

There is more to a session bean than just dependency injection and transaction management. For example, as we saw in Chapter 3, session beans can also take advantage of life cycle methods. Other services that are beyond the scope of this book include security management and interceptors.

The general rule is that in a test environment, you need to manually perform the work that would have otherwise been done automatically by the container. In the case of life cycle methods, for example, you will have to explicitly invoke these methods if they are required for a particular test. Given this requirement, it is a good idea to use package or protected scope methods so that they can be manually invoked by test cases.

That being said, be aggressive in determining the true number of things that have to occur in order for a test to succeed. Just because security roles have been declared for a session bean method doesn't mean that it actually has any effect on the test outcome. If it doesn't have to be invoked prior to the test, don't waste time setting up the test environment to make it happen.

Using Spring for Integration Testing

When multiple session beans collaborate together to implement a particular application use case, there can be a lot of scaffolding code required to get things up and running. If multiple test cases share similar graphs of session beans, then some or all of this code may have to be duplicated across multiple test cases. Ideally, we would like a framework to assist with issues like dependency injection in our test environment.

At this point in time there are no embeddable EJB 3.0 containers that we can use in an integration test, but there are several frameworks that can perform dependency injection without the need for an application server. One of these is the Spring framework, which maintains a stand-alone dependency-injection mechanism that can be integrated into any application. To demonstrate how to use Spring for integration testing with session beans and the entity manager, we will revisit the propagation test case from the preceding Container-Managed Entity Managers section and convert it to use Spring for dependency management.

■**Tip** This section is intended for readers already familiar with the Spring framework. Visit `http://www.springframework.org` to learn more.

Spring is designed to work with POJO service classes, and in most cases EJB 3.0 session beans are fully compatible with the format that it is expecting. Spring supports several different injection styles, but the one that is easiest to adapt to session beans is setter injection. So long as the bean class uses setter injection to acquire resources, no changes are required to use the bean with Spring.

One issue that we have to contend with is that by default Spring treats all managed beans as singletons. Therefore there is only one instance per named class type. How we configure the entity manager in the bean configuration file will determine whether or not it is shared between entity instances.

Before we can change our test case to use Spring, we need to establish a helper class that will let Spring create and manage entity manager instances. Listing 12-20 shows a bean class that bootstraps an `EntityManagerFactory` instance using the `Persistence` class and uses it to create and return new application-managed entity managers from the `createEntityManager()` method. The `unitName` field will be injected into this class using a value we configure in the XML bean configuration file. We will also configure the "em-factory" bean to invoke the `destroy()` method when the bean factory is destroyed so that the `EntityManagerFactory` instance will be closed correctly. Closing the factory will also close any entity managers that were created from it.

Listing 12-20. *Helper Class to Create Entity Manager Instances*

```
public class EntityManagerFactoryBean {
    String unitName;
    EntityManagerFactory emf;

    public void setUnitName(String unitName) {
        this.unitName = unitName;
    }

    public EntityManager createEntityManager() {
        if (emf == null) {
            emf = Persistence.createEntityManagerFactory(unitName);
        }
        return emf.createEntityManager();
    }

    public void destroy() {
        if (emf != null) {
            emf.close();
        }
    }
}
```

Next we need to configure this class in the bean configuration file and add two other dynamic bean definitions, one for shared (propagated) entity managers and one for private (non-propagated) entity managers. Listing 12-21 shows this configuration. Note that the "private-entity-manager" bean definition sets the `singleton` attribute to `false`, meaning that a new entity manager will be created every time a bean with this id is requested.

Listing 12-21. *Bean Configuration for Entity Managers*

```
<beans>
    <bean id="em-factory"
          class="examples.session.EntityManagerFactoryBean"
          destroy-method="destroy">
        <property name="unitName">
            <value>hr</value>
        </property>
    </bean>
    <bean id="shared-entity-manager"
          factory-bean="em-factory"
          factory-method="createEntityManager"/>
    <bean id="private-entity-manager"
          factory-bean="em-factory"
          factory-method="createEntityManager"
          singleton="false"/>
    ...
</beans>
```

So far we have the ability to create and manage entity managers using the Spring bean factory. We can access these objects directly in our test case or reference them from other beans to have the values injected automatically. The only step left before we get to our test case is to add in the configuration for our EJB 3.0 session beans. Listing 12-22 shows the remaining bean definitions for this test.

Listing 12-22. *Configuring Session Beans for Use with Spring*

```
<beans>
    ...
    <bean id="employee-service"
          class="examples.session.EmployeeServiceBean">
        <property name="entityManager">
            <ref bean="shared-entity-manager"/>
        </property>
        <property name="auditService">
            <ref bean="audit-service"/>
        </property>
    </bean>
    <bean id="audit-service"
          class="example.session.AuditServiceBean">
        <property name="entityManager">
            <ref bean="shared-entity-manager"/>
        </property>
    </bean>
</beans>
```

Because we are emulating propagation, both of the session beans in this test will use the same shared entity manager instance. To make this possible, we configure each bean to reference the "shared-entity-manager" bean for the "entityManager" property.

Finally we can modify the test case to use the dependency-injection features of Spring. Listing 12-23 shows the complete test case revised to use a dependency-injection framework. The propagated entity manager and `EmployeeService` session bean are both obtained from the `XmlBeanFactory` instance. Spring handles all of the dependency injection and ensures that both beans are sharing the correct entity manager instance. When the test is complete, we explicitly destroy the singleton objects in the `XmlBeanFactory` instance in order to ensure that the `EntityManagerFactory` will be closed before the next test.

Listing 12-23. *Test Case Using the Spring* `BeanFactory`

```java
public class TestEmployeeServiceBean extends TestCase {
    XmlBeanFactory factory;

    public void setUp() {
        ClassPathResource resource =
            new ClassPathResource("test-employee-service-bean.xml");
        factory = new XmlBeanFactory(resource);
    }

    public void tearDown() {
        factory.destroySingletons();
    }

    public void testCreateEmployee() throws Exception {
        EmployeeService bean =
            (EmployeeService) factory.getBean("employee-service");
        Employee emp = new Employee();
        emp.setId(99);
        emp.setName("Wayne");
        bean.createEmployee(emp);
        EntityManager em =
            (EntityManager) factory.getBean("shared-entity-manager");
        emp = em.find(Employee.class, 99);
        assertNotNull(emp);
        assertEquals(99, emp.getId());
        assertEquals("Wayne", emp.getName());
    }

    // ...
}
```

For two session beans this approach is arguably overkill compared to the same test case shown in Listing 12-19. But it should be easy to see even from this small example how complex bean relationships can be modeled and realized using a dependency-injection framework. In this example we have only focused on session bean classes, but many other resource types from the Java EE environment can be mocked or extended for testing and automatically managed by a dependency-injection framework for integration testing.

Best Practices

A full discussion of developer testing strategies is beyond the scope of this chapter, but to make testing of application code that uses entities easier, consider adopting the following best practices:

- **Avoid using the entity manager from within entity classes.** This creates a tight coupling between the domain object and the persistence API, making testing difficult. Queries related to an entity but not part of its object-relational mapping are better executed within a session façade or data access object.

- **Prefer dependency injection to JNDI lookups in session beans.** Dependency injection is a key technology for simplifying tests. Instead of mocking the JNDI interfaces to provide runtime support for testing, the required values can be directly assigned to the object using a setter method or field access. Note that accessing private fields from a test case is bad form. Either use package private fields as the target for injected objects or provide a setter method.

- **Isolate persistence operations.** Keeping `EntityManager` and `Query` operations separate in their own methods makes replacing them easier during unit testing.

- **Decouple with interfaces.** Just as the Java Persistence API uses interfaces to minimize dependencies on the persistence provider, loosely coupled objects with interfaces can help manage complex dependencies.

- **Refactor when necessary.** Don't be afraid to refactor application code to make it more test-friendly so long as the refactoring benefits the application as a whole. Method extraction, parameter introduction, and other refactoring techniques can help break down complex application logic into testable chunks, improving the overall readability and maintainability of the application in the process.

Note that everything we have described so far is just the beginning of a complete strategy for testing Java EE applications that use the Java Persistence API. As more developers gain experience with the Java Persistence API and learn how to take advantage of the simplifications brought about by EJB 3.0, we expect much more to be written on this subject.

Summary

In this chapter we started with an exploration of testing enterprise applications and the challenges that have traditionally faced developers. We also looked at the different types of testing performed by developers, quality engineers, and customers, and we refined our focus to look specifically at developer tests for EJB 3.0 and Java Persistence API applications.

In the section on unit testing, we looked at how to test entity classes and then pulled back to look at how to test session beans in combination with entities in a unit test environment. We introduced the concept of mock objects and explored how to test code that depends on the entity manager without actually using a real entity manager.

In our discussion of integration testing, we discussed how to get the entity manager up and running in JUnit tests in the Java SE environment and the situations where it makes sense to use this technique. We covered a number of issues related to the entity manager, including how to safely seed a database for testing, how to use multiple mapping files for different database configurations, and how to minimize the number of database connections required for a test suite.

We looked at how to use session beans in integration tests and how to deal with dependency-injection and transaction-management issues. For transaction management, we looked at how to emulate container-managed and bean-managed transactions, as well as how to simulate persistence context propagation in a test environment. We concluded with a summary of some best practices to consider when building Java EE applications using the Java Persistence API.

In the next chapter we will look at how to migrate existing EJB 2.1 and JDBC applications to the Java Persistence API.

CHAPTER 13

■ ■ ■

Migration

Now that the Java Persistence API has been explained in detail, the challenge is deciding how and when to adopt the new persistence model. For new applications, this is not an issue, but what about existing applications? In this chapter we will look at the challenges facing developers wishing to integrate the Java Persistence API into legacy applications and offer some solutions to help ease the transition.

Migrating from CMP Entity Beans

Until the publication of the EJB 3.0 specification and the Java Persistence API, the only persistence technology officially part of the Java EE platform was container-managed persistence using EJB entity beans. Ever since they were first required to be supported in EJB 1.1, entity beans have been criticized as being both too complex and lacking in features to handle the persistence requirements of real-world applications. But standards matter in the enterprise, so despite the availability of proven object-relational mapping solutions, both commercial and open source, companies have always found a way to work around the entity bean shortcomings and get the job done. As a result, there is a large installed base of applications based on CMP entity beans, and bringing them forward into the next generation of Java EE standards may be a task worth pursuing.

The complexity of entity beans lies not in the concept but in the implementation. Like session beans, entity beans are true EJB components, with separate classes for the bean implementation, home interface, and business interfaces. Entity beans also require a verbose XML deployment descriptor that describes the persistent properties of the bean, container-managed relationships between entities, and the EJB QL queries used to access the entities. Finally, many of the entity bean details require vendor-specific configuration to deploy and run. In response to these issues, the Java Persistence API offers a programming model that is easier to use, while offering a larger feature set with less vendor-specific configuration.

Although the Java Persistence API is the standard persistence model moving forward, the good news for companies that have made an investment in CMP entity beans is that the EJB 3.0 specification still fully supports container-managed persistence. Existing applications will work out of the box without changes and can expect to do so for years to come. The EJB 3.0 specification is only now deprecating version 1.1 of the entity bean model. All Java EE 5–compliant application servers must support EJB 2.0 and 2.1 CMP entity beans.

That's good news for applications that aren't likely to require much development going forward, but what about applications that are planning revisions? Is it feasible to move away from CMP and take advantage of the Java Persistence API? In many cases it will depend upon the design of your application. Only you can decide the most appropriate plan of action for your application. The following sections will lay out the issues and discuss potential strategies for migrating CMP applications to help you make your own decision.

▓**Note** This chapter assumes that you are familiar with EJB 2.1 container-managed entity bean implementation and configuration.

Scoping the Challenge

The challenge in moving from entity beans to entities is not the entity beans themselves. However complex they are to implement, they are relatively straightforward to use. The problem with entity beans is that the public API they expose is tightly coupled to the component model on which they are based. The principal issue facing any migration is the extent and manner in which application code interacts with entity bean interfaces. The more code that uses entity beans, the harder it is to migrate.

There are also some entity bean features that are not reflected in the Java Persistence API. Some of these features, such as container-managed relationships, can be worked around, while others are difficult if not impossible to replace.

The primary showstopper scenario is the use of remote entity bean interfaces. There is simply no equivalent to remote objects in the Java Persistence API. Entities are plain Java classes, not interface-based components that can be compiled down into RMI or Common Object Request Broker Architecture (CORBA) stubs. Entities are mobile in the sense that they can be serialized and transferred between client and server, but they are not network-aware. Ever since the EJB 2.0 specification introduced local interfaces, developers have been warned not to use remote interfaces on entity beans due to the overhead of the network infrastructure they require. If your application is one of the few, it is very unlikely that a migration would be possible until the application was refactored to use local interfaces.

▓**Tip** Often remote interfaces are used on entities only to facilitate transporting data off to a remote tier for presentation. Consider introducing the Transfer Object pattern (described later in this chapter) to remove remote interfaces in these cases. Transfer objects share a strong symmetry with serializable entities, making them good starting points for migration.

Applications that have isolated their persistence code, most likely through the use of one or more design patterns, present the least amount of effort to convert. Conversely, applications that sprinkle entity bean access across all tiers and are tightly coupled to the entity bean API present the greatest challenge. Refactoring to decouple business and presentation logic from persistence code is often a worthwhile exercise before attempting to migrate to the Java Persistence API.

Two levels of application migration are discussed next. The first, documented in Entity Bean Conversion, details the process of mapping an existing entity bean to a new entity. From there the developer can begin refactoring the application to introduce the entity manager and remove entity bean usage. The second level builds on the first by identifying business tier design patterns that present an opportunity to make a switch in persistence technologies with minimal impact to existing application code. Design patterns are discussed in the Leveraging Design Patterns section.

Entity Bean Conversion

When planning any conversion between entity beans and entities, it is useful to use the existing bean as a template for the new entity. The bean class, interfaces, and XML deployment descriptor describe the persistent fields used by the entity, the queries used by the application to find entity instances, and the container-managed relationships between entities. The following sections describe the process to convert an entity bean into an entity. Later sections will describe how to integrate these new entities into an existing application.

Converting the Business Interface

Entity beans are defined using a bean class, business interface, and home interface. When creating the initial entity version, the business interface or bean class can be used as a template. The business interface is often the best place to start as it defines the set of operations directly available on the entity as opposed to the bean class, which also includes home and finder methods specific to the home interface.

Migrating Properties

To demonstrate the process of migrating an entity bean to the Java Persistence API, we will look at converting an entity bean that stores information about a department. The business interface for the `Department` entity bean is shown in Listing 13-1.

Listing 13-1. *Department Business Interface*

```
public interface Department extends EJBLocalObject {
    public int getId();

    public String getName();
    public void setName(String name);

    public Collection getEmployees();
    public void setEmployees(Collection employees);

    public Employee getManager();
}
```

To begin converting this interface into an entity, a concrete implementation of the interface must be provided, removing the dependency on `EJBLocalObject` and providing a field to implement each of the persistent properties. The properties `id`, `name`, and `employees` all map to either persistent fields or relationships. The `getManager()` method is actually a non-persistent business method that searches for and returns the manager for the department. Therefore while the business interface is a good starting point, the bean implementation or the XML descriptor, which lists the persistent fields, must be consulted to determine the true meaning for each business method.

With the set of persistent properties identified, the next step is to determine how they map to the database. Unfortunately, this mapping was not standardized by the EJB specification, so vendor-specific XML descriptors will have to be checked. For this example, assume that the entity bean maps to the table DEPT, which has columns ID and NAME. Setting aside the getManager(), getEmployees(), and setEmployees() methods for now, the entity implementation with basic mappings is shown in Listing 13-2. Because the entity name and table name are different, the @Table annotation is required to override the default table name of the entity.

Listing 13-2. *Department Entity with Basic Mappings*

```
@Entity
@Table(name="DEPT")
public class Department {
    @Id
    private int id;
    private String name;

    public int getId () { return id; }
    public void setId(int id) { this.id = id; }

    public String getName() { return name; }
    public void setName(String name) { this.name = name; }
}
```

Migrating Business Methods

Non-persistent business methods may be a source of problems during entity bean conversion. Many business methods simply perform operations using the persistent state of the entity (using the persistent getter methods to obtain data) and these may be copied to the new entity as is. However, the EJB specification also allows for business methods to invoke select methods in order to issue queries and operate on the results. Listing 13-3 shows a fragment from the DepartmentBean class, which defines the implementation of the getManager() method.

Listing 13-3. *Business Method That Uses a Select Method*

```
public abstract class DepartmentBean implements EntityBean {
    // ...

    public abstract Employee ejbSelectManagerForDept(int deptId);

    public Employee getManager() {
        return ejbSelectManagerForDept(getId());
    }

    // ...
}
```

Select methods, which begin with the prefix "ejbSelect", are container-provided implementations of EJB QL queries. They may be called by home methods (described later) and business methods. Business methods that invoke "ejbSelect" methods pose a problem in entity bean conversion, as the entity manager required to execute the query is not typically available to entity bean instances. In this example, the select method issues the following query, which was defined in the XML descriptor:

```
SELECT OBJECT(e)
FROM Employee e
WHERE e.department.id = ?1 AND e.manager.department.id <> ?1
```

To execute these queries from within the entity class, the entity manager must be made available to the entity instance. Since the entity manager is not part of the persistent state of the entity, it is strongly discouraged that you store a reference to it. Instead, consider the Service Locator pattern so that the entity manager can be obtained from within the entity even though it is not part of the entity. The following implementation of getManager() uses this approach:

```
public Employee getManager() {
    EntityManager em =
        ServiceLocator.getInstance().getEntityManager("EmployeeService");
    return (Employee) em.createNamedQuery("Department.managerForDept")
                        .setParameter(1, getId())
                        .getSingleResult();
}
```

The ServiceLocator class looks up the entity manager from JNDI using the current environment naming context. The downside to this approach is that entities tend to get used in a lot of different components, each with its own set of environment references. To ensure portability, the same entity manager reference name must be used consistently in all components, or some vendor-specific approach must be used to acquire the entity manager independent of context.

Entity manager operations within an entity class are generally considered bad style as it introduces a dependency on the persistence runtime directly into the entity. This tightly couples the entity implementation to a particular persistence mechanism (the entity is no longer a plain Java object) and makes testing more difficult. Generally speaking, we recommend moving the business method to a session façade or other business-focused component instead of embedding entity manager operations within the entity class. The only consequence of moving the method to another class is that the entity needs to be passed as an argument to the method in its new location.

Migrating Container-Managed Relationships

CMP entity beans may make use of container-managed relationships. These relationships are called managed because the developer is required to update only one side of the relationship and the server will ensure that the other side of the relationship is updated automatically. Although there is no direct equivalent to container-managed relationships in the Java Persistence API, the XML descriptor for these relationships can guide the definition of entity relationships for object-relational mapping.

The Department entity bean has a one-to-many relationship with the Employee entity bean. Listing 13-4 shows the XML definition of the container-managed relationship between these two entity beans.

Listing 13-4. *XML Definition of a Container-Managed Relationship*

```
<ejb-relation>
    <ejb-relation-name>Dept-Emps</ejb-relation-name>
    <ejb-relationship-role>
        <ejb-relationship-role-name>Dept-has-Emps</ejb-relationship-role-name>
        <multiplicity>One</multiplicity>
        <relationship-role-source>
            <ejb-name>DepartmentBean</ejb-name>
        </relationship-role-source>
        <cmr-field>
            <cmr-field-name>employees</cmr-field-name>
            <cmr-field-type>java.util.Collection</cmr-field-type>
        </cmr-field>
    </ejb-relationship-role>
    <ejb-relationship-role>
        <ejb-relationship-role-name>Emps-have-Dept</ejb-relationship-role-name>
        <multiplicity>Many</multiplicity>
        <relationship-role-source>
            <ejb-name>EmployeeBean</ejb-name>
        </relationship-role-source>
        <cmr-field><cmr-field-name>department</cmr-field-name></cmr-field>
    </ejb-relationship-role>
</ejb-relation>
```

Each side of the relationship is defined using the ejb-relationship-role element. The relationship-role-source and cmr-field elements define the entity bean and relationship property being mapped. The multiplicity element defines the cardinality of that side of the relationship. There is a direct mapping between each ejb-relationship-role element and a relationship annotation, the choice of which is determined by the multiplicity elements from each end of the relationship.

Applying this pattern, the previous relationship descriptor maps to an @OneToMany annotation on the employees attribute of the Department entity and an @ManyToOne annotation on the department attribute of the Employee entity. Since the relationship is bi-directional, Employee will be the owner and Department the inverse, so the mappedBy element of the @OneToMany annotation is set to the name of the owning attribute, in this case department.

We can now complete our mapping for the Department entity by adding the relationships. Listing 13-5 shows the complete entity class.

Listing 13-5. Department *Entity with Relationship Mappings*

```java
@Entity
@Table(name="DEPT")
public class Department {
    @Id
    private int id;
    private String name;
    @OneToMany(mappedBy="department")
    private Collection<Employee> employees = new ArrayList<Employee>();

    public int getId () { return id; }
    public void setId(int id) { this.id = id; }

    public String getName() { return name; }
    public void setName(String name) { this.name = name; }

    public Collection<Employee> getEmployees() { return employees; }
}
```

Clients that used to use the relationship properties of the entity bean business interface require special attention when converted to use entities. Relationships that were previously managed by the container now require explicit maintenance to both sides of the relationship whenever a change occurs. In most cases, this amounts to one extra line of code. For example, adding an Employee entity bean to the employees property of the Department entity bean with container-managed relationships used to look like this:

```java
dept.getEmployees().add(emp);
```

Without container-managed relationships, an extra step is required:

```java
dept.getEmployees().add(emp);
emp.setDepartment(dept);
```

Rather than adding these statements directly throughout application code, a best practice to consider is the use of helper methods on entities to manage relationships. The following example demonstrates these same operations as they would be implemented on the Department entity:

```java
public void addEmployee(Employee emp) {
    getEmployees().add(emp);
    emp.setDepartment(this);
}
```

Converting the Home Interface

Creating an entity out of the entity bean business interface is often only the first step in conversion. Application code relies on the home interface to create new entity beans, find existing entity beans, and handle business methods that are related to an entity but not specific to any one entity bean instance.

The first choice to be made regarding the home interface is whether or not application code will be rewritten to work directly with the entity manager. Doing so obsoletes most of the home interface operations, but it may be challenging to implement depending on how tightly coupled the entity bean API is to the application code. Business methods on the home interface also must be accommodated.

If the home interface is still required, a stateless session bean may be used to provide equivalent methods to the home interface operations. The following sections continue the Department entity example by implementing a session façade for its business methods and finder operations.

Migrating Queries

EJB QL queries for CMP entity beans are defined in the deployment descriptor. Listing 13-6 shows two query definitions for the Department entity bean.

Listing 13-6. *EJB QL Query Definitions*

```
<query>
    <query-method>
        <method-name>findAll</method-name>
        <method-params/>
    </query-method>
    <ejb-ql>SELECT OBJECT(d) From Department d</ejb-ql>
</query>
<query>
    <query-method>
        <method-name>findByName</method-name>
        <method-params>
            <method-param>java.lang.String</method-param>
        </method-params>
    </query-method>
    <ejb-ql>SELECT OBJECT(d) FROM Department d WHERE d.name = ?1</ejb-ql>
</query>
```

To reuse these same queries with the converted entity bean, it is necessary to define named queries on the entity. Recall from Chapter 7 that every EJB QL query is a legal JPQL query; therefore existing EJB QL entity bean queries can be migrated without change to the Java Persistence API. The only thing we need to do is define a name for the query that will be unique across the persistence unit. To facilitate this we will prepend the query name with the name of the entity. The following @NamedQuery annotations mirror the XML versions:

```
@NamedQueries({
    @NamedQuery(name="Department.findAll",
                query="SELECT d FROM Department d"),
    @NamedQuery(name="Department.findByName",
                query="SELECT d FROM Department d WHERE d.name = ?1")
})
```

Migrating Home Methods

A home method is any method on the home interface that is not a finder (starts with "findBy") or a create method (starts with "create"). They are also typically the easiest to integrate into a session façade, because their implementation often relies only on select methods. Home methods are implemented on the bean class in methods prefixed with "ejbHome". Listing 13-7 shows a fragment of the DepartmentBean demonstrating a home method and the select method that it uses.

Listing 13-7. *Entity Bean Home Method*

```
public abstract class DepartmentBean implements EntityBean {
// ...

    public abstract Collection ejbSelectEmployeesWithNoDepartment()
        throws FinderException;

    public Collection ejbHomeUnallocatedEmployees() throws FinderException {
        return ejbSelectEmployeesWithNoDepartment();
    }

    // ...
}
```

Assuming that the entity manager has been injected into the session bean, we can use the EJB QL query definition from the XML descriptor to re-implement this method:

```
public Collection unallocatedEmployees() throws FinderException {
    try {
        return em.createQuery("SELECT e FROM Employee e WHERE e.dept IS NULL")
                .getResultList();
    } catch (PersistenceException e) {
        throw new FinderException(e.getMessage());
    }
}
```

Creating the Façade

With queries mapped and home methods ready for conversion, creating the façade is straight-forward. The advantage of a session bean is that it may be looked up from JNDI just as the entity home was previously and can use a similar interface in order to minimize application code changes. Listing 13-8 shows the home interface for the Department entity bean.

Listing 13-8. *The DepartmentHome Interface*

```
public interface DepartmentHome extends EJBLocalHome {
    public Department create(int id) throws CreateException;
    public Department findByPrimaryKey(int id) throws FinderException;
    public Collection findAll() throws FinderException;
    public Department findByName(String name) throws FinderException;
    public Collection unallocatedEmployees() throws FinderException;
}
```

The first step in this refactoring is to modify the home interface so that it does not extend `EJBLocalHome`. With this dependency removed, the interface is now suitable for use as a stateless session bean business interface. Listing 13-9 shows the converted interface.

Listing 13-9. *The* `DepartmentHome` *Business Interface*

```
public interface DepartmentHome {
    public Department create(int id) throws CreateException;
    public Department findByPrimaryKey(int id) throws FinderException;
    public Collection findAll() throws FinderException;
    public Department findByName(String name) throws FinderException;
    public Collection unallocatedEmployees() throws FinderException;
    public void remove (Object pk) throws RemoveException;
    public void remove (Department dept) throws RemoveException;
}
```

Note the addition of the `remove()` methods. The first is the standard `remove()` method that is part of the `EJBLocalHome` interface, and the second is a convenience method that does not require the user to extract the primary key from the entity. Since entities do not implement `EJBLocalObject`, application code will no longer be able to invoke the `remove()` method directly on the entity bean. Invoking these methods is a compromise that allows application code to avoid directly using the entity manager while maintaining the ability to remove an entity instance. Application code will need to be refactored to change all invocations of `remove()` on the entity bean to one of these new methods on the session bean home façade.

The next step is to create a session bean façade that implements the entity home interface. Using the techniques we have discussed so far, Listing 13-10 shows the complete stateless session bean implementation of the `DepartmentHome` interface. Note the use of checked exceptions on the bean methods. Until existing code is refactored to use the runtime exception model supported by the Java Persistence API, there may be client code that expects `CreateException` or `FinderException` exceptions to be thrown. We have also specified the `name` element for the `@PersistenceContext` annotation. This allows business methods such as the `getManager()` method we described earlier in the section Migrating Business Methods to access the entity manager from the "java:comp/env/EmployeeService" JNDI location.

Listing 13-10. *The* `DepartmentHome` *Session Bean*

```
@Stateless
public class DepartmentHomeBean implements DepartmentHome {
    @PersistenceContext(name="EmployeeService", unitName="EmployeeService")
    EntityManager em;

    public Department create(int id) throws CreateException {
        Department dept = new Department();
        dept.setId(id);
        try {
            em.persist(dept);
        } catch (PersistenceException e) {
            throw new CreateException(e.getMessage());
        } catch (IllegalArgumentException e) {
            throw new CreateException(e.getMessage());
```

```
        }
        return dept;
    }

    public Department findByPrimaryKey(int id) throws FinderException {
        try {
            return em.find(Department.class, id);
        } catch (PersistenceException e) {
            throw new FinderException(e.getMessage());
        }
    }

    public Collection findAll() throws FinderException {
        try {
            return em.createNamedQuery("Department.findAll")
                    .getResultList();
        } catch (PersistenceException e) {
            throw new FinderException(e.getMessage());
        }
    }

    public Department findByName(String name) throws FinderException {
        try {
            return (Department)
                em.createNamedQuery("Department.findByDepartmentName")
                  .setParameter(1, name)
                  .getSingleResult();
        } catch (PersistenceException e) {
            throw new FinderException(e.getMessage());
        }
    }

    public Collection unallocatedEmployees() throws FinderException {
        try {
            return em.createNamedQuery("Department.empsWithNoDepartment")
                    .getResultList();
        } catch (PersistenceException e) {
            throw new FinderException(e.getMessage());
        }
    }

    public void remove (Object pk) throws RemoveException {
        Department d = em.find(Department.class, pk);
        if (d == null) {
            throw new RemoveException("Unable to find entity with pk: " + pk);
        }
        em.remove(d);
    }
```

```
    public void remove(Department dept) throws RemoveException {
        Department d = em.find(Department.class, dept.getId());
        if (d == null) {
            throw new RemoveException("Unable to find entity with pk: " +
                                      dept.getId());
        }
        em.remove(d);
    }
}
```

Migrating from JDBC

The oldest and most basic form of relational persistence with Java is JDBC. A thin layer over the programming interfaces required for communicating with a database, JDBC operations are defined primarily in terms of SQL statements. Applications that make heavy use of JDBC may be more difficult to migrate to the Java Persistence API than applications that depend on entity beans.

As with entity beans, the complexity of migration depends on how tightly coupled the business logic is to the JDBC API. There are two basic issues that we need to be concerned with. The first is the amount of code that depends on the ResultSet or RowSet interfaces. The second is the amount of SQL and the role it plays in the application.

The ResultSet and RowSet interfaces are a concern because there is no logical equivalent to these structures in the Java Persistence API. Results from JPQL and SQL queries executed through the Query interface are basic collections. Even though we can iterate over a collection, which is semantically similar to the row position operations of the JDBC API, each element in the collection is an object or an array of objects. There is no equivalent to the column index operations of the ResultSet interface.

Emulating the ResultSet interface over the top of a collection is unlikely to be a worthwhile venture. Although some operations could be mapped directly, there is no generic way to map the attributes of an entity to the column positions needed by the application code. There is also no guarantee of consistency in how the column positions are determined; it may be different between two queries that achieve the same goal but have ordered the SELECT clause differently. Even when column names are used, the application code is referring to the column aliases of the query, not necessarily the true column names.

In light of these issues, our goal in planning any migration from JDBC is to isolate the JDBC operations so that they can be replaced as a group as opposed to accommodating business logic that depends on JDBC interfaces. Refactoring the existing application to break its dependencies on the JDBC interfaces is the easiest path forward.

With regards to the SQL usage in a JDBC application, we want to caution that though the Java Persistence API supports SQL queries, it is unlikely that this will be a major benefit to migration of an existing application. There are a number of reasons for this, but the first to consider is that most SQL queries in a JDBC application are unlikely to return results that map directly to the domain model of a Java Persistence API application. As we learned in Chapter 9, to construct an entity from a SQL query requires all of the data and foreign key columns to be returned, regardless of what will eventually be required by the application code at that point in time.

If the majority of SQL queries need to be expanded to add columns necessary to satisfy the requirements of the Java Persistence API and if they then need to be mapped before they can be used, then rewriting the queries in JPQL is probably a better investment of time. The syntax of a JPQL query is easier to read, easier to construct, and directly maps to the domain model you want to introduce to the application. The entities have already been mapped to the database, and the provider knows how to construct efficient queries to obtain the data you need. SQL queries have a role, but they should be the exception, not the rule.

There are many Java EE design patterns that can help in this exercise. We will be exploring several of these in detail later in the chapter, but it is worth mentioning at least a few now in the context of JDBC applications specifically. The first and most important pattern to consider is the Data Access Object pattern. This cleanly isolates the JDBC operations for a specific use case behind a single interface that we can migrate forward. Next consider the Transfer Object pattern as a way of introducing an abstraction of the row and column semantics of JDBC into a more natural object model. When an operation returns a collection of values, don't return the ResultSet to the client. Construct Transfer Objects and build a new collection similar to the results of the Query operations in the Java Persistence API. These steps can go a long way to creating boundary points where the Java Persistence API can be introduced without having a major impact on the application logic.

Migrating from Other ORM Solutions

Since the very beginnings of the Java programming language, object-relational mapping solutions have been available in one form or another, provided first by commercial vendors and later by a number of open source solutions. Transparent persistence was also standardized for Java as part of the Java Data Objects (JDO) specification, although object-relational mapping was not explicitly defined by JDO until version 2.0 of the specification. It was the growing popularity of the various proprietary solutions that pushed the EJB expert group to create the Java Persistence API and release it as part of the Java EE specification.

Fortunately, representatives from all major object-relational mapping providers (commercial and open source) contributed to the definition of the Java Persistence API specification. As a result, the Java Persistence API standardizes a decade of object-relational mapping techniques that are well understood and in production today. As participants in the process, existing object-relational mapping providers are also providing ways to move from their solution to the new standard while preserving features in their products outside the scope of the standard. It would be impractical for this book to describe the migration process for each product. Instead we invite you to contact your vendor for instructions on how to take advantage of the Java Persistence API.

Leveraging Design Patterns

For many years now, design patterns have been heavily promoted to help developers build better Java applications. For enterprise development in particular, using the proven solutions documented in design patterns has helped to manage the complexity of the Java EE platform. Ironically, patterns designed to help integrate entity beans and JDBC into enterprise applications are also the key to eliminating those technologies and introducing the Java Persistence API. This is because enterprise design patterns almost always point to solutions that isolate persistence code from the rest of the application. An enterprise application that has embraced common Java EE design patterns typically interacts only with session façades, data access objects, and transfer objects—perfect boundary points to safely make a switch in persistence technologies.

The following sections describe the design patterns that offer the greatest potential to replace container-managed entity beans and JDBC code with the lightweight entities of the Java Persistence API.

Transfer Object

The *Transfer Object*[1] pattern, also called the *Data Transfer Object* pattern, encapsulates the results of persistence operations in simple objects that are decoupled from the particular persistence implementation. Implemented in this way, transfer objects may be shared between application tiers without having dependencies on the entity bean API or requiring the use of remote entity beans. Although originally designed as a solution to avoid the poor performance of network calls for remote entity beans, they are widely used even in applications that do not have remote tiers in order to isolate business logic from the persistence API.

Fine-Grained Transfer Objects

When used with entity beans, transfer objects are typically implemented as a mirror of the entity data that is to be transported. For every persistent attribute on the entity bean, the same property is implemented on the transfer object. Listing 13-11 shows the business interface for the Address entity bean. It consists entirely of getter and setter methods to manage the persistent state of the entity bean.

Listing 13-11. *The Address Business Interface*

```
public interface Address extends EJBLocalObject {
    public int getId();
    public void setId(int id);

    public String getStreet();
    public void setStreet(String street);

    public String getCity();
    public void setCity(String city);

    public String getState();
    public void setState(String state);

    public String getZip();
    public void setZip(String zip);
}
```

---

1. Alur, Deepak, John Crupi, and Dan Malks. *Core J2EE Patterns: Best Practices and Design Strategies, Second Edition.* Upper Saddle River, N.J.: Prentice Hall PTR, 2003.

Using this business interface as a template, the transfer object corresponding to the Address business interface is shown in Listing 13-12. It is implemented using one field corresponding to each persistent property of the entity bean. This particular transfer object can also be used as a template for new entity bean instances or to capture changes that can be merged into an entity bean instance for updating. Transfer objects are often implemented as immutable objects if the client has no need to make changes and return the objects to the server for processing.

Listing 13-12. *The Address Transfer Object*

```
public class AddressTO implements Serializable {
    private int id;
    private String street;
    private String city;
    private String state;
    private String zip;

    public AddressTO() {}

    public AddressTO(int id, String street, String city,
                     String state, String zip) {
        this.id = id;
        this.street = street;
        this.city = city;
        this.state = state;
        this.zip = zip;
    }

    public int getId() { return id; }
    public void setId(int id) { this.id = id; }

    public String getCity() { return city; }
    public void setCity(String city) { this.city = city; }

    public String getState() { return state; }
    public void setState(String state) { this.state = state; }

    public String getStreet() { return street; }
    public void setStreet(String street) { this.street = street; }

    public String getZip() { return zip; }
    public void setZip(String zip) { this.zip = zip; }
}
```

This style of transfer object implementation, containing a one-to-one mapping of the persistent attributes from an entity bean, is considered *fine-grained*. The entire entity bean model used by the application is reflected in an identical, non-persistent model made up of transfer objects. When an application uses a fine-grained transfer object model, one option for migrating to the Java Persistence API is to convert the transfer objects into entities, by applying an object-relational mapping of the transfer objects to the database tables originally mapped by the entity beans. Even better, this can be accomplished with minimal impact to the business logic code that interacts with the transfer objects.

Compare the previous transfer object to the entity that follows:

```
@Entity
public class AddressTO implements Serializable {
    @Id
    private int id;
    private String street;
    private String city;
    private String state;
    @Column(name="ZIP_CODE")
    private String zip;

    // getter and setter methods
    // ...
}
```

The only difference between the original transfer object and this modified version is the addition of object-relational mapping annotations. Modified in this way, the transfer object, now an entity, is ready to be used with the entity manager to implement the persistence requirements of the application. If the Session Façade or Data Access Object patterns have been used, then this transformation is trivial. Instead of retrieving an entity and converting it into a transfer object, the entity manager and query interfaces can be used to retrieve the transfer object directly from the database.

Coarse-Grained Transfer Objects

A second type of transfer object is sometimes used that does not have a one-to-one correspondence with a particular entity bean. Instead, these transfer objects either collect data from multiple entities into a single transfer object or present a summarized view of overall entity state. This style of transfer object is *coarse-grained* and is sometimes called a view object since it presents a particular view of entity data that does not directly correspond to the entity bean implementation.

Listing 13-13 shows an example of this type of transfer object. Designed for distribution to the web tier for presentation on a web page, the transfer object stores summary information about the manager of a department. The managerName property is copied from the Employee entity bean, but the employeeCount and avgSalary properties are aggregate values computed by running summary queries.

Listing 13-13. *A Course-Grained Transfer Object*

```
public class ManagerStats {
    private String managerName;
    private int employeeCount;
    private double avgSalary;
```

```
    public ManagerStats(String managerName, int employeeCount, double avgSalary) {
        this.managerName = managerName;
        this.employeeCount = employeeCount;
        this.avgSalary = avgSalary;
    }

    public String getManagerName() { return managerName; }
    public int getEmployeeCount() { return employeeCount; }
    public double getAverageSalary() { return avgSalary; }
}
```

Fortunately, the Java Persistence API can often accommodate this style of transfer object through the constructor expressions in JPQL queries. The following query populates the transfer object shown previously:

```
SELECT NEW examples.ManagerStats(e.name, COUNT(d), AVG(d.salary))
FROM Employee e JOIN e.directs d
GROUP BY e.name
```

Constructor expression queries are also useful for composite transfer objects that simply combine the data from multiple entities into a single object. This style is sometimes used for entities that have a one-to-one relationship with other entities. The resulting transfer object flattens the object graph so that all reachable persistent fields become properties.

Despite the flexibility of JPQL expressions and native SQL query result set mapping, there will still be situations where transfer objects need to be manually constructed. However, the simplicity of working with entity classes can reduce the amount of code required to build transfer objects and reduce overall complexity as a result.

Session Façade

The *Session Façade*[2] pattern encapsulates business object access behind a session bean façade, typically implemented using stateless session beans. This business interface for the façade presents a coarse-grained view of the operations required on the business data, which may be implemented using entity beans, JDBC, or any other persistence technology.

Originally intended to define coarse-grained boundary operations for access by remote clients, the Session Façade pattern has evolved into a more general service façade, where remote access is no longer the driving factor. Decoupling enterprise applications into sets of collaborating services is a well-established best practice. Each service façade provides the business operations necessary to help realize one or more application use cases.

A key aspect of the Session Façade pattern that makes it appealing for introducing the Java Persistence API is the tendency to isolate persistence operations entirely behind the façade. The original use of transfer objects in the pattern stemmed from the need to prevent entity beans from being used remotely. Today, however, transfer objects are still widely used even for local services as a mechanism to abstract away the particular mechanics of persistence in the application.

---

2. Ibid.

Existing Java EE applications often use entity beans in the implementation of the Session Façade. Listing 13-14 shows a typical EJB 2.1 façade that provides business operations related to the management of `Project` entity beans.

Listing 13-14. *Session Façade with Entity Beans*

```
public class ProjectServiceBean implements SessionBean {
    private SessionContext context;
    private ProjectHome projectHome;
    private EmployeeHome empHome;

    public void setSessionContext(SessionContext context) {
        this.context = context;
    }

    public void ejbCreate() throws CreateException {
        try {
            Context ctx = new InitialContext();
            projectHome = (ProjectHome)
                ctx.lookup("java:comp/env/ejb/ProjectHome");
            empHome = (EmployeeHome)
                ctx.lookup("java:comp/env/ejb/EmployeeHome");
        } catch (NamingException e) {
            throw new CreateException(e.getMessage());
        }
    }

    public void addEmployeeToProject(int projectId, int empId)
        throws ApplicationException {
        try {
            Project project = projectHome.findByPrimaryKey(projectId);
            Employee emp = empHome.findByPrimaryKey(empId);
            project.getEmployees().add(emp);
        } catch (FinderException e) {
            throw new ApplicationException(e);
        }
    }

    // ...
}
```

Relying only on the primary key values as arguments, a service such as the one shown in Listing 13-14 would typically be invoked from a servlet, where the primary keys would have been obtained as part of an earlier display operation using transfer objects. With entity bean access isolated to the bean implementation, introducing entities is relatively straightforward. Listing 13-15 shows the service bean updated for EJB 3.0 and converted to use entities instead of entity beans. No change to existing clients of the service is necessary.

Listing 13-15. *Session Façade with Entities*

```
@Stateless
public class ProjectServiceBean {
    @PersistenceContext(name="EmployeeService")
    private EntityManager em;

    public void addEmployeeToProject(int projectId, int empId)
        throws ApplicationException {
        Project project = em.find(Project.class, projectId);
        if (project == null)
            throw new ApplicationException("Unknown project id: " + projectId);
        Employee emp = em.find(Employee.class, empId);
        if (emp == null)
            throw new ApplicationException("Unknown employee id: " + empId);
        project.getEmployees().add(emp);
        emp.getProjects().add(project);
    }

    // ...
}
```

Data Access Object

The *Data Access Object*[3] pattern, better known simply as the DAO pattern, presents a good
opportunity to introduce the Java Persistence API into an existing application. Indeed, the
pattern itself was designed on the premise that directly exposing persistence APIs to other
application tiers was something to be avoided. Therefore a well-designed data access object
implements a simple persistence manager interface by delegating to a particular persistence
technology.

The most common form of DAO delegates directly to JDBC, although other persistence
technologies are sometimes encountered. Data access objects are typically plain Java objects,
although other component types are sometimes used. When implemented as a session bean,
particularly when using entity beans, the lines between the data access object pattern and the
session façade pattern start to blur.

■**Note** Many DAO implementations use JDBC directly because it is often considered the "optimal" performance implementation by developers. As the Java Persistence API offers many benefits over direct JDBC,
including the potential for performance increases dues to caching, this pattern presents an opportunity to
introduce entities and see how they compare to traditional JDBC.

---

3. Ibid.

DAO implementations often use transfer objects to return results. For JDBC implementations, the use of transfer objects gives the illusion of an object-oriented domain model. Listing 13-16 shows a fragment of a DAO that uses JDBC for persistence and returns transfer objects to the client.

Listing 13-16. *DAO Using JDBC for Persistence*

```
public class AddressDAO {
    private static final String INSERT_SQL =
        "INSERT INTO address (id,street,city,state,zip) VALUES (?,?,?,?,?)";
    private static final String UPDATE_SQL =
        "UPDATE address SET street=?,city=?,state=?,zip=? WHERE id=?";
    private static final String DELETE_SQL =
        "DELETE FROM address WHERE id=?";
    private static final String FIND_SQL =
        "SELECT street,city,state,zip FROM address WHERE id=?";

    private DataSource ds;

    public AddressDAO(DataSource ds) {
        this.ds = ds;
    }

    public void create(AddressTO address) {
        Connection conn = null;
        PreparedStatement sth = null;
        try {
            conn = ds.getConnection();
            sth = conn.prepareStatement(INSERT_SQL);
            sth.setInt(1, address.getId());
            sth.setString(2, address.getStreet());
            sth.setString(3, address.getCity());
            sth.setString(4, address.getState());
            sth.setString(5, address.getZip());
            sth.execute();
        } catch (SQLException e) {
            throw new DAOException(e);
        } finally {
            if (sth != null) {
                try { sth.close(); } catch (SQLException e) {}
            }
            if (conn != null) {
                try { conn.close(); } catch (SQLException e) {}
            }
        }
    }
}
```

```
// ...

public AddressTO find(int id) {
    Connection conn = null;
    PreparedStatement sth = null;
    try {
        conn = ds.getConnection();
        sth = conn.prepareStatement(FIND_SQL);
        sth.setInt(1, id);
        ResultSet rs = sth.executeQuery();
        if (rs.next()) {
            AddressTO address = new AddressTO();
            address.setId(id);
            address.setStreet(rs.getString(1));
            address.setCity(rs.getString(2));
            address.setState(rs.getString(3));
            address.setZip(rs.getString(4));
            return address;
        } else {
            return null;
        }
    } catch (SQLException e) {
        throw new DAOException(e);
    } finally {
        if (sth != null) {
            try { sth.close(); } catch (SQLException e) {}
        }
        if (conn != null) {
            try { conn.close(); } catch (SQLException e) {}
        }
    }
}
}
```

One approach to conversion is to leave the transfer object as a non-persistent class while introducing a separate entity model. The DAO then converts back and forth between the two. Ideally the transfer object is replaced with the entity (see the following for an example of this approach), but preserving the transfer object allows developers to experiment with entities without disrupting the application in any way. Listing 13-17 demonstrates replacing the JDBC operations of a DAO with entities and an application-managed entity manager. Note the use of joinTransaction() in this example to ensure that the application-managed entity manager of the DAO class synchronizes itself with the active JTA transaction.

Listing 13-17. *DAO Using the Entity Manager for Persistence*

```
public class AddressDAO {
    private EntityManager em;

    public AddressDAO(EntityManager em) {
        this.em = em;
    }

    public void create(AddressTO address) {
        Address entity = createEntity(address);
        em.joinTransaction();
        em.persist(entity);
    }

    public void update(AddressTO address) {
        em.joinTransaction();
        em.merge(createEntity(address));
    }

    public void remove(int id) {
        em.joinTransaction();
        Address entity = em.find(Address.class, id);
        if (entity != null) {
            em.remove(entity);
        } else {
            throw new DAOException("No such address id: " + id);
        }
    }

    public AddressTO find(int id) {
        Address entity = em.find(Address.class, id);
        if (entity != null) {
            return createTO(entity);
        } else {
            return null;
        }
    }

    private Address createEntity(AddressTO address) {
        Address entity = new Address();
        entity.setId(address.getId());
        entity.setStreet(address.getStreet());
        entity.setCity(address.getCity());
        entity.setState(address.getState());
        entity.setZip(address.getZip());
        return entity;
    }
```

```
        private AddressTO createTO(Address entity) {
            AddressTO address = new AddressTO();
            address.setId(entity.getId());
            address.setStreet(entity.getStreet());
            address.setCity(entity.getCity());
            address.setState(entity.getState());
            address.setZip(entity.getZip());
            return address;
        }
    }
}
```

The symmetry between the transfer object and entity operations suggests a simpler implementation. If the transfer object has been migrated to be an entity, then this data access object can be simplified one further time. Listing 13-18 shows the final result.

Listing 13-18. *DAO Returning Entities*

```
public class AddressDAO {
    private EntityManager em;

    public AddressDAO(EntityManager em) {
        this.em = em;
    }

    public void create(Address address) {
        em.joinTransaction();
        em.persist(address);
    }

    public void update(Address address) {
        em.joinTransaction();
        em.merge(address);
    }

    public void remove(int id) {
        em.joinTransaction();
        Address entity = em.find(Address.class, id);
        if (entity != null) {
            em.remove(entity);
        } else {
            throw new DAOException("No such address id: " + id);
        }
    }
```

```
    public Address find(int id) {
        return em.find(Address.class, id);
    }
}
```

Business Object

The *Business Object*[4] pattern describes application object models that are conceptual rather than physical in nature. If the physical domain model is too fine-grained, a more abstract domain model is sometimes introduced that more closely represents the object model derived from use case modeling. This secondary model reflects the conceptual business objects of the system rather than the domain objects of the system and delegates to the physical domain model in its implementation. Application code typically interacts only with the business objects.

It is this delegation to the physical domain model that makes business objects candidates for migration to the Java Persistence API. Business objects are not directly persistent; instead they persist state using entity beans, Data Access Objects, or other persistence mechanisms. The choice of persistence mechanism is hidden from clients and therefore potentially replaceable.

There are several strategies for dealing with business objects. If the business object depends on a pattern such as Data Access Object, the business object can be ignored, and the application is migrated by virtue of tackling the underlying persistence pattern. If the business object directly uses a persistence mechanism such as entity beans, then an opportunity exists to change the persistence mechanism and rethink the physical domain model.

The advanced object-relational mapping features of the Java Persistence API may make it possible to map the business objects directly to the database, effectively turning the business objects into entities. Caution must be used in these situations, as business objects tend to contain more business logic and focus more on business use cases than persistence. This is not to say that it cannot be done, but the resulting entities are unlikely to be as lightweight as would normally be expected with the Java Persistence API.

Fast Lane Reader

The *Fast Lane Reader*[5] pattern uses JDBC directly instead of using entity beans to query large amounts of data for presentation. The theory behind this pattern is that entity beans are too expensive to create if the only purpose for retrieving the entity is to read some value from it and then discard the instance.

The Fast Lane Reader pattern is more a combination of two other existing patterns than a unique pattern of its own. The DAO pattern is used to collect the data for presentation, and the Transfer Object pattern is used to present the results in a format suitable for rendering in the presentation layer. We mention it distinct from other patterns only because it is one of the few cases where both DAO and entity bean implementations exist in the same application returning the same set of transfer objects.

---

4. Ibid.
5. See http://java.sun.com/blueprints/patterns/FastLaneReader.html for more information.

The result of a query with the Fast Lane Reader is either a set of transfer objects or basic collections containing entity fields. Therefore we can take advantage of the Fast Lane Reader pattern both at the DAO and transfer object levels. If the DAO is returning fine-grained transfer objects, then we can apply the techniques we described earlier in the chapter to change the implementation of the DAO to use the Java Persistence API and ideally return entities instead of transfer objects. Likewise, if the Fast Lane Reader is returning basic collections, we can use projection queries to produce the same results with no additional effort required to translate the JDBC result set.

Active Record

The *Active Record*[6] pattern describes classes that manage their own persistence, typically implemented using JDBC. The advantage of this approach is that the classes are not outwardly tied to any persistence implementation. However, the internal coupling presents difficulties, as a Service Locator must be used to access the data source, and testing may be difficult if the persistence occurs automatically as a side effect of mutating operations.

At first glance, migrating active record classes sounds easy—just map them as entities and get to work. Unfortunately, to be useful, entities require application code to work with the entity manager for all persistence operations. This requires the entity manager to be available in all cases where persistence of the active record needs to occur.

The amount of refactoring required to introduce the entity manager depends on the number of places where persistence operations occur as a side effect of public method calls on the active record object. This may be obvious if the active record exposes insert, update, and delete methods, or more subtle if a store occurs after every setter invocation. Before attempting to convert these classes to entities, ensure that the application persistence strategy is well understood, refactoring to simplify it before conversion if necessary.

Summary

Migrating the persistence layer of an application from one technology to another is rarely a trivial task. The differences between EJB container-managed entity beans and the lightweight entities of the Java Persistence API could make the task of migration tricky. And yet, despite these challenges, it is possible not only to extract enough information out of entity beans to bootstrap an object-oriented domain model but also to leverage the same design patterns that made entity beans easier to work with as the very tool to replace them.

In our discussion of entity beans, we looked at how to use the existing bean as a template for the new entity, using the business interface, bean class, and XML descriptor of the entity bean in the process. We also looked at the home interface and how we can introduce stateless session beans to emulate the functions of the home interface with minimal impact to application code.

---

6. Fowler, Martin. *Patterns of Enterprise Application Architecture*. Boston: Addison-Wesley, 2002.

We then touched on the migration of ORM and JDBC technologies to the Java Persistence API. While existing ORM migrations will largely depend on the support provided by the vendor, existing JDBC applications can be tackled by refactoring to existing Java EE design patterns before making the switch to the Java Persistence API.

Finally we looked at a catalog of Java EE design patterns related to persistence. Though not an exhaustive list, we looked at many of the major design patterns in use today and how they can be leveraged to safely introduce the Java Persistence API while minimizing the overall impact to the existing application.

■■■

Quick Reference

This appendix serves as a reference to those who may not have access to online Javadoc or who just can't otherwise tear themselves away from this book. The mapping annotations and XML mapping elements are included in this reference to further assist using one or the other, or both. We have also included the complete set of interfaces defined by the API.

Metadata Reference

The annotation definitions are useful in order to see which Java program elements may be annotated by a given annotation and to see the names and types of the annotation elements. Some cursory XML information is included to indicate the attributes and subelements of the XML elements.

@AttributeOverride

Description: Overrides an inherited or embedded basic mapping

```
@Target({TYPE, METHOD, FIELD}) @Retention(RUNTIME)
public @interface AttributeOverride {
    String name();
    Column column();
}
```

```
@Target({TYPE, METHOD, FIELD}) @Retention(RUNTIME)
public @interface AttributeOverrides {
    AttributeOverride[] value();
}
```

XML Element: annotation-override
XML Attributes: name
XML Subelements: column

@AssociationOverride

Description: Overrides an association mapping inherited from a mapped superclass

```
@Target({TYPE, METHOD, FIELD}) @Retention(RUNTIME)
public @interface AssociationOverride {
    String name();
    JoinColumn[] joinColumns();
}
```

```
@Target({TYPE, METHOD, FIELD}) @Retention(RUNTIME)
public @interface AssociationOverrides {
    AssociationOverride[] value();
}
```

XML Element: association-override
XML Attributes: name
XML Subelements: join-column

@Basic

Description: Simple mapped persistent attribute

```
@Target({METHOD, FIELD}) @Retention(RUNTIME)
public @interface Basic {
    FetchType fetch() default EAGER;
    boolean optional() default true;
}
```

XML Element: basic
XML Attributes: name, fetch, optional
XML Subelements: column, lob, temporal, enumerated

@Column

Description: Column to which entity attribute is mapped

```
@Target({METHOD, FIELD}) @Retention(RUNTIME)
public @interface Column {
    String name() default "";
    boolean unique() default false;
    boolean nullable() default true;
    boolean insertable() default true;
    boolean updatable() default true;
    String columnDefinition() default "";
    String table() default "";
    int length() default 255;
    int precision() default 0;
    int scale() default 0;
}
```

XML Element: column
XML Attributes: name, unique, nullable, insertable, updatable, column-definition, table,
length, precision, scale
XML Subelements: None

@ColumnResult

Description: Nested in @SqlResultSetMapping for mapping data projections

```
@Target({}) @Retention(RUNTIME)
public @interface ColumnResult {
    String name();
}
```

XML Element: column-result
XML Attributes: name
XML Subelements: None

@DiscriminatorColumn

Description: Column to store the entity type when a hierarchy of classes shares at least some of
the same table storage

```
@Target({TYPE}) @Retention(RUNTIME)
public @interface DiscriminatorColumn {
    String name() default "DTYPE";
    DiscriminatorType discriminatorType() default STRING;
    String columnDefinition() default "";
    int length() default 31;
}
```

XML Element: discriminator-column
XML Attributes: name, discriminator-type, column-definition, length
XML Subelements: None

@DiscriminatorValue

Description: The value used to represent a particular concrete entity class

```
@Target({TYPE}) @Retention(RUNTIME)
public @interface DiscriminatorValue {
    String value();
}
```

XML Element: discriminator-value
XML Attributes: None
XML Subelements: None

@Embeddable

Description: Denotes an object that may be embedded in an entity

```
@Target({TYPE}) @Retention(RUNTIME)
public @interface Embeddable {}
```

XML Element: embeddable
XML Attributes: class, access, metadata-complete
XML Subelements: attributes

@Embedded

Description: Embedded object that is stored in the same table as the embedding entity

```
@Target({METHOD, FIELD}) @Retention(RUNTIME)
public @interface Embedded {}
```

XML Element: embedded
XML Attributes: name
XML Subelements: attribute-override

@EmbeddedId

Description: Identifier attribute for compound primary key type stored in a single entity attribute

```
@Target({METHOD, FIELD}) @Retention(RUNTIME)
public @interface EmbeddedId {}
```

XML Element: embedded-id
XML Attributes: name
XML Subelements: attribute-override

@Entity

Description: Denotes object as being an entity

```
@Target(TYPE) @Retention(RUNTIME)
public @interface Entity {
    String name() default "";
}
```

XML Element: entity
XML Attributes: name, class, access, metadata-complete
XML Subelements: table, secondary-table, primary-key-join-column, id-class, inheritance, discriminator-value, discriminator-column, sequence-generator, table-generator, named-query, named-native-query, sql-result-set-mapping, exclude-default-listeners, exclude-superclass-listeners, entity-listeners, pre-persist, post-persist, pre-remove, post-remove, pre-update, post-update, post-load, attribute-override, association-override, attributes

@EntityListeners

Description: List of ordered entity listeners to be invoked on entity lifecycle events

```
@Target(TYPE) @Retention(RUNTIME)
public @interface EntityListeners {
    Class[] value();
}
```

XML Element: entity-listeners
XML Attributes: None
XML Subelements: entity-listener

@EntityResult

Description: Nested in @SqlResultSetMapping for mapping SQL results sets to entities

```
@Target({}) @Retention(RUNTIME)
public @interface EntityResult {
    Class entityClass();
    FieldResult[] fields() default {};
    String discriminatorColumn() default "";
}
```

XML Element: entity-result
XML Attributes: entity-class, discriminator-column
XML Subelements: field-result

@Enumerated

Description: Simple attribute that is an enumerated type

```
@Target({METHOD, FIELD}) @Retention(RUNTIME)
public @interface Enumerated {
    EnumType value() default ORDINAL;
}
```

XML Element: enumerated
XML Attributes: None
XML Subelements: None

@ExcludeDefaultListeners

Description: Cause default listeners to not be invoked on specifying entity

```
@Target({TYPE}) @Retention(RUNTIME)
public @interface ExcludeDefaultListeners {}
```

XML Element: exclude-default-listeners
XML Attributes: None
XML Subelements: None

@ExcludeSuperclassListeners

Description: Cause listener callbacks defined in superclasses to not be invoked on specifying entity

```
@Target({TYPE}) @Retention(RUNTIME)
public @interface ExcludeSuperclassListeners {}
```

XML Element: exclude-superclass-listeners
XML Attributes: None
XML Subelements: None

@FieldResult

Description: Nested in @EntityResult for mapping SQL results sets to entity fields

```
@Target({}) @Retention(RUNTIME)
public @interface FieldResult {
    String name();
    String column();
}
```

XML Element: field-result
XML Attributes: name, column
XML Subelements: None

@GeneratedValue

Description: Identifier attribute that is generated automatically

```
@Target({METHOD, FIELD}) @Retention(RUNTIME)
public @interface GeneratedValue {
    GenerationType strategy() default AUTO;
    String generator() default "";
}
```

XML Element: generated-value
XML Attributes: strategy, generator
XML Subelements: None

@Id

Description: Identifier attribute for simple primary key type

```
@Target({METHOD, FIELD}) @Retention(RUNTIME)
public @interface Id {}
```

XML Element: id
XML Attributes: name
XML Subelements: column, generated-value, temporal, table-generator, sequence-generator

@IdClass

Description: Compound primary key class spread across multiple entity attributes

```
@Target({TYPE}) @Retention(RUNTIME)
public @interface IdClass {
    Class value();
}
```

XML Element: id-class
XML Attributes: class
XML Subelements: None

@Inheritance

Description: Denotes an entity inheritance hierarchy

```
@Target({TYPE}) @Retention(RUNTIME)
public @interface Inheritance {
    InheritanceType strategy() default SINGLE_TABLE;
}
```

XML Element: inheritance
XML Attributes: strategy
XML Subelements: None

@JoinColumn

Description: Foreign key column that references the primary key of another entity

```
@Target({METHOD, FIELD}) @Retention(RUNTIME)
public @interface JoinColumn {
    String name() default "";
    String referencedColumnName() default "";
    boolean unique() default false;
    boolean nullable() default true;
    boolean insertable() default true;
    boolean updatable() default true;
    String columnDefinition() default "";
    String table() default "";
}

@Target({METHOD, FIELD}) @Retention(RUNTIME)
public @interface JoinColumns {
    JoinColumn[] value();
}
```

XML Element: join-column
XML Attributes: name, referenced-column-name, unique, nullable, insertable, updatable,
column-definition, table
XML Subelements: None

@JoinTable

Description: Association table to join two entity types in a many-valued relationship

```
@Target({METHOD, FIELD}) @Retention(RUNTIME)
public @interface JoinTable {
    String name() default "";
    String catalog() default "";
    String schema() default "";
    JoinColumn[] joinColumns() default {};
    JoinColumn[] inverseJoinColumns() default {};
    UniqueConstraint[] uniqueConstraints() default {};
}
```

XML Element: join-table
XML Attributes: name, catalog, schema
XML Subelements: join-column, inverse-join-column, unique-constraint

@Lob

Description: Simple attribute that is mapped to a large object (LOB) column

```
@Target({METHOD, FIELD}) @Retention(RUNTIME)
public @interface Lob {}
```

XML Element: lob
XML Attributes: None
XML Subelements: None

@ManyToMany

Description: Many-to-many association to another entity type

```
@Target({METHOD, FIELD}) @Retention(RUNTIME)
public @interface ManyToMany {
    Class targetEntity() default void.class;
    CascadeType[] cascade() default {};
    FetchType fetch() default LAZY;
    String mappedBy() default "";
}
```

XML Element: many-to-many
XML Attributes: name, target-entity, fetch, mapped-by
XML Subelements: order-by, map-key, join-table, cascade

@ManyToOne

Description: Many-to-one association to another entity type

```
@Target({METHOD, FIELD}) @Retention(RUNTIME)
public @interface ManyToOne {
    Class targetEntity() default void.class;
    CascadeType[] cascade() default {};
    FetchType fetch() default EAGER;
    boolean optional() default true;
}
```

XML Element: many-to-one
XML Attributes: name, target-entity, fetch, mapped-by
XML Subelements: join-column, join-table, cascade

@MapKey

Description: Entity attribute to act as the key value when storing target entities in a Map

```
@Target({METHOD, FIELD}) @Retention(RUNTIME)
public @interface MapKey {
    String name() default "";
}
```

XML Element: map-key
XML Attributes: name
XML Subelements: None

@MappedSuperclass

Description: Denotes an entity superclass that may contain mapped persistent state

```
@Target(TYPE) @Retention(RUNTIME)
public @interface MappedSuperclass {}
```

XML Element: mapped-superclass
XML Attributes: class, access, metadata-complete
XML Subelements: id-class, exclude-default-listeners, exclude-superclass-listeners,
entity-listeners, pre-persist, post-persist, pre-remove, post-remove, pre-update, post-
update, post-load, attributes

@NamedNativeQuery

Description: Defines a static query that uses SQL query criteria

```
@Target({TYPE}) @Retention(RUNTIME)
public @interface NamedNativeQuery {
    String name();
    String query();
    QueryHint[] hints() default {};
    Class resultClass() default void.class;
    String resultSetMapping() default "";
}
```

```
@Target({TYPE}) @Retention(RUNTIME)
public @interface NamedNativeQueries {
    NamedNativeQuery[] value ();
}
```

XML Element: named-native-query
XML Attributes: name, result-class, result-set-mapping
XML Subelements: query, hint

@NamedQuery

Description: Defines a static query that uses JPQL query criteria

```
@Target({TYPE}) @Retention(RUNTIME)
public @interface NamedQuery {
    String name();
    String query();
    QueryHint[] hints() default {};
}
```

```
@Target({TYPE}) @Retention(RUNTIME)
public @interface NamedQueries {
    NamedQuery[] value ();
}
```

XML Element: named-query
XML Attributes: name
XML Subelements: query, hint

@OneToMany

Description: One-to-many association to another entity type

```
@Target({METHOD, FIELD}) @Retention(RUNTIME)
public @interface OneToMany {
    Class targetEntity() default void.class;
    CascadeType[] cascade() default {};
    FetchType fetch() default LAZY;
    String mappedBy() default "";
}
```

XML Element: one-to-many
XML Attributes: name, target-entity, fetch, mapped-by
XML Subelements: order-by, map-key, join-table, join-column, cascade

@OneToOne

Description: One-to-one association to another entity type

```
@Target({METHOD, FIELD}) @Retention(RUNTIME)
public @interface OneToOne {
    Class targetEntity() default void.class;
    CascadeType[] cascade() default {};
    FetchType fetch() default EAGER;
    boolean optional() default true;
    String mappedBy() default "";
}
```

XML Element: one-to-one
XML Attributes: name, target-entity, fetch, mapped-by
XML Subelements: order-by, map-key, join-table, join-column, cascade

@OrderBy

Description: Entity attribute or attributes to order by when storing target entities in a List

```
@Target({METHOD, FIELD}) @Retention(RUNTIME)
public @interface OrderBy {
    String value() default "";
}
```

XML Element: order-by
XML Attributes: None
XML Subelements: None

@PostLoad

Description: Method invoked by provider after loading an entity

```
@Target({METHOD}) @Retention(RUNTIME)
public @interface PostLoad {}
```

XML Element: post-load
XML Attributes: method-name
XML Subelements: None

@PostPersist

Description: Method invoked by provider after persisting an entity

```
@Target({METHOD}) @Retention(RUNTIME)
public @interface PostPersist {}
```

XML Element: post-persist
XML Attributes: method-name
XML Subelements: None

@PostRemove

Description: Method invoked by provider after removing an entity

```
@Target({METHOD}) @Retention(RUNTIME)
public @interface PostRemove {}
```

XML Element: post-remove
XML Attributes: method-name
XML Subelements: None

@PostUpdate

Description: Method invoked by provider after updating an entity

```
@Target({METHOD}) @Retention(RUNTIME)
public @interface PostUpdate {}
```

XML Element: post-update
XML Attributes: method-name
XML Subelements: None

@PrePersist

Description: Method invoked by provider before persisting an entity

```
@Target({METHOD}) @Retention(RUNTIME)
public @interface PrePersist {}
```

XML Element: pre-persist
XML Attributes: method-name
XML Subelements: None

@PreRemove

Description: Method invoked by provider before removing an entity

```
@Target({METHOD}) @Retention(RUNTIME)
public @interface PreRemove {}
```

XML Element: pre-remove
XML Attributes: method-name
XML Subelements: None

@PreUpdate

Description: Method invoked by provider before updating an entity

```
@Target({METHOD}) @Retention(RUNTIME)
public @interface PreUpdate {}
```

XML Element: pre-update
XML Attributes: method-name
XML Subelements: None

@PrimaryKeyJoinColumn

Description: Foreign key column that is also a primary key

```
@Target({TYPE, METHOD, FIELD}) @Retention(RUNTIME)
public @interface PrimaryKeyJoinColumn {
    String name() default "";
    String referencedColumnName() default "";
    String columnDefinition() default "";
}

@Target({TYPE, METHOD, FIELD}) @Retention(RUNTIME)
public @interface PrimaryKeyJoinColumns {
    PrimaryKeyJoinColumn[] value();
}
```

XML Element: primary-key-join-column
XML Attributes: name, referenced-column-name, column-definition
XML Subelements: None

@QueryHint

Description: Nested in @NamedQuery and @NamedNativeQuery for vendor-specific behavior

```
@Target({}) @Retention(RUNTIME)
public @interface QueryHint {
    String name();
    String value();
}
```

XML Element: query-hint
XML Attributes: name, value
XML Subelements: None

@SecondaryTable

Description: Additional table or tables in which to store part of the entity state

```
@Target({TYPE}) @Retention(RUNTIME)
public @interface SecondaryTable {
    String name();
    String catalog() default "";
    String schema() default "";
    PrimaryKeyJoinColumn[] pkJoinColumns() default {};
    UniqueConstraint[] uniqueConstraints() default {};
}

@Target({TYPE}) @Retention(RUNTIME)
public @interface SecondaryTables {
    SecondaryTable[] value();
}
```

XML Element: secondary-table
XML Attributes: name, catalog, schema
XML Subelements: primary-key-join-column, unique-constraint

@SequenceGenerator

Description: Specifies a database sequence used for primary key generation

```
@Target({TYPE, METHOD, FIELD}) @Retention(RUNTIME)
public @interface SequenceGenerator {
    String name();
    String sequenceName() default "";
    int initialValue() default 1;
    int allocationSize() default 50;
}
```

XML Element: sequence-generator
XML Attributes: name, sequence-name, initial-value, allocation-size
XML Subelements: None

@SqlResultSetMapping

Description: Defines a mapping from a JDBC result set

```
@Target({TYPE}) @Retention(RUNTIME)
public @interface SqlResultSetMapping {
    String name();
    EntityResult[] entities() default {};
    ColumnResult[] columns() default {};
}
```

```
@Target({TYPE}) @Retention(RUNTIME)
public @interface SqlResultSetMappings {
    SqlResultSetMapping[] value();
}
```

XML Element: sql-result-set-mapping
XML Attributes: name
XML Subelements: entity-result, column-result

@Table

Description: Primary table in which state of a given entity type is stored

```
@Target({TYPE}) @Retention(RUNTIME)
public @interface Table {
    String name() default "";
    String catalog() default "";
    String schema() default "";
    UniqueConstraint[] uniqueConstraints() default {};
}
```

XML Element: table
XML Attributes: name, catalog, schema
XML Subelements: unique-constraint

@TableGenerator

Description: Specifies a table used for primary key generation

```
@Target({TYPE, METHOD, FIELD}) @Retention(RUNTIME)
public @interface TableGenerator {
    String name();
    String table() default "";
    String catalog() default "";
    String schema() default "";
    String pkColumnName() default "";
    String valueColumnName() default "";
    String pkColumnValue() default "";
    int initialValue() default 0;
    int allocationSize() default 50;
    UniqueConstraint[] uniqueConstraints() default {};
}
```

XML Element: table-generator
XML Attributes: name, table, catalog, schema, pk-column-name, value-column-name,
pk-column-value, initial-value, allocation-size
XML Subelements: unique-constraint

@Temporal

Description: Simple attribute that is a time-based type

```
@Target({METHOD, FIELD}) @Retention(RUNTIME)
public @interface Temporal {
    TemporalType value();
}
```

XML Element: temporal
XML Attributes: None
XML Subelements: None

@Transient

Description: Non-persistent attribute

```
@Target({METHOD, FIELD}) @Retention(RUNTIME)
public @interface Transient {}
```

XML Element: transient
XML Attributes: name
XML Subelements: None

@UniqueConstraint

Description: Nested in @Table and @SecondaryTable to specify columns having uniqueness constraints

```
@Target({}) @Retention(RUNTIME)
public @interface UniqueConstraint {
    String[] columnNames();
}
```

XML Element: unique-constraint
XML Attributes: None
XML Subelements: column-name

@Version

Description: Simple attribute that stores optimistic locking version

```
@Target({METHOD, FIELD}) @Retention(RUNTIME)
public @interface Version {}
```

XML Element: version
XML Attributes: name
XML Subelements: column, temporal

Enumerated Types

The following enumerated types are used in the annotations and API.

```
public enum GenerationType { TABLE, SEQUENCE, IDENTITY, AUTO };
```

```
public enum FetchType { LAZY, EAGER };
```

```
public enum TemporalType { DATE, TIME, TIMESTAMP };
```

```
public enum EnumType { ORDINAL, STRING };
```

```
public enum CascadeType { ALL, PERSIST, MERGE, REMOVE, REFRESH };
```

```
public enum InheritanceType { SINGLE_TABLE, JOINED, TABLE_PER_CLASS };
```

```
public enum DiscriminatorType { STRING, CHAR, INTEGER };
```

Mapping File-Level Metadata Reference

The XML elements in this section are default settings that apply only to the mapping file in which they are specified as subelements of the entity-mappings element. There are no corresponding annotations that apply to the same mapping file scope.

package

Description: Default package name for classes named in the XML mapping file
XML Attributes: None
XML Subelements: None

schema

Description: Default schema for tables of entities listed in the mapping file
XML Attributes: None
XML Subelements: None

catalog

Description: Default catalog for tables of entities listed in the mapping file
XML Attributes: None
XML Subelements: None

access

Description: Default access mode for managed classes in the mapping file for which there are
no annotations specified
XML Attributes: None
XML Subelements: None

Persistence-Unit-Level Metadata Reference

The XML elements in this section are default settings that apply to the entire persistence unit.
There are no corresponding annotations that apply to the same persistence-unit-level scope.

persistence-unit-metadata

Description: Top-level element for specifying mapping configuration for the entire
persistence unit
XML Attributes: None
XML Subelements: xml-mapping-metadata-complete, persistence-unit-defaults

xml-mapping-metadata-complete

Description: Setting to indicate that all annotation metadata in the persistence unit is to be
ignored
XML Attributes: None
XML Subelements: None

persistence-unit-defaults

Description: Parent element for default persistence unit settings
XML Attributes: None
XML Subelements: schema, catalog, access, cascade-persist, entity-listeners

schema

Description: Default schema for tables in the persistence unit for which there is no schema specified
XML Attributes: None
XML Subelements: None

catalog

Description: Default catalog for tables in the persistence unit for which there is no catalog specified
XML Attributes: None
XML Subelements: None

access

Description: Default access mode for managed classes in the persistence unit for which there are no annotations specified
XML Attributes: None
XML Subelements: None

cascade-persist

Description: Adds PERSIST cascade option to all relationships in the persistence unit
XML Attributes: None
XML Subelements: None

entity-listeners

Description: List of entity listeners to be invoked on every entity in the persistence unit
XML Attributes: None
XML Subelements: entity-listener

EntityManager Interface

The EntityManager interface is implemented by the persistence provider and proxied by the container in the server. Concrete instances are obtained from an EntityManagerFactory or from the container through injection or JNDI lookup.

```
public interface javax.persistence.EntityManager {

    public void persist(Object entity);

    public <T> T merge(T entity);

    public void remove(Object entity);
```

```
public <T> T find(Class<T> entityClass,
                  Object primaryKey);

public <T> T getReference(Class<T> entityClass,
                          Object primaryKey);

public void flush();

public void setFlushMode(FlushModeType flushMode);

public FlushModeType getFlushMode();

public void lock(Object entity, LockModeType lockMode);

public void refresh(Object entity);

public void clear();

public boolean contains(Object entity);

public Query createQuery(String qlString);

public Query createNamedQuery(String name);

public Query createNativeQuery(String sqlString);

public Query createNativeQuery(String sqlString,
                               Class resultClass);

public Query createNativeQuery(String sqlString,
                               String resultSetMapping);

public void joinTransaction();

public Object getDelegate();

public void close();

public boolean isOpen();

public EntityTransaction getTransaction();
}
```

Query Interface

The Query interface is implemented by the persistence provider. Concrete instances are obtained from the EntityManager query factory methods.

```
public interface javax.persistence.Query {

    public List getResultList();

    public Object getSingleResult();

    public int executeUpdate();

    public Query setMaxResults(int maxResult);

    public Query setFirstResult(int startPosition);

    public Query setHint(String hintName, Object value);

    public Query setParameter(String name, Object value);

    public Query setParameter(String name,
                              Date value,
                              TemporalType temporalType);

    public Query setParameter(String name,
                              Calendar value,
                              TemporalType temporalType);

    public Query setParameter(int position, Object value);

    public Query setParameter(int position,
                              Date value,
                              TemporalType temporalType);

    public Query setParameter(int position,
                              Calendar value,
                              TemporalType temporalType);

    public Query setFlushMode(FlushModeType flushMode);
}
```

EntityManagerFactory Interface

The EntityManagerFactory interface is implemented by the persistence provider. Concrete instances are obtained from the Persistence bootstrap class or from the container through injection or JNDI lookup.

```
public interface javax.persistence.EntityManagerFactory {

    public EntityManager createEntityManager();

    public EntityManager createEntityManager(Map map);

    public void close();

    public boolean isOpen();
}
```

EntityTransaction Interface

The EntityTransaction interface is implemented by the persistence provider. Concrete instances are obtained from the EntityManager.getTransaction() method.

```
public interface javax.persistence.EntityTransaction {

    public void begin();

    public void commit();

    public void rollback();

    public void setRollbackOnly();

    public boolean getRollbackOnly();

    public boolean isActive();
}
```

Index

Find it faster at http://superindex.apress.com

You Need the Companion eBook

PRISMATIC METROPOLIS

PRISMATIC METROPOLIS

Inequality in Los Angeles

Lawrence D. Bobo
Melvin L. Oliver
James H. Johnson Jr.
Abel Valenzuela Jr.

Editors

A VOLUME IN THE MULTI-CITY STUDY OF
URBAN INEQUALITY

Russell Sage Foundation | New York

The Russell Sage Foundation

The Russell Sage Foundation, one of the oldest of America's general purpose foundations, was established in 1907 by Mrs. Margaret Olivia Sage for "the improvement of social and living conditions in the United States." The Foundation seeks to fulfill this mandate by fostering the development and dissemination of knowledge about the country's political, social, and economic problems. While the Foundation endeavors to assure the accuracy and objectivity of each book it publishes, the conclusions and interpretations in Russell Sage Foundation publications are those of the authors and not of the Foundation, its Trustees, or its staff. Publication by Russell Sage, therefore, does not imply Foundation endorsement.

Library of Congress Cataloging-in-Publication Data

Prismatic metropolis : inequality in Los Angeles / edited by Lawrence D. Bobo
... [et al.].
    p. cm. — (The multi-city study of urban inequality)
    Includes bibliographical references and index.
    ISBN 0-87154-129-7
    1. Los Angeles County (Calif.)—Social conditions.   2. Los Angeles County
(Calif.)—Economic conditions.   3. Los Angeles County (Calif.)—Race
relations.   4. Discrimination in employment—California—Los Angeles
County.   5. Minorities—California—Los Angeles County—Social
conditions.   6. Minorities—California—Los Angeles County—Economic
conditions.   7. Equality—California—Los Angeles County.
8. Demographic surveys—California—Los Angeles County.   I. Bobo,
Lawrence D.   II. Series.

HN79.C22 L677 2000
305.8'.009794'94—dc21   00-027029

Text design by Suzanne Nichols.

RUSSELL SAGE FOUNDATION
112 East 64th Street, New York, New York 10021
10 9 8 7 6 5 4 3 2 1

The Multi-City Study of Urban Inequality

The Multi-City Study of Urban Inequality is a major social science research project designed to deepen the nation's understanding of the social and economic divisions that now beset America's cities. It is based on a uniquely linked set of surveys of employers and households in four major cities: Atlanta, Boston, Detroit, and Los Angeles. The Multi-City Study focuses on the effects of massive economic restructuring on racial and ethnic groups in the inner city, who must compete for increasingly limited opportunities in a shifting labor market while facing persistent discrimination in housing and hiring. Involving more than forty researchers at fifteen U.S. colleges and universities, the Multi-City Study has been jointly funded by the Ford Foundation and the Russell Sage Foundation. This volume is the fifth in a series of books reporting the results of the Multi-City Study to be published by the Russell Sage Foundation.

In memory of Bennett Harrison, scholar and friend

Contents

Contributors

LAWRENCE D. BOBO is professor of sociology and Afro-American studies at Harvard University.

MELVIN L. OLIVER is vice president of the Ford Foundation. He is responsible for overseeing the Asset Building and Community Development Program.

JAMES H. JOHNSON JR. is William Rand Kenan Jr. Distinguished Professor of Management, Sociology, and Public Policy and director of the Urban Investment Strategies Center in the Kenan Institute in the Kenan-Flager Business School at the University of North Carolina at Chapel Hill.

ABEL VALENZUELA JR. is assistant professor of urban planning and Chicana/o studies at the University of California, Los Angeles. He is also associate director of the Center for the Study of Urban Poverty, Institute for Social Science Research.

ELISA JAYNE BIENENSTOCK is assistant professor of sociology at Stanford University.

CAMILLE ZUBRINSKY CHARLES is assistant professor of sociology at the University of Pennsylvania. She is also research associate at the University of Pennsylvania's Population Studies Center.

WALTER C. FARRELL JR. is professor of social work and associate director of the Urban Investment Strategies Center at the University of North Carolina at Chapel Hill.

JENNIFER L. GLANVILLE is a doctoral candidate in the Sociology Department at the University of North Carolina at Chapel Hill.

ELIZABETH GONZALEZ is a doctoral candidate is the Department of Sociology at the University of California, Los Angeles. She is also a research fellow at the Center for the Study of Urban Poverty, Institute for Social Science Research.

DAVID M. GRANT is assistant professor of sociology at Cleveland State University.

TARRY HUM is assistant professor of urban studies at Queens College, City University of New York.

DEVON JOHNSON is a doctoral candidate in the Department of Sociology at the University of California, Los Angeles. She is also and a visiting fellow at Harvard University.

MICHAEL I. LICHTER is senior research analyst with the County of Los Angeles.

JULIE E. PRESS is assistant professor of sociology at Temple University. She is also faculty affiliate of the Temple University Women's Studies Program and research fellow at Temple's Center for Public Policy.

MICHAEL A. STOLL is assistant professor of public policy in the School of Public Policy and Social Research at the University of California, Los Angeles. He is also a research associate in the Center for the Study of Urban Poverty, Institute for Social Science Research.

SUSAN A. SUH is a doctoral candidate in the Department of Sociology at the University of California, Los Angeles.

JENNIFER A. STOLOFF is a doctoral candidate in the Department of Sociology at the University of North Carolina at Chapel Hill.

Acknowledgments

The starting point of this project is difficult to fix in time and place. In part, it traces back to the founding by James H. Johnson Jr., and Melvin L. Oliver of the Center for the Study of Urban Poverty (CSUP) at UCLA. In part, it traces to the partnership between CSUP and the Program on Poverty and Public Policy headed by Sheldon Danziger at the University of Michigan. In part, it traces to discussions between Reynolds Farley and Lawrence Bobo about a possible replication and expansion on the 1976 Detroit Area Study and Bobo's move to join the sociology department at UCLA at that time. In part, it traces to work inspired by the Social Science Research Council (SSRC) Committee on the Urban Underclass. These several strands of concern with poverty and inequality, residential segregation, and racial attitudes eventually were woven together by Johnson, Oliver, and Bobo, in consultation with many others, in the form of the Los Angeles Study of Urban Inequality (LASUI) project. From the outset, our goal was to craft a fresh and critical examination of the dynamics of inequality in Los Angeles. We sought to do so by linking more directly than has any previous research endeavor a concern with the labor market, the housing market, and patterns of intergroup identities, attitudes, and beliefs.

The vision and ultimate execution of the Los Angeles Study of Urban Inequality project took shape over a number of years. During this time, we were assisted in large and small ways by too many people to name and thank individually here. Among those who played critical roles in advancing our work were Sheldon Danziger at the University of Michigan and Alice O'Connor, originally senior staff to the SSRC Committee on the Urban Underclass and now at the University of California, Santa Barbara, who were instrumental in helping us conceptualize the research plan, develop the original proposal, stage a planning conference, and ultimately secure funding from both the Russell Sage and Ford Foundations to support the research. Marilynn Brewer, director of

UCLA's Institute for Social Science Research when the project began, and David O. Sears, ISSR director during the phase of data analysis, were always supportive of our efforts and established a nurturing working environment. Eve Fielder, director of the Survey Research Center at UCLA, and her able assistant, Tonya Hays, carried out with great skill and persistence the arduous task of fielding a 4,000-person household survey in five languages. We owe them more than words can convey. The inestimable Tana Wong, along with Deborah Potts, kept all the paperwork and paychecks flowing. Dean of Social Sciences at UCLA, Scott Waugh consistently supported the Center for the Study of Urban Poverty and the faculty and students who made it an intellectual home.

This project would not have been possible without the faith in us exhibited by Prudence Brown, program officer at the Ford Foundation when this project was launched, and Eric Wanner, president of the Russell Sage Foundation. We thank them both for the commitment they made to this project, their steadfast support of our efforts, and their trust in us to bring this very large endeavor to completion. Ron Mincy, our most recent program officer from the Ford Foundation, maintained an active interest in the project and provided both financial and intellectual assistance at just the right times. The National Advisory Group to the larger Multi-City Study of Urban Inequality project, composed of Robinson Hollister (chair), Jorge Chapa, Mary Jackman, Frank Levy, Seymour Sudman, and Franklin D. Wilson also deserve our thanks. We also thank the members of the Multi-City Study of Urban Inequality research teams, in Atlanta, Boston, and Detroit, who played a significant part in crafting the larger mission.

Certainly our greatest debt is owed to those who began their academic careers as graduate research assistants to the LASUI project. A number of these students, we are proud to note, are now independent scholars and researchers: Camille Z. Charles (University of Pennsylvania), David M. Grant (Cleveland State University), Tarry Hum (Queens College, CUNY), Michael I. Lichter (County of Los Angeles), and Julie Press (Temple University). Others are nearing that stage: Elizabeth Gonzalez, Devon Johnson, and Susan A. Suh. We thank them all for their dedication to this project, the intellectual and occasional sheer physical energy they devoted to it, and the seemingly inexhaustible spark of creativity each of them kept alive from start to finish.

We tested the commitment of these young scholars in many ways, not the least of which was the eventual departure of each of the principal investigators from UCLA during the course of the project. At the beginning of data collection, in 1993, Jim Johnson left UCLA to join the faculty at the University of North Carolina, Chapel Hill. In 1996, well into the analysis phase, Melvin Oliver left to join the Ford Foundation as vice president of the program on Asset Building and Community Development. And in 1997, as this volume was taking shape, Lawrence Bobo left UCLA to join the faculty at Harvard University. In some ways, as a result, this cadre of very capable and dedicated students became an important source of continuity in the project. Abel Valenzuela, now associate director of the CSUP, and Diego Vigil, who assumed the directorship upon Oliver's departure, played critical roles in sustaining the project. Diego has generously supported students and whatever other needs the project had in order to assure the completion of this volume. Abel became such a pivotal figure in our work that he quite simply earned a place as one of the editors of this volume.

All these people (and countless others) played a part in making this project happen. Race and ethnicity, space, gender and group identities and attitudes are linked in complex ways in the modern urban setting. We set about in this project, of which this volume is the culmination, to make those connections and how they structure urban inequality more explicit and understandable. We thank all of those who made this endeavor possible.

Lawrence D. Bobo
Melvin L. Oliver
James H. Johnson Jr.
Abel Valenzuela Jr.

Part I

INTRODUCTION:
FOUNDATIONS OF A
PRISMATIC METROPOLIS

1

ANALYZING INEQUALITY IN LOS ANGELES

Lawrence D. Bobo, Melvin L. Oliver, James H. Johnson Jr., and Abel Valenzuela Jr.

MANY scholars and policymakers are concerned that the nature and distribution of opportunity in our society is undergoing massive change. Owing in part to steady waves of immigration and differential rates of fertility, the United States is also rapidly becoming a more racially and ethically diverse nation (McDaniel 1995; Bean and Bell-Rose 1999). At the same time, processes of technological innovation, intensified global integration, deindustrialization, and industrial deconcentration are transforming the world of work. One central impact of these changes is a widening gap in pay between high-skill and low-skill workers (Danziger and Gottschalk 1995; Wilson 1996). This development has worsened the inequality in overall income distribution (Levy 1995).

With Los Angeles often seen as the signal case, many social commentators are concerned that American society is fragmenting. In addition to feeling the effects of these national trends, Los Angeles's unique geographic expanse, concentration of immigrants, and highly diversified labor market create sharply uneven outcomes for different segments of the population. The combination provides ample grounds for concern that deep economic inequality, coupled with persistent racial and ethnic divisions, made more complex and potentially roilsome by rapid immigration, constitute serious challenges to our institutions and social policy. The confluence of these transformations in urban settings such as Los Angeles points to a need for focused social scientific analysis. To understand the import of current social trends for future opportunities, we believe it essential to look in detail at how labor market processes, residential sorting processes, individual and group processes of adaptation, and patterns of intergroup attitude and relations play out in a modern urban setting. Los Angeles, we believe, provides an important and telling case of how these increasingly national challenges and transformations are unfolding.

With this volume, we aim to go further than most social science analysis, which is often constrained by reliance on the U.S. census and other highly standardized data sources. Like most major American metropolises, Los Angeles is ultimately defined by its people: where they live, how they make a living, whom they associate with in their daily lives, and how they make sense of the world in which they live. It is this story of neighborhoods, of work, of personal and social identity, and of patterns of interaction and meaning that we hope to tell here in new and revealing detail.

Contemporary analyses of the urban condition often focus on the processes and circumstances that have produced marginal and poor populations (Wilson 1987; Jencks and Peterson 1991; Massey and Denton 1993; Danziger, Sandefur, and Weinberg 1994; Holzer 1996; Jargowsky 1997). This research has examined the economic changes that result in divergent opportunities. Beginning with an emphasis on "Rustbelt" cities and the deindustrialization that accompanied changes in urban economics, analysts contended that economic opportunity for blue-collar workers declined as jobs with good pay and decent benefits in the manufacturing sector disappeared along with the factories (Harrison and Bluestone 1988). They investigated the divergent economic fortunes of the skilled and the unskilled. In the context of deindustrialization and the growth of jobs in the advanced service sector, skills (both "soft" and "hard") have become the differentiating marker of access to a comfortable place in the modern urban economy (Holzer 1996). Their research focused almost exclusively on deindustrializing, Rustbelt, urban centers of the Midwest and Northeast, thereby reinforcing an almost exclusively black-white lens on urban inequality and the notion that poverty and inequality are negligible in the West (Wilson 1987).

These explanations are not so much wrong as incomplete, lacking a fully developed perspective. Such a perspective would take into account not only the direct effects of each explanation separately, but their combined and interactive effects as well. By investigating mostly Rustbelt cities, the analysts missed a growing segment of urban America, where the racial dynamics were no longer simply black-white but increasingly multiracial and multiethnic. By focusing on skills, these explanations missed the fact that new immigrants with few skills were being absorbed economically in larger and larger numbers in the cities of the Sunbelt and elsewhere. By positing a set of structural forces ostensibly indifferent to race, these explanations were unable to provide compelling accounts for the resulting inequalities that were often strongly linked to race and ethnicity.

In addition, past studies rarely, if ever, took account of the social processes and interactions among and between recent arrivals and more established ethnic and minority groups (Wilson 1996 and Waldinger 1996c, provide recent important exceptions). As a result, a slice of the complex dynamics necessary to understanding inequality in cities went unexplained. This important factor, when coupled with an altogether different economic restructuring process in Los Angeles (and other Sunbelt regions), leaves unexamined many significant aspects of inequality in major urban centers.

The individual chapters in this book share a concern with urban inequality and a reliance on data from the Los Angeles Study of Urban Inequality to understand the dynamics of opportunity in the modern urban metropolis. We do not advance, nor is our work organized around, a single theoretical model or perspective. Nonetheless, viewed in its totality, our collective research implies that urban inequality is still heavily racialized (Sanjek 1994; Bonilla-Silva 1996; Sears et al. 2000). By racialization we mean that social inequality and the dynamics that produce (and reproduce) it are clearly related to racial and ethnic group distinctions. To be sure, we recognize that outcomes such as employment probabilities or earnings or risk of poverty are complex and multiply determined. But the overarching thrust of our research reveals that members of different racial and ethnic groups often start out with different opportunities, resources, and obstacles, and end with unequal outcomes in the quest for social and economic well-being.

Enduring racial residential segregation is one of the main underpinnings of the racialization of inequality. For example, the form of concentrated ghetto poverty so often associated with Rustbelt central cities would not have emerged in the absence of persistent racial bias in the housing market (Massey and Denton 1993; Yinger 1995). Research reported in this volume strongly pinpoints a racial preference hierarchy that permeates how individuals think about and make neighborhood location choices in Los Angeles. The matter of where people live, or even consider living, as well as where they feel welcomed or threatened is still powerfully influenced by racial and ethnic considerations. Where individuals live often has a direct impact on employment opportunities, information networks, services and amenities, and a host of other quality-of-life indicators (such as school quality, exposure to poverty and neighborhood decay, exposure to hazardous waste, and risk of criminal victimization).

Another telling example is the role that immigrants play in understanding differential economic opportunities and other outcomes for native-born and other groups. The increasing importance of the role of nativity in better explaining inequality in cities like Los Angeles and other metropolises points to complex layers of interactions, labor market opportunities, housing patterns, and racial bias. In this volume, we explore in several chapters how foreign-born status interacts with the native-born in different labor market contexts, racial bias in the housing market, travel patterns, and local economies. Clearly, the role of immigration takes on added significance in the interplay among race, opportunity structure, and inequality in immigrant-concentrated Los Angeles and, we argue, in other cities experiencing increasing rates of newcomers.

The Los Angeles Study of Urban Inequality

At the center of this project is a survey of adults living in households in Los Angeles County.[1] This survey is part of a larger multidisciplinary project known as the Multi-City Study of Urban Inequality. This study, of which LASUI is the largest and most complicated part, is the brain-child of an interdisciplinary team of researchers (see Johnson, Oliver, and Bobo 1994 and Oliver, Johnson, and Bobo 1994). The project is designed to broaden our knowledge and understanding of how three sets of forces—changing labor market dynamics, racial attitudes and relations, and residential segregation—interact to foster modern urban inequality.

Others provide detailed examinations of the historical emergence of Los Angeles as a major industrial center, cultural influence, and multiracial metropolis (Davis 1990; Dear 1996; Laslett 1996; Soja and Scott 1996). It is not our purpose to rehearse this history here. Instead, our aim is to take Los Angeles as an important case for examining the present-day features of economic and social inequality.

The LASUI survey instrument involved a long period of development. Prior to fielding the survey, we conducted a series of twelve focus groups: four involving Latinos (two of which were conducted in Spanish and two in English), two with Korean Americans (both of which were conducted in Korean), two with Chinese Americans (both of which were conducted in Mandarin Chinese), two with African Americans, and two with whites (see Bobo et al. 1994 and 1995 for fuller discussion). On the basis of these focus group discussions, input from a national advisory panel composed of distinguished social scientists,[2] and extensive literature search and instrument pretesting, we developed the final survey instrument.

The subject matter of the questionnaire was broad-ranging, reflecting serious investment in understanding labor market processes, residential segregation, and intergroup attitudes and relations. First and foremost, we obtained detailed information on the demographic background and labor market experiences of each respondent. The LASUI contained a full complement of the usual indicators of socioeconomic status: measures of educational attainment, employment status, labor force participation, earnings, occupational status, and authority in the workplace. But a variety of more detailed measures were obtained to facilitate more fine-grained analysis of labor market circumstances and economic well-being, including:

- Assets and debts
- Mode of transportation to and from work
- Actual commute time
- Reservation commute (that is, maximum tolerable travel time)
- Reservation wage (that is, lowest acceptable wage)
- Job-training experiences
- Job-search behavior and locations for those having recently sought work.

The study also obtained detailed information on current place of employment, including size of firm, race of co-workers, race of supervisor, sex of supervisor, and information on benefits packages and promotion opportunities. Personal background information that might bear on labor market outcomes was also obtained. In this category were such factors as:

- Social network characteristics
- Welfare receipt while growing up
- Public housing residence while growing up
- Prison record.

Because a large fraction of the working-age population in Los Angeles is of immigrant background, we also obtained information on nativity status, citizenship or residency status, length of time in the United States, and mastery of English. On this basis, the LASUI is unusually well positioned to perform comparative analyses of the labor market experiences of the multiracial population.

Second, we obtained detailed information on how people think about issues of neighborhood and community. Respondents gave us information on their actual housing expenditures, as well as on their beliefs about the cost of housing in many different parts of the metropolitan area. They were asked about the desirability of different neighborhoods and about how residents in strategically selected communities would react to the prospect of greater racial and ethnic integration. An extensive battery of questions, modeled on the pioneering 1976 Detroit

Area Study and subsequent replications (Farley et al. 1978; Farley et al. 1993), examines preferences for residential integration. We also asked about the perceived consequences of integration. As a result, we can provide a broad-gauge assessment of the processes that serve to reinforce or to break down patterns of racial residential segregation.

Third, the survey contained a number of questions on racial attitudes. Among the central subjects were a basic sense of group affiliation and identity (Tate 1993; Dawson 1994). We examined a number of racial stereotypes using a bipolar trait-rating procedure developed in the 1990 General Social Survey (Bobo and Kluegel 1997; Smith 1991; T. C. Wilson 1996). There were also measures of perceived competition between groups (Bobo and Hutchings 1996) and measures of perceptions about the extent of racial discrimination and the causes of racial and ethnic inequality (Kluegel and Smith 1986; Sigelman and Welch 1991). In addition, the survey contained measures of attitudes on affirmative action and immigration.

The multiracial character of Los Angeles presented special opportunities and challenges. The survey was designed to exploit the multiracial character of Los Angeles in three significant ways. First, the sample was designed to include large numbers of respondents from each of the four major racial and ethnic groupings, with majority versus non-majority status in a census tract for white, black, Latino, and Asian respondents used as one of the basic stratifying criteria. Second, the questionnaire content reached well beyond the traditional black-white dichotomy. Many of the attitudinal questions were posed in separate and specific reference to whites, blacks, Latinos, and Asians. Third, where it would have been redundant or tedious to repeat the same set of questions for each different racial group, or in some cases in order to test specific hypotheses, survey-based experimental manipulations were employed (Schuman and Bobo 1988). For example, a randomly selected subset of respondents were asked questions on residential integration involving whites and Latinos, or whites and Asians, or whites and blacks, and so on. This made it possible to examine several different types of integrated living settings and permitted a direct experimental test of whether individuals react in a uniform or racially discriminatory manner.

As designed, we sampled non-Hispanic white, Hispanic, black, and Asian adults, twenty-one years of age or older, living in households.[3] Due to the cost of multiple-language translation and interview staffing, we restricted the Asian sample to those of Japanese, Chinese, and Korean ancestry. Even with this restriction, the survey covers three of the four largest Asian ancestry groups in the Los Angeles area. These groups capture, furthermore, analytically important cases. Japanese-ancestry

TABLE 1.1   *Sample Characteristics by Race and Ethnicity*

	Whites	Blacks	Asians	Latinos
Total N	863	1118	1056	988
Sex				
Female	55%	57%	53%	52%
Male	45	43	47	48
Nativity				
Foreign-born	16%	8%	89%	74%
Native-born	84	92	12	26
Mean age	45.0	41.7	44.1	37.1
Mean years education	14.0	12.8	13.4	9.8
Mean family income	$64,387	$ 40,875	$46,236	$ 28,725
Employment status[a]				
Full- or part-time	68%	67%	65%	66%
Unemployed	10	15	7	16
Not in labor force	22	19	27	18
Neighborhood poverty				
Low poverty	96%	58%	77%	57%
Moderate poverty	4	36	22	38
High poverty	<1	6	<1	5

Source: Los Angeles Study of Urban Inequality 1994.
[a]Only for those age sixty-four or younger.

Asians are largely native-born and more affluent (see tables 1.1 and 1.2). Both the Korean- and Chinese-ancestry respondents are heavily composed of recent immigrants, but each has come to occupy a very different economic and cultural niche in the Los Angeles area. To accommodate the diversity of Los Angeles, the survey was fielded in five languages: English, Spanish, Mandarin, Cantonese, and Korean.

Since a core concern of the project is economic inequality, especially issues of poverty and joblessness, the sample design stratified on income levels in addition to race and ethnicity. Thus, census tracts were classified as to whether 40 percent or more of the residents were below the poverty level, from 20 to 39 percent below the poverty level, or 19 percent or fewer below the poverty level.

The field period for the 1993 to 1994 LASUI lasted nearly twelve months. We completed a total of 4,025 interviews. This reflects an overall response rate of 68 percent, a nonresponse adjusted rate of 71 percent, and an overall cooperation rate (ratio of completed interviews to interviews plus refusals) of 73 percent. Interviews averaged just under ninety minutes in length, and respondents were offered a ten-dollar in-

TABLE 1.2   *Sample Characteristics by National Ancestry for Asian and Latino Respondents*

| | Asians | | | Latinos | | |
	China	Japan	Korea	Mexico	Central America	Other
Total N	415	207	403	728	169	91
Sex						
Female	51%	60%	55%	51%	56%	54%
Male	49	40	45	49	44	46
Nativity						
Foreign-born	95%	54%	99%	68%	98%	73%
Native-born	5	46	1	32	2	28
Mean age	45.5	40.8	44.3	37.0	35.9	40.3
Mean years education	13.0	14.9	12.7	9.6	9.3	13.0
Mean family income	$41,321	$74,061	$35,663	$29,999	$20,771	$33,314
Language of interview						
English	34%	100%	28%	40%	18%	55%
Other	66	—	72	60	82	45

Source: Los Angeles Study of Urban Inequality 1994.

centive for their participation. Table 1.1 provides descriptive information, within racial and ethnic group categories, for distributions by sex, nativity, age, education, family income, employment status, and neighborhood poverty status. Table 1.2 reports whether the interview was conducted in English or another language for our Asian and Latino respondents, broken down by national ancestry.

Since the questionnaire covered many sensitive racial and ethnic issues, we attempted to match the race of the respondent to that of the interviewer and did so in 78 percent of the cases. The appendix tables provide more complete details about the characteristics of communities mentioned in the questionnaire, the sample design, the subgroup response rates, and the comparison to census data for 1990.

Because of the uniqueness of several key variables, our sampling frame, and our ability to compare different racial-ethnic groups across Los Angeles's metropolitan expanse, LASUI allows us to undertake statistical analyses never before attempted. As a result, new insights and hypotheses are being explored that allow us to better understand the complex and deep contours of urban and economic inequality that not only affect Los Angeles, but other cities and regions throughout the United States.

Race and Inequality in Los Angeles

Los Angeles, the "City of Angels," founded in 1781, has come of age in many respects and emerged as a mature economic center. Metropolitan Los Angeles is one of the largest industrial regions in the world.[4] If it were a separate nation, it would rank seventh in economic output. Since the 1960s it has experienced large economic growth, including the expansion of industrial production, manufacturing, and international corporate finance.

Los Angeles covers a vast physical space. From the city's downtown hub, its northernmost region includes the San Fernando Valley over twenty-five miles away, and the boundaries of the county include a wider area still. To the west and south, where sun, surf, and palm trees are found in abundance, are the popular Santa Monica and Venice beaches leading southward to the Palos Verdes peninsula. Farther south is the city of Long Beach, a major seaport and home to recent arrivals from Southeast Asia, Mexico, and Central America, as well as to many working-class African Americans and middle- to upper-middle-class whites. Immediately south of downtown is the beginning of the city's historic black community, encompassing South Central, Compton, Watts, and Inglewood. Finally, immediately east of downtown and east beyond Montebello and into Pico Rivera is the largest barrio outside Mexico City (see map 1.1).

We call Los Angeles a "prismatic metropolis" because of its many colors, hues, and cultures. Los Angeles now reflects in substantial numbers an enormous range of racial and ethnic groups. As Roger Waldinger has put it: "Los Angeles is now profoundly, irremediably ethnic. The issue confronting the region is whether this newly polyglot metropolis can work. And that is not a question for the region alone. In Los Angeles, late twentieth century America finds a mirror to itself" (Waldinger 1996a, 447). It is also a social prism, capturing and refracting much of the diversity of the modern American experience. Generally, there has been a rapid increase in the number of truly multiethnic urban areas in the United States. According to William Frey and Reynolds Farley: "The combined minority populations—Latinos, Asians and blacks—increased nationally at seven times the rate of non-Latino whites" (1996, 35). Their analysis of 1990 U.S. census data identified thirty-seven "multiethnic metros," where at least two of three minority groups exceeded their percentage in the U.S. population as a whole. Another way of appreciating the rapidly changing racial and ethnic makeup of the population is to consider a "diversity index," which indicates the proportion of times two randomly selected individuals in the United States would differ by race and ethnicity. In 1970, that figure was .29. It

MAP 1.1   *Los Angeles County with Selected Communities Identified*

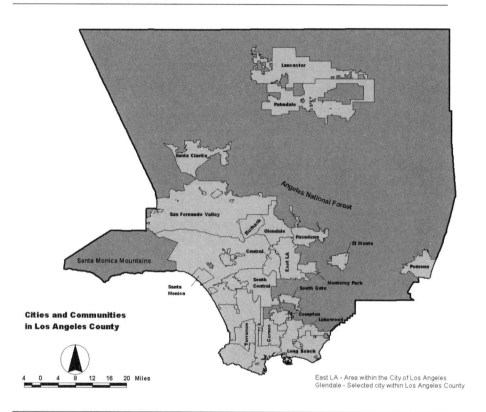

Source: 1990 U.S. Census STF3A.

rose to .35 in 1980 and to .40 in 1990. It is projected that this number will exceed .60 as early as 2020 and, furthermore, that by 2050 the U.S. population will be composed of roughly 50 percent those now classified as racial and ethnic minorities (all figures from Harrison and Bennett 1995, 142). Los Angeles is the quintessential multiethnic or prismatic metropolis. The diversification already accomplished there is spreading rapidly to other metropolitan areas and to other parts of the country.

Our account of the dynamics of inequality in Los Angeles focuses on four processes that prove to be important to the dynamics of social life in most large urban metropolitan areas: immigration and rapid population change; major economic transformations and widening inequality in life chances; persistent racial residential segregation; and persistent negative intergroup attitudes and beliefs. Although Los Angeles faces special challenges in each of these areas, this special character is more that of a bellwether than an exception to common patterns.

Immigration and Rapid Population Change

After the turn of the twentieth century and prior to the 1960s, immigration to Los Angeles mimicked that of the rest of the country but at a much smaller scale, with Europeans comprising the largest group of arrivals. Though Los Angeles has experienced continuous immigration from Mexico since its founding, Mexican immigration picked up after the Mexican revolution of 1910. The migration of Mexicans to the area was followed by declines of all immigrants at the onset of the Great Depression, until approximately 1965, when the National Origins Act was amended, allowing for easier immigration based on family reunification and other less stringent requirements. Those taking most advantage of this liberal policy were Asians and Latinos, the former bringing their families to join them after years of servitude and labor as coolies and war escapees, the latter as braceros bringing their families to settle permanently.[5] In 1970 there began a period of rapid immigration that continues today.

Indeed, a single year can do much to convey the scale of the changes being wrought by immigration. Table 1.3 shows immigration to California and Los Angeles during 1994. California was clearly the largest immigrant receiving state in the union with well over a quarter (26 percent) of all immigrants, followed by New York (18 percent) and Florida (7 percent). As a metropolitan area, Los Angeles ranks second to New York City in terms of the number of total immigrants who arrived in this region in 1994.[6] Los Angeles received thirty-seven percent of California's immigrant newcomers in 1994. The "prismatic metropolis" receives an heterogeneous mix of immigrants from all over the world, however, a few key sending countries stand out. It is not surprising, for example, that immigrants from Mexico constitute the largest number of arrivals of all immigrants, comprising one-quarter at the state level and one-fifth of new arrivals for the year in Los Angeles. Immigrants from Russia (10 percent), the Philippines (9.6 percent), China (8 percent), and El Salvador (7.7 percent) are also significant as a percentage of all newcomers to Los Angeles. These data however do not fully capture the magnitude of Los Angeles's immigration population. To do so requires a look at the unauthorized (illegal) immigrant population.

Table 1.4 presents data released from the INS detailing estimates of

TABLE 1.3   *Immigration to Los Angeles, 1994, by Selected Country of Birth and Area of Intended Residence*

	California	Los Angeles
All countries (total)	208,498	77,112
Canada	1,922	535
China Mainland	17,447	6,183
Colombia	665	316
Cuba	411	281
Dominican Republic	120	41
El Salvador	8,082	5,963
Germany	1,030	331
Guatemala	3,628	2,752
Guyana	141	60
Haiti	78	27
Hong Kong	3,359	1,067
India	7,085	1,339
Iran	6,302	3,723
Ireland	2,338	463
Jamaica	257	139
Japan	1,917	782
Korea	4,965	3,070
Mexico	52,088	15,605
Pakistan	1,389	347
Peru	1,619	661
Philippines	23,942	7,476
Poland	598	191
Soviet Union	14,542	7,710
Taiwan	4,862	2,342
Trinidad	147	79
United Kingdom	3,216	1,077
Vietnam	14,162	3,118
Other	32,186	11,228

Source: U.S. Immigration and Naturalization Service 1996, tables 17 and 19.

the undocumented immigrant population. According to the INS, about 3.4 million undocumented immigrants were residing in the United States in October 1992.[7] Two types of unauthorized immigrants exist. The most typical way of joining the illegal population is to obtain visas for temporary visits and stay beyond the authorized period of admission. This segment of the population constitutes roughly half of the illegal immigrant population residing in the United States. The second half are those that enter the country surreptitiously across land borders; these are referred to as EWIs (Entry Without Inspection). EWIs include persons from nearly every country, but a large majority are from Mexico; most of

TABLE 1.4   *Estimated Illegal Immigrant Population for Top Ten*
            Countries of Origin and Top Ten States of Residence,
            October 1992

Country of Origin	Population	State of Residence	Population
All countries	3,379,000	All states	3,379,000
Mexico	1,321,000	California	1,441,000
El Salvador	327,000	New York	449,000
Guatemala	129,000	Texas	357,000
Canada	97,000	Florida	322,000
Poland	91,000	Illinois	176,000
Philippines	90,000	New Jersey	116,000
Haiti	88,000	Arizona	57,000
Bahamas	71,000	Massachusetts	45,000
Nicaragua	68,000	Virginia	35,000
Italy	67,000	Washington	30,000

Source: U.S. Immigration and Naturalization Service 1996, table N.

the rest are from Central American countries (U.S. Immigration and Naturalization Service 1996).

By far, California received the largest share of unauthorized immigrants in 1992—well over 40 percent (43 percent). New York City follows Los Angeles with slightly more than 13 percent. The top five states with the largest number of unauthorized immigrants are the same as the top five states with the largest number of legal immigrants. Almost 40 percent of all unauthorized immigrants come from Mexico—no other country comes close to this figure. Included in the mix of unauthorized immigration are significant numbers from El Salvador, Canada, Poland, Philippines, and Italy. Using the percentage (37 percent) of all immigrants in Los Angeles relative to the state of California as a proxy, we estimate the number of unauthorized immigrants in Los Angeles as 532,947.

Perhaps what stands out the most about Los Angeles's population changes are not so much the rapidity as the transformation from a predominantly white European base to a majority people-of-color base. Of course, the pace and transformative character of this population change in part explains some of the unique contours of inequality described in this volume. At the very least, it provides us with a benchmark for thinking about massive and profound urban change in the face of an older (at least in terms of recency of arrival) African American, Mexican American, and white ethnic base. The implications of these changes for population characteristics, and economic outcomes are discussed in greater detail in chapter 2. Map 1.2 shows the racial and ethnic popula-

TABLE 1.5   *Percentage of Total Immigration Admitted by Metropolitan Area of Intended Residence, 1984 to 1997*

Year of Arrival	L.A. Metro[a]	New York	Chicago	Houston	Miami	Total (Top five cities)	Total Immigration
1984	11.4	16.9	4.1	1.4	2.1	35.9	543,903
1985	12.8	3.9	3.9	1.3	2.4	24.3	570,009
1987	12.9	16.2	3.4	1.9	6.3	40.7	601,516
1988	15.9	14.5	3.3	1.7	6.0	41.4	643,025
1989[b]	27.4	10.7	5.5	3.2	2.3	49.1	1,090,924
1990[b]	28.7	10.7	4.8	3.8	2.5	50.4	1,536,483
1991	17.3	8.9	3.3	2.9	3.2	35.7	1,827,167
1992	16.9	13.1	3.8	2.8	3.3	39.9	973,977
1993	14.6	14.2	4.9	2.5	3.4	39.6	904,292
1994	11.5	15.5	5.0	2.2	3.6	37.8	804,416
1995	10.1	15.5	4.4	2.0	4.3	36.3	720,461
1996	8.9	14.5	4.4	2.3	4.5	34.6	915,900
1997	10.1	13.5	4.4	2.2	5.7	35.9	796,378

Source: U.S. Immigration and Naturalization Service 1996.
[a]L.A. Metro includes the Los Angeles–Long Beach SMSA and Orange County.
[b]Part of what explains the large increase in immigration to Los Angeles in 1989 and 1990 is the large number of previously undocumented immigrants who became legalized through the Immigration Reform and Control Act of 1986. One of the act's provisions called for a general amnesty for those immigrants without documents who had been residing in the United States continuously prior to 1982.

tion distribution of Los Angeles County in 1990. It vividly captures the dramatic population change and distribution throughout the county, especially the rapid growth and spread of the Latino and Asian populations.

Economic Restructuring and Persistent Inequality

Over the past two and half decades, the gap between the economic haves and the have-nots in urban America has widened substantially (Phillips 1990; Michel 1991; Levy 1987; Burtless 1990; Harrison and Bluestone 1988). Recent studies have shown increasing polarization, especially in terms of employment prospects, earnings, and accumulated wealth (Michel 1991; Levy 1995; Harrison and Bluestone 1988; Oliver and Shapiro 1995). Other studies have drawn attention to the persistence of poverty and the increasing geographic isolation of the ghetto poor from mainstream American society (Wilson 1987; Jargowsky and Bane 1991; Mincy and Ricketts 1990; Jargowsky 1997). Here we discuss several measures of inequality for Los Angeles County.

Poverty has been more prevalently distributed in Los Angeles than in the United States as a whole. Table 1.6 provides poverty figures for

MAP 1.2   Distribution of Dominant Racial and Ethnic Groups in Los Angeles County

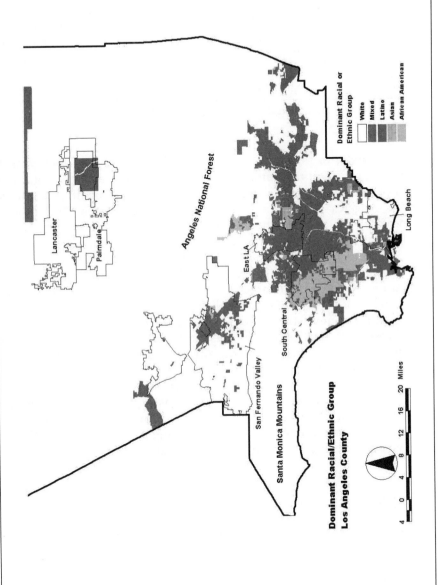

Source: 1990 U.S. Census STF3A.

TABLE 1.6   *Poverty in Los Angeles County and the United States*

| | Los Angeles County | | |
	Number of People in Poverty (All Ages)	Percentage	Percentage in the United States
1990	1,469,913	16.7	12.8
1993	2,164,629	23.8	15.1
1995	2,057,499	22.7	13.8

Source: United States Bureau of the Census, Current Population Survey.

the years prior to, during, and after the LASUI. During each year (1990, 1993, and 1995) the percentage figure that represents the total number of people in poverty relative to the nonpoor was significantly higher in Los Angeles than for the rest of the United States. This differential peaks in 1995, when the difference between the percent below poverty in Los Angeles and the rest of the United States is almost 9 points.

Table 1.7 provides perhaps the best-known measure of inequality: the gini coefficient or index. This widely used measure of income distribution—in which the larger the value, the greater the level of inequality (a value of 0 means no inequality and a value of 1 means extreme inequality)—shows that income inequality in Los Angeles increased between 1980 and 1990. This was especially true among Asians and Latinos and, to a lesser extent, African Americans. Whites also show greater inequality in Los Angeles County.

When analyzing salaried workers and incomes in Los Angeles County, we likewise see familiar patterns of growing inequality between different racial and ethnic groups. For example, Table 1.8 presents data on mean salary rates for workers during 1980 and 1990. Whites and Asians have higher mean salary rates than do African Americans and

TABLE 1.7   *Gini Index for Adults in Los Angeles County by Race (Income from All Sources)*

	1980	1990	Change
All	.544	.575	.031
White	.525	.536	.011
Black	.518	.524	.006
Latino	.541	.559	.017
Asian	.547	.573	.026

Source: 1980 and 1990 U.S. Census, 5 percent Public Use Microdata Samples.

TABLE 1.8   *Mean Salary for Workers in Los Angeles County by Year and Race*

	1980	1990	Change
All	21,857	24,258	2,401
White	24,822	31,017	6,195
Black	18,744	22,298	3,554
Latino	16,143	15,857	−286
Asian	20,549	23,354	2,805

Source: 1980 and 1990 U.S. Census, 5 percent Public Use Microdata Samples.

Latinos. Table 1.9 similarly presents data on mean income for adults in Los Angeles County. Once again, whites (not the case for Asians) have significantly higher mean income rates than do Asians, African Americans, and Latinos. Furthermore, the rate of change or growth between the two decennial periods (1980 and 1990) for Asians, African Americans, and Latinos is significantly lower than the rate of change for whites.

Two explanations of changing inequality highlight fundamental changes in the basic structure of the U.S. economy (Sassen 1990) and thus measures of inequality. These arguments hold that inequality is connected to the decline of central-city manufacturing employment and to the increasing polarization of the labor market into high-wage and low-wage sectors (Wilson 1987, 1996; Kasarda 1993). Accordingly, high rates of joblessness exist in central-city communities, especially among black males, in part as a consequence of the suburbanization of well-paying entry-level jobs (the spatial mismatch hypothesis) and in part due to the resulting gap between skills and types of employment opportunities available in central cities (on the skills mismatch hypothesis, see Kasarda 1989, 1992; Moore and Laramore 1990).

TABLE 1.9   *Mean Income from All Sources for Adults in Los Angeles County by Year and Race*

	1980	1990	Change
All	20,231	22,672	2,441
White	24,475	31,826	7,351
Black	15,607	18,576	2,969
Latino	13,174	13,126	−48
Asian	18,519	21,341	2,822

Source: 1980 and 1990 U.S. Census, 5 percent Public Use Microdata Samples.

The restructuring spin highlighted by Wilson (1987) and Kasarda (1993) is perhaps more readily applicable to Los Angeles than is the mismatch analysis. Goods-producing manufacturing in Los Angeles has been remarkably robust since World War II, and rivals historic growth periods in other regions of the United States (Scott 1996). At approximately the same time, Los Angeles began a downward spiral in the auto and auto-related branch plants and its aerospace and defense sectors, buffered to some extent by massive manufacturing growth. So, while the rest of the United States was reeling from manufacturing declines and horrendous Rustbelt-like economic conditions, Los Angeles was intensively manufacturing and only slightly headed toward becoming a Rustbelt.

The mismatch story also seems out of place in Los Angeles, where literally millions of low-skilled immigrants find jobs and consider the region a prime employment destination area. Roger Waldinger and Mehdi Bozorgmehr (1996) explain this theoretical contradiction by suggesting that "immigration is part of a fundamental process of urban economic restructuring, in which the growth of services breeds a demand for both high- and low-skilled labor while increasingly excluding workers with middle-level qualifications." (25) They further argue that by

> creating jobs for people with low skills, it also creates the demand for workers willing to work at low-status, low-paying jobs. While such low-wage jobs are increasingly found in the advanced services, the simultaneous proliferation of high-paid service workers adds further to the demand for immigrant workers. Once in place, the immigrants provide a cheap, easily managed labor force that can bolster the declining goods-producing sector and help revive sagging urban economies. (26)

As a result, unlike the mismatch explanation, this "immigrant restructured hypothesis" suggests that Los Angeles and other immigrant-rich regions retain and create many easy-entry jobs at the expense of creating better-paying and middle-skilled jobs, or jobs with well-developed internal labor markets.

Besides the typical industrial, manufacturing, and service type jobs found in Los Angeles, the area also boasts highly developed ethnic and immigrant employment niches spanning different occupations (such as domestics, gardeners, janitors, and restaurant workers). The growth of Los Angeles's ethnic economies has been profound. However, not all groups share in this growth equally. Perhaps even more daunting than the uneven participation rates is that these jobs tend to offer low wages, poor benefits packages, and few opportunities for upward mobility.

Racial Residential Segregation

Names of communities such as Harlem, South Chicago, East St. Louis, North Philadelphia, South Central Los Angeles, East Los Angeles, and Simi Valley are immediately and widely understood to have a particular racial and ethnic makeup. Terms such as Chinatown, Koreatown, or even Little Saigon remain in everyday parlance. Given the common-sense recognition of "racialized space," it is surprising that so much of the literature on economic restructuring and the dynamics of inequality ignored or downplayed the fact of racial residential segregation (Fainstein 1993). Indeed, both the hypothesis of the structural transformation of the economy and that of the culture of poverty came under sharp criticism for ignoring a central factor in modern urban inequality: patterns of racial residential segregation (Galster and Keeney 1988; Fainstein and Fainstein 1989; Massey and Denton 1993). According to this view, whites' unwillingness to share residential space with blacks and, to a lesser degree, with other minorities locks minorities into inner-city communities that are isolated from mainstream avenues of social and economic mobility (Massey and Denton 1993; Bickford and Massey 1991).

Three facts about racial residential segregation stand out. First, it can be quite extreme, as has long been the case for African Americans. Nationally, the black-white index of dissimilarity or segregation score stood at .69 in 1990, down only slightly from the 1980 figure of .74. This means that more than two-thirds of African Americans would have to change their current place of residence to accomplish a random distribution without regard to race. The comparable figure for Los Angeles in 1990 was .73, slightly above the national average. There is considerable variability depending upon the groups compared. Thus, the Hispanic–non-Hispanic-white segregation score was .50 nationally in 1990, and .61 in Los Angeles. The Asian-white figures were .41 and .46 nationally and in Los Angeles, respectively. One recent assessment of segregation patterns in the Los Angeles metropolitan area noted three important patterns: segregation tended to be higher and change less in Los Angeles County compared to Riverside, San Bernardino, Orange, and Ventura counties; the number of diverse neighborhoods was increasing substantially, but much of this involved black, Latino, and Asian mixtures, as opposed to extensive mixing with whites; and the level of Hispanic segregation was rising and threatening to create a "mega-barrio" (Clark 1996).

Second, where people live can have important effects on economic opportunities and overall quality-of-life experience. Neighborhoods vary tremendously in quality of services, amenities, and level of exposure to unwanted social conditions such as crime, severe unemployment and poverty, and failing schools (Bickford and Massey 1991; Massey, Condran, and Denton 1987; Massey and Fong 1990). Indeed, Douglas Massey and Nancy Denton (1993) make the powerful argument that economic restructuring and racial segregation interact in ways that can sharply increase the magnitude of economic dislocations and social ills associated with them. Furthermore, to the extent that minorities face racial discrimination and other constraints in the housing market, they are less likely to have ready access to areas rich in employment opportunities and less likely to form personal ties to individuals who can link them to important economic opportunities. Segregative processes in the housing market also lower the value of the homes minority individuals own, negatively affect the terms of mortgages and others loans they may obtain, and drive up the cost of insurance. All these factors play a part in undermining the accumulation of assets and wealth by African Americans and other racial minorities (Oliver and Shapiro 1995).

Third, although a complex array of factors, including economic resources and personal taste, seems to contribute to racial residential segregation, there is growing evidence that racial discrimination and prejudice are key elements in its perpetuation (Massey and Denton 1993; Yinger 1995). A number of auditing studies established that blacks and Latinos are likely to encounter considerably different treatment than whites in dealings with realtors, landlords, and homeowners (Yinger 1995). The forms of discrimination include: being shown fewer units; being lied to about the availability of units; being steered to particular neighborhoods or sites; being told discouraging things about a neighborhood, house, or apartment unit; and being offered less favorable terms. There is growing evidence of racial discrimination in access to home mortgage loans as well (Jackson 1995; Myers and Chan 1995).

Tension and Negative Intergroup Attitudes

Beneath the readily observable facts of changing demographic composition, economic restructuring, and residential segregation lie questions about the state of interethnic attitudes, identities, and tensions. It is one matter for a community to experience rapid immigration and economic dislocation in an environment of little or no segregation by race and ethnicity and a generally positive climate of interethnic attitudes. While there may be some friction and even conflict among groups, under such a scenario one should not see deep fissures of animosity and conflict emerge. It is an altogether different matter for a community to undergo major demographic and economic upheaval in a context of segregation, well-defined racial and ethnic identities, and interethnic attitudes characterized by mutual suspicion and hostility. This scenario opens the door to intense and sustained conflict and tension. Many suspect that Los Angeles tends toward the latter end of the continuum.

There are five aspects of the dynamics of interethnic attitudes that have immediate bearing on the dynamics of modern urban inequality. First, there is accumulating evidence that negative stereotypes about racial minorities remain widespread, particularly with regard to African Americans and Latinos (Smith 1991). Evidence on the persistence of negative stereotypes about African Americans has been found in laboratory experiments and college student samples (Devine and Elliot 1995), in ethnographic community studies (Anderson 1990), as well as in traditional large-scale surveys (Smith 1991; Sniderman and Piazza 1993; Bobo and Kluegel 1997). For example, data from the 1990 General Social Survey showed that better than 70 percent of whites perceived both blacks and Hispanics as more likely to "prefer living on welfare," that well over 60 percent perceived blacks and Hispanics as "tending to be lazy," and better than 50 percent rated blacks and Hispanics as less intelligent than whites. Whites' perceptions of Asians, while closer to their ratings of whites as a group, also tended to be negative, though not by the margins observed for blacks and Hispanics. Concerning our broad themes of inequality, Lawrence Bobo and James Kluegel's analysis of the 1990 GSS data found that whites' "negative ratings are most evident in the cases of traits related to work and socioeconomic success" (1997, 101).

To be sure, whites' attitudes toward African Americans have improved, especially with regard to support for broad goals of equality and equal treatment (Schuman et al. 1997). There has, likewise, been an increase in whites' openness to residential integration with blacks (Farley et al. 1993; Schuman et al. 1997). It should also be noted that even though stereotypes remain widespread, they are typically expressed with greater qualification now than in the past and, furthermore, tend to reflect cultural rather than biological assumptions about the nature of group differences (Jackman 1994). In addition, a major survey conducted by the National Conference of Christians and Jews suggested that blacks, Latinos, and Asians often hold negative stereotypes of one another (Smith 1998).

Second, there are often sharp differences in how the problems of racial inequality and discrimination are perceived (Jaynes and Williams 1989; Sigelman and Welch 1991; Hochschild 1995). Partly as a consequence, there is often racial and ethnic polarization concerning the types of social policies that individuals perceive as most appropriate to combat inequality, discrimination, and segregation. For example, results from the 1992 Detroit Area Study show that blacks are consistently more likely than whites to see racially discriminatory barriers in the housing market. In particular, African Americans were substantially more likely to see institutional actors, such as realtors and mortgage companies, as systematically discriminating (Farley et al. 1993). There is also evidence that Latinos and, to a lesser degree, Asians are inclined to understand racial and ethnic inequality in more structural terms than do whites (Hunt 1996).

Third, given the presence of well-rooted racial and ethnic identities (Dawson 1994; Espiritu 1992), negative stereotyping, and very different ways of understanding racial inequality, there is ample grounds to find that such attitudes influence broader community functioning and interaction (particularly under conditions of rapid social change). The clearest example involves the Los Angeles uprisings of 1992. Those riots were tied to tensions among racial minorities, tensions linked to a confluence of segregation, rapid population change, and economic restructuring (Johnson et al. 1992; Johnson and Farrell 1993). The deleterious effects of economic and demographic restructuring together with newly emerging housing market constraints have created a situation in which disadvantaged blacks and newly arrived immigrants are often forced to compete for scarce economic and social goods. The poorest of the newly arriving immigrant groups, particularly those entering the United States illegally, are affected by the same forces as blacks, but in different ways. Economic restructuring creates jobs for immigrant minorities, who become exploited workers in rapidly growing competitive sector industries. Working in unsafe and unregulated workplaces, making subminimum and minimum wages, these immigrants are forced to reside in some of the cheapest and most deteriorating sections of the Los Angeles metropolitan area—most of them formerly all-black communities. Since the late 1960s, for example, there has been a major influx of Spanish-speaking immigrants into the formerly all-black south central areas of Los Angeles (Oliver and Johnson 1984). Unable to find housing in the established East Los Angeles barrio, by 1970 approximately 50,000 Latinos had settled in the city's largest black ghetto, accounting for nearly 10 percent of the area's total population. During the 1970s, the number of Hispanics settling in the area doubled, totaling over 100,000, or nearly 21 percent of the population by decade's end (Johnson and Oliver 1989; see map 1.3).

At the same time that blacks have increasingly come to share residential space with newly arriving immigrants, they have also had to contend with the growth and spread of immigrant entrepreneurial activities. Rather than entering the primary or secondary labor markets, many newly arriving immigrants, particularly those from Korea, have elected to go into business for themselves.

These developments set the stage for considerable conflict and competition among people of color over jobs, housing, and such publicly provided resources as education, health, social welfare, and protective services (Johnson and Oliver 1989). Until recently, the occurrence of interethnic minority conflict had been limited to isolated incidents involving hostile verbal exchanges and group-based protests and boycotts against newly arriving Korean entrepreneurs. In the 1990s, however, interethnic minority conflict became more violent.

In addition to interethnic conflict, crimes of hate have also emerged as a major problem accompanying Los Angeles's transition to the status of prismatic metropolis. Hate crimes have been so prevalent in the Los Angeles metropolitan area that both the Los Angeles County Sheriff's Department and the Los Angeles City Police Department now systematically record statistics on the incidence of racially, ethnically, or religiously motivated crimes. Between 1985 and 1987, according to the Los Angeles Commission on Human Relations, there were 431 documented cases of such crimes—a 13 percent increase over the 1980 to 1984 period. The 1996 report documented a figure more than double the 1987 rate, with 995 officially classified hate crimes in the Los Angeles County area. This number reflects a 50 percent rise in the number of hate crimes directed at African Americans in just one year, from 196 in 1995 to 295 in 1996. (It should be noted that these data probably do not reflect the actual magnitude of the problem in Los Angeles, as it is likely that many such crimes, especially those perpetrated against new and undocumented immigrants, go unreported.)

There is suggestive evidence that these trends are profoundly reshaping how blacks, Latinos, and whites orient themselves toward one another. Neighborhood change is one of the central areas of conflict. Reacting to the growing influx of Hispanic immigrants, the president of a black homeowners' association complained that: "it's a different culture, a different breed of people. They don't have the same values. You can't get together with them. It's like mixing oil and water" (Frank Clifford, "Tension Among Minorities Upsets Old Rules of Politics," *Los Angeles Times*, August 11, 1991, p. A1). After a fire apparently set by angry drug dealers killed five Latinos in a public housing project, some in the Latino community raised the possibility of separating blacks and Latinos into different areas. As one Latina resident of the complex put it: "They're [the blacks] going to think we're racists. But we never do anything to defend ourselves . . . there's so few of us here. Maybe we would be better apart" ("Segregated Housing Sought at Jordan Downs," *Los Angeles Times*, September 10, 1991, p. B1).

Economic competition is also a concern. For example, Latinos in the city of Compton complain that the black-controlled local govern-

MAP 1.3   *Changing Dominant Ethnic Group in South Central Los Angeles*

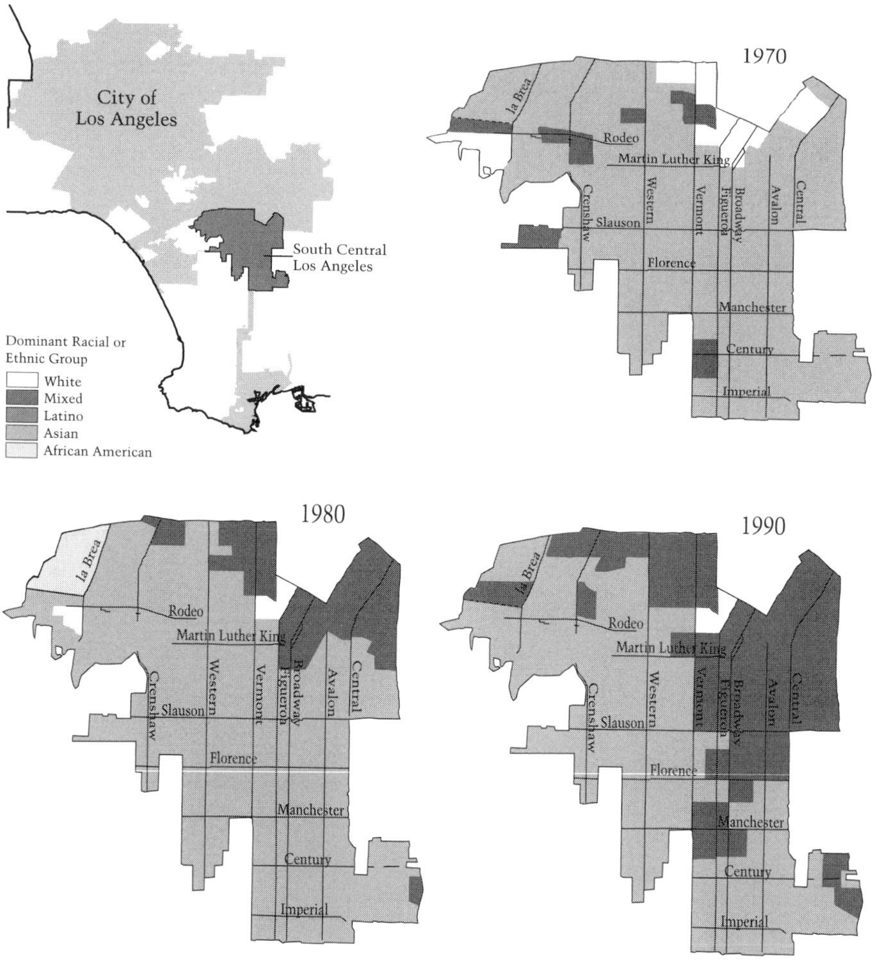

Source: U.S. Census 1970, 1980, 1990.

ment does nothing toward affirmative action for Latinos, despite tremendous growth in the proportion of Hispanics ("Latino Aspirations on Rise in Compton," *Los Angeles Times*, May 7, 1991, p. B1). There is also significant tension between blacks and Latinos over service delivery and especially employment at the Martin Luther King/Drew Medical Center in South Central Los Angeles. In the wake of the uprisings in Los Angeles and the initial wave of rebuilding efforts, significant tension flared between black residents and activists in South Central and the often overwhelmingly Latino work crews brought in to do the work.

There are also instances of conflict within groups. For example, many established Latino and Asian residents are troubled by the steady inflow of new immigrants. This conflict is often most evident among youngsters. As one reporter saw it: "The U.S.-born Latinos call the Mexican kids '*quebradita* people' because of their banda music and *quebradita* dances. They make fun of the immigrants' 'nerdy' Mickey Mouse–adorned backpacks and have even coined a term for them: 'Wetpacks'" ("The Great Divide," *Los Angeles Times*, November 11, 1995, p. E1). These types of underlying tensions no doubt played a part in the number of both Asians and Latinos who voted in favor of Proposition 187, which sought to make undocumented people ineligible for access to the public schools and to all but emergency medical care.

Fourth, interethnic attitudes and tensions influence the dynamics of both the labor market and the housing market. In-depth interviews with employers seeking to fill low-skill entry-level positions suggest that they often hold very negative stereotypical images of blacks, especially of young black men (Waldinger 1996b; W. J. Wilson 1996). In one early report, Joleen Kirschenman and Kathryn Neckerman (1990) conducted interviews with 185 employers representative of firms in Chicago and the surrounding Cook County area. Although their results were intermixed with ideas about the inner city versus the suburbs, and about class differences in values and behavior, they found powerful evidence that racial stereotyping informed employer preferences and decisions: "Chicago's employers did not hesitate to generalize about race or ethnic differences in the quality of the labor force. Most associated negative images with inner-city workers, and particularly with black men. 'Black' and 'inner city' were inextricably linked, and both were linked with 'lower class'" (230–31). These sorts of stereotypes do not merely operate at the low-skill end of the economic spectrum. Joe Feagin and Melvin Sikes (1994) conducted interviews with 209 middle-class African Americans. Their respondents reported frequent encounters with whites who held low expectations and/or behaved toward them in a discriminatory manner in the workplace, apparently, at least in part, as a result of negative stereotypes held about African Americans.

Stereotypes also matter for processes of racial residential segregation. Analyses of the 1992 DAS showed that whites' negative stereotypes about African Americans were strong predictors of willingness to live in integrated areas (Farley et al. 1994). Data from the 1992 Los Angeles County Social Survey, likewise, showed that negative stereotypes tended to decrease whites' openness to residential integration not just in the case of potential black neighbors, but also in the case of potential Latino or Asian neighbors (Bobo and Zubrinsky 1996). Both the DAS and LACSS results underscore that perceptions of differences in class standing and resources were far less important than negative racial stereotypes themselves in predicting whites' willingness to live in integrated areas.

Overview of the Volume

We have organized the research reported in this volume into three major components. In the first substantive component we address the "Foundations of a Prismatic Metropolis." Chapters 2 and 3 map the basic contours of population composition, racial and ethnic inequality, and intergroup attitudes. Taken together, these chapters make it clear that basic chances in life still vary substantially according to one's race, nativity, gender, and residential location and that most people definitely possess clear cognitive and socioemotional maps of Los Angeles that attend to racial group distinctions.

The second substantive section examines in greater depth the processes whereby economic opportunity and other life circumstances are divided along lines of race, ethnicity, and gender. Among the major questions addressed are: Is racial residential segregation in the process of breaking down or is it a self-reproducing social phenomenon? Do prejudice and discrimination play a major role in sustaining segregation, or are economic factors more important? Do black, white, Latino, and Asian men obtain employment and earnings through the same mechanisms? What is the role of social networks in obtaining employment and wages? How consequential is immigrant status for economic outcomes? Does it really benefit immigrants to work in the ethnic economic enclave? Chapter 4 carefully examines costs, perceptions, preferences, and prejudice as possible factors in the process of racial residential segregation. The analysis shows the centrality of race and racial prejudice in keeping racial minorities, especially the African American community, in segregated living conditions.

Chapter 5 focuses on labor force participation and joblessness among poorly educated white, black, Latino, and Asian men. Holding constant an array of individual labor market characteristics and contextual factors such as neighborhood poverty, the authors find that black men are unusually vulnerable to long-term joblessness. Their results run strongly against the idea that all low-skilled workers suffer equally in the restructured economy.

Two of the chapters tackle labor market circumstances. Chapter 6 examines earnings for Latinos and Latinas, with special attention on length of time in the United States and native versus foreign-born status. Chapter 7 examines the widely discussed hypothesis that ethnic economies provide "protective niches" for newcomers. Although the author does find significant participation by Latinos and Asians in ethnic economic niches, she also finds that employment in the ethnic enclave consists heavily of menial jobs in food and personal services, retail trade, and nondurable manufacturing. These jobs tend to offer low wages, poor benefits packages (if any), and little opportunity for training and promotion.

Chapter 8 looks at the labor market experiences of African Americans. The results show that African American men encounter disproportionately large employment and earnings penalties for low educational attainment and for having a criminal record. Having a dense social network facilitates higher rates of labor force participation and earnings for black men.

The economic and labor market experiences of racial and ethnic groups intersect with at least two other considerations: the dynamics of gender and issues of transportation to and from work. One of the principal ways that the labor market experiences of women tend to differ from that of men is the traditionally greater obligation for child care that falls to women. In a rigorous analysis, chapter 9 examines the impact of child-care constraints on women's labor force participation and poverty status. The increase in poverty risk as a result of child-care constraints is greatest for African American and immigrant Latina mothers. Chapter 10 examines the impact of social networks among women on employment prospects. The authors show that among black, Latina, and white women, having "bridging social capital" is more important than various forms of cultural capital.

One of the key questions that LASUI was designed to address is whether the spatial distance from employment opportunities is an important element in modern urban inequality. The economist John Kain (1968) argued that job opportunities, especially for low-skill but well-paying work, were shifting from traditional city core to suburban (or even ex-urban) locations. As a consequence, there was a growing mismatch between the skill levels of many minority inner-city residents and the available mix of jobs. Indeed, Wilson (1987) traced the rising level of black male joblessness, in part, to just this sort of industrial deconcentration. Although the subject of controversy and dispute, reviews of a wide body of evidence provide reasonably consistent support for the spatial mismatch hypothesis (Kain 1992). For example, Kasarda and Ting (1996) analyzed data on sixty-seven large cities, showing that the distance from jobs does increase joblessness, especially for African American men, and for women generally.

Two chapters examine how issues of race and gender intersect with transportation to and from work. Chapter 11 examines racial and ethnic group differences in commuting times and distances. The results partly run counter to the expectations of the spatial mismatch argument: minority workers tend to have shorter or equivalent commute distance, though they may take more commute time due to mode of transportation and need to travel particularly congested routes. The author also finds some evidence that it is racial discrimination or concern over the possibility of it that constrains the radius of job search. Chapter 12 examines the relationship between commute time and earnings, focusing special attention on the issue of whether women of color face "multiple jeopardy" in their journey to work. The results suggest that low-skill women may pay a "commute penalty": the longer the commute, the less the payoff. The author also finds that regardless of gender, African Americans commute more for less.

The third and final section examines in detail the interplay of group identity, attitudes, and the dynamics of workplace interaction and broader social relations. Among the key questions addressed are: Will negative racial stereotypes be carried into the workplace? Do racial and ethnic minorities perceive that they encounter discrimination in the workplace? Do women of color report more discrimination on the basis of race and ethnicity or on the basis of gender? Chapter 13 examines the racial attitudes of those with power in the workplace and finds that those who own businesses or who exert supervisory power are no more (or less) likely to hold negative stereotypes of blacks than are those who lack ownership or supervisory status. Chapter 14 investigates the LASUI questions concerned with subjective reports of discrimination in the workplace. Chapter 15 focuses on the intersection of subjective reports of racial and sexual discrimination among women. The author finds that the extent of reporting of racial and gender discrimination depends on racial background, with African American women most likely to report facing discrimination based on their racial group and gender. Both chapters underscore the significance of race and the complexity of interpreting behavior.

Conclusion

Our assessment of the research presented in this book points to a powerful and complicated nexus among the forces of economic restructuring, residential segregation, group relations, population change, and patterns of community and individual adaptation. These findings reflect a racialization in the way social and economic inequality is experienced (Gans 1999). Low wages and poor employment prospects continue to exist for those of limited skills and education, particularly immigrants and African Americans. Women, especially those from minority groups and with low skill levels, continue to confront barriers to the labor market, including the lack of affordable and dependable day care. Labor markets, despite the diversity of the workforce, remain profoundly segregated by race, gender, and immigration status.

The persistence of racial residential segregation deepens the overlap between economic disadvantage and race and ethnicity by serving to concentrate high rates of poverty and unemployment in communities of color. Racial residential segregation, in turn, is reinforced by group identities and negative racial attitudes—which are made harder to transform in a positive way while groups remain economically unequal and residentially separated. Such conditions provide both the kernel of truth and the motivation to sustain mutual suspicion and hostility.

Our first and more general conclusion is that despite the accomplishments of a variety of War on Poverty and Great Society programs and a generally expanding economy, both poverty in general and economic disadvantage in some segments of the population remain severe problems in Los Angeles. If we as a nation hope to ensure rising standards of living and greater equality, there is still enormous work that needs to be done.

To be sure, the percentage of residents in Los Angeles at or below the federally set poverty level of $16,534 (family of four) has fallen from a high of 23 percent in 1995 to the current 19 percent. Even with this decline in poverty as the economy improved, nearly 2 million Angelenos lived below the poverty level, with another 1.5 million just above the line. Perhaps most daunting is that this figure remains higher than the 16.7 percent level in 1990 at the beginning of California's economic downturn. The poor, especially the working poor, have lost ground, both in relative terms to other income groups and in absolute terms because of faster rises in the cost of living. Minimum-wage workers have seen their income remain stagnant over the past two years. Meanwhile, rents have increased at an average 6 percent a year, and the supply of affordable units has virtually disappeared. Wages for the lowest 10 percent of California wage earners have fallen steadily over the last thirty years, down 35 percent in real terms. The gap between the top 10 percent and bottom 10 percent of California wage earners has widened: in 1967, the wage ratio was about 5 to 1, it's almost 10 to 1 today. The percentage of Los Angeles households paying more than 35 percent of their income for rent—the threshold for affordable housing—has risen from 28 percent in 1970 to 41 percent today.

Second, economic hardship clearly has a strong racial and ethnic dimension, with segments of the African American and Latino communities bearing a heavily disproportionate burden of labor force nonparticipation, unemployment, poverty, and restricted life chances. For many blacks, especially black men, the central problem is joblessness. There are strong reasons to believe that this is fundamentally a racialized process, not merely a story of skill levels, or of values and group culture, or of proximity to employment opportunities. For many Latinos, economic disadvantage takes the form of low wages and constrained mobility prospects. However, we would be remiss if we were not to acknowledge that for many Latinos, discrimination in schools, housing opportunities, and work prospects, while not as pernicious as for African Americans, continues to constrain life opportunities. Again, these are racially and ethnically channeled experiences, not merely functions of other individual or contextual processes.

Our research suggests that both deep structural conditions and cultural-social psychological factors play an important part in sustaining a highly racialized urban environment. The structural factors are principally labor market privilege, racial residential segregation, and vast inequalities in accumulated wealth. The cultural and social psychological factors include widespread negative stereotyping of racial minorities and the behaviors of avoidance and discrimination they encourage. Thus, decades after the passage of the Civil Rights Act of 1964, the Voting Rights Act of 1965, the Immigration Act Amendments (Hart-Celler) of 1965, and the Fair Housing Act of 1968, our society continues to be riven by a historical legacy of deep racism, spasms of nativism, and the current condition of persistent racial and ethnic inequality in life chances.

Third, the economic fortunes of men continue to outstrip those of women. While we find women making inroads into all occupations, women of color remain primarily concentrated in poorly paid and low-skill work. This becomes even more profound among recent immigrant Latinas and Asians as they undertake roles as nannies, day care providers, housecleaners, manicurists and masseuses, and seamstresses.

Fourth, there is enormous variation in the conditions and trajectories facing members of different immigrant groups. For every high-skilled Iranian or Indian immigrant in Los Angeles, twenty-five Mexican, four Salvadorian, and three Filipino low-skill newcomers exist. Los Angeles businessmen seek out high-skill Asian immigrant engineers with zeal and then go home and hire, for mere pennies, low-skill immigrant Guatemalan or Oaxacan day laborers to work on a home repair or landscape project.

Los Angeles is a vast and complex megalopolis. For some, it can be a place of privilege and great opportunity. For others, it can be a place of disadvantage and constant struggle. Race continues to be an important dividing line. "To address these fundamental issues," Melvin Oliver and Thomas Shapiro argue, "to rejuvenate America's commitment to racial justice, we must first acknowledge the real nature of racial inequality in this country" (1995, 193). Our goal is to bring the nature of modern urban inequality into crisp descriptive and analytical focus. We do so by examining the interplay of labor market conditions, neighborhood and community makeup, and intergroup attitudes and beliefs in the prismatic metropolis of Los Angeles. We hope that this deepening of our knowledge and broadening of perspective moves us, collectively, further along the road toward social justice.

We wish to thank Camille Z. Charles, David M. Grant, and Devon Johnson for their comments and assistance with earlier versions of this chapter. The authors, of course, are responsible for any remaining errors or shortcomings. This research was party supported by NSF grant SBR9515183.

Appendix

TABLE 1A.1   *Final Disposition of Los Angeles Study of Urban Inequality Sample*

	JLo	KLo	KM	ChLo	ChM	BLo	BM
c NHW comp	46	29	7	141	1	27	7
c Hisp comp	28	1	48	60	17	34	43
c Black comp	2	1	54	3	2	285	300
c Asian comp	53	131	152	422	114	2	0
nr final refusal R	157	57	39	220	21	77	72
nr final refusal P	7	5	2	33	3	5	9
nr R not home	6	4	2	16	0	1	0
m not home	1	1	11	27	1	12	7
m no access	9	4	20	30	4	6	2
m screen refusal	8	11	8	66	12	44	24
ne R incapable	10	5	5	19	6	7	18
ne language barrier	1	3	5	6	2	0	0
ne vacant	39	82	107	104	21	34	42
ne not HU	42	3	6	8	12	0	6
ne n-elg all < twenty-one	0	0	1	9	1	1	1
nen-elg > twenty	639	404	507	1507	135	9	68
Total	1148	741	974	2671	352	544	599
Raw response rate	0.55	0.66	0.76	0.61	0.77	0.71	0.75
Adjusted response rate	0.56	0.70	0.82	0.67	0.81	0.71	0.77

J = Japanese K = Korean C = Chinese B = black H = Hispanic W = white
HU = housing unit R = respondent P = proxy Lo = Census tract < 20 percent
below poverty, M = Census tract $\geq$ 20 percent below poverty but $\leq$ 39 percent
below poverty, Hi = Census tract $\geq$ 40 percent below poverty
c = complete, nr = non-response, ne = not eligible, m = mixed nr and ne
Raw Response Rate = c/(c + nr + m)
Adjusted Response Rate = c/(c + nr + m(1-ne/(c + nr + ne)))

Source: Los Angeles Study of Urban Inequality 1994.
Note: The "adjusted response rate" assumes that some respondents in certain non-response categories (that is nobody home, no access, and screen refusal) would have been ineligible; appropriate adjustments are made based on stratum data.

TABLE 1A.1   *Continued*

BHi	HLo	HM	HHi	Wlo	WM	Mlo	MM	MHi	Total
9	23	9	15	346	52	69	65	14	860
9	72	223	252	58	7	101	35	7	995
180	0	6	47	27	12	29	83	86	1117
2	4	4	4	22	5	4	23	11	1053
22	25	26	21	137	17	43	35	8	977
0	1	7	4	5	0	3	3	1	88
0	1	0	0	9	1	0	0	0	40
5	1	0	2	19	2	1	1	0	91
5	1	1	10	27	11	3	18	0	151
13	34	32	23	97	24	76	31	9	513
4	5	6	7	26	7	5	6	4	140
0	5	3	0	13	18	1	25	0	82
43	13	33	77	99	23	65	60	10	852
1	0	4	15	5	7	1	6	11	127
4	0	1	5	2	0	0	0	0	25
108	15	19	10	60	32	41	223	50	3827
405	200	374	492	952	219	442	614	211	10938
0.82	0.61	0.79	0.84	0.61	0.58	0.62	0.70	0.87	0.68
0.85	0.64	0.80	0.86	0.63	0.66	0.67	0.77	0.89	0.73

TABLE 1A.2 *LASUI Sample and 1990 Census Data for Selected Demographic Characteristics*

Race-Ethnicity	LASUI Unweighted	LASUI Weighted	L.A. County Eligibles	L.A. County
Group				
White	21.4%	43.2%	49.4%	47.0%
Black	27.8	11.0	10.9	10.3
Asian	26.2	7.7	6.5	6.2
Latino	24.5	38.1	33.2	31.5
Other	—	—	—	5.0
Total	4,025	3,133	5,787,991	6,090,712
Age Group				
Twenty-one to thirty	24.6	27.7	28.3	28.2
Thirty-one to forty	27.6	26.5	25.1	25.3
Forty-one to fifty	19.9	20.1	16.7	16.9
Fifty-one to sixty	10.9	12.2	11.5	11.5
Sixty-one to seventy	9.1	8.1	9.8	9.7
Seventy-one to eighty	6.0	4.5	5.9	5.8
Eighty-one and over	1.8	0.9	2.7	2.6
Total	4,020	3,131	5,787,991	6,090,712
Sex				
Men	43.9	46.1	49.1	49.0
Women	56.1	53.9	50.9	51.0
Total	4,025	3,133	5,787,991	6,090,712
Nativity				
Native-born	53.2	57.4	64.3	62.0
Foreign-born	46.8	42.6	35.7	38.0
Total	4,017	3,126	5,787,991	6,090,712
Educational attainment				
Less than high school	25.6	23.7	30.7	30.2
H.S. grad, GED	26.1	24.5	21.3	21.0
H.S. + some college	11.1	12.4	20.5	20.4

Source: Los Angeles Study of Urban Inequality.

TABLE 1A.2   *Continued*

	Race-Ethnicity			
Assoc. degree	15.0	15.5	7.2	7.3
B.A.	16.5	17.0	13.2	13.9
Ph.D., M.A., Prof.	5.6	6.9	7.1	7.1
Total	4,022	3,133	5,787,991	6,090,712
Occupation				
Managerial, professional, specialist	25.8	29.9	27.4	27.4
Technical, sales, support	31.5	28.9	31.3	31.7
Service	17.7	15.2	12.4	12.3
Farm, forest, fish	0.9	0.9	1.3	1.2
Craft, repair	9.0	10.0	11.4	11.3
Operators, fabricators, laborers	15.2	15.1	16.2	15.9
Military	0	0	0.1	0.1
Total	2,990	2,569	4,563,593	4,806,492

TABLE 1A.3 *Characteristics of Housing Market Areas*

City	Total Population	Median Housing Value	Percentage Owner Occupied	Percentage White	Percentage Black	Percentage Latino	Percentage Asian-Pacific Islander
Alhambra	82,106	227,900	41	25	2	36	38
Baldwin Hills	15,254	224,600	59	21	59	12	8
Canoga Park	105,601	257,600	74	69	2	19	9
Culver City	38,793	329,400	56	58	10	19	12
Glendale	180,038	341,700	39	65	1	20	14
Palmdale	68,917	150,150	70	67	6	22	4
Pico Rivera	59,177	163,800	70	13	0.4	83	3
L.A. County	8,863,164	223,800	48	41	11	37	10

Source: 1990 U.S. Bureau of the Census, Census of Population and Housing, file STF3A.
Note: The median housing value, based on table H61A, is reported for owner-occupied housing units in each of the seven areas listed above. Baldwin Hills and Canoga Park are not incorporated areas, but neighborhoods within the City of Los Angeles. The median housing value reported above for these areas is the weighted average of the median housing value for each census tract in that neighborhood (weighted by the number of owner-occupied housing units in the tract).

TABLE 1A.4   *LASUI Sample and 1990 Census Data for*
Demographic Characteristics by Race

Panel A: Non-Hispanic Whites

	LASUI Raw	LASUI Weighted	L.A. County Eligible
Age			
Twenty-one to thirty	18%	19%	21.4%
Thirty-one to forty	24.4	25.4	22.6
Forty-one to fifty	22	23.1	17.5
Fifty-one to sixty	13	13.4	13
Sixty-one to seventy	11.5	11.1	12.8
Seventy-one to eighty	9	7.2	8.6
Eighty-one plus	2.1	0.9	4.1
Total	863	1,352	2,861,173
Education			
< high school	7	4.9	14.2
High school	24.6	23.5	22.9
Some college	34.4	35.5	33.2
B.A.	23.9	25.6	19.1
M.A., Ph.D., Prof	10.2	10.5	10.6
Total	863	1,352	2,861,173
Occupation			
Managerial, professional, specialist	43.1	46.1	39
Technical, sales, support	33.1	32.6	35.6
Service	9.7	7.9	7.7
Farm, forest, fish	1.0	0.9	0.6
Craft, repair	7.9	7.6	9.8
Operators, fabricators, laborers	5.2	4.9	7.4
Total	673	1,114	2,252,866
Nativity			
Native-born	85.6	84	86.1
Foreign-born	14.4	16	13.9
Sex			
Men	46.3	45.1	48.8
Women	53.7	54.9	51.2

(Table continues on p. 40.)

TABLE 1A.4   *Continued*

	Panel B: African Americans		
	LASUI Raw	LASUI Weighted	L.A. County Eligible
Age			
Twenty-one to thirty	23.2	28.5	27.6
Thirty-one to forty	27.5	26.7	25.9
Forty-one to fifty	18.6	18.4	17.4
Fifty-one to sixty	12.3	11.8	12.6
Sixty-one to seventy	10.5	7.8	9.3
Seventy-one to eighty	6	5.7	5.2
Eighty-one plus	1.9	1.2	1.9
Total	1,119	346	630,015
Education			
< high school	19	11.7	25.1
High school	33	32.6	24.9
Some college	37.1	40	35.9
B.A.	8.7	9.1	9.5
M.A., Ph.D., Prof.	2.2	6.4	4.5
Total	1,119	346	630,015
Occupation			
Managerial, professional, specialist	21.8	24.1	22.7
Technical, sales, support	36.5	40.5	36.5
Service	25.2	22.5	17.3
Farm, forest, fish	0.6	0.5	0.8
Craft, repair	6.1	4.8	8.4
Operators, fabricators, laborers	9.6	7.6	14.1
Total	783	273	479,538
Nativity			
Native-born	96.2	92.4	95.1
Foreign-born	3.8	7.6	4.9
Sex			
Men	34.8	43	45.4
Women	65.2	57	54.6

TABLE 1A.4   *Continued*

Panel C: Latinos			
	LASUI Raw	LASUI Weighted	L.A. County Eligible
Age			
Twenty-one to thirty	40.8	38.3	39.5
Thirty-one to forty	30.1	28.6	28.1
Forty-one to fifty	14.8	16.1	14.9
Fifty-one to sixty	8.6	11.1	8.6
Sixty-one to seventy	3.6	4.1	5.5
Seventy-one to eighty	1.2	0.9	2.5
Eighty-one plus	0.8	0.7	1.0
Total	988	1,195	1,921,170
Education			
< high school	57.8	50.1	59.5
High school	22.3	23.9	18.0
Some college	13.3	17.6	16.9
B.A.	5.3	6.7	3.7
M.A., Ph.D., Prof.	1.3	1.8	1.8
Total	988	1,195	1,921,170
Occupation			
Managerial, professional, specialist	9.8	11.9	10.7
Technical, sales, support	19.7	20.9	22.3
Service	22	21.1	18.2
Farm, forest, fish	1.4	1.1	2.4
Craft, repair	14.3	14.9	15.5
Operators, fabricators, laborers	32.9	30.1	30.9
Total	814	1,013	1,542,816
Nativity			
Native-born	19.7	26.3	29.6
Foreign-born	80.3	73.7	70.4
Sex			
Men	47.9	47.8	51
Women	52.1	52.2	49

(Table continues on p. 42.)

TABLE 1A.4 *Continued*

	LASUI Raw	LASUI Weighted	L.A. County Eligible
Panel D: Asians			
Age			
Twenty-one to thirty	16.3	21.9	24.4
Thirty-one to forty	27.8	22.2	27.2
Forty-one to fifty	24.4	26.1	18.7
Fifty-one to sixty	10	11.4	13
Sixty-one to seventy	10.8	11.1	10.3
Seventy-one to eighty	8.2	6.0	4.8
Eighty-one plus	2.5	1.2	1.6
Total	1,055	240	375,633
Education			
< high school	17.6	15.1	19.1
High school	23.8	20.8	19.5
Some college	19.8	19.8	26.1
B.A.	29.4	32	23.9
M.A., Ph.D., Prof.	9.3	12.2	11.4
Total	1,055	240	375,633
Occupation			
Managerial, professional, specialist	31.8	40	34
Technical, sales, support	38.1	33	38
Service	12.1	15.6	9.8
Farm, forest, fish	0.4	0.3	1.4
Craft, repair	7.2	5.7	7.5
Operators, fabricators, laborers	10.4	5.4	9.3
Total	720	170	288,373
Nativity			
Native-born	12.3	11.5	24.3
Foreign-born	87.7	88.5	75.7
Sex			
Men	48	46.7	47.3
Women	52	53.3	52.7

Source: Los Angeles Study of Urban Inequality 1994.

Notes

1. Los Angeles County, one of California's original 27 counties, was established February 18, 1850. Los Angeles County is one of the nation's largest counties, with 4,083 square miles, an area some 800 square miles larger than the combined area of the states of Delaware and Rhode Island. Los Angeles County includes the islands of San Clemente and Santa Catalina. It is bordered on the east by Orange and San Bernardino counties, on the north by Kern County, and on the west by Ventura County, and on the south by the Pacific Ocean. Its coastline is 76 miles long. It has the largest population (9.8 million in January 1999) of any county in the nation, and is exceeded by only eight states. Approximately 29 percent of California's residents live in Los Angeles County. There are 88 cities within the county, each with its own city council. We use the terms *Los Angeles* and *Los Angeles County* interchangeably.

2. The National Advisory Panel was chaired by Robinson Hollister. The other panel members were Mary R. Jackman, Jorge Chapas, Frank Levy, Seymour Sudman, and Franklin D. Wilson.

3. Social scientists have not reached complete consensus on how to define and use the terms *race* and *ethnicity*. Commonsense usage tends to understand race as biologically based differences between human social groups, differences that are typically observable in terms of skin color, hair texture, eye shape, and other physical attributes. Ethnicity tends to be understood in more cultural terms, pertaining to such factors as language, religion, and national origin. For most social scientists, the critical aspect of concepts of race and ethnicity for social, cultural, political, and economic interactions is that both are fundamentally social constructions. Throughout this volume we conceive of race as a special case of an ethnic distinction (See and Wilson 1989). We recognize that racial and ethnic categories and labels vary over time and place in meaning and in salience. We use the terms *white*, *black* or *African American*, *Asian* or *Asian American*, and *Hispanic* or *Latino* and *Latina*. It is important to stress that each of these broad social categories conceals important subgroup differences based in nativity, national ancestry, class, gender, and other social cleavages.

4. The greater "metropolitan Los Angeles" area in this context refers to a conglomeration of smaller cities that fills a sixty-mile circle around the downtown (civic center) hub, including all or parts of four counties (Orange, Riverside, San Bernardino, and Ventura).

5. The *Bracero Program*, a contractual agreement between the United States and Mexico, allowed for Mexican nationals to serve as guest workers in the United States from 1942 through 1964. During this period, close to 4.6 million braceros participated in this arrange-

ment, many of them settling and establishing ties in the United States. After the program ended, thousands sought permanent resident alien status and/or settled permanently in the United States without documentation.

6. County level data on immigration is unavailable for 1994. The dicennial census is able to capture this population every ten years during the census count, however, we have opted to use the Immigration and Naturalization Service (INS) records for 1994 for accuracy. The INS, however, does not collect data for Los Angeles by county but rather by the Los Angeles-Long Beach Metropolitan Statistical Area (MSA). The Los Angeles-Long Beach MSA is not identical, although similar, to Los Angeles County with regard to geographic expanse and population totals (see table 1.5).

7. These data represent estimates of the resident unauthorized immigrant population residing in the United States as of October 1992. No estimates of the unauthorized immigrant population were undertaken for the years 1993, 1994, and 1995.

References

Abramovitz, Mimi. 1992. "The New Paternalism." *The Nation* 255: 368–71.

Allport, Gordon W. 1954. *The Nature of Prejudice*. New York: Doubleday Anchor.

Anderson, Elijah. 1990. *Streetwise: Race, Class, and Change in an Urban Community*. Chicago: University of Chicago Press.

Apostle, R. A., C. Y. Glock, T. Piazza, and M. Suelzle. 1983. *The Anatomy of Racial Attitudes*. Berkeley: University of California Press.

Bean, Frank D., and Stephanie Bell-Rose. 1999. "Immigration and Its Relation to Race and Ethnicity in the United States." In *Immigration and Opportunity: Race, Ethnicity, and Employment in the United States*, edited by Frank D. Bean and Stephenie Bell-Rose. New York: Russell Sage.

Bickford, Alan, and Douglas S. Massey. 1991. "Segregation in the Second Ghetto: Racial and Ethnic Segregation in American Public Housing, 1977." *Social Forces* 69: 1011–36.

Bobo, Lawrence, and Vincent L. Hutchings. 1996. "Perceptions of Racial Group Competition: Extending Blumer's Theory of Group Position to a Multiracial Social Context." *American Sociological Review* 61: 951–72.

Bobo, Lawrence, and James R. Kluegel. 1993. "Opposition to Race-Targeting: Self-Interest, Stratification Ideology, or Racial Attitudes?" *American Sociological Review* 58: 443–64.

———. 1997. "Status, Ideology, and Dimensions of Whites' Racial Beliefs and Attitudes: Progress and Stagnation." In *Racial Attitudes in the 1990s: Continuity and Change*, edited by S. A. Tuch and J. K. Martin. Westport, Conn.: Praeger.

Bobo, Lawrence, and Camille L. Zubrinsky. 1996. "Attitudes on Residential Integration: Perceived Status Differences, Mere In-Group Preference, or Racial Prejudice?" *Social Forces* 74: 883–909.

Bobo, Lawrence, Camille L. Zubrinsky, James H. Johnson, and Melvin L. Oliver. 1994. "Public Opinion Before and After a Spring of Discontent." In *The Los Angeles Riots: Lessons for the Urban Future*, edited by M. Baldassare. Boulder, Colo.: Westview Press.

———. 1995. "Work Orientation, Job Discrimination, and Ethnicity: A Focus Group Perspective." *Research in the Sociology of Work* 5: 45–85.

Bonilla-Silva, Eduardo. 1996. "Rethinking Racism: Toward a Structural Interpretation."*American Sociological Review* 62: 465–80.

Burtless, Gary. 1990. *A Future of Lousy Jobs? The Changing Structure of U.S. Wages*. Washington, D.C.: Brookings Institution.

Carnoy, Martin I. 1994. *Faded Dreams: The Politics and Economics of Race in America*. New York: Cambridge University Press.

Chiswick, Barry R., and Teresa A. Sullivan. 1995. "The New Immigrants." In *State of the Union, America in the 1990s. Vol. I: Social Trends*, edited by R. Farley. New York: Russell Sage.

Clark, William A. V. 1986. "Residential Segregation in American Cities: A Review and Interpretation." *Population Research and Policy Review* 5: 95–127.

———. 1992. "Residential Preferences and Residential Choices in a Multiethnic Context." *Demography* 29: 451–66.

———. 1996. "Residential Patterns: Avoidance, Assimilation, and Succession." In *Ethnic Los Angeles*, edited by R. Waldinger and M. Bozorgmehr. New York: Russell Sage.

Danziger, Sheldon, and Peter Gottschalk. 1995. *America Unequal*. New York and Cambridge: Russell Sage and Harvard University Press.

Danziger, Sheldon, Gary Sandefur, and Daniel Weinberg, eds. 1994. *Confronting Poverty: Prescriptions for Change*. New York and Cambridge: Russell Sage and Harvard University Press.

Davis, Mike. 1990. *City of Quartz: Excavating the Future in Los Angeles*. New York: Verso.

Dawson, Michael C. 1994. *Behind the Mule: Race and Class in African-American Politics*. Princeton, N.J.: Princeton University Press.

Dear, Michael. 1996. "In the City, Time Becomes Visible: Intentionality and Urbanism in Los Angeles, 1781–1991." In *The City: Los Angeles and Urban Theory at the End of the 20th Century*, edited by A. J. Scott and E. W. Soja. Berkeley, Calif.: University of California Press.

Denton, Nancy A. 1994. "Are African Americans Still Hypersegregated?" In *Residential Apartheid: The American Legacy*, edited by E. Grigsby and R. Bullard. Los Angeles: UCLA Center for African American Studies.

Devine, Patricia G., and Andrew J. Elliot. 1995. "Are Racial Stereotypes Really Fading?: The Princeton Trilogy Revisited." *Personality and Social Psychology Bulletin* 21: 1139–50.

Espiritu, Yen Le. 1992. *Asian American Panethnicity: Bridging Institutions and Identities*. Philadelphia: Temple University Press.

Fainstein, Norman I. 1993. "Race, Class and Segregation: Discourses About African Americans." *International Journal of Urban and Regional Research* 17: 384–403.

Fainstein, Susan S., and Norman I. Fainstein. 1989. "The Racial Dimension in Urban Political Economy." *Urban Affairs Quarterly* 25: 187–99.

Farley, Reynolds, and William H. Frey. 1994. "Changes in the Segregation of Whites and Blacks During the 1980s: Small Steps Toward a More Integrated Society." *American Sociological Review* 59: 23–45.

Farley, Reynolds, Howard Schuman, Suzanne Bianchi, Diane Colasanto, and Shirley Hatchett. 1978. "Chocolate City, Vanilla Suburb: Will the Trend Toward Racially Separate Communities Continue?" *Social Science Research* 7: 319–44.

Farley, Reynolds, Charlotte Steeh, Tara Jackson, Maria Krysan, and Keith Reeves. 1993. "Continued Racial Residential Segregation." *Journal of Housing Research* 4: 1–38.

Farley, Reynolds, Charlotte Steeh, Maria Krysan, Tara Jackson, and Keith Reeves. 1994. "Stereotypes and Segregation: Neighborhoods in the Detroit Area." *American Journal of Sociology* 100: 750–80.

Feagin, Joe R., and Melvin P. Sikes. 1994. *Living with Racism: The Black Middle Class Experience.* Boston: Beacon Press.

Frey, William H., and Reynolds Farley. 1996. "Latino, Asian and Black Segregation in U.S. Metropolitan Areas; Are Multiethnic Metros Different?" *Demography* 33: 35–50.

Galster, George C., and W. Mark Keeney. 1988. "Race, Residence, Discrimination, and Economic Opportunity." *Urban Affairs Quarterly* 24: 87–117.

Gans, Herbert J. 1999. "The Possibility of a New Racial Hierarchy in the Twenty-First-Century United States." In *The Cultural Territories of Race: Black and White Boundaries,* edited by Michele Lamont, Chicago/New York: University of Chicago Press/Russell Sage.

Grant, David M., Melvin L. Oliver, and Angela D. James. 1996. "African Americans: Social and Economic Bifurcation." In *Ethnic Los Angeles,* edited by R. Waldinger and M. Bozorgmehr. New York: Russell Sage.

Harrison, Bennett, and Barry Bluestone. 1988. *The Great U-Turn: Corporate Restructuring and the Polarizing of America.* New York: Basic Books.

Harrison, Roderick, and Claudette E. Bennett. 1995. "Racial and Ethnic Diversity." In *State of the Union. America in the 1990s. Vol. II: Social Trends,* edited by R. Farley. New York: Russell Sage.

Hochschild, Jennifer L. 1995. *Facing Up to the American Dream: Race, Class and the Soul of the Nation.* Princeton, N.J.: Princeton University Press.

Holzer, Harry J. 1996. *What Employers Want: Job Prospects for the Less-Educated Workers.* New York: Russell Sage.

Hunt, Matthew O. 1996. "The Individual, Society, or Both?: A Comparison of Black, Latino, and White Beliefs About the Causes of Poverty." *Social Forces* 75: 293–322.

Jackman, Mary R. 1994. *The Velvet Glove: Paternalism and Conflict in*

Gender, Class, and Race Relations. Berkeley: University of California Press.

Jackson, William E. 1995. "Discrimination in Mortgage Lending Markets as Rational Economic Behavior: Theory, Evidence and Public Policy." In *African Americans and the New Policy Consensus: Retreat of the Liberal State?*, edited by M. E. Lashley and M. N. Jackson. Westport, Conn.: Greenwood.

Jargowsky, Paul A. 1997. *Poverty and Place: Ghettos, Barrios, and the American City.* New York: Russell Sage.

Jargowsky, Paul A., and Mary Jo Bane. 1991. "Ghetto Poverty in the United States: 1970 to 1980." In *The Urban Underclass*, edited by Christopher Jencks and Paul E. Peterson. Washington: Brookings Institution.

Jaynes, Gerald D., and Robin M. Williams, Jr. 1989. *A Common Destiny: Blacks and American Society.* Washington, D.C.: National Academy Press.

Jencks, Christopher, and Paul E. Peterson, eds. 1991. *The Urban Underclass.* Washington, D.C.: Brookings Institution.

Johnson, James H., and Walter C. Farrell. 1993. "The Fire This Time: The Genesis of the Los Angeles Rebellion of 1992." *North Carolina Law Review* 71: 1403–20.

Johnson, James H., Clyzelle K. Jones, Walter C. Farrell, and Melvin L. Oliver. 1992. "The Los Angeles Rebellion: A Retrospective View." *Economic Development Quarterly* 6: 356–72.

Johnson, James H., and Melvin L. Oliver. 1989. "Interethnic Minority Conflict in Urban America: The Effects of Economic and Social Dislocations." *Urban Geography* 10: 449–63.

———. 1991. "Economic Restructuring and Black Male Joblessness in U.S. Metropolitan Areas." *Urban Geography* 12: 542–62.

———. 1992. "Structural Changes in the Economy and Black Male Joblessness: A Reassessment." In *Urban Labor Markets and Job Opportunity*, edited by G. Peterson and W. Vrohman. Washington, D.C.: Urban Institute Press.

Johnson, James H., Melvin L. Oliver, and Lawrence D. Bobo. 1994. "Understanding the Contours of Deepening Urban Inequality: Theoretical Underpinnings and Research Design of a Multi-city Study." *Urban Geography* 15: 77–89.

Kain, John F. 1968. "Housing Segregation, Negro Employment and Metropolitan Decentralization." *Quarterly Journal of Economics* 82: 175–97.

———. 1992. "The Spatial Mismatch Hypothesis: Three Decades Later." *Housing Policy Debate* 3: 371–460.

Kasarda, John, 1988. "Jobs, Migration, and Emerging Urban Mismatches." In *Urban Change and Poverty*, edited by Laurence E. Lynn, Jr., and Michael G. H. McGeary. Washington: National Academy Press.

———. 1989. "Urban Industrial Transition and the Urban Underclass." *Annals of the American Academy of Political and Social Sciences* 501: 26–47.

———. 1993. "Cities as Places Where People Live and Work: Urban Change and Neighborhood Distress." In Henry Cisneros, *Interwoven Destinies: Cities and the Nation*. New York: Norton.

Kasarda, John D., and Kwok-fai Ting. 1996. "Joblessness and Poverty in America's Central Cities: Causes and Policy Prescriptions." *Housing Policy Debate* 7: 387–419.

Kirschenman, Joleen, and Kathryn M. Neckerman. 1990. "'We'd Love to Hire Them, But . . .': The Meaning of Race for Employers." In *The Urban Underclass*, edited by C. Jencks and P. Peterson. Washington, D.C.: Brookings Institute.

Kluegel, James R., and Eliot R. Smith. 1986. *Beliefs About Inequality: Americans' Views of What Is and What Ought to Be*. New York: Aldine de Gruyter.

Lacayo, Richard. 1993. "Los Angeles: Unhealed Wounds." *Time* 141: 26–32.

Laslett, John H. M. 1996. "Historical Perspectives: Immigration and the Rise of a Distinctive Urban Region, 1900–1970." In *Ethnic Los Angeles*, edited by Roger Waldinger and Mehdi Bozorgmehr. New York: Russell Sage.

Levy, Frank. 1987. *Dollars and Dreams: The Changing American Income Distribution*. New York: Russell Sage.

———. 1995. "Incomes and Income Inequality." In *State of the Union, America in the 1990s. Vol. I: Economic Trends*, edited by R. Farley. New York: Russell Sage.

Massey, Douglas S., Gretchen Condran, and Nancy A. Denton. 1987. "The Effects of Residential Segregation on Black Social and Economic Well-Being." *Social Forces* 66: 29–56.

Massey, Douglas S., and Nancy A. Denton. 1993. *American Apartheid: Segregation and the Making of the Underclass*. Cambridge, Mass.: Harvard University Press.

Massey, Douglas S., and Eric Fong. 1990. "Segregation and Neighborhood Quality: Blacks, Hispanics, and Asians in the San Francisco Metropolitan Area." *Social Forces* 69: 15–32.

McDaniel, Antonio. 1995. "The Dynamics of Racial Composition of the United States." *Daedalus* 124: 179–98.

Mead, Lawrence. 1992. *The New Politics of Poverty*. New York: Basic Books.

Michel, Richard. 1991. "Economic Growth and Income Inequality Since the 1982 Recession." *Journal of Policy Analysis and Management* 10: 181–203.

Mincy, Ronald, and Erol Ricketts. 1990. "Growth of the Underclass, 1970–1980." *Journal of Human Resources* 25(1): 137–45.

Moore, Thomas S., and Aaron Laramore. 1990. "Industrial Change and Urban Joblessness: An Assessment of the Mismatch Hypothesis." *Urban Affairs Quarterly* 25: 640–58.

Murray, Charles. 1984. *Losing Ground: American Social Policy, 1950–1980*. New York: Basic Books.

Myers, Samuel L., and Tsze Chan. 1995. "Racial Discrimination in Housing Markets: Accounting for Credit Risk." *Social Science Quarterly* 76: 543–61.

Oliver, Melvin L. 1988. "The Urban Black Community as Network: Toward a Social Network Perspective." *Sociological Quarterly* 29: 623–45.

Oliver, Melvin L., and James H. Johnson. 1984. "Interethnic Conflict in an Urban Ghetto: The Case of Blacks and Latinos in Los Angeles." *Research in Social Movements, Conflict and Change* 6: 57–94.

Oliver, Melvin L., James H. Johnson, and Lawrence Bobo. 1994. "Unraveling the Paradox of Deepening Urban Inequality: The Multi-City Survey of Urban Inequality." *African-American Research Perspectives* (Winter): 43–52.

Oliver, Melvin L., and Thomas M. Shapiro. 1989. "Race and Wealth." *Review of Black Political Economy* 17: 5–25.

———. 1990. "Wealth of a Nation: At Least One-third of Households Are Asset Poor." *American Journal of Economics and Sociology* 49: 129–51.

———. 1995. *Black Wealth/White Wealth: A New Perspective on Racial Inequality*. New York: Routledge.

Patterson, Orlando. 1997. *The Ordeal of Integration: Progress and Resentment in America's "Racial" Crisis*. Washington, D.C.: Counterpoint/Civitas.

Phillips, Kevin. 1990. *The Politics of Rich and Poor: Wealth and the American Electorate in the Reagan Aftermath*. New York: Random House.

Ryan, William. 1971. *Blaming the Victim*. New York: Vintage.

Sanjek, Roger. 1994. "The Enduring Inequalities of Race." In *Race*, edited by S. Gregory and Roger Sanjek. New Brunswick, N.J.: Rutgers University Press.

Sassen, Saskia. 1990. "Economic Restructuring and the American City." *Annual Review of Sociology* 16: 465–90.

Schuman, Howard, and Lawrence Bobo. 1988. "Survey-Based Experiments on White Racial Attitudes Toward Residential Integration." *American Journal of Sociology* 94: 273–99.

Schuman, Howard, Charlotte Steeh, Lawrence Bobo, and Maria Krysan. 1997. *Racial Attitudes in America: Trends and Interpretations, rev. ed.* Cambridge, Mass.: Harvard University Press.

Scott, Allen J. 1996. "The Manufacturing Economy: Ethnic and Gender Divisions of Labor." In Roger Waldinger and Mehdi Bozorgmehr, *Ethnic Los Angeles*. New York: Russell Sage.

Sears, David O., John J. Hetts, James Sidanius, and Lawrence Bobo. 2000. "Race in American Politics: Framing the Debates." In *Racialized Politics: The Debate About Racism in America*, edited by David O. Sears, James Sidanius, and Lawrence Bobo. Chicago: University of Chicago Press.

See, Katherine O'Sullivan, and William Julius Wilson. 1989. "Race and

Ethnicity." In *Handbook of Sociology*, edited by N. J. Smelser. New-bury Park, Calif.: Sage Publications.

Sigelman, Lee, and Susan Welch. 1991. *Black Americans' View of Racial Inequality: A Dream Deferred*. New York: Cambridge University Press.

Smith, Tom W. 1991. "Ethnic Images." General Social Survey Topical Report. NORC: University of Chicago.

———. 1998. "Intergroup Relations in Contemporary America: An Overview of Survey Research." In *Intergroup Relations in the United States: Research Perspectives*, edited by W. Winborne and R. Cohen.

Sniderman, Paul M., and Edward G. Carmines. 1997. *Reaching Beyond Race*. Cambridge, Mass.: Harvard University Press.

Sniderman, Paul M., and Thomas Piazza. 1993. *The Scar of Race*. Cambridge, Mass.: Harvard University Press.

Soja, Edward W., and Allen J. Scott. 1996. "Introduction to Los Angeles: City and Region." In *The City: Los Angeles and Urban Theory at the End of the 20th Century*, edited by Allen J. Scott and Edward W. Soja. Berkeley, Calif.: University of California Press.

Tate, Katherine. 1993. *From Protest to Politics*. New York and Cambridge: Russell Sage and Harvard University Press.

Thernstrom, Stephan, and Abigail Thernstrom. 1997. *America in Black and White: One Nation, Indivisible*. New York: Simon & Schuster.

Waldinger, Roger. 1989. "Immigration and Urban Change." *Annual Review of Sociology* 15: 211–32.

———. 1996a. "Ethnicity and Opportunity in the Plural City." In *Ethnic Los Angeles*, edited by R. Waldinger and M. Bozorgmehr. New York: Russell Sage.

———. 1996b. "Who Makes the Beds? Who Washes the Dishes?: Black/Immigrant Competition Reassessed." In *Immigrants and Immigration Policy: Individual Skills, Family Ties, and Group Identities*, edited by H. O. Dulup and P. V. Wannara. Greenwich, Conn.: JAI Press.

———. 1996c. *Still the Promised City?: Afro-Americans and New Immigrants in Post-Industrial New York*. Cambridge, Mass.: Harvard University Press.

Waldinger, Roger, and Mehdi Bozorgmehr. 1996. "The Making of a Multicultural Metropolis." In *Ethnic Los Angeles*, edited by Roger Waldinger and Mehdi Bozorgmehr. New York: Russell Sage.

Wilson, Thomas C. 1996. "Cohort and Prejudice: Whites' Attitudes Toward Blacks, Hispanics, Jews, and Asians." *Public Opinion Quarterly* 60: 253–74.

Wilson, William Julius. 1987. *The Truly Disadvantaged: The Inner-City, the Underclass and Public Policy*. Chicago: University of Chicago Press.

———. 1996. *When Work Disappears: The World of the New Urban Poor*. New York: Knopf.

Yinger, John. 1995. *Closed Doors, Opportunities Lost: The Continuing Cost of Housing Discrimination*. New York: Russell Sage.

2

A DEMOGRAPHIC PORTRAIT OF
LOS ANGELES COUNTY, 1970 TO 1990

David M. Grant

U NDERSTANDING inequality at the local level in Los Angeles County is a relatively complicated matter, due to the twin forces of demographic and economic restructuring. Indeed, few if any cities on the national or world stage can match the rapid recasting of Los Angeles's social and economic landscape. The Los Angeles Study of Urban Inequality (LASUI) was designed to capture the increasingly complex reality of urban inequality on the eve of the twenty-first century. Eliciting respondents' experiences and views on racial and ethnic attitudes, labor market dynamics, and housing segregation, this survey allows competing hypotheses about the causes and dimensions of inequality to be rigorously tested. Before turning to these analyses, this chapter seeks to provide some of the recent historical context of inequality and demographic change in Los Angeles County.

Population Characteristics

More than any other single factor, Los Angeles has been transformed by rapid and large population change. This change has been driven by several demographic forces: Asian and Latino immigration, white out-migration, and differential fertility rates among native and foreign-born residents (Johnson, Oliver, and Roseman 1989; Waldinger and Bozorg-mehr 1996). Between 1970 and 1990, the county's total population increased by nearly two million people while its white population decreased by 1.4 million. Of the four major racial groups, whites were the only group to undergo a decline (see figure 2.1). White population loss was due to out-migration, an older age structure, and a relatively low fertility rate. In addition, it may be related to immigration. Since 1980,

FIGURE 2.1   *Racial and Ethnic Composition of Los Angeles*
County, 1970 and 1990

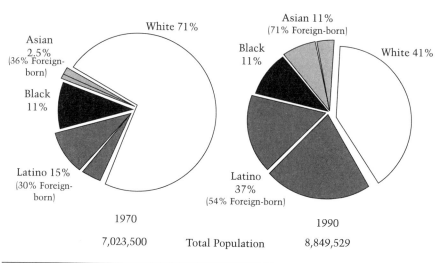

1970		1990
7,023,500	Total Population	8,849,529

Source: U.S. Department of Commerce 1970, 1990a.

it is the less-educated and skilled segments of the white population that have been leaving high-immigration metropolitan areas like Los Angeles, those most likely to compete for employment with new low-skilled immigrants (Frey 1994, 1996). Significant numbers of African Americans have left Los Angeles as well, but in-migration and natural increase have meant that African Americans remained a constant 10 percent of the county's population in 1970 and 1990, with a rate of growth equal to that of the county as a whole (26 percent). More than making up for the declining white population was the tremendous increase in the number of Asians and Latinos calling Los Angeles home. Between 1970 and 1990 the Latino population grew by more than 2.2 million (238 percent), and the Asian population by nearly 750,000 (426 percent).

Obviously, immigration has led to a substantial increase in the proportion of foreign-born persons now living in Los Angeles County. Less obvious is the impact of immigration on the age structure. Immigrants tend to migrate as young adults and have relatively high fertility rates when compared to native-born groups in Los Angeles.[1] The combination of these two factors has created a very young age structure for native-born Latinos and Asians, while their foreign-born counterparts domi-

FIGURE 2.2   *Age Structure of Racial-Ethnic Groups by Nativity,*
Los Angeles County, 1990

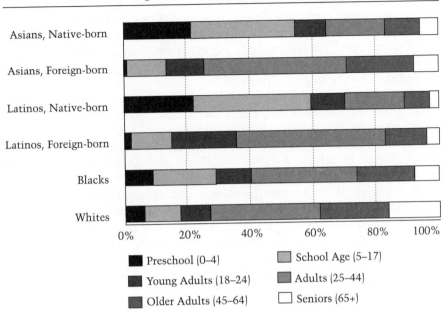

Source: U.S. Department of Commerce 1990a.

nated the adult population (see figure 2.2). In 1990, 54 percent of native-born Asians and 59 percent of native-born Latinos were under the age of eighteen, compared with 14 and 15 percent foreign-born Asians and Latinos, respectively. Conversely, among prime working-age adults (ages twenty-five to forty-four), foreign-born Latinos outnumbered native-born Latinos 3 to 1, and foreign-born Asians outnumbered native-born Asians by nearly six-to-one. These dramatic differences in age structure challenge the social structure in distinct ways. For example, the large youth population, predominantly the children of immigrants, has strained local institutions, particularly public schools, to adapt to their needs and characteristics. These current demographic forces will lead to a tremendous increase in the presence of native-born Asians and Latinos in the future labor force of Los Angeles.

The reasons people emigrate, and choose Los Angeles as a destination, are varied and complex. Immigration policy certainly plays a role in the ability of groups to enter the United States. The recent swelling of the immigrant population is in part due to the relaxation of immigration laws regarding family reunification and national origin quotas in 1965 (Waldinger 1989; Portes and Rumbaut 1996). Yet immigrants have come to the United States primarily for economic opportunity, and the strong economic performance of the region (discussed in the next section) provides a strong pull. Additionally, California's proximity to Asia and Central America has made it a magnet for political refugees fleeing war and repression. The rapidly growing immigrant population has impacted the county in profound ways.

The swift transformation of the racial composition of Los Angeles County due to internal migration and immigration has certainly not been lost on local residents. A 1992 survey of Los Angeles County found that most residents (56 percent) felt their neighborhood was experiencing a change in ethnic composition (Bobo and Zubrinsky 1996). This sentiment was most pronounced among African Americans; among those who felt their neighborhood was undergoing change, 78 percent reported that it was increasingly inhabited by Latinos. Demographic restructuring in Los Angeles has been dramatic and quick. The large scale out-migration of whites has more than been made up for by immigrants and their higher fertility rates. While immigrants are concentrated in the workforce, their children dominate Los Angeles's youth and portend continued population flux in the years ahead.

The Economy

Like its population, the Los Angeles economy is diverse. Economic change during the last several decades in Los Angeles includes Rustbelt deindustrialization and Sunbelt corporate boom alongside Third World sweatshops, street vendors, ethnic enclave entrepreneurs, and flexible forms of light manufacturing. The city is also home to Hollywood, several of the nation's leading defense and aerospace companies, and the world's largest entertainment industry. As an advertisement by a local telephone company boasts about its Yellow Pages, "If you can't find it here, it probably doesn't exist!"

Los Angeles was a small agricultural town until the discovery of oil in the 1890s initiated speculation and a land boom. As its population grew into the next century, the beginning of an industrial infrastructure emerged. World War II indelibly changed Los Angeles and the surrounding region into the nation's leader of military technology and production. Economic opportunities presented by wartime activities again brought migrants to Los Angeles; the mountains, beaches, Pacific Ocean, and temperate climate kept them there.

The center of manufacturing on the West Coast, Los Angeles was hard hit by the slowdown of manufacturing as the postwar boom came to a close in the 1970s. In this respect, Los Angeles in part follows the deindustrialization trajectory of the Rustbelt, with thousands of well-paying union jobs in the durable manufacturing sector, such as auto, glass, steel, and rubber, disappearing from the economy during the 1970s and 1980s (Harrison and Bluestone 1982; Soja, Morales, and Wolff 1983; Johnson and Oliver 1992). In 1970, one in five Angelenos was employed in durable manufacturing, easily dominating the County's industrial mix (see table 2.1).[2] By 1990, durables accounted for only 13 percent of employment among major industrial sectors of Los Angeles. Unlike in the Rustbelt, however, the cold war pumped millions of defense indus-

TABLE 2.1   *Percentage Distribution of Major Industrial Sectors, Los Angeles County, 1970, 1980, and 1990*

Industry	1970	1980	1990	Percentage Change, 1970 to 1990	Absolute Change, 1970 to 1990
Professional services	16.5	18.8	20.3	3.8	84
Retail trade	16.1	15.6	15.7	−0.4	46
Durable manufacturing	20.0	17.6	13.3	−6.7	−0.3
Nondurable manufacturing	8.2	8.4	7.5	−0.7	37
Financial, insurance, and real estate	6.0	6.9	7.5	1.5	88
Transportation, communications, and public utilities	6.7	7.1	6.9	0.2	55
Business and repair services	4.8	5.8	6.5	1.7	104
Construction	4.7	4.6	6.1	1.4	95
Wholesale trade	4.7	4.7	5.0	0.3	62
Personal services	4.1	3.1	3.7	−0.4	34
Entertaiment–recreation services	2.4	2.6	3.3	0.9	107
Public administration	4.7	3.4	2.8	−1.9	−9
Other	1.2	1.3	1.4	0.2	79
Total	100%	100%	100%	—	50
	2,906,800	3,557,540	4,357,033		

Source: U.S. Department of Commerce 1970, 1980, 1990a.

try dollars into the local economy and kept the Los Angeles growth machine on track. An influx of low-skill, low-wage immigrant labor also boosted manufacturing in industries such as garment, furniture, and electrical assembly (Levy 1987; Scott 1988). Thus, despite the decreasing importance of manufacturing to the economy as a whole, the number of Angelenos employed in manufacturing remained nearly unchanged from 1970 to 1990.

Replacing durable manufacturing atop the industrial hierarchy in 1990 was professional services. This sector, which includes industries such as medical, legal, and educational services, employed one in five Angelenos in 1990. In addition to durable manufacturing, other large industrial sectors were retail trade and nondurable manufacturing, which includes the production of garments and furniture. The fastest-growing industries during this period were entertainment and recreation services, business and repair services, and construction—a broad spectrum of economic activities that encompass a diverse mix of skills.

Occupationally, more Angelenos work in white-collar than in blue-collar jobs (see table 2.2). Although both sectors have experienced aggregate growth, white-collar occupations grew faster and accounted for nearly 60 percent of all jobs in 1990. Clerical and professional positions were the most abundant of white-collar jobs in all three decades, but declined in overall importance to the occupational structure over time. Managerial, finance and business sales, and the technical sector were the fastest-growing white-collar occupational categories. Blue-collar occupations employed more people in 1970 than in 1990, but proportionally declined from 46 percent of all occupations in 1970 to 41 percent in 1970. The core occupations of the blue-collar sector, craft and repair and operator-fabricator-laborer occupations, declined over time and failed to keep pace with the growth of the workforce in the county as a whole. Service jobs, such as household workers, food service, and protective service workers, accounted for an increasing percentage of blue-collar occupations over time.

These broad industrial and occupational designations show a growing and diverse economy that has remained heavily ensconced in goods production despite the net decline of the durable and nondurable manufacturing sectors. While the goods production sector continued to be a critical component of the Los Angeles economic structure, economic growth was principally due to the growth of managerial, technical, and finance and business sales in industries such as business services, finance-insurance-real estate (FIRE), and entertainment. There is an important caveat to consider, however, when interpreting these broad economic categories and how they have changed over time in Los Angeles: while the major industrial and occupational sectors portray a sense of

TABLE 2.2   *Percentage Distribution of Major Occupational Sectors, Los Angeles County, 1970, 1980, and 1990*

Occupation	1970	1980	1990	Percentage Change, 1970 to 1990	Absolute Change, 1970 to 1990
White-collar					
Managerial	8.6	11.4	12.7	4.1	121
Professional	15.2	12.6	13.8	−1.4	37
Technical	1.9	3.1	3.4	1.5	256
Finance and business sales	3.3	4.8	6.1	2.8	178
Retail sales	4.2	5.0	5.3	1.1	90
Clerical	21.1	19.5	17.3	−3.8	23
Total, white-collar	54.3	56.4	58.6	4.3	61.9
Blue-collar					
Craft and repair	13.2	12.4	11.4	−1.8	29
Operators, fabricators, and laborers	20.5	18.3	16.3	−4.2	19
Service	11.7	11.9	12.5	0.8	60
Farm, forest, fish	0.3	1.1	1.2	0.9	532
Total, blue-collar	45.7	43.7	41.4	−4.3	35.6
Total, all occupations	100% 2,906,800	100% 3,557,540	100% 4,357,239	—	50

Source: U.S. Department of Commerce 1970, 1980a, 1990a.

the macro-structure of the economy, they may mask much of the flux occurring within a given sector. The loss of high-wage union jobs in the auto industry along the Alameda corridor, for example, may be offset by the growth of low-wage electronic assembly jobs in the San Gabriel Valley; such a shift shows no net change in the census data on durable manufacturing as a major industrial sector, yet can have a profound effect on inequality due to differences in wages, benefits, job security, and opportunity for advancement.

The Labor Force

The population changes just discussed have had a tremendous impact on the composition of the labor supply in Los Angeles County. At a macro-level, economists understand employment as the nexus of the characteristics of the workforce, the demand for workers by employers, and institutional forces affecting employment regulation and organization. This section explores two dimensions of the changing labor force in Los Angeles County from 1970 to 1990: increasing racial-ethnic diversity and shifts in educational attainment.

The labor force in Los Angeles County added nearly 1.5 million people between 1970 and 1990, growing much faster (51 percent) than the total population (26 percent). (Throughout this chapter, *labor force* refers to those persons ages sixteen through sixty-five who were not in the military and were currently working or unemployed at the time of the census.) Slightly more women were added to the labor force than men during this time period, as the proportion of women increased from 40 percent to 43 percent. The major push behind the recasting of the workforce, however, was immigration.

In 1970, nearly three of four members of the labor force were white; this fell to less than one in two by 1990. African Americans remained a constant 10 percent of the labor force in each decade, just barely outpacing the growth rate for the county as a whole. If not for immigration, both the total population and the labor force in Los Angeles would have shrunk over time and quite possibly followed the declining fortunes of other large industrial metropolises. From 1970 to 1990, the Latino and Asian workforce grew by more than 300 percent and 463 percent, respectively. As noted previously, immigrants were particularly concentrated in the working-age population due to the age of emigration and their relatively high fertility rates (see figure 2.2). This means that diversity—in terms of national origin, language, educational attainment, orientation to the workplace, and so on—was also concentrated among the adult population and will likely decline over time as the children of recent immigrants, educated and acculturated predominantly in the United States, become adults. (Unless, of course, the tremendous levels of recent migration are not only sustained but significantly increased.)

The concentration of immigrants in the labor force in 1990 makes it an opportune site to reveal the increasingly variegated national origins behind the broad designations of "Asian" and "Latino." In 1970, four countries—(Philippines, China, Japan, and Korea)—accounted for over 90 percent of the 32,000 Asian immigrants in the Los Angeles work force. In 1990, these same countries were the origin of just 60 percent of Asian workers. The number of workers from Vietnam alone (over 37,000) in 1990 eclipsed the total number of foreign-born Asians working in Los Angeles in 1970. Furthermore, the country of origin for foreign-born Asian workers increased from twelve countries in 1970 to over ninety countries in 1990.[3] Mexico continues to be the dominant country of origin for Latinos in the workforce, accounting for 63 and 65 percent of all Latinos in 1970 and 1990, respectively. However, an increase in Latino diversity has occurred due to increased immigration from El Salvador and Guatemala. These two Central American countries accounted for 3 percent (4,700) of foreign-born Latino workers in 1970 and nearly 20 percent (205,875) in 1990.

Finally, rapid population change due to immigration and internal migration has had an impact on the age structure, work experience, and educational characteristics of the workforce in Los Angeles County. These factors are, of course, key components of a person's human capital and determine in large part one's occupational status and earnings. Given the strong relationship between human capital and wages, the reconfiguration of human capital within the labor force is an important part of inequality in Los Angeles.

As the single strongest predictor of income, educational attainment forms the foundation of a worker's human capital. Considering those in the labor force over the age of twenty-five, who for the most part have completed their schooling, the mean years of education increased very slightly among all workers in Los Angeles between 1970 and 1990, from 12.3 to 12.6 years. This constancy, however, masks large differences between groups as well as change within groups over time. With the exception of foreign-born Latinos, all major racial groups experienced an increase in the mean years of schooling over time (see figure 2.3). By 1990, native-born Asian and Pacific Islanders were the best-educated group among Los Angeles workers, with nearly 80 percent reporting some or more college education. All of the native-born groups experienced substantial educational upgrading between 1970 and 1990 as the proportion of workers with less than a high school diploma was at least cut in half, while the proportion receiving a college education doubled. The educational advances made by African Americans and native-born Latinos were especially impressive, given their low levels of educational attainment in 1970. Despite substantial improvement, however, years of completed schooling among these groups continued to trail that of whites and Asians in 1990. The substantial educational upgrading of native-born Latinos did not take place among foreign-born Latinos. The rapidly growing foreign-born Latino population that dominates the working-age Latino population showed little improvement over time, as fully two-thirds lacked a high school diploma in both 1970 and 1990.

Race and Gender in the Labor Market

How people find and get sorted into different jobs is a critical part of economic inequality and a major emphasis of the LASUI. As noted, hu-

FIGURE 2.3   *Educational Attainment Among the Los Angeles*
County Labor Force by Race and Nativity,
1970 and 1990

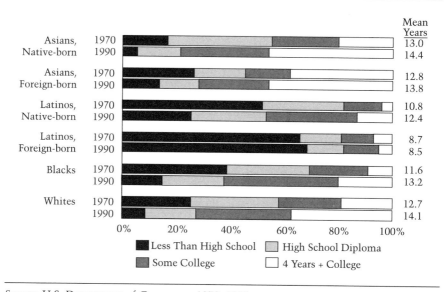

Source: U.S. Department of Commerce 1970, 1990a.

man capital is an important part of the person-to-job equation, yet racial and gender differences in employment rates, mobility, and wages persist. These differences remain when human capital factors are held constant and subsequent to civil rights legislation making racial, ethnic, religious, and gender discrimination in employment illegal (England and Browne 1992; Smith and Tienda 1988; Bound and Freeman 1992; Blau and Beller 1992). Subsequent chapters in this book explore the role race, space, gender, child-care responsibilities, and nativity play in the sorting of people into jobs. To provide a sense of the recent historical context surrounding these issues, we now turn our attention to the distribution of racial groups in the occupational structure and how they changed from 1970 to 1990.

In order to explore broad changes in the gender and racial occupational structure over time, the index of representation (Lieberson 1980; Waldinger 1996) was calculated for men and women of each major racial group (Asian, black, Latino or Latina, white).[4] Figures 2.4 and 2.5 show the representation in the occupational structure for women and men, respectively, of each racial group in 1970 and 1990. In both figures

FIGURE 2.4   *Women: Representation in Major Occupations,*
Los Angeles County, 1970 and 1990

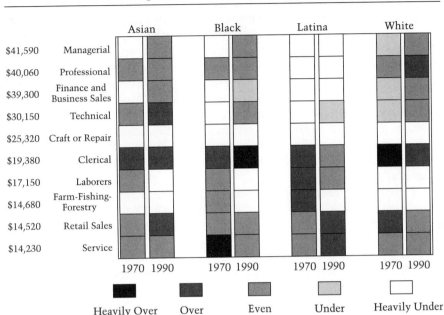

Source: U.S. Department of Commerce 1970, 1990a.

"heavily over-under" denotes over- or underrepresentation by a factor of 2 or greater, "over-under" denotes over- or underrepresentation by a factor of 1.5 to 1.9, and "even" designates a group being neither over- or underrepresented in an occupation by a factor of 1.4 or less. In addition, major occupational groups have been ordered based on the average earnings reported in each sector in 1989 and are listed next to each occupation.[5]

Levels of representation for women in major occupational sectors by race are presented in figure 2.4 for 1970 and 1990 and show substantial differences between groups and over time. In 1970, women of all groups were largely absent from the top-paying occupations. Among the twenty cells representing the five best-paying occupational sectors for each of the four racial groups, women were represented at a rate equal to their presence in the labor force in only four cells and were not over-represented in any of them. At the same time, women were underrepresented in only three cells among the five lowest-paying occupational sectors. The concentration of women in low-paying occupations and omission from the better-paying occupational sectors in 1970 is a major reason for the gender gap in earnings (to be discussed).

Twenty years later the occupational distribution of women had changed considerably for the better, but not for all groups. Asian, black, and white women all dramatically increased their share of employment in the top-paying occupational groups.[6] The representation of Asian and black women also decreased in lower-paying sectors such as laborer-operator-fabricator and service. White women were the most successful relative to other women in avoiding the lower tier of occupations in each decade. Latinas, however, were largely left out of the improving position of women in the occupational structure; they remained heavily underrepresented in the top occupational sectors in 1990 and became more entrenched over time in the worst-paying sectors, such as retail sales and service.

Figure 2.5 presents the levels of representation for racial groups among men in Los Angeles County in 1970 and 1990. Overall the distribution of men throughout the occupational structure was more stable

FIGURE 2.5   *Men: Representation in Major Occupations, Los Angeles County, 1970 and 1990*

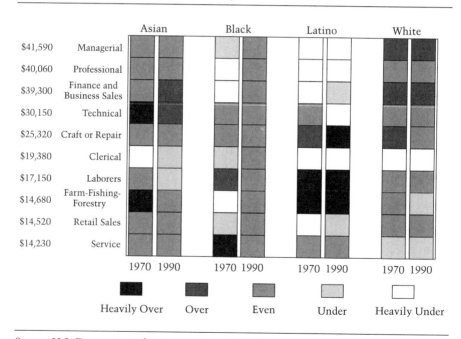

Source: U.S. Department of Commerce 1970, 1990a.

over time than it was for women. White men in particular showed little change, remaining overrepresented in two of the top three best-paying occupations, while sparsely distributed through the tier of lower-paying occupations. By 1990, Asian men, like white men, were well positioned in the occupational structure—even or overrepresented among the top five occupational sectors and even or underrepresented in the bottom five. Black men demonstrated an interesting pattern of change. In 1970 they were under to heavily underrepresented among the top of the occupational hierarchy and overrepresented only as laborer-fabricator-assembler and service workers. In 1990, they were evenly distributed in each of the major occupational groups. There is an up as well as a downside to this shift among black men, as they are evenly distributed among high, medium, and low-paying occupational groups. Nonetheless, for a group that was heavily or underrepresented in six of ten categories in 1970 to achieve representation even to their presence in the labor force suggests that significant occupational differentiation among black men has taken place (Grant, Oliver, and James 1996).

Differentiation cannot be associated with the occupational structuring of Latino men; in 1990 they were heavily overrepresented in three categories: craft and repair, laborer-fabricator-assembler, and farm-fishing-forestry. At the same time, they were underrepresented in all other occupational groups except the service sector. The underrepresentation of Latino men in well-paying occupations and their concentration in low-paying ones portend poorly for the economic well-being of this group.

In summary, some positive changes have occurred over time, but they have not been shared equally among men, women, and the various racial and ethnic groups; the occupational structure in Los Angeles remains heavily stratified along both dimensions. In 1990 whites and Asians were the groups best represented among the top-paying occupational categories, while African Americans showed the most improvement over time. Latinas and Latinos, however, are moored toward the bottom of the occupational hierarchy and exhibited little advancement between 1970 and 1990. Clearly, race and gender remain powerful forces in the sorting process of people to jobs.

Earnings

The sorting process of people to jobs has important consequences for economic inequality. All jobs are not, of course, equal; they differ in numerous ways, such as opportunity for advancement, industry, occupation, benefits, the presence or absence of unions, firm size, and skill, educational, training, and licensing requirements. And, most important in the context of economic inequality, jobs differ considerably by the wages they pay.

Following Frank Bean and Marta Tienda (1987), table 2.3 reports median earnings for men and women who worked full-time and full-year among the four major racial groups and also for the native- and foreign-born among Asian or Pacific Islanders and Latinos. Median wages are also reported within each group according to years of education completed. It is immediately apparent from the table that women earn considerably less than men. The gender gap in wages among full-time, full-year workers closed over the twenty-year period from .59 in 1970 to .76 in 1990; this convergence was due to the decline of men's median wage (12 percent) and a nearly identical increase in women's median wage (14 percent) during those years.

The decline in men's earnings was not shared among all ethnic-racial groups. Black and white men's median earnings increased overall, particularly among those with higher levels of education, while native- and foreign-born Latinos decreased; the decrease for foreign-born Latino men was especially pronounced ($5,900). Asian or Pacific Islander men's earnings were relatively constant over time, increasing slightly among both the native- and foreign-born. The stability in their earnings was due to a drop in earnings from 1970 to 1990 among all but the best educated, those with a college degree, whose earnings increased. Wage trends during this period for women were similar to those of men, with a few caveats. Black and white women, like men, experienced increased median earnings overall and at each level of education. Similar gains were recorded by native ($4,000) and foreign-born ($7,100) Asian or Pacific Islander women. Unlike their male counterparts, wages among native-born Latinas increased ($3,100), while foreign-born Latinas were the only group of women whose median wage declined ($1,500) during this twenty-year period. And although this decline was slight, foreign-born Latinas were least able to afford declining wages, as they were by far the lowest-paid group of workers in the county.

Labor Force Participation

As women and men of different racial backgrounds were moving up and down the occupational and wage hierarchy, others were either sorted out of a job altogether or not absorbed into the world of work. Unemployment and joblessness are critical dimensions of poverty and economic inequality (Wilson 1996). The employment rate of African American men, for example, has declined since the 1950s, and black men have experienced unemployment rates twice as high as those of their white counterparts since the 1960s (Cotton 1989). Scholars, however, disagree

TABLE 2.3 *Median Earnings Differentials of Individual Workers by Race, Gender, and Nativity, Los Angeles County, 1970 to 1990[a] (Full-Time, Full-Year Workers)*

Men	Total	Native-Born	Foreign-Born	Less Than Twelve	Twelve	Thirteen to Fifteen	Sixteen Plus
Los Angeles County							
1970	32.8	33.8	27.0	27.0	30.7	33.8	47.3
1990	29.0	35.0	19.2	16.0	25.0	31.0	45.0
Asian and Pacific Islanders							
1970	30.4	33.1	23.5	23.3	28.7	32.4	33.8
1990	30.0	35.0	28.0	18.0	22.0	26.5	36.0
Blacks							
1970	24.3	—	—	20.3	24.3	27.0	33.8
1990	27.8	—	—	20.5	24.0	28.0	39.0
Latinos							
1970	25.7	28.0	20.9	23.6	27.0	30.4	33.8
1990	18.0	27.0	15.0	14.5	20.0	25.0	35.0
Whites							
1970	33.8	—	—	30.4	33.8	33.8	50.7
1990	38.6	—	—	27.8	30.0	35.6	50.0

Women	Total	Native-Born	Foreign-Born	Less Than Twelve	Twelve	Thirteen to Fifteen	Sixteen Plus
Los Angeles County							
1970	19.3	19.9	16.9	16.9	18.9	20.3	27.0
1990	22.0	25.0	16.0	12.0	19.8	24.0	31.5
Asian and Pacific Islanders							
1970	20.3	23.0	13.5	13.5	21.3	21.6	27.0
1990	22.0	27.0	20.6	13.2	16.5	22.0	28.0
Blacks							
1970	16.9	—	—	13.5	16.9	19.3	23.6
1990	23.0	—	—	18.0	19.0	23.8	32.0
Latinas							
1970	15.5	16.9	13.5	13.5	16.9	18.6	17.6
1990	14.9	20.0	12.0	11.0	17.0	20.0	26.0
Whites							
1970	20.3	—	—	17.9	20.3	20.3	27.9
1990	26.0	—	—	19.0	22.0	25.0	34.0

Source: U.S. Department of Commerce 1970, 1990a.
[a]Based on 1969 and 1989 reported earnings in thousands of constant 1989 dollars.

as to the causes of labor market nonparticipation, and the LASUI hopes to inform these debates. Conservatives tend to blame the unemployed or jobless themselves for their condition. Authors such as Charles Murray (1984) and Lawrence Mead (1992) believe that welfare has created an inducement to being poor and destroyed the work ethic by giving the impoverished an easy alternative to the rigors of self-sufficiency through work. Liberal scholars, in contrast, argue that the economic structure has shifted to the disadvantage of low-skilled workers and that the War on Poverty was never actually fought, due to a lack of resources and political will (Wilson 1987; Harrington 1984). Beyond an emphasis on broad structural changes in the economy, however, liberals have had a difficult time sorting out the variety of obstacles that may explain declining rates of employment, such as discrimination, child care, the spatial diffusion of jobs out of the inner city to the suburbs, social networks, and skill or credential requirements for jobs in the growing sectors of the economy.

A number of these issues are explored in subsequent chapters of this volume. This section explores patterns of labor force participation in Los Angeles County. Figure 2.6 reports the rate of employment for

FIGURE 2.6   *Employment Rate of Young (Twenty-Five to Thirty-Four) Men and Women by Race and Educational Attainment, 1990*

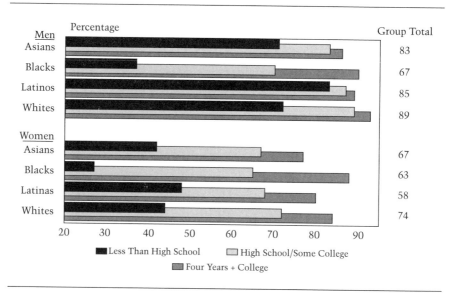

Source: U.S. Department of Commerce 1990.

young workers (age twenty-five to thirty-four) in 1990 by racial group and level of educational attainment for men and women. Employment rates are shown only for young workers, who have generally completed their education, since they more accurately reflect current labor market conditions than their more senior counterparts. Among men in 1990, educational attainment and employment demonstrated a modest relationship for most groups.[7] This relationship was most pronounced among young African American men; young college-educated black men had among the highest employment rate (90 percent) in Los Angeles County, while those without a high school education were by far the least likely to be employed (37 percent). Fortunately, as reported in the previous section, the educational upgrading of African Americans meant that those without a high school diploma were a small and declining proportion of black men. In contrast, the employment rate of young Latino men was high and differed little by level of education; fewer than 10 percentage points separated the employment rate among those with less than a high school education and college graduates. Although Latino men—particularly immigrants, who dominated the Latino population in the labor market in 1990—had very low levels of educational attainment relative to other groups, that did not pose an obstacle to their employment. Young white and Asian men show a marked decline in the rate of employment among the least educated, yet these declines were relatively modest when compared to African American men, and their overall employment levels were high.

The employment rate of young women increased substantially over recent decades, from 47 percent in 1970 to 66 percent in 1990. For women, employment rates in 1990 varied by level of education more so than those of men. While the employment rates of college-educated women were around 80 percent, those without a high school diploma hovered at about half that rate. Differential employment rates by educational attainment among African American women, like men, were extreme. And in contrast to Latino men, the rate of employment for Latinas was far more dependent on educational attainment. The strong relationship between education and employment among women meant that overall employment rates among young women largely mirrored levels of educational attainment and was highest among young white women, followed by Asian, black, and Latina women.

The employment rates of young men and women reveal an important dimension of inequality. The relationship between educational attainment and labor force participation is positive and strong, with the exception of young Latino men, who have very high rates of employment regardless of schooling. This relationship makes the educational upgrading of native-born groups over time, discussed previously, all the more important, and demonstrates the critical importance of education to employment.

Trends in Inequality Among Families and Households

The labor market is central to the shifting tides of inequality and a major focus of the LASUI, yet is by no means the only factor contributing to such trends, nor the only expression of inequality. Inequality, from the viewpoint of the authors of this volume, has a multitude of dimensions and causes. While the Census Bureau is limited in its ability to allow researchers to untangle the complex etiology of inequality (hence the need for projects such as LASUI), it does provide some useful measures of change in the social organization of the local population over time. This section explores some of these shifts by following recent trends in poverty rates, family structure, and wealth.

Poverty

The poverty line is a commonly used indicator of economic hardship, widely available through published census reports, and its calculus has remained the same since its creation in 1965 (adjusted for inflation), which makes it a comparable measure over time. The poverty threshold is based upon a household's size and income.[8] The proportion of households in Los Angeles below the poverty line remained constant at just under 12 percent between 1970 and 1990.[9] Figure 2.7 shows the percent of households below the poverty line among groups in Los Angeles County in both 1970 and 1990. In general, there was a slight reduction in the proportion of households below the poverty line for all racial and ethnic groups and among the native- and foreign-born, with the exception of foreign-born Latino households. Not only were foreign-born Latinos the only group whose proportion of households below the poverty line increased over time, but in 1990 they had the highest poverty rate, followed by African Americans, foreign-born Asians, native-born Latinos, whites, and native-born Asians.

Household and Family Structure

The structure of households and families in Los Angeles underwent steady change between 1970 and 1990. Most significantly, the proportion of households occupied by married couples declined, from 61 percent in 1970 to 50 percent in 1990, while other types of households

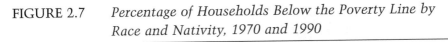

FIGURE 2.7   *Percentage of Households Below the Poverty Line by Race and Nativity, 1970 and 1990*

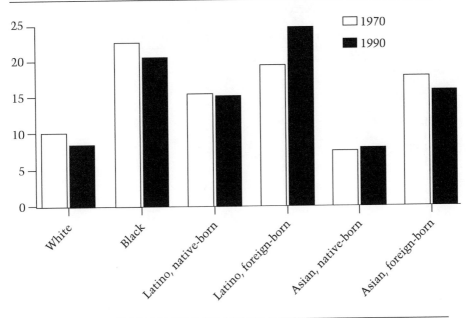

Source: U.S. Department of Commerce 1970, 1990a.

increased.[10] Among the increasing forms of family structure were single-headed households with children, which increased from 8 percent of all households in 1970 to 11 percent in 1990. The growth of single-headed households has elicited widespread concern due to the heightened potential risk for inadequate material and emotional resources for children in such families (Pearce 1978; Ellwood 1988; McLanahan and Casper 1995). At each decade point under review in this chapter, single-headed households in Los Angeles County were nearly three times more likely than other households to fall below the poverty line (table 2.4).

Among groups, black families were the most likely to be headed by a single parent, constituting nearly one in four black families by 1990 (see table). Latino families experienced the largest increase in the percent of families headed by a lone parent, nearly doubling from one in ten in 1970 to two in ten twenty years later. Single-parent households among Asians also nearly doubled, yet remained relatively low. And among whites, single-parent households accounted for a small proportion of households during this time period. Among all single-headed

TABLE 2.4   *Selected Characteristics of Single-Headed Households in Los Angeles County, 1970, 1980, 1990*

	Percentage of All Households	Percentage Below Poverty Line	Percentage Female	Percentage Ever Married
Asian and Pacific Islanders				
1970	4	n.a.	80	90
1980	4	25	79	91
1990	7	28	73	79
Blacks				
1970	19	46	92	84
1980	21	42	89	69
1990	23	39	87	60
Latinos				
1970	11	41	85	89
1980	12	44	84	76
1990	19	40	67	57
Whites				
1970	6	26	92	96
1980	6	21	83	92
1990	5	18	77	86
Los Angeles County				
1970	8	34	87	92
1980	9	34	85	80
1990	11	33	75	66

Source: U.S. Department of Commerce 1970, 1980a, 1990a.

households and all racial groups, the proportion of households headed by someone who had ever been married declined substantially, from over 90 percent in 1970 to just two-thirds in 1990. This latter trend was especially pronounced among African American and Latino households, less dramatic among whites and Asians. In part, the growth of single-headed households among Latinos and Asians was due to immigration patterns; as the proportion of single-headed households rose among Latinos and Asians, the proportion of them headed by women decreased, since migration streams tend to be male-dominant.

Wealth

Measures of income, such as earnings or family income, are commonly used in stratification analyses, yet have limits when relied upon exclusively. Income is only one dimension of economic well-being. Exploring differences in wealth, which includes financial holdings such as stocks, bonds, and real estate, adds the dimension of accumulated economic advantage-disadvantage to the picture of economic inequality in Los Angeles. Melvin Oliver and Thomas Shapiro argue that "the neglected wealth dimension of racial inequality and social justice must receive more attention if the notion of life chances, or even a broadened idea of economic well-being, is to be addressed seriously" (1989, 8). In contrast to income, wealth provides an indicator of a household's ability to, for example, put a child through college, start a business, or weather a period of income loss due to a major illness.

Data containing detailed information on wealth are sparse. This section relies on data reported by LASUI respondents. The LASUI asked respondents about the assets and debts of their households, allowing us to compare the wealth holdings of different groups. Homes and automobiles are the principal source of debt and assets. Because equity built up in the home is not easily transferable into cash, and a home or car is rarely sold to pay for a medical emergency, they are often omitted from measures of wealth to provide an indicator of net financial assets (NFA). In contrast to net worth (total assets minus total debt), NFA represents wealth that can be used to command future economic gain (Oliver and Shapiro 1989, 1995).

Among the LASUI sample, six in ten households reported having zero or negative NFA. While this seems stunningly high, it is on par with other national studies of wealth. Among households with positive NFA, slightly less than one-fifth reported moderate levels of NFA ($1,250 to 10,000) and slightly more than one-fifth had NFA in excess of $10,000. The economic well-being of households indicated by net financial assets demonstrates that the majority are asset-poor and, therefore, extremely dependent upon extant sources of income and limited in their ability to generate additional assets through, for example, more education or starting a business. Figure 2.8 presents three summary (mean) measures of wealth for each racial and ethnic group: debts, assets, and NFA. Whites and native-born Asians clearly top the wealth hierarchy, averaging asset-to-debt ratios in excess of 2:1, with mean NFA of nearly $10,000. Foreign-born Asians, native-born Latinos, and blacks rival whites and native-born Asians in terms of debt, but do not have anywhere near the amount of accumulated assets as the two wealthiest groups and fall substantially behind them in mean NFA. Foreign-born Asians average considerably more NFA ($5,505) than either native-born Latinos ($3,431) or African Americans ($1,980). Foreign-born Latinos have little debt or assets and average a minimal amount of NFA ($271).

The distribution of wealth by racial groups and nativity presents an interesting contrast to the earnings and poverty data just presented. Whites and native-born Asians top both measures of earnings and

FIGURE 2.8   *Mean Wealth Indicators in LASUI by Race-Ethnicity and Nativity*

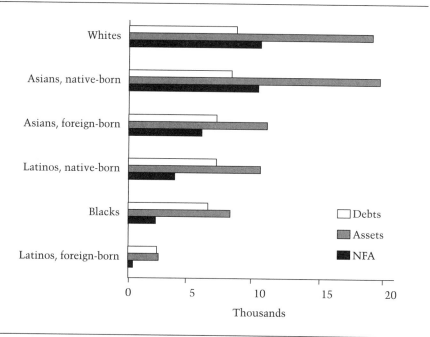

Source: Los Angeles Study of Urban Inequality 1994.

wealth. African Americans and native-born Latinos, despite substantial earnings growth and modest reductions in poverty over time, have not been able to turn their higher incomes into the security provided by wealth. And the scant and declining economic resources of foreign-born Latinos—despite remarkably high employment rates—is further corroborated by their near complete lack of wealth. Of all the major groups currently residing in Los Angeles County, foreign-born Latinos are by far the most economically marginal.

Residential Segregation

Residential segregation of whites and blacks remains one of the most persistent and pervasive forms of racial division in the United States. It has been called the "structural linchpin" of race relations (Pettigrew 1979; Bobo 1989). Physical separation of blacks and whites is so pronounced that Douglas Massey and Nancy Denton (1993) argue that a state of racial apartheid exists in our nation's cities. Although the sprawling urban form of Los Angeles is quite different from the "chocolate city, vanilla suburbs" (Farley et al. 1978) of the Midwest and Northeast, residential segregation in Los Angeles has been on par with, and in many cases has exceeded, rates of segregation in other parts of the country.

In 1970, the dissimilarity index for black and white residential segregation in Los Angeles ranked third nationally among major metropolitan areas in the United States, trailing only Chicago and Gary, Indiana (Massey and Denton 1993). The black-white dissimilarity index in 1970 was .90, meaning that whites and blacks were nearly completely separated residentially (see table 2.5).[11] Residential separation of blacks and whites declined in 1980 and again in 1990 relative to 1970, yet remains high. The decline was likely due to a combination of white and black out-migration from the county and the transformation of South Central Los Angeles from a nearly all-black ghetto in 1970 to equal proportions of blacks and Latinos in 1990. In 1990, as table 2.5 shows, blacks were the most residentially segregated group among the major racial groups in Los Angeles. On a positive note, the dissimilarity index for blacks with each other racial group has declined over time. The high rate of segregation among blacks is evident, as blacks are concentrated in South Central Los Angeles, Inglewood, and Compton, with smaller nodes in Pacoima, Altadena, and Pomona. Between 1980 and 1990, the concentration of African Americans in the heart of South Central diminished considerably as thousands of blacks left the area, most often migrating to neighboring Riverside and San Bernardino counties (Grant, Oliver, and James 1996).

Asian levels of residential segregation were low and stable, despite the tremendous growth of the Asian population in Los Angeles County. The Asian-white and Asian-Latino rates of dissimilarity were the lowest in the county in 1980 and 1990. In contrast with blacks, Asians' housing patterns do not demonstrate areas of heavy concentration;

TABLE 2.5   *Dissimilarity Indices of Major Racial-Ethnic Groups, Los Angeles County 1970, 1980, 1990 (Tract Level)*

	1970	1980	1990
Black–White	.901	.809	.730
Black–Asian	—	.761	.693
Black–Latino	.841	.724	.595
Latino–White	.458	.572	.611
Latino–Asian	—	.491	.511
Asian–White	—	.467	.462

Source: Clark 1996.

rather, the growing Asian population is widely spread throughout the county. The largest residential enclaves of Asians, which grew from 1980 to 1990, were in the San Gabriel Valley (especially in and around Monterey Park), downtown Los Angeles, Gardena and Carson, Cerritos and La Mirada along the Orange County border, and Diamond Bar.

While the segregation of whites and African Americans has diminished in recent decades, segregation between whites and Latinos rose. As the Latino population grew and the white population declined, these two groups, who together comprised nearly 80 percent of the Los Angeles population in 1990, have become less and less likely to share neighborhood space. These trends in the dissimilarity indices between groups over time suggest that the two fastest-growing populations, Asians and Latinos, have had differential success in their ability to penetrate white neighborhoods.

The residential distribution of whites and Latinos and are nearly mirror opposites of each other. That is, whites and Latinos, as the dissimilarity indices suggest, tend to be concentrated in almost entirely different neighborhoods throughout the county. While its mountainous geography and urban sprawl distinguish Los Angeles from traditional American urban form, the dearth of whites in and around the central core of Los Angeles is surprisingly consistent with other major metropolises. Between 1980 and 1990, that central region devoid of whites expanded. Latinos have become increasingly segregated from whites and Asians as they locate in a variety of areas throughout the county, among them South Central Los Angeles (Turner and Allen 1991). While part of this movement is economic in nature, as financially strapped foreign-born Latinos have sought housing in the oldest and cheapest housing stock south and east of downtown, racial attitudes play a critical role in the racial organization of neighborhoods in Los Angeles (Bobo and Zubrinsky 1996). Thus, as South Central and the surrounding area has become less inhabited by blacks, it nonetheless remains nonwhite.

Conclusion

This chapter has presented a bird's-eye view of demographic change in Los Angeles with information provided by the Census Bureau's 1970 to 1990 public use files. The central story that emerges from this analysis is of a robust economy and a rapidly shifting and economically stratified population. Immigration from Asia, Mexico, and Central America combined with white out-migration and aging has shifted the racial, ethnic, and national origin composition of Los Angeles from a predominantly white metropolis in 1970 to a diverse, multiethnic population in which no group constituted a majority of the population in 1990. Economically, Los Angeles became less dependent on industrial manufacturing as the principal source of jobs. While manufacturing remains a vital part of the economic mix, this sector experienced internal turmoil with heavy job losses in relatively high-wage industries such as auto, glass, and steel and growth in competitive, lower-wage industries.

The demographic and economic transformation of Los Angeles has had a widely differential impact on racial groups, as well as men and women, in the labor market. The employment rate among men declined slightly over time, but particularly among young, low-skilled black men. The employment rate of women, on the other hand, grew dramatically during this period, from 47 percent to 66 percent in 1990. The index of representation among occupations between 1970 and 1990 shows that white men remained concentrated among top-paying occupations, Asian and black men shifted into better-paying occupational categories, while Latino men remained concentrated in traditional blue-collar sectors. Asian, black, and white women all improved their distribution among the top tier of occupations, while Latina women were concentrated in the lowest-paying occupations in 1970 and 1990. The improved occupational status of most women was reflected in the declining gender gap in earnings among full-time, full-year workers. Nonetheless, with the ratio of women's to men's earnings at .76 in 1990, there remains a considerable gap to close.

Social change in Los Angeles has been rapid, challenging the population and local institutions to adapt and respond to the emergent new urban reality. Inequality runs deep in Los Angeles. And the diversity of peoples and activities in Los Angeles presents a complicated and multifaceted portrait of inequality, as this chapter documents. Subsequent chapters in this volume further illuminate the complex nature of urban inequality along the dimensions of racial attitudes, labor market dynamics, and residential segregation in Los Angeles.

Notes

1. Using the mean total fertility rate (the total number of lifetime births per woman) as a measure of fertility, in 1990 foreign-born Latinas had the highest total fertility rate in Los Angeles County (2.4), compared with a total fertility rate of less than two births for native-born Latinas. Native-born Asians had the lowest fertility rate (1.3), while the rate for foreign-born Asians was considerably higher (1.9).

2. The percent change from 1970 to 1990 reported in tables 2.1 through 2.5 is simply the difference between the percent a category

accounted for in the distribution in 1990 subtracted from the percent that category accounted for in 1970. The absolute change reported is the percentage change from 1970 to 1990 in the total number of a group in 1990, based on the number of that group in 1970. In table 2.1, for example, as a percent of all major industrial sectors, construction employed grew by 1.4 percent between 1970 (4.7) and 1990 (6.1). At the same time, in 1970 there were 136,900 and in 1990 267,292 people employed in construction; an absolute change of 95 percent. Whites comprised 71 percent of the population in 1970 and 41 percent in 1990, a percent change of −30. The number of whites in Los Angeles County was nearly 5 million in 1970 and 3.6 million in 1990, an absolute decline of 27 percent.

3. This increase is partly an artifact of the data due to greater detail in the 1990 census relative to 1970, yet less than 4 percent in 1970 reported "other Asian."

4. The index of representation is based on the percent that a group comprises of the occupational structure as a whole relative to the percentage rate that they are employed within a given occupational sector. The index of representation (IR) is 1.0 when a group is represented in an occupation and the labor force at the same rate, above 1.0 when it is overrepresented, and below 1.0 when underrepresented in a given occupational category. For example, in 1990, 5 percent of all workers were Asian women; 5 percent of Asian women were employed as managers, 8 percent as clericals, and 1.4 percent in craft and repair occupations. Thus, Asian women were evenly represented as managers (IR = 1), overrepresented as clericals by a factor of 1.6 (IR = 1.6), and underrepresented among craft and repair workers by a factor of 3.6 (IR = .28).

5. Mean earnings were calculated among all workers who reported positive earnings. The rank of occupations based on average earnings in 1969 was slightly different than in 1989. In 1969 the order was as follows, with constant 1989 dollars in parenthesis: managers ($44,840), finance and business sales ($38,590), professional ($38,480), technical ($33,230), craft and repair ($29,360), laborers-fabricators-operators ($19,770), clerical ($18,100), retail sales ($16,800), and service ($14,630).

6. When viewing figures 2.3 and 2.4 one should keep in mind that the movement of a group from one, and especially two, levels of representation to another over time can be immense; yet these large occupational categories can nonetheless be misleading. In general, the greater specificity in measurement of an occupation, the higher the level of gender or racial-ethnic segregation (King 1992). Consider, for example, the case of African American women in managerial occupations. In 1970 they were heavily underrepresented in the managerial sector, as only 1,500 black women worked in this

category, less than 1 percent of all black women, who comprised 4.3 percent of the workforce. In 1990 African American women were evenly represented in managerial occupations, with 24,594 employed in this sector (4.4 percent of black women, who comprised 4.9 percent of the workforce). This is a numeric increase of 1,540 percent between 1970 and 1990! However, within the managerial sector, African American women had an average annual income of $27,810 compared to $41,590 among all workers, suggesting that black women tend to be concentrated in relatively poor paying occupations and/or industries among managers.

7. Change in employment rates over time are not shown in figure 2.6, but for young men were generally high and stable, declining slightly over time from 88 percent in 1970 to 84 percent in 1990.

8. In 1990, the average poverty threshold for a family of four was $13,359 (U.S. Census Bureau, 1992).

9. The percent of persons below the poverty line, in contrast to households, increased from 11 percent in 1970 to 15 percent in 1990.

10. Other types of households include married-couple households, other family households (which include related persons), and non-family households (which include persons living alone or with other, nonrelated persons).

11. The dissimilarity index is a measure of segregation ranging from 0 (perfect integration) to 100 (complete segregation). It is a summary measure (mean) calculated by comparing the representation of two groups across neighborhoods (census tracts) with their representation in a larger area (such as a city or county).

References

Bean, Frank, and Marta Tienda. 1987. *The Hispanic Population of the United States.* New York: Russell Sage.

Blau, Francine, and Andrea Beller. 1992. "Black-White Earnings over the 1970s and 1980s: Gender Difference in Trends." *Review of Economics and Statistics* 74(2): 276–86.

Bobo, Lawrence. 1989. "Keeping the Linchpin in Place: Testing the Multiple Sources of Opposition to Residential Integration." *International Review of Social Psychology* 2: 305–23.

Bobo, Lawrence, and Camille Zubrinsky. 1996. "Attitudes on Residential Integration: Perceived Status Differences, Mere In-Group Preference, or Racial Prejudice?" *Social Forces* 74(3): 883–909.

Bound, John, and Richard Freeman. 1992. "What Went Wrong? The Erosion of Relative Earnings and Employment Among Young Black Men in the 1980s." *Quarterly Journal of Economics* 201(1): 201–32.

Clark, W.A.V. 1996. "Residential Patterns: Avoidance, Assimilation, and

Succession." In *Ethnic Los Angeles*, edited by Roger Waldinger and Mehdi Bozorgmehr. New York: Russell Sage.

Cotton, Jeremiah. 1989. "Opening the Gap: The Decline in Black Economic Indicators in the 1980s." *Social Science Quarterly* 40(4): 803–19.

Ellwood, David T. 1988. *Poor Support: Poverty in the American Family*. New York: Basic Books.

England, Paula, and Irene Browne. 1992. "Trends in Women's Economic Status." *Sociological Perspectives* 35: 17–51.

Farley, Reynolds, and Walter R. Allen. 1989. *The Color Line and the Quality of Life in America*. New York: Oxford University Press.

Farley, Reynolds, Howard Schuman, Suzanne Bianchi, Diane Colasanto, and Shirley Hackett. 1978. "Chocolate City, Vanilla Suburbs: Will the Trend Toward Racially Separate Communities Continue?" *Social Science Research* 7: 319–44.

Frey, William H. 1994. "The New White Flight." *American Demographics* 16(April): 40–48.

———. 1996. "Immigration, Domestic Migration, and Demographic Balkanization in America: New Evidence for the 1990s." *Population and Development Review* 22(4): 741–63.

Grant, David M., Melvin L. Oliver, and Angela D. James. 1996. "African Americans: Social and Economic Bifurcation." In *Ethnic Los Angeles*, edited by R. Waldinger and M. Bozorgmehr. New York: Russell Sage.

Harrington, Michael. 1984. *The New American Poverty*. New York: Harper & Row.

Harrison, Bennett, and Barry Bluestone. 1982. *The Deindustrialization of America*. New York: Basic Books.

Hochschild, Jennifer. 1996. *Race, Class, and the American Dream*. Princeton, N.J.: Princeton University Press.

Johnson, James H., Jr., and Melvin L. Oliver. 1992. "Structural Changes in the U.S. Economy and Black Male Joblessness: A Reassessment." In *Urban Labor Markets and Job Opportunity*, edited by G.E. Peterson and W. Vroman. Washington, D.C.: The Urban Institute Press.

Johnson, James H., Melvin L. Oliver, and Curtis C. Roseman. 1989. "Introduction: Ethnic Dilemmas in Comparative Perspective." *Urban Geography* 10: 425–33.

King, Mary C. 1992. "Occupational Segregation by Race and Sex, 1940–88." *Monthly Labor Review* 115(4): 30–36.

Levy, Frank. 1987. *Dollars and Dreams: The Changing American Income Distribution*. New York: Russell Sage.

Levy, Frank, and Richard J. Murnane. 1992. "U.S. Earnings Levels and Earnings Inequality: A Review of Recent Trends and Proposed Explanations." *Journal of Economic Literature* 30: 1333–81.

Lieberson, Stanley. 1980. *A Piece of the Pie: Black and White Immigrants Since 1880*. Berkeley: University of California Press.

Lopez, David, Eric Popkin, and Edward Telles. 1996. "Central Americas: At the Bottom, Struggling to Get Ahead." In *Ethnic Los Angeles*, edited by Roger Waldinger and Mehdi Bozorgmehr. New York: Russell Sage.

Massey, Douglas, and Nancy Denton. 1993. *American Apartheid: Residential Segregation and the Making of the Underclass.* Cambridge, Mass.: Harvard University Press.

McLanahan, Sarah, and Lynne Casper. 1995. "Growing Diversity and Inequality in the American Family." In *State of the Union: America in the 1990s,* edited by Reynolds Farley. New York: Russell Sage.

Mead, Lawrence. 1992. *The New Politics of Poverty: The Nonworking Poor in America.* New York: Basic Books.

Murray, Charles. 1984. *Losing Ground: American Social Policy, 1950–80.* New York: Basic Books.

Oliver, Melvin L., and Thomas Shapiro. 1989. "Race and Wealth." *Review of Black Political Economy* 17(4): 5–25.

———. 1995. *Black Wealth/White Wealth.* New York: Routledge.

Ortiz, Vilma. 1996. "The Mexican-Origin Population: Permanent Working Class or Emerging Middle Class?" In *Ethnic Los Angeles,* edited by R. Waldinger and M. Bozorgmehr. New York: Russell Sage.

Pearce, Diane. 1978. "The Feminization of Poverty: Women, Work, and Welfare." *Urban and Social Change Review* 11(1–2): 28–36.

Pettigrew, Thomas. 1979. "Racial Change and Social Policy." *Annals of the American Academy of Political and Social Science* 441:114–31.

Portes, Alejandro, and Rubin Rumbaut. 1996. *Immigrant America: A Portrait.* Berkeley, Calif.: University of California Press.

Scott, Alan J. 1988. "Flexible Production Systems and Regional Development: The Rise of New Industrial Spaces in North America and Western Europe." *International Journal of Urban and Regional Research* 12: 171–86.

Smith, Shelley, and Marta Tienda. 1988. "The Doubly Disadvantaged: Women of Color in the U.S. Labor Force." In *Women Working: Theories and Facts in Perspective,* 2d ed., edited by Ann Stromberg and Shirley Harkess. Mountain View, Calif.: Mayfield.

Soja, Ed, Rebecca Morales, and Goetz Wolff. 1983. "Urban Restructuring: An Analysis of Social and Spatial Change in Los Angeles." *Economic Geography* 58: 221–35.

Turner, Eugene, and James P. Allen. 1991. "An Atlas of Population Patterns in Metropolitan Los Angeles and Orange Counties, 1990." Occasional Publications in Geography No. 8. Northridge: California State University, Department of Geography.

U.S. Department of Commerce, Bureau of the Census. 1970. "Census of Population and Housing, 1970," Public Use Samples, County Group Samples, 5 percent, 1/100. Ann Arbor, Mich.: Inter-university Consortium for Political and Social Research.

———. 1980a. "Census of Population and Housing, 1980," Public Use Microdata Sample (A Sample), 5 percent. Ann Arbor, Mich.: Inter-university Consortium for Political and Social Research.

———. 1980b. "Census of Population and Housing, 1980." Summary Tape File 3A. Ann Arbor, Mich.: Inter-university Consortium for Political and Social Research.

————. 1990a. "Census of Population and Housing," Public Use Microdata Sample, 5 percent, 3rd release, 1995. Ann Arbor, Mich.: Inter-university Consortium for Political and Social Research.

————. 1990b. "Census of Population and Housing." Summary Tape File 3A. Ann Arbor, Mich.: Inter-university Consortium for Political and Social Research.

————. 1992. "Measuring the Effect of Benefits and Taxes on Income and Poverty: 1979 to 1991." Series P-60, no. 182. Washington: U.S. Government Printing Office.

Waldinger, Roger. 1989. "Immigration and Urban Change." *Annual Review of Sociology* 15:211–32.

————. 1996. *Still the Promised City? African Americans and New Immigrants in Postindustrial New York.* Cambridge, Mass.: Harvard University Press.

Waldinger, Roger, and Mehdi Bozorgmehr, eds. 1996. *Ethnic Los Angeles.* New York: Russell Sage.

Wilson, William J. 1987. *The Truly Disadvantaged.* Chicago: University of Chicago Press.

————. 1996. *When Work Disappears.* New York: Scribner.

3

RACIAL ATTITUDES IN A PRISMATIC METROPOLIS: MAPPING IDENTITY, STEREOTYPES, COMPETITION, AND VIEWS ON AFFIRMATIVE ACTION

Lawrence D. Bobo and Devon Johnson

How and why do racial attitudes influence patterns of urban inequality? At least since W. E. B. DuBois completed his pioneering study, *The Philadelphia Negro*, in 1899, students of urban social phenomena have tackled this question. In DuBois's era, the effects of racial prejudice and the necessity to incorporate them into any sensible social analysis were unambiguous. (For a fuller treatment of DuBois's discussion of racial prejudice in *The Philadelphia Negro*, see Bobo, 2000.) Contemporary scholars still face these questions, but the extent and effects of negative racial attitudes have become less transparent. Accordingly, examinations of job prospects for low-skilled workers (Holzer 1996) and of ghetto joblessness (Wilson 1996) pay close attention to employers' racial preferences and stereotypes as well as to points of racial friction in employer-worker interaction (Jencks 1992; Feagin and Sikes 1994). Similarly, assessments of urban housing market dynamics and residential segregation direct attention to racial preferences and attitudes (Massey and Denton 1993; Yinger 1995; Farley et al., 1994; Zubrinsky and Bobo 1996).

But simple generalizations about the nature and effects of racial identities, attitudes, and beliefs elude these analysts. Indeed, perhaps the only certain truth of race and ethnic relations in the modern urban metropolis is that they are complex and contradictory. In the broadest sense, our goal is to better inform structural analyses of modern urban labor and housing markets by providing a map of the basic contours of racial attitudes and beliefs in multiracial Los Angeles.

The general salience of racial attitudes and identities is undeniable. Scenes of misunderstanding, conflict, and even open bigotry in Los Angeles (or any major urban area in the United States), are not difficult to call to mind. Imagine a tense situation where angry words are exchanged in a housing project between the equally poor black and Latino residents, as some Latino residents fearful of victimization by blacks demand segregated units. Imagine the affluent black residents of Ladera Heights complaining of the litter, trespassing, and rude behavior of Latino day laborers who mill about each morning seeking work at a large household supply store in the area. Consider the mutual frustration of a struggling Latina housekeeper who comes up a few dollars short on the week's bag of groceries and has a hostile exchange with the Korean store owner who has just told her to leave if she doesn't have enough money. Imagine the circumstances of a black roofing contractor driving through the wealthy Encino area looking for the address of his next job when a white police officer pulls him over because neighbors have reported a suspicious-looking man in the area. Imagine tensions within the labor movement as older, traditional white leaders vie with younger Latinos for positions of power. Consider the general sense of unease with the racial divide conveyed in a front-page *Los Angeles Times* story written months before the 1992 riots:

> Cultural collisions, often violent, occasionally fatal, are occurring every day. Hostilities between black residents and Korean shop-keepers, Latinos and blacks vying for jobs at Martin Luther King Jr./Drew Medical Center, interracial fighting at Lawndale high school, and repeated charges of police brutality against minorities—all of this is disturbing the city's racial peace in a way that has some political analysts recalling Watts. [Frank Clifford, "Tension Among Minorities Upsets Old Rules of Politics." *Los Angeles Times*, August 11, 1991, p. A1]

The writer could not know how prophetic these words would prove to be.[1]

Conflict and division are only part of the story of race in Los Angeles. Imagine a situation where working-class Latino and African American neighbors join together to fight the dumping of hazardous waste in their community. Consider the case of Locke High School, where black and Latino students struggle both to excel academically and to build intergroup harmony. Envision the commitment of a trio of black, Latino, and Asian community leaders who draft a call for progressive leadership on race and found the Multicultural Collaborative. Imagine a prominent white female television newscaster serving, at first with trepidation, on a multiracial jury: "We were seven blacks, four

whites, and one Latino—nine women, and three men of diverse education, and of ages spanning six decades. I got the feeling that as a group
we probably would not be able to agree to walk out of a burning building
together." She subsequently leaves the experience feeling hopeful: "I
cannot explain the dynamic of that particular society of twelve—you
had to be there. Though we were a mixed batch, race was never an issue.
During the deliberations it was as if nobody had a life outside that room.
We were totally focused on the job we were there to do, and we did that
job" (Kelly Lange, "Strangers, 12 of Them, Reach Across Gulfs of Age,
Race and Experience," *Los Angeles Times*, June 7, 1995, p. B7). Imagine
black and Korean ministers facilitating group reconciliation or a Korean
American radio broadcast establishing a regular "Listening to African
American Voices" program. Picture the elderly Japanese American and
African American neighbors of Leimert Park getting together to go
bowling or marvel at the multiracial parade of "low-riders" cruising
down Crenshaw Boulevard on a Sunday evening. Take pride as the white
and Asian high school students on the Academic Decathlon team of the
affluent El Camino Real High School head off for the national competition.[2]

These scenes attest to the enormous range of situations and sample
some of the best and worst of all that is involved with racial and ethnic
"diversity." But perhaps most important, each of these scenes is real.
And each is refracted through social lenses that inevitably attend to the
racial and ethnic background of those involved. In this respect, at least,
the dynamics of urban life in Los Angeles resemble life in most of the
nation's major urban areas.

These scenes raise a number of analytical and substantive questions
about the nature of racial and ethnic attitudes and identities in Los Angeles. The purpose of this chapter is to provide a basic mapping of the
social psychological aspects of race that may impinge on the dynamics
of inequality. We are not concerned with a single domain such as the
labor market or the housing market, nor do we examine a single outcome (that is, wages) or specific research hypothesis (that is, spatial mismatch). Our objective is to take stock of the underlying potential for
racial and ethnic identifiers, or assumptions and preferences springing
from them, to affect social interaction across a wide array of settings
and situations. In this chapter we provide a portrait of the basic underlying contours of public thinking on the subject of race in Los Angeles.

Scenarios and Theoretical Background

Racial identities, attitudes, and beliefs are internally complex phenomena, and our empirical results reflect much of that complexity. In this

section we sketch two useful hypothetical or ideal scenarios for patterns of racial and ethnic attitudes and set what we do in the context of four core theoretical models of the nature of racial attitudes.

Possible Scenarios

As the magnitude, the reach across domains of life, and the stability of racial inequality vary, so too will the patterning of racial attitudes and belief that become bound up with those social circumstances (Jackman 1994). At least since the formulation of Robert E. Park's (1926) race relations cycle, social scientists have recognized stages or modalities to situations of interracial contact (Stone 1985). Thus, for example, comparative race and ethnic relations researchers have drawn a distinction between paternalistic social systems and competitive social systems (Van den Berghe 1967). Paternalistic systems (that is, slave or caste societies) typically involve extensive hierarchy and inequality between groups. The minority or subordinate group comes to be viewed as backward, childlike, suited only for lowly positions and in need of supervision and direction. Competitive systems (that is, industrializing free labor societies) place an increased emphasis on achievement and meritocratic advancement. The greater mobility and success enjoyed by minority or subordinate group members encourages dominant group members to view them as clannish, underhanded, and competitive threats. In a parallel fashion, social psychologists have long recognized a distinction between dominative racism (hot, close, direct, blatant, and aggressive expressions of prejudice) and aversive racism (cold, sophisticated, impersonal, and distancing expressions of prejudice [see Kovel 1970; Gaertner and Dovidio 1986]). And more proximate to our concern with contemporary urban inequality, William Julius Wilson's pathbreaking analysis of the changing structure of black-white relations stressed distinctive historical epochs defined by stable configurations of the economy and polity with respect to the status of blacks (Wilson 1978). Different structures of racial inequality set different patterns for attendant racial identities, attitudes, and beliefs.

To better anchor the analyses and interpretations discussed in this chapter, we consider some ideal-typical scenarios that might exist. At one extreme, there may be sharp and long-standing racial inequalities that structure the workplace, neighborhoods, family life, and the larger sociocultural environment. Under such conditions racial and ethnic identities are likely to be central to individuals' understandings of themselves. In addition, one might expect to find extreme negative out-group stereotyping, high perceptions of threat and competition from other groups, and highly polarized views on whether government is obligated to do anything about it. In sum, sharp and reinforcing structural cleavages between racial and ethnic groups in contact, all else equal, should manifest themselves in salient and polarized patterns of identity, attitude, and belief.

In contrast, the dynamics would be very different under conditions where racial inequalities are muted or nonexistent in the domains of work, neighborhood, family, and sociocultural environment. There would be little reason in such a structural setting to find highly salient racial group identities, and stereotypes would in all likelihood be quite muted themselves, if not obsolete. Similarly, there should be low or nonexistent concern about displacement by competitors from other racial groups. And to the extent that inequalities were still recognized as social problems, there might be a degree of consensus on the role that government should play in helping. Race would matter only when individuals wanted it to, and presumably this would be a freely exercised "option" that brought some enjoyment or benefit rather than misunderstanding, discrimination, and conflict (compare Waters 1990).

These two stylized extremes can be viewed as benchmarks against which to assess the meaning and implications of our results for Los Angeles. As we will show, Los Angeles of the 1990s falls in between the extreme scenarios of acute racial polarization and racial fluidity. Indeed, some elements of both types of scenarios operate depending on which set of group relations (such as, black and white as compared to Asian and white) and which particular indicator (perceptions of competition or opinions on affirmative action, for example) is under examination.

Theorizing Racial Attitudes

Substantive theories of racial attitudes can be usefully divided into four partially overlapping types, each of which tends to emphasize certain central variables or processes. The favored approach among sociologists can be labeled theories of intergroup ideology, dominance, and conflict (Jackman and Muha 1984; Jackman 1994; Sidanius and Pratto 1999; Bobo 1983; Bobo and Kluegel 1993). Approaches in this category tend to emphasize the implications of structured social inequality in access to valued social resources such as wealth, power, or prestige. The primary implication of such inequality is the development of self-interested or ideologically-based viewpoints that serve or favor the interests of one's own social group. The preeminent expositor of such a perspective is Herbert Blumer (1958), who developed a theory of prejudice as a sense of group position (see Bobo 1999). According to the theory, racial attitudes are not narrow individual expressions of like and dislike. Rather, they are preferences about the positional or status arrangement of racial groups in relation to one another. The concern with group entitlements, privileges, and threats to customary privileges encourage prejudiced acts in this framework. Racial attitudes in these formulations have substantially instrumental and reasoned components and may respond to more immediate situational or contextual factors (for example, the relative size of a minority group population [see Fossett and Kiecolt 1989; Glaser 1994; Taylor 1998]).

A second line of theorizing, favored among many social psychologists, can be labeled social learning models of prejudice (Allport 1954; Pettigrew 1982; Katz 1991; Sears 1988). From this perspective, individuals learn the prevailing social conceptions about members of other groups from significant figures (such as parents, peers, community leaders, and eventually the media) as they grow up. But important stages in the process of learning are typically held to occur early in life and to begin with a bedrock of emotional or affective tonality. That is, before a child has developed any elaborate informational or cognitive ideas about members of other racial groups, he or she attends to the emotional valence of remarks and behaviors of significant figures in the socializing environment. This process of social learning establishes deeply rooted inclinations of sympathy or aversion, fear or embrace, toward particular social categories. As the individual matures this emotional bedrock helps to channel subsequent information and experiences in a consistent manner. The end product is the acquisition of the images and inclinations toward members of other racial groups commonly held by members of the individual's own social background. Racial attitudes in this formulation are centrally emotional and unreasoned and linked to early childhood upbringing in racially biased and largely homogeneous socializing contexts.

A third approach may be labeled the cognitive information processing model (Ashmore and Del Boca 1981; Stephan and Rosenfield 1982; Stephan 1985). This approach is centrally concerned with the nature and effects of stereotyping. It begins with the assumption that categorization—the process of creating simplifying constructs that allow us to process the almost infinite flood of stimuli bombarding us—is a natural human activity. This activity has regularities to it that apply whether the object of attention is a piece of furniture or another human being. For example, once a set of categories becomes established, it is cognitively easier to exaggerate the degree of between-category difference and to minimize the degree of within-category variation. Such fundamental biases in information processing have strong implications for the development of ideas and beliefs about members of different racial and ethnic categories. Because the creation of categories and the rules that influence their operation are not specific to racial and ethnic phenomena, many cognitive psychologists do not accept a number of the common presumptions made about the notion of stereotyping. That is, many theorists do not assume that stereotypes are inherently inflexible, negative, nonresponsive to new information, or intrinsically bad.

The fourth type of theory involves personality models. Here the emphasis is on basic dynamics and motivational processes within the individual. The preeminent exemplar is *The Authoritarian Personality* (Adorno et al. 1950), which argues that racial and ethnic prejudice is most acute among those with broadly rigid, conventional, intolerant, unreflective personality styles or makeup. The authoritarian personality is predisposed to demeaning and aggressive behavior toward members of almost any out-group, not just those who might be realistic resource competitors or traditional objects of group socialization to dislike. Work in this tradition has faced severe methodological and conceptual problems (see Altemeyer 1988). However, there is a large body of evidence suggesting that the concept of authoritarianism, viewed as one of a range of social attitudes rather than as an aspect of deep Freudian personality structure, can give us a clue to why some individuals are particularly inclined to hostility toward racial and ethnic minorities (Altemeyer 1988; Duckitt 1992; Peffley and Hurwitz 1998).

For three reasons we adopt a catholic and descriptive approach for this chapter. First, although the LASUI measures are extensive, they are also limited in scope. The LASUI was designed to explore several complicated aspects of urban social life—the labor market, the housing market, and patterns of racial attitudes and beliefs. Though each domain received extensive coverage, none were exhaustively treated. An explicit decision was made in the design of the racial attitudes component of the questionnaire to emphasize measures of the most fundamental types of attitudes and beliefs (that is, identity), and those that had fairly direct implications for labor or housing market dynamics (stereotypes and group competition). As a result, many of the concepts and measures that might allow rigorous examination of competing theories of racial attitudes qua racial attitudes did not become elements of the LASUI survey (such as affect measures, general or abstract policy preferences, and other social and cultural value outlooks, such as individualism or egalitarianism; see Jackman 1977; Kluegel and Smith 1986).

Second, for the purpose of mapping the racial attitudes terrain, we share the analytical and theoretical eclecticism of Gordon Allport, who argued that: "There seems to be value in all of the . . . main approaches and some truth in virtually all of the resulting theories." Stating the case more concretely:

> A person acts with prejudice in the first instance because he perceives the object of prejudice in a certain way. But he perceives it in a certain way partly because his personality is what it is. And his personality is what it is chiefly because of the way he was socialized (training in family, school, neighborhood). The existing social situation is also a factor in his socialization and may also be a determinant of his perceptions. Behind these forces lie other valid but more remote causal influences. They involve the structure of society in which one lives, long-standing economic and cultural traditions, as well as national and historical influences of long duration. While these factors seem so remote as to be alien to the immediate psychological analysis of prejudiced acts, they are, nonetheless, important causal influences. [Allport 1954, 208]

This broad chain of logic remains apt today and undergirds all of the analyses and interpretations we present.

Third, our approach is to stress the multiracial character of Los Angeles and of the LASUI data, which provide an extraordinary opportunity to capture the dynamics of race in a heterogeneous urban environment. Theories of prejudice and racial attitudes were, overwhelmingly, developed with an eye toward understanding dominant group members' attitudes toward subordinate or minority group members. Prior theory and research thus provide little in the way of well-established guidance or expectations for situations as complex as those that exist in Los Angeles. Here we push the envelope by usually (though not always) asking parallel questions of members of each racial group.[3]

Analytical Focus and Strategy
Major Topical Domains

Our analysis focuses on measures of a sense of linked or common fate identity, on stereotypes, on perceptions of group competition for economic and political resources, and on opinions on affirmative action. By taking up these four outlooks, we address four core substantive questions:

(1) Do people see racial group membership as important in affecting outcomes in their own lives?

(2) What do people believe about the traits and predispositions of members of their own racial group and those of other groups?

(3) Are there weak or strong tendencies to see members of other racial and ethnic groups as competitive threats in the struggle for jobs and political influence?

(4) What social policies are people willing to support in order to ameliorate racial and ethnic inequality?

We structure our effort to address these questions around four analytical sets of questions:

(1) How sharply differentiated are members of the different racial and ethnic groups? That is, do white, black, Asian, and Latino respondents differ in the tendency to express a racial group attachment, to see other groups in negative terms, to perceive competitive group relations, or to support policies such as affirmative action?

(2) Are there other aspects of location in the social structure beyond race, such as economic status, gender, personal network, neighborhood, and workplace racial composition that shape racial attitudes and beliefs?

(3) Are there significant social psychological underpinnings of racial attitudes, such as broad political ideology or degree of religiosity?

(4) Does the immediate interview context influence the sorts of attitudes and beliefs that individuals express? That is, does the race of the interviewer or level of comfort talking about issues of race affect responses?

Our first and, in some sense, analytically most important task is to map and interpret group differences in attitudes and beliefs (question #1). The analytical primacy placed on group comparisons stems from our general concern with the structure and dynamics of group inequality wherein identities, attitudes, and beliefs lend meaning and coherence to the institutionalized or collective dimensions of social experience. As the sociologist Mary Jackman explained, such a focus

> draws attention to the structural conditions that encase an intergroup relationship and it underscores the point that individual actors are not free agents but are caught in an aggregate relationship. Unless we assume that the individual is socially atomized, her personal experiences constitute only one source of information that is evaluated against the backdrop of her manifold observations of the aggregated experiences (both historical and contemporaneous) of the group as a whole. [Jackman 1994, 119]

Group-level comparisons are central to but not exhaustive of our mission. Hence, as questions #2, 3, and 4 specify, we also examine critical sources of potential individual-level variation.

A bit more needs to be said about the issue of interview context. Survey researchers have long recognized that the interview setting, albeit stylized and more directed than most face-to-face encounters, is nonetheless a social interaction (Schuman and Kalton 1985). As such, it is subject to influence by a variety of factors that may impinge on any social interaction. Characteristics of the interviewer may influence the views respondents feel willing or constrained to express, and individual respondents may vary in their sensitivity to topics covered in the interview.

It is now widely recognized that the race of the interviewer may affect a respondent's expression of racial attitudes. We conducted extensive analysis of the LASUI data to assess the impact of interviewer race and of respondent comfort discussing racial issues (see appendix 3A). In brief, we found generally low to moderate effects of race of interviewer and of interviewer observations of respondent discomfort. These effects were largest among foreign-born Latinos. However, we found few if any other consistent patterns of relationships between interviewer race and patterns of response, between social background characteristics and susceptibility to influence based on interviewer race or observed discomfort in answering questions on racial topics. We did not find strong evidence of social desirability pressures on patterns of response. Nonetheless, we routinely control for aspects of the interview context in the analyses reported in this chapter.

Variables and Logic of the Analysis

Table 3.1 lists the core racial attitude dependent variables and the four groups of independent variables used in the analysis. The former have already been discussed. The independent variables include a set of social background characteristics, measures of religion and social values, measures of personal, work, and neighborhood context, and measures of the interview context.

A word on each. Education is often, though not uniformly (Jackman and Muha 1984) found to encourage both more tolerant racial outlooks and, among minority groups, a heightened sense of group identity. Men are often found to express more negative racial attitudes than women. Older respondents, presumably as a result of critical socialization during less tolerant eras (rather than due to aging per se), often express more negative racial attitudes than do younger people (Schuman et al. 1997). The impact of income is less consistent than that of education, but especially in terms of specifying, for example, which members of a group feel competitive threat from members of other racial groups, it is clear that income can have important effects (Bobo and Hutchings 1996). Given the complexity of the racial makeup of Los Angeles and the extent to which immigration from Asia and Latin America have transformed the metropolis, we routinely examine the possibility that native-

TABLE 3.1   *Core Dependent and Independent Variables*

Core dependent variables
  Common fate identity
  Stereotypes
  Perceived group competition (economic and political)
  Opposition to affirmative action

Core independent variables
  Social background characteristics
    Gender
    Age
    Education
    Income
    Asian ancestry (Chinese, Japanese, Korean, other)
    Latino ancestry (Central American, Mexican, other)
    Nativity

  Religion and social values
    Religious affiliation
    Church attendance
    Political ideology

  Personal, work, and neighborhood context
    Any friend of the target racial group?
    Coworkers mainly from target racial group?
    Percent of target racial group in census tract

  Interview context
    Not same-race interviewer
    Interviewer observations of the respondent

Source: authors' compilation.

versus foreign-born status as well as national ancestry may influence racial attitudes.

We also take into account the part that religion and social values may play in shaping racial attitudes. Some research suggests that there may be effects of religion on attitudes (for example, atheists often express liberal racial attitudes and individuals from more fundamentalist Protestant denominations more conservative views). In addition, those whose general political philosophy is liberal often express more tolerant racial attitudes than those who hold a more conservative political philosophy (Sears 1988; Sniderman and Piazza 1993).

Patterns of contact and interaction may also shape racial attitudes (Allport 1954; Jackman 1994). Individuals who have more diverse friendship networks, who work in more diverse environments, or who live in more diverse communities may, all else equal, be expected to express more liberal racial attitudes than those whose personal, work, and neighborhood context are more homogeneous. Finally, as already noted, we routinely control for aspects of the interview context. Since not all interviews could be matched on the basis of race, we control for exposure to an interviewer of a different race than that of the respondent. We also control for several interviewer observations of respondent behavior during the course of answering the racial attitudes section of the questionnaire.

Our analysis follows a logical progression of likely relationships, as depicted in figure 3.1. We allow for the possibility that the elements of the respondents' social background characteristics, religion and social values, personal, work, and neighborhood context, and interview context will exert influence on each of the racial identity, attitude, and belief measures. At the same time, we operate on the assumption that there is a sort of logical order or sequencing—not necessarily causal or temporal—to the attitude measures themselves. Accordingly, we begin with the extent of feelings of common fate racial identity and next consider racial stereotypes. In effect, we are positing that the degree of in-group attachment and out-group differentiation are, at least logically, prior to perceptions of racial group competition or particular social policy views. The stronger the sense of group identity and the more negative the views of out-groups, the more likely we are to find acute levels of perceived racial group competition. Finally, the extent of opposition to affirmative action for minorities should reflect the feelings of group competition most proximately, but also be shaped by the degree of negative stereotyping and strength of group attachments.

The Contours of Racial Attitudes
Common Fate Identity

Sociologists have long regarded racial and ethnic background as a core source of the individual's social identity. As Kathryn O'Sullivan See and William Julius Wilson put it: "A fundamental question in the study of intergroup relations is how ethnic identity arises, persists, and is altered" (1989, 224). The categories to which individuals are socially recognized as belonging are typically held to influence larger self-conceptions and feelings of self-worth. Under some circumstances a racial or ethnic identity can become a "master status" (Anderson 1990). Social psychologists emphasize that identities can be important bases for social action as well. Henri Tajfel and John Turner (1979) argue that categorization per se, even in the absence of face-to-face interaction with fellow group members or any real social ties, can result in consequential

FIGURE 3.1   *Heuristic Model of Racial Attitude Analysis*

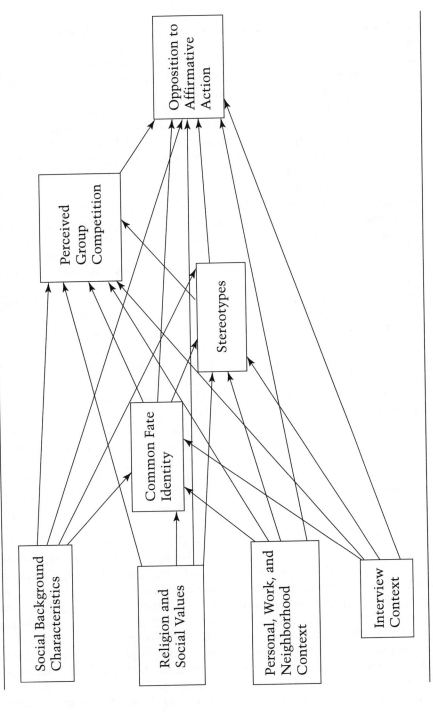

Source: authors' compilation.

social behavior favoring one's own group. We seek to determine the extent to which individuals see their own fate as bound up with that of the racial or ethnic group to which they belong and whether such identities are a product of the social background, values, and contextual influences impinging on the individual.

We used two steps to measure a sense of common fate racial identity. We first asked individuals, "Do you think what happens generally to [own racial group] people in this country will have something to do with what happens in your life?" For those respondents who answered positively, we then asked whether that racial group membership would "affect you a lot, some, or not very much." We are thus able to capture the intensity of feelings of common fate. Tajfel (1982) suggested that an assumption of common fate played a role in the pattern of in-group favoritism shown in his program of research on the impact of social categorization. Several studies have found that feelings of common fate are the most potent dimension of group consciousness among African Americans (Gurin, Hatchett, and Jackson 1989; Tate 1993; Dawson 1994). There is growing evidence of a sense of group identity and attachment among many Asian Americans as well (Espiritu 1992; Tuan 1999), and of important national ancestry attachments among Latinos (De la Garza, Falcon, and Garcia 1996).

Solid majorities—uniformly greater than two-thirds of white, black, Latino, and Asian respondents—expressed at least some degree of common fate racial identity. Figure 3.2 shows the results for the full four-category classification. There are highly significant racial group differences, with African Americans (40 percent) most likely to express "a lot" of common fate group identity. Whereas two out of five blacks express such a high level of common fate identity, only one out of four Latinos do so, and just one out of five whites and Asians do. Still, a nontrivial fraction of each group also denies that racial membership will have personal consequences, including 28 percent of Latinos and 27 percent of whites.

Table 3.2 reports mean scores on the common fate identity (1 = none, 4 = a lot) measured by race and by each of the independent variables. Among all groups there is a small but not monotonic trend for older respondents to express less sense of common fate identity. Although the effect of education emerges as significant only among African Americans, there is a trend for those with greater education, in particular for those with postgraduate training, to express higher levels of common fate identity. This is most clearly the case among African Americans, where those with postgraduate training have the single highest mean sense of common fate score (2.74). Among all groups we also find that self-identified political liberals tend to express higher

FIGURE 3.2   *Common Fate Identity by Race*

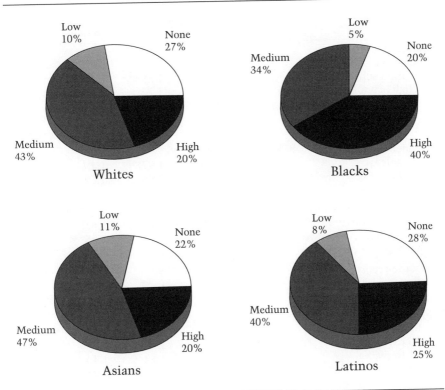

Source: Los Angeles Study of Urban Inequality 1994.

common fate identity than do self-identified conservatives. Only among Latinos is there a regular occurrence of significant relations between level of common fate identity and interview characteristics, with those interviewed by a Latino and those who had no objections to the racial attitude questions expressing higher levels of common fate identity than those interviewed by someone of another race or who did object.

Finally, national ancestry differences emerge among both Asians and Latinos. A weaker sense of common fate identity emerges among Chinese and Japanese ancestry respondents, as compared to Koreans and those from other Asian backgrounds. Among Latinos, those of Central American ancestry express a higher common fate identity than those of Mexican or other Hispanic origin. Both patterns imply that immigrants are taking the racial common fate identity question as an opportunity to express what is mainly a national ancestry or ethnic identity.

TABLE 3.2   *Mean Common Fate Identity by Independent Variables and Race*

	Whites	Blacks	Asians	Latinos
Social background				
Education				
< high school diploma	1.09	1.88***	1.28	1.69
High school diploma	1.50	1.73	1.73	1.41
Some college	1.51	2.05	1.69	1.51
Bachelor's degree	1.67	1.87	1.71	1.55
Postgraduate	1.78	2.74	1.78	1.64
Gender				
Female	1.63	1.97	1.49	1.59
Male	1.49	1.94	1.82	1.58
Age				
Twenty-one to twenty-nine years	1.26***	2.11***	1.89***	1.72***
Thirty to thirty-nine years	1.72	1.76	1.81	1.59
Forty to forty-nine years	1.60	2.20	1.85	1.55
Fifty plus years	1.57	1.83	1.29	1.34
Income report				
Reported	1.56	1.96	1.73	1.56
Did not report	1.51	1.93	1.44	1.72
Income				
Less than 20,000	1.32	1.78	1.75	1.62*
20 to 39,000	1.57	1.94	1.73	1.69
40 to 59,000	1.68	2.12	1.44	1.32
60,000+	1.57	2.17	1.98	1.12
Asian ancestry				
Chinese	—	—	1.54*	—
Japanese	—	—	1.40	—
Korean	—	—	1.86	—
Other	—	—	2.35	—
Latino ancestry				
Mexican	—	—	—	1.57**
Central American	—	—	—	1.85
Other	—	—	—	1.16
Nativity				
Foreign-born	—	—	1.68	1.68**
U.S. native	—	—	1.48	1.33
Religion and social values				
Religion				
Protestant	1.53	1.98	1.96**	1.51
Catholic	1.54	1.75	1.23	1.60
Jewish	1.79	—	—	—
Other	1.64	2.21	1.70	1.67
Agnostic or atheist	1.42	1.61	1.49	1.41

TABLE 3.2   *Continued*

	Whites	Blacks	Asians	Latinos
Political ideology				
Liberal	1.71**	2.17	1.90*	1.93***
Moderate or no thought	1.39	1.83	1.36	1.37
Conservative	1.58	1.75	1.74	1.58
Interview context				
Interviewer race				
Same as respondent	1.60	1.89	1.71	1.67**
Not same race	1.47	2.04	1.44	1.35
Pause				
No pausing	1.58	1.89	1.73	1.64
Paused	1.52	2.08	1.46	1.53
Justify				
No justifying	1.60	1.85**	1.67	1.54
Justified	1.43	2.30	1.50	1.78
Object				
Did not object	1.56	1.97	1.67	1.66**
Objected	1.53	1.61	1.45	1.23
Discomfort				
No discomfort	1.56	1.93	1.70*	1.62
Discomfort	1.54	2.18	1.07	1.42
Personal context				
Black friends				
None	1.55	1.83	1.66*	1.58
At least one	1.73	2.01	1.11	1.80
White friends				
None	1.33*	1.99	1.67	1.61
At least one	1.60	1.72	1.41	1.40
Asian friends				
None	1.57	1.92***	1.71	1.58
At least one	1.41	2.73	1.57	2.02
Latino friends				
None	1.56	1.93	1.66	1.47
At least one	1.54	2.34	1.50	1.67
Workplace context				
White coworkers				
Other	1.40*	1.96	1.63	1.56
Mainly white	1.65	1.94	1.73	1.74
Black coworkers				
Other	1.55	1.97	1.64	1.59
Mainly black	1.86	1.93	2.41	1.42

(Table continues on p. 98.)

TABLE 3.2   *Continued*

	Whites	Blacks	Asians	Latinos
Latino coworkers				
Other	1.56	1.95	1.65	1.44*
Mainly Latino	1.50	2.05	1.69	1.67
Asian coworkers				
Other	1.56	1.95	1.67	1.59
Mainly Asian	1.40	2.14	1.63	1.30
Neighborhood context				
Tract racial comp.				
<10 percent own race	.88*	2.00	1.59	.83**
10 to 19 percent own race	1.33	2.02	1.70	1.23
20+ percent own race	1.57	1.91	1.64	1.62

Source: Los Angeles Survey of Urban Inequality 1994.
*$p < .05$, **$p < .01$, ***$p < .001$

We also estimated full multivariate models of the determinants of common fate identity using ordinary least squares regression.[4] These results are reported separately by race in table 3.3. The first pattern to note is that overall the models are more successful among the racial minority respondents than for whites. (The model for whites yields a variance explained estimate of only .06 and the f-test for the full equation fails to reach conventional criteria for statistical discernibility.) That is, we cannot identify clear sources of individual variation in expression of common fate among whites.

The models are modestly more successful among blacks, Latinos, and Asians. Among African Americans we find an effect of education, with those who obtained postgraduate training scoring more than 1 point higher, net of all other variables in the model, than blacks at any other level of educational attainment. In addition, the model shows that two of the interview context variables had significant effects. Although the race of the interviewer was insignificant, those respondents rated as showing discomfort during the racial attitude section scored higher in common fate identity and those who objected to the racial attitude section scored lower.

Among the Asian respondents the level of expressed common fate identity was significantly tied to age, sex, income level, and aspects of the interview context. Younger respondents were more likely to express high common fate identity than were older respondents and women more so than men. Those of Korean ancestry expressed the highest level of common fate identity and those of Japanese ancestry the least.

TABLE 3.3   *Multivariate Models of Common Fate Identity*

	Whites	Blacks	Asians	Latinos
Constant	1.13 (.43)*	1.42 (.59)*	2.99 (.43)***	1.67 (.42)***
Social background				
Age	.00 (.00)	−.00 (.00)	−.02 (.00)**	−.01 (.00)**
Education				
No high school diploma	−.16 (.37)	.14 (.20)	−.26 (.27)	.28 (.11)
Some college	.02 (.14)	.16 (.13)	−.09 (.16)	.18 (.14)
Bachelor's degree	.19 (.14)	.08 (.19)	−.01 (.12)	.29 (.21)
Postgraduate	.23 (.18)	1.17 (.26)***	−.07 (.17)	.72 (.35)*
Gender	−.16 (.12)	−.11 (.13)	.34 (.11)**	−.03 (.11)
Income				
Did not report	.13 (.24)	.23 (.24)	−.63 (.14)***	.62 (.24)*
Low income	.00 (.23)	.02 (.23)	−.29 (.17)	.32 (.20)
Lower middle income	.09 (.17)	.20 (.22)	−.38 (.15)*	.45 (.17)*
Higher middle income	.13 (.14)	.34 (.20)	−.66 (.17)***	.20 (.24)
Not in work force	−.21 (.13)	−.00 (.15)	−.16 (.13)	.10 (.12)
Ancestry				
Korean	—	—	.39 (.18)*	—
Japanese	—	—	−.28 (.15)	—
Other Asian	—	—	.25 (.40)	—
Mexican	—	—	—	−.03 (.18)
Central American	—	—	—	.21 (.23)
U.S. native	—	—	.01 (.16)	−.10 (.15)
Religion and social values				
Protestant	.19 (.18)	.35 (.24)	.15 (.21)	.17 (.23)
Catholic	.20 (.18)	.14 (.29)	−.48 (.22)*	.14 (.19)
Jewish	.38 (.21)	—	—	—
Other religion	.35 (.19)	.49 (.37)	.23 (.12)	.43 (.29)
Church attendance	.00 (.03)	.02 (.04)	−.02 (.05)	−.02 (.03)
Political conservatism	−.04 (.03)	−.04 (.03)	.01 (.04)	−.08 (.04)*
Personal, work, and neighborhood context				
Has target group friend	.14 (.15)	.08 (.14)	−.10 (.11)	.24 (.10)*
Coworkers mainly target group	.17 (.13)	.05 (.13)	−.28 (.14)	.20 (.10)
Percentage target group in tract	−.00 (.00)	.00 (.00)	−.00 (.00)	−.00 (.00)
Interview context				
Not same-race interviewer	−.04 (.13)	−.03 (.29)	−.06 (.19)	−.30 (.13)*

(Table continues on p. 100.)

TABLE 3.3   *Continued*

	Whites	Blacks	Asians	Latinos
Paused before answering	−.08 (.12)	.23 (.12)	−.17 (.09)	−.22 (.11)*
Justified responses	−.19 (.12)	.17 (.11)	−.06 (.14)	.39 (.15)**
Showed discomfort	.05 (.15)	.35 (.15)*	−.37 (.25)	−.14 (.13)
Objected to section	.09 (.24)	−.63 (.23)**	.09 (.14)	−.66 (.16)**
R^2	.06	.11**	.27***	.14***
N	720	1061	1011	968

Source: Los Angeles Study of Urban Inequality 1994.
Note: Omitted categories for income, education, and religion are high-income, high school diploma, and agnostic or atheist, respectively. For the ancestry items, Chinese ancestry and other Latino ancestry were omitted.
*$p < .05$, **$p < .01$, ***$p < .001$

High-income Asian respondents tended to express higher levels of common fate identity.

For Latino respondents common fate identity was significantly related to age, education, income, political ideology, personal network composition, and several interview characteristic measures. Older respondents express less common fate identity than do younger respondents. Again, those with the very highest level of education are the most likely to express a sense of common fate identity. In contrast to the pattern observed among Asians, for Latinos it is lower-income individuals (and those who refused to report their income) who express higher levels of common fate identity. Politically conservative Latinos are less likely to express common fate identity than are political liberals.

Most striking is the number of interview context measures that influenced how Latinos responded to the common fate identity question. Those interviewed by a non-Latino, who paused during the racial section, who appeared uncomfortable with race questions, or who objected to the section express lower levels of common fate identity. In contrast, those whom interviewers rated as trying to "justify" their answers expressed higher levels of common fate identity than those who did not offer justifications. To us this implies that the idea of expressing a sense of *racial* common fate identity did not resonate with a goodly number of Latino respondents. This is not to say that such an identity has no meaning for Latino respondents, since in other ways—the effects of higher education, of age, and of political ideology—the results are all quite sensible. Rather, it suggests that common fate racial identity may not be the first nor even a highly salient group identity among Latinos.

National ancestry or a more distinctly ethnic attachment presumably takes a higher priority.

In sum, the vast majority of adults in Los Angeles County express some degree of common fate racial identity. This tendency is most pronounced among African Americans. Our results suggest not only racial group differences in the levels of common fate identity, but differences in the meaning and salience of such an identity as well. For white respondents, common fate identity does not appear to be strongly differentiated on the basis of individual characteristics. At least, there are no systematic sources of individual variation that we can detect. For African Americans and for Asians, the notion of a common racial fate does seem more firmly grounded in individual experiences. And as just noted, among Latinos there is some inclination to resist expression of a sense of common fate racial identity, but the notion clearly has some underlying patterning and roots for them.

Racial Stereotypes

What individuals think and believe about the members of other racial and ethnic groups—stereotypes—are commonly recognized as a critical factor in intergroup relations (Allport 1954; Ashmore and Del Boca 1981; Stephan 1985; Jackman 1994). The LASUI contained a large battery of 1- to 7-point bipolar trait rating items based on the model of the 1990 General Social Survey (see Smith 1991; Bobo and Kluegel 1993; Bobo and Kluegel 1997). The trait dimensions were: rich-poor, unintelligent-intelligent, prefer to be self-supporting–prefer to live off welfare, hard to get along with–easy to get along with, speak English poorly–speak English well, involved in drugs and gangs–not involved in drugs and gangs, tend to discriminate against members of other groups–tend to treat members of other groups equally. This set of traits reflects a mix of considerations. Some speak to core concerns in an achievement-oriented society as well as core elements of racial ideologies in the United States (that is, level of intelligence, welfare dependency). Other traits are included because they speak to potentially distinctive views of particular groups. For example, some segments of the Asian population (such as Korean store owners) have been stereotyped as brusque and difficult in social interaction (hard to get along with). And some traits seem to distinguish how racial minorities tend to view whites (such as tending to discriminate against others). This set of items was strongly suggested by our earlier multiethnic focus group discussions (Bobo et al. 1994 and 1995).

Are views of groups consensual or disputed? Are they extreme and categorical, or small and domain-specific? Does one group stand out as the subject of unusually negative stereotyping? In general, we should find a degree of consensus to stereotypes, since they tend to reflect the relative positioning of groups in the social structure (Eagly and Steffen 1984; Sigelman, Shockey and Sigelman 1993; Jackman 1994). However, some groups, due to historical experience or group resources and tradition, may be more effectively poised to challenge potentially negative perceptions of them than are members of other groups (Jackman and Senter 1983).

The racial stereotyping questions were asked as part of a three-way survey-based experiment (compare Schuman and Bobo 1988). This "split-ballot" experiment involved a manipulation wherein a randomly selected third of respondents were asked questions referring to broad racial and ethnic categories ("whites," "blacks," "Asians," or "Latinos"), a third were asked questions referring to males of each racial group, and a third were asked questions referring to females of each racial group. The basic distribution of responses for each item by race and by ballot are shown in table 3.4.

Two types of scores may be examined: absolute ratings in response to each question and a stereotype difference score (scores for any particular target group subtracted from those for the respondent's rating of his or her membership group). The difference scores provide a clearer depiction of whether other groups are seen as essentially no different from the in-group, superior to the in-group, or inferior to the in-group. For greater ease of interpretations we have rescored the absolute ratings so that they run from 0 to 50, with higher scores reflecting more negative ratings. The difference scores range from a low of -50 (most inferior in-group rating compared to out-group) to high of $+50$ (most superior in-group rating compared to out-group rating). A score of 25 is thus the midpoint, signaling moderate scores on the absolute rating scale, and a score of 0 indicates no perceived group difference for the difference score scale. For ease of interpretation, then, all else equal, the higher the score the more negative the stereotype rating.

Perceived Economic Status Differences   We begin with how respondents rated groups on the rich or poor trait dimension, and for now restrict our attention only to the one-third of the sample asked the general racial group category version of the questions (the first column and first row of each racial group block of figures in table 3.4). The results for the absolute ratings of each target group by race of respondent are shown in figure 3.3.

First, on average, all groups recognize some important racial group differences in economic standing. All respondents rate whites as the most affluent (lowest score), with no score exceeding 20 on a 50-point scale, and reaching lows (perception of greater affluence) of 16.25 among Latinos and of 13.02 among blacks. Whites see little difference economically between themselves as a group and Asians as a group, but Asians clearly perceive whites as slightly more affluent than themselves. On the whole, however, Asians are generally seen as close to whites in overall economic standing. Blacks and Latinos are uniformly seen as the most economically disadvantaged. Whites, Asians, and Latinos see Latinos as slightly more disadvantaged than blacks, whereas blacks see themselves as more disadvantaged than Latinos.

These results have important implications. First, it is evident that most adults in Los Angeles County recognize important racial group differences in economic standing. Second, the perception of differences is, by and large, a matter of mutual social recognition. We do not find sharp disagreement (the only exception is how blacks see themselves relative to Latinos) in the perception of group economic standing.

Group Self-Images We next consider how members of each group rated their own group on each of the personality or dispositional traits (intelligence, welfare, drugs and gangs, ability to get along with, tendency to discriminate, English). Among the six personality traits, only one rating tilts in the direction of an unfavorable self-rating among whites and that is on the "tends to discriminate against others" dimension (28.28). All the other absolute in-group ratings are less than 20 and some, like the "ability to speak English well" trait, are quite favorable (8.17). Whites give themselves, on average, the lowest (most favorable) overall stereotype rating (see figure 3.4).

Blacks give themselves ratings that tilt in an unfavorable direction (exceed 25 points) on the traits of welfare dependency and involvement with drugs and gangs, the latter being more extreme (30.96). The most favorable in-group rating among blacks emerges for English language ability (13.84) and the ability to get along with others (17.65).

For Latinos three of the dimensions tilt in the direction of negative in-group ratings: involvement with drugs and gangs (32.34), poor English ability (29.23), and welfare dependency (27.73). The most favorable in-group rating among Latinos is the ability to get along with others (14.75).

Among the Asian respondents we find that only one dimension, the tendency to discriminate against others, has an in-group rating that tilts in a negative direction (25.48), and even this just barely clears the midpoint of 25. The most favorable in-group rating occurs on the welfare dependency item (9.11), followed by intelligence (15.39).

Perceptions of Other Groups Figure 3.4 shows the average absolute stereotype score rating across the six personality dimensions (excluding

TABLE 3.4   *Mean Stereotype Ratings by Race and Target Group*

	All Whites	White Men	White Women	F	All Blacks	Black Men	Black Women	F
				Target Groups				
White respondents								
Rich-poor	19.47	19.34	25.81	45.12***	33.93	34.05	36.25	4.96**
Unintelligent	17.64	17.65	16.30	1.18	24.75	24.72	22.05	3.95*
Prefer welfare	11.95	10.32	13.50	4.69**	28.03	25.33	27.82	1.51
Hard to get along	17.64	18.36	18.71	.27	24.18	23.72	22.27	1.30
Poor English	8.17	9.21	6.19	6.20**	20.98	21.74	18.12	3.56*
Drugs-gangs	19.11	19.60	12.65	17.80***	34.70	30.49	26.68	16.07***
Discriminate	28.28	27.09	21.39	10.37***	33.20	31.57	28.38	6.05**
Absolute scale	17.20	16.96	14.77	5.35**	27.57	26.36	24.34	7.88***
Difference score	—	—	—	—	8.19	7.77	7.50	.35
SES difference	—	—	—	—	14.51	14.79	10.50	13.85***
Black respondents								
Rich-poor	13.02	16.84	18.79	7.13***	34.37	33.55	32.86	.39
Unintelligent	22.49	18.32	19.35	2.23	21.68	18.72	18.69	2.82
Prefer welfare	16.61	15.00	16.75	.49	26.79	24.72	23.63	1.22
Hard to get along	27.09	24.51	21.80	3.53*	17.65	18.60	16.59	.51
Poor English	8.33	8.22	7.82	.09	13.84	16.86	13.39	1.24
Drugs-gangs	27.07	27.06	20.13	10.45***	30.96	32.86	25.62	5.96**
Discriminate	38.37	34.41	33.23	6.02**	24.91	26.15	22.67	2.43
Absolute scale	23.50	21.31	19.77	10.11***	23.69	23.04	20.09	7.02***
Difference score	.56	−.87	.46	.97	—	—	—	—
SES difference	−21.33	−16.72	−14.02	3.81*	—	—	—	—
Asian respondents								
Rich-poor	16.78	16.85	16.47	.02	36.25	35.00	37.22	1.22
Unintelligent	17.70	18.97	15.97	.92	28.30	28.64	27.03	.28
Prefer welfare	11.57	15.59	14.74	3.00*	32.18	35.33	34.08	.83
Hard to get along	20.75	22.24	25.74	2.37	23.30	28.92	28.05	2.75
Poor English	3.85	4.06	2.05	2.79	9.71	9.54	8.77	.12
Drug-gangs	19.72	20.94	18.49	.49	34.78	33.91	31.45	1.97
Discriminate	32.71	27.88	31.80	2.85	27.87	25.10	29.44	3.02*
Absolute scale	17.81	18.83	18.48	.31	25.95	26.86	26.82	.27
Difference score	−.29	1.54	1.32	1.84	5.68	8.04	7.48	2.09
SES difference	−4.34	−3.21	−6.38	1.06	14.94	14.90	14.50	.03
Latino respondents								
Rich-poor	12.35	12.23	15.11	3.09*	34.16	31.77	33.36	2.26
Unintelligent	17.51	15.97	17.29	.55	24.67	24.30	24.04	.18
Prefer welfare	14.29	16.71	16.71	1.68	36.65	36.94	37.46	.14
Hard to get along	22.02	22.15	21.04	.27	27.64	26.85	27.90	.24
Poor English	5.59	4.45	3.15	2.16	16.01	13.64	14.64	.85
Drugs-gangs	21.82	22.13	20.00	.92	35.80	36.91	35.03	.84
Discriminate	33.06	33.72	31.52	.82	33.80	33.14	31.65	.83
Absolute scale	19.14	19.20	18.37	.72	29.30	28.49	28.17	1.22
Difference score	−4.36	−3.88	−3.32	.52	3.78	3.32	4.21	.97
SES difference	−24.12	−23.12	−19.84	2.76	−2.30	−3.65	−1.86	1.28

Source: Los Angeles Study of Urban Inequality 1994.
Note: Higher scores indicate more negative out-group ratings.
*p <.05, **p <.01, ***p <.001

the rich-poor dimension) by race and target group. It shows clearly that members of all racial groups perceive some degree of difference on these traits among and between racial groups, though none of the perceived differences are gaping or categorical. Among whites, the overall scores

				Target Groups			
All Latinos	Latino Men	Latina Women	F	All Asians	Asian Men	Asian Women	F
36.01	35.03	38.09	3.76*	19.60	20.08	25.12	22.75***
25.84	25.02	24.38	.76	15.33	15.92	15.49	.10
25.49	23.54	26.19	1.47	10.25	9.00	12.59	5.78**
21.52	22.03	21.57	.10	23.25	21.87	21.22	.75
31.73	31.33	30.93	.17	24.26	23.98	23.64	.10
33.99	29.13	26.70	14.76***	21.60	20.68	12.33	35.37***
29.70	28.91	26.54	3.30*	29.08	29.87	24.70	8.11***
27.88	26.78	26.31	1.71	20.61	20.18	18.02	6.14**
8.51	8.39	9.35	.78	3.05	3.06	3.32	.16
16.60	15.73	12.34	8.53***	.13	.89	−.55	1.10
26.22	34.49	34.35	.52	16.25	17.67	20.91	4.31**
25.51	23.59	22.62	1.81	21.34	17.02	19.09	2.06
27.03	27.27	26.07	.12	14.89	14.14	14.91	.10
21.09	21.21	17.06	2.79	31.75	28.48	23.83	5.02**
33.99	30.78	30.19	1.15	34.75	30.96	28.87	3.28*
31.04	32.56	27.45	2.86	26.46	27.99	18.96	13.36***
28.68	29.17	26.47	1.94	37.03	33.62	33.33	2.46
28.91	27.46	24.93	4.39**	27.95	25.44	22.99	14.18***
5.13	4.46	4.49	.26	5.36	3.15	3.82	1.95
1.86	.95	1.32	.27	−18.03	−15.89	−12.02	3.17*
37.69	36.21	38.46	1.07	21.23	20.14	22.76	1.39
28.95	30.00	27.91	.30	15.39	14.26	15.70	.67
32.18	35.62	33.16	.68	9.11	11.44	11.04	1.82
20.85	22.16	24.02	1.07	17.34	13.50	16.79	2.25
30.78	29.75	26.40	3.42*	21.82	22.44	20.92	.49
33.44	31.37	28.30	4.52**	16.13	13.07	11.85	1.75
23.66	19.76	23.09	2.41	25.48	19.78	22.09	2.54
28.39	28.04	27.33	.36	17.50	15.77	16.12	1.47
8.34	9.64	8.89	.70	—	—	—	—
16.47	16.05	15.55	.10	—	—	—	—
36.46	35.42	35.08	.68	17.58	14.90	17.39	2.36
22.84	21.31	21.23	1.17	16.35	14.64	14.57	.88
27.73	28.30	27.94	.07	13.65	16.43	14.85	2.19
14.75	15.59	12.71	2.02	25.70	27.41	24.82	1.40
29.23	27.88	27.92	.79	26.58	26.13	24.31	1.24
32.34	33.67	27.70	10.24***	21.24	21.59	16.06	7.80***
22.41	23.35	19.37	3.07*	29.13	30.77	29.00	.71
24.94	24.75	22.87	6.02**	22.07	22.64	20.65	4.23*
—	—	—	—	−1.27	−.50	−.53	.58
—	—	—	—	−18.89	−20.54	−17.35	1.88

for both blacks (25.95) and Latinos (28.39) exhibit a slight negative tilt. Among black respondents there is a similar slight overall negative tilt to their views of Asians (27.95) and Latinos (28.91). Latino respondents give the single highest negative absolute score for an out-group to blacks (29.30), but otherwise do not clearly swing in a negative direction for

FIGURE 3.3   *Perceived Socioeconomic Standing*

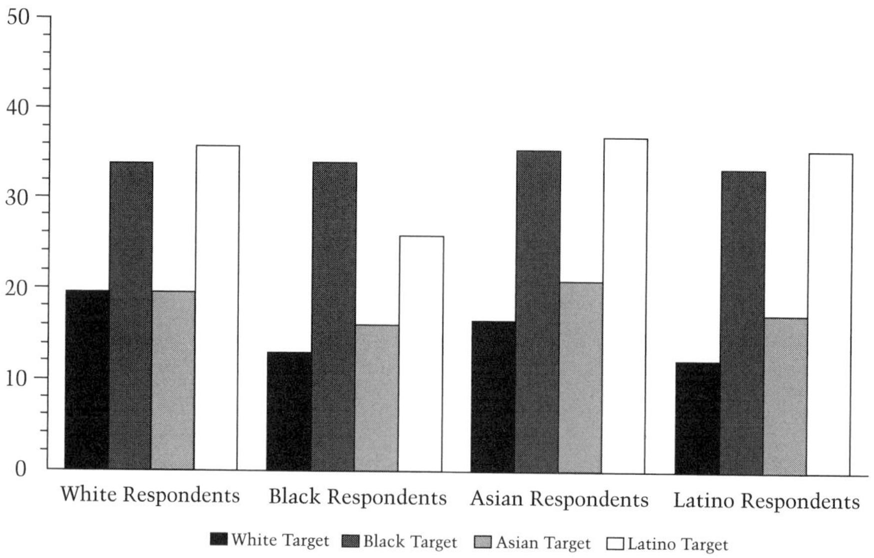

Source: Los Angeles Study of Urban Inequality 1994.

assessments of any other group. And Asian respondents give slightly negative overall ratings to Latinos (25.95) and to blacks (28.39).

It is worth commenting on the components of these ratings and what they may tell us about consensual or common stereotypical images. The only trait on which all three racial minorities tended to rate whites unfavorably was the tendency to discriminate against others, as expected. Otherwise, ratings of whites tilted in a neutral to favorable direction. There is quite a different story with regard to perceptions of blacks. Whites, Latinos, and Asians tended to have unfavorable ratings of blacks on the dimensions of welfare dependency, involvement with drugs and gangs, and the tendency to discriminate against others.

There is a tendency for whites, blacks, and Asians to give Latinos unfavorable ratings on the dimensions of drugs and gangs and English language ability. In addition, whites and blacks both give Latinos unfavorable ratings on the average with regard to discriminating against others. Blacks and Asians give Latinos unfavorable ratings on the welfare dependency dimension.

The clearest unfavorable rating that others give to Asians occurs on the tendency to discriminate against others, with whites, blacks, and

FIGURE 3.4   *Overall Stereotype Index Ratings by Race*

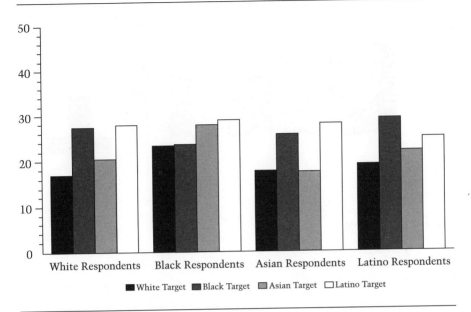

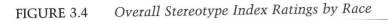

Source: Los Angeles Study of Urban Inequality 1994.

Latinos giving an overall unfavorable rating. In addition, both blacks and Latinos also rate Asians unfavorably on the English language ability and hard to get along with dimensions.

So far we have restricted our attention to the absolute ratings for individual dimensions and overall scores. There is also important information to be gleaned from examining difference score ratings. Figure 3.5 shows the overall difference score rating by respondent race and target group race. These scores may range from +50 (maximum possible superior rating of in-group) to −50 (maximum possible inferior rating of in-group). Four rather group-specific patterns stand out. First, whites clearly rate themselves as superior, on average, as compared to each of the racial minorities. All the scores are positive and usually exceed 3 points (on a 100-point scale). The consistency and size of the differentiation from other groups by whites is not matched by that of any other group.

Given the history of friction and negative exchanges between blacks and whites, especially in the wake of the riots of 1992 in Los Angeles, it was somewhat surprising that whites' ratings of Latinos were slightly more unfavorable than those given blacks. The scores might be unduly influenced by the negative perception whites have of Latinos' English language ability, due to their recent immigrant status. That is, whereas

FIGURE 3.5   *Stereotype Difference Score Ratings by Race*

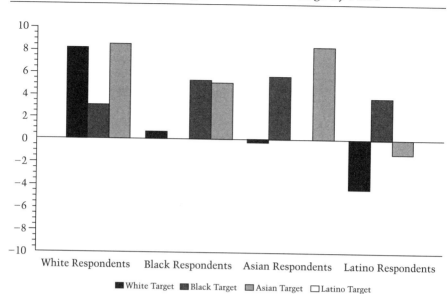

Source: Los Angeles Study of Urban Inequality 1994.

poor English ratings of blacks probably imply persistent failure to master the dominant English language dialect (white middle-class speech
patterns), as a result of recent heavy immigration a similar rating would
not imply the same degree of dispositional character for Latinos. Hence,
we recalculated whites' overall difference score, omitting the English
item; figure 3.6 shows these results. Here, the rating of blacks (7.30) is
less favorable than that given Latinos (5.58), and the perceived difference
from Asians vanishes almost entirely.

Second, black respondents essentially see themselves as no different
from whites, on average. However, blacks give themselves superior ratings compared to both Asians and Latinos. Third, a somewhat comple-
mentary pattern obtains among Asians. Overall for this set of dimensions, Asians see little difference between themselves and whites, but
clearly rate themselves as superior to blacks and (especially) Latinos.

Fourth, Latinos' scores are striking for the presence of a clear inferior group self-rating relative to whites and modestly negative group
self-rating relative to Asians. However, Latinos rate themselves as superior to blacks on average. We were struck by these negative in-group
ratings among Latinos and sought to determine whether they occurred
mainly among those of a particular national ancestry or more among the

FIGURE 3.6   *Whites' Stereotype Difference Scores (Omitting
English Language Ability)*

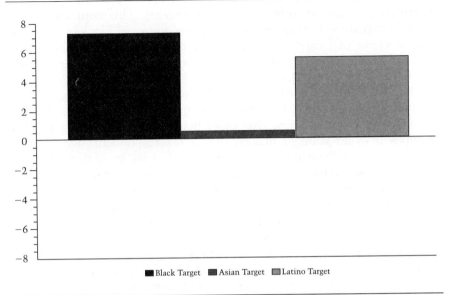

Black Target   Asian Target   Latino Target

Source: Los Angeles Study of Urban Inequality 1994.

foreign-born as compared to the native-born. We found that the negative
or inferior in-group rating tends to occur among Latinos irrespective of
national ancestry. And, with respect to the difference from whites, the
negative score occurs of roughly comparable magnitude among both the
native- and foreign-born. However, the negative rating relative to Asians
is mainly restricted to the foreign-born. Omitting the English language
item from the index does considerably mute the size of the favorable
out-group advantage among Latinos, but does not eliminate or reverse it.

We also estimated multivariate models of the determinants of stereotypes. Among white respondents, negative stereotypes of blacks rose
with age, political conservatism, and perceptions of black economic disadvantage. Stereotypes of blacks were more favorable among white
women as compared to white men, and among those with a black person in their personal network or who lived around more blacks compared to those lacking such contact. Whites' stereotypes of Latinos were
more negative among men as compared to women, for those who perceived Latinos as lagging behind whites economically, and among those
whites who had many Latino coworkers. However, white stereotypes of
Latinos tended to become more favorable among those with a Latino

friend (borderline, p = .055) and those who lived in a tract with a higher percentage of Latinos. Whites' views of Asians were not clearly tied to any of the variables we examined, with the model yielding a variance-explained estimate of only .05 (not significant). This contrasts to the variance-explained figures of .21 for whites' views of blacks and .19 for whites' views of Latinos. Perceptions of common fate identity had no discernible effect on any of whites' stereotype ratings of other groups. (See tables 3.5 through 3.8.)

Several variables consistently influence the extent of negative stereotyping among blacks. Whether the target group was whites, Latinos, or Asians, our results show that older blacks express less negative stereotypes than do younger blacks, that black respondents whom interviewers rated as "pausing" during the racial attitude section expressed more negative stereotypes than those who did not pause, and those blacks not currently in the labor force expressed more negative stereotypes than those in the labor force. There was also a tendency for other contextual variables to influence the proclivity to stereotype among blacks. Thus, blacks who had a white friend expressed more favorable views of whites. Yet those blacks with workplace contact with Asians expressed more negative views, whereas those with neighborhood contact expressed more favorable views of Asians. In addition, the more blacks perceived Latinos as economically disadvantaged, the more negative the stereotype rating. More politically conservative blacks also give Latinos more negative ratings.

Among Asians, national ancestry influenced stereotype perceptions of both whites and blacks but not Latinos. Korean, Japanese (especially), and Chinese respondents as compared to those of other Asian ancestry gave more favorable ratings to whites. A roughly similar pattern emerged in terms of ratings of blacks, though in this case respondents of Chinese ancestry gave the most favorable rating. In addition, the greater the perceived economic status gap, the more negative Asian respondents' views of whites, Latinos, and blacks. Better-educated Asians, especially those with postgraduate schooling, expressed more favorable stereotypes of all groups. Asian respondents interviewed by a non-Asian gave more favorable ratings to both blacks and Latinos than those interviewed by someone of the same race. Whereas stereotypes became less favorable as the percentage of blacks in an Asian respondent's tract rose, stereotype scores toward Latinos became more favorable as the percentage of Latinos in the tract rose. A sense of common fate identity never significantly influenced stereotype views among Asian respondents.

Latino respondents provide the one instance in which perceptions of common fate identity consistently related to stereotype ratings. The higher the level of common fate identity among Latinos, the more

TABLE 3.5   *Multivariate Models of Stereotype Difference Score, White Respondents*

	White-Black Stereotype Difference Score	White-Asian Stereotype Difference Score	White-Latino Stereotype Difference Score
Constant	−3.51 (2.51)	1.07 (2.13)	1.93 (2.49)
Experimental ballot			
Male ballot	−.38 (.73)	−.04 (.53)	−.43 (.73)
Female ballot	−.29 (.79)	.54 (.60)	.83 (.88)
Social background			
Age	.08 (.03)**	−.01 (.02)	.04 (.03)
Education			
No high school diploma	−1.22 (1.28)	1.55 (1.28)	−1.31 (1.61)
Some college	.62 (.90)	−.09 (.61)	.41 (.87)
Bachelor's degree	−.81 (1.17)	.17 (.76)	.17 (1.13)
Postgraduate	−1.79 (1.24)	−1.00 (.98)	−2.28 (1.27)
Gender	−1.38 (.68)*	.38 (.50)	−2.85 (.65)***
Income			
Did not report	1.57 (1.31)	1.88 (1.04)	2.58 (1.26)*
Low income	1.26 (1.05)	1.12 (.91)	2.26 (1.16)*
Lower middle income	.02 (.98)	.18 (.88)	.80 (.91)
Higher middle income	.45 (.89)	.25 (.83)	1.38 (.85)
Not in work force	−.23 (.79)	.79 (.66)	−.17 (.83)
Religion and social values			
Protestant	.46 (1.55)	.78 (.93)	1.68 (1.49)
Catholic	1.71 (1.50)	.76 (.98)	1.65 (1.54)
Jewish	3.41 (1.94)	.60 (1.09)	3.36 (1.81)
Other religion	−.18 (1.87)	1.25 (1.28)	.47 (1.83)
Attend	.28 (.20)	.13 (.19)	.18 (.18)
Political conservatism	1.33 (.28)***	.05 (.20)	.80 (.26)**
Personal work, and neighborhood context			
Has target group friend	−2.71 (1.24)*	−.08 (.86)	−1.21 (.79)
Coworkers mainly target group	3.43 (2.24)	−.60 (1.56)	4.06 (1.30)**
Percentage target group in tract	−:09 (.03)***	−.02 (.03)	−.06 (.02)**
Interview context			
Not same race interviewer	−.92 (.64)	−.56 (.66)	−.59 (.68)
Paused before answering	.19 (.98)	.38 (.64)	−.04 (.97)
Justified responses	.13 (1.13)	.12 (.75)	.17 (1.11)

(Table continues on p. 112.)

TABLE 3.5   *Continued*

	White-Black Stereotype Difference Score	White-Asian Stereotype Difference Score	White-Latino Stereotype Difference Score
Showed discomfort	−2.27 (1.21)	−1.57 (.79)*	−2.78 (1.14)*
Objected to section	2.17 (2.07)	.11 (1.57)	.49 (2.38)
Racial attitudes			
Common fate	.27 (.25)	.21 (.24)	−.07 (.33)
SES difference score	.13 (.04)***	.04 (.04)	.11 (.03)***
R^2	.21***	.05	.19***
N	761	740	757

Source: Los Angeles Study of Urban Inequality 1994.
Note: Omitted categories for income, education and religon are high income, high school diploma, and agnostic or atheist, respectively.
*$p < .05$, **$p < .01$, ***$p < .001$

negative the stereotypes of whites, blacks, and Asians. (Somewhat consistent with our earlier discussion, those Latinos who identified strongly as a racial group appeared to do so in part in contradistinction from other groups.) Otherwise, among Latinos the significant predictors of stereotype scores were target group–specific. Latinas have more negative views of whites than do Latino men. Being interviewed by a non-Latino also resulted in a more favorable rating of whites. Surprisingly, better-educated Latinos expressed strongly negative views of blacks (a difference of 4.4 points between those with postgraduate degrees and those with only a high school diploma). Having a black friend in one's network or being interviewed by a non-Latino resulted in more favorable ratings of blacks. Native-born Latinos expressed more negative views of Asians, as did politically liberal Latinos. But, again, being interviewed by a non-Latino resulted in more favorable ratings of Asians.

The Gendering of Stereotypes   Men typically face different expectations and experiences in the workforce than do women (Reskin, McBrier, and Kmec 1999). In particular, there is growing concern that black women are perceived more favorably by many potential employers than are black men (Holzer 1996; Wilson 1996). But also, even in the housing market, men are often differently positioned than women, with the latter more often perceived as lacking the resources, being burdened by children, or somehow less responsible for important household decisions than men, in the case of married couples. For these and other reasons the LASUI stereotype items included an experimental test of the

TABLE 3.6   *Multivariate Models of Stereotype Difference Score, Black Respondents*

	Black-White Stereotype Difference Score	Black-Asian Stereotype Difference Score	Black-Latino Stereotype Difference Score
Constant	3.16 (2.95)	7.67 (2.40)**	6.80 (1.98)***
Experimental ballot			
Male ballot	−1.83 (.98)	−2.09 (.87)*	−.41 (.78)
Female ballot	.06 (.95)	−1.17 (.95)	−.68 (.65)
Social background			
Age	−.07 (.03)*	−.10 (.02)***	−.08 (.02)***
Education			
No high school diploma	−2.07 (1.11)	−1.06 (1.19)	−.57 (.94)
Some college	−.60 (.94)	−.90 (.96)	−.37 (.67)
Bachelor's degree	1.13 (1.66)	−1.66 (1.25)	.05 (1.29)
Postgraduate	4.19 (2.15)*	1.86 (1.87)	−.95 (1.14)
Gender	1.38 (.85)	2.24 (.73)**	1.29 (.68)
Income			
Did not report	.07 (1.59)	−.55 (1.37)	−1.37 (1.12)
Low income	.30 (1.35)	.54 (.96)	1.15 (1.32)
Lower middle income	1.09 (1.42)	.74 (1.10)	.62 (1.09)
Higher middle income	.19 (1.42)	1.44 (1.48)	1.02 (1.26)
Not in work force	2.29 (.93)*	1.92 (.74)**	2.01 (.76)**
Religion and social values			
Protestant	−2.39 (1.55)	−1.75 (1.20)	−.77 (1.04)
Catholic	−2.89 (1.69)	−.80 (1.33)	−2.65 (1.21)*
Other religion	−.88 (2.15)	−1.80 (1.32)	−2.08 (1.25)
Attend	.07 (.20)	−.37 (.22)	−.07 (.15)
Political conservatism	.01 (.26)	.41 (.26)	.36 (.16)*
Personal, work, and neighborhood context			
Has target group friend	−3.44 (1.48)*	.00 (2.46)	−1.50 (1.25)
Coworkers mainly target group	.83 (.96)	4.39 (1.94)*	−.80 (.75)
Percentage target group in tract	−.03 (.03)	−.21 (.06)***	.00 (.02)
Interview context			
Not same-race interviewer	.49 (1.17)	1.60 (1.25)	−1.84 (.91)*

(Table continues on p. 114.)

113

TABLE 3.6   *Continued*

	Black-White Stereotype Difference Score	Black-Asian Stereotype Difference Score	Black-Latino Stereotype Difference Score
Paused before answering	1.99 (.90)*	2.06 (.72)**	1.23 (.66)
Justified responses	.19 (1.09)	1.08 (.77)	.91 (.65)
Showed discomfort	1.82 (1.47)	−.83 (1.20)	−.34 (1.07)
Objected to section	−5.60 (1.63)***	−2.95 (1.96)	−1.50 (1.34)
Racial attitudes			
Common fate	.38 (.36)	.53 (.33)	.17 (.33)
SES difference score	.01 (.03)	−.02 (.02)	.08 (.04)*
R^2	.14***	.16***	.16***
N	1037	999	1031

Source: Los Angeles Study of Urban Inequality 1994.
Note: Omitted categories for income, education, and religion are high income, high school diploma, and agnostic or atheist, respectively.
*$p < .05$, **$p < .01$, ***$p < .001$

impact of gender on racial stereotypes. The experiment suggests that gender definitely matters, but the perceived differences are often trait- and group-specific. The only broadly consistent patterns across race and racial target groups are the perception of women as less affluent than men and for men to be seen as more likely to engage in aggressive behaviors concerning involvement in drugs and gangs or exhibiting a tendency to discriminate against others. It should be stressed, however, that even these patterns do not appear with complete uniformity.

We begin this assessment by returning to the matter of group self-images in light of the gender experiment. Among white respondents we find significant experimental effects for five of the seven trait dimensions (see table 3.4). Among whites, men were seen as more difficult to get along with, as more likely to discriminate against others, as more likely to be involved in drugs and gangs, as more affluent and less likely to be on welfare as compared to women. We found no significant gender manipulation effect for the traits of intelligence or English language ability.

Among blacks rating themselves, only one significant gender difference emerged: men were rated as more likely to be involved in drugs and gangs than women. Among Latinos only two of the gender manipulations result in significant differences: men were seen as more involved in drugs and gangs than women and as more likely to discriminate

TABLE 3.7   *Multivariate Models of Stereotype Difference Score,*
             Asian Respondents

	Asian-White Stereotype Difference Score	Asian-Black Stereotype Difference Score	Asian-Latino Stereotype Difference Score
Constant	10.77 (3.03)***	7.37 (3.01)*	11.52 (2.45)***
Experimental ballot			
Male ballot	1.89 (.83)*	1.94 (.88)*	1.16 (.64)
Female ballot	2.06 (.84)*	1.74 (.73)*	.72 (.57)
Social background			
Age	−.03 (.02)	.00 (.03)	.02 (.02)
Education			
No high school diploma	.36 (1.01)	−.87 (.96)	.33 (.85)
Some college	−2.50 (1.19)*	−.37 (1.12)	−.66 (.92)
Bachelor's degree	−.93 (1.05)	−.95 (.79)	−.64 (.64)
Postgraduate	−2.79 (1.47)	−1.77 (.81)	−3.24 (.75)***
Gender	.96 (.61)	.43 (.63)*	.14 (.51)
Income			
Did not report	.83 (.93)	−.76 (1.07)	.06 (.85)
Low income	−.82 (.99)	−1.75 (1.28)	−.14 (.81)
Lower middle income	.46 (1.13)	.69 (1.02)	.87 (.85)
Higher middle income	−.94 (1.41)	1.89 (1.03)	1.11 (.76)
Not in work force	−1.33 (.84)	.41 (.70)	.01 (.52)
Ancestry			
Chinese	−5.34 (1.99)**	−3.73 (1.77)*	−.62 (1.12)
Japanese	−6.26 (2.37)**	−3.24 (1.64)*	−.73 (1.50)
Korean	−4.93 (2.12)*	−1.99 (1.88)	.74 (1.41)
U.S. native	.30 (1.18)	.26 (1.66)	−.78 (1.21)
Religion and social values			
Protestant	−1.99 (1.01)*	−1.33 (1.39)	−1.62 (1.07)
Catholic	−3.62 (1.29)**	−3.74 (1.82)*	−4.04 (1.27)**
Other religion	−1.30 (.75)	−1.20 (.94)	−.60 (.67)
Attend	−.29 (.24)	.03 (.31)	−.41 (.22)
Political conservatism	.22 (.24)	.34 (.27)	.06 (.20)
Personal, work, neighborhood context			
Has target group friend	−1.21 (.91)	−2.17 (2.09)	3.24 (1.27)**
Coworkers mainly target group	.35 (1.10)	−1.18 (1.90)	−.74 (.87)
Percentage target group in tract	−.02 (.02)	.13 (.07)	−.06 (.02)***

(Table continues on p. 116.)

TABLE 3.7   *Continued*

	Asian-White Stereotype Difference Score	Asian-Black Stereotype Difference Score	Asian-Latino Stereotype Difference Score
Interview context			
Not same-race interviewer	−.08 (.92)	−1.98 (.89)*	−2.46 (.68)***
Paused before answering	−.88 (.80)	−1.09 (.86)	−.41 (.63)
Justified responses	.13 (1.14)	−1.19 (1.06)	.07 (.56)
Showed discomfort	1.27 (1.21)	−1.01 (1.15)	−1.31 (.87)
Objected to section	−2.70 (1.00)**	−1.91 (.87)*	−.88 (.57)
Racial attitudes			
Common fate	−.16 (.34)	−.06 (.32)	−.06 (.25)
SES difference score	.08 (.03)**	.12 (.04)**	.10 (.03)***
R^2	.20***	.23***	.30***
N	712	723	721

Source: Los Angeles Study of Urban Inequality 1994.
Note: Omitted categories for income, education, and religion are high income, high school diploma, and agnostic or atheist, respectively.
*$p < .05$, **$p < .01$, ***$p < .001$

against others. And among Asians none of the trait dimensions showed a significant effect for the gender manipulations.

What about out-group views? White respondents did differentiate between black males and females on several dimensions. Whites saw black men as less intelligent, having a poorer command of the English language, and more involved with drugs and gangs than black women. But black women were seen as less affluent than black men. Surprisingly, whites did not see black women as more welfare-dependent. This may imply that the large number of jobless black men is roughly equated with welfare dependency among women. Among Latino and Asian respondents we found no significant effects of the gender manipulation in terms of ratings of blacks.

White respondents rated Latino men as significantly more likely to be involved in drugs and gangs and as more likely to discriminate against others than Latinas. Latinas were rated by whites as poorer than Latino men. Among black respondents we found no significant differences based on the gender manipulation. However, Asian respondents saw Latino men as having a poorer command of English and as being more involved in drugs and gangs than Latinas.

In terms of ratings of Asians, among white respondents Asian males

TABLE 3.8   *Multivariate Models of Stereotype Difference Scores,*
            Latino Respondents

	Latino-White Stereotype Difference Score	Latino-Black Stereotype Difference Score	Latino-Asian Stereotype Difference Score
Constant	−5.10 (3.24)	6.13 (1.93)**	−1.49 (2.58)
Experimental ballot			
Male ballot	.11 (.98)	−.37 (.69)	.36 (.77)
Female ballot	.37 (.99)	.05 (.59)	.30 (.81)
Social background			
Age	.01 (.03)	−.02 (.02)	.01 (.02)
Education			
No high school diploma	−1.41 (.88)	−.32 (.65)	.82 (.88)
Some college	−1.19 (1.20)	.13 (.80)	.57 (1.06)
Bachelor's degree	1.33 (1.38)	.33 (.93)	1.99 (1.20)
Postgraduate	1.06 (3.39)	4.38 (2.00)*	2.45 (1.94)
Gender	1.27 (.62)*	.15 (.55)	.49 (.68)
Income			
Did not report	−.81 (1.87)	1.05 (1.53)	−.31 (1.55)
Low income	−.55 (1.23)	−.03 (.91)	.47 (1.09)
Lower middle income	−.22 (1.11)	.31 (.91)	1.01 (1.04)
Higher middle income	−2.41 (1.52)	−.52 (1.02)	−1.36 (1.35)
Not in work force	.12 (.86)	.41 (.66)	.14 (.71)
Ancestry			
Mexican	.67 (1.94)	−1.60 (1.19)	.69 (1.50)
Central American	.20 (2.35)	−1.10 (1.28)	1.07 (1.44)
U.S. native	.01 (.97)	−1.08 (.66)	2.25 (.92)*
Religion and social values			
Protestant	2.72 (2.06)	1.53 (1.46)	2.18 (1.57)
Catholic	2.66 (1.43)	.26 (.84)	1.92 (1.07)
Other religion	3.95 (3.37)	.73 (1.89)	2.74 (1.81)
Attend	.23 (.27)	.06 (.20)	−.12 (.19)
Political conservatism	−.74 (.35)*	−.09 (.21)	−.70 (.29)**
Personal, work, and neighborhood context			
Has target group friend	−.07 (1.13)	−2.36 (.95)**	−.77 (2.33)
Coworkers mainly target group	1.09 (1.01)	−2.13 (1.70)	−2.53 (1.59)
Percentage target group in tract	−.01 (.03)	−.01 (.02)	−.03 (.03)
Interview context			
Not same-race interviewer	−1.88 (.88)*	−3.62 (.62)***	−3.08 (.85)***

(Table continues on p. 118.)

117

TABLE 3.8   *Continued*

	Latino-White Stereotype Difference Score	Latino-Black Stereotype Difference Score	Latino-Asian Stereotype Difference Score
Paused before answering	.87 (.65)	.94 (.50)	.32 (.67)
Justified responses	.82 (1.05)	−.81 (.55)	−.79 (.91)
Showed discomfort	−.59 (1.14)	−.34 (.71)	.96 (1.00)
Objected to section	2.10 (1.23)	−1.18 (.74)	1.62 (1.10)
Racial attitudes			
Common fate	.80 (.33)*	.64 (.28)*	.59 (.34)
SES difference score	.04 (.02)	.06 (.03)*	.04 (.02)
R^2	.09***	.14***	.11**
N	868	878	828

Source: Los Angeles Study of Urban Inequality 1994.
Note: Omitted categories for income, education, and religion are high income, high school diploma, and agnostic or atheist, respectively. The omitted category for ancestry is other Latino ancestry.
*$p < .05$, **$p < .01$, ***$p < .001$

were seen as more likely than Asian females to be involved in drugs and gangs and to discriminate against others. But Asian women were seen as more likely to be poor and to be welfare-dependent as compared to Asian men. Among blacks, Asian men as compared to Asian women were seen as more likely to be affluent, to be hard to get along with, to be involved with drugs and gangs, and to have poor English-speaking ability. Among Latino respondents only one significant gender difference emerged, with Asian men seen as more involved in drugs and gangs.

Summary Comments on Stereotyping   There are a few broad generalizations that can be made about stereotypes. And certainly everything we report must be conditioned by attention to the seven specific trait dimensions we focused on. Different patterns might emerge if a different set of traits had been examined. First, most adults in Los Angeles County do clearly differentiate the traits of the different racial groups. Second, these differences are never very large in magnitude, though they definitely vary from group to group and trait to trait. Third, there is some tendency for overlap in group self-images and rating by members of other groups. For example, whites are most likely to rate themselves negative on the "discriminate against others" dimension, and this is the dimension on which blacks, Latinos, and Asians also consistently rate whites negatively. Likewise, blacks rate themselves most negatively on involvement with drugs and gangs, a trait on which whites, Asians, and Latinos also give blacks unfavorable ratings.

Fourth, taking into account the special meaning of speaking "poor English" among a substantially immigrant group as compared to an overwhelmingly native-born group, there is a decided tendency for the most negative ratings to be applied to African Americans. Fifth, the determinants of stereotype perceptions tend be specific to a particular pairing of target group and respondent race. Here, a few interesting patterns emerge. The interview context measures often influence stereotype perceptions, though no one factor is consistently important among this set. Blacks not in the labor force are typically more hostile to each of the other racial groups in terms of stereotypes than those in the labor force. There are some patterns that may be interpreted as evidence of an incipient Chicano consciousness: the consistent effects of common fate identity on stereotypes of other groups, and the strong negative assessment of blacks by highly educated Latinos.

Perceived Group Competition

An immediate sociological concern raised by the growing heterogeneity of urban areas such as Los Angeles County is whether members of different groups view one another as direct competitors for scarce economic, political, and social resources. Such perceptions may influence the potential for coalition formation and cooperation among groups, as well as the prospects for open antagonism and conflict. We focus on two sets of questions from the LASUI that concern interracial competition. These questions attempted to gauge whether members of racial minority groups are viewed as zero-sum competitors for economic resources and political influence. Using a three-way split-ballot experiment, respondents were asked whether they strongly agreed to strongly disagreed with the statements that: "More good job for (blacks/Asians/Hispanics or Latinos) mean fewer good jobs for (respondent's racial-ethnic group)" and "The more political influence (blacks/Asians/Hispanics or Latinos) have in local politics, the less influence (respondent's racial-ethnic group) will have in local politics." Scores on each item range from a low perception of competition (score of 1) to a high perception of competition (score of 5). Consistent with prior research (Bobo and Hutchings 1996), since these items are highly intercorrelated, we also examine a group competition index reflecting a simple average score for the two items. The experimental design makes three types of comparisons possible: within race, we can determine whether a group perceives greater threat from one group as compared to others; within experimental ballot, we can determine whether one group perceives greater threat from a specific target group; and again within ballot, but also within race, we can determine whether a group feels more threatened economically or politically by another specific group.

Results for comparisons by experimental ballot and within ballot by respondent race are shown in table 3.9 for each individual item and the group competition index. In addition, figure 3.7 shows means scores on the group competition index by race of respondent and race of target group. The first and most general observation to make is that perceptions of competition range from low to moderate among racial minority group members and are quite discernible but low among whites. That is, for whites scores are uniformly above 2 on a 5-point scale, but never reach the midpoint of 3.

Second, only Latinos show responsiveness to the racial target group experimental manipulation. For both the political influence competition and the job opportunity competition items (and therefore the group competition index), Latinos perceive greater threat from Asians than from blacks. This is consistent with the results from a 1992 survey in Los Angeles County as well (Bobo and Hutchings 1996, esp. 958–59). However, neither blacks nor whites are affected by the target group race manipulation, and this is true for both the political influence and job opportunity items.

Third, considering the separate items, whites nonetheless express a slightly higher feeling of political threat than economic threat from minorities (significantly so when either blacks or Latinos are the target group). However, within the respective domains of political competition and economic competition, whites do not distinguish between the level of competition they perceive from blacks, Latinos, or Asians. A parallel pattern occurs among Asian respondents. Pairwise t-tests show that Asian respondents perceive greater political influence threat from blacks and Latinos than economic threat from either group. (This would be consistent with the earlier perceptions of group economic standing.)

Just the opposite patterns occur for blacks. Pairwise t-test results show that blacks feel significantly greater economic threat from both Asians and Latinos than political threat from either group. And Latinos express significantly higher political than economic threat from Asians, but do not differentiate between domains in their reactions to blacks.

We also estimate multivariate models of the determinants of perceptions of threat using the group competition index (see tables 3.10 through 3.13). Three broad patterns are worth noting at the outset. First, there is no single variable that operates to shape perceptions of group competition across respondent race and target group race. Second, in six of the nine equations predicting group competition index scores, the

TABLE 3.9   Perceptions of Group Competition by Race and Experimental Ballot

	Asian Economic Threat	Black Economic Threat	Latino Economic Threat	F
White respondents	2.79 (.11)	2.75 (.09)	2.76 (.09)	.03 ns
Black respondents	3.53 (.17)	—	3.38 (.15)	.46 ns
Asian respondents	—	2.69 (.14)	2.80 (.12)	.36 ns
Latino respondents	3.35 (.07)	3.09 (.07)	—	6.57**
F	11.75***	6.68***	94.41***	
	Asian Political Threat	Black Political Threat	Latino Political Threat	F
White respondents	2.85 (.11)	2.89 (.10)	2.93 (.09)	.20 ns
Black respondents	3.36 (.16)	—	3.17 (.14)	.84 ns
Asian respondents	—	2.93 (.12)	3.22 (.12)	2.82 ns
Latino respondents	3.46 (.07)	3.16 (.09)	—	7.12**
F	10.50***	2.83 ns	17.55***	
	Asian Group Threat Index	Black Group Threat Index	Latino Group Threat Index	F
White respondents	2.81 (.10)	2.82 (.08)	2.85 (.08)	.06 ns
Black respondents	3.44 (.16)	—	3.28 (.13)	.69 ns
Asian respondents	—	2.81 (.12)	3.01 (.10)	1.62 ns
Latino respondents	3.40 (.06)	3.13 (.07)	—	8.13**
F	13.26***	5.67***	4.02*	

Source: Los Angeles Study of Urban Inequality 1994.
*$p < .05$, **$p < .01$, ***$p < .001$

FIGURE 3.7   *Perceived Racial Group Competition Index by Race and Target Group*

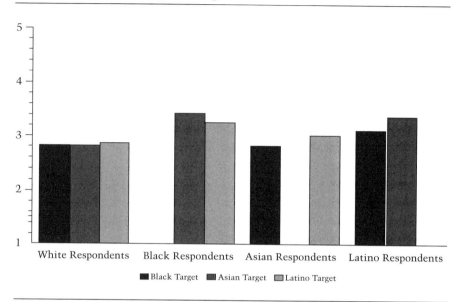

Source: Los Angeles Study of Urban Inequality 1994.

more negative the stereotypes of the target group, the higher the degree of perceived competition. This suggests that perceptions of group competition are at least partly based in more general prejudiced responses to an out-group. Third, with the significant exception of African Americans, we do not find that actual respondent economic status plays much of a role in perceptions of group competition. Otherwise, much of what we do find is specific to each pairing of respondent race and target group race.

In terms of perceived competition with blacks among white respondents, we find that in addition to negative racial stereotypes, the greater the perceived economic disadvantage of blacks the more the sense of threat. Surprisingly, however, the larger the percentage black in a respondent's census tract, the lower the perception of competition. This pattern contradicts the group-size-leads-to-threat hypothesis, but is consistent with the contact hypothesis and other recent findings (Ellison and Powers 1994; Kinder and Mendelberg 1995).

Among black respondents there are strong effects of income on perceptions of competition, with lower-income individuals scoring higher. Common fate identity also increased feelings of competition with

(Text continues on p. 127.)

TABLE 3.10   *Multivariate Models of Competitive Group Threat, White Respondents*

	Black Competitive Threat	Asian Competitive Threat	Latino Competitive Threat
Constant	2.31 (.61)***	.39 (.52)	2.63 (.55)***
Social background			
Age	.01 (.01)	.01 (.01)*	.00 (.00)
Education			
No high school diploma	1.11 (.31)***	−.14 (.47)	−.45 (.47)
Some college	−.01 (.18)	−.07 (.18)	−.01 (.21)
Bachelor's degree	−.07 (.19)	−.31 (.24)	−.27 (.20)
Postgraduate	−.24 (.24)	.05 (.30)	−.28 (.24)
Gender	.02 (.15)	−.24 (.16)	−.02 (.14)
Income			
Did not report	.28 (.26)	−.14 (.27)	.52 (.25)*
Low income	.09 (.22)	.19 (.24)	−.14 (.25)
Lower middle income	.16 (.25)	−.21 (.20)	−.09 (.18)
Higher middle income	.07 (.18)	−.07 (.27)	.11 (.19)
Not in work force	−.03 (.14)	.14 (.17)	.06 (.15)
Religion and social values			
Protestant	.04 (.25)	.32 (.25)	−.08 (.19)
Catholic	.24 (.24)	.32 (.25)	−.37 (.26)
Jewish	.35 (.25)	−.17 (.36)	−.15 (.28)
Other religion	.28 (.29)	.05 (.30)	.18 (.27)
Attend	−.01 (.04)	.21 (.05)***	−.07 (.04)
Political conservatism	.06 (.06)	.21 (.07)**	.08 (.05)
Personal, work, and neighborhood context			
Has target group friend	.23 (.21)	−.16 (.43)	.09 (.14)
Coworkers mainly target group	−.27 (.28)	.12 (.43)	−.55 (.20)**
Percentage target group in tract	−.02 (.01)*	−.00 (.01)	−.01 (.01)
Interview context			
Not same-race interviewer	−.08 (.15)	−.27 (.16)	.16 (.19)
Paused before answering	−.09 (.14)	.17 (.17)	.04 (.18)
Justified responses	.10 (.19)	.11 (.22)	.21 (.16)
Showed discomfort	−.24 (.20)	.14 (.25)	−.01 (.20)
Objected to section	−.04 (.64)	.28 (.38)	−.19 (.26)
Racial attitudes			
Common fate	−.13 (.07)	.09 (.07)	.17 (.05)***
Stereotype difference score	.05 (.01)***	.03 (.01)	.01 (.01)
SES difference score	−.02 (.01)**	.00 (.01)	.01 (.01)
R^2	.36***	.33***	.27***
N	255	233	253

Source: Los Angeles Study of Urban Inequality 1994.
Note: Omitted categories for income, education, and religion are high income, high school diploma, and agnostic or atheist, respectively.
*$p < .05$, **$p < .01$, ***$p < .001$

TABLE 3.11   *Multivariate Models of Competitive Group Threat,*
Black Respondents

	Asian Competitive Threat	Latino Competitive Threat
Constant	2.36 (.51)*	2.80 (.67)***
Social background		
Age	.01 (.00)**	.01 (.00)
Education		
No high school diploma	−.55 (.22)**	−.33 (.23)
Some college	−.37 (.17)*	−.31 (.21)
Bachelor's degree	−.50 (.32)	−.44 (.27)
Postgraduate	.37 (.33)	−1.29 (.46)**
Gender	−.35 (.13)**	−.17 (.18)
Income		
Did not report	.66 (.35)	.24 (.32)
Low income	.75 (.26)**	.10 (.25)
Lower middle inome	.39 (.27)	.12 (.29)
Higher middle income	.09 (.37)	.10 (.29)
Not in work force	−.22 (.14)	.22 (.18)
Religion and social values		
Protestant	.11 (.21)	.23 (.23)
Catholic	−.06 (.36)	.38 (.29)
Other religion	−.01 (.28)	−.32 (.32)
Attend	.06 (.04)	−.06 (.05)
Political conservatism	.06 (.05)	.08 (.06)
Personal, work, and neighborhood context		
Has target group friend	−.81 (.35)*	−.48 (.40)
Coworkers mainly target group	−.03 (.38)	−.18 (.24)
Percentage target group in tract	−.00 (.01)	.01 (.01)
Interview context		
Not same-race interviewer	−.77 (.21)***	−.36 (.19)
Paused before answering	−.06 (.12)	.06 (.19)
Justified responses	−.03 (.14)	−.12 (.18)
Showed discomfort	.31 (.24)	−.77 (.23)***
Objected to section	−.09 (.37)	.18 (.36)
Racial attitudes		
Common fate	.20 (.06)***	.08 (.07)
Stereotype difference score	.03 (.01)***	.02 (.01)**
SES difference score	−.01 (.00)	.01 (.01)
R^2	.42***	.36***
N	503	500

Source: Los Angeles Study of Urban Inequality 1994.
Note: Omitted categories for income, education, and religion are high income, high school diploma, and agnostic or atheist, respectively.
*$p < .05$, **$p < .01$, ***$p < .001$

TABLE 3.12   *Multivariate Models of Competitive Group Threat, Asian Respondents*

	Black Competitive Threat	Latino Competitive Threat
Constant	1.82 (.66)	1.07 (.47)*
Social background		
Age	.02 (.00)***	.01 (.00)
Education		
No high school diploma	−.26 (.20)	.33 (.22)
Some college	−.05 (.14)	.01 (.16)
Bachelor's degree	−.04 (.12)	.09 (.17)
Postgraduate	.30 (.18)	.07 (.21)
Gender	.13 (.11)	−.10 (.14)
Income		
Did not report	−.13 (.15)	.09 (.15)
Low income	−.29 (.17)	−.14 (.17)
Lower middle income	−.19 (.19)	.04 (.15)
Higher middle income	−.21 (.19)	−.06 (.13)
Not in work force	.01 (.12)	−.17 (.11)
Ancestry		
Chinese	.79 (.55)	.62 (.37)
Japanese	.61 (.55)	.52 (.38)
Korean	1.06 (.56)	1.15 (.38)**
U.S. native	−.39 (.17)*	−.20 (.17)
Religion and social values		
Protestant	−.12 (.23)	−.01 (.16)
Catholic	−.11 (.21)	−.12 (.20)
Other religion	−.19 (.15)	−.07 (.13)
Attend	−.04 (.05)	.07 (.03)*
Political conservatism	−.04 (.04)	.10 (.05)*
Personal, work, and neighborhood context		
Has target group friend	.10 (.19)	.20 (.26)
Coworkers mainly target group	.19 (.41)	−.25 (.19)
Percent target group in tract	−.00 (.01)	.00 (.00)
Interview context		
Not same-race interviewer	−.12 (.17)	−.07 (.17)
Paused before answering	.05 (.12)	.10 (.10)
Justified responses	−.07 (.14)	−.09 (.13)
Showed discomfort	−.22 (.19)	−.29 (.26)
Objected to section	−.04 (.22)	−.22 (.18)
Racial attitudes		
Common fate	−.03 (.05)	.08 (.06)
Stereotype difference score	.03 (.01)**	.03 (.01)***
SES difference score	−.01 (.01)	−.00 (.00)
R^2	.39***	.40***
N	358	340

Source: Los Angeles Study of Urban Inequality 1994.
Note: Omitted categories for income, education, and religion are high income, high school diploma, and agnostic or atheist, respectively. The omitted category for ancestry is other Asian ancestry.
*$p < .05$, **$p < .01$, ***$p < .001$

TABLE 3.13   *Multivariate Models of Competitive Group Threat,
Latino Respondents*

	Black Competitive Threat	Asian Competitive Threat
Constant	2.76 (.65)	3.93 (.54)
Social background		
Age	.01 (.01)	−.00 (.00)
Education		
No high school diploma	.17 (.18)	−.20 (.15)
Some college	.03 (.19)	−.50 (.25)*
Bachelor's degree	.10 (.31)	−.75 (.24)**
Postgraduate	−.41 (.40)	−.92 (.43)*
Gender	.05 (.12)	.02 (.14)
Income		
Did not report	.55 (.45)	.13 (.39)
Low income	.34 (.41)	−.13 (.32)
Lower middle income	.18 (.40)	.03 (.29)
Higher middle income	−.12 (.39)	−.16 (.32)
Not in work force	.05 (.14)	.30 (.14)*
Ancestry		
Mexican	−.23 (.22)	−.15 (.23)
Central American	−.40 (.23)	.06 (.26)
U.S. native	−.17 (.20)	.09 (.17)
Religion and social values		
Protestant	−.46 (.34)	−.48 (.34)
Catholic	.16 (.22)	.09 (.28)
Other religion	−.18 (.36)	−.42 (.55)
Attend	−.04 (.05)	−.03 (.03)
Political conservatism	−.01 (.04)	.03 (.04)
Personal, work, and neighborhood context		
Has target group friend	.18 (.30)	−.32 (.44)
Coworkers mainly target group	.12 (.33)	−.33 (.22)
Percent target group in tract	.00 (.00)	−.01 (.01)**
Interview context		
Not same-race inerviewer	−.11 (.18)	−.31 (.15)*
Paused before answering	−.06 (.14)	−.00 (.13)
Justified responses	−.31 (.21)	.04 (.16)
Showed discomfort	−.34 (.21)	−.17 (.18)
Objected to section	−.06 (.18)	−.20 (.17)
Racial attitudes		
Common fate	.22 (.06)***	−.00 (.05)
Stereotype difference score	−.00 (.01)	.01 (.01)
SES difference score	−.00 (.01)	−.01 (.00)
R^2	.20***	.21***
N	413	425

Source: Los Angeles Study of Urban Inequality 1994.
Note: Omitted categories for income, education, and religion are high income, high school diploma, and agnostic or atheist, respectively. The omitted category for ancestry is other Latino ancestry.
*$p < .05$, **$p < .01$, ***$p < .001$

Asians among blacks and, somewhat unexpectedly, the better-educated express a greater sense of competition with Asians as well. The pattern is different for blacks' responses to Latinos. In this case, feelings of competition are negatively related to education and show mild sensitivity to aspects of the interview context.

Among the Asian respondents there is a strong relationship between stereotypes and perceptions of group competition. This holds for perceptions of competition with both blacks and Latinos. In addition, national ancestry matters, with Koreans expressing significantly greater feelings of competition with Latinos than do Asians of other national origins, and there is an effect of borderline significance (p = .082) in the same direction with regard to competition with blacks.

Among Latinos, perceptions of threat from blacks are related only to common fate identity. The higher the level of expressed common fate identity, the greater the perceived competition with blacks. Latinos' perceptions of competition with Asians decline as education rises, as the percentage Asian in the respondent's census tract rises, and when the respondent has Asian coworkers.

Opposition to Affirmative Action

One of the primary reasons for an interest in studies of attitudes on race relations is that policy preferences that are widely shared and intensely felt in this domain are likely to find some expression in concrete social policy. Such preferences appear to provide some of the most compelling evidence of a meaningful connection between verbally expressed attitudes and overt social behavior (Schuman 1995). For example, survey data had for some time pointed in the direction of the passage of both Proposition 187, curtailing the social services that could be extended to undocumented immigrants, and subsequently Proposition 209, banning affirmative action in state contracts, hiring, and higher education.

The LASUI contained a set of questions on support for affirmative action. One set asked whether respondents favored or opposed "special training and educational assistance" programs for members of groups who have faced disadvantages in the past. The question referred separately to programs for blacks, for Latinos, and for Asians. The second set of questions, in reference to the same set of racial groups, asked about attitudes on affirmative action involving "preferences in hiring and promotion." These questions thus allow us to gauge how the content of the policy—mild versus fairly strong forms of affirmative action—influences responses.[5] Figures 3.8 and 3.9 show mean levels of opposition to affirmative action by race for "job training and educational assistance" and "preferences in hiring and promotion," respectively. As we will

FIGURE 3.8   *Mean Opposition to Race-Based "Special Job Training and Educational Assistance" Programs by Race*

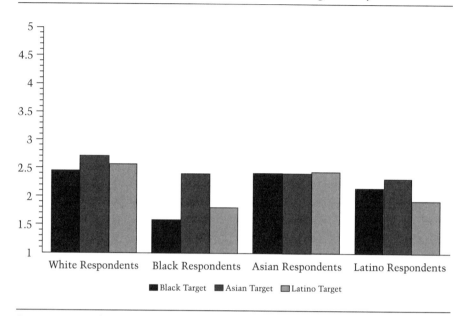

Source: Los Angeles Study of Urban Inequality 1994.

elaborate, the content of the policy, the racial target group, and respondent race all influence opinions on affirmative action.

Three patterns stand out immediately. First, the special job training and educational assistance version of affirmative action is consistently more popular than the preferences in hiring and promotion version. This result is consistent with the findings from many other studies (see Schuman et al. 1997; Steeh and Krysan 1996). Our results differ principally in moving beyond the usual black-white comparison in both question wording and samples. It is also worth noting that opinions do not indicate monolithic opposition to even the stronger version of affirmative action. Second, there are consistently significant racial group differences in opinion. Racial minorities, especially African Americans and Latinos, are less likely to oppose affirmative action than are whites and, to a lesser degree, Asians. Again, however, these differences cannot be read as enormous or gaping divides, even though they are quite real. Third, blacks and Latinos each express slightly lower levels of opposition to affirmative action when targeted on their own group as compared to the other.

The pattern of differential policy goal, racial target group, and re-

FIGURE 3.9   *Mean Opposition to Race-Based "Preferences in Hiring and Promotion" by Race*

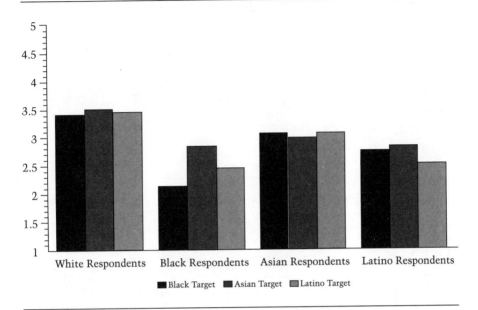

Source: Los Angeles Study of Urban Inequality 1994.

spondent race effects on the level of opposition to affirmative action carries over into the results of our multivariate analysis of individual variation in affirmative action opinions. The single most consistently influential variable is the perception of economic status differences between groups. This variable has significant effects for eight of the eighteen equations estimated in tables 3.14 through 3.17. Generally, the larger the perceived economic disadvantage of a racial minority group, the less the opposition to affirmative action. In effect, the greater the perceived neediness of a group, the less likely an individual is to object to affirmative action targeted at members of that group (Kluegel 1985). Beliefs about the degree of economic inequality between groups, as argued by the sociologist James Kluegel (Kluegel and Smith 1986; Kluegel 1990), play an important role in the policy debate about affirmative action. We find that negative stereotypes increased opposition to affirmative action in only four of the eighteen equations (most reliably so in the case of whites' opposition to preferences in hiring and promotion for blacks).

In addition, respondent age (seven of eighteen equations) and self-described political ideology (six of eighteen equations) also tended to

TABLE 3.14   Multivariate Models of Opposition to Affirmative Action, White Respondents

	Education and Training for Blacks	Education and Training for Asians	Education and Training for Latinos	Hiring and Promotion for Blacks	Hiring and Promotion for Asians	Hiring and Promotion for Latinos
Constant	3.78 (.77)***	2.12 (.54)***	2.06 (.66)**	4.81 (.58)***	3.21 (.45)	2.62 (.56)***
Social background						
Age	−.01 (.01)*	−.00 (.00)	−.01 (.01)	−.01 (.01)*	.00 (.01)	−.01 (.00)
Education						
No high school diploma	−1.11 (.30)***	−.48 (.30)	−.60 (.37)	−.16 (.40)	−.14 (.36)	.12 (.49)
Some college	−.38 (.17)*	.03 (.23)	.12 (.15)	.22 (.22)	−.12 (.20)	−.08 (.22)
Bachelor's degree	−.22 (.20)	.02 (.24)	−.26 (.21)	.02 (.19)	−.24 (.24)	−.08 (.21)
Postgraduate	−.49 (.26)	.05 (.29)	−.38 (.31)	.02 (.26)	−.67 (.28)*	−.22 (.28)
Gender	.36 (.15)*	.16 (.15)	.14 (.20)	.17 (.15)	.05 (.14)	.12 (.18)
Income						
Did not report	−.46 (.33)	−.40 (.25)	.14 (.44)	−.44 (.35)	−.94 (.34)**	.10 (.21)
Low income	−.66 (.23)**	−.25 (.23)	−.26 (.28)	−.52 (.26)*	−.74 (.31)*	−.65 (.32)*
Lower middle income	−.36 (.20)*	−.24 (.22)	−.19 (.24)	−.18 (.17)	−.62 (.20)**	−.37 (.18)*
Higher middle income	−.23 (.24)	.03 (.23)	−.28 (.21)	.08 (.19)	−.42 (.18)*	−.10 (.15)
Not in work force	.12 (.19)	.13 (.17)	−.06 (.21)	−.02 (.21)	−.06 (.19)	−.30 (.20)
Religion and social values						
Protestant	−.50 (.32)	.33 (.19)	−.38 (.32)	.10 (.24)	.07 (.23)	−.13 (.31)
Catholic	−.50 (.33)	.57 (.20)**	−.36 (.35)	.03 (.22)	.14 (.24)	−.31 (.34)
Jewish	−.64 (.32)*	.06 (.30)	−.54 (.39)	−.66 (.28)*	−.02 (.34)	−.07 (.36)
Other religion	−.48 (.41)	.01 (.31)	−.90 (.38)*	.25 (.26)	−.50 (.26)	−.29 (.36)
Attend	−.02 (.05)	.06 (.05)	.02 (.06)	−.09 (.04)*	−.00 (.05)	.10 (.04)*
Political conservatism	.04 (.08)	.10 (.05)*	.15 (.07)*	.08 (.06)	.12 (.05)	.25 (.05)***

	Model 1	Model 2	Model 3	Model 4	Model 5
Personal, work, and neighborhood context					
Has target group friend	−.10 (.17)	.46 (.27)	.24 (.27)	.03 (.20)	−.14 (.20)
Coworkers mainly target group	−.69 (.32)*	.48 (.34)	−.14 (.41)	−.32 (.35)	.07 (.49)
Percentage target group in tract	.02 (.01)**	−.02 (.07)	−.02 (.01)*	.00 (.01)	.01 (.01)
Interview context					
Not same-race interviewer	−.07 (.17)	−.36 (.14)**	−.02 (.14)	−.25 (.14)	.09 (.15)
Paused before answering	.10 (.17)	−.04 (.19)	−.03 (.17)	.12 (.21)	.09 (.19)
Justified responses	−.14 (.23)	−.23 (.28)	.03 (.21)	−.00 (.24)	.00 (.28)
Showed discomfort	−.17 (.22)	.03 (.20)	−.16 (.18)	−.12 (.20)	−.36 (.23)
Objected to section	−.32 (.29)	.47 (.45)	.21 (.48)	.49 (.54)	.75 (.27)**
Racial attitudes					
Common fate	−.05 (.06)	.15 (.07)*	−.06 (.09)	−.02 (.08)	−.10 (.08)
Stereotype difference score	.02 (.01)	.02 (.01)	.04 (.01)***	.03 (.02)	.00 (.01)
SES difference score	−.02 (.01)**	−.01 (.01)	−.03 (.01)***	−.00 (.01)	−.02 (.01)**
Threat from target group	.04 (.07)	−.02 (.07)	−.22 (.10)*	.18 (.07)**	.13 (.10)
R²	.28***	.33***	.31***	.23***	.26***
N	253	225	247	253	248

Source: Los Angeles Study of Urban Inequality 1994.
Note: Omitted categories for education, income, and religion are high school diploma, high income, and agnostic or atheist, respectively.
*$p < .05$, **$p < .01$, ***$p < .001$

TABLE 3.15   *Multivariate Models of Opposition to Affirmative Action,*
             Black Respondents

	Education and Training for Asians	Education and Training for Latinos	Hiring and Promotion for Asians	Hiring and Promotion for Latinos
Constant	2.54 (.51)***	1.84 (.56)***	3.58 (.49)***	2.33 (.64)***
Social background				
Age	−.01 (.00)	.01 (.00)	−.01 (.00)*	.00 (.00)
Education				
No high school diploma	−.26 (.23)	−.05 (.22)	−.32 (.23)	−.09 (.24)
Some college	−.25 (.16)	−.23 (.17)	−.18 (.17)	−.10 (.15)
Bachelor's degree	−.54 (.26)*	−.30 (.23)	−.02 (.25)	−.06 (.28)
Postgraduate	−.74 (.30)*	−.12 (.32)	−.26 (.24)	−.29 (.28)
Gender	.01 (.14)	.04 (.16)	.10 (.14)	−.11 (.16)
Income				
Did not report	−.24 (.31)	.33 (.19)	.08 (.31)	.26 (.25)
Low income	−.18 (.23)	.14 (.20)	−.04 (.23)	−.03 (.23)
Lower middle income	−.11 (.25)	.63 (.23)**	−.14 (.22)	.34 (.22)
Higher middle income	−.39 (.26)	.51 (.23)*	−.60 (.27)*	.10 (.21)
Not in work force	−.24 (.14)	−.30 (.16)	−.15 (.17)	−.35 (.13)**
Religion and social values				
Protestant	.09 (.18)	−.39 (.33)	.12 (.20)	−.07 (.23)
Catholic	.70 (.38)	−.38 (.32)	.36 (.33)	−.12 (.29)
Other religion	.34 (.32)	−.71 (.40)	.54 (.31)	−.16 (.32)
Attend	.09 (.04)	.01 (.03)	−.01 (.04)	−.01 (.04)
Political conservatism	−.04 (.04)	−.03 (.04)	−.05 (.05)	−.02 (.04)
Personal, work, and neighborhood context				
Has target group friend	−.55 (.34)	.09 (.32)	−.02 (.21)	.56 (.27)*
Coworkers mainly target group	.13 (.36)	−.17 (.18)	.76 (.27)**	.01 (.21)
Percentage target group in tract	−.00 (.01)	−.00 (.01)	−.01 (.00)	.00 (.01)
Interview context				
Not same-race interviewer	−.34 (.23)	.16 (.18)	−.10 (.25)	.22 (.16)

132

TABLE 3.15   *Continued*

	Education and Training for Asians	Education and Training for Latinos	Hiring and Promotion for Asians	Hiring and Promotion for Latinos
Paused before answering	−.04 (.15)	−.12 (.13)	.03 (.15)	.02 (.13)
Justified responses	−.11 (.15)	.05 (.19)	−.14 (.14)	−.01 (.16)
Showed discomfort	−.61 (.24)**	−.00 (.26)	−.44 (.27)	−.28 (.23)
Objected to section	−.35 (.32)	−.09 (.38)	−.06 (.29)	−.14 (.38)
Racial attitudes				
Common fate	−.08 (.07)	−.08 (.07)	.00 (.07)	−.11 (.07)
Stereotype difference score	.02 (.01)*	−.00 (.01)	.02 (.01)	.01 (.01)
SES difference score	−.01 (.00)**	−.01 (.01)	−.01 (.00)**	−.01 (.01)
Threat from target group	.09 (.07)	.15 (.05)***	−.07 (.07)	.12 (.06)
R^2	.25***	.16*	.17***	.13***
N	503	500	502	499

Source: Los Angeles Study of Urban Inequality 1994.
Note: Omitted categories for education, income, and religion are high school diploma, high income, and agnostic or atheist, respectively.
*$p < .05$, **$p < .01$, ***$p < .001$

influence views on affirmative action. Younger people and political liberals expressed less opposition to affirmative action than did their older and more conservative counterparts. Lastly, for ten of the eighteen affirmative action equations, we find some impact of income on opinions. However, this effect is not consistent in direction. Among white respondents, those in the highest income category tended to express the greatest opposition to affirmative action (four out of six equations). Among blacks, it is the middle-income categories who are more likely to oppose education and training affirmative action for Latinos. And among Asians, those in the middle-income categories are also more likely than those in the highest-income category to oppose preference in hiring and promotion for Latinos.

Perhaps more striking than these few consistent patterns of individual variation is the general absence of effects for many of the personal, work, and neighborhood context measures, for the interview context measures, and for the other racial attitude measures. With respect to this last, in only three instances do perceptions of threat have the ex-

TABLE 3.16   *Multivariate Models of Opposition to Affirmative Action,*
Asian Respondents

	Education and Training for Blacks	Education and Training for Latinos	Hiring and Promotion for Blacks	Hiring and Promotion for Latinos
Constant	3.01 (.60)	2.90 (.43)***	3.31 (.73)	3.31 (.46)***
Social background				
Age	−.01 (.00)*	−.01 (.01)	−.02 (.01)**	.01.(.00)***
Education				
No high school diploma	−.26 (.23)	.72 (.26)**	.25 (.26)	.49 (.18)**
Some college	−.17 (.16)	.16 (.19)	−.26 (.18)	.14 (.15)
Bachelor's degree	−.36 (.15)*	−.13 (.15)	−.44 (.15)**	.06 (.12)
Postgraduate	−.36 (.19)	−.07 (.22)	−.66 (.28)*	−.08 (.17)
Gender	.27 (.13)*	.29 (.12)*	.11 (.15)	.12 (.10)
Income				
Did not report	−.20 (.21)	.04 (.19)	−.54 (.19)**	.27 (.17)
Low income	−.24 (.21)	−.14 (.22)	−.55 (.23)*	−.12 (.20)
Lower middle income	−.57 (.21)**	.07 (.16)	−.91 (.24)***	.15 (.16)
Higher middle income	−.22 (.21)	.17 (.18)	−.30 (.22)	.56 (.15)***
Not in work force	.09 (.13)	.05 (.11)	−.27 (.15)	.05 (.10)
Ancestry				
Chinese	.37 (.40)	.54 (.36)	.85 (.49)	.14 (.35)
Japanese	.60 (.39)	.53 (.37)	1.43 (.47)**	.77 (.39)*
Korean	−.29 (.42)	.56 (.36)	.85 (.48)	.64 (.38)
U.S. native	−.76 (.21)***	.08 (.18)	−.48 (.21)*	−.02 (.16)
Religion and social values				
Protestant	−.02 (.20)	−.66 (.18)***	−.11 (.23)	−.09 (.18)
Catholic	.14 (.24)	−.21 (.21)	−.38 (.25)	−.28 (.19)
Other religion	−.17 (.19)	−.18 (.18)	−.27 (.20)	.06 (.15)
Attend	−.03 (.05)	−.06 (.04)	−.08 (.05)	−.03 (.03)
Political conservatism	.05 (.04)	.12 (.05)**	.18 (.05)***	.09 (.04)*
Personal, work, and neighborhood context				
Has target group friend	.32 (.21)	−.44 (.30)	.00 (.26)	−.41 (.29)
Coworkers mainly target group	−.22 (.21)	−.05 (.23)	.40 (.29)	−.23 (.17)
Percentage target group in tract	.00 (.01)	−.01 (.00)	.01 (.02)	−.01 (.00)*

TABLE 3.16 *Continued*

	Education and Training for Blacks	Education and Training for Latinos	Hiring and Promotion for Blacks	Hiring and Promotion for Latinos
Interview context				
Not same-race interviewer	.39 (.27)	−.08 (.23)	−.03 (.28)	.03 (.23)
Paused before answering	−.09 (.14)	.13 (.16)	−.17 (.20)	.52 (.13)***
Justified responses	−.02 (.17)	−.04 (.20)	.24 (.22)	−.43 (.18)*
Showed discomfort	−.63 (.25)**	−.24 (.32)	−.67 (.34)*	−.28 (.28)
Objected to section	.84 (.31)**	.11 (.25)	.62 (.30)*	.22 (.25)
Racial attitudes				
Common fate	−.02 (.07)	.24 (.06)***	.05 (.06)	−.16 (.05)**
Stereotype difference score	−.00 (.01)	.03 (.01)*	−.01 (.01)	.00 (.01)
SES difference score	−.02 (.00)***	−.02 (.01)**	−.00 (.01)	−.00 (.00)
Threat from target group	.00 (.06)	−.03 (.08)	−.02 (.07)	−.03 (.07)
R^2	.39***	.35***	.36***	.40***
N	355	340	355	340

Source: Los Angeles Study of Urban Inequality 1994.
Note: Omitted categories for education, income, religion, and ancestry are high school diploma, high income, agnostic or atheist, and other Asian ancestry, respectively.
*$p < .05$, **$p < .01$, ***$p < .001$

pected effect. Whites and blacks who perceive more threat from Latinos are more likely to oppose education and training programs for Latinos. In addition, there is a borderline effect of threat on blacks' opposition to preference in hiring and promotion for Latinos ($p = .06$).

These results prompt us to reiterate a point we made at the outset: often what is analytically most important about intergroup attitudes is the extent and nature of group differences in viewpoints, not the sources of individual variation within a group (see Jackman 1994). If, rather than examining within racial group determinants of affirmative action opinion, we pooled the data across race and estimated six equations (three racial minority target groups by two types of policies) and introduced race as a variable (a set of dummy coded variables with whites as the omitted category), the results speak plainly. There are highly significant racial group differences for all six equations net of all social background

TABLE 3.17   *Multivariate Models of Opposition to Affirmative Action, Latino Respondents*

	Education and Training for Blacks	Education and Training for Asians	Hiring and Promotion for Blacks	Hiring and Promotion for Asians
Constant	1.41 (.56)**	2.48 (.57)***	3.13 (.58)***	3.54 (.52)***
Social background				
Age	−.00 (.00)	−.00 (.00)	.00 (.00)	−.01 (.00)*
Education				
No high school diploma	.19 (.13)	−.03 (.13)	−.01 (.14)	−.39 (.14)**
Some college	.22 (.15)	.03 (.18)	.07 (.18)	−.08 (.17)
Bachelor's degree	.44 (.30)	.31 (.21)	−.10 (.32)	−.15 (.24)
Postgraduate	−.94 (.25)***	−.43 (.55)	.48 (.72)	.87 (.50)
Gender	.26 (.12)*	−.09 (.13)	−.10 (.10)	.19 (.10)
Income				
Did not report	.12 (.32)	−.75 (.28)**	−.11 (.30)	−.18 (.33)
Low income	−.13 (.24)	−.20 (.26)	−.18 (.22)	.10 (.22)
Lower middle income	−.36 (.23)	−.21 (.23)	−.11 (.23)	.02 (.23)
Higher middle income	−.19 (.27)	−.46 (.27)	−.26 (.23)	−.19 (.24)
Not in work force	−.07 (.10)	.19 (.14)	−.08 (.11)	.06 (.12)
Ancestry				
Mexican	.43 (.18)*	−.14 (.24)	−.34 (.27)	−.12 (.25)
Central American	.29 (.22)	−.14 (.28)	−.20 (.29)	−.23 (.26)
U.S. native	.04 (.16)	.06 (.16)	.02 (.15)	.11 (.20)
Religion and social values				
Protestant	.03 (.26)	.21 (.33)	−.25 (.28)	−.25 (.36)
Catholic	−.03 (.19)	−.05 (.26)	−.19 (.17)	−.14 (.23)
Other religion	−.40 (.33)	.33 (.36)	−.70 (.39)	−.29 (.30)
Attend	−.01 (.04)	.07 (.04)	−.04 (.04)	.00 (.04)
Political conservatism	.07 (.04)	−.03 (.04)	.07 (.04)	.02 (.05)
Personal, work, and neighborhood context				
Has target group friend	−.33 (.29)	.13 (.22)	−.09 (.44)	.60 (.38)
Coworkers mainly target group	−.08 (.27)	.04 (.28)	−.46 (.33)	.62 (.21)**
Percentage target group in tract	−.00 (.00)	−.01 (.00)	−.00 (.00)	.00 (.00)

TABLE 3.17   *Continued*

	Education and Training for Blacks	Education and Training for Asians	Hiring and Promotion for Blacks	Hiring and Promotion for Asians
Interview context				
Not same-race interviewer	.13 (.15)	.11 (.16)	−.02 (.15)	.02 (.15)
Paused before answering	.14 (.09)	.09 (.11)	.00 (.11)	−.14 (.09)
Justified responses	−.14 (.13)	.13 (.14)	−.02 (.15)	−.06 (.15)
Showed discomfort	.01 (.16)	−.24 (.18)	.05 (.20)	.16 (.16)
Objected to section	.45 (.19)*	−.25 (.16)	.37 (.19)*	.16 (.13)
Racial attitudes				
Common fate	−.07 (.05)	−.15 (.05)**	−.06 (.05)	−.01 (.04)
Stereotype difference score	.00 (.01)	.01 (.01)	−.00 (.01)	−.01 (.01)
SES difference score	−.00 (.00)	−.01 (.00)***	−.00 (.00)	−.00 (.00)
Threat from target group	.02 (.06)	.04 (.07)	.01 (.05)	−.08 (.05)
R^2	.21***	.18***	.13*	.21***
N	413	425	413	425

Source: Los Angeles Study of Urban Inequality 1994.
Note: Omitted categories for education, income, religion, and ancestry are high school diploma, high income, agnostic or atheist, and other Latino ancestry, respectively.
*$p < .05$, **$p < .01$, ***$p < .001$

measures, religion and social values measures, and interview context measures. Whites are uniformly the most likely to oppose affirmative action and blacks the least likely to do so. Asians do not differ significantly from whites in level of opposition to special education and training programs, irrespective of race of the target group, but express significantly less opposition to preferences in hiring and promotion.

Our results suggest that the debate over how the state should intervene to influence racial group positions in the labor market is most profoundly structured by the specific policy formulations or goal, by racial group membership and the interests attendant thereto, and the configuration of relations among particular groups (Bobo and Kluegel 1993). Each of these types of factors has a collective, institutional, and group-level center of concern. Still, policy goal and group membership do not exhaust the sources of opinion on affirmative action. At the individual level, we do find that the perceived neediness of a group, the ideological leanings of an individual, and, to a less consistent degree, stereotype beliefs, level of income, and perceptions of threat also play into opinions on affirmative action.

Conclusion

In imposing or drawing out some coherent threads or implications, it is useful to return to the opening juxtaposition of scenarios. Recall that we contrasted, at one extreme, a situation of contentious racial polarization to, at the other extreme, a situation of racial harmony and fluidity. In terms of the several types of attitudes we measured, it is fair to say that Los Angeles is not particularly close to either extreme, though the tilt, ever so mildly, would be in the direction of the latter state of affairs. In terms of major conclusions, we find that:

(1) The great majority of adults in Los Angeles do see their fate as individuals as bound up to some degree with that of others of similar race;

(2) Just about everyone sees and agrees on the presence of race-linked differences in economic standing;

(3) Just about everyone sees some noteworthy differences in behavioral predispositions among and between racial groups, though these differences are rarely seen as categorical or extreme and sometimes exhibit a degree of in-group and out-group consensus;

(4) Perceptions of racial group competition are common, though never acute; and

(5) There is a real and durable, if unremarkable, connection between racial group membership and how one is likely to feel about affirmative action.

The broadest implication of these results, as Cornel West (1993) put it so aptly, is that race matters! In an era when some scholars have announced the end of racism (D'Souza 1995) and others have suggested that we abandon talking about and measuring racial group differences (Thernstrom and Thernstrom 1997), this is an important point to reinforce and reinforce loudly. There are noteworthy racial group differences and group-specific patterning of results in each of the domains we examined. If, as Mary Jackman (1994) has persuasively argued, intergroup attitudes are centrally the property of groups and yield information about the dynamics of group relations, then these results point to a strong degree of racialization of the contemporary urban environment (Sanjek 1994).

Yet, we are prompted to temper this conclusion immediately with another observation. The heuristic model (recall figure 3.1) we structured our individual-level analysis around did not fare very well on the whole. That is, our results cannot be read as identifying a firmly and consistently socially rooted set of attitudes and beliefs that, among themselves, are also tightly interlaced. Instead, a second broad implication of our results is that there are often specific issues and sets of social relations and an emergent, often situational, and dynamic character to race relations (see Oliver and Johnson 1984). As Wilson has argued: "It is important to recognize that racial antagonisms, or the manifestation of racial tensions, are products of economic, political, and social situations" (1996, xx).

Even though race relations will play out in highly contingent and situationally specific ways, a third implication of our research is the expectation that the types of identities, attitudes, and beliefs we mapped here should hold transsituational relevance. We have charted important features of the cognitive, emotional, and identity-based considerations that individuals and groups will likely bring with them into a wide array of social situations. Thus, for example, as a person enters the housing market, it is reasonable to assume that he or she attends to social cues concerning the racial background of potential neighbors, holds distinct views of the characteristics of members of different racial groups, and expects different patterns of relation and interaction as a result. Likewise, in the workplace we should expect the same types of social lenses to be applied. None of these considerations ordains specific outcomes. But our results clearly show that racial considerations cannot be ignored across the domains of social life.

More than this, a fourth and final broad implication of our results is that elements of the classic American racial order or hierarchy, with whites still ensconced at the top, blacks still at the bottom, and the Asian and Latino populations arrayed in between, continues to exist (Gans 1999). White respondents perceive a sense of comfortable, but not categorical, superiority to racial minority group members and do not see themselves as being under acute competitive pressures. They are the most likely to consistently oppose affirmative action. The only stereotype personality trait for which minority group members consistently perceive whites in a poor light concerns a pattern of discriminating against others. African Americans, on the whole, are given the most negative stereotype ratings by others, are among those most likely to view race relations in competitive terms, most consistently express support for affirmative action, and are the most acutely race-conscious. The results for Latinos in some respects parallel those for African Americans but differ in noteworthy ways. Among these exceptions are greater concessions are made by Latinos to negative stereotypes held by the dominant group and a real strain of resistance to thinking of themselves in terms of racial group identity. Both Asians and Latinos exhibit tendencies for national ancestry–based attachments (rather than panethnic or racial attachments), and their experiences are variously conditioned by recency of immigration and class background.

There are those who may think the degree of racialized thinking is acutely high in Los Angeles, or that the dynamics are somehow importantly different from those in most other major metropolitan areas. Although possible, this is highly unlikely to be the case. In each of the major domains we examined, data on comparable measures in national samples are reassuringly similar. It is also unlikely that a number of local and potentially jarring race-related social events played a distorting role in our analysis. Thus, the initial airing of the infamous Rodney King beating video occurred more than two years prior to the start of LASUI data collection; the acquittal of the LAPD officers who beat King by a Simi Valley jury and the subsequent uprising in Los Angeles precede our survey by more than twelve months; and the highly divisive acquittal of O.J. Simpson in the criminal trial for the murders of Nicole Brown Simpson and Ronald Goldman occurred a year and a half after the completion of the LASUI field period. What is more, careful analyses conducted at the time of the rioting in Los Angeles make it clear that the impact of dramatic events on racial attitudes and beliefs is generally small to nonexistent (Bobo et al. 1994).

Our results are made all the more important, indeed, by virtue of focusing on a single, highly diverse metropolitan area. Unlike most studies of racial outlooks that draw on national data, it is safe to assume that our respondents constitute a more cohesive social community than is ordinarily examined in studies of racial attitudes. As residents of the same metropolis, they share a common environmental mix of racial and ethnic groups, a common set of broad economic conditions, a common media environment, and a common dependence on many of the same local and statewide institutions of government. Many of the vast array of factors ordinarily left uncontrolled (and often uncontrollable) in analyses of national data do not arise for our work. We are thus able to provide a sharp focus on processes of racial identity, attitude, and belief in a way that is not instantly rendered opaque by large differences in region, community size, institutions of local or state government, or other unique historical events and conditions. Furthermore, as we stress throughout this volume, Los Angeles is a crucial case for examining these processes, since it is at the leading edge of social trends now affecting most major metropolitan areas.

Crucially, with regard to the issues that will dominate our attention in this volume, we believe these results provide strong warrant for expecting racial identities, attitudes, and beliefs to influence—sometimes positively and sometimes negatively, sometimes weakly and sometimes powerfully—a range of key outcomes in the labor market and in the housing market. This will be so if for no other reason than that individuals very definitely hold identities, stereotypes, competitive apprehensions, and differing policy views that are linked to a racial mapping of the social world. It is a sociological truism that human action is guided by the meanings that other individuals and situations take on. In the prismatic metropolis of Los Angeles, as in the rest of the nation, the meanings that individuals bring to or create in many social settings are likely to reflect a racialized element.

A number of colleagues were generous enough to give this paper a careful reading. For their time and enormously helpful suggestions we wish to thank Camille Z. Charles, Jennifer L. Hochschild, Mary R. Jackman, Monica McDermott, Howard Schuman, David O. Sears, Jim Sidanius, Abel Valenzuela, Roger Waldinger, and William Julius Wilson. The authors are responsible for any remaining errors or problems. This research was partly supported by NSF grant # SBR9515183.

Appendix

TABLE 3A.1   Interviewer Ratings of Respondents' Behavior During Racial Attitudes Section by Race of Respondent

	Whites	Blacks	Native-Born Asians	Foreign-Born Asians	Native-Born Latinos	Foreign-Born Latinos	Design-Based F	Total
Hesitate or pause								
No	62%	67%	74%	70%	69%	49%	5.73***	61
Yes	38	33	26	30	31	51		40
	(860)	(1116)	(130)	(926)	(195)	(789)		(4016)
Justify or qualify								
No	78	77	89	89	91	78	3.21*	80
Yes	22	23	11	11	9	22		20
	(859)	(1114)	(129)	(925)	(195)	(789)		(4011)
Discomfort								
No	84	89	85	94	86	87	2.10 ns	86
Yes	16	11	15	6	14	13		14
	(856)	(1114)	(129)	(925)	(195)	(787)		(4006)
Object								
No	94	97	96	90	91	82	12.24***	91
Yes	06	03	4	10	9	18		09
	(855)	(1115)	(129)	(925)	(195)	(788)		(4007)
Summary count of ratings								
None	51	55	56	59	56	36	2.65**	49
Yes to one item	26	26	35	29	31	34		29
Yes to two items	15	14	4	10	10	19		15
Yes to three items	7	4	4	3	2[a]	9		6
Yes to four items	1	1	<1[a]	1	2	1		1
	(863)	(1118)	(130)	(926)	(195)	(793)		(4025)

Source: Los Angeles Study of Urban Inequality 1994.
[a]Cell count less than five.

TABLE 3A.2 *Percentage Summary of Race of Interviewer by Race of Respondent and Interviewer Ratings of Respondent Behavior by Race of Interviewer*

	Whites	Blacks	Asians	Latinos
Interviewer race				
White	71%	24%	14%	13%
Latino	6	12	6	74
Black	2	55	<1	2
Asian	21	10	80	11
	(863)	(1118)	(1056)	(988)
	Hesitate/ Pause	Justify/ Qualify	Show Discomfort	Object to Section
White respondents				
White interviewer	42%***	21%	16%	5%*
Nonwhite interviewer	26	23	17	10
	(859)	(858)	(855)	(854)
Black respondents				
Black interviewer	37	19	10	4
Nonblack interviewer	29	28	11	3
	(1115)	(1113)	(1113)	(1114)
Asian respondents				
Asian interviewer	24*	11	7	12
Non-Asian interviewer	52	12	9[a]	—
	(1052)	(1050)	(1050)	(1050)
Latino respondents				
Latino interviewer	52***	22***	13	18*
Non-Latino interviewer	29	10	14	8
	(983)	(983)	(981)	(982)

Source: Los Angeles Study of Urban Inequality 1994.
[a]Cell count less than five.
*$p < .05$, **$p < .01$, ***$p < .001$

143

TABLE 3A.3   *Percentage Summary of Interviewer Ratings of White Respondents' Behavior During the Racial Attitudes Section by Background Characteristics*

	Hesitate or Pause	Justify or Qualify	Show Discomfort	Object to Section
Sex				
Female	42%*	24%	21%**	8%
	(462)	(463)	(461)	(460)
Male	33	20	12	4
	(397)	(395)	(394)	(394)
Age				
Twenty-one–twenty-nine years	26*	21	15	4
	(138)	(137)	(137)	(137)
Thirty–thirty-nine years	33	14	12	4
	(204)	(205)	(204)	(204)
Forty–forty-nine years	41	24	18	7
	(187)	(187)	(185)	(184)
Fifty plus years	45	26	19	8
	(329)	(328)	(328)	(328)
Education				
< high school diploma	37	13	20	22**
	(61)	(61)	(61)	(61)
High school diploma	34	22	16	7
	(210)	(210)	(210)	(210)
Some college	36	19	13	3
	(294)	(295)	(293)	(293)
Bachelor's degree	40	23	20	8
	(206)	(204)	(203)	(202)
Postgraduate	44	31	20	3
	(88)	(88)	(88)	(88)
Family income				
< 20,000	35	27	11	4
	(195)	(195)	(195)	(195)
$20K to 39,000	41	23	17	2
	(220)	(220)	(219)	(219)
$40K to 59,000	34	16	14	3
	(164)	(164)	(162)	(161)
$60,000+	37	20	14	4
	(186)	(185)	(185)	(185)
Conservatism				
Liberal	43	26	16	7
	(253)	(252)	(251)	(250)
Moderate	32	17	17	6
	(313)	(314)	(313)	(313)
Conservative	39	22	17	5
	(290)	(289)	(288)	(288)

Source: Los Angeles Study of Urban Inequality 1994.
*p < .05, **p < .01

TABLE 3A.4   *Percentage Summary of Interviewer Ratings of Black Respondents' Behavior During the Racial Attitudes Section by Background Characteristics*

	Hesitate or Pause	Justify or Qualify	Show Discomfort	Object to Section
Sex				
Female	39%**	19%	12%	3%
	(728)	(727)	(727)	(727)
Male	27	27	10	4
	(387)	(386)	(386)	(387)
Age				
Twenty-one–twenty-nine years	20*	24	6	3
	(230)	(229)	(229)	(229)
Thirty–thirty-nine years	40	25	14	2
	(307)	(307)	(307)	(307)
Forty–forty-nine years	33	28	10	4
	(222)	(221)	(221)	(221)
Fifty plus years	40	18	12	5
	(354)	(354)	(354)	(355)
Education				
< high school diploma	57*	16	30***	5
	(213)	(212)	(212)	(212)
High school diploma	30	16	12	3
	(367)	(367)	(367)	(368)
Some college	31	32	05	2
	(413)	(412)	(412)	(412)
Bachelor's degree	36	20	11	3
	(96)	(96)	(96)	(96)
Postgraduate	20	24	1	7
	(25)	(25)	(25)	(25)
Family income				
< $20,000	37	20	15*	3*
	(556)	(555)	(555)	(555)
$20,000 to 39,000	33	23	8	2
	(248)	(248)	(248)	(249)
$40,000 to 59,000	40	23	15	4
	(95)	(95)	(95)	(95)
$60,000 +	26	35	3	<1[a]
	(83)	(83)	(83)	(83)
Conservatism				
Liberal	30	30	9	3
	(424)	(423)	(423)	(423)
Moderate	38	15	17	5
	(386)	(386)	(386)	(387)
Conservative	32	23	5	3
	(300)	(299)	(299)	(299)

Source: Los Angeles Study of Urban Inequality 1994.
[a]Cell count less than five.
*p < .05, **p < .01, ***p < .001

TABLE 3A.5   *Percentage Summary of Interviewer Ratings of Asian Respondents' Behavior During the Racial Attitudes Section by Background Characteristics*

	Hesitate or Pause	Justify or Qualify	Show Discomfort	Object to Section
Sex				
Female	25%	9%	11%**	10%
	(547)	(546)	(546)	(546)
Male	35	14	3	9
	(505)	(204)	(504)	(504)
Age				
Twenty-one to twenty-nine years	28	8	10	7
	(141)	(140)	(140)	(140)
Thirty to thirty-nine years	32	13	7	10
	(282)	(281)	(281)	(281)
Forty to forty-nine years	26	16	10	7
	(273)	(273)	(273)	(273)
Fifty plus years	32	9	4	12
	(354)	(354)	(354)	(354)
Education				
< high school diploma	25	8	8	19*
	(186)	(186)	(186)	(186
High school diploma	23	6	2	11
	(249)	(249)	(249)	(249)
Some college	19	7	4	10
	(207)	(207)	(207)	(207)
Bachelor's degree	39	14	10	6
	(309)	(308)	(308)	(308)
Postgraduate	41	24	11	4
	(99)	(98)	(98)	(98)
Family income				
<$20,000	25	13	6	9*
	(266)	(266)	(266)	(266)
$20,000 to 39,000	34	15	2	5
	(182)	(181)	(181)	(181)
$40,000 to 59,000	49	16	16	4
	(120)	(120)	(120)	(120)
$60,000+	25	6	10	2
	(149)	(148)	(148)	(148)
Conservatism				
Liberal	35	14	7	4***
	(257)	(256)	(256)	(256)
Moderate	28	11	8	16
	(394)	(393)	(393)	(393)
Conservative	26	9	7	5
	(374)	(374)	(374)	(374)

TABLE 3A.5   *Continued*

	Hesitate or Pause	Justify or Qualify	Show Discomfort	Object to Section
Ancestry				
Chinese	30	11	6	19***
	(524)	(522)	(522)	(522)
Japanese	35	12	16	3
	(165)	(165)	(165)	(165)
Korean	26	9	4	3
	(351)	(351)	(351)	(351)
Nativity				
Foreign-born	30	11	6	10*
	(923)	(922)	(922)	(922)
Native-born	25	11	15	4
	(129)	(128)	(128)	(128)

Source: Los Angeles Study of Urban Inequality 1994.
*p < .05, **p < .01, ***p < .001

TABLE 3A.6   *Percentage Summary of Interviewer Ratings of Latino Respondents' Behavior During the Racial Attitudes Section by Background Characteristics*

	Hesitate or Pause	Justify or Qualify	Show Discomfort	Object to Section
Sex				
Female	49%	19%	12%	18%
	(512)	(513)	(512)	(512)
Male	43	18	14	14
	(471)	(470)	(469)	(470)
Age				
Twenty-one to twenty-nine years	42	15	11	14
	(362)	(362)	(362)	(362)
Thirty to thirty-nine years	45	24	15	18
	(305)	(305)	(303)	(304)
Forty to forty-nine years	44	14	15	16
	(163)	(163)	(163)	(163)
Fifty plus years	56	22	15	15
	(152)	(152)	(152)	(152)
Education				
< high school diploma	52	20	14	22**
	(567)	(568)	(567)	(567)
High school diploma	38	15	11	9
	(219)	(218)	(217)	(218)
Some college	44	20	13	9
	(132)	(132)	(132)	(132)
Bachelor's degree	32	21	17	15
	(52)	(52)	(52)	(52)
Postgraduate	43	16[a]	—	4[a]
	(13)	(13)	(13)	(13)
Family income				
<$20,000	56**	20	13	19*
	(503)	(502)	(501)	(502)
$20,000 to 39,000	37	19	9	9
	(251)	(252)	(251)	(251)
$40,000 to 59,000	47	18	15	12
	(70)	(70)	(70)	(70)
$60,000+	34	3	9	6[a]
	(44)	(44)	(44)	(44)
Conservatism				
Liberal	45	20	10	7***
	(262)	(262)	(262)	(262)
Moderate	48	21	16	27
	(426)	(426)	(424)	(425)
Conservative	43	14	12	7
	(288)	(288)	(288)	(288)

TABLE 3A.6   *Continued*

	Hesitate or Pause	Justify or Qualify	Show Discomfort	Object to Section
Ancestry				
Mexican	42*	18	12	13*
	(671)	(671)	(670)	(670)
Central American	59	21	16	24
	(238)	(238)	(237)	(238)
Other	49	22	13	15
	(73)	(73)	(73)	(73)
Nativity				
Foreign-born	51***	22***	13	18*
	(788)	(788)	(786)	(787)
Native-born	31	9	14	9
	(195)	(195)	(195)	(195)

Source: Los Angeles Study of Urban Inequality 1994.
ᵃCell count less than five.
*p < .05, **p < .01, ***p < .001

TABLE 3A.7   Mean Summary of Independent Variables by Interviewer Race and Interviewer Observations for White Respondents

	Common Fate Identity	Black Stereotype Difference Score	Asian Stereotype Difference Score	Latino Stereotype Difference Score	Black Group Threat	Asian Group Threat	Latino Group Threat	Affirmative Action for Blacks	Affirmative Action for Asians	Affirmative Action for Latinos
Interviewer race										
Same race	1.58	7.96	3.28	9.10	2.83	2.87	2.81	2.95	3.15	3.03
	(.08)	(.45)	(.38)	(.51)	(.11)	(.14)	(.09)	(.05)	(.07)	(.06)
Different race	1.47	7.39	2.82	7.93	2.80	2.65	2.94	2.90	2.99	2.92
	(.08)	(.58)	(.54)	(.46)	(.10)	(.12)	(.14)	(.07)	(.06)	(.07)
Hesitate or pause										
No	1.58	7.64	3.11	8.69	2.81	2.68*	2.90	2.95	3.11	3.00
	(.08)	(.42)	(.35)	(.43)	(.08)	(.12)	(.10)	(.05)	(.06)	(.05)
Yes	1.52	8.06	3.23	8.92	2.84	3.11	2.79	2.89	3.09	2.99
	(.09)	(.60)	(.51)	(.72)	(.15)	(.15)	(.12)	(.08)	(.08)	(.07)
Justify or qualify										
No	1.60	7.84	3.17	8.84	2.81	2.75	2.80	2.94	3.13	3.00
	(.07)	(.37)	(.33)	(.40)	(.09)	(.11)	(.08)	(.04)	(.05)	(.05)
Yes	1.43	7.57	3.03	8.44	2.86	3.03	3.04	2.88	3.01	2.98
	(.11)	(.93)	(.60)	(.95)	(.17)	(.24)	(.16)	(.12)	(.13)	(.13)
Show discomfort										
No	1.56	8.08	3.33	9.11*	2.87	2.76	2.87	2.95	3.13	3.02
	(.07)	(.40)	(.33)	(.40)	(.09)	(.11)	(.08)	(.05)	(.05)	(.05)
Yes	1.54	6.24	2.18	6.71	2.52	3.09	2.83	2.82	2.96	2.84
	(.11)	(1.09)	(.51)	(1.08)	(.15)	(.25)	(.18)	(.08)	(.09)	(.08)
Object to section										
No	1.56	7.23	3.14	8.76	2.82	2.80	2.87	2.90*	3.08	2.98
	(.07)	(.36)	(.31)	(.39)	(.08)	(.10)	(.08)	(.04)	(.05)	(.05)
Yes	1.53	9.64	3.86	8.92	2.77	2.80	2.76	3.34	3.41	3.30
	(.20)	(2.63)	(1.54)	(2.69)	(.37)	(.58)	(.35)	(.22)	(.20)	(.21)

Source: Los Angeles Study of Urban Inequality 1994.
*p < .05

TABLE 3A.8 Mean Summary of Independent Variables by Interviewer Race and Interviewer Observations for Black Respondents

	Common Fate Identity	White Stereotype Difference Score	Asian Stereotype Difference Score	Latino Stereotype Difference Score	Asian Group Threat	Latino Group Threat	Affirmative Action for Blacks	Affirmative Action for Asians	Affirmative Action for Latinos
Interviewer race									
Same race	1.89	.11	4.00	5.56*	3.90***	3.60*	1.73*	2.57	2.14
	(.07)	(.47)	(.47)	(.36)	(.06)	(.10)	(.05)	(.06)	(.05)
Different race	2.04	−.24	3.93	3.49	2.90	2.90	1.97	2.64	2.09
	(.17)	(1.06)	(1.00)	(.79)	(.29)	(.28)	(.10)	(.15)	(.10)
Hesitate or pause									
No	1.90	−.71*	3.52	4.12*	3.40	3.13*	1.89	2.63	2.18
	(.12)	(.64)	(.66)	(.51)	(.23)	(.16)	(.07)	(.09)	(.07)
Yes	2.08	1.45	5.06	5.58	3.63	3.57	1.73	2.56	2.00
	(.12)	(.81)	(.62)	(.63)	(.11)	(.17)	(.06)	(.17)	(.08)
Justify or qualify									
No	1.85**	−.34	3.78	4.55	3.57	3.32	1.87	2.64	2.16*
	(.08)	(.58)	(.60)	(.47)	(.14)	(.17)	(.06)	(.08)	(.06)
Yes	2.30	.99	4.66	5.00	3.24	3.03	1.74	2.50	1.97
	(.16)	(1.29)	(.92)	(.74)	(.42)	(.17)	(.08)	(.10)	(.08)
Show discomfort									
No	1.93	−.21	3.96	4.60	3.47	3.24	1.86*	2.58	2.15*
	(.09)	(.56)	(.53)	(.42)	(.18)	(.13)	(.06)	(.07)	(.06)
Yes	2.17	2.02	4.22	5.19	3.54	3.58	1.64	2.80	1.90
	(.17)	(1.62)	(1.36)	(1.13)	(.20)	(.53)	(.08)	(.39)	(.10)
Object to section									
No	1.97*	.05*	4.04	4.68	3.47	3.27	1.84	2.61	2.12
	(.09)	(.54)	(.52)	(.42)	(.17)	(.14)	(.05)	(.08)	(.06)
Yes	1.59	−3.25	1.71	3.63	3.66	3.19	1.83	2.41	2.12
	(.17)	(1.44)	(1.71)	(1.11)	(.31)	(.23)	(.09)	(.15)	(.15)

Source: Los Angeles Study of Urban Inequality 1994.
*p < .05, **p < .01, ***p < .001

TABLE 3A.9   Mean Summary of Independent Variables by Interviewer Race and Interviewer Observations for Asian Respondents

	Common Fate Identity	Black Stereotype Difference Score	White Stereotype Difference Score	Latino Stereotype Difference Score	Black Group Threat	Latino Group Threat	Affirmative Action for Blacks	Affirmative Action for Asians	Affirmative Action for Latinos
Interviewer race									
Same race	1.71	7.95**	1.37	10.12***	2.97	3.09	2.77	2.71	2.78
	(.10)	(.39)	(.54)	(.41)	(.11)	(.09)	(.07)	(.06)	(.06)
Different race	1.44	4.774	-.44	5.85	2.59	2.70	2.61	2.59	2.61
	(.22)	(1.19)	(.82)	(.88)	(.29)	(.26)	(.22)	(.20)	(.22)
Hesitate or pause									
No	1.73	7.89*	1.33	9.66**	2.91	3.04	2.76	2.68	2.77
	(.12)	(.55)	(.60)	(.53)	(.12)	(.11)	(.09)	(.08)	(.08)
Yes	1.47	5.36	-.07	7.51	2.89	2.89	2.66	2.70	2.69
	(.12)	(.90)	(.72)	(.65)	(.23)	(.10)	(.13)	(.10)	(.12)
Justify or qualify									
No	1.67	7.40*	.92	9.16	2.89	3.04*	2.75	2.71	2.77
	(.10)	(.54)	(.51)	(.51)	(.12)	(.11)	(.08)	(.07)	(.08)
Yes	1.51	4.81	.71	7.83	2.97	2.72	2.58	2.49	2.57
	(.24)	(1.14)	(1.18)	(.96)	(.08)	(.10)	(.12)	(.12)	(.12)
Show discomfort									
No	1.70*	7.30***	.92	9.19**	2.96	3.03**	2.75	2.69	2.75
	(.10)	(.52)	(.49)	(.47)	(.11)	(.10)	(.08)	(.07)	(.07)
Yes	1.07	4.25	.46	6.15	2.42	2.57	2.53	2.67	2.70
	(.29)	(.66)	(.81)	(1.04)	(.33)	(.14)	(.21)	(.08)	(.08)
Object to section									
No	1.67	7.19	.97**	9.06	2.91	3.01	2.72	2.67	2.73
	(.10)	(.52)	(.48)	(.48)	(.12)	(.11)	(.08)	(.07)	(.08)
Yes	1.56	5.64	-.93	8.15	2.79	2.98	2.88	2.85	2.89
	(.13)	(.63)	(.56)	(.43)	(.10)	(.12)	(.08)	(.08)	(.08)

Source: Los Angeles Study of Urban Inequality 1994.
*p < .05, **p < .01, ***p < .001

TABLE 3A.10   Mean Summary of Independent Variables by Interviewer Race and Interviewer Observations for Latino Respondents

	Common Fate Identity	Black Stereotype Difference Score	Asian Stereotype Difference Score	White Stereotype Difference Score	Black Group Threat	Asian Group Threat	Affirmative Action for Blacks	Affirmative Action for Asians	Affirmative Action for Latinos
Interviewer race									
Same race	1.67**	4.75***	.06***	−3.31*	3.19	3.54***	2.43	2.54	2.11
	(.07)	(.39)	(.49)	(.55)	(.08)	(.07)	(.04)	(.05)	(.05)
Different race	1.35	1.31	−2.99	−5.34	2.97	3.01	2.43	2.56	2.31
	(.10)	(.66)	(.61)	(.82)	(.13)	(.11)	(.08)	(.08)	(.09)
Hesitate or pause									
No	1.64	3.22**	−1.02	−4.23	3.14	3.35	2.38	2.58	2.20
	(.08)	(.43)	(.41)	(.46)	(.11)	(.10)	(.05)	(.06)	(.06)
Yes	1.54	4.60	−.41	−3.28	3.11	3.43	2.49	2.53	2.19
	(.08)	(.44)	(.60)	(.73)	(.09)	(.09)	(.05)	(.05)	(.06)
Justify or qualify									
No	1.54	3.77	−.82	−4.19	3.16	3.36	2.44	2.54	2.22
	(.06)	(.39)	(.41)	(.46)	(.08)	(.08)	(.04)	(.05)	(.05)
Yes	1.79	4.02	−.64	−2.35	2.98	3.57	2.37	2.60	2.07
	(.17)	(.58)	(.82)	(1.04)	(.17)	(.12)	(.06)	(.07)	(.10)
Show discomfort									
No	1.63	3.96	−.84	−3.75	3.14	3.43	2.44	2.55	2.20
	(.06)	(.37)	(.41)	(.49)	(.08)	(.07)	(.04)	(.05)	(.05)
Yes	1.42	3.02	−.07	−4.18	2.96	3.17	2.41	2.58	2.19
	(.13)	(.69)	(.90)	(1.11)	(.15)	(.15)	(.07)	(.09)	(.08)
Object to section									
No	1.66**	3.93	−1.02	−4.12*	3.14	3.37	2.40**	2.53	2.15**
	(.06)	(.36)	(.41)	(.53)	(.08)	(.07)	(.04)	(.05)	(.05)
Yes	1.23	3.35	.90	−1.95	3.07	3.47	2.63	2.66	2.42
	(.13)	(.81)	(.99)	(.92)	(.13)	(.13)	(.07)	(.07)	(.07)

Source: Los Angeles Study of Urban Inequality 1994.
*p < .05, **p < .01, ***p < .001

TABLE 3A.11   *Frequencies for Independent Variables by Race*

	Whites	Blacks	Asians	Latinos	Total
Social background					
Education					
< high school diploma	5%	11%	15%	50%	20%
High school diploma	24	33	21	24	26
Some college	36	40	20	18	28
Bachelor's degree	26	9	32	7	18
Postgraduate	10	7	12	2	8
	(863)	(1117)	(1055)	(988)	(4023)
Gender					
Female	55	57	53	52	54
Male	45	43	47	48	46
	(863)	(1118)	(1056)	(988)	(4025)
Age					
Twenty-one to twenty-nine years	17	26	20	35	25
Thirty to thirty-nine years	25	28	23	29	26
Forty to forty-nine years	23	19	24	18	21
Fifty plus years	36	27	34	18	29
	(862)	(1117)	(1055)	(988)	(4022)
Income report					
Reported	91	87	74	86	84
Did not report	10	13	27	14	16
	(863)	(1118)	(1056)	(988)	(4025)
Income					
Less than 20,000	16	35	24	44	30
20,000 to 39,000	28	31	34	34	32
40,000 to 59,000	26	12	20	15	18
60,000 +	(781)	(969)	(776)	(854)	(3380)
Asian ancestry					
Chinese	—	—	40	—	—
Japanese	—	—	20	—	—
Korean	—	—	38	—	—
Other Asian	—	—	3	—	—
			(1055)		
Latino ancestry					
Mexican	—	—	—	72	—
Central American	—	—	—	19	—
Other Latino	—	—	—	9	—
				(988)	
Nativity					
Foreign-born	16	8	89	74	47
U.S. native	84	92	12	26	53
	(863)	(1118)	(1056)	(988)	(4025)

TABLE 3A.11   *Continued*

	Whites	Blacks	Asians	Latinos	Total
Religion and social values					
Religion					
Protestant	38	70	29	11	38
Catholic	27	12	13	77	31
Jewish	13	<1	—	<1	3
Other	9	12	28	5	14
Agnostic or atheist	12	6	31	7	14
	(860)	(1116)	(1057)	(987)	(4020)
Political Ideology					
Liberal	31	43	33	26	34
Moderate or no thought	34	32	35	44	37
Conservative	35	25	32	30	30
	(861)	(1111)	(1039)	(985)	(3996)
Interview context					
Interviewer race					
Same as respondent	70	60	78	73	70
Not same race	30	40	22	27	30
	(863)	(1118)	(1056)	(988)	(4025)
Pause					
No pausing	62	66	69	54	63
Paused	38	34	31	46	37
	(861)	(1117)	(1056)	(979)	(4013)
Justify					
No justifying	78	78	88	81	81
Justified	22	23	12	19	19
	(859)	(1116)	(1055)	(985)	(4015)
Object					
Did not object	93	97	91	85	91
Objected	7	3	9	16	9
	(854)	(1116)	(1055)	(978)	(4003)
Discomfort					
No discomfort	83	90	93	86	89
Discomfort	17	10	7	14	12
	(854)	(1116)	(1055)	(978)	(4003)
Personal context					
Black friends					
None	93	29	99	97	78
At least one	7	72	2	3	23
	(863)	(1118)	(1056)	(988)	(4025)
White friends					
None	16	88	91	86	72
At least one	83	12	9	14	27
	(863)	(1118)	(1056)	(988)	(4025)

(Table continues on page 156.)

TABLE 3A.11   *Continued*

	Whites	Blacks	Asians	Latinos	Total
Asian friends					
None	94	96	57	99	86
At least one	6	4	43	2	14
	(863)	(1118)	(1056)	(988)	(4025)
Latino friends					
None	85	93	97	44	80
At least one	15	7	3	56	20
	(863)	(1118)	(1056)	(988)	(4025)
Workplace context					
White coworkers					
Other	35%	75%	85%	86%	72%
Mainly white	65	25	15	15	28
	(863)	(1118)	(1056)	(988)	(4025)
Black coworkers					
Other	99	67	98	98	89
Mainly black	2	33	2	2	11
	(863)	(1119)	(1056)	(988)	(4026)
Latino coworkers					
Other	92	90	91	37	78
Mainly Latino	9	11	9	63	23
	(863)	(1118)	(1056)	(988)	(4025)
Asian coworkers					
Other	97	98	58	98	87
Mainly Asian	3	3	42	2	13
	(863)	(1118)	(1056)	(988)	(4025)
Neighborhood context					
Tract racial composition					
<10 percent own race	2	34	19	3	15
10 to 19 percent own race	3	6	33	4	12
20 + percent own race	95	61	49	94	73
	(863)	(1118)	(1056)	(988)	(4025)
<10 percent Asian	62	74	19	56	52
10 to 19 percent Asian	26	19	33	34	28
20 + percent Asian	12	7	49	11	20
	(863)	(1119)	(1056)	(988)	(4026)
<10 percent black	92	34	92	85	74
10 to 19 percent black	6	6	6	3	6
20 + percent black	2	61	2	12	21
	(863)	(1118)	(1057)	(988)	(4026)
<10 percent Latino	28	10	15	3	13
10 to 19 percent Latino	22	20	17	4	16
20 + percent Latino	50	70	68	94	71
	(863)	(1118)	(1056)	(988)	(4025)

TABLE 3A.11   *Continued*

	Whites	Blacks	Asians	Latinos	Total
<10 percent white	2	52	14	34	27
10 to 19 percent white	3	5	12	18	10
20+ percent white	95	43	74	47	64
	(863)	(1118)	(1056)	(988)	(4025)

Source: Los Angeles Study of Urban Inequality 1994.

Notes

1. Each example is drawn from an article in the *Los Angeles Times*. In the order in which scenarios are mentioned, see Katz and Serrano 1991; McDonnell 1994; Dunn 1992; Maher 1995; and Silverstein 1996.

2. Once again, each example is drawn from an article in the *Los Angeles Times*. In the order in which scenarios are mentioned in the text, see Hong 1995, 1996a, 1996b; Hicks, Kwoh, and Acosta 1996; Lange 1995; Kang 1996a, 1996b; Mitchell 1996; and Renwick 1997.

3. Our results thus speak to three shortcomings of the vast body of research on racial attitudes. First, we are not constrained to examining only the views of whites. Second, we are not asking only about black-white relations. Third, through focus groups (Bobo et al. 1994, 1995) and instrument pretesting, we took seriously the obligation to treat the experiences of racial minority group members as generative for the types of questions we would pose. That is, the LASUI measures are thoroughly multiracial in ambit.

4. All multiple regression models are estimated using STATA, thereby adjusting for sample design characteristics.

5. In practice, affirmative action does not involve the use of "preferences in hiring and promotion" (Reskin 1998). Much of the media discussion and elite discourse surrounding affirmative action, however, does invoke precisely this sort of language, and thus we employed it in our questions as well.

References

Adorno, Theodore, Elise Frenkel-Brunswik, Daniel J. Levinson, and R. Nevitt Sanford. 1950. *The Authoritarian Personality*. New York: Norton.

Allport, Gordon W. 1954. *The Nature of Prejudice*. Garden City, N.J.: Doubleday.

Altemeyer, Bob. 1988. *Enemies of Freedom: Understanding Right-Wing Authoritarianism*. San Francisco, Calif.: Jossey-Bass.

Anderson, Barbara A., Brian D. Silver, and Paul R. Abramson. 1988. "The Effects of Race of the Interviewer on Measures of Electoral Participation by Blacks in SRC National Election Studies." *Public Opinion Quarterly* 52: 53–83.

Anderson, Elijah. 1990. *Streetwise: Race, Class and Change in an Urban Community*. Chicago: University of Chicago Press.

Ashmore, Richard D., and Frances K. Del Boca. 1981. "Conceptual Approaches to Stereotypes and Stereotyping." In *Cognitive Processes in Stereotyping and Human Behavior*, edited by D. L. Hamilton. Hillsdale, N.J.: Erlbaum.

Blalock, Hubert M. 1965. *Toward a Theory of Minority Group Relations*. New York: Capricorn Books.

Blumer, Herbert. 1958. "Race Prejudice as a Sense of Group Position." *Pacific Sociological Review* 1: 3–7.

Bobo, Lawrence. 1983. "Whites' Opposition to Busing: Symbolic Racism or Realistic Group Conflict?" *Journal of Personality and Social Psychology* 45: 1196–1210.

———. 1999. "Prejudice as Group Position: Microfoundations of a Sociological Approach to Racism and Race Relations." *Journal of Social Issues* 55: 445–72.

———. 2000. "Reclaiming a DuBoisian Perspective on Racial Attitudes." *Annals of the American Academy of Political and Social Science* 568: 186–202.

Bobo, Lawrence, and Vincent L. Hutchings. 1996. "Perceptions of Racial Group Competition: Extending Blumer's Theory of Group Position to a Multiracial Social Context." *American Sociological Review* 61: 951–72.

Bobo, Lawrence, and James R. Kluegel. 1993. "Opposition to Race-Targeting: Self-Interest, Stratification Ideology, or Racial Attitudes." *American Sociological Review* 58: 443–64.

———. 1997. "Status, Ideology, and Dimensions of Whites' Racial Beliefs and Attitudes: Progress and Stagnation." In *Racial Attitudes in the 1990s: Continuity and Change*, edited by Steven A. Tuch and Jack K. Martin. Westport, Conn.: Praeger.

Bobo, Lawrence, and Camille L. Zubrinsky. 1995. "Attitudes on Residential Integration: Perceived Status Differences, Mere In-Group Preference, or Racial Prejudice?" *Social Forces* 74: 883–909.

Bobo, Lawrence, Camille L. Zubrinsky, James H. Johnson Jr., and Melvin L. Oliver. 1994. "Public Opinion Before and After a Spring of Discontent." In *The Los Angeles Riots: Lessons for the Urban Future*, edited by M. Baldassare. Boulder, Colo.: Westview.

———. 1995. "Work Orientation, Job Discrimination, and Ethnicity: A Focus Group Perspective." *Research in the Sociology of Work* 5: 45–85.

Broman, Clifford, Harold W. Neighbors, and James S. Jackson. 1988. "Racial Group Identification Among Black Adults." *Social Psychology Quarterly* 67: 146–58.

Davis, Darren W. 1997. "Nonrandom Measurement Error and Race of Interviewer Effects Among African Americans." *Public Opinion Quarterly* 61(1): 183–207.

Dawson, Michael C. 1994. *Behind the Mule: Race and Class in African-American Politics*. Princeton, N.J.: Princeton University Press.

De la Garza, Rudolfo, A. Falcon, and F. Chris Garcia. 1996. "Will the Real Americans Please Stand Up: Anglo and Mexican Support of Core American Political Values." *American Journal of Political Science* 40: 335–51.

Demo, David H., and Michael Hughes. 1990. "Socialization and Racial Identity Among Black Americans." *Social Psychology Quarterly* 53: 364–74.

D'Souza, Dinesh. 1995. *The End of Racism: Principles of a Multiracial Society*. New York: Free Press.

DuBois, W. E. B. 1996 (orig. pub. 1899). *The Philadelphia Negro: A Social Study*. Philadelphia: University of Pennsylvania Press.

Duckitt, John. 1992. *The Social Psychology of Prejudice*. New York: Praeger.

Dunn, Ashley. 1992. "Years of '2-cent' Insults Added Up to Rampage." *Los Angeles Times*, May 7, 1992, p. A1.

Eagly, Alice H., and Mary E. Kite. 1987. "Are Stereotypes of Nationalities Applied to Both Men and Women?" *Journal of Personality and Social Psychology* 53: 451–62.

Eagly, Alice H., and V. J. Steffen. 1984. "Gender Stereotypes Stem from the Distribution of Women and Men in Social Roles." *Journal of Personality and Social Psychology* 46: 735–54.

Ellison, Christopher G., and Daniel Powers. 1994. "The Contact Hypothesis and Racial Attitudes Among Black Americans." *Social Science Quarterly* 75: 385–400.

Espiritu, Yen Le. 1992. *Asian American Pan-Ethnicity: Bridging Institutions and Identities*. Philadelphia: Temple University Press.

Farley, Reynolds, Charlotte Steeh, Maria Krysan, Tara Jackson, and Keith Reeves. 1994. "Stereotypes and Segregation: Neighborhoods in the Detroit Area." *American Journal of Sociology* 100: 750–80.

Feagin, Joe R., and Melvin Sikes. 1994. *Living with Racism: The Black Middle Class Experience*. Boston: Beacon Press.

Finkel, Steven E., Thomas M. Guterbock, and Marian J. Borg. 1991. "Race-of-Interviewer Effects in a Preelection Poll: Virginia 1989." *Public Opinion Quarterly* 55(2): 313–30.

Fossett, Mark A., and K. Jill Kiecolt. 1989. "The Relative Size of Minority Populations and White Racial Attitudes." *Social Science Quarterly* 70: 820–35.

Gaertner, Samuel L., and John F. Dovidio. 1986. "The Aversive Form of Racism." In *Prejudice, Discrimination and Racism*, edited by J. F. Dovidio and S. L. Gaertner. New York: Academic Press.

Gans, Herbert J. 1999. "The Possibility of a New Racial Hierarchy in the Twenty-First-Century United States." In *The Cultural Territories of*

Race: Black and White Boundaries, edited by Michele Lamont. Chicago and New York: University of Chicago Press and Russell Sage.

Giles, Michael W., and Arthur Evans. 1986. "The Power Approach to Intergroup Hostility." *Journal of Conflict Resolution* 30: 469–86.

Glaser, James M. 1994. "Back to the Black Belt: Racial Environment and White Racial Attitudes in the South." *Journal of Politics* 56: 21–41.

Gurin, Patricia, Shirley Hatchett, and James S. Jackson. 1989. *Hope and Independence: Blacks' Response to Electoral and Party Politics*. New York: Russell Sage.

Gurin, Patricia, Arthur Miller, and Gerald Gurin. 1980. "Stratum Identification and Consciousness." *Social Psychology Quarterly* 43: 30–47.

Hatchett, Shirley, and Howard Schuman. 1975–76. "White Respondents and Race-of-Interviewer Effects." *Public Opinion Quarterly* 39: 523–28.

Hicks, Joe R., Stewart Kwoh, and Frank Acosta. 1996. "Where's the Leadership on Race Relations?" *Los Angeles Times*, March 29, 1996, p. B9.

Hochschild, Jennifer L. 1995. *Facing Up to the American Dream: Race, Class and the Soul of the Nation*. Princeton, N.J.: Princeton University Press.

Holzer, Harry J. 1996. *What Employers Want: Job Prospects for Less-Educated Workers*. New York: Russell Sage.

Hong, Peter Y. 1995. "New Activism Targets Waste Site." *Los Angeles Times*, September 4, 1995, p. B1.

———. 1996a. "Another Kind of Holiday Bowl Tradition." *Los Angeles Times*, January 2, 1996, p. B1.

———. 1996b. "Locke High Tries to Overcome Melee." *Los Angeles Times*, February 28, 1996, p. B1.

Jackman, Mary R. 1977. "Prejudice, Tolerance, and Attitudes Toward Ethnic Groups." *Social Science Research* 6: 145–69.

———. 1994. *The Velvet Glove: Paternalism and Conflict in Gender, Class, and Race Relations*. Berkeley: University of California Press.

Jackman, Mary R., and Michael J. Muha. 1984. "Education and Intergroup Attitudes: Moral Enlightenment, Superficial Democratic Commitment, or Ideological Refinement?" *American Sociological Review* 49: 751–69.

Jackman, Mary R., and Mary Scheuer Senter. 1983. "Different Therefore Unequal: Beliefs About Groups of Unequal Status." *Research in Social Stratification and Mobility* 2: 309–35.

Jencks, Christopher. 1992. *Rethinking Social Policy: Race, Poverty and the Underclass*. Cambridge, Mass.: Harvard University Press.

Kang, K. Connie. 1996a. "Black Pastor, Korean Shop Owner Resolve Racial Incident." *Los Angeles Times*, June 2, 1996, p. B1.

———. 1996b. "Airing Differences in Bid for Harmony." *Los Angeles Times*, July, 22, 1996, p. B1.

Katz, Irwin, 1991. "Gordon Allport's *The Nature of Prejudice*." *Political Psychology* 12: 25–57.

Katz, Jesse, and Richard A. Serrano. 1991. "Segregated Housing Sought at Jordan Downs." *Los Angeles Times*, September 10, 1991, p. B1.

Kinder, Donald R., and Tali Mendelberg. 1995. "Cracks in American Apartheid: The Political Impacts of Prejudice Among Segregated Whites." *Journal of Politics* 57: 402–24.

———. 1985. "If There Isn't a Problem, You Don't Need a Solution: The Bases for Contemporary Affirmative Action Attitudes." *American Behavioral Scientist* 28: 761–87.

Kluegel, James R. 1990. "Trends in Whites' Explanations of the Black-White Gap in Socioeconomic Status, 1977–1989." *American Sociological Review* 55: 512–25.

Kluegel, James R., and Eliot R. Smith. 1986. *Beliefs About Inequality: Americans' Views of What Is and What Ought to Be*. New York: Aldine de Gruyter.

Kovel, Joel. 1970. *White Racism: A Psychohistory*. New York: Columbia University Press.

Krysan, Maria. 1998. "Privacy and the Expression of White Racial Attitudes: A Comparison Across Three Contexts." *Public Opinion Quarterly* 62(4): 506–44.

Lange, Kelley. 1995. "Strangers, 12 of Them, Reach Across the Gulfs of Age, Race, and Experience." *Los Angeles Times*, June 7, 1995, p. B7.

Maher, Adrian. 1995. "Black Tradesmen Face a Daily Wall of Suspicion." *Los Angeles Times*, March 20, 1995, p. A1.

Massey, Douglas S., and Nancy A. Denton. 1993. *American Apartheid: Segregation and the Making of the Underclass*. Cambridge, Mass.: Harvard University Press.

McDonnell, Patrick J. 1994. "County Limits, But Does Not Ban, Day Laborers." *Los Angeles Times*, March 16, 1994, p. B1.

Mitchell, John L. 1996. "No Cruise Control." *Los Angeles Times*, August 18, 1996, p. B1.

Oliver, Melvin L., and James H. Johnson. 1984. "Inter-ethnic Conflict in an Urban Ghetto: The Case of Blacks and Latinos in Los Angeles." *Research in Social Movements, Conflict and Change* 6: 57–94.

Park, Robert E. 1926. *Race and Culture*. Glencoe, Ill.: Free Press.

Peffley, Mark, and Jon Hurwitz. 1998. "Stereotypes of Blacks: Sources and Political Consequences." In *Perception and Prejudice: Race and Politics in the United States*, edited by Jon Hurwitz and Mark Peffley. New Haven, Conn.: Yale University Press.

Pettigrew, Thomas F. 1979. "The Ultimate Attribution Error: Extending Allport's Cognitive Analysis of Prejudice." *Personality and Social Psychology Bulletin* 5: 461–76.

———. 1982. "Prejudice." In *Dimensions of Ethnicity*, edited by S. Thernstrom, A. Orlov, and O. Handlin. Cambridge, Mass.: Harvard University Press.

Renwick, Lucille. 1997. "Road Scholars." *Los Angeles Times*, April 16, 1997, p. B1.

Reskin, Barbara F. 1998. *The Realities of Affirmative Action.* Washington, D.C.: American Sociological Association.

Reskin, Barbara F., Debra B. McBrier, and Julie A. Kmec. 1999. "The Determinants and Consequences of Workplace Race and Sex Composition." *Annual Review of Sociology* 25: 335–61.

Sanjek, Roger. 1994. "The Enduring Inequalities of Race." In *Race*, edited by Steven Gregory and Roger Sanjek. New Brunswick, N.J.: Rutgers University Press.

Schaeffer, Nora Cate. 1980. "Evaluating Race-of-Interviewer Effects in a National Survey." *Sociological Methods and Research* 8(4): 400–19.

Schuman, Howard. 1982. "Artifacts Are in the Mind of the Beholder." *American Sociologist* 17(Feb.): 21–28.

———. 1985. "Attitudes, Beliefs and Behavior." In *Sociological Perspectives on Social Psychology*, edited by K. Cook, G. A. Fine, and J. S. House. Boston: Allyn and Bacon.

———. 1995. "Attitudes, Beliefs, and Behavior." In *Sociological Perspectives on Social Psychology*, edited by Karen S. Cook, Gary Alan Fine, and James S. House. Boston: Allyn and Bacon.

Schuman, Howard, and Lawrence Bobo. 1988. "Survey-Based Experiments on White Racial Attitudes Toward Residential Integration." *American Sociological Review* 94: 273–99.

Schuman, Howard, and Jean M. Converse. 1971. "The Effects of Black and White Interviewers on Black Responses." *Public Opinion Quarterly* 35(1): 44–68.

Schuman, Howard, and Graham Kalton. 1985. "Survey Methods." In *Handbook of Social Psychology, 3rd ed.*, edited by G. Lindzey and E. Aronson. New York: Random House.

Schuman, Howard, Charlotte Steeh, Lawrence Bobo, and Maria Krysan. 1997. *Racial Attitudes in America: Trends and Interpretations, rev. ed.* Cambridge, Mass.: Harvard University Press.

Sears, David O. 1988. "Symbolic Racism." In *Eliminating Racism: Profiles in Controversy*, edited by P. A. Katz, and D. A. Taylor. New York: Plenum.

See, Kathryn O'Sullivan, and William Julius Wilson. 1989. "Race and Ethnicity." In *Handbook of Sociology*, edited by N. Smelser. Newbury Park, Calif.: Sage.

Sidanius, Jim, and Felicia Pratto. 1999. *Social Dominance: An Intergroup Theory of Social Hierarchy and Oppression.* New York: Cambridge University Press.

Sigelman, Lee, James W. Shockey, and Carol K. Sigelman. 1993. "Ethnic Stereotyping: A Black-White Comparison." In *Prejudice, Politics, and the American Dilemma*, edited by Paul M. Sniderman, Philip E. Tetlock, and Edward G. Carmines. Stanford, Calif.: Stanford University Press.

Silverstein, Stuart. 1996. "L.A. Labor Federation Vote Divides Along Ethnic Lines." *Los Angeles Times*, April 4, 1996, p. D1.

Smith, Tom W. 1991. *Ethnic Images.* General Social Survey technical report, 19. Chicago: National Opinion Research Center, University of Chicago.

Sniderman, Paul M., and Thomas Piazza. 1993. *The Scar of Race*. Cambridge, Mass.: Harvard University Press.

Steeh, Charlotte, and Maria Krysan. 1996. "Trends: Affirmative Action and the Public, 1970–1995." *Public Opinion Quarterly* 60: 128–58.

Stephan, Walter G. 1985. "Intergroup Relations." In *The Handbook of Social Psychology*, vol. II, 3rd ed., edited by Gardner Lindzey and Elliot Aronson. New York: Random House.

Stephan, Walter G., and David Rosenfield. 1982. "Racial and Ethnic Stereotypes." In *In the Eye of the Beholder: Contemporary Issues in Stereotyping*, edited by A. G. Miller. New York: Praeger.

Stone, John. 1985. *Racial Conflict in Contemporary Society*. Cambridge, Mass.: Harvard University Press.

Tajfel, Henri. 1982. "Social Psychology of Intergroup Relations." *Annual Review of Psychology* 33: 1–39.

Tajfel, Henri, and John C. Turner. 1979. "An Integrative Theory of Intergroup Conflict." In *The Social Psychology of Intergroup Relations*, edited by W. G. Austin and S. Worchel. Monterey, Calif.: Brooks/Cole.

Tate, Katherine. 1993. *From Protest to Politics: The New Black Voters in American Elections*. Cambridge and New York: Harvard University Press and Russell Sage.

Taylor, Marylee C. 1998. "How White Attitudes Vary with the Racial Composition of Local Population: Numbers Count." *American Sociological Review* 63: 512–35.

Thernstrom, Stephan, and Abigail Thernstrom. 1997. *America in Black and White: One Nation, Indivisible, Race in Modern America*. New York: Simon & Schuster.

Tuan, Mia. 1999. *Forever Foreigners or Honorary Whites?: The Asian Ethnic Experience Today*. New Brunswick, N.J.: Rutgers University Press.

Turner, Margery Austin, Michael Fix, and Raymond J. Struyk. 1991. *Opportunities Denied, Opportunities Diminished: Racial Discrimination in Hiring*. Washington, D.C.: Urban Institute Press.

Van den Berghe, Pierre. 1967. *Race and Racism: A Comparative Perspective*. New York: Wiley.

Waters, Marcy C. 1990. *Ethnic Options: Choosing Identities in America*. Berkeley and Los Angeles: University of California Press.

West, Cornel. 1993. *Race Matters*. Boston: Beacon Press.

Wilson, William Julius. 1978. *The Declining Significance of Race*. Chicago: University of Chicago Press.

———. 1996. *When Work Disappears: The World of the New Urban Poor*. New York: Knopf.

Yinger, John. 1995. *Closed Doors, Opportunities Lost: The Continuing Cost of Housing Discrimination*. New York: Russell Sage.

Zubrinsky, Camille L., and Lawrence Bobo. 1996. "Prismatic Metropolis: Race and Residential Segregation in the City of Angels." *Social Science Research* 25: 335–74.

Part II

OPPORTUNITIES DIVIDED:
RACE, SPACE, AND
GENDER IN LOS ANGELES

4

RESIDENTIAL SEGREGATION IN LOS ANGELES

Camille Zubrinsky Charles

L os Angeles is one of the most ethnically and culturally diverse cities in the world. The public schools offer instruction in more than ninety different languages. Restaurants offer a wide variety of the world's cuisine. The political landscape is equally diverse, with local officeholders and prominent public figures whose surnames run from Hernandez to Ito to Yaroslavsky to Abramson to Bradley to Woo. Both residents and visitors to the city can take part in annual African Marketplace festivals, Cinco de Mayo and Dia de los Muertos commemorations, Chinese New Year, and the Korean Choosuk, a Thanksgiving celebration.

This diversity reflects a vast array of racial and ethnic communities and social structures in Los Angeles. The African American community, although perhaps associated by the rest of the world with the Watts uprising of 1965 and the more recent and destructive uprisings of 1992, possesses strong, vibrant institutions and neighborhoods. Broadway Federal Savings and Loan and Founders Bank and Trust are well-established, black-owned financial institutions. The Degnan Street area in Leimert Park has galleries, museums, bookstores, and import-export shops. "The World Stage," also on Degnan Street, is a place for up-and-coming jazz musicians to show their wares. There are at least two black newspapers, including the weekly *Los Angeles Sentinel*, serving the African American community for more than half a century. The "new Westside," for upwardly mobile blacks, includes Ladera Heights and Baldwin Hills (the "Black Beverly Hills") and the "tidy tractlands of suburban Inglewood and Carson" (Davis 1990, 304) (see figure 4.2).

Los Angeles is home to the largest Latino population in the country (3,350,638, according to the 1990 census; see Harrison and Weinberg

1992). Spanish-speaking television and radio station audiences rival those of mainstream electronic media, and the Spanish-language daily newspaper, *La Opinion*, thrives. East Los Angeles and, more recently, Pico Union are flourishing Latino communities. Businesses and churches cater to Mexican and Central American immigrants: posters, billboards, and store signs are in Spanish; loudspeakers broadcast Latin music into the streets; in the bars and restaurants of Boyle Heights, young children go from table to table selling novelties like those found in stalls in Tijuana; at parish fiestas, lottery jackpots are advertised in pesos (Skerry 1993).

Los Angeles is also home to the largest Korean settlement in the United States, as well as the most vital and profitable Korean economy (Min 1996). Commercial signs on this 1-mile strip near downtown Los Angeles are in Korean, with advertisements of "English spoken here." In addition to the plethora of ethnic restaurants and grocery stores, there are Korean banks, import-export houses, garment factories, real estate offices, and a wide variety of retail trade (Min 1996); the *Korea Times* is the newspaper of choice (Bobo et al. 1995). About 8 miles east of downtown Los Angeles is Monterey Park, a predominantly Chinese middle-class suburb that is home to a sizable number of Japanese as well (Horton 1995).

Finally, Brentwood, Bel Air, Beverly Hills, Hollywood, and Malibu: home of the rich and famous, land of beautiful people, shimmering surf, and big money. For many, these predominantly white areas *are* Los Angeles. As the center of the entertainment industry and a hub of Pacific Rim business and finance, this is the Los Angeles that entertainers, industry executives and hangers-on, and corporate employees call home, and that brings tourists and the up-and-coming in droves. The stars' homes, Universal Studios, the Hollywood Walk of Fame, the Sunset Strip, "The Tonight Show," Disneyland: this is the Los Angeles that visitors come to see.

But there is trouble here, and it has a structural basis and manifestation. Despite the increased presence of racial and ethnic minorities and the supposed softening of white attitudes toward minorities, the degree of residential segregation—particularly of whites from blacks—remains high in Los Angeles. Here, as in the rest of the nation, the degree of black isolation is so enduring that Douglas Massey and Nancy Denton labeled it "American apartheid" (1993), concluding that racial residential segregation is central to the development and persistence of ghetto populations. Understanding residential segregation is essential to understanding contemporary urban inequality in America (Farley 1987; Darden 1990; Massey and Gross 1991; Santiago and Wilder 1991; Massey and Denton 1993). Residential isolation, particularly among blacks, "contributes to the maintenance of subordinate status and has a definite impact on social contact between Whites and Blacks" as well (Marston and Van Valey 1979, 17).

These issues have interested scholars and policy analysts for decades. Despite antidiscrimination legislation and an expanding black middle class, African Americans continue to live in racially isolated neighborhoods, often twice as segregated from whites as are Latino and Asian Americans, regardless of socioeconomic and/or immigrant status (Massey and Denton 1987). In the United States as a whole, the black-white index of dissimilarity is a high .69, compared with the moderate Latino-white index of .51, and an even lower Asian-white index of .42.[1] Black and Latino segregation from whites in Los Angeles is well above these national figures (.728 and .611, respectively); Asian-white segregation is slightly higher there than the national average as well (.463) (Harrison and Weinberg 1992).

The overwhelming majority of research in this area has relied on a two-group model that focuses on the "ghettoization" of African Americans vis-à-vis whites. While a division of this sort has significant historical relevance and may still be useful in cities like Atlanta and Detroit, the same cannot be said of its applicability to Los Angeles, a city touted by some as the archetype of multiethnicity (Lee and Wood 1991; Wood and Lee 1991). It is possible, for instance, that with increasing ethnic diversity, whites will be less fixated on the proverbial tipping point—the point at which whites become uncomfortable with the level of integration and attempt to move away. In 1976, that tipping point was a 30 percent black neighborhood; by 1992, it was a 40 percent black neighborhood (Farley et al. 1993). This could create an opportunity for blacks and whites to increase their residential contact. Or, given the growing tensions between blacks and both Latinos and Asian Americans, blacks in a multiethnic setting may downplay the racism of whites, viewing them as relatively liberal.

Thirty-seven metropolitan areas in the United States are multiethnic, meaning that the proportion of two or more racial minorities exceeds their national representation (Farley and Frey 1993).[2] These cities span all regions of the country, highlighting the importance of moving beyond the traditional two-group, often black-white, analyses of racial phenomena: if we are to understand fully the dynamics of a multiethnic city, it is essential to conduct analyses that employ both minority-majority and minority-minority comparisons.

Is It Economic Differences?

Researchers have highlighted several individual-level factors as key to understanding racial residential segregation in the United States. Among these are socioeconomic differences, which have been convincingly discounted as a major determinant of black-white segregation; blacks are severely segregated from whites, irrespective of socioeconomic resources (Taeuber and Taeuber 1965; Schnare 1977; Kain 1986). Research on Latino and Asian segregation from whites, on the other hand, suggests that residential mobility and proximity to whites increase with improved socioeconomic status (Massey and Mullan 1984; Massey and Fong 1990; Alba and Logan 1993).

Despite the consistency of these results over time and across metropolitan areas, there is good reason to reexamine the role that socioeconomic status may play in shaping racial residential patterns, using Los Angeles as the case study. Los Angeles provides the opportunity for a full multiethnic analysis of whites, blacks, Latinos, and Asians in a single metropolitan area—something that previous research lacks.

Data from the 1990 Public Use Microdata Sample (PUMS) 5 percent File and a relatively simple but effective statistical method similar to those used in previous studies (Pascal 1967; Taeuber 1976; Schnare 1977; Farley 1986; Kain 1986) are employed to examine the contribution of several socioeconomic characteristics to current racial residential patterns in Los Angeles. How segregated would blacks, whites, Latinos, and Asians be if residential patterns were determined solely on the basis of income and household structure (that is, family type, family size, and age of household head)?

The geographical unit in the 1990 PUMS 5 percent File is a Public Use Microdata Sample Area (PUMA).[3] PUMAs are substantially larger than census tracts, used in many analyses of residential segregation (Denton and Massey 1988; Massey and Denton 1989): Los Angeles County has 1,642 census tracts, distributed among 58 PUMAs. This larger unit of aggregation results in somewhat lower indexes of dissimilarity (for a discussion of this effect, see Van Valey and Roof 1976). Still, a comparison of tract-level and PUMA-level indices located in table 4.1 reveals the same pattern and degree of residential segregation across racial groups. Black-white segregation in Los Angeles measured at the PUMA level (.613) remains high enough to be characterized as extreme (see Massey and Denton 1989; Denton 1994), while the segregation of Latinos (.458) and Asians (.344) from whites in Los Angeles is more accurately characterized as moderate.

PUMS data for Los Angeles County households are used with indirect standardization, a technique that "redistributes" the population of a metropolitan area based on a set of chosen characteristics (in this case, income, family type and size, and age of household head). This predicted population distribution is then used to compute expected segregation indexes based on the assumption that the chosen characteristics are the

TABLE 4.1   *Index of Dissimilarity for Blacks, Latinos, and Asians,*
             Computed by Census Tract and by PUMA

	Blacks	Latinos	Asians
Computed with 1990 tract-level data	.728	.611	.463
Computed with 1990 PUMA data	.613	.458	.344
Difference	−.115	−.153	−.118

Source: 1990 U.S. Bureau of the Census.
Note: Predicting degree of segregation from whites, where 0 indicates no segregation, and 1 complete segregation.

only cause of residential segregation.[4] Table 4.2 presents both actual and predicted levels of black, Latino, and Asian segregation from whites.

If residential patterns were based solely on the basis of income, family type and size, and age of household head, black-white segregation in Los Angeles County would be .110—more than five and a half times lower than it actually is (.613). Asian-white segregation would drop to .087, nearly four times lower than it is currently. In this analysis, Latinos are the only group for whom socioeconomic status characteristics and residential segregation from whites appear to be linked: the predicted level of Latino-white residential segregation (.191) remains substantially higher than for blacks and Asians. These results suggest that, at best, objective socioeconomic characteristics play only a small role in the segregation of Latinos from whites, but little or no role in the segregation of blacks and Asians from whites.

A simpler test of the role that socioeconomic differences play in understanding residential segregation is a straightforward, cross-racial comparison of monthly housing expenditures using the LASUI data. Monthly housing expenditures may vary greatly by homeownership sta-

TABLE 4.2   *Actual and Predicted Black, Latino, and Asian*
             Residential Segregation from Whites in Los Angeles
             County, 1990

Index of Dissimilarity	Blacks	Latinos	Asians
Actual	.613	.458	.344
Predicted	.110	.191	.087
Difference	−.503	−.267	−.257
Ratio	5.572	2.398	3.954

Source: U.S. Bureau of the Census, 1990 Public Use Microdata Sample, 5 percent file.
Note: Predicted index of dissimilarity accounts for income and household structure (family type, age of head, number of household members). A score of 0 indicates complete integration; 1 indicates complete segregation.

TABLE 4.3   *Housing Status by Race*

	Whites	Blacks	Latinos	Asians	Total
Housing Status					
Own or buying	52.6%	33.5%	27.3%	46.2%	40.6%
Renting	39.6	57.0	66.3	49.3	52.1
Other	7.8	9.5	6.5	4.5	7.3
Total	100%	100%	100%	100%	100%

Source: Los Angeles Study of Urban Inequality 1994.
$p < .001$

tus, and homeownership rates vary substantially across racial groups in Los Angeles: just over half of whites own their homes, as do 46.2 percent of Asians; however, rates of homeownership for both blacks (33.5 percent) and Latinos (27.3 percent) are substantially lower (see tables 4.3 and 4.4).

Among Latino and Asian respondents, immigrant status significantly impacts the likelihood of homeownership. Only 21.5 percent of foreign-born Latinos own their homes, compared with 43.3 percent of U.S.-born Latinos; among Asians, the rates of homeownership are 42 percent and 77.2 percent for foreign- and U.S.-born, respectively. For these reasons, monthly housing expenditures are measured separately for homeowners and renters, with distinctions being made between native- and foreign-born Latino and Asian respondents.

The top panel of figure 4.1 reports monthly mortgage payments, including taxes, insurance, and utilities. These figures show a great deal of overlap in such payments across groups, and suggest that a substantial number of all groups, including blacks and Latinos, have mortgage payments that would allow them to live in desirable white neighborhoods.

TABLE 4.4   *Housing Status of Native- and Foreign-Born Latinos and Asians*

	Foreign-Born Latinos	Native-Born Latinos	Foreign-Born Asians	Native-Born Asians	Total
Housing Status					
Own or buying	21.5%	43.3%	42.0%	77.2%	31.9%
Renting	74.4	43.5	54.0	14.5	63.7
Other	4.1	13.2	4.0	8.3	4.4
Total	100%	100%	100%	100%	100%

Source: Los Angeles Study of Urban Inequality 1994.
$p < .001$

FIGURE 4.1 *Housing Expenditures by Race, Nativity, and Tenure*

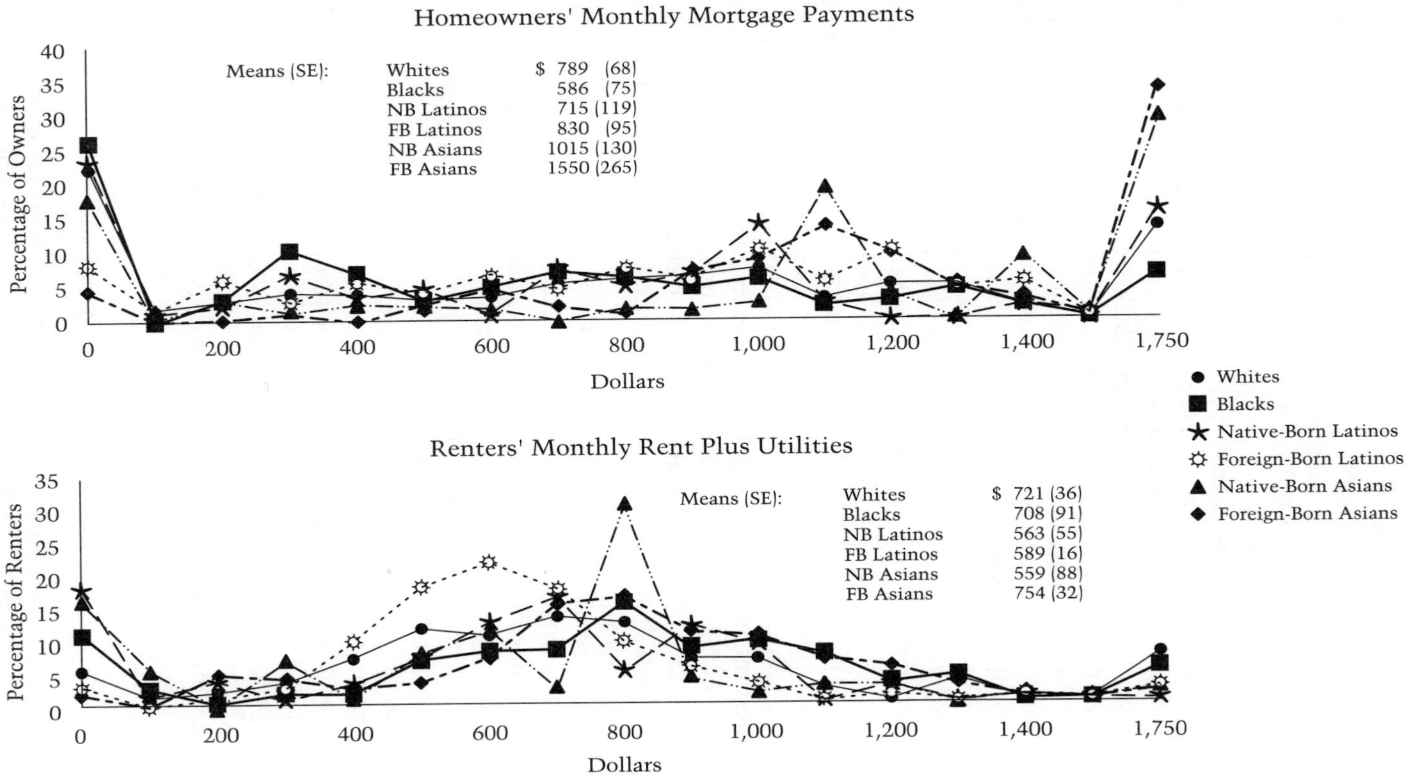

Homeowners' Monthly Mortgage Payments
Percentage of Owners
40
35
30
25
20
15
10
5
0
Means (SE):
Whites $ 789 (68)
Blacks 586 (75)
NB Latinos 715 (119)
FB Latinos 830 (95)
NB Asians 1015 (130)
FB Asians 1550 (265)
0
200
400
600
800
1,000
1,200
1,400
1,750
Dollars
Whites
Blacks
Native-Born Latinos
Foreign-Born Latinos
Native-Born Asians
Foreign-Born Asians
Renters' Monthly Rent Plus Utilities
Percentage of Renters
35
30
25
20
15
10
5
0
Means (SE):
Whites $ 721 (36)
Blacks 708 (91)
NB Latinos 563 (55)
FB Latinos 589 (16)
NB Asians 559 (88)
FB Asians 754 (32)
0
200
400
600
800
1,000
1,200
1,400
1,750
Dollars

Source: Los Angeles Study of Urban Inequality 1994.
Note: Means and standard errors rounded to whole dollars.
p = NS for owners; $p < .001$ for renters

Native- and foreign-born Asians report the highest monthly mortgage payments ($1,015 and $1,550, respectively). Interestingly, foreign-born Latinos report an average monthly mortgage payment of $830, slightly higher than the average mortgage payment of whites ($789). Foreign-born Latinos also spend more, on average, than their U.S.-born counterparts ($715). Black respondents spend the least each month, on average, to own their homes ($586); however, just over a quarter of blacks—compared with 27 percent of whites—report monthly mortgage payments between $600 and $1,000 per month. Blacks (26 percent) and U.S.-born Latinos (23 percent) are slightly more likely than whites (22 percent) and U.S.-born Asians (18 percent) to own their homes free and clear. Foreign-born homeowners, both Asian and Latino, are least likely to own their homes outright (4 percent and 8 percent, respectively).

The bottom panel of the figure reveals even greater overlap among renters. Fifty-two percent of blacks spend between $600 and $1,000 per month on rent and utilities, as do 52 percent of whites, 52 percent of U.S.-born Asians, and 58 percent of U.S.-born Latinos. Again, foreign-born Asians ($754) and Latinos ($589) spend more, on average, than their native-born counterparts to rent a place to live. At the same time, there are considerable racial differences. Foreign-born Asian respondents have the highest mean rent, at roughly $754 per month. The average monthly rent reported by white respondents is about $721, only $13 more than that of blacks. U.S.-born Latinos spend an average of $563 per month—$145 less than blacks, $158 less than whites, and roughly the same as U.S.-born Asians.

Whether renting or buying, foreign-born Latinos and Asians spend substantially more on housing than their U.S.-born counterparts. Foreign-born homeowners also spend more, on average, than whites to own their homes and are least likely to own their homes outright. The higher cost of homeownership found among the foreign-born may be the result of more recent home purchase. Foreign-born Asian and Latino homeowners report an average of six and eight years at their current addresses, respectively. For native-born homeowners, the average number of years at their current address ranges from twelve to twenty-two. Whatever, the cause, comparison of monthly housing expenditures indicates a great deal of overlap across racial (and immigrant status) categories. The results from these analyses strongly suggest that objective socioeconomic differences tell us comparatively little about racial residential segregation in Los Angeles.

Is It "Bad" Information?

It has also been suggested that differences in housing market perceptions and information across racial groups are responsible for racial residential patterns. That is, minorities, blacks in particular, are residentially isolated because they underestimate their access to desirable yet affordable housing. Despite a great deal of overlap in actual housing expenditures, groups may differ widely in their knowledge of housing costs. To investigate racial-group differences in knowledge and perceptions of the housing market, the LASUI asked all respondents about seven residential areas in Los Angeles County: Alhambra, Baldwin Hills, Canoga Park, Culver City, Glendale, Palmdale, and Pico Rivera. These areas, shown in map 4.1, were chosen to represent both appealing and important types of communities within the Los Angeles area; they share moderate housing prices and wide name recognition and are dispersed throughout the county. They also vary in historical reputations regarding integration and in their current racial composition.

Canoga Park, Palmdale, Glendale, and Culver City are predominantly white communities (69 percent, 67 percent, 65 percent, and 58 percent, respectively). Pico Rivera is predominantly Latino (83 percent). Baldwin Hills is a predominantly black (59 percent) middle-class community, and Alhambra is a mixed city of Asians (38 percent), Latinos (36 percent), and whites (25 percent). Glendale and Culver City have reputations for hostility toward blacks, but both have significant and growing Latino populations. In the past, the Culver City Police Department has had a reputation for mistreating blacks. And although still predominantly white, Culver City is adjacent to the heavily Latino and black community of South Central Los Angeles and is itself becoming increasingly diverse. Palmdale, in a newly developing area of the county, offers new and relatively inexpensive housing in an out-of-the-city atmosphere. Canoga Park is a white, working- and middle-class community in the west San Fernando Valley, a traditionally conservative stronghold with a growing minority representation.

Each respondent was asked to estimate the cost of an average home for each of the seven areas and was shown a map like the one here. The first panel of table 4.5 summarizes the demographics of each area, reporting both racial composition and total population. The middle section reports the average estimated cost of homes for each area across racial categories, as well as the actual mean housing values from the 1990 census.[5] The third and final section lists the ratio of estimated to actual housing costs for the seven communities, again by racial category. The closer the ratio is to 1, the more accurately a group has estimated the cost of the average home for that area.

Actual average home values range from a low of just over $150,000 in Palmdale, to approximately $342,000 in Glendale. In contrast to their variation in racial composition and disparate locations, Alhambra, Baldwin Hills, and Canoga Park are all moderately priced communities, with homes ranging from about $225,000 to $258,000. These prices are con-

MAP 4.1   *Map of Residential Search Areas*

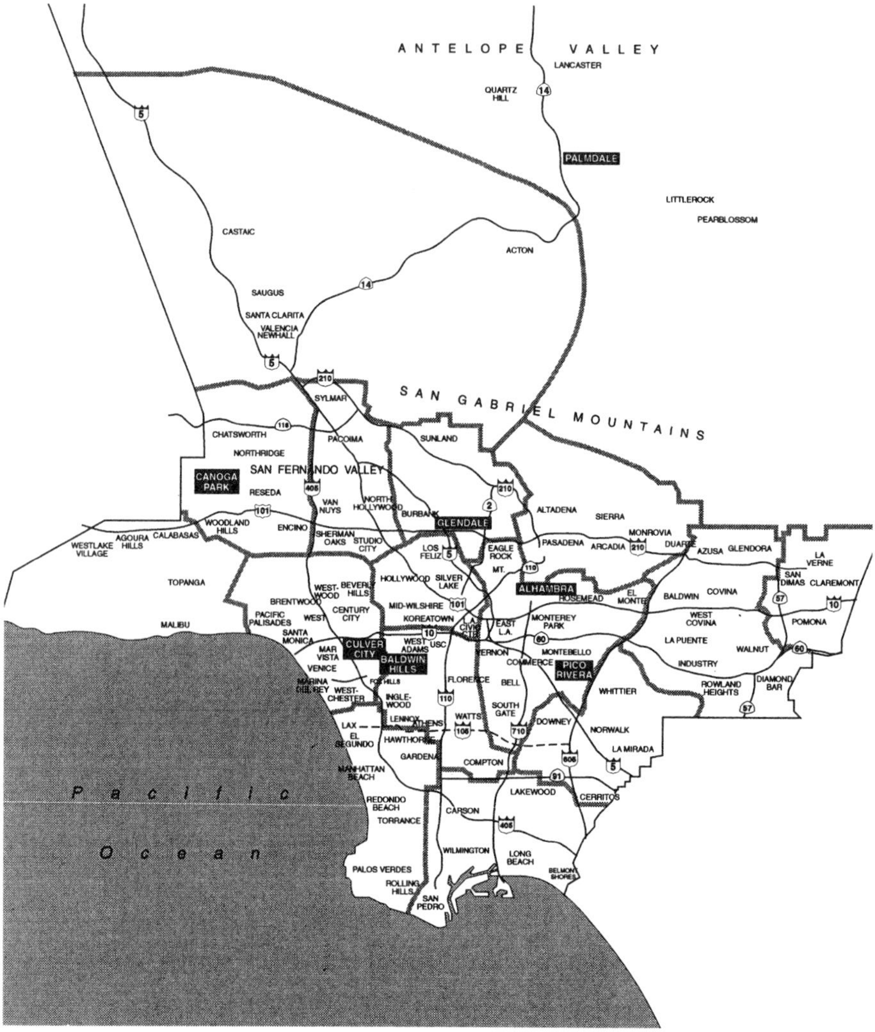

Source: Los Angeles Study of Urban Inequality 1994.

sistent with the average cost for Los Angeles County as a whole. The two most expensive neighborhoods, Glendale and Culver City, are also the two with the greatest reputations for hostility toward blacks. The two least expensive areas, Palmdale and Pico Rivera, have substantial Latino populations (22 percent and 84 percent, respectively). The significant presence of Latino residents in these lower-priced communities is consistent with their lower median income compared to other groups and with the sizable increase in Latino first-time homebuyers in recent years (O'Neill 1994).

Overall, respondents had reasonably accurate, although not precise, information about housing prices throughout Los Angeles County; this is true both within and across racial categories. Among the exceptions to this general pattern are that blacks significantly overestimated the cost of an average home in Baldwin Hills (a ratio of 1.18). This is rather surprising, given that blacks were attributing greater value to homes in the community with the largest same-race population (Baldwin Hills is nearly 60 percent black). Also, Latinos significantly underestimated the average home price in Canoga Park (.72), a community with substantial Latino representation (19 percent).

Inaccurate knowledge is also consistent across racial categories. Average housing costs in the two most expensive neighborhoods—Culver City and Glendale—were significantly underestimated across groups. Ratios of estimated to actual cost for Culver City ranged from .61 to .70. Respondents fared only slightly better in their knowledge of Glendale (from .69 to .75). Consistent with actual variations in housing prices, however, each group did perceive Glendale to be substantially more expensive than the other six communities: estimates for each group ranged from a low of $236,300 by Latinos to a high of just under $257,000 by whites.

This comparison of estimated to actual average housing prices indicates that Los Angeles–area residents generally have similar information regarding the cost of housing in a variety of communities. When respondents' perceptions are inaccurate, they are usually inaccurate across groups; no single group is informationally disadvantaged, compared to the others. And since misperceptions are typically on the low side, it seems reasonable to expect such misperceptions to encourage rather than discourage house hunting in these communities. Nonetheless, accurate information would mean little if racial-group members perceived others of their group as lacking the financial capacity to purchase homes in these areas, particularly those that are predominantly white. Individual minority group members with adequate information and resources may avoid communities if they believe that a majority of "people like them" cannot afford to live there. Moving into such communities might raise fears of being the "only one" on the block.

To examine perceptions of in-group minority affordability, we asked black, Latino, and Asian respondents whether "almost all," "many," "about half," "a few," or "just about no" members of their own racial group could afford to live in each of the seven communities. Figure 4.2

FIGURE 4.2   *Minority Respondents' Perception That "About Half," "Many," or "Almost All" Members of Their Group Can Afford Housing in Selected Areas*

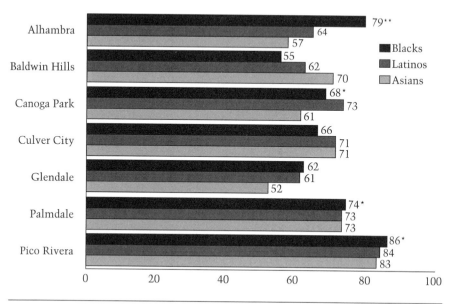

Source: Los Angeles Study of Urban Inequality 1994.
*$p < .05$, **$p < .001$

illustrates the percentage who responded that "about half," "many," or "almost all" of their group could afford to live in each area.

Clearly, blacks, Latinos, and Asians all have considerable confidence in the purchasing power of their co-ethnics; at least half of all three groups believed that half of their group could afford to live in each area. An apparent connection emerges between perceptions of the cost of housing in these areas (table 4.5) and perceptions of in-group ability to afford housing. Blacks are significantly more likely to perceive Alhambra (with an average home value of $228,000) as affordable for their group; however, they had the least accurate sense of the cost of housing there. Despite the concentration of blacks in Baldwin Hills, black respondents were least likely to view it as affordable to at least half of all blacks. They overestimated the cost of a home there by a substantial margin (18 percent), while Asian and Latino respondents were quite accurate. Sixty-six percent of blacks, and 71 percent of both Latinos and Asians, perceived Culver City—the most expensive of the seven areas

($342,000 mean home value)—as affordable to at least half of their group. All three groups (and whites) severely underestimated the cost of housing in Culver City. Palmdale and Pico Rivera, the two least expensive communities considered (and often the most accurately perceived with respect to price), were viewed as affordable by a sizable majority of blacks, Latinos, and Asians.

Among Latinos, there also appears to be a link between perceived group purchasing power and the proportion of Latinos already present in the community. Of the seven communities, Alhambra, Baldwin Hills, Culver City, and Glendale have the smallest Latino populations and/or some of the most expensive housing. Of these communities, Latinos were least likely to view Alhambra, Baldwin Hills, and Glendale as financially accessible to at least half the members of their group (64 percent, 62 percent, and 61 percent, respectively). Still, all seven communities were perceived to be affordable by a majority of Latinos. Taken as a whole, these results suggest that the housing-search behavior of Asians, Latinos, and blacks is not severely constrained by inaccurate housing market information relative to other groups, or the perception that in-group members are financially constrained.

Is It Different Housing Tastes?

Another potential explanation for relatively high rates of racial residential segregation is that racial-ethnic groups simply have different ideas about what constitutes a desirable place to live (Farley et al. 1978, 1993; Zubrinsky and Bobo 1996). To investigate perceptions of community desirability, all respondents were asked to rate each of the seven residential locations as "very desirable," "somewhat desirable," "somewhat undesirable," or "very undesirable" places to live. Figure 4.3 presents the percentage of positive responses by racial group.

Members of all groups expressed similar perceptions about the overall desirability of the seven communities. Regardless of the respondent's race, Pico Rivera was perceived as the least desirable area. Even though a clear majority (60 percent) of Latinos viewed Pico Rivera as at least somewhat desirable (compared with 37 percent of blacks, 26 percent of Asians, and a scant 19 percent of whites), it still ties with Palmdale as the community least desirable to this group. This low ranking by all groups is, no doubt, due to the combination of its high minority population, low socioeconomic status, and below average housing values.

Similarly, all groups perceived Glendale most favorably. Eighty-five percent of Latinos, 80 percent of Asians, and 76 percent of whites regarded it as a somewhat or very desirable place to live. Among blacks, the predominantly black, middle-class community of Baldwin Hills

TABLE 4.5   *Locations and Cost of Housing Estimated by Respondents of the Los Angeles Study of Urban Inequality and the 1990 Census of Housing*

	1990 Census Data			
	Population Size	Percentage Black	Percentage Latino	Percentage Asian
Alhambra	82,106	2	36	38
Baldwin Hills	15,254	59	12	8
Canoga Park	105,601	2	19	9
Culver City	38,793	10	19	12
Glendale	180,083	1	20	14
Palmdale	68,917	6	22	4
Pico Rivera	59,177	0.4	83	3
L.A. County	8,863,164	11	37	10

Sources: U.S. Bureau of the Census 1990; Los Angeles Study of Urban Inequality 1994.
$^*p < .05$, $^{**}p < .001$

FIGURE 4.3   *Respondents' Rating of Selected Areas as "Very Desirable" or "Somewhat Desirable" Places to Live, by Respondent Race*

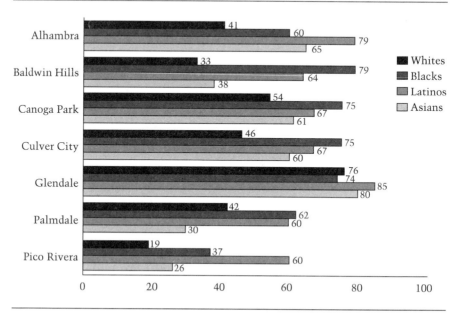

Source: Los Angeles Study of Urban Inequality 1994.
$p < .001$

Cost of Homes Estimated in LASUI (Reported in Thousands)				Mean Value 1990 Census (Thousands)	Ratio of Estimated to Actual Costs			
Blacks	Latinos	Asians	Whites		Black	Latino	Asian	White
$202.2	$209.8	$220.7	$197.5**	$227.9	0.89	0.92	0.97	0.87
265.6	220.9	218.6	217.4**	224.6	1.18	0.98	0.97	0.97
208.0	187.0	217.9	207.0*	257.6	0.81	0.72	0.84	0.80
230.0	202.8	224.0	211.5**	329.4	0.70	0.61	0.68	0.64
256.1	236.3	254.2	256.9*	341.7	0.75	0.69	0.74	0.75
157.8	151.4	168.3	136.5**	150.2	1.05	1.01	1.12	0.91
163.8	169.4	173.8	161.9	163.8	1.00	1.03	1.06	0.99
—	—	—	—	223.8	—	—	—	—

took top honors, seen favorably by 79 percent. Consistent with the other groups, however, 74 percent of blacks rated Glendale among the most desirable places to live.

Perceptions regarding the other areas take on an interesting pattern. For example, only the predominantly white and moderately to high-priced communities of Glendale and Canoga Park were viewed as desirable by more than half of whites (76 percent and 54 percent, respectively). These communities were followed in whites' perceptions by the racially mixed communities of Culver City (46 percent) and Alhambra (41 percent) and the distant but inexpensive community of Palmdale (42 percent). Finally, the heavily minority communities of Pico Rivera and Baldwin Hills were desirable to roughly one-fifth and one-third of whites, respectively. This is particularly telling in the case of Baldwin Hills relative to Palmdale, since home values in the former far exceed those of the latter.

Blacks, Latinos, and Asians were much more likely than whites to perceive areas with substantial numbers of minorities as desirable. Thus, while only two of the seven communities were perceived as desirable by a majority of whites, at least 60 percent of Latinos perceived each of the seven as desirable and only once did blacks' favorable perceptions fall below 60 percent (for Pico Rivera: 37 percent). Asians' perceptions more closely resembled those of whites. The only areas that less than 60 percent of Asians perceived favorably were Latino Pico Rivera (26 percent), black Baldwin Hills (38 percent), and working-class Palmdale (30 percent).

These results indicate general agreement across racial groups about the desirability of these communities as places to live. Whites, blacks, Latinos, and Asians all perceived Glendale to be a desirable place to live—much more desirable than Pico Rivera, Palmdale, and, except for blacks, Baldwin Hills. Among whites, a community with fewer racial minority group members was more desirable (refer to table 4.5 for specifics on the racial composition of each area); nonwhites also appreciated significant numbers of coethnics, but at the same time favored areas that were racially mixed.

As a whole, these results offer little support for the contention that group differences in perceptions of or information about the housing market explain current residential patterns. All groups had fairly accurate knowledge of housing costs throughout Los Angeles County; none of the racial minority groups perceived themselves as unable to afford housing in a wide variety of Los Angeles County areas—a perception that could constrain housing search behavior; and all groups shared similar perceptions of the selected communities as desirable places to live.

Is It Ethnocentric Preferences?

Previous research has also emphasized group differences in neighborhood racial composition preferences as a primary factor in persistent racial residential segregation (Clark 1986, 1989a, 1989b, 1991, 1992, and 1993). William Clark (1986, 1992) asserts that preferences for majority-same-race neighborhoods are universal, cutting across racial groups and reflecting positive feelings about one's own group, rather than prejudice or antipathy toward one or more out-groups.

Reynolds Farley and colleagues (1978, 1993) examined black-white differences in residential preferences using the showcard procedure originally designed for the Detroit Area Study. The experiment was expanded in this analysis to include Latinos and Asians; it uses a split-ballot format in which one-third of each racial group was asked to consider varying degrees of integration with a different one of the three remaining out-groups. The series of questions asked of white respondents differed slightly from the questions asked of blacks, Latinos, and Asians. Each respondent category is treated in turn.

White Preferences

To gauge the neighborhood preferences of whites, we presented respondents with a series of cards. Each card depicted fifteen houses with a particular degree of integration of whites with a single minority group (blacks, Latinos, or Asians). The respondent's home was said to be located in the middle of the card. Illustrations of all showcards are located in the appendix.

Respondents were shown the first card and asked to imagine that they lived in an all-white neighborhood. They were then shown the second card, with one minority home (black, Latino, or Asian) and fourteen white homes. Respondents were asked if they would feel "very comfortable," "somewhat comfortable," "somewhat uncomfortable," or "very uncomfortable" in this marginally integrated setting. Respondents who indicated some degree of comfort were then shown cards with increasing levels of integration until they either indicated discomfort or reached the end of the series—a neighborhood that is majority-outgroup. The left panel of Figure 4.4 summarizes white responses to each target group.

It is encouraging that most whites felt comfortable with some degree, even a substantial level, of integration. More than 90 percent of whites expressed comfort with the most marginal degree of integration—one nonwhite house—with only a slight decline when integration increased to three nonwhite houses. After this point, however, comfort with increasing numbers of black neighbors decreased markedly relative to potential Latino and Asian neighbors. White respondents felt more comfortable with Asians, slightly less comfortable with Latinos, and least so with blacks as neighbors. By the time white respondents reached the final scenario—a majority nonwhite neighborhood—comfort levels declined considerably for all out-groups, but especially for black neighbors. Over 70 percent of whites express comfort with a neighborhood that is one-third black; however, when asked to consider a neighborhood that is 53 percent black and 47 percent white, the percentage expressing comfort drops to 46 percent. This is a decrease of 24 percent, the largest drop in the chart. In contrast, 63 percent of whites felt comfortable in a majority-Latino neighborhood, and almost three-quarters expressed comfort with a majority-Asian neighborhood. Not only did whites express the least comfort with blacks, but their decline in comfort from one scenario to the next was always largest when potential neighbors were black.

This first set of questions assumes that white respondents are already living in an all-white neighborhood and tests comfort with neighborhood racial composition change. In essence, it tests the notion of "white flight": the point at which white residents become uncomfortable in their neighborhoods and, presumably, decide to move away. This is a long-standing explanation of residential segregation. It is also important, however, to know whether or not white residents would be willing to move into a neighborhood with more than token numbers of nonwhite, since this, too, affects racial residential patterns.

FIGURE 4.4 Attractiveness of Neighborhoods with Varying Degrees of Integration with Blacks, Latinos, and Asians

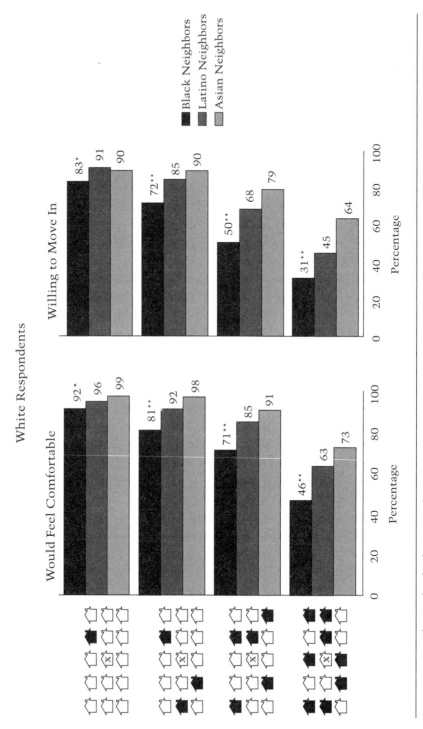

Source: Los Angeles Study of Urban Inequality 1994.
Note: Dark houses represent target group.
$*p < .05$, $**p < .001$

To measure whites' willingness to *enter* various integrated settings, we asked white respondents to consider a slightly different scenario, using the same set of cards:

> Suppose you have been looking for a house and have found one that you can afford. This house could be located in several different types of neighborhoods, as shown on these cards. Would you consider moving into any of these neighborhoods?

The split-ballot format used for the first scenario applied here as well. For example, white respondents revealing their comfort level with increasingly black neighborhoods then considered moving into a neighborhood with varying degrees of integration with blacks. Responses to this second scenario make up the right-hand panel in figure 4.4.

Not surprisingly, the two panels are quite similar. Nearly all whites said that they would be willing to move into a neighborhood with a single nonwhite family. As the percentage of nonwhites increased, though, willingness to move in decreased. However, the decline in willingness began much sooner than the decline in expressed comfort with neighborhood transition—especially for white-black integration. When whites were asked about their comfort with neighborhood change, the decline between the second and third neighborhoods for all target groups was 10 percent or less (see left panel, figure 4.4). On the other hand, the decline in whites' willingness to move into a neighborhood that is one-third minority ranged from 11 percent (Asian neighbors) to 22 percent (black neighbors). Whites' tolerance of majority-minority neighborhoods was much lower when they were considering a home in a new neighborhood, as opposed to undergoing racial transition in their current one.

These results suggest that whites' preferences for majority-same-race neighbors are conditioned by the race of potential neighbors. Whites are significantly more likely to feel comfortable with substantial integration when their nonwhite neighbors are Asian and, to a slightly lesser degree, Latino. Substantial integration with blacks appears to be much less desirable. This rank-ordering of out-groups as neighbors contradicts the view of residential preferences as a ubiquitous form of ethnocentrism: these preferences are quite race-specific.

Black Preferences

A slightly different experiment was used to test the neighborhood preferences of blacks. Instead of being asked about comfort levels in a neighborhood undergoing racial transition, black respondents were told to imagine that they had been looking for a house and had found a nice one that they could afford. They were told that the house could be located in any of several different types of neighborhoods and were shown a series of five cards. These five neighborhood showcards differ from the white respondents' cards, ranging from an all-black neighborhood to one that is entirely white, Latino, or Asian, except for the black respondent's home in the middle. In each set of cards, black homes were shaded black. The shading of out-group homes varied by race: white homes were left white, Latino homes were dark gray, and Asian homes were light gray. Next, respondents were instructed to arrange the five neighborhoods from most to least desirable. As with white respondents, a split-ballot form was used: one-third of black respondents contemplated integration with whites, one-third with Latinos, and one-third with Asians.

The left panel of figure 4.5 shows the percentage of black respondents selecting each of the five cards as either their first or second choice. The dark houses represent same-race neighbors, and the lighter houses represent out-group neighbors (white, Latino, or Asian).

There seems to be a desire among blacks not only for a substantial number of co-ethnics but for integration as well. The two most popular neighborhoods, regardless of target-group race, were between about one-quarter and one-half out-group. Again, target-group race mattered. The all-same-race alternative was more attractive when potential neighbors were white (29 percent) or Asian (33 percent) than when potential neighbors were Latino (27 percent). A neighborhood with twelve white and two black neighbors was roughly three times more attractive than one with twelve Latino and two black neighbors. The difference was slightly over five times with a predominantly Asian neighborhood. Finally, fewer than 5 percent of blacks found the single-black-on-the-block scenario to be attractive, regardless of the race of potential neighbors.

Black respondents were also asked if there were any neighborhoods into which they simply would not want to move. Similar to the follow-up question in the white respondents' experiment, this question was intended to glean information about blacks' potential behavior, rather than simply to indicate what they found attractive. Results are presented in the right-hand panel of figure 4.5. Consistent with the pattern of responses in the first panel, blacks indicated that they were most unwilling to move into a neighborhood where they would be the pioneer black family. A sizable majority of blacks (from 57 percent to 66 percent) said they would be unwilling to move into such a neighborhood, regardless of the race of their neighbors. This, along with the sizable minority (24 to 29 percent) of blacks who were unwilling to move into an all-black neighborhood, is consistent with blacks' historic desire for integration (Pettigrew 1973; Bobo, Schuman, and Steeh 1986; Farley et al. 1978, 1993). Overall, however, blacks' willingness to enter neighborhoods with varying degrees of integration does not differ significantly by target-group race.

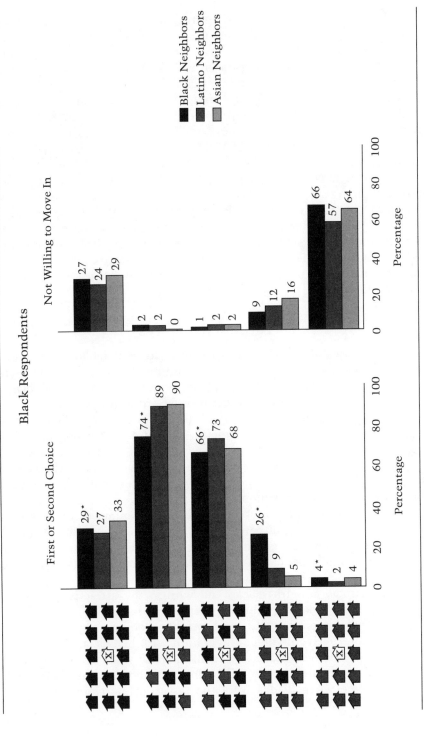

FIGURE 4.5   Attractiveness of Neighborhoods with Varying Degrees of Integration with Whites, Latinos, and Asians

Black Respondents

First or Second Choice

Not Willing to Move In

Black Neighbors
Latino Neighbors
Asian Neighbors

Percentage

Percentage

Source: Los Angeles Study of Urban Inequality 1994.
Note: Lighter houses represent target group.
*p < .05

Blacks in Los Angeles, like whites, seem to prefer neighborhoods that are integrated, but also where their own group predominates. Clear patterns of racial rank-ordering, however, are more difficult to pinpoint. In the most integrated settings (four or seven out-group houses), Latinos were the most-preferred out-group neighbors, and whites the least-preferred. Black respondents whose first or second most attractive neighborhood was majority out-group, however, showed preferences for white neighbors. The lower preference for white neighbors is not surprising when placed in the context of black perceptions of prejudice and discrimination (Farley et al. 1993; Zubrinsky and Bobo 1996). The lower ranking of Asians as potential neighbors may be indicative of the overt tensions in recent years between blacks and Asians (particularly Koreans) in Los Angeles County (Bobo et al. 1992, 1994; Johnson and Oliver 1989). It also reflects differing perceptions between blacks and whites: the latter respondents rank Asians as the most-desired potential neighbors. This is likely due to a perception of Asians as having similar socioeconomic status, as well as a strong work ethic (Bobo and Zubrinsky 1996).

Latino Preferences

The same series of questions and a similar set of neighborhood cards as for black respondents were used to examine the neighborhood preferences of Latinos. First, Latino respondents were asked to rearrange the five neighborhood cards from most to least attractive, and then to comment on their willingness to move into any of the five neighborhoods. Parallel to the previous experiment, one-third of Latinos considered varying degrees of integration with whites, one-third with blacks, and one-third with Asians. The shading of the showcards was the same as before: Latino houses were dark gray, blacks' homes black, whites' homes white, and Asians' homes light gray.

The left panel of figure 4.6 reports the percentage of Latinos rating each of the five cards as either their first or second choice for each of the three target groups. To emphasize the shift from all-same-race to all-other-race neighborhoods, the lighter homes represent same-race (Latino) homes.

For Latinos, as with blacks and whites, the attractiveness of the various neighborhoods appeared to depend in large part on the race of potential neighbors. An all-Latino neighborhood was most attractive when the alternative involved integration with blacks, and least attractive when it involved sharing residential space with whites. Nearly 80 percent of Latinos chose the all-Latino neighborhood as their first or second choice when blacks were the target group, compared with 21

FIGURE 4.6   *Attractiveness of Neighborhoods with Varying Degrees of Integration with Whites,*
              Blacks, and Asians

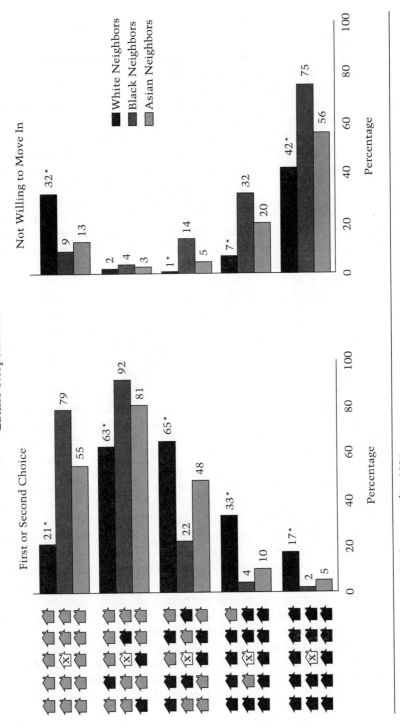

Source: Los Angeles Study of Urban Inequality 1994.
Note: Darker houses represent target group.
*p < .001

percent of Latinos receiving the Latino-white scenario, and 55 percent of those asked about Asians.

Like blacks, Latinos' most popular neighborhood overall was predominantly same-race but also populated with more than token numbers of whites, blacks, or Asians. The scenario closest to a 50/50 neighborhood was nearly three times more attractive with white neighbors (65 percent) than with black neighbors (22 percent). In fact, among Latinos rating the attractiveness of integration with whites, this was the most attractive choice. Latinos also found the all-white neighborhood more attractive than blacks did (17 percent of Latinos, compared with 4 percent of blacks). The twelve out-group and all-out-group neighborhoods were attractive to 33 percent and 17 percent of Latinos, respectively (compared with 26 percent and 4 percent of blacks), if their neighbors were white. The idea, however, of living in one of three Latino households or the only Latino home in the neighborhood in anything other than a predominantly white neighborhood was about as unappealing to Latinos as it was to blacks.

When asked which of the neighborhoods they were unwilling to move into, Latinos responded similarly to blacks: as the number of coethnics in an neighborhood decreased, Latino unwillingness to enter it increased, except when the neighborhood was white. When Latino respondents contemplated integration with whites, the all-same-race alternative was unacceptable to nearly a third.

Latinos, like blacks, have what appear to be conflicting desires for a strong coethnic presence as well as substantial integration. But their preferences, like those of blacks and whites, rise and fall with the race of their neighbors and present a clear rank-ordering of out-groups. If whites were clearly the most desirable neighbors, it was equally evident that blacks were the least desirable. Latino-Asian (again, particularly Korean) tension in Los Angeles (Bobo et al. 1994; Johnson and Farrell 1993; Johnson and Oliver 1989) and the role of Koreans as Latino employers (Kim 1999; Light et al. 1999) might explain why substantial Latino integration with Asians was also significantly less desirable to Latinos than integration with whites.

Finally, Latino respondents expressed a substantially higher preference for all-same-race neighborhoods than blacks did. This appears to be a manifestation of the comparatively high proportion of recent immigrants among Latinos (Ong et al. 1992). First- and second-generation Latinos have stronger desires for predominantly coethnic or all coethnic neighborhoods.[6] This may reflect the language barrier faced by new immigrants from Latin America and their initial need to rely on ethnic cultural institutions (churches, community organizations, grocery stores, and the like). Later generations might find the perceived improvement in social-class status and quality of life associated with predominantly white neighborhoods more attractive.

Asian Preferences

The investigation of Asian residential preferences used the same approach as that for blacks and Latinos. Asian respondents had much in common with other groups. As for blacks and Latinos, the all-same-race neighborhood was least attractive to Asians when the alternative involved integration with whites. Figure 4.7 summarizes the Asian respondents' first- and second-choice neighborhoods for each of the three target groups. Once again, the darker houses represent target-group homes. Only 17 percent of Asian respondents rated an all-Asian neighborhood among the two most attractive under the Asian-white scenario, compared with more than three-quarters in the Asian-black scenario and 55 percent of those shown the Asian-Latino neighborhood cards.

Another attribute that Asians shared with blacks and Latinos was their high regard for the second neighborhood scenario: nearly all Asian respondents rated this level of integration with blacks or Latinos as most attractive. But, like Latinos, the most desirable degree of integration with whites (80 percent) was the neighborhood closest to a 50/50 split. Moreover, Asians were the least likely to find predominantly outgroup neighborhoods attractive, except white ones. The Latino and black neighborhoods with only two other Asian homes were attractive to almost none of the Asian respondents, and the lone Asian-on-the-block situation was unattractive to all Asians presented with nonwhite neighborhoods.

As with Latinos, whites were far and away the most desirable neighbors among Asian respondents. And it is again clear that blacks were the least desirable neighbors. This pattern reappeared in responses to the question regarding willingness to move into each of the five neighborhoods. Asian respondents expressed the greatest resistance to all-Asian neighborhoods when considering integration with whites as the alternative (17 percent). Similarly, Asians were nearly two to three times more willing to be pioneers in an all-white neighborhood (73 percent) than in either an all-black (26 percent) or an all-Latino (44 percent) neighborhood. Willingness to enter neighborhoods with substantial numbers of blacks followed the expected pattern: only 3 percent of Asians refused the all-same-race alternative, and the percentage of Asians unwilling to enter a neighborhood increased as the neighborhood becomes blacker. In the Asian-black scenario, the refusal rates for neighborhoods 2 through 5 were 2 percent, 10 percent, 37 percent, and 74 percent, respectively—the highest rates of unwillingness for each

FIGURE 4.7 Attractiveness of Neighborhoods with Varying Degrees of Integration with Whites, Blacks, and Latinos

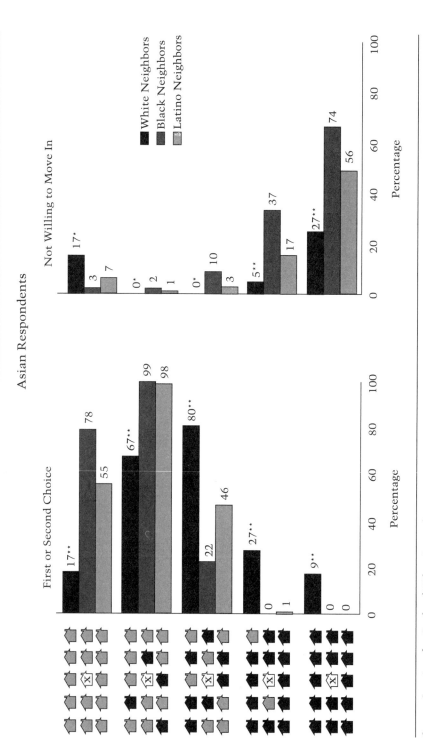

Asian Respondents

Source: Los Angeles Study of Urban Inequality 1994.
Note: Darker houses represent target group.
*p < .05, **p < .001

neighborhood. The pattern for the Asian-Latino scenarios is similar to—but less unfavorable than—that for potential black neighbors. Asian refusals of increasingly Latino neighborhoods rose steadily, from a low of 2 percent to a high of 56 percent.

Once again, it appears that neighborhood preferences are driven by the race of potential neighbors. Like Latinos (and, to a lesser extent, blacks), Asian respondents were much more open to integration with whites than with other nonwhites. And, like whites and Latinos, Asians were least inclined to find integration with blacks attractive. All groups did in fact express strong preferences for substantially same-race neighborhoods, but also desired a measure of integration. This was particularly true among racial minority-group members. Like those of Latinos, Asian preferences for substantial numbers of co-ethnic neighbors could be related to the relatively large numbers of recent immigrants among them and the need for parallel cultural institutions during the transitional period (Ong et al. 1992).[7]

Only in situations of complete segregation and isolation ("pioneers") were blacks unwilling to move into a neighborhood with nice homes within their price range. Blacks stood out as the group most likely to find substantial integration with all other groups to be desirable: over 65 percent of blacks found the 20 percent out-group neighborhood most attractive, regardless of the race of the target group (figure 4.6). Only in response to a white target group did at least 65 percent of Latinos or Asians find this neighborhood most appealing. White comfort in, or willingness to enter, a neighborhood that is just over half out-group was much more dependent on target-group race: when their current neighborhoods became 53 percent out-group (figure 4.4), a sizable percentage said they would still feel comfortable there. The percentage of whites willing to enter the most integrated neighborhood, however, was substantially lower for all out-groups, particularly blacks and, to a lesser extent, Latinos.

These results argue strongly against the idea that the high level of residential segregation experienced by blacks in Los Angeles is the result of black preferences for majority same-race neighborhoods. It is possible to conclude, on the other hand, that the low tolerance for integration with blacks expressed by all other groups functions as a significant barrier to increased integration. Across racial groups, blacks are indisputably the least-desired neighbors. It is equally clear that, among nonwhites, integration with whites is more favorable than integration with other nonwhites. The clear and persistent rank-ordering of out-groups across racial lines stands in sharp contrast to the assertion that blacks (particularly middle-class blacks) segregate themselves voluntarily (Patterson 1997; Thernstrom and Thernstrom 1997), or that neighborhood racial-composition preferences simply reflect a universal, and therefore innocent and inevitable, form of ethnocentrism.

Predicting Neighborhood Racial Composition Preferences

Since attitudes toward integration vary greatly, both within and across racial groups, it is important to determine whether other social-background factors beyond race itself are associated with the degree of tolerance for racial residential integration. To do this, a Racial Preference Index (RPI) similar to the one used by Farley et al. (1978) is employed in the multivariate analyses that follow.

For white respondents, the RPI has a range of 0 to 100, where the higher the score, the greater the acceptance of racial residential integration. A score of 25 was given for each of the four neighborhoods (white, black, Latino, and Asian) in which white respondents said they would feel "very comfortable"; a score of 20 was given for feeling "somewhat comfortable." If whites felt "somewhat uncomfortable" or "very uncomfortable" in a neighborhood but were willing to move into it, they received a score of 12.5. Whites who were "somewhat" or "very" uncomfortable and unwilling to move into a neighborhood received a score of 0. Finally, the scores for responses to all four neighborhoods were summed for each respondent.[8]

The RPI constructed for blacks, Latinos, and Asians is different, in that it is based on the series of neighborhood-preference questions and related showcards described and analyzed here. Scores for the nonwhites' RPI ranged from 12.5 to 100 (low to high acceptance, respectively). Nonwhite respondents were asked to arrange five neighborhood showcards, each representing a different degree of integration, from most to least attractive. The RPI was constructed first, by giving a score to each of the five choices; like the overall scale, high values indicate acceptance of integration and low ones the opposite. These scores were weighted according to respondents' expressed willingness or unwillingness to move into each neighborhood.[9] To arrive at a cumulative RPI score, the five weighted values were summed for each respondent.[10] Table 4.6 presents mean scores for the RPI by respondent- and target-group race.

Since the white RPI is based on a different set of questions from those used to compute the minority-respondent RPI, the high mean preference scores of whites do not permit the conclusion that whites are more open to integration than nonwhites. In fact, analysis of neighborhood racial preferences in the previous section suggests the opposite.[11] Upon examining mean scores by respondent and target-group race, the

TABLE 4.6   *Mean Racial-Preference Index Scores, by Race of Respondent and Race of Target Group*

	Respondent Race			
	Whites	Blacks	Latinos	Asians
Target group				
Whites	—	40.95	50.15	50.57
Blacks	69.62	—	27.95	25.83
Latinos	78.04	40.48	—	30.44
Asians	87.35	38.55	34.52	—
Overall mean	79.23	40.09	38.20	34.62
N	800	1091	978	1029
F	22.06*	0.54	45.86*	52.63*

Source: Los Angeles Study of Urban Inequality 1994.
Note: The racial preference index of whites is based on responses to cards showing neighborhoods of differing racial compositions. Scores range from 0 (indicating low acceptance of residential integration) to 100 (indicating high acceptance).

   The racial preference index for blacks, Latinos, and Asians is based on responses to a slightly different set of questions and neighborhood cards with different racial compositions from those for whites. Scores range from 12.5 (low acceptance of residential integration) to 100 (high acceptance).
*$p < .001$

racial-preference hierarchy observed throughout the analysis is immediately observable. Despite overall high scores, whites were most accepting of residential integration with Asians (87.35) and least accepting of residential integration with blacks (69.62). As anticipated, white acceptance of integration with Latinos fell in between, with a mean RPI score of 78.04.

   Latino and Asian preferences follow similar patterns: whites receive the highest mean racial-preference score—50.15 and 50.57, respectively. Consistent with the now familiar pattern of rank-ordering, blacks received the lowest racial-preference scores, averaging below 30 for both groups of respondents. Blacks were the only group whose mean racial-preference scores did not differ significantly across target groups. That is, they were the only group not to discriminate on the basis of race in their neighborhood-composition preferences.

   Attention now turns to OLS regression analysis. For each racial category, the RPI is the dependent variable. Independent variables always include the following demographic variables: sex, age, education, income, and immigrant status (immigrant status is included for Latino and Asian respondents only).[12] Model I includes independent effects for target-group race.[13] Model II adds interactions between target-group race and the five demographic characteristics. The results are shown in table 4.7.

TABLE 4.7 Multivariate Regression Coefficients Examining the Effects on Acceptance of Racial Residential Integration of Target-Group Race and Selected Social-Background Characteristics

	Whites		Blacks		Latinos		Asians	
	Model I	Model II	Model I	Model II	Model I	Model II	Model I	Model II
Constant	74.00***	81.92***	32.23***	16.96	31.21***	11.73	50.87***	54.45**
Demographics								
Sex (1 = male)	0.33	6.01	5.28**	3.69	1.29	3.18	-1.34	-4.21
Age	-0.17*	-0.31	0.08	0.25*	0.21**	0.32	-0.09	-0.26
Education	0.32	-0.04	0.17	0.74	0.59*	1.46**	0.11	0.21
Income	-0.03	-0.02	-0.04	-0.00	0.01	0.18	0.05*	0.12
U.S.-born (1 = yes)	—	—	—	—	-0.24	-2.14	2.56	5.01
Target group[a]								
Black neighbors	—	—	—	—	-19.89***	20.58*	-25.07***	-25.75
Latino neighbors	6.82*	3.17	0.51	21.88	—	—	-20.65***	-26.72
Asian neighbors	17.22***	0.25	-2.08	23.77	-13.15***	6.94	—	—
Interaction								
BN × sex	—	—	—	—	—	-3.66	—	4.94
BN × age	—	—	—	—	—	-0.23	—	0.24
BN × education	—	—	—	—	—	-2.24*	—	-0.49

BN × income	—	—	—	—	—	-0.28*	—	-0.11
BN × U.S.-born	—	—	—	—	—	3.33	—	-6.84
LN × sex	—	-7.30	—	2.17	—	—	—	6.11
LN × age	—	0.20	—	-0.29*	—	—	—	0.25
LN × education	—	0.19	—	-0.58	—	—	—	-0.28
LN × income	—	-0.07	—	-0.09	—	—	—	-0.08
LN × U.S.-born	—	—	—	—	—	—	—	-4.84
AN × sex	—	-6.30	—	1.19	—	-2.44	—	—
AN × age	—	0.21	—	-0.20	—	-0.14	—	—
AN × education	—	0.56	—	-1.27	—	-0.63	—	—
AN × income	—	0.06	—	-0.05	—	-0.24*	—	—
AN × nativity	—	—	—	—	—	2.64	—	—
R^2	0.11***	0.13***	0.06*	0.08**	0.26***	0.32***	0.43***	0.47***
Mean RPI	79.23		40.09		38.20		34.62	
N	701		965		864		703	

Source: Los Angeles Study of Urban Inequality 1994.

[a]The baseline experimental ballot for white respondents is black neighbors; for nonwhite respondents is black neighbors; white neighbors.

Note: Acceptance of integration is measured using the racial preference index (RPI). Whites' RPI scores range from 0 (low acceptance of racial residential integration) to 100 (high acceptance); nonwhites' RPI scores range from 12.5 to 100 (low to high acceptance, respectively, of racial residential integration), due to differences in the series of questions they were asked relative to whites.

*p < .05, **p < .01, ***p < .001

The first column for each respondent-race category reports regression coefficients for Model I, which includes demographic characteristics and target-group variables. Black respondents stand out as the only group for whom target-group race does not predict acceptance of racial residential integration. This is consistent with the previous observation that blacks are at once the most open to integration and most often seen as the least-desirable neighbors.

Among whites, Latinos, and Asians, by contrast, target-group race is a compelling predictor of attitudes toward residential integration. For all three groups, the pattern of rank-ordering is consistent and unmistakable, with blacks always at the end of the queue. White RPI scores for Latino and Asian neighbors are 6.82 and 17.22 points higher, respectively, than they are for black neighbors ($p < .001$). Even more striking is the power of target-group race in predicting Asian neighborhood preferences. Asian RPI scores drop at least 20 points when these respondents consider residential integration with either blacks (-25.07, $p < .001$) or Latinos (-20.65, $p < .001$).

The effect of demographic variables across respondent groups on RPI scores is inconsistent. The only instance of a significant sex effect is among blacks: black men have significantly higher RPI scores than black women (5.28, $p < .01$). Age has a small, negative effect on whites' RPI scores (-0.17, $p < .05$), and a positive effect on Latinos' RPI scores (0.21, $p < .001$). Latinos show a positive education effect (0.59, $p < .05$), and increased income has a small, positive effect on Asians' preferences. Immigrant status is not a significant predictor of neighborhood racial-composition preferences among Asians or Latinos, net of such factors as age, education, and income. Finally, the amount of variance explained for Latinos and Asians is substantially larger than for either whites or blacks. Standard demographic characteristics and target-group race explain 43 percent of the variation in Asians' neighborhood racial preferences. For Latinos, the comparable figure is 26 percent—roughly half the variance explained for Asians, but more than twice that explained by Model I for whites ($r^2 = .11$) or blacks ($r^2 = .06$).

Adding interactions between the five demographic characteristics and target-group race does not improve our understanding of tolerance for integration among whites or Asians; none of the interaction terms is statistically significant. Among blacks, only one of the interaction terms produces a significant effect: age has a more pronounced, negative effect on black RPI scores of their reaction to potential Latino neighbors than to potential white neighbors. This may be due, in part, to the large influx during the last decade of Latino immigrants into traditionally black communities (such as South Central Los Angeles), where many older blacks remain (Johnson et al. 1992). Finally, a total of three interactions are statistically significant among Latino respondents: education has a negative effect on Latino RPI scores when their potential neighbors are blacks; and income has a negative effect on Latino preferences for integration with both blacks and Asians. And, in this expanded model, immigrant status and target-group race do not produce significant effects for either Latino or Asian respondents. This suggests that the previously hypothesized relationship between preferences for majority same-race neighborhoods and immigrant status is, at least, complicated by other factors.

Multivariate analyses support bivariate patterns: a racial hierarchy that nearly always finds whites on top and blacks at the bottom. Consistent with previous results, both here and elsewhere (Bobo and Zubrinsky 1996), blacks demonstrate the greatest overall acceptance of racial residential integration, irrespective of target-group race or demographic characteristics. Finally, contrary to bivariate results, immigrant status and target-group race do not interact to significantly influence the neighborhood racial preferences of Latinos or Asians.

Do birds of a feather really prefer to flock together? Or are neighborhood racial-composition preferences better understood as expressions of negative racial attitudes (see Pettigrew 1973; Bobo 1989; Farley et al. 1978, 1993, 1994; Massey and Denton 1993; Bobo and Zubrinsky 1996)? The rank-ordering of preferences and the lack of support for nonracial explanations found in previous sections of this chapter lend credence to such an explanation. To test this, a final set of regression models examines the extent to which racial stereotypes affect neighborhood racial-composition preferences. Once again, the dependent variable is the Racial Preference Index (RPI). The independent variables consist of controls for the five demographic characteristics from the previous analysis (sex, age, education, income, and immigrant status), and political ideology (scaled 1 for liberal, 2 for moderate, and 3 for conservative).[14]

In addition to these controls, the models include indicators of the target-group racial composition of respondents' actual neighborhoods (measured at the tract level), a characteristic found to influence racial attitudes (Darden and Parsons 1981; Farley et al. 1994; Sigelman and Welch 1993). Finally, each model includes both a stereotype-difference score[15] and a perceived-socioeconomic-status-difference score.[16] These measures explore whether or not group members evaluate others as inferior relative to their own group and reveal the size of any perceived gap between the two groups (Bobo and Kluegel 1995; Jackman and Senter 1983). The stereotype and SES difference measures are summarized in table 4.8.

The importance of racial stereotyping to our understanding of neighborhood racial composition preferences is twofold, each related to

TABLE 4.8   *Summary Statistics, Stereotyping Measures*

Target Race	Respondent Race				F
	Whites	Blacks	Latinos	Asians	
Whites					
Hard to get along with	18.27	24.29	21.69	22.91	10.34***
Prefer welfare	11.98	16.08	15.85	14.08	13.79***
Unintelligent	17.16	19.79	16.98	17.62	3.43*
Poor English	7.77	8.08	4.39	3.32	21.61***
Stereotype rating	13.74	17.06	14.82	14.59	12.12***
Difference score	—	−3.72	−9.78	−2.67	84.00***
Poor	21.78	16.34	13.29	16.69	69.80***
SES difference	—	−17.21	−22.33	−4.58	102.58***
Blacks					
Hard to get along with	23.32	17.60	27.50	26.93	27.34***
Prefer welfare	27.06	24.98	37.00	33.96	67.62***
Unintelligent	23.55	19.52	24.35	28.00	20.10***
Poor English	20.17	14.79	14.82	9.34	29.81***
Stereotype rating	23.56	19.42	25.92	24.35	42.99***
Difference score	8.72	—	−0.01	6.29	146.15***
Poor	34.83	33.57	33.18	36.10	4.03**
SES difference	12.88	—	−2.52	14.61	275.56***
Latinos					
Hard to get along with	21.72	19.75	14.26	22.42	24.35***
Prefer welfare	25.10	26.80	27.96	33.77	13.05***
Unintelligent	25.03	23.79	21.82	28.97	12.08***
Poor English	31.30	31.44	28.36	28.97	5.56***
Stereotype rating	25.78	25.50	23.02	28.48	17.71***
Difference score	11.25	5.55	—	11.37	55.73***
Poor	36.44	34.95	35.66	37.40	1.52
SES difference	14.73	1.32	—	16.05	144.01***
Asians					
Hard to get along with	22.03	27.82	25.87	15.72	45.83***
Prefer welfare	10.69	14.69	14.88	10.60	11.94***
Unintelligent	15.60	18.77	15.22	15.10	4.22**
Poor English	23.93	31.38	25.66	21.75	25.35***
Stereotype rating	17.95	22.98	20.30	15.75	48.36***
Difference score	3.38	1.52	−5.25	—	180.25***
Poor	21.80	18.17	16.74	21.34	15.60***
SES difference	.01	15.56	−18.74	—	206.97***

Source: Los Angeles Study of Urban Inequality 1994.
Note: Individual traits and sterotype rating are means on a scale of 0 to 50; 50 is the negative end of a bipolar rating continuum. Stereotype- and SES-difference scores are means on a −50 to +50 scale, where positive scores reflect unfavorable ratings of out-groups relative to one's own group, negative scores reflect favorable ratings of out-groups relative to one's own group, and a score of 0 indicates no perceived difference between groups.
*p < .05, **p < .01, ***p < .001

prejudice. At its most basic level, prejudice is said to be heavily imbued with negative affect and negative stereotypes that are unreceptive to reason and new information (Jackman 1994). This understanding of racial stereotypes is consistent with the traditional definition of prejudice, which emphasizes simple out-group hostility (Allport 1954; Pettigrew 1982). As indicators of prejudice, racial stereotypes can also be examined in light of Blumer's (1958) theory of race prejudice as a sense of group position. From this perspective, prejudice has more to do with the socially learned commitments to maintaining a particular group status or relative group position. Groups that perceive little or no gap between themselves and another group will have higher racial-preference scores than groups that perceive sizable gaps and view the out-group unfavorably. Finally, the Latino and Asian respondent equations also include an interaction term for the stereotype-difference score and immigrant status, when this term yields a significant effect. The results are shown in table 4.9.

Consistent with expectations, the more negatively whites stereotype blacks and Latinos, the lower their preferences for integration with these groups are. Moreover, whites' stereotypes of blacks have a substantially larger impact on neighborhood racial preferences than their negative stereotypes of Latinos do (-1.88 and -1.04, respectively, $p < .001$). When considering integration with Asians—the so-called Model Minority—racial stereotypes are not a significant factor at all. There is, however, a comparatively small, negative effect for perceived SES differences ($-.29$, $p < .05$). Target-group neighborhood racial composition significantly impacts whites' racial-composition preferences only once: whites who live in a 20 to 30 percent black neighborhood have RPI scores that are 21 points lower than whites residing in neighborhoods with more or fewer blacks. This runs counter to the common belief that increased exposure results in more tolerant attitudes, suggesting that increased integration has a positive effect on attitudes—but only to a point.

Significant relationships between stereotypes and preferences are also present among black respondents. The patterns that emerge are again consistent with explanations based on prejudice (Blumer 1958; Bobo and Zubrinsky 1996; Farley et al. 1978, 1993, 1994; Massey and Denton 1993; Pettigrew 1973, 1979). It should be noted, however, that the influence of negative racial stereotypes among blacks is *always* substantially smaller than is true of whites. The more negative blacks' stereotypes of whites ($-.42$, $p < .05$) and Asians ($-.55$, $p < .001$) are, the less accepting they are of sharing residential space with members of these two groups. Racial stereotypes have no significant effect on blacks' preferences for sharing residential space with Latinos. Finally,

TABLE 4.9   *Multivariate Regression Coefficients Examining the Effects of Social Background and Stereotypes on Neighborhood Racial Preferences*

	White Respondents			Black Respondents		
	Blacks	Latinos	Asians	Blacks	Latinos	Asians
Constant	119.12***	108.78***	93.21***	27.10*	50.40***	35.23***
Demographics						
Scale (1 = male)	6.07	−7.43	2.59	0.38	6.64	3.68
Age	−0.22	−0.01	−0.11	0.18	−0.02	0.12
Education	−1.15	−0.10	0.51	−0.30	−0.52	−0.20
Income[a]	0.01	−0.09	0.02	0.04	−0.10	−0.04
Political ideology	−0.53	−4.23	−4.82*	2.73	−0.51	1.86
U.S.-born (1 = yes)	—	—	—	—	—	—
Tract racial composition						
LT 10 percent target race	−7.37	−2.90	−1.56	2.66	0.64	−1.52
10 to 20 percent target race	10.02	−6.64	0.18	7.54	−6.75	−2.55
20 to 30 percent target race	−21.04*	−0.80	4.20	7.47	−3.85	3.53
Racial attitudes[b]						
Stereotype	−1.88***	−1.04***	−1.60	−0.42*	−0.22	−0.55***
SES difference score	−0.29	0.12	−0.29*	0.20	0.04	0.05
Interactions						
Stereotype difference × U.S.-born	—	—	—	—	—	—
R²	0.37***	0.18**	0.15*	0.12*	0.14**	0.10***
Mean RPI	69.62	78.04	87.35	40.95	40.48	38.48
N	193	223	233	298	317	299

Source: Los Angeles Study of Inequality 1994.
Notes: The scale for difference scores ranges from −50 to +50, where positive scores indicate unfavorable ratings of out-groups. The racial preference index for white respondents is scaled from 0 to 100; for nonwhite respondents it is scaled 12.5 to 100. In both cases, low scores indicate low acceptance of integration, and high scores indicate high acceptance.
[a]Category midpoints divided by 1,000 to shift decimal places.
[b]Stereotype measures use a split-ballot format different from that used for the showcard experiment. For white respondents, one-third rated blacks as a group, one-third rated Latinos as a group, and the remaining one-third rated Asian females. For black respondents, one-third rated whites as a group, one-third rated Latino males, and the remaining one-third rated Asian females. For Latino respondents, one-third rated whites as a group, one-third rated black males, and the remaining one-third rated Asian females. For Asian respondents, one-third rated whites as a group, one-third rated black males, and the remaining one-third rated Latino females.
[c]The 20 to 30 percent Black tract variable drops out of this model.
*p < .05, **p < .01, ***p < .001

Latino Respondents			Asian Respondents		
Whites	Blacks	Asians	Whites	Blacks	Latinos
10.20	44.26***	25.33**	40.37**	27.93***	33.57***
3.94	−2.68	0.76	−4.85	−0.13	5.32***
0.30	0.11	0.14	−0.09	−0.02	−0.05
1.15*	−0.64	1.00**	0.06	−0.08	−0.30
0.14	−0.04	−0.07	0.04	0.00	−0.02
4.03	−0.03	1.48	7.57*	0.08	−0.57
−5.99	1.69	−2.53	6.21	−0.79	7.96
−7.91	−11.38***	−8.44	−21.18***	−0.88	0.84
1.08	−16.51***	−5.91	−16.23***	−1.86	5.43
−4.11	−11.59*	−11.83*	−0.07	c	−2.18
−0.26	−0.13	−0.19	0.05	0.16	0.06
0.09	0.17	0.11	0.09	−0.06	0.06
—	—	−0.89*	—	—	0.71*
0.29***	0.10***	0.23**	0.36***	0.03	0.41
50.15	27.95	38.20	50.57	25.83	30.44
275	245	264	186	187	177

target-group neighborhood racial composition does not significantly affect black preferences for integration with any of the three groups.

None of the direct effects of racial stereotyping is significant among either Latino or Asian respondents. For each group, only one significant immigrant-status-stereotyping interaction emerges, with both effects in the anticipated direction. The effect of stereotyping among native-born Latinos considering integration with Asians is −1.08 (−.19 + (1)(−.89), p <.05)—more than 5.5 times the effect of stereotyping among foreign-born Latinos (−.19). Conversely, the effect of stereotyping among native-born Asians considering integration with Latinos is $-.65$ $(.06 + (1)(-.71), p <.05)$.

The effect of target-group racial composition is also limited among Latino and Asian respondents. Latinos residing in tracts that are less than 10 percent black $(-11.38, p <.01)$, 10 to 20 percent black $(-16.51, p <.001)$, and 20 to 30 percent black $(-11.59, p <.05)$ all prefer significantly fewer black neighbors than Latinos residing in tracts that are more than 30 percent black. The effect of neighborhood racial composition on Latino preferences for Asian neighbors is slightly different, since RPI scores are significantly lower only among Latinos residing in neighborhoods that are 20 to 30 percent Asian $(-11.83, p <.05)$. Target-group racial composition does not significantly impact Latino preferences for white neighbors. This is, however, the only instance of a significant effect among Asian respondents: as the percentage white in Asian respondents' actual neighborhoods increases, so too do preferences for white neighbors.

Conclusion

Racial residential patterns are undoubtedly the result of a complex of factors, only some of which have been addressed here. Of the factors discussed in this analysis, however, the importance of race-related factors relative to socioeconomic status differences or differences in housing market perceptions and/or information is evident. The salience of race emerges in three important ways. First, in exploring group perceptions of community desirability, there is consistency across groups; however, there is some evidence that communities with higher minority populations (particularly blacks and Latinos) are significantly less desirable to whites. Asians also appear to find areas with high Latino and/or black populations less desirable. In both cases, this is true regardless of the average cost of housing.

Second, the clear and consistent rank-ordering of out-groups as neighbors suggests that racial-composition preferences are not benign, as has been suggested (Clark 1989, 1991, 1992; Patterson 1997; Thernstrom and Thernstrom 1997). *Whites are always the most desirable out-group*; this is true both in terms of the attractiveness of various types of neighborhoods to nonwhites and their willingness to enter particular neighborhoods—especially all out-group neighborhoods. Conversely, *blacks are always the least desirable out-group*; this is true with respect to whites' comfort levels and with respect to the attractiveness of various types of neighborhoods among other nonwhite groups. It is also clear that Asians and Latinos consistently fall between these extremes, in that order. This racial rank-ordering of preferences is supported in multivariate analyses. Not only are blacks least desired as neighbors, they are also the group demonstrating the greatest overall acceptance of integration, regardless of target-group race or sociodemographic characteristics.

Finally, the multivariate test of preferences was expanded to include measures of racial stereotypes, as well as actual neighborhood racial composition. These results, however, are mixed. Among whites and blacks, a pattern emerges emphasizing the importance of racial stereotypes to understanding neighborhood racial-composition preferences. As out-group stereotypes become increasingly negative, preferences for integration with members of those groups decline. This relationship is strongest among whites, but statistically significant only when the target group is blacks $(-1.88, p < .001)$ or Latinos $(-1.04, p < .001)$—again, the two groups at the bottom of the racial hierarchy. Moreover, exposure to minorities in whites' actual residential setting has almost no significant impact on preferences. The effect of stereotypes is always smaller among blacks, and significant only when the target group is whites or Asians. Actual neighborhood racial composition does not significantly affect blacks' preferences for integration. The effect of stereotyping is least consistent among Latino and Asian respondents, and linked to immigrant status; actual neighborhood racial composition is also most likely to matter for these two groups. Still, these effects vary by the race of the target group.

As a whole, these results lend limited support to the persistence of race prejudice as a sense of group position (Blumer 1958). The importance of race is not simply a matter of general out-group hostility. If this more straightforward version of prejudice were indicative of the dynamics described here, one would not expect to find such high levels of consensus when ranking out-groups as neighbors. It is because there is clear consensus regarding who the most and least desirable out-groups are that group position must be considered.

As the dominant group in American society, whites are at the top of the economic and social hierarchies; blacks, conversely, are at the bottom (Jaynes and Williams 1989; Massey and Denton 1993). Historically and in the present, socioeconomic advancement and assimilation for nonwhites is associated with greater proximity to whites. For whites, unfortunately, integration with any other group, but particularly with blacks, signals an unwelcome change in existing status relations of superiority (Bobo and Zubrinsky 1996). This helps us understand why the stereotype measure used here (emphasizing not just simple stereotypes, but the extent to which groups see each other as similar or different) has greater impact among whites compared to nonwhites. It may also explain why whites' preferences are rarely influenced by increased residential contact, as would be expected with a traditional prejudice argument (Allport 1954). And, because the top and bottom positions of the social hierarchy are common knowledge, it is plausible that Asians and Latinos—largely new immigrant populations looking for upward social and economic mobility—rank blacks least desirable for reasons similar to those of whites.

Policies designed to reduce racial residential segregation are said to be ineffective because people—particularly African Americans—are already living where they "choose" (Clark 1989, 1992; Patterson 1997; Thernstrom and Thernstrom 1997). Furthermore, whites' comparative lack of contact with concentrated urban poverty causes them to view issues of poverty and its resulting social dislocations as irrelevant to their immediate policy concerns—especially if the condition of black communities is believed to be the result of their own cultural inadequacies. Contextualizing the expressed preferences for same-race neighbors as part of a much larger, complex picture of intergroup relations—one that identifies the persistence of prejudice, discrimination, and racist ideology as critical elements of group relations and persistent inequality—moves us toward a more thorough understanding of the causes (and consequences) of racial residential segregation. This more thorough understanding of causes can, in turn, pave the way for developing more effective public policy strategies.

It was suggested earlier in this chapter that increased racial and ethnic diversity might create an environment where whites become less fixated on the number of blacks in the neighborhood, thereby expanding opportunities for residential integration between the races. This seemed a plausible expectation, given the generally high levels of acceptance of integration expressed by whites and the modest declines in segregation in 1990 reported for areas with comparatively large nonblack minority populations (Farley and Frey 1994). Despite lower overall black-white segregation in multiethnic areas, however, increased diversity did not produce substantial gains in black-white integration between 1980 and 1990 (Farley and Frey 1994). Moreover, blacks' location in the preference hierarchy has not improved with the increased presence of other racial minority groups (Jankowski 1995; Bobo and Zubrinsky 1996).

These results suggest that extreme black-white residential segregation is likely to persist, even in a metropolis as diverse as Los Angeles. The clear-cut racial hierarchy that emerges from these data suggests that the new prismatic metropolises offer the potential for greater residential diversity for some but not for others, and that race is critical to understanding who the winners and losers will be (Alba et al. 1995; Lee and Wood 1991; Wood and Lee 1991). Groups viewed more favorably (such as Asians)—especially by whites but also by other racial minorities—will have more and better opportunities for residential diversity than those who tend to be viewed unfavorably (such as blacks). Increased diversity may, therefore, simply add to the climate of resistance toward blacks as neighbors, rather than providing a buffer to it. Racial and ethnic diversity—offering opportunities for cultural enrichment and exposure to alternative perspectives, viewpoints, and experiences—is said to be what makes us strong as a nation. Unfortunately, increasing diversity in America is juxtaposed with persistent racial polarization, which undermines the benefits that pluralism is purported to offer. Racial residential segregation is an essential element of this polarization. Whether voluntary or involuntary, it has serious implications for the quality of American life.

Appendix

FIGURE 4A.1   Neighborhood Show Cards Used for White Respondents

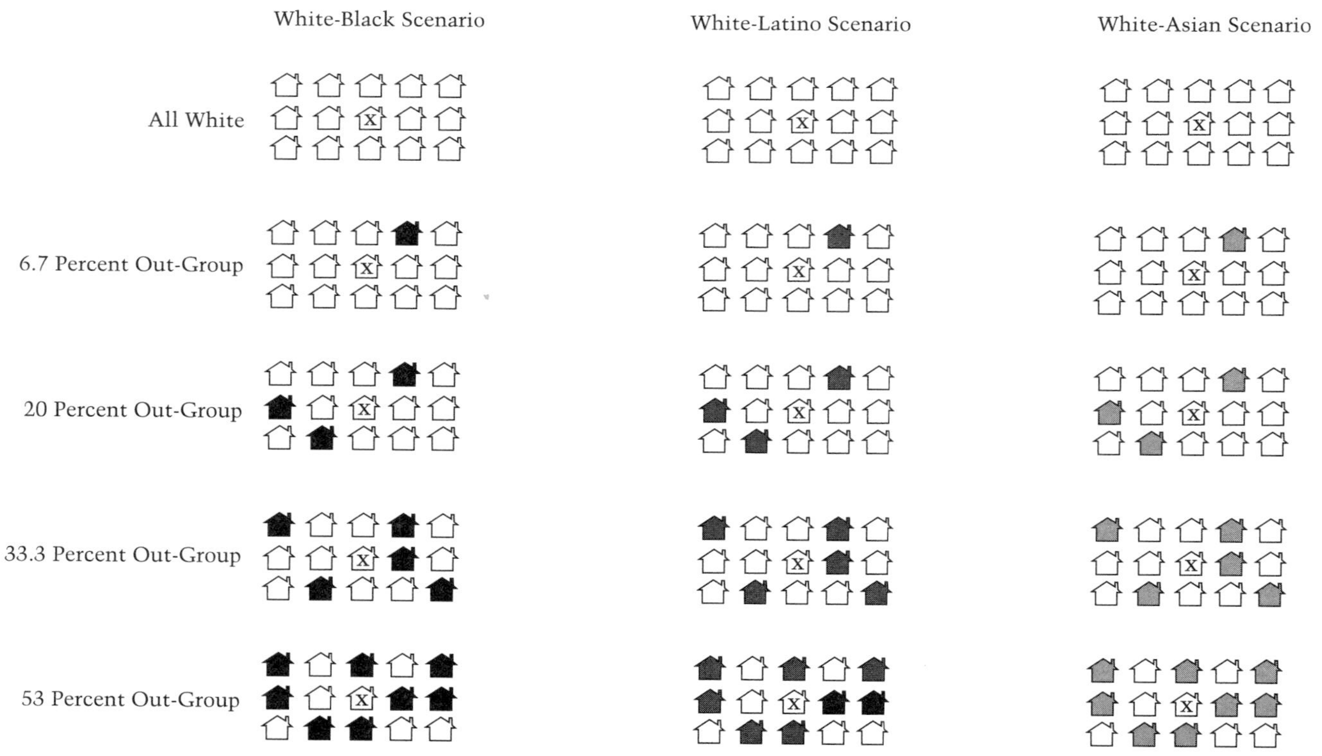

White-Black Scenario   White-Latino Scenario   White-Asian Scenario

All White

6.7 Percent Out-Group

20 Percent Out-Group

33.3 Percent Out-Group

53 Percent Out-Group

Source: Los Angeles Study of Urban Inequality 1994.

FIGURE 4A.2   Neighborhood Show Cards Used for Black Respondents

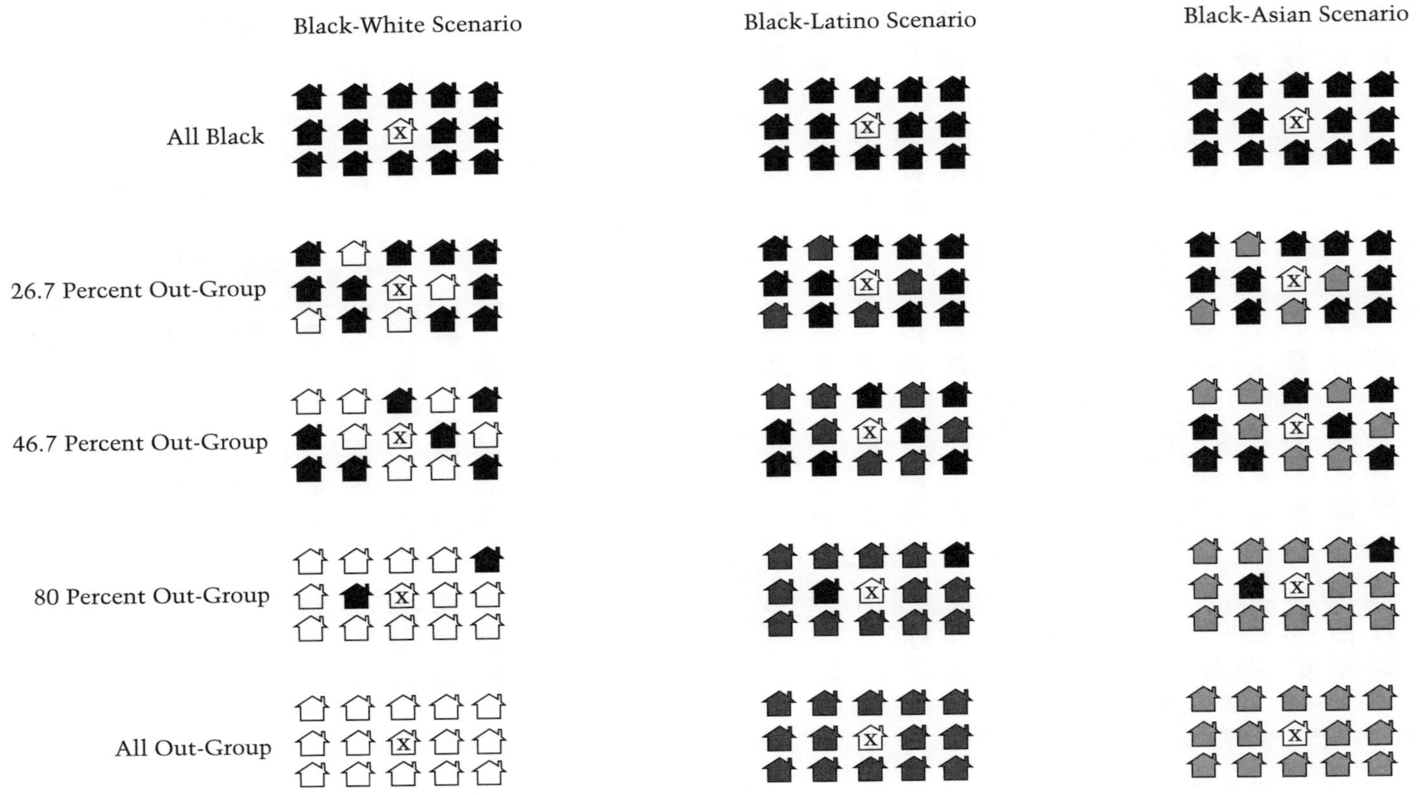

Source: Los Angeles Study of Urban Inequality 1994.

FIGURE 4A.3   Neighborhood Show Cards Used for Latino Respondents

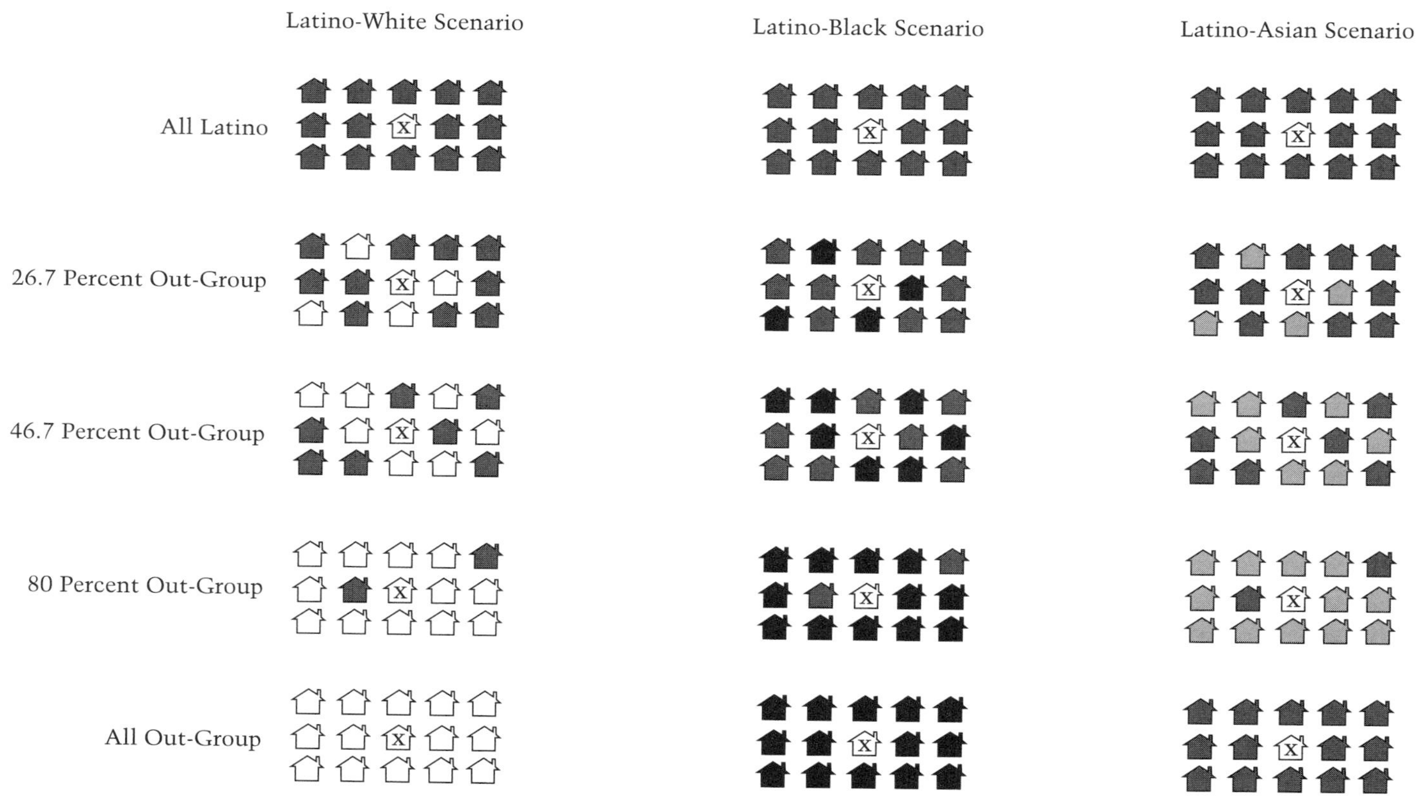

Source: Los Angeles Study of Urban Inequality 1994.

FIGURE 4A.4   Neighborhood Show Cards Used for Asian Respondents

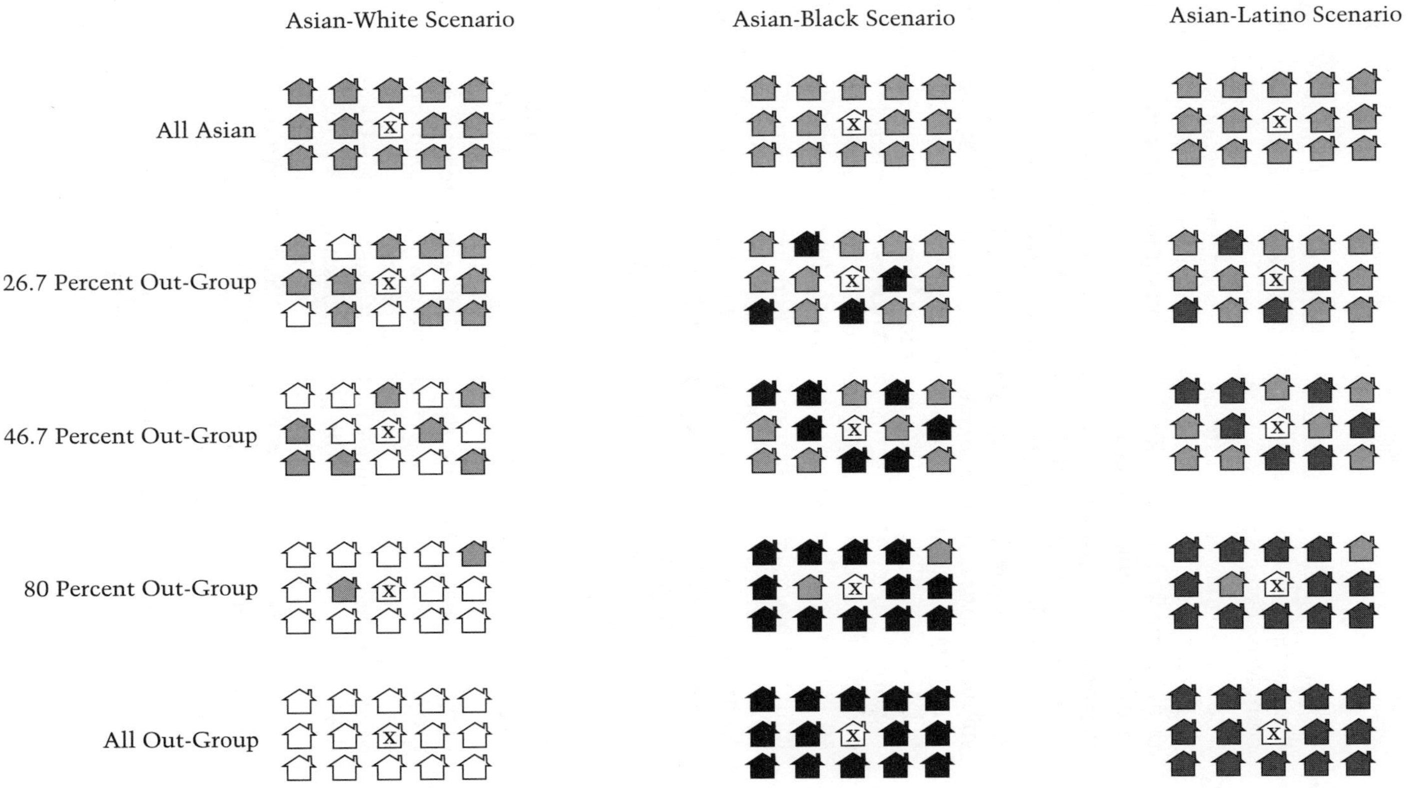

Asian-White Scenario   Asian-Black Scenario   Asian-Latino Scenario

All Asian

26.7 Percent Out-Group

46.7 Percent Out-Group

80 Percent Out-Group

All Out-Group

Source: Los Angeles Study of Urban Inequality 1994.

Notes

1. The scale for the index of dissimilarity ranges from 0 to 1. An index score of 0 represents complete integration, and an index of 1 complete segregation.

2. The conditions for multiethnicity used by Reynolds Farley and William Frey—that at least two racial minority groups exceed national representation—likely result in an understatement of multiethnicity in American cities.

3. PUMAs are census-defined areas with a minimum of 100,000 residents. PUMAs are designed to provide detailed information for areas as small as 100,000 people, while maintaining confidentiality. A single PUMA should not include both central-city and suburban areas, and non-central-city areas should not be broken into PUMAs (thus, all of Long Beach is one PUMA). Finally, PUMAs should be contiguous, unless that requires violating one of the other guidelines. For the Los Angeles–Long Beach PMSA, only one PUMA is seriously fragmented (6424). I decided to include all 58 PUMAs so that the analysis covers the entire county.

4. Kain (1986) used these categories. There are two categories for family type (children under eighteen present or not); five categories for family size (one, two, three, four to five, six and over); five income categories (under $15,000, $15,000–$28,339, $28,340–$43,499, $43,500–$66,999, $67,000 and over); and six age categories (under twenty-five, twenty-five–thirty-four, thirty-five–forty-four, forty-five–fifty-four, fifty-five–sixty-four, sixty-five and over). For more details see Charles, forthcoming.

5. The author considered the possibility that the results of this analysis could be affected by respondents' homeownership status. Specifically, renters may not be interested in the cost of owning a home. A comparison of the ratio of estimated to actual home prices between homeowners and nonowners produces only minor differences, and the overall pattern of results is unchanged. Moreover, a substantial number of LASUI nonhomeowners expressed a desire to own a home in the Los Angeles area (53 percent of whites, 68 percent of blacks, 44 percent of U.S.-born Asians, 42 percent of foreign-born Asians, 59 percent of U.S.-born Latinos, and 66 percent of foreign-born Latinos).

6. When whites were the potential neighbors, 27.2 percent of foreign-born Latinos regarded the all-same-race neighborhood as most attractive, compared with only 4.6 percent of native-born Latinos (p <.01). Foreign-born Latinos were also more likely than native-born Latinos (84.5 percent and 63.8 percent, respectively) to prefer an

all-same-race neighborhood to sharing residential space with blacks (p <.001). When considering residential integration with Asians, foreign-born Latinos were more likely than their native-born counterparts (58.7 percent and 45.5 percent, respectively) to express preferences for all coethnic neighborhoods (p <.001).

7. As was true of Latinos, there are statistically significant differences in the residential preferences of native- and foreign-born Asians. The latter are more likely to find the all-Asian neighborhood most attractive when responding to the Asian-white scenario (21 percent and 3 percent, respectively). These figures increase to 54 percent of foreign-born Asians preferring an all coethnic neighborhood when the alternative involves integration with Latinos (a difference of +10.4 percent). Finally, the importance of the race of potential neighbors is clear, irrespective of immigrant status: 83 percent of foreign-born Asians preferred the all-Asian neighborhood to any integration with blacks, as did 86 percent of native-born Asians.

8. A simple measure of favorability to residential integration was calculated for whites and correlated with the RPI to ensure that the concept being measured was not lost through the use of a scale. That measure is the total number of nonwhite houses pictured on each of the cards to which individuals gave favorable comfort ratings. The correlation between this simple measure and the RPI is .96 (p <.001). Therefore I am confident that the scale's construction did not obscure the meanings of individual responses (see Colasanto 1977, chap. 4).

9. Neighborhoods other than the all-same-race alternative were multiplied by a factor of 1 if the respondent would move in, and by a factor of .5 if the respondent would not move in. This weight was reversed for the all-same-race alternative. For more detailed information regarding the construction of the Racial Preference Index, see Colasanto 1977, chap. 4.

10. As with the white Racial Preference Index, a simple measure of acceptance of integration was correlated with the RPI for nonwhites to ensure that translating responses into a scaled item would not result in a loss of information. A count was made of responses favorable to the out-groups. The correlation between this simple measure and the nonwhite Racial Preference Index was .83 (p <.001). Once again, I am confident that the scale does not obscure information from individual responses.

11. The structure of white respondents' neighborhood-preference questions imposes a linearity that is not present in the structure of neighborhood-preference questions posed to nonwhites. Even more important are differences in the degree of integration that whites and nonwhites were asked to consider. The cards for white respon-

213

dents ranged from all-white neighborhoods to just over 50 percent other-race neighborhoods. Nonwhites, on the other hand, considered degrees of integration ranging from all-same-race to all-other-race. Thus, the apparently high acceptance could be attributed to the fact that whites were not asked to imagine a situation in which they were the only white family in the neighborhood (Colasanto 1977, 100).

12. Age and education are measured in years; income is measured in dollars divided by 1,000; sex and immigrant status are dummy variables (1 equals male and U.S.-born, respectively). All models also include a control for interviewer race that is not presented.

13. For white respondents, the baseline target group was blacks; for blacks Latinos, and for Asians whites.

14. Once again, a control for race of interviewer is included in the analysis, but not reported.

15. The original format of the stereotyping questions is a 1 to 7 scale taken directly from the 1990 General Social Survey (Bobo and Kluegel 1991; Smith 1991), which included a series of bipolar-trait rating items. This format has been shown to increase respondent comfort in expressing racial-ethnic group distinctions (Jackman and Senter 1983); produce evidence of much higher levels of negative stereotyping than do older, forced-choice formats (compare, Schuman, Steeh, and Bobo [1985] to Bobo and Kluegel [1991] and Smith [1991] as to reported levels of perceiving blacks as less intelligent); and yield reasonable, reliable, and valid measures of prejudice (Bobo and Kluegel 1993; Farley et al. 1994). The stereotype-difference score ranges from -50 to $+50$ and is computed by subtracting a respondent's rating of an out-group from his or her rating of his or her in-group. Higher (or positive) scores indicate favorable in-group ratings relative to out-groups; lower (or negative) scores indicate favorable out-group ratings relative to in-groups; and a score of 0 indicates no perceived difference between the two groups. The traits used for the stereotype-difference score are the following: difficulty to get along with socially; preference for welfare dependency; intelligence; and English language ability. For a detailed discussion of the trait selection process, see Bobo and Zubrinsky (1996).

16. The SES-difference score uses a single, bipolar-trait rating scale, which asks whether members of each group "tend to be rich" or "tend to be poor." The range and possible meaning of scores is identical to that of the stereotype-difference score; however, the rich-poor dimension is treated separately because it is not a personality or dispositional trait, like those used in the stereotype-difference score.

References

Alba, Richard D., Nancy A. Denton, Shu-yin J. Leung, and John R. Logan. 1995. "Neighborhood Change Under Conditions of Mass Immigration: The New York City Region, 1970–1990." *International Migration Review* 29: 625–56.

Alba, Richard D., and John R. Logan. 1993. "Minority Proximity to Whites in Suburbs: An Individual-Level Analysis of Segregation." *American Journal of Sociology* 98(6): 1388–1427.

Allport, Gordon W. 1954. *The Nature of Prejudice*. New York: Doubleday Anchor.

Blumer, Herbert. 1958. "Race Prejudice as a Sense of Group Position." *Pacific Sociological Review* 1: 3–7.

Bobo, Lawrence. 1989. "Keeping the Linchpin in Place: Testing the Multiple Sources of Opposition to Residential Integration." *International Review of Social Psychology* 2(3): 305–23.

Bobo, Lawrence, James H. Johnson Jr., Melvin L. Oliver, James Sidanius, and Camille L. Zubrinsky. 1992. "Public Opinion Before and After a Spring of Discontent: A Preliminary Report on the 1992 Los Angeles County Social Survey." *Occasional Working Paper Series* volume 3, number 1. Los Angeles, Calif.: UCLA Center for the Study of Urban Poverty.

Bobo, Lawrence, and James R. Kluegel. 1991. "Modern American Prejudice: Stereotypes, Social Distance, and Perceptions of Discrimination Toward Blacks, Hispanics, and Asians." Presented at the Meetings of the American Sociological Association, Cincinnati, Ohio (August 23–27, 1991).

———. 1993. "Opposition to Race-Targeting: Self-Interest, Stratification Ideology, or Racial Attitudes?" *American Sociological Review* 58(1): 443–64.

———. 1995. "Status, Ideology, and Dimensions of Whites' Racial Beliefs and Attitudes." In *Racial Attitudes in the 1990's: Continuity and Change*, edited by S. A. Tuch and J. K. Martin. Westport, Conn.: Praeger.

Bobo, Lawrence, Howard Schuman, and Charlotte Steeh. 1986. "Changing Attitudes Toward Residential Integration." In *Housing Desegregation and Federal Policy*, edited by John M. Goering. Chapel Hill: University of North Carolina Press.

Bobo, Lawrence, and Camille L. Zubrinsky. 1996. "Attitudes Toward Residential Integration: Perceived Status Differences, Mere In-Group Preference, or Racial Prejudice?" *Social Forces* 74(3): 883–909.

Bobo, Lawrence, Camille L. Zubrinsky, James H. Johnson Jr., and Melvin L. Oliver. 1995. "Work Orientation, Job Discrimination, and Ethnicity: A Focus Group Perspective." In *Research in the Sociology of Work*, volume 5, edited by Richard L. Simpson and Ida Harper Simpson. Greenwich, Conn.: JAI Press.

Bobo, Lawrence, Camille L. Zubrinsky, Melvin L. Oliver, and James H.

Johnson Jr. 1994. "Public Opinion Before and After a Spring of Discontent." In *The Los Angeles Riots: Lessons for the Urban Future*, edited by M. Baldassare. New York: Westview.

Charles, Camille Zubrinsky. Forthcoming. "Socioeconomic States and Segregation: African Americans, Hispanics, and the Century." In *Problem of the Century*; edited by Elijah Anderson and Douglas S. Massey. New York: Russell Sage.

Clark, W. A. V. 1986. "Residential Segregation in American Cities: A Review and Interpretation." *Population Research and Policy Review* 5: 95–127.

———. 1989a. "Residential Segregation in American Cities: Common Ground and Differences in Interpretation." *Population Research and Policy Review* 8: 193–97.

———. 1989b. "Revealed Preferences and Neighborhood Transitions in a Multiethnic Setting." *Urban Geography* 10(5): 434–48.

———. 1991. "Residential Preferences and Neighborhood Racial Segregation: A Test of the Schelling Segregation Model." *Demography* 28(1): 1–19.

———. 1992. "Residential Preferences and Residential Choices in a Multiethnic Context." *Demography* 29(3): 451–66.

———. 1993."Neighborhood Transitions in Multiethnic/Racial Contexts." *Journal of Urban Affairs* 15(2): 161–72.

Colasanto, Diane Lee. 1977. "The Prospects for Racial Integration in Neighborhoods: An Analysis of Residential Preferences in the Detroit Metropolitan Area." Ph.D. dissertation, University of Michigan.

Darden, Joe T. 1990. "Differential Access to Housing in the Suburbs." *Journal of Black Studies* 21(1): 15–22.

Darden, Joe T., and Margaret A. Parsons. 1981. "The Effect of Neighborhood Racial Composition on Black and White Attitudes." *Urban Review* 13(2): 103–9.

Davis, Mike. 1990. *City of Quartz*. New York: Vintage Books.

Denton, Nancy A. 1994. "Are African Americans Still Hypersegregated?" In *Residential Apartheid: The American Legacy*. Los Angeles: UCLA Center for African American Studies.

Denton, Nancy A., and Douglas S. Massey. 1988. "Residential Segregation of Blacks, Hispanics, and Asians by Socioeconomic Status and Generation." *Social Science Quarterly* 69: 797–817.

Farley, John E. 1986. "Segregated City, Segregated Suburbs: To What Extent Are They Products of Black-White Socioeconomic Differentials?" *Urban Geography* 7(2): 180–87.

———. 1987. "Disproportionate Black and Hispanic Unemployment in U.S. Metropolitan Areas: The Roles of Racial Inequality, Segregation and Discrimination in Male Joblessness." *American Journal of Economics and Sociology* 46(2): 129–50.

Farley, Reynolds, and William H. Frey. 1993. *Latino, Asian, and Black Segregation in Multi-Ethnic Metro Areas: Findings from the 1990*

Census. Report #93-278. University of Michigan: Population Studies Center Research.

———. 1994. "Changes in the Segregation of Whites from Blacks During the 1980s: Small Steps Toward a More Integrated Society." *American Sociological Review* 59(1): 23–45.

Farley, Reynolds, Maria Krysan, Tara Jackson, Charlotte Steeh, and Keith Reeves. 1993. "Causes of Continued Racial Residential Segregation in Detroit: 'Chocolate City, Vanilla Suburbs' Revisited." *Journal of Housing Research* 4(1): 1–38.

Farley, Reynolds, Howard Schuman, Suzanne Bianchi, Diane Colasanto, and Shirley Hatchett. 1978. "'Chocolate City, Vanilla Suburbs': Will the Trend Toward Racially Separate Communities Continue?" *Social Science Research* 7: 319–44.

Farley, Reynolds, Charlotte Steeh, Maria Krysan, Tara Jackson, and Keith Reeves. 1994. "Stereotypes and Segregation: Neighborhoods in the Detroit Area." *American Journal of Sociology* 100(3): 750–80.

Harrison, Roderick J., and Daniel H. Weinberg. 1992. "Racial and Ethnic Residential Segregation in 1990." Paper prepared for the Population Association of America Meetings. Denver (May 1992).

Horton, John. 1995. *The Politics of Diversity: Immigration, Resistance, and Change in Monterey Park, California.* Philadelphia: Temple University Press.

Jackman, Mary R. 1994. *The Velvet Glove: Paternalism and Conflict in Gender, Class, and Race Relations.* Berkeley, Calif.: University of California Press.

Jackman, Mary R., and Mary Scheuer Senter. 1983. "Different Therefore Unequal: Beliefs About Groups of Unequal Status." *Research in Social Stratification and Mobility* 2: 309–35.

Jankowski, Martin Sanchez. 1995. "The Rising Significance of Status in U.S. Race Relations." In *The Bubbling Cauldron: Race, Ethnicity, and the Urban Crisis,* edited by Michael Peter Smith and Joe R. Feagin. Minneapolis: University of Minnesota Press.

Jaynes, Gerald David, and Robin M. Williams Jr. 1989. *A Common Destiny: Blacks in American Society.* Washington, D.C.: National Academy Press.

Johnson, James H., Jr., and Walter C. Farrell, Jr. 1993. "The Fire This Time: The Genesis of the Los Angeles Rebellion of 1992." *North Carolina Law Review* 71(5): 1403–20.

Johnson, James H., Jr., Clyzelle K. Jones, Walter C. Farrell Jr., and Melvin L. Oliver. 1992. "The Los Angeles Rebellion: A Retrospective View." *Economic Development Quarterly* 6(4): 356–72.

Johnson, James H., Jr., and Melvin L. Oliver. 1989. "Interethnic Conflict in Urban America: The Effects of Economic and Social Dislocations." *Urban Geography* 10(5): 449–63.

Kain, John F. 1986. "The Influence of Race and Income on Racial Segregation and Housing Policy." In *Housing Desegregation and Federal*

217

Policy, edited by John M. Goering. Chapel Hill: University of North Carolina Press.

Kim, Dae Young. 1999. "Beyond Coethnic Solidarity: Mexican and Ecuadoran Employment in Korean-Owned Businesses in New York City." *Ethnic and Racial Studies* 22: 581–605.

Lee, B., and P. Wood. 1991. "Is Neighborhood Racial Succession Place-Specific?" *Demography* 28: 21–40.

Light, Ivan, Richard Bernard, and Rebecca Kim. 1999. "Immigrant Incorporation in the Garment Industry of Los Angeles." *International Migration Review* 33(1): 5–25.

Marston, W., and T. L. Van Valey. 1979. "The Role of Residential Segregation in the Assimilation Process." *Annals of the American Academy of Political and Social Science* 441: 13–25.

Massey, Douglas S., and Nancy A. Denton. 1987. "Trends in the Residential Segregation of Blacks, Hispanics, and Asians." *American Sociological Review* 52: 802–25.

———. 1989. "Hypersegregation in U.S. Metropolitan Areas: Black and Hispanic Segregation Along Five Dimensions." *Demography* 26(3): 373–92.

———. 1993. *American Apartheid*. Cambridge, Mass.: Harvard University Press.

Massey, Douglas S., and Eric Fong. 1990. "Segregation and Neighborhood Quality: Blacks, Hispanics, and Asians in the San Francisco Metropolitan Area." *Social Forces* 69(1): 15–32.

Massey, Douglas S., and Andrew B. Gross. 1991. "Segregation, the Concentration of Poverty, and the Life Chances of Individuals." *Social Science Research* 20: 397–420.

Massey, Douglas S., and Brendan P. Mullan. 1984. "Processes of Hispanic and Black Spatial Assimilation." *American Journal of Sociology* 89: 836–73.

Min, Pyong Gap. 1996. *Caught in the Middle*. Berkeley and Los Angeles: University of California Press.

O'Neill, Stephanie. 1994. "Casa, Sweet Casa: Latino Homebuyers Are the Fastest Growing Group in the Los Angeles County Real Estate Market." *Los Angeles Times*, December 4, 1994, p. K1.

Ong, Paul M., and Janette R. Lawrence, with Kevin Davidson. 1992. "Pluralism and Residential Patterns in Los Angeles." School of Architecture and Urban Planning, University of California, Los Angeles. Unpublished paper.

Pascal, H. A. 1967. *The Economics of Housing Segregation*. Los Angeles: Rand Corporation.

Patterson, Orlando. 1997. *The Ordeal of Integration: Progress and Resentment in America's "Racial" Crisis*. Washington, D.C.: Civitas/ Counterpoint.

Pettigrew, T. F. 1973. "Attitudes on Race and Housing: A Social Psychological View." In *Segregation in Residential Areas*, edited by A. H.

Hawley and V. P. Rock. Washington, D.C.: National Academy of Sciences Press.

———. 1979. "Racial Change and Social Policy." *Annals of the American Academy of Political and Social Science* 441: 114–31.

———. 1982. "Prejudice." In *Dimensions of Ethnicity: Prejudice,* edited by S. Thernstrom, A. Orlov, and O. Handlin. Cambridge, Mass.: Belknap.

Santiago, Anne M., and Margaret G. Wilder. 1991. "Residential Segregation and Links to Minority Poverty: The Case of Latinos in the United States." *Social Problems* 38(4): 492–513.

Schnare, Ann B. 1977. *Residential Segregation by Race in U.S. Metropolitan Areas: An Analysis Across Cities and over Time.* Washington, D.C.: Urban Institute.

Schuman, Howard, Charlotte Steeh, and Lawrence Bobo. 1985. *Racial Attitudes in America: Trends and Interpretations.* Cambridge, Mass.: Harvard University Press.

Sigelman, Lee, and Susan Welch. 1993. "The Contact Hypothesis Revisited: Black-White Interaction and Positive Racial Attitudes." *Social Forces* 71: 781–95.

Skerry, Peter. 1993. *Mexican Americans: The Ambivalent Minority.* Cambridge, Mass.: Harvard University Press.

Smith, Tom W. 1991. "Ethnic Images." GSS Technical Report 19. Chicago, Ill.: National Opinion Research Center.

Taeuber, Karl E. 1976. "The Effect of Income Redistribution on Racial Residential Segregation." *Urban Affairs Quarterly* 4: 5–15.

Taeuber, Karl E., and Alma F. Taeuber. 1965. *Negroes in the Cities: Residential Segregation and Neighborhood Change.* Chicago: Aldine.

Thernstrom, Stephen, and Abigail Thernstrom. 1997. *America in Black and White: One Nation, Indivisible, Race in Modern America.* New York: Simon & Schuster.

Van Valey, Thomas L., and Wade Clark Roof. 1976. "Measuring Residential Segregation in American Cities: Problems of Intercity Comparison." *Urban Affairs Quarterly* 11: 453–68.

Wood, Peter B., and Barrett A. Lee. 1991. "Is Neighborhood Racial Succession Inevitable?: Forty Years of Evidence." *Urban Affairs Quarterly* 26: 610–20.

Zubrinsky, Camille, and Lawrence Bobo. 1996. "Prismatic Metropolis: Race and Residential Segregation in the City of the Angels." *Social Science Research* 25: 335–74.

5

RACIAL DIFFERENCES IN LABOR FORCE PARTICIPATION AND LONG-TERM JOBLESSNESS AMONG LESS-EDUCATED MEN

Michael I. Lichter and Melvin L. Oliver

O NE OF the triumphs of William Julius Wilson's (1978, 1987) work has been an intellectual shift away from individualistic and toward more collective explanations of urban poverty and its correlates, including weak labor force attachment, crime, welfare dependency, and teen pregnancy. Wilson pointed to economic restructuring, a prospering and mobile black middle class, the resultant increase in residential segregation by class among blacks, and the rising concentration of poverty in ghetto neighborhoods as a set of interrelated changes that left some segments of the black formerly-working class socially isolated. Detached from the mainstream economy and bereft of traditional role models, the "ghetto underclass" has been caught in a cycle of increasing disadvantage. Their plight is due not only to their scarce resources and limited human capital, but also to their constant exposure to other people in a similarly weak structural position. As Wilson argues, "[the] issue is not simply that the underclass have a marginal position in the labor market similar to that of other disadvantaged groups, it is also that their economic position is uniquely reinforced by their social milieu" (Wilson 1991, 12).

Wilson's exposition on neighborhood effects has spawned an important and growing literature. Studies have convincingly linked juvenile delinquency, teen pregnancy, and to some extent school achievement to the neighborhood context in which children and adolescents grow up. Other studies have also shown links between neighborhood conditions and youth employment, but although much has been assumed about the relationship between neighborhood and the employment of adults, little has actually been demonstrated. This oversight has been due in part to thorny theoretical and practical problems, but also to a lack of appropriate data (Jencks and Mayer 1990; Tienda 1991). This chapter draws on the Los Angeles Survey of Urban Inequality (Bobo et al. 1995), which overcomes some of these problems, to explore the effects of neighborhood on one of the most extreme forms of weak labor market attachment: long-term labor market dropout.

Increases in Extended Joblessness

Contemporary American mores dictate that able-bodied adult men work for a living, and those who do not (even the independently wealthy) are looked upon as lazy and parasitic. Somehow, despite the lack of any apparent change in cultural values, levels of employment among working-age men have been falling steadily. Though the decline has been barely noticeable among the college-educated, it has been substantial among men who have had no education beyond high school, and even greater among those who did not finish high school. This should not be surprising to anyone who watches the news; for years the media have been broadcasting stories about the obsolescence of the poorly educated in our globalized, high-tech economy, a view that is supported by academic research. Employment among native-born nonwhites, African Americans in particular, has declined more steeply than among whites. This is probably no surprise either, given the well-known, long-standing employment problems of African American men. What has gotten less attention is growth in the proportion of men whose joblessness has become more or less permanent.

Although it has not attracted much attention, there has been a significant increase in extended joblessness among men over the past two or three decades. The 1990 U.S. Census tells us that in Los Angeles County, for instance, nearly 30 percent of African American men of working age (twenty-one to sixty-four) with no education beyond high school had not worked in at least five years. Just two decades earlier, only 6 percent of similarly educated, working-age African American men had been out of work for that long (see table 5.1). While they also evidenced increases in long-term joblessness, in 1990 only 8 percent of whites and 6 percent of Latinos in the same education range had dropped out of the labor force for similarly extended periods of time. Racial differences in labor force participation, while less extreme, tell a similar story. What accounts for these substantial racial differences in long-term joblessness and labor force participation? Can the differences be accounted for by race-neutral factors that just happen to affect African

TABLE 5.1   *Trends in Long-Term Joblessness for Less-Educated Men, 1970 to 1990, Los Angeles County and the U.S.*

Percentage who have not worked in . . .	Los Angeles County			United States
	1970	1980	1990	1990
White				
One year	5	10	13	11
Five years	2	6	8	6
African American				
One year	11	22	29	21
Five years	6	15	21	15
Asian American				
One year	3	14	19	15
Five years	1	10	15	11
Latino				
One year	5	8	9	10
Five years	2	6	6	7

Source: U.S. Census: 1970 PUMS 5 percent (1 in 100) sample; 1980 PUMS A 5 percent sample; 1990 PUMS A 5 percent sample.
Note: Less-educated men are males aged twenty-one to sixty-four with no education beyond high school.

Americans disproportionately, or is there a specifically racial dynamic involved? With the unraveling of the welfare state, labor market dropouts would appear to be increasingly at risk of living in poverty, suffering family dissolution, becoming homeless, or joining the ranks of the incarcerated. Uncovering the underlying processes is thus important for developing appropriate public policy.

Conservative analysts have long argued that poor labor market performance among ghetto-dwelling African Americans is due at least in part to a lack of adherence to core American values, in particular a commitment to moving steadily up the economic ladder through the exercise of hard work. They point to examples of apparently self-defeating behaviors as evidence of a self-perpetuating "culture of poverty." William Julius Wilson (1987) adapted these ideas in his research on the so-called urban underclass, a group in part defined by its "weak labor force attachment." Wilson turned the conservative position around, arguing that conditions in concentrated poverty neighborhoods were responsible for the observed "ghetto-related behaviors" (1996), and that these conditions were in turn the result of structural changes in the economy. While the ultimate causes of deteriorating ghetto conditions lay in economic restructuring, feedback effects developed in the ghetto, so that while past joblessness might be attributed purely to outside forces, future joblessness was in part due to the stultifying effects of "social isolation" built up over time. These effects could be partly undone by positive changes in the structure of the economy, almost certainly led by strong state policies, but not without extra efforts to address the complications of social isolation. Whatever the disagreements between Wilson and the conservatives, however, they concurred that the local neighborhood was a central locus for the development of persistent labor market troubles for African American men.

But what if neighborhood has little to do with the weak showing of African American men relative to others? Evidence suggests that many employers take a dim view of less-skilled black men, that blacks have relatively deficient social networks, and also that black men at any given level of education lag behind whites at the same level in cognitive and other skills. In this chapter, we examine the relative effects of the structure of local neighborhoods on the labor force participation and long-term joblessness of less-educated men. While studies on race and employment or wages abound, we believe that the following analysis of the effects of networks and neighborhoods, made possible by the Los Angeles Survey of Urban Inequality, is unique in this field.[1] Including data on individuals and yet able to control for neighborhood context, the survey enables us to move beyond the "underclass" studies of the 1980s, which were able to address only aggregate outcomes.

Theory

When we think about joblessness, we automatically think "unemployment." To be *unemployed* under the official definition, however, is not only to be without a job, but also to be actively searching for one. Adults who are either working or searching comprise the labor force; those who are doing neither are considered to be out of the labor force. Among the men and women who are not participating in the labor force we often distinguish between those who do not want a job or whose health prohibits their working, on one hand, and those who say they really would like to work but just cannot find anything. A great deal of discussion centers on how these "discouraged" workers differ from the unemployed, and whether or not they ought to be counted as unemployed in official statistics. The concept of *discouragement* rests on the premise that workers in this category had previously been unemployed, had conducted (what they considered to be) an exhaustive search, had been offered no satisfactory work (or had suffered through one or more bouts of unsatisfactory short-term employment), and had finally given up.

Critics argue that the existence in many firms of long vacant entry-level positions contradicts the perception that "there are no jobs out there." Instead, they find fault in the values of the long-term jobless, blame the alternative lures of welfare and criminal activity, or, as Lawrence Mead does, argue that it is (at least in part) the *perception* that there are no jobs that is the problem. Even those sympathetic to the plight of the long-term jobless have argued that availability of jobs is not a problem (Doeringer et al. 1972; Osterman 1980); it is rather the *kinds* of jobs that are most commonly available—with poor pay, benefits, and working conditions, low stability, and low advancement—that need to be addressed by public policy.

The quality of available jobs is, however, not a common object of study. Studies of income and earnings dominate the quantitative empirical literature on the labor market, partly because these are continuous variables and more easily modeled than discrete outcomes like labor force status; partly because income is more clearly related to human capital and demographic variables than is labor force status; and because there are agreed-upon ways of measuring wage discrimination. In quantitative studies of racial or gender differences in income, unequal returns to human capital typically are interpreted as discriminatory penalties (Oaxaca 1973).

Neoclassical economic theory links the "marginal productivity" of workers with wages, while human capital theory links measurable variables, education in particular, with productivity. Economic theory does not make predictions about employment separate from wages; employers will hire less-productive workers when their wage demands sink to a sufficiently low level. Thus many economists attribute the poor labor market performance of less-educated black men to unrealistic wage expectations or demands[2] relative to their human capital.[3] Some also cite the minimum wage as a barrier to hiring young blacks, in particular; their potential productivity is too low, in the employers' estimation, for employers to be able to "afford" them at the minimum wage.

Economists do, however, acknowledge that racial discrimination is often operative in labor markets, and that despite arguments predicting that market pressures will cause it to fade away (Becker 1957), it has proven very persistent. "Statistical discrimination," or the use of race as a proxy for differences in productivity between groups of workers is one proposed explanation for this persistence (Arrow 1973; Phelps 1972). A reluctance to invest in human capital or to take other steps to enhance personal productivity, however, can be a rational response to discrimination, reversing the direction of causality (Reder 1973). Labor force withdrawal is both a likely consequence of discrimination and an action that will lead to the understatement of discriminatory differentials in wages (since decreasing the pool of workers should raise wages).

All else being equal, however, economic theory leads us to expect that workers with higher levels of human capital should more readily find jobs than workers with lower levels. If we accept the view that the introduction of computers and other new technologies has led to up-skilling across the job spectrum, then the premium for human capital should be especially high. Our initial hypothesis, therefore, is that racial differences in long-term joblessness and labor force participation are explicable primarily in terms of human capital differences.

Acknowledging Barriers

Two things that are commonly overlooked in labor force studies are thought to be major barriers to employment: a history of criminal activity and medical conditions that limit a person's ability to work. Another labor market status, retirement, is also commonly overlooked, even though it is intimately linked with contemporaneous labor market conditions. The absence of criminal activity as an explanatory variable in typical models is due most simply to a lack of data. Yet a criminal history represents a significant stigma.[4] Many employers express reluctance to hire persons with a criminal history (Holzer 1996). Further, court appearances and jail time are likely to cause jobs to be lost, and create gaps in work records that are difficult to explain (Sullivan 1989). While native minorities do not commit more crimes than native whites from similar backgrounds (Harris 1993), the preponderance of evidence suggests that minorities are prosecuted more diligently and punished more harshly by the criminal justice system (Sullivan 1989).

Disability also carries a stigma, but the practical barriers posed to employment are probably more important (Oi 1992; U.S. Department of Labor 1992). Accommodating persons with disabilities often requires extra effort or flexibility on the part of the employer, and may affect the ability of a potential worker to seek employment in the first place. A body of literature shows that disabilities are suffered disproportionately by minorities and the poor, and such disabilities often have a more pronounced effect on employment when suffered by minorities. The disabled are commonly left out of employment and wage models because it is understood that their relationship to the labor market differs from that of able-bodied workers. We contend, however, that their numbers among minority communities demand that their behavior be examined along with that of the able-bodied. Beyond including them in our models, we also offer the hypothesis that having a criminal record or a work-limiting disability will significantly contribute to joblessness and labor force dropout, and to the differential joblessness and dropout of African Americans in particular.

Finally, those who declare themselves "retired" are normally omitted from models of economic activity. Retirement is often regarded as a sort of natural state that requires no explanation. Early retirement, however, is frequently a consequence of disability and/or the lack of labor market opportunity—a form of hidden labor market dropout. To avoid missing the determinants of this dropout, we included the working-age retired population in our analyses.

Social Networks and Social Resources

Recent studies on immigration have shown that social networks can be key to overcoming employment barriers such as poor English language ability and unfamiliarity with American culture (Massey et al. 1987; Portes and Bach 1985). The social structure of migration, in particular, is thought to create strong networks that facilitate economic actions like finding a job or founding small businesses (Granovetter 1995). These networks also engender obligations that reinforce pressures to comply with employers' wishes. At the same time that networks help locate opportunities for some workers, they are simultaneously cutting off opportunities for others (Waldinger 1996). Further, pervasive social segregation in the United States virtually guarantees that individuals' personal networks will be racially segregated, thus potentially cutting minorities off from opportunities that whites know about and may share information about among themselves (Braddock and McPartland 1987). In some cases, however, it is difficult to distinguish between the linking (and excluding) effects of networks and the discriminatory practices of employers, as when African Americans live right next to concentrations of jobs for which they are not normally considered or even informed about (Ellwood 1986; Kasinitz and Rosenberg 1996).

Having employed persons in one's social network may aid employment chances by providing information about job opportunities and exercising influence on behalf of the job seeker. Wilson (1987), however, sees employed members of a personal network more as enforcers of "mainstream" norms of appropriate behavior than as resources. Conversely, social ties with persons who have dropped out of the labor market and are depending on public assistance weaken the pressure to comply with mainstream norms while providing alternative role models. Likewise, participation in formal or volunteer organizations, such as churches, sports clubs, ethnic organizations (Massey et al. 1987), and so on are thought both to provide access to contacts and resources and to enforce mainstream values. Therefore we hypothesize that having working persons in one's network will increase the likelihood of labor force participation, as will participation in organizations. Having persons receiving public assistance in one's network, net of other factors, will, conversely, tend to increase the likelihood of joblessness and nonparticipation.

Both norms and resources are also at the core of our final hypotheses. Wilson (1987, 1991) has argued that with industrial relocation from inner cities to suburban (or more distant) areas (Kasarda 1989), the inner-city neighborhoods where many African Americans live have become jobless, and hence have become concentrated poverty neighborhoods. This trend has been reinforced by an out-migration of the middle class and stable working class. The residents of concentrated poverty neighborhoods suffer social isolation; they are surrounded by dysfunctional behaviors and divorced from mainstream institutions. The argument is not that many people in high poverty areas are jobless, which may be true, but that the context itself contributes to the problem, apart from the characteristics of the individuals living in the neighborhood. Poverty and high joblessness contribute to even higher poverty and joblessness (Wilson 1996).

Some scholars have suggested that social isolation can be alleviated in part through "mediating institutions" (Johnson and Oliver 1990), including neighborhood organizations, and through strong neighborhood-based social networks (Sampson and Groves 1989). Taking this into account, we hypothesize that neighborhood poverty should have an increasingly negative effect on labor force participation and encourage long-term joblessness.[5] Some neighborhoods are very poor, despite a high level of labor force engagement. If, as Wilson and others indicate, it is the concentration of many jobless adults that leads others to disengage from the labor market, then we should expect an independent negative effect from neighborhood joblessness. Finally, we hypothesize that the presence of mediating institutions in the neighborhood has an independent positive effect on the likelihood that residents will be in the labor force.

Data and Methods
Data Sources

The Los Angeles Study of Urban Inequality presents a unique combination of individual-level and neighborhood-level data with which we can make observations about the relationship between contextual effects and personal characteristics (including network ties). Aggregate data about the neighborhood context are drawn from the Summary Tape Files 3A of the 1990 U.S. Census of Population. Other tract-level measures, as described herein, were constructed by taking means of LASUI variables by census tract.

For several reasons, LASUI is more suitable to our purposes than more widely available surveys such as the U.S. Census or the Census Bureau's Current Population Survey (CPS). The census sample is much larger than ours is—including nearly 350,000 adults in Los Angeles County alone—but its labor market information is fairly limited, with little beyond employment status and wages. The CPS, on the other hand, gathers a larger array of labor market information than LASUI provides, and its 100,000 households nationally yields a Los Angeles–area sample similar in size to LASUI (4,068 adults in March 1994). The CPS is designed, however, so that subpopulations appear in the survey with roughly the same frequency as they appear in the general population. This means that the CPS in Los Angeles would include perhaps forty African Americans, forty Asians, and only a handful of people living in high poverty areas. The LASUI sample, in contrast, was designed so that there would be ample numbers of whites, Latinos, African Americans, and Asians, as well as large numbers of people living in moderate and high poverty areas. This means that LASUI is better suited for intergroup comparisons and for examining the effects of living in concentrated poverty areas. LASUI also contains much information not available in the CPS, such as network characteristics and links to geographical areas.[6]

LASUI's advantages do not come without cost. The sample comes from a complex stratified and clustered design. This means that our respondents came from a relatively limited set of areas in Los Angeles County—just ninety-eight tracts out of over one thousand. Picking census tracts at random from all over Los Angeles County would have given us substantially less variation in race, poverty levels, and other variables of interest. By aiming to increase variation, our clustered design has the unfortunate side effect of effectively increasing the variance around our statistical estimates, meaning that they are less precise than they would be if LASUI actually had come from a simple random sample. We have attempted to compensate properly for this loss of efficiency in regression estimates by using specialized statistical procedures.[7]

Population

We have chosen to focus on less-educated, working-age men in this chapter. "Less-educated" includes only those with no schooling beyond high school. Among the less-educated are those with no formal schooling at all, those who dropped out of high school (including those who successfully completed the General Educational Development exam, also known as the Graduate Equivalency Diploma), and those with diplomas who have not attended college. "Working age" starts at age twenty-one, when young people are expected to be "settling in" (Osterman 1980) to their future careers, and goes up to age sixty-five, the retirement age officially recognized by the Social Security Administration. The decision to consider only men is regrettable, but we feel justified by the significant differences in men's and women's labor market experiences and our desire to tell a coherent story. By looking primarily at the less-educated, we hold relatively constant what is thought to be one of the most important determinants of labor market success. By excluding the youngest and oldest workers we can also, for the most part, avoid the complexity of the school-to-work transition and the onset of mandatory retirement.

The less-educated men in our sample are broken down by race and nativity into five groups: native-born whites, native-born blacks, foreign-born Asians, native-born Latinos, and foreign-born Latinos. Note that LASUI targeted three Asian groups—Chinese, Japanese, and Koreans—to the exclusion of other Asian nationalities, so that the Asian subsample is not entirely representative of that population.[8]

Variables and Multivariate Analysis

In order to evaluate the hypotheses presented here, we chose to conduct a series of multivariate analyses with two different outcome variables: labor force participation and long-term joblessness. These are both binary ("yes" or "no") outcome variables, so the multivariate analysis was conducted using logistic regression, the most appropriate method. In logistic regression, the computed parameters are reported in either log odds or simple (antilogged) odds, neither of which is easily interpretable. We chose to report only in log odds, which has some intuitive advantages over simple odds. First, if a parameter expressed in log odds is negative, then the corresponding variable is negatively associated with the outcome variable. The opposite is also true. Second, a larger number means a larger effect, just as one might expect.

For each dependent variable, we computed a baseline model, including only demographic or human capital variables, and three additional models that included, respectively, barriers to employment, social ties or activities, and neighborhood characteristics. This allowed a contrast among the sets of variables that helped us evaluate our hypotheses.

The independent variables in the regressions were defined as follows. Men who reported a health problem that affected their ability to work were coded as having a Disability. Men who reported having been in reform school, jail, or prison were coded as having Criminal Justice Involvement. Respondents were asked whether they belonged to any of seven different types of organizations. For each person, Organizational Memberships represents the number of "yes" answers. Respondents were also asked to name up to three people "other than people living in your household, with whom you discussed matters important to you" during the past six months. If any of the people named were presently employed, it was noted that the respondent Has Working Ties. The variable Has Ties Receiving Public Assistance was created in the same way.

The neighborhood-level variable Organizational Density, which we use as a measure of the presence of mediating institutions, was constructed from the Organizational Memberships of all surveyed persons in the neighborhood and refers to the average number of organizational memberships held by persons in the neighborhood—including all adults, not just less-educated men.

The Labor Market Status and Characteristics of Less-Educated Men

The first step in our analysis is to examine the bivariate relationships between neighborhood poverty level, on one hand, and employment and long-term labor market dropout, on the other. The poverty level categories we use are somewhat arbitrary—low poverty areas are those where the proportion of families in poverty range from 0 to 19 percent, moderate poverty ranges from 20 to 39 percent, and high poverty is 40 percent and beyond.[9] Table 5.2 shows raw differences in employment by neighborhood, revealing an interesting pattern, or lack thereof. For whites, employment plummets drastically with increased neighborhood poverty. On average, blacks are much less likely to be employed than others, but though there is a large drop in employment between moderate and high poverty neighborhoods, there is no real difference in employment between low and moderate poverty neighborhoods. Asians seem to be following a pattern similar to whites, although a lack of data on high poverty areas makes it difficult to be certain. Finally, Latinos appear to be only very mildly impacted by neighborhood poverty, at least in their propensity to be employed.

All but the most disadvantaged whites in Los Angeles can usually avoid high poverty neighborhoods, which are mostly majority Latino or black. That whites who are found in high poverty neighborhoods do especially poorly is likely a result of the unusual circumstances that left them living there. For minorities, however, and especially for African

TABLE 5.2   *Employment Rate of Less-Educated Men, by Race and Neighborhood Poverty Rate*

	Low Poverty	Moderate Poverty	High Poverty
White	85%	23%	16%
	(44)	(24)	(8)
African American	54%	56%	34%
	(46)	(66)	(50)
Asian American	91%	75%	—
	(66)	(43)	—
Chicano-Latino	87%	80%	80%
	(111)	(132)	(128)

Source: Los Angeles Study of Urban Inequality 1994.
Note: Actual N in parentheses. Rate is number of employed men divided by total number of men. Less-educated men are males aged twenty-one to sixty-four with no education beyond high school.

Americans, discriminatory housing practices (discussed at length elsewhere in this volume) limit residential choice. If African Americans have fewer neighborhood choices than whites, and if more African Americans are poor, then we would expect African Americans to be more similar across neighborhood types than is the case for whites. This is what we see. Latinos, however, show even less variation in employment behavior than blacks across neighborhood types. This is at least partly explicable in terms of the notion that most immigrants see themselves as only temporary residents, dedicated to reaching a specific monetary goal before returning home. This orientation not only restricts the amount of money spent on housing—making residence in a poor neighborhood more likely—it limits the kinds of investments in work that would make upward mobility more likely (see, for example, Piore 1979).

Interestingly, patterns of long-term labor market dropout, as seen in table 5.3, are not entirely the inverse of employment patterns. While things do look much the same for whites, for whom almost all high poverty residents are dropouts, blacks are *more* likely to be dropouts in low poverty (35 percent) than in high poverty (20 percent) neighborhoods.[10] Asians again parallel whites, while Latinos, in contrast to the case with employment, show consistent (if not statistically significant) deterioration as poverty levels increase.

Will these patterns hold when we adjust for the characteristics of each group of less-educated men? One place to look is age: are less-educated blacks on average older than the other groups? We would suspect so, since education levels among natives, both black and white,

231

TABLE 5.3   *Labor Market Dropout Rate and Neighborhood Poverty Rate for Less-Educated Men*

	Low Poverty	Moderate Poverty	High Poverty
White	3%	13%	84%
	(44)	(24)	(8)
African American	35%	27%	20%
	(46)	(65)	(50)
Asian American	6%	13%	—
	(66)	(43)	—
Chicano-Latino	2%	4%	7%
	(111)	(132)	(128)

Source: Los Angeles Study of Urban Inequality 1994.
Note: Actual N in parentheses. Rate is number of men who have not been employed in five years divided by total number of men. Less-educated men are males aged twenty-one to sixty-four with no education beyond high school.

have improved significantly over the past few decades. Whites, however, are the oldest group on average, at 39.4 years old (see table 5.4), and the largest proportion in the 50-and-over age group is also among whites. Blacks are next, with an average age of 38.6, followed by Asians at 37 and foreign-born Latinos at 35.8. Over 40 percent of the Latinos are in the age group 21 to 29.

Among the least educated, whites and African Americans have very similar human capital and other background characteristics (see table 5.4). Not only do few of either group have less than a high school diploma, but both groups are surprisingly high in their incidence of disability and criminal justice system involvement. Latinos are next highest in incidence of disability, at only half as much. African Americans are by far the most likely to have close network ties receiving public assistance, and (also shown in the table) they live in neighborhoods with the highest levels of joblessness, but foreign-born Latinos live in neighborhoods with the highest levels of poverty, on average. Human capital seems to favor whites and blacks, while disability and criminal history plague both groups. Surprisingly, our network measures appear to favor natives over the foreign-born, with relatively few of the foreign-born reporting working ties. This may indicate that the foreign-born have looser network structures than natives, which is unlikely, or that they were more reluctant to tell us about their ties. Neighborhood quality appears to favor whites, who live in areas with the highest levels of organizational activity and the lowest levels of poverty and joblessness.

TABLE 5.4   *Means on Dependent and Independent Variables for Less-Educated Men, Individual Characteristics Only, Weighted*

	White Native-Born	Black Native-Born	Asian Foreign-Born	Latino Native-Born	Latino Foreign-Born
Employment					
Percentage employed	69%	53%	87%	68%	82%
	(0.10)	(0.08)	(0.04)	(0.12)	(0.03)
Percentage unemployed	16%	13%	3%	15%	5%
	(0.10)	(0.06)	(0.01)	(0.04)	(0.01)
Percentage not in labor force	15%	34%	10%	18%	13%
	(0.05)	(0.07)	(0.03)	(0.12)	(0.03)
Percentage in labor force	85%	66%	90%	82%	87%
	(0.05)	(0.07)	(0.03)	(0.12)	(0.03)
Worked in past five years	96%	68%	93%	98%	97%
	(0.02)	(0.08)	(0.04)	(0.01)	(0.01)
Education					
Zero to six years of school	2%	1%	7%	0%	35%
	(0.02)	(0.01)	(0.03)	(0.00)	(0.03)
Seven to eleven years of school	16%	15%	31%	17%	38%
	(0.06)	(0.04)	(0.15)	(0.06)	(0.03)
Twelve years of school	82%	84%	62%	83%	26%
	(0.06)	(0.04)	(0.14)	(0.06)	(0.03)
Demographics					
Age	39.4	38.6	37.0	34.0	35.8
	(1.70)	(2.15)	(3.32)	(2.27)	(0.59)
Married	51%	45%	64%	47%	62%
	(0.08)	(0.07)	(0.15)	(0.09)	(0.03)
Barriers					
Disability	22%	26%	5%	7%	12%
	(0.07)	(0.07)	(0.03)	(0.05)	(0.03)
Criminal justice involvement	30%	37%	0%	12%	10%
	(0.08)	(0.07)	(0.00)	(0.05)	(0.04)
Networks					
Organizational memberships	0.7	0.8	0.3	0.8	0.7
	(0.13)	(0.16)	(0.20)	(0.29)	(0.10)
Has working ties	73%	58%	11%	50%	50%
	(0.09)	(0.08)	(0.04)	(0.10)	(0.04)
Has ties receiving public assistance	10%	20%	1%	6%	4%
	(0.06)	(0.06)	(0.01)	(0.04)	(0.01)

(Table continues on p. 234.)

TABLE 5.4   *Continued*

	White Native-Born	Black Native-Born	Asian Foreign-Born	Latino Native-Born	Latino Foreign-Born
Neighborhood					
Organizational density	1.3	1.2	1.0	1.0	0.9
	(0.13)	(0.10)	(0.16)	(0.20)	(0.07)
Percentage in poverty	10.0	17.0	19.5	13.3	23.3
	(1.20)	(1.69)	(2.27)	(2.33)	(1.09)
Percentage not working	33.7	41.5	40.5	38.5	40.9
	(1.16)	(1.65)	(0.73)	(1.55)	(0.79)
Actual N	70	157	99	45	324
	10%	23%	14%	6%	47%
Weighted N	104	72	30	96	443
	14%	10%	4%	13%	59%

Source: Los Angeles Study of Urban Inequality 1994.
Note: Standard errors in parentheses. Less-educated men are males aged twenty-one to sixty-four with no education beyond high school.

Characteristics of Labor Force Dropouts

We have been discussing factors that might predispose group members to become labor force dropouts. We have not, however, discussed the characteristics of labor market dropouts themselves in any detail. Who are they? Of the less-educated men in our sample, dropouts are on average significantly older (forty-six versus thirty-six years), significantly more likely to have a criminal record (37 percent versus 14 percent), and vastly more likely to report some sort of work-limiting disability (56 percent versus 11 percent). They are also much more likely to report being retired (26 percent versus 2 percent), which is at least partly related to their greater age. Furthermore, 16 percent of those who have not worked in the past five years have never worked at all, and 3 percent are immigrants who have never worked in the United States. The vast majority have worked before, but less than half (41 percent) had worked through almost all the years since leaving school,[11] although another fifth reported having worked about three-quarters of that time. Four out of ten dropouts, then, have worked no more than half the time since they left school. This compares poorly with nondropouts, 78 percent of whom say that they have worked all of their adult lives.

When race is not taken into account, there is little difference in the propensity of dropouts to live in high versus moderate or low poverty tracts (a one way ANOVA and a Bonferroni multiple means comparison do not show any significant differences).

A legitimate concern may well be surfacing at this point: if dropouts are essentially the retired, the disabled, and the criminally active, does this analysis truly capture any significant labor market dynamics? We think so, but only if we conceive of labor market dynamics more broadly than is usual. The disabled, the prematurely retired, and those with criminal records are important segments of each group's potential workforce. That these statuses are not evenly spread across groups is partly a result of where each group fits into the larger economic structure. Disability can be a *result* of work, and it can also result from material deprivation. Furthermore, as we mentioned initially, we are focusing on long-term labor force dropouts because they are an extreme example of weak labor force attachment. Our presumption (which admittedly may not be correct) is that this extreme example should reveal most clearly what the "pressure points" are that lead to weak labor force attachment. If neighborhood context does not show up as an important cause here, it seems unlikely that it will be important in less serious problems. Our multivariate analysis should help clarify this question.

Multivariate Analysis

Our first logistic regression (see table 5.5) shows how neighborhood and other factors affect labor force participation. The model with human capital and demographic variables alone is not compelling. Having a sixth-grade education or less is a significant impediment, as is increasing age, while being married is associated with greater participation. In the second model, we add the barriers of disability and criminal justice system involvement. Disability does prove to be a major barrier, but crime apparently does not. Strikingly, being African American becomes more strongly negative and attains statistical significance in this model. Because whites are the reference group in this regression, and since whites share high levels of disability and crime with blacks, once those variables are controlled for the racial differences are able to come through more clearly. The addition of these two variables almost doubles the proportion of variance accounted for (from a reduction in log likelihood of 18 percent to a reduction of 33 percent).

In contrast, when we introduce our network variables in the next model, very little additional explanatory power is added. When we add neighborhood variables in the final model, the effect of the network variables essentially disappears. In its place, we find that increases in organizational density positively affect labor force participation, as, rather unexpectedly, does the poverty level of the tract. All else being

235

TABLE 5.5   Probability of Labor Force Participation for Less-Educated Men in Los Angeles County, 1993 to 1994

Variables	b	Standard Error	b	Standard Error	b	Standard Error	b	Standard Error
Demographic or human capital								
Black, native-born	-0.99	(0.52)	-1.21	(0.48)*	-1.47	(0.46)**	-1.75	(0.58)**
Asian, foreign-born	0.33	(0.67)	-0.34	(0.60)	-0.14	(0.72)	-0.30	(0.76)
Latino, native-born	-0.39	(1.11)	-1.11	(1.15)	-1.28	(1.36)	-1.07	(1.12)
Latino, foreign-born	0.52	(0.60)	-0.16	(0.54)	-0.36	(0.60)	-0.59	(0.78)
Zero to six years of education	-1.48	(0.47)**	-0.83	(0.48)	-0.43	(0.53)	-0.33	(0.54)
Seven to eleven years of education	0.06	(0.38)	0.08	(0.43)	0.14	(0.42)	-0.04	(0.46)
Age	0.18	(0.10)	0.30	(0.12)*	0.28	(0.12)*	0.28	(0.11)*
Age squared	0.00	(0.00)*	0.00	(0.00)**	0.00	(0.00)**	0.00	(0.00)**
Married	1.33	(0.40)**	1.10	(0.45)*	0.85	(0.50)	0.96	(0.55)
Barriers								
Disability			-2.71	(0.49)***	-2.95	(0.54)***	-3.29	(0.61)***
Criminal justice involvement			-0.28	(0.53)	-0.34	(0.53)	-0.13	(0.67)
Social ties or activities								
Organizational memberships					0.53	(0.27)*	0.34	(0.27)
Has working ties					0.55	(0.73)	0.91	(0.52)
Has ties receiving welfare					-0.06	(0.46)	-0.30	(0.46)
Neighborhood characteristics								
Organizational density							1.56	(0.45)**
Percentage in poverty							0.16	(0.05)**
Percentage in poverty, squared							0.00	(0.00)***
Percentage not working							0.01	(0.03)
Model								
Constant	-1.08	(1.81)	-2.36	(2.06)	-2.13	(2.26)	-5.15	(2.44)*
Pseudo R²	0.18	(N = 695)	0.33	(N = 692)	0.36	(N = 692)	0.40	(N = 692)

Source: Los Angeles Study of Urban Inequality 1994.
Note: Less-educated men are males aged twenty-one to sixty-four with no education beyond high school.
*p < .005; **p < 0.01; ***p < 0.001

equal, our model predicts that individuals are *more* likely to be in the labor force in higher poverty areas, up to a point. This is not easy to explain, but it does seem to contradict Wilson's model. We will return to this question after exploring the second regression. We should also note that there is a significant negative differential for African Americans in all but the first model, indicating that none of the included variables are able to adequately explain their low participation rates.

In summary, then, we see that human capital differences among less-educated men do little to distinguish them relative to labor force participation, but that disability status makes quite a large difference. Despite the high level of disability among African Americans, there is still a large unexplained racial residual. And neighborhood matters, but not entirely in the way we might have expected.

With the second logistic regression, we go on to see whether the factors that contribute to or impede labor market participation are the same as the factors that lead to long-term joblessness. We know from tables 5.1 and 5.4 that African Americans are overrepresented among those who have not worked in the past five years, so it is no surprise that, as in the labor force participation regressions, the coefficients for African Americans are large, negative, and significant (see table 5.6). Aside from the race variable, the human capital and demographic variables appear to contribute little. In contrast to the case for labor force participation, criminal justice system involvement does play a significant negative role in each of the models that it appears in here. Another contrast is that the social network variables here play their expected roles and are statistically significant. In the final model of the series, we see that the neighborhood coefficients look almost identical to those in the labor force participation model. The upshot is that human capital—relative to other less-educated men only—plays almost no role in determining long-term joblessness. Disability and prior involvement with the criminal justice system are important barriers to work, and contribute more to our understanding of long-term joblessness than do network or neighborhood variables. On the other hand, social networks do appear to play a positive role, as do the level of neighborhood organization and, perversely, the poverty level of the neighborhood.

Discussion

The relatively high employment rates of very poorly educated Latino immigrants have suggested to a number of scholars that something other than human capital must explain the relatively poor labor market performance of native minorities. Some have extolled the virtues of social networks, which they argue are much stronger and pervasive among

TABLE 5.6   Probability of Having Worked in Past Five Years for Less-Educated Men in Los Angeles County, 1993 to 1994

Variables	b	Standard Error	b	Standard Error	b	Standard Error	b	Standard Error
Demographic or human capital								
Black, native-born	-2.85	(0.61)***	-2.96	(0.78)***	-3.24	(0.86)***	-3.77	(1.00)***
Asian, foreign-born	-1.03	(0.72)	-1.99	(0.93)*	-1.72	(1.03)	-2.18	(0.99)*
Latino, native-born	0.36	(1.10)	-0.23	(1.20)	-0.25	(1.45)	-0.42	(1.25)
Latino, foreign-born	0.13	(0.72)	-0.62	(1.05)	-0.91	(1.11)	-1.31	(1.13)
Zero–six years of education	-1.01	(0.81)	-0.42	(1.07)	0.03	(1.08)	0.29	(1.11)
Seven–eleven years of education	-0.32	(0.53)	0.00	(0.72)	-0.11	(0.74)	-0.38	(0.75)
Age	0.19	(0.12)	0.39	(0.13)**	0.37	(0.13)**	0.37	(0.12)**
Age squared	0.00	(0.00)*	-0.01	(0.00)***	-0.01	(0.00)***	-0.01	(0.00)***
Married	0.28	(0.48)	0.26	(0.47)	-0.14	(0.50)	0.08	(0.45)
Barriers								
Disability			-1.89	(0.52)***	-1.95	(0.62)**	-2.24	(0.64)***
Criminal justice involvement			-1.46	(0.51)**	-1.38	(0.56)*	-1.14	(0.52)*
Social ties or activities								
Organizational memberships					0.65	(0.26)*	0.60	(0.28)*
Has Working Ties					1.37	(0.53)*	1.50	(0.53)**
Has ties receiving welfare					-1.67	(0.61)**	-2.02	(0.63)**
Neighborhood characteristics								
Organizational density							1.60	(0.50)**
Percentage in poverty							0.20	(0.06)**
Percentage in poverty, squared							0.00	(0.00)***
Percentage not working							0.02	(0.03)
Model								
Constant	1.32	(2.37)	-1.39	(2.89)	-1.10	(2.98)	-4.45	(2.90)
Pseudo R²	0.28	(N = 695)	0.38	(N = 692)	0.44	(N = 692)	0.49	(N = 692)

Source: Los Angeles Study of Urban Inequality 1994.
Note: Less-educated men are males aged twenty-one to sixty-four with no education beyond high school. Logistic regression.
*p < 0.05; **p < 0.01; ***p < 0.001.

immigrants than among natives. While we may well have missed important aspects of network quality and extent in our data collection, there is little here to indicate either that immigrants have superior networks or that networks make *the* difference in labor force participation and long-term joblessness. Others have argued that the differences are accounted for by unmeasured cognitive skills, a dysfunctional culture, poor motivation, or unreasonable expectations. We cannot address these contentions directly except to say that native-born African Americans are much more integrated into American society and have greater fluency in English, in reading and writing as well as speaking, than the great bulk of Latino or Asian immigrants. The strength of the African American variables in our regressions is not necessarily inconsistent with these other explanations, but we think that the cumulative effects of discrimination are more likely.

We believe that the positive direction of the tract poverty variable is an important finding. Roberto Fernandez and David Harris (1992) were unable to find much in the way of significant impacts on men from tract poverty (although they did find significant negative effects on women), but they were hindered by a sample design that did not include low poverty areas. We have both individual-level and contextual data and have found a small but positive effect of tract poverty on employment. To be sure, this effect decays as poverty increases (due to the squared term), so that labor force participation increases and joblessness decreases most in areas with moderate levels of poverty, and the areas with the very highest levels of poverty do affect residents negatively. Our interpretation is that there are relatively few opportunities for less-educated men in more affluent areas. Working-class men there are likely to be denied access to the organizational and network resources that middle-class residents share among themselves. This is especially true where residents are divided by race.

Finally, not only do African Americans disproportionately suffer from the two problems that most strongly handicap less-educated men—disability and criminal justice system involvement—but, controlling for other factors, only African Americans consistently do significantly worse than whites in labor force participation and long-term joblessness. This appears to be most consistent with radical claims that blacks have largely been consigned the role of excess labor (Marable 1983) not because of a lack of skills, but because they are black. This is a depressing finding, but it does fit the contemporary situation better than attempts to explain away poor labor market performance by black men as the result of impersonal shifts in the economy, or of dysfunctional ghetto culture.

Conclusion

Long-term joblessness is increasing among men, especially less-educated men. It has historically been highest among African American men, so that in Los Angeles in 1990, more than one-fifth of African American men who had no education beyond high school had been jobless for at least five years. This is more than two and a half times the rate among whites. Long-term joblessness among men is more pronounced in Los Angeles than in the nation as a whole. Long-term joblessness is an extreme form of the weak labor force attachment thought to characterize the urban underclass.

Most of the long-term jobless among the less-educated do not fit their "shiftless" image (Tienda and Stier 1991). The majority have worked most of their lives and have physical disabilities that limit their capacity to hold jobs. Nearly 60 percent are over the age of fifty, at a point in their careers where employers are increasingly reluctant to hire them because of their age. One-quarter are under the age of thirty, struggling to launch their work lives. When the long-term jobless are compared with other less-educated men using logistic regression, though one consistent finding stands out: African American men are a good deal more likely than whites and others to be among the long-term jobless. Being disabled, having a criminal record, and having network ties who receive welfare all make labor market dropout significantly more likely. Because African Americans are disproportionately likely to be disabled, to have a criminal record, or to have welfare recipients in their personal networks, they are doubly disadvantaged.

Consistent with Wilson's theory, the highest levels of concentrated poverty do encourage detachment from the labor market, all else being equal. Neighborhoods with extremely high levels of poverty are rare, however. In more commonplace neighborhoods, increasing poverty is associated with decreasing levels of labor market dropout. Whether the neighborhood has high or moderate levels of poverty, the effect of neighborhood context is weak. This suggests that *race* is the key, not space (or at least not this particular aspect of space).

Also consistent with Wilson's conception of the "institutional ghetto" and Robert Putnam's conceptualization of social capital, neighborhoods with higher institutional density (measured by the organizational memberships of surveyed residents) are associated with higher likelihood of employment and lower likelihood of long-term joblessness.

The upshot is that for reasons other than their personal characteristics or where they live, African Americans are more likely than others to drop out of the labor force for long periods of time.[12] This is consistent with the possibility that blacks are being squeezed out of the labor market by whites and Asians from "above" and Latino immigrants from "below," and inconsistent with the notion that less-educated workers all suffer equally in an environment of increasing skill requirements. Putting less-educated African Americans on an equal footing with others calls for efforts to build up trust between employers and black workers. If skill is not the most important factor keeping black men from finding and holding jobs, then just adding skills, through vocational programs, for example, is not likely to solve the problem.

Appendix: Questions from LASUI
Criminal History and Disability

Have you ever been in reform school, a detention center, jail, or prison?

1 YES
5 NO

Does your health or general condition limit the kind or amount of work you can do?

1 YES
5 NO

Social Networks

Now we have some questions about your social relationships and neighborhood activities.

From time to time, most people discuss important matters with other people. Looking back over the last six months—who are the people, other than people living in your household, with whom you discussed matters important to you?

Just tell me their first names or initials and how you know them.

If less than 3, probe: Anyone else? Only record first 3 names. Probe for sex and relationship—whether friend, relative, coworker, etc.

Enter "X" here if respondent mentions no one. Enter "C" to continue

Person 1:

1 MALE
2 FEMALE

Person 1:

1   Relative
2   Friend
3   Coworker
4   Other (specify)

[Repeat for Person 2 and Person 3]

Person 1:

Is married?

1   YES
5   NO

Person 1:

Lives in your neighborhood?

1   YES
5   NO

Person 1:

Is someone who during the past month you helped do everyday things like giving them a ride somewhere, lending them a little money, or running errands?

1   YES
5   NO

Person 1:

Is someone who you could count on for help in a major crisis, such as a serious illness or if you needed a place to stay?

1   YES
5   NO

Person 1:

Has a steady job?

1   YES
5   NO

Person 1:

Is receiving public aid or welfare?

1 YES
5 NO

[Repeat for Person 2 and Person 3]

Person 1:

1 Less than high school
2 Some high school
3 High school graduate
4 Technical or trade school
5 Some college
6 College graduate

[Repeat for Person 2 and Person 3]

Person 1:

1 White; Non-Hispanic
2 Black/African American
3 Hispanic
4 Asian
5 Other; (specify)

[Repeat for Person 2 and Person 3]

Now we would like to know something about the groups and organizations to which you belong. I will read a list of different types of organizations. Please tell me if you attended one or more of their meetings in the last twelve months.

1 YES
5 NO

Neighborhood or tenants' group or block association

PTA or school-related groups

Social clubs or sports teams

Political organizations

Business or professional organizations

Church related groups

Ethnic or cultural organizations

Notes

1. Although Roberto Fernandez and David Harris (1992) have in fact done something similar using data from Wilson's project in Chicago. Marta Tienda and Haya Stier (1991) conduct a rather different analysis, but with similar primary interests. They argue that only a vanishingly small fraction of the inner-city parents in their sample qualify as "shiftless," with most of the long-term jobless falling into the categories of "constrained" or "discouraged." We are less interested in determining whether the long-term jobless have an "excuse," though, than in understanding who becomes a long-term jobless person and why.

2. Or to the minimum wage, which, theoretically, artificially requires that low-quality workers be paid more than they are worth to employers.

3. For an interesting counterargument, see Stephen Petterson (1997). His contention is that what surveys measure when they collect data on reservation wages is what respondents think they ought to be worth, rather than the minimum they would truly accept for a job. While his data show that some blacks do have high reservation wages compared to what they are likely to earn, he also finds that those earning the lowest wages are those whose wage aspirations are most inflated relative to reality, and yet that this inflation is extremely modest.

4. Conversely, it has been argued that a criminal record in itself is not a barrier, but instead that it is associated with unacceptable behaviors that retard career progress.

5. It is important to note that if unemployment levels (or long-term joblessness levels) rise with increasing poverty, this does not in itself support the idea that the concentration of poverty has an independent effect on the outcomes of residents. Since joblessness can lead to poverty, it is only to be expected that high-poverty areas have many jobless people. High-poverty areas are also likely to have many people whose human capital and other characteristics are associated with negative outcomes. In this chapter, a neighborhood effect would be one that affects the likelihood of labor force participation or dropout *after* controlling for individual-level characteristics.

6. Also note that the LASUI questions about current employment status are different from those used by the census and CPS. We constructed what we feel to be a comparable measure, but some deviation from census and CPS figures is to be expected.

7. All LASUI-based tabulations and analyses were conducted using Stata™ (StataCorp 1997) statistical software. Huber/White corrections were used to adjust for geographical clustering of observations.

8. Filipinos, in particular, the second largest Asian origin group and quite distinctive from the East Asians, were not included. Southeast Asians, who are in general the least well educated of the Asian groups, are also omitted. Some men of Southeast Asian birth are represented among our sample, however: 23 of the 109 Asian men included reported being ethnic Chinese born in Vietnam, Cambodia, or Thailand.

9. It has been argued that areas with poverty levels of 40 percent and above "look like" underclass neighborhoods (see Bane and Jargowsky 1988).

10. The differences are not statistically significant, as determined by a Bonferroni multiple comparison test, but even the lack of significant differences is contrary to expectation.

11. Note that we are not counting those who have not been out of school for at least sixteen months.

12. The nature of the local postindustrial economy, with its emphasis on flexibility, (see, for example, Harrison 1994; Smith 1994) must be at least partly to blame. It might be helpful for future researchers to try to isolate those aspects of the local economy that make the situation worse for African Americans and others.

References

Arrow, Kenneth J. 1973. "The Theory of Discrimination." In *Discrimination in Labor Markets*, edited by O. Ashenfelter and A. Rees. Princeton, N.J.: Princeton University Press.

Bane, Mary Jo, and Paul A. Jargowsky. 1988. "Urban Poverty Areas: Basic Questions Concerning Prevalence, Growth, and Dynamics." In *Urban Change and Poverty*, edited by M. G. H. McGeary and L. E. Lynn, Jr. Washington, D.C.: National Academy Press.

Becker, Gary. 1957. *The Economics of Discrimination.* Chicago: University of Chicago Press.

Bobo, Lawrence, Eve Fielder, David Grant, James H. Johnson Jr., and Melvin L. Oliver. 1995. "The Los Angeles Study of Urban Inequality: Sample Report on the Household Survey." Center for the Study of Urban Poverty Occasional Working Papers Series. Vol. 5, no. 2. UCLA.

Braddock, Jomills Henry, II, and James M. McPartland. 1987. "How Minorities Continue to Be Excluded from Equal Employment Opportunities: Research on Labor Market and Institutional Barriers." *Journal of Social Issues* 43: 5–39.

Doeringer, Peter B., and U.S. Department of Labor Manpower Administration. 1972. "Low-Income Labor Markets and Urban Manpower Programs: A Critical Assessment." U.S. Department of Labor Manpower Administration, Research and Development Findings, no. 12. Washington: U.S. Department of Labor, Manpower Administration.

Ellwood, David. 1986. "The Spatial Mismatch Hypothesis: Are There Jobs Missing in the Ghetto?" In *The Black Youth Employment Crisis*, edited by R. B. Freeman and H. Holzer. Chicago: University of Chicago Press.

Fernandez, Roberto. 1992. "A Review of 'Why Black Men Are Doing Worse in the Labor Market.'" In *Conference on the Urban Underclass: Perspectives from the Social Sciences*. University of Michigan, Ann Arbor (June 8–10).

Fernandez, Roberto M., and David Harris. 1992. "Social Isolation and the Underclass." In *Drugs, Crime, and Social Isolation*, edited by A. V. Harrell and G. E. Peterson. Washington, D.C.: Urban Institute Press.

Granovetter, Mark. 1995. "The Economic Sociology of Firms and Entrepreneurs." In *The Economic Sociology of Immigration*, edited by A. Portes. New York: Russell Sage.

Harris, Ron. 1993. "Hand of Punishment Falls Heavily on Black Youths." *Los Angeles Times*, p. A1.

Harrison, Bennett. 1994. *Lean and Mean: The Changing Landscape of Corporate Power in the Age of Flexibility*. New York: Basic Books.

Holzer, Harry J. 1996. *What Employers Want: Job Prospects for Less-Educated Workers*. New York: Russell Sage.

Jencks, Christopher, and Susan E. Mayer. 1990. "Residential Segregation, Job Proximity, and Black Job Opportunities." In *Inner-City Poverty in the United States*, edited by L. E. Lynn, Jr., and M. G. H. McGeary. Washington, D.C.: National Academy Press.

Johnson, James H., Jr., and Melvin L. Oliver. 1990. "Modeling Urban Underclass Behavior: Theoretical Considerations." Occasional Working Paper Series. Vol. 1, no. 3. Los Angeles: UCLA Center for the Study of Urban Poverty.

Kasarda, John D. 1989. "Urban Industrial Transition and the Underclass." *Annals of the American Academy of Political and Social Science* 501: 26–47.

Kasinitz, Philip, and Jan Rosenberg. 1996. "Missing the Connection: Social Isolation and Employment on the Brooklyn Waterfront." *Social Problems* 43: 180–96.

Marable, Manning. 1983. *How Capitalism Underdeveloped Black America*. Boston: South End Press.

Massey, Douglas, Rafael Alarcón, Jorge Durand, and Humberto González. 1987. *Return to Aztlan: The Social Process of Migration from Western Mexico.* Berkeley: University of California Press.

Oaxaca, Ronald. 1973. "Male-Female Wage Differentials in Urban Labor Markets." *International Economic Review* 14: 693–709.

Oi, Walter Y. 1992. "Work for Americans with Disabilities." *Annals of the American Academy of Political and Social Science* 523: 159–74.

Osterman, Paul. 1980. *Getting Started: The Youth Labor Market.* Cambridge, Mass.: MIT Press.

Petterson, Stephen M. 1997. "Are Young Black Men Really Less Willing to Work?" *American Sociological Review* 62: 605–704.

Phelps, Edwin S. 1972. "The Statistical Theory of Racism and Sexism." *American Economic Review* 62: 659–61.

Piore, Michael. 1979. *Birds of Passage.* New York: Cambridge University Press.

Portes, Alejandro, and Robert Bach. 1985. *Latin Journey.* Berkeley: University of California Press.

Putnam, Robert D. 1996. "The Strange Disappearance of Civic America." *American Prospect* 24: 34–48.

Reder, Melvin W. 1973. "Comment." In *Discrimination in Labor Markets,* edited by O. Ashenfelter and A. Rees. Princeton, N.J.: Princeton University Press.

Sampson, Robert J., and W. Byron Groves. 1989. "Community Structure and Crime: Testing Social-Disorganization Theory." *American Journal of Sociology* 94: 774–802.

Smith, Vicki. 1994. "Institutionalizing Flexibility in a Service Firm: Multiple Contingencies and Hidden Hierarchies." *Work and Occupations* 21:284–307.

StataCorp. 1997. "Stata Statistical Software: Release 5.0." College Station, Tex.: Stata Corporation.

Sullivan, Mercer L., ed. 1989. *"Getting Paid": Youth Crime and Work in the Inner City.* Ithaca, N.Y.: Cornell University Press.

Tienda, Marta. 1991. "Poor People and Poor Places: Deciphering Neighborhood Effects on Poverty Outcomes." In *Macro-Micro Linkages in Sociology,* edited by J. Huber. Newbury Park Calif.: Sage Publications.

Tienda, Marta, and Haya Stier. 1991. "Joblessness and Shiftlessness: Labor Force Activity in Chicago's Inner City." In *The Urban Underclass,* edited by C. Jencks and P. E. Peterson. Washington, D.C.: Brookings Institution.

U.S. Department of Labor. 1992. "Developing Employment Policies for Persons with Disabilities." *Monthly Labor Review* 115: 35–36.

Waldinger, Roger. 1996. "The Jobs Immigrants Take." *New York Times,* Op-Ed. March 11, 1996.

Wilson, William Julius. 1978. *The Declining Significance of Race.* Chicago: University of Chicago Press.

———. 1987. *The Truly Disadvantaged: The Inner City, the Underclass, and Public Policy.* Chicago: University of Chicago Press.

———. 1991. "Studying Inner City Dislocations: The Challenge of Public Agenda Research." *American Review of Sociology* 56: 1–14.

———. 1996. *When Work Disappears: The World of the New Urban Poor.* New York: Knopf.

6

Latino Earnings Inequality: Immigrant and Native-Born Differences

Abel Valenzuela Jr. and Elizabeth Gonzalez

L ATINOS, immigrants and nonimmigrants alike, have become a formidable presence in Los Angeles. They, at least the Mexican ethnic subgroup, have been part of the Los Angeles landscape since the city was only a small pueblo, founded in 1581. As the city grew, so did the Mexican and, by extension, the Latino population. Early in the city's history (post–1848),[1] Mexicans clearly became a large part of the segregated, poor, and working-class segment of Los Angeles. Numerous factors, including migration from the Union and international immigration, industrial change, and the political and economic dominance by whites, contributed to the unequal economic outcomes experienced by Latinos. Even though their numbers were small at the turn of the nineteenth century (Laslett 1996), Mexican growth continued almost unabated as they ebbed and flowed in response to political and economic opportunities in the United States and Mexico.[2] By 1965, through the repeal of the National Origins Act, immigration increased significantly, signaling an even larger flow of Mexican and Latino migrants to Los Angeles. Economically, Mexicans and Latinos continue to be relegated to the worst jobs and to occupy a low level in the earnings distributions and in a host of other socioeconomic indicators.

Contemporary Latinos in Los Angeles include recent and older immigrants and their children. There is also a formidable native-born population. As a result, one can think of two Latino Los Angeleses (Ortiz 1996):[3] immigrant (foreign-born) Latinos, who comprise approximately 54 percent of all Latinos, and nonimmigrant (native-born) Latinos. Latinos born in the United States are skewed toward preschool and school-aged children. Latinos born outside the country are likewise skewed toward children, but have a larger percentage of working-age adults (see chapter 2). Mexicans, the largest subgroup under the Latino catchall term, are the most heterogeneous when it comes to generational mix. Native-born Mexicans are primarily made up of the children of the foreign-born—the largest single group—and a relatively small population of second-, third-, and higher-generation adults (Ortiz 1996).

To understand Latino economic inequality means understanding at least two important factors: their incorporation or progress in the labor market and the role of nativity. Both allow us to assess to what extent Latinos have made progress into perhaps the most important institution that mediates economic equality: the labor market. When analyzing progress among Latinos, it is likewise important to assess differences according to factors that make any ethnic group heterogeneous (such as gender and age). For Latinos, nativity is especially important because such a large part of their total population, especially in Los Angeles, is foreign-born. These factors are not mutually exclusive. In fact, when analyzing progress of nearly any type, ignoring differences by nativity results in inaccurate readings.

This chapter analyzes one type of economic inequality in the contemporary Latino population of Los Angeles—earnings—and is centered on a single question: How different are the factors that determine labor market opportunities for Latino immigrants and nonimmigrants? If the factors are significantly different, the argument that immigrants are suppressing the wages of domestic workers may have some validity. If, for example, immigrants earn lower wages due to inadequate human capital investments and because they have been in the labor market for only a few years relative to their native-born counterparts, then they may depress wages by concentrating in low skill or secondary labor markets.[4] Besides human capital, other factors such as living in poor neighborhoods and discrimination in hiring can also negatively impact earnings accumulation. These other factors further complicate the issue of why some groups of workers differ in their earnings capacity. On the other hand, if there are no notable differences in the factors that determine earnings between Latino immigrants and nonimmigrants, then placing the blame on immigrants for poor labor market performance by African Americans and other minority groups misses the point; structural forces may be the real culprit. What is perhaps most important is investigating the factors that differentially impact immigrant and nonimmigrant earnings to identify policy prescriptions for improving their labor market outcomes.

Utilizing a unique data set, we control for conventional human capital and demographic variables and regress several novel independent variables that theory predicts should significantly influence earnings for Latina and Latino immigrants. The Los Angeles Survey of Urban Inequality provides information on a number of factors that should help us better understand the processes contributing to labor market inequality among Latino subgroups. These factors include immigration status, year of immigration, living in poverty-concentrated neighborhoods, and the use of social networks for labor market success.

These factors are important for reasons not exclusively related to immigration. For example, research on urban inequality addresses several underlying themes on why urban minority residents, mostly African Americans, fare poorly in America's largest cities and labor markets. One area of research concentrates on factors that induce or hamper the labor market opportunities of black and other minority workers. Some of the most influential factors that researchers have attempted to analyze include the role of social networks in obtaining a job (Portes and Bach 1985; Granovetter 1974) and the labor market effect of living in areas concentrated with poor and/or racially isolated residents (Wilson 1987; Massey and Eggers 1990). Different groups of workers are studied to determine how these factors differ for male and female workers, minority laborers, and younger and older workers. Few, if any, studies look at these variables for immigrant groups, especially within the context of labor market participation.

Related research on immigration and Latinos has looked at how group adaptation strategies via social networks and neighborhood settlement patterns influence how immigrants become incorporated into the local economy and community. For example, the role of social networks in assisting immigrant groups obtain a job or find housing is well documented (Massey 1986, 1987; Massey et al. 1987; Chavez 1988; Hondagneu-Sotelo 1994). However, we know little about the role that social networks play in obtaining a good or bad job as reflected by earnings, and whether reliance on informal incorporation strategies such as the latter, persist after the initial immigration generation or after substantial years in the United States.

Even less studied for immigrants and Latinos is the deleterious impact of living in concentrated poverty areas. As first proposed by Wilson (1987), subsequent studies show that residential segregation by race along with increased poverty rates for groups results in cycles of social and economic ills at the neighborhood level (Massey and Denton 1993). While, overall, Latinos (with the exception of Puerto Ricans) are less concentrated in poor and/or minority communities compared to African Americans (Massey and Eggers 1990), it is well documented that immigrants have historically relied on ethnic and immigrant enclave neighborhoods to provide a modicum of incorporation (Massey 1986). However, the role of immigration, especially in the 1980s, in explaining residential segregation and its impacts is only beginning to surface.

Recent analysis of 1990 census data suggest that with increases in immigration, particularly Latino immigration, come increases in Latino residential segregation (Frey and Farley 1993; Denton and Massey 1991). Many of these immigrant neighborhoods exhibit the same characteristics as do black communities, being poor and residentially segregated, but differ in terms of the "social pathology" outcomes described by Wilson (1987) and others. How these residential patterns influence labor market outcomes is important in and of itself. However, assessing how residential patterns influence labor market outcomes according to nativity is key to uncovering some of the emerging cleavages between Latino immigrants and nonimmigrants and, similarly, to highlighting the commonalities shared by these two subgroups.

Driving our study is an analysis that differentiates between Latino immigrants and nonimmigrants, which we argue is important for at least two other reasons. First, the immigration debate described earlier is often posed in an immigrant and nonimmigrant and legal-illegal dichotomy, when "immigration," especially in California, is often code for Latino. Separating Latino immigrants from nonimmigrants allows us to measure differences between the two and, more important, to make the distinction between Latinos who are born in the United States and those who immigrated. As concern over immigration and population growth in California and other immigrant-receiving regions escalates, myth should be driven from reality by empirical analysis. Second, it is far from clear whether Latino native-born groups are faring better than their foreign-born counterparts. As the policy debate on welfare reform and other social policies continues and immigrants and others are targeted for nonparticipation, it becomes crucial to assess labor market and other social cleavages between and among different groups. This leads us to our primary research question: Given what research says about the primary determinants of Latino earnings, do immigrant and native-born Latinos have similar returns to human capital, social networks, and space?

At the outset, we should make clear that an understanding of the social and economic outcomes of Latinos is difficult because of several methodological issues and structural problems related to this population. For example, prior to contemporary immigration flows, the native-born Latino population (mostly Mexican American) was dubiously captured in the 1960 and 1970 censuses of population. The definition for categorizing people changed from having a Spanish surname in 1960, to people of Spanish origin in 1970, to Hispanic origin in 1980 and 1990. As a result, it becomes difficult to accurately measure and compare Latinos over time.

In addition, there are other methodological problems with researching Latinos. First is the fact that such a large proportion of their population is foreign-born (immigrant)—54 percent in Los Angeles—and, second, a large number of Latino immigrants are here illegally. This is why many studies either ignore nativity as a factor in Latino socioeconomic outcomes or oversimplify the impacts or effects that being an immigrant might have on their progress. To be fair, this problem is recent, given the massive inflows of Latino immigration to the United States during the 1980s and 1990s, which drastically altered the Latino population from a primarily U.S.-born population as early as 1960 to an almost majority immigrant population in 1990. Nevertheless, prevailing debates concerning Latinos in the United States lump together natives and immigrants, providing us with imprecise figures and socioeconomic outcomes for either group or the overall Latino population.

In addition, a large portion of the Latino population—those without papers—is relatively ignored in most scholarship on Latinos. While both issues are sampling-related, the former is more easily resolved by differentiating between immigrant and nonimmigrant status in survey samples. The problem of investigating documented and undocumented status, for any racial-ethnic group, is difficult because of the lack of studies and/or surveys that differentiate between these two populations and the fact that they are difficult to identify in any given setting.

We begin the chapter with a review of the theoretical arguments and empirical literature on factors influencing earnings. Where possible, we review the specific literature on this subject for Latinos and extrapolate from the findings and arguments for African Americans to Latinos. We then turn to our own approach by first laying out our research objectives, detailing the data used in our study, the equations to be estimated, and the various variables used in our analyses. We then review the results of our regression exercises and conclude by summarizing our argument and discussing the implications of our findings to larger theoretical issues.

Latinos and Labor Market Disadvantage

A review of the literature on Latino labor market disadvantage must include to some extent a summary of the important factors that contribute to labor market disadvantage among African Americans. Many of the same factors used to explain black and white earning differences may apply to Latinos as well (Moss and Tilly 1991). The scant literature on this subject for Latinos results from several technical and substantive problems related to their absence in major labor market–based surveys, such as the Current Population Survey, before the 1970s; their ethnic (national origin) diversity and geographic dispersion across regions, which contributes to heterogeneous outcomes; the immigrant status of a large proportion of the Latino population and their divergent assimilation patterns, which serve to bias predicted labor market outcomes for an entire ethnic group; and an overemphasis on black-white labor market difference in the literature. Here we sketch the major theoretical arguments and empirical evidence used to explain Latino labor market disadvantage.

As suggested earlier, the most widely used framework to explain the disadvantaged labor market status for Latinos focuses on the supply side of the labor market—that is, the characteristics or human capital endowments of this labor force. The basic assumption behind human capital theory is that each individual's decision or investment in schooling, job training, work experience, language proficiency, and age affects his or her labor market outcomes or, more specifically, earnings potential (Becker 1975). Much of the empirical research on wage differentials among racial-ethnic groups has focused on the disparity between African Americans and non-Hispanic white men (O'Neill 1990; Smith and Welch 1989). Some find that the racial gap between these two groups is closing due to improved educational attainment among African Americans (Smith and Welch 1977, 1989).

Research on the determinants of Latinos' earnings has established that most wage differentials between Latinos and whites are the result of poor human capital characteristics, such as education, language, work experience, and hours worked (Cotton 1985; Hirschman and Wong 1984; Reimers 1985). Most of these studies conclude that the unexplained variance of these models suggests that discrimination and other, perhaps institutional (for example, lack of union membership, being segmented into low- or minimum-wage jobs), factors play a role in wage inequality.

Institutional factors operate at a more aggregate level where race becomes a criterion for allocating labor in various segments of the labor market. One consequence is that a disproportionate number of minorities, including immigrants, is concentrated in the low-skill and low-pay secondary labor market, where employment is unstable at best and competitive forces exist (Ong and Valenzuela 1996).

Discrimination by employers against African Americans has long hurt their ability to enter many kinds of jobs and to earn equal pay with whites. Labor market discrimination is evident in the significant differences in wages or employment rates among races and ethnic groups that remain after factors such as education, experience, and skill are controlled. Today, race is as pervasive as ever in mediating job hiring (Kirschenman and Neckerman 1991; Waldinger 1995), setting wages (Smith and Welch 1989; Darity 1982), and concentrating workers in particular occupations (Reskin and Roos 1990; Tomaskovic-Devey 1993; Sokoloff 1992; Williams 1989; Gordon, Edwards, and Reich 1982). In addition, a labor market segmented by race, gender, and other factors (such as ethnicity, nativity status, and age) continues to concentrate African Americans and Latinos in low-paying and unstable jobs, where they more frequently come into contact with competitive sources of labor so that employers can more easily discriminate in their hiring and their pay rate.

The literature on human capital returns to earnings and employment, the effects of discrimination (both institutionally and at other levels, such as hiring), plus the concentration of minority workers in the secondary labor market fails to adequately capture nuances specific to Latinos in general and immigrant Latinos specifically in explaining their differential earnings and employment patterns. We argue that four important considerations, which we test in this study, help us better understand Latino labor market inequality: nativity status and the role of immigration (for example, year of arrival); geographic differences in place of residence; the use of social networks; and the poverty concentration where Latinos live.

Studies that consider nativity status as possible explanatory variables for inequality are sparse. If the immigrants of today are less skilled than immigrants of the past, their current or future labor market status (disadvantage) can be partially explained. Likewise, as other researchers have argued, foreign birth can be a disadvantage because it represents cultural and social differences related to preparation for the labor market in the United States, as well as differences in the transferability of specific employment skills (Bean and Tienda 1988, 395–96; Borjas 1987) and foreign certificates and degrees. Also, by measuring different rates of assimilation by country-of-origin groups, years of duration in the United States, and year of entry and age of immigrant, we can measure more accurately labor market progress of Latinos vis-à-vis other groups.

Often, multivariate models of immigrants in the urban economy fail to account for years of duration in the United States and year of entry, two important variables that can help us assess and predict assimilation patterns. When analyzing the Latino population in the United States—a large proportion of which is immigrant[5]—controlling for when an immigrant arrived and how many years he or she has been in the United States will yield better predictive models and account for more accurate determinants of labor market inequality because it takes into account processes of labor market incorporation, experience, assimilation, and familiarity with societal norms.

In addition to the role of immigration in explaining Latino labor market disadvantage, the regional dispersion of Latinos in the Southwest, the Midwest-Chicago area, the Northeast, and the Southeast may also contribute to differential earning and employment patterns. The Northeast, historically an immigrant entry point, is also home to the second largest U.S. Hispanic subgroup—Puerto Ricans—and an emerging Dominican population. Immigrant composition, coupled with economic restructuring in the New York metropolitan and Northeast region during the 1980s and early 1990s, resulted in disparate income and employment outcomes for these two groups and, indeed, the entire workforce. On the other hand, Los Angeles and other parts of the Southwest—home to the largest U.S. Hispanic subgroup, Mexicans—experienced a much different process of economic restructuring resulting in lower rates of unemployment, but similar rates of low earnings and high poverty rates. For these and other reasons, it is important to account for regional differences among earnings and employment in the Latino population.

Another important factor to consider in Latino labor market inequality is the role of social networks in immigrant settlement and job incorporation (Chavez 1991; Hondagneu-Sotelo 1994; Mines 1981; Massey et al. 1987; Portes and Bach 1985). Immigrants create layers of resources and strategies for dealing with a new and larger society. These levels or networks are based on the individual, on the family, and on a social network of extended relatives, comrades, paisanos (fellow country folk), trusted friends, and neighbors. By forming a network of family and friends in a region, local community, or neighborhood, immigrants increase the numbers of people they can turn to for help in securing a job or with other important problems such as crisis intervention, legal help, sickness, and short-term lending and borrowing of resources. Most immigrants know someone in their area of destination who can provide shelter and information on where to find a job and how to navigate the new city. This important factor usually means the difference between an immigrant acquiring a job, skirting shifts of unemployment, or returning to the country of origin jobless. Networks serve as a marker of sorts in segmenting workers into specific types of jobs, with immigrants often being concentrated in certain type jobs that offer no benefits, poor pay, and hard work. Factoring social networks into analysis of labor market inequality allow us to better distinguish the role of networks in job acquisition, and the types of jobs that networks provide.

Last, the concentration of Latino immigrants in high poverty areas may also contribute to higher rates of unemployment and poverty among the Latino population. Immigrants traditionally locate in areas where coethnics reside. Furthermore, because Latino immigrants tend to have poorer class backgrounds, these communities tend to be impoverished (Moore 1989). While substantial evidence (Portes and Bach 1985) suggests that immigrants locate to areas where ethnic enclaves provide substantial economic opportunities, it is not clear to what extent the concentration of Latino immigrants in a high poverty area compared to a low poverty area may have on their earnings.[6]

Los Angeles provides us with a unique historical and urban geography from which to begin an assessment of the effects of space on earnings. Because job opportunities rarely match place of residence, and commuting distances to and from work differ very little by group (see chapter 11), space between poor and nonpoor may matter very little when it comes to jobs. At the same time, living in poor neighborhoods usually means few resources and opportunities to escape the ravages of poverty—at least in the case of African Americans (Wilson 1987). This situation, however, is not readily apparent for Latinos who, because of continuous immigration flows, have the effect of rejuvenating poor communities. Immigrant-rich but income-poor communities in Los Angeles, such as Pico Union, Huntington Park, and South Gate, are vibrant and bustling neighborhoods replete with economic development, active parishes, community-based organizations, and busy streets full of vendors and other peddlers. As a result, living in one of these "impoverished" (that is, low-income) communities may not necessarily result in worsened labor market opportunities or diminished wages (Valenzuela 1995).

Research Objectives

Our review of the literature on labor market opportunities for Latinos tells us that human capital is an important predictor of earning differences. In addition, most empirical research on labor market outcomes also employs occupational characteristics in determining differences in earnings. However, what these analyses do not tell us is how nativity differences may result in differential returns to human capital characteristics. Additionally, how important are nativity status, social networks, and neighborhood-level variables such as the poverty or racial concentration of a census tract in differentiating between Latino subgroups in their labor market opportunities and influencing labor market success or failure?

We argue that central to any analysis on Latino labor market opportunities is the incorporation of immigrant characteristics and labor market processes that may or may not be unique to immigrants, such as social networks and neighborhood class and ethnic context. We know that immigrants, by their mere presence in the labor market, account for differences in their human capital acquisition vis-à-vis nonimmigrants. For example, depending on when an immigrant migrated to the United States, his or her educational attainment may differ substantially from the native-born or may have been acquired in the country of origin. Related to education are other immigrant-native differences that may also influence labor market disparities, such as language fluency, skills attainment, and labor market adaptation. Theory tells us that immigrants would be at a disadvantage to natives in this regard—that is, their lower educational levels, poor English fluency, and less work experience translate into higher unemployment and lower earnings. Given these immigrant characteristics, they are likely to live in high poverty-concentrated neighborhoods that can prove to be a further disadvantage to their employment and earnings. Possibly offsetting these negative factors, immigrants also have unique labor market processes (lower reservation wages and social networks) that allow them to better compete for jobs. Our objective is to disentangle these important immigrant variables and assess the relative significance of each in determining earnings inequality between the native and foreign-born Latino.

Data and Methods

We analyze data from the Los Angeles Study of Urban Inequality[7] to predict earning differences among Latinos by controlling for standard human capital variables (such as education, experience, age) and introducing four important independent variables unique to this survey: nativity status, poverty concentration, social networks, and experiences with discrimination.

Our unit of analysis is the Mexican and Central American populations captured by LASUI (N = 603). Table 6.1 describes the variables and models used in our study, while table 6.2 provides descriptive statistics by gender (N for males = 363; N for females = 245), nativity (N for native-born men = 92; N for native-born women = 66; N for foreign-born men = 266; N for foreign-born women = 179), and the key variables used in our analysis. Similar to other census-based classifications, our foreign-born variable refers to respondents who were born outside the United States.

Our analysis is restricted to Mexican and Central American employed male and female workers, age twenty-one to sixty-four, who reported earnings for the year (1993) in Los Angeles County. We began by examining differences (table 6.2) by nativity status for both men and women along socioeconomic outcomes and background characteristics as well as looking at differences in occupational and industry locations and neighborhood characteristics. We followed with a regression analysis to determine whether years in the United States, social networks, discrimination, racial and poverty concentration of area, net of other

TABLE 6.1   *Definitions of Variables*

Variable	Definition
Human capital characteristics (control)	
High school	1 if high school degree; 0 otherwise.
Less than high school	1 if less than high school; 0 otherwise.
Work experience	Continuous variable = number of years working.
Work experience²	Square of work experience.
If married	1 if living with spouse or partner; 0 otherwise.
With child, under age eighteen	1 if has a child under age eighteen; 0 otherwise.
English fluency	1 if speak English well or very well; 0 otherwise.
Hours worked per week	Continuous variable = number of hours worked.
Occupation	1 if low skill (that is, service, craft, and operators); 0 otherwise.
Immigrant characteristics	
Zero to four years in the United States	1 if zero to four years in the United States; 0 otherwise.
Five to nine years in the United States	1 if five to nine years in the United States; 0 otherwise.
Over ten years in the United States	1 if 10+ years in the United States; 0 otherwise.
Being Central American	1 if Central American; 0 otherwise
Social network	1 if one person in steady job; 0 otherwise.
Legal resident status	1 if has green card; 0 otherwise
Experienced discrimination on the job	1 if experienced discrimination; 0 otherwise.
Neighborhood characteristics	
Living in Southeast Los Angeles	1 if live in Southeast Los Angeles; 0 otherwise.
Living in South Central Los Angeles	1 if live in South Central Los Angeles; 0 otherwise.
Living in East Los Angeles	1 if live in East Los Angeles; 0 otherwise.
Living in medium and high poverty tract	1 if live in medium (21 to 39 percent) to high (40 percent or more) poverty tract; 0 otherwise.

Source: Los Angeles Study of Urban Inequality 1994.

TABLE 6.2   *Descriptive Statistics Means and Sample Size*

Gender Breakdown	All Latinas and Latinos		Foreign-Born		Native-Born	
	Men	Women	Men	Women	Men	Women
	60% (329)	40% (219)	61% (243)	39% (157)	58% (86)	42% (62)
General characteristics						
Married	67 (245)	55 (136)	3 (194)	58 (105)	52 (51)	47 (31)
Fluent in English	33 (118)	24 (60)	60 (23)	14 (25)	60 (58)	52 (34)
Social networks	58 (210)	59 (144)	56 (150)	54 (97)	62 (60)	72 (47)
Children under eighteen	46 (169)	61 (151)	55 (147)	65 (116)	22 (21)	53 (35)
Legal residence	—	—	79 (196)	72 (115)	—	—
Labor market characteristics						
Low skill	73 (263)	61 (149)	79 (210)	78 (140)	55 (53)	13 (9)
High skill	28 (100)	39 (96)	21 (56)	22 (39)	45 (44)	87 (57)
Job discrimination	13 (59)	9 (23)	19 (49)	8 (15)	11 (10)	13 (8)
Neighborhood characteristics						
Southeast Los Angeles	23 (85)	30 (72)	16 (42)	21 (38)	44 (43)	53 (35)
South Central Los Angeles	12 (43)	15 (37)	15 (39)	19 (35)	4 (3)	4 (2)
East Los Angeles	19 (70)	17 (42)	19 (50)	15 (27)	21 (20)	23 (15)
Poverty area	44 (160)	41 (100)	52 (138)	47 (85)	22 (22)	24 (16)
	Mean (S.D.)	Mean (S.D.)	Mean (S.D.)	Mean (S.D.)	Mean (S.D.)	Mean (S.D.)
Age	33.9 (9.9)	35.8 (10.4)	34.1 (9.5)	35.2 (9.6)	33.2 (11.2)	37.3 (12)
Income	$18,332 ($14,889)	$12,365 ($9,756)	$15,792 ($10,144)	$9,929 ($7,669)	$25,327 ($22,071)	$18,972 ($11,646)
Education	9.9 (4.1)	10.3 (3.8)	8.9 (4.1)	9.4 (3.9)	12.7 (2.5)	13.1 (1.5)

Source: Los Angeles Study of Urban Inequality 1994.
Note: Sample sizes are in parentheses.

variables (such as human capital and demographic) predicted earnings differences for Mexican and Central American respondents. We did this separately for native and foreign-born women and men. For the dependent earnings variable we used an ordinary least squares (OLS) regression. Within these two regression models, there are three different arrangements of the equation that represent three vectors of analysis: human capital and labor market characteristics; immigrant characteristics; and neighborhood-level characteristics. (See table 6.1 for listing and operationalization of variables.)

The primary independent variables are a series of dummy and continuous variables: ethnicity, nativity status, social networks, legal residency, racial and poverty concentration of respondent's census tract. Ethnicity was constructed as a dichotomous variable, with Central Americans given a value of 1 and persons of Mexican origin a value of 0. Nativity status was operationalized as three dummies: zero to four years in the United States, five to nine years, and ten and more years in the United States. Native-born was treated as the reference category.[8] The survey asked a series of questions regarding the quality of a respondent's network: education, job status, public aid use, and marital status. The social network variable was operationalized as a dummy, with those respondents who answered that they had at least one of three persons in their network who had a steady job assigned a value of 1 and those who did not a value of 0. Discrimination was constructed as a dummy variable, with those having responded affirmatively to the question of having experienced discrimination based on their race or ethnicity at work given the value of 1.[9] The final immigrant-related characteristic was operationalized as a dummy, with those reporting having a green card given the value of 1 and those without it treated as the reference group.[10]

Last, community-level variables were operationalized in two ways: with a two-category variable for poverty concentration; respondents who resided in a medium (21 to 39 percent) to high (40 percent or more) poverty census tract were assigned a value of 1 and those living in a low (less than 20 percent poverty tract a value of 0; and dummies for three geographic areas with varying concentrations of Latinos and specific histories: Southeast Los Angeles (less than 40 percent Latinos); South Central Los Angeles (greater than 40 percent but less than 51 percent Latino—a new neighborhood of recently arriving immigrants that was once predominantly African American); and East Los Angeles (greater than 51 percent Latino and a well-established Chicano barrio). The reference area are the remaining eleven geographic areas defined by the Los Angeles Study of Urban Inequality.

A series of standard control variables for human capital, household structure, and occupations were employed in the models: education, work experience, and hours worked were treated as continuous variables. Education was treated as a dummy, with those respondents who had a high school degree assigned a value of 1 and those without a value of 0. Similarly, those with less than a high school degree were assigned a value of 1 and those with high school or more were assigned a value of 0. Also included in the earnings model was work experience squared to capture the nonlinear relationship between work experience and income. English language fluency was constructed as a dummy variable, with those respondents who said they spoke English well or very well assigned a value of 1 and those who responded speaking no English, only a little, or just fair a value of 0. Marital status was operationalized as a dummy, with persons living with a spouse or partner given a value of 1 and everyone else a value of 0. A dummy variable for occupational skill was constructed. The occupation codes were assigned to all respondents who had worked in the past five years, implying that not all respondents with codes were presently in the labor force. However, all Latinos in the sample were presently in the labor force. Service, craft, and operators were classified as low skill and given a value of 1 and managers and professional were treated as the reference group of high-skill workers.

The first model poses the general question of what the effects of human capital and occupation are on earnings differences. The second model incorporates immigrant characteristics to determine the same labor market outcome on earnings. Last, model 3 adds the community-level variables East Los Angeles, South Central Los Angeles, and Southeast Los Angeles, and poverty tract, to determine the effect of living in a racially concentrated as well as high poverty tract, on earnings. The coefficients of our model can be interpreted roughly as percentage changes in the dependent variable in response to unit changes in the independent variables, or returns to investments in the case of such variables as education and fluency in English.

Hypotheses

We treat the human capital and occupation variables as controls for each model. Our primary interest lies with the immigrant-characteristics and neighborhood-level variables. Therefore, the crux of our analysis discussion deals with models 2 and 3. All dummies, these variables should have mixed impacts on earnings. We expect that being an early immigrant should have a negative impact on earnings for both men and women and that as years in United States increase, the gap between the earnings of native-born and immigrants should decrease. Second, we expect that social networks will have a positive effect for immigrants' earnings, but not on those of native-born because of their infrequent reliance on networks to get a good job. Third, obtaining permanent residency should have a positive impact because those with legal documents are able to obtain better jobs and confront exploitation and other workplace abuses with less tolerance. Fourth, experience with discrimination should have a negative impact on earnings for both groups (natives and foreign-born). Fifth, residing in a high poverty tract will be a disadvantage on earnings of both native and foreign-born men and women. Last, we expect that living in South Central Los Angeles should have a negative impact on earnings for both foreign and native-born workers. Living in East Los Angeles should have positive impact for immigrants because it has historically meant a move out of immigrant enclaves and into more established Chicano neighborhoods (Moore and Pinderhughes 1993; Ong and Lawrence 1992). Living in Southeast Los Angeles should have a positive effect for both nativity groups because it has meant a move into more integrated communities.

Findings

Descriptive Statistics

Table 6.2 tells us several important things about Latinos in Los Angeles. Women earn significantly less income (about $6,000) while having about the same level of education as men (about ten years). Once we control for nativity, we see that this gender-income difference holds between immigrants and native-born (over $6,000). Looking at differences between nativity groups, native-born men and women make more than their immigrant counterparts—at least $9,000 more. Similarly, the low educational attainment illustrated by the aggregate numbers shows marked change once we control for nativity. More specifically, immigrant educational attainment is considerably less, at nine years, than the native-born women and men, who on average hold a high school degree.

Immigrants are more likely to be married and, not surprisingly, less likely to be fluent in English than are nonimmigrants. Immigrants and nonimmigrants alike have job-connected networks. Latinos in our sample are most likely immigrants who have been in the United States for over ten years. Recent arrivals (zero to four years) are the smallest group of immigrants in this survey. As one might predict, immigrants are concentrated in low-skill occupations. For natives, there is a large gender difference in occupational skill. Native-born Latinas have a higher concentration in high-skill jobs than men—a 52 percent difference. Last, a majority of immigrant men and women live in areas in which 20 percent or more of the population is poor; less than one-quarter of native-born do. In addition, most immigrants are dispersed throughout Los Angeles, while the native-born are concentrated in Southeast and East Los Angeles.

Multivariate Analyses

As illustrated, there are significant differences along educational attainment, occupational skill, and geography among native and foreign-born Latinos. Our next step is to assess what explains differences in earnings, holding constant the latter factors. That is, how important were our immigrant related and neighborhood characteristics in predicting earnings net of human capital characteristics?

All Latinos

Tables 6.3 and 6.4 present the coefficients for all Latino men and women. We see that there are significant differences along nativity in both models. For men, differences between immigrants and natives decrease as time in the United States increases, net of neighborhood differences. More specifically, there is a $10,000 difference between natives and the most recent arrivals (0 to 4 years), while the most established immigrants (ten or more years) differ from the former by only a little

TABLE 6.3　*Selected OLS Coefficients for All Latino Earnings (Men Only, N = 328)*

Variables	Model 1	Model 2
Immigration characteristics		
Zero to four years in the United States	−10840.87***	−10133.56***
	(2949.37)	(2947.46)
Five to nine years in the United States	−8729.96***	−8168.29***
	(2475.93)	(2487.46)
Ten or more years in the United States	−3791.80*	−2333.74
	(1966.59)	(1973.59)
Central American	−2327.60	−618.96
	(1799.70)	(1826.52)
Network with a job	3385.58**	3149.43*
	(1360.70)	(1356.77)
Experienced discrimination	3757.69*	4412.76**
	(1799.30)	(1782.34)
Neighborhood characteristics		
Southeast Los Angeles		−3340.29
		(1940.91)
South Central Los Angeles		−3279.69
		(2209.80)
East Los Angeles		2161.69
		(2012.41)
Poverty rate > 20 percent		−5771.44***
		(1764.21)
Constant	17260.41	20701.39***
	(4110.25)	(4298.36)
R^2	.30	.32

Source: Los Angeles Study of Urban Inequality 1994.
Note: Control variables were included (education, work experience, work experience², being married [1], having children under eighteen years of age, being fluent in English [1], hours worked per week, and occupational skill [low skill = 1]).
*p < .05, **p <.01, ***p < .001

TABLE 6.4   *Selected OLS Coefficients for All Latino Earnings (Women Only, N = 219)*

Variables	Model 1	Model 2
Immigration characteristics		
Zero to four years in the United States	−11032.15***	−7921.41***
	(2554.30)	(2633.02)
Five to nine years in the United States	−10084.50***	−6865.07**
	(2340.38)	(2433.67)
Ten or more years in the United States	−6631.24***	−3843.61*
	(1857.54)	(2024.43)
Central American	1661.05	3307.37*
	(1371.77)	(1491.40)
Network with a job	−342.16	273.57
	(1217.58)	(1226.47)
Experienced discrimination	3270.13	4182.41*
	(2000.60)	(1964.04)
Neighborhood characteristics		
Southeast Los Angeles		5517.24***
		(1646.03)
South Central Los Angeles		430.91
		(1897.30)
East Los Angeles		634.74
		(1791.60)
Poverty rate > 20 percent		−604.70
		(1491.24)
Constant	8549.39	3791.31
	(3267.08)	(3535.26)
R^2		

Source: Los Angeles Study of Urban Inequality 1994.
Note: Control variables were included (education, work experience, work experience^2, being married [1], having children under eighteen years of age, being fluent in English [1], hours worked per week, and occupational skill [low skill = 1]).
*p < .05, **p < .01, ***p < .001

over $2,000. Among Latinas, the same pattern holds; however, the differences between immigrants and natives are not as stark and the decrease over time is not as large. That is, the earnings gap between immigrant and native women decreases by only $4,000 from the time they arrive to their tenth year in the United States. For men, the difference is twice as much—$8,000—illustrating a large payoff for prolonged time in the United States. The finding for women suggests a stagnation in earnings over time.

Having a job-connected network for men significantly increases income, by over $3,000, suggesting that Latinos connected to networks are

265

also tied to well-paying jobs. For women, there is no significant relationship between the two. Interestingly, having experienced racial and/or ethnic discrimination significantly affects wages by at least $4,000 for both men and women. One possible interpretation of this is that discrimination is a proxy for the differences in the types of jobs Latinas and Latinos hold. Last, in general, differences in neighborhood characteristics proved not to be a significant indicator of differences in earnings among Latino men and women. However, living in Southeast Los Angeles proved to be a highly significant advantage for Latinas—an increase in wages of about $5,500. The only significant neighborhood variable for men was living in a poverty-concentrated tract, which decreased earnings by over $5,700.

Immigrant Men and Women

Table 6.5 shows that the number of years in the United States is a significant determinant of earnings for immigrant men. Over time, the differences in earnings between the earliest arrivals and the most established decreases. This, of course, supports the well-honed argument that the incorporation of immigrants into better-paying jobs occurs as they become more permanent members of the Los Angeles labor market and society in general. The only other variable of interest that proved significant was social networks. Having at least one person in one's personal network connected to employment increased earnings by $2,658. Neighborhood differences (where one lives geographically and in terms of poverty concentration) were not significant in accounting for earnings differences.

Unlike their male counterparts, female immigrants (table 6.6) were not significantly different by years in the United States. In fact, the earnings gap between earliest and most established immigrants improve by a little over $1,100 once they add four years of residence in the United States. This suggests stagnation in immigrant women's earnings and little returns to their continued stay in the United States. This finding points to the continued concentration of immigrant women in low-paying jobs. Being Central American rather than Mexican also improves earnings by over $3,200, illustrating significant ethnic differences among Latina immigrants. Likewise, having a green card improves earnings by $2,500. One of the more interesting findings is related to our discrimination variable. Immigrant women who reported having experienced discrimination had a significant ($9,500) difference in their earnings compared to those who had not. One possible explanation for this is that this variable serves as a proxy for working with white employers and/or white employees. Working under or alongside whites would in-

TABLE 6.5   OLS Coefficients for Latino Foreign-Born Men
             (N = 243)

Variables	Model 1	Model 2	Model 3
Human capital (controls)			
High school	−376.52	−568.00	−2151.95
	(2787.33)	(2723.80)	(2770.90)
Less than high school	−1052.26	−1855.61	−3329.98
	(2791.84)	(2716.30)	(2766.63)
Work experience	2648.40*	1903.73	1551.74
	(1239.40)	(1252.68)	(1254.30)
Work experience^2	−.77	−3.05**	−3.35**
	(1.11)	(1.16)	(1.15)
Married	2063.47	916.84	334.07
	(1825.79)	(1769.59)	(1765.62)
Children under eighteen	4774.34**	4423.73**	5028.83***
	(1558.13)	(1487.78)	(1492.32)
English fluency	3704.13*	1347.86	1370.19
	(1767.94)	(1758.56)	(1740.63)
Hours worked	64.51	59.87	82.36
	(63.55)	(62.84)	(63.10)
Low skill	−5040.08**	−5462.03***	−5190.89***
	(1609.50)	(1581.88)	(1618.52)
Immigration characteristics			
Zero to four years in United States		−9324.31***	−9389.34***
		(2133.53)	(2131.58)
Five to nine years in United States		−5441.26***	−5536.98***
		(1558.77)	(1579.35)
Central American		−1963.05	−1109.93
		(1401.66)	(1414.31)
Network with job		1766.18	2657.24*
		(1266.42)	(1295.44)
Legal resident		−437.88	−773.14
		(1540.14)	(1531.39)
Experienced discrimination		1575.68	2076.73
		(1618.62)	(1618.12)
Neighborhood characteristics			
Southeast Los Angeles			2548.24
			(1817.98)
South Central Los Angeles			−1463.86
			(1846.98)
East Los Angeles			2158.71
			(1700.96)
Poverty rate (>20 percent)			−2228.04
			(1462.90)
Constant	12238.29	18324.07	19082.18
	(3901.00)	(4346.20)	(4415.25)
R^2	.19	.27	.29

Source: Los Angeles Study of Urban Inequality 1994.
*p < .05, **p < .01, ***p < .001

267

TABLE 6.6   OLS Coefficients for Latina Foreign-Born Women
(N = 157)

Variables	Model 1	Model 2	Model 3
Human capital (controls)			
High school	−2810.62	−1977.37	−1358.86
	(2350.72)	(2189.55)	(2094.43)
Less than high school	−4241.90	−3041.25	−3324.18
	(2476.32)	(2322.52)	(2239.65)
Work experience	812.52	1383.46	1421.36
	(1211.71)	(1153.94)	(1125.11)
Work experience^2	.72	−1.28	−1.46
	(1.19)	(1.21)	(1.17)
Married	1067.13	430.92	536.82
	(1289.26)	(1209.33)	(1177.68)
Children under eighteen	1900.66	839.96	1506.75
	(1345.84)	(1422.31)	(1393.00)
English fluency	3936.41**	3461.30*	3628.05*
	(1774.97)	(1720.05)	(1657.03)
Hours worked	263.02***	265.51***	257.20***
	(55.86)	(52.10)	(50.42)
Low skill	425.02	1633.34	998.14
	(1612.81)	(1504.77)	(1449.21)
Immigration characteristics			
Zero to four years in United		−4164.97*	−3419.07
States		(1922.95)	(1864.81)
Five to nine years in United		−2280.65	−2303.64
States		(1593.54)	(1602.97)
Central American		2157.41	3725.57**
		(1151.08)	(1235.87)
Network with job		1024.02	1875.21
		(1149.55)	(1156.22)
Legal resident		2343.97	2499.89*
		(1273.77)	(1230.49)
Experienced discrimination		8614.95***	9522.72***
		(2075.46)	(1995.98)
Neighborhood characteristics			
Southeast Los Angeles			5913.93***
			(1625.71)
South Central Los Angeles			1487.80
			(1557.68)
East Los Angeles			2353.11
			(1722.16)
Poverty rate (>20 percent)			−1124.11
			(1361.26)
Constant	801.24	−1780.37	−3910.32
	(2890.38)	(3007.17)	
R^2	.15	.29	.36

Source: Los Angeles Study of Urban Inequality 1994.
*p < .05, **p < .01, ***p < .001

crease instances of discrimination. By the same token, the increased wage differences account for the better wages that are generally paid in occupations that are not segregated by race and ethnicity. By procuring jobs in mixed (race-ethnicity) occupations, Latina immigrant workers confront discrimination but tolerate it in the face of increased wages. Given what we know about occupational concentrations of immigrant women in low-paying positions, the jobs with a mixed racial workforce are probably higher-paying. The only significant neighborhood variable is that of living in Southeast Los Angeles, where women earn significantly more than women elswhere in Los Angeles.

Native-Born Men and Women

Tables 6.7 and 6.8 present the regression coefficients for native-born Latino men and women. The variables of interest, specifically the role of networks and neighborhood characteristics, proved to hold little significance in explaining differences among the native-born. For native-born women, social networks and neighborhood-level characteristics made no significant impact on earnings. Native-born men, unlike immigrant men and women, experienced some negative repercussions to their earnings from living in Southeast Los Angeles, as well as living in poverty-concentrated areas. The model for native-born women was especially troubling, given the lack of significance for any of our variables of interest. One possible reason for this is the small sample size, which may have proved little variation among the cases.

Conclusion

What can we draw from these findings? Our work has sought to expand earnings models by looking beyond human capital variables and incorporating what immigrant theories have said about the importance of location, social networks, and the unique traits that immigrants possess. This chapter provides us with three major conclusions. First, when looking at all Latinos, time of immigration has a significant impact on earnings. The longer one has been in the United States, the greater one's earnings. This situation holds true for both men and women; however, while the decline in earnings lessens in significance for women over time, so does its magnitude, suggesting stagnation in earnings. Second, in our sample having social networks had a positive but insignificant effect on earnings. This finding may be related to the idea that networks are more important in acquiring a job and not necessarily to the type of job and what that job pays, as suggested by our model. Last, geographic location provided mixed findings in our models. For all Latino men and

TABLE 6.7   *OLS Coefficients for Latino Native-Born Men (N = 86)*

Variables	Model 1	Model 2	Model 3
Human capital (controls)			
High school	−13971.74**	−14383.62*	−15558.65**
	(5716.28)	(6432.32)	(6188.47)
Less than high school	−21810.84**	−21763.73*	26804.40**
	(8624.80)	(9736.38)	(9364.24)
Work experience	2361.44	2499.39	4705.95
	(3608.92)	(3627.26)	(3505.88)
Work experience^2	5.88	8.24	8.68
	(4.83)	(4.89)	(4.74)
Married	−12981.20**	−14925.47**	−15327.14**
	(5201.77)	(5465.04)	(5722.00)
Children under eighteen	20528.74***	19277.53***	16194.25**
	(5102.11)	(5067.81)	(5180.80)
English fluency	8244.88*	7602.44*	7313.74
	(3864.68)	(3820.85)	(4097.92)
Hours worked	1323.68***	1286.16***	1166.00***
	(206.94)	(206.40)	(223.15)
Low skill	7332.56*	−6300.91	−5492.56
	(3535.12)	(3562.24)	(3561.06)
Job place characteristics			
Network with job		2560.97	1371.91
		(4101.13)	(4338.13)
Experienced discrimination		10062.78	10110.98
		(5980.05)	(5663.56)
Neighborhood characteristics			
Southeast Los Angeles			−9965.60*
			(5118.79)
South Central Los Angeles			−8671.25
			(10164.37)
East Los Angeles			7385.07
			(8165.00)
Poverty rate (>20 percent)			−15389.72*
			(7274.76)
Constant	−14409.65	−15329.07	−3206.46
	(9880.09)	(11376.71)	(13579.87)
R^2	.55	.56	.61

Source: Los Angeles Study of Urban Inequality 1994.
*p < .05, **p < .01, ***p < .001

TABLE 6.8   OLS Coefficients for Latina Native-Born Women (N = 62)

Variables	Model 1	Model 2	Model 3
Human capital (controls)			
High school	−2578.82	−3044.15	−3700.79
	(4083.23)	(4147.04)	(4505.36)
Less than high school	−11907.09	−11969.52	−14618.14
	(7472.77)	(7676.35)	(8998.35)
Work experience	−4773.76*	−4250.22	−4943.74
	(2442.68)	(2540.36)	(2973.29)
Work experience^2	10.53***	10.34***	11.04***
	(2.82)	(2.86)	(3.24)
Married	−3681.21	−4057.54	−3889.06
	(2680.22)	(2817.75)	(3014.51)
Children under eighteen	5221.50	5127.68	6108.25
	(3234.53)	(3336.72)	(3650.42)
English fluency	−4525.27	−5944.12*	−6516.46*
	(2460.29)	(2974.93)	(3214.40)
Hours worked	496.81***	450.78**	393.60*
	(142.87)	(155.36)	(169.63)
Low skill	−820.69	−1428.36	−1126.08
	(4109.81)	(4175.33)	(4608.53)
Job place characteristics			
Network with job		−3296.37	−4138.38
		(3192.25)	(3708.15)
Experienced discrimination		−363.58	−1074.69
		(4090.91)	(4439.32)
Neighborhood characteristics			
Southeast Los Angeles			−3883.78
			(4142.26)
South Central Los Angeles			−3006.16
			(15375.74)
East Los Angeles			−1724.29
			(4052.48)
Poverty rate (>20 percent)			−1325.46
			(4169.04)
Constant	1548.46	6929.38	12909.26
	(6477.97)	(8100.55)	(10255.23)
R^2	.44	.43	.40

Source: Los Angeles Study of Urban Inequality 1994.
*p < .05, **p < .01, ***p < .001

women, living in poverty areas (more than 20 percent of the population poor) or in Southeast Los Angeles had a significantly negative effect on earnings. However, once we controlled for nativity status, these neighborhood effects became null for all respondents except for two locations. Southeast Los Angeles presented a positive impact on immigrant women's earnings but a negative one on native-born Latinos. In sum, what we can say with a large degree of confidence is that nativity, gender, and human capital matter most when looking at Latino labor market dynamics.

Our results provide support for the idea that nativity is an important distinction in Latino labor market opportunity. Furthermore, our findings show that our variables of interest differentially affect employment and earnings for immigrants versus natives and among men and women. What is important for increasing their earnings, however, is where immigrants live (that is, a high or low poverty area) and whether they are connected to social networks.

Research on urban poverty has long focused on its effects in communities—ghettos and barrios—across the United States. It has only been in the past decade or so that researchers have concentrated on the geography or space of concentrated and persistent poverty (Wilson 1987; Jargowsky and Bane 1991; Ricketts and Sawhill 1988). Indeed, one of the major facets of the underclass literature is its focus on space and the concentration of poor people in confined geographic areas. Wilson (1987) poignantly argues that labor market opportunities for African Americans are seriously curtailed in concentrated poverty areas, yet offers little proof that belonging in a poor community is causally related to increased unemployment. Related studies that attempt to model "underclass" traits and variables for the Latino population (Moore 1989; Cuitti and James 1990; Moore and Pinderhughes 1993) also fail to adequately connect the relationship between residing in high poverty areas and diminished employment opportunities and earnings. Our findings suggest that living in high concentrated poverty tracts negatively impacts employment opportunities and decreases wages for immigrant Latinos. This finding is particularly troublesome considering that immigrants cluster in poor communities filled with coethnics and earlier immigrant flows.

Because many Latino immigrants arrive in Los Angeles poor and in search of a job, it is only logical that they settle, at least initially, in communities that more often than not are poor but can aid them not only in their job search, but in other incorporation-assimilation strategies. In addition, immigrants also concentrate in specific (poor) communities for kinship, cultural, and survival reasons—often with little regard to a community's social or impoverished status. For these reasons, our finding that immigrants diminish their earnings potential by residing in high poverty tracts is perplexing and contrary to the notion that living in Latino immigrant-rich communities, most of which are poor, does not improve the earnings or, by extension, the employment prospects of recent arrivals.

Our finding that social networks are important to Latino immigrant increases in earnings is consistent with a large body of network and social capital literature. More specifically, social network literature on recent Latino immigrants (Massey et al. 1987; Chavez 1991; Hondagneu-Sotelo 1994; Romero 1992) shows its importance in mediating job searchers, providing information on local job opportunities at the spur of the moment, and strategizing for future employment down- or up-swings. That networks are insignificant in this study (statistically) for the native-born suggests only that other factors—such as human capital, fluency in English, and place of residence—are more important.

Notes

1. We use 1848 because that year marked the signing of the Treaty of Guadalupe Hidalgo, which seceded over half of Mexico's land to the United States as the result of losing the Mexican American War. The treaty in theory guaranteed the rights of Mexicans in the new territory and provided them with U.S. citizenship. Despite their newfound citizenship and ownership claims to large land areas in California and Los Angeles, even the most established and wealthy Mexicans lost their property interests.

2. The Great Depression led to a repatriation drive that forced about one-third of the city's Mexican population back to Mexico.

3. Actually, Vilma Ortiz (1996) states that Mexican Los Angeles can almost be split into two parts: those born in Mexico and those born in the United States to Mexican parents. We extend this argument to the entire Latino population, even though the figures show more foreign-born than native-born Latinos.

4. Segmentation theory divides the labor market into two parts: the core and peripheral, or the primary and secondary sectors. In the core sector, firms have oligopoly power (small number of large firms) in their product markets, employ large number of workers, have vast financial resources, are favored by government regulations and contracting, and workers are more likely to be in unions. These jobs offer a clear path for advancement, are better paid, and have a well-defined occupational structure. Firms in the periphery are smaller, have less influence over product markets, lack access to financial resources, and are usually dependent on subcontracting or retailing for larger firms. Jobs characterized in this category are low-paying, nonunion, and exhibit high levels of job turnover. Sec-

ondary jobs are described as the worst, employing low-educated workers, bad working conditions, and with very little upward integration (Doeringer and Piore 1971; Gordon, Edwards, and Reich 1982; Reich 1981; Freeman and Medoff 1979a, 1979b; Beck, Horan, and Tolbert 1978; Tolbert, Horan, and Beck 1980).

5. Recent data from the 1994 (March) Current Population Survey shows that immigrants account for 27 percent of the entire (United States) Hispanic population, 34 percent of California's Hispanic population, and 54 percent of Los Angeles County's population.

6. For purposes of this chapter, we define high poverty census tracts where 40 percent or more of the population fall below the official poverty threshold. A low poverty census tract is defined as 20 percent or less of the population falling below the official poverty threshold.

7. LASUI is a sample of single housing units (N = 4,025) with approximately equal proportions of the four racial-ethnic groups residing in Los Angeles County (approximately 1,000 from the white, black, Latino, and Asian populations). The survey is a stratified probability sample of households in the county by income-poverty level and racial-ethnic composition of census tracts undertaken in 1994. The LASUI data have been compared to 1990 census data within each major racial-ethnic category with respect to age, sex, nativity, education, and occupation. The sample data closely parallel census distribution for each variable within each racial-ethnic category (Bobo et al. 1995).

8. These dummies were entered in analyses that included all Latina and Latino respondents (see table 6.1) and for analyses with only foreign-born. In the latter case, ten or more years served as the reference category.

9. The actual wording of the question was as follows: During the (past year have you experienced racial or ethnic discrimination at your place of work) / (last year you worked did you experience racial or ethnic discrimination at your place of work) because of your race or ethnicity?

10. Legal residency was included only in models for the foreign-born (see tables 6.3 and 6.4).

References

Bean, Frank, and Marta Tienda. 1988. *Hispanic Population in the United States.* New York: Russell Sage.

Beck, E. M., Patrick M. Horan, and Charles M. Tolbert. 1978. "Satisfaction in a Dual Economy Approach." *American Sociological Review* 43 (October): 704–22.

Becker, Gary S. 1975. *Human Capital.* Chicago: University of Chicago Press.

Bergmann, Barbara. 1974. "Occupational Segregation, Wages and Profits When Employers Discriminate by Race or Sex." *Eastern Economic Journal* 1 (April/May): 103–10.

Bobo, Lawrence D., E. Fielder, D. M. Grant, H. James Johnson Jr., and Melvin H. Oliver. 1995. *The Los Angeles Survey of Urban Inequality Sample Report on the Household Survey.* Occasional working paper Series. Los Angeles, Calif.: UCLA Center for the Study of Urban Poverty.

Borjas, George. 1985. "Assimilation, Changes in Cohort Quality, and the Earnings of Immigrants." *Journal of Labor Economics* 3: 463–89.

———. 1987. "Self-Selection and the Earnings of Immigrants." *American Economic Review* 77 (September): 531–53.

———. 1990. *Friends or Strangers: The Impact of Immigrants on the U.S. Economy.* New York: Basic Books.

———. 1994. "The Economics of Immigration." *Journal of Economic Literature* 32(December): 1667–1717.

Borjas, George, and Marta Tienda. 1985. *Hispanics in the U.S. Economy.* Orlando, Fla.: Academic Press.

Chavez, Leo R. 1988. "Settlers and Sojourners: The Case of Mexicans in California." *Human Organization* 47: 95–108.

———. 1991. *Shadowed Lives: Undocumented Immigrants in American Society.* New York: Harcourt Brace Jovanovich.

Chiswick, B. R. 1978. "The Effects of Americanization on the Earnings of Foreign-Born Men." *Journal of Political Economy* 86: 897–921.

Cotton, J. 1985. "A Comparative Analysis of Black-White and Mexican-American–White Male Wage Differentials." *Review of Black Political Economy* (Spring): 51–69.

Cuitti, P., and F. James. 1990. "A Comparison of Black and Hispanic Poverty in Large Cities of the Southwest." *Hispanic Journal of Behavioral Sciences* 12: 50–75.

Darity, William A. 1982. "The Human Capital Approach to Black-White Earnings Inequality: Some Unsettled Questions." *Journal of Human Resources* 18: 72–93.

DeFreitas, George. 1991. *Inequality at Work: Hispanics in the U.S. Labor Force.* New York: Oxford University Press.

Denton, Nancy A., and Douglas S. Massey. 1991. "Patterns of Neighborhood Transition in a Multiethnic World." *Demography* 28: 41–64.

Doeringer, P. B., and Michael J. Piore. 1971. *Internal Labor Markets and Manpower Analysis.* Lexington, Mass.: Lexington Books.

Freeman, Richard B., and J. Medoff. 1979a. "New Estimates of Private Sector Unionism in the United States." *Industrial and Labor Relations Review* 32(January): 143–74.

———. 1979b. "The Two Faces of Unionism." *Public Interest* 57(Fall): 69–93.

Frey, William, and Reynolds Farley. 1993. "Latino, Asian and Black Segregation in Multiethnic Metro-areas: Findings from the 1990 Census." Research report 93-278. Ann Arbor, Mich.: Population Studies Center.

Gordon, D. M., R. Edwards, and Michael Reich. 1982. *Segmented Work, Divided Workers: The Historical Transformation of Labor in the United States*. New York: Cambridge University Press.

Granovetter, Mark. 1974. Getting a Job: A Study of Contacts and Careers. Chicago: University of Chicago Press.

Hirschman, Charles, and M. G. Wong. 1984. "Socio-economic Gains of Asian Americans, Blacks, and Hispanics: 1960–1976." *American Journal of Sociology* 90(3): 584–607.

Hondagneu-Sotelo, Pierrette. 1994. *Gendered Transitions: Mexican Experiences of Immigration*. Berkeley, Calif.: University of California Press.

Jargowsky, Paul A., and Mary Jo Bane. 1991. "Ghetto Poverty in the United States, 1970–1980." In *The Urban Underclass*, edited by Christopher Jencks and Paul E. Peterson. Washington, D.C.: Brookings Institution.

Kirschenman, Joleen, and Kathryn Neckerman. 1991. "'We'd Love to Hire Them, But . . . ': The Meaning of Race for Employers." In *The Urban Underclass*, edited by Christopher Jencks and Paul E. Peterson. Washington, D.C.: Brookings Institution.

Laslett, H. M. John. 1996. "Historical Perspectives: Immigration and the Rise of a Distinctive Urban Region, 1900–1970." In *Ethnic Los Angeles*, edited by Roger Waldinger and Mehdi Bozorgmehr. New York: Russell Sage.

Massey, Douglas S. 1986. "The Settlement Process among Mexican Migrants to the United States." American Sociological Review 51: 670–85.

———. 1987. "Understanding Mexican Migration to the United States." *American Journal of Sociology* 92: 1372–1403.

Massey, Douglas, Raphael Alarcon, Jorge Durand, and H. Gonzalez. 1987. *Return to Aztlan: The Social Process of International Migration from Western Mexico*. Berkeley, Calif.: University of California Press.

Massey, Douglas S., and Nancy A. Denton. 1993. *American Apartheid: Segregation and the Making of the Underclass*. Cambridge, Mass.: Harvard University Press.

Massey, Douglas S., and Mitchell L. Eggers. 1990. "The Ecology of Inequality: Minorities and the Concentration of Poverty." *American Journal of Sociology* (95): 1153–88.

Mines, R. 1981. *Developing a Community Tradition of Migration: A Field Study in Rural Zacatecas: Mexico and California Settlement Areas*. Monograph series 3. La Jolla, Calif.: Center for U.S.-Mexico Studies, University of California at San Diego.

Moore, Joan. 1989. "Is There a Hispanic Underclass?" *Social Science Quarterly* 70: 265–83.

Moore, Joan, and Raquel Pinderhughes, eds. 1993. *In the Barrios: Latinos and the Underclass Debate*. New York: Russell Sage.

Moreno-Evans, M. 1995. *Immigration Since 1990: U.S. and Local Trends.* Paper presented to the UCLA Lewis Center for Regional Policy Studies (May 19, 1995).

Moss, Philip, and Chris Tilly. 1991. *Why Black Men Are Doing Worse in the Labor Market: A Review of Supply-Side and Demand-Side Explanations.* Prepared for the Social Science Research Council Committee for Research on the Urban Underclass Working Group on Labor Market Research.

Ong, Paul, and Janet Lawrence. 1992. "Pluralism and Residential Patterns in Los Angeles." Los Angeles: UCLA School of Architecture and Urban Planning.

O'Neill, J. 1990. "The Role of Human Capital in Earnings Differences Between Black and White Men." *Journal of Economic Perspectives* (4): 25–46.

Ong, Paul, and Abel Valenzuela Jr. 1996. "The Labor Market: Immigrant Effects and Racial Disparities." In *Ethnic Los Angeles*, edited by Roger Waldinger, and Medhi Bozorgmehr. New York: Russell Sage Press.

Ortiz, Vilma. 1996. The Mexican-Origin Population: Permanent Working Class or Emerging Middle Class? In *Ethnic Los Angeles*, edited by Roger Waldinger, and Mehdi Bozorgmehr. New York: Russell Sage.

Portes, Alejandro, and Robert Bach. 1985. *Latin Journey: Cuban and Mexican Immigrants in the United States.* Berkeley, Calif.: University of California Press.

Reich, Michael. 1981. *Racial Inequality: A Political-Economic Analysis.* Princeton, N.J.: Princeton University Press.

Reimers, Cordelia. 1983. "Labor Market Discrimination Among Hispanic and Black Men." *Review of Economics and Statistics* 65(4): 570–79.

———. 1984a. "Sources of the Family Income Differentials Among Hispanics, Blacks and White Non-Hispanics." *American Journal of Sociology* 89(4): 889–903.

———. 1984b. "The Wage Structure of Hispanic Men: Implications for Policy." *Social Science Quarterly* 65(2): 401–16.

———. 1985. "A Comparative Analysis of the Wages of Hispanics, Blacks, and non-Hispanic Whites." In *Hispanics in the U.S. Economy*, edited by George Borjas and Marta Tienda. Orlando, Fla.: Academic Press.

Reskin, Barbara F., and Patricia A. Roos. 1990. *Job Queues, Gender Queues: Explaining Women's Inroads into Male Occupations.* Philadelphia: Temple University Press.

Rickets, E. R., and Isabelle V. Sawhill. 1988. "Defining and Measuring the Underclass." *Journal of Policy Analysis and Management* 7(Winter): 316–25.

Rodriguez, Clara. 1991. "The Effect of Race on Puerto Rican Wages." In *Hispanics in the Labor Force: Issues and Policies*, edited by Edwin Melendez, Clara Rodriguez, and Janis Berry Figueroa. New York: Plenum Press.

Romero, Mary. 1992. *Maid in the U.S.A.* New York: Routledge.

Smith, James P., and Finis R. Welch. 1977. "Black/White Male Earnings and Employment: 1960–70." In *The Distribution of Economic Well-Being*, edited by F. Thomas Juster. Cambridge, Mass.: Ballinger.

———. 1989. "Black Economic Progress After Myrdal." *Journal of Economic Literature* 27: 519–64.

Sokoloff, Natalie J. 1992. *Black Women and White Women in the Professions*. New York: Routledge.

Telles Edward E., and Edward Murguia. 1990. "Phenotypic Discrimination and Income Differences Among Mexican Americans." *Social Science Quarterly* 71(4): 682–97.

Tienda, Marta. 1983a. "Market Characteristics and Hispanic Earnings: A Comparison of Natives and Immigrants." *Social Problems* 31(1): 59–72.

———. 1983b. "Nationality and Income Attainment Among Native and Immigrant Hispanic Men in the United States." *Sociological Quarterly* 24: 253–373.

Tolbert, C., P. M. Horan, and E. M. Beck. 1980. "The Structure of Economic Segmentation: A Dual Economy Approach." *American Journal of Sociology* 85(5): 1095–1116.

Tomaskovic-Devey, Donald. 1993. *Gender and Racial Inequality at Work: The Sources and Consequences of Job Segregation.* Ithaca, N.Y.: ILR Press.

Torres, A. 1988. *"Human Capital, Labor Segmentation and Inter-Minority Relative Status: Blacks and Puerto Rican Labor in New York City, 1960–1980."* Ph.D. diss., New School for Social Research.

Valenzuela, Abel, Jr. 1993. *"Immigrants, Minority Workers, and Job Competition: A Comparative Analysis of New York and Los Angeles, 1970 to 1980."* Ph.D. diss., Massachusetts Institute of Technology, Department of Urban Studies and Planning.

———. 1995. "Job Competition Re-assessed: Regional and Community Impacts from Los Angeles." In *Immigration and Ethnic Communities: A Focus on Latinos*, edited by Refugio Rochin. Julian Samora Research Center. East Lansing, Mich.: Michigan State University Press.

Waldinger, Roger. 1995. "Black/Immigrant Competition Reassessed: New Evidence from Los Angeles." UCLA Department of Sociology. Unpublished paper.

Williams, Christine L. 1989. *Gender Differences at Work: Women and Men in Nontraditional Occupations*. Berkeley, Calif.: University of California Press.

Wilson, William Julius. 1987. *The Truly Disadvantaged: The Inner City and Public Policy*. Chicago: University of Chicago Press.

7

A PROTECTED NICHE? IMMIGRANT ETHNIC ECONOMIES AND LABOR MARKET SEGMENTATION

Tarry Hum

IMMIGRANT ethnic economies are a vibrant part of the urban economic and social landscape. Familiar to even the most casual observers, they are often spatially clustered and exhibit a distinct ethnic character. Historic enclaves such as Chinatown have been joined by newer ethnic concentrations including Koreatown, Pico Union, New Phnom Penh, and Little Saigon in Orange County. Other immigrant economies are distinguished by occupational and industrial niches, for example, South Asian–owned motels, newsstands, taxicabs, Cambodian doughnut shops, Korean and Vietnamese nail salons. Ethnic economic niches may also exhibit a regional specialization, as suggested by the agglomeration of Korean greengrocers and nail salons in New York City and Korean liquor stores, swap meets, and gas stations in Los Angeles. Aside from spatial concentration, economic niche, and regional specialization, the central quality that distinguishes immigrant ethnic economies from the mainstream economy is the co-ethnic nature of workplace relationships among employers, employees, and the self-employed (Bonacich and Modell 1980; Light and Bonacich 1988; Reitz 1990; Light and Karageorgis 1994; Waldinger 1996).

The growing literature on ethnic economies proposes that small, immigrant-owned firms that employ co-ethnics constitute a distinct labor market with characteristics of both the secondary and primary labor markets (Wilson and Portes 1980; Wilson and Martin 1982; Portes and Stepick 1985; Portes and Bach 1985; Bailey and Waldinger 1991; Light and Espiritu 1991). Although the quality of wage employment in the ethnic economy is similar to the secondary labor market and entails labor-intensive tasks, long hours, low wages, and poor work conditions, the ethnic economy also supports attributes of the primary labor market, namely, training and advancement opportunities. Ethnic-based networks and social ties transform typically "bad" jobs into ones that provide positive outcomes including privileged access to jobs, acquisition of skills, and protection from outside competition—benefits comparable to those provided by traditional institutional shelters such as unions (Portes and Bach 1985; Zhou 1992; Waldinger 1996).

The ethnic economy literature poses an important challenge to the current conceptualization of segmented labor markets. Immigrant workers in the ethnic economy engage in menial jobs but benefit from higher human capital returns, training, and promotions (Wilson and Martin 1982; Portes and Bach 1985; Portes and Stepick 1985; Portes and Jensen 1989; Zhou 1992; Bailey and Waldinger 1991). Ethnic economy employment is not only an alternative to joblessness but shelters immigrants from the typical processes of segmented labor markets: discrimination, instability, and barriers to mobility (Zhou 1992). The ethnic economy essentially serves as a "protected niche" for immigrant workers (Wilson and Portes 1980; Portes 1987). This optimistic profile of the ethnic economy is a stark contrast to the dominant projection of immigrant concentration in a highly exploitative, unstable, and dead-end secondary labor market (Piore 1979; DeFreitas 1988; Melendez 1992; Mar 1991).

With the exception of a few studies, such as Alejandro Portes's and Robert Bach's (1985) seminal work on Cubans in Miami, research on the ethnic economy has relied on census data utilizing place of residence, place of work, or industrial sector as rough approximations of ethnic economy participation (Nee and Sanders 1987; Model 1992, 1997; Logan, Alba, and McNulty 1994). Limited data have forced researchers to make assumptions about what constitutes an ethnic economy, thereby generating much debate on the methodological approaches to operationalizing and measuring the ethnic economy (see Nee and Sanders 1987; Portes and Jensen 1987, 1989, 1992; Sanders and Nee 1992). The co-ethnic nature of the work relationship is the key distinguishing quality of ethnic economy employment; however, relevant information is not available in most data sources.

This chapter evaluates the claims of the ethnic economy literature using data on Chinese, Korean, Mexican, and Central American immigrant workers in Los Angeles. A central contribution of this research is based on the original data generated by the Los Angeles Study of Urban Inequality and pertaining to the race of workplace supervisor and racial composition of coworkers.[1] These variables provide an improved measure of the ethnic economy by focusing on the fundamental issue of the ethnic economy debate—that is, the significance of co-ethnic employer and employee relations. Second, this chapter engages in a comparative analysis of four ethnoracial groups who largely comprise the mass immigrant influx to Los Angeles. A comparative approach provides insight on the prevalence of ethnically segregated work environments and the specific industrial and occupational contours of immigrant economic activity. Moreover, an interethnic comparison emphasizes the relative significance of co-ethnic work settings in shaping immigrant economic incorporation, labor market outcomes, and prospects for advancement.

While the ethnic economy is a central mode of immigrant incorporation in the labor market, the findings presented counter the sanguine picture of co-ethnic work relationships as depicted in the ethnic economy literature. Rather, they show sharp differences in the labor market positions and outcomes of immigrant groups, even among those within the same "racial" categories, in the Los Angeles economy. A number of findings cast doubt on the optimistic projection of the ethnic economy as a superior alternative to employment in the general economy. Just as it is imperative to reject a straight-line trajectory of immigrant assimilation, this chapter emphasizes the need for a more complex and comparative theory of the mediating role of immigrant ethnic economies.

Immigration and Ethnicity in Urban Labor Markets

The heterogeneity of post–1965 Asian and Latino immigrant labor market incorporation strategies and outcomes reinforces how current models of labor market segmentation and human capital are no longer adequate to address the increasing complexity in the economic significance of race and ethnicity. It appears that the structural segmentation of urban labor markets does not necessarily constrain the occupational status and mobility of some ethnic groups. Although the growing phenomenon of the immigrant self-employed is transforming the urban labor market, they do not fit neatly into the segmented labor market scheme. Human capital theory fails to account for "premarket" factors, such as informal networks and other social resources, which also facilitate labor market outcomes. Even accounting for differences in educational attainment and skills leaves an unexplained residual.

Rather than attributing uneven labor market outcomes to either institutional arrangements or human capital differentials, attention has increasingly focused on how ethnicity mediates labor market processes and outcomes through social networks, occupational and industrial niches, and economic enclaves (Model 1993; Light and Karageorgis 1994; Portes 1995; Waldinger 1996). Immigrant incorporation is mediated by a "context of reception" determined by labor market conditions, host government policies, and, most important, an ethnic community that supports the presence of entrepreneurs or the self-employed (Light 1972; Portes 1981; Portes and Rumbaut 1990). Central to the success of Cuban immigrants in Miami, Chinese and Dominican immigrants in New York City, and Iranian immigrants in Los Angeles is a vibrant ethnic economy (Portes and Bach 1985; Zhou 1992; Portes and Zhou 1992; Light et al. 1994; Waldinger 1996). The economic success of these immigrants has been contrasted to the persistent labor market inequality experienced by Mexican immigrants, Haitians, Puerto Ricans, and native-born African Americans—groups that supposedly lack viable ethnic economies (Model 1993; Portes and Zhou 1992).

Alejandro Portes's and Robert Bach's (1985) seminal study on Cubans and Mexicans in Miami argued that immigrant-owned firms present a superior mode of labor market integration. Cubans who worked for a co-ethnic employer did better than their counterparts in the secondary labor market. They received higher returns to their human capital and obtained jobs more closely commensurate with their educational levels. Ethnic economy workers were also sheltered from interracial competition and labor market discrimination. A comparison of Cuban and Mexican immigrants demonstrated that labor-intensive menial jobs were not dead-end when the person was working for a co-ethnic employer. The promise of mobility was evident in the Cuban workers who went on to establish their own businesses. In their statistical analysis, Portes and Bach found the most important predictor of self-employment to be prior employment in a Cuban-owned firm. These findings led to the conclusion that the agglomeration of immigrant-owned firms created an "ethnically controlled avenue of economic mobility" not available in the mainstream economy (Wilson and Portes 1980, 298; Portes and Bach 1985).

Ethnic economies are distinct, in part, because they depend on the mobilization of family and social ties (Portes 1995). Access to social and financial capital enables some immigrants to exploit marginal opportunities for self-employment. Through informal networks, many newcomers find jobs working for a co-ethnic employer (Portes and Bach 1985; Zhou 1992). Based on "bounded solidarity" cultivated by a collective identity as "foreigners" and outsiders, this shared experience, often grounded in experiences with discrimination, leads to mutual support among immigrant employers and employees (Portes and Sensenbrenner 1992). The social embeddedness of co-ethnic relations means that employment practices in the immigrant ethnic economy are not motivated solely by market—that is, profit-maximizing considerations—but are based on mutual obligations or reciprocity characteristic of a family enterprise (Portes 1995).

Immigrant employers have privileged access to low-wage co-ethnic labor and "protected" consumer markets. A common culture and language reduce operating, recruitment, and on-the-job communication costs, thereby benefiting employers (Ong 1984). Employers also appeal to ethnic solidarity to persuade workers to accept substandard conditions, but they are, in turn, bonded by obligations (Portes and Bach 1985). The exploitation of co-ethnic labor generates the marginal profit that typically enables immigrant firms to survive (Kim 1996; Kwong 1996). In exchange for substandard work conditions, employees benefit from a flexible work environment that provides cultural continuity, informal training, and promotion opportunities, as employers are obligated to reserve employment openings for their co-ethnic employees (Zhou 1992; Portes and Stepick 1985). While bounded solidarity and trust enable employers to demand greater discipline and effort, "obligations generated by social structures cut both ways" and employees' social capital "consist[s] of the ability to demand preferential treatment from owners when it comes to promotions and business training" (Portes 1995, 29).

Hence, immigrant-owned businesses facilitate broader group transformations by providing employment opportunities and avenues for upward mobility. Immigrant workers can achieve economic parity without joining the general labor market. Ethnicity is positive in the ethnic economy, whereas it reflects subordinance in the secondary labor market. Not only is employment in the ethnic economy often the sole option for new immigrants, but it is, in fact, a superior one. Social capital and ethnic resources have enabled these ethnic groups to overcome both institutionalized discrimination and human capital deficiencies.

Although ethnic economy workers typically hold jobs that resemble those in the secondary labor market, a principle tenet of the ethnic economy literature is that these jobs provide informal training, which subsequently leads to promotion and/or mobility into self-employment. Network hiring reproduces social relationships in the workplace, improving access to information about workers and employers. Based on community and social ties, the co-ethnic milieu in immigrant work settings cultivates "informal training systems" (Bailey and Waldinger 1991). The increase in both the quantity and quality of information available through informal networks enhances trust among workers and their employers, hence reducing the employers' investment risks in worker training. Moreover, the co-ethnic work setting facilitates social practices that enforce informal codes of behavior and provides the necessary mechanisms for sanction when these codes are violated (Portes 1995; Waldinger 1996).

The ethnic economy proposition of informal training and mobility poses an important challenge to labor market segmentation theory, since a central premise is that intersegment mobility is highly limited (Kerr 1954; Harrison and Sum 1979; Doeringer and Piore 1971; Gordon, Edwards, and Reich 1982). Despite the argument that training and advancement opportunities are key aspects of the superiority of ethnic economy employment, much of the empirical research on the benefits of socially embedded labor and capital relations has focused on human capital returns, which some scholars argue may, in fact, bias empirical studies in favor of ethnic economy claims (Gilbertson and Gurak 1993).

Ethnic economy research has focused on Cuban and Asian immigrants, who exhibit a high propensity for self-employment (Light and Bonacich 1988; Zhou 1992; Lee 1996; Huynh 1996; Min 1996); however, co-ethnic work environments are also significant for other Latino groups. The reproduction of the Cuban enclave experience among Mexicans and Dominicans has been debated (Villar 1994; Alvarez 1990; Gilbertson and Gurak 1993). Demographic trends, including self-employment rates and the prevalence of ethnic-based networks, suggest that ethnic economies are also a central labor market strategy for Latinos, although certainly not as extensive as for Asians (Mahler 1995; Logan, Alba, and McNulty 1994; Portes and Guarnizo 1991). Several conditions—including the overcrowding of employment niches, access to a ready labor supply, consolidation of a captive market for ethnic products and services, and access to informal sources of capital—have created important advantages for immigrant Latino entrepreneurs (Light and Roach 1996). These conditions contribute to the consolidation of emerging Latino ethnic economies.

As noted, a key contribution of this chapter is based on LASUI data, which allow for a test of the ethnic economy thesis. The key research objective is to examine whether ethnic economies serve as a protected niche, where socially embedded employment relations facilitate opportunities for workers' skill acquisition and advancement. This chapter tests two hypotheses that form the argument that ethnic economies represent a distinct and protected segment of the economy:

(1) The nature of ethnic economy employment is comparable to the secondary labor market, in that jobs are typically based in labor-intensive industries and are menial and low-paying, with few fringe benefits. Opportunities for training and advancement, and higher human capital returns, however, distinguish ethnic economy employment from the secondary labor market.

(2) Co-ethnic employment relationships mediate the work environment such that the immigrant ethnic economy constitutes a dis-

tinct labor market segment from the primary and secondary labor market.

Operational Measures

This chapter employs several improved operational approaches to test the claims of the ethnic economy literature. One improvement is the operationalization or measurement of the ethnic economy. LASUI provides information on the race of supervisor and coworkers, allowing for a closer approximation of participation in the immigrant ethnic economy.[2] A second improvement is that the analysis of labor market outcomes differentiates between employers and their employees. A central critique of the positive human capital returns proposed by Portes and his associates is based on the failure to separate ethnic economy employers and employees in the statistical analysis (Nee and Sanders 1987). Accordingly, this chapter focuses on the experiences of wage workers and their returns to ethnic economy employment. A related strength is an interethnic comparative approach that examines the relative significance of the ethnic economy in the economic integration of four immigrant groups: Chinese, Koreans, Mexicans, and Central Americans.

In addition to an improved measure of ethnic economy participation, this chapter operationalizes labor market segments according to criteria that are consistent with segmentation theory. Although the definition of *segmented labor markets* is generally agreed among its proponents, empirical testing and operationalization are problematic, and a consistent and universal definition does not exist (Reich 1984; Taubman and Wachter 1986; Rosenberg 1989; Gittleman and Howell 1995). The methods and criteria employed to test whether the immigrant ethnic economy is a distinct labor market segment reflect the lack of a standardized approach.

Empirical studies on ethnic economies as a distinct labor market segment have operationalized labor market segments based on the ethnicity of workplace relations (Portes and Bach 1985; Portes and Stepick 1985).[3] The emphasis on the ascriptive qualities of labor market participants is also reflected in Portes and his associates' discriminant analysis, which employed variables pertaining to labor supply characteristics (for example, sexual and racial composition, English language proficiency, knowledge of the host society, and job satisfaction) to differentiate labor market segments (Portes and Bach 1985; Portes and Stepick 1985). Labor market segmentation theory, however, proposes that labor markets are differentiated by wage-setting mechanisms, employment policies, work conditions, and mobility opportunities (Doeringer and Piore 1971; Gordon, Edwards, and Reich 1982; Harrison and Sum 1979).

Hence, this chapter adopts a modified version of the late David Gordon's (1986) operationalization of labor market segments based on industrial and occupational criteria (see appendix 7A).

In defining participation in the ethnic economy, two primary economic sectors are specified: the immigrant ethnic economy and the general labor market, which is further separated into the primary and secondary labor markets and the public sector (see table 7.1). Four variables were used to operationalize participation in the ethnic economy: class of worker, race of supervisor, race of coworkers, and firm size. Workers are considered in the ethnic economy if they have a co-ethnic supervisor and work primarily among co-ethnics in a private company with one hundred or fewer employees, or if they do not have a supervisor but work primarily among co-ethnics. The rationale to include these workers is based on the assumption that some respondents may have interpreted the question on race of supervisor literally to refer to a supervisor exclusive of the firm owner. Since many small businesses do not have a supervisor, I include these respondents. In addition to workers, those who are self-employed and have co-ethnic employees or no salaried employees are also included in defining the ethnic economy.[4]

The general labor market is divided into three sectors: primary, secondary, and public. Consistent with the theorization of labor market segmentation, jobs with internal labor markets, good wages, stability, on-the-job training, and advancement opportunities are allocated to the primary sector, while low-paying jobs with poor work conditions, high turnover, and no opportunity for on-the-job training or advancement are allocated to the secondary labor market. The following list defines the terms:

(1) *Primary*: White- and blue-collar jobs with internal labor markets, good wages and working conditions, stability, and advancement opportunities.

(2) *Secondary*: Low-paying jobs with poor working conditions, high turnover, and no opportunity for on-the-job training or advancement.

(3) *Ethnic Economy*: Immigrant wage workers with a co-ethnic supervisor and primarily co-ethnic coworkers in a firm of one hundred or fewer employees, and immigrant self-employed with co-ethnic employees or no salaried employees.

(4) *Public Sector*: Jobs in the government or nonprofit sectors.

Since this research emphasizes differences in the private sector, the public sector is not included in the analysis.

A Descriptive Profile of Immigrants in the Los Angeles Economy

The Centrality of Immigrant Ethnic Economies

Among immigrants, ethnic economies are clearly a central strategy for labor market incorporation (table 7.1). The ethnic economy is most important for Asian immigrants, Koreans in particular, as close to three-quarters (73 percent) are located in the ethnic economy. Well over half of Chinese (57 percent) and Central American (54 percent) labor force participants are also in the immigrant ethnic economy, while it is slightly less dominant for Mexican immigrants (45 percent). Although ethnic economies are a principal labor market segment for immigrants, the relative proportion of workers and employers indicates that ethnicity is an important marker in differentiating the class configuration of ethnic economies. More than two-thirds (68 percent) of Koreans in the ethnic economy are self-employed or employers.[5] Among Chinese, Mexicans, and Central Americans, the overwhelming majority are wage laborers, indicating that these immigrant economies provide a fairly extensive ethnic labor market.

Asians incorporated in the mainstream economy are likely to be employed in the primary labor market. In fact, fewer than one in ten Asian immigrants is employed in the secondary labor market. This observation not only reflects the class bifurcation of Asian immigration but emphasizes the centrality of the ethnic economy in absorbing low-skill immigrant wage workers. A bimodal labor market incorporation

TABLE 7.1   *Distribution of Immigrant Labor Force Participants Among Labor Market Segments*

	Chinese	Korean	Mexican	Central American
Ethnic economy	57%	73%	45%	54%
Workers	72	32	84	81
Employers	28	68	16	19
General economy	41	17	53	45
Primary	66	65	42	29
Secondary	14	13	47	63
Public sector	20	22	11	8
Self-employed	2	10	2	1
Total N	225	180	364	157

Source: Los Angeles Study of Urban Inequality 1994.

pattern is also found for Central American immigrants; however, those integrated in the mainstream economy are most likely to be employed in the secondary labor market. In contrast to the prevalent perception of unskilled Mexican immigrants and the dominance of the secondary labor market as their central mode of incorporation (Portes and Bach 1985), two-fifths (42 percent) of Mexican workers in the general economy are employed in the primary labor market. Not surprisingly, the public sector is the least prominent source of employment for immigrants, especially Latino immigrants.[6]

Ethnic-Racial Division of Labor

Immigrant ethnic economies are embedded in particular industrial and occupational niches (see tables 7.2 and 7.3).[7] Asian immigrant ethnic economies are concentrated in the trade industries, in particular, retail trade. In addition to the centrality of retail businesses, nondurable manufacturing, primarily apparel production, is important to the Chinese ethnic economy, while services, specifically professional services, constitute the second leading industry in the Korean ethnic economy.[8] Latino ethnic economies, on the other hand, are concentrated in manufacturing industries or personal services. Durable manufacturing is a key anchor of the Mexican ethnic economy. Rather than a concentration in one industry, the Central American ethnic economy is anchored by nondurable manufacturing, personal services, and construction.

The bimodal quality of Asian immigrant incorporation is especially salient for Chinese immigrants. While Chinese ethnic economy workers are concentrated in retail trade and nondurable manufacturing industries, their counterparts in the primary labor market are located in professional and related services, and FIRE industries: Finance, Insurance, and Real Estate. For Koreans in the primary sector, nondurable manufacturing industries are important, where they are employed as managers and supervisors, or craftsmen. In contrast, Mexican labor market location is not differentiated by industry, since manufacturing is central to Mexican wage employment across labor market segments (Scott 1996). Retail trade industries, however, are prominent for Latino workers in the secondary labor market.

The industrial niches of ethnic economies generate low-skill service and manufacturing jobs, especially for Latinos. A notable exception is the Korean ethnic economy, which exhibits a range of occupational types. Latinos in the ethnic economy are concentrated as service workers or operators and laborers. The occupational profile of Latino ethnic economies resembles that of the secondary labor market, also dominated by service and laborer jobs. Although service and manufacturing

TABLE 7.2   *Industry and Occupational Composition by Labor Market Segments, Immigrant Asian Wage Workers*

	Ethnic Economy	Primary
Chinese	N = 92	N = 62
Industry		
Manufacturing	23%	13%
Nondurable	85	25
Trade	56	12
Retail	88	86
Services	10	50
Professional	67	90
Business and repair	22	10
Personal	11	
Finance, insurance, and real estate	7	16
Other[a]	4	8
Occupation		
Managerial, professional	15%	65%
Technical, sales, and support	25	32
Service	43	
Craft	2	3
Operators, laborers	15	
Farm, forest, fishery	1	
Korean	N = 42	N = 20
Industry		
Manufacturing	8%	35%
Nondurable	67	86
Trade	48	27
Retail	80	67
Services	29	8
Professional	75	100
Business and repair	17	
Personal	8	
Finance, insurance, and real estate	9	10
Other[a]	6	20
Occupation		
Managerial, professional	25%	43%
Technical, sales, and support	31	36
Service	26	3
Craft	10	16
Operators, laborers	8	2

Source: Los Angeles Study of Urban Inequality 1994.
[a]"Other" industries include agriculture, forestry, and fishing; transportation, communications, and other public utilities; entertainment and recreation; and public adminstration.

TABLE 7.3   *Industry and Occupational Composition by Labor
Market Segments, Immigrant Latino Wage Workers*

	Ethnic Economy	Primary	Secondary
Mexican	N = 136	N = 82	N = 92
Industry			
Manufacturing	41%	34%	32%
Nondurable	36	46	47
Trade	24	8	33
Retail	82	67	97
Services	18	33	10
Professional	24	59	30
Business and repair	32	30	50
Personal	44	11	20
Construction	7	13	7
Other[a]	10	12	18
Occupation			
Managerial, professional	0%	12%	0%
Technical, sales, and support	11	17	22
Service	22	15	22
Craft	13	41	6
Operators, laborers	53	14	47
Farm, forest, fishery	1		3
Central American	N = 69	N = 21	N = 45
Industry			
Manufacturing	28%	20%	26%
Nondurable	63	80	73
Trade	17	51	40
Retail	73	100	95
Services	34	21	26
Professional	17	80	17
Business and repair	31	20	58
Personal	52		25
Construction	15	2	7
Other[a]	6	6	1
Occupation			
Managerial, professional	2%	39%	0%
Technical, sales, and support	8	26	18
Service	33	6	36
Craft	15	20	2
Operators, laborers	42	10	44

Source: Los Angeles Study of Urban Inequality 1994.
[a]"Other" industries include agriculture, forestry, and fishing; transportation, communications, and other public utilities; entertainment and recreation; and public administration.

jobs anchor the Chinese ethnic economy as well, a full quarter of Chinese ethnic economy workers hold technical, sales, or administrative support jobs.

Immigrants in the primary labor market are likely to be employed as managers and professionals. This is clearly the case for Chinese immigrants (65 percent). The notable exception are Mexican immigrants in the primary labor market, who are less likely than the other ethnic groups to be in white-collar occupations. Rather, Mexicans in the primary labor market are primarily employed as precision or craft production workers. In other words, labor market segment location differentiates Mexican production workers along skill levels rather than occupational or industrial types.

Immigrant Human Capital

The ethnic economy is proposed to be distinct in that workers have comparable human capital as those in the secondary labor market but reap rewards that resemble primary labor market employment (Portes and Bach 1985; Portes and Zhou 1992). The empirical evidence suggests that for some immigrant groups, the ethnic economy does provide gainful employment for those with minimal skills (see table 7.4). While the average human capital of Mexican immigrants in the ethnic economy and secondary labor market is fairly comparable, Central American immigrants in the ethnic economy are clearly disadvantaged relative to their counterparts in the mainstream economy, including the secondary labor market. For Central Americans, the ethnic economy is especially important in absorbing workers who might otherwise have no employment opportunities. The labor force characteristics that are statistically significant in differentiating immigrant wage workers in the labor market segments are English language ability, completed years of education, length of residence in the United States, and U.S. citizenship.

Among all immigrant ethnic economy workers, on average, Mexicans have resided in the United States for the greatest number of years. Their counterparts in the secondary labor market have also lived in the U.S. for an average of thirteen years. Despite the length of residence, few Mexican workers in the ethnic economy or secondary labor market are U.S. citizens. Mexican ethnic economy workers are disadvantaged in educational attainment and English language ability relative to their coethnics in the secondary labor market.

Central American ethnic economy workers are, however, the most disadvantaged of all immigrant workers. They compare poorly relative to their counterparts in the secondary labor market with respect to English language ability, years of education, and U.S. citizenship. Similar

TABLE 7.4   *Immigrant Workers in the Labor Force Average Human Capital Characteristics by Labor Market Segments*

	Ethnic Economy	Secondary	Primary
Chinese	N = 92		N = 69
Age	34***	—	42
Female	37%*	—	52%
Married	53%**	—	78%
Years in United States	6†	—	12
U.S. citizen	28%†	—	49%
No or little English	47%†	—	5%
Years of education	12†	—	15
Korean	N = 42		N = 20
Age	39	—	35
Female	55%	—	61%
Married	65%	—	58%
Years in United States	9	—	10
U.S. citizen	25%	—	18%
No or little English	39%	—	28%
Years of education	13	—	15
Mexican	N = 136	N = 82	N = 92
Age	35*	33	37
Female	36%	36%	42%
Married	70%	75%	63%
Years in United States	13*	13	16
U.S. citizen	4%†	7%	14%
No or little English	55%*	40%	35%
Years of education	8†	9	10
Central American	N = 69	N = 21	N = 45
Age	34	35	37
Female	48%	56%	56%
Married	49%	66%	64%
Years in United States	8*	15	15
U.S. citizen	1%*	11%	26%
No or little English	61%***	35%	17%
Years of education	9***	10	12

Source: Los Angeles Study of Urban Inequality 1994.
*p < .05, **p < .01, ***p < .001, †p < .0001

to Chinese workers in the ethnic economy, Central American ethnic economy workers are relatively newer immigrants, with an average length of U.S. residence of eight years compared with fifteen years for Central Americans employed in the primary and secondary labor markets. English language ability is extremely limited among Central American ethnic economy workers: 61 percent speak little or no English, compared with approximately one-third (35 percent) in the secondary labor market and less than one-fifth (17 percent) in the primary labor market. U.S. citizenship is an uncommon status for Central American ethnic economy workers.

Chinese wage workers in the ethnic economy are distinguished from their counterparts in the primary labor market in numerous human capital variables. Chinese ethnic economy workers are relatively younger, have little English-speaking ability, have resided in the United States for half the average number of years of their co-ethnics in the primary labor market, and are less likely to be married or a U.S. citizen. In contrast, Korean ethnic economy workers are not only less disadvantaged compared to Chinese and Latino workers, but their human capital is fairly comparable to their co-ethnics in the primary labor market. Human capital differentials are not statistically significant in distinguishing Korean wage workers among the labor market segments. Korean wage workers are typically in their mid-thirties, married, have lived in the United States for an average of ten years, are high school graduates, and have a fair command of English. Unlike the other immigrant groups, for which human capital variables are important in differentiating labor market location, Korean immigrants exhibit a high degree of homogeneity in their human capital endowment.

Employment Outcomes in Labor Market Segments

With the exception of Koreans, employment in the immigrant ethnic economy typically means menial work, lower earnings, fewer fringe benefits, and little opportunity for training or a promotion. Ethnic economy employment rarely entails supervisory duties, and even for Koreans, those in the ethnic economy are less likely than their counterparts in the primary labor market to hold a supervisory position.

A common measure of work quality is the socioeconomic index (SEI) or occupational prestige score (table 7.5). As expected, the mean occupational prestige score is statistically significant in differentiating the labor market segments for the four immigrant groups. The average SEI score for Koreans in the ethnic economy affirms the general observation of skilled employment relative to other immigrant groups. The mean SEI index for Mexicans and Central Americans is 20 compared with 28 for Chinese and 35 for Koreans. Moreover, the standard deviation of the SEI index for Latino ethnic economy workers is significantly smaller than for their Asian counterparts, suggesting less dispersion around the mean value—in other words, greater homogeneity in the quality or type of ethnic economy employment. The mean SEI scores for

TABLE 7.5   *Immigrant Workers in the Labor Force Employment Outcomes by Labor Market Segments*

	Ethnic Economy	Secondary	Primary
Chinese	N = 92		N = 9
Supervisory duties	18%†	—	65%
Mean SEI index	28†	—	50
Mean 1992 earnings	$15,095†	—	$31,552
Received benefits	31%**	—	90
Number of benefits	0.75	—	2.24
Received training	7%*	—	25%
Received promotion	17%	—	28%
Korean	N = 42		N = 20
Supervisory duties	33%**	—	70%
Mean SEI index	35**	—	49
Mean 1992 earnings	$19,462	—	$23,462
Received benefits	28%	—	68
Number of benefits	0.83	—	1.48
Received training	22%*	—	54%
Received promotion	9%*	—	29%
Mexican	N = 136	N = 82	N = 92
Supervisory duties	11%†	20%	29%
Mean SEI index	20†	20	29
Mean 1992 earnings	$11,058**	$12,143	$16,736
Received benefits	50%	57%	66%
Number of benefits	1	1.32	1.7
Received training	17%	21%	27%
Received promotion	12%†	26%	45%
Central American	N = 69	N = 21	N = 45
Supervisory duties	4%†	9%	39%
Mean SE index	20†	19	36
Mean 1992 earnings	$ 9,085**	$10,423	$16,865
Received benefits	36%***	41%	83%
Number of benefits	0.73	0.77	1.93
Received training	11%	18%	11%
Received promotion	10%***	27%	53%

Source: Los Angeles Study of Urban Inequality 1994.
*$p < .05$, **$p < .01$, ***$p < .001$, †$p < .0001$

Latinos in the ethnic economy and secondary labor market are comparable, indicating similar occupational types. Not surprisingly, the average SEI score for immigrant workers in the primary labor market is significantly higher than for their counterparts in the ethnic economy. A final note is that the mean SEI score for Asians in the primary labor market, at 48, is notably higher than that for Mexicans, at 36, and Central Americans, at 29, suggesting a higher premium for primary labor market employment, especially for Chinese immigrants.

An analysis of earnings and benefits provides further evidence that ethnic economy employment fares poorly relative to other labor market segments. With the exception of Koreans, the mean 1992 annual earnings are statistically significant in differentiating the labor market segments for Chinese, Mexican, and Central American immigrant workers. Employment in the Latino ethnic economies is the lowest-paying. Moreover, the salary payoff to Latino employment in the primary labor market is fairly modest, especially when compared to the experience of Chinese immigrants. Central Americans in the ethnic economy earn an average annual salary of $9,085, or an estimated hourly wage of $5.45.[9] The average 1992 annual earnings for Mexican ethnic economy workers were slightly higher, at $11,058. However, the key observation is that Latino immigrants employed in the secondary labor market earn, on average, a higher annual salary than those in the ethnic economy. Among Latinos, the earnings premium for primary labor market employment is greatest for Central American immigrants, indicated by the close to $8,000 dollar differential. Overall, the average annual earnings of Latino immigrants suggest the prevalence of working poverty.

Consistent with the profile of Korean exceptionalism, Korean immigrants in the ethnic economy earned, on average, the highest annual 1992 salary: $19,462. Asian immigrants, overall, receive higher average annual earnings than their Latino counterparts. Interestingly, the earnings payoff for primary labor market employment is smallest for Koreans, at only $4,000, and greatest for Chinese, as the average annual earnings of $31,000 for primary labor market employment are more than twice the average earnings of ethnic economy employees. For immigrant workers, annual earnings indicate that the payoff to ethnic economy employment is modest at best.

Nonmonetary benefits, such as health insurance and retirement pensions, can add as much as 23.7 to 14.6 cents for each dollar of wages to production workers in union and nonunion firms, respectively (Freeman and Medoff 1984). With the exception of Mexican workers, however, fewer than one in three ethnic economy workers receives health insurance, paid sick leave, or a retirement plan from their employer. Of those ethnic economy workers who receive benefits, on average, they receive only one benefit relative to their co-ethnics in the general economy, who have a significantly greater likelihood of receiving a comprehensive benefits package.

An exception to the virtual absence of nonmonetary benefits in the ethnic economy are Mexican workers, approximately two-fifths (41 percent) of whom receive health insurance. The greater probability of benefits for Mexican workers may be an outcome of the presence of unions—approximately one in ten (12 percent) workers in the Mexican ethnic economy is a union member or covered by a collective-bargaining agreement. This unionization rate may reflect the concentration of Mexicans in durable manufacturing industries, with a historical precedent of prominent union activism, and service industries such as janitorial services where contemporary worker-organizing efforts are frequently targeted.

Opportunities for Advancement?

LASUI data indicate that the probability of training and promotion is statistically significant in differentiating the labor market segments for immigrant workers. However, in contrast to the ethnic economy thesis, employment in the ethnic economy does not create improved opportunities for training or promotion.[10] In fact, ethnic economy workers are least likely to receive training or a promotion relative to their counterparts in the other labor market segments, including the secondary labor market. Among Asian and Latino immigrants, fewer than one in five workers in the ethnic economy (in many cases, the odds are even smaller) has received training or a promotion from their current employer. This finding substantiates the normative observation of menial and dead-end employment in the ethnic economy.

Interestingly, while the likelihood of training and promotions, in particular, is significantly greater in the primary labor market for Latino immigrants, labor market location is comparatively less significant for Asian immigrants. Approximately one in ten (11 percent) Latino ethnic economy workers received a promotion relative to more than one in four (27 percent) in the secondary labor market, and approximately one-half (49 percent) of those in the primary labor market. The difference in promotions is not as dramatic for Chinese and Korean immigrants in the primary labor market. This observation is consistent with the earlier finding on the occupational profile of Asian and Latino immigrants in the primary labor market. Asian immigrants are concentrated in professional and managerial jobs, indicating fairly senior or advanced positions, while their Latino counterparts are more likely to hold a craft-related occupation, which may be part of a defined mobility or career ladder.

These findings suggest that, with the exception of Koreans, the nature of ethnic economy employment is comparable to the secondary labor market in that work is typically menial and low-paying with few fringe benefits, and concentrated in labor-intensive industrial and occupational niches. Moreover, the empirical evidence for Los Angeles simply does not support the argument that ethnic economy workers benefit from improved opportunities for skill acquisition and advancement.

Is the Ethnic Economy a "Protected Niche"?

To test whether the labor market segments are empirically distinguishable—that is, whether the ethnic economy is a distinct labor market—this chapter replicates the statistical method employed by Alejandro Portes and his associates (Wilson and Portes 1980; Portes and Bach 1985; Portes and Stepick 1985). A discriminant analysis is conducted to determine whether the labor market segments are distinct based on a set of independent variables. However, as noted in the earlier discussion on operationalization, the independent variables employed reflect firm characteristics consistent with the theorization that structural qualities differentiate labor markets. Discriminant analysis forms a linear combination of independent or "predictor" variables, which then serve to classify cases (workers) into groups (labor market segments). Discriminant analysis identifies the variables that are important in differentiating labor market segments and helps determine whether the ethnic economy is distinct with respect to these characteristics.

The dependent variables are the labor market segments: primary, secondary, and the ethnic economy. The public sector is excluded from the analysis because it is the least significant for immigrant workers and, more important, the primary objective is to determine how the ethnic economy fares relative to other labor market segments in the private or market economy. The LASUI variables that serve as independent or "discriminating" variables pertain to the theorized differences among labor market segments: firm size, job stability, supervisory duties, work tasks, and opportunities for training and mobility. The objective of the discriminant analysis is to test whether the labor market segments are differentiated with respect to this set of independent or predictor variables. A central question is whether the ethnic economy emerges as an empirically distinct segment that approximates the characteristics of the primary sector, as proposed by Portes and his associates (Portes and Bach 1985; Wilson and Portes 1980).

The discriminant analysis results provide empirical evidence that the labor market segments—ethnic economy, primary, and secondary—are empirically distinguishable based on the independent or discriminating variables discussed (see tables 7.6 and 7.7). Since the dependent variable—labor market segment—has three categories, the maximum number of possible discriminant functions is two.[11] For Asians, the first canonical discriminant function is statistically significant, while the

TABLE 7.6   *Discriminant Analysis of Immigrant Asian Workers in Three Labor Market Segments*

	First Function	Second Function
Variable		
Number of employees in firm (N)	−0.34[a]	−0.08
Number of workplaces (N)[b]	0.12	−0.37
Months with current employer	−0.37	0.05
Training	0.02	0.32
Promotion	0.05	0.74
Supervisory duties	0.57	0.2
Union or collective bargaining agreement	−0.15	0.43
Experienced racial discrimination	0.09	0.08
Experienced sex discrimination	0.07	−0.07
Talk with customers or clients face to face	−0.38	0.08
Talk with customer or clients on phone	0.09	0.14
Read instructions or reports	0.62	−0.18
Write paragraphs	−0.14	0.08
Work on a computer	0.11	−0.75
Do arithmetic	−0.08	−0.01
Eigenvalue—relative percentage	93.82	12.02
Canonical correlation	0.69	0.32
X	124.77	18.27
p	0.0000	0.1946
Group centroids		
Ethnic economy	0.74	0.15
Primary labor market	−1.21	−0.01
Secondary labor market	0.88	−1.27
Percentage of cases correctly classified	73.59	73.59

Source: Los Angeles Study of Urban Inequality 1994.
[a]Figures above the double line are standardized canonical discriminant coefficients.
[b]Number of workplaces in the last five years.

second function is not, indicating that the significant information about labor market segment differences was absorbed by the first discriminant function and the remaining discrimination is insignificant. In other words, the second discriminant function does not contribute substantially to group differences, since a single dimension represents all the observed differences among the labor market segments (Klecka 1980, 41). This finding reinforces the bifurcated labor market experiences of immigrant Asians represented by the distinction between ethnic economy and primary labor market employment. The discriminant analysis for Latinos resulted in two significant discriminant functions; however, the significance level of the second discriminant function indicates that

TABLE 7.7   *Discriminant Analysis of Immigrant Latino Workers in Three Labor Market Segments*

Variable	First Function	Second Function
Number of employees in firm (N)	−0.38[a]	0.52
Number of workplaces (N)[b]	−0.15	−0.08
Months with current employer	0.2	0.3
Training	−0.33	0.04
Promotion	0.5	0.03
Supervisory duties	0.28	0.38
Union or collective bargaining agreement	0.13	0.02
Experienced racial discrimination	−0.05	−0.08
Experienced sex discrimination	−0.07	−0.49
Talk with customers or clients face to face	0.42	−0.4
Talk with customers or clients on phone	0.31	0.37
Read instructions or reports	−0.34	0.52
Write paragraphs	0.58	−0.15
Work on a computer	0.15	−0.13
Do arithmetic	−0.65	−0.5
Eigenvalue—relative percentage	43.76	11.11
Canonical correlation	0.55	0.31
X	109.46	24.62
p	0.0000	0.0385
Group centroids		
Ethnic economy	0.56	−0.22
Primary labor market	−1.09	−0.2
Secondary labor market	0.01	0.49
Percentage of cases correctly classified	58.98	58.98

Source: Los Angeles Study of Urban Inequality 1994.
[a]Figures above the double line are standardized canonical discriminant coefficients.
[b]Number of workplaces in the last five years.

it does not contribute as substantively to explaining labor market differences as the first discriminant function.

The standardized coefficients are a measure of the relative importance of the variables—the larger the magnitude, the greater that variable's contribution to differentiating labor market segments. For Asians, the most powerful discriminating variables between the ethnic economy and the primary labor market are supervisory duties and two work tasks: face-to-face interaction with customers or clients and reading instructions or reports. Employment in the primary labor market is positively associated with supervisory duties and reading instructions or reports, and negatively associated with face-to-face customer interaction. The variables that approximate mobility opportunities failed to be strong predictors, reinforcing the previous discussion that primary-sector employment for Asian immigrants is concentrated in professional and managerial positions reflecting fairly advanced or senior status. The strong association of supervisory duties in primary-sector employment further substantiates this observation.

The first and most important canonical discriminant function for Latinos differentiates the labor market segments according to different qualities compared to Asian immigrants. For Latinos, the strongest discriminating variables that differentiate the primary labor market from the ethnic economy and secondary labor market are promotion and such work-related tasks as writing paragraphs, doing arithmetic, and face-to-face customer interaction. For Latinos, the primary labor market is positively associated with promotions and writing, and negatively associated with doing arithmetic, which is typically required in retail-related occupations.

The eigenvalue and the canonical correlation coefficient indicate that there are significant differences among the labor market segments according to the measured dimensions of the independent or predictor variables.[12] The eigenvalue and canonical correlation coefficient for the first function in the discriminant analysis of Asian immigrant workers indicates that the fit of the first function is quite good and discriminates among the labor market segments well. In other words, the Asian ethnic economy is distinct from the primary and secondary labor markets, with the most powerful discriminating variables pertaining to work tasks, supervisory duties, and length of employment tenure. In fact, the first discriminant function successfully "explains" 68 percent of the variation among the labor market segments; moreover, the significance level indicates that it contributes to labor market segment differences. A final note is that the percentage of cases classified correctly is another indicator of the effectiveness of the discriminant function. The discriminant analysis for Asian immigrants resulted in 71 percent of the cases correctly classified by group membership (that is, labor market location).

The findings for the discriminant analysis of Latino immigrants also confirm that the labor market segments are distinct. The eigenvalue for the first discriminant function is 66.68 and the canonical correlation coefficient is .6, indicating that the first function is meaningful and significant in explaining group differences. Opportunities for mobility as measured by a promotion are a significant predictor variable in labor market segments for Latino immigrants. These findings affirm the theorized differences between labor market segments, in particular that the immigrant ethnic economy does not generate opportunities for advancement.

Finally, the group centroids are the average discriminant score for each group (that is, labor market segment) and represent the typical group position. For both Asian and Latino immigrants, the significant chi-square for the first discriminant function is due to the distance in the reduced function space between the primary labor market and the other two segments. In other words, immigrants in the ethnic economy and the secondary labor markets are indistinguishable in this function, but both are empirically distinct from immigrants in the primary labor market. Group centroids indicate that the first discriminant function best distinguishes employment in the primary labor market from the ethnic economy and secondary labor market. This result supports the earlier discussion of the univariate analysis findings, which suggests that the labor market segments are quite different and, more important, that immigrants in the ethnic economy fare poorly relative to their counterparts in the mainstream economy.

Earnings Returns to Labor Market Segments

The ethnic economy literature argues that the earnings returns to participants' human capital are higher than that of co-ethnics with comparable human capital but who work in the secondary labor market. The problem, however, with Portes's and Bach's (1985) analysis of human capital returns is that they defined *enclave participants* as all those who indicated employment in Cuban-owned firms, including a significant number of self-employed (217). In subsequent studies, separate analysis was conducted for employees and employers, with mixed results. Jimy Sanders and Victor Nee (1987) found that workers in the enclave received comparatively low returns to their human capital. They argued that the positive earnings returns were limited to ethnic entrepreneurs. Min Zhou and John Logan (1989) replicated the procedures employed by Sanders and Nee based on three definitions of the ethnic enclave economy—place of residence, place of work, and industrial sector—and found positive returns to human capital for male workers inside and outside the enclave.

Upon specifying the labor market sectors, an ordinary least squares (OLS) regression analysis was conducted to estimate the effects of individual human capital characteristics on logged annual earnings for Asian and Latino wage workers in the various labor market sectors. Earnings are regressed on human capital variables separately for ethnic economy, secondary-, and primary-sector workers.[13] A dummy variable for citizenship was left out of the model because it did not increase the explained variance. If the literature on the ethnic economy that emphasizes positive returns to human capital is true, we should find that immigrants in the secondary labor market have the least returns to prior human capital investments, while those in the primary and ethnic economy will exhibit similar or higher levels of return for past investments (Wilson and Portes 1980, 307).

The results of the OLS regression model with logged 1992 earnings as the dependent variable indicate that the earnings returns to years of completed education, while positive, is not statistically significant for Asian workers in the ethnic economy or the primary labor market (see tables 7.8 and 7.9). Labor market experience, which accounts for time in the United States and exposure to the labor market, is significant in the primary labor market. Not surprisingly, there is an earnings premium for English language ability in the ethnic economy. But clearly, for all

TABLE 7.8   *Earnings Regression Model for Immigrant Asian Workers Employed Full- or Part-Time*

Dependent Variable: 1992 Earnings (ln)	Ethnic Economy	Primary Labor Market
Intercept	.544	.099
	(.399)	(1.075)
Labor market experience	.012	.081*
	(.012)	(.031)
Labor market experience squared	−1.114	−.001
	(2.841)	(7.881)
Married	−.122	−.133
	(.078)	(.187)
Sex (male = 1)	.068	.06
	(.069)	(.122)
Years of education	.012	.006
	(.017)	(.03)
English language ability	.145**	.109
	(.048)	(.081)
Log-hours worked, 1992	.883†	.969**
	(.104)	(.305)
Professional, manager	.16	.022
	(.092)	(.241)
Technical, sales, and support	.013	−.048
	(.09)	(.262)
R^2	.60	.392
Number of cases	85	63

Source: Los Angeles Study of Urban Inequality 1994.
Note: Standard error in parentheses.
*$p < .05$, **$p < .01$, ***$p < .001$, †$p < .0001$

TABLE 7.9   *Earnings Regression Model for Immigrant Latino Workers Employed Full- or Part-Time*

Dependent Variable: 1992 Earnings (ln)	Ethnic Economy	Primary Labor Market	Secondary Labor Market
Intercept	1.732†	2.552*	1.53
		(1.067)	(.919)
Labor market experience	.016**	.069**	−.001
	(.005)	(.023)	(.016)
Labor market experience squared	−2.204*	−8.94	−1.209
	(1.015)	(4.949)	(3.652)
Married	.088*	.268	.23*
	(.036)	(.148)	(.019)
Sex (male = 1)	.144***	.233	.021
	(.034)	(.136)	(.089)
Years of education	.008	−.001	−.013
	(.005)	(.02)	(.013)
English language ability	.051*	.277***	.056
	(.02)	(.069)	(.039)
Log-hours worked, 1992	.535†	.673†	.724**
	(.064)	(.147)	(.272)
Professional, manager	−.159	.178	—
	(.147)	(.163)	
Technical, sales, and support	.032	−.066	−.14
	(.056)	(.144)	(.112)
R^2	.491	.645	.258
Number of cases	153	74	97

Source: Los Angeles Study of Urban Inequality 1994.
Note: Standard error in parentheses.
*$p < .05$, **$p < .01$, ***$p < .001$, †$p < .0001$

Asian immigrant wage workers, work effort as measured by logged hours worked in 1992 is statistically significant and accounts for much of the variance in immigrant earnings.

A similar dynamic shapes the earnings of Latino immigrants. As with their Asian counterparts, work effort is clearly a significant determinant of immigrant earnings, holding all human capital variables constant. Interestingly, earnings returns to the years of education completed in the country of origin is positive for Latino ethnic economy workers and negative for their counterparts in the primary and secondary labor markets. This finding may in fact support the ethnic economy thesis; however, this variable is not statistically significant in any of the labor market sectors. In addition to the key human capital factors that positively influence immigrant earnings—labor market experience, work effort, and English language ability—being married or having a partner also has a significant positive effect on earnings for Latino immigrant workers in the ethnic economy and secondary labor market. Finally, immigrant men tend to earn more than women regardless of labor market location, and the earnings premium for men is statistically significant for Latino immigrants.

Rather than superior payoffs to investments in education, as proposed in the literature, the results of this analysis emphasize the importance of work effort and labor market experience in shaping immigrant earnings—both factors that indicate the labor-intensiveness of immigrant work and the significance of accumulating U.S.-specific labor market skills and knowledge across all labor market segments.

Conclusion

Ethnic economies are vital centers of economic activity for immigrants in Los Angeles. The empirical data presented substantiates the general observation that a primary mode of labor market incorporation for new immigrants is employment in a small firm owned by a co-ethnic. Immigrant ethnic economies in Los Angeles are embedded in marginal industries and occupations that center on historic ethnic niches in food services, retail trade, and labor-intensive manufacturing. Although the ethnic economy is central to immigrant economic livelihood, ethnic economy employment is associated with menial jobs, few worker benefits, and little opportunity for mobility.

The empirical evidence presented fundamentally challenges the proposal that the ethnic economy is an "effective vehicle for upward mobility among immigrant minorities" (Portes and Jensen 1989, 930). Although ethnic economy employment is certainly preferable to joblessness, it promises little beyond minimal wages for most immigrant workers. Contrary to the literature, the empirical analysis of data for Los Angeles finds that ethnic economy employment does not result in higher returns to human capital or advancement opportunities, as measured by promotion or supervisory duties. While racially homogeneous work environments shelter workers from discrimination, the social and individual costs of segregated workplace environments are high. The prevalence of linguistic isolation hinders immigrant workers from acquiring the English language skills that are central to mainstream employment.

An interethnic comparative analysis of the experiences of the four immigrant groups elaborates how the nature and rewards of employment in the various labor market segments are mediated by ethnicity. First, it is notable that Asian immigrant workers exhibit a bimodal labor market incorporation strategy. For Chinese immigrants, this pattern not only highlights a class-bifurcated immigration flow, but the centrality of the ethnic economy for low-skill workers. The differences in labor market location are sharp for Chinese immigrants; clearly those with English language ability and educational credentials are employed in the primary labor market, where work is significantly superior in skill requirements, remuneration, and benefits.

The experience of Korean immigrants in the Los Angeles economy emphasizes the centrality of self-employment and co-ethnic work relationships, regardless of labor market location. Clearly, the quality of Korean ethnic economy employment stands out relative to the Chinese, Mexican, and Central American ethnic economies. Their generally superior human capital (with respect to educational attainment and English language proficiency) across labor market segments is key to Korean exceptionalism in that Korean immigrants are fairly homogeneous with respect to class position. This shared socioeconomic status may be a compelling factor in enforcing social sanctions against the labor exploitation of co-ethnics (Min 1996; Smith 1996). Hence, Korean entrepreneurs are increasingly turning to other labor sources, notably Latino immigrants (Kim 1996; Min 1996).

Contrary to the proposal that ethnic economy employment results in greater rewards, these findings indicate that for Latino immigrants, ethnic economy employment is relatively more menial and lower-paying than secondary labor market employment. This observation is most salient for Central American immigrants. The Latino ethnic economy absorbs immigrants with few transferable skills in labor-intensive service and manufacturing jobs. Although labor market location is significant in differentiating the quality and rewards of wage work, the relative payoffs to mainstream employment for Latinos are modest. The central observation for Latino immigrant workers is the concentration in low-skill, low-paying service and production jobs.

Discriminant analysis provides empirical evidence that the ethnic economy is distinct from the other labor market segments; however, the findings suggest that, at best, immigrant ethnic economies offer a cautionary alternative to the general economy. The claim that the ethnic economy is distinguished by opportunities for training and mobility—that is, that the boundaries of the ethnic economy are permeable—is key to its superiority relative to the secondary labor market. However, this study provides evidence that mobility opportunities are limited in the ethnic economy. Contrary to its projection as facilitating the assimilation and mobility of new immigrants, the immigrant ethnic economy does not typically provide a meaningful alternative to exploitative dead-end work.

The ethnic economy literature proposes that immigrant incorporation does not necessarily entail assimilation, since immigrants can do just as well or better by maintaining separate economies and communities. The formation of ethnic economies or economic niches "turns ethnic disadvantage to good account, enabling social outsiders to compensate for the background deficits of their groups and the discrimination they encounter" (Waldinger 1996, 23). LASUI findings suggest that while ethnic economies are certainly central in the incorporation of immigrant Asians and Latinos, the propensity of co-ethnic work environments to support worker training and mobility is unsubstantiated. The exceptional experience of Koreans suggests that the generally higher level of human capital indicates less social distance between ethnic economy workers and employers, which may in fact facilitate reciprocity and enforceable social obligations. Korean exceptionalism serves as a reminder that the meaning of ethnicity is mediated by other factors, such as social or class position.

The findings presented here for Los Angeles lead to the conclusion that for most immigrant workers, the ethnic economy is not a "protected niche" conferring economic advantages, as theorized. Rather, the absence of meaningful payoffs suggests that immigrant workers are in the ethnic economy because other alternatives are not available. Structural barriers and lack of English language proficiency continue to maintain a cheap labor supply, with few options. Ethnicity influences labor market processes such as job searches, as informal networks provide information and contacts for potential employment, and the co-ethnic workplace, by importing cultural norms and practices, helps facilitate aspects of firm operations. However, the empirical evidence indicates that the conditions and outcomes of ethnic economy employment in terms of skill acquisition, mobility, and benefits are constrained by their concentration in labor-intensive, low-skill service and manufacturing industries. In conclusion, there is little evidence that socially embedded employment relations can mediate the effects of marginal industries and hypercompetition in structuring labor market outcomes for low-skill Asian and Latino immigrants.

Appendix

TABLE 7A.1   *Labor Market Segment Composition 1990 Census, Occupation Codes*

Primary Labor Market

2–259	694–703
284	707
303–329	713
336–344	719
347	734–737
353–354	739
363	759
365–376	763
378–389	766
413–414	773–774
416–423	783
433	789
445–447	796–797
457–458	783
473–484	789
488–518	796–797
523–569	803
575–598	806–808
613–635	823–825
637	828–833
639	843–844
643	848–855
645–679	866–868
686–689	

Secondary Labor Market

263–283	693
285	704–706
335	708–709
345–346	714–717
348	723–733
355–359	738
364	743–758
377	764–765
403–407	768–769
415	777
424–427	779
434–444	784–787
448–456	793–795
459–469	798–799
485–487	804
519	809–814
573	826
599	834
636	845
644	856–865
683–684	869–889

Source: Los Angeles Study of Urban Inequality 1994.

Notes

1. While LASUI does not provide the supervisor or coworker ethnicity but rather the racial category—for example, Asian—Greta Gilbertson and Douglas Gurak (1993), in their survey on the Dominican and Colombian ethnic economy in New York City, faced similar limitations and operationalized enclave employment based on the race identity of a manager or owner.

2. Although the LASUI survey did not ask about the firm owner, the supervisor is a reliable proxy, especially for small firms, where the probability that the supervisor is the owner is quite high.

3. According to Alejandro Portes and his associates, the ethnic enclave is defined as employment in Cuban-owned firms, including those who are self-employed (Portes and Bach 1985, 218). The secondary labor market is defined by an Anglo employer and primarily minority coworkers, while the primary labor market is defined by an Anglo employer and primarily Anglo coworkers. This definition was later modified by the additional qualification of firm size (Portes and Stepick 1985).

4. Employers are included in the definition of the ethnic economy to measure its size—in other words, the relative proportion of immigrants in the labor force who are located in the ethnic economy either as employers or workers. However, consistent with the research objectives of this chapter, the empirical analysis pertains only to workers.

5. LASUI indicates that self-employment is prominent for Korean immigrants located in the general economy as well. Other studies also find high self-employment rates among Korean immigrants. See Kim and Hurh (1985), Illsoo Kim (1981, 1987), Dae Kim (1996), Min and Jaret (1984), and Min (1996).

6. Due to the small N for Asians in the secondary labor market, the comparative analysis of Asians in different labor market segments is limited to Asians in the ethnic economy and primary labor market. For all four ethnic groups, discussion of immigrants employed in the public sector is also limited due to the emphasis on immigrant workers in the private sector.

7. Roger Waldinger (1996) defines a *niche* as an industry or occupation in which groups are "overrepresented" with respect to their size in the labor force—at least 150 percent of the group's share of total employment (95). The use of *niche* in this chapter refers to this concept of concentration in specific industries and/or occupations.

8. Consistent with the Bureau of Labor Statistics' classifications, *durable* manufacturing industries refer to food and kindred products,

tobacco products, textile mill products, apparel products, paper and allied products, printing and publishing, petroleum refining and related industries, rubber and plastic products, and leather products. *Nondurable* manufacturing industries include primary metal industries, fabricated metal products, industrial and commercial machinery and computer equipment, electronic and other electrical equipment, transportation equipment, lumber products, furniture and fixtures, stone, clay, glass, and concrete products.

9. The estimated hourly wage was calculated by multiplying the average hours worked per week by the average number of weeks worked in 1992 and dividing the average hours worked in 1992 by the mean 1992 earnings.

10. The survey question asked whether the respondent had received any formal, classroom-style training.

11. Canonical discriminant functions are a linear combination of the discriminant variables formed to satisfy two conditions: (1) the coefficients derived for the first function maximize the differences between the group means, and (2) the coefficients for the second function are also derived to maximize the differences between the group means, but under the added condition that the second function is uncorrelated with the previous function, and so on. In other words, the first function is the most powerful and the second function provides the greatest discrimination after the first has done its best (Klecka 1980, 35). The maximum number of functions is one fewer than the number of subpopulations. If fewer than the maximum number of discriminant functions are significant, then some of the populations are empirically indistinguishable from each other with respect to the independent variables (Portes and Stepick 1985, 501).

12. The eigenvalue and canonical correlation coefficient indicate how meaningful the discriminant functions are, and how much utility they have in explaining group differences; that is, these coefficients indicate the model's goodness of fit (Klecka 1980, 38). The eigenvalue is the ratio of the between-groups to within-group sums of squares, and is converted to a relative percentage to indicate the total discriminating power of the discriminant function. Large eigenvalues are associated with "good" discriminating functions. A high canonical correlation coefficient indicates that a strong relationship exists between the groups (that is, labor market segments) and the discriminant function. If the groups were not very different on the variables being analyzed, then the correlation coefficient would be low.

13. The analysis for Asian workers did not include the secondary labor market because the sample size was too small (N = 16).

References

Alvarez, Robert M., Jr. 1990. "Mexican Entrepreneurs and Markets in the City of Los Angeles: A Case of an Immigrant Enclave." *Urban Anthropology* 19(1 & 2): 99–124.

Bailey, Thomas, and Roger Waldinger. 1991. "Primary, Secondary, and Enclave Labor Markets: A Training Systems Approach." *American Sociological Review* 56(August): 432–45.

Bates, Timothy. 1994. "An Analysis of Korean Immigrant–Owned Small Business Start-Ups with Comparison to African American and Non Minority-Owned Firms." *Urban Affairs Quarterly* 30(2): 227–48.

Bonacich, Edna, and John Modell. 1980. *The Economic Basis of Ethnic Solidarity: Small Business in the Japanese American Community.* Berkeley: University of California Press.

DeFreitas, Gregory. 1988. "Hispanic Immigration and Labor Market Segmentation." *Industrial Relations* 27(2): 195–214.

Doeringer, Peter B., and Michael Piore. 1971. *Internal Labor Markets and Manpower Analysis.* Lexington, Mass.: Heath.

Freeman, Richard, and James Medoff. 1984. *What Do Unions Do?* New York: Basic Books.

Gilbertson, Greta A., and Douglas T. Gurak. 1993. "Broadening the Enclave Debate: The Labor Market Experiences of Dominican and Colombian Men in New York City." *Sociological Forum* 8(2): 205–20.

Gittleman, Maury B., and David R. Howell. 1995. "Changes in the Structure and Quality of Jobs in the United States: Effects by Race and Gender, 1973–1990." *Industrial and Labor Relations Review* 48(3): 420–40.

Gordon, David. 1986. "Procedure for Allocating Jobs into Labor Segments." Unpublished paper.

Gordon, David, Richard Edwards and Michael Reich. 1982. *Segmented Work, Divided Workers: The Historical Transformation of Labor in the United States.* New York: Cambridge University Press.

Harrison, Bennett, and Andrew Sum. 1979. "The Theory of 'Dual' or Segmented Labor Markets." *Journal of Economic Issues* 13: 687–707.

Huynh, Craig. 1996. "Vietnamese-Owned Manicure Businesses in Los Angeles." In *Reframing the Immigration Debate*, edited by Bill Ong Hill and Ronald Lee. Los Angeles: LEAP Asian Pacific American Public Policy Institute and UCLA Asian American Studies Center.

Kaufman, Jonathan. 1995. "How Cambodians Come to Control California Doughnuts." *Wall Street Journal*, February 22, 1995.

Kerr, Clark. 1954. "The Balkanization of Labor Markets," reprinted in *Readings in Labor Economics and Labor Relations*, edited by Lloyd G. Reynolds, Stanley H. Masters, and Colletta H. Moser. Englewood Cliffs, N.J.: Prentice-Hall.

Kim, Dae Young. 1996. "The Limits of Ethnic Solidarity: Mexican and Ecuadorian Employment in Korean-Owned Businesses in New York

City." Paper presented to the American Sociological Association Conference, New York(August 16–20, 1996).

Kim, Illsoo. 1981. *New Urban Immigrants: The Korean Community in New York*. Princeton, N.J.: Princeton University Press.

———. 1987. "The Koreans: Small Business in an Urban Frontier." In *New Immigrants in New York*, edited by Nancy Foner, New York: Columbia University Press.

Kim, Kwang Chung, and Won Moo Hurh. 1985. "Ethnic Resources Utilization of Korean Immigrant Entrepreneurs in the Chicago Minority Area." *International Migration Review* 19(1): 82–111.

Klecka, William R. 1980. *Discriminant Analysis*. Newbury Park, Calif.: Sage Publications.

Kwong, Peter. 1996. *The New Chinatown*. New York: Hill and Wang.

Lee, Gen L. 1996. "Cambodian-Owned Donut Shops." In *Reframing the Immigration Debate*, edited by Bill Ong Hill and Ronald Lee. Los Angeles: LEAP Asian Pacific American Public Policy Institute and UCLA Asian American Studies Center.

Light, Ivan. 1972. *Ethnic Enterprise in America: Business and Welfare Among Chinese, Japanese and Blacks*. Berkeley: University of California Press.

Light, Ivan, and Edna Bonacich. 1988. *Immigrant Entrepreneurs: Koreans in Los Angeles, 1965–1982*. Berkeley and Los Angeles: University of California Press.

Light, Ivan, and Yen Espiritu. 1991. "The Changing Ethnic Shape of Contemporary Urban America." In *Urban Life in Transition*, edited by M. Gottdiener and Chris G. Pickvance. Vol. 39, *Urban Affairs Annual Reviews*. Newbury Park, Calif.: Sage Publications.

Light, Ivan, and Stavros Karageorgis. 1994. "The Ethnic Economy." In *The Handbook of Economic Sociology*, edited by Neil J. Smelser and Richard Swedberg. New York: Russell Sage.

Light, Ivan, and Elizabeth Roach. 1996. "Self-Employment: Mobility Ladder or Economic Lifeboat?" In *Ethnic Los Angeles*, edited by Roger Waldinger and Mehdi Bozorgmehr. New York: Russell Sage.

Light, Ivan, Georges Sabagh, Mehdi Bozorgmehr, and Claudia Der-Martirosian. 1994. "Beyond the Ethnic Enclave Economy." *Social Problems* 41(1): 65–80.

Logan, John R., Richard D. Alba, Thomas L. McNulty. 1994. "Ethnic Economies in Metropolitan Regions: Miami and Beyond." *Social Forces* 72(3): 691–724.

Mahler, Sara J. 1995. *American Dreaming: Immigrant Life on the Margins*. Princeton, N.J.: Princeton University Press.

Mar, Don. 1991. "Another Look at the Enclave Economy Thesis: Chinese Immigrants in the Ethnic Labor Market." *Amerasia Journal* 17(3): 5–21.

McDowell, Edwin. 1996. "Hospitality Is Their Business." *New York Times*, March 21, 1996.

Melendez, Edwin. 1992. "Labor Market Structure and Wage Differences in New York City: A Comparative Analysis of Hispanics and Non-Hispanic Blacks and Whites." In *Hispanics in the Labor Force,* edited by Edwin Melendez, Clara Rodriguez, and Janis Barry Figueroa. New York: Plenum Press.

Min, Pyong Gap. 1996. *Caught in the Middle: Korean Communities in New York and Los Angeles.* Berkeley: University of California Press.

Min, Pyong Gap, and Charles Jaret. 1984. "Ethnic Business Success: The Case of Korean Small Business in Atlanta." *Sociology and Social Research* 69: 412–35.

Model, Suzanne. 1992. "The Ethnic Economy—Cubans and Chinese Reconsidered." *Sociological Quarterly* 33(1): 63–82.

———. 1993. "The Ethnic Niche and the Structure of Opportunity: Immigrants and Minorities in New York City." In *The "Underclass" Debate: Views from History,* edited by Michael B. Katz. Princeton, N.J.: Princeton University Press.

———. 1997. "Ethnic Economy and Industry in Mid-Twentieth Century Gotham." *Social Problems* 44(4): 445–63.

Nee, Victor, and Jimy Sanders. 1987. "On Testing the Enclave-Economy Hypothesis, A Reply to Portes and Jensen." *American Sociological Review* 52(December): 771–73.

Ong, Paul. 1984. "Chinatown Unemployment and Ethnic Labor Markets." *Amerasia Journal* 11: 1.

Perez-Pena, Richard. 1996. "For 53, the Promise of America Fits on a Taxicab." *New York Times,* May 11, 1996.

Piore, Michael. 1979. *Birds of Passage.* New York: Cambridge University Press.

Portes, Alejandro. 1981. "Modes of Structural Incorporation and Present Theories of Labor Immigration." In *Global Trends in Migration,* edited by Mary Krtiz, Charles B. Keeley, and Silvano Tomasi. New York: Center for Migration Studies.

———. 1987. "The Social Origins of the Cuban Enclave Economy of Miami." *Sociological Perspectives* 30(4): 340–72.

———. 1995. "Economic Sociology and the Sociology of Immigration: A Conceptual Overview." In *The Economic Sociology of Immigration: Essays on Networks, Ethnicity, and Entrepreneurship,* edited by Alejandro Portes. New York: Russell Sage.

Portes, Alejandro, and Robert Bach. 1985. *Latin Journey: Cuban and Mexican Immigrants in the United States.* Berkeley: University of California Press.

Portes, Alejandro, and Luis E. Guarnizo. 1991. "Tropical Capitalists: U.S. Bound Immigration and Small Enterprise Development in the Dominican Republic." In *Migration, Remittances, and Small Business Development,* edited by Sergio Diaz-Briquets and Sidney Weintraub. Boulder, Colo.: Westview Press.

Portes, Alejandro, and Leif Jensen. 1987. "What's an Ethnic Enclave?

The Case for Conceptual Clarity, Comment on Sanders and Nee." *American Sociological Review* 52(December): 745–71.

———. 1989. "The Enclave and the Entrants: Patterns of Ethnic Enterprise in Miami Before and After Mariel." *American Sociological Review* 54(December): 929–49.

———. 1992. "Disproving the Enclave Hypothesis." *American Sociological Review* 57: 418–20.

Portes, Alejandro, and Ruben G. Rumbaut. 1990. *Immigrant America: A Portrait*. Berkeley: University of California Press.

Portes, Alejandro, and Julia Sensenbrenner. 1992. "Embeddedness and Immigration: Notes on the Social Determinants of Economic Action." John Hopkins University. Revised version of paper presented at American Sociological Association Conference (August 27, 1991).

Portes, Alejandro, and Alex Stepick. 1985. "Unwelcome Immigrants: The Labor Market Experiences of 1980 (Mariel) Cuban and Haitian Refugees in South Florida." *American Sociological Review* 50(August): 493–514.

Portes, Alejandro, and Min Zhou. 1992. "Gaining the Upper Hand: Economic Mobility Among Immigrant and Domestic Minorities." *Ethnic and Racial Studies* 15(4): 491–522.

Reich, Michael. 1984. "Segmented Labour: Time Series Hypothesis and Evidence." *Cambridge Journal of Economics* 8: 63–81.

Reitz, Jeffrey G. 1990. "Ethnic Concentrations in Labor Markets and Their Implications for Ethnic Inequality." In *Ethnic Identity and Equality: Varieties of Experience in a Canadian City*, edited by Raymond Breton, Wsevolod Isajiw, Warren E. Kalbach, and Jeffrey G. Reitz. Toronto: University of Toronto Press.

Rosenberg, Sam. 1979. "A Survey of Empirical Work on Labor Market Segmentation." Working paper series, 138. Davis, Calif.: Department of Economics, University of California, Davis.

Rumberger, Russell W., and Martin Carnoy. 1980. "Segmentation in the U.S. Labour Market: Its Effects on the Mobility and Earnings of Whites and Blacks." *Cambridge Journal of Economics* 4: 117–32.

Sanders, Jimy M., and Victor Nee. 1987. "Limits of Ethnic Solidarity in the Enclave Economy." *American Sociological Review* 52: 745–73.

———. 1992. "Comment: Problems in Resolving the Enclave Economy Debate." *American Sociological Review* 57(3): 415–18.

Scott, Allen. 1996. "The Manufacturing Economy: Ethnic and Gender Divisions of Labor." In *Ethnic Los Angeles*, edited by Roger Waldinger and Mehdi Bozorgmehr. New York: Russell Sage.

Sengupta, Somini. 1996. "Building Lives on Brooklyn's Scaffolds." *New York Times*, July 6, 1996.

Smith, Robert. 1996. "Mexicans in New York: Membership and Incorporation in a New Immigrant Community." In *Latinos in New York: Communities in Transition*, edited by Gabriel Haslip-Viera and Sherrie L. Baver. Notre Dame, Ind.: University of Notre Dame Press.

Taubman, Paul, and Michael L. Wachter. 1986. "Segmented Labor Markets." In *Handbook of Labor Economics, volume II*, edited by Orley Ashenfelter and Richard Layard. New York: Elesvier Science Publishers.

Tolbert, Charles, Patrick M. Horan, and E. M. Beck. 1980. "The Structure of Economic Segmentation: A Dual Economy Approach." *American Journal of Sociology* 85(5): 1095–1116.

Villar, DeLourdes Maria. 1994. "Hindrances to the Development of an Ethnic Economy Among Mexican Migrants." *Human Organizations* 53(3): 263–68.

Waldinger, Roger. 1992. "Who Makes the Beds? Who Washes the Dishes? Black/Immigrant Competition Reassessed." Discussion paper. University of California at Los Angeles.

———. 1996. *Still the Promised City? African-Americans and New Immigrants in Postindustrial New York*. Cambridge, Mass.: Harvard University Press.

Wilson, Kenneth, and W. Allen Martin. 1982. "Ethnic Enclaves: A Comparison of the Cuban and Black Economies in Miami." *American Journal of Sociology* 88: 135–60.

Wilson, Kenneth L., and Alejandro Portes. 1980. "Immigrant Enclaves: An Analysis of the Labor Market Experiences of Cubans in Miami." *American Journal of Sociology* 86: 295–319.

Zhou, Min. 1992. *Chinatown: The Socioeconomic Potential of an Urban Enclave*. Philadelphia: Temple University Press.

Zhou, Min, and John R. Logan. 1989. "Returns on Human Capital in Ethnic Enclaves: New York City's Chinatown." *American Sociological Review* 54: 809–20.

8

AFRICAN AMERICAN MALES IN DECLINE: A LOS ANGELES CASE STUDY

James H. Johnson Jr., Walter C. Farrell Jr., and Jennifer A. Stoloff

RESEARCH confirms that the social and economic status of the African American male has steadily deteriorated over the last quarter century. It is well documented that their rates of school failure, joblessness, homicide, incarceration, and other antisocial behaviors far exceed those for their white, Hispanic, and Asian male counterparts. In fact, the magnitude of these problems has led some researchers to characterize the African American male as an endangered species (Austin 1996; Cose 1995; Gibbs 1989; McCall 1995).

In an earlier article, we culled from the extant literature four schools of thought that have been advanced to explain the crisis of the black male in America (Johnson, Farrell, and Stoloff 1998; see also Johnson 1996). One school, the spatial isolation hypothesis, views it as essentially a structural problem, rooted primarily in the globalization of the economy and the persistence of racial discrimination in the U.S. housing market (Massey and Denton 1992; Wilson 1987, 1996). A second school of thought, the cultural capital–employer-preference hypothesis, characterizes the problem as "a crisis of values and morals," reflected in negative attitudes and behaviors that cause black males to be shunned in the mainstream labor market (Bennett, DiIulio, and Walters 1996; Harrison 1992; Lemann 1991; Mead 1992; Murray 1995; Sowell 1981, 1994; "Foul Shots," 1997). The third school of thought, the search-and-destroy hypothesis, views black males as the systematic target of discriminatory treatment, especially in the public education system, the labor market, and the criminal justice system (Miller 1996; Johnson and Oliver 1992; Oliver and Johnson 1989; Johnson, Farrell, and Sapp 1997). The fourth perspective, the social capital hypothesis, views the problems confronting black males as the result of a lack of embeddedness in individual and institutional networks that serve as "bridges" to the educational and economic mainstream (Braddock and McPartland 1987; Fernandez-Kelly 1995; Jarrett 1995; Johnson, Bienenstock, and Farrell 1999; Sullivan 1989).

In this chapter, we attempt to empirically assess the relative utility of each of these schools of thought in explaining the employment status and labor market experiences of African American males vis-à-vis their non-Hispanic white and Hispanic male counterparts in metropolitan Los Angeles in the early 1990s. After describing the data and methodology employed in the research, we present the results of our empirical test of these hypotheses. We conclude by discussing the implications of the findings for developing public policies to address the unique problems confronting African American males.

Research Design

To test the hypotheses that have been advanced to explain the declining economic and social fortunes of African American males in U.S. society (Johnson 1996; Johnson, Farrell, and Stoloff 1998), we focused on the subsample of white, black, and Hispanic men in the Los Angeles Survey of Urban Inequality. We extracted seven categories of data on the male respondents in each of these groups, which are divided into dependent and independent variables in table 8.1. Our dependent variable is a dichotomous measure of the employment status of men in the Los Angeles sample at the time the survey was conducted. After excluding men who were in school or retired, those who were employed either part-time or full-time, along with those who were temporarily laid off or on sick leave, were classified as working; those who indicated that they were unemployed were classified as not working.

For the purpose of our analyses, there are five categories of independent variables. The first set of variables is composed of measures that capture forces that supposedly shape an individual's morals, values, and work orientation—those "culturally derived" characteristics that purportedly explain who prospers and who does not in contemporary American society (Harrison 1992; Mead 1992; Sowell 1994). In an earlier article, we empirically derived measures of cultural background influences from a principal components analysis of the responses to fifteen questions in the LASUI—items designed to capture influences in the following domains: geographical, family background, religious, political, and linguistic (see Johnson, Bienenstock, and Stoloff 1995).

We employ five of those measures of cultural capital in this research. For our purposes here, they are operationalized as dichotomous indicators. The first, Third World socialization, distinguishes males who were born in a Third World country, lived in a Third World country most of the time before they were sixteen years old, and received most of their education outside the United States. Cultural capital theorists contend that such individuals possess attitudes and behavioral traits that are highly desirable in the labor market. The second measure, Southern roots, distinguishes Los Angeles men who were born in the southern United States and lived primarily in that region prior to age sixteen. According to cultural capital theorists, these men supposedly have poor attitudes toward work, especially if they are black (Lemann 1991).

The third cultural capital measure, ever lived in public housing, distinguishes men who live currently, or have lived, in public housing. In the eyes of cultural capital theorists, public housing environments are incubators of negative attitudes and behaviors that serve as impediments to work. The fourth measure, lived with both parents until age sixteen, distinguishes those males in our sample who spent their formative years with two parents from those who did not. Cultural capital theorists argue that these two contexts shape individual attitudes toward work, family, and community—the former positively and the latter negatively.

The final cultural capital measure, work status, distinguishes males in our sample who are U.S. citizens and documented aliens from those who are undocumented. Previous research indicates that this variable is a critical determinant of not only who gets a job in the Los Angeles economy but also how much they are likely to earn once employed (Johnson and Farrell 1998).

In this research, we employ two measures of spatial isolation, which constitute our second category of independent variables. One is a dichotomous measure of whether the males in our sample reside in East Los Angeles or South Central Los Angeles. Historically, these were the areas within which Los Angeles's Hispanic and black populations, respectively, concentrated, owing to widespread racial-ethnic discrimination in the broader metropolitan housing market (Oliver and Johnson 1984). Moreover, research indicates that, over the past two decades, these two communities have borne the brunt of high-wage job loss and of federal- and state-level cutbacks in funding for community and economic development (Grant and Johnson 1995; Johnson and Oliver 1992).

The second is a dichotomous measure of whether the males in our sample lived in a high poverty area at the time the LASUI was conducted. Following Wilson's (1987) definition, individuals who lived in a census tract with a poverty rate equal to or above 40 percent were assumed to be living in a high poverty area.

Our third category of independent variables is composed of four standard measures of human capital, which are typically included in statistical analyses of male employment: age, education, marital status, and work-limiting physical disability.

The fourth category of independent variables is composed of measures or indicators of social capital. In the LASUI, several questions were included pertaining to networks and social functioning. This series of questions was introduced with the following statement:

> From time to time, most people discuss important matters with other people. Looking back over the last six months, who are the people, other than people living in your household, with whom you discussed matters important to you?

For the first three names given, the following data were recorded: race or ethnicity, sex, level of education completed, relationship to respondent, marital status, and whether they lived in the respondent's neighborhood, had a steady job, and received public aid or welfare, as well as whether these individuals assisted with everyday activities and could be relied on for help in a major crisis.

From these data, we chose to dichotomize five variables as indicators of the presence of "bridging ties" for each survey respondent. If any member of a respondent's network was of a different race, then the respondent was assumed to have a *race bridge*. If a male respondent named at least one female, then he was assumed to have *a gender bridge*. Respondents were assumed to have a *neighborhood bridge* if any one of their network members was from a different neighborhood. If at least one person in the network had more than a high school education, then the respondent was assumed to have an *education bridge*. Finally, if at least one member of the network was currently receiving public assistance, a *welfare bridge* was assumed to exist. We should note here that, in contrast to the others, the latter is considered to be a non-employment-enhancing bridge (Johnson, Bienenstock, and Farrell 1999).

In addition to the foregoing measures of social capital, we included a measure of institutional embeddedness. For the purpose of this research, it is a dichotomous measure of whether the males in our sample belonged to at least one voluntary organization in 1992.

The fifth and final category of independent variables is composed of indicators of the domains in which black males are purported to be the targets of systematic discrimination. We included two such indicators in this research: whether the individual has a criminal record and whether he self-reported experiences of discrimination in the Los Angeles labor market.

Analyses and Findings

Our primary goal in attempting to empirically test the four hypotheses is to identify the attributes or factors that distinguish the experiences of African American males from other males in the Los Angeles labor market in the early 1990s. Toward this end, we present two types of findings.

In table 8.1, we present cross-tabulations of our operational measure of spatial isolation, cultural capital, human capital, and social capital, and the race-ethnic identity of our survey respondents. The results illustrate the extent to which men in our sample differed in terms of the skills and attributes that they brought to the Los Angeles labor market in the early 1990s.

In tables 8.2 and 8.3, we present the results of our multivariate statistical analyses, which seek to isolate the absolute and relative predictive power of the spatial isolation, cultural capital, human capital, and social capital attributes in explaining the employment status of white, black, and Hispanic men in our Los Angeles sample in the early 1990s. Because our dependent variable is dichotomous, we use the logit model to estimate the effects of the independent variables on the employment status of the survey respondents.

Bivariate Analysis

The cross-tabulations indicate that black men were more likely than their white and Hispanic counterparts to have lived or currently be living in public housing; to have spent their formative years in the South; to have a work-limiting disability; to be embedded in non-employment-enhancing networks (that is, those in which at least one person is on welfare); and to have a criminal record. Conversely, the black males were less likely to have grown up in a household with both biological parents, to be married, to be embedded in racially diverse networks, and to be working.

Because of the high concentration of recently arrived immigrants in

TABLE 8.1   *Descriptive Statistics*

Concept Variable/Specific Measure	All Men (N = 1,262)	White Men (N = 400)	Black Men (N = 388)	Hispanic Men (N = 474)	Chi-Square (p Value)
Independent variables					
Cultural capital-employer preference					
Third World socialization					
yes	34.0%	6.5%	5.9%	80.2%	721.4%
no	66.0	93.5	94.1	19.8	(.000)
Southern roots					
yes	12.1	6.0	32.5	0.6	223.7
no	87.9	94.0	67.5	99.4	(.000)
Ever lived in public housing					
yes	9.3	5.0	19.9	4.2	75.0
no	90.7	95.0	80.1	95.8	(.000)
Work status					
legal	91.1	98.0	99.5	78.4	151.0
illegal	8.9	2.0	0.5	21.6	(.000)
Spatial isolation					
East Los Angeles–South					
Central Los Angeles					
yes	31.9	24.0	35.6	35.7	17.0
no	68.1	76.0	64.4	64.3	(.000)
High poverty neighborhood					
yes	20.0	3.8	25.0	29.5	99.1
no	80.0	96.3	75.0	70.5	(.000)

Human capital

Age					
Eighteen to thirty-five	43.3	34.0	33.9	59.0	75.6
Thirty-five plus	56.7	66.0	66.1	41.0	(.000)
Education					
Less than high school	28.1	6.5	19.3	53.6	259.4
More than high school	71.9	93.5	80.7	46.4	(.000)
Marital status					
married	43.8	45.5	28.1	55.3	64.7
unmarried	56.2	54.5	71.9	44.7	(.000)
English proficiency					
yes	81.4	98.8	96.6	54.0	371.9
no	18.6	1.3	3.4	46.0	(.000)
Disability					
yes	20.9	22.8	31.5	10.8	56.7
no	79.1	77.3	68.5	89.2	(.000)
Self-employed					
yes	12.3	18.2	11.1	8.6	17.2
no	87.7	81.8	88.9	91.4	(.000)

Social capital

Welfare bridge					
yes	12.2	10.7	16.5	10.0	6.6
no	87.8	89.3	83.5	90.0	(.037)
Education bridge					
yes	61.7	84.2	61.6	34.1	154.4
no	38.3	15.8	38.4	65.9	(.000)

(*Table continues on p. 322.*)

TABLE 8.1   *Continued*

Concept	Variable/Specific Measure	All Men (N = 1,262)	White Men (N = 400)	Black Men (N = 388)	Hispanic Men (N = 474)	Chi-Square (p Value)
	Gender bridge					
	yes	55.7	65.4	60.9	40.0	44.5
	no	44.3	34.6	39.1	60.0	(.000)
	Neighborhood bridge					
	yes	74.3	78.0	77.4	67.2	11.3
	no	25.7	22.0	22.6	32.8	(.004)
	Race bridge					
	yes	26.3	33.1	18.0	26.3	17.2
	no	73.7	66.9	82.0	73.7	(.000)
	Institutional ties					
	yes	52.7	63.0	54.0	42.8	35.9
	no	47.3	37.0	46.0	57.2	(.000)
Search-and-destroy hypothesis						
	Criminal record					
	yes	18.0	17.5	28.6	9.7	51.8
	no	82.0	82.5	71.4	70.3	(.000)
	Self-report of job-related discrimination					
	yes	38.4	22.1	53.8	39.7	82.8
	no	61.6	77.9	46.2	60.3	(.000)
Dependent variables						
	Working					
	yes	84.1	87.7	76.8	85.9	14.2
	no	15.9	12.3	23.2	14.1	(.001)

Source: Los Angeles Study of Urban Inequality 1994.

Los Angeles's Hispanic population, the variables that distinguish Hispanic men from black and white men are fairly predictable. As table 8.1
shows, Hispanic men were more likely to have spent their formative
years (up to age sixteen) in a Third World country, to be undocumented,
to be young, and to have less than a high school education. They were,
on the other hand, less likely to be a member of at least one voluntary
organization, to be proficient in English, and to have a criminal record.

In comparison to their black and Hispanic male counterparts, white
males were less likely to report job-related discrimination and more
likely to be embedded in educationally diverse and institutionally (that
is, at least one voluntary organization) rich networks. They were also
more likely to be better-educated and to be working or self-employed.

Multivariate Analysis

The results of our logistic regression analyses for all men and for white,
black, and Hispanic men are summarized in table 8.2. Beginning with
column 1, eight of the independent variables proved to be statistically
significant determinants of labor force participation among our sample.
With respect to the four theoretical perspectives, one (high poverty area)
tests the spatial isolation hypothesis; one (Third World origin) is an
attribute of the cultural capital hypothesis; two are human capital attributes (education and work-limiting disability); two are attributes (education bridge and institutional embeddedness) of the social capital hypothesis; and two fall under the search-and-destroy hypothesis (criminal
record and job-related discrimination).

Among these variables, five exert a negative influence on the likelihood or odds of working. Men who lived in high poverty areas (b =
−0.83) were 56 percent less likely to be working than their counterparts
who lived outside such areas. Those with a work-limiting disability
(b = −.72) were 51 percent less likely to be working than their counterparts without such a disability. Having a criminal record (b = −0.65)
reduced the odds of working by 48 percent, and men who reported having experienced job-related discrimination (b = −1.06) were 66 percent
less likely to be working than their counterparts who did not report
such experiences.

On the other hand, being born and spending one's formative years
in a Third World country (b = 1.23), having an educational bridge
(b = 0.56), and being a member of at least one voluntary organization
(b = 0.64) enhanced the odds of working among our sample of Los Angeles men. Men who spent their formative years in a Third World country were 2.4 times more likely to be working than their counterparts.
And having at least one network member who had more than a high

TABLE 8.2 Logistic Regression Results

Independent Variables	All Men (1) β	odds ratio	White Men (2) β	odds ratio	Black Men (3) β	odds ratio	Hispanic Men (4) β	odds ratio
Constant	1.7		6.4		1.1		1.0	
Third World origin (yes)	1.23*** (.54)	3.4						
Southern roots (yes)					1.89** (.93)	6.7		
Age (under thirty-five)							1.06*** (.52)	2.90
Education (less than high school)	−0.86** (.43)	.42			−2.32** (.96)	.10		
Work-limiting disability (yes)	−0.72** (.34)	.49						
Education bridge (yes)	0.56*** (.30)	1.75						
Gender bridge (yes)			−1.27*** (.74)	.28				
Voluntary organization	0.64** (.27)	1.90	1.38** (.54)	4.00	1.10***	3.00		
Criminal record (yes)	−0.65** (.30)	.52			−1.47 (.57)	.23		
High poverty area (yes)	−0.83** (.36)	.44			−1.72** (.62)	.18		
Job-related discrimination (yes)	−1.06* (.28)	.34	−.97** (.57)	−.38			−1.31*** (.49)	.27
−2 log likelihood	425.8		132.0		107.8		140.4	
degrees of freedom	24		21		22		22	
x2	74.3		40.0		43.3		33.0	

Source: Los Angeles Study of Urban Inequality 1994.
Note: Standard errors appear in parentheses.
*p ≤ .0001, **p ≤ .05, ***p ≤ .10

school diploma increased the odds of working by 75 percent. Men who were actively involved in at least one voluntary association were 90 percent more likely to be working than their counterparts.

Even a cursory look at columns 2 through 4 in table 8.2 reveals that the determinants of who worked and who did not among Los Angeles males during the early 1990s varied substantially by race-ethnicity. For white men, as column 2 shows, only three variables emerged from our logistic regression analysis as statistically significant determinants of labor force participation; two of them are measures of the social capital hypothesis and the third is a domain of the search-and-destroy hypothesis. Among the three, being involved in at least one voluntary organization (b = 1.38) was the strongest predictor of the employment status of white men in our sample. Those who were institutionally embedded (that is, involved in at least one voluntary organization) were three times more likely to be working than those who were not actively involved in voluntary organizations. On the other hand, white males with networks that included at least one gender bridge (b = −1.27) were far less likely to be working than those without a gender bridge in their network. Having a female in the immediate network reduced the odds of working among our sample of white males by 72 percent.

In a similar vein, among the white males surveyed, self-reports of employment discrimination (b = −.97) reduced the odds of working by 62 percent. This finding, it should be noted, is inconsistent with the search-and-destroy hypothesis, which posits that black and other minority males are the ones who are systematically targeted for discrimination in the labor market and other walks of life. However, as we show, it reflects, in all likelihood, the growing preference among employers for immigrant and Hispanic workers over native workers—especially black males, but also increasingly white males—in the restructured U.S. economy (Kirschenman and Neckerman 1991).

The results for black men are reported in column 3. Five variables emerged from the logistic regression analysis as statistically determinant: one indicator (high poverty area) of the spatial isolation hypothesis, one measure (southern roots) of the cultural capital-employer-preference hypothesis, one indicator (education) of human capital, one variable (institutional embeddedness) of the social capital hypothesis, and one indicator (crime record) of the search-and-destroy hypothesis. Three of these variables exerted a negative effect on the employment status of black men in the LASUI sample. Residence in a high poverty area (b = −1.72), having completed fewer than twelve years of schooling (b = −2.32), and having a criminal record (b = −1.47) reduced the odds of working our sample of black men by 82 percent, 90 percent, and 77 percent, respectively.

The remaining two statistically significant determinants—southern roots (b = 1.89) and institutional embeddedness (b = 1.10)—enhanced the odds of working among our sample of black men. Proponents of the cultural capital-employer-preference hypothesis contend that blacks who were born and spent their formative years in the South, where the dependency systems of slavery and sharecropping prevailed, were more likely to rely on the governmental dole than to work when they migrated to the urban North (Lemann 1991). The findings of this research contradict that assertion. Black men who were born in the South and spent their formative years in the region were nearly six times more likely to be working than their counterparts. Similarly, black men who were embedded in a dense network of voluntary organizations were twice as likely to be working as their counterparts.

Finally, the findings for Hispanic males are presented in column 4 of table 8.2. Two variables achieved statistical significance in our logistic regression analysis. One is a human capital measure, age (b = 1.06), and it increased the odds of working. The other falls under the search-and-destroy hypothesis, self-reported job discrimination (b = −1.31), and it reduced the odds or likelihood of working among our sample. Young Hispanic males under the age of thirty-five were twice as likely as their older counterparts to be working. Those who reportedly encountered job-related discrimination were 73 percent less likely to working in comparison to their counterpart who did not report such experiences.

Our data suggest, in short, that radically different forces affected the employment status of black males compared to white and Hispanic males in Los Angeles in the early 1990s. Black males were seriously hampered in their efforts to secure a job in the local labor market if they had less than a high school education, if they lived in a high poverty area, and if they had a criminal record. To provide additional insights into the differential impacts of these constraints or deficits on the employment status of black, white, and Hispanic males in Los Angeles, we examined the predicted probabilities of working for all three groups through a transformation of the logit coefficients from the preceding analyses.

In this set of analyses, we assigned the three variables that seemed to disproportionately affect the employment status of black males—residence in a high poverty area, having a criminal record, and having less than a high school education—a score of 0, and all the other independent variables were assigned their most common value (that is, the mean or the mode). For our purposes, we refer to this first set of analyses as the average or base case. After estimating the predicted probabilities of working for the base case, we generated three subsequent runs to isolate the independent and cumulative effects of the constraining variables—high poverty area, criminal record, and low education level—on

TABLE 8.3   *Predicted Possibility of Working by Race-Ethnicity*

Race-Ethnicity	Base Case	High Poverty Area	High Poverty Area and Criminal Record	High Poverty Area and Criminal Record and Low Education
White male[a]	.96	.77	.68	.43
Black male[b]	.95	.78	.44	.07
Hispanic male[c]	.98	.97	.97	.97

[a]The base case is a white male, not from the Third World, documented, not from the south, does not live in East or South Central Los Angeles, never lived in public housing, lived with both parents as a child, is over age thirty-five, has at least a high school education, is not married, is proficient in English, does not have a work-related disability, is not self-employed, has an education bridge, has a gender bridge, has a neighborhood bridge, does not have a race bridge, has institutional ties, has no criminal record, does not live in a high poverty neighborhood, and has not experienced work-related discrimination.

[b]The base case is a black male, dark skin tone, not from the Third World, documented, not from the south, does not live in East or South Central Los Angeles, never lived in public housing, lived with both parents as a child, is over age thirty-five, has at least a high school education, is not married, is proficient in English, does not have a work-related disability, is not self-employed, has an education bridge, has a gender bridge, has a neighborhood bridge, does not have a race bridge, has institutional ties, has no criminal record, does not live in a high poverty neighborhood, and has experienced work-related discrimination.

[c]The base case is a Hispanic male, light or medium skin tone, from the Third World, documented, not from the south, does not live in East or South Central Los Angeles, never lived in public housing, lived with both parents as a child, is under age thirty-five, does not have an education bridge, does not have a gender bridge, has a neighborhood bridge, does not have a race bridge, does not have institutional ties, has no criminal record, does not live in a high poverty neighborhood, and has not experienced work-related discrimination.

the predicted probabilities of working for white males, black males, and Hispanic males. In these runs, the scores on the constraining variables were transformed from 0 to 1 when they were introduced into the model. The results are presented in table 8.3.

According to our model, a black male in Los Angeles who, in the language of the framers of the *Contract with America* (Gillespie and Shellhaus 1994), had played by the rules of American society (graduated from high school, avoided trouble with the law, and so on), had a predicted probability of working of .95 in the early 1990s—about the same as comparably situated white (.96) and Hispanic (.98) males. If that black male resided in a high poverty area, his predicted probability or working dropped to .78. If he lived in a high poverty area and had a criminal record, his predicted probability of working plummeted to .44. And if he lived in a high poverty area, had a criminal record, and had not graduated from high school—and had an average score on all the other independent variables in our model—his predicted probability of working fell all the way down to .07.

As the table shows, white males' participation in the Los Angeles labor market in the early 1990s was similarly constrained by these factors, but not nearly as dramatically. For a white male, the predicted probabilities of working were .77 (residence in a high poverty area), .68 (residence in a high poverty area and saddled with a criminal record), and .43 (high poverty area, criminal record, and failure to graduate from high school). A white male saddled with all three of these constraining attributes and average scores on all the other independent variables in our model still had a 43 percent chance of being employed in Los Angeles in 1992.

In contrast to black and white males, the predicted probabilities of working for Hispanic males were not affected by these factors. If a Hispanic male lived in a high poverty area, had a criminal record, and had less than a high school education—the worst-case scenario—his predicted probability of working in the early 1990s (.97) was roughly the same as it was for his counterpart who did not bear the burden of any of these constraints (.98). This individual's predicted probability of working was also the same as that of his Hispanic male counterpart who lived in a high poverty area (.97) and his counterpart who lived in a high poverty area and had a criminal record (.97). Our model suggests that a Hispanic male, irrespective of his place of residence, criminal history, or educational level, had a 97 percent chance or probability of being employed in Los Angeles in 1992. These results lend strong empirical support to the findings of recent surveys of private-sector employers who, in response to questions about their labor recruitment and screening practices, expressed a strong preference for Hispanic and immigrant labor over native-born, and especially black, labor to fill vacancies in their firms (Kirschenman and Neckerman 1991).

Conclusion

In terms of gaining access to jobs in the Los Angeles labor market, the results of our analyses indicate that black males, more so than their white and Hispanic male counterparts, were hurt tremendously by their residence in high poverty areas, their low levels of education, and their connection with the Los Angeles criminal justice system.

Our findings with regard to the effects of living in a high poverty area lend clear and convincing support to the validity of the spatial isolation hypothesis as an explanation for the low labor force participation rate of black males vis-à-vis other males in Los Angeles, especially their Hispanic counterparts, who are more likely to live in similar neighborhood contexts. While the predicted probability of working for a Hispanic male was largely unaffected by residence in a high poverty area, the predicted probability of working for a black male with comparable skills and background, who lived in such an area, was much lower.

The findings regarding the effects of low levels of education and a criminal record can be interpreted as lending support to either the cultural capital-employer-preference hypothesis or the search-and-destroy hypothesis. Based on our findings, proponents of the cultural capital-employer-preference hypothesis might argue that the lower labor force participation rates of African American males vis-à-vis their white and Hispanic male counterparts in Los Angeles is a "values and morals" problem. More specifically, they might argue that our findings support the notion that African American males do not "value" education and, therefore, end up dropping out of school before graduation and that they prefer to engage in criminal activities rather than pursue employment in the mainstream economy. We would caution against this interpretation for the following reasons.

First, it is well documented that both the Los Angeles Police Department and the Los Angeles Sheriff's Department have strategically targeted South Central Los Angeles, historically the heart of Los Angeles's black community, and young African American males within this community, in their war on gangs and drugs (see Klein 1994).

Second, it is also well documented that, in an effort to lure international capital to Los Angeles over the last quarter-century, city officials have pursued, consciously and aggressively, a strategy of downtown and Westside redevelopment, at the expense of the neighborhoods and communities that make up South Central Los Angeles (see Grant and Johnson 1995; Johnson and Farrell 1996). Partly as a function of the city's wholesale disinvestment in South Central Los Angeles communities, the area has become host to a disproportionate number of alcohol outlets and other locally unwanted land uses. Consider this comment on the impact of a high concentration of alcohol outlets in socially isolated and economically marginal communities like South Central Los Angeles:

> In economic terms, . . . high densities of alcohol outlets create negative "externalities" that compete against, cancel out, or overwhelm the positive "externalities" associated with traditional institutions and behaviors like churchgoing. Whether or not they themselves drink to excess, hang out in bars, or engage directly in related behaviors, it is probable that poor, inner city youths who grow up in places where drinking is common and liquor outlets are everywhere are more likely than otherwise comparable youths to have diminished life prospects that include joblessness, substance abuse, and getting into serious trouble with the law. [Bennett et al. 1996, 73–74]

Moreover, research shows that the city officials' neglect of South Central Los Angeles coincided with massive cuts in federal aid to cities

(NiBlack and Stan 1992). And both of these developments were occurring precisely at the time that the primary institutions in poor communities like South Central Los Angeles—families, schools, churches, and others—were being swamped with huge increases in the juvenile population. As William Bennett, John DiIulio, and John Walters point out, partly as a function of these cuts in local and federal government assistance, the primary institutions in South Central Los Angeles (and other inner-city communities) started "to crumble at the very moment when they were needed to be towers of strength" (1996, 74).

Research confirms that, in the past, such community-based institutions as the Boys' and Girls' Clubs, the YMCA, and the YWCA were successful mediators in poor inner-city environments; they encouraged disadvantaged youth to pursue mainstream avenues of social and economic mobility and discouraged them from engaging in antisocial or dysfunctional behavior (Oliver 1988). Today, owing to budget constraints occasioned by federal and local government cuts in financial support, these organizations are not as successful as they used to be (Farrell and Johnson 1994; Johnson and Farrell 1996).

Third, at the state level over this same period, there has been a drastic reallocation of resources from the public education system to the criminal justice system. Research shows that this reallocation process has been a double-edged sword for African American males. Cuts in education have contributed to their school failure, and the increased spending in "lock-them-up-and-throw-away-the-key" crime-control policies has been used to brand them with the scarlet letter of unemployability. As the data in table 8.3 illustrate, the employment prospects of African American males in Los Angeles have been devastated by these public policies.

In earlier studies, we presented the results of our retrospective analyses of the life courses of more than two dozen young black male violent offenders, who are now serving life sentences for murder. The findings of this research serve as a powerful illustration of what can happen to youth who grow up in communities where the social safety net has been systematically dismantled (see Johnson, Farrell, and Sapp 1996, 1997). Their childhoods were plagued by a common set of problems.

They grew up in families—in most cases two-parent families—in which there was a history of spousal and child abuse, alcohol and drug abuse, and chronic joblessness or, at best, weak attachment to the labor market. Moreover, they themselves suffered from undiagnosed and/or untreated learning disabilities, other mental problems, and alcohol and drug problems. They also were victimized by the discriminatory tracking and social promotion system in the Los Angeles public school system, which, in turn, led to school failure and involvement in gangs, drug dealing, and other criminal activities (see Johnson, Farrell, and Sapp 1997). It is clear from the retrospective data that these youth might be on a different life course trajectory today had they not been residents of high poverty areas in South Central Los Angeles, a community that is bereft of the kinds of social, psychological, and institutional supports that characterize working-class, middle-class, and upper-class communities.

Viewed within the context of the foregoing policy developments and the life course data for these violent offenders, we believe our findings lend support to the search-and-destroy hypothesis—the notion that African American males in Los Angeles have been the target of systematic exploitation.

On the positive side, the findings of this research lend limited support to the importance of social networks in terms of black males securing a place in the labor market. Black men who were embedded in a dense network of community-based organizations were twice as likely to be working as their counterparts. The results of this research suggest several policy directions that are worthy of consideration in our efforts to deal with the problems confronting contemporary African American males. The specific recommendations we propose here are designed to stem, simultaneously, the tide of crime and violence that currently plagues the African American community and to build bridges to the economic mainstream for African American males who are caught up in the criminal justice system.

In both the research community and the policy arena, it is typically assumed that unemployment leads to crime. However, recent ethnographic studies suggest that in inner-city communities, delinquency may occur before unemployment in the life course (Anderson 1990, 1994; Padilla 1992; Sullivan 1989). Based on his review of these ethnographic studies, John Hagan states that the evidence suggests that the "experience with crime precedes and sometimes entirely replaces conventional experiences with work, especially in the context of concentrated poverty that provided limited employment opportunities for minority youths" (1993, 469). He notes further that this early engagement in crime, especially among young black males, may constrain any effort later in life to connect with the labor market.

Hagan goes on to point out some of the avenues through which inner-city youth become criminally engaged at a relatively early age and some of the problems they pose later in life:

> involvement of parents in crime likely provide youth with more promising connections to illegal than legal labor markets. As well, contacts with

criminal friends are more likely to integrate youths into the criminal underworld than into referral networks for legal employment. And youth delinquent acts are likely to distance actors further from the job contacts that initiate and sustain legitimate occupational careers. Early crime contact may be especially damaging. Operating through the branching, snowballing, and multiplying processes . . . successive criminal acts and contact may further embed youths in criminal networks that are isolated from the personalized networks of job seeking. [1993, 469]

In order to prevent their active involvement in gangs and other illegal activities in the first instance, intervention programs will have to be devised that target young black males who are at risk of criminal behavior early in the life course—no later than sixth grade, earlier if possible. Building on the social capital hypothesis, the goal of these intervention programs must be to embed these young black males in a rich network of individual and institutional supports during the times when they are idle and thus subject to getting into trouble: after school on weekdays, on weekends, and during the summer months when school is out.

The Big Brother/Big Sister Program (BB/BS), which links inner-city youth with older mentors, is one example of the type of intervention that we advocate. Commenting on the powerful mediating role of this program in the lives of inner-city youth, Bennett, DiIulio, and Walters note:

> compared to otherwise comparable children not in the BB/BA program, Little Brothers and Little Sisters who met with their "Bigs" regularly for about a year were 46 percent less likely than their peers to start using illegal drugs, and 32 percent less likely than their peers to assault someone, not to mention less likely than their peers to skip school, get poor grades, or start drinking [1996, 59]

The Durham Scholars Program (DSP), which we recently established with support from a local philanthropist, is another example of an intervention designed to build social capital or institutional bridges to the mainstream for at-risk inner-city youth. It is designed to foster college access and matriculation for 240 youth from the six high-poverty neighborhoods in Durham, North Carolina. We recruit the youth as they are about to enter the sixth grade, and we work with them through high school. Those who manage to finish high school and gain acceptance to college will receive up to four years of postsecondary education at no cost.

The DSP is a twenty-year intervention. We recruit a cohort of 30 youth and their families each year, and we work with them in a wide range of academically and socially enriching activities in afterschool, weekend, and summer programs. The program participants and their families have access to three full-time social workers, three social work interns, a school psychologist, eight model teachers, and a steady flow of mentors and tutors from the University of North Carolina at Chapel Hill (Guill 1997). The students receive homework assistance on a daily basis, remedial training in subjects in which they are weak, and exposure to a wide range of culturally enriching extracurricular activities, including field trips, involvement in nontraditional sports activities (such as golf), and annual summer camp experiences. As the youth become older, the program will serve as their link or bridge to internship and employment opportunities.

Parental involvement is mandatory. Our staff of social workers and social work interns assist the parents in dealing with personal and family crises, and they host parent workshops twice a month. The themes of the workshops vary from month to month, but the basic goals are to foster effective parenting and child-rearing practices and to empower the parents to play a more active and central role in the education of their children.

Incorporated into the design of the program is a rigorous evaluation. For each cohort of program participants, we select a control group of youth from the same neighborhoods and track both groups over twenty years. Along the way, we issue periodic reports, which highlight the DSP's impact on the educational progress and academic performance of the program participants vis-à-vis the control group.

While the foregoing programs are designed to intervene early in the lives of young black males to prevent them from engaging in crime and other antisocial behaviors, what do we do about those prime working-age black males who are neither at work nor in school? Is it possible to build bridges to the mainstream for these individuals, most of whom have criminal records?

Our recent evaluation of the Milwaukee Midnight Basketball League suggests that the answer is yes (Farrell et al. 1996). Our evaluation suggested that the program improved the self-esteem and personal outlook of the league participants (N = 160), it provided scholarships that enabled a significant number of them to pursue additional education, and the private-sector sponsors used the league to recruit entry-level workers. Moreover, according to statistics compiled by the Milwaukee Police Department, crime rates dropped 30 percent in the target area during the first year of program operation. These outcomes, it should be noted, were achieved with a $70,000 investment—all from the private sector.

Was this a wise investment of corporate dollars? If one considers that the annual cost of incarceration is about $35,000 per person, the answer is a resounding yes. Basically, for the cost of incarcerating two young men for a year, Milwaukee's midnight basketball league was able to link a cadre of idle minority males to advanced education and employment opportunities while at the same time keeping them out of trouble with the law.

If we are to deal effectively with the seemingly intractable problems confronting the African American male, our greatest successes will not come from the "get tough" on education and crime polices of the past (Farrell and Johnson 1994; Soros 1997). Rather, they will likely come from social capital building programs like Big Brothers/Big Sisters, the Durham Scholars, and the Milwaukee Midnight Basketball League, which serve as bridges to the social and economic mainstream for the African American male (Farrell and Johnson 1994; Green 1993). Midnight basketball programs will be especially important for the 825,000 incarcerated young black males who have young children. Most of these men are locked up for petty drug offenses and will return to their communities in a short period of time. The future viability of the African American community, and the broader American society, will hinge on our ability to reconnect these individuals to the American mainstream.

The authors gratefully acknowledge the expert technical assistance of Cathy Mae Nelson of the University of Wisconsin-Milwaukee's School of Education word-processing pool. An earlier version of this chapter appeared in *Urban Affairs Review* 35(5): 695–716. Sage Publications, Inc. 2000.

References

Anderson, Elijah. 1990. *Streetwise: Race, Class, and Change in an Urban Community.* Chicago: University of Chicago Press.

———. 1994. "Code of the Streets." *Atlantic Monthly* (May): 81–94.

Austin, Bobby W., ed. 1996. *Repairing the Breach: Key Way to Support Family Life, Reclaim Our Streets, and Rebuild Civil Society in America's Communities.* Dillon, Colo.: Alpine Guild.

Bennett, William J., John J. DiIulio, Jr., and John P. Walters. 1996. *Body Count: Moral Poverty . . . and How to Win America's War Against Crime and Drugs.* New York: Simon & Schuster.

Braddock, J. H., II, and J. M. McPartland. 1987. "How Minorities Continue to Be Excluded from Equal Employment Opportunities: Research on Labor Markets and Institutional Barriers." *Journal of Social Issues* 43: 5–39.

Cose, Ellie. 1995. *A Man's World: How Real Is Male Privilege—and How High Is Its Price?* New York: HarperCollins.

Farrell, Walter C. Jr., James H. Johnson Jr., Marty Sapp, R. M. Pumphrey, and S. Freeman. 1996. "Redirecting the Lives of Urban Black Males: An Assessment of Milwaukee's Midnight Basketball League." *Journal of Community Practice* 2: 91–107.

Fernandez-Kelly, M. Patricia. 1995. "Towandas' Triumph: Social and Cultural Capital in the Urban Ghetto." In *Economic Sociology of Immigration*, edited by Alejandro Portes. New York: Russell Sage.

"Foul Shots." *The New Republic*, December 29, 1997, p. 11.

Gibbs, Jewelle Taylor. 1989. *Young, Black, and Male in America: An Endangered Species*. Dover, Mass.: Auburn House.

Gillespie, Ed, and Bob Shellhaus. 1994. *Contract with America: The Bold Plan by Rep. Newt Gingrich, Rep. Dick Armey, and the House Republicans to Change the Nation*. New York: Random House.

Grant, David, and James H. Johnson Jr. 1995. "Conservative Policymaking and Growing Urban Inequality in the 1980s." In *Research in Politics and Society*, edited by R. Ratcliff, Melvin Oliver, and T. Shapiro. Greenwich, Conn.: JAI Press.

Green, Michael B. 1993. "Chronic Exposure to Violence and Poverty: Interventions That Work for Youth." *Crime and Delinquency* 39(1): 106–24.

Guill, E. 1997. "Building Bridges." *Daily Tarheel*, February 14, 1997, pp. 1, 5.

Hagan, John. 1993. "The Social Embeddedness of Crime and Unemployment." *Criminology* 31(4): 465–91.

Harrison, Lawrence E. 1992. *Who Prospers? How Cultural Values Shape Economic and Political Success*. New York: Basic Books.

Holzer, Harry J., and Keith Ihlanfeld. 1996. "Customer Discrimination and Employment Outcomes for Minority Workers." Unpublished paper. Atlanta, Ga.: Georgia State University.

Jarrett, Robin. 1995. "Growing Up Poor: The Family Experiences of Socially Mobile Youth in Low Income African American Neighborhoods." *Journal of Adolescent Research* 10(1): 111–35.

Johnson, James H., Jr. 1996. "The Real Issues for Reducing Poverty." In *Reducing Poverty in America: Views and Approaches*, edited by Michael Darby. Thousand Oaks, Calif.: Sage Publications.

———. 1997. "Unraveling the Paradox of Deepening Urban Inequality: Theoretical Underpinnings, Research Design, and Preliminary Findings of a Multi-city Study." In *A Different Vision: Race and Public Policy*, edited by Thomas D. Boston. London and New York: Routledge.

Johnson, James H., Jr., Elisa J. Bienenstock, and Walter C. Farrell Jr. 1999. "Bridging Social Networks and Female Labor Force Participation in a Multi-Ethnic Metropolis." *Urban Geography* 20: 3–30.

Johnson, James H., Jr., E. Jennifer Bienenstock, and Jennifer A. Stoloff. 1995. "An Empirical Test of the Cultural Capital Hypothesis." *Review of Black Political Economy* 24: 7–27.

Johnson, James H., Jr., and Walter C. Farrell Jr. 1995. "Race Still Matters." *Chronicle of Higher Education*, July 7, p. A48.

———. 1996. "The Fire This Time: The Genesis of the Los Angeles Rebellion of 1992." In *Race, Poverty and American Cities*, edited by John Charles Boger and Judith W. Wegner. Chapel Hill: University of North Carolina Press.

———. 1998. "Growing Income Inequality in American Society: A Political Economy Perspective." In *The Inequality Paradox: Growth of Income Disparity*, edited by James A. Auerbach and Richard S. Belous. Washington, D.C.: National Policy Organization.

Johnson, James H., Jr., Walter C. Farrell Jr., and Marty Sapp. 1996. "The Daniel Green Case: A Death Penalty Mitigation Strategy." *Negro Education Review* 47(1–2): 94–115.

———. 1997. "African American Males and Capital Murder: A Death Penalty Mitigation Strategy." *Urban Geography* 18(5): 403–33.

Johnson, James H., Jr., Walter C. Farrell Jr., and Jennifer A. Stoloff. 1998. "The Declining Fortunes of African American Males: A Critical Assessment of Four Perspectives." *The Review of Black Political Economy* 25: 17–40.

Johnson, James H., Jr., and Melvin L. Oliver. 1992. "Structural changes in the U.S. Economy and Black Male Joblessness: A Reassessment." In *Urban Labor Markets and Job Opportunity*, edited by George E. Peterson and Wayne Vroman. Washington, D.C.: Urban Institute Press.

Johnson, James H., Jr., Melvin L. Oliver, and Lawrence M. Bobo. 1994. "Understanding the Contours of Deepening Urban Inequality." *Urban Geography* 15: 77–89.

Kirschenman, Joleen, and Kathryn Neckerman. 1991. "'We'd Love to Hire Them, But': The Meaning of Race for Employers." In *The Urban Underclass*, edited by Christopher Jencks and Paul E. Peterson. Washington, D.C.: Urban Institute Press.

Klein, Malcolm W. 1994. *The American Street Gang: Its Nature, Prevalence and Control*. New York: Oxford University Press.

Lemann, Nicholas. 1991. *The Promised Land*. New York: Knopf.

Massey, Douglas, and Nancy Denton. 1992. *American Apartheid: Segregation and the Making of the Underclass*. Cambridge, Mass.: Harvard University Press.

McCall, Nathan. 1995. *Makes Me Wanna Holler: A Young Black Man in America*. New York: Vintage Books.

Mead, Lawrence. 1992. *The New Politics of Poverty*. New York: Basic Books.

Miller, Jerome. 1996. *Search and Destroy: African American Males and the U.S. Criminal Justice System*. New York: Cambridge University Press.

Murray, Charles. 1995. "Reducing Poverty and Reducing the Underclass: Different Problems, Different Solutions." In *Reducing Poverty in America: Views and Approaches*, edited by Michael Darby. Newbury, Calif.: Sage Publications.

Neckerman, Kathryn, and Joleen Kirschenman. 1990. "Hiring Strategies, Racial Bias and Inner City Workers." *Social Problems* 38: 433–47.

NiBlack, P., and P. Stan. 1992. "Financing Public Services in Los Angeles." In *Urban America: Policy Choices for Los Angeles and the Nation*, edited by James Steinberg, David Lyon, and Mary Vaiana. Santa Monica, Calif.: Rand Corporation.

Oliver, Melvin L. 1988. "The Urban Black Community as Network: Towards a Social Network Perspective." *Sociological Quarterly* 29: 623–25.

Oliver, Melvin L., and James H. Johnson Jr. 1984. "Interethnic Minority Conflict in an Urban Ghetto: The Case of Blacks and Latinos in Los Angeles." *Research in Social Movements, Conflict and Change* 6: 57–94.

———. 1989. "The Challenge of Diversity in Higher Education." *Urban Review* 20: 139–45.

Padilla, Felix. 1992. *The Gang as an American Enterprise.* New Brunswick, N.J.: Rutgers University Press.

Soros, George. 1997. "Why the Drug War Cannot Be Won." *Washington Post National Weekly Edition*, February 10, 1997, p. 21.

Sowell, Thomas. 1981. *Ethnic America.* New York: Basic Books.

———. 1994. *Race and Culture: A World View.* New York: Basic Books.

Sullivan, Mercer. 1989. *Getting Paid: Youth Crime and Work in the Inner City.* Ithaca, N.Y.: Cornell University Press.

Wilson, William J. 1987. *The Truly Disadvantaged.* Chicago: University of Chicago Press.

———. 1996. *When Work Disappears.* New York: Knopf.

9

CHILD CARE AS POVERTY POLICY: THE EFFECT OF CHILD CARE ON WORK AND FAMILY POVERTY

Julie E. Press

WITH about two-thirds of mothers in the workforce, 21 million infants, toddlers, and preschoolers—and millions more school-age children—spend all or some of their day in the care of someone other than a parent. Another 5 million "latchkey" children are home alone after school while their parents work. Most child care facilities range from mediocre to poor, and children fall under the care of untrained, unlicensed, and poorly paid workers (the average salary is just above minimum wage). Even so, many families cannot find or afford dependable child care at all. According to findings from the 1990 National Child Care Survey, two-thirds of child care centers have waiting lists, and parents reported that it took five weeks to settle on a child care arrangement for their youngest child. Although there were three times as many child care centers in the early 1990s than there were in the 1970s, American families are still facing a child care shortage. Further, children are increasingly being placed in formal care at very young ages, and parents are paying more for lower-quality care (Willer et al. 1991).

The core issues are those of availability, quality, affordability, reliability, and convenience. But child care is also an important determinant of poverty and social inequality; the lack of affordable, good-quality child care keeps parents from working and contributes to social stratification in society by class, by gender, and by race-ethnicity and nativity by disproportionately affecting poor women of color. The National Child Care Survey also showed that poor families with a preschool-aged child and an employed mother who pay for child care spend 23 percent of their income on care, while similar nonpoor families spend only 9 percent (Hofferth et al. 1991). Of course, not all child care is paid for; friends, neighbors, and relatives care for children as well, especially in immigrant communities. According to Lynne Casper (1996) poor people and welfare recipients are disproportionately likely to rely on relative care because of the lack of affordable child care options. These relationships can be even less dependable and safe than more formal relationships, and usually involve costs in the form of some type of reciprocity.

Gender inequality is affected because women are much more likely than men to be influenced by lack of child care. Women are still predominantly responsible for the care of children, including the responsibility for finding outside care. Single mothers, whose ranks have been growing, epitomize this dilemma. Black and Latina women, who are disproportionately likely to be poor, single, and living in a neighborhood with fewer services and worse transportation, experience "multiple jeopardy" when it comes to child care (King 1988). They face the simultaneous barriers of race, gender, and class. According to Maria Cancian, Sheldon Danziger, and Peter Gottschalk (1993), while the level of income inequality between black and white married couples has worsened in recent years, this phenomenon is mitigated substantially by the increased earnings of wives. I suggest that this equalizing effect was made possible because alternative child care arrangements were found.

Although child care research during the past decade has analyzed the effects of various child care attributes on mothers' employment outcomes, child care's influence on poverty has not been measured directly. Barbara Bergmann (1996) argues eloquently that child care will help reduce poverty, but she does not make predictions about the *size* of the effect. Other recent studies focusing on poor single-mother families note that good-quality, affordable child care would have an important influence on reducing poverty (Edin and Lein 1997) and providing children with needed social resources (McLanahan and Sandefur 1996), but these studies do not quantify the effects, either. Further, research on urban poverty issues more generally focuses mainly on male employment issues, touching only tangentially on the subject of child care and neglecting it among the primary causes of or solutions to poverty. For example, a recent book by William Julius Wilson, *When Work Disappears* (1996), de-emphasizes women's employment issues and hardly mentions child care.

While child care as a public policy issue is suddenly gaining national attention at the federal level and scholarly attention as a "crisis" for all American families (for example, *The Silent Crisis in U.S. Child Care*, a special edition of the Annals of the American Academy of Political and Social Science, 1999), it is only very slowly being integrated into the discourse on fighting poverty.

In this chapter I argue that problems with child care keep mothers from working, that these problems are a significant cause of urban poverty in America as a result, and that this issue is of theoretical importance because it informs our understanding of the effects of multiple jeopardy on the mechanisms and contours of social stratification and inequality in American society. I use data from the Los Angeles Study of Urban Inequality to examine whether child care problems prevent mothers from entering the labor force and obtaining jobs. I also examine whether a lack of child care leads to poverty, how big the effects are, and how the effects differ for mothers from different racial-ethnic and nativity backgrounds. Lastly I estimate the effect on poverty of alleviating child care concerns.

Child Care and Material Well-Being

There are several theoretical perspectives in child care research. Developmental psychologists focus on the effects of child care on children's psychological and developmental well-being, while sociologists and labor economists are interested mainly in how factors such as the supply and affordability of child care affect women's labor force participation, fertility, and child care arrangements (Phillips 1992). The literature on the effect of child care on *parents'* well-being, however, either psychological or material, is scant. In a useful review of this problem, Karen Mason and Laura Duberstein (1992) argue that the "rare" research that does exist on this topic indicates that there are important links between parental well-being and child care problems, child care types, and child care quality (see White and Keith 1990 on marital relationships; Ross and Mirowsky 1988 on maternal depression). Research (discussed shortly) examines the effect of child care factors on mothers' labor force participation. This association points to, but does not measure, the relationship between child care and parental or familial economic well-being.

While we could take the intermediary evidence that child care affects labor force participation as an indicator of material well-being, I argue that there are two main problems with this approach. First, it goes only so far as investigating the association between child care and labor force participation—that is, mothers either working or looking for work. Yet, if child care impedes labor force participation, it seems likely to impede employment as well—that is, finding a job, given that one is searching for work. Second, labor force participation (and employment) is only an indicator—an intermediary measure. Knowing the change in number of hours worked or the decision about whether or not to work does not reveal the actual change in families' economic well-being that results from work gained through child care access.

I suggest that the effects of child care on families' socioeconomic well-being or poverty are fourfold. First, child care affects families' resources by enabling parents to enter the labor force, actively search for employment once in the labor force, increase work hours, or enter an education or training program. Work, in turn, provides income so families may survive. For single-parent families, the increase in income from working versus unemployment is clearly large if the parent can get a job that pays well enough to do more than cover child care costs. This feat is particularly difficult for single mothers, given the low wages typically earned by women relative to men. For two-parent families, the effects can also be significant, since men's real wages have fallen and rising inequality has made two incomes necessary for lower-income families. Without child care, neither single nor partnered mothers can earn a living. Second, child care expenses affect income by draining scarce resources, thereby reducing the family's material well-being. Third, the characteristics of child care itself—the quality—matters for the life chances of children reared in it. It affects how children perform in school, how happy and healthy they are, and how productive they are as adults (Burchinal 1999; Culkin, Howes, and Kagan 1999; Phillips 1995; Phillips and Bridgmann 1995). It therefore likely affects cycles of inter-generational poverty and could have the power to help break these cycles. Fourth, social inequality is affected because child care expenditures as a proportion of a family's income are much larger for low-income people than for others (Hofferth et al. 1991). In several ways, then, child care is an important factor in labor force attachment, poverty, and social inequality.

In this chapter I will focus on the effect of child care concerns on parental material well-being, as measured by family income below the poverty line. The poverty analysis is limited to household-level effects. That is, I will not measure possible differences in the household distribution of income benefits (from father to mother or parents to children), nor differences in other household distributions like marital power relations, the domestic division of labor, and in-home child care duties and prerogatives. However, I suggest that family income as a gross measure of the well-being of family members provides a useful account of the effect of child care concerns on material well-being.

I define *child care* by borrowing the words of Mason and Duberstein, whose definition is not limited to nonmaternal arrangements. Rather, it encompasses both informal arrangements and the whole domain of reproduction: "*Child care* refers to a division of labor through which dependent children are reared, where this division of labor may involve only members of the child's family or household, or may include other individuals and institutions, as well" (1992, 128).

341

Poverty is defined as income below the federal poverty line for a given family size. This measure is useful because it is used by the government for analyses of poverty and is therefore a standardized measure. It also has a drawback from my perspective, in that the poverty line is very low.[1] In 1994 the weighted average federal poverty threshold was $15,029 for a two-parent family of four—just $313 per person, per month (U.S. Census Bureau 1999). April Brayfield, Sharon Gennis Deich, and Sandra Hofferth (1993) found that poor families with a pre-school-age child spent an average of $33 each week on child care (27 percent of their income), while similar families earning 125 percent of the poverty line spent $38 each week (16 percent of their income).[2] These figures indicate that even many of those above the poverty line are suffering with the expense of child care costs. The federal poverty line does capture what is generally considered "poverty," but it ignores millions of others who, by other standards, one might consider as poor. This analysis will define *poverty* as those with incomes below the federal poverty standard, a choice that will yield conservative estimates of the relationship between child care and poverty. That is, if we were to expand the definition of poverty, the effects would probably be larger.

Figure 9.1 is a heuristic model of the relationships among child care, work, and poverty explored in this study. The diagram shows that problems with child care prevent parents from entering the labor force. Once in the labor force, child care problems may keep them from finding work, leading to unemployment. And even if a parent does find work, child care problems can force her to reduce work hours or take a lower-paying job because, for example, the job involves no work on weekends or at night, when dependable child care would be very difficult to get. Alternatively, problems with unreliable care may cause a parent to lose, miss, or quit work regularly, reducing annual income and making it harder to get a job because of an erratic work history and poor references. Lack of child care probably also leads directly to unemployment for the simple reason that one cannot easily go to a job interview with kids in tow. Finding out about job opportunities, obtaining applications, and writing resumes are difficult activities to do while taking care of children, especially very young ones. That is, the job search process itself may be severely hindered by concerns about child care. Therefore, child care directly affects labor force attachment (labor force participation, hours, employment, or unemployment). The arrows in the figure indicate that child care indirectly affects poverty through work.[3]

There is also some degree of feedback, as well: a higher income better allows families to purchase child care. However, I will bracket away this effect. It is methodologically too complex to model both simultaneously. Moreover, only some families use paid day care, so not all

FIGURE 9.1   *Model of How Child Care Problems Affect Poverty*

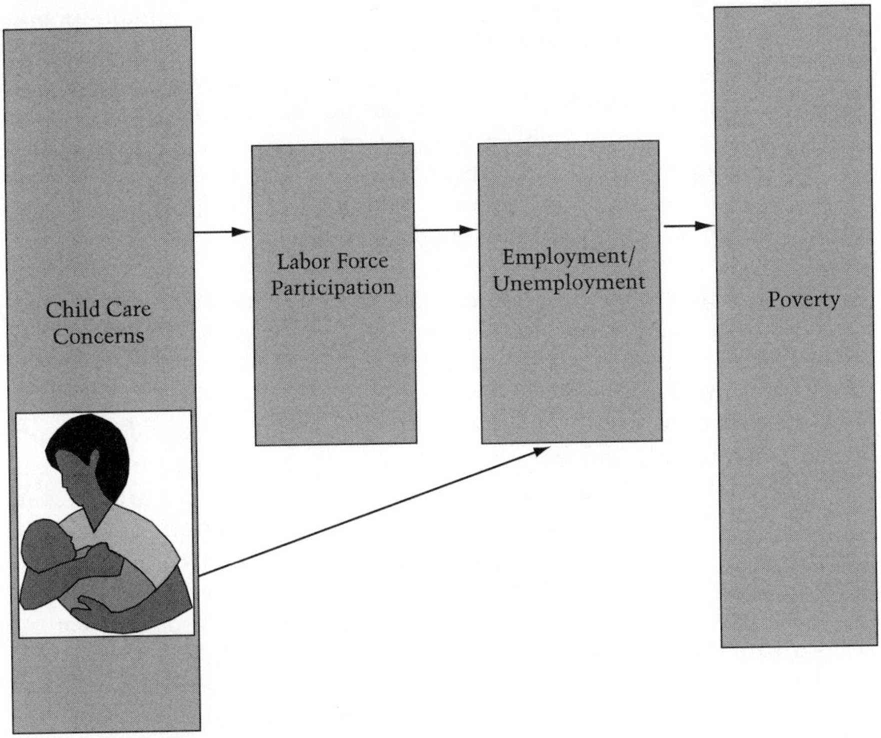

Source: Author's compilation.

respondents would be affected. Lastly, most other studies only take income as a predictor of child care usage, likewise bracketing away the effects I focus on here.

Quality, Affordability, and Availability

What child care concerns do parents have? Typically, they are concerned about a variety of issues, desiring care that is good, affordable, trustworthy, warm and loving, reliable and consistent, educational, with good social and physical programs, and convenient, both geographically and in relation to their work schedule. Parents vary in their perception of which of these and other characteristics are important. Most parents want their children to be safe and healthy at a minimum, while some want much more than that. Low-income parents tend to say they prefer

343

relatives to formal day care because the formal day care they can afford is often poor-quality (Brayfield, Deich, and Hofferth 1993; Hofferth 1992; Presser and Baldwin 1980). The reverse is true for middle-income parents, who tend to avoid family day care settings in favor of center-based care. Latino parents are far less likely to select center-based care compared with white or black parents. Latinos prefer caregivers who can speak Spanish and can teach Latino cultural values, such as respect for adults (Goldenberg and Gallimore 1995). In addition to income and race-ethnicity, parents' education level as well as many other factors determine what they consider to be good child care (Holloway and Fuller 1999).

Those who do opt for relative care face reliability problems that interfere with work when relatives are sick, too busy, late, or irresponsible. For higher-income families, the threshold level of acceptable child care may be higher, especially among parents whose cultural values tell them that mothers give the best care or that child care should be stimulating, educational, and entertaining as well as safe and convenient. High-quality full-time care (eight to ten hours, five days a week) costs from several hundred dollars to more than $1,000 a month (mainly because these child care centers pay higher wages for better workers and lower turnover rates). With women's documented lower average pay, many women in families with higher socioeconomic status still cannot afford the quality of child care they feel they can provide themselves.

Thus, what constitutes good-quality child care is highly contested by parents, child care professionals, policy makers, and scholars. While some still believe that only mothers ought to care for their children (Belsky 1986), a wide body of evidence is emerging in favor of other acceptable and desirable alternatives. For example, research shows that children who are in group day care do at least as well and sometimes better on several indices than those who are not (Clarke-Stewart 1992; Hayes, Palmer, and Zaslow 1990). While there are differences in the quality of paid child care that families receive, there are also differences in the quality of child care supplied by parents, relatives, and other non-paid providers, but this is a neglected area of research. We really do not know whether children being cared for by their own parents or other relatives are getting "quality" care, or even being supervised at all (Presser 1992, 30). We cannot assume that children are better off with their mothers.

Whether or not children in low-income families receive lower-quality care than children of other social classes is still unsettled. Some studies show that poorer families receive poorer quality care (Anderson et al. 1981; Goelman and Pence 1987; Howes and Stewart 1987). But more recent research finds a curvilinear relationship between family income and quality of child care (Voran and Whitebook 1991; Waite, Leibowitz, and Witsberger 1991; Whitebook, Howes, and Phillips 1989; Zaslow 1991), with children at low and high ends of the income distribution receiving relatively better care than children in the middle. Deborah Phillips and her colleagues (1994) compare the quality of care received by low-income children in Head Start, public school programs, and other community-based subsidized centers to a national sample of centers. Their results show that the quality of care provided in centers serving mainly low-income children was adequate but highly variable. Centers serving mainly higher-income children had the highest quality, and those serving primarily middle-income children provided the poorest quality of care, on indices ranging from teacher training to the appropriateness of the activities in preschool classrooms (489). The quality of care received by low-income children did not vary significantly from that received by high-income children on most indices.

In sum, a small but significant proportion of children are receiving poor quality care. It is difficult to assess because parents' attitudes are not conclusive and "experts'" opinions are not necessarily in consensus with parents. Parents who have their child(ren) in care tend to rate the quality of that care as good on average, even though more objective studies rate the typical care as mediocre (Holloway and Fuller 1999). This finding indicates that parents may have fewer concerns about child care than they should. However, Brayfield, Deich, and Hofferth (1993) found that although almost all low-income parents report satisfaction with their child care arrangements, a significant proportion want to change the arrangements for their youngest child. Quality, not cost, is the reason cited most often by low-income parents who would prefer to make a change.

Clearly, the concerns that parents cite when talking to survey takers include some intersection between quality and affordability: they cannot obtain acceptable quality care within their budget. Therefore, to allow parents across the socioeconomic spectrum to participate in the labor force without facing child care concerns, the level of care offered should be high and the cost low. This combination would require subsidized public provision to be economically viable.

Child Care and Work

Scholars disagree about which factors are instrumental to the assessment of child care and its impact on labor force participation and employment. Economists tend to stress the importance of cost, while sociologists tend to stress affordability, as well as other factors such as social networks, the noneconomic costs to relatives, and the effect on the household division of labor and work schedule shifts (for example, Presser 1989a, 1989b). The cost of child care is defined as the amount of money paid for child care services. *Affordability*, on the other hand, can be thought of as the cost of acceptable-quality child care as a proportion of a family's income, or the degree of burden of child care relative to a family's resources. Rachel Connelly (1991) argues from an economic perspective that the "trilogy of accessibility, affordability, and quality" are all fundamentally related to cost; cost, she says, is the important, underlying factor in understanding family decision making vis-à-vis the labor market.

On the other hand, Sandra Hofferth (1991) cautions that we should not focus only on the cost of care. Access to care, she says, is sometimes attained through the labor of unpaid relatives and is a function of family structure, and nonemployed mothers also utilize paid care. Further, there is evidence that cost is not, in fact, a good proxy for quality (Waite, Leibowitz, and Witsberger 1991; Hofferth and Wissoker 1990). Indeed, Presser says that "the little we know about the relationship between quality and price is unsettling" (1992, 29). Rather, Hofferth argues that quality, availability, accessibility, husband's earnings, and other factors have independent effects on work and should be considered separately. Moreover, even if we focus on affordability, "costs being what they are, little or no good quality care is for sale at the much lower price that it would be 'right' (morally, not economically) for parents to have to pay" (Bergmann 1994, 4).

Nearly all research on the effect of child care costs on labor force participation finds that net of other determining factors, the higher the cost of child care, the lower the probability of a mother's labor force participation (Blau and Robins 1988, 1989; Bloom and Steen 1990; Connelly 1991, 1992; Duberstein and Mason 1991; Mason and Kuhlthau 1992; Maume 1991; Ribar 1992). Estimates of the size of the cost effect on labor force participation differ widely. Connelly (1992) calculates that a 50 percent subsidy in costs to the average married mother in her sample (Survey of Income and Program Participation 1984) would increase labor force participation from 58.8 percent to 64 percent. Further, if nominally free, universal child care were offered, the participation rate would increase to 68.7 percent. These increases are much smaller than David Blau's and Philip Robins's (1988) very sensitive estimates suggesting that the availability of free child care would lead to an 87 percent labor force participation rate for married mothers.

In contrast, Karen Mason and Karen Kuhlthau (1992) argue that these economic studies are flawed because they make unwarranted assumptions about costs of care and the context of its use; they rely on areal measures of costs, and they define *child care* as extrafamilial or use data only from currently employed women or only married women. As an alternative method, they use a survey question that asked mothers whether they would work if satisfactory child care were available at a reasonable cost. One third of the Detroit-area mothers in their sample reported that child care concerns had constrained their employment. They found that whether women perceive child care problems to have affected their employment behavior depends largely on the supply of nonmarket child care available to them, their level of economic resources, and their attitudes about work and motherhood. Poor women and those without nearby relatives were especially likely to report this concern. Several other studies using comparable survey questions find about a 10 to 20 percent increase in labor force participation as a result of the availability of affordable child care (for example, Presser and Baldwin 1980). A recent qualitative study of low-income single mothers found that among 214 welfare-reliant mothers, the majority (57 percent) said they could not afford to work at least in part because they lacked low-cost child care (Edin and Lein 1997, 80).

In addition to the consideration of labor force participation as a binary outcome phenomenon, child care also affects the number of hours mothers work. According to Arleen Leibowitz and Linda Waite (1988), 20 percent of employed mothers in their sample from the National Longitudinal Survey of Youth, 1986, said they would work more hours if they could find child care. Further, among unemployed mothers, 40 percent said they would seek a job offering more hours if child care were available.

Access to child care includes availability and affordability, but also convenience. Using a sample of families living in public housing projects, Philip Robins (1988) compared labor market outcomes for families in projects with child care centers to families in projects without them. He found that the convenience of child care is an important factor in the ability of low-income families to achieve self-sufficiency. He argues that "reducing the time required to transport children to and from child-care facilities unambiguously leads to an increase in labor force participation" (135).

The structure of work is another factor that affects child care arrangements and labor. According to data from the National Child Care Survey, one-third of poor, working mothers and 25 percent of working-class mothers earning less than $25,000 worked weekends (Hofferth 1995; Phillips 1995), as is increasingly the case with the explosion of low-skill jobs in the service sector. Yet 10 percent or less of child care providers are open on weekends. Therefore, workers in low-wage sectors of the labor market are more constrained than other workers by child care arrangements, which become informal and less reliable. African Americans, Latinos, immigrants, and women are much more likely to work in these low-wage sectors.

In sum, parents are more likely to seek work and to seek more hours when they have acceptable, affordable, reliable, safe, convenient child care.[4] When this type of care is unavailable, they face concerns that limit or prevent their labor force activity. In the rest of this chapter I will analyze how these concerns affect work and poverty.

Hypotheses

Four main hypotheses are tested in these analyses. I hypothesize that net of other intervening factors:

(1)   Child care concerns will be negatively associated with labor force participation. That is, respondents who say they have concerns about child care will be less likely to work or be looking for work.

(2)   Child care concerns will be positively associated with unemployment. That is, respondents who say they have concerns about child care will be less likely to find work.

(3)   Child care concerns will be positively associated with poverty. That is, respondents who say they have concerns about child care will be more likely to have household income below the poverty line.

(4)   I expect several differences in these three phenomena by race/ethnicity, gender, and immigration status. First, because women and racial minorities are disadvantaged in the labor market in terms of hiring, promotion, wages, and gender and racial occupational segregation, I expect that these groups will be more likely to be unemployed and in poverty. Second, due to the gendered division of labor in society, I expect mothers to participate in the labor force at lower rates than fathers. Third, because women who are also racial minorities presumably suffer from multiple jeopardy—with their race/ethnicity, gender, and immigration constraints multiplying their disadvantages—I expect that white women will suffer lower unemployment and poverty and will have more freedom to stay out of the labor force than will other mothers in the sample. Fourth, because of cultural differences in the approach to family and parenting, we might expect immigrants, particularly Latinas, to have more concerns about child care and be less likely to pay for it. Finally, because the economic status of the immigrant Asians in the LASUI sample is not clearly disadvantaged, I think Asians will fare better than other women of color in the sample.

Data and Methods

The subsample of the Los Angeles Study of Urban Inequality used in this analysis is limited to respondents with at least one child under eighteen years old who lives in the household, and omits native-born Asians. There are very few native-born Asians in the parent sample, and limiting Asians to the foreign-born permits a direct comparison with immigrant Latinos that would otherwise be impossible.[5]

The basic research strategy proceeds in three steps. First, a logistic regression model estimates the effect of child care concerns on labor force participation, conditioning on gender, race-ethnicity-nativity, human capital or class, social and economic resources, neighborhood context and family characteristics. This sample includes all parents with at least one child under eighteen in the household. Second, the same set of explanatory variables is included in a logistic regression model estimating unemployment. This sample includes only parents in the labor force with at least one child under eighteen in the household, either employed or unemployed. Third, the explanatory factors are used to estimate poverty. This sample includes all parents with at least one child under eighteen in the household.

The main variable of interest in each analysis is whether or not child care concerns limited job search and job application. The other independent variables are included primarily as controls for better-known predictors of labor force activity and poverty. The set of controls is fixed across the models for simplicity of analysis.

Lastly, the poverty coefficients are used to estimate the probability of being poor for subgroups of mothers under two scenarios: with child care concerns that limit work and without those concerns. The difference in poverty risk under these two scenarios is then analyzed.

Measuring Child Care Concerns

The survey question used as a measure of child care problems states:

> In the past twelve months, has a concern about your child care needs caused you: (a) to not look or apply for work; (b) to turn down a job you were offered; (c) to not participate in school or a training program; and (d) to quit or be fired from your job?

The question was asked of all parents with at least one child under age eighteen living in the household. These four items are particularly useful for the analyses because they are not limited by respondents' employment status, and therefore allow for comparison across groups by work status to find out the answer to a counterfactual question: Who would be working, but isn't, as a result of child care problems? Some of the other child care variables in LASUI describe child care arrangements and other characteristics of those arrangements, but are asked only of working parents.

A sample of working parents allows us to assess the effect of child care problems on job characteristics and/or labor market situation, such as the hours worked, the pay rate, the degree of promotion, and so on. But it does not allow us to measure the risk of nonparticipation in the labor force. Further, it is important to have respondents who are employed, unemployed, and not in the labor force in the analysis of poverty because even those who have jobs may be underemployed, working at lower wages as a result of child care concerns that limit their work hours, location, or other job characteristics.

This study is limited to the first item of the survey question— whether child care concerns caused the respondent not to look or apply for work—in order to focus the analyses and elucidate the results. The use of all four items as a combined variable would confuse the nature of the effect, rendering even more ambiguous the definition of child care concerns and how exactly they affect work and poverty. The item about school concerns is particularly problematic in predicting poverty, since the benefits of education arguably reduce poverty at some future point. Moreover, the first item in the survey question is the only one that has a reasonably large number of eligible respondents (21 percent) who reported that they had been limited by child care.[6]

On the other hand, the survey question is slightly ambiguous because it does not further probe respondents about the nature of their child care concerns. Nonetheless, this is not an attitude question. It is a question about work-seeking behavior in which respondents report on what they did or did not *do.*

Table 9.1 presents the percentage of respondents answering yes to each of the four questions that asked about the impact of child care concerns on their labor force activity. It shows that mothers are more likely than fathers to report that child care concerns limited their employment chances in some way on all four measures, and that the largest effect for both genders is on job search. In fact, on all four questions, while the rates of child care concerns differ by race-ethnicity-nativity, the rate for mothers is always higher than the rate for fathers, so child care negatively affects mothers' work chances more than fathers, even when controlling for race-ethnicity (except in a single case, where immigrant Asian fathers were more likely than mothers to turn down a job). Among all groups, the problem of child care limiting job search is worst for immigrant Latina mothers, with a reported rate of almost 40 percent. The rest of the analyses use only the first measure of child care concerns

TABLE 9.1   *Parents' Reports of Child Care Problems*

	Total	White	African American	Foreign-Born Asian	Native-Born Latina or Latino	Foreign-Born Latina or Latino
In the past twelve months, has a concern about your child care needs caused you to						
Not look or apply for a job?[a]						
Mothers	30.4%	30.0%	15.1%	26.8%	15.7%	39.5%
Fathers	6.6	8.4	12.4	6.3	7.2	4.1
Turn down a job you were offered?						
Mothers	10.4	12.5	7.0	8.9	4.6	11.4
Fathers	3.1	4.4	2.4	11.6	0	1.8
Not participate in school or a training program?						
Mothers	15.1	18.8	10.7	9.8	14.5	14.1
Fathers	5.2	7.3	6.1	1.7	0.3	5.5
Quit or be fired from your job?						
Mothers	6.2	7.9	2.6	7.0	12.8	4.0
Fathers	1.1	1.8	1.2	0	0	1.1
Number of respondents[b]						
Mothers (unweighted)	(1163)	(157)	(379)	(257)	(52)	(318)
Fathers (unweighted)	(654)	(101)	(92)	(193)	(39)	(229)
Mothers (weighted)	(1149)	(387)	(127)	(82)	(113)	(440)
Fathers (weighted)	(749)	(222)	(62)	(53)	(88)	(324)

Source: Los Angeles Study of Urban Inequality 1994.

[a]The χ^2 test is significant at $p < .001$ for the overall gender difference and for the race-ethnicity difference among mothers, but not for the race-ethnicity difference among fathers.

[b]Percentages are based on weighted data for representativeness in Los Angeles County.

in the table: whether or not child care caused the respondent not to look or apply for work.

The number of fathers reporting that child care concerns limited their job search is non-negligible, but fairly small in absolute numbers. Based on raw, unweighted numbers, only a dozen or fewer fathers of each racial-ethnic group reported child care problems. These small sample sizes make it difficult to analyze the fathers in any detail. Therefore, fathers are included as controls in the regression analyses but are not used for further prediction or discussion.

While preliminary results show that about 30 percent of mothers report child care concerns that limited their job search, it is difficult to assess what sorts of child care are used by different women or to explain the racial-ethnic differences, because the survey questions about child care usage that LASUI provides are asked only of working parents. However, examining responses from working parents does provide a window, although somewhat incomplete, into child care usage.

Data from LASUI show that among parents who are currently working and have at least one preschool-aged child, the most common child care arrangement (32 percent) is the child's parent (or parent's spouse or partner) (see table 9.2). Other relatives and grandparents are utilized second most often (each used 16.8 percent of the time). However, when we break down these figures by poverty status, it is clear that families with income above the federal poverty line are much more likely than poor families to use nonrelative or institutional care like day care centers and nursery schools.

Further, among parents who are in the labor force and employed, low-wage workers are unlikely to let child care situations interfere with holding on to their job. Poor parents are less likely to be late for work than nonpoor parents because of child care problems (18.6 percent versus 28.8 percent). Low-income families are also much less likely to change their work hours as a result of child care concerns. This is probably due to less flexibility in their jobs, and it implies that children, rather than precarious jobs, suffer as a result of haphazard care situations as children are juggled around adult schedules. These results give a glimpse of some of the problems of low-wage workers with children that result from the current market-based system of child care in the United States.

Table 9.3 shows the child care arrangements and expenses for employed mothers with children under age six. The table indicates that Latinas are most likely to use relatives for child care, while black mothers are most likely to use center-based child care (43 percent). In addition, whites and Asians also use nonrelative child care much more than Latinas do.

TABLE 9.2   *Child Care Arrangements for Working Parents with a Child Under Age Six, and Child Care Problems for Parents of Children Under Eighteen Who Worked This Year*

Child Care Arrangement	Total	Not Poor	Poor
Nobody	3.8%	4.1%	2.3%
Myself	1.0	1.2	0.0
Spouse, partner, child's father	31.7	30.3	39.7
Child's grandparent	16.8	15.5	24.2
Other relative	16.8	15.8	22.4
Nonrelative	12.1	12.6	9.2
Day care center	9.7	11.3	1.2
Nursery school, preschool	7.8	9.0	1.0
Head Start	0.0	0.1	0.0
Other before-, after-school institutional care	0.2	0.3	0.0
n	(608)	(517)	(92)
In the past twelve months, has a concern about your child care needs caused you			
To be late for work?	27.2%	28.8%	18.6%
To be absent from work?	27.1	27.2	26.8
To change your hours of work?	22.3	25.3	6.3
To lose out on a promotion or a raise?	3.5	3.3	4.7
n	(1,272)	(1,072)	(200)

Source: Los Angeles Study of Urban Inequality 1994.

There are not large differences by race-ethnicity-nativity in the number of hours that children spend in child care. Most children spend an average of thirty to thirty-four hours a week, with a median of forty hours. However, there are differences in how much money is spent. White and immigrant Asian mothers, the two more affluent groups in the sample, pay substantially more than African American and Latina mothers. Asian mothers in the sample spend on average more than two times as much as black mothers, among those who reported paying for care at all. Just over half of all mothers surveyed reported paying for care, with only small differences by race-ethnicity.

Labor Market Status Predictors

Several other important explanatory factors are included in the regression analyses. First, race-ethnicity-nativity and gender are measured as a set of dummy variables with mothers, African Americans, native-born Latinos, foreign-born Latinos, and foreign-born Asians coded as 1, and fathers and whites coded as 0. Controls for human capital or class include education, measured as a set of dummy variables for degrees

TABLE 9.3   *Child Care Arrangements Among Working Mothers with a Child Under Six*

	White	Black	Foreign-Born Asian	Native-Born Latina	Foreign-Born Latina
Relative care					
Self	1.7%	0.1%	1.8%	0%	3.9%
Spouse, partner	23.7	6.9	7.3	9.3	2.1
Grandparent, other relative	28.4	40.3	44.3	67.1	61.0
Nonrelative care					
Nonrelative	18.4	7.8	11.9	19.6	12.8
Day care center, nursery school	20.8	43.4	30.4	0	7.3
Head Start	0	0.7	0	0	0
Other institutional care	0.3	0	0	0	0.8
Nobody	6.8	0.8	4.3	4.0	12.0
	100%	100%	100%	100%	100%
Hours with caregiver					
Mean	33.7	33.9	30.6	32.7	31.4
Standard deviation	18	14	20	17	16
Median	36	40	40	40	40
n	(44)	(70)	(45)	(17)	(63)
Weekly cost of care[a]					
Mean	$105	$61	$167	$60	$62
Standard deviation	76	35	106	52	32
Median	90	55	100	40	50
n[a]	(25)	(39)	(24)	(10)	(38)

Source: Los Angeles Study of Urban Inequality 1994.
[a]Among those paying for care.

earned, age, and age squared. For respondents who have had a consistent work history, age is associated with work experience.

Children in the household were divided into three age groups: preschool, preteen, and teenager. Then a dummy variable was created for each group to signify the presence of any children in the household belonging to that age group. Preteens (age six through twelve) were omitted as the reference category.

Social and economic resources are a set of measures for household structure, financial resources, and social capital or social resources.[7] The presence of a spouse or domestic partner is included because that person can act as a child care provider as well as a potential factor in social capital for job search. Spouse's earnings (continuous) are expected to affect labor market decisions, ability of respondents to pay for child care, and family poverty. Whether the respondent received alimony or child support should also affect poverty. Social resources that affect child care problems also include the number of adults in the household, other than the respondent and spouse, available to help with the kids.

Two variables tap respondents' social networks. There is a measure of the number of network ties and an index describing the quality of those ties. For the social network questions, respondents were asked to name up to three people, other than those in the household, with whom they discussed important matters in the last six months. Respondents reported some demographic information about these individuals, such as race-ethnicity, marital status, and education level, for example, and organizations to which they belong, as well as providing some idea of how close the ties are to them. The network quality index was computed as a weighted sum of these characteristics, with "positive" characteristics (like being employed) weighted more heavily than "negative" characteristics (like welfare recipiency).[8] Education, a continuous variable with many high values, was normalized so it would not weigh more heavily than other factors in the index. The resulting index produces a continuous variable that runs from −4 to +21, with a mean of 7.5. The higher the index, the better the quality of the respondent's social ties for aiding in job search. (The index was not designed to measure the quality of this network as a social support for child care provision, although the two types of networks are probably related.)

Last, residential neighborhood context is included to control for the underclass hypothesis (Massey and Denton 1993; Wilson 1987, 1996) that poor people, particularly African Americans and Latinos, suffer disproportionately from the negative effects of living in a racially and socially segregated, high-concentration poverty neighborhood. Wilson defines these "ghetto poverty census tracts" as tracts in which at least 40 percent of the people are poor by the federal poverty threshold (1996, 12). Neighborhood effects are operationalized using LASUI, with a three-level interval variable for increasing levels of poverty concentration in a respondent's census tract: low (less than 20 percent), medium (20 percent to 39 percent) and high (40 percent or more), coded 1, 2, 3.

Measuring Labor Market Outcomes

The three main dependent variables are 0-1 binary outcome measures. The labor force is defined as those who are either currently working or looking for a job. Stay-at-home mothers, disabled people, retired people, and full-time students are examples of respondents who are not participating in the labor force. All LASUI parents in the sample are included in the labor force analyses, with labor force participants coded as 1 (75.1 percent are in the labor force).

Unemployment is defined as the percent of people who are in the labor force but cannot find a job. The unemployment model only includes parents who are in the labor force, with unemployed respondents coded as 1 and employed respondents coded as 0 (12.7 percent are unemployed).

Poverty rates were constructed by comparing respondents' family income level to the federal poverty line for that household size. Respondents with incomes below that line were designated as poor. For example, in our survey year of 1994, the poverty line was $15,029 for a two-parent family of four. The poverty variable is coded 1 for respondents living in poor households and 0 for nonpoor respondents (23.2 percent of respondents are poor by this strict definition).

Description of the Sample

Table 9.4 describes the distribution of respondents on the explanatory variables for mothers and fathers. Because the subsample selected from LASUI for this study is limited to parents with children in the household, there is a higher percentage of women in this sample than men, since children living with only one parent are more likely to live with a mother. In fact, for African Americans, two-thirds of the sample are mothers and only one-third are fathers (not shown). Further, a sample of parents differs from society as a whole in that parents of minor children tend to be younger (thirty-seven is the average age in this sample) and more likely to be in the workforce. The labor force participation rate for American women is about 58 percent, compared with about 63 percent in the sample. Likewise, about three-fourths of men are employed or looking for work, while 94 percent of the fathers in the sample are in the labor force. Fathers with dependent children at home tend to work to support them, and at much higher levels than mothers in two-parent households because of the remaining gender division of domestic labor. In communities with high unemployment rates among working-age fathers, single parenthood is much more likely; these fathers are not in the sample because they don't have children in the household.

Table 9.4 provides evidence that the mothers and fathers are fairly similar in many ways, such as age, education, network ties, and neighborhood context. A main difference between respondents by gender, however, is that father-reported families are more likely to have a spouse or partner present (88 percent) than are mother-reported families (68 percent), many of whom are single parents. Mother-reported families also have higher rates of spousal or partner earnings, since men earn

TABLE 9.4   *Descriptive Statistics, Parents with Children Under Age Eighteen Living in the Household, by Gender*

	Total	Mothers	Fathers
Labor force participation	75.1% (1897)	62.9% (1149)	93.9% (749)
Unemployment rate	12.7% (1424)	16.0% (723)	9.3% (701)
Families below poverty line	23.2% (1703)	26.3% (1003)	18.7% (701)
Gender			
Mothers	60.5%	—	—
Fathers	39.5 (1897)	—	—
Race-ethnicity			
White	32.1%	33.7%	29.7%
African American	10.0	11.1	8.2
Native-born Latina or Latino	10.6	9.8	11.8
Foreign-born Latina or Latino	40.3	38.3	43.2
Foreign-born Asian	7.1 (1897)	7.1 (1149)	7.1 (749)
Child care caused respondent not to look or apply for work	21.0% (1897)	30.4% (1149)	6.6% (749)
Presence of children, by age			
Preschoolers	40.5%	40.6%	40.4%
Pre-teens	42.7	45.1	38.9
Teenagers	31.2 (1896)	32.5 (1149)	29.1 (749)
Education			
Less than high school	30.6%	32.1%	28.3%
High school or some college	51.7	53.8	48.5
College degree	12.4	10.8	15.0
More than college degree	5.2 (1897)	3.3 (1148)	8.2 (749)
Received child support or alimony	4.3% (1896)	6.7% (1148)	0.6% (748)
Married or living with partner	75.8% (1897)	67.6% (1149)	88.4% (749)
Index of social network quality			
0 or negative	30.7%	28.1%	34.7%
1 through 11	37.0	42.0	29.3
12 or more	32.3	29.9	36.0
mean	7.52 (1897)	7.48 (1149)	7.58 (749)

TABLE 9.4   *Continued*

	Total	Mothers	Fathers
Number of other adults in household			
Zero	61.2%	59.7%	63.6%
One	17.3	16.6	18.3
Two	11.1	11.1	11.0
Three	6.1	7.2	4.5
more than three	4.4	5.4	2.6
	(1897)	(1149)	(749)
Census tract relation to poverty line			
Low poverty	68.7%	69.1%	68.3%
Medium poverty	28.0	27.9	28.1
High poverty	3.3	3.1	3.6
	(1897)	(1149)	(749)
Age in years			
Twenty-one to thirty	28.7%	31.3%	24.8%
Thirty-one to forty	37.9	38.2	37.6
Forty-one to fifty	22.1	19.3	26.5
Over fifty	11.2	11.2	11.1
mean	37.1	36.4	38.1
	(1897)	(1149)	(748)
Spouse's Earnings			
0	51.0%	47.1%	56.6%
$1 to $20,000	24.4	23.1	26.2
$20,001 to $40,000	15.2	17.0	12.6
More than $40,000	9.5	12.8	4.6
mean	$13,582	$16,630	$9,157
	(1767)	(1046)	(721)
Number of network ties			
Zero	29.8%	27.1%	34.0%
One	6.7	8.0	4.6
Two	12.8	13.1	12.4
Three	50.7	51.8	49.0
	(1897)	(1149)	(749)

Source: Los Angeles Study of Urban Inequality 1994.
Note: Number of cases listed in parentheses.

more on average and are more likely to have a spouse at all (among a sample of parents). Further, there are important gender differences for each of the dependent variables. Nearly two-thirds of mothers are in the labor force, and they have higher unemployment and much higher poverty rates than fathers. These important differences suggest that gender should be accounted for in the analyses.

Table 9.5 describes the sample characteristics for mothers only, highlighting some important differences across racial groups on all three dependent variables and on most of the explanatory variables. Among mothers, about 40 percent of African Americans and immigrant Latinas

TABLE 9.5   *Descriptive Statistics, Mothers by Race-Ethnicity-Nativity*

	White	African American	Foreign-Born Asian	Native-Born Latina	Foreign-Born Latina
Labor force participation	65.8%	71.5%	34.5%	81.5%	58.5%
	(157)	(379)	(257)	(52)	(318)
Unemployment rate	14.7	19.1	5.4	17.5	17.0
	(107)	(241)	(135)	(38)	(174)
Families below poverty line	11.6	38.8	9.0	20.5	40.5
	(143)	(340)	(156)	(46)	(272)
Child care caused mother not to look or apply for work	30.0%	15.1%	26.8%	15.7%	39.5%
	(157)	(379)	(257)	(52)	(318)
Presence of children, by age					
Preschoolers	43.3%	32.1%	25.8%	31.8%	45.7%
Preteens	41.6	40.7	31.3	36.3	54.3
Teenagers	29.6	38.3	41.3	36.7	30.7
	(157)	(378)	(257)	(52)	(318)
Education					
Less than high school	5.8%	13.8%	24.7%	17.3%	65.7%
High school or some college	69.1	77.7	40.7	75.7	30.4
College degree	18.7	6.6	23.8	7.0	3.5
More than college degree	6.4	2.0	10.8	0.0	0.4
	(157)	(378)	(257)	(52)	(318)
Received child support or alimony	9.3%	9.2%	0.4%	10.8%	3.7%
	(157)	(377)	(257)	(52)	(318)
Married or living with partner	75.2%	46.7%	86.1%	48.3%	68.6%
	(157)	(379)	(257)	(52)	(318)
Number of network ties					
Zero	3.1%	28.3%	76.4%	16.7%	41.4%
One	10.5	12.1	1.7	10.9	5.1
Two	19.0	11.6	2.3	18.1	9.1
Three	67.4	48.0	19.7	54.3	44.4
	(157)	(379)	(257)	(52)	(318)
Index of social network quality					
0 or negative	4.3%	30.3%	77.1%	17.4%	42.1%
1 through 11	48.1	40.4	8.5	50.2	41.0
12 or more	47.6	29.3	14.4	32.3	16.9
mean	10.7	7.0	2.9	8.6	5.4
	(157)	(379)	(257)	(52)	(318)
Number of other adults in household					
Zero	71.5%	63.4%	66.8%	46.9%	44.3%
One	15.5	19.2	8.4	20.8	18.1
Two	4.9	10.5	8.8	9.0	20.8
Three or more	8.2	6.9	16.0	23.3	16.9
	(157)	(379)	(257)	(52)	(318)

(Table continues on p. 360.)

TABLE 9.5   *Continued*

	White	African American	Foreign-Born Asian	Native-Born Latina	Foreign-Born Latina
Census tract relation to poverty line					
Low poverty	97.0%	48.6%	83.2%	76.2%	46.0%
Medium poverty	2.8	44.9	16.7	22.8	48.3
High poverty	0.2	6.5	0.2	1.0	5.7
	(157)	(379)	(257)	(52)	(318)
Age in years					
Twenty-one to thirty	23.2%	35.2%	13.9%	30.9%	40.6%
Thirty-one to forty	40.7	41.5	28.9	34.1	37.8
Forty-one to fifty	26.2	12.4	29.6	13.3	14.8
Over fifty	9.8	10.9	27.6	21.7	6.9
mean	37.9	36.0	42.1	35.9	34.4
	(157)	(379)	(257)	(52)	(318)
Spouse's Earnings					
0	38.9%	70.4%	43.0%	64.9%	43.5%
$1 to $20,000	9.3	13.1	9.3	8.6	43.9
$20,001 to $40,000	29.3	7.9	13.9	14.6	10.0
More than $40,000	22.4	8.7	33.7	11.9	2.6
mean	$26,963	$8,171	$29,863	$13,206	$8,874
	(144)	(360)	(184)	(48)	(299)

Source: Los Angeles Study of Urban Inequality 1994.

live in poverty, which is two to four times as high as for whites, foreign-born Asians, and native-born Latinas. Unemployment is in the double digits for all groups except immigrant Asian mothers, who reported only 5 percent unemployment.[9] Foreign-born Asians also have the lowest labor force participation rate among mothers (one-third), compared with approximately two-thirds for the other mothers, whose rates are more in line with national averages. African American and native-born Latina mothers are much more likely to be single parents, and are less likely (together with immigrant Latinas) to have a college degree. Blacks and immigrant Latinas are also much more likely to live in a concentrated poverty neighborhood.

Results and Discussion
Estimating Labor Force Participation and Unemployment

The results of the first logistic regression, which models the relationship between child care concerns and labor force participation, are presented in table 9.6. As hypothesized, the effect of child care concerns is statistically significant, fairly large, and negative ($b = -1.62$). The odds

TABLE 9.6   *Logistic Regression Model Predicting Whether Respondent Is in the Labor Force*

	Coefficient	Standard Error	Odds Multiplier (e^b)
Child care			
Child care concerns caused respondent not to look or apply for work	−1.62***	0.16	0.20
Gender (mother = 1)	−1.84***	0.36	0.16
Race-ethnicity (reference = white)			
African American	−0.79	0.58	0.46
Asian immigrant	−0.90	0.65	0.40
Latino immigrant	0.84	0.47	2.32
Native-born Latino	0.70	0.66	2.01
Race-ethnicity × gender interactions			
African American × mother	0.87	0.64	2.38
Asian immigrant × mother	−0.23	0.72	0.79
Latino immigrant × mother	−0.57	0.48	0.57
Native-born Latino × mother	0.33	0.73	1.40
Human capital			
Less than high school	−2.50***	0.49	0.082
High school or some college	−1.59***	0.46	0.20
College degree	−0.77	0.49	0.46
Age	0.25***	0.05	1.28
Age squared	−3.60E-03***	6.00E-04	1.00
Presence of children by age (in reference to kids age six to twelve)			
Preschooler	−0.22	0.18	0.80
Teenager	−0.19	0.18	0.83
Social and economic resources			
Spouse or partner present	−0.15	0.19	0.86
Spouse earnings (= 0 if not present)	−1.50E-05***	3.71E-06	1.00
Number of ties	−0.088	0.10	0.92
Quality of network	0.058*	0.024	1.06
Number of adults in household, excluding respondent and spouse	0.23***	0.070	1.26
Received child support or alimony	0.044	0.34	1.04
Neighborhood context			
Census tract relation to poverty	−0.26	0.15	0.77
Constant	1.32	1.19	
Model χ^2 / df	626.9/24		
n	1639		

Source: Los Angeles Study of Urban Inequality 1994.
*$p < .05$, **$p < .01$, ***$p < .001$

of being in the labor force are 80 percent lower for parents who have experienced child care concerns, compared with parents who have not, net of other factors.[10] Second, gender matters.[11] Mothers are much less likely (84 percent) than fathers to participate in the labor force. It is not surprising that being female is associated with a lower odds of labor force participation, since mothers are more likely than fathers to stay home with children in families where that is socially and economically feasible. The mother's usual lower earnings capacity in the face of expensive child care options and her cultural association with caretaking of husbands and children make her more likely to stay out of the labor force.

We also find expected relationships among some of the other explanatory variables. As education increases, labor force participation increases; as age increases, labor force participation increases; as spouse's income increases, labor force participation decreases. Having other adults in the household is associated with higher labor force participation, perhaps because they provide child care, perhaps because larger households are associated with lower-income families that require everybody to contribute financially and fewer stay-at-home mothers.

While the labor force can be thought of as an activity one either does or does not participate in, we can also think of it as a continuum of degrees of participation, according to the number of hours worked. This is particularly true for women, who are more likely than men to work part-time. Therefore, as an additional check on the logit findings for labor force participation presented in table 9.6, the method of ordinary least squares was used to regress the same set of explanatory factors on the number of hours worked, with those not in the labor force coded as working 0 hours. The results of this procedure, presented in table 9.7, show that the association between child care concerns and hours worked is large. Child care concerns reduce work time by an average of 11.6 hours per week—enough to reduce full-time employment to part-time employment. This finding, as well as the finding from the logistic analysis of labor force participation, confirms that those who reported that child care limited their ability to find work do, indeed, work fewer hours than others.

Child care has an even larger effect on unemployment than on labor force participation. Table 9.8 shows the probability of being unemployed among those who are in the labor force—that is, either working or looking for work. Since the child care concerns survey question asks about concerns to both applying and looking for work, we could expect that even among parents who are in the labor force and actively seeking a job, child care problems could prevent them from acting on information about job opportunities. That is, jobs might be advertised, but because of

TABLE 9.7   *Ordinary Least Squares Regression Model Estimating Hours Worked*

	Coefficient	Standard Error
Child care		
Child care concerns caused respondent not to look or apply for work	−11.61***	1.04
Gender (mother = 1)	−16.86***	1.47
Race-ethnicity (reference = white)		
African American	−11.04***	2.45
Asian immigrant	−5.44*	2.74
Latino immigrant	−3.00	1.63
Native-born Latino	−1.44	2.11
Race-ethnicity × gender interactions		
African American × mother	12.20***	2.97
Asian immigrant × mother	−2.81	3.45
Latino immigrant × mother	4.98**	1.84
Native-born Latino × mother	8.95***	2.72
Human capital		
Less than high school	−11.83***	2.01
High school or some college	−7.71***	1.83
College degree	−5.04*	1.99
Age	2.22***	0.25
Age squared	−0.028***	0.0029
Presence of children by age (in reference to kids age six to twelve)		
Preschooler	−0.15	0.93
Teenager	−4.21***	0.96
Social and economic resources		
Spouse or partner present	1.58	1.11
Spouse earnings (= 0 if not present)	−1.05E-04***	2.10E-05
Number of ties	−1.27*	0.61
Quality of network	0.53***	0.13
Number of adults in household, excluding respondent and spouse	1.67***	0.36
Received child support or alimony	5.36**	1.95
Neighborhood context		
Census tract relation to poverty	−1.37	0.82
Constant	11.16	5.88
Adjusted R²	36.4	
F	43.0***	
n	1763	

Source: Los Angeles Study of Urban Inequality 1994.
*p < .05, **p < .01, ***p < .001

TABLE 9.8   *Logistic Regression Model Predicting Whether Respondent Is Unemployed, Given Labor Force Participation*

	Coefficient	Standard Error	Odds Multiplier (e^b)
Child care			
Child care concerns caused respondent not to look or apply for work	1.20***	0.23	3.32
Gender (mother = 1)	1.14**	0.38	3.12
Race-ethnicity (reference = white)			
African American	0.57	0.54	1.76
Asian immigrant	−1.75	1.17	0.17
Latino immigrant	−0.31	0.42	0.73
Native-born Latino	0.91*	0.45	2.49
Race-ethnicity × gender interactions			
African American × mother	−0.44	0.64	0.64
Asian immigrant × mother	0.25	1.50	1.29
Latino immigrant × mother	−0.69	0.45	0.50
Native-born Latino × mother	−0.81	0.56	0.44
Human capital			
Less than high school	−0.08	0.44	0.93
High school or some college	−0.81*	0.39	0.45
College degree	−0.76	0.46	0.47
Age	−0.06	0.071	0.94
Age squared	1.10E-03	9.00E-04	1.00
Presence of children by age (in reference to kids age 6–12)			
Preschooler	−0.27	0.22	0.76
Teenager	−0.074	0.21	0.93
Social and economic resources			
Spouse or partner present	0.31	0.24	1.37
Spouse earnings (= 0 if not present)	−2.60E-05***	7.48E-06	1.00
Number of ties	0.42**	0.13	1.52
Quality of network	−0.13***	0.03	0.87
Number of adults in household, excluding respondent and spouse	−0.010	0.08	0.99
Received child support or alimony	−0.76	0.52	0.47
Neighborhood context			
Census tract relation to poverty	0.12	0.18	1.13
Constant	−1.13	1.51	
Model χ^2 / df	122.7/24		
n	1170		

Source: Los Angeles Study of Urban Inequality 1994.
*p < .05, **p < .01, ***p < .001

child care responsibilities a parent cannot go to the employer to obtain an application or have an interview. Parents might also be limited in their ability to find out about jobs in the first place if they are taking care of children. The results show a positive and statistically significant child care concern coefficient of 1.2. The odds of being unemployed are 3⅓ times greater for parents who experienced child care concerns than for those who did not. The odds of unemployment are also 3 times greater for mothers in the labor force than for fathers.

The odds multiplier of 3.32 for unemployment resulting from child care concerns is a measure that tells us the relative difference in the odds of poverty between respondents with concerns and those without. To render this relative measure meaningful, we need to contextualize the findings by providing a baseline of how likely a parent is to be unemployed in the first place. Likewise, the odds multiplier for labor force participation is a relative measure. Further, the coefficients from logistic regression models are difficult to interpret directly because they are nonlinear, changing at every level of the respondent's characteristics. Therefore, in order to provide a more meaningful interpretation of the results, the logistic regression models were used to make predictions about labor force participation and unemployment for mothers by race-ethnicity, simulating the rates with and without child care concerns. This is a statistical simulation experiment that assumes that we could somehow remove all the respondent's child care concerns and that appropriate jobs would be available. To make these predictions, I multiplied each estimated coefficient by the mean value for each explanatory variable. The result was summed (plus the constant) and substituted into the logit equation (9.1).[12]

(9.1) Predicted Probability of Labor Force Participation $= 1 / [1 + e^{(-b\ell X\ell)}]$

(9.2) Predicted Probability of Unemployment $= 1 / [1 + e^{(-buXu)}]$,

where $b\ell$ and bu are the vectors of estimated coefficients for labor force participation and unemployment, respectively, and $X\ell$ and Xu are the mean values of the vectors of explanatory variables for the labor force participation and unemployment models.

These predictions were calculated for mothers of each racial-ethnic group using the mean value for that group. For example, to estimate labor force participation for Asian mothers, the "typical" Asian mother in the sample was used. I substituted the mean level of education, age, marital status, and so on for the group of Asian mothers into the regression model. For African American mothers, the average values for African American women were used, and so on for each race-gender grouping.

TABLE 9.9 *Predicted Labor Force Participation and Unemployment Rates for Mothers, With and Without Child Care Concerns*

	With Child Care Concerns	Without Child Care Concerns	Improvement Factor
Labor force participation			
White	37.4%	70.8%	0.89
African American	40.3	73.6	0.83
Foreign-born Asian	2.2	38.9	16.68
Native-born Latina	75.6	81.9	0.08
Foreign-born Latina	29.1	66.0	1.27
Unemployment			
White	33.8%	9.9%	2.4
African American	38.8	13.1	2.0
Foreign-born Asian	12.6	0.50	24.2
Native-born Latina	42.8	16.4	1.6
Foreign-born Latina	27.6	9.8	1.8

Source: Los Angeles Study of Urban Inequality 1994.

Table 9.9 shows the estimated labor force participation rates and the estimated unemployment rates, first under a scenario in which everyone in the group has child care concerns and then under a scenario in which nobody has them. The third column shows the factor of potential improvement in predicted labor force participation (unemployment) that could be achieved by removing mothers' child care concerns (the percent change from having child care problems to not having problems).

The table makes clear that the difference in mothers' labor force participation rates with child care concerns and without is quite large for all the racial-ethnic groups. Participation rates could almost double for black and white mothers, more than double for immigrant Latinas, and increase by sixteen-fold for immigrant Asian mothers. There is a small significant improvement for native-born Latinas as well. The impact on mothers' unemployment risk by "removing" child care concerns is even greater than the effects on labor force participation. Holding other factors constant, unemployment rates are more than double for mothers with child care concerns than they are for mothers without them.

To sum up, the first two logistic regression models demonstrate that, as hypothesized, *child care concerns have a sizable depressive effect on both labor force participation and employment.* This is true net of other factors typically used to predict labor force participation and unemployment, such as human capital and social factors.

Child Care and Poverty

Recall from figure 9.1 that the effect of child care on poverty is indirect (child care affects work, which affects income and poverty), so a single equation model is not the only framework with which to estimate it. However, given that the intermediate consequences of child care concerns on labor force participation and unemployment have been demonstrated, I argue that using child care concerns to predict poverty directly produces a reasonable estimate, without leaving unanswered questions— that is, a "black box"—about how and why it has this effect.[13] Further, including a variable to measure child care concerns in a model of poverty produces a regression coefficient that can then be used to easily analyze the effects of removing child care concerns on poverty.

The results of the logistic regression model predicting poverty (table 9.10) show that, as hypothesized, child care concerns have a positive, statistically significant effect of 0.71 ($p < .001$) on a family's risk of being poor, net of the other factors (poor = 1 in the model). Specifically, experiencing child care concerns that caused a respondent not to look or apply for work increased the odds of poverty by more than two times compared with parents who did not experience such concerns, even when controlling for many other factors. The size of the child care concerns effect is of the same order of magnitude as the neighborhood effect (0.59, $p < .001$), the variable included to account for Wilson's (1987) underclass hypothesis about the effect of concentrated poverty neighborhoods on individual chances of poverty.[14] The gender by race-ethnicity-nativity coefficients are positive and large, indicating that white fathers are much less likely to be poor than are women and people of color. (The statistically insignificant coefficient for native-born Latinos is probably a result of the small number of cases included in the regression, but in any case the sign is positive.)

Since the survey question wording about child care concerns is vague, because we do not know exactly what "concerns" respondents have, I analyze working mothers separately. This acts as a check on the possibility that parents who are not working for some other reason use the child care concerns item to explain their situation to survey interviewers.

The coefficient for child care concerns (1.1, $p < .01$) in table 9.11 indicates that working mothers who reported child care concerns are significantly more likely to have family income below the poverty line than similar women who did not experience child care problems. In fact, such problems increase their odds of poverty by nearly three times, which is even larger than the effect found for the whole sample. For working mothers, child care problems may reduce their income because

TABLE 9.10   *Logistic Regression Model Predicting Whether Family Income Is Below the Poverty Level*

	Coefficient	Standard Error	Odds Multiplier (e^b)
Child care			
Child care concerns caused respondent not to look or apply for work	0.71***	0.19	2.04
Neighborhood context			
Census tract relation to poverty	0.59***	0.13	1.81
Gender (mother = 1)	4.01***	1.10	55.25
Race-ethnicity (reference = white)			
African American	3.24**	1.16	25.63
Asian immigrant	3.23**	1.18	25.22
Latino immigrant	3.51**	1.10	33.53
Native-born Latino	2.25	1.20	9.45
Race-ethnicity × gender interactions			
African American × mother	−2.63*	1.20	0.07
Asian immigrant × mother	−3.72**	1.34	0.02
Latino immigrant × mother	−3.52**	1.11	0.03
Native-born Latino × mother	−2.46*	1.24	0.09
Human capital			
Less than high school	0.69	0.49	2.00
High school or some college	−0.079	0.49	0.92
College degree	0.043	0.52	1.04
Age	0.00150	0.043	1.00
Age squared	1.25E-05	5.00E-04	1.00
Presence of children by age (in reference to kids age six to twelve)			
Preschooler	0.16	0.18	1.18
Teenager	0.58**	0.18	1.78
Social and economic resources			
Spouse or partner present	0.63**	0.20	1.88
Spouse earnings (= 0 if not present)	−1.00E-04***	1.11E-05	1.00
Number of ties	0.27*	0.11	1.31
Quality of network	−0.10***	0.026	0.90
Number of adults in household, excluding respondent and spouse	0.20***	0.06	1.23
Received child support or alimony	−1.21**	0.43	0.30
Constant	−6.08	1.55	
Model χ^2 / df	572.5/24		
n	1473		

Source: Los Angeles Study of Urban Inequality 1994.
*$p < .05$, **$p < .01$, ***$p < .001$

TABLE 9.11   *Logistic Model of Poverty for Employed Mothers*

	Coefficient	Standard Error	Odds Multiplier e^b
Child care			
Child care concerns caused respondent not to look or apply for work	1.070**	0.42	2.9
Neighborhood context			
Census tract relation to poverty	0.19	0.30	1.2
Social and economic resources			
Spouse earnings (= 0 if not present)	−0.00010***	0.000028	1.0
Received child support or alimony	−0.84	0.79	0.43
Spouse or partner present	0.83*	0.41	2.3
Number of ties	−0.041	0.23	1.0
Quality of network	0.0032	0.05	1.0
Number of adults in household, excluding respondent and spouse	0.18	0.12	1.2
Presence of children by age (in reference to kids age six to twelve)			
Preschooler	−0.33	0.40	0.7
Teenager	1.19**	0.43	3.3
Race-ethnicity (reference = white)			
African American	0.81	0.58	2.2
Asian immigrant	−0.16	1.4	0.8
Latino immigrant	1.41***	0.54	4.1
Native-born Latino	0.86	0.59	2.4
Constant	−3.11	16.2	
Model χ^2/df	142/19		
n	551		

Source: Los Angeles Study of Urban Inequality 1994.
*$p < .05$, **$p < .01$, ***$p < .001$

they are out of work for periods during the year or because they are underemployed. That is, problems with child care may prevent them from taking the best possible job. These mothers could be limited to days of the week and hours of the day that are convenient for child care, or to jobs that are more flexible about work hours. For example, more highly paid shift work that requires evenings is very difficult to combine with children's schedules. This strong result for working mothers demonstrates that the child care concerns variable has real effects on the work and poverty chances of parents who responded "yes"—it is *not* only a device for the unemployed to justify their lack of work.

Reducing Mothers' Poverty Risk

As with the models of labor force participation and unemployment, the comparison of poverty odds between parents with child care concerns that limit work and those without is a relative measure that is better interpreted in the context of predicted probabilities. The prediction equation (9.3) is below.

(9.3) Predicted Probability of Poverty $= 1 \, / \, [1 \, + \, e^{(-b_p X_p)}]$,

where b_p is the vector of estimated coefficients from table 9.10, and X_p are the mean values of the vector of explanatory variables in the poverty model. The predictions were calculated for mothers of each racial-ethnic group using the mean values for that group.

The difference in mothers' poverty risk under the two child care scenarios is presented in figure 9.2. Controlling for other important factors, figure shows that black and immigrant Latina mothers have the highest probability of poverty in Los Angeles County, regardless of

FIGURE 9.2   *Predicted Poverty Rates for Mothers*

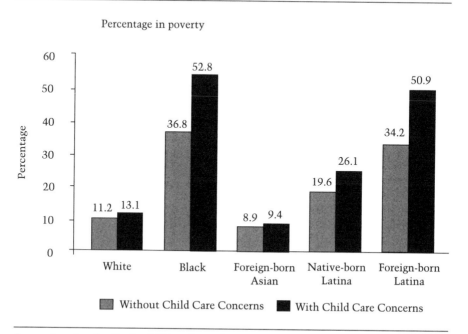

Source: Los Angeles Study of Urban Inequality 1994.

child care problems. That is, even *without* child care problems, these two groups are more likely to be poor than the other three groups *with* child care problems. This merely demonstrates that factors other than child care lead to poverty—not a surprising finding. What is interesting, however, is that poverty is lower for all the mothers when child care problems do not impede work. For example, 13.1 percent of white mothers would live below the poverty line if child care constrained their job search, while only 11.2 percent would live in poverty if child care were not a problem.

The size of the gap for each category of mother is quantified in figure 9.3, helping to answer the question: By how much could we reduce poverty if the child care concerns preventing work were somehow removed? Again using white women as the example, the percent improvement in poverty risk is calculated as (13.1 − 11.2)/13.1. (Dividing by 11.2 instead of 13.1 produces even larger estimates, but I have chosen to present the more conservative estimates for argument's sake.)

The first thing to notice in figure 9.3 is that alleviating child care concerns that limit work could potentially reduce the chance of poverty by almost one-third for immigrant Latina and African American mothers,

FIGURE 9.3   *Percentage Change in Mothers' Poverty Rate*

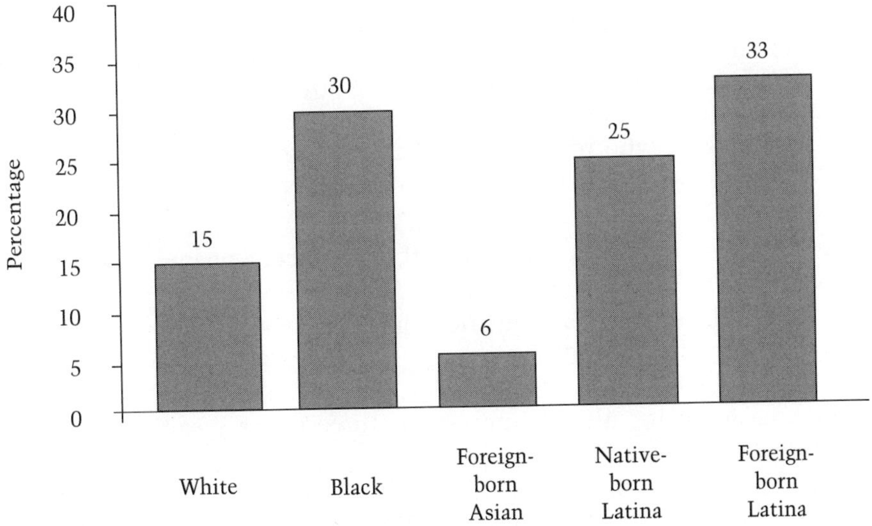

Source: Los Angeles Study of Urban Inequality 1994.

the groups most likely to be poor. Eliminating restrictive child care concerns would also reduce poverty for groups with a lower risk. Native-born Latinas are predicted to reduce their chance of poverty by one-fourth, while white and immigrant Asian mothers could reduce their risk by 15 percent and 6 percent, respectively. In the context of the millions of mothers in Los Angeles County represented in the LASUI survey, even 6 percent is a very large and sociologically significant improvement in poverty chances.

Thus, among many of the mothers in this study, the inability to find or keep adequate child care prevented them from paid work at least once during the year. And this paid work would make the difference between poverty earnings and above-poverty earnings. The working poor are the group particularly affected by this predicament since they typically cycle in and out of poverty. When a child care situation fails, women may lose their job or be forced to quit. It is then difficult to find another job and another child care arrangement. When this pattern repeats itself through the course of the year, lost wages—enough to push the family into poverty—result.

Conclusion

In this chapter I have argued that while income is usually used to explain problems with child care that prevent parents from entering the labor force or limit their labor force attachment, the plight of poverty as a *result* of child care concerns has been neglected in empirical analyses. Since child care enables work, it thereby generates income and has a measurable effect on individual chances of poverty.

My estimates from the Los Angeles Study of Urban Inequality suggest that parents who report having had concerns about child care that caused them not to look or apply for work have:

- an odds of being in the labor force that is 80 percent lower than other parents;

- a level of labor force participation that is nearly twelve hours a week fewer than other parents;

- an odds of being unemployed, given that they desire and are actively looking for work, that is more than three times greater than other parents; and

- an odds of living in poverty that is more than two times greater than other parents, even when conditioning on important social and economic factors; *further,*

- while there are differences in magnitude, the direction of these findings holds across racial and immigrant groups and for both mothers and fathers with children;
- by eliminating child care concerns, labor force participation could increase and unemployment could decrease so that poverty could potentially be reduced by one-quarter for the poorest groups and by nontrivial amounts for mothers across racial-ethnic groups.

While others have suggested that child care is a prerequisite to reducing poverty through economic self-sufficiency, the size of the effect has not been measured. Further, while there is an existing literature on the effect of child care characteristics on labor force participation, the notion that child care constrains the job search itself, resulting in unemployment among parents who are actively seeking work, has not been explored in the literature.

In fact, the size of the effect of child care concerns on poverty that I estimate is large enough to be of the same order of magnitude as concentrated poverty neighborhood effects, Wilson's "underclass" hypothesis. This implies that child care has a place in theoretical discussions about urban poverty, male unemployment, housing segregation, family structure, and other macro-level phenomena known to be associated with urban poverty.

These findings also suggest that lack of access to child care is a major component and mechanism of social stratification through class, gender, and race inequality. Since child care *is* education, it can have the intergenerational inequality effects that result when children are poorly educated. Recent biological research on the development of babies' brains in the first three years of life shows how small children need stimulation to grow and develop, and that if they fail to get it during the first three years, the brain synapses—and the opportunity—are lost forever. In this context, high-quality child care, especially for infants and toddlers, is even more important than previously thought for the provision of equal life chances (Barnett 1995). Inequality by gender is affected because women are more likely to be responsible for the care of children, so it is more likely to be their earnings and employment situation that are negatively impacted by child care problems. Racial stratification also results because black and immigrant Latina mothers are most severely penalized by child care. The multiple jeopardy of gender, race, class, and nativity best explains their situation.

The work of William Julius Wilson, which has arguably defined the agenda for poverty research in American sociology for the past twenty years, is focused on the labor market situation of men. Clearly this is an important issue. However, I argue that we should also bring women as workers to the center of the analysis. This has been a period in which women have entered the labor force in record numbers for wages that are still only about three-quarters of men's wages, on average. Divorce rates are high for the whole population, and there has been a growing feminization of poverty, with women and children now the largest poverty population. These effects are exacerbated for black and Latina women, who have high rates of heading families—44 percent and 23 percent, respectively, as of the 1990 census. In that year, almost half of all African American children lived in poverty. While women have played a prominent role in the assessment of poverty policy, they have often been relegated to the issue of family structure, in particular the pitfalls of single motherhood for children's development, achievement, and criminal behavior. Sara McLanahan and Gary Sandefur (1996) argue that children raised with single parents are worse off than other children because they are deprived of economic, parental, and community resources that undermine their chances of future success. However, they also suggest that in the long run, employment for single mothers is the best solution. If children are placed in good child care and have mothers who earn sufficient income and are good parents, then single-mother families can provide a viable future for their children.

Further, with low wages, benefits, and job security for low-skilled fathers and mothers, and with a good job or two incomes required to stay afloat, mother's work is now central to a family's survival even in two-parent families. That is, while poverty policies designed to help men gain employment are imperative, even if single mothers could suddenly marry employed men, one income would not be enough to make ends meet, especially for low-skilled working families. Only fairly affluent families can now afford a stay-at-home mother, and the majority of those women elect to work. The problem of poverty needs to be tackled from many angles and child care is a missing piece of that puzzle.

I suggest that to help remedy the problems with child care that I uncovered in this study, the United States needs an optional, but universally available, high-quality child care system for the benefit of all parents and children, as several European countries (notably France and Sweden) have had for years. Such a policy should also be a cornerstone of antipoverty policy. Child care subsidies are provided in limited ways, along with the 1996 Temporary Assistance to Needy Families program. In 1996 the Child Care and Development Fund (CCDF) (formerly the Child Care and Development Block Grant) combined three major federal child care programs to provide federal funds allowing states to subsidize child care for working or preparing-for-work families with income up to

85 percent of state median income. Subsidies to families vary by state because states are not required to provide subsidies at this level of eligibility. In fact, while Rhode Island, Illinois, and Wisconsin have used these funds to provide child care subsidies to welfare families as well as low-wage working families, all but five states disqualify families for help at lower threshold levels. As of January 1998, three out of five states would not have provided any child care assistance to a family of three earning $25,000, which is slightly over 185 percent of the poverty line, but not enough to afford the high costs of quality child care (Children's Defense Fund 1999). Even for parents who do receive subsidies, in many states the amounts are so low that many providers refuse these children or accept them only when parents make up the difference in cost. As a result, parents are forced to choose low-quality care. These gaps in care contribute to the well-known cycling in and out of work and poverty that welfare and low-wage mothers do. A more comprehensive child care program would be universally available, that is, open to all parents, regardless of income level so that parents may work and children may be cared for properly. A universal program could aid poverty, the overburdened American family, and our early childhood education needs simultaneously.

Additional research on this topic should explore and uncover the nature of the child care concerns expressed in the LASUI survey and the mechanisms by which these concerns inhibit labor force participation and employment. It also would be useful to study fathers as well as mothers, since preliminary evidence from Los Angeles indicates that fathers also experience child care concerns that limit work. Lastly, I suggest that future work should use longitudinal data to better unpack the process of child care and work search over the course of a job search.

Notes

1. The poverty line, originated by Mollie Orshansky in the mid-1960s (Orshansky 1963, 1965) is defined by assessing the market value of the minimal adequate nutritional standard a person could live on temporarily. Then, assuming that food expenditures are one-third of after-tax income, the value of this food is then multiplied by 3 to get the appropriate income. Then several adjustments are made for items like the number of adults and children in the household. (Weinberg 1995).

2. These dollar figures probably seem low because parents who do not pay for care are included in the average.

3. The *direct* expenses of paid child care can thrust a family into poverty as well, but those direct effects, which would increase the size of the findings of this study, are not measured here.

4. These characteristics may also affect the number of children a family will have and the number of mouths it must feed. Research on the effect of maternal employment and child care costs on fertility is inconclusive because of endogeneity problems. Do women who feel childbearing will interfere with labor force attachment have fewer children, or are women who have fewer children better able to work? Several studies show that fertility is probably constrained by child care or labor force participation (Connelly 1992; Mason and Kuhlthau 1992; Lehrer and Nerlove 1986; Lehrer and Kawasaki 1985; Cramer 1980; Presser and Baldwin 1980), but the effects found were not large.

5. The number of eligible cases is then 1,817 unweighted and 1,897 weighted for representativeness in Los Angeles County.

6. Note that while the data are cross-sectional and the employment outcomes are current, the question about child care is retrospective. That is, respondents were asked about the effect of child care on work during the *past twelve months*. So it is possible that a respondent had a child care concern a few months ago but is working now without such a concern. This set of responses would generate a result that child care concerns do not lead to unemployment for this respondent. However, the finding operates *against* my hypothesis, so if anything, bias from the question wording destroys rather than bolsters my argument. Further, there is only a potential gap between past and present if child care concerns are reported. Thus, if the opposite occurred—if no child care concerns were reported but the respondent is not working—there would not be a bias; the relationship between child care concerns and work would be accurate. Lastly, note that the poverty measure is based on family income in 1992, so any gap between past income and current child care concerns affects all respondents equally on average, since income is measured at the same point for every respondent.

7. According to Pierre Bourdieu:

> Social capital is the aggregate of the actual or potential resources which are linked to possession of a durable network of more or less institutionalized relationships of mutual acquaintance and recognition—or in other words, to membership in a group—which provides each of its members with the backing of the collectivity-owned capital, a "credential" which entitles them to credit, in the various senses of the word. . . . The volume of the social capital possessed by

a given agent thus depends on the size of the network of connections he can effectively mobilize and on the volume of the capital (economic, cultural or symbolic) possessed in his own right by each of those to whom he is connected. [1983, 248–49]

James Coleman (1988) applies the concept of social capital to the creation of human capital, hypothesizing that those with the most social capital are likely to accumulate more human and physical capital and thus reap the corresponding material rewards in society.

8. The index of network quality was conceived and operationalized by Michael Lichter, University of California, Los Angeles, Center for the Study of Urban Poverty.

9. Recall that LASUI was fielded in 1993 and 1994, during or just after a severe recession. The high unemployment and poverty rates reflect this economic downturn, which affected white- and blue-collar employment.

10. The odds are computed from the Odds Multiplier column. Logit coefficients (b) are interpreted as the log odds of the event being modeled, for a unit change in the independent variable. The odds multiplier merely converts log odds (b) into odds (e^b), which are easier to interpret because of the nonlinear effects of each coefficient. The odds multiplier is a positive number, with 1.0 meaning even odds (no effect). To compute the percentage effect for numbers less than 1, subtract the odds multiplier from 1 if the coefficient is negative. If the coefficient is positive, the percentage effect can be read as is. In the first line of table 9.6, for example, the odds multiplier of 0.20 translates into an odds of $1.00 - 0.20 = 0.80$, or 80%. For odds multipliers greater than 1, the percentage effect is the percentage amount above 1 (for example, 1.29 for age in the table is 29 percent higher for each additional year). An odds of 3.0 is 3 times or 3:1 odds.

11. Note from table 9.1 that there are 654 fathers. Only 6.6 percent of them (43 fathers) reported child care concerns. While this is a meaningful percentage in a substantive discussion of fathers and child care, the number of cases is insufficient to run separate logit models by gender. The samples for each racial group are also too small, especially given the number of other explanatory variables, to estimate separate models by race-ethnicity. In a gender- and race-ethnicity-pooled regression, however, we can get reasonable estimates for gender and by racial groups by including dummy variables for these categories; what is lost in richness is gained in consistency of the estimates.

12. The resulting predictions were also bias-adjusted due to the nonlinear nature of the logistic function.

13. There is a certain degree of endogeneity resulting from the effect of income on child care. I suggest that a more complex multi-equation method would not necessarily avoid this endogeneity or provide a better assessment. That is, endogeneity is one essential element of the substantive phenomenon. Simple unidirectional models are typically used to predict child care usage from income without explanation. Using longitudinal data could improve the analysis if adequate data sources were available. Moreover, by my definition, child care includes all forms of child rearing, not only market-based sources. Therefore, income has perhaps less of an impact on child care arrangements than one would initially think.

14. Coding the neighborhood effects as a dummy variable rather than a three-level variable does not alter the results of the regression or any of the analyses that follow.

References

Anderson, C. W., J. R. Nagle, W. A. Roberts, and J. W. Smith. 1981. "Attachment to Substitute Caregivers as a Function of Center Quality and Caregiver Involvement." *Child Development* 52: 53–61.

Barnett, W. Steven. 1995. "Long-Term Effects of Early Childhood Programs on Cognitive and School Outcomes." *The Future of Children* 5(3): 25–50.

Belsky, Jay. 1986. "Infant Day Care: A Cause for Concern?" *Zero to Three* 6: 1–7.

Bergmann, Barbara R. 1994. "Child Care: The Key to Ending Child Poverty." Paper presented at the conference on *Social Policies for Children*, Woodrow Wilson School of Public and International Affairs, Princeton University. Princeton, N.J. (May 25–27, 1994).

———. 1996. *Saving Our Children from Poverty: What the United States Can Learn from France.* New York: The Russell Sage Foundation.

Blau, David, and Philip K. Robins. 1988. "Child-Care Costs and Family Labor Supply." *Review of Economics and Statistics* 70(August): 374–81.

———. 1989. "Fertility, Employment, and Child Care Costs." *Demography* 26(May): 287–99.

Bloom, David E., and T. P. Steen. 1990. "The Labor Force Implications of Expanding the Child Care Industry." *Population Research and Policy Review* 9: 25–44.

Bobo, Lawrence D., Eve Fielder, David M. Grant, James H. Johnson Jr., and Melvin L. Oliver. 1995. "The Los Angeles Survey of Urban Inequality: Sample Report on the Household Survey." UCLA Center for the Study of Urban Poverty Occasional Working Paper Series. Los Angeles: University of California.

Bourdieu, Pierre. 1983. "Forms of Capital." In *Handbook of Theory and*

Research for the Sociology of Education, edited by J. Richardson. Westport, Conn.: Greenwood.

Brayfield, April A., Sharon Gennis Deich, and Sandra L. Hofferth. 1993. *Caring for Children in Low-Income Families: A Substudy of the National Child Care Survey, 1990*. Washington, D.C.: Urban Institute Press.

Burchinal, Margaret R. 1999. "Child Care Experiences and Developmental Outcomes." In *The Silent Crisis in U.S. Child Care*, special ed. of *The Annals of the American Academy of Political and Social Science*, edited by Suzanne W. Helburn, 563: 73–97 (May 1999).

Cancian, Maria, Sheldon Danziger, and Peter Gottschalk. 1993. "Working Wives and Family Income Inequality Among Married Couples." In *Uneven Tides: Rising Inequality in America*, edited by Sheldon Danziger and Peter Gottschalk. New York: Russell Sage.

Casper, Lynne M. 1996. "Who's Minding Our Preschoolers?" March *Current Population Reports*, U.S. Bureau of the Census, P70–53. Washington: U.S. Government Printing Office.

Children's Defense Fund. 1998. "Facts About Child Care in America." Washington, D.C.: Children's Defense Fund, March 10, 1998.

———. 1999. "Child Care Helps Families Work and Learn," testimony of the Children's Defense Fund before the House Ways and Means Committee, March 16, 1999.

Clarke-Stewart, Alison. 1992. "Consequences of Child Care for Children's Development." In *Child Care in the 1990s: Trends and Consequences*, edited by Alan Booth. Hillsdale, N.J.: Lawrence Erlbaum.

Coleman, James S. 1988. "Social Capital in the Creation of Human Capital." *American Journal of Sociology* 94, suppl. (July 15, 1988): S95–S120.

Connelly, Rachel. 1991. "The Importance of Child Care Costs to Women's Decision Making." In *The Economics of Child Care*, edited by David Blau. New York: Russell Sage.

———. 1992. "The Effect of Child Care Costs on Married Women's Labor Force Participation." *Review of Economics and Statistics* 74(1): 83–90.

Cramer, James. 1980. "Fertility and Female Employment: Problems of Causal Direction," *American Sociological Review* 45: 167–90.

Culkin, Mary L., Carollee Howes, and Sharon Lynn Kagan. 1999. "The Children of the Cost, Quality, and Outcomes Study Go to School," executive summary. National Center for Early Development Learning, University of North Carolina, Chapel Hill.

Duberstein, L., and K.O. Mason. 1991. "The Impact of Child Care Costs on Women's Work Plans." Paper presented at the annual meeting of the Population Association of America, Washington, D.C.

Edin, Kathryn, and Laura Lein. 1997. *Making Ends Meet: How Low Income Mothers Survive Welfare and Low Wage Work*. New York: Russell Sage.

Goelman, H., and A. R. Pence. 1987. "Effects of Child Care, Family, and Individual Characteristics on Children's Language Development: The

Victoria Day Care Research Project." In *Quality in Child Care: What Does Research Tell Us?*, edited by Deborah A. Phillips. Washington, D.C.: National Association for the Education of Young Children.

Goldenberg, Claude, and Ronald Gallimore. 1995. "Immigrant Latino Parents' Values and Beliefs About Their Children's Education: Continuities and Discontinuities Across Cultures and Generations." *Advances in Motivation and Achievement* 9: 183–228.

Hayes, Cheryl D., John L. Palmer, and Martha J. Zaslow, eds. 1990. *Who Cares for America's Children?: Child Care Policy for the 1990s*. Washington, D.C.: National Academy Press.

Hofferth, Sandra L. 1991. "The Importance of Child Care to Women's Decision Making." In *The Economics of Child Care*, edited by David Blau. New York: Russell Sage.

———. 1992. "The Demand for and Supply of Child Care in the 1990s." In *Child Care in the 1990s: Trends and Consequences*, edited by Alan Booth. Hillsdale, N.J.: Lawrence Erlbaum.

———. 1995. "Caring for Children at the Poverty Line." *Children and Youth Services Review.* 17(1/2): 1–31.

Hofferth, Sandra L., April Brayfield, Sharon Deich, and Pamela Holcomb. 1991. *The National Child Care Survey, 1990*. Washington, D.C.: Urban Institute Press.

Hofferth, Sandra, and D. Wissoker. 1990. "Quality, Price and Income in Child Care Choice." Paper presented at the annual meeting of the Population Association of America. Toronto, Canada (May 1990).

Holloway, Susan D., and Bruce Fuller. 1999. "Families and Child Care: Divergent Viewpoints." In *The Silent Crisis in U.S. Child Care*, special ed. of *The Annals of the American Academy of Political and Social Science*, edited by Suzanne W. Helburn, 563: 98–115 (May 1999).

Howes, C., and P. Stewart. 1987. "Child's Play with Adults, Toys, and Peers: An Examination of Family and Child Care Influences." *Developmental Psychology* 23: 423–30.

Kamerman, Sheila B., and C. D. Hayes, eds. 1982. *Families That Work: Children in a Changing World*. Panel on Work, Family and Community, Committee on Child Development Research and Public Policy, Commission on Behavior and Social Sciences and Education, National Research Council. Washington, D.C.: National Academy Press.

King, Deborah. 1988. "Multiple Jeopardy, Multiple Consciousness: The Context of a Black Feminist Ideology." *SIGNS: Journal of Women in Culture and Society* 14(1): 42–72.

Lehrer, E. L., and S. Kawasaki. 1985. "Child Care Arrangements and Fertility: An Analysis of Two-Earner Households." *Demography* 22: 499–513.

Lehrer, E. L., and M. Nerlove. 1986. "Female Labor Force Behavior and Fertility in the United States." *Annual Review of Sociology* 12: 181–204.

Leibowitz, Arleen, and Linda J. Waite. 1988. "The Consequences for

Women of the Availability and Affordability of Child Care." RAND Paper P-7525. New York: RAND.

Mason, Karen O., and Laura Duberstein. 1992. "Consequences of Child Care for Parents' Well-Being." In *Child Care in the 1990s: Trends and Consequences*, edited by Alan Booth. Hillsdale, N.J.: Lawrence Erlbaum.

Mason, Karen O., and Karen Kuhlthau. 1992. "The Perceived Impact of Child Care Costs on Women's Labor Supply and Fertility." *Demography* 29(4): 523–43.

Massey, Douglas S., and Nancy A. Denton. 1993. *American Apartheid: Segregation and the Making of the Underclass*. Cambridge, Mass.: Harvard University Press.

Maume, David J., Jr. 1991. "Child Care Expenditures and Women's Employment Turnover." *Social Forces* 70(2): 495–508.

McLanahan, Sara, and Gary Sandefur. 1996. *Growing Up with a Single Parent: What Hurts, What Helps*. Cambridge, Mass.: Harvard University Press.

Orshansky, Mollie. 1963. "Child of the Poor." *Social Security Bulletin* v. 26 (July): 3–13.

———. 1965. "Counting the Poor." *Social Security Bulletin* v. 28 (January): 3–29.

Phillips, Deborah A. 1992. "Child Care and Parental Well-Being: Bringing Quality of Care into the Picture." In *Child Care in the 1990s: Trends and Consequences*, edited by Alan Booth. Hillsdale, N.J.: Lawrence Erlbaum.

———. ed. 1995. "Child Care for Low Income Families." Steering Committee on Child Care Workshops, Board on Children and Families. Commission on Behavioral and Social Sciences and Education; National Research Council; Institute of Medicine. Washington, D.C.: National Academy Press.

Phillips, Deborah A., and Anne Bridgmann, eds. 1995. "New Findings on Children, Families, and Economic Self-Sufficiency: Summary of a Research Briefing." National Academy of Sciences. Washington, D.C.: National Academy Press.

Phillips, Deborah A., Miriam Voran, Ellen Kisker, Carollee Howes, and Marcy Whitebook. 1994. "Child Care for Children in Poverty: Opportunity or Inequity?" *Child Development* 65(2): 472–92.

Presser, Harriet B. 1989a. "Can We Make Time for Children? The Economy, Work Schedules and Child Care." *Demography* 26: 523–43.

———. 1989b. "Some Economic Complexities of Child Care Provided by Grandmothers." *Journal of Marriage and the Family* 51(3): 581–91.

———. 1992. "Child Care Supply and Demand: What Do We Really Know?" In *Child Care in the 1990s: Trends and Consequences*, edited by Alan Booth. Hillsdale, N.J.: Lawrence Erlbaum.

Presser, Harriet B., and Wendy Baldwin. 1980. "Child Care as a Constraint on Employment: Prevalence, Correlates, and Bearing on the Work and Fertility Nexus." *American Journal of Sociology* 85: 1202–13.

Ribar, David C. 1992. "Child Care and the Labor Supply of Married Women: Reduced Form Evidence." *Journal of Human Resources* 27: 135–65.

Robins, Philip K. 1988. "Child Care and Convenience: The Efforts of Labor Market Entry Costs on Economic Self-Sufficiency Among Public Housing Residents." *Social Science Quarterly* 69(1): 122–36.

Ross, Catherine E., and John Mirowsky. 1988. "Child Care and Emotional Adjustment to Wives' Employment." *Journal of Health and Social Behavior* 29(2): 127–38.

U.S. Department of Commerce. U.S. Bureau of the Census. 1999. "Poverty Thresholds in 1994: Poverty Thresholds in 1994, by Size of Family and Number of Related Children Under 18 Years." Washington: U.S. Government Printing Office.

Voran, Miriam J., and Marcy Whitebook. 1991. "Inequality Begins Early: The Relationship Between Day Care Quality and Family Social Class." Paper presented at the meetings of the Society for Research in Child Development. Seattle, Wash. (April 1991).

Waite, Linda J., Arleen Leibowitz, and Christina Witsberger. 1991. "What Parents Pay For: Child Care Characteristics, Quality and Costs." *Journal of Social Issues* 47(2): 33–48.

Weinberg, Daniel H. 1995. "Measuring Poverty: Issues and Approaches." Poverty Measurement Working Papers, U.S. Bureau of the Census. Washington: U.S. Government Printing Office.

White, L., and B. Keith. 1990. "The Effect of Shift Work on the Quality and Stability of Marital Relations." *Journal of Marriage and the Family* 52: 453–62.

Whitebook, Marcy, Carollee Howes, and Deborah Phillips. 1989. "Who Cares? Child Care Teachers and the Quality of Care in America." Final report of the National Child Care Staffing Study. Oakland, Calif.: Child Care Employee Project.

Willer, Barbara, Sandra L. Hofferth, Ellen Eliason Kisker, Patricia Divine-Hawkins, Elizabeth Farquhar, and Frederic B. Glantz. 1991. "The Demand and Supply of Child Care in 1990: Joint Findings from the National Child Care Survey 1990 and a Profile of Child Care Settings." Washington, D.C.: National Association for the Education of Young Children.

Wilson, William Julius. 1987. *The Truly Disadvantaged*. Chicago: University of Chicago Press.

———. 1996. *When Work Disappears: The World of the New Urban Poor*. New York: Knopf.

Zaslow, Martha J. 1991. "Variation in Child Care Quality and Its Implications for Children." *Journal of Social Issues: Child Care Policy Research* 47: 125–38.

10

BRIDGING SOCIAL NETWORKS AND FEMALE LABOR FORCE PARTICIPATION IN A MULTIETHNIC METROPOLIS

James H. Johnson Jr., Elisa Jayne Bienenstock, Walter C. Farrell Jr., and Jennifer L. Glanville

I N ACADEMIC circles, the policy arena, and the popular press, consider-able attention has been devoted to the unprecedented rise in ille-gitimacy and in the growth of welfare-dependent, female-headed households in urban America during the past five decades (Garfinkel and McLanahan 1994; Usdansky 1996). This demographic change has been popularly characterized as the "feminization of poverty," and both cultural and structural explanations have been advanced as a basis for proposed policy prescriptions to remedy the situation. The main cul-tural explanation derives primarily from the culture of poverty thesis, which posits that deviant cultural values, especially negative attitudes toward work, are perpetuated generation after generation in a cycle of welfare dependency (Mead 1992; Murray 1984). In contrast, the struc-tural explanations typically underscore the negative effects of social and spatial isolation from mainstream education and employment oppor-tunities on female labor force participation (Massey and Denton 1992; Wilson 1987).

Research indicates that the policy prescriptions that have emanated from this discussion of the underlying causes of the feminization of pov-erty range from the enormously punitive (abolish welfare) to the seem-ingly paternalistic (Learnfare, Workfare, and Bridefare), and include an array of strategies in between (such as, placing time limits on receipt of welfare (Abramovitz 1992; Bloom and Butler 1995; Darby 1995; Farrell and Johnson 1994; General Accounting Office 1995). Moreover, studies show that, irrespective of whether the underlying causes are perceived to be culturally based or structurally induced, proponents have expressed "ideological certainty" about the utility of their specific proposals to reduce the cost of welfare, discourage illegitimacy and long-term welfare dependency, and transition poor women from welfare to work (Darby 1995; Moynihan 1996).

In reality, however, no such certainty exists, as U.S. Senator Daniel Patrick Moynihan (1996) has noted. He shows how desperately little we know about illegitimacy and argues, forcefully and convincingly, that we do not fully understand the unique challenges and constraints that women in general, and poor women in particular, face as they attempt to enter the U.S. labor market. For these reasons, Moynihan concludes that the proposed remedies for the feminization of poverty, advanced by cultural and structural theorists alike, may do more harm than good, especially to poor children.

In this chapter, which focuses on the labor market experiences of women in a major U.S. metropolitan area, our goal is "to expand the current state of knowledge and understanding of the critical issues that need to be considered in developing effective policy to transition poor women from welfare to work" (Stoloff et al. 1996, 2). In an earlier paper, we began the task of empirically exploring the absolute and relative weight of cultural versus structural explanations of female labor force participation and nonparticipation. Building on this earlier work, in these pages we develop a model that specifies how both cultural and structural forces influence female labor force participation through a complex web of interactions, and present preliminary results of our exploratory analyses of the hypothesized linkages in the model that pertain to the role of social networks.

Our specific objective is to assess the effects on female labor force participation of what has been referred to as "bridging social networks," which are ties that connect individuals—in this instance, women in general and poor women in particular—to a different world of information, resources, and opportunities (Fernandez-Kelly 1995). We assess this impact for all women in our sample and for the different race-ethnic groups to see if bridging social networks affect these groups differentially. Further, we explore how the women in our sample used their social networks in obtaining jobs.

A Model of Female Labor Force Participation

Our conceptual model of female labor force participation is depicted in figure 10.1. In formulating the model, we have drawn on recent research

FIGURE 10.1   *A Model of Female Labor Force Participation*

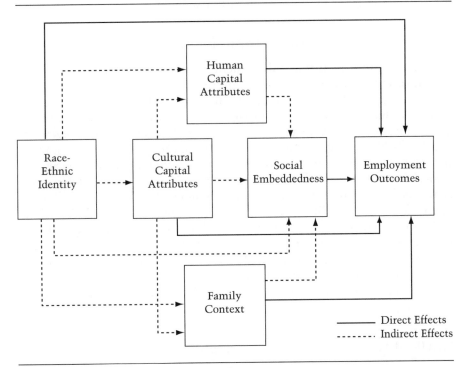

Source: Los Angeles Study of Urban Inequality 1994.

on employer preferences in the U.S. labor market (Neckerman and Kirschenman 1991); cultural versus structural explanations for growing inequality in American society (Danziger and Gottschalk 1993; Freeman 1991, 1992; Harrison 1992; Johnson, Oliver, and Bobo 1994; Mead 1992; Murray 1984, 1995; Wilson 1987); the unique opportunity costs that females face as they attempt to enter the labor market (Apter 1993; Berrick 1991; Felmlee 1995; Harlan 1985; Maume 1991; Osterman 1993); and the roles that social networks and, more broadly, social capital play in determining who has access to mainstream education and employment opportunities as well as other social goods (for example, housing) in American society (Boxman, De Graaf, and Flap 1991; Braddock and McPartland 1987; Browne and Hewitt 1995; Coleman 1988; Granovetter 1973, 1974; Jarrett 1995; Laumann 1973; Lin 1982; Marsden 1987). While our main focus here is on social embeddedness, we cannot ignore these other factors, since we wish to provide a sense of the relative importance of social networks. First we discuss how each set of variables influences the labor market outcomes of women.

Race-Ethnic Identity

That race-ethnic identity, independent of other factors, plays a major role in terms of not only access to employment but also wages for those who manage to find work is well documented in the literature. Focusing on black and white women who were not ill, not in school, not in the armed forces, and not keeping house, Barry Bluestone, Mary Stevenson, and Chris Tilly (1992), using Current Population Survey data, showed that the racial gap in female joblessness grew dramatically between the mid-1960s and the mid-1980s. In the mid-1960s, black women were twice as likely to be jobless as white women, but by 1980 they were nearly four times as likely. As figure 10.2 shows, the growth in the racial gap is evident in the data for all white and black women and for their counterparts who are high school dropouts. Other research indicates that the so-called racial divide in female employment is related, at least in part, to employers' expressed preference for immigrant and white female labor over black female labor, especially for jobs that re-

FIGURE 10.2   *U.S. Joblessness, Twenty-Year-Old Females*

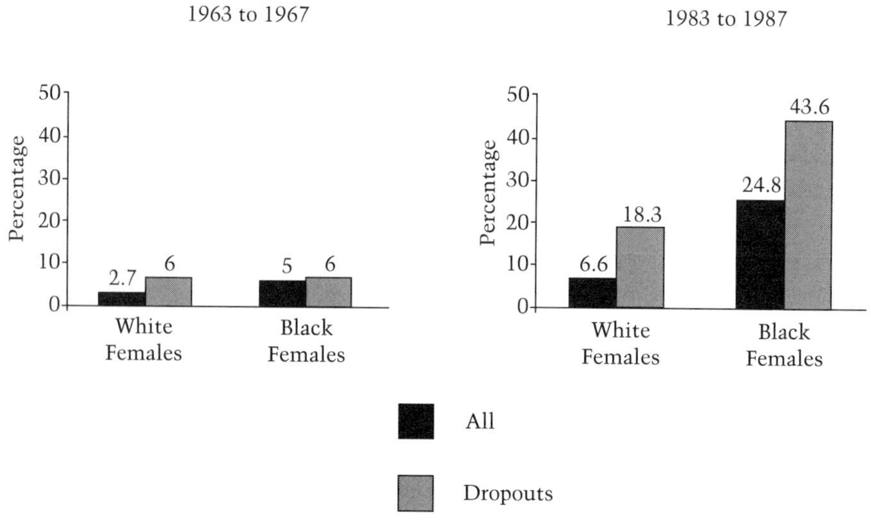

Source: Bluestone, Stevenson, and Tilly 1992.

quire direct interface with the public (see Neckerman and Kirschenman 1991).

Cultural Capital

Cultural capital theorists attribute the contemporary feminization of poverty to the deterioration in individual responsibility and family morals and values in American society (Gillespie and Schellhaus 1994). They argue that the "values" problem is rooted principally in the liberal social welfare policies of the 1960s (Wilson 1992; Woodson 1995). Contrary to their original intent, they contend that the Great Society programs, accompanying President Lyndon Johnson's War on Poverty, created a culture of dependency among women who receive governmental assistance, encouraging them to have children outside of marriage and discouraging the fathers of these children from working to support their offspring (Mead 1992; Murray 1984). They further assert that these deviant values are being transmitted intergenerationally.

In the case of blacks, some conservative policy analysts have argued that the culture of dependency that exists in urban ghettos today is not solely a function of contemporary liberal social policy, but is also an extension of the debilitating influences of slavery and Jim Crowism in the South (Mead 1992; Sowell 1981, 1994). Both of these systems, they contend, forced blacks to rely on "the man" for their livelihood and thereby inculcated in blacks "values that are impediments to work, saving, education, and upward mobility" (Harrison 1992, 194). Nicholas Lemann (1991) insists that blacks who migrated to the urban North brought with them from the rural South a set of deviant behavioral traits (such as lack of initiative, evasion of work, and unpredictable absenteeism). The liberal social welfare policies of the 1960s, according to Lemann (1991) and Lawrence Mead (1992), have simply served to reinforce these "bad" behaviors.

In a similar vein, proponents of the culture of poverty thesis also argue that Mexican immigrants arrive in this country with deviant cultural values and behavioral traits. Lawrence Harrison states, "Mexicans who migrate to the United States bring with them a repressive [Iberian] culture that is disconcertingly persistent" (1992, 223). Thomas Sowell (1994) contends that the goals and values of Mexican Americans have never been centered on education, and Mead (1992) argues that they have less industrious work attitudes than most Asian immigrants and Americans of European descent.

Thus, in the eyes of the proponents of these cultural explanations, blacks who migrated from the South and immigrants who enter the United States from Mexico have a propensity to rely on the government dole rather than to be self-supporting (Lemann 1991; Mead 1992). Cultural capital theorists also reason that while there is plenty of work out there, these people are not motivated to take advantage of what is available; they simply do not possess a strong work ethic (Mead 1992, 1995; Murray 1984, 1995). As noted previously, the policy prescriptions emanating from this school of thought generally focus on programs that would force people who currently rely on government support to work (Gueron 1995; Harlan 1985).

Family Context

Research confirms that the family context has a major impact on female labor force participation—far greater than it does for men. Despite recent changes in social norms resulting in a sharp increase in females as paid workers in the U.S. labor market, research shows that women remain either principally (two-parent families) or solely (single-mother families) responsible for child care in their households. As Terri Apter (1993) points out in her provocatively titled book, *Working Women Don't Have Wives*, this reality represents a major barrier to female labor force participation, in large measure because most workplaces in both the private and the public sectors are not family-friendly. Previous research indicates that the lack of access to affordable child care is one reason women are more likely to work part-time or to drop out of the labor force from time to time (Maume 1991). Further, studies show that such family-related breaks in employment adversely affect wages, other types of compensation, and occupational attainment (Felmlee 1995). In the current climate of downsizing, right-sizing, and reengineering, such behavior also may be grounds for termination (Grimsley 1995).

Even programs specifically designed to draw women into the labor force do not adequately take child care into account (Harlan 1985). They generally do not accurately estimate the costs in terms of ability to pay and time off work for children's illnesses. Child care arrangements are particularly problematic for low-income, female-headed families. In a national survey, Sandra Hoffert (1989, cited in Berrick 1991) found that 54.7 percent of nonworking, low-income single mothers said they would seek employment if adequate and affordable child care arrangements were available. In Hoffert's study, employed females who were poor spent about 32 percent of their income on child care, which resulted in less buying power for their families. In a study of Boston-area women with a high school education or less, conducted at the peak of the so-called Massachusetts Miracle of the late 1980s, Paul Osterman also found that the need for child care was a significant impediment to female employment. Being single with one or more dependent children decreased the odds of a woman working, but living in an extended family offset this effect by enabling single mothers to participate in the workforce (Osterman 1993).

Human Capital

Traditionally, women in U.S. society had been expected to perform two primary roles: homemaker and caretaker of children. Over the last half century, however, social norms have changed dramatically, resulting in a sharp increase in female participation in the labor market. The women's rights movement has been principally responsible for both changes in attitudes toward women and the enactment of laws designed to protect and enhance their status in the employment arena and other walks of life since World War II. In part as a result of these forces, the labor force participation rates of men and women have narrowed steadily over the last fifty years, and recent studies indicate that the gender wage gap narrowed during the 1980s (Bianchi 1995).

According to Suzanne Bianchi (1995), the convergence in labor force participation and wages is due in large part to the increased education of the baby boom cohort of women. Women born after World War II, she notes, were raised by parents whose "ability to finance a college education for their sons and daughters was unprecedented" (107). Further, research indicates that many went on to earn graduate degrees and then joined the professional and managerial ranks in both the public and private sectors. According to Bianchi:

> they inundated executive offices, law firms, hospitals, and finally the armed forces, voicing great skepticism as to whether they would be the exception rather than the rule. If they worked assertively, diligently, and continuously, the inherently sexist, unfair system would somehow recognize their individual talent and would promote them as readily as their equally well trained male counterparts . . . the gamble that unfairness and discrimination would not impede their progress—or at least would deter them much less than it had in the past—ultimately paid off. [1995, 108]

The narrowing of the gender wage gap during the 1980s was partly a function of the baby boom generation of young women moving into mid-career and partly a result of their mothers' (who were paid much less than their daughters) retirement from the labor market.

In addition to the baby boomers, there is a second group of women for whom life did not seem so fair in the 1980s: working women with a high school education or less. Research reveals that the gender wage gap closed for these women but not for the same reason as their better-educated counterparts (Bianchi 1995). The narrowing of the wage gap for these women was due, somewhat, to stagnating and declining wages among their male counterparts, to the fact that their male counterparts were concentrated in the declining blue-collar manufacturing sector, and to the fact that these women were concentrated in the expanding service sector of the economy (particularly in health care). Working long hours (much longer than their male counterparts) in mostly part-time and temporary jobs, these women and their families have become members of the working poor in America—that growing class of individuals and families whose earnings are insufficient to lift them above the official poverty line (Cancian, Danziger, and Gottschalk 1993; Hayghe and Bianchi 1994; Newman 1993; Sheenan 1995).

But it is the third group of women who have evoked the ire of policy makers at all levels of government: single mothers with dependent children who are disconnected from the labor market and who rely, primarily, on welfare for survival. Studies show that a majority of these women possess neither the "hard" human capital skills nor the "soft" cultural capital skills to compete for jobs in the existing labor market. They are the target of the previously mentioned punitive and paternalistic policies that seek to "change welfare as we know it" (Abramovitz 1992; Gillespie and Schellhaus 1994; Jost 1992; Katz 1995; Moynihan 1996), including the Personal Responsibility and Work Reconciliation Act of 1996 (U.S. Congress 1996).

Social Embeddedness

Whereas the aforementioned cultural explanations emphasize individual failings or shortcomings, structural explanations—advocated by liberal and progressive policy analysts—focus on broader societal forces or constraints that hamper the labor market participation of women, especially those who are poor. They argue, for example, that as living-wage jobs have fled the nation's cities, those left behind have become socially and spatially isolated and economically marginalized from mainstream education and employment opportunities (Wilson 1987, 1996). While much of the research has focused on the impact of central-city job loss by inner-city males, there is no question that women residing in these communities also have been adversely affected, not only in terms of the shrinking pool of marriageable men (which William Julius Wilson [1987] argues is largely responsible for the feminization of poverty), but also in terms of the disappearance of mainstream employment opportunities nearby and the lack of information about jobs elsewhere (Wilson 1996).

Previous research documents that job attainment is highly dependent on the extent to which individuals are embedded in a set of employment-enhancing social networks. These networks are composed of individuals and institutions that act as conduits through which information about jobs is passed. Jobs may be available and individuals may have the requisite qualifications, but unless the potential employer or job seeker has access to information, the match cannot be made. Because so many people find their jobs through social networks, liberal scholars have concluded that welfare-dependent mothers and other mothers who have operated outside the normal workings of the labor market are at a substantial disadvantage in the job search process.

Studies have shown that the structure of an individual's social network has an impact on his or her attitudes (Bienenstock, Bonacich, and Oliver 1990; Bott 1957; Laumann 1973) and job search outcomes, including the number of job offers, type of job, and wages (Boxman, De Graaf, and Flap 1991; Braddock and McPartland 1987; Browne and Hewitt 1995; Granovetter 1973; Lin 1982). Further, there are three structural elements of social networks that have been found to influence employment outcomes.

The first is the *size* of the network, that is, the number of people in it. Ed Boxman, Paul De Graaf, and Hendrik Flap (1991) found that people who have larger networks attain higher-paying jobs. The second critical element is the *composition* of the network, that is, whether it is composed of a homogeneous or heterogeneous group of individuals. A homogeneous network is one in which all the members are the same on a particular characteristic (for example, race, gender, or class). A heterogeneous network, by contrast, is one in which members differ on such characteristics as place of residence, race, gender, or class. Research shows that network composition, and more specifically network heterogeneity, has an impact on both attitudes (Bienenstock, Bonacich, and Oliver 1990) and employment outcomes (Braddock and McPartland 1987).

In their study of job outcomes for African Americans, Jomills Braddock and James McPartland (1987) found that blacks who were embedded in racially segregated networks had lower incomes and were much less likely to have white coworkers than their counterparts who were embedded in racially heterogeneous networks. Braddock and McPartland concluded that, because they contain less beneficial information about jobs, racially homogeneous networks disadvantage blacks in the labor market. Based on these findings, it is reasonable to expect women who are embedded in racially and otherwise diverse networks (in terms of things like gender, education, and class) to be employed at a higher rate than those who are embedded in homogeneous networks.

The third structural element that has been shown to influence employment outcomes is the *strength of ties* in the network. Mark Granovetter (1973) defines the strength of a tie as "(probably a linear) combination of the amount of time, the emotional intensity, the intimacy (mutual confiding), and reciprocal services which characterize the tie" (1,361). Using this formulation, he found in a study of white males that those who utilized weak ties in their job search earned higher wages. He argued that weak ties were beneficial because they were more likely than strong ties to expose job seekers to new information.

Other research suggests, however, that the benefits of weak ties are not constant across social groups. More specifically, the evidence suggests that using a personal contact to obtain a job is not necessarily beneficial for all social groups, particularly the disadvantaged. For example, Irene Browne and Cynthia Hewitt (1995), in a study of African Americans in the Atlanta area, observed that those who acquired their jobs through personal contacts were more likely to have segregated jobs than those who used formal means. In contrast to Granovetter's (1973) finding for white men, their study implies that blacks who use weak ties to find jobs are not employed in the higher-paying jobs because predominantly black jobs tend to pay less.

Thus, it is important to recognize that not all weak ties are advantageous. Advantageous weak ties are those that bridge distinct social worlds—what we defined earlier as bridging social networks. Having access to many diverse social worlds increases access to information about jobs, which, in turn, increases the likelihood or probability of acquiring a good job. White males typically have weak ties that bridge divergent social worlds more often than do women and minorities. Members of disadvantaged groups are more likely to be embedded in homogeneous social networks. Hence, for them, weak ties may not be advantageous, and may be of no utility in terms of accessing employment opportunities precisely because they do not bridge social worlds.

Indeed, research on persistent poverty and the urban underclass has demonstrated that women who find themselves in highly segregated and ghetto environments are more likely to encounter difficulty in the labor market than their counterparts in more socially diverse and economically residential environments (Massey and Denton 1992; Wilson 1987, 1996). This difficulty is related, at least in part, to the fact that the women are more likely to have truncated social networks, which diminishes their capacity to gain access to resources controlled by larger social networks (Fernández-Kelly 1995).

But not all women in poor ghetto neighborhoods have truncated social networks. Ethnographic research by Robin Jarrett (1995) has shown, for example, that some poor women manage to develop social networks that connect them, and especially their children, with individuals and institutions beyond the boundaries of their own neighborhoods. Further, Jarrett demonstrates that the children of these women are more likely to manifest "community-bridging behaviors," including high aspirations and interest in formal education, than the children of their counterparts who were not embedded in bridging social networks. The latter group of youth were more likely to engage in what Jarrett terms "community-specific behaviors"—that is, antisocial or dysfunctional behaviors consistent with those described in the literature on the urban underclass (Wilson 1987, 1996).

Thus, for women in general, and minority and poor women in particular, we posit that bridging social networks can mediate the potential negative effects of what otherwise might be perceived or construed in the labor market as inadequate or inappropriate cultural capital, human capital, and family context attributes. Conversely, the absence of bridging social networks can make securing employment difficult even for women who have the appropriate set of cultural and human capital attributes and who are not hindered by family context–induced constraints.

Research Design

Using data from the LASUI, we explore in the remainder of this chapter, first, a wide array of bivariate relationships among the final dependent variable, employment status, and all the other variables in our model to determine which forces impede and which forces foster female labor force participation. We then specify a set of logistic regression models that are designed to assess the absolute and relative effects of both cultural and structural factors, including network composition, on the employment status of our diverse sample of Los Angeles women. Finally, we explore the use of social ties and their characteristics in job searches.

Because the level of residential segregation and the incidence of poverty vary markedly from one racial or ethnic group to the next and from one location to the next, at each step in the analyses that follow we report findings for the entire sample and then for three race-ethnic groups separately. We exclude Asian women because our initial exploratory analyses revealed that their network data are unreliable.

For the purpose of this research, we selected six different categories of data from the Los Angeles survey. The variables are divided into dependent and independent variables in table 10.1, which also includes descriptive statistics for each of the variables. The dependent variable is a dichotomous measure of the employment status of women in the Los Angeles sample at the time the survey was conducted. After excluding women who were in school, disabled, or retired, those who were employed either part-time or full-time along with those who were temporarily laid off, on maternity leave, or on sick leave were classified as

TABLE 10.1　Variables Used in the Analysis, Descriptive Statistics (N = 968)

Type of Variable	Attributes	Variable	n	Percentage Working	Percentage Not Working
Independent	Race-ethnicity	Black (yes)	411	59.4	40.6
		Hispanic (yes)	263	55.9	44.1
		White (yes)	294	69.0	31.0
	Cultural background	Family dependency (yes)	257	44.4	56.6
		English proficiency (yes)	830	64.3	35.7
		Legal working status (yes)	797	64.1	35.9
		Third World socialization (yes)	227	51.5	48.5
		Other foreign country for early years (yes)	32	68.8	31.1
		Southern roots (yes)	127	63.8	36.2
	Human capital	Age (< forty)	569	56.6	43.4
		Education (≥ high school diploma)	755	68.9	31.1
	Family context	Living with parents (yes)	74	74.3	25.7
		Single mom (yes)	358	51.1	48.9
		Child ≤ three (yes)	222	40.5	59.5
		Child care constraints (yes)	243	30.5	69.5
		Married (yes)	358	58.9	41.1
	Social embeddedness	AFDC bridge (yes)[a]	214	39.7	60.3
		Education bridge (yes)	618	69.9	30.1
		Gender bridge (yes)	697	63.6	36.4
		Race bridge (yes)	252	70.2	29.8
		Neighborhood bridge (yes)	773	64.4	35.6
		Job bridge (yes)	825	64.7	35.3
Dependent	Employment status	Working	968	61.4	38.6

Source: Los Angeles Study of Urban Inequality 1993.
[a] Aid to Families with Dependent Children.

working; those who indicated that they were unemployed or house-wives were classified as not working. For the purpose of the analyses that follow, there are five categories of independent variables.

The first category is composed of self-identification measures of race-ethnicity. The second set is composed of measures that capture the forces that supposedly shape an individual's morals, values, and work orientation—those "culturally derived" characteristics that purportedly explain who prospers and who does not in contemporary American society (Harrison 1992; also Mead 1992; Sowell 1994). In an earlier paper, we empirically derived our measures of these cultural background influences from a principal components analysis of the responses to fifteen questions in the LASUI—items designed to capture geographical influences, family background influences, religious influences, and linguistic influences (see Johnson, Bienenstock, and Stoloff 1995).

We employ six dichotomous measures of cultural capital attributes that correspond to the measures that were empirically derived in our earlier work (Johnson, Bienenstock, and Stoloff 1995; Stoloff et al. 1996). The first of these measures, *family dependency*, distinguishes women who lived in public housing as children and/or grew up in a family that received Aid to Families with Dependent Children from other women in the Los Angeles sample. If the culture of poverty theorists are correct (Lemann 1991; Mead 1992; Sowell 1994), these women should have low rates of labor force participation. The second measure, *English proficiency*, distinguishes those women who speak and understand standard English from those who do not, while the third, *legal working status*, distinguishes U.S. citizens and documented aliens from those who are undocumented or illegal aliens. The fourth cultural background variable, *Third World early socialization*, distinguishes individuals who were born in a Third World country, who lived in a Third World country most of the time before they were sixteen years old, and who received most of their education outside the United States, from other women in the Los Angeles sample. The final cultural component, *Southern roots*, distinguishes Los Angeles women who were born in the southern United States and who lived primarily in that region prior to age six-teen—those females who, according to cultural capital theorists, have poor attitudes toward work, especially if they are black (Lemann 1991) —from women who were born elsewhere.

Our third category of independent variables is composed of two measures of human capital: age and years of school completed. Because it is difficult to measure for women, we opted not to include the other standard human capital variable typically included in statistical analyses of male employment: prior work experience. As noted previously, due to their child-rearing and other domestic responsibilities, women, in contrast to men, are more likely to experience either long or periodic spells of nonwork or part-time work. In analyses of male employment such a work history is typically interpreted as evidence of a major skills deficit or a poor work ethic. For women, such an interpretation would be inappropriate and misleading. Thus, in an effort to address this problem, we drew on the economic concept of opportunity cost in deciding which additional variables to include in our analysis.

Opportunity cost refers to the lost opportunity for labor force participation due to competing responsibilities such as childbearing or housework. Having children, especially young children, presents a large opportunity cost to women with or without a spouse (Felmlee 1995; Garfinkel and McLanahan 1994; Hayghe and Bianchi 1994; Maume 1991; Osterman 1993), but especially for single mothers, although previous research suggests that living with immediate or extended family may offset this effect for unwed mothers (Osterman 1993). Further, whereas being married acts as a motivating factor for men to participate in the paid labor force, marriage could present an opportunity cost for women because it creates competing responsibilities in the household (Apter 1993).

Thus, in order to capture the unique opportunity costs that confront women in the labor market, we include five *family context* indicators as the fourth set of independent variables: marital status, single-mother status, whether the respondent has a child three years of age or younger (when child care is especially problematic), respondent's self-report that lack of child care has impeded her participation in the labor market, and whether the respondent lives with her parents (a proxy measure for extended family).

Our final category of independent variables is composed of social network indicators. In the LASUI, several questions pertained to networks and social functioning. This series of questions were introduced with the following statement:

> From time to time, most people discuss important matters with other people. Looking back over the last six months—who are the people, other than people living in your household, with whom you discussed matters important to you?

The following data were recorded for the first three names that each respondent gave: race or ethnicity, sex, level of education completed, relationship to respondent, marital status, and whether they lived in respondent's neighborhood, had a steady job, and received public aid or welfare, as well as whether these individuals assisted with everyday activities and could be relied on for help in a major crisis.

From these data we chose to dichotomize six variables as indicators of the presence of "bridging ties" for each survey respondent. If any member of a respondent's network was of a different race, then the respondent was assumed to have a race bridge. If at least one male was named by a female respondent, then she was assumed to have a gender bridge. Respondents were assumed to have a neighborhood bridge if any one of their network members lived in a different neighborhood. If at least one person in the network had more than a high school education, then the respondent was assumed to have an education bridge.

Similarly, if one person in the network was employed, then a job bridge was assumed to exist. Finally, if at least one member of the network was currently receiving public assistance or welfare, an AFDC bridge was assumed to exist. Unlike the other bridge variables, an AFDC bridge is hypothesized to have a negative effect on the likelihood of working.

Findings

The findings of our bivariate statistical analyses are presented in tables 10.2 and 10.3. In these tables we have included only those bivariate relationships that proved to be statistically significant at the 95 percent confidence level. The results of our multivariate statistical analysis are presented in table 10.4.

Bivariate Analyses

Table 10.2 illustrates the relationship between race-ethnic identity and labor force participation among Los Angeles women. The results suggest that there are indeed statistically significant group differences in the incidence of employment. While nearly two-thirds of all women in the

TABLE 10.2   *Cross-Tabulation of Race-Ethnic Identity and Employment Status*

Working	All Women	White Women	Black Women	Hispanic Women
Yes	594 (61.4)	203 (69.0)	244 (59.4)	147 (55.9)
No	374 (38.6)	91 (31.0)	167 (40.6)	116 (44.1)
Total	968	294	411	263

Source: Los Angeles Study of Urban Inequality 1994.
$\chi^2 = 27.1, p < .0001$

sample (61.4 percent) were employed at the time the LASUI was conducted, white women were employed at a higher rate (69.0 percent) than either black (59.4 percent) or Hispanic women (55.9 percent). Table 10.3 provides insights into those factors that might account for these racial differences; it highlights statistically significant relationships among the dependent variable, employment status, and the cultural capital, human capital, family context, and social network variables in our proposed model of female labor force participation.

Four of the cultural capital indicators—family dependency, Third World early socialization, English proficiency, and legal work status— are associated with the employment status of the women in our sample. To the extent that these variables are related to female labor force participation, that is principally because of the unique cultural background influences of black and Hispanic women. As table 10.3 shows, cultural capital variables do not affect the employment status of white women.

Consistent with the views of the cultural capital theorists, women, in general (53.1 percent), and black women, in particular (48.4 percent), who grew up in a public housing environment or in a family that was dependent on welfare, are less likely to be employed than all females (69.0 percent) and black females (75.7 percent) who did not grow up under such conditions. Also consistent with the views of Harrison (1992) and others (Mead 1992; Sowell 1994), women who spent their formative years in a Third World country and who received most of their formal education in that country (58.0 percent) are less likely to be working than their counterparts who were born and educated elsewhere (65.2 percent). However, this effect was not discernible for any specific race-ethnic group of women in our sample.

Employment status among our sample of Los Angeles women is also associated with level of English proficiency and citizenship status. Women who do not speak or understand standard English (45.7 percent) and who are undocumented aliens (51.6 percent) are less likely to be working than their counterparts who are proficient in the English language (66.5 percent) and who are U.S. citizens (66.2 percent). While these factors do not constrain the labor force participation of white and black women, they pose major obstacles for Hispanic women. As table 10.3 shows, Hispanic women who do not speak or understand standard English (43.8 percent) and who are undocumented aliens (45.3 percent) are less likely to be employed than their counterparts who are English-proficient (66.2 percent) and citizens of the United States (66.9 percent).

Female labor force participation is also statistically associated with the human capital attributes of our sample. Black women with at least a high school diploma (66.1 percent) are significantly less likely to be em-

TABLE 10.3 Bivariate Relationships Between Employment Status and Cultural Capital, Family Context, Human Capital, and Social Network Variables

	All Women		White Women		Black Women		Hispanic Women	
	N	Percentage Working	N	Percentage Working	N	Percentage Working	N	Percentage Working
Family dependency								
Yes	473	53.1	—	—	252	48.4	—	—
No	735	69.0	—	—	169	75.7	—	—
χ²		30.4***				31.3***		
English proficiency								
Yes	989	66.5	—	—	—	—	139	66.2
No	219	45.7	—	—	—	—	153	43.8
χ²		32.2***						14.7***
Legal working status								
Yes	931	66.2	—	—	—	—	124	66.9
No	277	51.6	—	—	—	—	172	45.3
χ²		19.3***						13.5
Third World early socialization								
Yes	409	58.0	—	—	—	—	—	—
No	800	65.2	—	—	—	—	—	—
χ²		5.9***						
Age								
< forty	528	67.2	—	—	163	70.6	—	—
> forty	677	59.2	—	—	258	52.3	—	—
χ²		8.1***				13.8***		

(Table continues on p. 400.)

TABLE 10.3 Continued

	All Women		White Women		Black Women		Hispanic Women	
	N	Percentage Working	N	Percentage Working	N	Percentage Working	N	Percentage Working
Education								
At least high school degree								
Yes	941	70.1	285	71.2	360	66.1	135	70.4
No degree	267	37.1	17	41.2	61	19.7	161	41.0
χ^2		97.3***		6.8***		46.6***		25.5***
Living with parents								
Yes	101	73.3		—		—	28	75.0
No	1107	61.9		—		—	268	52.2
χ^2		5.14***		—		—		5.29***
Single mother								
Yes	414	52.7		—	201	44.8		—
No	794	68.1		—	220	72.7		—
χ^2		27.9***		—		34.0***		—
Child under three								
Yes	257	43.6		—	83	32.5	107	40.2
No	951	68.0		—	338	66.0	189	62.4
χ^2		51.8***		—		30.9***		13.6***
Child care								
Yes	294	31.6	59	45.8	89	23.6	109	26.6
No	914	72.9	243	75.3	332	69.0	187	70.6
χ^2		161.94***		19.6***		59.9***		53.9***
Married								
Yes		—	156	59.6	94	71.3	128	47.7
No		—	146	80.1	326	55.8	168	59.5
χ^2		—		14.9***		7.2***		4.12***

AFDC bridge										
Yes	—	—	—	—	—	115	30.4	71	39.4
No	—	—	—	—	—	306	70.3	224	58.9
χ^2	—			—		19.6***		8.3***	
Education bridge										
Yes	—	—	253	71.9	261	67.8	113	70.0
No	—	—	47	55.3	157	45.9	155	45.2
χ^2	—		5.15***		19.6***		17.4***	
Gender bridge										
Yes	—	—	164	76.2	—	—	144	61.8
No	—	—	138	61.6	—	—	152	47.4
χ^2	—		7.57***		—		6.2***	
Race bridge										
Yes	—	—	—	—	—	—	115	61.7
No	—	—	—	—	—	—	181	49.7
χ^2	—		—		—		4.1***	
Neighborhood bridge										
Yes	—	—	241	71.8	353	61.8	207	59.9
No	—	—	61	60.7	68	47.1	89	41.6
χ^2	—		2.85		5.66***		8.4***	
Job bridge										
Yes	—	—	258	71.3	348	62.9	254	58.3
No	—	—	38	55.3	74	41.9	40	27.5
χ^2	—		4.01***		11.1***		13.2***	

Source: Los Angeles Study of Urban Inequality 1994.
Note: — Variable did not achieve statistical significance ($p < .05$).
$*p < .05$, $**p < .01$, $***p < .0001$

ployed than are all women (70.1 percent) and white (71.2 percent) and Hispanic (70.4 percent) women with a comparable education. In a similar vein, black women with no diploma (19.7 percent) are signficantly less likely than their white (41.2 percent) and Hispanic (41.0 percent) counterparts to be working. As expected, older women (59.2 percent) are less likely to be working than younger women (67.2 percent) in the sample, but the difference is only statistically significant for one racial group: young black women (70.6 percent) are substantially more likely to be working than their over-forty-year-old counterparts (52.3 percent).

Previous research has documented the constraining effects of family context–related opportunity costs on female labor force participation (Felmlee 1995; Maume 1991). Our findings support the results of these earlier studies. In general, single motherhood, having a child under age three, and, especially, self-reported child care problems all constrain labor force participation among our sample of women. Being a single mother is especially problematic for black women—less than half of them work (44.8 percent), compared with 73 percent of their counterparts who are not single mothers. Having a dependent child under age three is a problem for both black (32.5 percent) and Hispanic (40.2 percent) women, who are far less likely to be working than their black (66.0 percent) and Hispanic (62.4 percent) counterparts who do not have a young child to support. Self-reported child care problems are significantly associated with white, black, and Hispanic female labor force participation, but they constrain the employment of the latter two groups (23.6 percent and 26.6 percent, respectively) far greater than the former (45.8 percent).

As table 10.3 shows, marriage has an interesting impact on female labor force participation, which varies significantly by race-ethnic identity. While marriage seems to lower labor force participation for white women, it has the opposite effect for black women. Nearly three-fourths (71.3 percent) of married black women work, while only 60 percent of married white women work. In all probability, this finding reflects the fact that white women, who are more likely to be married to men who are employed in well-paying jobs, have more of a choice in their employment decision than minority women, who are more likely to be married to men who are either unemployed or underemployed. For unmarried women, a polar opposite pattern emerges. Nearly 80 percent of white women work, while slightly more than half of their black (55.8 percent) and Hispanic (59.5 percent) counterparts participate in the labor market.

What impact does bridging social networks have on labor force participation among our sample of Los Angeles women? Our findings indicate that black (30.4 percent) and Hispanic (39.4 percent) women who have at least one individual in their networks who receives AFDC are less likely to be working than their counterparts who do not have such an individual in their networks (70.3 percent and 58.9 percent, respectively). We found no association between an AFDC bridge and white labor force participation. In all likelihood that is because nonpoor whites are highly segregated from poor people of any race or ethnicity, especially in Los Angeles.

While linkages with AFDC recipients appear to adversely impact labor force participation, other social network indicators appear to enhance employment among our sample of Los Angeles women. White (71.9 percent), black (67.8 percent), and Hispanic (70.0 percent) women whose networks are educationally diverse are more likely to be employed than their counterparts who do not have at least one individual in their network with more than a high school diploma (55.3 percent, 45.9 percent, and 45.2 percent, respectively). White (76.2 percent) and Hispanic (61.8 percent) women with gender-diverse networks are more likely to be employed than their counterparts who have gender-homogeneous networks (61.6 percent and 47.4 percent, respectively). We found no significant association between black female employment and gender-based network diversity.

Race-baced network diversity is significantly associated with employment for Hispanic women only. Nearly two-thirds (61.7 percent) of Hispanic women who are embedded in racially diverse networks are employed, compared with half of their counterparts who are embedded in racially homogeneous social networks.

While race-based network diversity appears to benefit only Hispanic women, neighborhood-based network diversity is significantly associated with employment outcomes for all three race/ethnic groups. As table 10.3 shows, white, black, and Hispanic women whose social networks transcend their local neighborhood boundaries are more likely to be employed than their counterparts whose networks are limited to individuals within their local neighborhoods.

Finally, women who have at least one member of their social network who is employed are themselves more likely to be employed than women who do not have at least one employed individual in their network. This finding holds for white, black, and Hispanic women in our Los Angeles sample.

Multivariate Analyses

In this section we attempt to assess the absolute and relative effects of the cultural capital, human capital, family context, and social network variables on female labor force participation in Los Angeles. Since our dependent variable is dichotomous, we use binomial regression analyses to test our model of employment outcomes. The results of our logit regression analyses for all women and for white, black, and Hispanic women are summarized in table 10.4. In this table we have included only variables that were statistically significant at the 95 percent confidence level for one or more groups of women. However, all the other variables discussed in our conceptual framework have been controlled.

Nine of the independent variables proved to be statistically significant determinants of labor force participation among our sample of Los Angeles women. Three of the variables fall under the family context rubric (child care, married, and single mother), three are social network indicators (education bridge, job bridge, and neighborhood bridge), and the remaining three are single measures of human capital (education), cultural capital (family dependency), and race-ethnic identity (Hispanic).

Among these variables, self-reported child care problems (b = -1.41), being married (b = -.480, being a single mother (b = -.423), or having grown up in a welfare-dependent family (b = -.358) all exert a negative influence on the likelihood or odds of working. Women who said that lack of access to affordable child care is an impediment to labor force participation are 75 percent less likely to be working than their female counterparts who do not report such problems. Women who spent their formative years in public housing and/or in families that received public assistance are 30 percent less likely to be working than their counterparts who did not have these experiences. And being married or a single mother reduces the odds of working by 38 percent and 34 percent, respectively.

On the other hand, having at least a high school diploma (b = 1.13), a job bridge (.701), an education bridge (.313), or a neighborhood bridge (b = .416) appear to enhance the odds of employment among our sample of Los Angeles women. Women with twelve or more years of education are 38 percent more likely to be working than their female counterparts who did not finish high school. Those who have at least one employed network member are 100 percent more likely to be employed than their counterparts who do not have such an individual in their network. And having at least one network member who lives beyond the boundaries of one's own neighborhood or who has more than a high school diploma increased the odds of working among our sample of Los Angeles women, in comparison to their counterparts who have homogeneous networks along these two dimensions, by 52 percent and 38 percent, respectively. Finally, our results indicate that Hispanic women (b = .671) are 96 percent more likely to be employed than white women, net of the other explanatory variables included in the model.

Even a cursory look at columns 2 through 4 in table 10.4 reveals that the determinants of who works and who does not among Los Angeles women vary substantially by race-ethnicity. For white women, as column 2 shows, only three variables emerged from our logistic regres-

TABLE 10.4 *Logistic Regression Results*

Independent Variables	All Women (1) β	All Women (1) odds ratio	White Women (2) β	White Women (2) odds ratio	Black Women (3) β	Black Women (3) odds ratio	Hispanic Women (4) β	Hispanic Women (4) odds ratio
Constant	−1.24	1.96	−1.12		−1.26		−1.13	
Hispanic	.671* (.321)	1.96						
Family dependency	−.358* (.163)	.70			−.758** (.262)	.47		
High school degree or better	1.13*** (.222)	3.11	1.75** (.549)	5.81	1.64*** (.379)	5.15	.623† (.360)	1.86
Living with parents							1.07† (.612)	2.92
Single mother	−.423* (.209)	.66			−.643* (.306)	.53		
Married	−.480* (.194)	.62	−1.08** (.356)	.34				
Child under three					−.744* (.352)	.48		
Child care	−1.41*** (.201)	.25	−1.50*** (.416)	.22	−1.17*** (.330)	.31	−1.84*** (.361)	.16
Education bridge	.313† (.177)	1.38						
Job bridge	.701** (.224)	2.01			.618† (.345)	1.86	1.37** (.514)	3.95
Neighborhood bridge	.416* (.194)	1.52			.633† (.336)	1.88		
−2 Log likelihood	1051.2		321.2		422.3		273.9	
Degrees of freedom	5		5		5		5	
χ^2	27.8***		35.3***		13.2*		13.4*	

Source: Los Angeles Study of Urban Inequality 1994.
Note: Only those variables whose coefficients were statistically significant in one or more of the models are shown. Standard errors appear in parentheses.

*$p \leq .05$, **$p \leq .01$, ***$p \leq .0001$, †$p \leq .10$

sion analysis as statistically significant determinants of labor force participation: two family context indicators (being married and child care) and one human capital attribute (education). Among these three predictors, years of school completed (b = 1.75) is the most important. Educated white women are roughly five times more likely to be working than their counterparts with less than a high school education. Self-reported child care constraints (b = −1.50) is the second most important variable. Women who note child care constraints are 78 percent less likely to be working than their counterparts who do not report such problems. In comparison to their unmarried counterparts, married white women (b = −1.08) were 66 percent less likely to be working. In contrast to white women who expressly indicate that lack of access to affordable child care has constrained their ability to work, we believe that not working for this latter group is more a matter of choice than constraint. In all likelihood, these women are in family contexts with adequate financial resources to preclude them from having to work.

The results for black women in the Los Angeles sample are reported in column 3. Seven variables emerged as statistically significant predictors: one cultural capital indicator (family dependency), one human capital measure (education), three family context variables (child care, child younger than three, and being a single mother), and two social network variables (neighborhood bridge and job bridge). Self-reported child care constraints (b = −1.17), family dependency (b = −.758), child under age three (b = −.744), and being a single mother (b = −.643) all have a negative impact on the odds of working among our black female subsample. Black women who report child care access problems were 69 percent less likely to be working than their counterparts who did not report such problems. Black women with a dependent child under age three, in comparison to their counterparts who do not have dependent children of this age, are 52 percent less likely to be working. Black women who grew up in a welfare-dependent family are 53 percent less likely to be working, in comparison to black women who did not grow up in a household that was dependent on public assistance. Black single mothers are 47 percent less likely to be employed, compared to black women who are not the sole caretakers of their children.

On the other hand, black women with at least a high school diploma are three times more likely to be employed than black women who do not manage to finish high school. And those embedded in neighborhood (b = .633) or job (b = .618) bridging social networks are 88 percent and 86 percent, respectively, more likely to be working than their counterparts who are not involved in such networks.

Finally, the results for Hispanic women can be found in column 4. Only four of our independent variables achieved statistical significance in our logistic regression analysis: two family context indices (living with parents and child care), one network measure (job bridge), and one human capital attribute (education). Moreover, only one of these variables has a negative impact on Hispanic female labor force participation: self-report of child care accessibility problems ($b = -1.84$). Hispanic women who report child care constraints, in comparison to their counterparts who did not report such problems, were 96 percent less likely to be working.

For Hispanic women the other three statistically significant determinants are employment-enhancing forces. Those who have at least one employed individual in their network are three times more likely to be working than their counterparts who do not have a working person in their network. Similarly, Hispanic women who live with their parents are nearly twice as likely to be working as their counterparts who live independent of their parents. Educated Hispanic women ($b = .623$) are 86 percent more likely to be working than their poorly educated counterparts.

Social Networks and Job Search

Information extracted from the LASUI on the job search behavior of those women in the sample who have looked for work within the last five years provides additional insights into how bridging social networks influence female employment outcomes in Los Angeles. Over half of these women (51 percent) indicate that they found their last-present job through friends-relatives or other personal contact (see table 10.5). (The remainder, as the table shows, indicate that they found their jobs through newspaper ads and other sources.) There are, however, notable race-ethnic differences in the use of such personal networks. Hispanic women (71.8 percent) are significantly more likely than their black (50.7 percent) and white (49.5 percent) counterparts to have found their jobs through personal ties.

TABLE 10.5   *Person(s) Who Assisted Respondents in Finding Last-Present Job*

	All (N = 515)	White (N = 107)	Black (N = 191)	Hispanic (N = 149)
Friends or relatives	50.0	43.0	40.8	69.8
Other person	6.0	6.5	9.9	2.0
Newspaper ad	21.2	21.5	23.0	10.1
Other source	21.6	27.1	25.1	18.1

Source: Los Angeles Study of Urban Inequality 1994.

The individual who provides the direct employment assistance for these women is more likely to be a friend than a relative, and this finding holds across all three race-ethnic groups (see table 10.6). For a smaller group—17 percent of all women, 22 percent of white women, 19 percent of black women, and 14 percent of Hispanic women—the person who most directly helped them get their last-present job is an acquaintance or other person (table 10.6). In contrast to their counterparts who relied on friends or relatives, this latter group of women, in all likelihood, took advantage of what Granovetter (1973) defines as "weak" ties to land their current-last jobs.

For Los Angeles women who have searched for work within the last five years, what appears to have mattered most, as table 10.7 shows, is being embedded in either a job-based or a neighborhood-based bridging social network, which is consistent with the finding of our logistic regression analyses. More than two-thirds of all women (67.1 percent), white women (67 percent), and black women (67.2 percent), and nearly three-quarters of Hispanic women (72 percent) who engaged in job searches within the last five years indicate that the individual who helped them land their last-present job actually worked in the firm in which they themselves ultimately secured employment (table 10.6). This individual was either the primary source of information about the job (55 percent) or talked to the employer about the hiring decision (26 percent). Similarly, over half of all women (53 percent) and roughly two-thirds of the white (67 percent) and black women (61 percent) who searched for jobs over the last five years indicated that the person who most directly helped them get their last-present job lived outside their own neighborhoods.

Also consistent with our logistic regression findings, race-based bridging social networks were found to be relatively unimportant in the

TABLE 10.6   *Respondents' Relationship to the Person(s) Most Helpful in Helping Them Get Their Last-Current Job*

	All (N = 295)	White (N = 55)	Black (N = 99)	Hispanic (N = 107)
Relative	25.1	18.2	23.2	31.8
Friend	56.6	56.4	55.6	53.3
Acquaintance	11.2	10.9	14.1	11.2
Other person	5.4	10.9	5.1	2.8

Source: Los Angeles Study of Urban Inequality 1994.
Note: Due to rounding, percentages do not add up to 100 percent.

TABLE 10.7   *Selected Characteristics of Person Who Most Directly Helped Respondents Get Their Last-Current Job*

	All (N = 295)	White (N = 55)	Black (N = 99)	Hispanic (N = 107)
Different race (yes)	11.5	12.8	11.0	11.2
Different gender (yes)	23.1	34.5	23.2	24.3
Lived in different neighborhood (yes)	52.9	67.3	61.6	40.2
Worked at firm (yes)	67.1	67.3	67.7	72.0
Told respondent about job (yes)	54.9	49.1	67.7	43.0
Hired respondent (yes)	6.8	10.9	8.1	2.8
Talked to employee (yes)	25.8	18.2	14.1	43.9
Gave respondent a reference (yes)	7.8	7.3	5.1	10.3

Source: Los Angeles Study of Urban Inequality 1994.
Note: Percentages exceed 100 percent in each racial category because an individual may be counted in more than one characteristic.

job search outcomes of this subset of women in our sample. Gender-based bridging networks were somewhat more important than race-based bridging networks, especially for white women.

Conclusion

In this chapter, we have sought to expand the current state of knowledge regarding the determinants of female employment in a multiethnic metropolitan community. Using a model of female labor force participation as our theoretical guide, we have been concerned with the relative utility of cultural versus structural explanations of labor force participation and nonparticipation in the employment experience of women in Los Angeles. We have devoted specific attention to the role of bridging social networks in the labor market experiences of white, black, and Hispanic women. Our main findings are summarized in table 10.8.

As this table illustrates, the mix of factors that influence female labor force participation varies substantially by race-ethnicity. It is clear from the summary data in these tables that Hispanic and black women are confronted with a much broader set of obstacles to employment than their white counterparts. More specifically, black and Hispanic women are more likely than white women to be constrained by opportunity costs or family context factors. Moreover, given these obstacles, bridging social networks are far more important for Hispanic and black women than for white women. Such networks are less important to

TABLE 10.8 *Summary of Statistically Significant Determinants of Employment Status of Women in Los Angeles*

	Positive Effects			Negative Effects		
	Variable	β	odds	Variable	β	odds
All women						
Race-ethnicity	Hispanic	.676	1.96			
Cultural background influences				Family dependency	−.358	.70
Human capital	Education	1.13	3.11			
Family context				Child care	−1.44	.25
				Married	−.480	.62
				Single mother	−.423	.66
Social embeddedness	Job bridge	.701	2.01			
	Neighborhood bridge	.416	1.52			
	Education bridge	.313	1.38			
White women						
Cultural background influences						
Human capital	Education	1.75	5.81			
Family context				Child care	−1.50	.22
				Married	−1.08	.34
Social embeddedness						

Hispanic women				
Cultural background influences				
Human capital	Education	.623	1.86	
Family context	Living with parents	1.07	2.92	
Social embeddedness	Job bridge	1.37	3.95	
	Child care			−1.84	.16
Black women				
Cultural background influences				
Human capital	Education	1.64	5.15	
Family context				Child care	−1.17	.31
				Child under three	−.744	.48
				Single mother	−.643	.53
Social embeddedness	Neighborhood bridge	.633	1.88	
	Job bridge	.618	1.86	

Source: Los Angeles Study of Urban Inequality 1994.

most white women because they are already embedded, either by birth or marriage, in mainstream networks (that is, predominantly white networks) that provide access to information about job opportunities and other valuable resources.

In terms of constraints on labor market participation, our research confirms that women who have grown up in a dependency situation are hampered by this experience, especially black women, but this variable is much less important than child care constraints and other family context factors that represent major barriers for women trying to enter the labor market. This is true for all women and for white, black, and Hispanic women.

On the positive side, education matters a great deal in terms of female labor force participation: only child care constraints are more important than schooling. Moreover, it is clear from our research that bridging social networks matter for women in Los Angeles, and they are far more important than the kinds of cultural forces that serve as the foundation of much of contemporary conservative social policy making in the United States (see table 10.7).

Based on the findings presented here and in an earlier study (Stoloff et al. 1996), in order to successfully transition poor women from welfare to work, the federal government's top priority should be to ensure that both public-sector organizations and private-sector companies become more family-friendly—that is, that they reengineer their organizations by implementing and enforcing policies that acknowledge that women are biologically different from men and take into account the unique needs of women for access to affordable child care, flexible working arrangements, and so forth. Also, it will be necessary to extend such benefits to men so that single fathers, married couples, and unmarried partners can share responsibility for child care. Given that in excess of one-quarter of prime working-age African American males are connected with the criminal justice system, it is unrealistic, at least in the near term, to view greater enforcement of child-support statutes as a viable solution to the feminization of poverty.

Thus, in addition to promoting and enforcing family-friendly employment policies, especially the provision of child care, considerable resources must be invested in mending the social fabric of poor ghetto neighborhoods, where most welfare-dependent mothers and their children live. This will require serious policy discussions about the best ways that poor women in these neighborhoods can be ensured greater access to bridging social networks, that is, a diverse set of ties in terms of race, gender, education, neighborhood, and so forth, that lead to greater access to education and employment opportunities for both the women and their children. If we are to break the cycle of poverty and dependency for women, such efforts must be part of a larger initiative designed to reestablish the civic community in American society (Putnam, Leonardi, and Nanetti 1993; Putnam 1995).

An earlier version of this chapter appeared in *Urban Geography* 20(1): 3–30. © V. H. Wiston & Son, Inc. Reprinted with permission.

References

Abramovitz, M. 1992. "The New Paternalism." *The Nation* 225: 368–71.

Apter, Terri. 1993. *Working Women Don't Have Wives: Professional Success in the 1990s.* New York: St. Martin's Press.

Berrick, J. D. 1991. "Welfare and Child Care: The Intricacies of Competing Social Values." *Social Work* 36: 345–51.

Bianchi, Suzanne. 1995. "Changing Economic Roles of Women and Men. In *State of the Union: America in the 1990s,* edited by R. Farley. New York: Russell Sage.

Bienenstock, Elisa J., P. Bonacich, and Melvin Oliver. 1990. "The Effect of Network Density and Homogeneity on Attitude Polarization." *Social Networks* 12: 153–72.

Bloom, Dan, and David Butler. 1995. *Implementing Time-limited Welfare: Early Experiences in Three States.* New York: Manpower Demonstration Research Corporation.

Bluestone, Barry, Mary Stevenson, and Chris Tilly. 1992. *An Assessment of the Impact of "Deindustrialization" and the Spatial Mismatch in the Labor Market: Outcomes of Young White, Black, and Latino Men and Women Who Have Limited Schooling.* Boston: Johns McCormick Institute of Public Affairs.

Bott, Elizabeth. 1957. *Family and Social Networks: Roles, Norms and External Relationships in Ordinary Urban Families.* New York: Free Press.

Boxman, Ed A. W., Paul M. De Graaf, and Hendrik D. Flap. 1991. "The Impact of Social and Human Capital on the Income Attainment of Dutch Managers." *Social Networks* 13: 51–73.

Braddock, J. H., and J. M. McPartland, 1987. "How Minorities Continue to Be Excluded from Equal Employment Opportunities: Research on Labor Market and Institutional Barriers." *Journal of Social Issues* 43: 5–39.

Browne, Irene, and Cynthia Hewitt. 1995. "Networks, Discrimination or Location? Explaining Job Segregation Among African Americans." Emory University, Department of Sociology. Unpublished paper.

Cancian, Mary, Sheldon Danziger, and Peter Gottschalk. 1993. "Working Wives and Family Income Inequality Among Married Couples." In *Uneven Tides: Rising Inequality in America,* edited by Sheldon Danziger and Peter Gottschalk. New York: Russell Sage.

Coleman, James S. 1988. "Social Capital in the Creation of Human Capital." *American Journal of Sociology* 94: 95–120.

Danziger, Sheldon, and Peter Gottschalk. 1993. *Uneven Tides: Rising Inequality in America.* New York: Russell Sage.

Darby, Michael R., ed. 1995. *Reducing Poverty in America.* Thousand Oaks, Calif.: Sage Publications.

Farrell, Walter C., Jr., and James H. Johnson Jr. 1994. "Access to Local Resources Is Key to Problems in the Inner City." *Wisconsin Review* 2: 23.

Felmlee, Diane H. 1995. "Causes and Consequences of Women's Employment Discontinuity, 1967–1973." *Work and Occupations* 22(2): 167–87.

Fernández-Kelly, Patricia. 1995. "Towanda's Triumph: Social and Cultural Capital in the Urban Ghetto." In *The Economic Sociology of Immigration,* edited by Alejandro Portes. New York: Russell Sage.

Freeman, Richard B. 1991. "Employment and Earnings of Disadvantaged Young Men in a Labor Shortage Economy. In *The Urban Underclass,* edited by Chrisopher Jencks and Paul E. Peterson. Washington, D.C.: Brookings Institution.

———. 1992. "Crime and Punishment of Disadvantaged Youth." In *Urban Labor Markets and Job Opportunity,* edited by George E. Peterson and Wayne Vroman. Washington, D.C.: The Urban Institute Press.

Garfinkel, Irvin, and Sara McLanahan. 1994. "Single-Mother Families, Economic Insecurity, and Government Policy." In *Confronting Poverty: Prescriptions for Change,* edited by Sheldon Danziger, Gary D. Sandefur, and Daniel H. Weinberg. New York: Russell Sage.

General Accounting Office. 1995. *Welfare to Work: Approaches That Help Teenage Mothers Complete High School.* Washington: U.S. General Accounting Office, Health, Education, and Human Services Division.

Gillespie, Ed, and Bob Schellhaus. 1994. *Contract with America: The Bold Plan by Rep. Newt Gingrich, Rep. Dick Armey, and the House Republicans to Change the Nation.* New York: Random House.

Granovetter, Mark. 1973. "The Strength of Weak Ties." *American Journal of Sociology* 78:1360–80.

———. 1974. *Getting a Job.* Cambridge, Mass.: Harvard University Press.

Grimsley, K. D. 1995. "The Human Cost of Downsizing." *Washington Post National Weekly Edition,* November 13–19, pp. 16–17.

Gueron Judith. 1995. "Welfare and Poverty: Strategies to Increase Work." In *Reducing Poverty in America: Views and Approaches,* edited by Michael Darby. Thousand Oaks, Calif.: Sage Publications.

Harlan, S. L. 1985. "Federal Job Training Policy and Economically Disadvantaged Women." *Women and Work* 1: 282–311.

Harrison, Lawrence E. 1992. *Who Prospers? How Cultural Values Shape Economic and Political Success.* New York: Basic Books.

Hayghe, Howard V., and Suzanne Bianchi. 1994. "Married Mothers' Work Patterns: The Job-Family Compromise." *Monthly Labor Review* 117(6): 24–30.

Jarrett, Rob. 1995. "Growing Up Poor: The Family Experiences of Socially Mobile Youth in Low Income African American Neighborhoods." *Journal of Adolescent Research* 10: 111–35.

Johnson, James H., Jr., Elisa J. Bienenstock, and Jennifer A. Stoloff. 1995. "An Empirical Test of the Cultural Capital Hypothesis." *Review of Black Political Economy* 23(4): 7–27.

Johnson, James H., Jr., Melvin L. Oliver, and Lawrence Bobo. 1994. "Unraveling the Paradox of Deepening Urban Inequality: Theoretical Underpinnings and Research Design of a Multi-city Study." *Urban Geography* 15: 77–89.

———. 1995. *The Los Angeles Study of Urban Inequality: Theoretical Underpinnings, Research Design, and Preliminary Findings*, app. A. Los Angeles: UCLA Center for the Study of Urban Poverty.

Jost, K. 1992. "Welfare Reform: The Issues." *Congressional Quarterly Researcher* 2: 315–30.

Katz, J. L. 1995. "GOP Welfare Plan: Self Help, and Leave It to the States." *Congressional Quarterly Weekly* 53: 613–19.

Laumann, Edward O. 1973. *Bonds of Pluralism: The Form and Substance of Urban Social Networks*. New York: Wiley Interscience.

Lemann, Nicholas. 1991. *The Promised Land*. New York: Knopf.

Lin, Nan. 1982. "Social Resources and Instrumental Action." In *Social Structure and Network Analysis*, edited by Peter V. Marsden and Nan Lin. Beverly Hills, Calif.: Sage Publications.

Marsden, Peter V. 1987. "Core Discussion Networks of Americans." *American Sociological Review*, 52: 122–31.

Massey, Douglas, and Nancy Denton. 1992. *American Apartheid*. Cambridge, Mass.: Harvard University Press.

Maume, David J. 1991. "Child-care Expenditures and Women's Employment Turnover." *Social Forces* 70(2): 495–508.

Mead Lawrence. 1992. *The New Politics of Poverty*. New York: Basic Books.

———. 1995. "Raising Work Levels Among the Poor." In *Reducing Poverty in America: Views and Approaches*, edited by Michael Darby. Thousand Oaks, Calif.: Sage Publications.

Moynihan, Daniel P. 1996. "Congress Builds a Coffin." *New York Review of Books* 43: 33–36.

Murray, Charles. 1984. *Losing Ground*. New York: Basic Books.

———. 1995. "Reducing Poverty and Reducing the Underclass: Different Problems, Different Solutions." In *Reducing Poverty in America: Views and Approaches*, edited by Michael Darby. Thousand Oaks, Calif.: Sage Publications.

Neckerman, Kathryn, and Joleen Kirschenman. 1991. "Hiring Strategies, Racial Bias and Inner City Workers." *Social Problems* 38: 433–47.

Newman, Katherine S. 1993. *Declining Fortunes: The Withering of the American Dream.* New York: Basic Books.

Osterman, Paul. 1993. "Why Don't 'They' Work? Employment Patterns in a High Pressure Economy." *Social Science Research* 22(2): 115–30.

Putnam, Robert C. 1995. "Bowling Alone." *Journal of Democracy* (January): 65–88.

Putnam, Robert C., with Robert Leonardi and Raffaella Y. Nanetti. 1993. *Making Democracy Work: Civic Traditions in Modern Italy.* Princeton, N.J.: Princeton University Press.

Roberts, S. 1995. "Alone in the Vast Wasteland." *New York Times*, December 24, 1995, p. E3.

Sheenan, S. 1995. "Ain't No Middle Class." *The New Yorker*, December 11, 1995, 82–93.

Sowell Thomas. 1981. *Ethnic America.* New York: Basic Books.

———. 1994. *Race and Culture: A World View.* New York: Basic Books.

Stoloff, Jennifer, J. Glanville, James H. Johnson Jr., and Elisa J. Bienenstock. 1996. "Determinants of Female Employment in a Multiethnic Labor Market." University of North Carolina, Chapel Hill. Unpublished paper.

U.S. Congress. 1996. *The Personal Responsibility and Work Opportunity Reconciliation Act of 1996.* Washington: U.S. Government Printing Office, August 13, 1996.

Usdansky, M. L. 1996. "Single Motherhood: Stereotypes vs. Statistics." *New York Times*, February 11, 1996, p. 4E.

Wilson, James Q. 1992. "How to Teach Better Values in the Inner Cities." *Wall Street Journal*, June 1, 1992, p. A12.

Wilson, William Julius. 1987. *The Truly Disadvantaged.* Chicago: University of Chicago Press.

———. 1996. *When Work Disappears: The World of the New Urban Poor.* New York: Knopf.

Woodson, R. L. 1995. "What We Can Learn from Grassroots Leaders." In *Reducing Poverty in America: Views and Approaches*, edited by Michael Darby. Thousand Oaks, Calif.: Sage Publications.

11

SEARCH, DISCRIMINATION, AND THE TRAVEL TO WORK

Michael A. Stoll

THE QUESTION of space has become an important component of labor market analysis. Where workers live in relation to where jobs are located indicates to a large extent how much time and how far workers search for and travel to work, among other things. For urban blacks, and to a lesser extent Latinos, the question of space has become central to the story of their labor market difficulties. For the past three decades, the employment difficulties of blacks have been much more severe than those of whites. Even in the good economic times of 1999, the unemployment rate of white adults in metropolitan areas was 3.6 percent, while that for blacks stood at 8.1 percent (U.S. Bureau of Labor Statistics 1999). John Kain (1968) proposed that persistent housing market discrimination practices that restrict blacks' residential choices to the central city combined with the increasing suburbanization of jobs, particularly low-skill ones, act to undermine blacks' employment opportunities in metropolitan areas. This jobs-housing (spatial) mismatch for blacks, and to a lesser extent Latinos, therefore may be partly responsible for their labor market difficulties.

The empirical basis for the spatial mismatch hypothesis is well supported. Housing market discrimination continues to play a role in restricting blacks' residential locations in metropolitan areas to central cities (Yinger 1995; Zubrinsky and Bobo 1996; Massey and Denton 1993). Indeed, in 1990, while 68.9 percent of blacks in metropolitan areas lived in central cities, only 34.1 percent of whites did. At the same time, employment opportunities, as measured by added new jobs, continue to locate in suburbs. Employment growth from 1990 to 1993 in U.S. metropolitan areas was much greater in suburbs than in central cities, and this pattern was much more true for low- than high-skill jobs

(U.S. Department of Housing and Urban Development 1997). However, there is still controversy about whether this spatial division of people and jobs negatively impacts labor market outcomes.

Studies using more recent data and more sophisticated methodologies are more consistent with spatial mismatch than previous ones.[1] These studies usually focus on employment and wages. Measures of physical job access are created and then job access is examined to see if it affects individual or geographic labor market outcomes. The spatial mismatch hypothesis is supported if job access is found to affect these outcomes and if blacks are found to have worse job access than whites.

This study takes a different approach to investigate the spatial mismatch hypothesis, by examining racial differences in commuting distance and time and in geographic job search. In studies of this nature, it is generally assumed that if the mismatch hypothesis is to hold true, blacks and other minorities living in racially segregated areas should work farther from home and take more time to get to work than other commuters, controlling for relevant factors. This finding would indicate that blacks are farther from job opportunities than other groups and thus are likely to incur more travel-related costs in searching for and getting to work. These higher travel costs resulting from longer commutes negatively impact blacks' labor market outcomes by lowering their real wage. On the other hand, if it is found that blacks' commutes to work are shorter than those of other groups, it is generally assumed that the mismatch hypothesis is not supported, since such evidence seems to suggest that blacks are closer than other groups to job opportunities. In this instance, blacks are unlikely to suffer any negative, spatially related labor market consequences.

In this chapter, I argue that the spatial mismatch hypothesis need not be disconfirmed if blacks are found to travel shorter distances or take less time to get to work than other commuters, controlling for relevant factors. Spatial mismatch could explain blacks' shorter commutes to work. This is because the additional travel costs, such as increased time and money costs as a result of traveling far distances, and the increased information costs of learning about distant jobs for those who live far from them, could prohibit them from keeping such jobs if they were to attain them. Moreover, these additional costs could cause such workers to forgo searching far distances and instead look for work only in their immediate residential areas. Competition for jobs in these job poor areas would likely be stiff. Those who are unable to find jobs in close proximity may become discouraged and leave the labor force, while those who find jobs are likely to work near their homes.

It is equally likely that if blacks live in job-poor areas, they will likely compensate for this fact by adjusting their search behavior to search farther distances or more areas than other groups (Stoll, forthcoming). Increasing their "search net" is likely to increase the probability of attaining employment. Such actions are behavioral responses consistent with spatial mismatch. However, other factors, such as increased employment discrimination against blacks in nonminority areas, could prevent blacks from getting distant jobs. Thus, even if blacks searched farther than other groups for jobs as a result of living in job-poor areas, it is likely that they will work closer to their residential areas than other groups if social factors such as race discrimination limit their access to distant jobs. Such evidence would also be consistent with the spatial mismatch hypothesis.

The results of this chapter are consistent with this position. While low-skill blacks, and to a lesser extent Latinos, are found to commute shorter distances and take less time to get to work than comparable whites, they travel longer distances during their search for work. Race discrimination in areas outside predominantly minority, residential locations is found to be a plausible reason why low-skill blacks are unable to attain jobs distant from their residential locations. However, differences in geographic job search, mode of transportation, and personal characteristics explain all the differences in commuting time and distance between low-skill Latinos and whites.

Treating Space in
Spatial Mismatch Research

The dynamics of demographic and economic geography across metropolitan areas make the analysis of large, aggregated spatial units within these areas difficult and problematic. Many use broad geographic categories such as "central city" and "suburbs" as the spatial unit of analysis to examine whether space affects labor market outcomes (Stoll 1999a; Raphael 1998; Holzer, Ihlanfeldt, and Sjoquist 1994; Cooke and Shumway 1991; Ihlanfeldt and Sjoquist 1990; Price and Mills 1985; Vrooman and Greenfield 1980; and Harrison 1974). However, such spatial categories are difficult to impose on all metropolitan areas for the following reasons.

First, the central city–suburban distinction cannot adequately describe all U.S. cities. The notion of an older, more dense central core that is in decline and a newer, more dispersed periphery that is growing is based primarily on older Eastern and Midwestern cities that have evolved fairly closely along these dimensions. However, the urban sprawl in some newer cities of the South and West has less distinguishable zones. Los Angeles has a unique urban topography that does not have a traditional central-city core, but instead has numerous suburbanlike nodes spread throughout a large urban land mass.

Second, the central city–suburban dichotomy is sometimes incorrectly used to describe the particular economic health of areas within metropolitan areas. Generally, central cities are assumed to be in decline and contain all or most of the metropolitan area's high poverty districts, while suburbs are thought to be growth areas where few if any poverty areas exist. However, in Los Angeles, as with other Southern and Western cities, this typology does not always fit. East Los Angeles, which is predominantly Latino, is classified as a suburban area, although it has serious poverty problems and other characteristics that resemble those of an inner city. On the other hand, the low population and employment densities and low poverty rates of some central-city areas in Los Angeles, in particular the San Fernando Valley and the Westside, are more analogous to those in the suburbs.

But although differences in economic health may exist within cities and suburbs, what seems true is that black residential areas in either area lack employment opportunities (Stoll, Holzer, and Ihlanfeldt 2000). In Los Angeles, tremendous economic jolts during the 1970s and early 1980s caused approximately 70,000 manufacturing jobs to leave (Soja, Morales, and Wolff 1983). Moreover, much of this job loss was concentrated in the historically black community of South Central Los Angeles. Table 11.1 shows total employment and population growth from 1980 to 1990 in Los Angeles County (see figure 11.1 for the location of these areas).[2] Population growth data is included to provide information on the degree of local competition for jobs in these areas. The table shows that net job growth has been substantially lower in the predominantly minority areas of South Central and East Los Angeles, a predominantly Latino area, than other areas (except downtown), though employment levels there are relatively high. Likewise, though employment levels are high in downtown, which borders the minority areas of South Central and East Los Angeles, employment growth between 1980 and 1990 in this area was stagnant. Population growth in the predominantly minority areas of South Central and East Los Angeles has far outpaced employment growth, while employment growth has either been even with or outpaced population growth in all other areas in Los Angeles. This is particularly true in San Fernando, Covina-Industry, and Pasadena, that is, in areas distant from black residential areas. Taken together, these results imply that employment opportunities appear to be much greater outside the predominantly black and Latino areas of Los Angeles.

Third, the central city–suburban dichotomy may not fairly represent the nature of residential segregation in urban areas. The spatial mismatch hypothesis is predicated on the existence of racial residential segregation. This implies that those who are hurt most by the movement of

TABLE 11.1   *Total Employment and Population Growth in Los Angeles, 1980 to 1990*

	1980 Level	1990 Level	Change, 1980 to 1990	Percentage Change, 1980 to 1990
Employment				
San Fernando Valley	465,616	611,348	145,732	31.30
Westside	383,445	443,604	60,159	15.69
Downtown	554,686	557,560	2,874	0.52
South Bay	341,794	361,294	19,500	5.71
Harbor-Long Beach	288,696	354,608	65,912	22.84
Burbank-Glendale	167,971	211,018	43,047	25.63
Covina-Industry	170,927	262,964	92,037	53.81
South Central	389,204	406,615	17,411	4.47
East Los Angeles	556,396	554,171	−2,225	−0.40
Southeast	233,423	286,410	52,987	22.70
Pomona	60,615	80,841	20,226	33.37
Pasadena	159,451	190,439	30,988	19.43
Agoura Hills-Malibu	12,800	46,919	34,119	266.55
Total	3,786,024	4,367,791	581,767	15.37
Population				
San Fernando Valley	979,668	1,177,517	197,849	20.20
Westside	543,676	563,290	19,614	3.61
Downtown	621,961	726,307	104,346	16.78
South Bay	494,527	528,293	33,766	6.83
Harbor-Long Beach	713,019	850,102	137,083	19.23
Burbank-Glendale	314,173	371,155	56,982	18.14
Covina-Industry	509,021	625,504	116,483	22.88
South Central	924,757	1,079,130	154,373	16.69
East Los Angeles	1,044,846	1,280,591	235,745	22.56
Southeast	519,033	628,282	109,249	21.05
Pomona	179,315	235,343	56,028	31.25
Pasadena	367,074	398,532	31,458	8.57
Agoura Hills-Malibu	59,259	80,459	21,200	35.78
Total	7,270,329	8,544,505	1,274,176	17.53

Source: Employment: Southern California Association of Governments. Population: U.S. Census.

jobs to suburban areas may not be blacks living in an urban area, but those who are concentrated in large racially segregated areas. However, the use of "central city" in spatial mismatch studies is mistakenly used synonymously with black (Latino) residence and segregation. Although most blacks, and to a lesser extent Latinos, live in residentially segregated central-city areas, many also live in suburbs. However, many of the suburban areas in which minorities live are themselves segregated, and most are extensions of central-city segregated areas. Thus, racial

FIGURE 11.1   Search Areas and Racial-Ethnic Composition of
               Los Angeles County, 1994

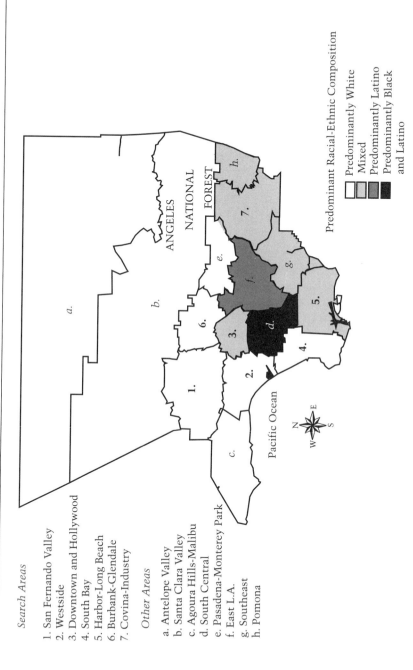

Search Areas

1. San Fernando Valley
2. Westside
3. Downtown and Hollywood
4. South Bay
5. Harbor-Long Beach
6. Burbank-Glendale
7. Covina-Industry

Other Areas

a. Antelope Valley
b. Santa Clara Valley
c. Agoura Hills-Malibu
d. South Central
e. Pasadena-Monterey Park
f. East L.A.
g. Southeast
h. Pomona

Predominant Racial-Ethnic Composition

☐ Predominantly White
☐ Mixed
☐ Predominantly Latino
■ Predominantly Black
   and Latino

Source: Los Angeles Study of Urban Inequality 1994; U.S. Census 1990.

segregation is not limited to central cities, but can also be found in the inner suburbs as well (Galster 1991; Massey and Denton 1988; Kain 1985). It is important in spatial mismatch studies, then, to examine blacks and Latinos who live in racially segregated areas independent of central city–suburban boundaries.

Not only must questions of urban geography be treated with caution in spatial mismatch studies, so too must other variables that have a spatial component. Commuting time measures, which provide a sense of how far workers commute to work, cannot be interpreted correctly without controlling for mode of transportation used. Marcus Alexis and Nancy DiTomaso (1983), using data from the 1970s, found that blacks had longer commuting times to work than whites in Chicago, suggesting that a spatial mismatch of black residential locations and employment centers negatively impacts blacks' labor market outcomes. However, mode of transportation, or the fact that blacks were more likely to use slower modes of travel to work, such as public transit, was responsible for these longer commuting times, rather than the absence of job opportunities near black residential areas. Others also using older data have found that blacks, and to a lesser extent Latinos, experienced longer commuting times to work than similar whites even after controlling for mode of transit to work (Ihlanfeldt 1993; Ihlanfeldt and Sjoquist 1991; Leonard 1987; Ellwood 1986), but it is not agreed that these longer commuting times to work are responsible for their lower employment and wages in urban areas.

The difficulties of interpreting commuting time measures suggests that commuting distance variables should also be included in spatial mismatch studies. The spatial mismatch hypothesis is in part a story about how far certain groups of workers are located from jobs. Commuting time measures give us a sense of how far workers commute, but they are not a perfect measure of distance, since they are confounded by differential travel times of various modes of transit that workers use and by the degree of traffic congestion workers experience while traveling to work. Harry J. Holzer, Keith R. Ihlanfeldt, and David L. Sjoquist (1994) included distance in their analysis of youth and found that whites' commuting distances, but not commuting times, to work were longer than those of blacks in metropolitan areas. Blacks' greater commuting time to work was partially explained by their greater reliance on slower transportation modes. However, little is known about whether these results hold for adults. Similarly, Brian D. Taylor and Paul Ong (1995), improving spatial mismatch research by defining space by racial composition and using more recent data, found that commuters living in predominantly minority areas had shorter average commute distances and times than other commuters. The shorter commuting distances and times of minority workers, particularly those living in minority areas, led them to conclude that a spatial mismatch did not exist for these workers. However, this conclusion is questionable because an analysis of the geographic dimensions of job search by such groups was not included in their study.

Methodological Approach and Definition of Main Variables

This analysis examines racial differences in commuting distance and time and in geographic job search patterns. For this analysis, the sample consists of those non-Latino whites, non-Latino blacks, and Latinos between the ages of twenty-one and sixty-five who indicated that they had searched for work within five years prior to the survey and who did not have a disability that prevented them from working. This sample selection allows for the examination of unique spatial job search questions and includes both those who are employed and those who are unemployed.[3] For the unemployed, we used their previous employment location, provided that they had not moved from their current residence prior to becoming unemployed.[4] These restrictions result in a sample of n = 1,291.[5]

To overcome the difficulties of interpreting central city–suburban dichotomies in spatial mismatch studies, Los Angeles is categorized into areas defined by their racial concentration. First, Los Angeles is divided into fifteen well-established areas.[6] These areas are fairly large and include populations from as low as 70,000 to as high as 1.1 million. Next, we used the 1990 U.S. Census Summary Tape File (STF) for Los Angeles County to examine the racial compositions within each of these fifteen areas. Then, similar to Taylor and Ong (1995), we categorized four more general areas: predominantly white, mixed, predominantly Latino, and predominantly black-Latino. Areas where 50 percent or more of the population was one ethnic or racial group were defined as predominantly that group. Areas where no group represented more than 40 percent of the population were defined as mixed, while areas where blacks and Latinos each represented at least 40 percent of the population were defined as predominantly black-Latino.[7] This approach, which defines large, racially segregated areas within metropolitan areas, is more in keeping with the motivations of the spatial mismatch hypothesis.

Based on criticisms of commuting time measures, in this analysis both commuting distance and time are used as the main dependent variables. Commuting distance to work is measured using Geographic Information Systems (GIS) techniques as the straight-line distance, in miles, between a respondent's residential and employment address. Commuting time to work is asked of each respondent for their current or last job.[8] Thus, commuting time is self-reported and is therefore subject to response bias.

The main independent variables in the analysis include average and farthest distance searched for work. LASUI is unique in that it provides information on the geographic locations of search for workers who looked for work in the last five years. These spatial job search variables are constructed from seven questions that asked respondents if they had ever searched for work in each of the seven LASUI defined areas.[9] Figure 11.1 provides a geographic map of these search areas, as well as the other, major residential areas identified in the analysis. It also provides shading that indicates the racial composition of these areas in Los Angeles County. GIS is used to estimate the straight-line distance, in miles, between i's residential location and the centroid of the k areas searched by i. The farthest distance searched variable is measured by identifying the farthest k area searched by i. This variable provides information about the absolute distance that individuals are willing to travel to get to work. On the other hand, the average distance searched variable is measured by taking the average distance in miles for the k areas that i searched. This variable provides an alternative measure of the distance that individuals are willing to travel to get to work. These measures are highly correlated with one another (above .80).

The Analysis: The Travel to Work in Los Angeles
Travel by Race and Gender

Table 11.2 shows the average commute to work—in time, distance, and speed per mile traveled—for racial and gender groups.[10] For men, the average distance traveled to work by blacks and Latinos is over two miles shorter than that of whites, while their commuting time to work is significantly longer. Thus, the speed per mile traveled by blacks and Latino men is slower than that for white men, most probably due to black and Latino men's greater reliance on slower modes of transportation. These findings are consistent with recent research (Taylor and Ong 1995; Holzer, Ihlanfeldt, and Sjoquist 1994).

The same patterns are true for women, expect that the distances traveled are not statistically different among racial groups. In addition, for each racial group, women travel less distance to work than men.

TABLE 11.2   Travel Means by Race and Gender in Los Angeles, 1994

	Men			Women		
	White	Black	Latino	White	Black	Latina
Travel						
Miles traveled to work	11.0	8.7[a]	8.6[a]	7.5	7.1	6.8
	(10.0)	(6.8)	(8.0)	(7.4)	(4.9)	(6.0)
Commuting time to work	25.1	32.4[a]	30.5[a]	22.2	28.2[a]	25.8
	(17.3)	(27.8)	(19.5)	(17.9)	(19.0)	(14.6)
Time/miles	4.1	5.1[a]	4.8[a]	4.3	4.9[a]	4.5
	(5.3)	(6.6)	(5.8)	(8.1)	(5.2)	(4.3)
Travel mode						
Own car	.88	.76[a]	.78[a]	.87	.77[a]	.63[a]
Public	.02	.11[a]	.07[a]	.03	.09[a]	.09[a]
Carpool	.05	.04	.06	.03	.06[a]	.14[a]
Walk	.02	.03	.06[a]	.03	.01	.08[a]
Other	.03	.05	.03	.03	.08[a]	.07[a]
N	(184)	(248)	(228)	(193)	(295)	(143)

Source: Los Angeles Study of Urban Inequality 1994.
[a]Statistically different from whites within gender groups at the 5 percent level of significance.
Note: Standard deviations in parentheses.

This finding is consistent with previous research (McLafferty and Preston 1992), and is likely caused by a number of factors, including family responsibilities that cause women to work closer to home (Hanson and Pratt 1991), employers' choice to locate near specific race-gender groups for a particular labor supply (Nelson 1986), or labor market segmentation of women into "female occupations" restricting women to work closer to home (see chapter 12).

Thus, black and Latino men and women travel shorter distances to work than their white counterparts. The shorter distances are likely caused in part by the greater time cost per mile traveled as a result of the greater percentage of blacks and Latinos who travel by slower modes of transit. Since blacks and Latinos pay more during travel with respect to time as compared to whites, economic theory suggests that they should travel less distance. Whether the use of slower modes of transit can explain these racial differences in commuting distance and time will be examined later in this chapter. Because racial differences in travel patterns are similar for men and women, for the remainder of this analysis the sample is pooled across gender groups.

Skill Levels and the Travel to Work

Table 11.2 includes both high- and low-skill workers. The standard urban model predicts that the former should have longer commutes to work than the latter because employers may be more willing to compensate them for the longer commute (Heilbrun 1987). Table 11.3 shows the means for commuting distance and time for high- and low-skill workers who travel to work by car.[11] There are two major findings. First, the results confirm the general predictions of urban economic theory and show that low-skill workers' commuting time and distance to work are generally longer for each racial group than that of their high-skill counterparts. This is consistent with Martin Wachs et al. (1993), who find that 39.4 percent of workers making over $15.00 an hour traveled over 10 or more miles to work, while only 26.9 percent of workers making less than $15.00 an hour did.

Second, the same racial patterns of commute for the sample as a whole are found for the low-skill worker group. That is, for low-skill workers, blacks and Latinos travel fewer miles and take more time to get to work than their white counterparts. Since there are no significant racial differences in travel for high-skill workers, we focus for the rest of the chapter on low-skill workers. Moreover, this is more in keeping with the spatial mismatch hypothesis, since low-skill workers are the group of greatest concern and most likely to be harmed by the movement of jobs to the suburbs (Kasarda 1989).

427

TABLE 11.3   *Travel Means by Skill and Race in Los Angeles, 1994*

	White	Black	Latino
Low-Skill			
Own car			
Miles traveled to work	9.5	8.1[a]	7.9[a]
Commuting time to work	23.8	28.4[a]	25.9[a]
Time/miles	4.3	6.1[a]	5.8[a]
N	(95)	(182)	(235)
High-skill			
Own car			
Miles traveled to work	10.8	8.5	8.1
Commuting time to work	29.4	28.2	25.2
Time/miles	4.1	4.5	4.6
N	(293)	(363)	(143)

Source: Los Angeles Study of Urban Inequality 1994.
[a]Statistically different from whites at the 5 percent level of significance.

Residential Location and the Travel to Work

This section examines the travel means of residents who live in areas with different racial composition, since the spatial mismatch hypothesis implies that residents in racially segregated areas are disadvantaged in the labor market. Table 11.4 shows the travel means for low-skilled workers who live in areas of different racial composition. Two major findings stand out. First, the group of greatest concern (residents in minority areas) travel the shortest distances to work, though their commuting time is very similar to workers living in nonminority areas. This implies, as the data confirm, that residents in minority areas have higher time costs per mile traveled. Moreover, these higher time costs may explain part of the shorter miles traveled to work by these groups.

Second, low-skill blacks and Latinos who live in predominantly white and mixed areas travel only slightly shorter distances to work than their white counterparts in these areas. However, their commuting time to work is much longer than their white counterparts. This is likely due to blacks' and Latinos' greater reliance on slower, public modes of transportation, resulting in higher time costs per mile traveled. These results are consistent with recent research (Taylor and Ong 1995).

TABLE 11.4   *Travel Means by Residence and Race for*
Low-Skill Workers in Los Angeles, 1994

	Commuting Miles	Commuting Time	Time/ Miles
Commuters from predominantly white areas			
White	8.9	24.0	4.4
Black	8.4	27.8	6.1
Latino	8.8	26.9	5.7
Commuters from racially mixed areas			
White	10.2	23.5	4.3
Black	9.9	29.9	6.0
Latino	9.9	26.0	5.8
Commuters from predominantly black-Latino areas			
White	a	a	a
Black	7.4	27.7	6.4
Latino	6.7	24.4	6.2
Commuters from predominantly Latino areas			
White	a	a	a
Black	a	a	a
Latino	7.2	23.7	5.9

Source: Los Angeles Study of Urban Inequality 1994.
[a]Fewer than twenty cases in cell.

The Geography of Low-Skill Workers' Residential and Work Locations

Figures 11.3, 11.4, and 11.5 show the residential and employment locations of low-skill white, black, and Latino workers, respectively, in Los Angeles County, to confirm the findings in table 11.4. These maps should be analyzed with reference to figure 11.2, which shows the boundaries of areas defined by racial composition. In reviewing these maps, note that the large areas due west and north of the Angeles National Forest are desert areas containing sparse population and development. Northwest of the Angeles National Forest are the expanding areas of Palmdale and Lancaster.

These maps reveal that, compared to other groups, low-skill whites' employment and residential locations are more dispersed, while low-skill blacks' employment locations are much more contained around their residential locations. This should be expected, given the findings that low-skill whites travel longer distances to work than other groups. Note also that low-skill whites are more likely to work in predomi-

(Text continues on p. 434.)

429

FIGURE 11.2 Racial-Ethnic Composition of Los Angeles County, 1990

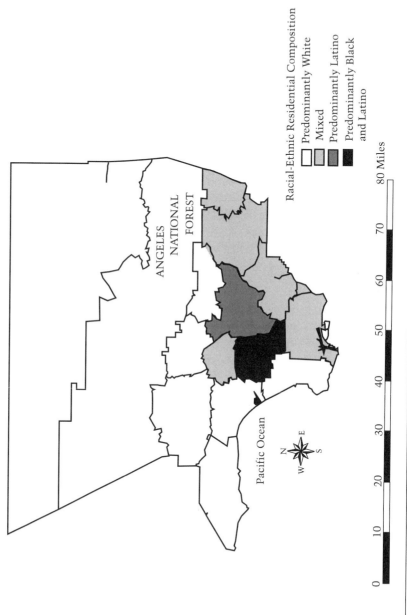

Source: 1990 U.S. Census.

FIGURE 11.3   Low-Skill Whites' Residential and Employment Locations in Los Angeles County, 1994

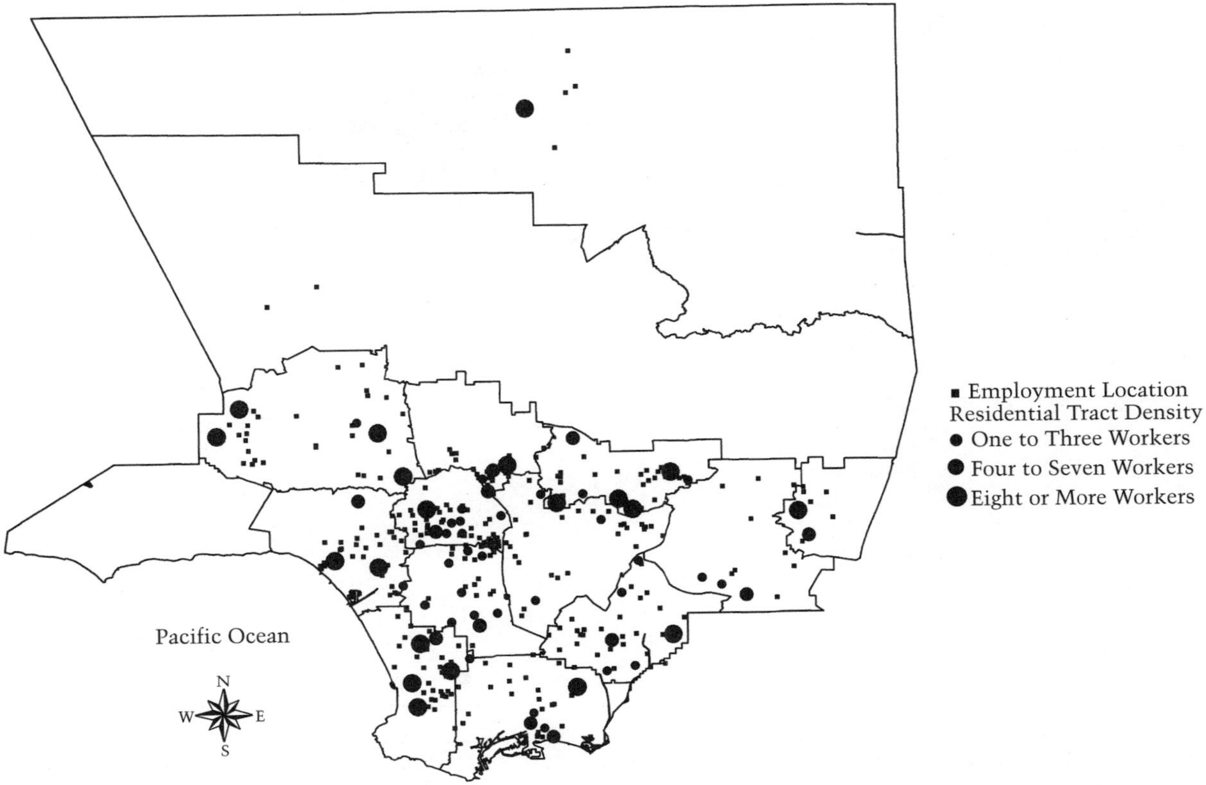

Employment Location
Residential Tract Density
● One to Three Workers
● Four to Seven Workers
● Eight or More Workers

Pacific Ocean

Source: Los Angeles Study of Urban Inequality 1994.

FIGURE 11.4   Low-Skill Blacks' Residential and Employment Locations in Los Angeles County, 1994

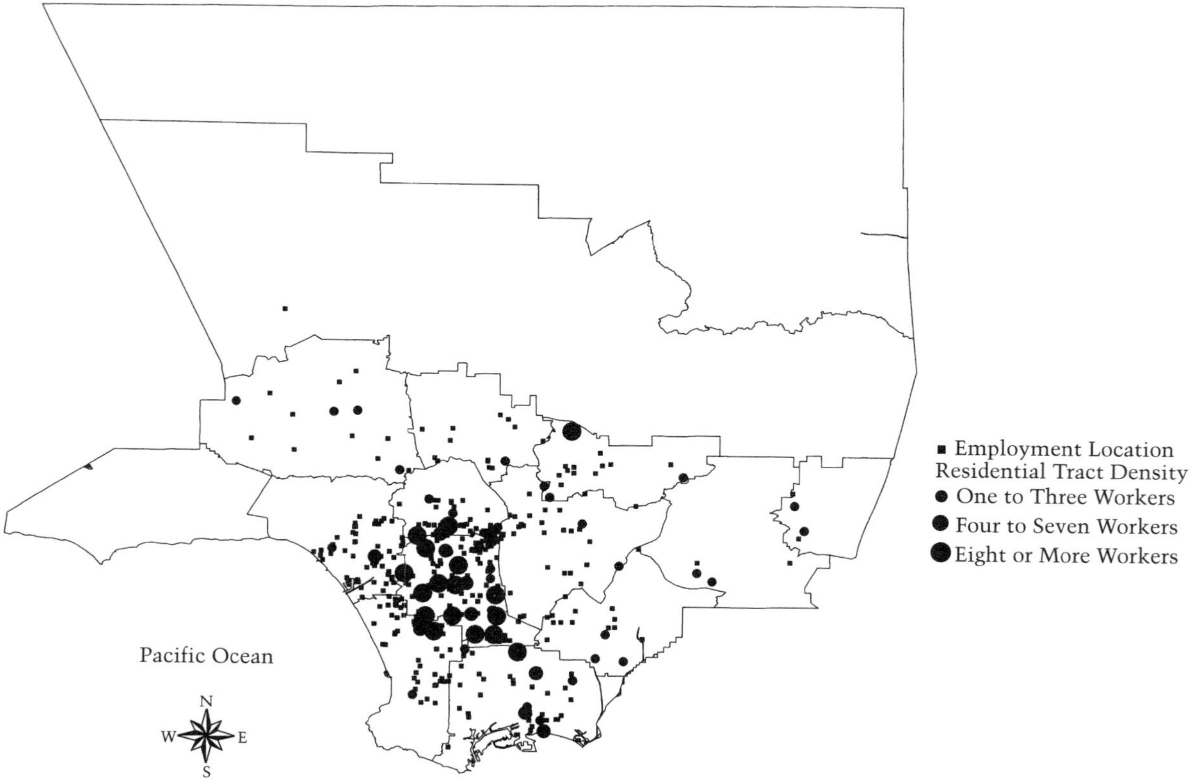

- ■ Employment Location
  Residential Tract Density
- ● One to Three Workers
- ● Four to Seven Workers
- ● Eight or More Workers

Pacific Ocean

Source: Los Angeles Study of Urban Inequality 1994.

FIGURE 11.5 *Low-Skill Latinos' Residential and Employment Locations in Los Angeles County, 1994*

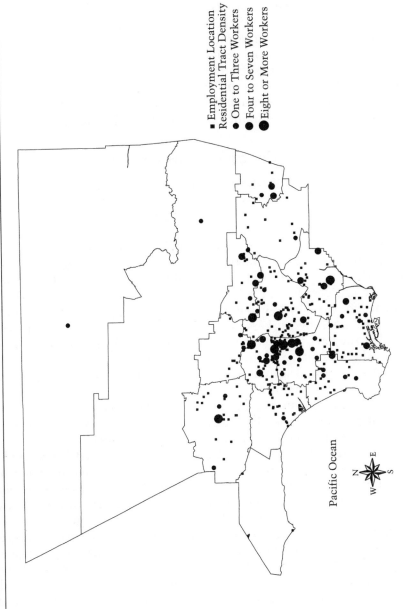

Employment Location
Residential Tract Density
● One to Three Workers
● Four to Seven Workers
● Eight or More Workers

Pacific Ocean

Source: Los Angeles Study of Urban Inequality 1994.

nantly white and mixed areas than are low-skilled blacks and Latinos. The maps also show that low-skilled whites' residential locations are more dispersed in Los Angeles and are found in predominantly white areas such as San Fernando Valley, Burbank-Glendale, Pasadena, the Westside, and South Bay. At the same time, low-skilled blacks' residential locations are concentrated in the black-Latino area of South Central, while low-skilled Latinos' residences are concentrated in downtown South Central, a racially mixed area, and East Los Angeles, the predominantly Latino area. Moreover, in comparison to similar whites, low-skilled blacks', and to a much lesser extent Latinos', employment locations are much more contained to their residential areas.

The Geographic Search for Work

The observed shorter work trips by minority workers, particularly those who live in heavily minority areas, need not imply that such workers are closer to jobs than other groups or that they are unaffected by a spatial mismatch. As noted earlier, this is a difficult conclusion to reach without an analysis of workers' geographic search patterns. This is particularly true since the employment data provided in table 11.1 indicate that little or no job growth has occurred in minority areas of Los Angeles over the last decade. But before comparisons are made of the distances searched for work by low-skilled workers, it is important to examine the degree of search by workers in the LASUI defined search areas, to gather whether they are less likely to search in more distant areas. Table 11.5 shows the percentage of low-skilled workers who searched for work in the LASUI defined search areas.[12] The search areas are categorized by their direction from downtown (see figure 11.1 for a map of these areas). An estimate of the distance, in miles, that these search areas are located from minority areas is also included. The results are reported by the racial composition of the respondent's residential area.[13]

The results in table 11.5 indicate that low-skilled blacks and Latinos are more likely to search in areas nearer to minority residential locations. For example, while 21.1 percent of blacks living in the black-Latino area searched in San Fernando, which is nearly 21.5 miles away, 72.4 percent of this group searched for work in downtown, an area only 8.9 miles from the black-Latino area. These same patterns with respect to whites' residential locations are also generally true for low-skilled whites. Table 11.5 shows that low-skilled whites are more likely to search in areas that are characterized by predominantly white residential compositions. The one exception is downtown, which is a mixed residential area, but where the highest percentage (nearly 50 percent) of low-skilled whites searched for work.

TABLE 11.5   Percentage of Low-Skill Workers Who Search in LASUI Search Areas and Distance of Search Areas from Minority Residential Areas, 1994

Search areas	Distance		White			Black			Latino		
	Miles from Black-Latino Area	Miles from Latino Area	White and Mixed Areas	Black-Latino Area	Latino Area	White and Mixed Areas	Black-Latino Area	Latino Area	White and Mixed Areas	Black-Latino Area	Latino Area
North											
San Fernando (w)	21.5	28.2	42.9	a	a	25.7	21.1	a	20.5	25.0	16.5
Burbank-Glendale (w)	19.3	22.0	44.0	a	a	43.9	34.1	a	35.1	30.1	27.8
East											
Covina-Industry (m)	25.3	16.5	28.1	a	a	46.5	18.7	a	19.0	13.2	37.1
South											
Harbor-Long Beach (m)	15.0	18.4	37.2	a	a	49.6	46.8	a	32.7	29.6	24.0
South Bay (w)	9.1	16.4	29.0	a	a	45.9	75.0	a	33.7	7.9	30.8
West											
Westside (w)	9.1	16.1	45.1	a	a	70.4	63.5	a	32.7	23.4	29.2
Center City											
Downtown (m)	8.9	7.4	48.9	a	a	66.9	72.4	a	39.7	70.8	58.7

Source: Los Angeles Study of Urban Inequality 1994.
Notes: (w) indicates predominantly white area. (m) indicates mixed area.
[a]Fewer than twenty cases in cell.

TABLE 11.6   *Average and Farthest Distance Searched (in Miles) for Low-Skill Workers in Los Angeles by Racial Concentration of Residence, 1994*

	All Areas			White Areas		
	White	Black	Latino	White	Black	Latino
Actual distance searched						
Average distance	10.9	12.6	12.0	10.0	11.2	8.9
searched	(6.2)	(8.3)	(6.7)	(6.4)	(6.6)	(7.2)
Farthest distance	14.0	17.9	16.5	13.1	14.1	13.3
searched	(11.7)	(9.1)	(8.7)	(9.1)	(8.6)	(10.0)
Physical distance from search area						
Average distance from	18.1	16.8	15.0	20.1	16.2	16.1
search areas	(10.6)	(8.2)	(7.5)	(10.1)	(2.2)	(2.5)
Farthest distance from	28.3	26.7	24.9	31.4	27.2	27.3
search areas	(13.3)	(8.4)	(9.2)	(10.6)	(2.1)	(3.8)

Source: Los Angeles Study of Urban Inequality 1994.
Notes: Standard deviations in parentheses.
 [a] Fewer than twenty cases in cell.

In general, these results indicate that low-skilled workers are more likely to search in areas that are closer to their residential locations. These results confirm the predictions of general search theory and are consistent with previous research (Stoll 1999b). They suggest that search costs, which stem from the additional time, money, and information costs of traveling during the search, limit the distance traveled. However, it is difficult to generalize from these results whether low-skilled blacks and Latinos cover more distance during search than their white counterparts. To the extent that they do, this would imply a behavioral response consistent with being located farther from job opportunities than other groups.

Table 11.6 is provided to show the average and farthest distance searched by low-skilled workers. The results are summarized by the race and residential location of low-skilled workers so that comparisons can be made across the groups of interest. However, because of the incomplete coverage of the LASUI defined search areas, it is difficult to interpret these data alone. This is because the search areas do not cover the heavily minority areas of South Central and East Los Angeles, or the predominantly mixed areas of Southeast Los Angeles and Pomona. Because of this, bias is introduced into the measures of average and farthest distances searched. Those who are physically closer to these LASUI defined search areas will likely have shorter average and farthest distances searched than those who are physically farther from them. To

TABLE 11.6   *Continued*

	Mixed Areas			Black-Latino Areas			Latino Areas	
White	Black	Latino	White	Black	Latino	White	Black	Latino
11.6	12.1	12.2	[a]	13.8	11.3	[a]	[a]	12.7
(5.8)	(5.7)	(6.5)		(3.4)	(3.1)			(4.4)
14.4	17.4	17.1	[a]	18.6	14.6	[a]	[a]	16.6
(9.4)	(9.4)	(9.9)		(6.3)	(6.7)			(5.7)
21.1	21.9	17.8	[a]	15.5	15.6	[a]	[a]	15.4
(6.9)	(6.9)	(4.3)		(2.7)	(3.1)			(2.6)
32.7	32.4	29.5	[a]	25.3	25.0	[a]	[a]	23.4
(7.2)	(7.4)	(5.4)		(4.4)	(4.9)			(2.1)

overcome this bias, measures indicating the average and farthest physical distance from the search areas are included in table 11.6.[14] These measures provide information about how far respondents are from the LASUI defined search areas, so that their actual distance-searched measures can be compared meaningfully.

There are three major findings in table 11.6. First, for all residential areas combined, low-skilled blacks cover more geographic space during search than either low-skilled whites or Latinos. For example, the average and farthest distance searched by low-skilled blacks is over a mile and a half and nearly four miles longer, respectively, that those of their white counterparts. As noted earlier, these comparisons may mean little, given the bias in the coverage of the LASUI defined search areas. However, an analysis of the physical distance from search areas shows that, for all residential areas combined, low-skilled whites are located farther from the search areas than all other groups. Thus, low-skill whites have greater opportunities to indicate that they searched farther for work than other groups. This result supports the first of our conclusions. Moreover, to the extent that respondents who live farther from search areas are likely to have longer average and farthest distance searched measures, the observed, longer distances searched for work by low-skilled blacks, and to a lesser extent Latinos, are likely underestimated.

Second, low-skilled blacks living in the predominantly black-Latino area travel the longest distances during search than any other group. This is true despite the fact that search costs limit the distances searched for work and despite the fact that they live closer to the LASUI defined search areas than any other group. Third, low-skill Latinos living in the predominantly black-Latino area travel significantly shorter distances during search than their black counterparts in this area.

These results suggest that low-skilled blacks, particularly those who live in the predominantly black-Latino area, have greater difficulty than other groups obtaining employment near their residential areas. The greater geographic search by this group is a behavioral response consistent with living far from job opportunities or having less access to jobs near their residential areas. These factors appear less true for low-skill Latinos. The results for this group are inconsistent and suggest both behavioral responses consistent with living far from jobs, as is the case for those living in Latino areas, and responses consistent with having greater access to jobs nearby, as is the case of those living in black-Latino areas. The difference in distance searched between low-skilled Latinos and blacks in the black-Latino areas suggests that of the jobs available there, low-skilled Latinos may have greater access to them than low-skilled blacks. This result is consistent with recent research that indicates that, controlling for application rates and distance to jobs, low-skilled blacks have less access to low-skill jobs than similar Latinos (Stoll, Holzer, and Ihlanfeldt, 2000). The extent to which low-skilled Latinos' greater access to nearby jobs than similar blacks is due to their lower reservation wages, more effective social networks in particular industries (Waldinger 1993), or the perception that members of many immigrant groups are harder workers (Wilson 1996; Kirschenman and Neckerman 1991) is not clear from these data.

Does Geographic Job Search Affect the Travel to Work?

In this section, regression analysis is used to examine the factors that predict commuting distance and time and that explain racial differences in these measures. Regression models are developed to control for personal characteristics that also affect travel patterns and behavior (see, for example, Taylor and Ong 1995). The central concern in these models is whether racial differences in geographic search can explain the observed racial differences in commuting distance and time. To examine these questions, OLS regression analysis is used.[15] These models are captured by the following equations:

$$\text{MILES}_i = f(\text{RACE}_i, \text{RL}_i, \text{MODE}_i, \text{TM}_i, \text{SEARCH}_i, X_i) + u_1 \quad (11.1)$$

$$\text{TIME}_i = f(\text{RACE}_i, \text{RL}_i, \text{MODE}_i, \text{TM}_i, \text{MILES}_i, \text{SEARCH}_i, X_i) + u_2 \quad (11.2)$$

where MILES is defined as the distance to work in miles and TIME is the commuting time to work in minutes; RACE corresponds to the commuter's race; RL represents residential location in areas defined by racial composition; MODE identifies the mode of transportation used to get to work; TM captures the time cost per mile traveled; SEARCH represents the average- and farthest-distance-searched variables[16] and X represents a vector of personal characteristic control variables that include age (in years), gender, education, annual earned income (log), and school enrollment status (1 = yes) for the ith individual.[17]

The variables indicating race for blacks and Latinos are interacted with the variables identifying residential location in the heavily minority areas to examine whether search or other factors can explain the shorter distances traveled by these groups. Because of the focus on these groups and since none of other race-residential location interacted effects are significant, only the interactions for low-skilled blacks and Latinos living in the minority residential areas are shown.

The presentation of regression results highlights the sensitivity of the interacted race-residential location effect on commuting distance and time to the inclusion of geographic search variables into the equation. Thus, only the results of the main variables are show here.[18] The empirical strategy is to estimate a baseline race-residential location effect on commuting distance and time while controlling only for personal characteristics, then to systematically add time/miles, mode of transportation, and geographic search variables into the equation. Examination of the change in magnitude of the race-residential location coefficient after the geographic search variables are entered will determine whether and to what extent geographic search can account for the observed race-residential location effect on commuting distance and time.

Models 1 through 5 in table 11.7 show the regression results for commuting distance. Note that all models include the personal control variables described earlier. In this MILES equation, low-skilled blacks and Latinos who live in minority residential areas travel nearly 2 miles less to work than other workers, even after controlling for personal characteristics. These results confirm the earlier findings. Model 2 adds time cost per mile traveled to the equation. Its effect on commuting distance is of the expected sign and is statistically significant. However, time cost per mile traveled, which reflects both choice of transportation mode to get to work and the degree of traffic congestion experienced during the journey to work, explains only about 5 percent of the differences in commuting distance between those who live in minority versus nonminority areas.

Model 3 adds the mode of transportation variables into the equation. On average, travel mode explains about 20 percent of the com-

TABLE 11.7 Determinants of Commuting Miles and Time to Work for Low-Skill Workers in Los Angeles

	Commuting Miles					Commuting Time				
	(1)	(2)	(3)	(4)	(5)	(6)	(7)	(8)	(9)	(10)
Race × area										
Black × black and Latino	-1.98*** (0.74)	-1.87*** (0.70)	-1.67*** (0.72)	-1.92*** (0.79)	-2.02*** (0.80)	-2.57** (0.99)	-2.01* (1.05)	-1.82* (1.07)	-2.68** (1.12)	-2.83** (1.15)
Latino × black and Latino	-1.87*** (0.72)	-1.75** (0.71)	-1.49** (0.76)	-1.31 (0.81)	-1.29 (0.83)	-2.31** (0.92)	-1.93** (0.95)	-1.69** (0.96)	-1.26 (1.01)	-1.04 (1.06)
Latino × Latino	-1.78*** (0.81)	-1.71*** (0.79)	-1.31 (0.82)	-1.39 (0.86)	-1.40 (0.88)	-0.94 (0.90)	0.72 (0.93)	1.12 (0.95)	0.97 (0.97)	0.89 (1.01)
Mode										
Own Car	—	—	4.89*** (1.03)	4.84*** (1.04)	4.82*** (1.03)	—	—	3.87* (2.10)	4.08* (2.19)	3.97* (2.23)
Public	—	—	4.12** (1.27)	4.09*** (1.29)	4.10*** (1.28)	—	—	17.4*** (2.29)	17.1*** (2.33)	17.0*** (2.34)
Carpool	—	—	4.65*** (1.23)	4.62*** (1.24)	4.63*** (1.24)	—	—	2.58 (1.91)	2.24 (1.98)	2.17 (2.06)
Travel										
Miles	—	—	—	—	—	—	3.91*** (0.12)	3.86*** (0.13)	3.87*** (0.13)	3.88*** (0.13)
Time/miles	—	-0.23*** (0.03)	—	—	—	—	1.64*** (0.11)	—	—	—
Search										
Average distance searched	—	—	—	0.28*** (0.08)	—	—	—	—	1.72*** (0.03)	—
Farthest distance searched	—	—	—	—	0.35*** (0.04)	—	—	—	—	2.15*** (0.05)
Adj. R²	.18	.24	.44	.51	.51	.22	.45	.54	.59	.60
N	614	614	614	599	599	601	601	601	577	577

Source: Los Angeles Study of Urban Inequality 1994.
Notes: *p < 0.10, **p < 0.05, ***p < 0.01
[a] All models include control variables for age, gender, education (in years), annual earned income, school enrolled status, and main effects for race and residence. Standard errors in parentheses.

muting miles difference between those who live in minority versus nonminority areas. Indeed, mode of transit explains all the remaining significant differences of commuting distance by low-skilled Latinos who live in Latino areas. Moreover, the impact of mode of transportation on distance to work is of the expected direction. Those who travel by car or carpools travel longer distances to work than those who travel by bus, in part because of the greater time costs imposed by riding buses.

Models 4 and 5 add the geographic job search variables into the equation. The effects of average and farthest distance searched on commuting distance are significant and positive, although not nearly 1 to 1. However, while geographic job search explains the remaining significant differences in commuting distance for low-skilled Latinos living in black-Latino areas, it does not do so for low-skilled blacks living there. Indeed, after taking geographic job search into account, low-skilled blacks living in minority areas travel even shorter distances to work, about two miles, than others living in nonminority areas. This result is anticipated, since average and farthest distance searched for work are found to increase commuting distance and since low-skilled blacks living in this area are found to search the greatest distances for work.

The regression results for commuting time presented in models 6 through 10 are qualitatively similar to those for commuting miles. Model 7 indicates that commuting miles and time cost per mile traveled to work increase commuting time and that they explain part of the commuting time difference between those living and not living in minority areas. Moreover, as indicated in model 8, differences in the mode of transportation used to get to work explain about 30 percent of the commuting time differences between low-skilled blacks and Latinos who live in predominantly black-Latino areas and those who live in nonminority areas. Use of public modes of transportation significantly increases commuting times to work.

In models 9 and 10, the geographic job search variables are added to the equation. The effects of average and farthest distance searched on commuting time are positive and significant. Geographic job search explains the remaining significant differences in commuting time for low-skilled Latinos living in black-Latino areas, but does not do so for low-skilled blacks living there. Low-skilled blacks living in black-Latino areas take even less time to get to work than others living in nonminority areas, after taking geographic job search into account.

The results from these commuting distance and time regressions indicate that the reasons low-skilled blacks and Latinos living in minority areas travel less distance and take less time to get to work than others in nonminority areas are very different. For low-skilled Latinos, the greater use of slower modes of transportation to get to work, the higher time cost per mile traveled, and the shorter distances traveled during search explain all of their shorter commuting distances and times. This is not the case for low-skilled blacks living in these areas. While the greater use of public modes of transportation to get to work and the higher time cost per mile traveled helps explain part of their shorter commuting distance and time to work, geographic job search does not. Given that low-skilled blacks, particularly those living in black-Latino areas, travel longer distances during search but have shorter commuting distances and times to work than others, these results imply that low-skilled blacks have difficulty getting jobs in areas near or distant from their residential locations.

Likelihood of Working in Areas Given Search for Work There

One way to analyze the possible difficulties that low-skilled blacks have in getting jobs in distant suburban areas is to examine the likelihood that low-skilled workers are working in these areas, given that they searched for work there. Table 11.8 shows the percent of low-skilled workers who are working in one of the LASUI defined job search areas, given that they searched for work there. The search areas are again categorized by their direction from downtown. Note also that those in the north and east are the most distant from minority, in particular black-Latino, residential areas (see table 11.5).

The results in table 11.8 indicate clear patterns. Low-skilled blacks, and to a much lesser extent Latinos, who search for work in the predominantly white northern and mixed eastern search areas are much less likely than low-skilled whites to find work there.[19] However, this pattern is not true in the remaining search areas, as there are no statistical racial differences in working in these areas conditional on search. These results are consistent with previous research that finds that blacks' hire rates decrease with distance from black populations (Stoll, Holzer, and Ihlanfeldt 2000, Holzer and Ihlanfeldt 1996). Whether low-skilled blacks' access to jobs in white and mixed suburban areas distant from black residential areas is limited because of distance-related problems, skills, perceptions of hostility, or employer discrimination is not clear from the data presented here, though there is evidence to support each of these claims (Holzer 1996; Holzer and Ihlanfeldt 1998; Sjoquist 1997; Turner, Fix, and Struyk 1991).

TABLE 11.8   *Probability of Working in LASUI Search Area Conditional on Searching for Work There, 1994*

	White	Black	Latino
Search areas			
North	31.1	6.9[a]	13.7[a]
San Fernando (w)	30.0	5.0[a]	14.8[a]
Burbank-Glendale (w)	35.9	8.4[a]	11.8[a]
East			
Covina-Industry (m)	9.2	1.0[a]	6.2
South	20.5	15.1	17.6
South Bay (w)	23.7	18.3	14.0[a]
Harbor-Long Beach (m)	16.5	12.4	19.3
West			
Westside (w)	15.7	15.2	9.9
Center City			
Downtown (m)	14.5	12.8	10.1

Source: Los Angeles Study of Urban Inequality 1994.
Notes: (w) indicates predominantly white area. (m) indicates mixed area.
[a]Chi-squared test statistically different than whites at the 5 percent level of significance.

The Problem of Race in Constraining Space

As noted, greater employer discrimination in hiring against blacks in distant suburban areas is one reason low-skilled blacks' access to distant suburban jobs may be limited. If racial discrimination is more intense in more distant suburban areas, low-skilled blacks would have greater difficulty getting jobs there, even if they overcame the additional travel, information, and search costs associated with getting jobs in these distant areas. More intense discrimination in these areas could stem from increased contact with white employers and coworkers, or from increased consumer discrimination on the part of whites (Holzer and Ihlanfeldt 1996).

Table 11.9 provides some evidence on this question by summarizing self-reports of job discrimination by low-skilled blacks and Latinos across employment areas of different racial composition. It also provides information on the percentage of workers' supervisors and coworkers who are white. Because self-reports on discrimination do not prove prima facie employment discrimination, they must be interpreted with caution.[20] However, answers to these questions can shed important light on the treatment of blacks in the workplace. LASUI asked respondents whether during the past year they experienced racial or ethnic discrimi-

TABLE 11.9   Reports of Job Discrimination by Low-Skill Black and Latino Workers in Employment Location, 1994 Percentage

Employment Areas	Black			Latino		
	Experienced Discrimination	Supervisor (Percentage White)	Coworkers (Percentage White)	Experienced Discrimination	Supervisor (Percentage White)	Coworkers (Percentage White)
Predominantly black-Latino	11.8	18.2	10.2	11.1	10.6	1.0
Predominantly Latino	a	a	a	16.7	35.1	6.1
Mixed	13.9	41.2	11.1	21.2	34.8	7.5
Covina-Industry	a	a	a	a	a	a
Downtown	16.2	54.6	11.0	27.6	14.8	8.1
Harbor-Long Beach	11.2	21.5	17.2	29.4	62.0	1.5
Predominantly white	48.1	64.5	55.3	12.7	54.1	29.4
San Fernando	54.6	75.1	63.1	40.0	61.3	51.4
Burbank-Glendale	53.3	78.5	65.2	9.8	58.2	59.1
South Bay	44.7	31.6	13.5	10.2	30.9	5.1
Westside	42.3	74.4	51.1	30.3	43.1	27.7

Source: Los Angeles Study of Urban Inequality 1994.
[a]Fewer than twenty cases in cell.

nation on the job. The responses to these questions are summarized by the racial composition of the respondent's last or current employment location. The definitions of the employment locations are the same as those for residential locations. Note that the predominantly white and mixed employment areas are also the LASUI defined search areas.

Table 11.9 shows that low-skilled blacks report higher incidences of racial discrimination on the job when they work in predominantly white and mixed areas than in the black-Latino area. This is likely due in part to greater contact with white supervisors and, to a lesser extent, coworkers. However, the source of racial discrimination need not be limited to just white supervisors and coworkers. Given the multiracial, multiethnic labor force in Los Angeles, discrimination can originate among and between many different racial-ethnic groups. These same patterns are less true for low-skilled Latinos. Their reports of discrimination on the job are higher in mixed than in minority or white areas. However, they are more likely to work under white supervisors and with white coworkers in white than other areas. Nevertheless, the evidence here suggests that it is difficult to rule out the possibility that low-skilled blacks are more likely to be discriminated against in hiring by employers in more distant white areas. These results are supported by recent research that indicates that employers in more white areas are much more likely to discriminate against blacks in hiring than those near black residential areas (Stoll 1999a, Holzer 1996; Bendick Jr., Jackson, and Reinoso 1994).

Conclusion

In this chapter, I have examined racial differences in commuting time and distance and in geographic job search in Los Angeles to assess the spatial mismatch hypothesis. The analysis reveals that low-skilled blacks, particularly those living in heavily minority areas, travel significantly shorter distances and take less time to get to work than low-skilled whites. These same patterns are generally true when low-skilled Latinos are compared to similar whites, but the differences are not as stark as those between blacks and whites. These patterns are consistent with findings from recent research.

However, as argued here, these results are not necessarily supportive of the spatial mismatch hypothesis. To draw firm conclusions, racial differences in geographic job search patterns must be examined. The analysis of geographic job search patterns reveals that low-skilled blacks, particularly those living in minority areas, search significantly greater distances for work than comparable Latinos and whites. These results imply a behavioral response by low-skilled blacks consistent with living in job-poor areas, or spatial mismatch. Moreover, differences in geographic job search patterns between low-skilled blacks and whites do not explain these racial differences in commute time and distance, even after controlling for differences in mode of transportation and personal characteristics. However, this is not true for low-skilled Latinos, as the statistically significant differences in commute distance and time between low-skill Latinos and whites are entirely explained by differences in geographic job search, mode of transportation, and personal characteristics.

These results for low-skilled blacks indicate that they have difficulty attaining or keeping jobs distant from their residential locations. In fact, the results further indicate that low-skilled blacks are less likely than other groups to work in white and mixed suburban areas, areas distant from minority residential locations, given search for work in these areas. It is not clear from these data whether the access of low-skilled blacks to jobs in white and mixed suburban areas distant from black residential areas is limited because of distance-related problems such as the increased time and money costs of working far from home, skills, or perceptions of hostility.

An equally plausible hypothesis is that increased racial discrimination in hiring against low-skilled blacks in more distant, predominantly white areas limits low-skilled blacks' access to distant, suburban jobs, though they search for work there. The analysis reveals that low-skilled blacks who worked in distant, predominantly white areas of Los Angeles report greater experiences of being discriminated against on the job than their counterparts who worked in mixed or minority areas. These results suggest that racial discrimination in hiring against low-skilled blacks is greater in these more distant, predominantly white areas. This greater discrimination may serve to reduce blacks' spatial, employment sphere, thereby helping explain why low-skilled blacks travel shorter distances to work than other groups. If this is true, space should be viewed not only as a representation of distance, transportation, and job information problems in labor markets, but also as a representation of the continuing problem of race in society.

This research was supported in part by a grant from the Russell Sage Foundation. I thank Abel Valenzuela Jr. and David Grant for their technical assistance, Gerardo Ramirez and Julian Ware for their Geographic Information Systems expertise, and Carlos Torres for his research assistance. Many thanks also to Sheldon Danziger and the Center for the Study of Urban Poverty working group for comments on earlier drafts.

Notes

1. See Ihlanfeldt and Sjoquist (1998), Stoll (1996), Kain (1992), and Holzer (1991) for comprehensive reviews of the spatial mismatch literature.

2. The population data come from the U.S. Census STF3 data files, and the employment data come from the Southern California Association of Governments (SCAG) and are geo-coded to census tracts. The SCAG data record all businesses in the state of California through employment counts furnished by Dun and Bradstreet and American Business Information (ABI). SCAG data may not record all businesses, such as small neighborhood stores or businesses that exhibit rapid turnover. However, unlike other data on employment, for example, the U.S. Census and the U.S. Census County Business Patterns, these data provide employment counts at the census-tract level rather than by large geographical areas such as central cities–suburbs, PUMAs, or counties, thus allowing for geographic detail. SCAG data also record these employment counts by industry for 1990, but not 1980. Therefore, only total employment counts are shown in table 11.1, though industry employment distributions could vary by region and over time.

3. Problems of sample selectivity could bias the results. However, comparisons of the means for variables measuring education, occupation, gender, and age between the full LASUI sample and the selected sample here did not reveal any statistically significant differences. Thus, any possible sample selectivity bias is likely to be minimal.

4. Only a few cases of the unemployed were lost as a result of imposing this condition. Thus, the exclusion of these cases is unlikely to affect the main findings in this chapter.

5. The total number of cases for this five-year search sample was 1,386. Of this sample, 95 cases were eliminated because the employment location of the respondent was unable to be verified. These missing cases, however, were not biased toward any particular racial group or skill level. With the remaining sample, only those cases that had both commuting time and distance data were selected. The resulting sample is n = 1,291.

6. The fifteen defined areas include Antelope Valley, Santa Clarita-Valencia, San Fernando Valley, Agoura-Malibu, Burbank-Glendale, the West Side, Downtown, Pasadena-Monrovia, Covina-Industry, Pomona-Claremont, East Los Angeles, Southeast, Long Beach-Harbor, South Bay, and South Central.

7. Of the fifteen areas, predominantly white areas include Antelope Valley, Santa Clarita-Valencia, San Fernando Valley, Agoura-Mal-

447

ibu, the West Side, South Bay, Burbank-Glendale, and Pasadena-Monrovia. Mixed areas include Long Beach-Harbor, Downtown, Covina-Industry, Southeast, and Pomona. The predominantly Latino area includes East Los Angeles, while the predominantly black-Latino area includes South Central.

8. This chapter follows the conventional research reporting in this area and analyzes travel means. However, means have a disadvantage in that a very small number of very long or short trips could significantly bias the mean upward or downward, respectively. On the other hand, the median can be misleading because it cannot take into account such long or short trips that might, in fact, be the result of spatial mismatch.

9. Over 97 percent of the sample searched in at least one of the LASUI defined job search areas. Those who did not search were not included in the analysis when search variables were analyzed. The elimination of respondents who did not search in at least one search area is not likely to affect the results of the analysis.

10. Time cost per mile traveled is determined by dividing commuting time by commuting distance. This measure indicates the speed with which workers commute 1 mile. Thus, it reflects not only the speed of the transportation mode used to get to work, but also the degree of traffic congestion faced during travel.

11. Low-skill workers are defined as being in service, farm, craft, or labor occupations, while high-skill workers are defined as being in managerial, professional, technical, and sales occupations. Alternatively, following Wachs et al. (1993), high-skill workers are defined as those making over $15 per hour, with low-skill workers defined as those making less than this amount. However, the results of this analysis using this alternative definition of skill based on wages were not qualitatively different from those shown in table 11.3. Thus, only the results based on the occupational definition of skill are reported here.

12. The search areas are categorized by their direction from downtown (center city) Los Angeles.

13. The distance between the search areas and minority residential areas is calculated using Geographic Information Systems (GIS) and is measured as the straight-line distance, in miles, between the centroid of each search area and the centroid of each predominantly minority area.

14. The average physical distance from search area variable is measured as the average distance, in miles, of i from the k search areas, where distance is measured using GIS as the straight-line distance, in miles, from i's residential location (street address) to the centroid of the k spatial search areas. The farthest physical distance

from search area variable is measured as the farthest distance in miles of i from one of the k search areas.

15. Models were also estimated to examine factors related to the time cost per mile traveled to work, that is, time/miles. About 50 percent of the racial differences in time cost per mile traveled is explained by mode of transportation. This is because low-skill blacks and Latinos are much more likely than low-skill whites to use slower public transit modes. However, significant racial differences in time cost per mile traveled still remain, especially for those blacks and Latinos who live in the heavily minority areas, suggesting that traffic congestion in central-city areas also explains these race differences in time costs per mile traveled.

16. To minimize measurement bias, it is assumed in these models that the measures of search distance are constant over time. Geographic search could have occurred anytime within five years prior to the survey, while the commuting time and distance variables could be measured for jobs that respondents had anytime during this five-year period. As a check for this assumption, the average and farthest distance during search was measured for a more recent search sample (within the last year). Comparisons of the average and farthest distance searched between the five- and one-year search samples revealed no statistically significant differences.

17. Variables for occupation and industry were also experimented with and included in other models. However, these variables were inconsistently significant and did not change the basic results shown here. Thus, they are not included in the models reported in table 11.7.

18. Complete results are available upon request.

19. Regression analysis was conducted to control for other factors that might affect the results shown in this section. A series of logit models were estimated to predict the probability of working in a particular LASUI defined search area as a function of searching for work in that area, controlling for residence, race, and a vector of personal, human capital, and family background control variables. The results of these logit equations confirmed the basic results shown in table 11.8; low-skill whites are much more likely to work in distant, predominantly white search areas than are comparable blacks or Latinos, given that each group searched for work there.

20. Because self-reports of discrimination are very subjective, they can be criticized for not recording actual incidences of job discrimination. Chapter 15 explores the limits of interpreting self-reported job discrimination experiences and the contexts in which this discrimination is likely to be reported. However, these responses can be

taken as a minimum indicator of the extent of job discrimination (see Bobo 1992).

References

Alexis, Marcus, and Nancy DiTomaso. 1983. "Transportation, Race, and Employment: In Pursuit of the Elusive Triad." *Journal of Urban Affairs* 5(2): 81–94.

Bendick, Marc, Jr., Charles W. Jackson, and Victor A. Reinoso. 1994. "Measuring Employment Discrimination Through Controlled Experiments." *Review of Black Political Economy* 23(1) (Summer): 25–48.

Bobo, Larry D. 1992. "Prejudice and Alternative Dispute Resolution." *Studies in Law, Politics, and Society* 12: 147–76.

Cooke, Thomas J., and J. Matthew Shumway. 1991. "Developing the Spatial Mismatch Hypothesis: Problems of Accessibility to Employment for Low-Wage Central City Labor." *Urban Geography* 12(4): 310–23.

Ellwood, David. 1986. "The Spatial Mismatch Hypothesis: Are There Teenage Jobs Missing in the Ghetto?" In *The Black Youth Employment Crises*, edited by Richard Freeman and Harry Holzer. Chicago: University of Chicago Press.

Galster, George. 1991. "Black Suburbanization: Has It Changed the Relative Location of the Races?" *Urban Affairs Quarterly* 26: 621–28.

Hanson, Susan, and Geraldine Pratt. 1991. "Job Search and the Occupational Segregation of Women." *Annals of the Association of American Geographers* 81: 229–53.

Harrison, Bennett. 1974. "The Intrametropolitan Distribution of Minority Economic Welfare." *Journal of Regional Science* 12: 23–43.

Heilbrun, James. 1987. *Urban Economics and Public Policy*. New York: St. Martin's Press.

Holzer, Harry J. 1991. "The Spatial Mismatch Hypothesis: What Has the Evidence Shown?" *Urban Studies* 28(1): 105–22.

———. 1996. *What Employers Want: Job Prospects for Less-Educated Workers*. New York: Russell Sage.

Holzer, Harry J., and Keith R. Ihlanfeldt. 1996. "Spatial Factors and the Employment of Blacks at the Firm Level." *New England Economic Review* (May/June): 65–86.

———. 1998. "Customer Discrimination and Employment Outcomes for Minority Workers," *Quarterly Journal of Economics*, v113(n3): 835–67.

Holzer, Harry J., Keith R. Ihlanfeldt, and David L. Sjoquist. 1994. "Work, Search, and Travel Among White and Black Youth." *Journal of Urban Economics* 35: 320–45.

Ihlanfeldt, Keith R. 1993. "Intra-Urban Job Accessibility and Hispanic Youth Employment Rates." *Journal of Urban Economics* 33: 254–71.

Ihlanfeldt, Keith R., and David L. Sjoquist. 1990. "The Effect of Residential Location on the Probability of Black and White Teenagers Having a Job." *Review of Regional Studies* 20(1): 10–20.

———. 1991. "The Effect of Job Access on Black and White Youth Employment: A Cross-Section Analysis." *Urban Studies* 28: 255–65.

———. 1998. "The Spatial Mismatch Hypothesis: A Review of Recent Studies and Their Implications for Welfare Reform." *Housing Policy Debate* 9(4): 849–92.

Kain, John F. 1968. "Housing Segregation, Negro Employment and Metropolitan Decentralization." *Quarterly Journal of Economics* 82: 175–97.

———. 1985. "Black Suburbanization in the Eighties: A New Beginning or a False Hope?" In *American Domestic Priorities: An Economic Appraisal*, edited by John M. Quigley and Daniel L. Rubinfeld. University of California Press.

———. 1992. "The Spatial Mismatch Hypothesis: Three Decades Later." *Housing Policy Debate* 3(2): 371–460.

Kasarda, John. 1989. "Urban Industrial Transition and the Underclass." *Annals of the American Academy of Political and Social Science* 501: 26–47.

Kirschenman, Joleen, and Kathryn M. Neckerman. 1991. " 'We'd Love to Hire Them, But . . . ': The Meaning of Race for Employers." In *The Urban Underclass*, edited by Christopher Jencks and Paul E. Peterson. Washington, D.C.: Brookings Institution.

Leonard, Jonathan S. 1987. "The Interaction of Residential Segregation and Employment Discrimination." *Journal of Urban Economics* 21: 323–46.

Massey, Douglas, and Nancy A. Denton. 1988. "Suburbanization and Segregation in U.S. Metropolitan Areas." *American Journal of Sociology* 94(3): 592–626.

———. 1993. *American Apartheid: Segregation and the Making of the Underclass*. Cambridge, Mass.: Harvard University Press.

McLafferty, Sara, and Valerie Preston. 1992. "Spatial Mismatch and Labor Market Segmentation for African-American and Latina Women." *Economic Geography* 68(4): 406–31.

Nelson, K. 1986. "Female Labor Force Supply Characteristics and the Suburbanization of Low-Wage Office Work." In *Production, Work, and Territory*, edited by Allan J. Scott and Michael Storper. London: Allen and Unwin.

Price, Richard, and Edwin S. Mills. 1985. "Race and Residence in Earnings Determination." *Journal of Urban Economics* 17: 1–18.

Raphael, Steve. 1998. "Inter- and Intra-Ethnic Comparisons of the Central City–Suburban Youth Employment Differential: Evidence from the Oakland Metropolitan Area." *Industrial and Labor Relations Review* 51: 505–25.

Sjoquist, David. 1997. "Spatial Mismatch and Social Acceptability." Working Paper. Policy Research Center, Georgia State University.

Soja, Ed, Rebecca Morales, and Goetz Wolff. 1983. "Urban Restructuring: An Analysis of Social and Spatial Change in Los Angeles." *Economic Geography* 58: 221–35.

Stoll, Michael A. 1996. "Distance or Discrimination? The Convergence of Space and Race in Understanding Racial Differences in Employment." *Sage Race Relations* 21: 3–25.

———. 1999a. "Spatial Mismatch, Discrimination and Male Youth Employment in the Washington, D.C., Area: Implications for Residential Mobility Programs." *Journal of Policy Analysis and Management* 18: 77–98.

———. 1999b. "Spatial Job Search, Spatial Mismatch and the Employment and Wages of Racial and Ethnic Groups in Los Angeles." *Journal of Urban Economics* 46: 129–55.

Stoll, Michael A., Harry J. Holzer, and Keith R. Ihlanfeldt. 2000. "Within Cities and Suburbs: Racial Residential Concentration and the Distribution of Employment Opportunities Across Sub-Metropolitan Areas." *Journal of Policy Analysis and Management* 19(2).

Taylor, Brian D., and Paul Ong. 1995. "Spatial Mismatch or Automobile Mismatch? An Examination of Race, Residence and Commuting in U.S. Metropolitan Areas." *Urban Studies* 32(9): 1453–73.

Turner, Margery Austin, Michael Fix, and Raymond J. Struyk. 1991. *Opportunities Denied, Opportunities Diminished: Racial Discrimination in Hiring*. Washington, D.C.: Urban Institute Press.

U.S. Department of Labor. U.S. Bureau of Labor Statistics. 1999. *Employment and Earnings*. Washington: U.S. Government Printing Office (March).

U.S. Department of Housing and Urban Development. 1997. *The State of Cities*. Washington: U.S. Department of Housing and Urban Development.

Vrooman, John, and Stuart Greenfield. 1980. "Are Blacks Making It in the Suburbs? Some New Evidence on Intrametropolitan Spatial Segmentation." *Journal of Urban Economics* 7: 155–67.

Wachs, Martin, Brian D. Taylor, Ned Levine, and Paul Ong. 1993. "The Changing Commute: A Case-Study of the Jobs-Housing Relationship over Time." *Urban Studies* 30(10): 1711–29.

Waldinger, Roger. 1993. "The Ethnic Enclave Debate Revisited." *International Journal of Urban and Regional Research* 3: 444–52.

Wilson, William J. 1996. *When Work Disappears: The World of the New Urban Poor*. New York: Knopf.

Yinger, John. 1995. *Closed Doors, Opportunities Lost: The Continuing Costs of Housing Discrimination*. New York: Russell Sage.

Zubrinsky, C., and L. Bobo. 1996. "Prismatic Metropolis: Race and Residential Segregation in the City of Los Angeles." *Social Science Research* 25: 335–75.

12

SPATIAL MISMATCH OR MORE OF A MISHMASH? MULTIPLE JEOPARDY AND THE JOURNEY TO WORK

Julie E. Press

THE JOURNEY to work is a crucial factor in the operation of urban labor markets. Time spent commuting is the tie that binds residential location, job location, and transportation. This relationship is a dynamic system that structures and shapes the character of labor pools and job pools, determining many important social and economic outcomes for metropolitan workers and firms. Analyses of commuting emerging from the early neoclassical economic perspective (for example, Alonso 1964) assume that workers freely choose their commute between home and work, with higher wages justifying longer commute times. Social scientists now understand that many factors differentially restrict the residential location and employment characteristics of many groups of urban workers, and that these restrictions make understanding the journey to work much more complex than earlier thought. Consequential elements of inequality in urban labor markets that are manifest in the commute time to work include racial residential segregation, employer preferences for certain gender and racial-ethnic groups, gender relations in families, class factors like poverty and job skills, macroeconomic phenomena like deindustrialization and globalizing markets, and state policy like welfare reform, as well as many other factors. The friction of time and distance is intimately related to the opportunity and reward structure for women and men in society. But how is commute time related to these structures for different social groups?

Most studies of urban inequality and the journey to work have focused either on the effects of race or on the effects of gender. It is well established, for example, that women as a group work closer to home and commute a shorter time than do men in modern industrial cities. Several factors are thought to explain this phenomenon: earnings/income, labor market structure, the domestic division of labor, transportation/mobility, and socio-spatial dimensions such as employer location. However, while these gender studies do differentiate among women based on class, household, and other characteristics, they tend to neglect racial-ethnic factors and have typically analyzed whites.

There is also a large body of research in the field of urban inequality on the spatial mismatch between suburbanized jobs and impoverished urban black communities. But gender relations have been largely absent from that debate, which focuses on suburban employment practices and job search conditions for low-skilled black men. Spatial mismatch studies typically include only men, or else add in women without theorizing gender relations in society per se. The intersections of gender, race, and class relations are rarely analyzed jointly in this context.

This neglect implies that we do not understand well the journey to work for women of color, who may experience multiple jeopardy in trying to negotiate urban labor markets. Are commuting and earnings for black women (or Latinas, or Asian women, and so on) better explained by our theories about black men or our theories about white women? Or is there a unique set of social relations that describes black women's situation vis-à-vis the journey to work? These questions are at the core of this chapter.

The scarcity of research about the work-home relationship for African American, Latina, and Asian women is problematic because the earnings and employment situation of black and Latina women, in particular, is disproportionately important for their families' well-being, relative to white women. White women are less likely to be single mothers, their income is a lower percentage of household income, on average, and the near parity we once saw between white and black women's earnings has recently given way to higher relative earnings for white women heading families (Browne 1997). Moreover, economic restructuring since the 1970s has produced job growth in the service sector and in contingent work jobs that is disproportionately occupied by low-skilled women of color. The gender and racial division of labor are part and parcel of the industrial restructuring process that continues to affect, even during these good economic times, the opportunity structure for all urban workers, not just whites or the middle class. As America moves forward with the 1996 welfare reform policy, Temporary Assistance for Needy Families (TANF), more poor mothers are thrust into urban labor markets, whether they like it or not and whether or not they have skills, transportation, or the resources to relocate to areas with better job opportunities. These mothers are disproportionately likely to be black and Latina, and their ability to support financially and otherwise care for families without husbands is paramount. For all these reasons, the necessity of understanding the intersections of gender, race, and class relations in the context of spatial location and the journey to work is increasingly important. Longer commute times and, even more important, their association with wages marks a crucial piece of the urban labor markets and inequality puzzle.

In this chapter I invoke the theory of multiple jeopardy to analyze the journey to work for women of color, asking whether race or gender is more salient or whether a combination of race, gender, and class act in concert to describe commute time and earnings in the new urban landscape of Los Angeles. This analysis will enrich the spatial mismatch debate by highlighting the employment situation of women, and particularly women of color. It will also contribute to this debate by focusing on Los Angeles, a metropolis largely unexplored in this debate thus far.

Los Angeles has a substantively different urban geography and multiethnic texture than the Rustbelt cities usually analyzed in research about the work-home relationship. For example, the urban-suburban dichotomy is much less pronounced in Los Angeles, where technopoles, mini-downtowns, commercial services, industrial production, and residential communities are strewn across the megalopolis of the five-county Los Angeles region stretching roughly 150 × 150 miles.[1] The financial center is in a different location from the core of Hollywood's entertainment industry; Los Angeles really has no center to speak of. Further, public transportation is much less convenient in Los Angeles than in other major cities. There is no convenient subway system to date, and most public transportation riders must rely on slow-moving buses that travel in bustling traffic over surface streets. Moreover, since Los Angeles is so spread out spatially, a bus trip across town could easily take over two hours. On the other hand, since the sprawling Los Angeles region was built up during the twentieth century to accommodate the automobile, freeways and freeway access ramps are plentiful, well-marked, and fairly quick during nonpeak hours. It is common wisdom among car-driving Angelenos that "you can get anywhere in Los Angeles in twenty minutes." Therefore, in Los Angeles, far more than most other cities in the world, access to a car and the ability to get where one needs to go become important aspects of social inequality.

Los Angeles has large Asian and Latino populations, both native and immigrant, so that it is not a black-white racial landscape. In fact, Los Angeles is the most ethnically diverse city in the world; some estimates put the number of languages spoken in Los Angeles at 133. One thing that Los Angeles does have in common with other American cities is a high level of racial residential segregation, especially between whites and nonwhites (discussed in depth in other chapters in this volume). Thus, in many ways, Los Angeles is a new and unique location in which to analyze multiple jeopardy and the journey to work.

This chapter applies the theory of multiple jeopardy to the LASUI data, first, to analyze how established findings about gender differences in commute time fare for women of color in Los Angeles County. What factors determine the journey to work for women and men who are white, black, Asian, and Latino? Second, I explore the relationship between commute time and earnings. How do race relations and gender relations act together in local housing and labor markets to produce multiple jeopardy effects in the relationship between commute time and earnings? Are longer commute times good or bad for wages, or does it depend on who is doing the commuting? I find that for more marginalized workers, including low-skilled women and African Americans of both sexes, longer commute times are actually associated with *lower* wages, even after controlling for bus usage. This finding is counter to neoclassical economic predictions and indicates the paucity of job opportunities for African Americans and low-skilled women.

Multiple Jeopardy and the Journey to Work

The concept of "multiple jeopardy" (King 1988) or "triple oppression" refers to the "interplay among class, race, and gender, whose cumulative effects place women of color in a subordinate social and economic position relative to men of color and the majority White population" (Segura 1990, 48). According to Denise Segura, no single element of the three is sufficient to explain the pervasiveness of the social inequality of women of color.[2] Their inferior status, she says, is reproduced in the home and in all other social arenas. I invoke this notion here to argue that it is theoretically insufficient to study *either* gender and work trips *or* race and work trips. Rather, men and women, blacks and whites, and others commuting to work are simultaneously embedded in gender, race, and class relations in society; where people live and what jobs they have are both structured by these relations. If we collapse these categories, we are likely to miss salient distinctions *among* women or men, blacks, whites, Asians, or Latinos.

Recent studies find consistently that women in modern industrial cities have a shorter average journey to work than men do (Fagnani 1983; Hanson and Johnston 1985; Hanson and Pratt 1995; Hecht 1974; Howe and O'Connor 1982; Madden 1981). However, these findings mask large differences among women of different racial-ethnic groups. The theory of multiple jeopardy predicts that negative gender effects of lower wages and occupational segregation (for example), together with negative racial effects of housing segregation and employment discrimination (for example), will lead women of color to experience more severe effects of and on the journey to work than white women and men of color. When analysts take account of both race and gender, they find that there are indeed strong race effects that are analytically distinct from the gender effects (Johnston-Anumonwo 1992, 1995a, 1995b; McLafferty and Preston 1991, 1992). Yet, despite this evidence, research on gender and the spatial aspects of employment continues to focus on whites. Susan Hanson and Geraldine Pratt (1995, 97), for example, in their otherwise thorough analysis, acknowledge that "we now know that this frequently documented gender difference [in work-trip length] holds only for Whites," but they nonetheless select a sample of women for their study that is 90 percent white.

The literature on gender and the journey to work offers five broad hypotheses to explain the gender gap in commute time: labor market segmentation and occupational gender segregation, the gendered division of labor in households, gender differences in mobility, the spatial distribution of jobs and residences, and the lower earnings associated with female-typed occupations. These hypotheses are detailed in this chapter, including connected racial-ethnic hypotheses from the literature where appropriate.

Labor Market Structure

Labor market structures such as occupational gender segregation, work-status differences, and ethnic economies have been associated with journey-to-work time. First, workers in female-dominated occupations commute a shorter time than other women and men (Hanson and Johnston 1985; Hanson and Pratt 1995, 1991, 1988; Singell and Lillydahl 1986). This results in a gender gap because certain labor market sectors, such as clerical, sales, and services, are more localized geographically (Cubukgil and Miller 1982) and because women are segregated in these occupations. Hanson and Pratt (1991) argue that women in female-dominated occupations prefer to be closer to home and therefore seek employment nearby. A related hypothesis suggests that employment status affects commute. Because women are more likely to work part-time, and because part-time work is associated with shorter commutes, women will have shorter commutes.

These theories are not supported by the data in Sara McLafferty's and Valerie Preston's (1991) comparison of blacks, whites, and Hispanics in New York. They found that not only do the usually large gender differences documented for whites disappear for blacks and Hispanics, but both men and women of these two groups commute significantly longer than whites, even when examining service-sector workers per se. In their 1992 paper, they go on to argue that minority women have less access to localized labor markets, but better spatial access than minority men (McLafferty and Preston 1992).

Another facet of labor market segmentation that may explain the relationship of work location to residential location is employment in the ethnic economy. Ethnic economies can be defined as production relations in which the owner or controller of a firm has the same ethnicity as the employees (see, for example, Portes and Bach 1985; Portes and Jensen 1992). Immigrant communities tend to cluster spatially into "enclaves" of workers, who, by virtue of their cultural isolation from the preexisting society, have fewer resources with which to obtain work in the primary or secondary labor market sectors.[3] They may also gain social mobility benefits from participating in a sector from which others are excluded. Therefore, ethnic economies provide a link to employment for these types of immigrant workers.

Ethnic economies may be significant in the current analysis because workers and employers who participate in the ethnic economy are more likely to live relatively close to their place of employment. This is particularly true for the Asian sample, who are largely foreign-born and have the highest rates of membership in the ethnic economy, and for the Latinos. Tarry Hum used the LASUI data to estimate that 57 percent of Chinese and 73 percent of Koreans in Los Angeles participate in the ethnic economy as either workers or employers (Hum, this volume). Based on distance data from LASUI, she also found that immigrant workers in the ethnic economy tend to work near where they live (Hum, this volume). Since Hum's analysis of commuting distance and ethnic economy participation is not disaggregated by gender, and analyzes distance rather than time, the relationship between gender, the ethnic economy, and commuting behavior is still a question that requires further research. These findings do, however, indicate that Asians and Latinos in Los Angeles may commute short distances as a result of membership in the ethnic economy located in their communities.

Socio-Spatial Relations

A second hypothesis is the spatial dimension of home-to-work trips. First, employers may intentionally locate near desirable workers or services. According to Nelson (1986), some clerical offices locate their firms in the suburbs in order to take advantage of the captive labor pool of suburbanized women. This close proximity may help explain women's shorter commute. If firms prefer captive (presumably white) female labor in the suburbs, however, then by definition they are avoiding less desirable labor elsewhere. A recent multivariate study using employer interview data from the Multi-City Study of Urban Inequality finds that employers in Los Angeles exhibit a distaste for locating in neighborhoods with growing African American populations, even when conditioning on many firm characteristics (Iceland and Harris 1998).

Second, the spatial mismatch hypothesis, first proposed by John Kain in 1968, suggests that the suburbanization of white households and many businesses during the post–World War II period left African Americans in the inner cities spatially and socially isolated from employment opportunities in the suburbs. Since racial residential segregation persists in American cities, black migration to white neighborhoods has been difficult, if not impossible (Massey and Denton 1993). Therefore, commuting and search costs are more expensive for urban blacks than for suburbanites; a mismatch between black workers in urban cores and job opportunities in the suburban periphery results (Ellwood 1986; Wilson 1987).

However, with few exceptions the spatial mismatch is primarily an argument about high unemployment rates among minority men. McLafferty and Preston (1992, 1997) tested the spatial mismatch hypothesis for women in New York and found that while African American and Latina women have poorer spatial access to jobs than do white women, they have better spatial access than minority men. They also found that the mismatch is worst for African American women, who tend to use public transportation. But although Latinas commute shorter distances, they work locally for lower pay, highlighting the lack of access to *well-paying* jobs as their main problem. Overall, however, the evidence for a spatial mismatch among women is sparser and even more ambiguous than it is for men.

The Gendered Division of Household Labor

The third hypothesis suggests that the gender gap in the journey to work is explained by the gendered division of household labor. Evidence for this theory is mixed. Women with more household responsibility have been found to work closer to home (Ericksen 1977; Madden 1981; Madden and White 1980; Fagnani 1983; Guest and Cluett 1976). However, commute time measures are also invariant to class and family structure. According to Hanson and Pratt, "the fundamental gender difference in travel time to work is robust across various household configurations and age cohorts and across most social class groups" (1995, 100). On the other hand, in the same study, when Hanson and Pratt specifically asked

women why they work close to home, the women cited household responsibility (table 3).

African American and Latina women are less likely than white
women to be affected by household labor requirements because they
have had historically higher levels of labor force participation, typically
in low-wage sectors, and regardless of family structure (Brewer 1988).
Since their income has been a vitally important contribution to the family's resources, they do not have the same freedom to accommodate
their domestic duties at the expense of paid work. The quality of jobs is
therefore of primary importance for women of color, especially for working-class families.

Transportation or Mobility

Transportation mode is the fourth explanation for women's shorter commute (Giuliano 1979; Hanson and Johnston 1985). Women are more
likely to use public transportation or to walk than men, who tend to
drive or ride in a car. Since women have reduced access to cars, they are
limited in their job search and employment location, which results in
their shorter commuting distances. However, public transportation, particularly buses that rely on surface streets, may take longer than a car
to go the same distance, which is probably not true for rapid-transit
subways.[4]

When racial differences are also accounted for, Ipipo Johnston-
Anumonwo (1995a) finds that poor access to automobiles among blacks
causes them to spend longer in the journey to work and that there is no
gender gap in commuting for African Americans. Black, Latina, and
Asian women in Los Angeles are much more likely than white women
to travel to work by bus. In fact, white women in Los Angeles, unlike
other, less car-intensive cities, have a very high rate of car commuting
(91 percent). The transportation theory of women's commute predicts
that white women commute less time than white men and men of
color, and similarly that women of color commute longer than white
women and men of color.

Earnings and Social Class

Women's jobs are not only segregated from men's, but they are concentrated in lower status, lower authority occupations, often in the secondary labor market segment that has lower associated commute times and
significantly lower pay (Bergmann 1996; Bielby and Baron 1984; Fagnani
1983; Gordon, Kumar, and Richardson 1989; Reskin and Hartmann
1986; Wheeler 1967, 1969). Since occupational gender segregation limits
women's job opportunities so strongly to lower-paid work with little
room for advancement, race differences in earnings among women are

much less pronounced than among men. However, the simultaneous effects of racial segregation in occupations and hiring queues result in an intricate structure in which white women are preferred to women of color. Therefore, multiple jeopardy may affect black and Latina women by lowering their wages relative to white women.

There is also a complex association among earnings, gender, and commute time. First, women's lower earning levels make longer work-trip lengths less worthwhile (Madden 1981). In a study of the extra income women obtain for extra commute distance, Brent Rutherford and Gerda Wekerle (1988) found that women earned only one-third of what men did for the same additional commute. However, there is an issue of endogeneity between job location and its associated wage rate, and residential location. That is, it is unclear which comes first—the selection of housing or the selection of a job—commute being literally the difference between the two. This issue is itself gendered. Married households are very unlikely to change location for the sake of a wife's job. While an increase in husband's income induces families to relocate, wives tend to be "trapped" in space, tethered to home, and constrained to find a job in the immediate area, often at a lower wage than they would have otherwise received (Hanson and Pratt 1995). Thus, wives' shorter commute is associated with lower earnings. This effect is racialized for women of color, since their families are constrained residentially by housing segregation, particularly for blacks, that separates them from jobs. Therefore, women of color may experience multiple jeopardy by being tethered to husbands who are themselves residentially constrained.

Second, there is a nonlinear relationship between earnings and commute that is mediated by social class. If low-income households of racial minorities are located farther from jobs, households with higher incomes also tend to locate farther from employment in low-density residential neighborhoods (McLafferty and Preston 1992). In Los Angeles, this means that professional women who work in the financial center downtown or in Hollywood's studios in the San Fernando Valley can afford to buy expensive homes on Malibu Beach and have the option to voluntarily commute ninety minutes into the city every day. Latinas living in East Los Angeles, on the other hand, make the same ninety-minute (or more) commute by bus to clean houses and mind children on the West Side. These long commutes are associated with high earnings and low earnings, respectively. Thus, unless we analyze commute time taking account of social class, the answer to whether long commutes are good or bad is not obvious.

Studies of gender and the journey to work often use income as an explanatory variable in commute equations. This method is more sensible for men, who have more control than women over their residential location. That is, for men, the causal arrow from job (income) selection to commute is stronger. But for women, I suggest that there is a lower degree of simultaneity. When seeking employment, each potential job is characterized by a number of attributes, such as the wage rate and the associated commute time that women are constrained to take as given. Therefore, in the context of the other constraints on women that lead them to have shorter commutes than men (household responsibilities, transportation, localized labor markets, and so on), I argue that earnings are an outcome rather than a precursor to the journey to work. In qualitative interviews where women discussed this question, Hanson and Pratt (1995) found them to report that "their incomes are lower because their work trips are shorter," rather than the other way around. The question, then, is how much lower are their earnings?

To answer this question, I estimate earnings in a second analysis, separate from the determinants of commute time, in which earnings are a function of commute time. I also account for the nonlinear relationship of commute time to earnings by interacting commute with social class, operationalized as "skill."

Research Strategy

The journey to work is analyzed first by using ordinary least squares regression to estimate commute time for men and women and for four racial-ethnic groups. Second, commute time and its interaction with skill level are regressed on the natural log of earnings to assess the costs associated with commute time, conditioning on race, gender, and social class. In these equations, earnings are the dependent variable, and the main variable of interest is the interaction between skill level–class and commute time as it affects earnings. There are ten explanatory variables in the first stage of the analysis: gender, race, percent female in the occupation, skill level or class, work status, marital status, majority black census tract (as a measure of residential segregation), public transportation usage, residential location, and participation in an ethnic economic sector. The second stage of the analysis uses a subset of these factors.

The LASUI data subset used in this analysis is limited to employed respondents with a valid commute time. There are 2,194 cases unweighted, and 2,446 cases weighted, or about 55 percent of the total LASUI sample.

Measuring the Journey to Work

The survey question in LASUI about commuting asks: "How much time do you usually spend traveling to work each (one) way?" Respondents who reported working at home or living at their workplace were coded as spending zero commuting minutes (the minimum possible).

The maximum commute time for the sample and for each race by sex group was two hours each way. The mean commute time for the sample was 24.6 minutes one way each day, with a standard deviation of twenty minutes. The median commute was only twenty minutes. While these figures may seem short to those unfamiliar with Los Angeles, this average is consistent with CPS results as well as the conventional wisdom among Angelenos that "you can get anywhere in Los Angeles in twenty minutes." Los Angeles's convenient freeway system and wide, modern boulevards, and the fact that employment is decentralized and interspersed throughout residential spaces, means that the traditional suburban-to-downtown commute is much less common in the Los Angeles area than in older American cities that expanded from a core. For those who ride in cars, average commutes are fairly short.

Studies of the journey to work vary in whether they analyze distance or time to measure the outcome. Distance is a useful measure because it is fixed from day to day. However, I argue that commuting time is a much better measure of the typical "costs" incurred to workers from time spent on their journey, even though it varies with traffic, weather, and the like. For example, two workers commuting from and to the same location but using different transportation modes would have the same commute distance but very different commute time distributions. To understand the real impact on families of the journey to work, distance is not a sensible measure. There is also a practical reason for using commute time in this study; the data on distance in LASUI were calculated based on respondents who volunteered their employers' address. In that portion of the survey, respondents were asked first whether they would allow the surveyors to contact and interview their employer about a range of issues. If the household respondent agreed, information was gathered about the employer location. Consequently, only 52 percent of the respondents for whom a commute time was available gave an associated employer location, and therefore a computed spatial distance from work.[5] Commute time, on the other hand, was obtained directly from respondents' self-reports of time spent in the journey to work. Only 1 percent of eligible cases were missing this piece of information. Results from studies using time are consistent with those using distance in revealing that women's commute is shorter than men's, on average.

Discussion

A Profile of Workers in Los Angeles

Table 12.1 describes the sample by race and gender. Gender was coded 1 for male (54 percent) and 0 for female (46 percent). Women's lower rates

TABLE 12.1 Description of Sample by Gender and Race-Ethnicity

	Total	Women	Men	White	Black	Asian	Latino
Mean percentage female in occupation	47.3	66.0	31.6	47.7	54.3	49.1	44.7
(standard deviation)	(29.2)	(24.6)	(22.9)	(27.7)	(28.6)	(24.0)	(31.4)
Full-time worker (≥ thirty-five hours)	81.2	73.4	87.7	81.1	78.0	82.8	81.9
High skill (> high school education)	58.0	59.5	56.8	77.5	67.5	72.4	31.6
Spouse or partner present	61.3	56.8	65.0	61.2	42.5	74.6	64.1
Transportation to work							
Own car	78.2	78.4	78.1	83.0	81.6	81.8	71.5
Carpool	6.2	5.3	6.9	5.0	4.7	5.2	8.0
Public transportation	6.0	7.8	4.6	2.7	5.8	2.7	10.4
Other	9.6	8.5	10.4	9.4	7.8	10.3	10.1
Majority-black census tract	7.1	9.0	5.4	0.5	46.9	0.3	4.5
Asian ethnic economy	2.3	2.7	2.0	0	0	32.3	0
Latino ethnic economy	12.8	9.9	15.2	0	0	0	32.6
Percentage of sample	100.0	45.7	54.3	42.8	10.8	7.1	39.3
Weighted n	2446	1118	1328	1046	265	174	961
Unweighted n[a]	2194	1050	1144	502	500	601	591

	White Men	White Women	Black Men	Black Women	Asian Men	Asian Women	Latino Men	Latina Women
Mean percentage female in occupation	32.5	64.5	38.4	67.1	36.1	63.1	28.6	68.0
(standard deviation)	(20.9)	(24.3)	(24.3)	(25.3)	(18.9)	(20.9)	(24.5)	(25.2)
Full-time worker (≥ thirty-five hours)	90.1	71.2	78.6	77.4	90.9	74.0	86.8	74.7
High skill (> high school education)	83.6	70.8	65.0	69.4	69.7	75.2	27.1	38.1
Spouse or partner present	60.7	61.7	49.0	37.2	78.1	70.8	70.4	54.9
Transportation to work								
Own car	75.9	90.9	86.9	77.4	87.2	76.1	77.0	63.5
Carpool	8.0	1.7	3.9	5.3	2.3	8.4	7.3	9.1
Public transportation	3.3	1.9	3.7	7.5	0.9	4.5	6.5	16.0
Other transportation	12.8	5.5	5.5	9.7	9.7	11.0	9.2	11.3
Majority-black census tract	0.5	0.5	37.0	54.8	0.3	0.3	4.5	4.5
Asian ethnic economy	0	0	0	0	29.5	35.4	0	0
Latino ethnic economy	0	0	0	0	0	0	35.5	28.4
Percentage of sample	22.5	20.2	4.8	6.0	3.7	3.4	23.3	16.0
Weighted n	551	495	118	147	90	84	569	392
Unweighted n[a]	264	238	184	316	333	268	363	228

Source: Los Angeles Study of Urban Inequality 1994.
[a] Percentages are based on weighted data.

of labor force participation explain why this sample of workers has fewer women then men. Race is operationalized as white, black, Asian, or Latino. Recall from earlier discussions that Asians and Asian Americans in the LASUI survey were limited to people of Chinese, Japanese, and Korean descent. Latinos included those of Hispanic descent who also said that others perceive them as Latino. Respondents of Hispanic origin who reported being perceived by others as black, white, or Asian were coded as such in order to maintain a measure of race that portrays the way an individual is treated by the society at large. (For ease of exposition, I use *race* and *ethnicity* interchangeably.)

As a measure of occupational gender segregation, the percent female in the respondent's occupation was calculated by computing the percent of female workers for every three-digit occupation code in the 1990 Public Use Microdata Sample (PUMS) (U.S. Bureau of the Census 1990) for Los Angeles County. These percentages were then ascribed to each respondent according to his or her occupation. LASUI uses the same three-digit codes as the Census Bureau.[6] The average woman works in an occupation that is two-thirds female, while the average man works in an occupation that is two-thirds male. Breaking the sample down by race does not alter this result significantly.

Employment status is operationalized as a dummy variable for full-time work. Full-time work is coded 1 and is defined as thirty-five hours or more at the main job, while part-time work is coded as 0. In the earnings equations, work hours are measured as a continuous variable to allow for the fact that many workers are paid hourly wages. Most respondents in the sample work full-time (81 percent). But, as expected, there is a gender gap, with over one-quarter of women working part-time while only about 12 percent of men work part-time. For whites, Asians, and Latinos, this pattern is very similar. Black men, however, have a much lower rate of full-time work than other groups of men, with a rate of 79 percent compared with 90 percent for white men. For blacks, there is no significant gender difference in full-time work. The gender gap in work status is substantially smaller in LASUI than in Hanson's and Pratt's (1995) study of commuting in Worcester, Massachusetts. They found that 35.7 percent of women and less than 4 percent of men worked part-time, and that this fact accounted for a substantial portion of the gender gap in commuting.

Social class is defined using years of education. A dummy variable measuring "high skill" level is coded 1 for respondents with more than a high school degree (58 percent of respondents). Those with a high school degree or less were coded as 0 and referred to as "low skill." Education levels are distributed very unevenly among racial groups. Fewer than one-third of Latinos in the sample have more than a high school education, compared with two-thirds to three-fourths of blacks, Asians, and whites.

Marital status is accounted for with a dummy variable coded 1 for those with a spouse or partner present in the household and 0 otherwise. Overall about 61 percent of workers have a spouse or partner at home. Among women, the rate is 57 percent and among men it is 65 percent. There are also significant differences in marital status among races. African Americans have a low rate of coupling (42.5 percent), while Asians are much more likely to live with a spouse or partner (75 percent).

Transportation to work is measured with a dummy variable coded 1 for respondents who reported getting to work on public transportation (6 percent). In Los Angeles, this usually means travel by bus, since Los Angeles does not yet have a popular subway or commuter train system like other major cities. (I use the terms "bus" and "public transportation" interchangeably throughout the analysis.) Other methods of transportation to work, such as driving in one's own car (78 percent) or participating in a carpool (6 percent) are pooled and coded 0. Women disproportionately use the bus (7.8 percent, compared with 4.6 percent for men), as do Latinos (10.4 percent). These differences are even more pronounced when race and gender are considered simultaneously. First, women of color are more likely than men of the same race to use the bus, but this is not true among whites. Nearly all white women commute by car (91 percent); less than 2 percent of them use public transport; White men are more likely than white women to take the bus. Latina women depend heavily on bus transportation to work (16 percent) and also are most dependent on carpooling. Aside from the education gap between Latinas and all other women, the biggest difference *among* women is in their access to automobiles, a staple of all aspects of life in Southern California. On this dimension, white women are much better off than women of color.

A variable for majority-black census tract assesses the level of racial residential segregation for African Americans (and small numbers of others). For this test I computed a dummy variable coded 1 for census tracts that are at least 50 percent black. Since there is a persistently high degree of racial segregation, practically no white or Asian respondents live in such neighborhoods. Almost half of black respondents live in majority-black tracts. In recent years, however, Latinos have migrated into formerly black neighborhoods in and around the South Central portion of Los Angeles. This helps account for the small but significant numbers of Latinos living in majority-black tracts (4.5 percent).

Two dummy variables were computed to test the ethnic economy hypothesis for Asians and Latinos. Respondents working for a supervisor of the same race-ethnicity were coded as participants in their ethnic economy. For both groups, about one-third work in the ethnic sector of the labor market.

Lastly, thirteen dummy variables mark the geographic location of respondents' residence within Los Angeles County (Antelope Valley, San Fernando Valley, West Side, South Bay, South Central Los Angeles, Harbor-Long Beach, Downtown, Burbank-Glendale, Pasadena-Monterey Park, East Los Angeles, Southeast, Covina-Industry, and Pomona). These residential locations were aggregated from tract-level data.

How Much Time Do Workers Spend Commuting?

As in other metropolitan areas, the gender gap in commute time holds for Los Angeles County, where women travel only forty-four minutes to work round trip, while men average fifty-four minutes, a difference ($p < .001$) of 10 minutes daily (see table 12.2). There are also significant differences by race, particularly between African Americans (fifty-six minutes) and the other groups: whites (forty-eight minutes), Asians (forty-four minutes), and Latinos (fifty minutes). Disaggregating by gender, white women have the shortest commute (forty minutes), shorter than the women of color, and much shorter than black women (fifty-two minutes). The gap between black and white women is even larger than between men and women. The longest average commute among men is traveled by black men, at an hour each day. The gender gap in commute time holds *within* each racial group, so that Latinas have a shorter commute than Latinos, white women commute less than white men, and so on. These preliminary data suggest that multiple jeopardy is in operation, so that women of color commute less than men in their own ethnic group (associated with gendered disadvantage in jobs, transportation, and so on), but that racialized minority women commute longer than white women (associated with disadvantage in housing and employment opportunities).

Table 12.2 presents the average travel times by gender for each of the hypothesized effects.[7] The bivariate analysis indicates that in some ways, Los Angeles is different from other cities. For example, women of color commute less time on average than most men in Los Angeles, whereas that was not true in New York (McLafferty and Preston 1991). Notably, the largest difference in average work trips is for public transportation usage. Women who ride the bus incur an extra half-hour trip on average, compared with other women. For men, buses cost an additional twenty-five minutes. The mean differences in table 12.2 that are especially large for men include a much *longer* commute for part-time work or for living in Covina-Industry. There is also a much shorter com-

TABLE 12.2   *Gender Differences in Travel Time to Work
(One Way, Per Day)*

	Women			Men		
	Mean Travel Time (Minutes)	Standard Deviation	n	Mean Travel Time (Minutes)	Standard Deviation	n
Total	21.9	17.4	1,050	26.9	21.5	1144
Race-ethnicity						
White	19.8	15.6	238	27.4	21.9	264
Black	26.0	19.7	316	30.4	27.8	184
Asian	20.3	15.4	268	24.4	17.4	333
Latino	23.2	19.6	228	26.1	20.0	363
Marital status						
Spouse or partner absent	22.9	17.6	530	24.8	20.4	441
Spouse or partner present	21.1	17.9	518	28.0	22.0	703
Education or social class						
Low-skill	21.7	20.2	419	25.8	20.2	490
High-skill	22.0	15.9	631	27.7	22.4	654
Hours worked						
Part-time	20.7	16.8	227	34.6	28.6	149
Full-time	22.3	18.0	921	25.8	20.1	993
Occupation type						
Not female-dominated	20.9	17.4	531	27.5	21.9	1050
Female-dominated	22.8	18.1	519	19.2	13.3	94
Race of tract						
Not majority-black	21.7	17.6	771	27.2	21.8	979
Majority-black	23.6	18.9	279	22.2	15.0	165
Public transportation						
No	19.5	13.9	941	25.8	20.7	1074
Yes	49.4	30.8	109	50.1	24.3	69
Asian ethnic economy						
No	21.9	17.8	935	27.0	21.6	1024
Yes	20.5	14.2	115	20.2	14.7	120
Latino ethnic economy						
No	21.9	18.06	982	27.0	21.3	1015
Yes	21.9	14.64	68	26.4	22.4	129
Earnings quintile						
Lowest	23.2	21.1	219	30.0	28.2	151
Low-middle	20.7	17.9	189	25.7	18.6	207
Middle	22.6	16.6	191	23.8	17.5	197
Middle-high	21.8	15.7	185	28.1	19.0	207
Highest	21.2	13.6	119	30.3	25.1	226

(Table continues on p. 470.)

TABLE 12.2   *Continued*

	Women			Men		
	Mean Travel Time (Minutes)	Standard Deviation	n	Mean Travel Time (Minutes)	Standard Deviation	n
Residential location						
Antelope Valley	22.2	21.8	12	38.3	30.0	15
San Fernando Valley	24.0	17.4	39	26.4	23.9	58
West Side	20.4	9.7	34	25.1	18.6	30
South Bay	22.3	17.2	82	26.7	20.4	91
Harbor-Long Beach	19.6	17.4	57	22.6	18.3	72
South Central	24.9	21.1	303	23.1	16.6	226
Downtown	29.8	25.9	159	24.6	20.4	221
Burbank-Glendale	21.8	19.0	30	21.9	21.8	39
Pasadena-Monterey Park	19.2	16.3	137	33.3	22.7	143
East Los Angeles	25.7	25.9	68	26.3	18.6	102
Southeast	18.8	11.0	69	26.3	18.0	58
Covina-Industry	22.2	20.5	41	53.5	41.1	60
Pomona	19.3	16.6	19	32.3	17.6	29
Number of kids under five						
Zero	22.6	18.2	861	26.8	21.2	914
One	17.6	14.2	155	28.2	23.9	173
Two	21.3	14.5	29	24.1	16.9	53
Three	62.5	67.0	4	16.3	45.1	4
Any kids at home						
No	22.2	17.6	531	26.1	20.0	665
Yes	21.4	17.9	518	28.2	23.5	479

Source: Los Angeles Study of Urban Inequality 1994.

mute for single men, those working in female-dominated occupations, living in majority-black census tracts, or working in the Asian ethnic economy. The mean differences for women on all these factors, except public transportation, are small: only about two minutes difference. However, an analysis of the multiple regression results is fruitful.

Explaining the Journey to Work in Los Angeles

Ordinary least squares regression tests simultaneously the theories expected to explain racial-ethnic and gender differences in the journey to work. A model based on the whole sample (table 12.3) confirms the established finding that white women commute about five fewer minutes

TABLE 12.3   *OLS Coefficients (Standard Error) Estimating Commute Time in Los Angeles County*

	Model 1	Model 2
Gender and race (white men = reference)		
White woman	−5.09***	−5.03***
	(1.27)	(1.26)
Black woman	4.84*	5.46**
	(2.08)	(2.07)
Latina woman	−3.64*	−2.77
	(1.47)	(1.54)
Asian woman	−5.22*	−5.21*
	(2.48)	(2.48)
Black man	6.76***	6.56**
	(2.00)	(1.99)
Latino man	−0.46	1.01
	(1.28)	(1.33)
Asian man	−1.66	−1.42
	(2.29)	(2.33)
Spouse or partner present	2.70***	1.90*
	(0.79)	(0.79)
Public transportation	29.33***	30.34***
	(1.62)	(1.64)
High-skill	2.90***	3.05***
	(0.86)	(0.86)
Full-time worker	−2.18*	−2.15*
	(0.98)	(0.98)
Percentage female in occupation	−6.88***	−6.58***
	(1.61)	(1.61)
Majority-black census tract	−7.91***	−5.42*
	(1.76)	(2.38)
Asian ethnic economy	−1.79	−2.62
	(3.02)	(2.98)
Latino ethnic economy	−1.32	−1.34
	(1.29)	(1.28)
Residential location (Covina-Industry = reference)		
Antelope Valley	—	−8.57*
		(3.75)
San Fernando Valley	—	−17.44***
		(3.46)
West Side	—	−19.24***
		(3.46)
South Bay	—	−17.37***
		(3.49)
South Central Los Angeles	—	−20.57***
		(3.78)
Harbor-Long Beach	—	−21.71***
		(3.52)

(Table continues on p. 472.)

TABLE 12.3   *Continued*

	Model 1	Model 2
Downtown	—	−18.86***
		(3.62)
Burbank-Glendale	—	−20.96***
		(3.52)
Pasadena-Monterey Park	—	−15.02***
		(3.52)
East Los Angeles	—	−17.40***
		(3.55)
Southeast	—	−17.97***
		(3.40)
Pomona	—	−14.37***
		(3.63)
Constant	26.64***	43.86***
	(1.55)	(3.58)
N	2444	2444
Adjusted R^2	0.15	0.17
F	28.96***	19.53***

Source: Los Angeles Study of Urban Inequality 1994.
*$p < .05$, **$p < .01$, ***$p < .001$

than white men and indicates the appropriateness of modeling men and women separately. Black women commute almost 5 minutes longer than white men, while black men spend an extra 6.8 minutes relative to white men. This analysis shows that gender is statistically significant in explaining work trip, but race is significant only for African Americans. In other words, Asians' and Latinos' trip lengths cannot be distinguished from whites'. Further, the interaction of race and gender for blacks is not statistically significant, indicating that black women's commute time is more closely associated with black men's than with white women's, once we condition on other factors. It is more appropriate to model men and women separately and blacks and nonblacks separately, especially since we expect the other major hypotheses to affect commute differently by race and gender. Table 12.4 presents the results of the commute time regressions broken down by gender. Table 12.5 models African Americans.

In table 12.3, model 2 includes dummy variables for places of residence in Los Angeles County. The reference category for location is Covina-Industry; therefore the coefficients represent the (statistically significant) difference in commute time between each location and this area, located about twenty miles east of downtown Los Angeles. Includ-

TABLE 12.4   Selected OLS Coefficients (Standard Error)
Estimating Commute Time in Los Angeles County,
by Gender

	Women	Men
Race (white = reference)		
Black	8.43***	6.59*
	(1.92)	(2.30)
Latino and Latina	1.86	0.72
	(1.34)	(1.66)
Asian	−0.47	−0.49
	(2.31)	(2.75)
Spouse or partner present	0.25	4.40***
	(1.00)	(1.20)
Public transportation	31.51***	28.27***
	(1.89)	(2.68)
High-skill	3.36**	2.20
	(1.06)	(1.33)
Full-time worker	1.27	−8.95***
	(1.09)	(1.76)
Percentage female in occupation	−2.22	−11.02***
	(1.95)	(2.53)
Majority-black census tract	−4.91	−4.58
	(2.80)	(3.78)
Asian ethnic economy	−0.88	−5.47
	(3.63)	(4.58)
Latino ethnic economy	−4.55*	0.32
	(1.81)	(1.76)
Constant	19.64***	56.78***
	(5.08)	(4.89)
N	1117	1327
Adjusted R^2	0.22	0.16
F	15.00***	11.91***

Source: Los Angeles Study of Urban Inequality 1994.
Note: Residential location coefficients included but not shown.
*p < .05, **p < .01, ***p < .001

ing location does not alter substantially the magnitudes of other coefficients in the model.

Table 12.4 shows that, as predicted, use of public transportation increases women's daily commutes by over half an hour each way, by far the largest effect in the model. Higher-skilled women have longer commute times by about 3 minutes each way, conditioning on other factors, and women working in the Latino ethnic economy work closer to home than other women. Black women spend an additional 8.4 minutes each way getting to work compared with white women, even when controlling for transportation mode. Latinos and Asians are not statistically different than whites.

However, the other hypotheses are rejected. Household characteristics (spouse present) have no significant effect for women, in keeping with Hanson's and Pratt's (1995) findings. (Models run including various measures of the number and ages of children also showed no effect.) But having a spouse present *increases* men's commutes, perhaps because male "breadwinners" travel farther in order to gain additional income, perhaps because they have a woman at home taking care of household responsibilities. Perhaps, then, women's commutes are not shorter if they are married, but the fact that men's are longer increases the *difference* between men's and women's commute—that is, the gender gap in commuting. We must reject the hypothesis, however, that women travel less because of their marital status.

Labor market structures as measured in this model have no significant effect either. It does not matter (statistically) whether women's employment status is part-time or full-time. It does not matter whether they work in predominantly female, segregated occupations. Additional models specifying a dummy variable for female-typed work, measured as 70 percent female or more, also showed no effect on commute time and explained less of the variance. For men, on the other hand, working in female-dominated occupations did increase the work-trip length. This effect is large and is not explained by too few men in female-typed jobs. Working part-time is associated with a *longer* commute for men. Again, we must reject the hypothesis that the gender gap is explained by occupational segregation or employment status.

Living in a black census tract is insignificant for women, probably because it is highly correlated with being African American. We can also see more clearly in this model that Latinas and Asian women do not have significantly different commute behavior than white women when other factors are controlled. Although more factors determine commute times for men than for women, the adjusted R^2 is smaller for men. This indicates that explaining women's journey to work is more straightforward than explaining men's. I suggest that this phenomenon is due to the endogeneity of men's employment and residence location; women have fewer choices, so there is less variance for them.[8]

The separate model for blacks (table 12.5) confirms that gender is not a significant predictor; race is more salient in explaining black women's commute time. In fact, the only statistically significant predictor in the model is transportation to work, which adds twenty-six minutes each way. The other hypotheses are rejected. In a model run exclu-

TABLE 12.5   OLS Coefficients (Standard Errors) Estimating
Commute Time in Los Angeles County,
by Race

	Blacks	Non-blacks
Gender (male = 1)	−1.37	2.51*
	(1.99)	(1.09)
Spouse or partner present	−0.99	2.44**
	(1.72)	(0.94)
Public transportation	26.00***	27.00***
	(2.68)	(1.78)
High-skill	0.37	3.99***
	(1.74)	(0.93)
Full-time worker	0.61	0.92
	(2.15)	(1.22)
Percentage female in occupation	−4.83	−6.00**
	(3.31)	(1.98)
Majority-black census tract	−2.62	−1.29
	(1.88)	(2.26)
Constant	27.62	18.88
	(3.69)	(1.92)
n	498	1690
Adjusted R^2	0.17	0.13
F	15.22***	35.84***

Source: Los Angeles Study of Urban Inequality 1994.
$*p < .05$, $**p < .01$, $***p < .001$

sively on black women (not shown), residence in a majority-black census tract reduced commute time by five minutes each way. This result suggests not a spatial mismatch for black women, but that black women living in black neighborhoods have an easier time finding work nearby than black women living in mixed-race neighborhoods. This effect was not apparent for black men.

In sum, the multivariate analysis of commute time supports the hypothesis that non-black women have a shorter journey to work than men. For black women, work trip is better explained by their race than their gender, however, since black men and women are difficult to distinguish statistically. There is little evidence for any of the hypothesized determinants of the gender gap in commute time, except the large effect of public transportation usage and a small class effect.

Are Shorter Commutes Better?
Earnings, Class, and the
Commute Penalty

Although we saw little evidence for the interaction of race and gender in explaining commute times, the evidence thus far is not sufficient to say that multiple jeopardy is not operating. The length of the journey to work is not necessarily a good or bad outcome unless it is associated with negative job characteristics. (Of course, wasting time is in and of itself a negative outcome.) I will present an analysis of earnings to assess the impact of the journey to work on one characteristic of job quality. Table 12.6 shows multiple regression equations predicting the natural log of weekly earnings for the pooled sample and separately by gender. (I transform earnings using logarithms in order to normalize the distribution, which is otherwise truncated at zero.)

In this stage of the analysis, we are interested in the effect of commute time, skill-class, and the interaction of the two on earnings. Other variables are included as controls. For example, blacks earn approximately 22 percent less than whites, and Latinos earn approximately 41 percent less than whites.[9] For men, there is a marriage premium—that is, being married is associated with higher earnings. For women, marriage is associated with slightly lower earnings.

The women's equation shows a negative coefficient for the effect of commute minutes on wages of -0.0032; the longer a woman travels, the *less* she earns. This finding is counter to the notion that women have shorter commutes because their wages are lower. The effect is tempered when combined with the commute-skill interaction, which is significant and positive at 0.0037. These two coefficients are essentially inverses of each other. Therefore, if a woman is high-skilled, her commute time's negative drag on wages is canceled out and her skill, together with other factors, determines her earnings. If she is low-skilled, however, then the interaction term is zero and commute time does have a negative association with earnings, which I will refer to as a *commute penalty*. In other words, longer commute times are associated with lower earnings for low-skilled women, but not high-skilled women. Men as a group do not suffer a commute penalty.

At first glance this seems counterintuitive. If low-skilled women can earn more by staying closer to home, then why not do so? One possible explanation is that low-skilled women are constrained from taking jobs in their neighborhoods, perhaps because there are no jobs available nearby. A second explanation is that low-skilled women are more likely to ride the bus, which is associated with a much longer travel time. Table 12.7 shows earnings estimates for men and

TABLE 12.6   OLS Coefficients (Standard Errors) Estimating Log of
Individual Weekly Earnings

	Total	Women	Men
Commute time	−0.0032*	−0.0032*	0.19
	(0.0013)	(0.0013)	(0.13)
High-skill	0.35***	0.32***	0.34***
	(0.042)	(0.057)	(0.062)
Commute × high-skill	0.0036*	0.0037*	0.000097
	(0.0017)	(0.0020)	(0.0017)
Race (relative to whites)			
Black	−0.22***	−0.26***	−0.22***
	(0.044)	(0.056)	(0.068)
Latino	−0.41***	−0.44***	−0.46***
	(0.030)	(0.041)	(0.045)
Asian	−0.093	−0.029	−0.18*
	(0.055)	(0.074)	(0.078)
Spouse or partner present	0.091***	−0.069*	0.29***
	(0.026)	(0.036)	(0.038)
Hours worked	0.032***	0.038***	0.024***
	(0.0011)	(0.0015)	(0.0017)
Gender (male = 1)	0.48**	—	—
	(0.18)		
Commute × gender	0.57***	—	—
	(0.16)		
Commute × skill × gender	−0.0036*	—	—
	(0.0017)		
Constant	4.25***	4.52***	4.98***
	(0.18)	(0.076)	(0.096)
n	2243	1046	1197
Adjusted R^2	0.44	0.49	0.38
F	163.6***	124.6***	94.6***

Source: Los Angeles Study of Urban Inequality 1994.
*$p < .05$, **$p < .01$, ***$p < .001$

women with the addition of a dummy variable for public transportation usage.

Bus ridership reduces women's earnings by about 24 percent and men's by even more. Once we include public transportation, the commute penalty for women is no longer statistically significant. The coefficient is still negative, however, while it is positive for men. Buses are much slower than other transportation modes, so bus usage and commute time are highly correlated (0.5 for women, which is particularly high for a dummy variable). This multicollinearity probably accounts for the statistical insignificance of commute time in the women's regression. What is interesting is that the sign is negative—still a counter-

TABLE 12.7   OLS Coefficients (Standard Errors) Estimating
Log of Individual Weekly Earnings, Including
Public Transportation

	Total	Women	Men
Commute time	0.0031**	−0.0011	0.0036**
	(0.0010)	(0.0015)	(0.0014)
High-skill	0.36***	0.32***	0.36***
	(0.042)	(0.057)	(0.061)
Commute × high-skill	2.36847E-04	0.0028	−0.0012
	(0.0013)	(0.0020)	(0.0017)
Public transportation	−0.41***	−0.24**	−0.43***
	(0.058)	(0.075)	(0.090)
Race (relative to whites)			
Black	−0.24***	−0.26***	−0.22***
	(0.044)	(0.056)	(0.067)
Latino	−0.38***	−0.42***	−0.46***
	(0.030)	(0.041)	(0.045)
Asian	−0.090	−0.021	−0.18*
	(0.056)	(0.074)	(0.079)
Spouse or partner present	0.081**	−0.076*	0.26***
	(0.026)	(0.035)	(0.038)
Hours worked	0.034***	0.038***	0.024***
	(0.0011)	(0.0015)	(0.0017)
Constant	4.56***	4.50***	5.00***
	(0.059)	(0.076)	(0.095)
n	2243	1046	1197
Adjusted R^2	0.44	0.49	0.40
F	196.28***	112.91***	88.23***

Source: Los Angeles Study of Urban Inequality 1994.
*$p < .05$, **$p < .01$, ***$p < .001$

intuitive finding. To investigate further, I condition on bus ridership, estimating separate equations for riders and nonriders (see table 12.8). Once we condition on public transportation, is there still a negative relationship between women's travel time and earnings? What explains it?

The models for public and private transportation users show that women's journey time is still negatively associated with earnings, although the main effects are not statistically significant (for bus riders, the samples are quite small, which reduces the probability of reaching significance). Even so, low-skilled women who ride the bus still have a commute penalty to their earnings that is *not* explained away by transportation (we are already conditioning on transportation). Men still gain more earnings from longer travel times.

TABLE 12.8   OLS Coefficients (Standard Errors) Estimating Log of Individual Weekly Earnings, Conditioning on Public Transportation

	Public Transportation		Private Transportation	
	Women	Men	Women	Men
Commute time	−7.68677E-04	0.0015	−0.0025	0.0044**
	(0.0014)	(0.0023)	(0.0022)	(0.0015)
High-skill	0.075	0.075	0.31***	0.38***
	(0.18)	(0.34)	(0.066)	(0.064)
Commute × high-skill	0.0063*	0.0041	0.0040	−0.0021
	(0.0031)	(0.0054)	(0.0028)	(0.0018)
Race (relative to whites)				
Black	−0.63***	−0.66**	−0.26***	−0.20**
	(0.16)	(0.23)	(0.060)	(0.070)
Latino	−0.84***	−0.62**	−0.41***	−0.45***
	(0.14)	(0.21)	(0.043)	(0.046)
Asian	−0.20	−0.46	−0.020	−0.17*
	(0.23)	(0.36)	(0.077)	(0.081)
Spouse or partner present	0.22**	0.16	−0.096*	0.26***
	(0.082)	(0.13)	(0.038)	(0.039)
Hours worked	0.033***	0.022***	0.038***	0.024***
	(0.0043)	(0.0029)	(0.0016)	(0.0018)
Constant	4.67***	4.91***	4.52***	4.95***
	(0.22)	(0.24)	(0.085)	(0.10)
n	85	53	961	1145
Adjusted R^2	0.63	0.61	0.46	0.37
F	19.28***	10.98***	105.38***	64.33***

Source: Los Angeles Study of Urban Inequality 1994.
*$p < .05$, **$p < .01$, ***$p < .001$

A comparison of the effect of race on earnings in these models shows that for private transportation users, the earnings cost of being African American or Latino is about the same as in the full model (about 20 to 25 percent for blacks and approximately 40 percent for Latinos). But for bus riders, these coefficients jump enormously to over 0.6 for blacks and up to 0.8 for Latina women. This difference alone, we could speculate, is enough to purchase a car. The results of this exercise strongly suggest that race per se, that is, racial discrimination, plays an important role in preventing black and Latina women from working near their homes. Thus, there is indeed a multiple jeopardy effect in operation in which all women are constrained from working profitably near to home, but for which the penalty is particularly severe for women of color.

Table 12.9 analyzes the relationship between travel time and earnings for blacks separately, to measure the size of the commute penalty for them. The negative relationship between work-trip time and wages is nearly three times as large for African Americans (-0.0084) as it is for the pooled sample (-0.0032). Further, the interaction term for commute with skill is not statistically significant. Regardless of skill level, African Americans' commute penalty is not canceled out; blacks experience a reduction in earnings the longer they commute, even if they have a college degree and even controlling for bus usage. Further, it holds for both men and women. Nonblack men earn more for longer travel times. The commute penalty to the earnings of black men and women is evidence that they cannot work near their homes.

The literature responding to the spatial mismatch debate suggests that lack of employment in proximity to residential location results

TABLE 12.9   *OLS Coefficients (Standard Errors) Estimating Log of Individual Weekly Earnings for Blacks*

	Total	Women	Men
Commute time	−0.0084*	−0.0084[a]	−0.0030
	(0.0038)	(0.0049)	(0.0073)
High-skill	0.55***	0.59**	0.54*
	(0.15)	(0.22)	(0.22)
Commute × high-skill	0.0042	0.0060	0.0022
	(0.0042)	(0.0062)	(0.0075)
Public transportation	−0.097	0.0012	−0.62
	(0.19)	(0.26)	(0.33)
Spouse or partner present	−0.066	−0.070	−0.060
	(0.087)	(0.13)	(0.12)
Hours worked	0.043***	0.044***	0.039***
	(0.0039)	(0.0050)	(0.0067)
Gender (male = 1)	0.21*	—	—
	(0.090)		
Constant	4.02***	3.94***	4.41***
	(0.22)	(0.29)	(0.36)
n	230	133	98
Adjusted R^2	0.49	0.50	0.40
F	32.33***	22.88***	11.64***

Source: Los Angeles Study of Urban Inequality 1994.
[a]The *p*-value for this coefficient is .09.
*$p < .05$, **$p < .01$, ***$p < .001$.

from racial residential segregation as well as racial discrimination in hiring and racial preferences in firm location. The results presented here are also suggestive of these problems facing African Americans and Latinos in Los Angeles and other American cities.

Conclusion

This analysis has combined hypotheses about gender and the journey to work with hypotheses about race and local labor markets to investigate the question of whether race or gender or the interaction of the two with other factors such as class, space, and place best explains commuting and earnings differences in Los Angeles. Do women of color experience multiple jeopardy in their journey to work?

Evidence from regression analysis shows, first, that dependence on public transportation is the most important single factor shaping the journey to work, adding half an hour each way to the journeys of workers in Los Angeles. Net of this and other factors, non-black women commute fewer minutes than men, blacks commute longer than whites, but black women's commute is very similar to black men's; for black women, gender relations alone cannot explain the journey to work. Asian and Latina women do not differ significantly from white women in commute times.

Analysis of earnings shows a positive association with commute time for men as a group. Low-skilled women, however, suffer a commute penalty to their earnings. That is, they receive *lower* wages for longer trip times, even when conditioning on the mode of transportation—a finding inverse to the results of previous studies that find a positive association between commute time and earnings. For nonblack, high-skilled women, the effect of commute time is substantially canceled out by the interaction between skill and commute; their longer commutes are voluntary.

Further, there is a commute penalty for African Americans, regardless of their skill level or gender, that is more than twice as large as the penalty for all women. This penalty is also not explained by the longer time it takes to ride the bus. Since we can presume that spending additional time commuting is undesirable, this statistical evidence indicates that employed blacks are constrained from living in close proximity to their place of employment, whether they are high-skilled or low-skilled. This constraint may be attributable to a combination of factors found in previous studies that include racial residential segregation, racial discrimination in employment, racial preferences in employers' selection of firm location, and race and gender differences in job search social

481

networks. It is difficult to unpack gender effects for black women in this study.

The results suggest that the theory of multiple jeopardy holds for the journey to work, but not as neatly as anticipated; race is more salient than gender for black women, gender is more salient than race for Asian, white, and Latina women, and gender negatively affects all groups of women relative to white men.

The theory of multiple jeopardy is a rather crude instrument; it uses large concepts like race and gender to help explain complex social, political, and economic outcomes. It points us in the right direction. By trying actually to measure and account for race-ethnic, class, and gender interactions and intersections, it makes clear that the ways that multiple jeopardy operates on different categories of people depend on the ongoing social relations among groups. This study shows that in the context of racial residential segregation and labor markets in Los Angeles, gender differences pale in comparison to the racial component for black women, while the reverse is true to some degree for other women. Multiple jeopardy will produce different outcomes in different contexts. Therefore, as a theory of the subordination of women of color, it still needs substantial refinement.

Further research into questions posed in this chapter could explore how commuting affects the job search, how employer practices construct race-gender differences in the socio-spatial topography of employment opportunities, and how transportation constraints are related to unemployment. Further, in Los Angeles there is clearly a substantial difference in the social and economic outlook for immigrant Latinos and Latinas relative to native Latinos and Latinas that was bracketed for this study.

The study results are suggestive of several remedies to the myriad problems that face low-skilled women, and particularly black women, in Los Angeles in terms of commuting to work. The scope of this chapter is insufficient to address them, particularly the employment inequities facing women and people of color more generally. But one clear suggestion for low-skilled women (over and above the obvious need for higher skills and better-paying jobs) is that they need better access to transportation. Only 9 percent of white women in this study commute to work without a car, compared with about one-quarter to one-third of black and Latina women, respectively. A fast, inexpensive subway or regional rail system with many stations is warranted in Los Angeles, as is available in other major metropolitan areas. London would be the example since it, too, is spread over a vast area. Unfortunately, although the system that Los Angeles County is currently installing will help, current plans do not include enough stations to get people to their destination without also taking above-ground transportation, that is, buses. Many Angelenos are doubtful the new and extremely expensive-to-build subway system will fulfill the needs of commuters in an efficient and affordable way. Until it does, tax incentives or other incentives, perhaps through employers, to help low-skilled women acquire and maintain cars would undoubtedly have an impact.

This research was supported by the UCLA Center for the Study of Urban Poverty through a generous grant from the Ford Foundation. I thank Lawrence Bobo, Ruth Milkman, Simon Potter, Michael Stoll, Abel Valenzuela Jr., and three anonymous reviewers for their comments and suggestions.

Notes

1. Counties include Los Angeles, Orange, Riverside, San Bernardino, and Ventura.

2. The term *women of color* connotes women who are not of European or "white" ancestry.

3. Ethnic economies are not necessarily concentrated geographically, although they are in Los Angeles County in areas such as Koreatown.

4. Several studies of time found that public transportation usage yields both shorter times and shorter distances for women (Ericksen 1977; Fagnani 1983; Madden 1977).

5. Note further that analyses of the missing data for distance from home to work reveal large and statistically significant differences between the group of respondents with an employer address and those without one. In particular, 70 percent of Asian men and 61 percent of Asian women were missing distance data, compared with only 44 percent of white women, for example. There were also significant differences by occupation and industry. The main analytic cost resulting from the use of time as a measure is the loss of the *direct* spatial element that would permit the mapping of commuting patterns and the distribution of employment around Los Angeles County.

6. Some studies include a variable for female-dominated jobs measured with a dummy variable for occupations that are 70 percent or more women (for example, Hanson and Johnston 1985). By using a continuous measure of the percent female, rather than an arbitrary 50 or 70 percent threshold, I allow for a linear relationship between degree of occupational segregation of women and work-trip length. I also ran models using the 70 percent female dummy variable and found that while other relationships in the model were left unchanged, the

overall explanatory power of the model is better with the continuous rather than the discrete measure of occupational segregation.

7. The bivariate effect of the explanatory variables on commute time by race and gender simultaneously is too complex to present here. It is more fruitful to confine that analysis to the regression framework.

8. While the gender models include dummy variables for location of residence, the significant effects are highly unstable and depend on which community is left out as the reference variable. For Covina-Industry, all the location variables are significant for men but none is significant for women, indicating that place does not matter for women's commute. This interesting finding only holds, however, for locations relative to Covina-Industry. Altering the reference community does not alter any of the other coefficients or standard errors of the models, as it should not.

9. With a logged dependent variable, the coefficients can be interpreted approximately as percentages. As the coefficient magnitude diverges from 0, the approximation becomes much less reliable. A coefficient of 0.22 can thus be loosely interpreted as 22 percent, but a coefficient of .50 or .75 has a smaller percentage effect than 50 percent or 75 percent. These approximations should not be used literally but seen as ballpark figures.

References

Alexis, M., and N. DiTomaso. 1983. "Transportation, Race and Employment: In Pursuit of the Elusive Triad." *Journal of Urban Affairs* 5(2): 81–94.

Alonso, W. 1964. *Location and Land Use*. Cambridge, Mass.: Harvard University Press.

Bergmann, Barbara. 1996. *Saving Our Children from Poverty: What the United States Can Learn from France*. New York: The Russell Sage Foundation.

Bielby, William T., and James N. Baron. 1984. "A Woman's Place Is with Other Women: Sex Segregation Within Organizations." In *Sex Segregation in the Workplace: Trends, Explanations, Remedies*, edited by Barbara F. Reskin. Washington, D.C.: National Academy Press.

Bobo, Lawrence D., Eve Fielder, David M. Grant, James H. Johnson Jr., and Melvin L. Oliver. 1995. "The Los Angeles Survey of Urban Inequality: Sample Report on the Household Survey." UCLA Center for the Study of Urban Poverty Occasional Working Paper Series. Los Angeles: University of California.

Brewer, Rose. 1988. "Black Women in Poverty: Some Comments on Female-Headed Households." *Signs: Journal of Women in Culture and Society* 13: 331–39.

Browne, Irene. 1997. "Explaining the Black-White Gap in Labor Force Participation Among Women Heading Households." *American Sociological Review* 62: 236–52.

Cubukgil, A., and E. J. Miller. 1982. "Occupational Status and the Journey-to-Work." *Transportation* 11: 251–76.

Ellwood, David. 1986. "The Spatial Mismatch Hypothesis: Are There Teenage Jobs Missing in the Ghetto?" In *The Black Youth Employment Crisis*, edited by Richard Freeman and Harry J. Holzer. Chicago: University of Chicago Press.

Ericksen, Julia. 1977. "An Analysis of the Journey-to-Work for Women." *Social Problems* 24: 428–35.

Fagnani, J. 1983. "Women's Commuting Patterns in the Paris Region." *Tijdschrift voor Economische en Sociale Geographie* 74: 12–24.

Giuliano, G. 1979. "Public Transportation and the Travel Needs of Women." *Traffic Quarterly* 33: 607–16.

Goodman, J., and M. Berkman. 1977. "Racial Differences in Commuting Behavior from the Panel Study of Income Dynamics." *Review of Public Data Use* 5(4): 29–36.

Gordon, Peter, and Ajay Kumar. 1989. "The Spatial Mismatch Hypothesis: Some New Evidence." *Urban Studies* 26: 315–26.

Gordon, Peter, Ajay Kumar, and Harry W. Richardson. 1989. "Gender Differences in Metropolitan Travel Behavior." *Regional Studies* 23(6): 32–39.

Gordon, Peter, Harry W. Richardson, and Myung-Jin Jun. 1991. "The Commuting Paradox: Evidence from the Top Twenty." *Journal of the American Planning Association* 57(4): 416–20.

Guest, Avery M., and Christopher Cluett. 1976. "Workplace and Residential Location: A Push-Pull Model." *Journal of Regional Science* 16 (3): 399–410.

Hanson, Susan, and Ipipo Johnston. 1985. "Gender Differences in Work-Trip Length: Explanations and Implications." *Urban Geography* 6: 193–219.

Hanson, Susan, and Geraldine Pratt. 1988. "Spatial Dimensions of the Gender Division of Labor in a Local Labor Market." *Urban Geography* 9: 180–202.

———. 1991. "Job Search and the Occupational Segregation of Women." *Annals of the Association of American Geographers* 81: 229–53.

———. 1995. *Gender, Work, and Space*. London and New York: Routledge. Janet Momsen and Janet Monk, series editors. *International Studies of Women and Place*.

Hecht, A. 1974. "The Journey-to-Work Distance in Relation to the Socioeconomic Characteristics of Workers." *Canadian Geographer* 18: 367–78.

Holzer, Harry, and W. Vroman. 1992. "Mismatches and the Urban Labor Market." In *Urban Labor Markets and Job Opportunity*, edited by

George E. Peterson and Wayne Vroman. Washington, D.C.: Urban Institute Press.

Howe, A., and K. O'Connor. 1982. "Travel to Work and Labor Force Participation of Men and Women in an Australian Metropolitan Area." *Professional Geographer* 34: 50–64.

Iceland, John, and David R. Harris. 1998. "Why Work Disappears: Neighborhood Racial Composition and Employers' Relocation Intentions." Evanston, Ill.: Joint Center for Poverty Research. Working Paper. October 1998.

Ihlanfeldt, Keith R., and David L. Sjoquist. 1989. "The Impact of Job Decentralization on the Economic Welfare of Central City Blacks." *Journal of Urban Economics* 26: 110–30.

———. 1990. "Job Accessibility and Racial Differences in Youth Employment Rates." *American Economic Review* 80(1): 266–76.

Jencks, Christopher, and Susan Mayer. 1991. "Residential Segregation, Job Proximity, and Black Job Opportunities: The Empirical Status of the Spatial Mismatch Hypothesis." In *Concentrated Urban Poverty in America*, edited by M. McGeary. Washington, D.C.: National Academy Press.

Johnston-Anumonwo, I. 1992. "The Influence of Household Type on Gender Differences in Work Trip Distance." *Professional Geographer* 44: 161–69.

———. 1995a. "Gender, Race, and the Spatial Context of Women's Employment." In *Gender in Urban Research*, edited by Judith A. Garber and Robyne S. Turner. Thousand Oaks, Calif.: Sage Publications.

———. 1995b. "Locational Access to Employment: Comparing the Work Trips of African Americans and European Americans." *21st Century Afro Review* 1(3) Spring: 107–44.

Kain, J. 1968. "Housing Segregation, Negro Employment, and Metropolitan Decentralization." *Quarterly Journal of Economics* 82: 175–97.

King, Deborah. 1988. "Multiple Jeopardy, Multiple Consciousness: The Context of a Black Feminist Ideology." *Signs: Journal of Women in Culture and Society* 14(1): 42–72.

Madden, Janice F. 1977. "A Spatial Theory of Sex Discrimination." *Journal of Regional Science* 17: 369–80.

———. 1981. "Why Women Work Closer to Home." *Urban Studies* 18: 181–94.

Madden, Janice F., and Michelle White. 1980. "Spatial Implications of Increases in the Female Labor Force: A Theoretical and Empirical Synthesis." *Land Economics* 56(4): 432–46.

Massey, Douglas, and Nancy Denton. 1993. *American Apartheid*. Cambridge, Mass.: Harvard University Press.

McLafferty, Sara, and Valerie Preston. 1991. "Gender, Race and Commuting Among Service Sector Workers." *Professional Geographer* 43: 1–14.

————. 1992. "Spatial Mismatch and Labor Market Segmentation for African-American and Latina Women." *Economic Geography* 68(4): 406–31.

————. 1996. "Spatial Mismatch and Employment in a Decade of Restructuring." *Professional Geographer* 48(4): 420–31.

————. 1997. "Gender, Race, and the Determinants of Commuting: New York in 1990." *Urban Geography* 18(3): 192–212.

Moore, Thomas, and Aaron Laramore. 1990. "Industrial Change and Urban Joblessness: An Assessment of the Mismatch Hypothesis." *Urban Affairs Quarterly* 25(4): 640–58.

Moss, Philip, and Chris Tilly. 1991. *Why Black Men Are Doing Worse in the Labor Market: A Review of Supply-Side and Demand-Side Explanations*. Report. New York: Social Science Research Council Committee for Research on the Urban Underclass Working Group on Labor Market Research (August).

Nee, Victor, and Jimy Sanders. 1987. "On Testing the Enclave-Economy Hypothesis: A Reply to Portes and Jensen." *American Sociological Review* 52: 771–73.

Nelson, K. 1986. "Female Labor Supply Characteristics and the Suburbanization of Low-Wage Office Work." In *Production, Work and Territory*, edited by Allan Scott and Michael Storper. London: Allen and Unwin.

Portes, Alejandro, and Robert Bach. 1985. *Latin Journey: Cuban and Mexican Immigrants in the United States*. Berkeley: University of California Press.

Portes, Alejandro, and Leif Jensen. 1987. "What's an Ethnic Enclave? The Case for Conceptual Clarity, Comment on Sanders and Nee." *American Sociological Review* 52: 745–71.

————. 1989. "The Enclave and the Entrants: Patterns of Ethnic Enterprise in Miami Before and After Mariel." *American Sociological Review* 54: 929–49.

————. 1992. "Reply: Disproving the Enclave Hypothesis." *American Sociological Review* 57(3): 418–20.

Reskin, Barbara F., and Heidi I. Hartmann. 1986. *Women's Work, Men's Work: Sex Segregation on the Job*. Washington, D.C.: National Academy Press.

Rutherford, Brent M., and Gerda R. Wekerle. 1988. "Captive Rider, Captive Labor: Spatial Constraints on Women's Employment." *Urban Geography* 9: 173–93.

Sanders, Jimy, and Victor Nee. 1992. "Limits of Ethnic Solidarity in the Enclave Economy." *American Sociological Review* 57: 745–74.

Segura, Denise. 1990. "Chicanas and Triple Oppression in the Labor Force," in *Chicana Voices: Intersections of Class, Race, and Gender*, edited by Teresa Córdova. Colorado Springs, Colo.: National Association for Chicano Studies.

Singell, L., and J. Lillydahl. 1986. "An Empirical Analysis of the Commute to Work Pattern of Males and Females in Two-Earner Households." *Urban Studies* 23: 119–29.

Stolz, Barbara Ann. 1985. *Still Struggling: America's Low Income Working Women Confront the 80s.* Lexington, Mass.: D. C. Heath.

Taylor, Brian, and Paul Ong. 1995. "Spatial Mismatch or Automobile Mismatch? An Examination of Race, Residence and Commuting in U.S. Metropolitan Areas." *Urban Studies* 32(9): 1453.

U.S. Department of Commerce. U.S. Bureau of the Census. 1990. *Census of Population and Housing, 1990: Public Use Microdata Samples Technical Documentation.* Washington: U.S. Government Printing Office.

Wheeler, James O. 1967. "Occupational Status and Work Trips: A Minimum Distance Approach." *Social Forces* 45: 508–15.

———. 1969. "Some Effects of Occupational Status on Work Trips." *Journal of Regional Science* 19: 41–52.

Wilson, William Julius. 1987. *The Truly Disadvantaged: The Inner City, the Underclass, and Public Policy.* Chicago: The University of Chicago Press.

PART III

UNDERSTANDING
PROCESSES OF
DISCRIMINATION

13

RACIAL ATTITUDES AND POWER IN THE WORKPLACE: DO THE HAVES DIFFER FROM THE HAVE-NOTS?

Lawrence D. Bobo, Devon Johnson, and Susan A. Suh

WITHIN the social sciences there has been a strong tendency to assume that the logic and demands of a competitive industrial economy would, in the long run, work against racial inequality. Many students of race relations, however, argue that racialized social conditions and identities can powerfully affect market dynamics. In light of these differing perspectives, one hypothesis worthy of careful investigation springs from Herbert Blumer's analyses of "Industrialization and Race Relations" (1965a) and "The Future of the Color Line" (1965b). In these essays he argued that the larger social relations of race will carry over into market relations of the economy. Accordingly, it is a mistake to assume that racial inequality and racial dynamics will be undone by some putatively deeper economic reality or dynamic. Although we do not presume to have the data to resolve this perennial debate, we examine several important aspects of Blumer's proposition that are directly related to it.

The broad purpose of this research is to assess whether whites with power in the workplace differ in their racial attitudes from white workers who lack it. We consider four specific empirical questions: Do whites with power in the workplace hold more or less negative stereotypes of African Americans than those lacking power? Do whites with power in the workplace form and express their stereotypes of African Americans in a different way from those lacking workplace power? Does holding stereotypes of African Americans have consequential effects on other political outlooks among those with workplace power? And, how does this compare to those who lack it?

The answer to each of these questions bears on the deeper issue of whether the presumed rationalizing and productivity-driven demands of the market weaken a sensitivity to factors presumably as unrelated to worker productivity as race. We focus on stereotypes because such expectations of behavior have the closest connections to judgments of potential worker productivity (Jackman and Senter 1983). We focus on whites' views of African Americans because of the many indicators of unique economic disadvantage and vulnerability among African Americans and the many indicators of considerable white advantage and power in the workplace, especially as supervisors and those empowered to make hiring decisions. Before turning to the data and analyses, we develop in detail Blumer's argument.

Theoretical Foundations
Race as Subordinate
to Market Dynamics

Scholars from the left and the right, within both economics and sociology, have expected market dynamics to wipe away anachronistic racial attachments, or at least have maintained that what appears racial on the surface only masks a more important underlying economic or class dynamic. As an example of the former line of reasoning, M.D.R. Evans and Jonathan Kelley have argued that:

> neoclassical economic theory implies that discrimination cannot exist in advanced industrial societies' largely free and competitive labor markets. . . . Unless discrimination can be enforced on every single employer (e.g., by legislation, boycotts, or threat of violence), it cannot long endure in a competitive market, save in very special circumstances. Discrimination by workers or customers leads to the same result. (1991, 723)

In assessing the large body of literature on urban political economy, Susan Fainstein and Norman Fainstein concluded:

> participants in the debates about urban restructuring focus on the interaction between economic processes and social organization. To the extent that political economists examine social groups as actors and mediating forces, they define the relevant groups by those interests that arise directly out of economic processes—for example, the owners of capital, real estate

developers, the professional-managerial class, redundant workers, gentrifiers, displaced households, in-migrants. (1989, 187–88)

Distinctly racial dynamics are pushed to the margins in such analyses.

Certainly within sociology there is a strong tradition of theoretical inattention to race or of subordinating race to market dynamics. For example, none of the founding figures of sociology—Emile Durkheim, Karl Marx, or Max Weber—devoted sustained analytical attention to race or posited race as a central theoretical aspect to larger social processes (see reviews in Blauner 1972; Omi and Winant 1986; Stone 1985).[1] Even some of the most eminent figures in the sociology of race and ethnic relations have argued pointedly for viewing "racial dynamics" as having deeper economic foundations. For example, Edna Bonacich writes:

> while race and ethnicity may appear to be primordial attachments, in fact they reflect a deeper reality, namely, class relations and dynamics. I believe that class approaches are the most fruitful way to study ethnicity and race. Not only are they more in accord with a "deeper" level of reality that enables us to understand phenomena at the surface of society, but they also provide us with the tools for changing that reality. [1991, 59]

The economist Michael Reich (1981) fashioned a similar analysis, arguing that only capitalists benefit from a racially divided economy. A theoretical emphasis on the power of markets to undo racial and ethnic attachments is also evident in the emerging economic sociology of immigration. As Victor Nee, Jimy Sanders, and Scott Sernau argue:

> market relations encourage open social relationships. For this reason, markets function as an integrative institution. Workers gradually adapt their behavior to gain advantages in the labor market, shopkeepers customize their services and products to meet consumer tastes, and firms seek the best qualified and least expensive workers, regardless of ethnicity. (1994, 870)

It is not our objective here to review in detail the various market dynamic approaches to matter of race. Rather, we wish to explore several testable hypotheses that bear on how and why race might come to assert itself within market relations. A strong version of a market dynamic argument should be uncomfortable with each of the core hypotheses we specify here. But, in order to develop those hypotheses we need to flesh out the theoretical framework and specific reasons why we believe that race is likely to express itself in economic relations.

Markets as Accommodating a Racial Group Dynamic

Students of racial relations often assume that racial prejudice leads to discrimination (Merton 1949)—or as some have put it, that "a taste for discrimination" leads to discrimination (Becker 1957; Arrow 1973). From our vantage point, it is important to be clear about what one means by *prejudice*. Further, it is important to be clear about the reasons racial prejudice is likely to influence economic and market dynamics.

We adopt a view developed in the work of Herbert Blumer (1958a) and subsequently elaborated by Bobo (1999). He believed that there is an intrinsically collective or group-based dimension to racial prejudice. Blumer maintained that racial prejudice was best understood as a general attitude or orientation involving normative ideas about where one's own group should stand in the social order vis-à-vis an out-group.

He argued that the fully developed sense of group position involved a belief that the dominant group was superior to the subordinate group, that subordinate group members were alien and different, that dominant group members were duly entitled to enjoy rights of first access or proprietary claim over a range of valued social resources, and a perception that subordinate racial group members were threatening to infringe on the proprietary claims of dominant group members (Blumer 1958a). This sense of group position is historically rooted and collectively developed, and thus becomes a widely shared set of ideas among dominant group members about appropriate relations to subordinate group members.

Most research has focused on Blumer's argument about the perception of threat (Bobo 1983; Bobo and Hutchings 1996; Bobo and Kluegel 1997; Fossett and Kiecolt 1989; Quillian 1995; Wellman 1977). For the present purposes, there are two features of Blumer's ideas that should be made more explicit in the group position model. The first concerns the nature and effects of racial identities. The second concerns the role of affect and emotions in the sense of group position.

Race as a Fundamental Cleavage   Blumer's work indicates that racial identities are quasi-autonomous forces, ranking with economic and other institutional dynamics in shaping human social organization. He makes this point most directly in his essay on "Industrialization and Race Relations" (1965a). After reviewing the transformations in market relations brought about by industrialization and the presumed broader social effects thereof, Blumer's work debunks one of the claims made by many economists and sociologists then and today: namely, that industrialization would inevitably erode the parochial and anachronistic effects of racial-ethnic ties in ordering social life.

Prior modes of social organization constrain the presumed rationalizing force of economic modernization. This is especially likely to happen where patterns of racial identity, belief, and social organization have been institutionalized. Indeed, accommodation to an established racial order may become economically rational under such conditions:

> rational operation of industrial enterprises which are introduced into a racially ordered society may call for a deferential respect for the canons and sensitivities of that racial order. This observation is not a mere a priori speculation. It is supported by countless instances of such decisions in the case of industrial enterprises in the Southern region of the United States, in South Africa and in certain colonial areas. . . . It is a mistake, accordingly, to assume that the rational motif of industrialism signifies an automatic undermining of a racial order into which industrialism enters. To the contrary, the rational imperative in industrial operations may function to maintain and reinforce the established racial order. [Blumer 1965a, 233]

Blumer thus credited race with a powerful capacity to influence, shape, and condition the economic and class dynamics of a society. He did so, it should be emphasized, without denying the importance of economic and class dynamics. Instead, he avoided the conventional error of reducing race to merely its economic manifestations.

None of this, however, amounts to adopting a primordial or essentialist view of racial identities. Blumer was explicit about the socially constructed nature of racial identities. That a social process or phenomena rests on constructed meaning in no way reduces its importance as a patterned and recurrent—indeed, structural—dimension of human social experience (Sewell 1992). Blumer was equally explicit about the potential for change in a racial order. He argued that change in a racial order would spring from a direct assault on that racial order from largely noneconomic and political forces: "The evidence seems to me to lead overwhelmingly to the conclusion that such changes do not arise from inner considerations of industrial efficiency. Instead they arise from outside pressure, chiefly political pressures" (1965a, 247).

The Role of Affect in the Sense of Group Position   Blumer recognized that racial attachments and the sense of group position have core nonrational or socio-emotional elements. The historical origins and tenacity of racial attachments cannot be accounted for in terms of purely rational, material, and structural forces. First and foremost, attachment to a particular set of socially constructed racial identities cannot be taken as given in nature or as a purely rational phenomenon (Stone 1985).

Blumer expressly argued that the sense of group position is a normative construct:

> Sociologically it is not a mere reflection of the objective relations between racial groups. Rather it stands for "what ought to be" rather than for "what is." It is a sense of where the two racial groups *belong*. . . . In its own way, the sense of group position is a norm and imperative—indeed a very powerful one. It guides, incites, cows, and coerces. It should be borne in mind that this sense of group position stands for and involves a fundamental kind of group affiliation for the members of the dominant racial group. (Blumer 1958a, 5; emphasis in original)

This normative character to the sense of group position immediately separates it from a purely instrumental basis. The normative dimension is also part of the reason prejudice is an active, adaptive social force. It is infused with a moral imperative.

Blumer also argued that the sense of group position functioned along two important axes. One involved the more obvious dimension of domination and oppression, of hierarchical ordering and positioning. A second critical axis, however, involved a dimension of exclusion and inclusion, of socioemotional embrace or recoil. The exclusion and inclusion dimension, again, invokes an affective or emotional basis to the sense of group position. He also held that "on the social psychological side [the sense of group position] cannot be equated to a sense of social status as ordinarily conceived, for it refers not merely to vertical positioning but to many other lines of position independent of the vertical dimension" (1958a, 5).

Part of the point Blumer makes here is that restrictions imposed on a subordinate group reach beyond the conventional status dimensions defined by rank within the economy or polity. His argument was that even profound change in some aspects of a racial order, and the sense of group position surrounding it, may not erode other core aspects of the sense of dominant group position.

He suggested that the color line had many layers. The layers of economic status and political status were themselves complex and multilayered. Thus, for example, the elimination of racial exclusion policies in access to employment hardly meant that blacks would find an easy route to positions of high pay, authority, and prestige. More important, the economic and political dimensions of the racial order did not exhaust either the forms of restricted life chances facing African Americans or those undergirding racial prejudice as a social force.

Blumer argued that for this reason the civil rights movement had failed to accomplish a fundamental change in "the color line":

> The contested area of civil rights is . . . but the outer band of the color line. Inside it lies the crucial area of economic subordination and opportunity restriction—an area of debarment of Negroes which is exceedingly tough because it is highly complicated by private and quasi-private property rights, managerial rights, and organizational rights. Still further inside the color line are the varied circles of private associations from which the Negro is grossly excluded. Thus, the successful achievement of civil rights merely peels off, so to speak, the outer layer of the color line. (Blumer 1965b, 30)

That is, he expected that whites' sense of racial group position would continue to assert itself. There had been only partial success in changing the color line in the political and economic spheres. Moreover, how the color line affected the private spheres of community, friends, home, and family ties had not been touched at all.

Conceptually, Blumer thus recognized an "inner citadel of the color line." The inner citadel involved the exclusion-inclusion dimension of the sense of dominant group position. He held that this inner citadel was "a matter of personal attitudes and thus falls inside the area of individual determination" (1965b, 335). As such, it would prove unusually resistant to external pressure for change.

Implications and Hypotheses

The central implication of the group position framework is that race will assert itself in economic arrangements so long as important status, affective, and social organizational supports (that is, racially segregated communities, friendship networks, and family structures) exist as bulwarks for a racialized social order (see also Sanjek 1994; Gans 1999). The mechanism that Blumer's analysis underscores is that individuals are not merely business owners, line supervisors, or workers, but social beings embedded in an array of relationships, experiences, and ties. As such, they form identities, outlooks, and expectations that accompany them into many different settings, including racialized identities and expectations that they are likely to carry with them into a specific workplace and in the market more generally.

First, the group position framework hypothesizes no meaningful differences in the overall tenor of the racial stereotypes of whites with power in the workplace from those who lack power (hypothesis 1).

Second, the group position framework hypothesizes that racial stereotypes among those with power in the workplace and those lacking power in the workplace will exhibit a similar degree of rootedness in such indicators of race-relevant cultural exposure and socialization as age, education, and region of upbringing (hypothesis 2).

Third, the group position framework hypothesizes that racial stereotypes among whites with power in the workplace and those lacking it will exhibit a similar degree of rootedness in such other psychological and general value orientations as ideological self-identification and religiosity (hypothesis 3).

Fourth, the group position framework hypothesizes that the effect of racial stereotypes on other political outlooks will be the same among those with power in the workplace and those without (hypothesis 4).

Analysis and Results
Underlying Social Organization of Race

In the group position framework, racial dynamics are likely to assert themselves in the workplace, irrespective of the basic form of economic organization, because a set of racialized identities and status relations permeate many other domains of social life. In particular, if the neighborhood, friendship, and family circles of individuals continue to be organized or circumscribed by race, then those racialized patterns of interaction and likely self-conception should influence preferences and behavior in the work setting. Thus, a basic precondition in order for Blumer's argument to hold is that neighborhood, friendship, and family ties remain sharply divided by race. In order to establish the prima facie plausibility of the group position framework, we first examine the racial makeup of these important domains of life.

Residential Space   A substantial body of research documents the extreme and slowly changing pattern of black-white residential segregation in the United States (Massey and Denton 1993; Farley and Frey 1994). Los Angeles continues to rank as "hypersegregated," even using 1990 census data (Denton 1994). Only a very small component of the black-white division into separate neighborhoods can be attributed to differences in income or household composition. Camille Zubrinsky's analyses of PUMA data for Los Angeles County, which adjusted residential segregation indices for household income and composition, concluded: "If Black households could be distributed throughout the Los Angeles area on the basis of socioeconomic characteristics alone, Black-White residential segregation would be roughly 5.5 times lower than it actually is. Class or economic resources, most emphatically, are not the reason for high Black concentration in just a few areas, and severe underrepresentation in others" (Zubrinsky 1996, 102–3).

In addition, it is clear that whites express significantly greater aversion to residential integration when asked about contact with blacks as compared to other racial minority groups (Bobo and Zubrinsky 1996; Zubrinsky and Bobo 1996; Farley et al. 1994). Black-white separation into distinct, segregated neighborhoods remains the common pattern in Los Angeles. This segregation appears to have more to do with race and racial prejudice than with class status differences or other factors.

Social Networks National studies of network ties show substantial racial homogeneity of personal networks. For example, Peter Marsden's analysis of data from the 1985 General Social Survey showed that: "The race-ethnic homogeneity of the networks is most pronounced: only 96 respondents (8 percent of those with networks of size 2 or greater) cite alters with any racial-ethnic diversity" (1987, 126). A recent detailed investigation in the Detroit metropolitan area reports an increase between the late 1960s and the early 1990s in the amount of contact between blacks and whites. However, much of this contact was restricted to very brief, superficial, public encounters. As these researchers explained: "Nearly half of city's black residents do not have a single white friend, and almost the same proportion of whites in the Detroit suburbs have neither a friend nor a social acquaintance who is black" (Sigelman et al. 1996, 1,326).

As for our Los Angeles County data, only 6.6 percent of whites named one or more black persons as a member of their social network. Importantly, there was no difference in the likelihood of having African Americans in the social networks of whites with power in the workplace as compared to whites lacking power in the workplace. The social sphere of friendship ties is even more starkly segregated than the apartheid-like character of residential communities.

Family Ties Black-white intermarriage, although on the rise, remains extremely uncommon, both in absolute and relative terms compared to that observed among other racial minority groups. As Belinda Tucker and Claudia Mitchell-Kernan explained:

> Virtually all U.S. subpopulations that might be defined as "ethnic minorities" have interracial marriage rates that are considerably higher than those for the general population or those of Whites. Yet, interracial marriage among Japanese and Native American women is now practically normative (40.6% and 53.7%, respectively) while such behavior is still rather rare among Blacks (1.2% for Black women and 3.6% for Black men). Fur-

thermore, female outmarriage is higher than male outmarriage for every major racial ethnic group *except* Blacks. (Tucker and Mitchell-Kernan 1990, 209; emphasis in original)

They report higher rates of intermarriage among blacks in Los Angeles as compared to the national figures, but both sets of figures remain very low (well below 10 percent of all black marriages). Naturally, the proportion of white marriages involving blacks is lower still.

In sum, race continues to structure where people live and with whom they share residential space, whom they interact with on a close and regular basis, and to whom they have blood ties. The social organization of race has a number of bases above and beyond those extant in the economic market. Indeed, they are so many and profound, as Blumer argued, that one might well develop the strong a priori expectation that these patterns would come to shape what happens in workplaces and market relations more broadly.

Blacks, Whites, and Power in the Workplace

Our analysis focuses on two key measures of workplace power. First, we distinguish between business owners and nonowners, or workers. Whites and blacks differ considerably in levels of workplace power. We found that 18 percent of whites in our Los Angeles sample are business owners, compared to 9 percent of blacks, a difference of 9 percentage points (see appendix tables). This gap is perhaps better understood in ratio terms, since whites are twice as likely as blacks to be business owners. Black-owned businesses also differ from white-owned businesses in industrial-sector locations, size of firm, and owner earnings. Blacks are less likely than whites to own retail establishments (5 percent versus 15 percent), to own business and repair services (9 percent versus 13 percent), professional service businesses (18 percent versus 27 percent), and less likely to be involved in durable manufacturing (less than 1 percent versus 6 percent). Black business owners are more likely than whites to be found in construction (22 percent versus 11 percent), finance, insurance, and real estate (12 percent versus 6 percent), personal service (9 percent versus 4 percent), and in entertainment and recreation (21 percent versus 11 percent). The differences in firm size are even more striking, with the average number of workers in white-owned firms being 10 compared with 2 in black-owned firms.

Our second measure of workplace power is supervisory authority (Dahrendorf 1959). As was true of business ownership, blacks are also less likely to hold supervisory positions compared to whites: 29 percent versus 42 percent, for a white-to-black ratio of 1.45. In terms of firm size, black and white supervisors are in firms of comparable size (480 versus 399 employees, on average). In addition, there is a large difference in average personal income between black and white supervisors ($62,232 versus $86,035). However, black and white supervisors do appear to be located in very different types of work. Black supervisors are concentrated in a few industrial sectors, with the majority in just two: professional and related services (41 percent) and retail trade (13 percent). Whites with supervisory authority are more evenly spread across industrial sectors, with the four largest categories being: professional and related services (28 percent), retail trade (13 percent), durable manufacturing (12 percent), and business and repair services (9 percent).

Stereotyping and Power in the Workplace   We measure stereotypes of blacks with four bipolar trait rating items: intelligent to unintelligent, prefer to be self-supporting to prefer to live off welfare, easy to get along with to hard to get along with, and speak English well to speak English poorly.[2] We use stereotype difference scores, which show whether respondents see blacks as no different from whites, superior to whites, or inferior to whites. We calculate stereotype difference scores by subtracting the respondent's rating of blacks from the respondent's rating of whites. The difference scores range from a low of −50 (most inferior in-group rating compared to out-group) to a high of +50 (most superior in-group rating compared to out-group rating). A score of zero indicates no perceived difference between the two groups, while higher scores indicate more negative ratings of blacks relative to whites.

We address three possible sources of the tendency to hold negative stereotypical views of African Americans. First, several factors tap exposure to distinctive forms or eras of cultural learning and socialization with regard to race. Older individuals experienced critical life events and perspectives at a time when very different, more overtly antiblack and segregationist ideas were more common (Bobo, Kluegel, and Smith 1997; Schuman et al. 1997). Individuals with more formal education have been exposed to different norms with regard to race and presumably have been either trained or selected for thinking with greater complexity and sophistication. Individuals who had early socializing experiences in the American South are likely to have been exposed to a more overtly antiblack set of ideas and outlooks.

Second, some psychological orientations, or other bases of social identity, frequently have a connection to views toward subordinate racial groups. Specifically, those with more conservative political identi-

TABLE 13.1   *White-Black Stereotype Difference Score Means by Social Background Characteristics*

	Not Intelligent	Prefer Welfare	Hard to Get Along With	Poor English Ability	Stereotype Scale
Overall mean	6.37	15.06	5.13	12.39	9.84
Education					
Less than high school diploma	5.51***	11.3***	5.51***	9.26***	7.59***
High school diploma	5.65	16.11	3.98	11.88	9.64
Some college	7.75	16.35	5.58	12.69	10.67
Bachelor's degree	5.64	13.64	6.00	13.16	9.69
Post-graduate	5.34	13.59	3.76	12.01	8.69
Gender					
Female	7.08	16.08	5.84	12.85	10.59
Male	5.65	14.03	4.60	11.92	9.07
Age					
Twenty-one to twenty-nine years	4.42***	12.66***	5.44***	10.61***	8.08***
Thirty to thirty-nine years	5.31	15.13	2.93	11.50	8.72
Forty to forty-nine years	5.03	12.44	3.16	11.43	8.21
Fifty plus years	8.90	17.80	7.76	14.44	12.57
Conservatism					
Liberal	5.04*	10.71***	2.58**	10.13***	7.21***
Moderate or no thought	5.62	15.67	4.68	12.23	9.74
Conservative	8.32	18.44	7.87	14.63	12.36

Religion					
Protestant	7.12*	15.78	4.53	12.42	9.95
Catholic	7.01	14.85	5.76	13.89	10.57
Other religion	6.73	16.70	5.36	12.04	10.54
Agnostic or atheist	2.29	10.91	4.57	10.08	6.93
Religious attendance					
More than once a week	3.93*	13.94*	4.03	10.66	7.59*
Once a week	8.71	17.80	5.57	12.84	11.56
Almost once a week	9.01	20.17	5.39	14.13	12.02
Few times a month	7.21	18.20	3.39	14.01	10.88
Few times a year	5.93	14.40	5.72	13.35	10.03
Never	2.58	13.00	2.08	10.70	8.61
Residence at age sixteen					
Non-South	6.59	15.22	4.84	12.13	9.82
Southern resident	8.28	16.91	8.00	14.48	11.98
Business ownership					
Worker	6.13	14.90	5.48	11.84	9.71
Owner	7.20	15.93	3.93	11.09	9.54
Job authority					
Not supervisor	6.24	15.45	5.23	11.48	9.81
Supervisor	6.42	14.57	5.17	12.01	9.49

Source: Los Angeles Study of Urban Inequality 1994.
*$p < .05$, **$p < .01$, ***$p < .001$

ties often adopt a traditional, status-hierarchy maintenance orientation that readily embraces more hostile outlooks toward racial minorities (Sidanius, Pratto, and Bobo 1996). There are often differences in the level of prejudice attributable to differences in religious denomination and, especially, to religiosity (frequency of church attendance). Third, we also examine whether those with power in the workplace exhibit more or less antiblack stereotyping than those lacking such power.

Table 13.1 presents mean difference scores on the four stereotype trait dimensions—intelligence, welfare dependency, ease of interracial interaction, and poor English-speaking ability—as well as for an average score across the four items.[3] Concentrating on the overall mean differences, it is clear that whites rate blacks as inferior to whites on each of the four dimensions. The difference is at its largest on the welfare dependency dimension, with a difference of comparable magnitude also occurring on the English-speaking-ability trait. There is a consistent tendency to see blacks as more likely to possess negative attributes than whites. Education, age, and conservatism exhibit the most consistent connection to the individual trait dimensions and the overall stereotype index. There are less consistent effects for the religion measures. As the table shows, there is no overall mean difference in antiblack stereotyping between those with workplace power and those lacking it, whether considering the supervisory authority dimension or the ownership dimension.

We conducted three further tests to determine whether the pattern of stereotyping among those with workplace power differed from those who neither owned nor exerted control in the work setting. Under a strong version of the market dynamic perspective, we might expect to find that those with power in the workplace less readily engage in negative stereotyping. To assess this possibility we, first, examined whether there was a difference in the likelihood of offering a "don't know" response to any of the stereotype trait rating items by workplace power. Table 13.2 shows there is no difference, with one exception. Owners are significantly more likely than workers to offer a "don't know" response to the intelligence item, although a small cell count indicates that this finding should be interpreted with caution. Second, we examined whether workplace power affected the chances of using the midpoint response of 4 on the original 1 to 7 stereotype trait rating scales. Again, we saw that it did not. Third, we examined interviewer debriefing ratings of respondent behavior concerning the racial attitudes section of the questionnaire. Interviewers were asked to indicate whether a respondent had hesitated during the racial attitudes section, consistently attempted to qualify or justify his or her answers, showed signs of dis-

TABLE 13.2   Whites' Stereotypes of Blacks by Ownership and Job Authority

	Ownership		Authority	
	Worker	Owner	No	Yes
Unintelligent				
Neutral response	46%	42%	42%	49%
Non-neutral	54	58	58	51
Do not know	1*	5[a]	2	2[a]
Valid response	99	95	98	98
Prefer welfare				
Neutral response	23	20	23	22
Non-neutral	77	80	77	78
Do not know	1[a]	2[a]	1[a]	1[a]
Valid response	99	98	99	99
Hard to get along with				
Neutral response	38	41	40	37
Non-neutral	62	59	60	63
Do not know	2	1[a]	1	2[a]
Valid response	98	99	99	98
Poor English				
Neutral response	23	17	21	22
Non-neutral	77	83	79	78
Do not know	—	1[a]	1[a]	1[a]
Valid response	100	99	99	99

Source: Los Angeles Study of Urban Inequality 1994.
[a] Cell count less than ten.
*$p < .05$

comfort, or objected to the entire section. As table 13.3 shows, only one of the eight tests (four debriefing items by two dimensions of workplace power) met conventional criteria of statistical significance. We find that supervisors are less likely to show discomfort than those without supervisory authority. The summary count mean significantly differs by job authority, indicating that, overall, interviewers rated nonsupervisors as more sensitive to the racial attitudes section of the survey than supervisors, a trend opposite to the pattern that the market dynamics hypothesis would have predicted.

TABLE 13.3   *Interviewer Observations of Whites by Ownership and Job Authority*

	Ownership		Authority	
	Worker	Owner	No	Yes
Interviewer observations				
Paused or hesitated	38%	28%	40%	31%
Justified or qualified answers	21	19	23	17
Showed discomfort	16	12	18*	11
Objected to section	5	3ª	5	3
Summary count				
None	51	64	78	61
Yes to one item	27	18	28	22
Yes to two items	15	11	16	12
Yes to three items	6	5ª	7	4
Yes to four items	1ª	2ª	1ª	1ª
Mean of summary count	.80	.69	.85**	.66

Source: Los Angeles Study of Urban Inequality 1994.
ª Cell count less than 10.
*p < .05, **p < .001

In sum, we find not only no difference in the overall level of negative stereotyping by power in the workplace, but no apparent difference in readiness to stereotype. The results of our test of hypothesis 1 favor the group position over the market dynamic framework. The degree and character of whites' stereotypes of African Americans are held largely without regard to the level of power a white individual holds in the workplace.

The analyses shown in table 13.4 involve tests of hypotheses 2 and 3, which speak to the determinants of racial stereotypes. Recall that hypothesis 2 concerned whether the cultural socializing factors of age, education, and region of upbringing had differential effects on negative stereotyping depending on level of workplace power. Hypothesis 3 concerned whether the psychological orientation factors of conservatism and religiosity had differential effects on stereotyping depending on the level of workplace power. To test these hypotheses, we estimated three OLS regression models in nested steps. At step 1, stereotyping is specified as a function of age, education, gender (male = 1), region of upbringing (South = 1), conservatism (high score = extreme conservatism), religiosity, and a series of dummy variables for religious denomination. At step 2, we add dummy variables representing the workplace power measures for ownership (owner = 1) and for supervisory authority (supervisor = 1). At step 3, we test for interactions between each of

TABLE 13.4   *Whites' Stereotyping of Blacks (Difference Score)*

	Model 1	Model 2	Model 3
Constant	−3.64	−.27	−5.88
	(3.87)	(3.92)	(6.71)
Background characteristics			
Age	.08	.10*	.08
	(.04)	(.05)	(.07)
Education	.19	−.02	.39
	(.18)	(.20)	(.28)
Gender	−1.49	−1.40	−1.49
	(1.08)	(1.04)	(1.00)
South at sixteen	1.89	−.52	−.30
	(1.97)	(1.36)	(1.64)
Conservatism	1.49*	1.64*	1.88*
	(.40)	(.39)	(.57)
Church attendance	.32	−.04	−.15
	(.31)	(.34)	(.44)
Catholic	1.82	.99	1.11
	(1.31)	(1.26)	(1.25)
Other religion	1.73	1.97	2.56
	(1.34)	(1.57)	(1.52)
Agnostic or atheist	−2.04	−1.37	−1.29
	(2.29)	(2.42)	(2.29)
Workplace power			
Owner	—	.41	−6.54
		(1.47)	(7.12)
Supervisor	—	−.09	12.01
		(1.10)	(10.01)
Interactions			
Age × Owner	—	—	.05
			(.10)
Age × Supervisor	—	—	.04
			(.09)
Education × Owner	—	—	−.32
			(.36)
Education × Supervisor	—	—	−.54
			(.38)
Conservatism × Owner	—	—	.72
			(.71)
Conservatism × Supervisor	—	—	−.82
			(.73)
Attendance × Owner	—	—	1.49
			(.91)
Attendance × Supervisor	—	—	−.60
			(.76)
Region × Owner	—	—	4.76
			(3.03)

(Table continues on p. 508.)

TABLE 13.4   *Continued*

	Model 1	Model 2	Model 3
Region × Supervisor	—	—	−2.22
			(2.49)
R squared	.10	.13	.15
N	613	473	473

Source: Los Angeles Study of Urban Inequality 1994.
*p < .001

the workplace power measures and age, education, conservatism, religiosity, and region of upbringing.[4]

In the multivariate framework, only age and conservatism prove to be significant direct determinants of antiblack stereotyping. Model 2 shows that older whites and those with more conservative ideological outlooks tend to hold more derogatory views of African Americans. These are important results, especially the effect of ideology, since it underscores that such stereotypes are, at least in part, a reflection of cultural learning and filtered through other psychological predispositions. Model 2 makes it clear that there is no significant difference in the level of stereotyping, net of these other factors, based on either ownership or supervisory authority. Model 3 introduces all the interaction terms. Collectively, adding the interaction terms increases the variance explained from .13 to .15. However inspection of the individual coefficients indicates that none of the interactions is significant.

These results tend to suggest, consistent with the group position framework, that the underpinnings of the racial attitudes of those with power in the workplace do not differ appreciably from those lacking such power. Table 13.1 showed no difference at the bivariate level in the degree of antiblack stereotyping by workplace power. Table 13.4 adds three further pieces of information. No difference in stereotyping emerges after controlling for such other variables as education, age, gender, region of upbringing, conservatism, and religion. In the main, the process of stereotyping does not appear to be contingent on level of power in the workplace.

Our final hypothesis concerned the effects of stereotypes on other outcomes. The other outcomes of interest are, first, perceptions of zero-sum competition with blacks for economic and political resources and, second, level of support for affirmative action. The substantive question is whether those with workplace power are any less likely to translate antiblack stereotypes into other hostile orientations. Once again, we estimated three models in nested steps. The first model contains age, education, region of upbringing, gender, conservatism, religiosity, religion, and the stereotyping index. The second model then introduces the workplace power variables. The third model tests for an interaction between stereotyping and workplace power.

Table 13.5 examines the possible differential effect of workplace power and antiblack stereotyping on perceptions of zero-sum group competition with blacks.[5] As model 1 shows, the more negative a white respondent's stereotypes of blacks, the more likely the individual is to perceive blacks as zero-sum competitive threats. Perceptions of threat also increase with age and political conservatism. Model 2 shows neither workplace power variable exhibiting a significant relationship to perceptions of threat. The introduction of the workplace power measures in model 2 reduces the effects of conservatism to insignificance. However, the individual interaction coefficients are insignificant, indicating that workplace power does not interact with stereotyping to influence perceptions of competitive threat (model 3).

Our second effort to examine the potentially differential consequences of stereotyping involves levels of opposition to affirmative action in the workplace for blacks.[6] In this case, Model 1 shows that as political conservatism rises, so too does opposition to affirmative action. In addition, opposition to affirmative action is significantly lower among those from "other" religions than among Protestants. Negative stereotyping of blacks has a significant effect on opposition to affirmative action for blacks. Introducing the workplace power variables (model 2) shows that supervisors are significantly more likely than nonsupervisors to oppose affirmative action. Allowing workplace power and stereotyping to interact (model 3) provides more information. In this instance we find a significant interaction between ownership and negative stereotyping: owners are less likely to translate antiblack stereotypes into opposition to affirmative action.

Conclusion

We began this investigation with the general question of whether the racial attitudes of whites with power in the workplace differed from the racial attitudes of those lacking such power. Our results suggest that they do not. At one level, these results can be read as beginning to fill in an important gap in our knowledge. Discrimination by employers and others with power in the workplace may occur, in part, because these individuals tend to hold the same antiblack stereotypes, for the same reasons, and generalize them to other issues in much the same fashion as everyone else. At least for these data and measures, we can find little

TABLE 13.5   *Whites' Perceived Competitive Threat from Blacks and Opposition to Affirmative Action for Blacks*

	Perceived Competitive Threat			Opposition to Affirmative Action		
	Model 1	Model 2	Model 3	Model 1	Model 2	Model 3
Constant	1.52*	.95	1.06	2.26***	2.09***	2.13***
	(.74)	(.83)	(.81)	(.32)	(.37)	(.37)
Background characteristics						
Age	.01*	.02*	.02*	−.00	−.00	−.00
	(.01)	(.01)	(.01)	(.02)	(.00)	(.00)
Education	−.03	.00	.00	−.00	−.01	−.00
	(.03)	(.04)	(.04)	(.02)	(.02)	(.02)
Gender	.09	.04	.02	.10	.09	.08
	(.17)	(.19)	(.18)	(.09)	(.11)	(.11)
South at sixteen	−.39	−.55	−.62	.08	−.07	−.08
	(.36)	(.33)	(.36)	(.16)	(.16)	(.17)
Conservatism	.14**	.08	.05	.17***	.19***	.18***
	(.05)	(.06)	(.06)	(.03)	(.04)	(.04)
Church attendance	.05	.09	.08	.01	.01	.01
	(.06)	(.06)	(.06)	(.03)	(.04)	(.03)
Catholic	.29	.29	.27	−.03	−.02	−.03
	(.21)	(.24)	(.25)	(.11)	(.12)	(.12)
Other religion	.30	.20	.16	−.23	−.20*	−.21*
	(.21)	(.25)	(.26)	(.09)	(.10)	(.10)
Agnostic or atheist	−.12	−.22	−.26	.09	.14	.14
	(.31)	(.33)	(.33)	(.16)	(.16)	(.16)
Stereotype scale	.03***	.03***	.03**	.01*	.01	.00
	(.01)	(.01)	(.01)	(.01)	(.01)	(.01)
Workplace power						
Owner	—	−.05	−.33	—	−.24	−.32*
		(.22)	(.27)		(.14)	(.16)
Supervisor	—	.09	.28	—	.25**	.20
		(.15)	(.18)		(.09)	(.13)
Interactions						
Stereotype × Owner	—	—	.03	—	—	.01
			(.02)			(.01)
Stereotype × Supervisor	—	—	−.02	—	—	.00
			(.01)			(.01)
R^2	.24	.27	.29	.14	.17	.17
N	199	156	156	612	473	473

Source: Los Angeles Study of Urban Inequality 1994.
*$p < .05$, **$p < .01$, ***$p < .001$

sign that whites with power in the workplace differ in their attitudes toward blacks from those lacking such power.

Does it matter to know that those with power in the workplace adopt and apparently use racial stereotypes in much the same fashion as those without such power? In a context of intense concern about labor market outcomes for subordinate racial groups, especially for African Americans, we think it does. First, there is strong reason to expect such perceptions to exert a diffuse effect on behavior (Schuman 1995). There is now a wide body of social psychological research suggesting that group stereotypes can influence consequential social judgments, even in the presence of important "individuating" information (see reviews in Brewer and Kramer 1985; Brown 1995, esp. 90–99; Duckitt 1992, 81–84).

Second, there is wide latitude for such stereotypes to influence decisions in the workplace in particular. Employers rarely have information to make strong or conclusive judgments about the likely productivity of a potential new hire and are frequently surprised by the outcomes of their choices (Bishop 1993). Hence, as the economist Harry Holzer explained: "Under these circumstances there is considerable room for discriminatory judgments about who will be competent in performing a variety of job-specific tasks" (1996, 83).

Social psychological research on stereotyping provides important leverage here. Perhaps the single most consistent finding of stereotyping research is that stereotypes lead to selective information processing in a manner that tends to confirm the existing stereotype (Duckitt 1992, 82; Stephan 1985). What is more, considerable research suggests that one of the social conditions most likely to activate and encourage reliance on a group stereotype is the arousal of feelings of discomfort (Brown 1995, 104–5). Given the relative infrequency of black-white social interaction generally, especially as status equals or in close casual acquaintances, it is likely that workplace encounters arouse a degree of uncertainty and discomfort for both blacks and whites.

This may be particularly true in the types of encounters that occur at the point of a hiring decision. The African American job applicant may be particularly eager to behave in ways that do not conform to stereotypes and to monitor for any signs of racial bias. The white business owner or supervisor is engaging in a comparatively novel interracial interaction and may be eager to avoid conveying the impression that race is in any way influencing his or her thinking. Ironically, rather than curbing the operation of stereotypes, it is exactly this mix of pressures that may exaggerate the adverse effects of stereotypes.[7]

Third, there is a growing body of evidence to suggest that employers probably do act on racial stereotypes. For example, Holzer's large-scale surveys of employers in Atlanta, Boston, Detroit, and Los Angeles found that: "even after controlling for racial differences in educational attainment, employer perceptions of racial and gender differences in abilities to perform tasks, in certain credentials, and in the preferences of their customers apparently lead them to hire blacks (and Hispanics) much less frequently in some jobs than others" (1996, 103). The evidence on this point is even more direct from in-depth interview studies of employers. Joleen Kirschenman and Kathryn Neckerman write: "Chicago's employers did not hesitate to generalize about race or ethnic differences in the quality of the labor force. Most associated negative images with inner-city workers, and particularly with black men. 'Black' and 'inner city' were inextricably linked, and both were linked with lower class" (1991, 230–31).

Our research thus helps fill in another important piece of the puzzle of how and why blacks remain disadvantaged in the modern urban labor market. Whites with power in the workplace appear to arrive at and draw inferences from their stereotypes of blacks in much the same fashion as those lacking such workplace power. There is a larger historical and contemporaneous social organization to race that supports a set of racial stereotypes—persistent black-white economic inequality, sharp racial residential segregation, racially homogeneous social networks and family structures—all of which facilitate the likelihood that race and racial stereotypes will operate in the economic arena.

There may, of course, be many who argue that racial stereotypes include a large element of truth (compare Sniderman and Piazza 1993). A number of labor market differences between blacks and whites appear to involve noteworthy differences in skill levels (for reviews, see Ferguson 1995; Holzer 1996). Hence, it is often argued that most of what flows from stereotypes is "statistical discrimination," where, given the costs of obtaining more detailed diagnostic information, it is sensible and legitimate for employers to act on their knowledge of meaningful aggregate differences in key potential productivity-related attributes between blacks and other groups.

We believe this analysis is mistaken at several levels. To be sure, we share with most social psychologists the assumption that stereotypes often reflect the actual distribution of social groups into differently valued social roles and structural positions in society (Eagly and Steffen 1984; Duckitt 1992; Brown 1995). We also share two further assumptions about stereotypes typically made by social psychologists: that this "realistic" social basis to stereotypes provides no more than the kernel of truth to a stereotype; and that the operation of stereotypes, in this case racial stereotypes, remains inherently problematic and thus cannot be excused. This is so because they facilitate categorical and discriminatory treatment and because they usually involve the attribution of group differences to individual dispositions rather than to social processes and circumstances (Pettigrew 1981; Duckitt 1992). There may well be a meaningful difference, on average, between blacks and whites on such traits as "commitment to work," especially among young, low-skilled African Americans compared to white middle-class expectations. But, such differences neither justify shortchanging a real assessment of individual potential in any particular situation, nor make legitimate the common assumption that the onus for change rests on the stereotyped individual rather than on the social structures and conditions that created the difference. As the economist Ronald Ferguson has cogently argued:

> Substantially reducing racial disparity among young adults in the labor market requires supporting *and* holding accountable the institutions that should inspire, educate, and nurture African American children. In addition, it requires continued vigilance against racial bias in the workplace that validates young people's expectations that the game is rigged against them even when they do their part to prepare and perform. Given the complexity of the social forces that affect the acquisition of skill and success in labor markets, and given that social forces are malleable, this author rejects any assertion that the remaining differences in skill among blacks and whites . . . are genetically predetermined . . . or that society should acquiesce and be content to tolerate them. (1995, 39; emphasis in original)

In this regard, it is interesting to note that William Julius Wilson's (1996) interviews with both black and white employers show the former to hire blacks more often, despite sharing with their white counterparts a stereotype of low-skilled blacks. The crucial difference appears to be that for black employers, this stereotype is understood as having malleable social causes as opposed to the more dispositional assumption made by the white employers. Thus, while from the purview of much economistic reasoning, there is an important logical distinction between pure and statistical discrimination, it should be equally borne in mind that from the purview of much social psychologistic reasoning, the categorical treatment of individual members of a socially defined racial group is intrinsically problematic.

Lastly, we should be clear about the scope of the implications to be drawn from these results. Nothing we have found or argued implies that stereotyping or racial dynamics completely overwhelm market forces, situation-specific interactions, or information about an individual. Indeed, phenomena such as the Massachusetts Miracle, which involved such tight labor markets that even segments of the population normally confronting very bleak employment opportunities found work (that is, young, low-skilled, black males), plainly suggest otherwise. The work of

Evans and Kelley (1991) with respect to recent immigrants in the Australian labor market makes the same point. Our point is that as long as stereotypes persist and are widely shared, especially by those with power in the workplace, economic conditions and roles alone are not enough to account for the range of conditions and experiences blacks are highly likely to encounter in the labor market. As a result, meaningful social analyses must engage, directly and substantively, the matter of race.

Our central message, therefore, is that scholars attempting to understand group inequality in modern urban labor markets need to adjust some central or baseline theoretical and empirical expectations. This adjustment involves a reframing of analyses in a manner that the ex ante expectation is that—in addition to conventional human capital, class analytic and institutional or organization variables—negative stereotypes of African Americans matter in the workplace, and matter for a variety of labor market dynamics (such as hiring decisions, and raise and promotion decisions). Furthermore, in all likelihood these stereotypes function to create higher, more difficult, and recurrent constraints to black success in the labor market. They are likely to introduce a powerful set of irreducibly race-linked and noneconomic factors into marketplace dynamics.

Appendix

TABLE 13A.1   *Workplace Power by Race of Respondent*

	Whites	Blacks	Asians	Latinos	Total	F
Business Ownership						
Worker	82%	91%	71%	91%	86%	9.75*
Owner	18	9	29	9	14	
Job Authority						
Not Supervisor	58	71	90	76	67	14.92*
Supervisor	42	29	40	24	33	

Source: Los Angeles Study of Urban Inequality 1994.
*$p < .001$

TABLE 13A.2   *Mean Firm Size and Mean Family Income by Race of Respondent*

	Whites	Blacks	Asians	Latinos	F
Firm size					
Owners	10	2	6	406	4.46**
Supervisors	399	480	193	279	2.85*
Family income					
Owners	$89,082	$81,702	$80,546	$35,665	5.34***
Supervisors	$86,035	$62,232	$46,126	$42,987	6.75***

Source: Los Angeles Study of Urban Inequality 1994.
*$p < .05$, **$p < .01$, ***$p < .001$

TABLE 13A.3   *Industrial Sector for Owners by Race*

	Whites	Blacks	Asians	Latinos	Total
Agricultural, forestry, fish	4%	2%	1%	—	3%
Construction	11	22	3	17	13
Nondurable manufacturing	1	1	11	17	6
Durable manufacturing	6	<1	3	2	4
Transportation, communication, other public utility	—	<1	2	5	1
Wholesale trade	2	—	7	3	2
Retail trade	15	5	30	15	16
Finance, insurance, real estate	6	12	9	3	6
Business and repair services	13	9	14	7	11
Personal services	4	9	2	19	8
Entertainment and recreation	11	21	2	5	9
Professional and related services	27	18	16	8	20

Source: Los Angeles Study of Urban Inequality 1994.

TABLE 13A.4   *Industrial Sector for Supervisors by Race*

	Whites	Blacks	Asians	Latinos	Total
Agricultural, forestry, fish	1%	<1%	<1%	3%	1%
Construction	8	3	4	11	8
Nondurable manufacturing	3	3	15	16	7
Durable manufacturing	12	6	5	11	10
Transportation, communication, other public utility	8	5	7	11	9
Wholesale trade	1	1	9	2	2
Retail trade	13	13	21	18	15
Finance, insurance, real estate	6	7	5	6	6
Business and repair services	9	8	8	6	8
Personal services	1	1	6	3	2
Entertainment and recreation	6	6	1	<1	4
Professional and related services	28	41	18	11	24
Public administration	4	4	1	3	3

Source: Los Angeles Study of Urban Inequality 1994.

TABLE 13A.5   *Occupation for Owners by Race*

	Whites	Blacks	Asians	Latinos	Total
Managerial and professional	50%	48%	52%	17%	42%
Technical, sales	25	13	35	15	23
Service	12	10	5	28	15
Other	13	29	9	39	20

Source: Los Angeles Study of Urban Inequality 1994.

TABLE 13A.6   *Occupation for Supervisors by Race*

	Whites	Blacks	Asians	Latinos	Total
Managerial and professional	53%	38%	61%	23%	44%
Technical, sales	24	32	29	22	24
Service	8	19	4	11	10
Other	16	11	6	44	22

Source: Los Angeles Study of Urban Inequality 1994.

TABLE 13A.7   *Workplace Power of Whites by Gender, Nativity, and Conservatism*

	Ownership		Authority		
	Worker	Owner	No	Yes	N
Gender					
Women	86%	14%	68%**	32%	(324)
Men	79	21	50	50	(344)
Nativity					
Foreign born	69*	31	64	36	(94)
Native	85	15	57	43	(574)
Conservatism					
Liberal	76	24	55	45	(211)
Moderate or no thought	85	15	62	38	(234)
Conservative	85	15	57	43	(220)

Source: Los Angeles Study of Urban Inequality 1994.
*$p < .01$, **$p < .001$

TABLE 13A.8   *Mean Education, Age, Family Income, and Conservatism for Whites by Workplace Power*

	Ownership			Authority		
	Worker	Owner	F	No	Yes	F
Education	14.1	15.0	3.43 ns	14	14.7	7.68**
Age	41.8	45.6	3.61 ns	41.8	43.4	1.33 ns
Family income	$61,617	$89,082	3.87*	$52,465	$86,035	11.70***
Conservatism	4.04	3.69	1.85 ns	3.65	4.00	.13 ns

Source: Los Angeles Study of Urban Inequality 1994.
*$p < .05$, **$p < .01$, ***$p < .001$

Notes

1. To be sure, Weber's important conceptual recognition of "status" groups provides a theoretical entrée for a discussion of race, but this did not become a major project for Weber himself.

2. In order to maintain the potential for comparability to other sites in the Multi-City Study of Urban Inequality, we restrict our analysis to the four trait dimensions that appeared in all four household surveys.

3. The four items constitute a reasonable scale with a Cronbach's alpha of .70.

4. In preliminary analyses, we entered each of the interaction terms into the equation separately. In no instance were there significant effects.

5. Respondents were asked whether they agreed or disagreed with each of the following statements: "More good jobs for blacks mean fewer good jobs for whites" and "The more influence blacks have in local politics the less influence whites will have in local politics." The two items are highly correlated $(r = .57)$, and though composed of only two items, Cronbach's alpha for a simple additive scale of the two items is also quite high (alpha = .73). See Bobo and Hutchings (1996) for analyses of closely similar items. Because of a split-ballot experiment, the perceived group competitive threat items were asked only of a randomly selected third of the sample.

6. Respondents were asked whether they favored or opposed each of two forms of affirmative action for blacks: "Some people feel that because of past disadvantages there are some groups in society that should receive special job training and educational assistance. Others say that it is unfair to give these groups special job training and educational assistance. What about you?" and "Some people feel that because of past disadvantages there are some groups in society that should be given preference in hiring and promotion. Others say that it is unfair to give these groups special preferences. What about you?" The two questions are highly interrelated $(r = .45)$ and, though composed of only two items, the Cronbach's alpha for a simple additive scale of the two items is reasonable (alpha = .62).

7. Indeed, this sort of process of stereotypes having heightened effects in an interview situation casts a very different light on the finding of greater racial discrimination by employers in suburban as compared to central-city areas (Holzer 1996). Rather than reflecting more negative attitudes on the part of employers or suburban customers, it may reflect the more infrequent, and therefore anxiety-producing and stereotype-enhancing, character of black-white interactions in suburban work settings. Suburbs are settings that may increase the

correspondence between stereotypes and behavior or likelihood of the expression of underlying stereotypes in overt behavior.

References

Arrow, Kenneth. 1973. "The Theory of Discrimination." In *Discrimination in Labor Markets*, edited by O. Aschenfelter and A. Rees. Princeton, N.J.: Princeton University Press.

Becker, Gary S. 1957. *The Economics of Discrimination*. Chicago: University of Chicago Press.

Bishop, John. 1993. "Improving Job Matches in the U.S. Labor Market." *Brookings Papers on Economic Activity—Microeconomics* 1: 375–90.

Blauner, Robert A. 1972. *Racial Oppression in America*. New York: Harper & Row.

Blumer, Herbert. 1958a. "Race Prejudice as a Sense of Group Position." *Pacific Sociological Review* 1: 3–7.

———. 1958b. "Recent Research on Race Relations: United States of America." *International Social Science Bulletin* 10: 403–77.

———. 1965a. "Industrialization and Race Relations." In *Industrialization and Race Relations: A Symposium*, edited by G. Hunter. New York: Oxford University Press.

———. 1965b. "The Future of the Color Line." In *The South in Continuity and Change*, edited by J. C. McKinney and E. T. Thompson. Durham, N.C.: Seeman.

Bobo, Lawrence. 1983. "Whites' Opposition to Busing: Symbolic Racism or Realistic Group Conflict?" *Journal of Personality and Social Psychology* 45: 1196–1210.

———. 1999. "Prejudice as Group Position: Microfoundations of a Sociological Approach to Racism and Race Relations. *Journal of Social Issues* 55: 445–72.

Bobo, Lawrence, and Vincent L. Hutchings. 1996. "Perceptions of Racial Group Competition: Extending Blumer's Theory of Group Position to a Multiracial Social Context." *American Sociological Review* 61: 951–72.

Bobo, Lawrence, and James R. Kluegel. 1993. "Opposition to Race-Targeting: Self-Interest, Stratification Ideology, or Racial Attitudes." *American Sociological Review* 58: 443–64.

———. 1997. "Status, Ideology, and Dimensions of Whites' Racial Beliefs and Attitudes: Progress and Stagnation." In *Racial Attitudes in the 1990s: Continuity and Change*, edited by S. A. Tuch and J. K. Martin. Westport, Conn.: Praeger.

Bobo, Lawrence, James R. Kluegel, and Ryan A. Smith. 1997. "Laissez-Faire Racism: The Crystallization of a 'Kinder, Gentler' Anti-Black Ideology." In *Racial Attitudes in the 1990s: Continuity and Change*, edited by S. A. Tuch and J. K. Martin. Westport, Conn.: Praeger.

Bobo, Lawrence, and Camille L. Zubrinsky. 1996. "Attitudes on Residential Integration: Perceived Status Differences, Mere In-Group Preference, or Racial Prejudice?" *Social Forces* 74: 883–909.

Bondach, Edna. 1991 (orig. pub. 1980). "Class Approaches to Ethnicity and Race." In *Majority and Minority: The Dynamics of Race and Ethnicity in American Life*, edited by Norman R. Yetman. Boston: Allyn and Bacon.

Brewer, Marilynn B., and Roderick M. Kramer. 1985. "The Psychology of Intergroup Attitudes and Behavior." *Annual Review of Psychology* 36: 219–41.

Brown, Rupert. 1995. *Prejudice: Its Social Psychology*. Cambridge, Mass.: Blackwell.

Dahrendorf, Ralf. 1959. *Class and Class Conflict in Industrial Society*. Stanford, Calif.: Stanford University Press.

Denton, Nancy A. 1994. "Are African Americans Still Hypersegregated in 1990?" In *Residential Apartheid: The American Legacy*, edited by Robert Ballard, Charles Lee, and J. Eugene Grisly. Los Angeles: UCLA Center for Afro-American Studies.

Duckitt, John H. 1992. *The Social Psychology of Prejudice*. New York: Praeger.

Eagly, Alice H., and Valerie J. Steffan. 1984. "Gender Stereotypes, Occupational Roles, and Beliefs about Part-Time Employees." *Psychology of Women Quarterly* 10: 252–62.

Evans, M.D.R., and Jonathan Kelley. 1991. "Prejudice, Discrimination, and the Labor Market: Attainments of Immigrants in Australia." *American Journal of Sociology* 97: 721–59.

Fainstein, Susan S., and Norman I. Fainstein. 1989. "The Racial Dimension in Urban Political Economy." *Urban Affairs Quarterly* 25: 187–99.

Farley, Reynolds, and William H. Frey. 1994. "Changes in the Segregation of Whites from Blacks During the 1980s: Small Steps Toward a More Integrated Society." *American Sociological Review* 59: 23–45.

Farley, Reynolds, Charlotte Steeh, Maria Krysan, Tara Jackson, and Keith Reeves. 1994. "Stereotypes and Segregation: Neighborhoods in the Detroit Area." *American Journal of Sociology* 100: 750–80.

Ferguson, Ronald F. 1995. "Shifting Challenges: Fifty Years of Economic Change Toward Black-White Earnings Inequality." *Daedalus* 124: 16–45.

Fossett, Mark A., and K. Jill Kiecolt. 1989. "The Relative Size of Minority Populations and White Racial Attitudes." *Social Science Quarterly* 70: 820–35.

Gans, Herbert J. 1999. "The Possibility of a New Racial Hierarchy in the Twenty-First-Century United States." In *The Cultural Territories of Race: Black and White Boundaries*, edited by Michéle Lamont. Chicago and New York: University of Chicago Press and Russell Sage.

Holzer, Harry J. 1996. *What Employers Want*. New York: Russell Sage Foundation.

Jackman, Mary R., and Mary S. Senter. 1983. "Different, Therefore Un-equal: Beliefs About Trait Differences Between Groups of Unequal Status." *Research in Social Stratification and Mobility* 2: 309–35.

Kirschenman, Joleen, and Kathryn M. Neckerman. 1991. "'We'd Love to Hire Them, But . . .': The Meaning of Race for Employers." In *The Urban Underclass*, edited by C. Jencks and P. Peterson. Washington, D.C.: Brookings Institution.

Marsden, Peter V. 1987. "Core Discussion Networks of Americans." *American Sociological Review* 52: 122–31.

Massey, Douglas S., and Nancy A. Denton. 1993. *American Apartheid: Segregation and the Making of the Underclass*. Cambridge, Mass.: Harvard University Press.

Merton, Robert K. 1949. "Discrimination and the American Creed." In *Discrimination and National Welfare*, edited by R. M. MacIver. New York: Harper & Row.

Nee, Victor, Jimy M. Sanders, and Scott Sernau. 1994. "Job Transitions in an Immigrant Metropolis: Ethnic Boundaries and the Mixed Econ-omy. *American Sociological Review* 59: 849–72.

Omi, Michael, and Howard Winant. 1986. *Racial Formation in the United States: From the 1960s to the 1980s*. New York: Routledge.

Pettigrew, Thomas F. 1981. "The Ultimate Attribution Error: Extending Allport's Cognitive Analysis of Prejudice. *Personality and Social Psy-chology Bulletin* 5: 461–76.

Quillian, Lincoln. 1995. "Prejudice as a Response to Perceived Group Threat: Population Composition and Anti-Immigrant and Racial Prej-udice in Europe." *American Sociological Review* 60: 586–611.

Reich, Michael. 1981. *Racial Inequality: A Political-Economic Anal-ysis*. Princeton, N.J.: Princeton University Press.

Sanjek, Roger. 1994. "The Enduring Inequalities of Race." In *Race*, edi-ted by S. Gregory and R. Sanjek. New Brunswick, N.J.: Rutgers Uni-versity Press.

Schuman, Howard. 1995. "Attitudes, Beliefs, and Behaviors." In *Socio-logical Perspectives on Social Psychology*, edited by Karen Cook, Gary Alan Fine, and James S. House. Boston: Allyn & Bacon.

Schuman, Howard, Charlotte Steeh, Lawrence Bobo, and Maria Krysan. 1997. *Racial Attitudes in America: Trends and Interpretations*. Cam-bridge, Mass.: Harvard University Press.

Sewell, William H. 1992. "A Theory of Structure: Duality, Agency, and Transformation." *American Journal of Sociology* 98: 1–29.

Sidanius, Jim, Felicia Pratto, and Lawrence Bobo. 1996. "Racism, Con-servatism, Affirmative Action, and Intellectual Sophistication: A Mat-ter of Principled Conservatism or Group Dominance?" *Journal of Per-sonality and Social Psychology* 70: 476–90.

Sigelman, Lee, Timothy Bledsoe, Susan Welch, and Michael W. Combs. 1996. "Making Contact? Black-White Social Interaction in an Urban Setting." *American Journal of Sociology* 5: 1306–32.

Sniderman, Paul, and Thomas Piazza. 1993. *The Scar of Race*. Cambridge, Mass.: Harvard University Press.

Stephan, Walter G. 1985. "Intergroup Relations." In *Handbook of Social Psychology, Volume II*, 3rd edition, edited by Gardner Lindzey and Elliott Aronson. New York: Random House.

Stone, John. 1985. *Racial Conflict in Contemporary Society*. Cambridge, Mass.: Harvard University Press.

Tucker, M. Belinda, and Claudia Mitchell-Kernan. 1990. "New Trends in Black American Interracial Marriage: The Social Structural Context." *Journal of Marriage and the Family* 52: 209–18.

Wellman, David T. 1977. *Portraits of White Racism*. New York: Cambridge University Press.

Wilson, William Julius. 1996. *When Work Disappears: The World of the New Urban Poor*. New York: Knopf.

Zubrinsky, Camille L. 1996. *"I Have Always Wanted to Have a Neighbor, Just Like You . . .": Race and Residential Segregation in the City of Angels*. Ph.D. diss., Department of Sociology, University of California, Los Angeles.

Zubrinsky, Camille L., and Lawrence Bobo. 1996. "Prismatic Metropolis: Race and Residential Segregation in the City of the Angels." *Social Science Research* 25: 335–74.

14

SURVEYING RACIAL DISCRIMINATION: ANALYSES FROM A MULTIETHNIC LABOR MARKET

Lawrence D. Bobo and Susan A. Suh

T HE DEBATE over the extent, nature, and consequences of modern racial-ethnic discrimination continues to grow. Social science research has not yielded simple answers to the question of the current potency of race-based discrimination in the workplace. On the one hand, the growth of the black middle class (Landry 1987), significant affirmative action and antidiscrimination enforcement efforts (Burstein 1985; Jaynes and Williams 1989), and more positive racial attitudes (Firebaugh and Davis 1988; Schuman, Steeh, and Bobo 1985) all point toward a potentially diminishing problem of labor market discrimination (Wilson 1978). On the other hand, systematic social science investigations of actual forms of discrimination have become a surprising new area of active inquiry (Reskin, forthcoming).[1] Research over the past decade spanning auditing studies (Turner et al. 1991), in-depth interviews (Feagin and Sikes 1994; Kirschenman and Neckerman 1991), organizational surveys (Braddock and McPartland 1987), as well as social psychological (Pettigrew and Martin 1987) and sociopolitical analyses (Carnoy 1994; Waldinger and Bailey 1991), all tend to suggest that racial-ethnic discrimination remains a common problem, especially for African Americans.

Attitude studies complicate the picture further by partly confirming positions on both sides of the discrimination debate. Many sample surveys suggest that blacks and other minorities generally perceive high rates of collective or group discrimination (Jaynes and Williams 1989, 131–36; Kluegel and Smith 1986). Nonetheless, many of these same studies tend to elicit very low levels of personal reports of experiences with discrimination (Sigelman and Welch 1991). For example, national surveys from the mid-1980s showed that 61 percent of blacks felt that blacks as a group faced discrimination in wages and 68 percent felt that blacks faced discrimination in gaining managerial positions. Yet, only 39 percent of black respondents to the same survey reported that they had personally faced discrimination in the labor market (Sigelman and Welch 1991, 55–57).

Our broad objective is to examine the utility of general population surveys for illuminating personal reports of labor market discrimination. Our specific analytical purposes in this chapter are threefold. First, we analyze data expressly designed to contain multiple-item measures of possible encounters with racial discrimination in the workplace, as well as a detailed open-ended description of one of these encounters. We suspect that the relatively low rates of reported personal encounters with discrimination found in many surveys reflect reliance on responses to one question or a small number of general items. Second, we analyze data from a multiethnic labor market. The great bulk of social research on the problem of racial discrimination has focused on the black experience. Although important in its own right, this focus is constraining in at least two ways. The U.S. population is far more racially diverse. But also, given the concentration of many recent Asian and Hispanic-Latino immigrants in major urban centers with large black populations (Waldinger 1989), even those primarily interested in the status of African Americans must increasingly pay attention to the altered dynamics of workplaces and larger labor markets in the newly multiethnic social context. Third, we also assess the impact of personal encounters with discrimination on a broader sense of racial-ethnic identity and attachment. What constitutes discrimination can be a matter of judgment. It thus seems important to determine how closely connected the personal reporting of discrimination is to other indicators of ethnic awareness.

Background

There is no uniformly accepted definition of *discrimination* in the social sciences. The social processes involved in discrimination are enormously complex. It may take direct and indirect forms, involve blatant or subtle acts, have both immediate and longer-term effects on individuals and on broader social relations between groups. Students of discrimination also differ in the research questions they examine, the levels of analyses they conduct (for example, interpersonal versus macrosocial), and the political values they hold. All these considerations have made arriving at a single conceptualization of discrimination difficult (see Pettigrew and Taylor 1990).

Our interest is in learning what individuals can relate to us about their own encounters with discrimination. For this purpose a service-able definition conceives of discrimination as "involving actions that serve to limit the social, political, or economic opportunities of particular groups" (Fredrickson and Knobel 1982, 31). Our focus is thus on the interpersonal, observable experience of discrimination. We are concerned with discrimination that individuals are aware of and can thus potentially relate to an interviewer when asked about it.

Even when the term is defined in this manner, however, many researchers remain skeptical of the utility of general population surveys (and possibly any quantitatively oriented methodology) for illuminating processes of discrimination. Writing two decades ago, Joe Feagin and Douglas Lee Eckberg argued that: "By emphasizing census data, survey data, laboratory settings, and the mathematical analysis of existing data, social science will not deal with phenomena such as discrimination that might occur in natural settings" (1980, 18). This reservation doubtless played a part in the reliance on 209 snowball sample in-depth interviews in a major study of the black middle class conducted by Joe Feagin and Melvin Sikes, who emphasize that such data provide a "richness of material unavailable in surface-level analyses based on surveys and opinion polls" (1994, x). An element of this skepticism is hinted at in the important analyses of surveys of employers that have largely stressed patterns derived from in-depth interviews (Kirschenman and Neckerman 1991; Neckerman and Kirschenman 1991).

To our knowledge, Lee Sigelman and Susan Welch (1991) provide the only in-depth survey-based effort to map and model personal reports of discrimination. Analyzing national data on African Americans, they found that 60 percent reported at least one encounter with discrimination spanning the life domains of work, housing, and education. The main determinants of reports of discrimination were sex, age, education, subjective class identification, and subjective feelings of economic insecurity. Men were slightly more likely to report discrimination than women, older blacks more than the young, the highly educated more than the poorly educated, and those identifying with the working class and feelings of economic insecurity.[2]

Previous research points to a number of workplace characteristics and dynamics that are likely to influence the odds of encountering discrimination. Public-sector employment is often seen as a site of less discrimination at point of entry and a generally more hospitable climate for minorities than the private sector (Bean and Tienda 1987; Farley 1984). Smaller firms often have less formal recruitment and hiring procedures than do large firms, which may open the door wider to processes of discrimination (Waldinger 1986). The racial-ethnic background of an individual's coworkers and supervisors can also influence the likelihood of encountering discrimination in the workplace (Pettigrew and Martin 1987).

Previous research suggests that one of the principal mechanisms of discrimination is informal social networks (Feagin and Sikes 1994). Within larger industrial sectors (Waldinger and Bailey 1991) and within specific work sites or locations (Braddock and McPartland 1987), it is the patterns of interaction, association, and information sharing that play a critical role in who gets extended opportunities for employment, pay raises, and promotions. If this is true, we should find that when called upon to describe discriminatory experiences, respondents identify exclusion from important information and decision-making networks as a key factor.[3]

Results
Reports of Discrimination

In interviews with respondents to the Los Angeles Study of Urban Inequality, we asked four questions about personal experience with racial-ethnic discrimination in the labor market. The percentage answering yes to each possible form of discrimination is shown by race of respondent in table 14.1. With only one exception, African Americans and Latinos were the most likely to report direct personal experience with discrimination in the workplace. White and Asian American respondents were usually less likely to report such experiences. The one exception occurs for reports that a supervisor has used racial or ethnic slurs during the past year, where we find that whites (11.5 percent) reported a higher rate of hearing such comments than did blacks (7.9 percent) or Asian Americans (3.5 percent). This instance, however, may deviate from the pattern observed for the other items because white subordinates were hearing their white supervisors use racial epithets or slurs directed against other racial minorities and not at themselves.[4]

In general, the reported rates of experience with discrimination were low. None of the four individual items yields as much as 50 percent of the respondents of any race indicating that they experienced a particular form of discrimination. The single most frequently cited form of discrimination involves perhaps the most extreme form: refusal of employment. Reports of having been refused employment were given by more than two out of five African Americans, 16 percent of Latinos, and approximately one in ten white and Asian American respondents.

The relatively low rates of response to any single item, however, would surely underestimate the likelihood that any given individual has

TABLE 14.1   *Personal Experience of Racial Discrimination in the Workplace, by Respondent Race*

| | Respondent Race and Percentage "Yes" | | | |
Type of Discrimination	White	African American	Asian American	Latino
Supervisor used racial slurs	11.5%	7.9%	3.5%	12.0%*
General racial discrimination	8.5	22.6	6.9	13.3*
Pay or promotion slower	6.2	16.7	2.8	8.6*
Refused a job	11.0	44.7	11.6	16.0*

QUESTION WORDING: (1) During the (past year/last year you worked) has/did your supervisor or boss ever use racial slurs; (2) During the (past year/last year you worked) have/did you experience racial or ethnic discrimination at your place of work because of your race or ethnicity?; (3) Have you ever felt at any time in the past that others at your place of employment got promotions or pay raises faster than you did because of your race or ethnicity?; and (4) Have you ever felt at any time in the past that you were refused a job because of your race or ethnicity?

Source: Los Angeles Study of Urban Inequality 1994.
Note: Base Ns for whites range from 531 to 790; for African Americans, from 765 to 1,059; for Asian Americans, from 459 to 821; and for Latinos, from 692 to 900. These ranges reflect different skip patterns for each question asked.
*$p < .001$

encountered discrimination in the workplace. A somewhat more robust gauge of its overall likelihood can be obtained by examining the cumulative frequency of discrimination (see table 14.2). Far and away, African Americans were the most likely to report encountering racial discrimination. Just under 60 percent (58.9 percent) responded positively to at least one of the personal experience of discrimination items. In addition, African Americans were the most likely to encounter multiple forms of discrimination. Approximately 30 percent reported experiencing two or more forms of discrimination, with one in ten responding positively to three or more of the four items. Latinos followed blacks in the personal experience of discrimination queue, with 30.9 percent reporting encounters with at least one type of discrimination. One in four whites reported encountering some form of discrimination, while Asian Americans reported the least, at 21.6 percent. Asian Americans, it should be noted, are the minority group most likely to have supervisors of the same race (56.2 percent; see table 14A.2). Hence, the relatively low rates of personal discrimination reported by Asian Americans may be partly attributable to their greater immersion in an ethnic economic enclave.

TABLE 14.2   *Cumulative Frequency of Personal Experience of Racial Discrimination in the Workplace, by Respondent Race*

Cumulative Frequency	White	African American	Asian American	Latino
0	74.9%	41.1%	78.4%	69.1%
1	15.4	30.4	13.5	18.8
2	6.0	20.1	6.8	6.1
3	3.6	6.8	1.1	4.4
4	0.1	1.6	0.1	1.5
Percentage reporting any discrimination	25.1	58.9	21.6	30.9*
Mean	.39	.97	.31	.50*

Source: Los Angeles Study of Urban Inequality 1994.
*p < .001

Social Background and Workplace Factors

Table 14.3 shows the percentage of respondents reporting any experience of racial discrimination by respondent race and the social background factors of nativity, sex, age, education, occupation, and income. The largest and most consistent effects are found for level of education. As education levels increase, so do the percentages reporting discrimination among both African American and Asian American respondents. The gradient for both groups is quite sharp, with a 50-plus percentage point difference separating those who did not finish high school from those with postgraduate training. The importance of postgraduate training emerged sharply for both blacks and Asian Americans. Virtually all African Americans (98 percent) in the highest educational category reported experiencing at least one form of racial discrimination in the workplace. Sixty-four percent of the most highly educated (postgraduate training) Asian Americans did so, a rate nearly three times that for Asian respondents who had only completed college.

Aside from the education effects observed among the African American and Asian American respondents, the social background variables do not have strong connections to the likelihood of encountering workplace discrimination. Among the black and Asian American respondents, there is a tendency for the reported experience of discrimination to rise with increasing occupational standing, but this presumably reflects the strong effect of education. The weak or nonexistent effects of occupation and income strongly suggest that the experience of discrimi-

TABLE 14.3   *Percentage Reporting Any Personal Experience of Racial Discrimination in the Workplace, by Social Background Factors and Respondent Race*

	White	African American	Asian American	Latino
Nativity				
United States	24.9	62.4***	21.8	25.5
Foreign	26.3	28.8	21.6	33.1
Sex				
Male	29.2*	58.2	28.4**	35.0**
Female	21.0	59.5	17.0	25.7
Age				
Twenty-one to thirty-five	27.5	53.8**	19.2*	29.0
Thirty-six to fifty	26.8	68.4	28.7	31.5
Fifty-one to sixty-five	17.3	58.5	17.0	38.1
Sixty-six or more	20.4[a]	49.3	—	46.3[a]
Education				
Zero to eleven years	15.7[a]	46.8***	2.6[a]***	32.7
Twelve	28.0	53.4	16.3	31.9
Thirteen to fifteen	25.9	51.6	18.3	28.1
Sixteen	23.1	79.9	23.1	21.3
Sixteen plus or more	24.1	98.0	63.6	51.1[a]
Occupation				
Lower-blue-collar	25.1*	58.2	5.2[a]***	32.6
Upper-blue-collar	38.4	56.0	5.8[a]	33.7
Lower-white-collar	26.3	56.5	35.4	28.2
Upper-white-collar	20.5	67.3	23.9	24.5
Income				
< $5,999	27.9	56.4	17.4***	30.8
$6,000 to 16,999	34.6	56.5	9.2[a]	34.4
$17,000 to 31,999	24.5	58.5	12.4	21.9
$32,000 or more	22.9	64.3	46.8	36.4

Source: Los Angeles Study of Urban Inequality 1994.
Note: Base Ns for whites range from 515 to 517; for African Americans, from 757 to 758; for Asian Americans, from 442 to 446; and for Latinas and Latinos, from 675 to 679.
[a]Cell count less than 10.
*$p < .05$, **$p < .01$, ***$p < .001$.

nation in the workplace tends to occur across the class spectrum. There is also a tendency among the African American and Asian American respondents for reports of discrimination to be highest in the prime working-age category of thirty-six to fifty years old. White, Latino, and Asian American males are slightly more likely to report discrimination than are their female counterparts. Native-born blacks are substantially more likely to report discrimination than are foreign-born blacks. Surprisingly, there is little evidence of an effect of nativity on reports of discrimination among Latino or Asian American respondents.

It is important to determine whether certain types of workplace characteristics contribute to the likelihood of reporting discrimination. Hence, table 14.4 reports the experience of any discrimination by the workplace characteristics of type of employment (public or private sector), size of firm, race of supervisor, sex of supervisor, and racial mix of coworkers. In general, workplace characteristics that bring increased chances of interethnic contact, especially contact with other-race authority figures, appear to be associated with higher rates of reported discrimination. Race of supervisor and race of coworkers most consistently affect the likelihood that a respondent will report having encountered discrimination. Indeed, the relative rates of reported discrimination closely parallel the likelihood of having a supervisor of another race. The two groups most likely to report discrimination, African Americans and Latinos, are also the two groups most likely to have other race supervisors (69.7 percent and 57.1 percent, respectively; see table 14A.2). Likewise, the significant affect of public-sector employment among black and Asian respondents, for the latter in particular, suggests that movement out of private and presumably co-ethnic-owned enterprises increases the chances of experiencing discrimination.

In order to better understand the likely social processes involved with reports of discrimination, we estimated a series of multivariate logit models predicting the log-odds of reporting any experience of discrimination using both the social background variables and workplace characteristic measures. The results are shown separately by race in table 14.5 for the full model. We estimated the logit models in a three-step process. At the first stage, the models fit only a constant term. At the second stage, we introduce all the social background variables. At the third stage, we introduce all the workplace characteristic variables. With the exception of white respondents, two patterns hold: introducing the set of social background variables always brings a significant improvement in fit for the model; and introducing the workplace variables always brings an improvement in fit over a model including only the social background variables. Only the latter pattern holds among whites.

The odds of reporting discrimination by whites does not hinge to a significant degree on nativity, age, education, occupation, or income, though there is a borderline effect in the full model for men as contrasted to women. As a result, the second-stage model including only these variables is not a significant improvement over the constant model (difference chi-square = 23.42, d.f. = 15, ns). Although the third stage, or full model, which introduces the workplace variables is a sig-

TABLE 14.4   *Percentage Reporting Any Personal Experience of*
Racial Discrimination in the Workplace, by
Characteristics of the Workplace and Respondent Race

	White	African American	Asian American	Latina or Latino
Type of company				
Private	25.4	56.5*	19.9**	31.6
Public	23.4	66.1	39.2	22.2
Size				
very small (<10)	25.4	46.1**	7.8[a]***	30.6
small or mid (10 to 49)	24.4	59.1	15.5	34.6
medium (50 to 499)	28.0	65.6	37.0	30.1
large (500+)	20.5	54.7	31.0	25.1
Race of coworkers				
White	22.2*	73.0***	31.0***	31.4
African American	46.3[a]	53.7	90.2	41.4
Asian American	38.3[a]	86.2	10.0	29.6[a]
Latino	33.4	65.7	16.7[a]	29.5
Race of supervisor				
White	22.3**	57.5*	25.9**	35.6*
African American	35.6[a]	53.2	54.1[a]	18.2[a]
Asian American	53.0	70.4	16.9	34.0
Latino	34.0	73.2	23.7[a]	26.4
Sex of supervisor				
Male	27.2	67.2***	23.4	33.1
Female	20.7	48.4	16.4	25.5

Source: Los Angeles Study of Urban Inequality 1994.
Note: Base Ns for whites range from 510 to 515; for African Americans, from 752 to 758;
for Asian Americans, from 436 to 446; and for Latinos, from 665 to 679.
[a]Cell count less than ten.
*$p < .05$, **$p < .01$, ***$p < .001$

nificant improvement in fit (difference chi-square = 21.48, d.f. = 9, $p < .05$), only one variable has a significant effect: whites with Asian American supervisors were more likely to report discrimination. It is worth noting that there is an effect of borderline significance for having African American coworkers (b = 1.20, s.e. = .68, p = .075).

Among African Americans we found a significant curvilinear effect of age, with discrimination highest in the middle age ranges and lower for younger and older blacks. In addition, there are clear education effects, with reports of discrimination increasing in monotonic fashion with increasing education. Although adding the workplace variables brought a significant improvement in fit of the model (difference chi-

TABLE 14.5   Logit Models of Reports of Personal Experience of Racial Discrimination in the Workplace, by Respondent Race

	Race of Respondent							
	White		African American		Asian American		Latino	
Independent Variables	B	S.E.	B	S.E.	B	S.E.	B	S.E.
Constant	-1.09	(1.43)	2.15	(1.24)	-3.05	(2.22)	-1.22	(1.52)
Background variables								
Nativity	.15	(.34)	-.73	(.57)	-.35	(.47)	.86**	(.27)
Sex	.47	(.27)	.05	(.24)	.84*	(.39)	.43	(.23)
Age	<-.01	(.07)	.10*	(.05)	.12	(.11)	-.17**	(.06)
Age squared	<-.01	(<.01)	<-.01*	(<.01)	<-.01	(<.01)	<-.01**	(<.01)
Education								
Zero to eleven years	-.88	(.94)	-4.48***	(1.02)	-2.59*	(1.02)	1.25	(.97)
Twelve	-.36	(.52)	-4.61***	(.99)	-.74	(.66)	1.40	(.97)
Thirteen to fifteen	-.43	(.46)	-4.36***	(.97)	-1.74***	(.52)	1.24	(.99)
Sixteen	-.55	(.46)	-3.44***	(1.00)	-1.56**	(.52)	.94	(1.03)
Occupation								
Lower-blue-collar	.27	(.46)	.06	(.38)	-2.06*	(1.02)	.38	(.40)
Upper-blue-collar	.66	(.39)	-.07	(.29)	-1.08	(.64)	.56	(.39)
Lower-white-collar	.18	(.30)	.03	(.26)	.29	(.38)	.47	(.38)

	Model 1		Model 2		Model 3		Model 4	
Income								
$6,000 to $16,999	.45	(.39)	.23	(.28)	-.68	(.62)	.14	(.25)
$17,000 to $31,999	.09	(.36)	.44	(.27)	-.88	(.50)	-.49	(.32)
$32,000 or more	-.19	(.38)	-.24	(.32)	-.22	(.50)	.74	(.41)
refused to answer	-1.04	(.75)	-.29	(.38)	-1.79*	(.78)	-1.02	(.70)
Workplace variables								
Sector	-.40	(.36)	.38	(.23)	-.13	(.58)	-.10	(.40)
Firm size	<-.01	(<.01)	<.01	(<.01)	<-.01	(<.01)	<-.01	(<.01)
Coworkers' race								
White	—	—	.30	(.23)	1.12	(.60)	.38	(.27)
African American	1.20	(.68)	—	—	4.43***	(.99)	1.54**	(.58)
Asian American	.94	(.59)	1.06	(.59)	—	—	.69	(.57)
Latino	.27	(.39)	.12	(.30)	.51	(.61)	—	—
Supervisor's race								
White	—	—	.18	(.23)	-.71	(.58)	.44*	(.22)
African American	.33	(.69)	—	—	-.80	(1.19)	-.87	(.69)
Asian American	1.34**	(.48)	.44	(.64)	—	—	.18	(.44)
Latino	.61	(.47)	.73	(.41)	-.24	(.89)	—	—
Supervisor's sex	.25	(.29)	.62**	(.21)	.61	(.47)	.44	(.25)
Model chi-square	21.48		29.22		42.39		19.34	
Base Ns	(442)		(576)		(380)		(581)	

Source: Los Angeles Study of Urban Inequality 1994.
Note: Cell entries are unstandardized regression coefficients. Figures in parentheses are standard errors.
*p < .05, **p < .01, ***p < .001

square = 29.21, d.f. = 9, $p < .001$), only sex of supervisor (male) significantly increased reports of discrimination.

Among Asian Americans, we found that the most highly educated group reported substantially more discrimination than did those with less education. Likewise, Asians in upper-white-collar occupations reported more discrimination than did those in blue-collar occupations. Both of these patterns suggest that high-status Asian Americans are striving to assimilate and move out of the ethnic enclave economy but encountering greater discrimination when they do so. Men reported more discrimination than women. And those with African American coworkers reported very high levels of discrimination.

For our Latino respondents, we found that the foreign-born were more likely to report discrimination than the native-born. There is also a significant effect of age, with younger and older Latinos reporting more discrimination than those in the middle age range. In addition, those with African American coworkers or white supervisors tended to report more discrimination.

It is worth noting that size of firm never has a significant effect on the odds of reporting discrimination. Similarly, the public- versus private-sector distinction does not influence the odds of reporting discrimination.[5] To the extent that workplace factors matter for personal reports of discrimination, they seem largely to involve something about the mix and characteristics of coworkers and supervisors.

Open-Ended Descriptions

In order to develop a richer sense of what the experience of discrimination involves, we asked one open-ended question seeking a fuller description of the discrimination experience. This question, which asked "What happened that made you feel that way?" followed the item on whether the respondent had ever faced racial discrimination in terms of rates of pay or promotion. Generally, we think, the open-ended responses substantially clarify and flesh out the closed-ended reports of discrimination, though it is important to emphasize that the open-ended question followed the item on pay and promotion differences. This probably somewhat narrows the base of possible reports of discrimination, and as a result may point to dynamics a bit different from those suggested when analyzing overall rates of exposure to discrimination. Table 14.6 shows the distribution of responses among white respondents, while table 14.7 shows the responses of African American, Asian American, and Latino respondents. It was necessary to separate responses in this fashion due to the largely nonoverlapping character of the answers given by white as contrasted to racial minority respondents.

TABLE 14.6   *Distribution of Open-Ended Descriptions of Pay or Promotion Discrimination Among White Respondents*

Major Reasons (and Subcategories)	Percentage	Frequency
Reverse discrimination	71.4	(35)
(more promotion chances)	(26.5)	
(minority quotas)	(20.4)	
(general minority favoritism)	(14.3)	
(higher minority pay)	(10.2)	
Other white ethnicity favored	10.2	(5)
Gender discrimination	8.1	(4)
Other nonracial (for example, age nepotism, favoritism)	10.2	(4)
Not ascertained	2.0	(1)

Source: Los Angeles Study of Urban Inequality 1994.

On the whole, recall that fewer than one in ten white respondents reported experiencing pay or promotion discrimination. As table 14.6 shows, of this number, nearly three-fourths (71.4 percent) complained of some form of reverse discrimination involving a preference for racial minorities over whites (though only one respondent actually used the phrase "reverse discrimination"). The table also shows a more detailed specification of the reverse discrimination complaints into assertions that minorities have easier chances for promotion (26.5 percent), the use of minority quotas (20.4 percent), wage differentials (10.2 percent), or general remarks about favoritism toward minorities (14.3 percent).

Multiple Ethnic Cleavages   One of the immediately striking qualities to the open-ended comments is the extent to which whites reported experiences of discrimination in relation to Latinos and Asians and not merely in relation to blacks. For example, a thirty-six-year-old white woman who worked as a clerk explained that: "I went on jury duty in November and returned demoted and a Hispanic got my job. Also a lady two people above me is Hispanic. She promotes Hispanics to higher-position pay raises over whites who have seniority and are also very qualified for those jobs." According to a thirty-two-year-old white woman who worked as a stationary engineer in a plant: "My supervisor was a Filipino man and when a Filipino girl came [she] got a lot of privileges and he didn't blame her for anything. But me? I was blamed."

Specificity of Accounts   Sometimes these descriptions of the discrimination experience, though usually brief, spoke directly to a particu-

535

lar incident. For example, a thirty-six-year-old white man who worked as a computer systems analyst explained that: "Another Hispanic employee was promoted ahead of me. He had less experience with the company." Likewise, a thirty-nine-year-old white woman who worked as a manager in a food service establishment claimed that: "There were all Hispanics. During promotion the supervisor gave promotions to every Hispanic, but not me. That's the reason I quit." "They preferred a black woman because they need racial balance in the office where I worked," according to a thirty-four-year-old white female account auditor. Or, in the case of a twenty-seven-year-old white woman who worked in an office support capacity: "Another girl who arrived at the same time [I did] [was] Filipino and most of the people at higher levels are either of different origin, Filipino or Asian men. She's in line for a promotion."

General Resentments Many of the comments, however, were less concrete or did not seem to speak to a direct personal experience of discrimination at all. Sometimes respondents spoke of a general perception of how the work situation in their field was operating. For instance, a forty-nine-year-old white man working as an electrician in the entertainment industry said: "Different types of shows that are happening. With black television series, they prefer you to hire black employees if you can. When I first started on this job, you'd rarely see women working or Asians or Latinos." These more generalized perceptions often involve negative references to affirmative action or quotas, such as the response of a twenty-six-year-old white man who works as a guard: "Courtappointed standards make unfair standards for different races."

Similar remarks were made by a sixty-two-year-old white man who worked as an educational administrator: "Race and gender preference in civil rights legislation. Blacks and females got jobs faster and got promoted more." One respondent simply stated: "The politics." When asked, "Can you be more specific?" by the interviewer, she responded: "Just general perception." And when asked if there was "anything else," the forty-year-old who worked in the clergy simply said: "No." The one instance among white respondents of using the phrase "reverse discrimination" also was a vague reference to general conditions rather than a description of a direct personal experience: "A case of reverse discrimination. Universities are in the main 'race-sensitive.' Prefer minorities over whites," explained a forty-six-year-old white male office supervisor. Thus, in a number of cases, the claim of experiencing direct personal discrimination among our white respondents appears to involve a more generalized discontent or grievance against at least affirmative action pressures if not also against minorities more broadly.[6]

A few respondents pointed to instances of discrimination among whites based on religion or national origin. Some also took the question as an opportunity to speak to other forms of discrimination involving gender, sexual preference or orientation, or age. A few respondents spoke to such other factors as nepotism or playing to personal favorites.

The distribution of responses among racial minority respondents is shown in table 14.7. The overwhelming fraction of African American (82.6 percent), Asian American (86.8 percent), and Latino (78.6 percent) respondents reported that the pay or promotion discrimination they encountered involved a form of white preference. Among the black and Asian respondents, the bulk of these open-ended accounts dealt squarely with pay or promotion preferences for whites. The responses more evenly covered other possible forms of discrimination, such as lower starting salaries or demotions, among our Latino respondents.

As was true of the white respondents, our minority respondents frequently recounted fairly concrete situations of discrimination:

TABLE 14.7   *Distribution of Open-Ended Descriptions of Pay or Promotion Discrimination Among African American, Asian American, and Latino Respondents*

Major Reasons (and Subcategories)	African American	Asian American	Latino
White preference	82.6%	86.8%	78.6%
(more promotion chances)	(40.3)	(39.5)	(15.5)
(more pay raises)	(12.8)	(18.4)	(15.5)
(general white favoritism)	(12.1)	(23.7)	(23.8)
(higher starting salary)	(11.4)	(2.6)	(17.9)
(preference in hiring)	(5.4)	(2.6)	(4.8)
(demotions)	(0.7)	—	(1.2)
Other nonwhites favored	22.8	15.8	23.8
(Latinos and Latinas);	(13.4)	(10.5)	—
(Asian Americans)	(9.4)	—	(17.9)
(African Americans)	—	(5.3)	(6.0)
Other ethnicity favored (same race as respondent)	1.3	5.3	2.4
Gender discrimination	3.4	13.2	1.2
Other nonracial	4.3	—	1.2
Not ascertained	2.0	5.3	1.2
Base N	(149)	(38)	(84)

Source: Los Angeles Study of Urban Inequality 1994.

I had worked at a job for three years already and when an English guy came after a month he got promoted. Although he always wanted for me to help him out. This was at a clinic. I felt that this was very unfair. The guy didn't know anything about the job, yet he had preference over the others and myself.—thirty-two-year-old Latina, property manager

I was more experienced. I was on the job longer and I trained a white male for the job. He was promoted before me.—forty-three-year-old African American woman, legal assistant

You see one white nurse who doesn't have the experience that other Asian or Hispanic nurse[s have] but she got promoted to charge nurse job.— thirty-six-year-old Asian American woman, registered nurse

Five years ago I had a prejudiced white female supervisor. Others got a pay raise, while I did not. So I went to her supervisor and complained and later I received a raise comparable to the others.—forty-year-old African American woman, licensed practical nurse

Although minority respondents were significantly more likely to offer concrete descriptions of discrimination than were white respondents, there are a number of accounts that are less concrete.[7] Unlike the vague explanations offered by some white respondents, however, the vague accounts offered by minority respondents did not involve broad resentments of affirmative action pressures. Instead, they involved general reference to favoritism toward specific groups, disadvantages confronted by members of the respondent's racial group, or a blunt assertion of discrimination:

They have special preferences to [whites]. They get more money.—thirty-four-year-old Latino, drafting technician

I feel the whites got promoted more often because they were white.—seventy-year-old African American man, tool and die maker

Whites get promoted faster.—fifty-year-old Asian American man, civil engineer

The Generality of Ethnocentrism and Bias   A common thread linking the responses of our white, African American, Asian American, and Latino respondents was the perception of general ethnocentric bias. If the ranks of supervisory positions and/or owners were filled by members of a different racial-ethnic group, there was a possibility of ethnic favoritism:

Supervisors seem to push/promote their own kind.—thirty-seven-year-old African American man, distribution clerk

Hispanics are always paid the lowest wages. Others get more on any jobs.—thirty-two-year-old Latino, real estate manager

In [the] sixties and seventies at [my] former job, all white people got promotions and very few Asians got promotions.—sixty-eight-year-old Asian American man, truck driver

The suggestion of general ethnocentrism comes through as well in reference to a great variety of bases of preference other than race, such as national origin or religion. The apparent universal sensitivity to the prospect of ethnocentric bias in the workplace may signal an important part of the processes by which groups come to specialize in particular economic niches and act to achieve "occupational closure" (Waldinger 1986).

Many respondents offered only brief descriptions. Some of the brevity in the remarks of minority respondents in answer to our request to describe the discrimination they had experienced appeared to reflect genuine exasperation at having to explain repeatedly experienced problems of discrimination that to them seemed obvious. For example, when asked the open-ended follow-up question, a forty-year-old African American man who worked as a machinist initially refused to answer the question. But then he asserted: "It's obvious. People with less time come in and get promoted over you because they are white."[8]

The Importance of Networks   Many of the open-ended comments from minority respondents strongly suggest that the process of discrimination is played out through networks of information sharing and interaction. From the vantage point of many of our minority respondents, the crucial decision-making ranks are overwhelmingly staffed by whites who come to favor other whites at pay or promotion time, either through greater trust, comfort and familiarity, or friendship, or direct family ties:

All the higher positions are white.—twenty-nine-year-old Asian American woman, registered nurse

Supervisor usually promote[s] relative or somebody he knows. One time, [a] white male supervisor said, "I hate men and Orientals," and told me, "You'll never make it." He promoted [a] white woman he was seeing.—thirty-two-year-old Asian American man, postal worker

There were positions with the organization that have never been filled by a Hispanic. I was qualified but denied the position.—fifty-one-year-old Latino, manager in a service organization

Because my boss gets along better with people of his own race.—thirty-three-year-old Latina, food preparer

The most clear-cut descriptions of network connections working in a discriminatory fashion tended to come from the African American respondents:

> Hispanics promoted other Hispanics because they were Hispanic. Blacks were not informed on what was available for promotion.—twenty-seven-year-old African American woman, billing clerk

> I see some people that are not qualified for the job get promoted, and I feel they have a stronger support group.—forty-seven-year-old African American man, social worker

> People under me, after my date of hire, got promoted faster and their pay increase was higher than mine, and I did more than they did. They was white and they were family members.—thirty-one-year-old African American man, order clerk

> When I worked as a programmer at a manufacturing plant, whites were promoted faster and received pay raises faster than I did. I found out by talking with people and discussing their salaries.—forty-nine-year-old African American woman, elementary school teacher

> I found out that the white employees were making more money than I was, and I found out from these same white employees.—forty-two-year-old African American woman, dental hygienist

Group-Specific Experiences   There are also some types of complaints of discrimination revealed in the open-ended accounts that are unique to specific groups. Blacks are the main group to complain of bilingual ability as a factor that sometimes disadvantages them in the workplace relative to Latinos. Latinos complained of restrictions they face because they lacked citizenship (which led to advantages for whites and for African Americans) or because they are monolingual Spanish speakers. A number of Latinos, consistent with the results of our earlier focus group research, complained of confronting a general expectation that they would work for less and have no aspirations for upward mobility in the workplace (see Bobo et al. 1995).

Also consistent with our earlier focus group research, Latinos and Asian Americans voiced grievances against one another in the workplace that did not arise with the same degree of frequency relative to African Americans (Bobo et al. 1994). For example, a thirty-four-year-old Latino production checker stated: "I used to work with Koreans and I noticed that as soon as they got their job they gave them a raise and not to me." Or, as a forty-four-year-old Latino who worked as a textile sewing machine operator puts it: "Korean owners give the best jobs to Koreans than to us. If someone comes and is the same race, they give them the best-paid jobs." In contrast, a thirty-nine-year-old Asian American woman who worked as a cook complained: "Overtime is paid to Hispanics, but not to Koreans." Or, as a thirty-three-year-old Asian American male secretary said: "[The] manager is Hispanic. For new jobs she advertises only in *La Opinion* [the largest Spanish-language paper in Los Angeles]. Hispanics are allowed to work overtime for one hour but paid for the whole day on Saturdays."

Emotional Impact One of the concerns of recent research on discrimination is the emotional impact it may have on those who experience it. At one level, any claim of experience with discrimination denotes an encounter with perceived unfair treatment and is thus potentially upsetting. At another level, however, review of the open-ended accounts suggested considerable variability in the explicitness of emotional upset or anger. The overwhelming fraction of respondent remarks reflect some degree of emotional upset.[9] Nonetheless, by a slight margin, signs of emotional upset were more often manifest in the comments of our African American (87.7 percent), Asian American (75.0 percent), and Latino respondents (89.2 percent) than among white respondents (57.4 percent, chi-square = 26.51, df. = 3, $p < .001$).

The Connection to Ethnic Awareness

Interpreting experiences in the workplace as discrimination may be bound up with or contribute to a broader sense of ethnic awareness. We conceive of ethnic awareness as concerning the degree of feelings of attachment and significant subjective involvement with others sharing a common racial-ethnic background. We employ two indicators of the degree of ethnic awareness: a measure of "common fate ethnic identity," and a measure of the degree of perceived labor market discrimination against members of one's racial-ethnic group generally. A sense of common fate is a critical element of group identity formation (Tajfel 1982) and powerfully affects the political attitudes and behaviors of African Americans (Gurin, Hatchett, and Jackson 1989; Tate 1993; Dawson 1994). Perceptions of discrimination, likewise, are regarded as core elements in a potentially politicized sense of group awareness (Gurin, Miller, and Gurin 1980). Distributions by race for these two items are shown in table 14.8.

In general, the ethnic awareness measures suggest that African Americans and Latinos, the two groups most likely to report personal experiences of discrimination in the labor market, were also the most ethnically aware. To be sure, most respondents expressed some degree of common fate identity with their racial group as a whole. But this ten-

TABLE 14.8   *Ethnic Awareness by Respondent Race*

	White	African American	Asian American	Latino
Common fate ethnic identity				
A lot	20.2	39.5	20.3	27.0
Some	43.2	34.8	46.3	35.9
Not much	9.2	5.4	11.8	5.6
None	27.3	20.3	21.7	31.5
Totals	99.9%	100.0%	100.1%	100.0%
N	(855)	(1,111)	(1,050)	(983)
Collective labor market discrimination				
A lot	3.7	67.1	3.0	57.0
Some	27.8	29.4	49.7	30.0
Only a little	39.0	2.8	37.4	9.2
None	29.5	0.7[a]	9.9	3.8
Totals	100.0%	100.0%	100.0%	100.0%
N	(850)	(1,112)	(1,005)	(986)

QUESTION WORDING: (1) Do you think what happens generally to [respondent's race] people in this county will have something to do with what happens in your life? [If yes,] Will it affect you . . . ?; and (2) In general, how much discrimination is there that hurts the chances of [Hispanics, blacks, Asians, women, whites] to get good-paying jobs? Do you think there is a lot, some, only a little, or none at all?

Source: Los Angeles Study of Urban Inequality 1994.
[a]Cell count less than ten.

dency was strongest among the African American and Latino respondents, where 39.5 percent and 27.0 percent, respectively, felt the strongest possible ("a lot" response) connection between their circumstances as individuals and the fate of the group as a whole. In terms of collective perceptions of discrimination, we again found that African Americans and Latinos, by lopsided margins compared to whites and Asian Americans, saw their own groups as tending to face "a lot" of discrimination in getting jobs. In contrast, nearly a third of white respondents (29.5 percent) said their group faced no labor market discrimination versus less than 5 percent of Latinos and less than 1 percent of African Americans who gave such responses.

In tables 14.9 and 14.10 we examine the connection between reports of personal discrimination and each of the ethnic awareness measures separately by race in a multivariate framework. There is usually a significant positive association between reporting any workplace experience of discrimination and ethnic awareness, net of controls for respondent social background and workplace characteristics. In six of the eight tests, the impact of personal discrimination was significant. Both of the exceptions came when predicting the ethnic common fate identity measure. One of these exceptions occurred among white respondents, where the effect of personal discrimination was in the right direction but barely of borderline significance ($b = .16$, s.e. $= .11$, $p = .11$). The other occurred among Latinos ($b = .14$, s.e. $= .10$, n.s.).

Personal discrimination is associated with increasing strength of common fate ethnic identity among blacks ($b = .40$, s.e. $= .09$, $p < .001$) and among Asians ($b = .37$, s.e. $= .13$, $p < .01$). With respect to perceived discrimination against one's group, we find a significant net association, regardless of race. Among the white ($b = .21$, s.e. $= .09$, $p < .05$), African American ($b = .22$, s.e. $= .05$, $p < .001$), Asian American ($b = .30$, s.e. $= .09$, $p < .01$), and Latino respondents ($b = .33$, s.e. $= .07$, $p < .001$), as personal reports of discrimination increased so too did the likelihood of perceiving one's group as collectively facing discrimination.

Given the cross-sectional nature of the data it is, of course, impossible to specify in which direction the causality flows. For that reason we are careful to discuss the effects observed in tables 14.9 and 14.10 as "associations" rather than as cause-and-effect relations. Over the life-course there are almost certainly reciprocal effects between an individual's interpretation of direct personal experiences of discrimination and his or her sense of ethnic awareness. Greater ethnic awareness, all else equal, probably increases the chances of interpreting certain workplace experiences and conditions as constituting discrimination based on race. Conversely, concluding that one has experienced racial discrimination at work probably deepens a sense of ethnic awareness.

We are reassured about the likely flow of effects as we have specified them by the significant impact of personal discrimination on ethnic awareness *net of respondent education* among our African American and Asian American respondents. It seems clear that the highly educated are unusually well adept at interpreting certain experiences as constituting racial discrimination, at least among blacks and Asians (see tables 14.3 and 14.5). But education is not the whole story. There appears to be something about interpreting an experience as involving discrimination that carries over for measures of ethnic awareness above and beyond whatever it is that greater education does to increase sensitivity to discrimination.

We took one further step to verify our specification of the models that assume that personal discrimination is likely to contribute to a sense of ethnic awareness. Each of the models in tables 14.9 and 14.10 involving significant effects for personal discrimination were re-estimated, including either the group discrimination variable when pre-

(Text continues on p. 548.)

TABLE 14.9 Multivariate OLS Models of the Relation of Ethnic Awareness and Reports of Personal Discrimination by Respondent Race

	Race of Respondent						
	White		African American		Asian American		Latino
Independent Variables	B	S.E.	B	S.E.	B	S.E.	B
Constant	1.85***	(.28)	2.16***	(.30)	1.87	(.34)	1.94***
Background variables							
Nativity	−.06	(.14)	.01	(.20)	.22	(.15)	.43***
Sex	−.04	(.11)	.10	(.10)	.47***	(.11)	−.14
Age	<.01	(<.01)	<−.01	(<.01)	−.02***	(<.01)	<−.01
Education							
Zero to eleven years	−.45	(.37)	−.90***	(.25)	−.11	(.24)	−1.02*
Twelve	−.30	(.22)	−.66***	(.20)	−.28	(.22)	−1.02*
Thirteen to fifteen	−.17	(.19)	−.70***	(.18)	−.30	(.18)	−.78
Sixteen	−.17	(.18)	−.61**	(.20)	−.15	(.18)	−.79
Occupation							
Lower blue-collar	−.34	(.20)	.16	(.18)	.23	(.21)	.45*
Upper blue-collar	−.16	(.17)	.08	(.13)	−.29	(.17)	.55**
Lower white-collar	−.05	(.12)	.15	(.11)	−.26*	(.12)	.31

Income								
$6,000 to $16,999	−.26	(.17)	.47***	(.13)	.77***	(.13)	.29*	(.15)
$17,000 to $31,999	<.01	(.14)	.30*	(.13)	.61***	(.13)	−.11	(.14)
$32,000 or more	.07	(.14)	.41**	(.15)	.72***	(.15)	.21	(.15)
refused to answer	.63**	(.23)	.76***	(.18)	.56**	(.18)	.82**	(.20)
Workplace variables								
Sector	.26	(.13)	.10	(.10)	−.13	(.10)	.35*	(.17)
Firm size	<.01	(<.01)	<.01	(<.01)	<.01	(<.01)	<.01	(<.01)
Different race Coworkers	.08	(.13)	−.10	(.10)	.29*	(.10)	−.03	(.14)
Different race Supervisor	.09	(.14)	−.05	(.10)	−.10	(.10)	−.05	(.14)
Supervisor's sex	−.18	(.11)	−.19	(.09)	−.04	(.09)	.10	(.12)
Personal discrimination	.16	(.11)	.40***	(.09)	.37**	(.09)	.14	(.13)
Model R²	.085		.148		.348		.094	
Base N	(461)		(617)		(403)		(615)	

Source: Los Angeles Study of Urban Inequality 1994.
Note: Cell entries are unstandardized regression coefficients. Figures in parentheses are standard errors.
*p < .05, **p < .01, ***p < .001

TABLE 14.10   Multivariate OLS Models of the Relation of Group Discrimination and Reports of Personal Discrimination, by Respondent Race

				Race of Respondent			
	White		African American		Asian American		Latino
Independent Variables	B	S.E.	B	S.E.	B	S.E.	B
Constant	.95***	(.23)	2.56***	(.16)	1.61***	(.25)	2.50***
Background variables							
Nativity	−.34**	(.11)	−.33**	(.11)	−.03	(.11)	.25**
Sex	−.14	(.09)	−.08	(.05)	−.03	(.09)	−.26***
Age	<.01	(<.01)	<.01	(<.01)	<.01	(<.01)	<−.01*
Education							
Zero to eleven years	<.01	(.30)	.08	(.13)	−.36	(.19)	−.41
Twelve	−.13	(.18)	−.07	(.10)	−.26	(.16)	−.44
Thirteen to fifteen	.12	(.15)	−.15	(.09)	−.45***	(.13)	−.48
Sixteen	−.04	(.15)	−.21*	(.10)	−.04	(.13)	−.31
Occupation							
Lower blue-collar	.11	(.16)	−.26**	(.09)	−.05	(.16)	.64***
Upper blue-collar	.22	(.14)	−.10	(.07)	−.29*	(.12)	.58***
Lower white-collar	.04	(.10)	−.06	(.06)	.08	(.09)	.32**

Income								
$6,000–$16,999	-.04	(.14)	-.01	(.07)	.16	(.13)	.04	(.07)
$17,000–$31,999	-.04	(.12)	-.02	(.07)	.11	(.11)	-.19*	(.07)
$32,000 or more	.06	(.11)	.02	(.07)	-.12	(.12)	.01	(.07)
refused to answer	.11	(.19)	.16	(.09)	.06	(.15)	-.06	(.09)
Workplace variables								
Sector	<-.01	(.11)	-.02	(.05)	.28*	(.13)	.19	(.05)
Firm size	<.01	(<.01)	<-.01	(<.01)	<.01*	(<.01)	<.01*	(<.01)
Different race								
Coworkers	.26*	(.11)	-.03	(.05)	-.28**	(.10)	<-.01	(.05)
Different race								
Supervisor	.11	(.12)	-.02	(.05)	.13	(.11)	.01	(.05)
Supervisor's sex	-.17	(.09)	.13**	(.05)	-.10	(.09)	-.12	(.05)
Personal discrimination	.21*	(.09)	.22***	(.09)	.30**	(.05)	.33***	(.09)
Model R²	.090		.107		.223		.201	
Base N	(464)		(621)		(380)		(619)	

Source: Los Angeles Study of Urban Inequality 1994.
Note: Cell entries are unstandardized regression coefficients. Figures in parentheses are standard errors.
* p < .05, ** p < .01, *** p < .001

dicting common fate ethnic identity or the common fate identity variable when predicting group discrimination. In every instance, the personal discrimination variable continued to have a significant net association, and the size of the coefficient changed only trivially. Taken as a whole, then, these results suggest that personal reports of discrimination are not merely the interpretive product of ethnic awareness. Experiencing discrimination personally seems to reinforce or enhance common fate ethnic identity (net of education and general perceptions of group discrimination) and to increase perceptions of group discrimination (net of education and of common fate ethnic identity).

Conclusion

Examinations of racial attitudes are among the most enduring topics of survey-based research in the United States (Converse 1987; Hyman 1991; Smith 1987). The issue of race was an important concern in the classic *American Soldier* studies (Stouffer 1949) and was the subject of a series of pioneering surveys conducted by NORC in the 1940s (Hyman and Sheatsley 1956; Taylor, Greeley, and Sheatsley 1978). Despite this distinguished and ongoing tradition of research (Schuman, Steeh, and Bobo 1985; Niemi, Mueller, and Smith 1989), Feagin and others are right to note the lack of sustained survey-based research on discrimination per se. Our aim has been to begin to fill this critical lacuna and to stem the growing impression that general population samples cannot meaningfully illuminate actual social processes of discrimination. We believe that they can and in ways that allow one to exploit the other strengths of large systematic sample surveys.

These analyses support five noteworthy conclusions about the personal experience of racial discrimination in a major multiethnic labor market. First, there were substantial group differences in levels of reported experiences of discrimination. In general, minority respondents reported more encounters with discrimination than did whites. Minorities were also more likely to relate concrete instances of discrimination when asked an open-ended follow-up than did whites and more often did so in a fashion suggestive of emotional distress or upset. African Americans clearly reported the highest levels of encounters with discrimination in the workplace. Latinos followed blacks in the discrimination queue, though the two are separated by an order of magnitude difference. This discrimination can take strong forms, with the most frequently cited type involving the denial of employment. We found little evidence that the experience of discrimination in the workplace was concentrated at a particular place in the class hierarchy. Save for the substantial differences by level of education, discrimination appears to occur across the class spectrum.

Our analyses are based on respondent reports of personal experiences, neither controlled experiments or auditing methodology nor based on an observer's judgments of actual behaviors or situations.[10] That is, we measured the subjective individual salience of workplace racial discrimination. This is a different type of outcome than probabilities of employment, wage rates, or occupational standing and mobility. It is thus not surprising that personal discrimination of this type may have roots in a somewhat different mix of individual and workplace characteristics than do these other types of outcomes (for example, the relative lack of importance of the public- versus private-sector distinction).

We take any claim of having experienced discrimination seriously. Feagin (1991) rightly reminds us that the experience of discrimination is painful and rarely an eagerly embraced interpretation of one's experiences. More important, in some respects what individuals believe about the experiences of discrimination is of great social consequence. As we have shown, personal discrimination reinforces a sense of common fate ethnic identity and increases the perception of collective discrimination against members of one's group. It may also affect other workplace and labor market–relevant behaviors (such as job change and job search behavior), though this is a matter for future research.

In addition, the overall levels of discrimination we found are best regarded as lower-bound estimates of the likelihood that individuals of any given race encounter discrimination in the workplace. Some types of discrimination are difficult to observe by the individual and thus could not be taken into account in a self-report. Most important, we asked only four questions, and could have addressed a number of other potential forms of bias. The weight of both considerations, we believe, leans in the direction of regarding our reported levels of discrimination as lower- rather than upper-bound estimates.

Second among our major conclusions: across race-ethnicity there was a strong expectation and reported experience of ethnocentric bias in the workplace. The thread that most strongly connects the open-ended responses of our white, African American, Asian American, and Latino respondents is mutual sensitivity to in-group favoritism that may occur when coworkers, supervisors, those with decision-making authority, or owners are of a different racial-ethnic background.

One immediate implication of these results is that there are a number of points of potential racial-ethnic group conflict in the workplace, as opposed to one great overwhelmingly salient divide. That is, there are as many potential sources of conflict as there are possible pairings of workers of different racial-ethnic group backgrounds. Two that bear close watching in the future are the Latino and Asian American case and the white and Asian American case. These two types of pairings are increasingly common and, our results indicate, far from free of feelings of racial discrimination, competition, and conflict.

Third among our major conclusions: many of the African American, Asian American, and Latino respondents who reported discrimination share a perception of the current ubiquity of white privilege in the workplace:

[It's a] race problem. Whites get promoted faster.—thirty-three-year-old Asian American man, financial manager

What happens is that they favor white people.—forty-five-year-old Latino truck driver

Whites are always over blacks. They got promotions and I didn't.—forty-three-year-old African American man, social worker

White guys always receive higher wages and more jobs than the Latinos and blacks.—thirty-nine-year-old Latino carpenter

Well, ah, whites just get special treatment.—twenty-nine-year-old African American woman, police officer

As discussed, our open-ended responses suggest that the ubiquitous perception of white advantage rests in the subtle operation of informal networks of communication and interaction among whites in the workplace. African Americans, Asian Americans, and Latinos frequently feel excluded from these networks. Whites may well feel equally excluded from minority social networks. But minority social networks are a good deal less likely to include supervisory personnel, business owners, or others with workplace authority. The ubiquity of this perception among those minority respondents who had reported discrimination may also be traced to the observation of few minorities in positions of authority, and to repeated observation of promotions and pay raises going to whites with less seniority or less apparent qualification.

Fourth, and perhaps most important, it is often the case that what constitutes discrimination is a complex interpretative process. This is most immediately indicated by the powerful impact of level of education on the likelihood of reporting discrimination among our African American and Asian American respondents. The impact of education points up one possible danger in generalizing too broadly from samples of well-educated minorities (compare Feagin and Sikes 1994). Without questioning the validity of any claim of discrimination, it is clear that the less well educated among African Americans and Asian Americans *reported* far less discrimination than did the well educated. Indeed, among blacks virtually every respondent with postgraduate training reported experiencing at least one form of workplace racial discrimination, as did nearly two-thirds of comparably well educated Asian Americans. Reports of experience of workplace discrimination would appear far less common among a sample composed exclusively of poor and working-class respondents.

Fifth and last among our major conclusions, our results suggest that the gap in levels of discrimination between survey-based reports of personal encounters (low) and those obtained from in-depth interviews (high), or even within surveys when comparing questions concerning the individual (low) versus the group (high), may be more apparent than real (compare Schuman 1972). That is, the disjuncture may reflect the limited number and often vague character of the questions typically used in surveys to tap personal encounters with discrimination. Questions referring to concrete types of situations and, critically, multiple-item measures of possible forms of discrimination can produce quite high overall rates of reported encounters with discrimination. In this regard, the ubiquity of the experience of discrimination suggested in several recent nonsample survey studies of the black middle class is directly mirrored in results for our highly educated black and Asian respondents (see, for example, Cose 1993; Feagin and Sikes 1994; Zweigenhaft and Domhoff 1991).

If surveys are to better measure and provide a basis for systematic research on the relative frequency, form, and processes of modern racial-ethnic discrimination, then our research suggests that it is important to draw on multiple-item measures of discrimination. Our questions dealt exclusively with discrimination in the workplace, yet we found an overall rate of encounters with discrimination among African Americans equivalent to that reported by Sigelman and Welch for measures that covered, in addition to the workplace, the domains of education and housing (Sigelman and Welch 1991, 55–56). Multiple-item measures spanning a number of major life domains, especially when supplemented by open-ended questions, may go even further toward erasing the apparent gap between survey-based assessments of discrimination and those obtained through in-depth interview and other procedures.

Future survey-based research should do more on several fronts. It is essential to collect fuller open-ended accounts about the discrimination experience. Direct probes for the impact of perceived discrimination on the individual's emotional state and work productivity need to be examined. Likewise, explicit examination of the types of responses to discrimination, including the possible pursuit of formal grievances, needs to be undertaken (see Bobo 1992, 170–71). In all of this, the design and execution of surveys will surely be improved by a constant dialogue with research based in other methodologies, whether it be auditing studies, in-depth interviews, laboratory experiments, or case studies of particular industries.

This research bears on matters of much broader scope as well. These results have implications for the intensifying debate over affirmative action and antidiscrimination efforts. Like an accumulating body of work using a variety of methods, our data call into question the popular assumption that racial discrimination against minorities is now a relatively infrequent problem in the workplace. The data also cast strong doubt on the validity of the perception of widespread minority preference over whites in the workplace.

The authors wish to thank Harry Holzer, Melvin L. Oliver, and Roger Waldinger for their helpful comments on an earlier draft of this chapter. This research was partly supported by NSF grant SBR9515183.

Appendix

TABLE 14A.1   *Background Variables, by Respondent Race*

	White	African American	Asian American	Latinas and Latinos
Nativity				
U.S.-born	84.0%	92.4	11.5	26.3
Foreign-born	16.0	7.6	88.5	73.7
Total N	(863)	(1119)	(1055)	(988)
Sex				
Male	45.1	43.0	46.7	47.8
Female	54.9	57.0	53.3	52.2
Total N	(863)	(1119)	(1055)	(988)
Age				
Twenty-one to thirty-five	33.3	44.9	34.9	53.3
Thirty-six to fifty	34.2	28.6	35.4	29.8
Fifty-one to sixty-five	20.3	16.4	15.3	14.0
Sixty-six or more	12.3	10.1	14.4	3.0
Total N	(862)	(1118)	(1054)	(987)
Education				
Zero to eleven years	4.9	11.7	15.1	50.1
Twelve	23.5	32.7	20.9	23.9
Thirteen to fifteen	35.5	40.0	19.8	17.5
Sixteen	25.6	9.1	32.0	6.7
Over sixteen	10.5	6.5	12.2	1.8
Total N	(863)	(1117)	(1054)	(988)

TABLE 14A.1   *Continued*

	White	African American	Asian American	Latinas and Latinos
Occupation				
Lower blue-collar	7.6	9.6	7.4	35.3
Upper blue-collar	13.7	25.9	19.6	31.8
Lower white-collar	32.6	40.4	33.0	20.9
Upper white-collar	46.1	24.1	40.0	11.9
Total N	(711)	(882)	(748)	(837)
Income				
< $6,000	21.3	22.6	24.7	27.9
$6,000 to $16,999	13.3	21.0	18.0	41.5
$17,000 to $31,999	26.2	29.1	29.5	21.4
$32,000 or more	39.2	27.4	27.8	9.1
Total N	(659)	(787)	(591)	(804)

Source: Los Angeles Study of Urban Inequality 1994.

TABLE 14A.2   *Characteristics of the Workplace, by Respondent Race*

	White	African American	Asian American	Latino
Type of company				
Private	85.6%	76.7	94.0	91.6
Public	14.4	23.3	6.0	8.4
Total N	(711)	(883)	(754)	(839)
Size				
very small (<10)	27.3	19.9	43.4	26.4
small or mid (10 to 49)	25.8	24.4	28.7	33.2
medium (50 to 499)	32.5	33.2	21.5	33.0
large (500+)	14.4	22.5	6.5	7.2
Total N	(700)	(875)	(723)	(820)
Race of coworkers				
White	83.5	34.5	22.0	18.4
African American	2.2	46.7	3.1	3.0
Asian American	3.4	4.1	61.5	2.6
Latino	10.8	14.7	13.3	76.1
Total N	(673)	(789)	(728)	(814)
Race of supervisor				
White	86.3	58.7	37.8	46.4
African American	2.9	30.3	2.9	4.6
Asian American	4.8	2.2	56.2	6.1
Latino	5.9	8.7	3.1	42.9
Total N	(518)	(747)	(457)	(683)

(Table continues on p. 554.)

TABLE 14A.2   *Continued*

	White	African American	Asian American	Latino
Sex of supervisor				
Male	67.8	55.5	73.6	71.7
Female	32.2	44.5	26.4	28.3
Total N	(529)	(766)	(459)	(690)

Source: Los Angeles Study of Urban Inequality 1994.

Notes

1. The most prominent research on discrimination has involved analyses of large-scale quantitative data sources. In such analyses, for example, models of income determination are compared for blacks and whites who have been equated on major human capital and labor force experience variables. The remaining black-white gap in earnings (or occupational status or probability of employment or job authority), after holding the other relevant variables constant, is typically interpreted as evidence of discrimination. Mary Corcoran and Greg Duncan (1978) and Reynolds Farley (1984) provide excellent examples and reviews of such research (but see also Duncan 1969; Featherman and Hauser 1978; Kluegel 1978; Lieberson and Fuguitt 1967; Siegel 1970). Some research in this vein is beginning to pursue multiethnic comparisons (Tienda and Lii 1987) or to examine how discrimination confronts Latinos (Telles and Murgia 1990) and Asian Americans (Duleep and Sanders 1992; Kim and Lewis 1994; Tang 1993). Unfortunately, multiethnic analyses remain the exception rather than the rule, and we know of no other research examining direct reports on the experience of discrimination.

2. The conceptual and theoretical reasons for a connection between personal reports of discrimination and both subjective social class identity and subjective economic insecurity are unclear. For that reason we do not pursue analyses using such measures here. However, the effects of such factors reinforce the important interpretative aspect of any reported experience of discrimination. We take up this issue by examining the connection between reports of discrimination and other measures of subjective ethnic awareness (see rest of chapter, especially the discussion of tables 14.7 and 14.8).

3. Several other variables, most notably length of time in the United States and English language mastery, have been found to affect labor market outcomes for immigrant groups (Bean and Tienda 1987). We chose to examine those factors likely to operate among each of the four racial-ethnic groups.

4. As can be seen in appendix table 14A.2, 86.3 percent of our white respondents had white supervisors and 83.5 percent had mainly white coworkers, leaving a comparatively small fraction of whites in work settings where they were likely to hear racial epithets directed at them by minorities.

5. We were surprised by the absence of an effect of the public- versus private-sector distinction. One possible reason for this may be that we have pooled the "refused a job" item, which assesses point of entry discrimination, with the other three items that assess on-the-job discrimination. A separate analysis of the "refused a job" item, however, still shows no significant effect for the public- versus private-sector distinction at the bivariate level or in the full multivariate models for white, African American, and Latino respondents. Among Asian Americans, we do find a significant bivariate association, but it shows greater discrimination in the public sector and does not survive controls in the multivariate model. We discuss in the conclusion how the subjective personal salience of discrimination of the type we measure here differs from more routinely studied labor market outcomes of employment probabilities, earnings, and occupational standing.

6. Despite the considerable media attention given to claims of "reverse discrimination" (Gamson and Modigliani 1987) and the perception that blacks and other minorities receive significant preferential treatment (Kluegel and Smith 1982), the vague character of the claims of discrimination from many of our white respondents is consistent with a growing body of evidence challenging the claim of significant bias against whites (Reskin 1998). For example, data from the 1990 General Social Survey found that 70 percent of whites believed it "very likely" or "somewhat likely" that due to affirmative action whites lose out to "equal or less well qualified" blacks. However, when asked why they felt this way, only 6.9 percent spoke in terms of a direct personal experience; the great bulk of responses fell into the "heard about from others" (35 percent) or "heard about it in the media" (42 percent) categories (Davis and Smith 1990). Along the same lines, a major study found that "reverse discrimination" complaints were an extremely small fraction of all discrimination claims filed, and that only a handful of these were found to have merit ("Reverse Discrimination Complaints Rare, a Labor Study Reports," New York Times, March 31, 1995, p. A10). Similarly, the Urban Institute employer auditing study found three times as much discrimination against blacks as they did preference in favor of blacks over whites (Turner et al. 1991, 62–63).

7. We classified all the open-ended comment in terms of the presence or absence of a direct, personally experienced event or action. Gen-

eral comments and responses that are not racial in nature were counted as lacking concreteness. We found that 42.6 percent of the white responses contained such a concrete reference, compared with 65.8 percent among African Americans, 58.3 percent among Asian Americans, and 60.2 percent among Latinos (chi-square = 8.01, d.f. = 3, $p < .05$).

8. This sense of exasperation was hinted at in our earlier focus group research. It was sometimes difficult, especially among the African American participants, to initiate discussion of personal encounters with discrimination. Once the moderator made it clear that we were seriously interested in obtaining detailed reports, the participants were far more forthcoming. One reason for the initial hesitance seemed to be an assumption that the pervasiveness of discrimination was obvious. "The experience of discrimination was considered so common, especially among the Blacks, that one person joked 'Where do you want me to start?'" (Bobo et al. 1995, 82).

9. We defined signs of emotional upset as the explicit use of charged terms such as "unfair," "get away with," "not qualified," "discriminated," "forced" (as in "forced to quit" or "forced to implement quotas"), or the use of extreme words to describe promotion or raise practices by race, such as "always" and "never." For these purposes, responses that are not racial in nature are counted as lacking emotional content.

10. There is no single best way to gauge discrimination in the labor market. Other methodologies have weaknesses as well when it comes to judging the extent of discrimination. For example, even in cases where trained observers judge a behavior, there can be substantial ambiguities of interpretation and judgment (see Schuman et al. 1983). And the degree of "control" achieved in auditing studies is seldom perfect. Indeed, the closer such research comes to perfect experimental control, the more artificial the test may become. For instance, black and white job applicants with absolutely no apparent difference in taste in clothing, spoken English, hairstyle, and other subtle cultural attributes that might become salient in the course of self-presentation in a job interview (that is, ability to engage in everyday conversation about favorite musicians) would be virtually impossible to find. The more the research pressed toward an exactly identical stimulus save for race, the greater the problem of external validity would become.

References

Bean, Frank D., and Marta Tienda. 1987. *The Hispanic Population of the United States.* New York: Russell Sage.

Bobo, Lawrence. 1992. "Prejudice and Alternative Dispute Resolution." *Studies in Law, Politics, and Society* 12: 147–76.

Bobo, Lawrence, Camille L. Zubrinsky, James H. Johnson, and Melvin L. Oliver. 1994. "Public Opinion Before and After a Spring of Discontent." In *The Los Angeles Riots: Lessons for the Urban Future*, edited by M. Baldassare. Boulder, Colo.: Westview Press.

———. 1995. "Work Orientation, Job Discrimination, and Ethnicity: A Focus Group Perspective." *Research in the Sociology of Work* 5: 45–85.

Braddock, JoMills H., and James M. McPartland. 1987. "How Minorities Continue to Be Excluded from Equal Employment Opportunities: Research on Labor Market and Institutional Barriers." *Journal of Social Issues* 43: 5–39.

Burstein, Paul. 1985. *Discrimination, Jobs and Politics: The Struggle for Equal Employment Opportunity in the United States Since the New Deal*. Chicago: University of Chicago Press.

Carnoy, Martin. 1994. *Faded Dreams: The Politics and Economics of Race in America*. New York: Cambridge University Press.

Converse, Jean M. 1987. *Survey Research in the United States: Roots and Emergence 1890–1960*. Berkeley and Los Angeles: University of California Press.

Corcoran, Mary, and Greg J. Duncan. 1978. "Work History, Labor Force Attachment, and Earning Differences Between Races and Sexes." *Journal of Human Resources* 14: 3–20.

Cose, Ellis. 1993. *The Rage of a Privileged Class*. New York: Harper-Collins.

Davis, James A., and Tom W. Smith. 1990. *General Social Surveys, 1972–1990: Cumulative Codebook*. Chicago: National Opinion Research Center.

Dawson, Michael C. 1994. *Behind the Mule: Race and Class in African American Politics*. Princeton, N.J.: Princeton University Press.

Duleep, Harriet Orcutt, and Seth Sanders. 1992. "Discrimination at the Top: American-born Asian and White Men." *Industrial Relations* 31: 416–32.

Duncan, Otis Dudely. 1969. "Inheritance of Poverty or Inheritance of Race?" In *On Understanding Poverty*, edited by D. P. Moynihan. New York: Basic Books.

Farley, Reynolds. 1984. *Blacks and Whites: Narrowing the Gap?* Cambridge, Mass.: Harvard University Press.

Feagin, Joe R. 1991. "The Continuing Significance of Race: Antiblack Discrimination in Public Places." *American Sociological Review* 56: 101–16.

Feagin, Joe R., and Douglas Lee Eckberg. 1980. "Discrimination: Motivation, Action, Effects, and Context." *Annual Review of Sociology* 6: 1–20.

Feagin, Joe R., and Melvin P. Sikes. 1994. *Living with Racism: The Black Middle Class Experience*. Boston: Beacon Press.

Featherman, David L., and Robert M. Hauser. 1978. *Opportunity and Change*. New York: Academic Press.

Firebaugh, Glenn, and Kenneth E. Davis. 1988. "Trends in Antiblack Prejudice, 1972–1984: Region and Cohort Effects." *American Journal of Sociology* 94: 251–72.

Fredrickson, George M., and Dale T. Knobel. 1982. "A History of Discrimination." In *Prejudice: Dimensions of Ethnicity*, edited by S. Thernstrom, A. Orlov, and O. Handlin. Cambridge, Mass.: Harvard University Press.

Gamson, William, and Andre Modigliani. 1987. "The Changing Culture of Affirmative Action." *Research in Political Sociology* 3: 137–77.

Gurin, Patricia, Shirley Hatchett, and James S. Jackson. 1989. *Hope and Independence: Blacks' Response to Electoral and Party Politics*. New York: Russell Sage.

Gurin, Patricia, Arthur H. Miller, and Gerald Gurin. 1980. "Stratum Identification and Consciousness." *Social Psychology Quarterly* 43: 30–47.

Hyman, Herbert H. 1991. *Taking Society's Measure: A Personal History of Survey Research*. New York: Russell Sage.

Hyman, Herbert H., and Paul B. Sheatsley. 1956. "Attitudes Towards Desegregation." *Scientific American* 195: 35–39.

Jaynes, Gerald D., and Robin M. Williams, Jr. 1989. *A Common Destiny: Blacks and American Society*. Washington, D.C.: National Academy Press.

Johnson, James H., Melvin L. Oliver, and Lawrence Bobo. 1994. "Understanding the Contours of Deepening Urban Inequality: Theoretical Underpinnings and Research Design of a Multi-city Study." *Urban Geography* 15: 78–90.

Kim, Pan Suk, and Gregory B. Lewis. 1994. "Asian Americans in the Public Service: Success, Diversity and Discrimination." *Public Administration Review* 54: 285–90.

Kirschenman, Joleen, and Kathryn M. Neckerman. 1991. "'We'd Love to Hire Them, But . . .': The Meaning of Race for Employers." In *The Urban Underclass*, edited by C. Jencks and P. E. Peterson. Washington, D.C.: Brookings Institute.

Kluegel, James R. 1978. "The Causes and Cost of Racial Exclusion from Job Authority." *American Sociological Review* 43: 285–301.

Kluegel, James R., and Eliot R. Smith. 1982. "Whites' Beliefs About Blacks' Opportunity." *American Sociological Review* 47: 518–32.

———. 1986. *Beliefs About Inequality: Americans' Views of What Is and What Ought to Be*. New York: Aldine de Gruyter.

Landry, Bart. 1987. *The New Black Middle Class*. Berkeley and Los Angeles: University of California Press.

Lieberson, Stanley. 1980. *A Piece of the Pie: Blacks and White Immigrants Since 1880*. Berkeley and Los Angeles: University of California Press.

Lieberson, Stanley, and Glen Fuguitt. 1967. "Negro-White Occupational Differences in the Absence of Discrimination." *American Journal of Sociology* 73: 188–200.

Neckerman, Kathryn M., and Joleen Kirschenman. 1991. "Hiring Strategies, Racial Bias, and Inner-City Workers." *Social Problems* 38: 433–47.

Niemi, Richard G., John Mueller, and Tom W. Smith. 1989. *Trends in Public Opinion: A Compendium of Survey Data*. Westport, Conn.: Greenwood Press.

Oliver, Melvin L., James H. Johnson, and Lawrence Bobo. 1994. "Unraveling the Paradox of Deepening Urban Inequality: The Multi-city Survey of Urban Inequality." *African American Research Perspectives* (Winter): 43–52.

Pettigrew, Thomas F., and Joanne Martin. 1987. "Shaping the Organizational Context for Black Inclusion." *Journal of Social Issues* 43: 41–78.

Pettigrew, Thomas F., and Marylee C. Taylor. 1990. "Discrimination." In *Encyclopedia of Sociology*. Vol. 1, edited by E. F. Borgatta and M. L. Borgatta. New York: Macmillan.

Reskin, Barbara F. 1998. *The Realities of Affirmative Action*. Washington, D.C.: American Sociological Association.

———. Forthcoming. "Employment Discrimination and Its Remedies." In *Handbook on Labor Market Research*, edited by I. Berg and A. Kalleberg. New York: Plenum.

Schuman, Howard. 1972. "Attitudes vs. Actions versus Attitudes vs. Attitudes." *Public Opinion Quarterly* 36: 347–54.

Schuman, Howard, Eleanor Singer, Rebecca Donovan, and Claire Selltiz. 1983. "Discriminatory Behavior in New York Restaurants: 1950 and 1981." *Social Indicators Research* 13: 69–83.

Schuman, Howard, Charlotte Steeh, and Lawrence Bobo. 1985. *Racial Attitudes in America: Trends and Interpretations*. Cambridge, Mass.: Harvard University Press.

Siegel, Paul M. 1970. "On the Cost of Being Negro." In *The Logic of Social Hierarchies*, edited by E. O. Laumann, P. M. Siegel, and R. Hodge. New York: Routledge.

Sigelman, Lee, and Susan Welch. 1991. *Black American's Views of Racial Inequality: The Dream Deferred*. New York: Cambridge University Press.

Smith, A. Wade. 1987. "Problems and Progress in the Measurement of Black Public Opinion." *American Behavioral Scientist* 30: 441–55.

Stone, Jonathan. 1985. *Racial Conflict in Contemporary Society*. Cambridge, Mass.: Harvard University Press.

Stouffer, Samuel A. 1949. *The American Soldier: Studies in Social Psychology in World War II*. Princeton, N.J.: Princeton University Press.

Tajfel, Henri. 1982. "Social Psychology of Intergroup Relations." *Annual Review of Psychology* 33: 1–39.

Tang, Joyce. 1993. "The Career Attainment of Caucasian and Asian Engineers." *Sociological Quarterly* 34: 467–97.

Tate, Katherine. 1993. *From Protest to Politics: The New Black Voters in American Elections*. New York: Russell Sage.

Taylor, D. Garth, Andrew M. Greeley, and Paul B. Sheatsley. 1978. "Attitudes Toward Racial Integration." *Scientific American* 238: 42–50.

Telles, Edward E., and Edward Murgia. 1990. "Phenotypic Discrimination and Income Differences Among Mexican Americans." *Social Science Quarterly* 71: 682–97.

Tienda, Marta, and Ding-Tzann Lii. 1987. "Minority Concentration and Earnings Inequality: Blacks, Hispanics, and Asians Compared." *American Journal of Sociology* 93: 141–65.

Turner, Margery Austin, Michael Fix, and Raymond J. Struyk. 1991. *Opportunities Denied, Opportunities Diminished: Racial Discrimination in Hiring*. Washington, D.C.: Urban Institute Press.

Waldinger, Roger. 1986. "Changing Ladders and Musical Chairs: Ethnicity and Opportunity in Post-Industrial New York." *Politics and Society* 15: 369–401.

———. 1989. "Immigration and Urban Change." *Annual Review of Sociology* 15: 211–32.

Waldinger, Roger, and Tom Bailey. 1991. "The Continuing Significance of Race: Racial Conflict and Racial Discrimination in Construction." *Politics and Society* 19: 291–323.

Waters, Mary C. 1990. *Ethnic Options: Choosing Identities in America*. Berkeley and Los Angeles: University of California Press.

Wilson, William Julius. 1978. *The Declining Significance of Race*. Chicago: University of Chicago Press.

Zweigenhaft, Richard L., and G. William Domhoff. 1991. *Blacks in the White Establishment?: A Study of Race and Class in America*. New Haven, Conn.: Yale University Press.

15

WOMEN'S PERCEPTIONS OF WORKPLACE DISCRIMINATION: IMPACTS OF RACIAL GROUP, GENDER, AND CLASS

Susan A. Suh

Fᴿᴏᴍ 1950 to 1990, women of color have doubled their representation in the paid workforce, and are projected to increase their participation through the next century (Federal Glass Ceiling Commission 1991), but their self-described experiences in the workplace
have often been neglected.[1] This gap in knowledge is especially noticeable regarding Asian Americans, even though there has been a doubling
of their representation in the paid workforce between 1980 and 1990.
This paucity hinders the development of more rigorous theory building,
hypothesis testing, and research designs that incorporate women in the
workforce, especially those who are neither white nor African American.

Workers' perceptions of discrimination in the workplace are salient,
regardless of whether formal documentation was filed at the time of the
experience. Consequences of the belief that discrimination has occurred
easily extend beyond an individual concern to a societal one, when one
interprets these reports as conservative estimates of all occurrences.[2]
Importantly, the extent of perceptions of discrimination against oneself
is an indication of the climate of racial group and gender relations in the
multiracial and bigendered workplaces of today.

To this end, I use data from LASUI to explore the self-reporting of
workplace discrimination for African American, East Asian American,
Latina, and white women. I employ a double jeopardy framework, which
emphasizes the simultaneous effects of racial group and gender in the
lives of women of color. By focusing on the following questions within a

double jeopardy framework, I seek to further develop our understanding of what women in various occupations and workplaces face as workers:

(1) To what extent do women in the workforce perceive discrimination against themselves? Does this perception differ by racial group, by socioeconomic characteristics, and/or by the degree of group consciousness?

(2) What specific forms does this discrimination take? Whom do workers think is doing the discriminating?

(3) Why do some workers report having experienced discrimination, while others do not?

These data allow me to contribute to the discrimination literature by focusing on women in the workforce across racial groups; extending analysis beyond black and white by including East Asian Americans and Latinas; documenting quantitative and qualitative measures of workers' perceptions of discrimination across racial groups; and analyzing a relatively large sample of workers across various occupations and industries. Since findings include analyses of closed- and open-ended responses, the inclusion of the latter in this survey gives us a rare opportunity to combine the strengths of survey data analysis (such as capturing experiences and profiles of large numbers of respondents) with open-ended interviews (such as allowing for more detailed accounts of experiences).

Background

For the most part, contemporary quantitative research on workplace discrimination has focused on investigating readily quantified outcomes like wage differentials[3] and occupational segregation[4] (Tang 1993; Tomaskovic-Devey 1993; Telles and Murguia 1990; Tienda and Lii 1987; Yamanaka and McClelland 1994). Much of these studies have made racial comparisons between African Americans vis-à-vis whites (as in Lieberson and Fuguitt 1967; Braddock and McPartland 1987), or "women" vis-à-vis "men" (as in Hartmann 1976; England et al. 1988; Reskin and Roos 1990), thereby focusing on either racial group or gender discrimination separately.[5] In either case, separating the potential primacy of racial group and of gender tends to shift attention away from how the intersection of these two social markers influence or dictate the workplace experiences for women in the workforce. In addition, exploring mechanisms of discrimination has meant focusing more on employer practices of economic discrimination, such as occupational segregation and job exclusion, and less on actual workers' perspectives (see, for example, Kirschenman and Neckerman 1991).[6]

How racial group and class inform the positioning and day-to-day work experiences of different women has only recently been addressed, and then only in a few ethnographic works, each usually limited to one racial or ethnic group, a small sample size, and one specific firm or industry (see Chow 1994; Glenn 1986; Hossfeld 1994; Segura 1994).

A theoretical framework of double jeopardy or multiple jeopardy has been proposed by Deborah King (1988) and others (see Collins 1990) to describe discrimination that women of color face based on the combination of their racial group and gender. This framework acknowledges the primacy that such interconnected social factors as racial group, gender, and class hold in orienting people's realities. There have been some empirical studies prior to this decade that have worked within a double jeopardy framework; that is, these works have helped capture experiences specifically defined by one's racial group and gender. However, most empirical studies that use this theoretical framing have come out only in the last few years in such disciplines as education and psychology.[7]

Given that prejudice, often acted out through discriminatory actions, has been found to be "top of the list" of barriers for corporate advancement, and that whites, especially white men, make up the overwhelming majority of higher-level managers across all occupations and industries (Federal Glass Ceiling Commission 1991),[8] this can translate into seriously deleterious results for women of color in the workforce. Explicitly, because women of color have more strikes against them, according to the double jeopardy argument, they are anticipated to face different discrimination than white women, since the former group must face racism and forms of racialized sexism as well.

Once an establishment of the importance of racial differences in perceptions of discrimination experiences is made, it is conceivable to further determine whether there are differences within racial group as well. For example, we might expect that differences in class position and nativity could potentially differentiate people of the same gender and racial group from each other in terms of the labor market in which they work and the people with whom they interact at work. Taking the double jeopardy argument a step further, I would like to explore how these other socioeconomic class factors affect discrimination outcomes for women of different racial groups in the labor force.

The Population

The appendix summarizes characteristics such as social background and workplaces of the respondents of this survey by racial group.[9] Although there are similarities in populations across racial groups, significant differences justify keeping these groups distinct. The African American

563

and white groups are primarily native-born and primarily English speakers, compared to the East Asian American and Latina groups. However, whites are more likely than African Americans to have higher levels of formal education, income, and upper-white-collar jobs. Moreover, African Americans are almost twice as likely to work in the public sector than whites, as well as to work with coworkers and supervisors of a different racial group.

Blacks and Latinas are the two racial groups with lower levels of formal education compared to whites and East Asian Americans, but Latinas are substantially poorer as a group, predominantly foreign-born, the most represented in blue-collar jobs, and much more likely than blacks to work with coworkers of the same racial group.

Similarly, Asian Americans and whites are often compared for their similar class standings of higher levels of education and income, as opposed to other racial groups. However, women of Chinese, Japanese, and Korean descent in Los Angeles are predominantly foreign-born, resulting in a higher percentage of those with limited English language ability. Furthermore, about 50 percent more East Asian Americans than whites earn below $6,000 a year or have no more than high school–level education.

In addition, differences within racial groups justify disaggregating beyond racial group. For example, we might suspect that the two-thirds of Latinas who have no more than a high school diploma would fare very differently in the labor force than their more highly educated sisters, or that there might be differences in discrimination patterns for those one-third of African American women who have supervisors who are also black, compared to the majority of black women, who have white supervisors.

Once the main concepts are operationalized in the next section, several research questions that explore this diversity across and within racial groups will follow, framing the direction of inquiry in this chapter.

Data and Measures

This chapter uses a subsample of the original LASUI dataset, composed of respondents who have worked for pay at some point in their lives and have or had a supervisor in their current or last jobs.[10] Four broad racial categories are represented: African American (N = 245), East Asian American (N = 177), Latina (N = 205), and white (N = 152), for a total of 779 women, age twenty-one and over, residing in Los Angeles County.

Six closed-ended and two open-ended questions were asked of respondents to determine recent experiences of racial discrimination in their workplaces: four gender-based and four racial group–based. Each question focused on a specific form of discrimination (see bottom of table 15.1 for exact wording): two on racist or sexist speech by a supervisor, one on general racial discrimination, one on sexual harassment, and two on promotion or pay discrimination against one's racial group or gender. Possible answers to these questions were in a "yes-no" format. Respondents who answered affirmatively to the questions of promotion or pay discrimination were asked to further specify ("What happened that made you feel that way?").

Double jeopardy is measured by an affirmative answer to at least one of the racial discrimination *and* at least one of the gender discrimination questions. Although this does not exactly capture the interactive effects of racial group and gender explicitly (that is, there is no discrimination question wording such as, "Because you are a (black/East Asian American/Latina) woman . . . "), we may believe that all the questions *combined* give us some sense of this, since the same women are asked to answer questions regarding discrimination based on their racial group and based on their gender.

I also include three measures for group consciousness: two racial group–based, one gender-based. Two questions that measure perceptions of discrimination against one's group were asked of all respondents about their own racial and gender group: "In general, how much discrimination is there that hurts the chances of [*your racial group/women*] to get good-paying jobs?" Multiple-answer choices were on a four-point scale of "a lot, some, only a little, or none at all." One question measured the strength of identity to one's racial group on the same four-point scale.

The responses examined here should be taken as a *minimum* indicator of the extent of discrimination in workplace settings, for a number of reasons (see Bobo 1992). First, the survey did not ask the frequency of occurrence of discriminatory behavior, but rather whether or not it had occurred at all.[11] Second, not reporting could be a coping mechanism for the psychological pain and frustration of acknowledging recurring and/ or obvious discriminatory practices (see Bobo and Suh 1995; Feagin 1991). Third, discouragement (by employers, coworkers, family) from pointing out occurrences might have successfully deterred workers from acknowledging discriminatory actions at the time they occurred.[12] Fourth, especially for those women for whom cultural norms (both in the United States and otherwise) dictate less openly assertive behavior, self-imposed restraints of speech and behavior can occur (Chow 1994) that might effectively lower discrimination reporting. Finally, it should be kept in mind that naming discrimination as such, thereby separating a particular act or situation from the rest of daily life, is an outlook that not all women have. Immigrants, for example, often see their lives not as specifically and particularly oppressed, but as filled with hardships and negotiated by employing various forms of survival tactics. The focus could then be away from naming particular instances of discrimination, and toward day-to-day survival (Glenn 1986).

Reported accounts of discrimination may be criticized for not being valid or accurate records of "actual" incidents, because of their highly subjective nature. Some would even argue that a survey question allows the respondent to vent contrived grievances of discrimination in lieu of shouldering responsibility for personal failures. However, reports of discrimination are not conducive to facile interpretations, insofar as people's definitions and perceptions of what constitutes discrimination vary widely. Whether or not a situation is described as discriminatory is dependent on how it is defined by the subject and society (as is anything that is social or political in nature). No social event is conceived in absolute terms, but rather reflects the point of view of the subject at the time of its telling and the perspective of the intended audience. This is why, for example, respondents and interviewers are consciously matched by racial group.[13]

With this in mind, analyzing reports of discrimination should include a combination of factors. They indicate the extent of historical precedence of racist sexism the particular group has (or has not) faced, the extent of discrimination one may face as a particular racialized and gendered person in a *specific* work situation, and one's level of consciousness of the existence (or nonexistence) of structural discrimination against one's group.

Analyses and Discussion

Since the concept of double jeopardy has been theorized to explain outcomes and experiences of women of color, all analyses in the following discussion will compare their responses with each other. At the end of each section, I will analyze the responses of the white respondents for comparison.[14]

Do Women of Color Report a Double Jeopardy Liability in Their Workplaces?

How do reports compare in relation to each other? Because African American women have arguably the longest and most severe history of oppression in the United States compared to the other women in this survey and are the least likely to work with coworkers and supervisors who are also black, one might reason that they will be the most likely to report double jeopardy. One might also argue that the mostly immigrant populations of East Asian American and Latina workers would perceive discrimination against themselves, in light of the racialized anti-immigrant and English-only message that has been prevalent, especially in the Los Angeles region, over the last decade.

However, these groups might report less than other racialized ethnic groups, for as we found earlier, East Asian Americans are the most likely among women of color to have co-ethnic supervisors,[15] while Latina respondents are the most likely among women of color to work in co-ethnic workplaces. In addition, it might be argued that immigrants might attribute unfair treatment to other characteristics (for example, their immigrant status, language barriers) rather than discrimination based on their racial group and/or gender.

Table 15.1 summarizes who reports double jeopardy discrimination and shows a breakdown of the "yes" responses to the individual closed-ended questions by racial group of respondent. Looking at the top half of the table, we see that women of all racial groups reported some level of gender and racial group–based discrimination. However, all except one of the questions show significant differences across racial groups.[16] The questions with the largest differences across racial groups are the general racial discrimination, sexual harassment, and gender bias in raise and promotion distribution questions. African Americans were much more likely to report having experienced racial discrimination (24.9 percent) and sexual harassment (13.5 percent) on the job than all other working women. In fact, African American workers compared to all other women reported the most gender and racial group–based discrimination of all types, except for slow raises or promotions because of gender, in which case white women (16.4 percent) reported more than black women (10.2 percent).

East Asian American women were the least likely to report discrimination in receiving raises and promotions based on racial group or gender, experiences with sexual harassment, and witnessing a supervisor using racial slurs (all less than 5 percent). They were as likely to report being generally discriminated against based on their racial group or ethnic group as Latinas (11.3 percent versus 11.8 percent, respectively), and more likely to report witnessing a supervisor using sexist speech (13.0 percent), compared with Latinas (6.8 percent) or whites (9.2 percent). However, these findings, and all subsequent analyses regarding East Asian American and Latina workers, should be read cautiously. As mentioned earlier, these groups had the highest percentage of male interviewers of all groups, which indicates that an interviewer effect might be at work here.

TABLE 15.1 *Reports of Racial and Gender Discrimination in the Workplace, by Racial Group of Respondent, Women in Los Angeles, 1993 to 1994*
(N = 779)

| | Respondent Racial Group and Percentage "Yes" | | | |
Type of Discrimination	African American	East Asian American	Latina	White
Racial group discrimination				
Supervisor used racial slurs	10.2%	3.4%	8.3%	7.9%
General racial-ethnic discrimination	24.9	11.3	11.8	7.9***
Slow raises and promotions	13.5	3.4	6.8	7.8**
Gender discrimination				
Supervisor used sexist speech	16.7	13.0	6.8	9.2**
Sexual harassment	13.5	1.1	7.3	10.5***
Slow raises and promotions	10.2	1.1	5.4	16.4***
Double jeopardy	24.8	9.0	6.8	8.6***
Only gender discrimination	6.9	5.6	8.3	15.1
Only racial group discrimination	12.6	6.8	10.2	10.5

RACIAL DISCRIMINATION QUESTIONS WORDING: (1) During the (past year/last year you worked) has/did your supervisor or boss ever use racial slurs?; (2) During the (past year/last year you worked) have/did you experience racial or ethnic discrimination at your place of work because of your racial group or ethnicity?; and (3) Have you ever felt at any time in the past that others at your place of employment got promotions or pay raises faster than you did because of your racial group or ethnicity?

GENDER DISCRIMINATION QUESTIONS WORDING: (1) During the (past year/last year you worked) (has/did) your supervisor or boss ever (made/make) insulting comments about women?; (2) During the (past year/last year you worked) did you experience sexual harassment at your place of work?; and (3) Have you ever felt at any time in the past that others at your place of employment got promotions or pay raises faster than you did because of your gender (sex)?

Source: Los Angeles Study of Urban Inequality 1994.
$*p < .05$, $**p < .01$, $***p < .001$

I next look at the aggregated distribution of double jeopardy, only gender-based, and only racial discrimination by racial group (see bottom third of the table). Here we see overwhelming differences across racial groups, with African Americans most likely to report double jeopardy.[17] Although it is clear from this table that a fraction of workers within each racial group reported experiencing double jeopardy at work, this includes close to *one in four* black workers reporting that they have experienced gender- *and* racial group–based discrimination in the workplace. This is a serious concern, for it points to widespread discrimination, on the one hand, and widespread perceptions of workplace unfairness and mistreatment, on the other. This suggests that the notion of double jeopardy can be applied most strongly for black women, and is apparent for a number of Latinas (6.8 percent) and East Asian Americans (9.0 percent).

Respondents were given a chance to elaborate on their experiences of racial group– and gender-based discrimination if they answered "yes" to the two questions of whether they felt others got promotions or raises faster than themselves. African Americans were most likely to answer these open-ended questions at all (N = 60). They were also the respondents most likely to elaborate on the racial discrimination question (N = 42); that is, there were over 2.5, 3, and 4.5 times more responses by African American women than Latina, white, and Asian American respondents, respectively.

It is clear through the open-ended responses that some women do see themselves in double jeopardy in the workplace, and that this occurs across racial groups. Although the racial group and gender discrimination questions were asked separately, some workers answered for each question that both their racial group and gender were relevant to their experiences, pointing to the interaction of racial group and gender:

Really it was an advertising company and advertising is dominated by white males.—thirty-three-year-old African American worker's answer to gender question

For example, a Latino employer was prejudiced against women. He felt women were inferior. I was twice discriminated [against] because I was a woman and a Latina.—thirty-two-year-old Latina worker's answer to gender question

How did white workers respond to the racial-based and gender discrimination questions? Regarding only gender discrimination, white workers were the most likely to report discrimination in raises and promotions (16.4 percent compared with 10.2 percent of African American workers, the next highest). Their reporting of dealing with sexist speech or dealing with sexual harassment on the job was between the levels of reporting for African Americans on the high end and Latinas or East Asian Americans on the other, and are nonzero. Around these issues in common, then, women of color and white women can hope to work together in the workplace in support of each other.

However, about as often as white workers reported dealing with sexist speech from their supervisors (9.2 percent), they reported experiencing racial group and gender discrimination (8.6 percent)—about as much as Latina (6.8 percent) and East Asian American workers (9.0 percent) did. Responses to the three individual racial discrimination questions also hovered at about 8 percent. Fortunately, white workers' perceptions that hinge on "color-conscious racist ideologies" (Weber and Higginbotham 1995) like reverse discrimination were in the minority in these findings.[18] Although it could be argued that workers bring to the work site ideologies that are learned from and encouraged by the larger U.S. society, it appears that they are reinforced at the work site as well. Some employers, for example, play a role in disseminating ideas about racial quotas that increase distrust and scapegoating of visible workers of color in today's economic reality of countrywide "downsizing":

When they started hiring on the basis of quotas, they told us not to expect raises or promotions. They even said specifically because I was white.—fifty-nine-year-old computer systems analyst with white female supervisor

In civil service exams, minorities got 10 points extra. We were told that, which led to them getting faster promotions from civil service list.—sixty-three-year-old secretary with white male supervisor

How Does Socioeconomic Status Impact Perceptions of Double Jeopardy Discrimination?

Social class markers, such as higher levels of formal education and occupations, could be linked to lower levels of discrimination or less identifiable instances of it. This line of reasoning assumes that people with higher education exhibit less prejudice and less blatant discriminatory actions; and/or when discrimination does occur, it occurs in more subtle forms and therefore is not as easily recognizable as such (Moghissi 1994). Although discrimination might be more subtle and harder to prove in work settings of the highly educated, the claim that it exists only in some areas of our society is a weak one. Since racism and sexism are practiced in and perpetuated from arenas that go beyond purely logical or academic ones (such as symbolic, sexual, psychological, emotional, and cultural terrains), hanging the eradication of racism and sexism on the peg of "higher education" seems unconvincing.

In contrast, higher educational levels have been linked to higher reporting of discrimination (see previous chapter and Bobo and Suh 1995), such that individuals with more formal education and who work in higher-status occupations are more likely to know their rights in relation to discrimination in general and thus be in better positions to report it. Further, those with higher formal education might work in environments that increase the likelihood of experiencing racial and gender discrimination, that is, where they are more likely to work with people of other racial groups and to work with men, who may be antagonistic (if not hostile) to them (Braddock and McPartland 1987).

To see whether there is a relationship between class status and reporting of discrimination, I next look at the sociodemographic profile of the respondents by the type of discrimination they report. Those who report no experiences of discrimination in the workplace based on gender or racial group constitute the omitted column of data.

There are some stark contrasts in the profiles of those respondents who report having experienced double jeopardy in the workplace with those who report otherwise. Table 15.2 shows that a class difference is apparent. Those with the highest levels of education and income and working in white-collar jobs tended to report double jeopardy more than those of the working class. Twenty percent of those with at least a bachelor's degree reported double jeopardy, compared with 10.2 percent of those with no more than a high school degree. Over 30 percent of white-collar workers reported it, while a little under 14 percent of blue-collar workers did. There is some support, then, to the claim that racism and sexism do not disappear or lessen in environments where people with higher levels of education work, especially given the fact that this difference by class of those who reported double jeopardy also applies to those who reported only gender or racial group–based discrimination.

We see this reflected in the open-ended responses as well. A majority of the responses came from workers with white-collar jobs (92 out of 136 responses). It is interesting to note, though, that the following comments came from respondents working in very different occupations, albeit white-collar ones:

> Hired white people off the streets to be head cashier when there were qualified black people for the job already working there.—thirty-year-old African American, general office clerk

> I felt I was discriminated for my race. I was working longer than a white person and she got more benefits than me.—fifty-two-year-old Latina, bookkeeper

There are a few differences between those who reported double jeopardy and those who reported having experienced only one type of discrimination. As we might expect, white women (15.1 percent) were much more likely to report only gender discrimination compared to women of color (for example, the second highest to report only gender

TABLE 15.2   *Sociodemographic Profile of Respondents by Reports of Discrimination, Women in Los Angeles, 1993 to 1994 (N = 779)*

Variable	Racial Only	Gender Only	Double Jeopardy
(All respondents)	10.3%	8.6%	13.3%***
Racial group			
African American	12.6	6.9	24.8***
East Asian American	6.8	5.6	9.0
Latina	10.2	8.3	6.8
white	10.5	15.1	8.6
Age			
Twenty-one to twenty-nine	9.4	7.1	12.6***
Thirty to thirty-nine	13.4	9.7	19.8
Forty to forty-nine	8.7	13.9	8.7
Fifty and over	7.3	5.5	5.5
Formal education			
High school or less	9.1	5.7	10.2**
Some college	10.4	11.2	12.0
Bachelor's or higher	13.0	11.3	20.3
Income			
< $6,000	8.7	5.2	10.1***
$6,000 to $16,999	7.2	7.7	12.4
$17,000 to $31,999	18.5	13.2	7.3
$32,000 or more	9.8	17.1	41.5
Occupation			
Lower blue-collar	8.3	7.1	3.6***
Upper blue-collar	6.1	7.3	10.1
Lower blue-collar	13.8	7.5	17.6
Upper white-collar	8.2	13.5	12.9
Year of immigration			
Native-born	11.1	9.1	17.3***
Before 1985	5.0	13.2	4.4
1985 to 1994	12.1	3.6	10.9
English speaking ability			
Little or none	8.4	3.1	3.1***
Fair	9.3	7.0	17.4
Well	10.7	10.2	14.8

Source: Los Angeles Study of Urban Inequality 1994.
Note: Omitted column is of those who reported no discrimination by each variable. Including omitted column, rows total to 100 percent (± 1 percent due to rounding).
*p < .05, **p < .01, ***p < .001

discrimination was 8.3 percent of Latinas). Also, those who reported only gender-based discrimination were more likely to be older than those who reported double jeopardy or only racial group discrimination. For example, while close to one in five of those in their thirties (19.8 percent) reported having experienced double jeopardy compared with less than one in ten of those in their forties (8.7 percent), women in their forties (13.9 percent) were more likely to report having experienced only gender-based discrimination compared with women in their thirties (9.7 percent).

Does Nativity Affect Perceptions of Discrimination?

Negatively perceived attributes of lack of English-speaking ability, lower formal education and "class," and lower levels of acculturation could be attributed to certain immigrants and result in more discrimination against them. On the other hand, immigrants (especially newly arrived folks) might be less inclined to report their experiences as unfair and discriminatory for a number of reasons. First, East Asian Americans and Latinas are most likely to work in small businesses among people of the same racial group, compared with African Americans and whites, which would decrease the likelihood of facing racial discrimination by a supervisor or coworkers. Second, as discussed earlier, because they are working in an adopted country and not their native one, they might anticipate some higher level of hardship in their daily lives that comes from being an immigrant.

As we see in table 15.2, there are some differences by nativity in who reports experiencing only one type of discrimination. About 13 percent of those who immigrated earlier reported having experienced only gender-based discrimination, compared with 3.6 percent of those who immigrated more recently and 9.1 percent of those who were born in the United States. However, more recently arrived immigrants reported having experienced only racial group–based discrimination by about the same percentage as those born in this country (12.1 percent and 11.1 percent, respectively).

There is also a difference by nativity and English-speaking ability in who reports double jeopardy. Of those who were native-born, 17.3 percent reported having experienced double jeopardy, compared with 4.4 percent of immigrants who arrived prior to 1985. Of those who spoke English fairly or well, 17.4 percent and 14.8 percent reported double jeopardy, respectively, while only 3.1 percent of those who self-described their English language ability as little or none reported it. It appears, then, that immigrants, but especially those who arrived before 1985 (before the recent decade of a strongly anti-immigrant climate), are less likely to report experiencing double jeopardy compared to those who were born in the United States. This might suggest either that earlier immigrants were more politically conservative as a group upon entry and/or that growth of a racial consciousness was suppressed for survival upon arrival and has carried forth even (or especially) in today's climate.

It appears that immigrants are more likely to report having faced gender discrimination or racial group discrimination (depending on whether they emigrated recently or earlier) than U.S.-born workers, while those born in the United States are more likely to report having faced double jeopardy.

How Does Workplace Affect
Perceptions of Double Jeopardy
Discrimination?

In addition to SES and nativity, characteristics of workplaces might also affect whether one reports experiencing double jeopardy discrimination. For example, previous studies have found that public sector jobs and those with co-racial coworkers and supervisors were found to be less discriminatory worksites (for example, Pettigrew and Martin 1987). Because the data allow for comparison across various occupations and work sites in public and private sectors, this question can be tested here.

The top half of table 15.3 examines how workplace characteristics (such as public or private sector, racial group and gender of supervisor and coworkers) might be associated with reporting patterns. Crosstabular analysis seems to refute previous scholarship that anticipates less discriminatory behavior in public-sector workplaces compared to private-sector ones. There appears to be no significant difference between public- and private-sector worker responses; for example, 13.4 percent of private-sector workers compared with 12.4 percent of public-sector workers reported having experienced both their gender and their racial group as a liability in the workplace.

In contrast, there are significantly larger differences when looking at differing workplace demographics. First, racially, whom you work with and for makes a difference. About 7 percent of workers with coworkers mainly of the same racial group reported double jeopardy, compared with close to one in four of workers who worked predominantly with coworkers of a different racial group. Second, gender of your boss makes a difference.[19] Having a male supervisor of any racial group corresponds to higher reporting of gender discrimination and double jeopardy than if one has a female supervisor of any racial group (see middle column of table 15.3).

TABLE 15.3   *Workplace and Group Consciousness Profile of Respondents, by Discrimination Reporting, Women in Los Angeles, 1993 to 1994 (N = 779)*

Variable	Racial Only	Gender Only	Double Jeopardy
Sector			
Private	9.7	8.6	13.4
Public	13.5	10.1	12.4
Racial Group of Coworkers			
Different	13.7	10.2	23.9***
Same	7.9	7.9	7.2
Gender and Racial Group of Supervisor			
Male of different racial group	16.6	9.9	27.2***
Female of different racial group	13.2	3.7	10.6
Male of same racial group	5.2	11.6	10.4
Female of same racial group	7.8	8.9	7.3
Racial Identity			
Some or lot	11.4	9.1	13.0
Little or none	8.1	8.5	11.9
Racial Group Discrimination			
Some or lot	11.6	9.4	15.2**
Little or none	7.4	6.9	8.7
Gender Discrimination			
Some or lot	9.7	8.9	15.3
Little or none	11.7	7.3	9.5

RACIAL GROUP IDENTITY QUESTION WORDING: Do you think what happens generally to [racial group] people in this country will have something to do with what happens in your life? Will it affect you: a lot, some, or not very much?

RACIAL/GENDER DISCRIMINATION OF GROUP QUESTIONS WORDING: In general, how much discrimination is there that hurts the chances of [racial group]/women to get good-paying jobs? Do you think there is a lot, some, only a little, or none at all?

Source: Los Angeles Study of Urban Inequality 1994.
Notes: Omitted column is of those who reported no discrimination by each variable. Including omitted column, rows total to 100 percent (± 1 percent due to rounding).
*p < .05, **p < .01, ***p < .001

Racial Discrimination   Although white preferencing was the form of discrimination given most often by women of color, some women of color working in multiracial environments named other coworkers of color who were preferred and/or had social networks that excluded them. For example, African American workers secondarily mentioned favoritism toward Latinas and Latinos and, thirdly, favoritism toward Asian Americans. For Latinas, competition with Asian Americans was mentioned second most often, and competition with blacks was mentioned third. East Asian American workers were much more likely to name white preferencing than other nonwhite favoritism.

General comments concerning favoritism of other people of color outside the respondent's own racial group mention unfair advantage of Asian Americans or Latinas specifically. These are usually terse, blunt comments, that indicate the perceived pervasiveness of the inequality:

> Overtime is paid to Hispanics, but not to Koreans.—thirty-nine-year-old Korean American cook

> Asians get less work and make more money. They get promotions faster.—thirty-nine-year-old Latina textile sewing machine operator

> Now, [Hispanics and Filipinos] just move up and I've been there before them.—twenty-seven-year-old African American data-entry worker

It is clear that these impressions are occurring at the same time as increased representation and visibility of growing Latina and Asian-Pacific Islander (API) populations are taking place in Los Angeles. For example, Latinas and APIs were mentioned by African American workers as having a ready-made workplace network based on shared ethnicity that these workers can rely on to get promotions and pay raises:

> Spanish people—they help each other. . . . They just look out for each other.—thirty-eight-year old bus driver with Latino supervisor

> Hispanics got raises faster than me because of racism. All management was Hispanic.—forty-six-year-old cashier with Latina supervisor.

> Because a girl came in after me on transitional basis; I was there four months and she was always late and I was not. She was picked because she was Asian. We were both trained for the machine. . . . The supervisor was Asian.—thirty-year-old occupation unknown with Asian American male supervisor

With demographic changes come changes in markets. The following quote demonstrates how the needs (and purchasing power) of a large and visible community might influence the need for co-ethnic workers, and especially bilingual workers:

Tried to keep the Hispanics because they had Hispanic accounts . . . they paid them more and promoted them faster.—twenty-four-year-old African American data-entry worker

In my department, when you are bilingual you are given consideration over straight-speaking English [sic] people when it comes to certain promotions and filling vacancies.—thirty-seven-year-old African American secretary

They hired a Spanish [sic] girl right after me and paid her $2.00 more an hour because she was bilingual.—forty-two-year-old African American food counter worker

Conversely, when black workers are specifically mentioned as being unfairly advantaged in the workplace, it is because of their native-born status:

When I worked at a company I saw that black and American citizens were paid more than us and we all [did] the same job.—forty-two-year-old Latina housekeeper

Some East Asian Americans reported being penalized by people of the same racial group but different ethnic group, which speaks to the complexity of racial and ethnic relations that is oftentimes overlooked when API and Latina communities are seen erroneously as monolithic:

There's a Cantonese person, his raise and promotion is faster than [mine] because he came from that kind of environment.—forty-six-year-old Japanese American financial officer

Boss is unfair, promotes the Taiwanese. I worked for him for ten years, but not promoted.—thirty-six-year-old Chinese American receptionist

Because of some village relations, some get promoted and pay raises faster than me.—thirty-three-year-old Chinese American, in sales

Gender Discrimination Similar to the general responses we have seen to the racial group discrimination open-ended question, a general acknowledgment of the extent of sexism operating in the workplace is apparent. Paralleling findings in a study of black and white women in professional and managerial jobs (Weber and Higginbotham 1995), this is most often mentioned as discrimination in raise and promotion distributions, rather than from pay differences with men (although this too is mentioned by some workers). The difference here is that these responses are coming from workers from various levels of occupations:

The men received pay raises and women didn't.—fifty-one-year-old African American police officer

Because somebody started to work after me and he got a raise. This person and I do the same job.—forty-year-old Latina dressmaker

Male nurse, with no more experience than me, got promoted within two years to a supervisor position.—fifty-nine-year-old white, registered nurse

Responses to the gender discrimination question focused less on an "old boys' network" or gendered connections, and more on the lack of representation in higher levels of organization hierarchies, due to occupational sex segregation and explicit preferencing of male workers in higher-ranked positions:

It's a hierarchy. Everyone in upper management is a man. Even the man who works under me is given special preference in anything he does or says, before me.—twenty-seven-year-old white, administrative support

In the company I work in, the field supervisors are male, not female.— thirty-five-year-old African American guard

Running airline stations is seen as a male position.—thirty-year-old Latina manager

They were paid more anyway, from the start. When I was a TV producer, I was the only female. I was paid 50 to 60 percent less than the males. When I got promoted I needed to fight tooth and nail for them, whereas the males didn't. I won Emmys and they didn't—and it was still harder for me to get a promotion.—thirty-four-year-old white director

It is clear from their sometimes detailed and lengthy responses that they also faced demoralizing work environments:

Somebody got promoted to a much higher level who's much younger and it just seemed that the men are valued. They make more money and they're taken more seriously. [Whenever] the woman is in the office, she's always the secretary or she always has to answer the phone, because she's the woman.—thirty-one-year-old white, door-to-door sales worker

Excluding women from pay increases and promotions cannot be based solely on the ability of employers to do so. The unusually lengthy response of this next respondent makes clear that economics is only one part of the reason to discriminate: it seems that there is a "taste" for male workers (Reskin and Roos 1990)—especially in positions of power and prestige—that also must be taken into account:

> First of all, a man was hired to be the Director of Development. He couldn't do it. I was doing it all. For that whole year, I did the work and he did nothing, so she decided to promote me and fire him. I know what he made because I was responsible for the contracts . . . after she fired him, she offered me the job but she offered me $20,000 when he was hired at $50,000. Then, she decided she wanted me to do more of the pitching, so we hired a guy as the administrative assistant. He was full of crap. He'd been there two weeks, hadn't been doing anything, and went to her and said, "If I'm going to meetings, I should be given the Director of Development title." So she called me and told me this. She gave him the title and I went on doing the work. And this is a woman doing this to me. I just can't believe it. Then we ended up hiring another guy. This guy couldn't do what I was doing, [but] they gave these guys more money. Finally, I quit.—thirty-eight-year-old white manager with white female supervisor

Reasons for discriminating against women that rely on family obligations seem to have changed with the times. As economic imperatives and access to more jobs have led more women into the paid workforce, using the stereotype of male workers as sole financial supporters of families to justify higher wages for men is no longer an option. However, this stereotype of financially dependent women seems hard to shake, while the same argument of family obligations equaling more pay does not seem to apply for the gander as it did for the goose:

> Back in the 60s, a man doing less work got pay raises and it was even acknowledged [by] management because he had a wife and child to support.—fifty-nine-year-old white, computer systems analyst

> I was told that I do not need the extra commission because I had a male partner at that time who also had an income.—thirty-five-year-old Chinese American guide

> When I was pregnant with my youngest son, I worked as a manager and hired someone to take my place while I was on maternity leave. When I returned to work, the person I hired, a man, had been made my supervisor. He had a better position and more money. I was told that he was made supervisor because he was a man, and men need to earn more money than women.—thirty-one-year-old white, registered nurse

In fact, men are sometimes not seen as having the "problem" of raising children who might interfere with putting work first, while this does not seem to be the case for perceptions of women's roles in the family:

Data-processing department only hired men to do the job because they could come at any odd hour. They didn't have to worry about their kids.— African American door-to-door salesperson

Do Higher Levels of Racial Group and Gender Consciousness Increase the Likelihood of Perceiving Double Jeopardy Discrimination?

Level of identification with a woman's racial group may also be associated with the level of discrimination she identifies as occurring against her racial group. Joe Feagin and Melvin Sikes found that (contrary to popular misconception) African Americans who perceived a general reality of racial discrimination were found to be *less* likely to attribute racial motivation to incidences of ill treatment toward them in public spaces (Feagin and Sikes 1994). This dataset allows us to examine this statistically. Moreover, we can see how a gendered consciousness might affect reporting of gender discrimination as well.

The bottom half of table 15.3 summarizes some indicators of racial and gender group consciousness. One question was asked of the respondents that reveals the strength of connectedness one feels with a larger racial group community (see bottom of table for exact wording). A stronger racial identity is not associated with reporting any type of discrimination: the small differences in cell percentage are not statistically significant. In other words, whether or not one believes her fate is tied to the fate of her racial group has no effect on whether she will report experiencing racial discrimination herself.

However, those who see more discrimination against their own racial group are more likely to report that they themselves have experienced some form of discrimination in the workplace. This is most apparent for those who report double jeopardy: 8.7 percent of those who think little or no discrimination occurs against their racial group have, however, experienced double jeopardy discrimination themselves, while 15.2 percent of those who think some or a lot of discrimination occurs in general report the same. That is, if one is aware of racial discrimination against her racial group as a whole, she is more likely to be aware of it in her own individual life. This points to the fact that incidents of racial discrimination are far-reaching, impacting not only individuals in isolated cases but the collective history of a people, which in turn impacts the individuals of that community (Scott 1991; Feagin 1991).

The last two variables in table 15.3 compare those who believe that extensive racial and gender discrimination exist in the working world with those who see little or none of it there. Although there are no significant differences in how workers reported based on whether they believe gender discrimination exists or not, those who believe that there is "some" or "a lot" of racial group discrimination are almost twice as likely to report experiencing double jeopardy (15.2 percent) as those who believe that there is "only a little" or "none at all" (8.7 percent). That almost 1 in 10 of the former group still report experiencing it themselves suggests that any relationship between perceived personal discrimination and perceived group discrimination is a complicated one.

Logistic Regression Analyses

In order to determine which factors analyzed in the preceding sections are significant predictors of reporting discrimination, net of all others, I ran four logistic regression models. These models estimate the log odds of reporting discrimination as a function of the independent variables used in the previous cross-tabulations.[20] Each dependent variable is dichotomous and differentiates between those who reported some form of discrimination and those who reported no discriminatory experiences.

Model 1: Reporting of Some Form of Discrimination The first model has as the dependent variable reporting of any type of discrimination and uses all the independent variables described in the previous section. In the end, with this analysis we can estimate the probability of reporting discrimination for different profiles of workers.

Table 15.4 shows coefficients (b), standard errors, and the odds multipliers (e^b). There are several factors that stand up to statistical scrutiny. First, it appears that racial group sometimes helps us to determine the odds of someone reporting discrimination. Holding all other variables constant, the odds of East Asian American and Latinas reporting are .3 times less than the odds that white women will report. That is, white workers are more likely to report any type of workplace discrimination against themselves than are East Asian American and Latina women. However, the odds of African American and white women reporting some type of discrimination are indistinguishable from each other, net of all other factors.

Education and income seem to have effects on the odds of reporting also, net of all other factors. Each year of education increases the odds of reporting discrimination by 1.2 times, so that the net odds of reporting discrimination for those with a bachelor's degree are about 2.2 times larger than for those with only a high school degree. Similarly, those who get paid more for their work have higher odds of reporting than those who get paid less (for example, the odds of those who make

TABLE 15.4   *Effect Parameters for a Model Predicting Reporting of Any Form of Workplace Discrimination, Women in Los Angeles (N = 584) (Standard Errors in Parentheses)*

Independent Variable	b		e^b
Racial group (white omitted)			
African American	−.0853	(.3560)	.9183
East Asian American	−1.2146**	(.4385)	.2968
Latina	−1.1079*	(.4604)	.3303
Years of formal education	.2026**	(.0651)	1.2246
Income (dollars)	6.81E-06*	(3.473E-06)	1.0000
Occupation (lower-blue-collar omitted)			
Upper-blue-collar	−.1964	(.4487)	.8217
Lower-white-collar	.2349	(.4182)	1.2648
Upper-white-collar	−.2149	(.4631)	.8066
Native-born	−.4232	(.3484)	.6549
Public-sector	−.1590	(.3140)	.8530
Coworkers of different racial group	.8778***	(.2356)	2.4056
Supervisor (same racial group and gender omitted)			
Male supervisor of different racial group	.8208**	(.3184)	2.2722
Female supervisor of different racial group	−.0581	(.3266)	.9435
Male supervisor of same racial group	.1538	(.2865)	1.1662
Racial group identity (little or none omitted)	.0491	(.2204)	1.0203
Racial group discrimination (little or none omitted)	.5785*	(.2967)	1.7834
Gender group discrimination (little or none omitted)	−.6746**	(.2518)	.5094
Interviewer effects (male of different racial group omitted)			
Female interviewer of same racial group	.5311	(.3174)	1.7008
Female interviewer of different racial group	1.6142***	(.3806)	5.0237
Male interviewer of same racial group	.7322	(.3991)	2.0797
Intercept	−2.2590	(.8901)	

Source: Los Angeles Study of Urban Inequality 1994.
Note: Controls: age, English language ability, employment status, and years employed for pay.
*p < .05, **p < .01, ***p < .001.

$60,000 reporting discrimination are about 1.4 times larger than those who make $15,000 a year).

A worker's work site characteristics also matter. Having most of your coworkers of a different racial group or groups increases the odds of reporting 2.4 times, compared with having coworkers of same racial group, net of all other variables. Similarly, having a male supervisor of a different racial group increases the odds of reporting discrimination 2.3 times, compared to having a female supervisor of the same racial group (holding all other variables constant).

Believing that one's own racial group suffers discrimination as a whole increases the odds of reporting by 1.8 times compared with those who don't believe it happens more than a little. Conversely, believing that women as a group suffer gender discrimination decreases the odds of reporting any discrimination experiences by about half, compared with women who believe it doesn't happen or happens "a little."

The strongest effect, though, seems to come from a gendered interviewer.[21] Having a female interviewer of a different racial group increases the odds of reporting five times, compared with having a male interviewer of a different racial group. Curiously, no significant difference in odds of reporting is seen when comparing interviewers of the same racial group and gender with interviewers of a different racial group and gender than the respondent. This might indicate a reluctance to admit information that might make the respondent appear to be weak or a victim when she is speaking with her racial and gendered peer, which does not come into play when she is speaking with a woman of another racial group. All other factors do not significantly alter the odds of reporting discrimination.

Among those who do report some type of discrimination experience, I next examine whether different types of discrimination have different predictors. I do this by running models on only those who have reported any type of discrimination. The subsequent three models have the following three dependent variables: reporting of any racial discrimination, reporting of any gender discrimination, and reporting of double jeopardy (see table 15.5).

Model II: Reporting of Racial Discrimination   The only factors that test significant predictors are who one's supervisor is in relation to the respondent and an interviewer effect.

The odds of those with male supervisors of a different racial group reporting racial discrimination are 4.8 times greater than the odds of those with female supervisors of the same racial group. More striking is that there is a gender difference: the increase in the odds of those with *female* supervisors of a different racial group reporting racial discrimina-

TABLE 15.5   *Effect Parameters for Models Predicting Reporting of Different Forms of Workplace Discimination, Women in Los Angeles Who Report Some Form of Discrimination (N = 209) (Standard Errors in Parentheses)*

Independent Variable	Racial Only		Gender Only		Double Jeopardy	
	logit coefficients					
Racial group (white omitted)						
African American	.9257	(.5710)	.5385	(.5843)	1.2266*	(.5649)
East Asian American	.6594	(.7485)	.0261	(.6948)	.7083	(.7036)
Latina	−.3085	(.7492)	.7806	(.7330)	.5667	(.7310)
Years of formal education	−.0940	(.0802)	.0917	(.0744)	.0150	(.0733)
Native-born	.0886	(.5559)	−.7570	(.5041)	−.7562	(.5301)
Public-sector	−.4808	(.5255)	−.5969	(.4671)	−.7973	(.4673)
Coworkers of different racial group	.0779	(.4450)	.5524	(.4189)	.5402	(.3969)
Supervisor (same racial group and gender omitted)						
Male supervisor of different racial group	1.5712*	(.6700)	−1.0458	(.5991)	.0912	(.5686)
Female supervisor of different racial group	1.9879**	(.7115)	−1.3184*	(.5870)	.0951	(.5629)
Male supervisor of same racial group	−.6758	(.4896)	.8650	(.5346)	.0695	(.5063)
Racial group identity (little or none omitted)	.6384	(.4355)	−.4483	(.3711)	.0645	(.3757)
Racial group discrimination (little or none omitted)	−.4613	(.4985)	−.2150	(.5076)	−.5759	(.5100)
Gender group discrimination (little or none omitted)	−.6022	(.4551)	.6601	(.3998)	.0784	(.4234)
Interviewer effects (male of different racial group omitted)						
Female interviewer of same racial group	2.4567***	(.6873)	−.6784	(.5688)	1.6263*	(.7404)
Female interviewer of different racial group	2.9585***	(.7260)	−.0465	(.6407)	2.6713***	(.7813)
Male interviewer of same racial group	2.6963***	(.8187)	−.8610	(.7340)	1.7197*	(.8957)
Intercept	1.9760	(1.1298)	−.7434	(1.0449)	−1.4275	(1.0486)

TABLE 15.5 Continued

Independent Variable	Racial Only	Gender Only	Double Jeopardy
	Odds Multipliers, e^b		
Racial group (white omitted)			
African American	2.5237	1.7134	3.4096
East Asian American	1.9337	1.0265	2.0306
Latina	.7345	2.1827	1.7625
Years of formal education	.9103	1.0960	1.0151
Native-born	1.0926	.4691	.4694
Public-sector	.6183	.5505	.4506
Coworkers of different racial group	1.0810	1.7375	1.7163
Supervisor (same racial group and gender omitted)			
Male supervisor of different racial group	4.8122	.3514	1.0955
Female supervisor of different racial group	7.3003	.2676	1.0998
Male supervisor of same racial group	.5087	2.3750	1.0719
Racial group identity (little or none omitted)	1.8934	.6387	1.0666
Racial group discrimination (little or none omitted)	.6305	.8065	.5622
Gender group discrimination (little or none omitted)	.5476	1.9350	1.0816
Interviewer effects (male of different racial group omitted)			
Female interviewer of same racial group	11.6659	.5074	5.0851
Female interviewer of different racial group	19.2694	.9546	14.4586
Male interviewer of same racial group	14.8254	.4227	5.5827

Source: Los Angeles Study of Urban Inequality 1994.
*p < .05, **p < .01, ***p < .001

tion is even greater—7.3 times greater than the odds of those with male supervisors of a different racial group.

Interviewer effects are very strong here, with a gender difference again. The odds of reporting racial discrimination by respondents with female interviewers of the same racial group are over 11 times greater than respondents who had a male interviewer of a different racial group.

However, this effect is even stronger when the interviewer is male and of the same racial group (14.8 times increase), and stronger still when the interviewer is also female but of a different racial group (19.3 times increase).

The implications of these findings are twofold. First, when interviewing female respondents about a sensitive and controversial topic such as racial discrimination, not matching the interviewer's racial group *and* gender effectively silences their voices. Second, although matching both racial group and gender is effective in encouraging respondent participation, women are most free when speaking with women of a different racial group. This is encouraging, for it implies that women across racial boundaries can talk freely about racial issues.

Of those who report any form of discrimination, race of respondent turns out not to be a significant predictor of the odds of reporting racial discrimination, specifically. None of the other determinants significantly affect the odds of reporting racial discrimination.

Model III: Reporting Gender Discrimination Only one variable is a significant predictor of whether those who report any type of discrimination report having experienced gender-based discrimination. The odds of reporting gender discrimination by those with female supervisors of a different racial group are .3 times less than the odds of reporting by those with male supervisors of a different racial group. Having a male supervisor of the same racial group does not seem to affect the odds of reporting when compared to those with male supervisors of a different racial group. That is, racial group of supervisor seems to play no significant role in determining the odds of reporting gender discrimination, but gender doesn't either if you're comparing male and female supervisors of the same racial group as the worker. Having a female supervisor decreases the odds of reporting only when the supervisor is of a different racial group than the worker. (These findings are net of all other variables.)

Unlike in the previous model, who interviews you seems to have no significant effects on the odds of reporting gender discrimination. This seems to suggest that in this day and age, gender issues are not as "loaded" as racial ones.

Model IV: Reporting Double Jeopardy This is the only full logistic model that concluded that racial group of respondent had a significant effect on the odds of reporting discrimination. The odds of African American workers reporting double jeopardy discrimination experiences are 3.4 times greater than the odds of white workers reporting having experienced it.

Similar to what we observed in the racial discrimination model, there are strong interviewer effects here. The strongest lie in the odds of respondents with female interviewers of a different racial group reporting double jeopardy: 14.5 times greater than the odds of respondents with male interviewers of a different racial group reporting it. Having a female interviewer of a different racial group increases the odds of reporting much more than having a female interviewer of the *same* racial group, and much more than having a *male* interviewer of the same racial group.

Conclusion

There are several implications to be derived from these findings. First, a percentage of all women across racial groups reported experiencing some form of discrimination in the workplace. All women of color also reported some level of double jeopardy discrimination. This commonality can be used to unify all workers and workers of color, respectively, toward collective actions that challenge these practices.

However, there are important differences across these racial groups that must be taken into consideration. African American workers were much more likely than all other women to articulate discriminatory experiences at all, as well as most likely to recognize their experiences as double jeopardy. Since one in four of these workers reported direct experiences with discrimination, this translates into a seriously high level of dissatisfaction and work environments at odds with many of its African American female workers.

Second, it is also clear that the workplaces of today form complicated social settings. The racial and gendered profiles of coworkers and bosses can send strong messages to workers of who is racially and gender "appropriate" for better pay, raises, and promotions. How multiracial workplaces are defined by coworkers and bosses can contribute to reinforcing racist or prejudicial thinking about other groups and their opportunities in relation to one's own. If workers, and especially employers, make no visible and effective efforts toward racial and gender equality, the simmering racial, ethnic, and gendered antagonisms apparent in today's workplaces are likely to increase in the new millennium.

Third, perceptions of discrimination in one's paid work life are dependent on a few, but not many, individual attributes as well. Higher levels of formal education and awareness of racial discrimination against one's racial group both increase the likelihood of reporting some form of personal experiences of discrimination, net of all other variables. Higher education and racialized awareness, however, do not affect which type of discrimination one is likely to report.

Fourth, differences in gender and racial group between interviewer and respondent can create significant discrepancies in responses to sensitive topics, such as racial discrimination experiences. Specifically, having a female interviewer of a different racial group than one's own increases the odds of reporting some form of discrimination substantially. This remains true for those who report racial discrimination or double jeopardy.

Finally, although the majority of workers of all racial groups reported having experienced no gender or racial discrimination, we should keep in mind that if zero tolerance is our goal, these findings point to a significant degree of discrimination experiences that women in the workforce still face. The belief that racial and gender barriers are commonplace in the workplace is a serious concern, not only in the obvious instance of the discriminatory work environments that workers face, but also in terms of producing discouraged workers and self-induced barriers to seeking jobs and advancement within an organization.

The author would like to thank the following people for their invaluable input and support: Lawrence Bobo, Roger Waldinger, Min Zhou, Elizabeth González, Nelson Lim, Julie Press, Dean Toji, Donald Treiman, and three anonymous reviewers.

Appendix

TABLE 15A.1   *Descriptive Data by Racial Group, Women in Los Angeles, 1993 to 1994*

Variable	African American	East Asian American	Latina	White
Age				
Twenty-one to twenty-nine	39.2%	32.2%	54.4%	29.6%
Thirty to thirty-nine	39.2	28.2	27.0	29.6
Forty to forty-nine	12.7	14.1	11.3	23.7
Fifty and over	9.0	25.4	7.4	17.1
Formal education				
High school or less	37.1	45.8	64.4	31.1
Some college	48.6	14.7	29.9	35.8
Bachelor's degree or higher	14.3	39.6	10.8	33.2
Income				
< $6,000	33.8	45.6	49.5	27.3
$6,000 to $16,999	34.6	13.1	38.8	22.3
$17,000 to $31,999	20.9	22.5	8.2	36.7
$32,000 or more	10.7	18.8	3.6	13.7

TABLE 15A.1   Continued

Variable	African American	East Asian American	Latina	White
Year of immigration				
Native-born	97.6	11.9	30.0	86.2
Before 1985	2.0	34.5	38.4	10.5
1985 to 1994	0.4	53.7	31.5	3.3
English-speaking ability				
Little or none	—	31.1	37.6	—
Fair	—	25.4	19.0	1.3
Well	100.0	43.5	43.4	98.7
Total N	(245)	(177)	(205)	(152)

Source: Los Angeles Study of Urban Inequality 1994.
Note: Columns for each variable total to 100 percent (± 1 percent due to rounding).

TABLE 15A.2   Workplace Setting Data by Racial Group, Women in Los Angeles, 1993 to 1994

Variable	African American	East Asian American	Latina	White
Occupation				
Lower blue-collar	4.1%	7.4%	27.9%	2.6%
Upper blue-collar	24.0	31.3	24.0	9.9
Lower white-collar	52.4	42.6	37.7	43.4
Upper white collar	19.5	18.8	10.3	44.1
Sector				
Private	82.9	94.4	88.7	90.2
Public	17.1	5.6	11.3	9.8
Racial group of most coworkers				
African American	41.4	9.7	3.0	4.1
Asian American	4.3	67.6	4.0	6.1
Latina and Latino	10.8	9.7	70.6	12.2
White	43.5	13.1	22.4	77.6
Racial group of supervisor				
African American	30.3	2.9	3.5	2.7
Asian American	1.6	73.1	5.0	2.7
Latina and Latino	10.2	2.3	50.0	10.0
White	57.8	21.7	41.5	84.7

(Table continues on p. 590.)

TABLE 15A.2   *Continued*

Variable	African American	East Asian American	Latina	White
Gender of supervisor				
Woman	55.7	30.7	49.8	52.0
Man	44.3	69.3	50.2	48.0
Gender and racial group of supervisor				
Male of different racial group	34.0	10.8	16.4	11.3
Female of different racial group	35.2	16.5	33.8	4.6
Male of same racial group	10.2	58.5	32.8	37.1
Female of same racial group	20.5	14.2	16.9	47.0
Total N	(245)	(177)	(205)	(152)

Source: Los Angeles Study of Urban Inequality 1994.
Note: Columns for each variable total to 100 percent (± 1 percent due to rounding).

Notes

1. Given the primacy of racial group in the United States as a historical, psychological, political, and sociological marker of an individual and the group to which that individual belongs, it warrants a
careful choice of terms to describe these groups. Although there are
problems of exclusion in their use, because of the historical and
political meanings inscribed to them in the U.S. context, I will use
"black" and "African American" interchangeably to describe peoples of African and Caribbean descent. "Latina" will refer to the
women of this sample who are Mexicanas, women of Mexican descent, Central Americans, and South Americans. "East Asian
American," will include women of Chinese, Japanese, and/or Korean ancestry. To refer to commonalities across these broad racial
groupings, I will use the term "women of color." Although the
term is problematic, because of its historical and sociological importance, I will use "white" to indicate people of European ancestry who make up the dominant racial grouping in the United
States.

2. Although it has been argued that self-reporting of discrimination
can include false reports, I do not count any that might exist as
significant for two reasons. First, there are serious and weighty
considerations that discourage reporting, given the likelihood of
negative repercussions when one publicly identifies having faced
discrimination, that would far outweigh any "positive gain" a false
reporter might plan to receive (such as remuneration, revenge

against disliked boss). These can include retaliatory moves on the part of the employer (such as labeling worker as "troublemaker" or "not a team player," a cutback in hours, further and/or more aggressive harassment, demotion, loss of job) or other employees (avoidance of or hostility toward disfavored worker, new harassment from other workers for causing trouble that might negatively affect them) to a general loss of credibility as a reliable worker and a general social stigma attached to whistleblowers. Although for respondents to a general survey such as LASUI, these negative repercussions in reporting would not apply, neither would the positive gains. Second, there is evidence to suggest that even if false reports do occur, the numbers are small. For example, in the case of reporting another highly sensitive and controversial charge, the level of false reporting of rape has been found to be comparable to the level of false reporting of any other violent crime, which in all cases is less than 5 percent (Brownmiller 1975, 387). (Also see the end of the section entitled "Measuring Racial and Gender Discrimination" in this chapter.)

3. For example, Donald Tomaskovic-Devey (1993) looked at a 1989 survey of North Carolina employees, to explore gender and racial wage inequality. This was the first study of a general population survey to include gender and racial composition in the interviewee's workplace. Joyce Tang (1993) went a step beyond comparing earnings by looking at occupational status and promotion attainment for Asian American and white engineers. She found that Asian American engineers (except recent immigrants) had attained income parity with whites, but lagged behind in occupational status and upward mobility, given comparable backgrounds.

4. A study showed that even in occupations that have been historically "female" professions, such as nursing, elementary school teaching, librarianship, and social work, men in these professions do not face discrimination, and in fact "encounter structural advantages in these occupations which tend to enhance their careers" (Williams 1992).

5. For example, consider the popular term "women and minorities," which implies that the two are mutually exclusive. However, some recent social scientists have made efforts not to disassociate racial group and gender in their analysis (see, for example, Carlson 1992).

6. Even when workers' points of view are addressed, the previously mentioned paucity of focus on people of color beyond African Americans still applies (Sigelman and Welch 1991; Feagin and Sikes 1994).

7. For example, see Wade Smith's 1988 study of black and white college students' goals and achievements by racial group and gender, or Anita Pak, Kenneth Dion, and Karen Dion's 1991 study of Chi-

nese Canadian women who were doubly disadvantaged when comparing their social-psychological effects of dealing with discrimination with those of their male counterparts.

8. For example, 3 to 5 percent of all senior-level jobs in major corporations are filled by women; of these, only 5 percent are filled by women of color.

9. Comparisons of the percent distributions of several demographic indicators such as age, nativity, educational attainment, and occupational category from LASUI to the 1990 U.S. census indicate that the population represented in the survey is very similar to the target population. The largest discrepancies (within racial group) lie in LASUI respondents being slightly (7 percent) more likely to be foreign-born and less likely to be among the least educated than the 1990 census reveals.

10. All cross-tabular analyses in this report reflect the use of weights that correct for oversampling of poverty tracts and household size. The weights are used normalized to the sample size, so that cases are not lost and does not normalize to the population of Los Angeles County. Therefore, the proportions of workers by racial group cited in this chapter do not reflect their respective proportions in the population. Sample size for all logistic regression models are unweighted.

11. The wording of each question of discrimination analyzed here had the same time frame: within the last year of their current job or within the last year of their most recent job (whichever was applicable to their current employment status).

12. For example, women in the workforce who had been sexually harassed at the work site felt "economic and social pressures against taking any action" (Schneider 1991). Of course, this discouragement can come from an employer and/or coworker within the work site.

13. In contrast, gender matching was not done systematically. Fortunately, a majority of African American and white respondents had female interviewers (74.8 percent and 66.4 percent, respectively). However, the lack of systematic gender matching of respondent and interviewer is something to keep in mind when reviewing the Latina and East Asian American responses: each group had mostly male interviewers (74.1 percent and 62.5 percent, respectively). This point will be broached later, in the logistic analysis.

14. In any instances of white women reporting experiencing both racial- and gender-based discrimination, I take this to mean the belief that whites might have of being "reversely discriminated" against because they are *not* people of color. The possibility of this belief by white women is not addressed in the double jeopardy literature,

for it can be argued that "reverse discrimination" of whites is an illogical concept to consider, when compared to the systematic and institutional nature of racial discrimination against people of color throughout this nation's history, as well as its tenacious presence today. Thus, while this question focuses on determining whether I can quantify any difference in reporting discrimination between women of color and whites, the meaning of the answers to the racial group-based discrimination questions will be different for these two groups.

15. Although the survey question regarding race-ethnicity of supervisor does not allow for any ethnic group distinctions in the Asian category, so that a pan-Asian identity and solidarity between worker and management seems to be assumed, it might be more appropriate to point to the fact that Asian Americans usually are situated in the workplace in one of the following two ways: either working among co-ethnics or in a co-ethnic business in the "ethnic economy," or working in a workplace with a dearth of Asian Americans of any ethnicity. In the former case, racial discrimination by supervisor does not apply; in the latter case, it seems most likely that even those East Asian American workers with an Asian American supervisor of a different ethnicity would not be considered a different racial group to that supervisor when compared to non–Asian American workers.

16. The question of whether their supervisor had made racial slurs in their presence was the most consistent across racial groups, all between 3.4 percent and 10.2 percent reporting yes with a range of 6.8 percentage points. However, it is unclear in the original question wording whether the respondent understood the question to mean racial slurs directed at her own racial group, or directed at another racial group but in the worker's presence.

17. Separate analysis of cumulative frequencies of reporting individual items by racial group also shows African American women reporting the largest number. Black workers also account for the largest percentage of those who have experienced any of the six discrimination items analyzed here.

18. However, they do signal a challenge against coalition building across racial lines. Eight out of the twelve white respondents who answered in the affirmative to the open-ended general racial discrimination question work in white-collar jobs. Half work in jobs where white workers are dominant.

19. The LASUI survey does not have a corresponding question that asks for the gender of the majority of coworkers.

20. All logistic regression models were determined by a stepwise method. That is, each model started from a model where racial

group was the only independent variable. Subsequent models were generated by introducing groups of independent variables into the previous model. Each likelihood ratio χ^2 was compared to determine whether or not the introduction of the new variables led to a better model. Each model shown in tables 15.4 and 15.5 is the final model, which corresponded to the lowest likelihood ratios.

21. Since it was clear from the outset that there were large differences in the level of success of gender matching between interviewer and respondent across racial groups, I ran all logistic regression models with a dummied variable for interviewer's gender and racial group vis-à-vis the respondent.

References

Bobo, Lawrence. 1992. "Prejudice and Alternative Dispute Resolution." *Studies in Law, Politics, and Society* 12: 147–76.

Bobo, Lawrence, and Susan A. Suh. 1995. "Surveying Racial Discrimination: Analyses from a Multiethnic Labor Market." Presented at the Russell Sage MCSUI Conference on "Searching for Work/Searching for Workers." New York (September 28–29, 1995).

Braddock, Jomills H., and James M. McPartland. 1987. "How Minorities Continue to Be Excluded from Equal Employment Opportunities: Research on Labor Market and Institutional Barriers." *Journal of Social Issues* 43: 5–39.

Brownmiller. Susan. 1975. *Against Our Will: Men, Women and Rape.* New York: Simon & Schuster.

Carlson, Susan M. 1992. "Trends in Racial Group/Sex Occupational Inequality: Conceptual and Measurement Issues." *Social Problems* 39: 268–85.

Chow, Esther Ngan-Ling. 1994. "Asian American Women at Work." In *Women of Color in U.S. Society*, edited by Maxine Baca Zinn and Bonnie Thornton Dill. Philadelphia: Temple University Press.

Collins, Patricia Hill. 1990. *Black Feminist Thought: Knowledge, Consciousness, and the Politics of Empowerment.* New York: Routledge.

England, Paula, George Farkas, Barbara Stanek Kilbourne, and Thomas Dou. 1988. "Explaining Occupational Sex Segregation and Wages: Findings from a Model with Fixed Effects." *American Sociological Review* 53: 544–58.

Feagin, Joe R. 1991 "The Continuing Significance of Race: Antiblack Discrimination in Public Places." *American Sociological Review* 56: 101–16.

Feagin, Joe R., and Melvin P. Sikes. 1994. *Living with Racism: The Black Middle Class Experience.* Boston: Beacon Press.

Federal Glass Ceiling Commission. 1991. *Good for Business: Making Full Use of the Nation's Human Capital.* Washington: U.S. Department of Labor.

Glenn, Evelyn Nakano. 1986. *Issei, Nisei, Warbride: Three Generations of Japanese American Women in Domestic Service*. Philadelphia: Temple University Press.

Hartmann, Heidi. 1976. "Capitalism, Patriarchy, and Job Segregation by Sex." In *Women and the Workplace: The Implications of Occupational Segregation*, edited by Martha Blaxall and Barbara Reagan. Chicago: University of Chicago Press.

Hossfeld, Karen J. 1994. "Hiring Immigrant Women: Silicon Valley's 'Simple Formula.'" In *Women of Color in U.S. Society*, edited by Maxine Baca Zinn and Bonnie Thornton Dill. Philadelphia: Temple University Press.

King, Deborah 1988. "Multiple Jeopardy, Multiple Consciousness: The Context of a Black Feminist Ideology." *Signs: Journal of Women in Culture and Society* 14(1): 42–72.

Kirschenman, Joleen, and Kathryn M. Neckerman. 1991. "'We'd Love to Hire Them, But . . . ': The Meaning of Race for Employers." In *The Urban Underclass*, edited by C. Jencks and P. E. Peterson. Washington, D.C.: Brookings Institution.

Lieberson, Stanley, and Glen Fuguitt. 1967. "Negro-White Occupational Differences in the Absence of Discrimination." *American Journal of Sociology* 73: 188–200.

Moghissi, Haideh. 1994. "Racism and Sexism in Academic Practice: A Case Study." In *The Dynamics of "Race" and Gender: Some Feminist Interventions*, edited by Haleh Afshar and Mary Maynard. London: Taylor and Francis.

Pak, Anita Wan-Ping, Kenneth L. Dion, and Karen K. Dion. 1991. "Social-Pychological Correlates of Experienced Discrimination: Test of the Double Jeopardy Hypothesis." *International Journal of Intercultural Relations* 15: 243–54.

Pettigrew, Thomas F., and Joanne Martin. 1987. "Shaping the Organizational Context for Black Inclusion." *Journal of Social Issues* 43: 41–78.

Reskin, Barbara F., and Patricia A. Roos. 1990. *Job Queues, Gender Queues: Explaining Women's Inroads into Male Occupations*. Philadelphia: Temple University Press.

Schneider, Beth E. 1991. "Put Up and Shut Up: Workplace Sexual Assaults." *Gender and Society* 5 (4): 533–49.

Scott, Kesho Yvonne. 1991. *The Habit of Surviving: Black Women's Strategies for Life*. New Brunswick, N.J.: Rutgers University Press.

Segura, Denise A. 1994. "Inside the Work Worlds of Chicana and Mexican Immigrant Women." In *Women of Color in U.S. Society*, edited by Maxine Baca Zinn and Bonnie Thornton Dill. Philadelphia: Temple University Press.

Sigelman, Lee, and Susan Welch. 1991. *Black Americans' Views of Racial Inequality: The Dream Deferred*. Cambridge, England: Cambridge University Press.

Smith, A. Wade. 1988. "In Double Jeopardy: Collegiate Academic Outcomes of Black Females vs. Black Males." *National Journal of Sociology* (Spring): 3–31.

Tang, Joyce. 1993. "The Career Attainment of Caucasian and Asian Engineers." *Sociological Quarterly* 34 (3): 467–97.

Telles, Edward E., and Edward Murguia. 1990. "Phenotypic Discrimination and Income Differences Among Mexican Americans." *Social Science Quarterly* 71 (4): 682–97.

Tienda, Marta, and Ding-Tzann Lii. 1987. "Minority Concentration and Earnings Inequality: Blacks, Hispanics, and Asians Compared." *American Journal of Sociology* 93: 141–65.

Tomaskovic-Devey, Donald. 1993. "The Gender and Racial Composition of Jobs and the Male/Female, White/Black Pay Gaps." *Social Forces* 72 (1): 45–77.

Weber, Lynn, and Elizabeth Higginbotham. 1995. "Perceptions of Workplace Discrimination Among Black and White Professional-Managerial Women." Memphis, Tenn.: Center for Research on Women.

Williams, Christine L. 1992. "The Glass Escalator: Hidden Advantages for Men in the 'Female' Professions." *Social Problems* 39: 253–80.

Yamanaka, Keiko, and Kent McClelland. 1994. "Earning the Model-Minority Image: Diverse Strategies of Economic Adaptation by Asian-American Women." *Ethnic and Racial Studies* 17 (1): 79–114.

Index

Numbers in **boldface** refer to figures and tables.